Oxford Essential

French Dictionary

Oxford
Essential
French
Dictionary

FRENCH-ENGLISH

ENGLISH-FRENCH

FRANÇAIS-ANGLAIS

ANGLAIS-FRANÇAIS

OXFORD
UNIVERSITY PRESS

OXFORD
UNIVERSITY PRESS

Great Clarendon Street, Oxford OX2 6DP

Oxford University Press is a department of the University of Oxford.
It furthers the University's objective of excellence in research, scholarship,
and education by publishing worldwide in

Oxford New York

Auckland Cape Town Dar es Salaam Hong Kong Karachi
Kuala Lumpur Madrid Melbourne Mexico City Nairobi
New Delhi Shanghai Taipei Toronto

With offices in

Argentina Austria Brazil Chile Czech Republic France Greece
Guatemala Hungary Italy Japan Poland Portugal Singapore
South Korea Switzerland Thailand Turkey Ukraine Vietnam

Oxford is a registered trade mark of Oxford University Press
in the UK and in certain other countries

British Library Cataloguing in Publication Data

Data available

Library of Congress Cataloging in Publication Data

Data available

ISBN 978-0-19-957638-8

12

Typeset by Interactive Sciences Ltd, Gloucester
Printed in Great Britain by Clays Ltd, St Ives plc

Contents/**Table des matières**

Introduction/Introduction   viii–ix

Pronunciation/Prononciation
    French/français   x
    English/anglais   xi

French–English/français–anglais   **1**

English–French/anglais–français   **241**

French Verbs   467

Verbes irréguliers anglais   477

Numbers/Les nombres   479

Proprietary terms

This dictionary includes some words which are, or are asserted to be, proprietary terms or trademarks. The presence or absence of such assertions should not be regarded as affecting the legal status of any proprietary name or trademark. In cases where the editorial staff has evidence that a word is used as a proprietary name or trademark, this is indicated by the symbol ®. No judgement concerning the legal status of such words is made or implied thereby.

Les marques déposées

Les mots qui, à notre connaissance, sont considérés comme des marques ou des noms déposés sont signalés dans cet ouvrage par ®. La présence ou l'absence de cette mention ne peut pas être considérée comme ayant valeur juridique.

Contributors/Collaborateurs

Michael Janes
Dora Latiri-Carpenter
Edwin Carpenter
Isabelle Stables-Lemoine
Marianne Chalmers
Rosalind Combley
Catherine Roux
Laura Wedgeworth
Hélène Haenen
Neil and Roswitha Morris
Nicholas Rollin
Jean Benoit Ormal-Grenon
Susan Wilkin
Meic Haines
Mary O'Neill

Introduction

The *Oxford Essential French Dictionary* has been designed to be a practical reference tool for the student, adult learner, traveller and business professional. It provides user-friendly treatment of core vocabulary across a broad spectrum of written and spoken language.

Enhanced coverage

The wordlist has been revised to reflect recent additions to both languages.

The more complex grammatical words, or *function words*, are given special treatment in highlighted entries to make them easily accessible. All verbs in the French-English section are cross-referenced to the verb tables at the end of the book. Here information is given on regular, irregular and reflexive verbs as well as the translation of French verb tenses.

Easy reference

The dictionary layout has been designed to be clear, streamlined and easy to use. Bullet points separate each new part of speech within an entry. Nuances of meaning or usage are pinpointed by semantic indicators or by typical collocates with which the headword frequently occurs. Extra help is given with symbols to mark the register of language. A boxed exclamation mark ☒ indicates colloquial language and a cross ☒ indicates slang.

The pronunciation of French is given in the International Phonetic Alphabet. Irregular parts of French verbs appear as headwords with a cross-reference to the main entry of the verb.

Introduction

L'*Oxford Essential French Dictionary* a été conçu comme un outil de référence practique destiné aux étudiants, aux touristes et aux professionnels. Il offre un traitement convivial du vocabulaire de base représentatif de la langue écrite et parlée.

Une édition augmentée

La nomenclature a été revisée de façon à refléter les récents apports de vocabulaire dans les deux langues.

Les mots grammaticaux, qui forment les structures de base des deux langues, font l'objet d'une présentation distincte qui les rend rapidement accessibles, les choix de traduction et des exemples étant clairement signalés. De courtes notes d'usage indiquent les pièges éventuels. Une liste de verbes irréguliers anglais se trouve à la fin de l'ouvrage.

Une consulatation facilitée

La présentation du dictionnaire a été conçue de façon à être claire, simplifiée et à faciliter la consultation de l'ouvrage. Des *puces* séparent chaque nouvelle partie du discours à l'intérieur d'une entrée, ce qui facilite leur repérage. Les nuances de sens ou d'usage sont marquées au moyen d'indicateurs sémantiques ou par des collocateurs types avec lesquels le mot s'emploie fréquemment, guidant ainsi rapidement l'utilisateur à la traduction appropriée. Un point d'exclamation ▣ indique un niveau de langue familier et une croix ▣ indique un niveau argotique.

Les symboles utilisés pour la prononciation sont ceux de l'Alphabet Phonétique International. Les pluriels irréguliers ainsi que les conjugaisons ou les formes du comparatif et du superlatif irrégulières anglaises sont indiqués entre parenthèses.

Pronunciation of French

Vowels

a	*as in*	patte	/pat/		ɑ	*as in*	pâte	/pɑt/
ɑ̃		clan	/klɑ̃/		e		dé	/de/
ɛ		belle	/bɛl/		ɛ̃		lin	/lɛ̃/
ə		demain	/dəmɛ̃/		i		gris	/gRi/
o		gros	/gRo/		ɔ		corps	/kɔR/
ɔ̃		long	/lɔ̃/		œ		leur	/lœR/
œ̃		brun	/bRœ̃/		ø		deux	/dø/
u		fou	/fu/		y		pur	/pyR/

Semi-Vowels

j	*as in*	fille	/fij/
ɥ		huit	/ɥit/
w		oui	/wi/

Consonants

Aspiration of 'h'

Where it is impossible to make a liaison this is indicated by /'/ immediately after the slash e.g. *haine* /'ɛn/.

b	*as in*	bal	/bal/		ŋ	*as in*	camping	/kɑ̃piŋ/
d		dent	/dɑ̃/		p		porte	/pɔRt/
f		foire	/fwaR/		R		rire	/RiR/
g		gomme	/gɔm/		s		sang	/sɑ̃/
k		clé	/kle/		ʃ		chien	/ʃjɛ̃/
l		lien	/ljɛ̃/		t		train	/tRɛ̃/
m		mer	/mɛR/		v		voile	/vwal/
n		nage	/naʒ/		z		zèbre	/zɛbR/
ɲ		oignon	/ɲɔ̃/		ʒ		jeune	/ʒœn/

....

La prononciation de l'anglais

....

Voyelles et diphtongues

i:	see	ɔː	saw	eɪ	page	ɔɪ	join
ɪ	sit	ʊ	put	əʊ	home	ɪə	near
e	ten	uː	too	aɪ	five	eə	hair
æ	hat	ʌ	cup	aɪə	fire	ʊə	poor
ɑː	arm	ɜː	fur	aʊ	now		
ɒ	got	ə	ago	aʊə	flour		

Consonnes

p	pen	tʃ	chin	s	so	n	no
b	bad	dʒ	June	z	zoo	ŋ	sing
t	tea	f	fall	ʃ	she	l	leg
d	dip	v	voice	ʒ	measure	r	red
k	cat	θ	thin	h	how	j	yes
g	got	ð	then	m	man	w	wet

L'accent d'intensité

L'accent d'intensité est indiqué au moyen du signe / ' /, placé devant la syllabe qu'il affecte.

a /a/ →AVOIR **5**.

à /a/
● préposition

à+le = au
à+les = aux

····▶ (avec verbe de mouvement) to.

····▶ (pour indiquer où l'on se trouve) ~ **la maison** at home; ~ **Nice** in Nice.

····▶ (âge, date, heure) ~ **l'âge de...** at the age of...; **au XIXe siècle** in the 19th century; ~ **deux heures** at two o'clock.

····▶ (description) with; **aux yeux verts** with green eyes.

····▶ (appartenance) ~ **qui est ce stylo?** whose pen is this?; **c'est ~ vous?** is this yours?

····▶ (avec nombre) ~ **90 km/h** at 90 km per hour; ~ **10 minutes d'ici** 10 minutes from here; **des tomates ~ 2 euros le kilo** tomatoes at 2 euros a kilo; **un timbre ~ 2 euros** a 2-euro stamp; **nous avons fait le travail ~ deux** two of us did the work; **mener 5 ~ 4** to lead 5 (to) 4.

····▶ (avec être) **c'est ~ moi** it's my turn; **je suis ~ vous tout de suite** I'll be with you in a minute; **c'est ~ toi de décider** it's up to you to decide.

····▶ (hypothèse) ~ **ce qu'il paraît** apparently; ~ **t'entendre** to hear you talk.

····▶ (exclamatif) ~ **ta santé!** cheers!; ~ **demain/bientôt!** see you tomorrow/soon!

····▶ (moyen) ~ **la main** by hand; ~ **vélo** by bike; ~ **pied** on foot; **chauffage au gaz** gas heating.

abaissement /abɛsmã/ nm (de taux, de prix) cut; (de seuil) lowering.

abaisser /abese/ **1** vt lower; (levier) pull ou push down; (fig) humiliate. □ **s'~** vpr go down, drop; (fig) demean oneself; **s'~ à** to stoop to.

abandon /abãdɔ̃/ nm abandonment; (de personne) desertion; (de course) withdrawal; (naturel) abandon; **à l'~** in a state of neglect.

abandonner /abãdɔne/ **1** vt abandon; (épouse, cause) desert; (renoncer à) give up, abandon; (céder) give (à to); (course) withdraw from; (Ordinat) abort. □ **s'~ à** vpr give oneself up to.

abasourdir /abazuʀdiʀ/ **2** vt stun.

abat-jour /abaʒuʀ/ nm inv lampshade.

abats /aba/ nmpl offal.

abattement /abatmã/ nm dejection; (faiblesse) exhaustion; (Comm) reduction; ~ **fiscal** tax allowance.

abattre /abatʀ/ **11** vt knock down; (arbre) cut down; (animal) slaughter; (avion) shoot down; (affaiblir) weaken; (démoraliser) demoralize; **ne pas se laisser ~** not let things get one down. □ **s'~** vpr come down, fall (down).

abbaye /abei/ nf abbey.

abbé /abe/ nm priest; (supérieur d'une abbaye) abbot.

abcès /apsɛ/ nm abscess.

abdiquer /abdike/ **1** vt/i abdicate.

abdomen /abdɔmɛn/ nm abdomen.

abdominal (pl -aux) /abdɔminal/ adj abdominal. **abdominaux** nmpl (Sport) stomach exercises.

abeille /abɛj/ nf bee.

aberrant, ~e /abɛʀã, -t/ adj absurd.

abêtir /abetiʀ/ **2** vt turn into a moron.

abîme /abim/ nm abyss.

abîmer /abime/ **1** vt damage, spoil. □ **s'~** vpr get damaged ou spoilt.

ablation /ablasjɔ̃/ nf removal.

aboiement /abwamã/ nm bark, barking; ~**s** barking.

abolir /abɔliʀ/ **2** vt abolish.

abondance /abɔ̃dãs/ nf abundance; (prospérité) affluence. **abondant**, ~e adj abundant, plentiful.

abonder /abɔ̃de/ **1** vi abound (en in); ~ **dans le sens de qn** agree wholeheartedly with sb.

abonné, ~e /abɔne/ *nm, f* (*lecteur*) subscriber; (*voyageur, spectateur*) season-ticket holder.

abonnement /abɔnmɑ̃/ *nm* (à un journal) subscription; (de bus, Théât) season-ticket; (au gaz) standing charge.

abonner (s') /(s)abɔne/ **1** *vpr* subscribe (à to).

abord /abɔʀ/ *nm* access; **~s** surroundings; **d'~** first.

abordable /abɔʀdabl/ *adj* (*prix*) affordable; (*personne*) approachable; (*texte*) accessible.

aborder /abɔʀde/ **1** *vt* approach; (*lieu*) reach; (*problème*) tackle. ● *vi* reach land.

aborigène /abɔʀiʒɛn/ *nm* aborigine.

aboutir /abutiʀ/ **2** *vi* succeed, achieve a result; **~ à** end (up) in, lead to; **n'~ à rien** come to nothing.

aboutissement /abutismɑ̃/ *nm* outcome; (de carrière, d'évolution) culmination.

aboyer /abwaje/ **31** *vi* bark.

abrégé /abʀeʒe/ *nm* summary.

abréger /abʀeʒe/ **14 40** *vt* (*texte*) shorten, abridge; (*mot*) abbreviate, shorten; (*visite*) cut short.

abreuver /abʀœve/ **1** *vt* water; (fig) overwhelm (de with). □ **s'~** *vpr* drink.

abréviation /abʀevjasjɔ̃/ *nf* abbreviation.

abri /abʀi/ *nm* shelter; **à l'~** under cover; (en lieu sûr) safe; **à l'~ de** sheltered from; **se mettre à l'~** take shelter.

abricot /abʀiko/ *nm* apricot.

abriter /abʀite/ **1** *vt* shelter; (recevoir) house. □ **s'~** *vpr* (take) shelter.

abrupt, ~e /abʀypt/ *adj* steep, sheer; (fig) abrupt.

abruti, ~e /abʀyti/ *nm, f* **1** idiot.

absence /apsɑ̃s/ *nf* absence; **il a des ~s** sometimes his mind goes blank.

absent, ~e /apsɑ̃, -t/ *adj* (*personne*) absent, away; (*chose*) missing; **il est toujours ~** he's still away; **d'un air ~** absently. ● *nm, f* absentee.

absenter (s') /(s)apsɑ̃te/ **1** *vpr* go *ou* be away; (sortir) go out, leave.

absolu, ~e /apsɔly/ *adj* absolute.

absorbant, ~e /apsɔʀbɑ̃, -t/ *adj* (travail) absorbing; (matière) absorbent.

absorber /apsɔʀbe/ **1** *vt* absorb; **être absorbé par qch** be engrossed in sth.

abstenir (s') /(s)apstəniʀ/ **58** *vpr* abstain; **s'~ de** refrain from.

abstrait, ~e /apstʀɛ, -t/ *adj & nm* abstract.

absurde /apsyʀd/ *adj* absurd.

abus /aby/ *nm* abuse, misuse; (injustice) abuse; **~ de confiance** breach of trust.

abuser /abyze/ **1** *vt* deceive. ● *vi* go too far; **~ de** abuse, misuse; (profiter de) take advantage of; (alcool) overindulge in. □ **s'~** *vpr* be mistaken.

abusif, -ive /abyzif, -v/ *adj* excessive; (impropre) wrong; (injuste) unfair.

académie /akademi/ *nf* academy; (circonscription) local education authority.

> **Académie française** A scholarly body composed of 40 life members selected on the basis of their contribution to scholarship or literature. It monitors developments in the French language and rules on French usage, as encoded in the *Dictionnaire de l'Académie française* (which is not always taken seriously by the public at large).

acajou /akaʒu/ *nm* mahogany.

accablant, ~e /akablɑ̃, -t/ *adj* (chaleur) oppressive; (fait, témoignage) damning.

accabler /akable/ **1** *vt* overwhelm; **~ d'impôts** burden with taxes; **~ d'injures** heap insults upon.

accéder /aksede/ **14** *vi* **~ à** (lieu) reach; (pouvoir, trône) accede to; (requête) grant; (Ordinat) access; **~ à la propriété** become a homeowner.

accélérateur /akseleʀatœʀ/ *nm* accelerator.

accélérer /akseleʀe/ **14** *vt/i* accelerate. □ **s'~** *vpr* speed up.

accent /aksɑ̃/ *nm* accent; (sur une syllabe) stress, accent; **mettre l'~ sur** stress; **~ aigu/grave/circonflexe** acute/grave/circumflex accent.

accentuer /aksɑ̃tɥe/ **1** *vt* (lettre, syllabe) accent; (fig) emphasize, accentuate. □ **s'~** *vpr* become more pronounced, increase.

accepter /aksɛpte/ **1** *vt* accept; ~ **de faire** agree to do.

accès /aksɛ/ *nm* access; (porte) entrance; (de fièvre) bout; (de colère) fit; (d'enthousiasme) burst; (Ordinat) access; **les ~ de** (voies) the approaches to; **facile d'~** easy to get to.

accessoire /aksɛswaʀ/ *adj* secondary, incidental. ● *nm* accessory; (Théât) prop.

accident /aksidɑ̃/ *nm* accident; ~ **de train/d'avion** train/plane crash; **par ~** by accident. **accidenté, ~e** *adj* (*personne*) injured (in an accident); (*voiture*) damaged; (*terrain*) uneven, hilly. **accidentel, ~le** *adj* accidental.

acclamer /aklame/ **1** *vt* cheer, acclaim.

accommoder /akɔmɔde/ **1** *vt* adapt (à to); (cuisiner) prepare; (assaisonner) flavour. □ **s'~ de** *vpr* make the best of.

accompagnateur, -trice /akɔ̃paɲatœʀ, -tʀis/ *nm, f* (Mus) accompanist; (guide) guide; ~ **d'enfants** accompanying adult.

accompagner /akɔ̃paɲe/ **1** *vt* accompany. □ **s'~ de** *vpr* be accompanied by.

accomplir /akɔ̃pliʀ/ **2** *vt* carry out, fulfil. □ **s'~** *vpr* take place, happen; (*vœu*) be fulfilled.

accord /akɔʀ/ *nm* agreement; (harmonie) harmony; (Mus) chord; **être d'~** agree (**pour** to); **se mettre d'~** come to an agreement, agree; **d'~!** all right 🔲, OK!

accorder /akɔʀde/ **1** *vt* grant; (*couleurs*) match; (Mus) tune; (attribuer) (*valeur, importance*) assign. □ **s'~** *vpr* (se mettre d'accord) agree; (s'octroyer) allow oneself; **s'~ avec** (s'entendre avec) get on with.

accotement /akɔtmɑ̃/ *nm* verge; ~ **non stabilisé** soft verge.

accouchement /akuʃmɑ̃/ *nm* childbirth; (travail) labour.

accoucher /akuʃe/ **1** *vi* give birth (**de** to); (être en travail) be in labour. ● *vt* deliver. **accoucheur** *nm* **médecin ~** obstetrician.

accoudoir /akudwaʀ/ *nm* arm-rest.

accoupler /akuple/ **1** *vt* (Tech) couple. □ **s'~** *vpr* mate.

accourir /akuʀiʀ/ **20** *vi* run up.

accoutumance /akutymɑ̃s/ *nf* familiarization; (Méd) addiction.

accoutumer /akutyme/ **1** *vt* accustom. □ **s'~** *vpr* get accustomed.

accro /akʀo/ *nmf* 🔲 (drogué) addict; (amateur) fan.

accroc /akʀo/ *nm* tear, rip; (fig) hitch.

accrochage /akʀɔʃaʒ/ *nm* hanging; hooking; (Auto) collision; (dispute) clash; (Mil) encounter.

accrocher /akʀɔʃe/ **1** *vt* (suspendre) hang up; (attacher) hook, hitch; (déchirer) catch; (heurter) hit; (attirer) attract. □ **s'~** *vpr* cling, hang on (à to); (se disputer) clash.

accroissement /akʀwasmɑ̃/ *nm* increase (de in).

accroître /akʀwatʀ/ **24** *vt* increase. □ **s'~** *vpr* increase.

accroupir (s') /(s)akʀupiʀ/ **2** *vpr* squat.

accru, ~e /akʀy/ *adj* increased, greater.

accueil /akœj/ *nm* reception, welcome.

accueillant, ~e /akœjɑ̃, -t/ *adj* friendly, welcoming.

accueillir /akœjiʀ/ **25** *vt* receive, welcome; (*film, livre*) receive; (prendre en charge) (*réfugiés, patients*) take care of, cater for.

accumuler /akymyle/ **1** *vt* (*énergie*) store up; (*capital*) accumulate. □ **s'~** *vpr* (*neige, ordures*) pile up; (*dettes*) accrue.

accusation /akyzasjɔ̃/ *nf* accusation; (Jur) charge; **l'~** (magistrat) the prosecution.

accusé, ~e /akyze/ *adj* marked. ● *nm, f* defendant, accused.

accuser /akyze/ **1** *vt* accuse (**de** of); (blâmer) blame (**de** for); (Jur) charge (**de** with); (fig) emphasize; ~ **réception de** acknowledge receipt of.

acharné, ~e /aʃaʀne/ *adj* relentless, ferocious. **acharnement** *nm* (énergie) furious energy; (ténacité) determination.

acharner (s') /(s)aʃaʀne/ **1** *vpr* persevere; **s'~ sur** set upon; (poursuivre) hound; **s'~ à faire** (s'évertuer) try desperately; (s'obstiner) keep on doing.

achat /aʃa/ nm purchase; ~s shopping; **faire l'**~ **de** buy; **faire des** ~s do some shopping.

acheminer /aʃ(ə)mine/ **1** vt dispatch, convey; (*courrier*) handle. □ **s'**~ **vers** vpr head for.

acheter /aʃ(ə)te/ **6** vt buy; ~ **qch à qn** (pour lui) buy sth for sb; (chez lui) buy sth from sb. **acheteur, -euse** nm, f buyer; (client de magasin) shopper.

achèvement /aʃɛvmɑ̃/ nm completion.

achever /aʃ(ə)ve/ **6** vt finish (off). □ **s'**~ vpr end.

acide /asid/ adj acid, sharp. ● nm acid.

acier /asje/ nm steel.

acné /akne/ nf acne.

acompte /akɔ̃t/ nm deposit, part-payment.

à-côté (pl ~s) /akote/ nm side issue; ~s (argent) extras.

acoustique /akustik/ nf acoustics (+ sg). ● adj acoustic.

acquéreur /akerœr/ nm purchaser, buyer.

acquérir /akerir/ **7** vt acquire, gain; (*biens*) purchase, acquire.

acquis, ~e /aki, -z/ adj acquired; (*fait*) established; **tenir qch pour** ~ take sth for granted. ● nm experience. **acquisition** nf acquisition; purchase.

acquitter /akite/ **1** vt acquit; (*dette*) settle. □ **s'**~ **de** vpr (*promesse*) fulfil; (*devoir*) discharge.

âcre /ɑkr/ adj acrid.

acrobatie /akrɔbasi/ nf acrobatics (+ pl); ~ **aérienne** aerobatics (+ pl).

acte /akt/ nm act, action, deed; (Théât) act; (Jur) deed; ~ **de naissance/mariage** birth/marriage certificate; ~s (compte rendu) proceedings; **prendre** ~ **de** note.

acteur /aktœr/ nm actor.

actif, -ive /aktif, -v/ adj active; (*population*) working. ● nm (Comm) assets; **avoir à son** ~ have to one's credit ou name.

action /aksjɔ̃/ nf action; (Comm) share; (Jur) action; (effet) effect; (initiative) initiative. **actionnaire** nmf shareholder.

activer /aktive/ **1** vt speed up; (*feu*) boost. ● **s'**~ vpr hurry up; (s'affairer) be very busy.

activité /aktivite/ nf activity; **en** ~ (*volcan*) active; (*fonctionnaire*) working; (*usine*) in operation.

actrice /aktris/ nf actress.

actualité /aktʃalite/ nf topicality; **l'**~ current affairs; **les** ~s news; **d'**~ topical.

actuel, ~le /aktʃɛl/ adj current, present; (d'actualité) topical. **actuellement** adv currently, at the present time.

acupuncture /akypɔ̃ktyr/ nf acupuncture.

adaptateur /adaptatœr/ nm (Électr) adapter.

adapter /adapte/ **1** vt adapt; (fixer) fit. □ **s'**~ vpr adapt (oneself); (Tech) fit.

additif /aditif/ nm (note) rider; (substance) additive.

addition /adisjɔ̃/ nf addition; (au café) bill; (US) check. **additionner** **1** vt add; (totaliser) add (up).

adepte /adɛpt/ nmf follower; (d'activité) enthusiast.

adéquat, ~e /adekwa, -t/ adj suitable; (suffisant) adequate.

adhérent, ~e /aderɑ̃, -t/ nm, f member.

adhérer /adere/ **14** vi adhere, stick (à to); ~ **à** (club) be a member of; (s'inscrire à) join.

adhésif, -ive /adezif, -v/ adj adhesive; **ruban** ~ sticky tape.

adhésion /adezjɔ̃/ nf membership; (soutien) support.

adieu (pl ~x) /adjø/ interj & nm goodbye, farewell.

adjectif /adʒɛktif/ nm adjective.

adjoint, ~e /adʒwɛ̃, -t/ nm, f assistant; ~ **au maire** deputy mayor. ● adj assistant.

adjuger /adʒyʒe/ **40** vt award; (aux enchères) auction. □ **s'**~ vpr take (for oneself).

ADM abrév fpl (armes de destruction massive) WMD.

admettre /admɛtr/ **42** vt let in, admit; (tolérer) allow; (reconnaître) admit, acknowledge; (candidat) pass.

administrateur, -trice /administratœr, -tris/ nm, f administrator, director; (Jur) trustee; ~ **de site Internet** Webmaster.

administratif, -ive /administʀatif, -v/ adj administrative; (*document*) official. **administration** nf administration; (*gestion*) management; **l'A**~ Civil Service.

administrer /administʀe/ **1** vt run, manage; (*justice, biens, antidote*) administer.

admirateur, -trice /admiʀatœʀ, -tʀis/ nm, f admirer.

admiration /admiʀasjɔ̃/ nf admiration.

admirer /admiʀe/ **1** vt admire.

admission /admisjɔ̃/ nf admission.

ADN abrév m (**acide désoxyribonucléique**) DNA.

adolescence /adɔlesɑ̃s/ nf adolescence. **adolescent, ~e** nm, f adolescent, teenager.

adopter /adɔpte/ **1** vt adopt. **adoptif, -ive** adj (*enfant*) adopted; (*parents*) adoptive.

adorer /adɔʀe/ **1** vt love; (*plus fort*) adore; (*Relig*) worship, adore.

adosser /adɔse/ **1** vt lean (**à, contre** against). □ **s'**~ vpr lean back (**à, contre** against).

adoucir /adusiʀ/ **2** vt soften; (*boisson*) sweeten; (*chagrin*) ease. □ **s'**~ vpr soften; (*chagrin*) ease; (*temps*) become milder. **adoucissant** nm (fabric) softener.

adresse /adʀɛs/ nf address; (*habileté*) skill; ~ **électronique** email address.

adresser /adʀese/ **1** vt send; (*écrire l'adresse sur*) address; (*remarque*) address; ~ **la parole à** speak to. □ **s'**~ **à** address; (*aller voir*) (*personne*) go and ask ou see; (*bureau*) enquire at; (*viser, intéresser*) be directed at.

adroit, ~e /adʀwa, -t/ adj skilful, clever.

ADSL abrév m (asymmetrical digital subscriber line) ADSL.

adulte /adylt/ nmf adult. ● adj adult; (*plante, animal*) fully grown.

adultère /adyltɛʀ/ adj adulterous. ● nm adultery.

adverbe /advɛʀb/ nm adverb.

adversaire /advɛʀsɛʀ/ nmf opponent, adversary.

aérer /aeʀe/ **1** vt air; (*texte*) space out. □ **s'**~ vpr get some air.

aérien, ~ne /aeʀjɛ̃, -jɛn/ adj air; (*photo*) aerial; (*câble*) overhead.

aérobic /aeʀɔbik/ nm aerobics (+ sg).

aérogare /aeʀɔgaʀ/ nf air terminal.

aéroglisseur /aeʀɔglisœʀ/ nm hovercraft.

aérogramme /aeʀɔgʀam/ nm airmail letter; (US) aerogram.

aéronautique /aeʀɔnotik/ adj aeronautical. ● nf aeronautics (+ sg).

aéroport /aeʀɔpɔʀ/ nm airport.

aérospatial, ~e (mpl **-iaux**) /aeʀɔspasjal, -jo/ adj aerospace.

affaiblir /afebliʀ/ **2** vt weaken. □ **s'**~ vpr get weaker.

affaire /afɛʀ/ nf affair, matter; (Jur) case; (*histoire, aventure*) affair; (*occasion*) bargain; (*entreprise*) business; (*transaction*) deal; (*question, problème*) matter; ~**s** (Comm) business; (Pol) affairs; (*problèmes personnels*) business; (*effets personnels*) things; **c'est mon** ~ that's my business; **avoir** ~ **à** deal with; **ça fera l'**~ that will do the job; **ça fera leur** ~ that's just what they need; **tirer qn d'**~ help sb out of a tight spot; **se tirer d'**~ get out of trouble.

affairé, ~e /afeʀe/ adj busy.

affaisser (s') /(s)afese/ **1** vpr (*terrain, route*) sink, subside; (*poutre*) sag; (*personne*) collapse.

affamé, ~e /afame/ adj starving.

affectation /afɛktasjɔ̃/ nf (nomination) (à une fonction) appointment; (dans un lieu) posting; (de matériel, d'argent) allocation; (comportement) affectation.

affecter /afɛkte/ **1** vt (feindre) affect; (toucher, affliger) affect; (destiner) assign; (nommer) appoint, post.

affectif, -ive /afɛktif, -v/ adj emotional.

affection /afɛksjɔ̃/ nf affection; (maladie) complaint.

affectueux, -euse /afɛktɥø, -z/ adj affectionate.

affichage /afiʃaʒ/ nm billposting; (électronique) display.

affiche /afiʃ/ nf (public) notice; (publicité) poster; (Théât) bill; **être à l'**~ (*film*) be showing; (*pièce*) be on.

afficher /afiʃe/ **1** vt (annonce) put up; (événement) announce; (sentiment) dis-

affirmatif | ai

a

play; (Ordinat) display.

affirmatif, -ive /afiʀmatif, -v/ *adj* affirmative. **affirmation** *nf* assertion.

affirmer /afiʀme/ **1** *vt* assert; (soutenir) maintain.

affligé, ~e /afliʒe/ *adj* distressed; ~ **de** afflicted with.

affluer /aflye/ **1** *vi* flood in; (*sang*) rush.

affolant, ~e /afɔlɑ̃, -t/ *adj* alarming.

affoler /afɔle/ **1** *vt* throw into a panic. □ **s'~** *vpr* panic.

affranchir /afʀɑ̃ʃiʀ/ **2** *vt* stamp; (à la machine) frank; (*esclave*) emancipate; (fig) free. **affranchissement** *nm* (tarif) postage.

affreux, -euse /afʀø, -z/ *adj* (laid) hideous; (mauvais) awful.

affrontement /afʀɔ̃tmɑ̃/ *nm* confrontation.

affronter /afʀɔ̃te/ **1** *vt* confront. □ **s'~** *vpr* confront each other.

affûter /afyte/ **1** *vt* sharpen.

afin /afɛ̃/ *prép & conj* ~ **de faire** in order to do; ~ **que** so that.

africain, ~e /afʀikɛ̃, -ɛn/ *adj* African. **A~, ~e** *nm, f* African.

Afrique /afʀik/ *nf* Africa. ~ **du Sud** South Africa.

agacer /agase/ **10** *vt* irritate, annoy.

âge /aʒ/ *nm* age; (vieillesse) (old) age; **quel ~ avez-vous?** how old are you?; ~ **adulte** adulthood; ~ **mûr** maturity; **d'un certain ~** middle-aged.

âgé, ~e /aʒe/ *adj* elderly; ~ **de cinq ans** five years old.

agence /aʒɑ̃s/ *nf* agency, bureau, office; (succursale) branch; ~ **d'interim** employment agency; ~ **de voyages** travel agency; ~ **publicitaire** advertising agency.

agenda /aʒɛ̃da/ *nm* diary; ~ **électronique** electronic organizer.

agent /aʒɑ̃/ *nm* agent; (fonctionnaire) official; ~ **(de police)** policeman; ~ **de change** stockbroker; ~ **commercial** sales representative.

agglomération /aglɔmeʀasjɔ̃/ *nf* town, built-up area.

aggraver /agʀave/ **1** *vt* aggravate, make worse. □ **s'~** *vpr* get worse.

agile /aʒil/ *adj* agile, nimble.

agir /aʒiʀ/ **2** *vi* act; (se comporter) behave; (avoir un effet) work, take effect. □ **s'~ de** *vpr* (être nécessaire) **il s'agit de faire** we/you *etc.* must do; (être question de) **il s'agit de faire** it is a matter of doing; **dans ce livre il s'agit de** this book is about; **dont il s'agit** in question; **il s'agit de ton fils** it's about your son; **de quoi s'agit-il?** what is it about?

agitation /aʒitasjɔ̃/ *nf* bustle; (trouble) agitation; (malaise social) unrest.

agité, ~e /aʒite/ *adj* restless, fidgety; (troublé) agitated; (mer) rough.

agiter /aʒite/ **1** *vt* (bras, mouchoir) wave; (liquide, boîte) shake; (troubler) agitate; (discuter) debate. □ **s'~** *vpr* bustle about; (enfant) fidget; (foule, pensées) stir.

agneau (*pl* ~**x**) /aɲo/ *nm* lamb.

agrafe /agʀaf/ *nf* hook; (pour papiers) staple. **agrafeuse** *nf* stapler.

agrandir /agʀɑ̃diʀ/ **2** *vt* enlarge; (maison) extend. □ **s'~** *vpr* expand, grow. **agrandissement** *nm* extension; (de photo) enlargement.

agréable /agʀeabl/ *adj* pleasant.

agréé, ~e /agʀee/ *adj* (agence) authorized; (nourrice, médecin) registered; (matériel) approved.

agréer /agʀee/ **15** *vt* accept; ~ **à** please; **veuillez ~, Monsieur, mes salutations distinguées** (personne non nommée) yours faithfully; (personne nommée) yours sincerely.

agrégation /agʀegasjɔ̃/ *nf highest examination for recruitment of teachers.* **agrégé, ~e** *nm, f* teacher (*who has passed the agrégation*).

agrément /agʀemɑ̃/ *nm* charm; (plaisir) pleasure; (accord) assent.

agresser /agʀese/ **1** *vt* attack; (pour voler) mug.

agressif, -ive /agʀesif, -v/ *adj* aggressive. **agression** *nf* attack; (pour voler) mugging; (Mil) aggression.

agricole /agʀikɔl/ *adj* agricultural; (ouvrier, produit) farm. **agriculteur, -trice** *nm, f* farmer. **agriculture** *nf* agriculture, farming.

agripper /agʀipe/ **1** *vt* grab. □ **s'~** *vpr* cling (à to).

agroalimentaire /agʀɔalimɑ̃tɛʀ/ *nm* food industry.

agrumes /agʀym/ *nmpl* citrus fruit(s).

ai /e/ →**avoir** **5**.

aide /ɛd/ nf help, assistance; (en argent) aid; **à l'~ de** with the help of; **venir en ~** à help; **~ à domicile** carer, home help; **~ familiale** mother's help; **~ sociale** social security; (US) welfare. ● nmf assistant. **aide-éducateur, -trice** nm, f classroom assistant. **aide-mémoire** nm inv handbook of key facts.

aider /ede/ **1** vt/i help, assist; (subventionner) aid, give aid to; **~ à faire** help to do. □ **s'~ de** vpr use.

aïeul, **~e** /ajœl/ nm, f grandparent.

aigle /ɛgl/ nm eagle.

aigre /ɛgʀ/ adj sour, sharp; (fig) sharp.

aigrir /egʀiʀ/ **2** vt embitter. □ **s'~** vpr turn sour; (personne) become embittered.

aigu, ~ë /egy/ adj (douleur, problème) acute; (objet) sharp; (voix) shrill; (Mus) high(-pitched); (accent) acute.

aiguille /egɥij/ nf needle; (de montre) hand; (de balance) pointer; **~ à tricoter** knitting needle.

aiguilleur /egɥijœʀ/ nm pointsman; **~ du ciel** air traffic controller.

aiguiser /eg(ɥ)ize/ **1** vt sharpen; (fig) stimulate.

ail (pl **~s** ou **aulx**) /aj, o/ nm garlic.

aile /ɛl/ nf wing.

ailier /elje/ nm winger; (US) end.

aille /aj/ →ALLER **8**.

ailleurs /ajœʀ/ adv elsewhere, somewhere else; **d'~** besides, moreover; **nulle part ~** nowhere else; **par ~** moreover, furthermore; **partout ~** everywhere else.

aimable /ɛmabl/ adj kind.

aimant /ɛmɑ̃/ nm magnet.

aimer /eme/ **1** vt like; (d'amour) love; **j'aimerais faire** I'd like to do; **~ bien** quite like; **~ mieux** ou **autant** prefer.

aîné, ~e /ene/ adj eldest; (de deux) elder. ● nm, f eldest (child); (premier de deux) elder (child); **~s** elders; **il est mon ~** he is older than me ou my senior.

ainsi /ɛ̃si/ adv like this, thus; (donc) so; **et ~ de suite** and so on; **pour ~ dire** so to speak, as it were; **~ que** as well as; (comme) as.

air /ɛʀ/ nm air; (mine) look, air; (mélodie) tune; **~ conditionné** air-conditioning; **avoir l'~** look, appear;

avoir l'~ de look like; **avoir l'~ de faire** appear to be doing; **en l'~** (up) in the air; (promesses) empty; **prendre l'~** get some fresh air.

aire /ɛʀ/ nf area; **~ d'atterrissage** landing-strip; **~ de pique-nique** picnic area; **~ de repas** rest area; **~ de services** (motorway) services.

aisance /ɛzɑ̃s/ nf ease; (richesse) affluence.

aise /ɛz/ nf joy; **à l'~** (sur un siège) comfortable; (pas gêné) at ease; (fortuné) comfortably off; **mal à l'~** uncomfortable; ill at ease; **aimer ses ~s** like one's creature comforts; **mettre qn à l'~** put sb at ease; **se mettre à l'~** make oneself comfortable.

aisé, ~e /eze/ adj easy; (fortuné) well-off.

aisselle /ɛsɛl/ nf armpit.

ait /ɛ/ →AVOIR **5**.

ajourner /aʒuʀne/ **1** vt postpone; (débat, procès) adjourn.

ajout /aʒu/ nm addition.

ajouter /aʒute/ **1** vt add (à to); **~ foi à** lend credence to. □ **s'~** vpr be added.

ajuster /aʒyste/ **1** vt adjust; (cible) aim at; (adapter) fit; **~ son coup** adjust one's aim.

alarme /alaʀm/ nf alarm; **donner l'~** raise the alarm.

alarmer /alaʀme/ **1** vt alarm. □ **s'~** vpr become alarmed (de at).

Albanie /albani/ nf Albania.

alcool /alkɔl/ nm alcohol; (eau de vie) brandy; **~ à brûler** methylated spirit. **alcoolique** adj & nmf alcoholic. **alcoolisé, ~e** adj (boisson) alcoholic. **alcoolisme** nm alcoholism.

alcootest /alkɔtɛst/ nm breath test; (appareil) Breathalyser®.

aléa /alea/ nm hazard. **aléatoire** adj unpredictable, uncertain; (Ordinat) random.

alentours /alɑ̃tuʀ/ nmpl surroundings; **aux ~ de** (de lieu) around; (de chiffre, date) about, around.

alerte /alɛʀt/ adj (personne) alert; (vif) lively. ● nf alert; **~ à la bombe** bomb scare. **alerter 1** vt alert.

algèbre /alʒɛbʀ/ nf algebra.

Algérie /alʒeʀi/ nf Algeria.

a

algue /alg/ *nf* seaweed; **les** ~**s** (Bot) algae.

aliéné, ~e /aljene/ *nm, f* insane person.

aliéner /aljene/ **14** *vt* alienate; (céder) give up. □ **s'**~ *vpr* alienate.

aligner /alipe/ **1** *vt* (objets) line up, make lines of; (chiffres) string together; ~ **sur** bring into line with. □ **s'**~ *vpr* line up; **s'**~ **sur** align oneself on.

aliment /alimã/ *nm* food.

alimentaire /alimãtɛʀ/ *adj* (industrie) food; (habitudes) dietary; **produits** ~**s** foodstuffs.

alimentation /alimãtasjɔ̃/ *nf* feeding, supply(ing); (régime) diet; (aliments) food; **magasin d'**~ grocery shop *ou* store.

alimenter /alimãte/ **1** *vt* feed; (fournir) supply; (fig) sustain. □ **s'**~ *vpr* eat.

allaiter /alete/ **1** *vt* (bébé) breast-feed; (US) nurse; (animal) suckle.

allée /ale/ *nf* path, lane; (menant à une maison) drive(way); (dans un cinéma, magasin) aisle; (rue) road; ~**s et venues** comings and goings.

allégé, ~e /aleʒe/ *adj* diet; (beurre, yaourt) low-fat.

alléger /aleʒe/ **14 40** *vt* make lighter; (fardeau, chargement) lighten; (fig) (souffrance) alleviate.

allégresse /alegʀɛs/ *nf* gaiety, joy.

alléguer /alege/ **14** *vt* (exemple) invoke; (prétexter) allege.

Allemagne /almaɲ/ *nf* Germany.

allemand, ~e /almã, -d/ *adj* German. ● *nm* (Ling) German. **A~, ~e** *nm, f* German.

---

aller /ale/ **8**

● *verbe auxiliaire*

····▸ **je vais l'appeler** I'm going to call him; **j'allais partir** I was about to leave; **va savoir!** who knows?; ~ **en s'améliorant** be improving.

● *verbe intransitif*

····▸ (se déplacer) go; **allons-y!** let's go!; **allez!** come on!

····▸ (se porter) **comment allez-vous?, comment ça va?** how are you?; **ça va (bien)** I'm fine;

qu'est-ce qui ne va pas? what's the matter?; **ça ne va pas la tête?** 🛈 are you mad? 🛈.

····▸ (mettre en valeur) ~ **à qn** suit sb; **ça te va bien** it really suits you.

····▸ (convenir) **ça va ma coiffure?** is my hair OK?; **ça ne va pas du tout** that's no good at all.

□ **s'en aller** *verbe pronominal*

····▸ go; **va-t'en!** go away!; **ça ne s'en va pas** (tache) it won't come out.

● *nom masculin*

····▸ outward journey; ~ **(simple)** single (ticket); (US) one-way (ticket); ~ **retour** return (ticket); (US) round trip (ticket); **à l'**~ on the way out.

---

allergie /alɛʀʒi/ *nf* allergy. **allergique** *adj* allergic (**à** to).

alliance /aljãs/ *nf* alliance; (bague) wedding-ring; (mariage) marriage.

allier /alje/ **45** *vt* combine; (Pol) ally. □ **s'**~ *vpr* combine; (Pol) form an alliance; (famille) become related (**à** to).

allô /alo/ *interj* hallo, hello.

allocation /alɔkasjɔ̃/ *nf* allowance; ~ **chômage** unemployment benefit; ~**s familiales** family allowance.

allonger /alɔ̃ʒe/ **40** *vt* lengthen; (bras, jambe) stretch (out); (coucher) lay down. □ **s'**~ *vpr* get longer; (s'étendre) lie down; (s'étirer) stretch (oneself) out.

allouer /alwe/ **1** *vt* allocate; (prêt) grant.

allumer /alyme/ **1** *vt* (bougie, gaz) light; (lampe, appareil) turn on; (pièce) switch the light(s) on in; (fig) arouse. □ **s'**~ *vpr* (lumière, appareil) come on.

allumette /alymɛt/ *nf* match.

allure /alyʀ/ *nf* speed, pace; (démarche) walk; (apparence) appearance; **à toute** ~ at full speed; **avoir de l'**~ have style; **avoir des** ~**s de** look like; **avoir une drôle d'**~ be funny-looking.

allusion /alyzjɔ̃/ *nf* allusion (**à** to); (implicite) hint (**à** at); **faire** ~ **à** allude to; hint at.

alors /alɔʀ/ *adv* (à ce moment-là) then; (de ce fait) so; (dans ce cas-là) then; **ça** ~**!** well!; **et** ~**?** so what? ● *conj* ~

que (pendant que) while; (tandis que) when, whereas.

alouette /alwɛt/ nf lark.

alourdir /aluʀdiʀ/ **2** vt weigh down; (rendre plus important) increase.

aloyau (pl ~x) /alwajo/ nm sirloin.

Alpes /alp/ nfpl les ~ the Alps.

alphabet /alfabɛ/ nm alphabet. **alphabétique** adj alphabetical.

alphabétiser /alfabetize/ **1** vt teach to read and write.

alpinist /alpinist/ nmf mountaineer.

altérer /alteʀe/ **14** vt (fait, texte) distort; (abîmer) spoil; (donner soif à) make thirsty. □ **s'~** vpr deteriorate.

alternance /altɛʀnɑ̃s/ nf alternation; en ~ alternately.

altitude /altityd/ nf altitude, height.

amabilité /amabilite/ nf kindness.

amaigrir /amegʀiʀ/ **2** vt make thin(ner).

amande /amɑ̃d/ nf almond; (d'un fruit à noyau) kernel.

amant /amɑ̃/ nm lover.

amarre /amaʀ/ nf (mooring) rope; ~s moorings.

amas /amɑ/ nm heap, pile.

amasser /amɑse/ **1** vt amass, gather; (empiler) pile up. □ **s'~** vpr pile up; (gens) gather.

amateur /amatœʀ/ nm amateur; ~ de lover of; **d'~** amateur; (péj) amateurish.

ambassade /ɑ̃basad/ nf embassy. **ambassadeur, -drice** nm, f ambassador.

ambiance /ɑ̃bjɑ̃s/ nf atmosphere. **ambiant, ~e** adj surrounding.

ambigu, ~ë /ɑ̃bigy/ adj ambiguous.

ambitieux, -ieuse /ɑ̃bisjø, -z/ adj ambitious. **ambition** nf ambition.

ambulance /ɑ̃bylɑ̃s/ nf ambulance.

ambulant, ~e /ɑ̃bylɑ̃, -t/ adj itinerant, travelling.

âme /ɑm/ nf soul; ~ **sœur** soul mate.

amélioration /ameljɔʀasjɔ̃/ nf improvement.

améliorer /ameljɔʀe/ **1** vt improve. □ **s'~** vpr improve.

aménagement /amenaʒmɑ̃/ nm (de magasin) fitting out; (de grenier) conversion; (de territoire) development; (de cuisine) equipping.

aménager /amenaʒe/ **40** vt (magasin) fit out; (transformer) convert; (territoire) develop; (cuisine) equip.

amende /amɑ̃d/ nf fine; **faire ~ honorable** make amends.

amener /am(ə)ne/ **6** vt bring; (causer) bring about; ~ **qn à faire** cause sb to do. □ **s'~** vpr **1** turn up.

amer, -ère /amɛʀ/ adj bitter.

américain, ~e /ameʀikɛ̃, -ɛn/ adj American. **A~, ~e** nm, f American.

Amérique /ameʀik/ nf America; ~ **centrale/latine** Central/Latin America; ~ **du Nord/Sud** North/South America.

amertume /amɛʀtym/ nf bitterness.

ami, ~e /ami/ nm, f friend; (amateur) lover; **un ~ des bêtes** an animal lover. ● adj friendly.

amiable /amjabl/ adj amicable; **à l'~** (divorcer) by mutual consent; (se séparer) on friendly terms; (séparation) amicable.

amical, ~e (mpl **-aux**) /amikal, -o/ adj friendly.

amiral (pl **-aux**) /amiʀal, -o/ nm admiral.

amitié /amitje/ nf friendship; ~s (en fin de lettre) kind regards; **prendre qn en ~** take a liking to sb.

amnistie /amnisti/ nf amnesty.

amoindrir /amwɛ̃dʀiʀ/ **2** vt reduce.

amont: en ~ /ɑ̃amɔ̃/ loc upstream.

amorcer /amɔʀse/ **10** vt start; (hameçon) bait; (pompe) prime; (arme à feu) arm.

amortir /amɔʀtiʀ/ **2** vt (choc) cushion; (bruit) deaden; (dette) pay off; ~ **un achat** make a purchase pay for itself.

amortisseur /amɔʀtisœʀ/ nm shock absorber.

amour /amuʀ/ nm love; **pour l'~ de** for the sake of.

amoureux, -euse /amuʀø, -z/ adj (personne) in love; (relation, regard) loving; (vie) love; ~ **de qn** in love with sb. ● nm, f lover.

amour-propre /amuʀpʀɔpʀ/ nm self-esteem.

amphithéâtre /ɑ̃fiteatʀ/ nm amphitheatre; (d'université) lecture hall.

a

ampleur /ɑ̃plœʀ/ nf extent, size; (de vêtement) fullness; **prendre de l'~** spread, grow.

amplifier /ɑ̃plifje/ 45 vt amplify; (fig) expand, develop. □ s'~ vpr (son) grow; (scandale) intensify.

ampoule /ɑ̃pul/ nf (électrique) bulb; (sur la peau) blister; (Méd) phial, ampoule.

amusant, ~e /amyzɑ̃, -t/ adj (blague) funny; (soirée) enjoyable, entertaining.

amuse-gueule /amyzgœl/ nm inv cocktail snack.

amusement /amyzmɑ̃/ nm amusement; (passe-temps) entertainment.

amuser /amyze/ 1 vt amuse; (détourner l'attention de) distract. □ s'~ vpr enjoy oneself; (jouer) play.

amygdale /amidal/ nf tonsil.

an /ɑ̃/ nm year; **avoir dix ~s** be ten years old; **un garçon de deux ~s** a two-year-old boy; **à soixante ~s** at the age of sixty; **les moins de dix-huit ~s** under eighteens.

analogie /analɔʒi/ nf analogy.

analogue /analɔg/ adj similar, analogous (à to).

analphabète /analfabɛt/ adj & nmf illiterate.

analyse /analiz/ nf analysis; (Méd) test. **analyser** 1 vt analyse; (Méd) test.

ananas /anana(s)/ nm pineapple.

anarchie /anaʀʃi/ nf anarchy.

anatomie /anatɔmi/ nf anatomy.

ancêtre /ɑ̃sɛtʀ/ nm ancestor.

anchois /ɑ̃ʃwa/ nm anchovy.

ancien, ~ne /ɑ̃sjɛ̃, -jɛn/ adj old; (de jadis) ancient; (meuble) antique; (précédent) former, ex-, old; (dans une fonction) senior; **~ combattant** veteran. ● nm, f senior; (par l'âge) elder. **anciennement** adv formerly. **ancienneté** nf age, seniority.

ancre /ɑ̃kʀ/ nf anchor; **jeter/lever l'~** cast/weigh anchor.

andouille /ɑ̃duj/ nf sausage (filled with chitterlings); (idiot 🔲) fool; **faire l'~** fool around.

âne /ɑn/ nm donkey, ass; (imbécile 🔲) dimwit 🔲.

anéantir /aneɑ̃tiʀ/ 2 vt destroy; (exterminer) annihilate; (accabler) overwhelm.

anémie /anemi/ nf anaemia.

ânerie /ɑnʀi/ nf stupid remark.

anesthésie /anɛstezi/ nf (opération) anaesthetic.

ange /ɑ̃ʒ/ nm angel; **aux ~s** in seventh heaven.

angine /ɑ̃ʒin/ nf throat infection.

anglais, ~e /ɑ̃glɛ, -z/ adj English. ● nm (Ling) English. **A~, ~e** nm, f Englishman, Englishwoman.

angle /ɑ̃gl/ nm angle; (coin) corner.

Angleterre /ɑ̃glətɛʀ/ nf England.

anglophone /ɑ̃glɔfɔn/ adj English-speaking. ● nmf English speaker.

angoissant, ~e /ɑ̃gwasɑ̃, -t/ adj alarming; (effrayant) harrowing. **angoisse** /ɑ̃gwas/ nf anxiety. **angoissé, ~e** adj anxious. **angoisser** 1 vi worry.

animal (pl **-aux**) /animal, -o/ nm animal; **~ familier, ~ de compagnie** pet. ● adj (mpl **-aux**) animal.

animateur, -trice /animatœʀ, -tʀis/ nm, f organizer, leader; (TV) host, hostess.

animation /animasjɔ̃/ nf liveliness; (affairement) activity; (au cinéma) animation; (activité dirigée) organized activity.

animé, ~e /anime/ adj lively; (affairé) busy; (être) animate.

animer /anime/ 1 vt liven up; (débat, atelier) lead; (spectacle) host; (pousser) drive; (encourager) spur on. □ s'~ vpr liven up.

anis /ani(s)/ nm (Culin) aniseed; (Bot) anise.

anneau (pl **~x**) /ano/ nm ring; (de chaîne) link.

année /ane/ nf year; **~ bissextile** leap year; **~ civile** calendar year.

annexe /anɛks/ adj (document) attached; (question) related; (bâtiment) adjoining. ● nf (bâtiment) annexe; (US) annex; (document) appendix; (électronique) attachment. **annexer** 1 vt annex; (document) attach.

anniversaire /anivɛʀsɛʀ/ nm birthday; (d'un événement) anniversary. ● adj anniversary.

annonce /anɔ̃s/ nf announcement; (publicitaire) advertisement; (indice) sign.

annoncer /anɔ̃se/ **10** *vt* announce; (prédire) forecast; (être l'indice de) herald. □ **s'~** *vpr* (crise, tempête) be brewing; **s'~ bien/mal** look good/bad. **annonceur** *nm* advertiser.

annuaire /anɥɛʀ/ *nm* year-book; **~ (téléphonique)** (telephone) directory.

annuel, ~le /anɥɛl/ *adj* annual, yearly.

annulation /anylasjɔ̃/ *nf* cancellation; (de sanction, loi) repeal; (de mesure) abolition.

annuler /anyle/ **1** *vt* cancel; (contrat) nullify; (jugement) quash; (loi) repeal. □ **s'~** *vpr* cancel each other out.

anodin, ~e /anɔdɛ̃, -in/ *adj* insignificant; (sans risques) harmless, safe.

anonymat /anɔnima/ *nm* anonymity; **garder l'~** remain anonymous. **anonyme** *adj* anonymous.

anorexie /anɔʀɛksi/ *nf* anorexia.

anormal, ~e (*mpl* **-aux**) /anɔʀmal, -o/ *adj* abnormal.

anse /ɑ̃s/ *nf* handle; (baie) cove.

Antarctique /ɑ̃taʀktik/ *nm* Antarctic.

antenne /ɑ̃tɛn/ *nf* aerial; (US) antenna; (d'insecte) antenna; (succursale) agency; (Mil) outpost; **à l'~** on the air; **~ chirurgicale** mobile emergency unit; **~ parabolique** satellite dish.

antérieur, ~e /ɑ̃teʀjœʀ/ *adj* previous, earlier; (placé devant) front; **~ à** prior to.

antiaérien, ~ne /ɑ̃tiaeʀjɛ̃, -ɛn/ *adj* anti-aircraft; **abri ~** air-raid shelter.

antiatomique /ɑ̃tiatɔmik/ *adj* **abri ~** nuclear fall-out shelter.

antibiotique /ɑ̃tibjɔtik/ *nm* antibiotic.

anticipation /ɑ̃tisipasjɔ̃/ *nf* **d'~** (livre, film) science fiction; **par ~** in advance.

anticiper /ɑ̃tisipe/ **1** *vt* **~ (sur)** anticipate; (effectuer à l'avance) bring forward.

anticorps /ɑ̃tikɔʀ/ *nm* antibody.

antidater /ɑ̃tidate/ **1** *vt* backdate, antedate.

antigel /ɑ̃tiʒɛl/ *nm* antifreeze.

Antilles /ɑ̃tij/ *nfpl* **les ~** the West Indies.

antipathique /ɑ̃tipatik/ *adj* unpleasant.

antiquaire /ɑ̃tikɛʀ/ *nmf* antique dealer.

antiquité /ɑ̃tikite/ *nf* (objet) antique; **l'A~** antiquity.

antisémite /ɑ̃tisemit/ *adj* anti-Semitic.

antiseptique /ɑ̃tisɛptik/ *adj & nm* antiseptic.

antivirus /ɑ̃tiviʀys/ *nm inv* (Ordinat) antivirus software.

antivol /ɑ̃tivɔl/ *nm* anti-theft device; (Auto) steering lock.

anxiété /ɑ̃ksjete/ *nf* anxiety.

anxieux, -ieuse /ɑ̃ksjø, -z/ *adj* anxious. ● *nm, f* worrier.

août /u(t)/ *nm* August.

apaiser /apeze/ **1** *vt* calm down; (colère, militant) appease; (douleur) soothe; (faim) satisfy. □ **s'~** *vpr* (tempête) die down.

apathie /apati/ *nf* apathy. **apathique** *adj* apathetic.

apercevoir /apɛʀsəvwaʀ/ **52** *vt* see. □ **s'~ de** *vpr* notice; **s'~ que** notice *ou* realize that.

aperçu /apɛʀsy/ *nm* (échantillon) glimpse, taste; (intuition) insight.

apéritif /apeʀitif/ *nm* aperitif, drink.

aphte /aft/ *nm* mouth ulcer.

apitoyer /apitwaje/ **31** *vt* move (to pity). □ **s'~** *vpr* **s'~ sur (le sort de) qn** feel sorry for sb.

aplanir /aplaniʀ/ **2** *vt* level; (fig) iron out.

aplatir /aplatiʀ/ **2** *vt* flatten (out). □ **s'~** *vpr* (s'immobiliser) flatten oneself.

aplomb /aplɔ̃/ *nm* balance; (fig) self-confidence; **d'~** (en équilibre) steady; **je ne suis pas bien d'~** **1** I don't feel very well.

apogée /apɔʒe/ *nm* peak.

apologie /apɔlɔʒi/ *nf* panegyric.

apostrophe /apɔstʀɔf/ *nf* apostrophe; (remarque) remark.

apothéose /apɔteoz/ *nf* high point; (d'événement) grand finale.

apparaître /apaʀɛtʀ/ **18** *vi* appear; **il apparaît que** it appears that.

appareil /apaʀɛj/ *nm* device; (électrique) appliance; (Anat) system; (téléphone) phone; (avion) plane; (Culin) mixture; (système administratif) apparatus; **~ (dentaire)** brace; (dentier) dentures; **~ (photo)** camera; **c'est**

a

Gabriel à l'∼ it's Gabriel on the phone; **∼ auditif** hearing aid; **∼ électroménager** household electrical appliance.

appareiller /apaʀeje/ **1** vi (navire) cast off, put to sea.

apparemment /apaʀamɑ̃/ adv apparently.

apparence /apaʀɑ̃s/ nf appearance; **en ∼** outwardly; (apparemment) apparently.

apparent, ∼e /apaʀɑ̃, -t/ adj apparent; (visible) conspicuous.

apparenté, ∼e /apaʀɑ̃te/ adj related; (semblable) similar.

apparition /apaʀisjɔ̃/ nf appearance; (spectre) apparition.

appartement /apaʀtəmɑ̃/ nm flat; (US) apartment.

appartenir /apaʀtəniʀ/ **58** vi belong (**à** to); **il lui appartient de** it is up to him to.

appât /apɑ/ nm bait; (fig) lure.

appauvrir /apovʀiʀ/ **2** vt impoverish. □ **s'∼** vpr become impoverished.

appel /apɛl/ nm call; (Jur) appeal; (supplique) appeal, plea; (Mil) call-up; (US) draft; **faire ∼** appeal; **faire ∼ à** (recourir à) call on; (invoquer) appeal to; (évoquer) call up; (exiger) call for; **faire l'∼** (Scol) call the register; (Mil) take a roll-call; **∼ d'offres** (Comm) invitation to tender; **faire un ∼ de phares** flash one's headlights.

appeler /aple/ **38** vt call; (téléphoner) phone, call; (nécessiter) call for; **en ∼ à** appeal to; **appelé à** (destiné) destined for. □ **s'∼** vpr be called; **il s'appelle Tim** his name is Tim ou he is called Tim.

appellation /apɛlasjɔ̃/ nf name, designation.

appendice /apɛ̃dis/ nm appendix. **appendicite** nf appendicitis.

appesantir /apəzɑ̃tiʀ/ **2** vt weigh down. □ **s'∼** vpr grow heavier; **s'∼ sur** dwell upon.

appétissant, ∼e /apetisɑ̃, -t/ adj appetizing.

appétit /apeti/ nm appetite; **bon ∼!** enjoy your meal!

applaudir /aplodiʀ/ **2** vt/i applaud. **applaudissements** nmpl applause.

application /aplikasjɔ̃/ nf (soin) care; (de loi) (respect) application; (mise en œuvre) implementation; (Ordinat) application program.

appliqué, ∼e /aplike/ adj (travail) painstaking; (sciences) applied; (élève) hard-working.

appliquer /aplike/ **1** vt apply; (loi) enforce. □ **s'∼** vpr apply oneself (**à** to), take great care (**à faire** to do); **s'∼ à** (concerner) apply to.

appoint /apwɛ̃/ nm support; **d'∼** extra; **faire l'∼** give the correct money.

apport /apɔʀ/ nm contribution.

apporter /apɔʀte/ **1** vt bring; (aide, précision) give; (causer) bring about.

appréciation /apʀesjasjɔ̃/ nf estimate, evaluation; (de monnaie) appreciation; (jugement) assessment.

apprécier /apʀesje/ **45** vt appreciate; (évaluer) assess; (objet) value, appraise.

appréhender /apʀeɑ̃de/ **1** vt dread, fear; (arrêter) apprehend.

apprendre /apʀɑ̃dʀ/ **50** vt learn; (être informé de) hear, learn; (de façon indirecte) hear of; **∼ qch à qn** teach sb sth; (informer) tell sb sth; **∼ à faire** learn to do; **∼ à qn à faire** teach sb to do; **∼ que** learn that; (être informé) hear that.

apprenti, ∼e /apʀɑ̃ti/ nm, f apprentice. **apprentissage** nm apprenticeship; (d'un sujet) learning.

apprêter /apʀete/ **1** vt prepare; (bois) prime; (mur) size. □ **s'∼ à** vpr prepare to.

apprivoiser /apʀivwaze/ **1** vt tame.

approbation /apʀɔbasjɔ̃/ nf approval.

approchant, ∼e /apʀɔʃɑ̃, -t/ adj close, similar.

approcher /apʀɔʃe/ **1** vt (objet) move near(er) (**de** to); (personne) approach; **∼ de** get nearer ou closer to. ● vi approach. □ **s'∼ de** vpr approach, move near(er) to.

approfondir /apʀɔfɔ̃diʀ/ **2** vt deepen; (fig) (sujet) go into sth in depth; (connaissances) improve.

approprié, ∼e /apʀɔpʀije/ adj appropriate.

approprier (s') /(s)apʀɔpʀije/ **45** vpr appropriate.

approuver /apʀuve/ **1** *vt* approve; (trouver louable) approve of; (soutenir) agree with.

approvisionner /apʀovizjɔne/ **1** *vt* supply (**en** with); (*compte en banque*) pay money into. □ **s'~** *vpr* stock up.

approximatif, -ive /apʀɔksimatif, -v/ *adj* approximate.

appui /apɥi/ *nm* support; (de fenêtre) sill; (pour objet) rest; **à l'~ de** in support of; **prendre ~ sur** lean on.

appui-tête (*pl* **appuis-tête**) /apɥitɛt/ *nm* headrest.

appuyer /apɥije/ **31** *vt* lean, rest; (presser) press; (soutenir) support, back. ● *vi* **~ sur** press (on); (fig) stress. □ **s'~ sur** *vpr* lean on; (compter sur) rely on.

après /apʀɛ/ *prép* after; (au-delà de) after, beyond; **~ avoir fait** after doing; **~ tout** after all; **~ coup** after the event; **d'~** (selon) according to; (en imitant) from; (adapté de) based on. ● *adv* after(wards); (plus tard) later; **le bus d'~** the next bus. ● *conj* **~ qu'il est parti** after he left. **aprèsdemain** *adv* the day after tomorrow. **après-guerre** (*pl* **~s**) *nm ou f* postwar period. **après-midi** *nm ou f inv* afternoon. **après-rasage** (*pl* **~s**) *nm* aftershave. **après-shampooing** *nm* conditioner. **après-ski** *nm inv* moon boot. **après-vente** *adj inv* after-sales.

a priori /apʀijɔʀi/ *adv* (à première vue) offhand, on the face of it; (sans réfléchir) out of hand. ● *nm* preconception.

à-propos /apʀopo/ *nm* timing, timeliness; (fig) presence of mind.

apte /apt/ *adj* capable (**à** of); (ayant les qualités requises) suitable (**à** for); (en état) fit (**à** for).

aptitude /aptityd/ *nf* aptitude, ability.

aquarelle /akwaʀɛl/ *nf* water-colour.

aquatique /akwatik/ *adj* aquatic; (Sport) water.

arabe /aʀab/ *adj* Arab; (Ling) Arabic; (désert) Arabian. ● *nm* (Ling) Arabic. **A~** *nmf* Arab.

Arabie /aʀabi/ *nf* **~ Saoudite** Saudi Arabia.

arachide /aʀaʃid/ *nf* groundnut; **huile d'~** groundnut oil.

araignée /aʀeɲe/ *nf* spider.

arbitraire /aʀbitʀɛʀ/ *adj* arbitrary.

arbitre /aʀbitʀ/ *nm* referee; (au cricket, tennis) umpire; (expert) arbiter; (Jur) arbitrator. **arbitrer** **1** *vt* (*match*) referee, umpire; (Jur) arbitrate in.

arbre /aʀbʀ/ *nm* tree; (Tech) shaft.

arbuste /aʀbyst/ *nm* shrub.

arc /aʀk/ *nm* (arme) bow; (courbe) curve; (voûte) arch; **~ de cercle** arc of a circle.

arc-en-ciel (*pl* **arcs-en-ciel**) /aʀkɑ̃sjɛl/ *nm* rainbow.

arche /aʀʃ/ *nf* arch; **~ de Noé** Noah's ark.

archéologie /aʀkeɔlɔʒi/ *nf* archaeology.

archevêque /aʀʃəvɛk/ *nm* archbishop.

architecte /aʀʃitɛkt/ *nmf* architect. **architecture** *nf* architecture.

Arctique /aʀktik/ *nm* Arctic.

ardent, ~e /aʀdɑ̃, -t/ *adj* burning; (passionné) ardent; (foi) fervent. **ardeur** *nf* ardour; (chaleur) heat.

ardoise /aʀdwaz/ *nf* slate; **~ électronique** notepad computer.

arène /aʀɛn/ *nf* arena; **~s** amphitheatre; (pour corridas) bullring.

arête /aʀɛt/ *nf* (de poisson) bone; (bord) ridge.

argent /aʀʒɑ̃/ *nm* money; (métal) silver; **~ comptant** cash; **prendre pour ~ comptant** take at face value; **~ de poche** pocket money.

argenté, ~e /aʀʒɑ̃te/ *adj* silver(y); (métal) (silver-)plated.

argenterie /aʀʒɑ̃tʀi/ *nf* silverware.

Argentine /aʀʒɑ̃tin/ *nf* Argentina.

argile /aʀʒil/ *nf* clay.

argot /aʀgo/ *nm* slang.

argument /aʀgymɑ̃/ *nm* argument; **~ de vente** selling point. **argumenter** **1** *vi* argue.

aristocratie /aʀistɔkʀasi/ *nf* aristocracy.

arithmétique /aʀitmetik/ *nf* arithmetic. ● *adj* arithmetical.

armature /aʀmatyʀ/ *nf* framework; (de tente) frame.

arme /aʀm/ *nf* arm, weapon; **~ à feu** firearm; **~s** (blason) coat of arms; **~s**

a

de destruction massive weapons of mass destruction.

armée /aʀme/ *nf* army; ∼ **de l'air** Air Force; ∼ **de terre** Army.

armer /aʀme/ **1** *vt* arm; (*fusil*) cock; (*navire*) equip; (renforcer) reinforce; (Photo) wind on. □ **s'∼ de** *vpr* arm oneself with.

armoire /aʀmwaʀ/ *nf* cupboard; (penderie) wardrobe; (US) closet; ∼ **à pharmacie** medicine cabinet.

armure /aʀmyʀ/ *nf* armour.

arnaque /aʀnak/ *nf* **1** swindling; **c'est de l'∼** it's a swindle**1**.

arobas(e) /aʀɔbas, aʀɔbaz/ *nm* at sign.

aromate /aʀɔmat/ *nm* herb, spice.

aromatisé, ∼e /aʀɔmatize/ *adj* flavoured.

arôme /aʀom/ *nm* aroma; (additif) flavouring.

arpenter /aʀpɑ̃te/ **1** *vt* pace up and down; (*terrain*) survey.

arqué, ∼e /aʀke/ *adj* arched; (*jambes*) bandy.

arrache-pied: d'∼ /daʀaʃpje/ *loc* relentlessly.

arracher /aʀaʃe/ **1** *vt* pull out *ou* off; (*plante*) pull *ou* dig up; (*cheveux, page*) tear *ou* pull out; (par une explosion) blow off; ∼ **à** (enlever à) snatch from; (fig) force *ou* wrest from. □ **s'∼ qch** *vpr* fight over sth.

arranger /aʀɑ̃ʒe/ **40** *vt* arrange, fix up; (réparer) put right; (régler) sort out; (convenir à) suit. □ **s'∼** *vpr* (se mettre d'accord) come to an arrangement; (se débrouiller) manage (**pour** to).

arrestation /aʀɛstasjɔ̃/ *nf* arrest.

arrêt /aʀɛ/ *nm* stopping; (de combats) cessation; (de production) halt; (lieu) stop; (pause) pause; (Jur) ruling; **aux ∼s** (Mil) under arrest; **à l'∼** (véhicule) stationary; (*machine*) idle; **faire un ∼** (make a) stop; **sans ∼** (sans escale) nonstop; (sans interruption) constantly; ∼ **maladie** sick leave; ∼ **de travail** (grève) stoppage; (Méd) sick leave.

arrêté /aʀete/ *nm* order; ∼ **municipal** bylaw.

arrêter /aʀete/ **1** *vt* stop; (date) fix; (*appareil*) turn off; (renoncer à) give

up; (appréhender) arrest. ● *vi* stop. □ **s'∼** *vpr* stop; **s'∼ de faire** stop doing.

arrhes /aʀ/ *nfpl* deposit; **verser des ∼** pay a deposit.

arrière /aʀjɛʀ/ *adj inv* back, rear. ● *nm* back, rear; (football) back; **à l'∼** in *ou* at the back; **en ∼** behind; (marcher, tomber) backwards; **en ∼ de** behind. **arrière-boutique** (*pl* ∼s) *nf* back room (of the shop). **arrière-garde** (*pl* ∼s) *nf* rearguard. **arrière-goût** (*pl* ∼s) *nm* aftertaste. **arrière-grand-mère** (*pl* **arrière-grands-mères**) *nf* great-grandmother. **arrière-grand-père** (*pl* **arrière-grands-pères**) *nm* great-grandfather. **arrière-pays** *nm inv* backcountry. **arrière-pensée** (*pl* ∼s) *nf* ulterior motive. **arrière-plan** *nm* (*pl* ∼s) background.

arrimer /aʀime/ **1** *vt* secure; (*cargaison*) stow.

arrivage /aʀivaʒ/ *nm* consignment.

arrivée /aʀive/ *nf* arrival; (Sport) finish.

arriver /aʀive/ **1** *vi* (aux être) arrive, come; (réussir) succeed; (se produire) happen; ∼ **à** (atteindre) reach; ∼ **à faire** manage to do; **je n'arrive pas à faire** I can't do; **en ∼ à faire** get to the stage of doing; **il arrive que** it happens that; **il lui arrive de faire** he (sometimes) does.

arriviste /aʀivist/ *nmf* go-getter, self-seeker.

arrondir /aʀɔ̃diʀ/ **2** *vt* (make) round; (*somme*) round off. □ **s'∼** *vpr* become round(ed).

arrondissement /aʀɔ̃dismɑ̃/ *nm* district.

Arrondissement A subdivision of a *département*. Each *arrondissement* has a *sous-préfet* representing the state administration at local level. In Paris, Lyons and Marseilles, an *arrondissement* is a subdivision of the commune, and has its own *maire* and local council.

arroser /aʀoze/ **1** *vt* water; (*repas*) wash down (with a drink); (*rôti*) baste; (*victoire*) drink to. **arrosoir** *nm* watering can.

art /aʀ/ *nm* art; (don) knack (**de faire** of doing); **∼s et métiers** arts and crafts; **~s ménagers** home economics (+ *sg*).

artère /aʀtɛʀ/ *nf* artery; **(grande)** ~ main road.

arthrite /aʀtʀit/ *nf* arthritis.

arthrose /aʀtʀoz/ *nf* osteoarthritis.

artichaut /aʀtiʃo/ *nm* artichoke.

article /aʀtikl/ *nm* article; (Comm) item, article; **à l'~ de la mort** at death's door; **~ de fond** feature (article); **~s de voyage** travel goods.

articulation /aʀtikylasjɔ̃/ *nf* articulation; (Anat) joint.

articuler /aʀtikyle/ **1** *vt* articulate; (structurer) structure; (assembler) connect (**sur** to).

artificiel, ~le /aʀtifisjɛl/ *adj* artificial.

artisan /aʀtizɑ̃/ *nm* artisan, craftsman; **l'~ de** (fig) the architect of.

artisanal, ~e (*mpl* **~aux**) /aʀtizanal/ *adj* craft; (*méthode*) traditional; (*amateur*) home-made; **de fabrication ~e** hand-made, hand-crafted.

artiste /aʀtist/ *nmf* artist. **artistique** *adj* artistic.

as¹ /a/ ➞AVOIR **5**.

as² /as/ *nm* ace.

ascenseur /asɑ̃sœʀ/ *nm* lift; (US) elevator.

ascension /asɑ̃sjɔ̃/ *nf* ascent; **l'A~** Ascension.

aseptiser /asɛptize/ **1** *vt* disinfect; (stériliser) sterilize; **aseptisé** (péj) sanitized.

asiatique /azjatik/ *adj* Asian. **A~** *nmf* Asian.

Asie /azi/ *nf* Asia.

asile /azil/ *nm* refuge; (Pol) asylum; (pour malades, vieillards) home; **~ de nuit** night shelter.

aspect /aspɛ/ *nm* appearance; (facettes) aspect; (perspective) side; **à l'~ de** at the sight of.

asperge /aspɛʀʒ/ *nf* asparagus.

asperger /aspɛʀʒe/ **40** *vt* spray.

asphyxier /asfiksje/ **45** *vt* (personne) asphyxiate; (entreprise, réseau) paralyse. □ **s'~** *vpr* suffocate; gas oneself; (entreprise, réseau) become paralysed.

aspirateur /aspiʀatœʀ/ *nm* vacuum cleaner.

aspirer /aspiʀe/ **1** *vt* inhale; (liquide) suck up. ● *vi* **~ à** aspire to.

aspirine® /aspiʀin/ *nf* aspirin.

assainir /aseniʀ/ **2** *vt* clean up.

assaisonnement /asɛzɔnmɑ̃/ *nm* seasoning.

assassin /asasɛ̃/ *nm* murderer; (Pol) assassin. **assassiner** **1** *vt* murder; (Pol) assassinate.

assaut /aso/ *nm* assault, onslaught; **donner l'~ à, prendre d'~** storm.

assemblage /asɑ̃blaʒ/ *nm* assembly; (combinaison) collection; (Tech) joint.

assemblée /asɑ̃ble/ *nf* meeting; (gens réunis) gathering; (Pol) assembly.

Assemblée nationale The lower house of the French parliament, in which 577 *députés* are elected for a five-year term. *Députés* sit in parties in the semi-circular chamber, with the most left-wing to the extreme left and the most right-wing to the extreme right. The *Assemblée nationale* passes laws, votes on the Budget, and questions ministers.

assembler /asɑ̃ble/ **1** *vt* assemble, put together; (réunir) gather. □ **s'~** *vpr* gather, assemble.

asseoir /aswaʀ/ **9** *vt* sit (down), seat; (bébé, malade) sit up; (affermir) establish; (baser) base. □ **s'~** *vpr* sit (down).

assez /ase/ *adv* (suffisamment) enough; (plutôt) quite, fairly; **~ grand/rapide** big/fast enough (**pour** to); **~ de** enough; **j'en ai (~ de)** I've had enough (of).

assidu, ~e /asidy/ *adj* (zélé) assiduous; (régulier) regular; **~ auprès de** attentive to. **assiduité** *nf* assiduousness, regularity.

assiéger /asjeʒe/ **14** **40** *vt* besiege.

assiette /asjɛt/ *nf* plate; (équilibre) seat; **~ anglaise** assorted cold meats; **~ creuse/plate** soup-/ dinner-plate; **ne pas être dans son ~** feel out of sorts.

assigner /asiɲe/ **1** *vt* assign; (limite) fix.

assimilation /asimilasjɔ̃/ *nf* assimilation; (comparaison) likening, comparison.

assimiler /asimile/ **1** *vt* **~ à** liken to; (classer) class as. □ **s'~** *vpr* assimilate;

(être comparable) be comparable (à to).

assis, ~e /asi, -z/ *adj* sitting (down), seated. ● →ASSEOIR 9.

assise /asiz/ *nf* (base) foundation; ~s (tribunal) assizes; (congrès) conference, congress.

assistance /asistɑ̃s/ *nf* audience; (aide) assistance; **l'A~ (publique)** welfare services.

assistant, ~e /asistɑ̃, -t/ *nm, f* assistant; (Scol) foreign language assistant; ~s (spectateurs) members of the audience; **~e sociale** social worker; **~ personnel numérique** personal digital assistant, PDA.

assister /asiste/ 1 *vt* assist; **~ à** attend, be (present) at; (*accident*) witness; **assisté par ordinateur** computer-assisted.

association /asɔsjasjɔ̃/ *nf* association.

associé, ~e /asɔsje/ *nm, f* partner, associate. ● *adj* associate.

associer /asɔsje/ 45 *vt* associate; (mêler) combine (à with); **~ qn à** (*projet*) involve sb in; (*bénéfices*) give sb a share of. □ **s'~** *vpr* (*sociétés, personnes*) become associated, join forces (à with); (s'harmoniser) combine (à with); **s'~ à** (*joie, opinion de qn*) share; (*projet*) take part in.

assommer /asɔme/ 1 *vt* knock out; (*animal*) stun; (fig) overwhelm; (ennuyer 1) bore.

Assomption /asɔ̃psjɔ̃/ *nf* Assumption.

assortiment /asɔʀtimɑ̃/ *nm* assortment.

assortir /asɔʀtiʀ/ 2 *vt* match (à with, to); **~ de** accompany with. □ **s'~** *vpr* match; **s'~ à** qch match sth.

assoupir (s') /(s)asupiʀ/ 2 *vpr* doze off; (s'apaiser) subside.

assouplir /asupliʀ/ 2 *vt* make supple; (fig) make flexible.

assourdir /asuʀdiʀ/ 2 *vt* (*personne*) deafen; (*bruit*) muffle.

assouvir /asuviʀ/ 2 *vt* satisfy.

assujettir /asyʒetiʀ/ 2 *vt* subjugate, subdue; **~ à** subject to.

assumer /asyme/ 1 *vt* assume; (*coût*) meet; (accepter) come to terms with, accept.

assurance /asyʀɑ̃s/ *nf* (self-) assurance; (garantie) assurance; (contrat)

insurance; **~s sociales** social insurance; **~ automobile/maladie** car/health insurance.

assuré, ~e /asyʀe/ *adj* certain, assured; (sûr de soi) confident, assured. ● *nm, f* insured party.

assurer /asyʀe/ 1 *vt* ensure; (fournir) provide; (exécuter) carry out; (Comm) insure; (stabiliser) steady; (*frontières*) make secure; **~ à qn que** assure sb that; **~ qn de** assure sb of; **~ la gestion/défense de** manage/defend. □ **s'~** *vpr* take out insurance; **s'~ de/que** make sure of/that; **s'~ qch** (se procurer) secure sth. **assureur** *nm* insurer.

astérisque /asteʀisk/ *nm* asterisk.

asthmatique /asmatik/ *adj & nmf* asthmatic.

asthme /asm/ *nm* asthma.

asticot /astiko/ *nm* maggot.

astreindre /astʀɛ̃dʀ/ 22 *vt* **~ qn à qch** force sth on sb; **~ qn à faire** force sb to do.

astrologie /astʀɔlɔʒi/ *nf* astrology. **astrologue** *nmf* astrologer.

astronaute /astʀonot/ *nmf* astronaut.

astronomie /astʀonomi/ *nf* astronomy.

astuce /astys/ *nf* smartness; (truc) trick; (plaisanterie) wisecrack.

astucieux, -ieuse /astysjø, -z/ *adj* smart, clever.

atelier /atəlje/ *nm* (local) workshop; (de peintre) studio; (séance de travail) workshop.

athée /ate/ *nmf* atheist. ● *adj* atheistic.

athlète /atlɛt/ *nmf* athlete. **athlétisme** *nm* athletics.

Atlantique /atlɑ̃tik/ *nm* Atlantic (Ocean).

atmosphère /atmɔsfɛʀ/ *nf* atmosphere.

atomique /atɔmik/ *adj* atomic; (*énergie, centrale*) nuclear.

atomiseur /atɔmizœʀ/ *nm* spray.

atout /atu/ *nm* trump (card); (avantage) asset.

atroce /atʀɔs/ *adj* atrocious.

attabler (s') /(s)atable/ 1 *vpr* sit down at table.

attachant, ~e /ataʃɑ̃, -t/ *adj* charming.

attache /ataʃ/ *nf* (agrafe) fastener; (lien) tie.

attaché, ~e /ataʃe/ *adj* **être ~ à** (aimer) be attached to. ● *nm, f* (Pol) attaché.

attacher /ataʃe/ **1** *vt* tie (up); (ceinture, robe) fasten; (bicyclette) lock; **~ à** (attribuer à) attach to. ● *vi* (Culin) stick. □ **s'~** *vpr* fasten, do up; **s'~ à** (se lier à) become attached to; (se consacrer à) apply oneself to.

attaquant, ~e /atakɑ̃, -t/ *nm, f* attacker; (au football) striker; (au football américain) forward.

attaque /atak/ *nf* attack; **~ (cérébrale)** stroke; **il va en faire une ~** he'll have a fit; **~ à main armée** armed attack.

attaquer /atake/ **1** *vt* attack; (banque) raid. ● *vi* attack. □ **s'~ à** *vpr* attack; (problème, sujet) tackle.

attardé, ~e /atarde/ *adj* backward; (idées) outdated; (en retard) late.

attarder (s') /(s)atarde/ **1** *vpr* linger.

atteindre /atɛ̃dʀ/ **22** *vt* reach; (blesser) hit; (affecter) affect.

atteint, ~e /atɛ̃, -t/ *adj* **~ de** suffering from.

atteinte /atɛ̃t/ *nf* attack (à on); **porter ~ à** attack; (droit) infringe.

atteler /atle/ **38** *vt* (cheval) harness; (remorque) couple. □ **s'~ à** *vpr* get down to.

attelle /atɛl/ *nf* splint.

attenant, ~e /atnɑ̃, -t/ *adj* **~ (à)** adjoining.

attendant: en ~ /ɑ̃natɑ̃dɑ̃/ *loc* meanwhile.

attendre /atɑ̃dʀ/ **3** *vt* wait for; (bébé) expect; (être le sort de) await; (escompter) expect; **~ que qn fasse** wait for sb to do. ● *vi* wait; (au téléphone) hold. □ **s'~ à** *vpr* expect.

attendrir /atɑ̃dʀiʀ/ **2** *vt* move (to pity). □ **s'~** *vpr* be moved to pity.

attendu¹ /atɑ̃dy/ *prép* given, considering; **~ que** considering that.

attendu², ~e /atɑ̃dy/ *adj* (escompté) expected; (espéré) long-awaited.

attentat /atɑ̃ta/ *nm* assassination attempt; **~ (à la bombe)** (bomb) attack.

attente /atɑ̃t/ *nf* wait(ing); (espoir) expectations (+ *pl*).

attenter /atɑ̃te/ **1** *vi* **~ à** make an attempt on; (fig) violate.

attentif, -ive /atɑ̃tif, -v/ *adj* attentive; (scrupuleux) careful; **~ à** mindful of; (soucieux) careful of.

attention /atɑ̃sjɔ̃/ *nf* attention; (soin) care; **~ (à)!** watch out (for)!; **faire ~ à** (écouter) pay attention to; (prendre garde à) watch out for; (prendre soin de) take care of; **faire ~ à faire** be careful to do. **attentionné, ~e** *adj* considerate.

attentisme /atɑ̃tism/ *nm* wait-and-see policy.

atténuer /atenɥe/ **1** *vt* (violence) reduce; (critique) tone down; (douleur) ease; (faute) mitigate. □ **s'~** *vpr* subside.

atterrir /ateʀiʀ/ **2** *vi* land. **atterrissage** *nm* landing.

attestation /atɛstasjɔ̃/ *nf* certificate.

attester /atɛste/ **1** *vt* testify to; **~ que** testify that.

attirant, ~e /atiʀɑ̃, -t/ *adj* attractive.

attirer /atiʀe/ **1** *vt* draw, attract; (causer) bring. □ **s'~** *vpr* bring upon oneself; (amis) win.

attiser /atize/ **1** *vt* (feu) poke; (sentiment) stir up.

attitré, ~e /atitʀe/ *adj* accredited; (habituel) usual, regular.

attitude /atityd/ *nf* attitude; (maintien) bearing.

attraction /atʀaksjɔ̃/ *nf* attraction.

attrait /atʀɛ/ *nm* attraction.

attraper /atʀape/ **1** *vt* catch; (corde, main) catch hold of; (habitude, accent) pick up; (maladie) catch; **se faire ~** **1** get told off.

attrayant, ~e /atʀɛjɑ̃, -t/ *adj* attractive.

attribuer /atʀibɥe/ **1** *vt* allocate; (prix) award; (imputer) attribute. □ **s'~** *vpr* claim (for oneself). **attribution** *nf* awarding, allocation.

attrouper (s') /(s)atʀupe/ **1** *vpr* gather.

au /o/ ⇒**À**.

aubaine /obɛn/ *nf* godsend, opportunity.

aube /ob/ *nf* dawn, daybreak.

auberge /obɛʀʒ/ *nf* inn; **~ de jeunesse** youth hostel.

aubergine /obɛRʒin/ nf aubergine; (US) eggplant.

aucun, ∼e /okœ̃, okyn/ adj (dans une phrase négative) no, not any; (positif) any. ● pron (dans une phrase négative) none, not any; (positif) any; ∼ des deux neither of the two; d'∼s some. **aucunement** adv not at all, in no way.

audace /odas/ nf daring; (impudence) audacity.

audacieux, -ieuse /odasjø, -z/ adj daring.

au-delà /od(ə)la/ adv beyond. ● prép ∼ de beyond.

au-dessous /od(ə)su/ adv below. ● prép ∼ de below; (couvert par) under.

au-dessus /od(ə)sy/ adv above. ● prép ∼ de above.

au-devant /od(ə)vɑ̃/ prép aller ∼ de qn go to meet sb; aller ∼ des désirs de qn anticipate sb's wishes.

audience /odjɑ̃s/ nf audience; (d'un tribunal) hearing; (succès, attention) success.

audimat® /odimat/ nm l'∼ the TV ratings.

audiovisuel, ∼le /odjovizɥɛl/ adj audio-visual.

auditeur, -trice /oditœR, -tris/ nm, f listener.

audition /odisjɔ̃/ nf hearing; (Théât, Mus) audition.

auditoire /oditwaR/ nm audience.

augmentation /ogmɑ̃tasjɔ̃/ nf increase; ∼ (de salaire) (pay) rise; (US) raise.

augmenter /ogmɑ̃te/ **1** vt/i increase; (employé) give a pay rise ou raise to.

augure /ogyR/ nm (devin) oracle; être de bon/mauvais ∼ be a good/ bad sign.

aujourd'hui /oʒuRdɥi/ adv today.

auparavant /opaRavɑ̃/ adv (avant) before; (précédemment) previously; (en premier lieu) beforehand.

auprès /opRɛ/ prép ∼ de (à côté de) beside, next to; (comparé à) compared with; s'excuser/se plaindre ∼ de apologize/complain to.

auquel /okɛl/ ➡LEQUEL.

aura, aurait /oRa, oRɛ/ ➡AVOIR **5**.

aurore /oRɔR/ nf dawn.

aussi /osi/ adv (également) too, also, as well; (dans une comparaison) as; (si, tellement) so; ∼ bien que as well as. ● conj (donc) so, consequently.

aussitôt /osito/ adv immediately; ∼ que as soon as, the moment; ∼ arrivé as soon as he arrived.

austère /ostɛR/ adj austere.

Australie /ostRali/ nf Australia.

australien, ∼ne /ostRaljɛ̃, -ɛn/ adj Australian. A∼, ∼ne nm, f Australian.

autant /otɑ̃/ adv (travailler, manger) as much (que as); ∼ (de) (quantité) as much (que as); (nombre) as many (que as); (tant) so much, so many; ∼ faire one had better do; d'∼ plus que all the more than; en faire ∼ do the same; pour ∼ for all that.

autel /otɛl/ nm altar.

auteur /otœR/ nm author; l'∼ du crime the perpetrator of the crime.

authentifier /otɑ̃tifje/ **45** vt authenticate.

authentique /otɑ̃tik/ adj authentic.

auto /oto/ nf car; ∼ tamponneuse dodgem, bumper car.

autobus /otobys/ nm bus.

autocar /otokaR/ nm coach.

autochtone /otokton/ nmf native.

autocollant, ∼e /otokolɑ̃, -t/ adj self-adhesive. ● nm sticker.

autodidacte /otodidakt/ nmf self-taught person.

auto-école (pl ∼s) /otoekɔl/ nf driving school.

automate /otomat/ nm automaton, robot.

automatique /otomatik/ adj automatic.

automatisation /otomatizasjɔ̃/ nf automation.

automne /oton/ nm autumn; (US) fall.

automobile /otomobil/ adj motor, car; (US) automobile. ● nf (motor) car; l'∼ the motor industry; (Sport) motoring. **automobiliste** nmf motorist.

autonome /otonom/ adj autonomous; (Ordinat) stand-alone.

autoradio /otoRadjo/ nm car radio.

autorisation /otoRizasjɔ̃/ nf permission, authorization; (permis) permit.

autorisé, ∼e /otoRize/ adj (opinions) authoritative; (approuvé) authorized.

autoriser /otɔRize/ **1** vt authorize, permit; (rendre possible) allow (of); (donner un droit) ~ qn à faire entitle sb to do.

autoritaire /otɔRitɛR/ adj authoritarian.

autorité /otɔRite/ nf authority; **faire ~** be authoritative.

autoroute /otɔRut/ nf motorway; (US) highway; **~ de l'information** (Ordinat) information superhighway.

auto-stop /otɔstɔp/ nm hitch-hiking; **faire de l'~** hitch-hike; **prendre qn en ~** give a lift to sb.

autour /otuR/ adv around; **tout ~** all around. ● prép **~ de** around.

autre /otR/ adj other; **un ~ jour/livre** another day/book; **~ chose/part** something/somewhere else; **quelqu'un/rien d'~** somebody/nothing else; **quoi d'~?** what else?; **d'~ part** on the other hand; (de plus) moreover, besides; **vous ~s Anglais** you English. ● pron **un ~, une ~** another (one); **l'~** the other (one); **les ~s** the others; (autrui) others; **d'~s** (some) others; **l'un l'~** each other; **l'un et l'~** both of them; **d'un jour à l'~** (bientôt) any day now; **entre ~s** among other things.

autrefois /otRəfwa/ adv in the past; (précédemment) formerly.

autrement /otRəmã/ adv differently; (sinon) otherwise; (plus **1**) far more; **~ dit** in other words.

Autriche /otRiʃ/ nf Austria.

autrichien, ~ne /otRiʃjɛ̃, -jɛn/ adj Austrian. **A~, ~ne** nm, f Austrian.

autruche /otRyʃ/ nf ostrich.

autrui /otRɥi/ pron others, other people.

aux /o/ **➡À**.

auxiliaire /oksiljɛR/ adj auxiliary. ● nmf (assistant) auxiliary. ● nm (Gram) auxiliary.

auxquels, -quelles /okɛl/ **➡LEQUEL**.

aval: en ~ /ãnaval/ loc downstream.

avaler /avale/ **1** vt swallow.

avance /avãs/ nf advance; (sur un concurrent) lead; **~ (de fonds)** advance; **à l'~** in advance; **d'~** already; **en ~** early; (montre) fast; **en (~ sur)** (menant) ahead (of).

avancement /avãsmã/ nm promotion.

avancé, ~e /avãse/ adj advanced.

avancer /avãse/ **10** vi move forward, advance; (travail) make progress; (montre) be fast; (faire saillie) jut out. ● vt move forward; (dans le temps) bring forward; (argent) advance; (montre) put forward. □ **s'~** vpr move forward, advance; (se hasarder) commit oneself.

avant /avã/ nm front; (Sport) forward. ● adj inv front. ● prép before; **~ de faire** before doing; **en ~ de** in front of; **~ peu** shortly; **~ tout** above all. ● adv (dans le temps) before, beforehand; (d'abord) first; **en ~** (dans l'espace) forward(s); (dans le temps) ahead; **le bus d'~** the previous bus. ● conj **~ que** before; **~ qu'il (ne) fasse** before he does.

avantage /avãtaʒ/ nm advantage; (Comm) benefit.

avantager /avãtaʒe/ **40** vt favour; (embellir) show off to advantage.

avantageux, -euse /avãtaʒø, -z/ adj advantageous, favourable; (prix) attractive.

avant-bras /avãbRa/ nm inv forearm.

avant-centre (pl **avants-centres**) /avãsãtR/ nm centre forward.

avant-coureur (pl **~s**) /avãkuRœR/ adj precursory, foreshadowing.

avant-dernier, -ière (pl **~s**) /avãdɛRnje, -jɛR/ adj & nm, f last but one.

avant-goût (pl **~s**) /avãgu/ nm foretaste.

avant-hier /avãtjɛR/ adv the day before yesterday.

avant-poste (pl **~s**) /avãpɔst/ nm outpost.

avant-première (pl **~s**) /avãpRəmjɛR/ nf preview.

avant-propos /avãpRopo/ nm inv foreword.

avare /avaR/ adj miserly; **~ de** sparing with. ● nmf miser.

avarié, ~e /avaRje/ adj (aliment) spoiled.

avatar /avataR/ nm misfortune.

avec /avɛk/ prép with. ● adv **1** with it ou them.

a

avènement /avɛnmɑ̃/ *nm* advent; (d'un roi) accession.

avenir /avniʀ/ *nm* future; **à l'~** in future; **d'~** with (future) prospects.

aventure /avɑ̃tyʀ/ *nf* adventure; (sentimentale) affair. **aventureux, -euse** *adj* adventurous; (hasardeux) risky.

avérer (s') /(s)aveʀe/ 14 *vpr* prove (to be).

averse /avɛʀs/ *nf* shower.

avertir /avɛʀtiʀ/ 2 *vt* inform; (mettre en garde, menacer) warn. **avertissement** *nm* warning.

avertisseur /avɛʀtisœʀ/ *nm* alarm; (Auto) horn; **~ d'incendie** fire-alarm; **~ lumineux** warning light.

aveu (*pl* **~x**) /avø/ *nm* confession; **de l'~ de** by the admission of.

aveugle /avœgl/ *adj* blind. ● *nmf* blind man, blind woman.

aviateur, -trice /avjatœʀ, -tʀis/ *nm, f* aviator.

aviation /avjasjɔ̃/ *nf* flying; (industrie) aviation; (Mil) air force.

avide /avid/ *adj* greedy (**de** for); (anxieux) eager (**de** for); **~ de faire** eager to do.

avion /avjɔ̃/ *nm* plane, aeroplane, aircraft; (US) airplane; **~ à réaction** jet.

aviron /aviʀɔ̃/ *nm* oar; **l'~** (Sport) rowing.

avis /avi/ *nm* opinion; (conseil) advice; (renseignement) notification; (Comm) advice; **à mon ~** in my opinion; **changer d'~** change one's mind; **être d'~ que** be of the opinion that; **~ au lecteur** foreword.

avisé, ~e /avize/ *adj* sensible; **être bien/mal ~** de be well-/ill-advised to.

aviser /avize/ 1 *vt* advise, notify. ● *vi* decide what to do. □ **s'~ de** *vpr* suddenly realize; **s'~ de faire** take it into one's head to do.

avocat, ~e /avɔka, -t/ *nm, f* barrister; (US) attorney; (fig) advocate; **~ de la défense** counsel for the defence. ● *nm* (fruit) avocado (pear).

avoine /avwan/ *nf* oats (+ *pl*).

---

avoir /avwaʀ/ 5

● *verbe auxiliaire*
····▸ have; **il nous a appelés hier** he called us yesterday.

● *verbe transitif*
····▸ (possession) have (got).
····▸ (obtenir) get; (au téléphone) get through to.
····▸ (duper) 1 have; **on m'a eu!** I've been had!
····▸ **~ chaud/faim** be hot/hungry.
····▸ **~ dix ans** be ten years old.

● **avoir à** *verbe + préposition*
····▸ to have to; **j'ai beaucoup à faire** I have a lot to do; **tu n'as qu'à leur écrire** all you have to do is write to them.

● **en avoir pour** *verbe + préposition*
····▸ **j'en ai pour une minute** I will only be a minute; **j'en ai eu pour 100 euros** it cost me 100 euros.

● **il y a** *verbe impersonnel*
····▸ there is; (pluriel) there are; **qu'est-ce qu'il y a?** what's the matter?; **il est venu il y a cinq ans** he came here five years ago; **il y a au moins 5 km jusqu'à la gare** it's at least 5 km to the station.

● *nom masculin*
····▸ (dans un magasin) credit note.
····▸ (biens) asset (+ *pl*).

---

avortement /avɔʀtəmɑ̃/ *nm* (Méd) abortion.

avorter /avɔʀte/ 1 *vi* (projet) abort; **(se faire) ~** have an abortion.

avoué, ~e /avwe/ *adj* avowed. ● *nm* solicitor; (US) attorney.

avouer /avwe/ 1 *vt* (amour, ignorance) confess; (crime) confess to, admit. ● *vi* confess.

avril /avʀil/ *nm* April.

axe /aks/ *nm* axis; (essieu) axle; (d'une politique) main line(s), basis; **~ (routier)** main road.

ayant /ɛjɑ̃/ →**AVOIR** 5.

azote /azɔt/ *nm* nitrogen.

azur /azyʀ/ *nm* sky-blue.

Bb

baba /baba/ *nm* ~ **(au rhum)** (rum) baba; **en rester** ~ 🔲 be flabbergasted.

babillard /babijaʀ/ *nm* ~ **électronique** (Internet) bulletin board system, BBS.

babines /babin/ *nfpl* **se lécher les** ~ lick one's chops.

babiole /babjɔl/ *nf* trinket.

bâbord /babɔʀ/ *nm* port (side).

baby-foot /babifut/ *nm inv* table football.

bac /bak/ *nm* (Scol) ➡**BACCALAURÉAT**; (bateau) ferry; (récipient) tub; (plus petit) tray.

baccalauréat /bakalɔʀea/ *nm* school leaving certificate.

> **Baccalauréat** Known informally as *le bac*, the *Baccalauréat* is an examination taken in the final year of the *lycée* (*la terminale*). Students sit exams in a broad range of subjects in a particular category: the *bac S* emphasises science subjects, for example, while the *bac L* has a literary bias.

bâche /baʃ/ *nf* tarpaulin.

bachelier, -ière /baʃəlje, -jɛʀ/ *nm, f* holder of the *baccalauréat*.

bachoter /baʃɔte/ 🔳 *vi* cram (for an exam).

bâcler /bakle/ 🔳 *vt* botch (up).

bactérie /bakteʀi/ *nf* bacterium; ~**s** bacteria.

badaud, ~e /bado, -d/ *nm, f* onlooker.

badigeonner /badiʒɔne/ 🔳 *vt* whitewash; (barbouiller) daub.

badiner /badine/ 🔳 *vi* banter.

baffe /baf/ *nf* 🔲 slap.

baffle /bafl/ *nm* speaker.

bafouiller /bafuje/ 🔳 *vt/i* stammer.

bagage /bagaʒ/ *nm* bag; (connaissances) knowledge; ~**s** luggage; ~ **à main** hand luggage.

bagarre /bagaʀ/ *nf* fight.

bagatelle /bagatɛl/ *nf* trifle; (somme) trifling amount.

bagnard /baɲaʀ/ *nm* convict.

bagnole /baɲɔl/ *nf* 🔲 car.

bague /bag/ *nf* (bijou) ring.

baguette /bagɛt/ *nf* stick; (de chef d'orchestre) baton; (chinoise) chopstick; (pain) baguette; ~ **magique** magic wand; ~ **de tambour** drumstick.

baie /bɛ/ *nf* (Géog) bay; (fruit) berry; ~ **(vitrée)** picture window; (Ordinat) bay.

baignade /bɛɲad/ *nf* swimming.

baigner /beɲe/ 🔳 *vt* bathe; (enfant) bath. ● *vi* ~ **dans l'huile** swim in grease. ☐ **se** ~ *vpr* have a swim. **baigneur, -euse** *nm, f* swimmer.

baignoire /bɛɲwaʀ/ *nf* bath(tub).

bail (*pl* **baux**) /baj, bo/ *nm* lease.

bâiller /baje/ 🔳 *vi* yawn; (être ouvert) gape.

bailleur /bajœʀ/ *nm* ~ **de fonds** (Comm) sleeping partner.

bain /bɛ̃/ *nm* bath; (baignade) swim; **prendre un** ~ **de soleil** sunbathe; ~ **de bouche** mouthwash; **être dans le** ~ (fig) be in the swing of things; **se remettre dans le** ~ get back into the swing of things; **prendre un** ~ **de foule** mingle with the crowd.

bain-marie (*pl* **bains-marie**) /bɛ̃maʀi/ *nm* double boiler.

baiser /beze/ 🔳 *vt* (main) kiss; ✖ screw ✖. ● *nm* kiss.

baisse /bɛs/ *nf* fall, drop; **être en** ~ be going down.

baisser /bese/ 🔳 *vt* lower; (radio, lampe) turn down. ● *vi* (niveau) go down, fall; (santé, forces) fail. ☐ **se** ~ *vpr* bend down.

bal (*pl* ~**s**) /bal/ *nm* dance; (habillé) ball; (lieu) dance-hall; ~ **costumé** fancy-dress ball.

balade /balad/ *nf* stroll; (en auto) drive.

balader /balade/ 🔳 *vt* take for a stroll. ☐ **se** ~ *vpr* (à pied) (go for a) stroll; (en voiture) go for a drive; (voyager) travel.

baladeur /baladœʀ/ *nm* personal stereo.

balafre /balafʀ/ *nf* gash; (cicatrice) scar.

b

b

balai /balɛ/ *nm* broom.

balance /balɑ̃s/ *nf* scales (+ *pl*); **la B∼** Libra.

balancer /balɑ̃se/ 🔟 *vt* swing; (doucement) sway; (lancer ▯) chuck!; (se débarrasser de ▯) chuck out ▯. ● *vi* sway. □ **se ∼** *vpr* swing; sway; **s'en ∼** ▯ not to give a damn ▯.

balancier /balɑ̃sje/ *nm* (d'horloge) pendulum; (d'équilibriste) pole.

balançoire /balɑ̃swaʀ/ *nf* swing.

balayage /baleja3/ *nm* sweeping; (cheveux) highlights.

balayer /baleje/ 🔢 *vt* sweep (up); (vent) sweep away; (se débarrasser de) sweep aside.

balbutiement /balbysimɑ̃/ *nm* stammering; **les ∼s** (fig) the first steps.

balcon /balkɔ̃/ *nm* balcony; (Théât) dress circle.

baleine /balɛn/ *nf* whale.

balise /baliz/ *nf* beacon; (bouée) buoy; (Auto) (road) sign. **baliser** 🔟 *vt* mark out (with beacons); (route) signpost; (sentier) mark out.

balivernes /balivɛʀn/ *nfpl* nonsense.

ballant, ∼e /balɑ̃, -t/ *adj* dangling.

balle /bal/ *nf* (projectile) bullet; (Sport) ball; (paquet) bale.

ballerine /balʀin/ *nf* (danseuse) ballerina; (chaussure) ballet pump.

ballet /balɛ/ *nm* ballet.

ballon /balɔ̃/ *nm* (Sport) ball; **∼ (de baudruche)** balloon; **∼ de football** football.

ballonné, ∼e /balɔne/ *adj* bloated.

balnéaire /balneɛʀ/ *adj* seaside.

balourd, ∼e /baluʀ, -d/ *nm, f* oaf. ● *adj* uncouth.

balustrade /balystʀad/ *nf* railing.

ban /bɑ̃/ *nm* round of applause; **∼s** (de mariage) banns; **mettre au ∼ de** cast out from.

banal, ∼e (*mpl* **∼s**) /banal/ *adj* commonplace, banal.

banane /banan/ *nf* banana.

banc /bɑ̃/ *nm* bench; (de poissons) shoal; **∼ des accusés** dock; **∼ d'essai** (test) testing ground.

bancaire /bɑ̃kɛʀ/ *adj* (secteur) banking; (chèque) bank.

bancal, ∼e (*mpl* **∼s**) /bɑ̃kal/ *adj* wobbly; (solution) shaky.

bande /bɑ̃d/ *nf* (groupe) gang; (de papier) strip; (rayure) stripe; (de film) reel; (pansement) bandage; **∼ dessinée** comic strip; **∼ (magnétique)** tape; **∼ sonore** sound-track.

> **Bande dessinée** More than *i* just a comic book, this form of popular literature (known as the *neuvième art*) plays a significant cultural role in France and is celebrated annually at the Festival d'Angoulême. Cartoon characters such as *Astérix*, *Lucky Luke* and *Tintin* are household names, and older *BD* are often collectors' items.

bande-annonce (*pl* **bandes-annonces**) /bɑ̃danɔ̃s/ *nf* trailer.

bandeau (*pl* **∼x**) /bɑ̃do/ *nm* headband; (sur les yeux) blindfold; **∼ publicitaire** (Ordinat) banner.

bander /bɑ̃de/ 🔟 *vt* bandage; (arc) bend; (muscle) tense; **∼ les yeux à** blindfold.

banderole /bɑ̃dʀɔl/ *nf* banner.

bandit /bɑ̃di/ *nm* bandit. **banditisme** *nm* crime.

bandoulière: en ∼ /ɑ̃bɑ̃duljɛʀ/ *loc* across one's shoulder.

banlieue /bɑ̃ljø/ *nf* suburbs; **de ∼** suburban. **banlieusard, ∼e** *nm, f* (suburban) commuter.

bannir /baniʀ/ 🛮 *vt* banish.

banque /bɑ̃k/ *nf* bank; (activité) banking; **∼ de données** databank.

banqueroute /bɑ̃kʀut/ *nf* bankruptcy.

banquet /bɑ̃kɛ/ *nm* banquet.

banquette /bɑ̃kɛt/ *nf* seat.

banquier, -ière /bɑ̃kje, -jɛʀ/ *nm, f* banker.

baptême /batɛm/ *nm* baptism, christening. **baptiser** 🔟 *vt* baptize, christen; (nommer) call.

bar /baʀ/ *nm* (lieu) bar.

baragouiner /baʀagwine/ 🔟 *vt/i* gabble; (langue) speak a few words of.

baraque /baʀak/ *nf* hut, shed; (maison ▯) house.

baratin /baʀatɛ̃/ *nm* ▯ sweet *ou* smooth talk.

barbare /baʀbaʀ/ *adj* barbaric. ● *nmf* barbarian.

barbe /baʀb/ *nf* beard; **∼ à papa** candy-floss; (US) cotton candy; **quelle**

~! ⊡ what a drag! ⊡.

barbelé /baʀbəle/ *adj* **fil** ~
barbed wire.

barber /baʀbe/ ◼ *vt* ⊡ bore.

barboter /baʀbɔte/ ◼ *vi* (dans l'eau)
paddle, splash. ● *vt* (voler ⊡) pinch.

barbouiller /baʀbuje/ ◼ *vt* (souiller)
smear (**de** with); **tu es tout bar-
bouillé** your face is all dirty; **être bar-
bouillé** feel queazy.

barbu, ~e /baʀby/ *adj* bearded.

barème /baʀɛm/ *nm* list, table;
(échelle) scale.

baril /baʀil/ *nm* barrel.

bariolé, ~e /baʀjɔle/ *adj* multicoloured.

baromètre /baʀɔmɛtʀ/ *nm* barometer.

baron, ~ne /baʀɔ̃, -ɔn/ *nm, f* baron,
baroness.

barque /baʀk/ *nf* (small) boat.

barrage /baʀaʒ/ *nm* dam; (sur route)
roadblock.

barre /baʀ/ *nf* bar; (trait) line, stroke;
(Naut) helm; ~ **de boutons** (Ordinat)
toolbar.

barreau (*pl* ~x) /baʀo/ *nm* bar; (d'é-
chelle) rung; **le** ~ (Jur) the bar.

barrer /baʀe/ ◼ *vt* block; (*porte*) bar;
(rayer) cross out; (Naut) steer. ☐ **se** ~
vpr ⊡ leave.

barrette /baʀɛt/ *nf* (hair) slide.

barrière /baʀjɛʀ/ *nf* (porte) gate, (clôture) fence; (obstacle) barrier.

bar-tabac (*pl* **bars-tabac**) /baʀtaba/
nm café (*selling stamps and cigarettes*).

bas, basse /ba, bas/ *adj* (niveau, table)
low; (action) base; **au** ~ **mot** at the
lowest estimate; **en** ~ **âge** young; ~
morceaux (viande) cheap cuts. ● *nm*
bottom; (chaussette) stocking; ~ **de
laine** (fig) nest-egg. ● *adv* low; **en** ~
down below; (dans une maison)
downstairs; **en** ~ **de la page** at the
bottom of the page; **plus** ~ further
ou lower down; **mettre** ~ give birth
(to). **bas de casse** *nm inv* lower case.

bas-côté (*pl* ~s) *nm* (de route) verge;
(US) shoulder.

bascule /baskyl/ *nf* (balance) scales (+
pl); **cheval/fauteuil à** ~ rocking-
horse/-chair.

basculer /baskyle/ ◼ *vi* topple over;
(*benne*) tip up.

base /baz/ *nf* base; (fondement) basis;
(Pol) rank and file; **de** ~ basic. **base
de données** *nf* database.

baser /baze/ ◼ *vt* base. ☐ **se** ~ **sur** *vpr*
go by.

bas-fonds /bafɔ̃/ *nmpl* (eau) shallows;
(fig) dregs.

basilic /bazilik/ *nm* basil.

basilique /bazilik/ *nf* basilica.

basque /bask/ *adj* Basque. **B**~ *nmf*
Basque.

basse /bas/ ➥**BAS.**

basse-cour (*pl* **basses-cours**)
/baskuʀ/ *nf* farmyard.

bassesse /basɛs/ *nf* baseness; (action)
base act.

bassin /basɛ̃/ *nm* (pièce d'eau) pond;
(de piscine) pool; (Géog) basin; (Anat)
pelvis; (plat) bowl; ~ **houiller**
coalfield.

bassine /basin/ *nf* bowl.

basson /basɔ̃/ *nm* bassoon.

bas-ventre (*pl* ~s) /bavɑ̃tʀ/ *nm* lower
abdomen.

bat /ba/ ➥**BATTRE** ◼.

bataille /bataj/ *nf* battle; (fig) fight.

bâtard, ~e /bataʀ, -d/ *adj* (solution)
hybrid. ● *nm, f* bastard.

bateau (*pl* ~x) /bato/ *nm* boat; ~
pneumatique rubber dinghy. **bateau-
mouche** (*pl* **bateaux-mouches**) *nm*
sightseeing boat.

bâti, ~e /bati/ *adj* **bien** ~ well-built.

bâtiment /batimɑ̃/ *nm* building; (industrie) building trade; (navire) vessel.

bâtir /batiʀ/ ◼ *vt* build.

bâton /batɔ̃/ *nm* stick; **conversation à**
~**s rompus** rambling conversation; ~
de rouge lipstick.

battant /batɑ̃/ *nm* (vantail) flap; **porte
à deux** ~**s** double door.

battement /batmɑ̃/ *nm* (de cœur)
beat(ing); (temps) interval; (Mus) beat.

batterie /batʀi/ *nf* (Mil, Électr) battery;
(Mus) drums; ~ **de cuisine** pots
and pans.

batteur /batœʀ/ *nm* (Mus) drummer;
(Culin) whisk.

battre /batʀ/ ◼ *vt/i* beat; (*cartes*) shuffle; (Culin) whisk; (l'emporter sur)
beat; ~ **des ailes** flap its wings; ~
des mains clap; ~ **des paupières**

b

blink; ∼ **en retraite** beat a retreat; ∼ **la semelle** stamp one's feet; ∼ **son plein** be in full swing. □ **se** ∼ *vpr* fight.

baume /bom/ *nm* balm.

bavard, ∼e /bavaʀ, -d/ *adj* talkative. ● *nm, f* chatterbox.

bavardage /bavaʀdaʒ/ *nm* chatter, gossip. **bavarder** 🗌 *vi* chat; (jacasser) chatter, gossip.

bave /bav/ *nf* dribble, slobber; (de limace) slime. **baver** 🗌 *vi* dribble, slobber. **baveux, -euse** *adj* dribbling; (omelette) runny.

bavoir /bavwaʀ/ *nm* bib.

bavure /bavyʀ/ *nf* smudge; (erreur) blunder; ∼ **policière** police blunder.

bazar /bazaʀ/ *nm* bazaar; (objets 🗌) clutter.

BCBG *abrév mf* (**bon chic bon genre**) posh.

BD *abrév f* (**bande dessinée**) comic strip.

béant, ∼e /beã, -t/ *adj* gaping.

béat, ∼e /bea, -t/ *adj* (hum) blissful; ∼ **d'admiration** wide-eyed with admiration.

beau (**bel** before vowel or mute h), **belle** (*mpl* ∼**x**) /bo, bɛl/ *adj* beautiful; (femme) beautiful; (homme) handsome; (temps) fine, nice. ● *nm* beauty. ● *adv* **il fait** ∼ the weather is nice; **au** ∼ **milieu** right in the middle; **bel et bien** well and truly; **de plus belle** more than ever; **faire le** ∼ sit up and beg; **on a** ∼ **essayer/insister** however much one tries/insists.

beaucoup /boku/ *adv* a lot, very much; ∼ **de** (nombre) many; (quantité) a lot of; **pas** ∼ **(de)** not many; (quantité) not much; ∼ **plus/mieux** much more/better; ∼ **trop** far too much; **de** ∼ by far.

beau-fils (*pl* **beaux-fils**) /bofis/ *nm* (remariage) stepson.

beau-frère (*pl* **beaux-frères**) /bofʀɛʀ/ *nm* brother-in-law.

beau-père (*pl* **beaux-pères**) /bopɛʀ/ *nm* father-in-law; (remariage) step-father.

beauté /bote/ *nf* beauty; **finir en** ∼ end magnificently.

beaux-arts /bozaʀ/ *nmpl* fine arts.

beaux-parents /bopaʀã/ *nmpl* parents-in-law.

bébé /bebe/ *nm* baby. **bébé-éprouvette** (*pl* **bébés-éprouvette**) *nm* test-tube baby.

bec /bɛk/ *nm* beak; (de théière) spout; (de casserole) lip; (bouche 🗌) mouth; ∼ **de gaz** gas street-lamp.

bécane /bekan/ *nf* 🗌 bike.

bêche /bɛʃ/ *nf* spade.

bégayer /begeje/ 🗌 *vt/i* stammer.

bègue /bɛg/ *nmf* stammerer. ● *adj* **être** ∼ stammer.

bégueule /begœl/ *adj* prudish.

beige /bɛʒ/ *adj & nm* beige.

beignet /bɛɲɛ/ *nm* fritter.

bel /bɛl/ →**BEAU**.

bêler /bele/ 🗌 *vi* bleat.

belette /bəlɛt/ *nf* weasel.

belge /bɛlʒ/ *adj* Belgian. **B**∼ *nmf* Belgian.

Belgique /bɛlʒik/ *nf* Belgium.

bélier /belje/ *nm* ram; **le B**∼ Aries.

belle /bɛl/ →**BEAU**.

belle-fille (*pl* **belles-filles**) /bɛlfij/ *nf* daughter-in-law; (remariage) step-daughter.

belle-mère (*pl* **belles-mères**) /bɛlmɛʀ/ *nf* mother-in-law; (remariage) stepmother.

belle-sœur (*pl* **belles-sœurs**) /bɛlsœʀ/ *nf* sister-in-law.

belliqueux, -euse /belikø, -z/ *adj* warlike.

bémol /bemɔl/ *nm* (Mus) flat.

bénédiction /benediksjõ/ *nf* blessing.

bénéfice /benefis/ *nm* (gain) profit; (avantage) benefit.

bénéficiaire /benefisjɛʀ/ *nmf* beneficiary.

bénéficier /benefisje/ 🗌 *vi* ∼ **de** benefit from; (jouir de) enjoy, have.

bénéfique /benefik/ *adj* beneficial.

Bénélux /benelyks/ *nm* Benelux.

bénévole /benevɔl/ *adj* voluntary.

bénin, -igne /benɛ̃, -iɲ/ *adj* minor; (tumeur) benign.

bénir /beniʀ/ 🗌 *vt* bless. **bénit, ∼e** *adj* (eau) holy; (pain) consecrated.

benjamin, ∼e /bɛ̃ʒamɛ̃, -in/ *nm, f* youngest child.

benne /bɛn/ *nf* (de grue) scoop; ∼ à **ordures** (camion) waste disposal truck; (conteneur) skip; ∼ **(basculante)** dump truck.

béquille /bekij/ *nf* crutch; (de moto) stand.

berceau (*pl* ∼x) /bɛʀso/ *nm* (de bébé, civilisation) cradle.

bercer /bɛʀse/ **10** *vt* (balancer) rock; (apaiser) lull; (leurrer) delude.

béret /beʀɛ/ *nm* beret.

berge /bɛʀʒ/ *nf* (bord) bank.

berger, -ère /bɛʀʒe, -ɛʀ/ *nm, f* shepherd, shepherdess.

berne: en ∼ /ũbɛʀn/ *loc* at halfmast.

berner /bɛʀne/ **1** *vt* fool.

besogne /bəzɔɲ/ *nf* task, job.

besoin /bəzwɛ̃/ *nm* need; **avoir** ∼ **de** need; **au** ∼ if need be; **dans le** ∼ in need.

bestiole /bɛstjɔl/ *nf* 🔢 bug.

bétail /betaj/ *nm* livestock.

bête /bɛt/ *adj* stupid. ● *nf* animal; ∼ **noire** pet hate; ∼ **sauvage** wild beast; **chercher la petite** ∼ be overfussy.

bêtise /betiz/ *nf* stupidity; (action) stupid thing.

béton /betɔ̃/ *nm* concrete; ∼ **armé** reinforced concrete; **en** ∼ (mur) concrete; (argument 🔢) watertight. **bétonnière** *nf* concrete mixer.

betterave /bɛtʀav/ *nf* beet; ∼ **rouge** beetroot.

beugler /bøgle/ **1** *vi* bellow; (radio) blare out.

beur /bœʀ/ *nmf & adj* 🔢 second-generation North African living in France.

beurre /bœʀ/ *nm* butter. **beurré,** ∼e *adj* buttered; 🔢 drunk. **beurrier** *nm* butter-dish.

bévue /bevy/ *nf* blunder.

biais /bjɛ/ *nm* (moyen) way; **par le** ∼ **de** by means of; **de** ∼**, en** ∼ at an angle.

bibelot /biblo/ *nm* ornament.

biberon /bibʀɔ̃/ *nm* (feeding) bottle; **nourrir au** ∼ bottle-feed.

bible /bibl/ *nf* bible; **la B**∼ the Bible.

bibliographie /biblijɔgʀafi/ *nf* bibliography.

bibliothécaire /biblijɔtekɛʀ/ *nmf* librarian.

bibliothèque /biblijɔtɛk/ *nf* library; (meuble) bookcase.

bic® /bik/ *nm* biro®.

bicarbonate /bikaʀbɔnat/ *nm* ∼ **(de soude)** bicarbonate (of soda).

biceps /bisɛps/ *nm* biceps.

biche /biʃ/ *nf* doe; **ma** ∼ darling.

bichonner /biʃɔne/ **1** *vt* pamper.

bicyclette /bisiklɛt/ *nf* bicycle.

bide /bid/ *nm* (ventre 🔢) paunch; (échec 🔢) flop.

bidet /bidɛ/ *nm* bidet.

bidon /bidɔ̃/ *nm* can; (plus grand) drum; (ventre 🔢) belly; **c'est du** ∼**!** it's a load of hogwash 🔢. ● *adj inv* 🔢 phoney.

bidonville /bidɔ̃vil/ *nm* shanty town.

bidule /bidyl/ *nm* 🔢 thing.

Biélorussie /bjelɔʀysi/ *nf* Byelorussia.

bien /bjɛ̃/ *adv* well; (très) quite, very; ∼ **des** (nombre) many; **tu as** ∼ **de la chance** you are very lucky; **j'aimerais** ∼ I would like to; **ce n'est pas** ∼ **de** it is not nice to; ∼ **sûr** of course. ● *nm* good; (patrimoine) possession; ∼**s de consommation** consumer goods. ● *adj inv* good; (passable) all right; (en forme) well; (à l'aise) comfortable; (beau) attractive; (respectable) nice, respectable. ● *conj* ∼ **que** (al-)though; ∼ **que ce soit** although it is. **bien-aimé,** ∼e *adj & nm, f* beloved. **bien-être** *nm* wellbeing.

bienfaisance /bjɛ̃fəzɑ̃s/ *nf* charity; **fête de** ∼ charity event. **bienfaisant,** ∼e *adj* beneficial.

bienfait /bjɛ̃fɛ/ *nm* (kind) favour; (avantage) beneficial effect. **bienfaiteur, -trice** *nm, f* benefactor.

bien-pensant, ∼e /bjɛ̃pɑ̃sɑ̃, -t/ *adj* right-thinking.

bienséance /bjɛ̃seɑ̃s/ *nf* propriety.

bientôt /bjɛ̃to/ *adv* soon; **à** ∼ see you soon.

bienveillance /bjɛ̃vɛjɑ̃s/ *nf* kind-(li)ness.

bienvenu, ∼e /bjɛ̃vny/ *adj* welcome. ● *nm, f* **être le** ∼**, être la** ∼e be welcome.

b

bienvenue /bjɛ̃vny/ *nf* welcome; **souhaiter la ~ à** welcome.

bière /bjɛʀ/ *nf* beer; (cercueil) coffin; **~ blonde** lager; **~ brune** ≈ stout; **~ pression** draught beer.

bifteck /biftɛk/ *nm* steak.

bifurquer /bifyʀke/ **1** *vi* branch off, fork.

bigarré, ~e /bigaʀe/ *adj* motley.

bigoudi /bigudi/ *nm* curler.

bijou (*pl* **~x**) /biʒu/ *nm* jewel; **~x en or** gold jewellery. **bijouterie** *nf* (boutique) jewellery shop; (Comm) jewellery. **bijoutier, -ière** *nm, f* jeweller.

bilan /bilɑ̃/ *nm* outcome; (d'une catastrophe) (casualty) toll; (Comm) balance sheet; **faire le ~ de** assess; **~ de santé** check-up.

bile /bil/ *nf* bile; **se faire de la ~** 🛈 worry.

bilingue /bilɛ̃g/ *adj* bilingual.

billard /bijaʀ/ *nm* billiards (+ *pl*); (table) billiard-table.

bille /bij/ *nf* (d'enfant) marble; (de billard) billiard-ball.

billet /bijɛ/ *nm* ticket; (lettre) note; (article) column; **~ (de banque)** (bank) note; **~ de 50 euros** 50-euro note.

billetterie /bijɛtʀi/ *nf* cash dispenser.

billion /biljɔ̃/ *nm* billion; (US) trillion.

bimensuel, ~le /bimɑ̃sɥɛl/ *adj* fortnightly, bimonthly.

binette /binɛt/ *nf* hoe; (visage) face; (Internet) smiley.

biochimie /bjoʃimi/ *nf* biochemistry.

biodégradable /bjodegʀadabl/ *adj* biodegradable.

biographie /bjogʀafi/ *nf* biography.

biologie /bjɔlɔʒi/ *nf* biology. **biologique** *adj* biological; (produit) organic.

bioterrorisme /bjotɛʀɔʀism/ *nm* bioterrorism.

bis /bis/ *nm & interj* encore.

biscornu, ~e /biskɔʀny/ *adj* crooked; (bizarre) cranky 🛈.

biscotte /biskɔt/ *nf* continental toast.

biscuit /biskɥi/ *nm* biscuit; (US) cookie; **~ salé** cracker; **~ de Savoie** sponge-cake.

bise /biz/ *nf* 🛈 kiss; (vent) north wind.

bison /bizɔ̃/ *nm* buffalo.

Bison Futé Devised by the French traffic information service, *Bison Futé* reports on travel conditions nationally and recommends alternative routes (*les itinéraires 'bis'*) for travellers wishing to avoid traffic jams. *Bison Futé* traffic tips are made known through the media and appear on road signs in yellow on a green background.

bisou /bizu/ *nm* 🛈 kiss.

bistro(t) /bistʀo/ *nm* 🛈 café, bar.

bit /bit/ *nm* (Ordinat) bit.

bitume /bitym/ *nm* asphalt.

bizarre /bizaʀ/ *adj* odd, strange. **bizarrerie** *nf* peculiarity.

blafard, ~e /blafaʀ, -d/ *adj* pale.

blague /blag/ *nf* 🛈 joke; **sans ~!** no kidding! 🛈.

blaguer /blage/ **1** 🛈 *vi* joke.

blaireau (*pl* **~x**) /blɛʀo/ *nm* shaving-brush; (animal) badger.

blâmer /blame/ **1** *vt* criticize.

blanc, blanche /blɑ̃, blɑ̃ʃ/ *adj* white; (papier, page) blank. ● *nm* white; (espace) blank; **~ d'œuf** egg white; **~ de poireau** white part of the leek; **~ (de poulet)** chicken breast; **le ~** (linge) whites; **laisser en ~** leave blank. **B~, Blanche** *nm, f* white man, white woman. **blanche** *nf* (Mus) minim.

blanchiment /blɑ̃ʃimɑ̃/ *nm* (d'argent) laundering.

blanchir /blɑ̃ʃiʀ/ **2** *vt* whiten; (personne: fig) clear; (argent) launder; (Culin) blanch; **~ (à la chaux)** whitewash. ● *vi* turn white.

blanchisserie /blɑ̃ʃisʀi/ *nf* laundry.

blason /blazɔ̃/ *nm* coat of arms.

blasphème /blasfɛm/ *nm* blasphemy.

blé /ble/ *nm* wheat.

blême /blɛm/ *adj* pallid.

blessant, ~e /blesɑ̃, -t/ *adj* hurtful.

blessé, ~e /blese/ *nm, f* casualty, injured person.

blesser /blese/ **1** *vt* injure, hurt; (par balle) wound; (offenser) hurt. □ **se ~** *vpr* injure *ou* hurt oneself. **blessure** *nf* wound.

bleu, ~e /blø/ *adj* blue; (Culin) very rare; **~ marine/turquoise** navy blue/turquoise; **avoir une peur ~e** be

scared stiff. ● *nm* blue; (contusion)
bruise; ~ **(de travail)** overalls (+ *pl*).
bleuet /blœ/ *nm* cornflower.
blindé, ~e /blɛ̃de/ *adj* armoured; (fig)
immune (**contre** to); **porte ~e** security car. ● *nm* armoured car, tank.
blinder /blɛ̃de/ **1** *vt* armour; (fig)
harden.
bloc /blɔk/ *nm* block; (de papier) pad;
serrer à ~ tighten hard; **en ~** (matériau) in a block; (nier) outright.
blocage /blɔkaʒ/ *nm* (des prix) freeze,
freezing; (des roues) locking; (Psych)
block.
bloc-notes (*pl* **blocs-notes**) /blɔknɔt/
nm note-pad.
blocus /blɔkys/ *nm* blockade.
blond, ~e /blɔ̃, -d/ *adj* fair, blond.
● *nm, f* fair-haired man, fairhaired
woman.
bloquer /blɔke/ **1** *vt* block; (*porte,
machine*) jam; (roues) lock; (prix, crédits) freeze. □ **se ~** *vpr* jam; (roues)
lock; (freins) jam; (ordinateur) crash;
bloqué par la neige snowbound.
blottir (se) /(sə)blɔtiʀ/ **2** *vpr* snuggle, huddle (**contre** against).
blouse /bluz/ *nf* overall. **blouse blanche** *nf* white coat.
blouson /bluzɔ̃/ *nm* jacket, blouson.
bluffer /blœfe/ **1** *vt/i* bluff.
bobine /bɔbin/ *nf* (de fil, film) reel;
(Électr) coil.
bobo /bobo/ *nm* **1** sore, cut; **avoir ~**
have a pain.
bocal (*pl* **-aux**) /bɔkal, -o/ *nm* jar.
bœuf (*pl* **~s**) /bœf, bø/ *nm* bullock;
(US) steer; (viande) beef; **~s** oxen.
bogue /bɔg/ *nm* (Ordinat) bug.
bohème /bɔɛm/ *adj & nmf* bohemian.
boire /bwaʀ/ **12** *vt/i* (personne, plante)
drink; (argile) soak up; **~ un coup** **1**
have a drink.
bois /bwa/ ➞**BOIRE 12**. ● *nm* (matériau,
forêt) wood; **de ~, en ~** wooden.
● *nmpl* (de cerf) antlers.
boiseries /bwazʀi/ *nfpl* panelling.
boisson /bwasɔ̃/ *nf* drink.
boit /bwa/ ➞**BOIRE 12**.
boîte /bwat/ *nf* box; (de conserves) tin,
can; (entreprise **1**) firm; **en ~** tinned,
canned; **~ à gants** glove compartment; **~ aux lettres** letterbox; **~ aux**

lettres électronique mailbox; **~ de
nuit** night-club; **~ postale** post-office
box; **~ de vitesses** gear box.
boiter /bwate/ **1** *vi* limp. **boiteux,
-euse** *adj* lame; (raisonnement) shaky.
boîtier /bwatje/ *nm* case.
bol /bɔl/ *nm* bowl; **~ d'air** abreath of
fresh air; **avoir du ~!** be lucky.
bolide /bɔlid/ *nm* racing car.
Bolivie /bɔlivi/ *nf* Bolivia.
bombardement /bɔ̃baʀdəmɑ̃/ *nm*
bombing; shelling.
bombarder /bɔ̃baʀde/ **1** *vt* bomb;
(par obus) shell; **~ qn de** (fig) bombard sb with. **bombardier** *nm* (Aviat)
bomber.
bombe /bɔ̃b/ *nf* bomb; (atomiseur)
spray, aerosol.
bombé, ~e /bɔ̃be/ *adj* rounded;
(route) cambered.
bon, bonne /bɔ̃, bɔn/ *adj* good; (qui
convient) right; **~ à/pour** (approprié)
it to/for; **bonne année** happy New
Year; **~ anniversaire** happy birthday;
~ appétit/voyage enjoy your meal/
trip; **bonne chance/nuit** good luck/
night; **~ sens** common sense; **bonne
femme** (péj) woman; **de bonne heure**
early; **à quoi ~?** what's the point?
● *adv* **sentir ~** smell nice; **tenir ~**
stand firm; **il fait ~** the weather is
mild. ● *interj* right, well. ● *nm* (billet)
voucher, coupon; **~ de commande**
order form; **pour de ~** for good.
bonne *nf* (domestique) maid.
bonbon /bɔ̃bɔ̃/ *nm* sweet; (US) candy.
bonbonne /bɔ̃bɔn/ *nf* demijohn; (de
gaz) cylinder.
bond /bɔ̃/ *nm* leap; **faire un ~** (de surprise) jump.
bonde /bɔ̃d/ *nf* plug; (trou) plughole.
bondé, ~e /bɔ̃de/ *adj* packed.
bondir /bɔ̃diʀ/ **2** *vi* leap; (de surprise) jump.
bonheur /bɔnœʀ/ *nm* happiness;
(chance) (good) luck; **au petit ~** haphazardly; **par ~** luckily.
bonhomme (*pl* **bonshommes**)
/bɔnɔm, bɔzɔm/ *nm* fellow; **~ de
neige** snowman. ● *adj inv* good
hearted.
bonifier (se) /(sə)bɔnifje/ **45** *vpr*
improve.

b

b

bonjour /bɔ̃ʒuʀ/ *nm & interj* hallo, hello, good morning *ou* afternoon.

bon marché /bɔ̃maʀʃe/ *adj inv* cheap. ● *adv* cheap (ly)

bonne /bɔn/ →**BON**.

bonne-maman (*pl* **bonnes-mamans**) /bɔnmamɑ̃/ *nf* 🔢 granny.

bonnement /bɔnmɑ̃/ *adv* **tout** ~ quite simply.

bonnet /bɔnɛ/ *nm* hat; (de soutien-gorge) cup; ~ **de bain** swimming cap. **bonneterie** *nf* hosiery.

bonsoir /bɔ̃swaʀ/ *nm* good evening; (en se couchant) good night.

bonté /bɔ̃te/ *nf* kindness.

bonus /bɔnys/ *nm* (Auto) no-claims bonus.

boots /buts/ *nmpl* ankle boots.

bord /bɔʀ/ *nm* edge; (rive) bank; **à** (~ **de**) on board; **au** ~ **de la mer** at the seaside; **au** ~ **des larmes** on the verge of tears; ~ **de la route** road-side.

bordeaux /bɔʀdo/ *adj inv* maroon. ● *nm inv* Bordeaux.

bordel /bɔʀdɛl/ *nm* brothel; (désordre 🔢) shambles.

border /bɔʀde/ 🔢 *vt* line, border; (tissu) edge; (*personne, lit*) tuck in.

bordereau (*pl* ~**x**) /bɔʀdəʀo/ *nm* (document) slip.

bordure /bɔʀdyʀ/ *nf* border; **en** ~ **de** on the edge of.

borgne /bɔʀɲ/ *adj* one-eyed.

borne /bɔʀn/ *nf* boundary marker; (pour barrer le passage) bollard; ~ **(kilométrique)** ≈milestone; ~**s** limits.

borné, ~e /bɔʀne/ *adj* (esprit) narrow; (*personne*) narrow minded.

borner (se) /(sə)bɔʀne/ 🔢 *vpr* confine oneself (à to).

bosniaque /bɔsnjak/ *adj* Bosnian. **B**~ *nmf* Bosnian.

Bosnie /bɔsni/ *nf* Bosnia.

bosse /bɔs/ *nf* bump; (de chameau) hump; **avoir la** ~ **de** 🔢 have a gift for; **avoir roulé sa** ~ have been around. **bosselé, ~e** *adj* dented; (terrain) bumpy.

bosser /bɔse/ 🔢 *vi* 🔢 work (hard).

bossu, ~e /bɔsy/ *adj* hunchbacked. ● *nm, f* hunchback.

botanique /bɔtanik/ *nf* botany.● *adj* botanical.

botte /bɔt/ *nf* boot; (de fleurs, légumes) bunch; (de paille) bundle, bale; ~**s de caoutchouc** wellingtons.

botter /bɔte/ 🔢 *vt* **ça me botte** I like the idea.

bottin® /bɔtɛ̃/ *nm* phone book.

bouc /buk/ *nm* (billy-)goat; (barbe) goatee; ~ **émissaire** scapegoat.

boucan /bukɑ̃/ *nm* 🔢din.

bouche /buʃ/ *nf* mouth; (lèvres) lips; ~ **bée** open-mouthed; ~ **d'égout** manhole; ~ **d'incendie** (fire)hydrant; ~ **de métro** entrance to the underground *ou* subway (US). **bouche-à-bouche** *nm inv* mouth-to-mouth resuscitation. **bouche-à-oreille** *nm inv* word of mouth.

bouché, ~e /buʃe/ *adj* (*profession, avenir*) oversubscribed; (stupide: péj) stupid.

bouchée /buʃe/ *nf* mouthful.

boucher¹ /buʃe/ 🔢 *vt* block; (bouteille) cork. ❑ **se** ~ *vpr* get blocked; **se** ~ **le nez** hold one's nose.

boucher², -ère /buʃe, -ɛʀ/ *nm, f* butcher. **boucherie** *nf* butcher's (shop); (carnage) butchery.

bouchon /buʃɔ̃/ *nm* stopper; (en liège) cork; (de stylo, tube) cap; (de pêcheur) float; (embouteillage) traffic jam; ~ **de cérumen** plug of earwax.

boucle /bukl/ *nf* (de ceinture) buckle; (de cheveux) curl; (forme) loop; ~ **d'oreille** earring. **bouclé, ~e** *adj* (cheveux) curly.

boucler /bukle/ 🔢 *vt* fasten; (enfermer 🔢) shut up; (encercler) seal off; (budget) balance; (terminer) finish off. ● *vi* curl.

bouclier /buklije/ *nm* shield.

bouddhiste /budist/ *adj & nmf* Buddhist.

bouder /bude/ 🔢 *vi* sulk. ● *vt* stay away from.

boudin /budɛ̃/ *nm* black pudding.

boue /bu/ *nf* mud.

bouée /bwe/ *nf* buoy; ~ **de sauvetage** lifebuoy.

boueux, -euse /buø, -z/ *adj* muddy.

bouffe /buf/ *nf* 🔢 food, grub.

bouffée /bufe/ *nf* puff, whiff; (d'orgueil) fit; ~ **de chaleur** (Méd) hot flush.

bouffi, ~**e** /bufi/ *adj* bloated.

bouffon, ~**ne** /bufɔ̃, -ɔn/ *adj* farcical. ● *nm* buffoon.

bougeoir /buʒwaʀ/ *nm* candlestick.

bougeotte /buʒɔt/ *nf* **avoir la** ~ 🔲 have the fidgets.

bouger /buʒe/ 🔟 *vt/i* move. ◻ **se** ~ *vpr* 🔲 move.

bougie /buʒi/ *nf* candle; (Auto) spark(ing)-plug.

bouillant, ~**e** /bujɑ̃, -t/ *adj* boiling; (très chaud) boiling hot.

bouillie /buji/ *nf* (pour bébé) baby cereal; (péj) mush; **en** ~ crushed, mushy.

bouillir /bujiʀ/ 🔢 *vi* boil; (fig) seethe; **faire** ~ boil.

bouilloire /bujwaʀ/ *nf* kettle.

bouillon /bujɔ̃/ *nm* (de cuisson) stock; (potage) broth.

bouillonner /bujɔne/ 🔟 *vi* bubble.

bouillotte /bujɔt/ *nf* hot-water bottle.

boulanger, **-ère** /bulɑ̃ʒe, -ɛʀ/ *nm, f* baker. **boulangerie** *nf* bakery. **boulangerie-pâtisserie** *nf* bakery (selling cakes andpastries).

boule /bul/ *nf* ball; (jeu) boules; **jouer aux** ~**s** play boules; **une** ~ **dans la gorge** a lump in one's throat; ~ **de neige** snowball.

Boules A form of bowls, played on rough, dry ground with metal balls. The aim is to throw the balls to land as near as possible to a smaller target ball called the *cochonnet*. In the South of France, *boules* is often called *pétanque*. *i*

---

bouleau (*pl* ~**x**) /bulo/ *nm* (silver) birch.

boulet /bulɛ/ *nm* (de forçat) ball and chain; ~ **(de canon)** cannonball; ~ **de charbon** coal nut.

boulette /bulɛt/ *nf* (de pain, papier) pellet; (bévue) blunder; ~ **de viande** meat ball.

boulevard /bulvaʀ/ *nm* boulevard.

bouleversant, ~**e** /bulvɛʀsɑ̃, -t/ *adj* deeply moving. **bouleversement** *nm* upheaval. **bouleverser** 🔟 *vt* turn upside down; (*pays, plans*) disrupt; (*émouvoir*) upset.

boulimie /bulimi/ *nf* bulimia.

boulon /bulɔ̃/ *nm* bolt.

boulot, ~**te** /bulo, -ɔt/ *adj* (rond 🔲) dumpy. ● *nm* (travail 🔲) work.

boum /bum/ *nm & interj* bang. ● *nf* (fête 🔲) party.

bouquet /bukɛ/ *nm* (de fleurs) bunch, bouquet; (d'arbres) clump; **c'est le** ~**!** 🔲 that's the last straw!

bouquin /bukɛ̃/ *nm* 🔲book. **bouquiner** 🔟 *vt/i* 🔲read. **bouquiniste** *nmf* second-hand bookseller.

bourbier /buʀbje/ *nm* mire; (fig) tangle.

bourde /buʀd/ *nf* blunder.

bourdon /buʀdɔ̃/ *nm* bumble bee. **bourdonnement** *nm* buzzing.

bourg /buʀ/ *nm* (market) town (centre), village centre.

bourgeois, ~**e** /buʀʒwa, -z/ *adj & nm,f* middle-class (person); (péj) bourgeois. **bourgeoisie** *nf* middle class(es).

bourgeon /buʀʒɔ̃/ *nm* bud.

bourgogne /buʀgɔɲ/ *nm* Burgundy.

bourlinguer /buʀlɛ̃ge/ 🔟 *vi* 🔲 travel about.

bourrage /buʀaʒ/ *nm* ~ **de crâne** brainwashing.

bourratif, **-ive** /buʀatif, -v/ *adj* stodgy.

bourreau (*pl* ~**x**)/buʀo/ *nm* executioner; ~ **de travail** (fig) workaholic.

bourrelet /buʀlɛ/ *nm* weather strip, draught excluder; (de chair) roll of fat.

bourrer /buʀe/ 🔟 *vt* cram (**de** with); (*pipe*) fill; ~ **de** (*nourriture*) stuff with; ~ **de coups** thrash; ~ **le crâne à qn** brainwash sb.

bourrique /buʀik/ *nf* donkey; 🔲 pigheaded person.

bourru, ~**e** /buʀy/ *adj* gruff.

bourse /buʀs/ *nf* purse; (subvention) grant; **la B**~ the Stock Exchange.

boursier, **-ière** /buʀsje, -jɛʀ/ *adj* (valeurs) Stock Exchange. ● *nm, f* grant holder.

boursoufler /buʀsufle/ 🔟 *vt* (visage) cause to swell; (peinture) blister.

bousculade /buskylad/ *nf* crush; (précipitation) rush. **bousculer** 🔟 *vt* (pousser) jostle; (presser) rush; (renverser) knock over.

bousiller /buzije/ **1** vt **1** wreck.

boussole /busɔl/ nf compass.

bout /bu/ nm end; (de langue, bâton) piece; (morceau) bit; **à ~** exhausted; **à ~ de souffle** out of breath; **à ~ portant** point-blank; **au ~ de** (après) after; **venir à ~ de** (finir) manage to finish; **d'un ~ à l'autre** throughout; **au ~ du compte** in the end; **~ filtre** filtertip.

bouteille /butɛj/ nf bottle; **~ d'oxygène** oxygen cylinder.

boutique /butik/ nf shop; (de mode) boutique.

bouton /butɔ̃/ nm button; (sur la peau) spot, pimple; (pousse) bud; (de porte, radio) knob; **~ de manchette** cufflink. **boutonner** **1** vt button (up). **boutonnière** nf buttonhole. **bouton-pression** (pl **boutons-pression**) nm press-stud; (US) snap.

bouture /butyʀ/ nf cutting.

bovin, ~e /bɔvɛ̃, -in/ adj bovine. **bovins** nmpl cattle (pl).

box (pl **~ ou boxes**) /bɔks/ nm lock-up garage; (de dortoir) cubicle; (d'écurie) (loose) box; (Jur) dock.

boxe /bɔks/ nf boxing.

boyau (pl **~x**) /bwajo/ nm gut; (corde) catgut; (galerie) gallery; (de bicyclette) tyre; (US) tire.

boycotter /bɔjkɔte/ **1** vt boycott.

BP abrév f (**boîte postale**) PO Box.

bracelet /bʀaslɛ/ nm bracelet; (de montre) watchstrap.

braconnier /bʀakɔnje/ nm poacher.

brader /bʀade/ **1** vt sell off. **braderie** nf clearance sale.

braguette /bʀagɛt/ nf fly.

braille /bʀaj/ nm & adj Braille.

brailler /bʀaje/ **1** vt/i bawl.

braise /bʀɛz/ nf embers (+ pl).

braiser /bʀeze/ **1** vt (Culin) braise.

brancard /bʀɑ̃kaʀ/ nm stretcher; (de charrette) shaft.

branche /bʀɑ̃ʃ/ nf branch.

branché, ~e /bʀɑ̃ʃe/ adj **1** trendy.

branchement /bʀɑ̃ʃmɑ̃/ nm connection. **brancher** **1** vt (prise) plug in; (à un réseau) connect.

brandir /bʀɑ̃diʀ/ **2** vt brandish.

branler /bʀɑ̃le/ **1** vi be shaky.

braquer /bʀake/ **1** vt (arme) aim; (regard) fix; (roue) turn; (banque: **1**) hold up; **~ qn contre** turn sb against. ● vi (Auto) turn (the wheel). □ **se ~** vpr dig one's heels in.

bras /bʀa/ nm arm; (de rivière) branch; (Tech) arm; **~ dessus ~ dessous** arm in arm; **~ droit** (fig) right hand man; **~ de mer** sound; **en ~ de chemise** in one's shirtsleeves. ● nmpl (fig) labour, hands.

brasier /bʀazje/ nm blaze.

brassard /bʀasaʀ/ nm armband.

brasse /bʀas/ nf breast-stroke; **~ papillon** butterfly (stroke).

brasser /bʀase/ **1** vt mix; (bière) brew; (affaires) handle a lot of. **brasserie** nf brewery; (café) brasserie.

brave /bʀav/ adj (bon) good; (valeureux) brave. **braver** **1** vt defy.

bravo /bʀavo/ interj bravo. ● nm cheer.

bravoure /bʀavuʀ/ nf bravery.

break /bʀɛk/ nm estate car; (US) station-wagon.

brebis /bʀəbi/ nf ewe.

brèche /bʀɛʃ/ nf gap, breach; **être sur la ~** be on the go.

bredouille /bʀəduj/ adj emptyhanded.

bredouiller /bʀəduje/ **1** vt/i mumble.

bref, brève /bʀɛf, -v/ adj short, brief. ● adv in short; **en ~** in short.

Brésil /bʀezil/ nm Brazil.

Bretagne /bʀətaɲ/ nf Brittany.

bretelle /bʀətɛl/ nf (de sac, maillot) strap; (d'autoroute) access road; **~s** (pour pantalon) braces; (US) suspenders.

breton, ~ne /bʀətɔ̃, -ɔn/ adj & nm (Ling) Breton. **B~, ~ne** nm, f Breton.

breuvage /bʀœvaʒ/ nm beverage.

brève /bʀɛv/ →**BREF**.

brevet /bʀəvɛ/ nm **~ (d'invention)** patent; (diplôme) diploma.

breveté, ~e /bʀəvte/ adj patented.

bribes /bʀib/ nfpl scraps.

bricolage /bʀikɔlaʒ/ nm do-it yourself (jobs).

bricole /bʀikɔl/ nf trifle.

bricoler /bʀikɔle/ **1** vi do DIY; (US) fix things, tinker with.

bricoleur, -euse /bʀikɔlœʀ, -øz/ nm, f handyman, handywoman.

bride /bʀid/ nf bridle.

bridé | bruyère

bridé, ~e /bʀide/ adj yeux ~s slant-ing eyes.

brider /bʀide/ **1** vt (cheval) bridle; (fig) keep in check.

brièvement /bʀijɛvmɑ̃/ adv briefly.

brigade /bʀigad/ nf (de police) squad; (Mil) brigade; (fig) team. **brigadier** nm (de gendarmerie) sergeant.

brigand /bʀigɑ̃/ nm robber.

brillant, ~e /bʀijɑ̃, -t/ adj (couleur) bright; (luisant) shiny; (remarquable) brilliant. ● nm (éclat) shine; (diamant) diamond.

briller /bʀije/ **1** vi shine.

brimade /bʀimad/ nf vexation. **bri-mer 1** vt bully, harass; **se sentir brimé** feel put down.

brin /bʀɛ̃/ nm (de muguet) sprig; (d'herbe) blade; (de paille) wisp; **un ~ de** (un peu) a bit of.

brindille /bʀɛ̃dij/ nf twig.

brioche /bʀijɔʃ/ nf brioche, sweet bun; (ventre **1**) paunch.

brique /bʀik/ nf brick.

briquet /bʀikɛ/ nm (cigarette-)lighter.

brise /bʀiz/ nf breeze.

briser /bʀize/ **1** vt break. □ **se** ~ vpr break.

britannique /bʀitanik/ adj British. **B**~ nmf Briton; **les B**~s the British.

brocante /bʀɔkɑ̃t/ nf bric-à-brac trade; (marché) flea market.

broche /bʀɔʃ/ nf brooch; (Culin) spit; **à la** ~ spit-roasted.

broché, ~e /bʀɔʃe/ adj paperback.

brochet /bʀɔʃɛ/ nm pike.

brochette /bʀɔʃɛt/ nf skewer.

brochure /bʀɔʃyʀ/ nf brochure, booklet.

broder /bʀɔde/ **1** vt/i embroider. **bro-derie** nf embroidery.

broncher /bʀɔ̃ʃe/ **1** vi **sans** ~ with-out turning a hair.

bronchite /bʀɔ̃ʃit/ nf bronchitis.

bronze /bʀɔ̃z/ nm bronze.

bronzé, ~e /bʀɔ̃ze/ adj (sun-) tanned.

bronzer /bʀɔ̃ze/ **1** vi (personne) get a (sun-)tan.

brosse /bʀɔs/ nf brush; ~ **à dents** toothbrush; ~ **à habits** clothes brush; **en** ~ (coiffure) in a crew cut.

brosser /bʀɔse/ **1** vt brush; (fig) paint. □ **se** ~ vpr se ~ **les dents/les che-**

veux brush one's teeth/hair.

brouette /bʀuɛt/ nf wheelbarrow.

brouhaha /bʀuaa/ nm hubbub.

brouillard /bʀujaʀ/ nm fog.

brouille /bʀuj/ nf quarrel.

brouiller /bʀuje/ **1** vt (vue) blur; (œufs) scramble; (amis) set at odds; ~ **les pistes** cloud the issue. □ **se** ~ vpr (ciel) cloud over; (amis) fall out.

brouillon, ~ne /bʀujɔ̃, -ɔn/ adj un-tidy. ● nm (rough) draft.

brousse /bʀus/ nf **la** ~ the bush.

brouter /bʀute/ **1** vt/i graze.

broyer /bʀwaje/ **31** vt crush; (moudre) grind.

bru /bʀy/ nf daughter-in-law.

bruine /bʀɥin/ nf drizzle.

bruissement /bʀɥismɑ̃/ nm rustling.

bruit /bʀɥi/ nm noise; ~ **de couloir** (fig) rumour.

bruitage /bʀɥitaʒ/ nm sound effects.

brûlant, ~e /bʀylɑ̃, -t/ adj burning (hot); (sujet) red-hot; (passion) fiery.

brûlé /bʀyle/ nm burning; **ça sent le** ~ I can smell something burning. ● →BRÛLER **1**.

brûler /bʀyle/ **1** vt/i burn; (essence) use (up); (cierge) light (à to); ~ **un feu (rouge)** jump the lights; ~ **d'en-vie de faire** be longing to do. □ **se** ~ vpr burn oneself.

brûlure /bʀylyʀ/ nf burn; ~s **d'esto-mac** heartburn.

brume /bʀym/ nf mist. **brumeux, -euse** adj misty; (esprit) hazy.

brun, ~e /bʀœ̃, -yn/ adj brown, dark. ● nm brown. ● nm, f dark haired per-son. **brunir 2** vi turn brown; (bron-zer) get a tan.

brushing /bʀœʃiŋ/ nm blow-dry.

brusque /bʀysk/ adj (personne) ab-rupt; (geste) violent; (soudain) sudden.

brusquer /bʀyske/ **1** vt be abrupt with; (précipiter) rush.

brut, ~e /bʀyt/ adj (diamant) rough; (champagne) dry; (pétrole) crude; (Comm) gross.

brutal, ~e (mpl -aux) /bʀytal, -o/ adj brutal. **brutalité** nf brutality.

brute /bʀyt/ nf brute.

Bruxelles /bʀysɛl/ npr Brussels.

bruyant, ~e /bʀɥijɑ̃, -t/ adj noisy.

bruyère /bʀyjɛʀ/ nf heather.

bu /by/ →**BOIRE** 12.

bûche /byʃ/ *nf* log; ~ **de Noël** Christmas log; **ramasser une** ~ 1 fall.

bûcher /byʃe/ 1 *vt/i* 1 slog away (at) 1. ● *nm* (supplice) stake.

bûcheron /byʃRɔ̃/ *nm* lumberjack.

budget /bydʒɛ/ *nm* budget. **budgétaire** *adj* budgetary.

buée /bɥe/ *nf* condensation.

buffet /byfɛ/ *nm* sideboard; (table garnie) buffet.

buffle /byfl/ *nm* buffalo.

buisson /bɥisɔ̃/ *nm* bush.

buissonnière /bɥisɔnjɛR/ *adj* **faire l'école** ~ play truant.

bulbe /bylb/ *nm* bulb.

bulgare /bylgaR/ *adj & nm* Bulgarian. **B**~ *nmf* Bulgarian.

Bulgarie /bylgaRi/ *nf* Bulgaria.

bulldozer /byldozɛR/ *nm* bulldozer.

bulle /byl/ *nf* bubble.

bulletin /byltɛ̃/ *nm* bulletin, report; (Scol) report; ~ **d'information** news bulletin; ~ **météorologique** weather report; ~ **(de vote)** ballot-paper; ~ **de salaire** pay-slip.

buraliste /byRalist/ *nmf* tobacconist.

bureau (*pl* ~**x**) /byRo/ *nm* office; (meuble) desk; (comité) board; ~ **d'études** design office; ~ **de poste** post office; ~ **de tabac** tobacconist's (shop); ~ **de vote** polling station.

bureaucrate /byRokRat/ *nmf* bureaucrat. **bureaucratie** *nf* bureaucracy. **bureaucratique** *adj* bureaucratic.

bureautique /byRotik/ *nf* office automation.

burlesque /byRlɛsk/ *adj* (histoire) ludicrous; (film) farcical.

bus /bys/ *nm* bus.

business /biznɛs/ *nm inv* (affaires commerciales) business; (affaires privées) affairs.

buste /byst/ *nm* bust.

but /by(t)/ *nm* target; (dessein) aim, goal; (football) goal; **avoir pour** ~ **de** aim to; **de** ~ **en blanc** point-blank; **dans le** ~ **de** with the intention of; **aller droit au** ~ go straight to the point.

butane /bytan/ *nm* butane, Calor gas®.

buté, ~**e** /byte/ *adj* obstinate.

buter /byte/ 1 *vi* ~ **contre** knock against; (problème) come up against. ● *vt* antagonize. □ **se** ~ *vpr* (s'entêter) become obstinate.

buteur /bytœR/ *nm* (au football) striker.

butin /bytɛ̃/ *nm* booty, loot.

butte /byt/ *nf* mound; **en** ~ **à** exposed to.

buvard /byvaR/ *nm* blotting-paper.

buvette /byvɛt/ *nf* (refreshment) bar.

buveur, -euse /byvœR, -øz/ *nm, f* drinker.

Cc

c' /s/ →**CE**.

ça /sa/

● *pronom démonstratif*

⋯▸ (sujet) it; that; ~ **flotte** it floats; ~ **suffit!** that's enough!; ~ **y est!** that's it!; ~ **sent le brûlé** there's a smell of burning; ~ **va?** how are things?

⋯▸ (objet) (proche) this; (plus éloigné) that; **c'est** ~ that's right.

⋯▸ (dans expressions) **où** ~? where?; **quand** ~? when?; **et avec** ~? anything else?

çà /sa/ *adv* ~ **et là** here and there.

cabane /kaban/ *nf* hut; (à outils) shed.

cabaret /kabaRɛ/ *nm* cabaret.

cabillaud /kabijo/ *nm* cod.

cabine /kabin/ *nf* (à la piscine) cubicle; (de bateau) cabin; (de camion) cab; (d'ascenseur) cage; ~ **d'essayage** fitting room; ~ **de pilotage** cockpit; ~ **de plage** beach hut; ~ **(téléphonique)** phone booth, phone box.

cabinet /kabinɛ/ *nm* (de médecin) surgery; (US) office; (d'avocat) office; (clientèle) practice; (cabinet collectif) firm; (Pol) Cabinet; (pièce) room; ~**s** (toilettes) toilet; (US) bathroom; ~ **de toilette** bathroom.

câble /kɑbl/ *nm* cable; (corde) rope; (TV) cable TV. **câbler** *vt* 1 cable; (TV) install cable television in.

cabosser /kabɔse/ **1** vt dent.

cabotage /kabɔtaʒ/ nm coastal navigation.

cabrer (se) /(sə)kabʀe/ **1** vpr (cheval) rear; **se ~ contre** rebel against.

cabriole /kabʀijɔl/ nf **faire des ~s** caper about.

cacahuète /kakawɛt/ nf peanut.

cacao /kakao/ nm cocoa.

cachalot /kaʃalo/ nm sperm whale.

cache /kaʃ/ nm mask. ● nf hiding place; **~ d'armes** arms cache.

cache-cache /kaʃkaʃ/ nm inv hide-and-seek.

cache-nez /kaʃne/ nm inv scarf.

cacher /kaʃe/ **1** vt hide, conceal (à from). □ **se ~** vpr hide; (se trouver caché) be hidden.

cachet /kaʃɛ/ nm (de cire) seal; (à l'encre) stamp; (de la poste) postmark; (comprimé) tablet; (d'artiste) fee; (chic) style, cachet.

cachette /kaʃɛt/ nf hiding-place; **en ~** in secret.

cachot /kaʃo/ nm dungeon.

cachottier, -ière /kaʃɔtje, -jɛʀ/ adj secretive.

cacophonie /kakɔfɔni/ nf cacophony.

cactus /kaktys/ nm cactus.

cadavérique /kadaveʀik/ adj (teint) deathly pale.

cadavre /kadavʀ/ nm corpse; (de victime) body.

caddie /kadi/ nm (de supermarché®) trolley; (au golf) caddie.

cadeau (pl ~x) /kado/ nm present, gift; **faire un ~ à qn** give sb a present.

cadenas /kadna/ nm padlock.

cadence /kadɑ̃s/ nf rhythm, cadence; (de travail) rate; **en ~** in time; (marcher) in step.

cadet, ~te /kadɛ, -t/ adj youngest; (entre deux) younger. ● nm, f youngest (child); younger (child).

cadran /kadʀɑ̃/ nm dial; **~ solaire** sundial.

cadre /kɑdʀ/ nm frame; (lieu) setting; (milieu) surroundings; (limites) scope; (contexte) framework; **dans le ~ de** (à l'occasion de) on the occasion of; (dans le contexte de) in the framework of. ● nm (personne) executive;

les **~s** the managerial staff.

cadrer /kadʀe/ **1** vi **~ avec** tally with. ● vt (photo) centre.

cafard /kafaʀ/ nm (insecte) cockroach; **avoir le ~** ① be down in the dumps.

café /kafe/ nm coffee; (bar) café; **~ crème** espresso with milk; **~ en grains** coffee beans; **~ au lait** white coffee.

cafetière /kaftjɛʀ/ nf coffee-pot; **~ électrique** coffee machine.

cage /kaʒ/ nf cage; **~ d'ascenseur** lift shaft; **~ d'escalier** stairwell; **~ thoracique** rib cage.

cageot /kaʒo/ nm crate.

cagibi /kaʒibi/ nm storage room.

cagneux, -euse /kaɲø, -z/ adj **avoir les genoux ~** be knock-kneed.

cagnotte /kaɲɔt/ nf kitty.

cagoule /kagul/ nf hood; (passe-montagne) balaclava.

cahier /kaje/ nm notebook; (Scol) exercise book; **~ de textes** homework notebook; **~ des charges** (Tech) specifications (+ pl).

cahot /kao/ nm bump, jolt. **cahoteux, -euse** adj bumpy.

caïd /kaid/ nm ① big shot.

caille /kɑj/ nf quail.

cailler /kɑje/ **1** vi curdle; **ça caille** ① it's freezing. □ **se ~** vpr (sang) clot; (lait) curdle. **caillot** nm (blood) clot.

caillou (pl ~x) /kaju/ nm stone; (galet) pebble.

caisse /kɛs/ nf crate, case; (tiroir, machine) till; (guichet) cash desk; (au supermarché) check-out; (bureau) office; (Mus) drum; **~ enregistreuse** cash register; **~ d'épargne** savings bank; **~ de retraite** pension fund. **caissier, -ière** nm, f cashier.

cajoler /kaʒɔle/ **1** vt coax.

calcaire /kalkɛʀ/ adj (sol) chalky; (eau) hard.

calciné, ~e /kalsine/ adj charred.

calcul /kalkyl/ nm calculation; (Scol) arithmetic; (différentiel) calculus; **~ biliaire** gallstone.

calculatrice /kalkylatʀis/ nf calculator. **calculer** **1** vt calculate. **calculette** nf (pocket) calculator.

cale /kal/ nf wedge; (pour roue) chock; (de navire) hold, **~ sèche** dry dock.

calé, ~e /kale/ adj ① clever.

caleçon /kalsɔ̃/ nm boxer shorts (+ pl); underpants (+ pl); (de femme) leggings.

calembour /kalɑ̃buʀ/ nm pun.

calendrier /kalɑ̃dʀije/ nm calendar; (fig) schedule, timetable.

calepin /kalpɛ̃/ nm notebook.

caler /kale/ **1** vt wedge. ● vi stall; (abandonner **1**) give up.

calfeutrer /kalføtʀe/ **1** vt (fissure) stop up; (porte) draught proof.

calibre /kalibʀ/ nm calibre; (d'un œuf, fruit) grade.

calice /kalis/ nm (Relig) chalice; (Bot) calyx.

califourchon: à ~ /akalifuʀʃɔ̃/ loc astride.

câlin, ~e /kɑlɛ̃, -in/ adj (regard, ton) affectionate; (personne) cuddly.

calmant /kalmɑ̃/ nm sedative.

calme /kalm/ adj calm. ● nm peace; calm; (maîtrise de soi) composure; **du ~!** calm down!

calmer /kalme/ **1** vt (personne) calm down; (situation) defuse; (douleur) ease; (soif) quench. □ **se ~** vpr (personne, situation) calm down; (agitation, tempête) die down; (douleur) ease.

calomnie /kalɔmni/ nf (orale) slander; (écrite) libel. **calomnier 45** vt slander; libel. **calomnieux, -ieuse** adj slanderous; libellous.

calorie /kalɔri/ nf calorie.

calque /kalk/ nm tracing; **(papier)** ~ tracing paper; (fig) exact copy.

calquer /kalke/ **1** vt trace; (fig) copy; ~ **qch sur** model sth on.

calvaire /kalvɛʀ/ nm (croix) Calvary; (fig) suffering.

calvitie /kalvisi/ nf baldness.

camarade /kamaʀad/ nmf friend; (Pol) comrade; ~ **de jeu** playmate. **camaraderie** nf friendship.

cambouis /kɑ̃bwi/ nm dirty oil.

cambrer /kɑ̃bʀe/ **1** vt arch. □ **se ~** vpr arch one's back.

cambriolage /kɑ̃bʀijɔlaʒ/ nm burglary. **cambrioler 1** vt burgle. **cambrioleur, -euse** nm, f burglar.

camelot /kamlo/ nm **1** street vendor.

camelote /kamlɔt/ nf **1** junk.

caméra /kameʀa/ nf (cinéma, télévision) camera.

caméscope® /kameskɔp/ nm camcorder.

camion /kamjɔ̃/ nm lorry, truck. **camion-citerne** (pl **camions-citernes**) nm tanker. **camionnage** nm haulage. **camionnette** nf van. **camionneur** nm lorry ou truck driver; (entrepreneur) haulage contractor.

camisole /kamizɔl/ nf ~ **(de force)** straitjacket.

camoufler /kamufle/ **1** vt camouflage.

camp /kɑ̃/ nm camp; (Sport, Pol) side.

campagnard, ~e /kɑ̃paɲaʀ, -d/ adj country. ● nm, f countryman, countrywoman.

campagne /kɑ̃paɲ/ nf country; countryside; (Mil, Pol) campaign.

campement /kɑ̃pmɑ̃/ nm camp, encampment.

camper /kɑ̃pe/ **1** vi camp. ● vt (esquisser) sketch. □ **se ~** vpr plant oneself. **campeur, -euse** nm, f camper.

camping /kɑ̃piŋ/ nm camping; **faire du ~** go camping; **(terrain de)** ~ campsite. **camping-car** (pl ~**s**) nm camper-van; (US) motorhome. **camping-gaz®** nm inv (réchaud) camping stove.

Canada /kanada/ nm Canada.

canadien, ~ne /kanadjɛ̃, -ɛn/ adj Canadian. **C~, ~ne** nm, f Canadian. **canadienne** nf (veste) fur-lined jacket; (tente) ridge tent.

canaille /kanɑj/ nf rogue.

canal (pl **-aux**) /kanal, -o/ nm (artificiel) canal; (bras de mer) channel; (Tech, TV) channel; (moyen) channel; **par le ~ de** through. **canalisation** nf (tuyaux) mains (+ pl). **canaliser 1** vt (eau) canalize; (fig) channel.

canapé /kanape/ nm sofa.

canard /kanaʀ/ nm duck; (journal **1**) rag.

canari /kanaʀi/ nm canary.

cancans /kɑ̃kɑ̃/ nmpl **1** gossip.

cancer /kɑ̃sɛʀ/ nm cancer; **le C~** Cancer. **cancéreux, -euse** adj cancerous. **cancérigène** adj carcinogenic.

cancre /kɑ̃kʀ/ nm dunce.

candeur /kɑ̃dœʀ/ nf ingenuousness.

candidat, ~e /kɑ̃dida, -t/ nm, f (à un examen, Pol) candidate; (à un poste) applicant, candidate (**à** for).

candidature /kɑ̃didatyʀ/ nf application; (Pol) candidacy; **poser sa ∼ à un poste** apply for a job.

candide /kɑ̃did/ adj ingenuous.

cane /kan/ nf (female) duck. **caneton** nm duckling.

canette /kanɛt/ nf (bouteille) bottle; (boîte) can.

canevas /kanva/ nm canvas; (ouvrage) tapestry; (plan) framework, outline.

caniche /kaniʃ/ nm poodle.

canicule /kanikyl/ nf scorching heat; (vague de chaleur) heatwave.

canif /kanif/ nm penknife.

canine /kanin/ nf canine (tooth).

caniveau (pl ∼x) /kanivo/ nm gutter.

cannabis /kanabis/ nm cannabis.

canne /kan/ nf (walking) stick; **∼ à pêche** fishing rod; **∼ à sucre** sugar cane.

cannelle /kanɛl/ nf cinnamon.

cannibale /kanibal/ adj & nmf cannibal.

canoë /kanɔe/ nm canoe; (Sport) canoeing.

canon /kanɔ̃/ nm (blg) gun; (ancien) cannon; (d'une arme) barrel; (principe, règle) canon.

canot /kano/ nm dinghy, (small) boat; **∼ de sauvetage** lifeboat; **∼ pneumatique** rubber dinghy. **canotier** nm boater.

cantatrice /kɑ̃tatʀis/ nf opera singer.

cantine /kɑ̃tin/ nf canteen.

cantique /kɑ̃tik/ nm hymn.

cantonner /kɑ̃tɔne/ ❶ vt (Mil) billet. □ **se ∼ dans** vpr confine oneself to.

canular /kanylaʀ/ nm hoax.

caoutchouc /kautʃu/ nm rubber; (élastique) rubber band; **∼ mousse** foam rubber.

cap /kap/ nm cape, headland; (direction) course; (obstacle) hurdle; **franchir le ∼ de la cinquantaine** pass the fifty mark; **mettre le ∼ sur** steer a course for.

capable /kapabl/ adj capable (de of); **∼ de faire** able to do, capable of doing.

capacité /kapasite/ nf ability; (contenance, potentiel) capacity.

cape /kap/ nf cape; **rire sous ∼** laugh up one's sleeve.

capillaire /kapilɛʀ/ adj (lotion, soins) hair; (vaisseau) ∼ capillary.

capitaine /kapitɛn/ nm captain.

capital, ∼e (mpl **-aux**) /kapital,-o/ adj key, crucial, fundamental; (peine, lettre) capital. ● nm (pl **-aux**) (Comm) capital; (fig) stock; **capitaux** (Comm) capital; **∼-risque** venture capital; **∼-risqueur** venture capitalist. **capitale** nf (ville, lettre) capital.

capitalisme /kapitalism/ nm capitalism.

capitonné, ∼e /kapitɔne/ adj padded.

capituler /kapityle/ ❶ vi capitulate.

caporal (pl **-aux**) /kapɔʀal, -o/ nm corporal.

capot /kapo/ nm (Auto) bonnet; (US) hood.

capote /kapɔt/ nf (Auto) hood; (US) top; (préservatif 🄸) condom.

capoter /kapɔte/ ❶ vi overturn; (fig) collapse.

câpre /kɑpʀ/ nf (Culin) caper.

caprice /kapʀis/ nm whim; (colère) tantrum; **faire un ∼** throw a tantrum. **capricieux, -ieuse** adj capricious; (appareil) temperamental.

Capricorne /kapʀikɔʀn/ nm **le ∼** Capricorn.

capsule /kapsyl/ nf capsule; (de bouteille) cap.

capter /kapte/ ❶ vt (eau) collect; (émission) get; (signal) pick up; (fig) win, capture.

captif, -ive /kaptif, -v/ adj & nm, f captive.

captiver /kaptive/ ❶ vt captivate.

capturer /kaptyʀe/ ❶ vt capture.

capuche /kapyʃ/ nf hood. **capuchon** nm hood; (de stylo) cap.

car /kaʀ/ conj because, for. ● nm coach; (US) bus.

carabine /kaʀabin/ nf rifle.

caractère /kaʀaktɛʀ/ nm (lettre) character; (nature) nature; **∼s d'imprimerie** block letters; **avoir bon/mauvais ∼** be good-natured/bad-tempered; **avoir du ∼** have character.

caractériel, ∼le /kaʀakteʀjɛl/ adj (trait) character; (enfant) disturbed.

caractériser /kaʀakteʀize/ ❶ vt characterize. □ **se ∼ par** vpr be characterized by. **caractéristique** adj & nf characteristic.

carafe /kaʁaf/ nf carafe.

Caraïbes /kaʁaib/ nfpl les ~ the Caribbean.

carambolage /kaʁɑ̃bɔlaʒ/ nm pile-up.

caramel /kaʁamɛl/ nm caramel; (bonbon) toffee.

carapace /kaʁapas/ nf shell.

caravane /kaʁavan/ nf (Auto) caravan; (US) trailer; (convoi) caravan.

carbone /kaʁbɔn/ nm carbon; **(papier)** ~ carbon (paper). **carboniser** 🔳 vt burn (to ashes).

carburant /kaʁbyʁɑ̃/ nm (motor) fuel.

carburateur /kaʁbyʁatœʁ/ nm carburettor; (US) carburetor.

carcan /kaʁkɑ̃/ nm constraints (+ pl).

carcasse /kaʁkas/ nf (squelette) carcass; (armature) frame; (de voiture) shell.

cardiaque /kaʁdjak/ adj heart. ● nmf heart patient.

cardinal, ~e (mpl -aux) /kaʁdinal, -o/ adj & nm cardinal.

Carême /kaʁɛm/ nm le ~ Lent.

carence /kaʁɑ̃s/ nf shortcomings (+ pl); inadequacy; (Méd) deficiency; (absence) lack.

caresse /kaʁɛs/ nf caress; (à un animal) stroke. **caresser** 🔳 vt caress, stroke; (espoir) cherish.

cargaison /kaʁgɛzɔ̃/ nf cargo.

cargo /kaʁgo/ nm cargo boat.

caricature /kaʁikatyʁ/ nf caricature.

carie /kaʁi/ nf (trou) cavity; **la ~ (dentaire)** tooth decay.

carillon /kaʁijɔ̃/ nm chimes (+ pl); (horloge) chiming clock.

caritatif, **-ive** /kaʁitatif, -v/ adj **association caritative** charity.

carnage /kaʁnaʒ/ nm carnage.

carnassier, **-ière** /kaʁnasje, -jɛʁ/ adj carnivorous.

carnaval (pl ~s) /kaʁnaval/ nm carnival.

carnet /kaʁnɛ/ nm notebook; (de tickets, timbres) book; ~ **d'adresses** address book; ~ **de chèques** chequebook.

carotte /kaʁɔt/ nf carrot.

carpe /kaʁp/ nf carp.

carré, ~e /kaʁe/ adj (forme, mesure) quare; (fig) straightforward; **un mètre** ~ one square metre. ● nm square; (de terrain) patch.

carreau (pl ~x) /kaʁo/ nm (window) pane; (par terre, au mur) tile; (dessin) check; (aux cartes) diamonds (+ pl); **à** ~**x** (tissu) check(ed); (papier) squared.

carrefour /kaʁfuʁ/ nm crossroads (+ sg).

carrelage /kaʁlaʒ/ nm tiling; (sol) tiles.

carrément /kaʁemɑ̃/ adv (complètement) completely; (stupide, dangereux) downright; (dire) straight out; **elle a** ~ **démissionné** she went straight ahead and resigned.

carrière /kaʁjɛʁ/ nf career; (terrain) quarry.

carrossable /kaʁɔsabl/ adj suitable for vehicles.

carrosse /kaʁɔs/ nm (horse-drawn) coach.

carrosserie /kaʁɔsʁi/ nf (Auto) body(work).

carrure /kaʁyʁ/ nf shoulders; (fig) necessary qualities, calibre.

cartable /kaʁtabl/ nm satchel.

carte /kaʁt/ nf card; (Géog) map; (Naut) chart; (au restaurant) menu; ~**s** (jeu) cards; **à la** ~ (manger) à la carte; (horaire) personalized; **donner** ~ **blanche à** give a free hand to; ~ **bleue®** credit card; ~ **de crédit** credit card; ~ **de fidélité** loyalty card; ~ **grise** (car) registration document; ~ **d'identité** identity card; ~ **magnétique** swipe card; ~ **de paiement** debit card; ~ **postale** postcard; ~ **à puce** smart card; ~ **de séjour** resident's permit; ~ **SIM** SIM card; ~ **des vins** wine list; ~ **de visite** (business) card; ~ **vitale** social insurance smart card.

Carte d'identité Not to be confused with a passport, this is a proof of identity carried by French citizens. It is issued by the préfecture and is valid for ten years. Though not compulsory, it is used to guarantee payments by cheque and is accepted as a travel document within the EU.

cartilage /kaʀtilaʒ/ nm cartilage.

carton /kaʀtɔ̃/ nm cardboard; (boîte) (cardboard) box; ~ **à dessin** portfolio; **faire un** ~ 🔳 do well.

cartonné, -e /kaʀtɔne/ adj **livre** ~ hardback.

cartouche /kaʀtuʃ/ nf cartridge; (de cigarettes) carton. **cartouchière** nf cartridge-belt.

cas /kɑ/ nm case; **au** ~ **où** in case; ~ **urgent** emergency; **en aucun** ~ on no account; **en** ~ **de** in the event of, in case of; **en tout** ~ in any case; (du moins) at least; **faire** ~ **de** set great store by; ~ **de conscience** moral dilemma.

casanier, -ière /kazanje, -jɛʀ/ adj home-loving.

cascade /kaskad/ nf waterfall; (au cinéma) stunt; (fig) spate, series (+ sg).

cascadeur, -euse /kaskadœʀ, øz/ nm, f stuntman, stuntwoman.

case /kɑz/ nf hut; (de damier) square; (compartiment) pigeon-hole; (sur un formulaire) box.

caser /kaze/ 🔳 vt 🔳 (mettre) put; (loger) put up; (dans un travail) find a job for; (marier: péj) marry off.

caserne /kazɛʀn/ nf barracks; ~ **de sapeurs-pompiers** fire station.

casier /kazje/ nm pigeon-hole, compartment; (à chaussures) rack; ~ **judiciaire** criminal record.

casque /kask/ nm (de motard) crash helmet; (de cycliste) cycle helmet; (chez le coiffeur) (hair-)drier; ~ **(à écouteurs)** headphones; ~ **anti-bruit** ear defenders; ~ **de protection** safety helmet.

casquette /kaskɛt/ nf cap.

cassant, -e /kasɑ̃, -t/ adj brittle; (brusque) curt.

cassation /kasasjɔ̃/ nf **cour de** ~ appeal court.

casse /kɑs/ nf (objets) breakages; (lieu) breaker's yard; **mettre à la** ~ scrap.

casse-cou /kasku/ nmf inv daredevil.

casse-croûte /kaskʀut/ nm inv snack.

casse-noix /kasnwa/ nm inv nutcrackers (+ pl).

casse-pieds /kaspje/ nmf inv 🔳 pain (in the neck) 🔳.

casser /kase/ 🔳 vt break; (annuler) annul; ~ **les pieds à qn** 🔳 annoy sb.

● vi break. ◻ **se** ~ vpr break; (partir) 🔳 be off 🔳.

casserole /kasʀɔl/ nf saucepan.

casse-tête /kastɛt/ nm inv (problème) headache; (jeu) brain teaser.

cassette /kasɛt/ nf casket; (de magnétophone) cassette, tape; (de vidéo) video tape; ~ **audio numérique** ~ digital audio tape.

cassis /kasi(s)/ nm inv blackcurrant.

cassure /kasyʀ/ nf break.

castor /kastɔʀ/ nm beaver.

castration /kastʀasjɔ̃/ nf castration.

catalogue /katalɔg/ nm catalogue.

catalyseur /katalizœʀ/ nm catalyst; (Auto) catalytic convertor.

catastrophe /katastʀɔf/ nf disaster, catastrophe. **catastrophique** adj catastrophic.

catch /katʃ/ nm (all-in) wrestling.

catéchisme /kateʃism/ nm catechism.

catégorie /kategɔʀi/ nf category. **catégorique** adj categorical.

cathédrale /katedʀal/ nf cathedral.

catholique /katɔlik/ adj Catholic; **pas très** ~ a bit fishy.

catimini: en ~ /ɑ̃katimini/ loc on the sly.

cauchemar /koʃmaʀ/ nm nightmare.

cause /koz/ nf cause; (raison) reason; (Jur) case; **à** ~ **de** because of; **en** ~ (en jeu, concerné) involved; **pour** ~ **de** on account of; **mettre en** ~ implicate; **remettre en** ~ call into question.

causer /koze/ 🔳 vt cause; (discuter de 🔳) ~ **travail** talk shop; ~ **de** talk about. ● vi chat. **causerie** nf talk.

causette /kozɛt/ nf (Internet) chat; **faire la** ~ have a chat.

caution /kosjɔ̃/ nf surety; (Jur) bail; (appui) backing; (garantie) deposit; **libéré sous** ~ released on bail. **cautionner** 🔳 vt guarantee; (soutenir) back.

cavalcade /kavalkad/ nf stampede, rush.

cavalier, -ière /kavalje, -jɛʀ/ adj offhand; **allée cavalière** bridle path. ● nm, f rider; (pour danser) partner. ● nm (aux échecs) knight.

cave /kav/ nf cellar. ● adj sunken.

caveau (pl ~x) /kavo/ nm vault.

caverne /kavɛʀn/ nf cave.

CCP abrév m (**compte chèque postal**) post office account.

CD abrév m (**compact disc**) CD.

CD-ROM abrév m inv (**compact disc read only memory**) CD-ROM.

---

ce, c', cet, cette (pl **ces**) /sə, s, sɛt, se/

c' before e. **cet** before vowel or mute h.

● **ce, cet, cette** (pl **ces**) adjectif démonstratif

····▸ this; (plus éloigné) that; **ces** these; (plus éloigné) those; **cette nuit** (passée) last night; (à venir) tonight.

● **ce, c'** pronom démonstratif

····▸ **c'est** it's ou it is; **c'est un policier** he's a policeman; ~ **sont eux qui l'ont fait** they did it; **qui est- ~?** who is it?

····▸ **ce que/qui** what; ~ **que je ne comprends pas** what I don't understand; **elle est venue, ~ qui est étonnant** she came, which is surprising; ~ **que tu as de la chance!** how lucky you are! **tout ~ qu'elle trouve/peut** everything she finds/can

---

CE abrév f (**Communauté européenne**) EC.

CEAM abrév f (**Carte européenne d'assurance maladie**) EHIC.

ceci /səsi/ pron this.

cécité /sesite/ nf blindness.

céder /sede/ 🔢 vt give up; ~ **le passage** give way; (vendre) sell. ● vi (se rompre) give way; (se soumettre) give in.

cédérom /sedeʀɔm/ nm CD-ROM.

cédille /sedij/ nf cedilla.

cèdre /sɛdʀ/ nm cedar.

CEI abrév f (**Communauté des États indépendants**) CIS.

ceinture /sɛ̃tyʀ/ nf belt; (taille) waist; ~ **de sauvetage** lifebelt; ~ **de sécurité** seatbelt.

cela /səla/ pron it, that; (pour désigner) that; ~ **va de soi** it is obvious; ~ **dit/fait** having said/done that.

célèbre /selɛbʀ/ adj famous. **célébrer** 🔢 vt celebrate. **célébrité** nf fame; (personne) celebrity.

céleri /sɛlʀi/ nm (en branches) celery. **céleri-rave** (pl **célerisraves**) nm celeriac.

célibat /seliba/ nm celibacy; (état) single status.

célibataire /selibatɛʀ/ adj single. ● nm bachelor. ● nf single woman.

celle, celles /sɛl/ ➡CELUI.

cellulaire /selylɛʀ/ adj cell; **emprisonnement** ~ solitary confinement; **fourgon** ou **voiture** ~ prison van; **téléphone** ~ cellular phone.

cellule /selyl/ nf cell; ~ **souche** stem cell.

celui, celle (pl **ceux, celles**) /səlɥi, sɛl, sø/ pron the one; ~ **de mon ami** my friend's; ~**-ci** this (one); ~**-là** that (one); **ceux-ci** these (ones); **ceux-là** those (ones).

cendre /sɑ̃dʀ/ nf ash.

cendrier /sɑ̃dʀije/ nm ashtray.

censé, ~e /sɑ̃se/ adj être ~ **faire** be supposed to do.

censeur /sɑ̃sœʀ/ nm censor; (Scol) administrator in charge of discipline.

censure /sɑ̃syʀ/ nf censorship. **censurer** 🔢 vt censor; (critiquer) censure.

cent /sɑ̃/ adj (a) hundred; **20 pour** ~ 20 per cent.● n (quantité) hundred; ~ **un** a hundred and one;)**centième d'euro**) cent.

centaine /sɑ̃tɛn/ nf hundred; **une** ~ **(de)** (about) a hundred.

centenaire /sɑ̃tnɛʀ/ nm (anniversaire) centenary.

centième /sɑ̃tjɛm/ adj & nmf hundredth.

centimètre /sɑ̃timɛtʀ/ nm centimetre; (ruban) tape-measure.

central, ~e (mpl **-aux**) /sɑ̃tʀal,-o/ adj central. ● nm (pl **-aux**) ~ (**téléphonique**) (telephone) exchange. **centrale** nf power-station.

centre /sɑ̃tʀ/ nm centre; ~ **commercial** shopping centre; (US) mall; ~ **d'appels** call centre; ~ **de formation** training centre; ~ **hospitalier** hospital. **centrer** 🔢 vt centre. **centre-ville** (pl **centres-villes**) nm town centre.

centuple /sãtypl/ *nm* le ~ de a hundred times; **au** ~ a hundredfold.

cep /sɛp/ *nm* vine stock.

cépage /sepaʒ/ *nm* grape variety.

cèpe /sɛp/ *nm* cep.

cependant /səpãdã/ *adv* however.

céramique /seramik/ *nf* ceramic; (art) ceramics (+ *sg*).

cercle /sɛʀkl/ *nm* circle; (cerceau) hoop; (association) society, club; ~ **vicieux** vicious circle.

cercueil /sɛʀkœj/ *nm* coffin.

céréale /seʀeal/ *nf* cereal; ~**s** (Culin) (breakfast) cereal.

cérébral, ~e (*mpl* **-aux**) /seʀebʀal, -o/ *adj* cerebral.

cérémonie /seʀemɔni/ *nf* ceremony; **sans** ~**s** (*repas*) informal; (*recevoir*) informally.

cerf /sɛʀ/ *nm* stag.

cerfeuil /sɛʀfœj/ *nm* chervil.

cerf-volant (*pl* **cerfs-volants**) /sɛʀvɔlã/ *nm* kite.

cerise /s(ə)ʀiz/ *nf* cherry. **cerisier** *nm* cherry tree.

cerner /sɛʀne/ **1** *vt* surround; (*question*) define; **avoir les yeux cernés** have rings under one's eyes.

certain, ~e /sɛʀtɛ̃, -ɛn/ *adj* certain; (*sûr*) certain, sure (**de** *of*; **que** that); **d'un** ~ **âge** no longer young; **un** ~ **temps** some time. **certainement** *adv* (probablement) most probably; (avec certitude) certainly. **certains, -es** *pron* some people.

certes /sɛʀt/ *adv* (sans doute) admittedly; (bien sûr) of course.

certificat /sɛʀtifika/ *nm* certificate.

certifier /sɛʀtifje/ **45** *vt* certify; ~ **qch à qn** assure sb of sth; **copie certifiée conforme** certified true copy.

certitude /sɛʀtityd/ *nf* certainty.

cerveau (*pl* ~**x**) /sɛʀvo/ *nm* brain.

cervelle /sɛʀvɛl/ *nf* (Anat) brain; (Culin) brains.

ces /se/ ➡CE.

césarienne /sezaʀjɛn/ *nf* Caesarean (section).

cesse /sɛs/ *nf* **n'avoir de** ~ **que** have no rest until; **sans** ~ constantly, incessantly.

cesser /sese/ **1** *vt* stop; ~ **de faire** stop doing. ● *vi* cease; **faire** ~ put an end to.

cessez-le-feu /seselfø/ *nm inv* ceasefire.

cession /sɛsjõ/ *nf* transfer.

c'est-à-dire /setadiʀ/ *conj* that is (to say).

cet, cette /sɛt/ ➡CE.

ceux /sø/ ➡CELUI.

chacun, ~e /ʃakœ̃, -yn/ *pron* each (one), every one; (tout le monde) everyone; ~ **d'entre nous** each (one) of us.

chagrin /ʃagʀɛ̃/ *nm* sorrow; **avoir du** ~ be sad.

chahut /ʃay/ *nm* row, din.

chahuter /ʃayte/ **1** *vi* make a row. ● *vt* (enseignant) be rowdy with; (orateur) heckle.

chaîne /ʃɛn/ *nf* chain; (de télévision) channel; ~ **(d'assemblage)** assembly line; ~**s** (Auto) snow chains; ~ **de montagnes** mountain range; ~ **de montage/fabrication** assembly/production line; ~ **hi-fi** hi-fi system; ~ **laser** CD player; **en** ~ (accidents) multiple; (réaction) chain. **chaînette** *nf* (small) chain. **chaînon** *nm* link.

chair /ʃɛʀ/ *nf* flesh; **bien en** ~ plump; **en** ~ **et en os** in the flesh; ~ **à saucisses** sausage meat; **la** ~ **de poule** goose pimples. ● *adj inv* (couleur) ~ flesh-coloured.

chaire /ʃɛʀ/ *nf* (d'église) pulpit; (Univ) chair.

chaise /ʃɛz/ *nf* chair; ~ **longue** deckchair.

châle /ʃɑl/ *nm* shawl.

chaleur /ʃalœʀ/ *nf* heat; (moins intense) warmth; (d'un accueil, d'une couleur) warmth. **chaleureux, -euse** *adj* warm.

chalumeau (*pl* ~**x**) /ʃalymo/ *nm* blowtorch.

chalutier /ʃalytje/ *nm* trawler.

chamailler (se) /(sə)ʃamɑje/ **1** *vpr* squabble.

chambre /ʃɑ̃bʀ/ *nf* (bed) room; (Pol, Jur) chamber; **faire** ~ **à part** sleep in separate rooms; ~ **à air** inner tube; ~ **d'amis** spare *ou* guest room; ~ **de commerce (et d'industrie)** Chamber of Commerce; ~ **à coucher** bedroom;

~ à un lit/deux lits single/twin room; **~ pour deux personnes ~** double room; **~ forte** strong-room; **~ d'hôte** bed and breakfast. **chambrer ⬛ 1** vt (vin) bring to room temperature.

chameau (pl **~x**) /ʃamo/ nm camel.

chamois /ʃamwa/ nm chamois.

champ /ʃɑ̃/ nm field; **~ de bataille** battlefield; **~ de courses** racecourse; **~ de tir** firing range.

champêtre /ʃɑ̃pɛtʀ/ adj rural.

champignon /ʃɑ̃piɲɔ̃/ nm mushroom; (moisissure) fungus; **~ de Paris** button mushroom.

champion, ~ne /ʃɑ̃pjɔ̃, -ɔn/ nm, f champion. **championnat** nm championship.

chance /ʃɑ̃s/ nf (good) luck; (possibilité) chance; **avoir de la ~** be lucky; **quelle ~!** what luck!

chanceler /ʃɑ̃sle/ 38 vi stagger; (fig) falter, waver.

chancelier /ʃɑ̃səlje/ nm chancellor.

chanceux, -euse /ʃɑ̃sø, -z/ adj lucky.

chandail /ʃɑ̃daj/ nm sweater.

chandelier /ʃɑ̃dəlje/ nm candlestick.

chandelle /ʃɑ̃dɛl/ nf candle; **dîner aux ~s** candlelight dinner.

change /ʃɑ̃ʒ/ nm (foreign) exchange; (taux) exchange rate.

changement /ʃɑ̃ʒmɑ̃/ nm change; **~ climatique** climate change; **~ de vitesse** (dispositif) ears.

changer /ʃɑ̃ʒe/ 40 vt change; **~ qch de place** move sth; (échanger) change (pour, contre for); **~ de nom/voiture** change one's name/car; **~ de place/train** change places/trains; **~ de direction** change direction; **~ d'avis** ou **d'idée** change one's mind; **~ de vitesse** change gear. □ **se ~** vpr change, get changed.

chanson /ʃɑ̃sɔ̃/ nf song.

chant /ʃɑ̃/ nm singing; (chanson) song; (Relig) hymn.

chantage /ʃɑ̃taʒ/ nm blackmail.

chanter /ʃɑ̃te/ 1 vt sing; **si cela vous chante** 1 if you feel like it. ● vi sing; **faire ~** (délit) blackmail. **chanteur, -euse** nm, f singer.

chantier /ʃɑ̃tje/ nm building site; **~ naval** shipyard; **mettre en ~** get under way, start.

chaos /kao/ nm chaos.

chaparder /ʃapaʀde/ 1 vt 1 pinch 1, filch.

chapeau (pl **~x**) /ʃapo/ nm hat; **~!** well done!

chapelet /ʃaplɛ/ nm rosary; (fig) string.

chapelle /ʃapɛl/ nf chapel.

chapelure /ʃaplyʀ/ nf (Culin) breadcrumbs.

chaperonner /ʃapʀɔne/ 1 vt chaperone.

chapiteau (pl **~x**) /ʃapito/ nm marquee; (de cirque) big top; (de colonne) capital.

chapitre /ʃapitʀ/ nm chapter; (fig) subject.

chaque /ʃak/ adj every, each.

char /ʃaʀ/ nm (Mil) tank; (de carnaval) float; (charrette) cart; (dans l'antiquité) chariot.

charabia /ʃaʀabja/ nm 1 gibberish.

charade /ʃaʀad/ nf riddle.

charbon /ʃaʀbɔ̃/ nm coal; (Méd) anthrax; **~ de bois** charcoal.

charcuterie /ʃaʀkytʀi/ nf pork butcher's shop; (aliments) (cooked) pork meats. **charcutier, -ière** nm, f pork butcher.

chardon /ʃaʀdɔ̃/ nm thistle.

charge /ʃaʀʒ/ nf load, burden; (Mil, Électr, Jur) charge; (responsabilité) responsibility; **avoir qn à ~** be responsible for; **~s** expenses; (de locataire) service charges; **être à la ~ de** (personne) be the responsibility of; (frais) be payable by; **~s sociales** social security contributions; **prendre en ~** take charge of.

chargé, ~e /ʃaʀʒe/ adj (véhicule) loaded; (journée, emploi du temps) busy; (langue) coated. ● nm, f **~ de mission** head of mission; **~ d'affaires** chargé d'affaires; **~ de cours** lecturer.

chargement /ʃaʀʒəmɑ̃/ nm loading; (objets) load.

charger /ʃaʀʒe/ 40 vt load; (Ordinat, Photo) load; (attaquer) charge; (batterie) charge; **~ qn de** (fardeau) weigh sb down with; (tâche) entrust sb with; **~ qn de faire** make sb responsible for doing. ● vi (attaquer) charge. □ **se ~ de** vpr take charge ou care of.

chariot /ʃaʀjo/ nm (à roulettes) trolley; (US) cart; (charrette) cart.

charitable /ʃaʀitabl/ *adj* charitable.

charité /ʃaʀite/ *nf* charity; **faire la ~ à** give (money) to.

charlatan /ʃaʀlatɑ̃/ *nm* charlatan.

charmant, ~e /ʃaʀmɑ̃, -t/ *adj* charming.

charme /ʃaʀm/ *nm* charm; (qui envoûte) spell. **charmer** ❶ *vt* charm. **charmeur, -euse** *nm, f* charmer.

charnel, ~le /ʃaʀnɛl/ *adj* carnal.

charnière /ʃaʀnjɛʀ/ *nf* hinge; **à la ~ de** at the meeting point between.

charnu, ~e /ʃaʀny/ *adj* plump, fleshy.

charpente /ʃaʀpɑ̃t/ *nf* framework; (carrure) build.

charpentier /ʃaʀpɑ̃tje/ *nm* carpenter.

charrette /ʃaʀɛt/ *nf* cart.

charrue /ʃaʀy/ *nf* plough.

chasse /ʃas/ *nf* hunting; (au fusil) shooting; (poursuite) chase; (recherche) hunt(ing); **~ (d'eau)** (toilet) flush; **~ sous-marine** harpoon fishing.

chasse-neige /ʃasnɛʒ/ *nm inv* snow plough.

chasser /ʃase/ ❶ *vt* hunt; (au fusil) shoot; (faire partir) chase away; (odeur, employé) get rid of. ● *vi* go hunting; (au fusil) go shooting.

chasseur, -euse /ʃasœʀ, -øz/ *nm, f* hunter. ● *nm* bellboy, (US) bellhop; (avion) fighter plane.

châssis /ʃasi/ *nm* frame; (Auto) chassis.

chasteté /ʃastəte/ *nf* chastity.

chat¹ /ʃa/ *nm* cat; (mâle) tomcat.

chat² /tʃat/ *nm* (Internet) chat.

châtaigne /ʃatɛɲ/ *nf* chestnut. **châtaignier** *nm* chestnut tree. **châtain** *adj inv* chestnut (brown).

château (pl **~x**) /ʃato/ *nm* castle; (manoir) manor; **~ d'eau** water tower; **~ fort** fortified castle.

châtiment /ʃatimɑ̃/ *nm* punishment.

chaton /ʃatɔ̃/ *nm* (chat) kitten.

chatouillement /ʃatujmɑ̃/ *nm* tickling. **chatouiller** ❶ *vt* tickle. **chatouilleux, -euse** *adj* ticklish; (susceptible) touchy.

châtrer /ʃatʀe/ ❶ *vt* castrate; (chat) neuter.

chatte /ʃat/ *nf* female cat.

chaud, ~e /ʃo, -d/ *adj* warm; (brûlant) hot; (vif: fig) warm. ● *nm* heat; **au ~**

in the warm(th); **avoir ~** be warm; be hot; **il fait ~** it is warm; it is hot; **pour te tenir ~** to keep you warm. **chaudement** *adv* warmly; (disputé) hotly.

chaudière /ʃodjɛʀ/ *nf* boiler.

chaudron /ʃodʀɔ̃/ *nm* cauldron.

chauffage /ʃofaʒ/ *nm* heating; **~ central** central heating.

chauffard /ʃofaʀ/ *nm* (péj) reckless driver.

chauffer /ʃofe/ ❶ *vt/i* heat (up); (moteur, appareil) overheat. □ **se ~** *vpr* warm oneself (up).

chauffeur /ʃofœʀ/ *nm* driver; (aux gages de qn) chauffeur.

chaume /ʃom/ *nm* (de toit) thatch.

chaussée /ʃose/ *nf* road (way).

chausse-pied /ʃospje/ (pl **~s**) /ʃospje/ *nm* shoehorn.

chausser /ʃose/ ❶ *vt* (chaussures) put on; (enfant) put shoes on (to). ● *vi* **~ bien** (aller) fit well; **~ du 35** take a size 35 shoe. □ **se ~** *vpr* put one's shoes on.

chaussette /ʃosɛt/ *nf* sock.

chausson /ʃosɔ̃/ *nm* slipper; (de bébé) bootee; **~ de danse** ballet shoe; **~ aux pommes** apple turnover.

chaussure /ʃosyʀ/ *nf* shoe; **~ de ski** ski boot; **~ de marche** hiking boot.

chauve /ʃov/ *adj* bald.

chauve-souris (pl **chauves-souris**) /ʃovsuʀi/ *nf* bat.

chauvin, ~e /ʃovɛ̃, -in/ *adj* chauvinistic. ● *nm, f* chauvinist.

chavirer /ʃaviʀe/ ❶ *vt* (bateau) capsize; (objets) tip over.

chef /ʃɛf/ *nm* leader, head; (supérieur) boss, superior; (Culin) chef; (de tribu) chief; **architecte en ~** chief ou head architect; **~ d'accusation** (Jur) charge; **~ d'équipe** foreman; (Sport) captain; **~ d'État** head of State; **~ de famille** head of the family; **~ de file** (Pol) leader; **~ de gare** stationmaster; **~ d'orchestre** conductor; **~ de service** department head; **~ de train** guard; (US) conductor.

chef-d'œuvre (pl **chefs-d'œuvre**) /ʃedœvʀ/ *nm* masterpiece.

chef-lieu (pl **chefs-lieux**) /ʃefljø/ *nm* county town, administrative centre.

chemin /ʃəmɛ̃/ nm road; (étroit) lane; (de terre) track; (pour piétons) path; (passage) way; (direction, trajet) way; **avoir du ~ à faire** have a long way to go; **~ de fer** railway; **par ~ de fer** by rail; **~ de halage** towpath; **~ vicinal** country lane.

cheminée /ʃəmine/ nf chimney; (intérieure) fireplace; (encadrement) mantelpiece; (de bateau) funnel.

cheminot /ʃəmino/ nm railwayman; (US) railroad man.

chemise /ʃəmiz/ nf shirt; (dossier) folder; (de livre) jacket; **~ de nuit** nightdress. **chemisette** nf short-sleeved shirt. **chemisier** nm blouse.

chêne /ʃɛn/ nm oak.

chenil /ʃəni(l)/ nm (pension) kennels (+ sg).

chenille /ʃənij/ nf caterpillar; **véhicule à ~s** tracked vehicle.

cheptel /ʃɛptɛl/ nm livestock.

chèque /ʃɛk/ nm cheque; **~ sans provision** bad cheque; **~ de voyage** traveller's cheque. **chéquier** nm chequebook.

cher, chère /ʃɛʀ/ adj (coûteux) dear, expensive; (aimé) dear; (dans la correspondance) dear. ● adv (coûter, payer) a lot (of money); (en importance) dearly. ● nm, f **mon ~, ma chère** my dear.

chercher /ʃɛʀʃe/ **1** vt look for; (aide, paix, gloire) seek; **aller ~** go and get ou fetch, go for; **~ à faire** attempt to do; **~ la petite bête** be finicky.

chercheur, -euse /ʃɛʀʃœʀ, -øz/ nm, f research worker.

chèrement /ʃɛʀmɑ̃/ adv dearly.

chéri, ~e /ʃeʀi/ adj beloved. ● nm, f darling.

chérir /ʃeʀiʀ/ **2** vt cherish.

chétif, -ive /ʃetif, -v/ adj puny.

cheval (pl -**aux**) /ʃəval, -o/ nm horse; **à ~** on horseback; **à ~ sur** astride, straddling; **faire du ~** ride, go horse-riding.

chevalerie /ʃəvalʀi/ nf chivalry.

chevalet /ʃəvalɛ/ nm easel; (de menuisier) trestle.

chevalier /ʃəvalje/ nm knight.

chevalière /ʃəvaljɛʀ/ nf signet ring.

cheval-vapeur (pl **chevaux-vapeur**) /ʃəvalvapœʀ/ nm horsepower.

chevaucher /ʃəvoʃe/ **1** vt sit astride. □ **se ~** vpr overlap.

chevelu, ~e /ʃəvly/ adj (péj) long-haired; (Bot) hairy.

chevelure /ʃəvlyʀ/ nf hair.

chevet /ʃəvɛ/ nm **au ~ de** at the bed-side of; **livre de ~** bedside book.

cheveu (pl ~**x**) /ʃəvø/ nm (poil) air; **~x** (chevelure) hair; **avoir les ~x longs** have long hair.

cheville /ʃəvij/ nf ankle; (fiche) peg, pin; (pour mur) (wall) plug.

chèvre /ʃɛvʀ/ nf goat.

chevreuil /ʃəvʀœj/ nm roe (deer); (Culin) venison.

chevron /ʃəvʀɔ̃/ nm (poutre) rafter; **à ~s** herringbone.

chez /ʃe/ prép (au domicile de) at the house of; (parmi) among; (dans le caractère ou l'œuvre de) in; **aller ~ qn** go to sb's house; **~ le boucher** at ou to the butcher's; **~ soi** at home; **rentrer ~ soi** go home. **chez-soi** nm inv home.

chic /ʃik/ adj inv smart; (gentil) kind. ● nm style; **avoir le ~ pour** have a knack for; **~ (alors)!** great!

chicane /ʃikan/ nf double bend; **chercher ~ à qn** pick a quarrel with sb.

chiche /ʃiʃ/ adj mean (de with); **~ que je le fais!** **1** I bet you I can do it.

chichis /ʃiʃi/ nmpl **1** fuss.

chicorée /ʃikɔʀe/ nf (frisée) endive; (à café) chicory.

chien /ʃjɛ̃/ nm dog; **~ d'aveugle** guide dog; **~ de garde** watch-dog. **chienne** nf dog, bitch.

chiffon /ʃifɔ̃/ nm rag; (pour nettoyer) duster; **~ humide** damp cloth. **chiffonner** **1** vt crumple; (préoccuper **1**) bother.

chiffre /ʃifʀ/ nm figure; (numéro) number; (code) code; **~s arabes/romains** Arabic/Roman numerals; **~s (statistiques)** statistics; **~ d'affaires** turnover.

chiffrer /ʃifʀe/ **1** vt put a figure on, assess; (texte) encode. □ **se ~ à** vpr come to.

chignon /ʃiɲɔ̃/ nm bun, chignon.

Chili /ʃili/ nm Chile.

chimère /ʃimɛʀ/ nf fantasy.

chimie /ʃimi/ nf chemistry. **chimique** adj chemical. **chimiste** nmf chemist.

chimpanzé /ʃɛ̃pɑze/ nm chimpanzee.

Chine /ʃin/ nf China.

chinois, ~e /ʃinwa, -z/ adj Chinese.
● nm (Ling) Chinese. **C~, ~e** nm, f
Chinese.

chiot /ʃjo/ nm pup(py).

chipoter /ʃipɔte/ **1** vi (manger) pick
at one's food; (discuter) quibble.

chips /ʃips/ nf inv crisp; (US) chip.

chirurgie /ʃiryrʒi/ nf surgery; **~ es-**
thétique plastic surgery. **chirurgien**
nm surgeon.

chlore /klɔr/ nm chlorine.

choc /ʃɔk/ nm (heurt) impact, shock;
(émotion) shock; (collision) crash; (affrontement) clash; (Méd) shock; **sous**
le ~ in shock.

chocolat /ʃɔkɔla/ nm chocolate; (à
boire) drinking chocolate; **~ au lait**
milk chocolate; **~ chaud** hot chocolate; **~ noir** plain ou dark chocolate.

chœur /kœr/ nm (antique) chorus;
(chanteurs, nef) choir; **en ~** in chorus.

choisir /ʃwazir/ **2** vt choose, select.

choix /ʃwa/ nm choice, selection; **fro-**
mage ou dessert au ~ a choice of
cheese or dessert; **de ~** choice; **de**
premier ~ top quality.

chômage /ʃomaʒ/ nm unemployment;
au ~, en ~ unemployed; **mettre en**
~ technique lay off.

chômeur, -euse /ʃomœr, -øz/ nm, f
unemployed person; **les ~s** the unemployed.

choquer /ʃɔke/ **1** vt shock; (commo-
tionner) shake.

choral, ~e (mpl **~s**) /kɔral/ adj choral.
chorale nf choir, choral society.

chorégraphie /kɔregrafi/ nf chore-
ography.

choriste /kɔrist/ nmf (à l'église) chor-
ister; (à l'opéra) member of the
chorus ou choir.

chose /ʃoz/ nf thing; **(très) peu de ~**
nothing much; **pas grand ~**
not much.

chou (pl **~x**) /ʃu/ nm cabbage; **~ (à la**
crème) cream puff; **~ de Bruxelles**
Brussels sprout; **mon petit ~** 🅸
my dear.

chouchou, ~te /ʃuʃu, -t/ nm, f (de
professeur) pet; (du public) darling.

choucroute /ʃukrut/ nf sauerkraut.

chouette /ʃwɛt/ nf owl. ● adj 🅸 super.

chou-fleur (pl **choux-fleurs**) /ʃuflœr/
nm cauliflower.

choyer /ʃwaje/ 🛐 vt pamper.

chrétien, ~ne /kretjɛ̃, -jɛn/ adj & nm,
f Christian.

Christ /krist/ nm le **~** Christ.

chrome /krom/ nm chromium,
chrome.

chromosome /krɔmozom/ nm
chromosome.

chronique /krɔnik/ adj chronic. ● nf
(rubrique) column; (nouvelles) news;
(annales) chronicle.

chronologique /krɔnɔlɔʒik/ adj
chronological.

chronomètre /krɔnɔmɛtr/ nm stop-
watch. **chronométrer** 🔢 vt time.

chrysanthème /krizɑ̃tɛm/ nm chrysanthemum.

chuchoter /ʃyʃɔte/ **1** vt/i whisper.

chut /ʃyt/ interj shh, hush.

chute /ʃyt/ nf fall; (déchet) offcut; **~**
(d'eau) waterfall; **~ de pluie** rainfall;
~ des cheveux hair loss; **~ des ven-**
tes ~ drop in sales; **~ de 5%** 5%
drop. **chuter** **1** vi fall.

Chypre /ʃipr/ nf Cyprus.

ci /si/ adv here; **~-gît** here lies; **cet**
homme-~ this man; **ces maisons-~**
these houses.

ci-après /siaprɛ/ adv below.

cible /sibl/ nf target.

ciboulette /sibulɛt/ nf (Culin) chives
(+ pl).

cicatrice /sikatris/ nf scar.

cicatriser /sikatrize/ **1** vt heal. ▢ **se**
~ vpr heal.

ci-dessous /sidəsu/ adv below.

ci-dessus /sidəsy/ adv above.

cidre /sidr/ nm cider.

ciel (pl **cieux, ciels**) /sjɛl, sjø/ nm sky;
(Relig) heaven; **cieux** (Relig) heaven.

cierge /sjɛrʒ/ nm (church) candle.

cigale /sigal/ nf cicada.

cigare /sigar/ nm cigar.

cigarette /sigarɛt/ nf cigarette.

cigogne /sigɔɲ/ nf stork.

ci-joint /siʒwɛ̃/ adv enclosed.

cil /sil/ nm eyelash.

cime /sim/ nf peak, tip.

ciment /simɑ̃/ nm cement.

cimetière /simtjɛʀ/ *nm* cemetery, graveyard; ~ **de voitures** breaker's yard.

cinéaste /sineast/ *nmf* film-maker.

cinéma /sinema/ *nm* cinema; (US) movie theater. **cinémathèque** *nf* film archive; (salle) film theatre. **cinématographique** *adj* cinema.

cinéphile /sinefil/ *nmf* film lover.

cinglant, ~**e** /sɛ̃glɑ̃, -t/ *adj* (vent) biting; (remarque) scathing.

cinglé, ~**e** /sɛ̃gle/ *adj* ◩ crazy.

cinq /sɛ̃k/ *adj & nm* five.

cinquante /sɛ̃kɑ̃t/ *adj & nm* fifty.

cinquième /sɛ̃kjɛm/ *adj & nmf* fifth.

> **Cinquième République** As ℹ️ established by the constitution of 1958 and still in force today, the *Cinquième République* refers to the system of government established by Charles de Gaulle, enshrining a strong executive and institutions to guarantee stability.

cintre /sɛ̃tʀ/ *nm* coat-hanger; (Archit) curve.

cirage /siʀaʒ/ *nm* polish.

circoncision /siʀkɔ̃sizjɔ̃/ *nf* circumcision.

circonflexe /siʀkɔ̃flɛks/ *adj* circumflex.

circonscription /siʀkɔ̃skʀipsjɔ̃/ *nf* district; ~ **électorale** constituency; (US) district; (de conseiller, maire) ward.

circonscrire /siʀkɔ̃skʀiʀ/ ⻏ *vt* (incendie, épidémie) contain; (sujet) define.

circonspect, ~**e** /siʀkɔ̃spɛkt/ *adj* circumspect.

circonstance /siʀkɔ̃stɑ̃s/ *nf* circumstance; (situation) situation; (occasion) occasion; ~**s atténuantes** mitigating circumstances.

circuit /siʀkɥi/ *nm* circuit; (trajet) tour, trip.

circulaire /siʀkylɛʀ/ *adj & nf* circular.

circulation /siʀkylasjɔ̃/ *nf* circulation; (de véhicules) traffic.

circuler /siʀkyle/ ◧ *vi* (se répandre, être distribué) circulate; (aller d'un lieu à un autre) get around; (en voiture) travel; (piéton) walk; (être en service) (bus, train) run; **faire** ~ (badauds)

move on; (rumeur) spread.

cire /siʀ/ *nf* wax.

ciré /siʀe/ *nm* oilskin.

cirer /siʀe/ ◧ *vt* polish.

cirque /siʀk/ *nm* circus; (arène) amphitheatre; (désordre: fig) chaos; **faire le** ~**!** make a racket ◩.

ciseau (pl ~**x**) /sizo/ *nm* chisel; ~**x** scissors.

ciseler /sizle/ ⑥ *vt* chisel.

citadelle /sitadɛl/ *nf* citadel.

citadin, ~**e** /sitadɛ̃, -in/ *nm, f* city-dweller. ● *adj* city.

citation /sitasjɔ̃/ *nf* quotation; (Jur) summons.

cité /site/ *nf* city; (logements) housing estate; ~ **universitaire** (university) halls of residence.

citer /site/ ◧ *vt* quote, cite; (Jur) summon.

citerne /sitɛʀn/ *nf* tank.

citoyen, ~**ne** /sitwajɛ̃, -ɛn/ *nm, f* citizen.

citron /sitʀɔ̃/ *nm* lemon; ~ **vert** lime. **citronnade** *nf* lemon squash, (still) lemonade.

citrouille /sitʀuj/ *nf* pumpkin.

civet /sivɛ/ *nm* stew; ~ **de lièvre** jugged hare.

civière /sivjɛʀ/ *nf* stretcher.

civil, ~**e** /sivil/ *adj* civil; (non militaire) civilian; (poli) civil. ● *nm* civilian; **dans le** ~ in civilian life; **en** ~ in plain clothes.

civilisation /sivilizasjɔ̃/ *nf* civilization.

civiliser /sivilize/ ◧ *vt* civilize. ☐ **se** ~ *vpr* become civilized.

civique /sivik/ *adj* civic.

clair, ~**e** /klɛʀ/ *adj* clear; (éclairé) light, bright; (couleur) light; **le plus** ~ **de** most of. ● *adv* clearly; **il faisait** ~ it was already light. ● *nm* ~ **de lune** moonlight; **tirer une histoire au** ~ get to the bottom of things. **clairement** *adv* clearly.

clairière /klɛʀjɛʀ/ *nf* clearing.

clairsemé, ~**e** /klɛʀsəme/ *adj* sparse.

clamer /klame/ ◧ *vt* proclaim.

clameur /klamœʀ/ *nf* clamour.

clan /klɑ̃/ *nm* clan.

clandestin, ~**e** /klɑ̃dɛstɛ̃, -in/ *adj* secret; (journal) underground; (immigra-

tion, travail) illegal; **passager** ~ stowaway.

clapier /klapje/ *nm* (rabbit) utch.

clapoter /klapɔte/ **1** *vi* lap.

claquage /klakaʒ/ *nm* strained muscle; **se faire un** ~ pull a muscle.

claque /klak/ *nf* slap.

claquer /klake/ **1** *vi* bang; (*porte*) slam, bang; (*fouet*) crack; (*se casser* ⚡) conk out; (*mourir* ⚡) snuff it!; ~ **des doigts** snap one's fingers; ~ **des mains** clap one's hands; **il claque des dents** his teeth are chattering. ● *vt* (*porte*) slam, bang; (*dépenser* ⚡) blow; (*fatiguer* ⚡) tire out.

claquettes /klaket/ *nfpl* tapdancing.

clarifier /klaʁifje/ **45** *vt* clarify.

clarinette /klaʁinɛt/ *nf* clarinet.

clarté /klaʁte/ *nf* light, brightness; (*netteté*) clarity.

classe /klas/ *nf* class; (*salle: Scol*) classroom; (*cours*) class, lesson; **aller en** ~ go to school; **faire la** ~ teach; ~ **ouvrière/moyenne** working/middle class.

classement /klasmã/ *nm* classification; (*d'élèves*) grading; (*de documents*) filing; (*rang*) place, grade; (*de coureur*) placing.

classer /klase/ **1** *vt* classify; (*par mérite*) grade; (*papiers*) file; (*Jur*) (*affaire*) close. □ **se** ~ *vpr* rank.

classeur /klasœʁ/ *nm* (*meuble*) filing cabinet; (*chemise*) file; (*à anneaux*) ring binder.

classification /klasifikasjɔ̃/ *nf* classification.

classique /klasik/ *adj* classical; (*de qualité*) classic; (*habituel*) classic, standard. ● *nm* classic; (*auteur*) classical author.

clavecin /klavsɛ̃/ *nm* harpsichord.

clavicule /klavikyl/ *nf* collarbone.

clavier /klavje/ *nm* keyboard; ~ **numérique** keypad.

clé, clef /kle/ *nf* key; (*outil*) spanner; (*Mus*) clef; ~ **anglaise** (monkey-)wrench; ~ **de contact** ignition key; ~ **à molette** adjustable spanner; ~ **de voûte** keystone. ● *adj inv* key.

clémence /klemãs/ *nf* (*de climat*) mildness; (*indulgence*) leniency.

clergé /klɛʁʒe/ *nm* clergy.

clérical, ~**e** (*mpl* **-aux**) /kleʁikal, -o/ *adj* clerical.

clic /klik/ *nm* (Ordinat) click.

cliché /kliʃe/ *nm* cliché; (Photo) negative.

client, ~**e** /klijã, -t/ *nm, f* customer; (*d'un avocat*) client; (*d'un médecin*) patient; (*d'hôtel*) guest; (*de taxi*) passenger.

clientèle /klijãtɛl/ *nf* customers, clientele; (*d'un avocat*) clients, practice; (*d'un médecin*) patients, practice; (*soutien*) custom.

cligner /kliɲe/ **1** *vi* ~ **des yeux** blink; ~ **de l'œil** wink.

clignotant /kliɲɔtã/ *nm* (Auto) indicator, turn.

clignoter /kliɲɔte/ **1** *vi* blink; (*lumière*) flicker; (*comme signal*) flash.

climat /klima/ *nm* climate.

climatisation /klimatizasjɔ̃/ *nf* air-conditioning.

clin d'œil /klɛ̃dœj/ *nm* wink; **en un** ~ in a flash.

clinique /klinik/ *adj* clinical. ● *nf* (*private*) clinic.

clinquant, ~**e** /klɛ̃kã, -t/ *adj* showy.

clip /klip/ *nm* video.

cliquer /klike/ **1** *vi* (Ordinat) click (**sur** on).

cliqueter /klikte/ **38** *vi* (*couverts*) clink; (*clés, monnaie*) jingle; (*ferraille*) rattle.

cliquetis /klikti/ *nm* clink(ing), jingle, rattle.

clivage /klivaʒ/ *nm* divide.

clochard, ~**e** /klɔʃaʁ, -d/ *nm, f* tramp.

cloche /klɔʃ/ *nf* bell; (*imbécile* ⚡) idiot; ~ **à fromage** cheese-cover.

cloche-pied: à ~ /aklɔʃpje/ *loc* **sauter à** ~ hop on one leg.

clocher /klɔʃe/ *nm* bell-tower; (*pointu*) steeple; **de** ~ parochial.

cloison /klwazɔ̃/ *nf* partition; (fig) barrier.

cloître /klwatʁ/ *nm* cloister. **cloîtrer (se)** **1** *vpr* shut oneself away.

clonage /klonaʒ/ *nm* clonage.

cloner /klone/ **1** *vt* clone.

cloque /klɔk/ *nf* blister.

clos, ~**e** /klo, -z/ *adj* closed.

clôture /klotyʁ/ *nf* fence; (*fermeture*) closure; (*de magasin, bureau*) closing; (*de débat; liste*) close; (*en Bourse*) close of trading. **clôturer** **1** *vt* enclose, fence in; (*festival, séance*) close.

clou /klu/ *nm* nail; (furoncle) boil; (de spectacle) star attraction; **les ~s** (passage) pedestrian crossing; (US) crosswalk.

clouer /klue/ **1** *vt* nail down; (fig) pin down; **être cloué au lit** be confined to one's bed; **~ le bec à qn** shut sb up.

cloué, ~e /klute/ *adj* studded; **passage ~** pedestrian crossing; (US) crosswalk.

CMU *abrév f* free health care for people on low incomes.

coaliser (se) /(sə)kɔalize/ **1** *vpr* join forces.

coalition /kɔalisjɔ̃/ *nf* coalition.

cobaye /kɔbaj/ *nm* guinea-pig.

cocaïne /kɔkain/ *nf* cocaine.

cocasse /kɔkas/ *adj* comical.

coccinelle /kɔksinɛl/ *nf* ladybird; (US) ladybug.

cocher /kɔʃe/ **1** *vt* tick (off), check. ● *nm* coachman.

cochon, ~ne /kɔʃɔ̃, -ɔn/ *nm, f* (personne 🄸) pig. ● *adj* 🄸 filthy. ● *nm* pig. **cochonnerie** *nf* (saleté 🄸) filth; (marchandise 🄸) rubbish, junk.

cocon /kɔkɔ̃/ *nm* cocoon.

cocorico /kɔkɔʀikɔ/ *nm* cock-a-doodle-doo.

cocotier /kɔkɔtje/ *nm* coconut palm.

cocotte /kɔkɔt/ *nf* (marmite) casserole; **~ minute®** pressure-cooker; **ma ~** 🄸 my dear.

cocu, ~e /kɔky/ *nm, f* 🄸 deceived husband, deceived wife.

code /kɔd/ *nm* code; **~s** dipped headlights; **se mettre en ~s** dip one's headlights; **~ (à) barres** bar code; **~ confidentiel (d'identification)** PIN number; **~ postal** post code; (US) zip code; **~ de la route** Highway Code. **coder** **1** *vt* code, encode.

coéquipier, -ière /kɔekipje, -jɛʀ/ *nm, f* team mate.

cœur /kœʀ/ *nm* heart; (aux cartes) hearts (+ *pl*); **~ d'artichaut** artichoke heart; **~ de palmier** palm heart; **à ~ ouvert** (*opération*) open-heart; (*parler*) freely; **avoir bon ~** be kind-hearted; **de bon ~** willingly; (*rire*) heartily; **par ~** by heart; **avoir mal au ~** feel sick *ou* nauseous; **je veux en avoir le**

net I want to be clear in my own mind (about it).

coffre /kɔfʀ/ *nm* chest; (pour argent) safe; (Auto) boot; (US) trunk. **coffre-fort** (*pl* **coffres-forts**) *nm* safe.

coffret /kɔfʀɛ/ *nm* casket, box; (de livres, cassettes) boxed set.

cogner /kɔɲe/ **1** *vt/i* knock. □ **se ~** *vpr* knock oneself; **se ~ la tête** bump one's head.

cohabitater /kɔabite/ **1** *vi* live together.

cohérent, ~e /kɔeʀɑ̃, -t/ *adj* coherent; (homogène) consistent.

cohue /kɔy/ *nf* crowd.

coi, ~te /kwa, -t/ *adj* silent.

coiffe /kwaf/ *nf* headgear.

coiffer /kwafe/ **1** *vt* do the hair of; (*chapeau*) put on; (surmonter) cap; **~ qn d'un chapeau** put a hat on sb; **coiffé de** wearing; **être bien/mal coiffé** have tidy/untidy hair. □ **se ~** *vpr* do one's hair.

coiffeur, -euse /kwafœʀ, -øz/ *nm, f* hairdresser. **coiffeuse** *nf* dressing-table.

coiffure /kwafyʀ/ *nf* hairstyle; (métier) hairdressing; (chapeau) hat.

coin /kwɛ̃/ *nm* corner; (endroit) spot; (cale) wedge; **au ~ du feu** by the fireside; **dans le ~** locally; **du ~** local.

coincer /kwɛ̃se/ **10** *vt* jam; (caler) wedge; (attraper 🄸) catch. □ **se ~** *vpr* get jammed.

coïncidence /kɔɛ̃sidɑ̃s/ *nf* coincidence.

coing /kwɛ̃/ *nm* quince.

coït /kɔit/ *nm* intercourse.

col /kɔl/ *nm* collar; (de bouteille) neck; (de montagne) pass; **~ blanc** white-collar worker; **~ roulé** polo-neck; (US) turtle-neck; **~ de l'utérus** cervix; **se casser le ~ du fémur** break one's hip.

colère /kɔlɛʀ/ *nf* anger; (accès) fit of anger; **en ~** angry; **se mettre en ~** lose one's temper; **faire une ~** throw a tantrum.

coléreux, -euse /kɔleʀø, -z/ *adj* quick-tempered.

colin /kɔlɛ̃/ *nm* (merlu) hake; (lieu noir) coley.

colique /kɔlik/ *nf* diarrhoea; (Méd) colic.

colis /kɔli/ nm parcel.

collaborateur, -trice /kɔlabɔratœr, -tris/ nm, f collaborator; (journaliste) contributor; (collègue) colleague.

collaboration /kɔlabɔrasjɔ̃/ nf collaboration (**à** on); (à ouvrage, projet) contribution (**à** to).

collaborer /kɔlabɔre/ **1** vi collaborate (**à** on); ~ **à** (journal) contribute to.

collant, ~e /kɔlɑ̃, -t/ adj (moulant) kin-tight; (poisseux) sticky. ● nm (bas) tights; (US) panty hose.

colle /kɔl/ nf glue; (en pâte) paste; (problème 🔢) poser; (Scol 🔢) detention.

collecter /kɔlɛkte/ **1** vt collect.

collectif, -ive /kɔlɛktif, -v/ adj collective; (billet, voyage) group.

collection /kɔlɛksjɔ̃/ nf collection; (ouvrages) series (+ sg); (du même auteur) set. **collectionner** **1** vt collect. **collectionneur, -euse** nm, f collector.

collectivité /kɔlɛktivite/ nf community; ~ **locale** local authority.

collège /kɔlɛʒ/ nm secondary school (up to age 15); (US) junior high school; (assemblée) college. **collégien, ~ne** nm, f schoolboy, schoolgirl.

collègue /kɔlɛg/ nmf colleague.

coller /kɔle/ **1** vt stick; (avec colle liquide) glue; (affiche) stick up; (mettre 🔢) stick; (par une question 🔢) stump; (Scol 🔢) **se faire** ~ get a detention; **je me suis fait** ~ **en maths** I failed ou flunked maths. ● vi stick (à to); (être collant) be sticky; ~ **à** (convenir à) fit, correspond to.

collet /kɔlɛ/ nm (piège) snare; ~ **monté** prim and proper; **mettre la main au** ~ **de qn** collar sb.

collier /kɔlje/ nm necklace; (de chien) collar.

colline /kɔlin/ nf hill.

collision /kɔlizjɔ̃/ nf (choc) collision; (lutte) clash; **entrer en** ~ **(avec)** collide (with).

collyre /kɔlir/ nm eye drops (+ pl).

colmater /kɔlmate/ **1** vt plug, seal.

colombe /kɔlɔ̃b/ nf dove.

Colombie /kɔlɔ̃bi/ nf Colombia.

colon /kɔlɔ̃/ nm settler.

colonel /kɔlɔnɛl/ nm colonel.

colonie /kɔlɔni/ nf colony; ~ **de vacances** children's holiday camp.

> **Colonie de vacances** A holiday village or summer camp where children take part in a variety of outdoor activities. Originally set up to give poorer children a means of getting out into the countryside, they are still largely state-subsidized. Colloquially they are referred to as la/une colo.

colonne /kɔlɔn/ nf column; ~ **vertébrale** spine; **en** ~ **par deux** in double file.

colorant /kɔlɔrɑ̃/ nm colouring.

colorier /kɔlɔrje/ **45** vt colour (in).

colosse /kɔlɔs/ nm giant.

colza /kɔlza/ nm rape(-seed).

coma /kɔma/ nm coma; **dans le** ~ in a coma.

combat /kɔ̃ba/ nm fight; (Sport) match; ~**s** fighting. **combatif, -ive** adj eager to fight; (esprit) fighting.

combattre /kɔ̃batr/ **11** vt/i fight.

combien /kɔ̃bjɛ̃/ adv ~ **(de)** quantité) how much; (nombre) how many; (temps) how long; ~ **il a changé!** (comme) how he has changed!; ~ **y a-t-il d'ici à...?** how far is it to...?; **on est le** ~ **aujourd'hui?** what's the date today?

combinaison /kɔ̃binɛzɔ̃/ nf combination; (de femme) slip; (bleu de travail) boiler suit; (US) overalls; ~ **d'aviateur** flying-suit; ~ **de plongée** wetsuit.

combine /kɔ̃bin/ nf trick; (fraude) fiddle; (intrigue) scheme.

combiné /kɔ̃bine/ nm (de téléphone) receiver, handset.

combiner /kɔ̃bine/ **1** vt (réunir) combine; (calculer) devise; ~ **de faire** plan to do.

comble /kɔ̃bl/ adj packed. ● nm height; ~**s** (mansarde) attic, loft; **c'est le** ~**!** that's the (absolute) limit!

combler /kɔ̃ble/ **1** vt fill; (perte, déficit) make good; (désir) fulfil; ~ **qn de cadeaux** lavish gifts on sb.

combustible /kɔ̃bystibl/ nm fuel.

comédie /kɔmedi/ nf comedy; (histoire🔢) fuss; ~ **musicale** musical; **jouer la** ~ put on an act. **comédien,**

c

~ne *nm, f* actor,actress.

comestible /kɔmɛstibl/ *adj* edible.

comète /kɔmɛt/ *nf* comet.

comique /kɔmik/ *adj* comical, funny; (*genre*) comic. ● *nm* (acteur) comic; (comédie) comedy; (côté drôle) comical aspect.

commandant /kɔmɑ̃dɑ̃/ *nm* commander; (dans l'armée de terre) major; ~ **(de bord)** captain; ~ **en chef** Commander-in-Chief.

commande /kɔmɑ̃d/ *nf* (Comm) order; (Tech) control; **~s** (d'avion) controls.

commandement /kɔmɑ̃dmɑ̃/ *nm* command; (Relig) commandment.

commander /kɔmɑ̃de/ **1** *vt* command; (acheter) order; (*étude, œuvre d'art*) commission; ~ **à** (maîtriser) control; ~ **à qn de** command sb to. ● *vi* be in command.

comme /kɔm/ *adv* ~ **c'est bon!** it's so good!; ~ **il est mignon!** isn't he sweet! ● *conj* (dans une comparaison) as; (dans une équivalence, illustration) like; (en tant que) as; (puisque) as, since; (au moment où) as; **vif ~ l'éclair** as quick as a flash; **travailler ~ sage-femme** work as a midwife; ~ **ci ~ ça** so-so; ~ **il faut** properly; ~ **pour faire** as if to do; **jolie ~ tout** as pretty as anything; **qu'est-ce qu'il y a ~ légumes?** what is there in the way of vegetables?

commencer /kɔmɑ̃se/ **10** *vt/i* begin, start; ~ **à faire** begin ou start to do.

comment /kɔmɑ̃/ *adv* how; **~?** (répétition) pardon?; (surprise) what?; ~ **est-il?** what is he like?; **le ~ et le pourquoi** the whys and wherefores.

commentaire /kɔmɑ̃tɛʁ/ *nm* comment; (d'un texte, événement) commentary. **commentateur, -trice** *nm, f* commentator.

commenter /kɔmɑ̃te/ **1** *vt* comment on; (*film, visite*) provide a commentary for; (radio,TV) commentate.

commérages /kɔmeʁaʒ/ *nmpl* gossip.

commerçant, ~e /kɔmɛʁsɑ̃, -t/ *adj* (rue) shopping; (personne) business-minded. ● *nm, f* shopkeeper.

commerce /kɔmɛʁs/ *nm* trade, commerce; (magasin) business; **faire du ~** be in business; ~ **électrique** e-commerce; ~ **équitable** fair trade.

commercial, ~e (*mpl* **-iaux**) /kɔmɛʁsjal, -jo/ *adj* commercial. **commercialiser** **1** *vt* market.

commettre /kɔmɛtʁ/ **42** *vt* commit.

commis /kɔmi/ *nm* (de magasin) assistant; (de bureau) clerk.

commissaire /kɔmisɛʁ/ *nm* commissioner; (Sport) steward; ~ **(de police)** (police) superintendent. **commissaire-priseur** (*pl* **commissaires-priseurs**) *nm* auctioneer.

commissariat /kɔmisaʁja/ *nm* ~ **(de police)** police station.

commission /kɔmisjɔ̃/ *nf* commission; (course) errand; (message) message; **~s** shopping.

commode /kɔmɔd/ *adj* handy; (facile) easy; **il n'est pas ~** he's a difficult customer. ● *nf* chest (of drawers). **commodité** *nf* convenience.

commotion /kɔmosjɔ̃/ *nf* ~ **(cérébrale)** concussion.

commun, ~e /kɔmœ̃, -yn/ *adj* common; (effort, action) joint; (frais, pièce) shared; **en ~** jointly; **avoir** ou **mettre en ~** share; **le ~ des mortels** ordinary mortals. **communal, ~e** (*mpl* **-aux**) *adj* of the commune, local.

communauté /kɔmynote/ *nf* community.

commune /kɔmyn/ *nf* (circonscription, collectivité) commune.

> **Commune** The smallest administrative unit in France, headed by a *maire* and a *conseil municipal*. Each village, town and city is a *commune*, of which there are 36,000 throughout the country.

communicatif, -ive /kɔmynikatif, -v/ *adj* (personne) talkative; (gaieté) infectious.

communication /kɔmynikasjɔ̃/ *nf* communication; (téléphonique) call; **~s** (relations) communications (+ *pl*); **voies** ou **moyens de ~** communications (+ *pl*).

communier /kɔmynje/ **45** *vi* (Relig) receive communion; (fig) commune.

communiqué /kɔmynike/ *nm* statement; (de presse) communiqué.

communiquer /kɔmynike/ **1** *vt* pass on, communicate; (date, décision) an-

nounce. ● *vi* communicate. □ **se ~ à**
vpr spread to.

communiste /kɔmynist/ *adj & nmf*
communist.

commutateur /kɔmytatœʀ/ *nm*
(Électr) switch.

compagne /kɔpaɲ/ *nf* companion.

compagnie /kɔpaɲi/ *nf* company;
tenir ~ à keep company; **en ~ de**
together with; **~ aérienne** airline.

compagnon /kɔpaɲɔ̃/ *nm* companion.

comparable /kɔpaʀabl/ *adj* comparable (**à** to). **comparaison** *nf* comparison; (littéraire) simile.

comparaître /kɔpaʀɛtʀ/ 18 *vi* (Jur)
appear (**devant** before).

comparatif, -ive /kɔpaʀatif, -v/ *adj &
nm* comparative.

comparer /kɔpaʀe/ 1 *vt* compare (**à**
with). □ **se ~** *vpr* compare oneself;
(être comparable) be comparable.

compartiment /kɔpaʀtimɑ̃/ *nm* compartment.

comparution /kɔpaʀysjɔ̃/ *nf* (Jur) appearance.

compas /kɔpa/ *nm* (pair of) com-
passes; (boussole) compass.

compassion /kɔpasjɔ̃/ *nf* compassion.

compatible /kɔpatibl/ *adj* compatible.

compatir /kɔpatiʀ/ 2 *vi* sympathize;
~ à share in.

compatriote /kɔpatʀijɔt/ *nmf* com-
patriot.

compensation /kɔpɑ̃sasjɔ̃/ *nf* compensation. **compenser** 1 *vt* compensate for, make up for.

compère /kɔpɛʀ/ *nm* accomplice.

compétence /kɔpetɑ̃s/ *nf* competence; (fonction) domain, sphere; **entrer dans les ~s de qn** be in sb's domain. **compétent, ~e** *adj* competent.

compétition /kɔpetisjɔ̃/ *nf* competition; (sportive) event; **de ~** competitive.

complaire (se) /(sə)kɔplɛʀ/ 47 *vpr* se
~ dans delight in.

complaisance /kɔplɛzɑ̃s/ *nf* kindness;
(indulgence) indulgence.

complément /kɔplemɑ̃/ *nm* supplement; (Gram) complement; **~ (d'objet)** (Gram) object; **~ d'information**
further information. **complémentaire**
adj complementary; (renseignements)
supplementary.

complet, -ète /kɔplɛ, -t/ *adj* complete;
(train, hôtel) full. ● *nm* suit.

compléter /kɔplete/ 14 *vt* complete;
(agrémenter) complement. □ **se ~** *vpr*
complement each other.

complexe /kɔplɛks/ *adj* complex. ●
nm (sentiment, bâtiments) complex.

complexé, ~e /kɔplekse/ *adj* **être ~**
have a lot of hang-ups.

complice /kɔplis/ *nm* accomplice.

compliment /kɔplimɑ̃/ *nm* compliment; **~s** (félicitations) compliments,
congratulations.

compliquer /kɔplike/ 1 *vt* complicate. □ **se ~** *vpr* become complicated.

complot /kɔplo/ *nm* plot.

comportement /kɔpɔʀtəmɑ̃/ *nm* behaviour; (de joueur, voiture) performance.

comporter /kɔpɔʀte/ 1 *vt* (être composé de) comprise; (inclure) include;
(risque) entail. □ **se ~** *vpr* behave;
(joueur, voiture) perform.

composant /kɔpozɑ̃/ *nm* component.

composé, ~e /kɔpoze/ *adj* composite;
(salade) mixed; (guindé) affected.
● *nm* compound.

composer /kɔpoze/ 1 *vt* make up,
compose; (chanson, visage) compose;
(numéro) dial; (page) typeset. ● *vi*
(transiger) compromise. □ **se ~ de**
vpr be made up *ou* composed of.
compositeur, -trice *nm, f* (Mus)
composer.

composter /kɔpɔste/ 1 *vt* (billet)
punch.

compote /kɔpɔt/ *nf* stewed fruit; **~
de pommes** stewed apples.

compréhensible /kɔpʀeɑ̃sibl/ *adj*
understandable; (intelligible) compre-
hensible.

compréhensif, -ive /kɔpʀeɑ̃sif, -v/
adj understanding.

compréhension /kɔpʀeɑ̃sjɔ̃/ *nf*
understanding, comprehension.

comprendre /kɔpʀɑ̃dʀ/ 50 *vt* understand; (comporter) comprise, be made
up of. □ **se ~** *vpr* (personnes) understand each other; **ça se comprend**
that is understandable.

compresse /kɔpʀɛs/ *nf* compress.

comprimé /kɔpʀime/ *nm* tablet.

comprimer /kɔpʀime/ 1 *vt* compress; (réduire) reduce.

compris, ~e /kɔ̃pRi, -z/ adj included; (d'accord) agreed; ~ **entre** (contained) between; **service (non)** ~ service (not) included; **tout** ~ (all) inclusive; **y** ~ including.

compromettre /kɔ̃pRɔmɛtR/ 42 vt compromise. **compromis** nm compromise.

comptabilité /kɔ̃patibilite/ nf accountancy; (comptes) accounts; (service) accounts department.

comptable /kɔ̃tabl/ adj accounting. ● nmf accountant.

comptant /kɔ̃tɑ̃/ adv (payer) (in) cash; (acheter) for cash.

compte /kɔ̃t/ nm count; (facture, comptabilité) account; (nombre exact) right number; ~ **bancaire,** ~ **en banque** bank account; **prendre qch en** ~, **tenir** ~ **de qch** take sth into account; **se rendre** ~ realize; **demander/rendre des** ~s ask for/ give an explanation; **à bon** ~ cheaply; **s'en tirer à bon** ~ get off lightly; **travailler à son** ~ be self-employed; **faire le** ~ **de** count; **pour le** ~ **de** on behalf of; **sur le** ~ **de** about; **au bout du** ~ all things considered; ~ **à rebours** countdown.

compte-gouttes /kɔ̃tgut/ nm inv (Méd) dropper; **au** ~ (fig) in dribs and drabs.

compter /kɔ̃te/ 1 vt count; (prévoir) allow, reckon on; (facturer) charge for; (avoir) have; (classer) consider; ~ **faire** intend to do. ● vi (calculer, importer) count; ~ **avec** reckon with; ~ **parmi** (figurer) be considered among; ~ **sur** rely on, count on.

compte(-)rendu /kɔ̃tRɑ̃dy/ nm report; (de film, livre) review.

compteur /kɔ̃tœR/ nm meter; ~ **de vitesse** speedometer.

comptine /kɔ̃tin/ nf nursery rhyme.

comptoir /kɔ̃twaR/ nm counter; (de café) bar.

comte /kɔ̃t/ nm count.

comté /kɔ̃te/ nm county.

comtesse /kɔ̃tɛs/ nf countess.

con, ~**ne** /kɔ̃, kɔn/ adj 🅧 bloody stupid 🅧. ● nm, f 🅧 bloody fool 🅧.

concentrer /kɔ̃sɑ̃tRe/ 1 vt concentrate. □ **se** ~ vpr be concentrated.

concept /kɔ̃sɛpt/ nm concept.

concerner /kɔ̃sɛRne/ 1 vt concern; **en ce qui me concerne** as far as I am concerned.

concert /kɔ̃sɛR/ nm concert; **de** ~ in unison.

concerter /kɔ̃sɛRte/ 1 vt organize, prepare. □ **se** ~ vpr confer.

concession /kɔ̃sesjɔ̃/ nf concession; (terrain) plot.

concevoir /kɔ̃svwaR/ 52 vt (imaginer, engendrer) conceive; (comprendre) understand; (élaborer) design.

concierge /kɔ̃sjɛR/ nmf caretaker.

concilier /kɔ̃silje/ 45 vt reconcile. □ **se** ~ vpr (s'attirer) win (over).

concis, ~**e** /kɔ̃si, -z/ adj concise.

conclure /kɔ̃klyR/ 16 vt conclude; ~ **à** conclude in favour of. ● vi ~ **en faveur de/contre** find in favour of/against. **conclusion** nf conclusion.

concombre /kɔ̃kɔ̃bR/ nm cucumber.

concordance /kɔ̃kɔRdɑ̃s/ nf agreement.

concourir /kɔ̃kuRiR/ 20 vi compete. ● vt ~ **à** contribute towards.

concours /kɔ̃kuR/ nm competition; (examen) competitive examination; (aide) help; (de circonstances) combination.

concret, -ète /kɔ̃kRɛ, -t/ adj concrete.

concrétiser /kɔ̃kRetize/ 1 vt give concrete form to. □ **se** ~ vpr materialize.

conçu, ~**e** /kɔ̃sy/ adj **bien/mal** ~ well/badly designed.

concubinage /kɔ̃kybinaʒ/ nm cohabitation; **vivre en** ~ live together, cohabit.

concurrence /kɔ̃kyRɑ̃s/ nf competition; **faire** ~ **à** compete with; **jusqu'à** ~ **de** up to a limit of.

concurrencer /kɔ̃kyRɑ̃se/ 10 vt compete with.

concurrent, ~e /kɔ̃kyRɑ̃, -t/ nm, f competitor; (Scol) candidate. ● adj rival.

condamnation /kɔ̃danasjɔ̃/ nf condemnation; (peine) sentence; ~ **centralisée des portières** central locking. **condamné,** ~**e** nm, f condemned man, condemned woman. **condamner** 1 vt (censurer, obliger) condemn; (Jur) sentence; (porte) block up.

condition /kɔ̃disjɔ̃/ *nf* condition; ∼s (prix) terms; **à** ∼ **de** *ou* **que** provided (that); **sans** ∼ unconditional(ly); **sous** ∼ conditionally.

conditionnel, ∼le /kɔ̃disjɔnɛl/ *adj* conditional. ● *nm* conditional (tense).

conditionnement /kɔ̃disjɔnmɑ̃/ *nm* conditioning; (emballage) packaging.

condoléances /kɔ̃dɔleɑ̃s/ *nfpl* condolences.

conducteur, -trice /kɔ̃dyktœʀ, -tʀis/ *nm, f* driver.

conduire /kɔ̃dɥiʀ/ **17** *vt* take (à to); (guider) lead; (Auto) drive; (affaire) conduct; ∼ **à** (faire aboutir) lead to. ● *vi* drive. □ **se** ∼ *vpr* behave.

conduit /kɔ̃dɥi/ *nm* duct.

conduite /kɔ̃dɥit/ *nf* conduct, behaviour; (Auto) driving; (tuyau) pipe; **voiture avec** ∼ **à droite** right-hand drive car.

confection /kɔ̃fɛksjɔ̃/ *nf* making; **de** ∼ ready-made; **la** ∼ the clothing industry.

conférence /kɔ̃feʀɑ̃s/ *nf* conference; (exposé) lecture; ∼ **au sommet** summit meeting. **conférencier, -ière** *nm, f* lecturer.

confesser /kɔ̃fese/ **1** *vt* confess. □ **se** ∼ *vpr* go to confession.

confiance /kɔ̃fjɑ̃s/ *nf* trust; **avoir** ∼ **en** trust.

confiant, ∼e /kɔ̃fjɑ̃, -t/ *adj* (assuré) confident; (sans défiance) trusting.

confidence /kɔ̃fidɑ̃s/ *nf* confidence.

confidentiel, ∼le /kɔ̃fidɑ̃sjɛl/ *adj* confidential.

confier /kɔ̃fje/ **45** *vt* ∼ **à qn** entrust sb with; ∼ **un secret à qn** tell sb a secret. □ **se** ∼ **à** *vpr* confide in.

configuration /kɔ̃figyʀasjɔ̃/ *nf* configuration.

configurer/kɔ̃figyʀe/*vt* configure.

confiner /kɔ̃fine/ **1** *vt* confine; ∼ **à** border on. □ **se** ∼ *vpr* confine oneself (à, **dans** to).

confirmation /kɔ̃fiʀmasjɔ̃/ *nf* confirmation. **confirmer** **1** *vt* confirm.

confiserie /kɔ̃fizʀi/ *nf* sweet shop; ∼s confectionery.

confisquer /kɔ̃fiske/ **1** *vt* confiscate.

confit, ∼e /kɔ̃fi, -t/ *adj* candied; (fruits) crystallized. ● *nm* ∼ **de ca-** nard confit of duck.

confiture /kɔ̃fityʀ/ *nf* jam.

conflit /kɔ̃fli/ *nm* conflict.

confondre /kɔ̃fɔ̃dʀ/ **3** *vt* confuse, mix up; (étonner) confound. □ **se** ∼ *vpr* merge; **se** ∼ **en excuses** apologize profusely.

conforme /kɔ̃fɔʀm/ *adj* **être** ∼ **à** comply with; (être en accord) be in keeping with.

conformer /kɔ̃fɔʀme/ **1** *vt* adapt. □ **se** ∼ **à** *vpr* conform to.

conformité /kɔ̃fɔʀmite/ *nf* compliance, conformity; **agir en** ∼ **avec** act in accordance with.

confort /kɔ̃fɔʀ/ *nm* comfort; **tout** ∼ with all mod cons. **confortable** *adj* comfortable.

confrère /kɔ̃fʀɛʀ/ *nm* colleague.

confronter /kɔ̃fʀɔ̃te/ **1** *vt* confront; (textes) compare. □ **se** ∼ **à** *vpr* be confronted with.

confus, ∼e /kɔ̃fy, -z/ *adj* confused; (gêné) embarrassed.

congé /kɔ̃ʒe/ *nm* holiday; (arrêt momentané) time off, leave; (avis de départ) notice; **en** ∼ on holiday *ou* leave; ∼ **de maladie/maternité** sick/maternity leave; **jour de** ∼ day off; **prendre** ∼ **de** take one's leave of.

congédier /kɔ̃ʒedje/ **45** *vt* dismiss.

congélateur /kɔ̃ʒelatœʀ/ *nm* freezer.

congeler /kɔ̃ʒle/ **6** *vt* freeze.

congère /kɔ̃ʒɛʀ/ *nf* snowdrift.

congrès /kɔ̃gʀɛ/ *nm* conference; (Pol) congress.

conjoint, ∼e /kɔ̃ʒwɛ̃, -t/ *nm, f* spouse. ● *adj* joint.

conjonctivite /kɔ̃ʒɔ̃ktivit/ *nf* conjunctivitis.

conjoncture /kɔ̃ʒɔ̃ktyʀ/ *nf* situation; (économique) economic climate.

conjugaison /kɔ̃ʒygɛzɔ̃/ *nf* conjugation.

conjugal, ∼e (mpl **-aux**) /kɔ̃ʒygal, -o/ *adj* conjugal, married.

conjuguer /kɔ̃ʒyge/ **1** *vt* (Gram) conjugate; (efforts) combine. □ **se** ∼ *vpr* (Gram) be conjugated; (facteurs) be combined.

conjurer /kɔ̃ʒyʀe/ **1** *vt* (éviter) avert; (implorer) beg.

connaissance /kɔnɛsɑ̃s/ nf knowledge; (personne) acquaintance; ~s (science) knowledge; **faire la ~ de** meet; (apprécier une personne) get to know; **perdre/reprendre ~** lose/regain consciousness; **sans ~** unconscious.

connaisseur /kɔnɛsœʀ/ nm expert, connoisseur.

connaître /kɔnɛtʀ/ 18 vt know; (difficultés, faim, succès) experience; **faire ~** make known. □ **se ~** vpr (se rencontrer) meet; **s'y ~ en** know (all) about.

connecter /kɔnɛkte/ 1 vt connect; **être/ne pas être connecté** be on-/off-line. □ **se ~ à** vpr (Ordinat) log on to.

connerie /kɔnʀi/ nf ⊠ **faire une ~** do something stupid; **dire des ~s** talk rubbish.

connexion /kɔnɛksjɔ̃/ nf (Ordinat) connection.

connu, ~e /kɔny/ adj well-known.

conquérant, ~e /kɔ̃keʀɑ̃, -t/ nm, f conqueror.

conquête /kɔ̃kɛt/ nf conquest.

consacrer /kɔ̃sakʀe/ 1 vt devote; (Relig) consecrate; (sanctionner) sanction. □ **se ~ à** vpr devote oneself to.

conscience /kɔ̃sjɑ̃s/ nf conscience; (perception) awareness; (de collectivité) consciousness; **avoir/prendre ~ de** be/become aware of; **perdre/reprendre ~** lose/regain consciousness; **avoir bonne/mauvaise ~** have a clear/guilty conscience.

conscient, ~e /kɔ̃sjɑ̃, -t/ adj conscious; **~ de** aware ou conscious of.

conseil /kɔ̃sɛj/ nm (piece of) advice; (assemblée) council, committee; (séance) meeting; (personne) consultant; **~ d'administration** board of directors; **~ en gestion** management consultant; **~ des ministres** Cabinet; **~ municipal** town council.

conseiller¹ /kɔ̃seje/ 1 vt advise; **~ à qn de** advise sb to; **~ qch à qn** recommend sth to sb.

conseiller,² -ère /kɔ̃seje, -jɛʀ/ nm, f adviser, counsellor; **~ municipal** town councillor; **~ d'orientation** careers adviser.

consentement /kɔ̃sɑ̃tmɑ̃/ nm consent.

conséquence /kɔ̃sekɑ̃s/ nf consequence; **en ~** (comme il convient) accordingly; **en ~ (de quoi)** as a result of which.

conséquent, ~e /kɔ̃sekɑ̃, -t/ adj consistent, logical; (important) substantial; **par ~** consequently, therefore.

conservateur, -trice /kɔ̃sɛʀvatœʀ, -tʀis/ adj conservative. ● nm, f (Pol) conservative; (de musée) curator. ● nm preservative.

conservation /kɔ̃sɛʀvasjɔ̃/ nf preservation; (d'espèce, patrimoine) conservation.

conservatoire /kɔ̃sɛʀvatwaʀ/ nm academy.

conserve /kɔ̃sɛʀv/ nf tinned ou canned food; **en ~** tinned, canned; **boîte de ~** tin, can.

conserver /kɔ̃sɛʀve/ 1 vt keep; (en bon état) preserve; (Culin) preserve. □ **se ~** vpr (Culin) keep.

considérer /kɔ̃sideʀe/ 14 vt consider; (respecter) esteem; **~ comme** consider to be.

consigne /kɔ̃siɲ/ nf (de gare) left-luggage office; (US) baggage checkroom; (somme) deposit; (ordres) orders; **~ automatique** left-luggage lockers; (US) baggage lockers.

consistance /kɔ̃sistɑ̃s/ nf consistency; (fig) substance, weight. **consistant, ~e** adj solid; (épais) thick.

consister /kɔ̃siste/ 1 vi **~ en/dans** consist of/in; **~ à faire** consist in doing.

consoler /kɔ̃sɔle/ 1 vt console. □ **se ~** vpr find consolation; **se ~ de qch** get over sth.

consolider /kɔ̃sɔlide/ 1 vt strengthen; (fig) consolidate.

consommateur, -trice /kɔ̃sɔmatœʀ, -tʀis/ nm, f (Comm) consumer; (dans un café) customer.

consommation /kɔ̃sɔmasjɔ̃/ nf consumption; (accomplissement) consummation; (boisson) drink; **de ~** (Comm) consumer.

consommer /kɔ̃sɔme/ 1 vt consume, use; (manger) eat; (boire) drink; (mariage) consummate. □ **se ~** vpr (être mangé) be eaten; (être utilisé) be used.

consonne /kɔ̃sɔn/ nf consonant.

constat /kɔsta/ nm (official) report; ~ (à l')amiable accident report drawn up by those involved.

constatation /kɔstatasjɔ̃/ nf observation, statement of fact. **constater** ❶ vt note, notice; (certifier) certify.

consternation /kɔstɛʀnasjɔ̃/ nf dismay.

constipé, ~e /kɔstipe/ adj constipated; (fig) uptight.

constituer /kɔstitɥe/ ❶ vt (composer) make up, constitute; (organiser) form; (être) constitute; **constitué de** made up of. □ **se ~ vpr se ~ prisonnier** give oneself up.

constitution /kɔstitysjɔ̃/ nf formation, setting up; (Pol, Méd) constitution.

constructeur /kɔstʀyktœʀ/ nm manufacturer, builder.

construction /kɔstʀyksjɔ̃/ nf building; (structure, secteur) construction; (fabrication) manufacture.

construire /kɔstʀɥiʀ/ ⓱ vt build; (système, phrase) construct.

consulat /kɔsyla/ nm consulate.

consultation /kɔsyltasjɔ̃/ nf consultation; (réception: Méd) surgery; (US) office; **heures de ~** surgery ou office (US) hours.

consulter /kɔsylte/ ❶ vt consult. ● vi (médecin) hold surgery, see patients. □ **se ~** vpr consult together.

contact /kɔtakt/ nm contact; (toucher) touch; **au ~ de** on contact with; (personne) by contact with, by seeing; **mettre/couper le ~** (Auto) switch on/off the ignition; **prendre ~ avec** get in touch with. **contacter** ❶ vt contact.

contagieux, -ieuse /kɔtaʒjø, -z/ adj contagious.

conte /kɔt/ nm tale; ~ **de fées** fairy tale.

contempler /kɔtɑ̃ple/ ❶ vt contemplate.

contemporain, ~e /kɔtɑ̃pɔʀɛ̃, -ɛn/ adj & nm,f contemporary.

contenance /kɔt(ə)nɑ̃s/ nf (volume) capacity; (allure) bearing; **perdre ~** lose one's composure.

contenir /kɔt(ə)niʀ/ ⓹⓼ vt contain; (avoir une capacité de) hold. □ **se ~** vpr contain oneself.

content, ~e /kɔtɑ̃, -t/ adj pleased, happy (**de** with); ~ **de faire** pleased ou happy to do.

contenter /kɔtɑ̃te/ ❶ vt satisfy. □ **se ~ de** vpr content oneself with.

contenu /kɔt(ə)ny/ nm (de récipient) contents (+ pl); (de texte) content.

conter /kɔte/ ❶ vt tell, relate.

contestation /kɔtɛstasjɔ̃/ nf dispute; (opposition) protest.

contester /kɔtɛste/ ❶ vt question, dispute; (s'opposer) protest against. ● vi protest.

conteur, -euse /kɔtœʀ, -øz/ nm, f storyteller.

contigu, ~ë /kɔtigy/ adj adjacent (à to).

continent /kɔtinɑ̃/ nm continent.

continu, ~e /kɔtiny/ adj continuous.

continuer /kɔtinɥe/ ❶ vt continue. ● vi continue, go on; ~ **à** ou **de faire** carry on ou go on ou continue doing.

contorsionner (se) /(sə) kɔtɔʀsjɔne/ ❶ vpr wriggle.

contour /kɔtuʀ/ nm outline, contour; ~**s** (d'une route) twists and turns, bends.

contourner /kɔtuʀne/ ❶ vt go round, by-pass; (difficulté) get round.

contraceptif, -ive /kɔtʀasɛptif, -v/ adj contraceptive. ● nm contraceptive. **contraception** nf contraception.

contracter /kɔtʀakte/ ❶ vt (maladie) contract; (dette) incur; (muscle) tense; (assurance) take out. □ **se ~** vpr contract.

contractuel, -le /kɔtʀaktɥɛl/ nm, f (agent) traffic warden.

contradictoire /kɔtʀadiktwaʀ/ adj contradictory; (débat) open.

contraignant, ~e /kɔtʀɛɲɑ̃, -t/ adj restricting.

contraindre /kɔtʀɛdʀ/ ⓶⓶ vt force, compel (**à faire** to do).

contrainte /kɔtʀɛt/ nf constraint.

contraire /kɔtʀɛʀ/ adj opposite; ~ **à** contrary to. ● nm opposite; **au ~** on the contrary; **au ~ de** unlike.

contrarier /kɔtʀaʀje/ ⓸⓹ vt annoy; (projet, volonté) frustrate; (chagriner) upset.

contraste /kɔtʀast/ nm contrast.

contrat /kɔtʀa/ nm contract.

contravention /kɔ̃tʀavɑ̃sjɔ̃/ nf (parking) ticket; **en ~** in breach (à of).

contre /kɔ̃tʀ(ə)/ prép against; (en échange de) for; **par ~** on the other hand; **tout ~** close by. **contreattaque** (pl **~s**) nf counterattack. **contre-attaquer** 🔟 vt counter-attack. **contre-balancer** 🔟 vt counterbalance.

contrebande /kɔ̃tʀəbɑ̃d/ nf contraband; **faire la ~ de** smuggle.

contrebas: en ~ /ɑ̃kɔ̃tʀəbɑ/ loc below.

contrebasse /kɔ̃tʀəbas/ nf double bass.

contrecœur: à ~ /akɔ̃tʀəkœr/ loc reluctantly.

contrecoup /kɔ̃tʀəku/ nm effects, repercussions.

contredire /kɔ̃tʀədiʀ/ 🔢 vt contradict. □ **se ~** vpr contradict oneself.

contrée /kɔ̃tʀe/ nf region; (pays) land.

contrefaçon /kɔ̃tʀəfasɔ̃/ nf (objet imité, action) forgery.

contre-indiqué, ~e /kɔ̃tʀɛ̃dike/ adj (Méd) contra-indicated; (déconseillé) not recommended.

contre-jour: à ~ /akɔ̃tʀəʒuʀ/ loc against the light.

contrepartie /kɔ̃tʀəparti/ nf compensation; **en ~** in exchange, in return.

contreplaqué /kɔ̃tʀəplake/ nm plywood.

contresens /kɔ̃tʀəsɑ̃s/ nm misinterpretation; (absurdité) nonsense; **à ~** the wrong way.

contretemps /kɔ̃tʀətɑ̃/ nm hitch; **à ~** (fig) at the wrong time.

contribuable /kɔ̃tʀibɥabl/ nmf taxpayer.

contribuer /kɔ̃tʀibɥe/ 🔟 vt contribute (à to, towards).

contrôle /kɔ̃tʀol/ nm (maîtrise) control; (vérification) check; (des prix) control; (poinçon) hallmark; (Scol) test; **~ continu** continuous assessment; **~ des changes** exchange control; **~ des naissances** birth control; **~ de soi-même** self-control; **~ technique (des véhicules)** MOT (test).

contrôler /kɔ̃tʀole/ 🔟 vt (vérifier) check; (surveiller, maîtriser) control. □ **se ~** vpr control oneself.

contrôleur, -euse /kɔ̃tʀolœʀ, -øz/ nm, f inspector.

convaincre /kɔ̃vɛ̃kʀ/ 🔢 vt convince; **~ qn de faire** persuade sb to do.

convalescence /kɔ̃valesɑ̃s/ nf convalescence; **être en ~** be convalescing.

convenable /kɔ̃vnabl/ adj (correct) decent, proper; (approprié) suitable; (acceptable) reasonable, acceptable.

convenance /kɔ̃vnɑ̃s/ nf **à ma ~** to my satisfaction; **les ~s** convention.

convenir /kɔ̃vniʀ/ 🔢 vt/i be suitable; **~ à** suit; **~ que** admit that; **~ de qch** (avouer) admit sth; (s'accorder sur) agree on sth; **~ de faire** agree to do; **il convient de** it is advisable to; (selon les bienséances) it would be right to.

convention /kɔ̃vɑ̃sjɔ̃/ nf agreement, convention; (clause) article, clause; **~s** (convenances) convention; **de ~** conventional; **~ collective** industrial agreement.

convenu, ~e /kɔ̃vny/ adj agreed.

conversation /kɔ̃vɛʀsasjɔ̃/ nf conversation.

convertir /kɔ̃vɛʀtiʀ/ 🔢 vt convert (à to; en into). □ **se ~** vpr be converted, convert.

conviction /kɔ̃viksjɔ̃/ nf conviction; **avoir la ~ que** be convinced that.

convivial, ~e (mpl **-iaux**) /kɔ̃vivjal, -jo/ adj convivial; (Ordinat) userfriendly.

convocation /kɔ̃vɔkasjɔ̃/ nf (Jur) summons; (d'une assemblée) convening; (document) notification to attend.

convoi /kɔ̃vwa/ nm convoy; (train) train; **~ (funèbre)** funeral procession.

convoquer /kɔ̃vɔke/ 🔟 vt (assemblée) convene; (personne) summon; **être convoqué pour un entretien** be called for interview.

coopération /kɔɔpeʀasjɔ̃/ nf cooperation; (Mil) civilian national service abroad.

coordination /kɔɔʀdinasjɔ̃/ nf coordination. **coordonnées** nfpl coordinates; (adresse) address and telephone number.

copain /kɔpɛ̃/ nm friend; (petit ami) boyfriend.

copie /kɔpi/ nf copy; (Scol) paper; **~ d'examen** exam paper ou script; **~**

de sauvegarde back-up copy.

copier /kɔpje/ 45 vt/i copy; ~ **sur** (Scol) copy ou crib from.

copieux, -ieuse /kɔpjø, -z/ adj copious.

copine /kɔpin/ nf friend; (petite amie) girlfriend.

coq /kɔk/ nm cockerel.

coque /kɔk/ nf shell; (de bateau) hull.

coquelicot /kɔkliko/ nm poppy.

coqueluche /kɔklyʃ/ nf whooping cough.

coquet, ~te /kɔkɛ, -t/ adj flirtatious; (élégant) pretty; (somme 𝟏) tidy.

coquetier /kɔktje/ nm eggcup.

coquillage /kɔkijaʒ/ nm shellfish; (coquille) shell.

coquille /kɔkij/ nf shell; (faute) misprint; ~ **Saint-Jacques** scallop.

coquin, ~e /kɔkɛ̃, -in/ adj mischievous. ● nm, f rascal.

cor /kɔr/ nm (Mus) horn; (au pied) corn.

corail (pl **-aux**) /kɔraj, -o/ nm coral.

corbeau (pl ~**x**) /kɔrbo/ nm (oiseau) crow.

corbeille /kɔrbɛj/ nf basket; ~ **à papier** waste-paper basket.

corbillard /kɔrbijar/ nm hearse.

cordage /kɔrdaʒ/ nm rope; ~**s** (Naut) rigging.

corde /kɔrd/ nf rope; (d'arc, de violon) string; ~ **à linge** washing line; ~ **à sauter** skipping-rope; ~ **raide** tightrope; ~**s vocales** vocal cords.

cordon /kɔrdɔ̃/ nm string, cord; ~ **de police** police cordon.

cordonnier /kɔrdɔnje/ nm cobbler.

Corée /kɔre/ nf Korea.

coriace /kɔrjas/ adj tough.

corne /kɔrn/ nf horn.

corneille /kɔrnɛj/ nf crow.

cornemuse /kɔrnəmyz/ nf bagpipes (+ pl).

corner /kɔrne/ 𝟏 vt (page) turn down the corner of; **page cornée** dog-eared page. ● vi (Auto) hoot, honk.

cornet /kɔrnɛ/ nm (paper) cone; (crème glacée) cornet, cone.

corniche /kɔrniʃ/ nf cornice; (route) cliff road.

cornichon /kɔrniʃɔ̃/ nm gherkin.

corporel, ~le /kɔrpɔrɛl/ adj bodily; (châtiment) corporal.

corps /kɔr/ nm body; (Mil) corps; **combat ~ à ~** hand-to-hand combat; ~ **électoral** electorate; ~ **enseignant** teaching profession.

correct, ~e /kɔrɛkt/ adj proper, correct; (exact) correct.

correcteur, -trice /kɔrɛktœr, -tris/ nm, f (d'épreuves) proofreader; (Scol) examiner; ~ **liquide** correction fluid; ~ **d'orthographe** spell-checker.

correction /kɔrɛksjɔ̃/ nf correction; (d'examen) marking, grading; (punition) beating.

correspondance /kɔrɛspɔ̃dɑ̃s/ nf correspondence; (de train, d'autobus) connection; **vente par** ~ mail order; **faire des études par** ~ do a correspondence course.

correspondant, ~e /kɔrɛspɔ̃dɑ̃, -t/ adj corresponding. ● nm, f correspondent; penfriend; (au téléphone) **votre** ~ the person you are calling.

correspondre /kɔrɛspɔ̃dr/ 𝟑 vi (s'accorder, écrire) correspond; (chambres) communicate. ● v + prép ~ **à** (être approprié à) match, suit; (équivaloir à) correspond to. □ **se** ~ vpr correspond.

corrida /kɔrida/ nf bullfight.

corriger /kɔriʒe/ 40 vt correct; (devoir) mark, grade, correct; (punir) beat; (guérir) cure.

corsage /kɔrsaʒ/ nm bodice; (chemisier) blouse.

corsaire /kɔrsɛr/ nm pirate.

Corse /kɔrs/ nf Corsica. ● nmf Corsican. **corse** adj Corsican.

corsé, ~e /kɔrse/ adj (vin) full-bodied; (café) strong; (scabreux) racy; (problème) tough.

cortège /kɔrtɛʒ/ nm procession; ~ **funèbre** funeral procession.

corvée /kɔrve/ nf chore.

cosmonaute /kɔsmonot/ nmf cosmonaut.

cosmopolite /kɔsmopolit/ adj cosmopolitan.

cosse /kɔs/ nf (de pois) pod.

cossu, ~e /kɔsy/ adj (gens) well-to-do; (demeure) opulent.

costaud, ~e /kɔsto, -d/ 𝟏 adj strong. ● nm strong man.

costume /kɔstym/ nm suit; (Théât) costume.

cote /kɔt/ nf (classification) mark; (en Bourse) quotation; (de cheval) odds (**de** on); (de candidat, acteur) rating; **~ d'alerte** danger level; **avoir la ~** be popular.

côte /kot/ nf (littoral) coast; (pente) hill; (Anat) rib; (Culin) chop; **~ à ~** side by side; **la C~ d'Azur** the (French) Riviera.

côté /kote/ nm side; (direction) way; **à ~** nearby; **voisin d'à ~** next-door neighbour; **à ~ de** next to; (comparé à) compared to; **à ~ de la cible** wide of the target; **aux ~s de** by the side of; **de ~** (regarder) sideways; (sauter) to one side; **mettre de ~** put aside; **de ce ~** this way; **de chaque ~** on each side; **de tous les ~s** on every side; (partout) everywhere; **du ~ de** (vers) towards; (proche de) near.

côtelette /kotlɛt/ nf chop.

coter /kote/ **1** vt (Comm) quote; **coté en Bourse** listed on the Stock Exchange; **très coté** highly rated.

cotiser /kotize/ **1** vi pay one's contributions (**à** to); (à un club) pay one's subscription. □ **se ~** vpr club together.

coton /kotɔ̃/ nm cotton; **~ hydrophile** cotton wool.

cou /ku/ nm neck.

couchant /kuʃɑ̃/ nm sunset.

couche /kuʃ/ nf layer; (de peinture) coat; (de bébé) nappy; (US) diaper; **~s** (Méd) childbirth; **~s sociales** social strata.

coucher /kuʃe/ **1** vt put to bed; (loger) put up; (étendre) lay down; **~ (par écrit)** set down. ● vi sleep. □ **se ~** vpr go to bed; (s'étendre) lie down; (soleil) set. ● nm **~ de soleil** sunset.

couchette /kuʃɛt/ nf (de train) couchette; (Naut) berth.

coude /kud/ nm elbow; (de rivière, chemin) bend; **~ à ~** side by side.

cou-de-pied (pl **cous-de-pied**) /kudpje/ nm instep.

coudre /kudʀ/ **19** vt/i sew.

couette /kwɛt/ nf duvet, quilt.

couler /kule/ **1** vi flow, run; (fromage, nez) run; (fuir) leak; (bateau) sink; (entreprise) go under; **faire ~ un bain** run a bath. ● vt (bateau) sink; (sculp-

ture, métal) cast. □ **se ~** vpr slip (**dans** into).

couleur /kulœʀ/ nf colour; (peinture) paint; (aux cartes) suit; **~s** (teint) colour; **de ~** (homme, femme) coloured; **en ~s** (télévision, film) colour.

couleuvre /kulœvʀ/ nf grass snake.

coulisse /kulis/ nf (de tiroir) runner; **à ~** (porte, fenêtre) sliding; **~s** (Théât) wings; **dans les ~s** (fig) behind the scenes.

couloir /kulwaʀ/ nm corridor; (Sport) lane; **~ de bus** bus lane.

coup /ku/ nm blow; (choc) knock; (Sport) stroke; (de crayon, chance, cloche) stroke; (de fusil, pistolet) shot; (fois) time; (aux échecs) move; **donner un ~ de pied/poing à** kick/punch; **à ~ sûr** definitely; **après ~** after the event; **boire un ~** 🔢 have a drink; **~ sur ~** in rapid succession; **du ~** as a result; **d'un seul ~** in one go; **du premier ~** first go; **sale ~** dirty trick; **sous le ~ de la fatigue/colère** out of tiredness/anger; **sur le ~** instantly; **tenir le ~** hold out; **manquer son ~** 🔢 blow it!; **~ de chiffon** wipe (with a rag); **~ de coude** nudge; **~ de couteau** stab; **~ d'envoi** kick-off; **~ d'État** (Pol) coup; **~ franc** free kick; **~ de main** helping hand; **~ d'oeil** glance; **~ de soleil** sunburn; **~ de téléphone** telephone call; **~ de vent** gust of wind.

coupable /kupabl/ adj guilty.

coupe /kup/ nf cup; (de champagne) goblet; (à fruits) dish; (de vêtement) cut; (dessin) section; **~ de cheveux** haircut.

couper /kupe/ **1** vt cut; (arbre) cut down; (arrêter) cut off; (voyage) break up; (appétit) take away; (vin) water down; **~ par** take a short cut via; **~ la parole à qn** cut sb short. ● vi cut. □ **se ~** vpr cut oneself; **se ~ le doigt** cut one's finger; (routes) intersect; **se ~ de** cut oneself off from.

couple /kupl/ nm couple; (d'animaux) pair.

coupure /kupyʀ/ nf cut; (billet de banque) note; (de presse) cutting; (pause, rupture) break; (**~ de courant**) power cut.

cour /kuʀ/ nf (court) yard; (du roi) court; (tribunal) court; (**~ de récréa-**

tion) playground; ~ **martiale** court-martial; **faire la ~ à** court.

courageux, -euse /kuraʒø, -z/ adj courageous.

couramment /kuramã/ adv frequently; (parler) fluently.

courant, ~e /kurã, -t/ adj standard, ordinary; (en cours) current. ● nm current; (de mode, d'idées) trend; ~ **d'air** draught; **dans le ~ de** in the course of; **être/mettre au ~ de** know/tell about; (à jour) be/bring up to date on.

courbature /kurbatyr/ nf ache; **avoir des ~s** be stiff, ache.

courber /kurbe/ **1** vt bend.

coureur, -euse /kurœr, -øz/ nm, f (Sport) runner; ~ **automobile** racing driver; ~ **cycliste** racing cyclist. ● nm womanizer.

courgette /kurʒɛt/ nf courgette; (US) zucchini.

courir /kurir/ **20** vi run; (se hâter) rush; (nouvelles) go round; ~ **après qn/qch** chase after sb/ sth. ● vt (risque) run; (danger) face; (épreuve sportive) run ou compete in; (fréquenter) do the rounds of; (filles) chase (after).

couronne /kurɔn/ nf crown; (de fleurs) wreath.

couronnement /kurɔnmã/ nm coronation, crowning; (fig) crowning achievement.

courriel /kurjɛl/ nm email.

courrier /kurje/ nm post, mail; (à écrire) letters; ~ **du cœur** problem page; ~ **électronique** email.

cours /kur/ nm (leçon) class; (série de leçons) course; (prix) price; (cote) (de valeur, denrée) price; (de devises) exchange rate; (déroulement, d'une rivière) course; (allée) avenue; **au ~ de** in the course of; **avoir ~** (monnaie) be legal tender; (fig) be current; (Scol) have a lesson; ~ **d'eau** river, stream; ~ **du soir** evening class; ~ **particulier** private lesson; ~ **magistral** (Univ) lecture; **en ~** current; (travail) in progress; **en ~ de route** along the way.

course /kurs/ nf running; (épreuve de vitesse) race; (activité) racing; (entre rivaux: fig) race; (de projectile) flight; (voyage) journey; (commission) errand; ~s (achats) shopping; (de che-

vaux) races; **faire la ~ avec qn** race sb.

coursier, -ière /kursje, -jɛr/ nm, f messenger.

court, ~e /kur, -t/ adj short. ● adv short; **à ~ de** short of; **pris de ~** caught unawares. ● nm ~ **(de tennis)** (tennis) court.

courtier, -ière /kurtje, -jɛr/ nm, f broker.

courtiser /kurtize/ **1** vt woo, court.

courtois, ~e /kurtwa, -z/ adj courteous. **courtoisie** nf courtesy.

cousin, ~e /kuzɛ̃, -in/ nm, f cousin; ~ **germain** first cousin.

coussin /kusɛ̃/ nm cushion.

coût /ku/ nm cost; **le ~ de la vie** the cost of living.

couteau (pl ~x) /kuto/ nm knife; ~ **à cran d'arrêt** flick knife.

coûter /kute/ **1** vt/i cost; **coûte que coûte** at all costs; **au prix coûtant** at cost (price).

coutume /kutym/ nf custom.

couture /kutyr/ nf sewing; (métier) dressmaking; (points) seam. **couturier** nm fashion designer. **couturière** nf dressmaker.

couvée /kuve/ nf brood.

couvent /kuvã/ nm convent.

couver /kuve/ **1** vt (œufs) hatch; (personne) overprotect, pamper; (maladie) be coming down with, be sickening for. ● vi (feu) smoulder; (mal) be brewing.

couvercle /kuvɛrkl/ nm (de marmite, boîte) lid; (qui se visse) screwtop.

couvert, ~e /kuvɛr, -t/ adj covered (de with); (habillé) covered up; (ciel) overcast. ● nm (à table) place setting; (prix) cover charge; ~s (couteaux etc.) cutlery; **mettre le ~** lay the table; (abri) cover; **à ~** (Mil) under cover; **à ~ de** (fig) safe from.

couverture /kuvɛrtyr/ nf cover; (de lit) blanket; (toit) roofing; (dans la presse) coverage; ~ **chauffante** electric blanket.

couvre-feu (pl ~x) /kuvrəfø/ nm curfew.

couvre-lit (pl ~s) /kuvrəli/ nm bedspread.

couvrir /kuvrir/ **21** vt cover. □ **se ~** vpr (s'habiller) wrap up; (se coiffer) put one's hat on; (*ciel*) become overcast.

covoiturage /kɔvwatyʀaʒ/ *nm* car sharing.

cracher /kʀaʃe/ **1** *vi* spit; (*radio*) crackle. ● *vt* spit (out); (*fumée*) belch out.

crachin /kʀaʃɛ̃/ *nm* drizzle.

craie /kʀɛ/ *nf* chalk.

craindre /kʀɛ̃dʀ/ **22** *vt* be afraid of, fear; (être sensible à) be easily damaged by.

crainte /kʀɛ̃t/ *nf* fear (**pour** for); **de ~ de/que** for fear of/that. **craintif, -ive** *adj* timid.

crampon /kʀɑ̃pɔ̃/ *nm* (de chaussure) stud.

cramponner (se) /(sə)kʀɑ̃pɔne/ **1** *vpr* se ~ à cling to.

cran /kʀɑ̃/ *nm* (entaille) notch; (trou) hole; (courage 🆃) guts 🆃, courage; **~ de sûreté** safety catch.

crâne /kʀɑn/ *nm* skull.

crapaud /kʀapo/ *nm* toad.

craquer /kʀake/ **1** *vi* crack, snap; (plancher) creak; (couture) split; (fig) (personne) break down; (céder) give in. ● *vt* (allumette) strike; (vêtement) split.

crasse /kʀas/ *nf* grime.

cravache /kʀavaʃ/ *nf* (horse) whip.

cravate /kʀavat/ *nf* tie.

crayon /kʀɛjɔ̃/ *nm* pencil; **~ de couleur** coloured pencil; **~ à bille** ballpoint pen; **~ optique** light pen.

créateur, -trice /kʀeatœʀ, -tʀis/ *adj* creative. ● *nm, f* creator, designer.

crèche /kʀɛʃ/ *nf* day nursery, crèche; (Relig) crib.

crédit /kʀedi/ *nm* credit; (somme allouée) funds; **à ~** on credit; **faire ~** give credit (à to).

créer /kʀee/ **15** *vt* create; (produit) design; (société) set up.

crémaillère /kʀemajɛʀ/ *nf* **pendre la ~** have a housewarming party.

crème /kʀɛm/ *adj inv* cream. ● *nm* (café) ~ espresso with milk. ● *nf* cream; (dessert) cream dessert; **~ anglaise** egg custard; **~ fouettée** whipped cream; **~ pâtissière** confectioner's custard. **crémerie** *nf* dairy. **crémeux, -euse** *adj* creamy. **crémier, -ière** *nm, f* dairyman, dairywoman.

créneau (*pl* ~**x**) /kʀeno/ *nm* (trou, moment) slot, window; (dans le marché) gap; **faire un ~** to parallel-park.

crêpe /kʀɛp/ *nf* (galette) pancake. ● *nm* (tissu) crêpe; (matière) crêpe (rubber).

crépitement /kʀepitmɑ̃/ *nm* crackling; (d'huile) sizzling.

crépuscule /kʀepyskyl/ *nm* twilight, dusk.

cresson /kʀəsɔ̃/ *nm* (water) cress.

crête /kʀɛt/ *nf* crest; (de coq) comb.

crétin, ~e /kʀetɛ̃, -in/ *nm, f* 🆃 moron 🆃.

creuser /kʀøze/ **1** *vt* dig; (évider) hollow out; (fig) go into in depth. □ **se ~** *vpr* (écart) widen; **se ~ (la cervelle)** 🆃 rack one's brains.

creux, -euse /kʀø, -z/ *adj* hollow; (heures) off-peak. ● *nm* hollow; (de l'estomac) pit; **dans le ~ de la main** in the palm of the hand.

crevaison /kʀəvɛzɔ̃/ *nf* puncture.

crevasse /kʀəvas/ *nf* crack; (de glacier) crevasse; (de la peau) chap.

crevé, ~e /kʀəve/ *adj* 🆃 worn out.

crever /kʀəve/ **1** *vt* burst; (pneu) puncture, burst; (exténuer 🆃) exhaust; (œil) put out. ● *vi* (pneu, sac) burst; (mourir 🆃) die.

crevette /kʀəvɛt/ *nf* **~ grise** shrimp; **~ rose** prawn.

cri /kʀi/ *nm* cry; (de douleur) scream, cry; **pousser un ~** cry out, scream.

criard, ~e /kʀijaʀ, -d/ *adj* (couleur) garish; (voix) shrill.

crier /kʀije/ **45** *vi* (fort) shout, cry (out); (de douleur) scream; (grincer) creak. ● *vt* (ordre) shout (out).

crime /kʀim/ *nm* crime; (meurtre) murder.

criminel, ~le /kʀiminɛl/ *adj* criminal. ● *nm, f* criminal; (assassin) murderer.

crinière /kʀinjɛʀ/ *nf* mane.

crise /kʀiz/ *nf* crisis; (Méd) attack; (de colère) fit; **~ cardiaque** heart attack; **~ de foie** bilious attack; **~ de nerfs** hysterics (+ pl).

crisper /kʀispe/ **1** *vt* tense; (énerver 🆃) irritate. □ **se ~** *vpr* tense; (mains) clench.

critère /kʀitɛʀ/ *nm* criterion.

critique /kʀitik/ *adj* critical. ● *nf* criticism; (article) review; (commentateur)

critic; **la** ∼ (personnes) the critics. **critiquer** 🔟 *vt* criticize.

Croate /kʀɔat/ *adj* Croatian. **C**∼ *nmf*
Croatian.

Croatie /kʀɔasi/ *nf* Croatia.

croche /kʀɔʃ/ *nf* quaver.

croche-pied (*pl* ∼**s**) /kʀɔʃpje/ *nm* 🔟
faire un ∼ à trip up.

crochet /kʀɔʃɛ/ *nm* hook; (détour) detour; (signe) (square) bracket; (tricot)
crochet; **faire au** ∼ crochet.

crochu, ∼e /kʀɔʃy/ *adj* hooked.

crocodile /kʀɔkɔdil/ *nm* crocodile.

croire /kʀwaʀ/ 🈷 *vt* believe (**à, en** in);
(estimer) think, believe (**que** that).
● *vi* believe.

croisade /kʀwazad/ *nf* crusade.

croisement /kʀwazmɑ̃/ *nm* crossing;
(fait de passer à côté de) passing;
(carrefour) crossroads.

croiser /kʀwaze/ 🔟 *vi* (bateau) cruise.
● *vt* cross; (passant, véhicule) pass; ∼
les bras fold one's arms; ∼ **les jambes** cross one's legs; (animaux) cross-
breed. ▫ **se** ∼ *vpr* (véhicules, piétons)
pass each other; (lignes) cross. **croisière** *nf* cruise.

croissance /kʀwasɑ̃s/ *nf* growth.

croissant, ∼e /kʀwasɑ̃, t/ *adj* growing. ● *nm* crescent; (pâtisserie)
croissant.

croix /kʀwa/ *nf* cross; ∼ **gammée**
swastika; **C**∼**-Rouge** Red Cross.

croquant, ∼e /kʀɔkɑ̃, -t/ *adj* crunchy.

croque-monsieur /kʀɔkməsjø/ *nm*
inv toasted ham and cheese sandwich.

croque-mort (*pl* ∼**s**) /kʀɔkmɔʀ/ *nm*
🔟 undertaker.

croquer /kʀɔke/ 🔟 *vt* crunch; (dessiner) sketch; **chocolat à** ∼ plain chocolate. ● *vi* be crunchy.

croquis /kʀɔki/ *nm* sketch.

crotte /kʀɔt/ *nf* dropping.

crotté, ∼e /kʀɔte/ *adj* muddy.

crottin /kʀɔtɛ̃/ *nm* (horse) dropping.

croupir /kʀupiʀ/ 🔢 *vi* stagnate.

croustillant, ∼e /kʀustijɑ̃, -t/ *adj*
crispy; (pain) crusty; (fig) spicy.

croûte /kʀut/ *nf* crust; (de fromage)
rind; (de plaie) scab; **en** ∼ (Culin) in
pastry.

croûton /kʀutɔ̃/ *nm* (bout de pain)
crust; (avec potage) croûton.

CRS *abrév m* (**Compagnie républicaine
de sécurité**) French riot police; **un** ∼
a member of the French riot police.

cru¹ /kʀy/ ➡**CROIRE** 🈷.

cru², ∼e /kʀy/ *adj* raw; (lumière) harsh;
(propos) crude. ● *nm* vineyard; (vin)
vintage wine.

crû /kʀy/ ➡**CROÎTRE** 🈢.

cruauté /kʀyote/ *nf* cruelty.

cruche /kʀyʃ/ *nf* jug, pitcher.

crucial, ∼e (*mpl* **-iaux**) /kʀysjal, -jo/
adj crucial.

crudité /kʀydite/ *nf* (de langage)
crudeness; ∼**s** (Culin) raw vegetables.

crue /kʀy/ *nf* rise in water level; **en** ∼
in spate.

crustacé /kʀystase/ *nm* shellfish.

cube /kyb/ *nm* cube. ● *adj* (mètre)
cubic.

cueillir /kœjiʀ/ 🈯 *vt* pick, gather;
(personne 🔟) pick up.

cuiller, cuillère /kɥijɛʀ/ *nf* spoon; ∼ à
soupe soup spoon; (mesure) table-
spoonful.

cuir /kɥiʀ/ *nm* leather; ∼ **chevelu**
scalp.

cuire /kɥiʀ/ 🈁 *vt* cook; ∼ (**au four**)
bake. ● *vi* cook; **faire** ∼ cook.

cuisine /kɥizin/ *nf* kitchen; (art) cookery, cooking; (aliments) food; **faire la**
∼ cook.

cuisiner /kɥizine/ 🔟 *vt* cook; (interroger 🔟) grill. ● *vi* cook.

cuisinier, -ière /kɥizinje, -jɛʀ/ *nm, f*
cook. **cuisinière** *nf* (appareil) cooker,
stove.

cuisse /kɥis/ *nf* thigh; (de poulet)
thigh; (de grenouille) leg.

cuisson /kɥisɔ̃/ *nf* cooking.

cuit, ∼e /kɥi, -t/ *adj* cooked; **bien** ∼
well done *ou* cooked; **trop** ∼
overdone.

cuivre /kɥivʀ/ *nm* copper; ∼ (**jaune**)
brass; ∼**s** (Mus) brass.

cul /ky/ *nm* (derrière 🈲) backside, bottom, arse 🈲.

culbuter /kylbyte/ 🔟 *vi* (personne)
tumble; (objet) topple (over). ● *vt*
knock over.

culminer /kylmine/ 🔟 *vi* reach its
highest point *ou* peak.

culot /kylo/ *nm* (audace 🔟) nerve,
cheek; (Tech) base.

culotte /kylɔt/ nf (de femme) pants (+ pl), knickers (+ pl); (US) panties (+ pl); ∼ de cheval riding breeches; en ∼ courte in short trousers.

culpabilité /kylpabilite/ nf guilt.

culte /kylt/ nm cult, worship; (religion) religion; (office protestant) service.

cultivateur, -trice /kyltivatœr, -tris/ nm, f farmer.

cultiver /kyltive/ **1** vt cultivate; (plantes) grow.

culture /kyltyr/ nf cultivation; (de plantes) growing; (agriculture) farming; (éducation) culture; (connaissances) knowledge; ∼s (terrains) lands under cultivation; ∼ physique physical training.

culturel, ∼le /kyltyrɛl/ adj cultural.

cumuler /kymyle/ **1** vt accumulate; (fonctions) hold concurrently.

cure /kyr/ nf (course of) treatment.

curé /kyre/ nm (parish) priest.

cure-dent (pl ∼s) /kyrdã/ nm toothpick.

curer /kyre/ **1** vt clean. □ se ∼ vpr se ∼ les dents/ongles clean one's teeth/nails.

curieux, -ieuse /kyrjø, -z/ adj curious. ● nm, f (badaud) onlooker.

curiosité /kyrjozite/ nf curiosity; (objet) curio; (spectacle) unusual sight.

curriculum vitae /kyrikylɔm vite/ nm inv curriculum vitae; (US) résumé.

curseur /kyrsœr/ nm cursor.

cutané, ∼e /kytane/ adj skin.

cuve /kyv/ nf vat; (à mazout, eau) tank.

cuvée /kyve/ nf (de vin) vintage.

cuvette /kyvɛt/ nf bowl; (de lavabo) (wash) basin; (des cabinets) pan, bowl.

CV abrév m (**curriculum vitae**) CV.

cyberbranché, ∼e /siberbrãʃe/ adj cyberwired.

cybercafé /siberkafe/ nm cybercafe.

cyberespace /sibersɛpas/ nm cyberspace.

cybernaute /sibernot/ nmf Netsurfer.

cybernétique /sibernetik/ nf cybernetics (+ pl).

cyclisme /siklism/ nm cycling.

cycliste /siklist/ nmf cyclist. ● nm cycling shorts. ● adj cycle.

cyclone /siklon/ nm cyclone.

cygne /siɲ/ nm swan.

cynique /sinik/ adj cynical. ● nm cynic.

Dd

d' /d/ ➡DE.

d'abord /dabɔr/ adv first; (au début) at first.

dactylo /daktilo/ nf typist. **dactylographier** **45** vt type.

dada /dada/ nm hobby-horse.

daim /dɛ̃/ nm (fallow) deer; (cuir) suede.

dallage /dalaʒ/ nm paving. **dalle** nf slab.

daltonien, ∼ne /daltɔnjɛ̃, -ɛn/ adj colour-blind.

dame /dam/ nf lady; (cartes, échecs) queen; ∼s (jeu) draughts; (US) checkers.

damier /damje/ nm draught board; (US) checker-board; à ∼ chequered.

damner /dane/ **1** vt damn.

dandiner (se) /(sə)dãdine/ **1** vpr waddle.

Danemark /danmark/ nm Denmark.

danger /dãʒe/ nm danger; en ∼ in danger; mettre en ∼ endanger.

dangereux, -euse /dãʒ(ə)rø, -z/ adj dangerous.

danois, ∼e /danwa, -z/ adj Danish. ● nm (Ling) Danish. D∼, ∼e nm, f Dane.

dans /dã/ prép in; (mouvement) into; (à l'intérieur de) inside, in; être ∼ un avion be on a plane; ∼ dix jours in ten days' time; boire ∼ un verre drink out of a glass; ∼ les 10 euros about 10 euros.

danse /dãs/ nf dance; (art) dancing.

danser /dãse/ **1** vt/i dance. **danseur, -euse** nm, f dancer.

darne /darn/ nf steak (of fish).

date /dat/ nf date; ∼ limite deadline; ∼ limite de vente sell-by date; ∼ de

péremption use-by date.

dater /date/ **1** vt/i date; **à ∼ de** as from.

datte /dat/ nf (fruit) date.

daube /dob/ nf casserole.

dauphin /dofɛ̃/ nm (animal) dolphin.

davantage /davɑ̃taʒ/ adv more; (plus longtemps) longer; **∼ de** more; **je n'en sais pas ∼** that's as much as I know.

---

de, **d'** /də, d/

d' before vowel or mute h.

● *préposition*

····▸ of; **le livre ∼ mon ami** my friend's book; **un pont ∼ fer** an iron bridge.

····▸ (provenance) from.

····▸ (temporel) from; **∼ 8 heures à 10 heures** from 8 till 10.

····▸ (mesure, manière) **dix mètres ∼ haut** ten metres high; **pleurer ∼ rage** cry with rage.

····▸ (agent) by; **un livre ∼ Marcel Aymé** a book by Marcel Aymé.

● **de, de l', de la, du,** (pl **des**) *déterminant*

····▸ some; **du pain** (some) bread; **des fleurs** (some) flowers; **je ne bois jamais ∼ vin** I never drink wine.

de + le = du
de + les = des

---

dé /de/ nm (à jouer) dice; (à coudre) thimble; **∼s** (jeu) dice.

débâcle /debɑkl/ nf (Géog) breaking up; (Mil) rout.

déballer /debale/ **1** vt unpack; (révéler) spill out.

débarbouiller /debarbuje/ vt wash the face of. □ **se ∼** vpr wash one's face.

débarcadère /debarkadɛr/ nm landing-stage.

débardeur /debardœr/ nm (vêtement) tank top.

débarquement /debarkəmɑ̃/ nm disembarkation. **débarquer** **1** vt/i disembark, land; (arriver **1**) turn up.

débarras /debara/ nm junk room; **bon ∼!** good riddance!

débarrasser /debarase/ **1** vt clear (de of); **∼ qn de** relieve sb of; (défaut, ennemi) rid sb of. □ **se ∼ de** vpr get rid of.

débat /deba/ nm debate.

débattre /debatr/ **11** vt debate. ● vi **∼ de** discuss. □ **se ∼** vpr struggle (to get free).

débauche /deboʃ/ nf debauchery; (fig) profusion.

débaucher /deboʃe/ **1** vt (licencier) lay off; (distraire) tempt away.

débile /debil/ adj weak; **1** stupid. ● nmf moron **1**.

débit /debi/ nm (rate of) flow; (élocution) delivery; (de compte) debit; **∼ de tabac** tobacconist's shop; **∼ de boissons** bar; **haut ∼** broadband.

débiter /debite/ **1** vt (compte) debit; (fournir) produce; (vendre) sell; (dire: péj) spout; (couper) cut up.

débiteur, -trice /debitœr, -tris/ nm, f debtor. ● adj (compte) in debit.

déblayer /debleje/ **31** vt clear.

déblocage /deblɔkaʒ/ nm (de prix) deregulating. **débloquer** **1** vt (prix, salaires) unfreeze.

déboiser /debwaze/ **1** vt clear (of trees).

déboîter /debwate/ **1** vi (véhicule) pull out. ● vt (membre) dislocate.

débordement /debɔrdəmɑ̃/ nm (de joie) excess.

déborder /debɔrde/ **1** vi overflow. ● vt (dépasser) extend beyond; **∼ de** (joie etc.) be brimming over with.

débouché /debuʃe/ nm opening; (carrière) prospect; (Comm) outlet; (sortie) end, exit.

déboucher /debuʃe/ **1** vt (bouteille) uncork; (évier) unblock. ● vi come out (de from); **∼ sur** (rue) lead into.

débourser /deburse/ **1** vt pay out.

debout /dəbu/ adv standing; (levé, éveillé) up; **être ∼, se tenir ∼** be standing, stand; **se mettre ∼** stand up.

déboutonner /debutɔne/ **1** vt unbutton. □ **se ∼** vpr unbutton oneself; (vêtement) come undone.

débrancher /debrɑ̃ʃe/ **1** vt (prise) unplug; (système) disconnect.

débrayer /debreje/ **31** vi (Auto) declutch; (faire grève) stop work.

débris /debʀi/ *nmpl* fragments; (détritus) rubbish (+ *sg*); debris.

débrouillard, ~e /debʀujaʀ, -d/ *adj* 🔟 resourceful.

débrouiller /debʀuje/ 🔟 *vt* disentangle; (*problème*) solve. □ **se ~** *vpr* manage.

début /deby/ *nm* beginning; **faire ses ~s** (en public) make one's début; **à mes ~s** when I started out. **débutant, ~e** *nm*, *f* beginner. **débuter** 🔟 *vi* begin; (dans un métier etc.) start out.

déca /deka/ *nm* 🔟 decaf.

deçà: en ~ /ɑ̃dəsa/ *loc* this side. ● *prép* **en ~ de** this side of.

décacheter /dekaʃte/ 🔟 *vt* open.

décade /dekad/ *nf* ten days; (décennie) decade.

décadent, ~e /dekadɑ̃, -t/ *adj* decadent.

décalage /dekalaʒ/ *nm* (écart) gap; **~ horaire** time difference. **décaler** 🔟 *vt* shift.

décalquer /dekalke/ 🔟 *vt* trace.

décamper /dekɑ̃pe/ 🔟 *vi* clear off.

décanter /dekɑ̃te/ *vt* allow to settle. □ **se ~** *vpr* settle.

décapant /dekapɑ̃/ *nm* chemical agent; (pour peinture) paint stripper. ● *adj* (*humour*) caustic.

décapotable /dekapɔtabl/ *adj* convertible.

décapsuleur /dekapsylœʀ/ *nm* bottle-opener.

décédé, ~e /desede/ *adj* deceased. **décéder** 🔟 *vi* die.

déceler /desle/ 🔟 *vt* detect; (démontrer) reveal.

décembre /desɑ̃bʀ/ *nm* December.

décemment /desamɑ̃/ *adv* decently. **décence** *nf* decency. **décent, ~e** *adj* decent.

décennie /deseni/ *nf* decade.

décentralisation /desɑ̃tʀalizasjɔ̃/ *nf* decentralization. **décentraliser** 🔟 *vt* decentralize.

déception /desɛpsjɔ̃/ *nf* disappointment.

décerner /desɛʀne/ 🔟 *vt* award.

décès /desɛ/ *nm* death.

décevant, ~e /des(ə)vɑ̃, -t/ *adj* disappointing. **décevoir** 🔟 *vt* disappoint.

déchaîner /deʃene/ 🔟 *vt* (enthousiasme) rouse. □ **se ~** *vpr* go wild.

décharge /deʃaʀʒ/ *nf* (de fusil) discharge; **~ électrique** electric shock; **~ publique** municipal dump.

décharger /deʃaʀʒe/ 🔟 *vt* unload; **~ qn de** relieve sb from. □ **se ~** *vpr* (*batterie, pile*) go flat.

déchausser (se) /(sə)deʃose/ 🔟 *vpr* take off one's shoes; (*dent*) work loose.

dèche /dɛʃ/ *nf* 🔟 **dans la ~** broke.

déchéance /deʃeɑ̃s/ *nf* decay.

déchet /deʃɛ/ *nm* (reste) scrap; (perte) waste; **~s** (ordures) refuse.

déchiffrer /deʃifʀe/ 🔟 *vt* decipher.

déchiqueter /deʃikte/ 🔟 *vt* tear to shreds.

déchirement /deʃiʀmɑ̃/ *nm* heartbreak; (conflit) split.

déchirer /deʃiʀe/ 🔟 *vt* (par accident) tear; (lacérer) tear up; (arracher) tear off *ou* out; (diviser) tear apart. □ **se ~** *vpr* tear. **déchirure** *nf* tear.

décibel /desibɛl/ *nm* decibel.

décidément /desidemɑ̃/ *adv* really.

décider /deside/ 🔟 *vt* decide on; (persuader) persuade; **~ que/de** decide that/to; **~ de qch** decide on sth. □ **se ~** *vpr* make up one's mind (à to).

décimal, ~e (*mpl* **~aux**) /desimal, -o/ *adj* & *nf* decimal.

décisif, -ive /desizif, -v/ *adj* decisive.

décision /desizjɔ̃/ *nf* decision.

déclaration /deklaʀasjɔ̃/ *nf* declaration; (commentaire politique) statement; **~ d'impôts** tax return.

déclarer /deklaʀe/ 🔟 *vt* declare; (naissance) register; **déclaré coupable** found guilty; **~ forfait** (Sport) withdraw. □ **se ~** *vpr* (*feu*) break out.

déclencher /deklɑ̃ʃe/ 🔟 *vt* (Tech) set off; (conflit) spark off; (avalanche) start; (rire) provoke. □ **se ~** *vpr* (Tech) go off. **déclencheur** *nm* (Photo) shutter release.

déclic /deklik/ *nm* click.

déclin /deklɛ̃/ *nm* decline.

déclinaison /deklinɛzɔ̃/ *nf* (Ling) declension.

décliner /dekline/ 🔟 *vt* (refuser) decline; (dire) state; (Ling) decline.

décocher /dekɔʃe/ 🔟 *vt* (coup) fling; (regard) shoot.

décollage /dekɔlaʒ/ nm take-off.

décoller /dekɔle/ **1** vt unstick. ● vi (avion) take off. □ **se ~** vpr come off.

décolleté, ~e /dekɔlte/ adj lowcut. ● nm low neckline.

décolorer /dekɔlɔʀe/ **1** vt fade; (cheveux) bleach. □ **se ~** vpr fade.

décombres /dekɔ̃bʀ/ nmpl rubble.

décommander /dekɔmɑ̃de/ **1** vt cancel.

décomposer /dekɔ̃poze/ **1** vt break up; (substance) decompose. □ **se ~** vpr (pourrir) decompose.

décompte /dekɔ̃t/ nm deduction; (détail) breakdown.

décongeler /dekɔ̃ʒle/ **6** vt thaw.

déconseillé, ~e /dekɔ̃seje/ adj not recommended, inadvisable.

déconseiller /dekɔ̃seje/ **1** vt ~ qch à qn advise sb against sth.

décontracté, ~e /dekɔ̃tʀakte/ adj relaxed.

déconvenue /dekɔ̃vny/ nf disappointment.

décor /dekɔʀ/ nm (paysage) scenery; (de cinéma, théâtre) set; (cadre) setting; (de maison) décor.

décoratif, -ive /dekɔʀatif, -v/ adj decorative.

décorateur, -trice /dekɔʀatœʀ, -tʀis/ nm, f (de cinéma) set designer. **décoration** nf decoration. **décorer** **1** vt decorate.

décortiquer /dekɔʀtike/ **1** vt shell; (fig) dissect.

découdre (se) /(sə)dekudʀ/ **19** vpr come unstitched.

découler /dekule/ **1** vi ~ de follow from.

découper /dekupe/ **1** vt cut up; (viande) carve; (détacher) cut out.

découragement /dekuʀaʒmɑ̃/ nm discouragement.

décourager /dekuʀaʒe/ **40** vt discourage. □ **se ~** vpr become discouraged.

décousu, ~e /dekuzy/ adj (vêtement) which has come unstitched; (idées) disjointed.

découvert, ~e /dekuvɛʀ, -t/ adj (tête) bare; (terrain) open. ● nm (de compte) overdraft; **à ~** exposed; (fig) openly.

découverte /dekuvɛʀt/ nf discovery; **à la ~ de** in search of.

découvrir /dekuvʀiʀ/ **21** vt discover; (voir) see; (montrer) reveal. □ **se ~** vpr (se décoiffer) take one's hat off; (ciel) clear.

décrasser /dekʀase/ **1** vt clean.

décrépit, ~e /dekʀepi, -t/ adj decrepit. **décrépitude** nf decay.

décret /dekʀɛ/ nm decree. **décréter** **14** vt order; (dire) declare.

décrié, ~e /dekʀije/ adj criticized.

décrire /dekʀiʀ/ **30** vt describe.

décroché, ~e /dekʀɔʃe/ adj (téléphone) off the hook.

décrocher /dekʀɔʃe/ **1** vt unhook; (obtenir **1**) get. ● vi (abandonner **1**) give up; **~ (le téléphone)** pick up the phone.

décroître /dekʀwatʀ/ **24** vi decrease.

déçu, ~e /desy/ adj disappointed.

décupler /dekyple/ **1** vt/i increase tenfold.

dédaigner /dedeɲe/ **1** vt scorn.

dédain /dedɛ̃/ nm scorn.

dédale /dedal/ nm maze.

dedans /dədɑ̃/ adv & nm inside; **en ~** on the inside.

dédicacer /dedikase/ **10** vt dedicate; (signer) sign.

dédier /dedje/ **45** vt dedicate.

dédommagement /dedɔmaʒmɑ̃/ nm compensation. **dédommager** **40** vt compensate (**de** for).

déduction /dedyksjɔ̃/ nf deduction; **~ d'impôts** tax deduction.

déduire /deduiʀ/ **17** vt deduct; (conclure) deduce.

déesse /deɛs/ nf goddess.

défaillance /defajɑ̃s/ nf (panne) failure; (évanouissement) blackout. **défaillant, ~e** adj (système) faulty; (personne) faint.

défaire /defɛʀ/ **33** vt undo; (valise) unpack; (démonter) take down. □ **se ~** vpr come undone; **se ~ de** rid oneself of.

défait, ~e /defɛ, -t/ adj (cheveux) ruffled; (visage) haggard; (nœud) undone. **défaite** nf defeat.

défaitiste /defetist/ adj & nmf defeatist.

défalquer /defalke/ **1** vt (somme) deduct.

défaut /defo/ nm fault, defect; (d'un verre, diamant, etc.) flaw; (pénurie) shortage; **à ∼ de** for lack of; **pris en ∼** caught out; **faire ∼** (*argent etc.*) be lacking; **par ∼** (Jur) in one's absence; **∼ de paiement** non-payment.

défavorable /defavɔrabl/ *adj* unfavourable.

défavoriser /defavɔrize/ **1** *vt* discriminate against.

défectueux, -euse /defɛktɥø, -z/ *adj* faulty, defective.

défendre /defɑ̃dr/ **3** *vt* defend; (interdire) forbid; **∼ à qn de** forbid sb to. □ **se ∼** *vpr* defend oneself; (se protéger) protect oneself; (se débrouiller) manage; **se ∼ de** (refuser) refrain from.

défense /defɑ̃s/ *nf* defence; **∼ de fumer** no smoking; (d'éléphant) tusk. **défenseur** *nm* defender. **défensif, -ive** *adj* defensive.

déferler /defɛrle/ **1** *vi* (*vagues*) break; (*violence*) erupt.

défi /defi/ *nm* challenge; (provocation) defiance; **mettre au ∼** challenge.

déficience /defisjɑ̃s/ *nf* deficiency. **déficient, ∼e** *adj* deficient.

déficit /defisit/ *nm* deficit. **déficitaire** *adj* in deficit.

défier /defje/ **45** *vt* challenge; (braver) defy.

défilé /defile/ *nm* procession; (Mil) parade; (fig) (continual) stream; (Géog) gorge; **∼ de mode** fashion parade.

défiler /defile/ **1** *vi* march; (*visiteurs*) stream; (*images*) flash by; (*chiffres, minutes*) add up. □ **se ∼** *vpr* **1** sneak off.

défini, ∼e /defini/ *adj* (Ling) definite.

définir /definir/ **2** *vt* define.

définitif, -ive /definitif, -v/ *adj* final, definitive; **en définitive** in the end.

définition /definisjɔ̃/ *nf* definition; (de mots croisés) clue.

définitivement /definitivmɑ̃/ *adv* definitively, permanently.

déflagration /deflagrasjɔ̃/ *nf* explosion.

déflation /deflasjɔ̃/ *nf* deflation. **déflationniste** *adj* deflationary.

défoncé, ∼e /defɔ̃se/ *adj* (*terrain*) full of potholes; (*siège*) broken; (*drogué*: **1**) high.

défoncer /defɔ̃se/ **10** *vt* (*porte*) break down; (*mâchoire*) break. □ **se ∼** *vpr* **1** to give one's all.

déformation /defɔrmasjɔ̃/ *nf* distortion. **déformer** **1** *vt* put out of shape; (*faits, pensée*) distort.

défouler (se) /(sə)defule/ **1** *vpr* let off steam.

défrayer /defreje/ **31** *vt* (payer) pay the expenses of; **∼ la chronique** be the talk of the town.

défricher /defriʃe/ **1** *vt* clear.

défroisser /defrwase/ **1** *vt* smooth out.

défunt, ∼e /defœ̃, -t/ *adj* (mort) late. ● *nm, f* deceased.

dégagé, ∼e /degaʒe/ *adj* (*ciel*) clear; (*front*) bare; **d'un ton ∼** casually.

dégagement /degaʒmɑ̃/ *nm* clearing; (football) clearance.

dégager /degaʒe/ **40** *vt* (exhaler) give off; (désencombrer) clear; (faire ressortir) bring out; (*ballon*) clear. □ **se ∼** *vpr* free oneself; (*ciel, rue*) clear; (*odeur*) emanate.

dégarnir (se) /(sə)degarnir/ **2** *vpr* clear, empty; (*personne*) be going bald.

dégâts /degɑ/ *nmpl* damage (+ *sg*).

dégel /deʒɛl/ *nm* thaw. **dégeler** **6** *vi* thaw (out).

dégénéré, ∼e /deʒenere/ *adj & nm,f* degenerate.

dégivrer /deʒivre/ **1** *vt* (Auto) de-ice; (*réfrigérateur*) defrost.

déglinguer /deglɛ̃ge/ **1** **1** *vt* bust. □ **se ∼** *vpr* break down.

dégonflé, ∼e /degɔ̃fle/ *adj* (*pneu*) flat; (lâche **1**) yellow.

dégonfler /degɔ̃fle/ **1** *vt* deflate. ● *vi* (*blessure*) go down. □ **se ∼** *vpr* **1** chicken out.

dégouliner /deguline/ **1** *vi* trickle.

dégourdi, ∼e /degurdi/ *adj* smart.

dégourdir /degurdir/ **2** *vt* (*membre, liquide*) warm up. □ **se ∼** *vpr* **se ∼ les jambes** stretch one's legs.

dégoût /degu/ *nm* disgust.

dégoûtant, ∼e /degutɑ̃, -t/ *adj* disgusting.

dégoûter /degute/ **1** *vt* disgust; **∼ qn de qch** put sb off sth.

dégradant, ∼e /degradɑ̃, -t/ *adj* degrading.

dégradation /degʀadasjɔ̃/ nf damage; **commettre des ~s** cause damage.

dégrader /degʀade/ **1** vt (abîmer) damage. □ **se ~** vpr (se détériorer) deteriorate.

dégrafer /degʀafe/ **1** vt unhook.

degré /dəgʀe/ nm degree; (d'escalier) step.

dégressif, -ive /degʀesif, -v/ adj graded; **tarif ~** tapering charge.

dégrèvement /degʀɛvmɑ̃/ nm ~ **fiscal** ou **d'impôts** tax reduction.

dégringolade /degʀɛ̃gɔlad/ nf tumble.

dégrossir /degʀosiʀ/ **2** vt (bois) trim; (projet) rough out.

déguerpir /degɛʀpiʀ/ **2** vi clear off.

dégueulasse /degœlas/ adj ⊠ disgusting, lousy.

dégueuler /degœle/ **1** vt ⊠ throw up.

déguisement /degizmɑ̃/ nm (de carnaval) fancy dress; (pour duper) disguise.

déguiser /degize/ **1** vt dress up; (pour duper) disguise. □ **se ~** vpr (au carnaval etc.) dress up; (pour duper) disguise oneself.

déguster /degyste/ **1** vt taste, sample; (savourer) enjoy.

dehors /dəɔʀ/ adv en ~ de outside; (hormis) apart from; **jeter/ mettre ~** throw/put out. ● nm outside. ● nmpl (aspect de qn) exterior.

déjà /deʒa/ adv already; (avant) before, already.

déjeuner /deʒœne/ **1** vi have lunch; (le matin) have breakfast. ● nm lunch; **petit ~** breakfast.

delà /dəla/ adv & prép **au ~ (de) par ~** beyond.

délai /delɛ/ nm time-limit; (attente) wait; (sursis) extension (of time); **sans ~** immediately; **dans un ~ de 2 jours** within 2 days; **finir dans les ~s** finish within the deadline; **dans les plus brefs ~s** as soon as possible.

délaisser /delese/ **1** vt (négliger) neglect.

délassement /delasmɑ̃/ nm relaxation.

délation /delasjɔ̃/ nf informing.

délavé, ~e /delave/ adj faded.

délayer /deleje/ **31** vt mix (with liquid); (idée) drag out.

délecter (se) /(sə)delɛkte/ **1** vpr se ~ **de** delight in.

délégué, ~e /delege/ nm, f delegate.

délibéré, ~e /delibeʀe/ adj deliberate; (résolu) determined.

délicat, ~e /delika, -t/ adj delicate; (plein de tact) tactful. **délicatesse** nf delicacy; (tact) tact. **délicatesses** nfpl (kind) attentions.

délice /delis/ nm delight. **délicieux, -ieuse** adj (au goût) delicious; (charmant) delightful.

délier /delje/ **45** vt untie; (délivrer) free. □ **se ~** vpr come untied.

délimiter /delimite/ **1** vt determine, demarcate.

délinquance /delɛ̃kɑ̃s/ nf delinquency. **délinquant, ~e** adj & nm, f delinquent.

délirant, ~e /deliʀɑ̃, -t/ adj delirious; (frénétique) frenzied; ⊞ wild.

délire /deliʀ/ nm delirium; (fig) frenzy. **délirer** **1** vi be delirious (de with); ⊞ be off one's rocker ⊞.

délit /deli/ nm offence.

délivrance /delivʀɑ̃s/ nf release; (soulagement) relief; (remise) issue. **délivrer** **1** vt free, release; (pays) liberate; (remettre) issue.

déloyal, ~e (mpl **-aux**) /delwajal, -jo/ adj disloyal; (procédé) unfair.

deltaplane /dɛltaplan/ nm hangglider.

déluge /delyʒ/ nm downpour; **le D~** the Flood.

démagogie /demagɔʒi/ nf demagogy. **démagogue** nmf demagogue.

demain /dəmɛ̃/ adv tomorrow.

demande /dəmɑ̃d/ nf request; ~ **d'emploi** job application; ~ **en mariage** marriage proposal.

demander /dəmɑ̃de/ **1** vt ask for; (chemin, heure) ask; (nécessiter) require; ~ **que/si** ask that/if; ~ **qch à qn** ask sb sth; ~ **à qn de** ask sb to; ~ **en mariage** propose to. □ **se ~** vpr **se ~ si/où** wonder if/where.

demandeur, -euse /dəmɑ̃dœʀ, -øz/ nm, f ~ **d'emploi** job seeker; ~ **d'asile** asylum-seeker.

démangeaison /demɑ̃ʒɛzɔ̃/ nf itch(ing).

démanteler /demɑ̃tle/ **6** vt break up.

d

démaquillant /demakijɑ̃/ nm make-up remover. **démaquiller (se)** **1** vpr remove one's make-up.

démarchage /demaʀʃaʒ/ nm door-to-door selling.

démarche /demaʀʃ/ nf walk, gait; (procédé) step.

démarcheur, -euse /demaʀʃœʀ, -øz/ nm, f (door-to-door) canvasser.

démarrage /demaʀaʒ/ nm start.

démarrer /demaʀe/ **1** vi (moteur) start (up); (partir) move off; (fig) get moving. ● vt **1** get moving.

démarreur /demaʀœʀ/ nm starter.

démêlant /demelɑ̃/ nm conditioner. **démêler** **1** vt disentangle.

déménagement /demenaʒmɑ̃/ nm move; (transport) removal.

déménager /demenaʒe/ **40** vi move (house). ● vt (meubles) remove.

déménageur /demenaʒœʀ/ nm removal man.

démence /demɑ̃s/ nf insanity.

démener (se) /(sə)demne/ **6** vpr move about wildly; (fig) put oneself out.

dément, ~e /demɑ̃, -t/ adj insane. ● nm, f lunatic.

démenti /demɑ̃ti/ nm denial.

démentir /demɑ̃tiʀ/ **46** vt deny; (contredire) refute; **~ que** deny that.

démerder (se) /(sə)demɛʀde/ **1** vpr 🗙 manage.

démettre /demɛtʀ/ **42** vt (poignet etc.) dislocate; **~ qn de** relieve sb of. ▢ **se ~** vpr resign (de from).

demeure /dəmœʀ/ nf residence; **mettre en ~ de** order to.

demeurer /dəmœʀe/ **1** vi live; (rester) remain.

demi, ~e /dəmi/ adj half(-). ● nm, f half. ● nm (bière) (half-pint) glass of beer; (football) half-back. ● adv **à ~** half; (ouvrir, fermer) halfway; **à la ~e** at half past; **une heure et ~e** an hour and a half; (à l'horloge) half past one; **une ~-journée/-livre** half a day/pound. **demi-cercle** (pl ~s) nm semicircle. **demi-finale** (pl ~s) nf semifinal. **demi-frère** (pl ~s) nm half-brother, stepbrother. **demi-heure** (pl ~s) nf half-hour, half an hour. **demi-litre** (pl ~s) nm half a litre. **demi-mesure** (pl ~s) nf half-measure.

à demi mot adv without having to express every word. **demi-pension** nf half-board. **demi-queue** nm boudoir grand piano.

demi-sel adj inv slightly salted.

demi-sœur (pl ~s) nf half-sister, stepsister.

démission /demisjɔ̃/ nf resignation.

demi-tarif (pl ~s) /dəmitaʀif/ nm half-fare.

demi-tour (pl ~s) /dəmituʀ/ nm about turn; (Auto) U-turn; **faire ~** turn back.

démocrate /demɔkʀat/ nmf democrat. ● adj democratic. **démocratie** nf democracy.

démodé, ~e /demɔde/ adj old-fashioned.

demoiselle /dəmwazɛl/ nf young lady; (célibataire) single lady; **~ d'honneur** bridesmaid.

démolir /demɔliʀ/ **2** vt demolish.

démon /demɔ̃/ nm demon; **le D~** the Devil. **démoniaque** adj fiendish.

démonstration /demɔ̃stʀasjɔ̃/ nf demonstration; (de force) show.

démonter /demɔ̃te/ **1** vt take apart, dismantle; (installation) take down; (fig) disconcert. ▢ **se ~** vpr come apart.

démontrer /demɔ̃tʀe/ **1** vt demonstrate; (indiquer) show.

démoraliser /demɔʀalize/ **1** vt demoralize.

démuni, ~e /demyni/ adj impoverished; **~ de** without.

démunir /demyniʀ/ **2** vt **~ de** deprive of. ▢ **se ~ de** vpr part with.

dénaturer /denatyʀe/ **1** vt (faits) distort.

dénigrement /denigʀəmɑ̃/ nm denigration.

dénivellation /denivɛlasjɔ̃/ nf (pente) slope.

dénombrer /denɔ̃bʀe/ **1** vt count.

dénomination /denɔminasjɔ̃/ nf designation.

dénommé, ~e /denɔme/ nm, f **le ~ X** the said X.

dénoncer /denɔ̃se/ **10** vt denounce. ▢ **se ~** vpr give oneself up. **dénonciateur, -trice** nm, f informer.

dénouement /denumɑ̃/ nm outcome; (Théât) dénouement.

dénouer /denwe/ **1** *vt* undo. □ **se ~** *vpr* (*nœud*) come undone.

dénoyauter /denwajote/ **1** *vt* stone.

denrée /dɑ̃ʀe/ *nf* **~ alimentaire** foodstuff.

dense /dɑ̃s/ *adj* dense. **densité** *nf* density.

dent /dɑ̃/ *nf* tooth; **faire ses ~s** teethe; **~ de lait** milk tooth; **~ de sagesse** wisdom tooth; (*de roue*) cog. **dentaire** *adj* dental.

denté, ~e /dɑ̃te/ *adj* (*roue*) toothed

dentelé, ~e /dɑ̃tle/ *adj* jagged.

dentelle /dɑ̃tɛl/ *nf* lace.

dentier /dɑ̃tje/ *nm* dentures (+ *pl*), false teeth (+ *pl*).

dentifrice /dɑ̃tifʀis/ *nm* toothpaste.

dentiste /dɑ̃tist/ *nmf* dentist.

dentition /dɑ̃tisjɔ̃/ *nf* teeth, dentition.

dénudé, ~e /denyde/ *adj* bare.

dénué, ~e /denɥe/ *adj* **~ de** devoid of.

dénuement /denymɑ̃/ *nm* destitution.

déodorant /deɔdɔʀɑ̃/ *nm* deodorant.

dépannage /depanaʒ/ *nm* repair; (Ordinat) troubleshooting. **dépanner** **1** *vt* repair; (*fig*) help out. **dépanneuse** *nf* breakdown lorry.

déparellé, ~e /depaʀeje/ *adj* odd, not matching.

départ /depaʀ/ *nm* departure; (Sport) start; **au ~ de Nice** from Nice; **au ~** (d'abord) at first.

département /depaʀtəmɑ̃/ *nm* department.

> **Département** An administrative unit, of which there   *i* are 96 in Metropolitan France, most are named after rivers or mountains within their borders. Each *département* has a number which appears as the first two digits in postcodes for addresses within the *département* and as the final two-digit number in vehicle registration numbers. See ▷**Région**.

dépassé, ~e /depase/ *adj* outdated.

dépasser /depase/ **1** *vt* go past, pass; (*véhicule*) overtake; (*excéder*) exceed; (*rival*) surpass; **ça me dépasse** **1** it's beyond me. ● *vi* stick out.

dépaysement /depeizmɑ̃/ *nm* change of scenery; (désagréable) disorientation.

dépêche /depɛʃ/ *nf* dispatch.

dépêcher /depeʃe/ **1** *vt* dispatch. □ **se ~** *vpr* hurry (up).

dépendance /depɑ̃dɑ̃s/ *nf* dependence; (à une drogue) dependency; (bâtiment) outbuilding.

dépendre /depɑ̃dʀ/ **3** *vt* take down. ● *vi* depend (**~ de** on); **~ de** (appartenir à) belong to.

dépens /depɑ̃/ *nmpl* **aux ~ de** at the expense of.

dépense /depɑ̃s/ *nf* expense; expenditure.

dépenser /depɑ̃se/ **1** *vt/i* spend; (*énergie etc.*) use up. □ **se ~** *vpr* get some exercise.

dépérir /depeʀiʀ/ **2** *vi* wither.

dépêtrer (se) /(sə)depetʀe/ **1** *vpr* get oneself out (**de** of).

dépeupler /depœple/ **1** *vt* depopulate. □ **se ~** *vpr* become depopulated.

déphasé, ~e /defaze/ *adj* **1** out of step.

dépilatoire /depilatwaʀ/ *adj & nm* depilatory.

dépistage /depistaʒ/ *nm* screening. **dépister** **1** *vt* detect; (*criminel*) track down.

dépit /depi/ *nm* resentment; **par ~** out of pique; **en ~ de** despite; **en ~ du bon sens** in a very illogical way. **dépité, ~e** *adj* vexed.

déplacé, ~e /deplase/ *adj* (*remarque*) uncalled for.

déplacement /deplasmɑ̃/ *nm* (*voyage*) trip.

déplacer /deplase/ **10** *vt* move. □ **se ~** *vpr* move; (*voyager*) travel.

déplaire /deplɛʀ/ **47** *vi* **~ à** (irriter) displease; **ça me déplaît** I don't like it.

déplaisant, ~e /deplɛzɑ̃, -t/ *adj* unpleasant, disagreeable.

dépliant /deplijɑ̃/ *nm* leaflet.

déplier /deplije/ **45** *vt* unfold.

déploiement /deplwamɑ̃/ *nm* (démonstration) display; (militaire) deployment.

déplorable /deplɔʀabl/ *adj* deplorable. **déplorer** **1** *vt* (trouver regrettable) deplore; (*mort*) lament.

déployer /deplwaje/ 31 vt (ailes, carte) spread; (courage) display; (armée) deploy.

déportation /depɔrtasjɔ̃/ nf (en 1940) internment in a concentration camp.

déposer /depoze/ 1 vt put down; (laisser) leave; (passager) drop; (argent) deposit; (plainte) lodge; (armes) lay down. ● vi (Jur) testify. □ se ~ vpr settle.

dépositaire /depoziter/ nmf (Comm) agent.

déposition /depozisjɔ̃/ nf (Jur) statement.

dépôt /depo/ nm (entrepôt) warehouse; (d'autobus) depot; (particules) deposit; (garantie) deposit; **laisser en ~** give for safe keeping; **~ légal** formal deposit of a publication with an institution.

dépouille /depuj/ nf skin, hide; (~ **mortelle**) mortal remains.

dépouiller /depuje/ 1 vt (courrier) open; (scrutin) count; (écorcher) skin; **~ qn de** strip sb of.

dépourvu, ~e /depurvy/ adj **~ de** devoid of; **prendre au ~** catch unawares.

déprécier /depresje/ 45 vt depreciate. □ se ~ vpr depreciate.

déprédations /depredasjɔ̃/ nfpl damage (+ sg).

dépression /depresjɔ̃/ nf depression; **~ nerveuse** nervous breakdown.

déprimer /deprime/ 1 vt depress.

---

depuis /dəpɥi/

● préposition

····▸ (point de départ) since; **~ quand attendez-vous?** how long have you been waiting?

····▸ (durée) for; **~ toujours** always; **~ peu** recently.

● adverbe

····▸ since; **il a eu une attaque le mois dernier, ~ nous sommes inquiets** he had a stroke last month and we've been worried ever since.

● **depuis que** conjonction

····▸ since, ever since; **Sophie a beaucoup changé depuis que Camille est née** Sophie has

---

changed a lot since Camille was born.

député /depyte/ nm ≈ Member of Parliament.

déraciné, -e /derasine/ nm, f rootless person.

déraillement /derajmɑ̃/ nm derailment.

dérailler /deraje/ 1 vi be derailed; (fig 1) be talking nonsense; **faire ~** derail. **dérailleur** nm (de vélo) derailleur.

déraisonnable /derɛzɔnabl/ adj unreasonable.

dérangement /derɑ̃ʒmɑ̃/ nm bother; (désordre) disorder, upset; **en ~** out of order; **les ~s** the fault reporting service.

déranger /derɑ̃ʒe/ 40 vt (gêner) bother, disturb; (dérégler) upset, disrupt. □ se ~ vpr (aller) go; (fig) put oneself out; **ça te dérangerait de...?** would you mind...?

dérapage /derapaʒ/ nm skid. **déraper** 1 vi skid; (fig) (prix) get out of control.

déréglé, ~e /deregle/ adj (vie) dissolute; (estomac) upset; (mécanisme) (that is) not running properly.

dérégler /deregle/ 14 vt make go wrong. □ se ~ vpr go wrong.

dérision /derizjɔ̃/ nf mockery; **tourner en ~** ridicule.

dérive /deriv/ nf **aller à la ~** drift.

dérivé /derive/ nm by-product.

dériver /derive/ 1 vi (bateau) drift; **~ de** stem from.

dermatologie /dermatɔlɔʒi/ nf dermatology.

dernier, -ière /dernje, -jɛr/ adj last; (nouvelles, mode) latest; (étage) top. ● nm, f last (one); **ce ~** the latter; **le ~ de mes soucis** the least of my worries.

dernièrement /dernjɛrmɑ̃/ adv recently.

dérober /derɔbe/ 1 vt steal. □ se ~ vpr slip away; **se ~ à** (obligation) shy away from.

dérogation /derɔgasjɔ̃/ nf special authorization.

déroger /derɔʒe/ 40 vi **~ à** depart from.

déroulement /deʀulmã/ *nm* (d'une action) development.

dérouler /deʀule/ **1** *vt* (*fil etc.*) unwind. □ **se ∼** *vpr* unwind; (avoir lieu) take place; (*récit, paysage*) unfold.

déroute /deʀut/ *nf* (Mil) rout.

dérouter /deʀute/ **1** *vt* disconcert.

derrière /dɛʀjɛʀ/ *prép & adv* behind. ● *nm* back, rear; (postérieur 🔲) behind 🔲; **de ∼** (*fenêtre*) back, rear; (*pattes*) hind.

des /de/ ➡**DE**.

dès /dɛ/ *prép* (right) from; **∼ lors** from then on; **∼ que** as soon as.

désabusé, **∼e** /dezabyze/ *adj* disillusioned.

désaccord /dezakɔʀ/ *nm* disagreement.

désaffecté, **∼e** /dezafɛkte/ *adj* disused.

désagréable /dezagʀeabl/ *adj* unpleasant.

désagrément /dezagʀemã/ *nm* annoyance, inconvenience.

désaltérer (se) /(sə)dezalteʀe/ **14** *vpr* quench one's thirst.

désamorcer /dezamɔʀse/ **10** *vt* (*situation, obus*) defuse.

désapprobation /dezapʀɔbasjõ/ *nf* disapproval. **désapprouver** **1** *vt* disapprove of.

désarçonner /dezaʀsɔne/ **1** *vt* throw.

désarmement /dezaʀməmã/ *nm* (Pol) disarmament.

désarroi /dezaʀwa/ *nm* distress.

désastre /dezastʀ/ *nm* disaster. **désastreux, -euse** *adj* disastrous.

désavantage /dezavãtaʒ/ *nm* disadvantage. **désavantager** **40** *vt* put at a disadvantage.

désaveu (*pl* **∼x**) /dezavø/ *nm* denial. **désavouer** **1** *vt* deny.

descendance /desãdãs/ *nf* descent; (enfants) descendants (+ *pl*). **descendant, ∼e** *nm, f* descendant.

descendre /desãdʀ/ **3** *vi* (*aux être*) go down; (venir) come down; (*passager*) get off *ou* out; (*nuit*) fall; **∼ à pied** walk down; **∼ par l'ascenseur** take the lift down; **∼ de** (être issu de) be descended from; **∼ à l'hôtel** go to a hotel; **∼ dans la rue** (Pol) take to the streets. ● *vt* (*aux avoir*) (*escalier etc.*) go *ou* come down; (*objet*) take

down; (abattre 🔲) shoot down.

descente /desãt/ *nf* descent; (à ski) downhill; (raid) raid; **dans la ∼** going downhill; **∼ de lit** bedside rug.

descriptif, -ive /dɛskʀiptif, -v/ *adj* descriptive. **description** *nf* description.

désemparé, **∼e** /dezãpaʀe/ *adj* distraught.

désendettement /dezãdɛtmã/ *nm* reduction of the debt.

déséquilibré, **∼e** /dezekilibʀe/ *adj* unbalanced; 🔲 crazy. ● *nm, f* lunatic. **déséquilibrer** **1** *vt* throw off balance.

désert, **∼e** /dezɛʀ, -t/ *adj* deserted. ● *nm* desert.

déserter /dezɛʀte/ **1** *vt/i* desert. **déserteur** *nm* deserter.

désertique /dezɛʀtik/ *adj* desert.

désespérant, **∼e** /dezɛspeʀã, -t/ *adj* utterly disheartening.

désespéré, **∼e** /dezɛspeʀe/ *adj* in despair; (*état, cas*) hopeless; (*effort*) desperate.

désespérer /dezɛspeʀe/ **14** *vt* drive to despair. ● *vi* despair, lose hope; **∼ de** despair of. □ **se ∼** *vpr* despair.

désespoir /dezɛspwaʀ/ *nm* despair; **en ∼ de cause** as a last resort.

déshabillé, **∼e** /dezabije/ *adj* undressed. ● *nm* negligee.

déshabiller /dezabije/ **1** *vt* undress. □ **se ∼** *vpr* get undressed.

désherbant /dezɛʀbã/ *nm* weedkiller.

déshérité, **∼e** /dezeʀite/ *adj* (*région*) deprived; (*personne*) the underprivileged.

déshériter /dezeʀite/ **1** *vt* disinherit.

déshonneur /dezɔnœʀ/ *nm* disgrace.

déshonorer /dezɔnɔʀe/ **1** *vt* dishonour.

déshydrater /dezidʀate/ **1** *vt* dehydrate. □ **se ∼** *vpr* get dehydrated.

désigner /dezine/ **1** *vt* (montrer) point to *ou* out; (élire) appoint; (signifier) designate.

désillusion /dezilyzjõ/ *nf* disillusionment.

désinence /dezinãs/ *nf* (Gram) ending.

désinfectant /dezɛ̃fɛktã/ *nm* disinfectant. **désinfecter** **1** *vt* disinfect.

désintéressé, **∼e** /dezɛ̃teʀese/ *adj* (*personne, acte*) selfless.

d

désintéresser (se) | détachant

désintéresser (se) /(sə)dezɛ̃terese/
1 *vpr* **se ~ de** lose interest in.

désintoxiquer /dezɛ̃tɔksike/ **1** *vt*
detoxify; **se faire ~** to undergo detoxification.

désinvolte /dezɛ̃vɔlt/ *adj* casual. **désinvolture** *nf* casualness.

désir /deziʀ/ *nm* wish, desire; (convoitise) desire.

désirer /dezire/ **1** *vt* want; (sexuellement) desire; **vous désirez?** what would you like?

désireux, -euse /deziʀø, -z/ *adj* **~ de faire** anxious to do.

désistement /dezistəmɑ̃/ *nm* withdrawal.

désobéir /dezɔbeiʀ/ **2** *vi* (**~ à**) disobey. **désobéissant, ~e** *adj* disobedient.

désobligeant, ~e /dezɔbliʒɑ̃, -t/ *adj* disagreeable, unkind.

désodorisant /dezodoʀizɑ̃/ *nm* air freshener.

désodoriser /dezodoʀize/ **1** *vt* freshen up.

désœuvré, ~e /dezœvʀe/ *adj* at a loose end. **désœuvrement** *nm* lack of anything to do.

désolation /dezɔlasjɔ̃/ *nf* distress.

désolé, ~e /dezɔle/ *adj* (au regret) sorry; (région) desolate.

désoler /dezɔle/ **1** *vt* distress. □ **se ~** *vpr* be upset (**de qch** about sth).

désopilant, ~e /dezɔpilɑ̃, -t/ *adj* hilarious.

désordonné, ~e /dezɔʀdɔne/ *adj* untidy; (mouvements) uncoordinated.

désordre /dezɔʀdʀ/ *nm* untidiness; (Pol) disorder; **en ~** untidy.

désorganiser /dezɔʀganize/ **1** *vt* disorganize.

désorienter /dezɔʀjɑ̃te/ **1** *vt* disorient.

désormais /dezɔʀmɛ/ *adv* from now on.

desquels, desquelles /dekɛl/ →LEQUEL.

dessécher /deseʃe/ **1** *vt* dry out. □ **se ~** *vpr* dry out, become dry; (plante) wither.

dessein /desɛ̃/ *nm* intention; **à ~** intentionally.

desserrer /desere/ **1** *vt* loosen; **il n'a pas desserré les dents** he never once

opened his mouth. □ **se ~** *vpr* come loose.

dessert /desɛʀ/ *nm* dessert; **en ~** for dessert.

desservir /desɛʀviʀ/ **46** *vt/i* (débarrasser) clear away; (autobus) serve.

dessin /desɛ̃/ *nm* drawing; (motif) design; (discipline) art; (contour) outline; **professeur de ~** art teacher; **~ animé** (cinéma) cartoon; **~ humoristique** cartoon.

dessinateur, -trice /desinatœʀ, -tʀis/ *nm, f* artist; (industriel) draughtsman.

dessiner /desine/ **1** *vt/i* draw; (fig) outline. □ **se ~** *vpr* appear, take shape.

dessoûler /desule/ **1** *vt/i* sober up.

dessous /dəsu/ *adv* underneath. ● *nm* underside, underneath. ● *nmpl* underwear; **les ~ d'une histoire** what is behind a story; **du ~** bottom; (voisins) downstairs; **en ~, par-~** underneath. **dessous-de-plat** *nm inv* (heat resistant) table-mat. **dessous-de-table** *nm inv* backhander. **dessous-de-verre** *nm inv* coaster.

dessus /dəsy/ *adv* on top (of it), on it. ● *nm* top; **du ~** top; (voisins) upstairs; **avoir le ~** get the upper hand. **dessus-de-lit** *nm inv* bedspread.

destabiliser /destabilize/ **1** *vt* destabilize, unsettle.

destin /dɛstɛ̃/ *nm* (sort) fate; (avenir) destiny.

destinataire /dɛstinatɛʀ/ *nmf* addressee.

destination /dɛstinasjɔ̃/ *nf* destination; (fonction) purpose; **vol à ~ de** flight to.

destinée /dɛstine/ *nf* destiny.

destiner /dɛstine/ **1** *vt* **~ à** intend for; (vouer) destine for; **le commentaire m'est destiné** this comment is aimed at me; **être destiné à faire** be intended to do; (obligé) be destined to do. □ **se ~ à** *vpr* (carrière) intend to take up.

destituer /dɛstitɥe/ **1** *vt* discharge.

destructeur, -trice /dɛstʀyktœʀ, -tʀis/ *adj* destructive. **destruction** *nf* destruction.

désuet, -ète /dezɥɛ, -t/ *adj* outdated.

détachant /detaʃɑ̃/ *nm* stain remover.

détacher /detaʃe/ **1** vt untie; (ôter) remove, detach; (déléguer) second. □ se ~ vpr come off, break away; (nœud etc.) come undone; (ressortir) stand out.

détail /detaj/ nm detail; (de compte) breakdown; (Comm) retail; **au ~** (vendre etc.) retail; **de ~** (prix etc.) retail; **en ~** in detail; **entrer dans les ~s** go into detail.

détaillant, ~e /detajɑ̃, -t/ nm, f retailer.

détaillé, ~e /detaje/ adj detailed.

détailler /detaje/ **1** vt (rapport) detail; **~ ce que qn fait** scrutinize what sb does.

détaler /detale/ **1** vi **1** bolt.

détartrant /detartrɑ̃/ nm descaler.

détecter /detɛkte/ **1** vt detect. **détecteur** nm detector.

détective /detɛktiv/ nm detective.

déteindre /detɛ̃dʀ/ **22** vi (dans l'eau) run (sur on to); (au soleil) fade; **~ sur** (fig) rub off on.

détendre /detɑ̃dʀ/ **3** vt slacken; (ressort) release; (personne) relax. □ se ~ vpr (ressort) slacken; (personne) relax. **détendu, ~e** adj (calme) relaxed.

détenir /det(ə)niʀ/ **58** vt hold; (secret, fortune) possess.

détente /detɑ̃t/ nf relaxation; (Pol) détente; (saut) spring; (gâchette) trigger; **être lent à la ~** **1** be slow on the uptake.

détenteur, -trice /detɑ̃tœʀ, -tʀis/ nm, f holder.

détention /detɑ̃sjɔ̃/ nf detention; **~ provisoire** custody.

détenu, ~e /detny/ nm, f prisoner.

détergent /detɛʀʒɑ̃/ nm detergent.

détérioration /deteʀjɔʀasjɔ̃/ nf deterioration; (dégât) damage.

détériorer /deteʀjɔʀe/ **1** vt damage. □ se ~ vpr deteriorate.

détermination /detɛʀminasjɔ̃/ nf determination. **déterminé, ~e** adj (résolu) determined; (précis) definite. **déterminer** **1** vt determine.

déterrer /detɛʀe/ **1** vt dig up.

détestable /detɛstabl/ adj (caractère, temps) foul.

détester /detɛste/ **1** vt hate. □ se ~ vpr hate each other.

détonation /detɔnasjɔ̃/ nf explosion, detonation.

détour /detuʀ/ nm (crochet) detour; (fig) roundabout means; (virage) bend.

détournement /detuʀnəmɑ̃/ nm hijack(ing); (de fonds) embezzlement.

détourner /detuʀne/ **1** vt (attention) divert; (tête, yeux) turn away; (avion) hijack; (argent) embezzle. □ se ~ de vpr stray from.

détraquer /detʀake/ **1** vt make go wrong; (estomac) upset. □ se ~ vpr (machine) go wrong.

détresse /detʀɛs/ nf distress; **dans la ~, en ~** in distress.

détritus /detʀity(s)/ nmpl rubbish (+ sg).

détroit /detʀwa/ nm strait.

détromper /detʀɔ̃pe/ **1** vt set straight. □ se ~ vpr **détrompe-toi!** you'd better think again!

détruire /detʀɥiʀ/ **17** vt destroy.

dette /dɛt/ nf debt.

deuil /dœj/ nm (période) mourning; (décès) bereavement; **porter le ~** be in mourning; **faire son ~ de qch** give sth up as lost.

deux /dø/ adj & nm two; **~ fois** twice; **tous (les ~)** both. **deuxième** adj & nmf second. **deux-pièces** nm inv (maillot de bain) two-piece; (logement) two-room flat. **deux-points** nm inv (Gram) colon. **deux-roues** nm inv two-wheeled vehicle.

dévaliser /devalize/ **1** vt rob, clean out.

dévalorisant, ~e /devalɔʀizɑ̃, -t/ adj demeaning.

dévaloriser /devalɔʀize/ **1** vt (monnaie) devalue. □ se ~ vpr (personne) put oneself down.

dévaluation /devaluasjɔ̃/ nf devaluation.

dévaluer /devalue/ **1** vt devalue. □ se ~ vpr devalue.

devancer /dəvɑ̃se/ **10** vt be ou go ahead of; (arriver) arrive ahead of; (prévenir) anticipate.

devant /d(ə)vɑ̃/ prép in front of; (distance) ahead of; (avec mouvement) past; (en présence de) in front of; (face à) in the face of; **avoir du temps ~ soi** have plenty of time. ● adv in front; (à distance) ahead; **de**

$\sim$ front. ● nm front; **prendre les** $\sim$**s** take the initiative.

devanture /dəvɑ̃tyʀ/ nf shop front; (vitrine) shop window.

développement /devlɔpmɑ̃/ nm development; (de photos) developing.

développer /devlɔpe/ **1** vt develop. □ **se** $\sim$ vpr (corps, talent) develop; (entreprise) grow, expand.

devenir /dəvniʀ/ **58** vi (aux être) become; **qu'est-il devenu?** what has become of him?

dévergondé, $\sim$**e** /deveʀɡɔ̃de/ adj & nm,f shameless (person).

déverser /deveʀse/ **1** vt (liquide) pour; (ordures, pétrole) dump. □ **se** $\sim$ vpr (rivière) flow; (égout, foule) pour.

dévêtir /devetiʀ/ **61** vt undress. □ **se** $\sim$ vpr get undressed.

déviation /devjasjɔ̃/ nf diversion.

dévier /devje/ **45** vt divert; (coup) deflect. ● vi (ballon, balle) veer; (personne) deviate.

devin /dəvɛ̃/ nm soothsayer.

deviner /dəvine/ **1** vt guess; (apercevoir) distinguish.

devinette /dəvinɛt/ nf riddle.

devis /dəvi/ nm estimate, quote.

dévisager /devizaʒe/ **40** vt stare at.

devise /dəviz/ nf motto; $\sim$**s** (monnaie) (foreign) currency.

dévisser /devise/ **1** vt unscrew.

dévitaliser /devitalize/ **1** vt (dent) carry out root canal treatment on.

dévoiler /devwale/ **1** vt reveal.

---

devoir /dəvwaʀ/ **26**
● verbe auxiliaire
····▸ $\sim$ **faire** (obligation, hypothèse) must do; (nécessité) have got to do; **je dois dire que...** I have to say that...; **il a dû partir** (nécessité) he had to leave; (hypothèse) he must have left.
····▸ (prévision) **je devais lui dire** I was to tell her; **elle doit rentrer bientôt** she's due back soon.
····▸ (conseil) **tu devrais** you should.
● verbe transitif
····▸ (argent, excuses) owe; **combien je vous dois?** (en achetant) how much is it?
□ **se devoir** verbe pronominal

····▸ **je me dois de le faire** it's my duty to do it.
● nom masculin
····▸ duty; **faire son** $\sim$ do one's duty.
····▸ (Scol) $\sim$ **(surveillé)** test; **les** $\sim$**s** homework (+ sg); **faire ses** $\sim$**s** do one's homework.

---

dévorer /devɔʀe/ **1** vt devour.

dévot, $\sim$**e** /devo, -ɔt/ adj devout.

dévoué, $\sim$**e** /devwe/ adj devoted. **dévouement** nm devotion.

dévouer (se) /(sə)devwe/ **1** vpr devote oneself (à to); (se sacrifier) sacrifice oneself.

dextérité /dɛksteʀite/ nf skill.

diabète /djabɛt/ nm diabetes. **diabétique** adj & nmf diabetic.

diable /djɑbl/ nm devil.

diagnostic /djagnɔstik/ nm diagnosis. **diagnostiquer** **1** vt diagnose.

diagonal, $\sim$**e** (mpl -aux) /djagɔnal, -o/ adj diagonal. **diagonale** nf diagonal; **en** $\sim$**e** diagonally.

diagramme /djagʀam/ nm diagram; (graphique) graph.

dialecte /djalɛkt/ nm dialect.

dialogue /djalɔɡ/ nm dialogue. **dialoguer** **1** vi have talks, enter into a dialogue.

diamant /djamɑ̃/ nm diamond.

diamètre /djamɛtʀ/ nm diameter.

diapositive /djapozitiv/ nf slide.

diarrhée /djaʀe/ nf diarrhoea.

dictateur /diktatœʀ/ nm dictator.

dicter /dikte/ **1** vt dictate. **dictée** nf dictation.

dictionnaire /diksjɔnɛʀ/ nm dictionary.

dicton /diktɔ̃/ nm saying.

dièse /djɛz/ nm (Mus) sharp.

diesel /djezɛl/ nm & adj inv diesel.

diète /djɛt/ nf restricted diet.

diététicien, $\sim$**ne** /djetetisjɛ̃, -ɛn/ nm, f dietician.

diététique /djetetik/ nf dietetics. ● adj **produit** ou **aliment** $\sim$ dietary product; **magasin** $\sim$ health food shop ou store.

dieu (pl $\sim$**x**) /djø/ nm god; **D**$\sim$ God.

diffamation /difamasjɔ̃/ nf slander; (par écrit) libel. **diffamer** **1** vt slander; (par écrit) libel.

différé: en ~ /ãdifeʀe/ *loc* (*émission*) pre-recorded.

différemment /difeʀamã/ *adv* differently.

différence /difeʀãs/ *nf* difference; **à la ~ de** unlike.

différencier /difeʀãsje/ 🟦 *vt* differentiate. □ **se ~** *vpr* differentiate oneself; **se ~ de** (différer de) differ from.

différend /difeʀã/ *nm* difference (of opinion).

différent, ~e /difeʀã, -t/ *adj* different (**de** from).

différer /difeʀe/ 🟦 *vt* postpone. ● *vi* differ (**de** from).

difficile /difisil/ *adj* difficult; (exigeant) fussy. **difficilement** *adv* with difficulty.

difficulté /difikylte/ *nf* difficulty; **faire des ~s** raise objections.

diffus, ~e /dify, -z/ *adj* diffuse.

diffuser /difyze/ 🟦 *vt* (*émission*) broadcast; (*nouvelle*) spread; (*lumière, chaleur*) diffuse; (Comm) distribute. **diffusion** *nf* broadcasting; diffusion; distribution.

digérer /diʒeʀe/ 🟦 *vt* digest; (endurer 🟦) stomach. **digeste** *adj* digestible.

digestif, -ive /diʒɛstif, -v/ *adj* digestive. ● *nm* after-dinner liqueur.

digital, ~e (*mpl* **-aux**) /diʒital, -o/ *adj* digital.

digne /diɲ/ *adj* (noble) dignified; (approprié) worthy; **~ de** worthy of; **~ de foi** trustworthy.

digue /dig/ *nf* dyke; (US) dike.

dilater /dilate/ 🟦 *vt* dilate. □ **se ~** *vpr* dilate; (*estomac*) distend.

dilemme /dilɛm/ *nm* dilemma.

dilettante /diletãt/ *nmf* amateur.

diluant /dilɥã/ *nm* thinner.

diluer /dilɥe/ 🟦 *vt* dilute.

dimanche /dimãʃ/ *nm* Sunday.

dimension /dimãsjɔ̃/ *nf* (taille) size; (mesure) dimension; (aspect) dimension.

diminuer /diminɥe/ 🟦 *vt* reduce, decrease; (*plaisir, courage*) dampen; (dénigrer) diminish. ● *vi* (se réduire) decrease; (faiblir) (*bruit, flamme*) die down; (*ardeur*) cool. **diminutif** *nm* diminutive; (surnom) pet name. **diminution** *nf* decrease (**de** in); (réduction)

reduction; (affaiblissement) diminishing.

dinde /dɛ̃d/ *nf* turkey.

dîner /dine/ 🟦 *vi* have dinner. ● *nm* dinner.

dingue /dɛ̃g/ *adj* 🟦 crazy.

dinosaure /dinozɔʀ/ *nm* dinosaur.

diphtongue /diftɔ̃g/ *nf* diphthong.

diplomate /diplɔmat/ *nmf* diplomat. ● *adj* diplomatic. **diplomatique** *adj* diplomatic.

diplôme /diplom/ *nm* certificate, diploma; (Univ) degree. **diplômé, ~e** *adj* qualified.

dire /diʀ/ 🟦 *vt* say; (*secret, vérité, heure*) tell; (penser) think; **~ que** say that; **~ à qn que** tell sb that; **~ à qn de** tell sb to; **ça me dit de faire** I feel like doing; **on dirait que** it would seem that, it seems that; **dis/dites donc!** hey! □ **se ~** *vpr* (*mot*) be said; (penser) tell oneself; (se prétendre) claim to be. ● *nm* **au ~ de, selon les ~s de** according to.

direct, ~e /diʀɛkt/ *adj* direct. ● *nm* (train) express train; **en ~** (*émission*) live.

directeur, -trice /diʀɛktœʀ, -tʀis/ *nm, f* director; (chef de service) manager, manageress; (de journal) editor; (d'école) headteacher; (US) principal; **~ de banque** bank manager; **~ commercial** sales manager; **~ des ressources humaines** human resources manager.

direction /diʀɛksjɔ̃/ *nf* (sens) direction; (de société) management; (Auto) steering; **en ~ de** (going) to.

dirigeant, ~e /diʀiʒã, -t/ *nm, f* (Pol) leader; (Comm) manager. ● *adj* (*classe*) ruling.

diriger /diʀiʒe/ 🟦 *vt* (*service, école, parti, pays*) run; (*entreprise, usine*) manage; (*travaux*) supervise; (*véhicule*) steer; (*orchestre*) conduct; (braquer) aim; (tourner) turn. □ **se ~** *vpr* (s'orienter) find one's way; **se ~ vers** head for, make for.

dis /di/ → DIRE 🟦.

discernement /disɛʀnəmã/ *nm* discernment.

disciplinaire /disiplinɛʀ/ *adj* disciplinary. **discipline** *nf* discipline.

discontinu, ~e /diskõtiny/ *adj* intermittent.

discordant, ~e /diskɔrdã, -t/ *adj* discordant.

discothèque /diskɔtɛk/ *nf* record library; (boîte de nuit) disco- (thèque).

discours /diskur/ *nm* speech; (propos) views.

discret, -ète /diskrɛ, -t/ *adj* discreet.

discrétion /diskresjõ/ *nf* discretion; à ~ (*vin*) unlimited; (*manger, boire*) as much as one desires.

discrimination /diskriminasjõ/ *nf* discrimination. **discriminatoire** *adj* discriminatory.

disculper /diskylpe/ **1** *vt* exonerate. □ **se ~** *vpr* vindicate oneself.

discussion /diskysjõ/ *nf* discussion; (querelle) argument.

discutable /diskytabl/ *adj* debatable; (critiquable) questionable.

discuter /diskyte/ **1** *vt* discuss; (contester) question. ● *vi* (parler) talk; (répliquer) argue; **~ de** discuss.

disette /dizɛt/ *nf* food shortage.

disgrâce /disgras/ *nf* disgrace.

disgracieux, -ieuse /disgrasjø, -z/ *adj* ugly, unsightly.

disjoindre /diʒwɛ̃dr/ **22** *vt* take apart. □ **se ~** *vpr* come apart.

disloquer /dislɔke/ **1** *vt* (*membre*) dislocate; (*machine*) break (apart). □ **se ~** *vpr* (*parti, cortège*) break up; (*meuble*) come apart.

disparaître /disparɛtr/ **18** *vi* disappear; (mourir) die; **faire ~** get rid of.
disparition *nf* disappearance; (mort) death.

disparate /disparat/ *adj* illassorted.

disparu, ~e /dispary/ *adj* missing.
● *nm, f* missing person; (mort) dead person.

dispensaire /dispãsɛr/ *nm* clinic.

dispense /dispãs/ *nf* exemption.

dispenser /dispãse/ **1** *vt* exempt (de from). □ **se ~ de** *vpr* avoid.

disperser /dispɛrse/ **1** *vt* (éparpiller) scatter; (répartir) disperse. □ **se ~** *vpr* disperse.

disponibilité /disponibilite/ *nf* availability. **disponible** *adj* available.

dispos, ~e /dispo, -z/ *adj* **frais et ~** fresh and alert.

disposé, ~e /dispoze/ *adj* **bien/mal ~** in a good/bad mood; **~ à** prepared to; **~ envers** disposed towards.

disposer /dispoze/ **1** *vt* arrange; **~ à** (engager à) incline to. ● *vi* **~ de** have at one's disposal. □ **se ~ à** *vpr* prepare to.

dispositif /dispozitif/ *nm* device; (ensemble de mesures) operation.

disposition /dispozisjõ/ *nf* arrangement, layout; (tendance) tendency; **~s** (humeur) mood; (préparatifs) arrangements; (mesures) measures; (aptitude) aptitude; **mettre à la ~ de** place *ou* put at the disposal of.

disproportionné, ~e /disprɔpɔrsjɔne/ *adj* disproportionate; **~ à** out of proportion with.

dispute /dispyt/ *nf* quarrel.

disputer /dispyte/ **1** *vt* (match) play; (course) run in; (prix) fight for; (gronder **1**) tell off. □ **se ~** *vpr* quarrel; (se battre pour) fight over; (match) be played.

disquaire /diskɛr/ *nmf* record dealer.

disque /disk/ *nm* (Mus) record; (Sport) discus; (cercle) disc, disk; (Ordinat) disk; **~ compact** compact disc; **~ dur** hard disk; **~ optique compact** CD-ROM; **~ souple** floppy disk.

disquette /diskɛt/ *nf* floppy disk, diskette; **~ de sauvegarde** back-up disk.

disséminer /disemine/ **1** *vt* spread, scatter.

dissertation /disɛrtasjõ/ *nf* essay, paper.

disserter /disɛrte/ **1** *vi* **~ sur** speak about; (par écrit) write about.

dissident, ~e /disidã, -t/ *adj & nm, f* dissident.

dissimulation /disimylasjõ/ *nf* concealment; (fig) deceit.

dissimuler /disimyle/ **1** *vt* conceal (à from). □ **se ~** *vpr* conceal oneself.

dissipé, ~e /disipe/ *adj* (élève) unruly.

dissiper /disipe/ **1** *vt* (fumée, crainte) dispel; (fortune) squander; (personne) distract. □ **se ~** *vpr* disappear; (élève) grow restless.

dissolvant /disɔlvã/ *nm* solvent; (pour ongles) nail polish remover.

dissoudre /disudr/ **53** *vt* dissolve. □ **se ~** *vpr* dissolve.

dissuader | doléances

dissuader /disɥade/ **1** *vt* dissuade (**de** from).

dissuasion /disɥazjɔ̃/ *nf* dissuasion; **force de** ∼ deterrent force.

distance /distɑ̃s/ *nf* distance; (*écart*) gap; **à** ∼ **at** *ou* from a distance.

distancer /distɑ̃se/ **10** *vt* outdistance.

distendre /distɑ̃dʀ/ **3** *vt* (*estomac*) distend; (*corde*) stretch.

distinct, -e /distɛ̃(kt) , -ɛkt/ *adj* distinct.

distinctif, -ive /distɛ̃ktif, -v/ *adj* (*trait*) distinctive; (*signe, caractère*) distinguishing.

distinction /distɛ̃ksjɔ̃/ *nf* distinction; (*récompense*) honour.

distinguer /distɛ̃ge/ **1** *vt* distinguish.

distraction /distʀaksjɔ̃/ *nf* absent-mindedness; (*passe-temps*) entertainment, leisure; (*détente*) recreation.

distraire /distʀɛʀ/ **29** *vt* amuse; (*rendre inattentif*) distract; ∼ **qn de qch** take sb's mind off sth. □ **se** ∼ *vpr* amuse oneself.

distrait, -e /distʀɛ, -t/ *adj* absent-minded; (*élève*) inattentive.

distrayant, -e /distʀɛjɑ̃, -t/ *adj* entertaining.

distribuer /distʀibɥe/ **1** *vt* hand out, distribute; (*répartir*) distribute; (*tâches, rôles*) allocate; (*cartes*) deal; (*courrier*) deliver.

distributeur /distʀibytœʀ/ *nm* (Auto, Comm) distributor; ∼ **(automatique)** vending-machine; ∼ **de billets (de banque)** cash dispenser. **distribution** *nf* distribution; (*du courrier*) delivery; (*acteurs*) cast; (*secteur*) retailing.

district /distʀikt/ *nm* district.

dit¹, dites /di, dit/ ➡**DIRE** **27**.

dit², -e /di, dit/ *adj* (*décidé*) agreed; (*surnommé*) known as.

diurne /djyʀn/ *adj* diurnal; (*activité*) daytime.

divagations /divagasjɔ̃/ *nfpl* ravings.

divergence /divɛʀʒɑ̃s/ *nf* divergence. **divergent, -e** *adj* divergent. **diverger** **40** *vi* diverge.

divers, -e /divɛʀ, -s/ *adj* (*varié*) diverse; (*différent*) various; (*frais*) miscellaneous; **dépenses** ∼**es** sundries. **diversifier** **45** *vt* diversify.

diversité /divɛʀsite/ *nf* diversity, variety.

divertir /divɛʀtiʀ/ **2** *vt* amuse, entertain. □ **se** ∼ *vpr* amuse oneself; (*passer du bon temps*) enjoy oneself. **divertissement** *nm* amusement, entertainment.

dividende /dividɑ̃d/ *nm* dividend.

divin, -e /divɛ̃, -in/ *adj* divine. **divinité** *nf* divinity.

diviser /divize/ **1** *vt* divide. □ **se** ∼ *vpr* become divided; **se** ∼ **par sept** be divisible by seven. **division** *nf* division.

divorce /divɔʀs/ *nm* divorce.

divorcé, -e /divɔʀse/ *adj* divorced. ● *nm, f* divorcee.

divorcer /divɔʀse/ **10** *vi* (**d'avec**) divorce.

dix /dis/ (/di/ before consonant, /diz/ before vowel) *adj & nm* ten.

dix-huit /dizɥit/ *adj & nm* eighteen.

dixième /dizjɛm/ *adj & nmf* tenth.

dix-neuf /diznœf/ *adj & nm* nineteen.

dix-sept /disɛt/ *adj & nm* seventeen.

docile /dɔsil/ *adj* docile.

docteur /dɔktœʀ/ *nm* doctor.

doctorat /dɔktɔʀa/ *nm* doctorate, PhD.

document /dɔkymɑ̃/ *nm* document. **documentaire** *adj & nm* documentary.

documentaliste /dɔkymɑ̃talist/ *nmf* information officer; (Scol) librarian.

documentation /dɔkymɑ̃tasjɔ̃/ *nf* information, literature; **centre de** ∼ resource centre.

documenté, -e /dɔkymɑ̃te/ *adj* well-documented.

documenter /dɔkymɑ̃te/ **1** *vt* provide with information. □ **se** ∼ *vpr* collect information.

dodo /dodo/ *nm* **faire** ∼ (*langage enfantin*) sleep.

dodu, -e /dody/ *adj* plump.

dogmatique /dɔgmatik/ *adj* dogmatic. **dogme** *nm* dogma.

doigt /dwa/ *nm* finger; **un** ∼ **de** a drop of; **montrer qch du** ∼ point at sth; **à deux** ∼**s de** a hair's breadth away from; ∼ **de pied** toe. **doigté** *nm* (Mus) fingering, touch; (*diplomatie*) tact.

dois, doit /dwa/ ➡**DEVOIR** **26**.

doléances /dɔleɑ̃s/ *nfpl* grievances.

dollar /dɔlaʀ/ *nm* dollar.

domaine /dɔmɛn/ *nm* estate, domain; (fig) domain, field.

domestique /dɔmɛstik/ *adj* domestic. ● *nmf* servant. **domestiquer** **1** *vt* domesticate.

domicile /dɔmisil/ *nm* home; **à ~** at home; (*livrer*) to the home.

domicilié, **~e** /dɔmisilje/ *adj* resident; **être ~ à Paris** live *ou* be resident in Paris.

dominant, **~e** /dɔminã, -t/ *adj* dominant. **dominante** *nf* dominant feature.

dominer /dɔmine/ **1** *vt* dominate; (*surplomber*) tower over, dominate; (*sujet*) master; (*peur*) overcome. ● *vi* dominate; (*équipe*) be in the lead; (*prévaloir*) stand out.

domino /dɔmino/ *nm* domino.

dommage /dɔmaʒ/ *nm* (tort) harm; (**~s**) (dégâts) damage; **c'est ~** it's a pity *ou* shame; **quel ~** what a pity *ou* shame. **dommages-intérêts** *nmpl* (Jur) damages.

dompter /dõte/ **1** *vt* tame. **dompteur**, **-euse** *nm, f* tamer.

DOM-TOM /dɔmtɔm/ *abrév mpl* (**départements et territoires d'outre-mer**) French overseas departments and territories.

don /dõ/ *nm* (cadeau, aptitude) gift. **donateur**, **-trice** *nm, f* donor. **donation** *nf* donation.

donc /dõk/ *conj* so, then; (par conséquent) so, therefore; **quoi ~?** what did you say?; **tiens ~!** fancy that!

donjon /dõʒõ/ *nm* (tour) keep.

donné, **~e** /dɔne/ *adj* (fixé) given; (pas cher **11**) dirt cheap; **étant ~ que** given that.

donnée /dɔne/ *nf* (élément d'information) fact; **~s** data.

donner /dɔne/ **1** *vt* give; (*vieilles affaires*) give away; (distribuer) give out; (*fruits, résultats*) produce; (*film*) show; (*pièce*) put on; **ça donne soif/faim** it makes one thirsty/hungry; **~ qch à réparer** take sth to be repaired; **~ lieu à** give rise to. ● *vi* **~ sur** look out on to; **~ dans** tend towards. □ **se ~ à** *vpr* devote oneself to; **se ~ du mal** go to a lot of trouble (**pour faire** to do).

dont /dõ/

● *pronom*

····▸ (personne) **la fille ~ je te parlais** the girl I was telling you about; **l'homme ~ la fille a dit...** the man whose daughter said...

····▸ (chose) which, **l'affaire ~ il parle** the matter which he is referring to; **la manière ~ elle parle** the way she speaks; **ce ~ il parle** what he's talking about

····▸ (provenance) from which.

····▸ (parmi lesquels) **deux personnes ~ toi** two people, one of whom is you; **plusieurs thèmes ~ l'identité et le racisme** several topics including identity and racism.

dopage /dɔpaʒ/ *nm* (de cheval) doping; (d'athlète) illegal drug-use.

doper /dɔpe/ **1** *vt* dope. □ **se ~** *vpr* take drugs.

doré, **~e** /dɔre/ *adj* (couleur d'or) golden; (qui rappelle de l'or) gold; (avec de l'or) gilt; **la jeunesse ~e** gilded youth.

dorénavant /dɔrenavã/ *adv* henceforth.

dorer /dɔre/ **1** *vt* gild; (Culin) brown.

dormir /dɔrmir/ **46** *vi* sleep; (être endormi) be asleep; **~ debout** be asleep on one's feet; **une histoire à ~ debout** a cock-and-bull story.

dortoir /dɔrtwar/ *nm* dormitory.

dorure /dɔryr/ *nf* gilding.

dos /do/ *nm* back; (de livre) spine; **à ~ de** riding on; **au ~ de** (chèque) on the back of; **de ~** from behind; **~ crawlé** backstroke.

dosage /dozaʒ/ *nm* (mélange) mixture; (quantité) amount, proportions. **dose** *nf* dose. **doser** **1** *vt* measure out; (contrôler) use in a controlled way.

dossier /dosje/ *nm* (documents) file; (Jur) case; (de chaise) back; (TV, presse) special feature.

dot /dɔt/ *nf* dowry.

douane /dwan/ *nf* customs.

douanier, **-ière** /dwanje, -jɛr/ *adj* customs. ● *nm* customs officer.

double /dubl/ *adj & adv* double. ● *nm* (copie) duplicate; (sosie) double; **le ~ (de)** twice as much *ou* as many (as);

le ~ messieurs the men's doubles.

double-cliquer /dublklike/ **1** vt double-click.

doubler /duble/ **1** vt double; (dépasser) overtake; (vêtement) line; (film) dub; (classe) repeat; (cap) round. ● vi double.

doublure /dublyʀ/ nf (étoffe) lining; (acteur) understudy.

douce /dus/ ➡DOUX.

doucement /dusmã/ adv gently; (sans bruit) quietly; (lentement) slowly.

douceur /dusœʀ/ nf (mollesse) softness; (de climat) mildness; (de personne) gentleness; (friandise) sweet; (US) candy; **en ~** smoothly.

douche /duʃ/ nf shower.

doucher (se) /duʃe/ **1** vpr have ou take a shower.

doudoune /dudun/ nf 🔢 down jacket.

doué, ~e /dwe/ adj gifted; **~ de** endowed with.

douille /duj/ nf (Électr) socket.

douillet, ~te /dujɛ, -t/ adj cosy, comfortable; (personne: péj) soft.

douleur /dulœʀ/ nf pain; (chagrin) sorrow, grief. **douloureux, -euse** adj painful.

doute /dut/ nm doubt; **sans ~** no doubt; **sans aucun ~** without doubt.

douter /dute/ **1** vt **~ de** doubt; **~ que** doubt that. ● vi doubt. ◻ **se ~ de** vpr suspect; **je m'en doutais** I thought so.

douteux, -euse /dutø, -z/ adj dubious, doubtful.

Douvres /duvʀ/ npr Dover.

doux, douce /du, dus/ adj (moelleux) soft; (sucré) sweet; (clément, pas fort) mild; (pas brusque, bienveillant) gentle.

douzaine /duzɛn/ nf about twelve; (douze) dozen; **une ~ d'œufs** a dozen eggs.

douze /duz/ adj & nm twelve. **douzième** adj & nmf twelfth.

doyen, ~ne /dwajɛ̃, -ɛn/ nm, f dean; (en âge) most senior person.

dragée /dʀaʒe/ nf sugared almond.

draguer /dʀage/ **1** vt (rivière) dredge; (filles 🔢) chat up.

drainer /dʀene/ **1** vt drain.

dramatique /dʀamatik/ adj dramatic; (tragique) tragic. ● nf (television) drama.

dramatiser /dʀamatize/ **1** vt dramatize.

dramaturge /dʀamatyʀʒ/ nmf dramatist.

drame /dʀam/ nm (genre) drama; (pièce) play; (événement tragique) tragedy.

drap /dʀa/ nm sheet; (tissu) (woollen) cloth.

drapeau (pl ~x) /dʀapo/ nm flag.

drap-housse (pl **draps-housses**) /dʀaus/ nm fitted sheet.

dressage /dʀɛsaʒ/ nm training; (compétition équestre) dressage.

dresser /dʀese/ **1** vt put up, erect; (tête) raise; (animal) train; (liste, plan) draw up; **~ l'oreille** prick up one's ears. ◻ **se** ~ vpr (bâtiment) stand; (personne) draw oneself up. **dresseur, -euse** nm, f trainer.

dribbler /dʀible/ **1** vi (Sport) dribble.

drive /dʀajv/ nm (Ordinat) drive.

drogue /dʀɔg/ nf drug; **la ~** drugs.

drogué, ~e /dʀɔge/ nm, f drug addict.

droguer /dʀɔge/ **1** vt (malade) drug heavily; (victime) drug. ◻ **se** ~ vpr take drugs.

droguerie /dʀɔgʀi/ nf hardware shop. **droguiste** nmf owner of a hardware shop.

droit, ~e /dʀwa, -t/ adj (contraire de gauche) right; (non courbe) straight; (loyal) upright; **angle ~** right angle. ● adv straight. ● nm right; **~(s)** (taxe) duty; **le ~** (Jur) law; **avoir le ~ de** be entitled to; **avoir le ~ à** be allowed to; **être dans son ~** be in the right; **~ d'auteur** copyright; **~ d'inscription** registration fee; **~s d'auteur** royalties.

droite /dʀwat/ nf (contraire de gauche) right; **à ~** on the right; (direction) (to the) right; **la ~** the right (side); (Pol) the right (wing); (ligne) straight line. **droitier, -ière** adj right-handed.

drôle /dʀol/ adj (amusant) funny; (bizarre) funny, odd. **drôlement** adv funnily; (très 🔢) really.

dru, ~e /dʀy/ adj thick; **tomber ~** fall thick and fast.

drugstore /dʀœgstɔʀ/ nm drugstore.

d

DTD *abrév m* (**document type definition**) DTD.

du /dy/ →DE.

dû, due /dy/ *adj* due. ● *nm* due; (argent) dues; ~ à due to. ● →DEVOIR 26.

duc, duchesse /dyk, dyʃɛs/ *nm, f* duke, duchess.

duo /dɥo/ *nm* (Mus) duet; (fig) duo.

dupe /dyp/ *nf* dupe.

duplex /dyplɛks/ *nm* split-level apartment; (US) duplex; (émission) link-up.

duplicata /dyplikata/ *nm inv* duplicate.

duquel /dykɛl/ →LEQUEL.

dur, ~e /dyʀ/ *adj* hard; (sévère) harsh, hard; (viande) tough; (col, brosse) stiff; ~ **d'oreille** hard of hearing. ● *adv* hard. ● *nm, f* tough nut 1; (Pol) hardliner.

durable /dyʀabl/ *adj* lasting.

durant /dyʀɑ̃/ *prép* (au cours de) during; (avec mesure de temps) for; ~ **des heures** for hours; **des heures** ~ for hours and hours.

durcir /dyʀsiʀ/ 2 *vt* harden. ● *vi* (terre) harden; (ciment) set; (pain) go hard. □ **se** ~ *vpr* harden.

durée /dyʀe/ *nf* length; (période) duration; **de courte** ~ short-lived; **pile longue** ~ long-life battery.

durer /dyʀe/ 1 *vi* last.

dureté /dyʀte/ *nf* hardness; (sévérité) harshness.

duvet /dyvɛ/ *nm* down; (sac) sleeping-bag.

DVD *abrév m* (**digital versatile disc**) DVD.

dynamique /dinamik/ *adj* dynamic.

dynamite /dinamit/ *nf* dynamite.

dynamo /dinamo/ *nf* dynamo.

• •

Ee

• •

eau (*pl* ~x) /o/ *nf* water; ~ **courante** running water; ~ **de mer** seawater; ~ **de source** spring water; ~ **douce/salée** fresh/salt water; ~ **de pluie** rainwater; ~ **potable** drinking water; ~ **de javel** bleach; ~ **minérale** min-

eral water; ~ **gazeuse** sparkling water; ~ **plate** still water; ~ **de toilette** eau de toilette; ~**x usées** dirty water; ~**x et forêts** forestry commission (+ *sg*); **tomber à l'**~ (fig) fall through; **prendre l'**~ take in water.

eau-de-vie (*pl* **eaux-de-vie**) *nf* brandy.

ébahi, ~e /ebai/ *adj* dumbfounded.

ébauche /eboʃ/ *nf* (dessin) sketch; (fig) attempt.

ébéniste /ebenist/ *nm* cabinet-maker.

éblouir /ebluiʀ/ 2 *vt* dazzle.

éboueur /ebwœʀ/ *nm* dustman.

ébouillanter /ebujɑ̃te/ 1 *vt* scald.

éboulement /ebulmɑ̃/ *nm* landslide.

ébouriffé, ~e /eburife/ *adj* dishevelled.

ébrécher /ebreʃe/ 14 *vt* chip.

ébruiter /ebrɥite/ 1 *vt* spread about. □ **s'**~ *vpr* get out.

ébullition /ebylisjɔ̃/ *nf* boiling; **en** ~ boiling.

écaille /ekaj/ *nf* (de poisson) scale; (de peinture, roc) flake; (matière) tortoiseshell.

écarlate /ekaʀlat/ *adj* scarlet.

écarquiller /ekaʀkije/ 1 *vt* ~ **les yeux** open one's eyes wide.

écart /ekaʀ/ *nm* gap; (de prix) difference; (embardée) swerve; ~ **de conduite** lapse in behaviour; **être à l'**~ be isolated; **se tenir à l'**~ **de** stand apart from; (fig) keep out of the way of.

écarté, ~e /ekaʀte/ *adj* (lieu) remote; **les jambes** ~**es** (with) legs apart; **les bras** ~**s** with one's arms out.

écarter /ekaʀte/ 1 *vt* (séparer) move apart; (membres) spread; (branches) part; (éliminer) dismiss; ~ **qch de** move sth away from; ~ **qn de** keep sb away from. □ **s'**~ *vpr* (s'éloigner) move away; (quitter son chemin) move aside; **s'**~ **de** stray from.

ecchymose /ekimoz/ *nf* bruise.

écervelé, ~e /esɛʀvəle/ *adj* scatterbrained. ● *nm, f* scatterbrain.

échafaudage /eʃafodaʒ/ *nm* scaffolding; (amas) heap.

échalote /eʃalɔt/ *nf* shallot.

échancré, ~e /eʃɑ̃kʀe/ *adj* lowcut.

échange /eʃɑ̃ʒ/ *nm* exchange; **en** ~ (**de**) in exchange (for). **échanger** 40 *vt* exchange (**contre** for).

échangeur /eʃɑ̃ʒœʀ/ *nm* (Auto) interchange.

échantillon /eʃɑ̃tijɔ̃/ *nm* sample.

échappatoire /eʃapatwaʀ/ *nf* way out.

échappement /eʃapmɑ̃/ *nm* exhaust.

échapper /eʃape/ **1** *vi* **à** escape; (en fuyant) escape (from); ~ **des mains de** slip out of the hands of; **ça m'a échappé** (fig) it just slipped out; **l'~ belle** have a narrow *ou* lucky escape. □ **s'~** *vpr* escape.

écharde /eʃaʀd/ *nf* splinter.

écharpe /eʃaʀp/ *nf* scarf; (de maire) sash; **en ~** (bras) in a sling.

échasse /eʃɑs/ *nf* stilt.

échauffement /eʃofmɑ̃/ *nm* (Sport) warm-up.

échauffer /eʃofe/ **1** *vt* heat; (fig) excite. □ **s'~** *vpr* warm up.

échéance /eʃeɑ̃s/ *nf* due date (for payment); (délai) deadline; (obligation) (financial) commitment.

échéant: le cas ~ /ləkazeʃeɑ̃/ *loc* if need be.

échec /eʃɛk/ *nm* failure; **~s** (jeu) chess; **~ et mat** checkmate.

échelle /eʃɛl/ *nf* ladder; (dimension) scale.

échelon /eʃlɔ̃/ *nm* rung; (hiérarchique) grade; (niveau) level.

échevelé, ~e /eʃəvle/ *adj* dishevelled.

écho /eko/ *nm* echo; **~s** (dans la presse) gossip.

échographie /ekɔgʀafi/ *nf* (ultra-sound) scan.

échouer /eʃwe/ **1** *vi* (bateau) run aground; (ne pas réussir) fail; **~ à un examen** fail an exam. ● *vt* (bateau) ground. □ **s'~** *vpr* run aground.

échu, ~e /eʃy/ *adj* (délai) expired.

éclabousser /eklabuse/ **1** *vt* splash.

éclair /eklɛʀ/ *nm* (flash of) lightning; (fig) flash; (gâteau) éclair. ● *adj inv* (visite) brief.

éclairage /eklɛʀaʒ/ *nm* lighting.

éclaircie /eklɛʀsi/ *nf* sunny interval.

éclaircir /eklɛʀsiʀ/ **2** *vt* lighten; (mystère) clear up. □ **s'~** *vpr* (ciel) clear; (mystère) become clearer. **éclaircissement** *nm* clarification.

éclairer /eklɛʀe/ **1** *vt* light (up); (personne) (fig) enlighten; (situation) throw light on. ● *vi* give light. □ **s'~** *vpr* become clearer.

éclaireur, -euse /eklɛʀœʀ, -øz/ *nm, f* (boy) scout, (girl) guide.

éclat /ekla/ *nm* fragment; (de lumière) brightness; (splendeur) brilliance; **~ de rire** burst of laughter.

éclatant, ~e /eklatɑ̃, -t/ *adj* brilliant; (soleil) dazzling.

éclater /eklate/ **1** *vi* burst; (exploser) go off; (verre) shatter; (guerre) break out; (groupe) split up; **~ de rire** burst out laughing.

éclipse /eklips/ *nf* eclipse.

éclosion /eklozjɔ̃/ *nf* hatching, opening.

écluse /eklyz/ *nf* (de canal) lock.

écœurant, ~e /ekœʀɑ̃, -t/ *adj* (gâteau) sickly; (fig) disgusting. **écœurer** **1** *vt* sicken.

éco-guerrier, -ière /ekogɛʀje, jɛʀ/ *nmf* eco-warrior.

école /ekɔl/ *nf* school; **~ maternelle/primaire/secondaire** nursery/primary/secondary school; **~ normale** teachers' training college. **écolier, -ière** *nm, f* schoolboy, schoolgirl.

écologie /ekɔlɔʒi/ *nf* ecology. **écologique** *adj* ecological, green. **écologiste** *nmf* (chercheur) ecologist; (dans l'âme) environmentalist; (Pol) Green.

économie /ekɔnɔmi/ *nf* economy; (discipline) economics; **~s** (argent) savings; **une ~ de** (gain) a saving of. **économique** *adj* (Pol) economic; (bon marché) economical.

économiser /ekɔnɔmize/ **1** *vt/i* save.

écorce /ekɔʀs/ *nf* bark; (de fruit) peel.

écorcher /ekɔʀʃe/ **1** *vt* (genou) graze; (animal) skin. □ **s'~** *vpr* graze oneself. **écorchure** *nf* graze.

écossais, ~e /ekɔsɛ, -z/ *adj* Scottish. **É~, ~e** *nm, f* Scot.

Écosse /ekɔs/ *nf* Scotland.

écoulement /ekulmɑ̃/ *nm* flow.

écouler /ekule/ **1** *vt* dispose of, sell. □ **s'~** *vpr* (liquide) flow; (temps) pass.

écourter /ekuʀte/ **1** *vt* shorten.

écoute /ekut/ *nf* listening; **à l'~ (de)** listening in (to); **heures de grande ~** prime time; **~s téléphoniques** phone tapping.

écouter /ekute/ **1** *vt* listen to. ● *vi* listen; ~ **aux portes** eavesdrop. **écouteur** *nm* earphones (+ *pl*); (de téléphone) receiver.

écran /ekʀɑ̃/ *nm* screen; ~ **total** sunblock.

écraser /ekʀɑze/ **1** *vt* crush; (*piéton*) run over; (*cigarette*) stub out. □ **s'**~ *vpr* crash (**contre** into).

écrémé, ~**e** /ekʀeme/ *adj* skimmed; **demi-**~ semi-skimmed.

écrevisse /ekʀəvis/ *nf* crayfish.

écrier (s') /(s)ekʀije/ **45** *vpr* exclaim.

écrin /ekʀɛ̃/ *nm* case.

écrire /ekʀiʀ/ **30** *vt/i* write; (orthographier) spell. □ **s'**~ *vpr* (*mot*) be spelt.

écrit /ekʀi/ *nm* document; (*examen*) written paper; **par** ~ in writing.

écriteau (*pl* ~**x**) /ekʀito/ *nm* notice.

écriture /ekʀityʀ/ *nf* writing; ~**s** (Comm) accounts.

écrivain /ekʀivɛ̃/ *nm* writer.

écrou /ekʀu/ *nm* (Tech) nut.

écrouler (s') /(s)ekʀule/ **1** *vpr* collapse.

écru, ~e /ekʀy/ *adj* (*couleur*) natural; (*tissu*) raw.

écueil /ekœj/ *nm* reef; (fig) danger.

éculé, ~e /ekyle/ *adj* (*soulier*) worn at the heel; (fig) well-worn.

écume /ekym/ *nf* foam; (Culin) scum.

écumer /ekyme/ **1** *vt* skim. ● *vi* foam.

écureuil /ekyʀœj/ *nm* squirrel.

écurie /ekyʀi/ *nf* stable.

écuyer, -ère /ekɥije, -jɛʀ/ *nm, f* (horse) rider.

eczéma /ɛgzema/ *nm* eczema.

EDF *abrév f* (**Électricité de France**) *French electricity board*.

édifice /edifis/ *nm* building.

édifier /edifje/ **45** *vt* construct; (porter à la vertu) edify.

Édimbourg /edɛ̃buʀ/ *npr* Edinburgh.

édit /edi/ *nm* edict.

éditer /edite/ **1** *vt* publish; (annoter) edit. **éditeur, -trice** *nm, f* publisher; (réviseur) editor.

édition /edisjɔ̃/ *nf* (activité) publishing; (livre, disque) edition.

éditique /editik/ *nf* electronic publishing.

éditorial, ~e (*pl* -**iaux**) /editoʀjal, -jo/ *adj & nm* editorial.

édredon /edʀədɔ̃/ *nm* eiderdown.

éducateur, -trice /edykatœʀ, -tʀis/ *nm, f* youth worker.

éducatif, -ive /edykatif, -v/ *adj* educational.

éducation /edykasjɔ̃/ *nf* (façon d'élever) upbringing; (enseignement) education; (manières) manners; ~ **physique** physical education.

éduquer /edyke/ **1** *vt* (élever) bring up; (former) educate.

effacé, ~e /efase/ *adj* (modeste) unassuming.

effacer /efase/ **10** *vt* (gommer) rub out; (à l'écran) delete; (*souvenir*) erase. □ **s'**~ *vpr* fade; (s'écarter) step aside.

effarer /efaʀe/ **1** *vt* alarm; **être effaré** be astounded.

effaroucher /efaʀuʃe/ **1** *vt* scare away.

effectif, -ive /efɛktif, -v/ *adj* effective. ● *nm* (d'école) number of pupils; ~**s** numbers. **effectivement** *adv* effectively; (en effet) indeed.

effectuer /efɛktɥe/ **1** *vt* carry out, make.

efféminé, ~e /efemine/ *adj* effeminate.

effervescent, ~e /efɛʀvesɑ̃, -t/ *adj* **comprimé** ~ effervescent tablet.

effet /efɛ/ *nm* effect; (impression) impression; ~**s** (habits) clothes, things; **sous l'**~ **d'une drogue** under the influence of drugs; **en** ~ indeed; **faire de l'**~ have an effect, be effective; **faire bon/ mauvais** ~ make a good/ bad impression; **ça fait un drôle d'**~ it feels strange.

efficace /efikas/ *adj* effective; (personne) efficient. **efficacité** *nf* effectiveness; (de personne) efficiency.

effleurer /eflœʀe/ **1** *vt* touch lightly; (sujet) touch on; **ça ne m'a pas effleuré** it did not cross my mind.

effondrement /efɔ̃dʀəmɑ̃/ *nm* collapse. **effondrer (s')** **1** *vpr* collapse.

efforcer (s') /(s)efoʀse/ **10** *vpr* try (hard) (**de** to).

effort /efoʀ/ *nm* effort.

effraction /efʀaksjɔ̃/ *nf* **entrer par** ~ break in.

effrayant, ~e /efʀejɑ̃, -t/ *adj* frightening; (fig) frightful.

effrayer /efʀeje/ 🕱 vt frighten; (dé-courager) put off. □ **s'~** vpr be frightened.

effréné, ~e /efʀene/ adj wild.

effriter (s') /(s)efʀite/ 🕱 vpr crumble.

effroi /efʀwa/ nm dread.

effronté, ~e /efʀɔ̃te/ adj cheeky. ● nm, f cheeky boy, cheeky girl.

effroyable /efʀwajabl/ adj dreadful.

égal, ~e (mpl **-aux**) /egal, -o/ adj equal; (surface, vitesse) even. ● nm, f equal; **ça m'est/lui est ~** it is all the same to me/him; **sans ~** matchless; **d'~ à ~** between equals. **également** adv equally; (aussi) as well. **égaler** 🕱 vt equal.

égaliser /egalize/ 🕱 vt/i (Sport) equal-ize; (niveler) level out; (cheveux) trim.

égalitaire /egalitɛʀ/ adj egalitarian.

égalité /egalite/ nf equality; (de sur-face) evenness; **être à ~** be level.

égard /egaʀ/ nm consideration; **~s** re-spect (+ sg); **par ~ pour** out of con-sideration for; **à cet ~** in this respect; **à l'~ de** with regard to; (envers) towards.

égarer /egaʀe/ 🕱 vt mislay; (tromper) lead astray. □ **s'~** vpr get lost; (se tromper) go astray.

égayer /egeje/ 🕱 vt (personne) cheer up; (pièce) brighten up.

église /egliz/ nf church.

égoïsme /egoism/ nm selfishness, egoism.

égoïste /egoist/ adj selfish. ● nmf egoist.

égorger /egɔʀʒe/ 🕱 vt slit the throat of.

égout /egu/ nm sewer.

égoutter /egute/ 🕱 vt drain. □ **s'~** vpr (vaisselle) drain; (lessive) drip dry. **égouttoir** nm draining-board.

égratigner /egʀatiɲe/ 🕱 vt scratch. **égratignure** nf scratch.

Égypte /eʒipt/ nf Egypt.

éjecter /eʒɛkte/ 🕱 vt eject.

élaboration /elabɔʀasjɔ̃/ nf elabor-ation. **élaborer** 🕱 vt elaborate.

élan /elɑ̃/ nm (animal) moose; (Sport) run-up; (vitesse) momentum; (fig) surge.

élancé, ~e /elɑ̃se/ adj slender.

élancement /elɑ̃smɑ̃/ nm twinge.

élancer (s') /(s)elɑ̃se/ 🔟 vpr leap for-ward, dash; (arbre, édifice) soar.

élargir /elaʀʒiʀ/ 🕑 vt (route) widen; (connaissances) broaden. □ **s'~** vpr (famille) expand; (route) widen; (écart) increase; (vêtement) stretch.

élastique /elastik/ adj elastic. ● nm elastic band; (tissu) elastic.

électeur, -trice /elɛktœʀ, -tʀis/ nm, f voter. **élection** nf election. **électoral, ~e** (mpl **-aux**) adj (réunion) election. **électorat** nm electorate, voters (+ pl).

électricien, ~ne /elɛktʀisjɛ̃, ɛn/ nm, f electrician. **électricité** nf electricity.

électrifier /elɛktʀifje/ 🕮 vt electrify.

électrique /elɛktʀik/ adj electric; (ins-tallation) electrical.

électrocuter /elɛktʀɔkyte/ 🕱 vt elec-trocute.

électroménager /elɛktʀɔmenaʒe/ nm **l'~** household appliances (+ pl).

électron /elɛktʀɔ̃/ nm electron. **élec-tronicien, ~ne** nm, f electronics en-gineer.

électronique /elɛktʀɔnik/ adj elec-tronic. ● nf electronics.

élégance /elegɑ̃s/ nf elegance. **élé-gant, ~e** adj elegant.

élément /elemɑ̃/ nm element; (meu-ble) unit. **élémentaire** adj elementary.

éléphant /elefɑ̃/ nm elephant.

élevage /ɛlvaʒ/ nm (stock-) breeding.

élévation /elevasjɔ̃/ nf rise; (hausse) rise; (plan) elevation; **~ de terrain** rise in the ground.

élève /elɛv/ nmf pupil.

élevé, ~e /ɛlve/ adj high; (noble) ele-vated; **bien ~** well-mannered.

élever /ɛlve/ 🔟 vt (lever) raise; (en-fants) bring up, raise; (animal) breed. □ **s'~** vpr rise; (dans le ciel) soar up; **s'~ à** amount to. **éleveur, -euse** nm, f (stock-)breeder.

éligible /eliʒibl/ adj eligible.

élimination /eliminasjɔ̃/ nf elim-ination.

éliminatoire /eliminatwaʀ/ adj quali-fying. ● nf (Sport) heat.

éliminer /elimine/ 🕱 vt eliminate.

élire /eliʀ/ 🕬 vt elect.

elle /ɛl/ pron she; (complément) her; (chose) it. **elle-même** pron herself; it-self. **elles** pron they; (complément) them. **elles-mêmes** *pron* themselves.

élocution /elɔkysjɔ̃/ *nf* diction.

éloge /elɔʒ/ *nm* praise; **faire l'~ de** praise; **~s** praise (+ *sg*).

éloigné, ~e /elwaɲe/ *adj* distant; **~ de** far away from; **parent ~** distant relative.

éloigner /elwaɲe/ **1** *vt* take away *ou* remove (**de** from); (*danger*) ward off; (*visite*) put off. □ **s'~** *vpr* go *ou* move away (**de** from); (*affectivement*) become estranged (**de** from).

élongation /elɔ̃gasjɔ̃/ *nf* strained muscle.

éloquent, ~e /elɔkɑ̃, -t/ *adj* eloquent.

élu, ~e /ely/ *adj* elected. ● *nm, f* (*Pol*) elected representative.

élucider /elyside/ **1** *vt* elucidate.

éluder /elyde/ **1** *vt* evade.

> **Élysée** The *palais de l'Élysée* is the official residence of the *Président de la République*, not far from the *Champs Élysées* in central Paris. The word *Élysée* is often used to refer to the president's office. See ▷**MATIGNON**. *i*

émacié, ~e /emasje/ *adj* emaciated.

e-mail /imɛl/ *nm* email; **envoyer un ~ a qn** email sb.

émail (*pl* **-aux**) /emaj, -o/ *nm* enamel.

émanciper /emɑ̃sipe/ **1** *vt* emancipate. □ **s'~** *vpr* become emancipated.

émaner /emane/ **1** *vi* emanate.

emballage /ɑ̃balaʒ/ *nm* (*dur*) packaging; (*souple*) wrapping.

emballer /ɑ̃bale/ **1** *vt* pack; (*en papier*) wrap; **ça ne m'emballe pas** 🗉 I'm not really taken by it. □ **s'~** *vpr* (*moteur*) race; (*cheval*) bolt; (*personne*) get carried away; (*prices*) shoot up.

embarcadère /ɑ̃baʀkadɛʀ/ *nm* landing-stage.

embarcation /ɑ̃baʀkasjɔ̃/ *nf* boat.

embardée /ɑ̃baʀde/ *nf* swerve.

embarquement /ɑ̃baʀkəmɑ̃/ *nm* (*de passagers*) boarding; (*de fret*) loading.

embarquer /ɑ̃baʀke/ **1** *vt* take on board; (*frêt*) load; (*emporter* 🗉) cart off. ● *vi* board. □ **s'~** *vpr* board; **s'~ dans** embark upon.

embarras /ɑ̃baʀa/ *nm* (*gêne*) embarrassment; (*difficulté*) difficulty.

embarrasser /ɑ̃baʀase/ **1** *vt* (*encombrer*) clutter (up); (*fig*) embarrass. □ **s'~ de** *vpr* burden oneself with.

embauche /ɑ̃boʃ/ *nf* hiring. **embaucher** **1** *vt* hire, take on.

embaumer /ɑ̃bome/ **1** *vt* (*pièce*) fill; (*cadavre*) embalm. ● *vi* be fragrant.

embellir /ɑ̃beliʀ/ **2** *vt* make more attractive; (*récit*) embellish.

embêtant, ~e /ɑ̃betɑ̃, -t/ *adj* 🗉 annoying.

embêter /ɑ̃bete/ **1** *vt* bother. □ **s'~** *vpr* be bored.

emblée: d'~ /dɑ̃ble/ *loc* right away.

emblème /ɑ̃blɛm/ *nm* emblem.

emboîter /ɑ̃bwate/ **1** *vt* fit together; **~ le pas à qn** (*imiter*) follow suit. □ **s'~** *vpr* fit together; (**s'**)**~ dans** fit into.

embonpoint /ɑ̃bɔ̃pwɛ̃/ *nm* stoutness.

embourber (s') /(s)ɑ̃buʀbe/ **1** *vpr* get stuck in the mud; (*fig*) get bogged down.

embouteillage /ɑ̃butɛjaʒ/ *nm* traffic jam.

emboutir /ɑ̃butiʀ/ **2** *vt* (*Auto*) crash into.

embraser (s') /(s)ɑ̃bʀɑze/ **1** *vpr* catch fire.

embrasser /ɑ̃bʀase/ **1** *vt* kiss; (*adopter, contenir*) embrace. □ **s'~** *vpr* kiss.

embrayage /ɑ̃bʀɛjaʒ/ *nm* clutch. **embrayer** 🗷 *vi* engage the clutch.

embrouiller /ɑ̃bʀuje/ **1** *vt* confuse; (*fils*) tangle. □ **s'~** *vpr* become confused.

embryon /ɑ̃bʀijɔ̃/ *nm* embryo.

embûches /ɑ̃byʃ/ *nfpl* traps.

embuer(s') /(s)ɑ̃bɥe/ **1** *vpr* mist up.

embuscade /ɑ̃byskad/ *nf* ambush.

émeraude /ɛmʀod/ *nf* emerald.

émerger /emɛʀʒe/ 🗷 *vi* emerge; (*fig*) stand out.

émeri /emʀi/ *nm* emery.

émerveillement /emɛʀvejmɑ̃/ *nm* amazement, wonder.

émerveiller /emɛʀveje/ **1** *vt* fill with wonder. □ **s'~** *vpr* marvel at.

émetteur /emɛtœʀ/ *nm* transmitter.

émettre /emɛtʀ/ 🗷 *vt* (*son*) produce; (*message*) send out; (*timbre, billet*) issue; (*opinion*) express.

émeute /emøt/ nf riot.

émietter /emjete/ **1** vt crumble. □ **s'~** vpr crumble.

émigrant, ~e /emigʀɑ̃, -t/ nm, f emigrant. **émigration** nf emigration. **émigrer** **1** vi emigrate.

émincer /emɛ̃se/ **10** vt cut into thin slices.

éminent, ~e /eminɑ̃, -t/ adj eminent.

émissaire /emisɛʀ/ nm emissary.

émission /emisjɔ̃/ nf (programme) programme; (de chaleur, gaz) emission; (de timbre) issue.

emmagasiner /ɑ̃magazine/ **1** vt store.

emmanchure /ɑ̃mɑ̃ʃyʀ/ nf armhole.

emmêler /ɑ̃mele/ **1** vt tangle. □ **s'~** vpr get mixed up.

emménager /ɑ̃menaʒe/ **40** vi move in; **~ dans** move into.

emmener /ɑ̃mne/ **6** vt take; (comme prisonnier) take away.

emmerder /ɑ̃mɛʀde/ **1** ✕ vt **~ qn** get on sb's nerves. □ **s'~** vpr be bored.

emmitoufler /ɑ̃mitufle/ **1** vt wrap up warmly. □ **s'~** vpr wrap oneself up warmly.

émoi /emwa/ nm turmoil; (plaisir) excitement.

émotif, -ive /emɔtif, -v/ adj emotional. **émotion** nf emotion; (peur) fright. **émotionnel, ~le** adj emotional.

émousser /emuse/ **1** vt blunt.

émouvant, ~e /emuvɑ̃, -t/ adj moving.

empailler /ɑ̃paje/ **1** vt stuff.

empaqueter /ɑ̃pakte/ **38** vt package.

emparer (s') /(s)ɑ̃paʀe/ **1** vpr **s'~ de** get hold of.

empêchement /ɑ̃pɛʃmɑ̃/ nm **avoir un ~** to be held up.

empêcher /ɑ̃peʃe/ **1** vt prevent; **~ de faire** prevent ou stop (from) doing; **(il) n'empêche que** still. □ **s'~** vpr **il ne peut pas s'en ~** he cannot help it.

empereur /ɑ̃pʀœʀ/ nm emperor.

empester /ɑ̃pɛste/ **1** vt stink out; (essence) stink of. ● vi stink.

empêtrer (s') /(s)ɑ̃petʀe/ **1** vpr become entangled.

empiéter /ɑ̃pjete/ **14** vi **~ sur** encroach upon.

empiffrer (s') /(s)ɑ̃pifʀe/ **1** vpr **1** stuff oneself.

empiler /ɑ̃pile/ **1** vt pile up. □ **s'~** vpr pile up.

empire /ɑ̃piʀ/ nm empire.

emplacement /ɑ̃plasmɑ̃/ nm site.

emplâtre /ɑ̃plɑtʀ/ nm (Méd) plaster.

emploi /ɑ̃plwa/ nm (travail) job; (embauche) employment; (utilisation) use; **un ~ de chauffeur** a job as a driver; **~ du temps** timetable. **employé, ~e** nm, f employee.

employer /ɑ̃plwaje/ **31** vt (personne) employ; (utiliser) use. □ **s'~** vpr be used; **s'~ à** devote oneself to. **employeur, -euse** nm, f employer.

empoigner /ɑ̃pwaɲe/ **1** vt grab. □ **s'~** vpr come to blows.

empoisonnement /ɑ̃pwazɔnmɑ̃/ nm poisoning.

empoisonner /ɑ̃pwazɔne/ **1** vt poison; (embêter **1**) annoy. □ **s'~** vpr to poison oneself.

emporter /ɑ̃pɔʀte/ **1** vt take (away); (entraîner) sweep away; (arracher) tear off. □ **s'~** vpr lose one's temper; **l'~** get the upper hand (**sur** of); **plat à ~** take-away.

empoté, ~e /ɑ̃pote/ adj clumsy.

empreinte /ɑ̃pʀɛ̃t/ nf mark; **~ (digitale)** fingerprint; **~ écologique** carbon footprint; **~ de pas** footprint.

empressé, ~e /ɑ̃pʀese/ adj attentive.

empresser (s') /(s)ɑ̃pʀese/ **1** vpr **s'~ de** hasten to; **s'~ auprès de** be attentive to.

emprise /ɑ̃pʀiz/ nf influence.

emprisonnement /ɑ̃pʀizɔnmɑ̃/ nm imprisonment. **emprisonner** **1** vt imprison.

emprunt /ɑ̃pʀœ̃/ nm loan; **faire un ~** take out a loan.

emprunté, ~e /ɑ̃pʀœ̃te/ adj awkward.

emprunter /ɑ̃pʀœ̃te/ **1** vt borrow (**à** from); (route) take; (fig) assume. **emprunteur, -euse** nm, f borrower.

ému, ~e /emy/ adj moved; (intimidé) nervous.

émule /emyl/ nmf imitator.

en /ɑ̃/

➡ Pour les expressions comme **en principe, en train de, s'en aller,** etc. ➡**principe, train, aller,** etc.

● *préposition*

····▸ (lieu) in.

····▸ (avec mouvement) to.

····▸ (temps) in.

····▸ (manière, état) in; **~ faisant** by *ou* while doing; **je t'appelle ~ rentrant** I will call you when I get back.

····▸ (en qualité de) as.

····▸ (transport) by.

····▸ (composition) made of; **table ~ bois** wooden table.

● *pronom*

····▸ **en avoir/vouloir** have/want some; **ne pas ~ avoir/vouloir** not have/want any; **j'~ ai deux** I've got two; **prends-~ plusieurs** take several; **il m'~ reste un** I have one left; **j'~ suis content** I am pleased with him/her/it/them; **je m'~ souviens** I remember it.

····▸ **~ êtes-vous sûr?** are you sure?

encadrement /ɑ̃kadʀəmɑ̃/ *nm* framing; (de porte) frame. **encadrer 1** *vt* frame; (entourer d'un trait) circle; (superviser) supervise.

encaisser /ɑ̃kese/ **1** *vt* (*argent*) collect; (*chèque*) cash; (*coups* **1**) take.

encart /ɑ̃kaʀ/ *nm* **~ publicitaire** (advertising) insert.

en-cas /ɑ̃kɑ/ *nm* (stand-by) snack.

encastré, ~e /ɑ̃kastʀe/ *adj* built-in.

encaustique /ɑ̃kostik/ *nf* wax polish.

enceinte /ɑ̃sɛ̃t/ *adj f* pregnant; **~ de 3 mois** 3 months pregnant. ● *nf* enclosure; **~ (acoustique)** speaker.

encens /ɑ̃sɑ̃/ *nm* incense.

encercler /ɑ̃sɛʀkle/ **1** *vt* surround.

enchaînement /ɑ̃ʃɛnmɑ̃/ *nm* (suite) chain; (d'idées) sequence.

enchaîner /ɑ̃ʃene/ **1** *vt* chain (up); (*phrases*) link (up). ● *vi* continue. ◻ **s'~** *vpr* follow on.

enchanté, ~e /ɑ̃ʃɑ̃te/ *adj* (ravi) delighted. **enchanter 1** *vt* delight; (ensorceler) enchant.

enchère /ɑ̃ʃɛʀ/ *nf* bid; **mettre** *ou* **vendre aux ~s** sell by auction.

enchevêtrer /ɑ̃ʃəvetʀe/ **1** *vt* tangle. ◻ **s'~** *vpr* become tangled.

enclave /ɑ̃klav/ *nf* enclave.

enclencher /ɑ̃klɑ̃ʃe/ **1** *vt* engage.

enclin, ~e /ɑ̃klɛ̃, -in/ *adj* **~ à** inclined to.

enclos /ɑ̃klo/ *nm* enclosure.

enclume /ɑ̃klym/ *nf* anvil.

encoche /ɑ̃kɔʃ/ *nf* notch.

encolure /ɑ̃kɔlyʀ/ *nf* neck.

encombrant, ~e /ɑ̃kɔ̃bʀɑ̃, -t/ *adj* cumbersome.

encombre /ɑ̃kɔ̃bʀ/ *nm* **sans ~** without any problems.

encombrement /ɑ̃kɔ̃bʀəmɑ̃/ *nm* (Auto) traffic congestion; (volume) bulk.

encombrer /ɑ̃kɔ̃bʀe/ **1** *vt* clutter (up); (obstruer) obstruct. ◻ **s'~ de** *vpr* burden oneself with.

encontre: à l'~ de /alɑ̃kɔ̃tʀədə/ *loc* against.

encore /ɑ̃kɔʀ/ *adv* (toujours) still; (de nouveau) again; (de plus) more; (aussi) also; **~ plus grand** even larger; **~ un café** another coffee; **pas ~** not yet; **si ~** if only; **et puis quoi ~?** **1** what next?

encouragement /ɑ̃kuʀaʒmɑ̃/ *nm* encouragement. **encourager** **40** *vt* encourage.

encourir /ɑ̃kuʀiʀ/ **20** *vt* incur.

encrasser /ɑ̃kʀase/ **1** *vt* clog up (with dirt).

encre /ɑ̃kʀ/ *nf* ink. **encrier** *nm* ink-well.

encyclopédie /ɑ̃siklɔpedi/ *nf* encyclopaedia.

endettement /ɑ̃dɛtmɑ̃/ *nm* debt.

endetter /ɑ̃dɛte/ **1** *vt* put into debt. ◻ **s'~** *vpr* get into debt.

endiguer /ɑ̃dige/ **1** *vt* dam; (fig) curb.

endimanché, ~e /ɑ̃dimɑ̃ʃe/ *adj* in one's Sunday best.

endive /ɑ̃div/ *nf* chicory.

endoctriner /ɑ̃dɔktʀine/ **1** *vt* indoctrinate.

endommager /ɑ̃dɔmaʒe/ **40** *vt* damage.

endormi, ~e /ɑ̃dɔʀmi/ *adj* asleep; (apathique) sleepy.

endormir /ɑ̃dɔʀmiʀ/ 46 vt send to sleep; (médicalement) put to sleep; (duper) dupe (**avec** with). □ **s'~** vpr fall asleep.

endosser /ɑ̃dose/ 1 vt (vêtement) put on; (assumer) take on; (Comm) endorse.

endroit /ɑ̃dʀwa/ nm place; (de tissu) right side; **à l'~** the right way round; **par ~s** in places.

enduire /ɑ̃dɥiʀ/ 17 vt coat. **enduit** nm coating.

endurance /ɑ̃dyʀɑ̃s/ nf endurance. **endurant, ~e** adj tough.

endurcir /ɑ̃dyʀsiʀ/ 2 vt strengthen. □ **s'~** vpr become hard (hardened).

endurer /ɑ̃dyʀe/ 1 vt endure.

énergétique /enɛʀʒetik/ adj energy; (food) high-calorie. **énergie** nf energy; (Tech) power. **énergique** adj energetic.

énervant, ~e /enɛʀvɑ̃, -t/ adj irritating, annoying.

énerver /enɛʀve/ 1 vt irritate. □ **s'~** vpr get worked up.

enfance /ɑ̃fɑ̃s/ nf childhood; **la petite ~** infancy.

enfant /ɑ̃fɑ̃/ nmf child. **enfantillage** nm childishness. **enfantin, ~e** adj simple, easy; (puéril) childish; (jeu, langage) children's.

enfer /ɑ̃fɛʀ/ nm (Relig) Hell; (fig) hell.

enfermer /ɑ̃fɛʀme/ 1 vt shut up. □ **s'~** vpr shut oneself up.

enfiler /ɑ̃file/ 1 vt (aiguille) thread; (vêtement) slip on; (rue) take.

enfin /ɑ̃fɛ̃/ adv (de soulagement) at last; (en dernier lieu) finally; (résignation, conclusion) well; **~ presque** well nearly.

enflammé, ~e /ɑ̃flame/ adj (Méd) inflamed; (discours) fiery; (lettre) passionate.

enflammer /ɑ̃flame/ 1 vt set fire to. □ **s'~** vpr catch fire.

enfler /ɑ̃fle/ 1 vt (histoire) exaggerate. ● vi (partie du corps) swell (up); (mer) swell; (rumeur, colère) spread. □ **s'~** vpr (colère) mount; (rumeur) grow.

enfoncer /ɑ̃fɔ̃se/ 10 vt (épingle) push ou drive in; (chapeau) push down; (porte) break down. ● vi sink. □ **s'~** vpr sink (**dans** into).

enfouir /ɑ̃fwiʀ/ 2 vt bury.

enfourcher /ɑ̃fuʀʃe/ 1 vt mount.

enfreindre /ɑ̃fʀɛ̃dʀ/ 22 vt infringe, break.

enfuir (s') /(s)ɑ̃fɥiʀ/ 35 vpr run away.

enfumé, ~e /ɑ̃fyme/ adj filled with smoke.

engagé, ~e /ɑ̃gaʒe/ adj committed.

engagement /ɑ̃gaʒmɑ̃/ nm (promesse) promise; (Pol, Comm) commitment.

engager /ɑ̃gaʒe/ 40 vt (lier) bind, commit; (embaucher) take on; (commencer) start; (introduire) insert; (investir) invest. □ **s'~** vpr (promettre) commit oneself; (commencer) start; (soldat) enlist; (concurrent) enter; **s'~ à faire** undertake to do; **s'~ dans** (voie) enter.

engelure /ɑ̃ʒlyʀ/ nf chilblain.

engendrer /ɑ̃ʒɑ̃dʀe/ 1 vt (causer) generate.

engin /ɑ̃ʒɛ̃/ nm device; (véhicule) vehicle; (missile) missile.

engloutir /ɑ̃glutiʀ/ 2 vt swallow (up).

engouement /ɑ̃gumɑ̃/ nm passion.

engouffrer /ɑ̃gufʀe/ 1 vt 1 gobble up. □ **s'~ dans** vpr rush in.

engourdir /ɑ̃guʀdiʀ/ 2 vt numb. □ **s'~** vpr go numb.

engrais /ɑ̃gʀɛ/ nm manure; (chimique) fertilizer.

engrenage /ɑ̃gʀənaʒ/ nm gears (+ pl); (fig) spiral.

engueuler /ɑ̃gœle/ 1 ✖ vt shout at. □ **s'~** vpr have a row.

enhardir (s') /(s)ɑ̃aʀdiʀ/ 2 vpr become bolder.

énième /ɛnjɛm/ adj umpteenth.

énigmatique /enigmatik/ adj enigmatic. **énigme** nf enigma; (devinette) riddle.

enivrer /ɑ̃nivʀe/ 1 vt intoxicate. □ **s'~** vpr get intoxicated.

enjambée /ɑ̃ʒɑ̃be/ nf stride. **enjamber** 1 vt step over; (pont) span.

enjeu (pl **~x**) /ɑ̃ʒø/ nm stake.

enjoué, ~e /ɑ̃ʒwe/ adj cheerful.

enlacer /ɑ̃lase/ 10 vt entwine.

enlèvement /ɑ̃lɛvmɑ̃/ nm (de colis) removal; (d'ordures) collection; (rapt) kidnapping.

enlever /ɑ̃lve/ 6 vt remove (**à** from); (vêtement) take off; (tache, organe)

e

take out, remove; (kidnapper) kidnap; (gagner) win.

enliser (s') /(s)ālize/ **1** vpr get bogged down.

enneigé, ~e /āneʒe/ adj snow-covered.

ennemi, ~e /ɛnmi/ adj & nm enemy; **~ de** (fig) hostile to.

ennui /ānɥi/ nm problem; (tracas) boredom; **s'attirer des ~s** run into trouble.

ennuyer /ānɥije/ **31** vt bore; (irriter) annoy; (préoccuper) worry; **si cela ne t'ennuie pas** if you don't mind. ☐ **s'~** vpr get bored.

ennuyeux, -euse /ānɥijø, -z/ adj boring; (fâcheux) annoying.

énoncé /enõse/ nm wording, text; (Gram) utterance.

énoncer /enõse/ **10** vt express, state.

enorgueillir (s') /(s)ānɔʀɡœjiʀ/ **2** vpr **s'~ de** pride oneself on.

énorme /enɔʀm/ adj enormous.

enquête /ākɛt/ nf (Jur) investigation, inquiry; (sondage) survey; **mener l'~** lead the inquiry. **enquêter** **1** vi **~ (sur)** investigate. **enquêteur, -euse** nm, f investigator.

enquiquinant, ~e /ākikinā, -t/ adj **1** irritating.

enraciné, ~e /āʀasine/ adj deep rooted.

enragé, ~e /āʀaʒe/ adj furious; (chien) rabid; (fig) fanatical.

enrager /āʀaʒe/ **40** vi be furious; **faire ~ qn** annoy sb.

enregistrement /āʀ(ə)ʒistʀəmã/ nm recording; (des bagages) check-in. **enregistrer** **1** vt (Mus, TV) record; (mémoriser) take in; (bagages) check in.

enrhumer (s') /(s)āʀyme/ **1** vpr catch a cold.

enrichir /āʀiʃiʀ/ **2** vt enrich. ☐ **s'~** vpr grow rich(er). **enrichissant, ~e** adj (expérience) rewarding.

enrober /āʀɔbe/ **1** vt coat (**de** with).

enrôler /āʀole/ **1** vt recruit. ☐ **s'~** vpr enlist, enrol.

enroué, ~e /āʀwe/ adj hoarse.

enrouler /āʀule/ **1** vt wind, wrap. ☐ **s'~** vpr wind; **s'~ dans une couverture** roll oneself up in a blanket.

ensanglanté, ~e /āsāglāte/ adj bloodstained.

enseignant, ~e /āsɛɲā, -t/ nm, f teacher. ● adj teaching.

enseigne /āsɛɲ/ nf sign.

enseignement /āsɛɲəmã/ nm (profession) teaching; (instruction) education.

enseigner /āsɛɲe/ **1** vt/i teach; **~ qch à qn** teach sb sth.

ensemble /āsābl/ adv together. ● nm group; (Mus) ensemble; (vêtements) outfit; (cohésion) unity; (maths) set; **dans l'~** on the whole; **d'~** (idée) general; **l'~ de** (totalité) all of, the whole of.

ensevelir /āsəvliʀ/ **2** vt bury.

ensoleillé, ~e /āsɔleje/ adj sunny.

ensorceler /āsɔʀsəle/ **38** vt bewitch.

ensuite /āsɥit/ adv next, then; (plus tard) later.

ensuivre (s') /(s)āsɥivʀ/ **57** vpr follow; **et tout ce qui s'ensuit** and all the rest of it.

entaille /ātaj/ nf cut; (profonde) gash; (encoche) notch.

entamer /ātame/ **1** vt start; (inciser) cut into; (ébranler) shake.

entasser /ātase/ **1** vt (livres) pile; (argent) hoard; (personnes) cram (**dans** into). ☐ **s'~** vpr (objets) pile up (**dans** into); (personnes) squeeze (**dans** into).

entendement /ātādmã/ nm understanding; **ça dépasse l'~** it's beyond belief.

entendre /ātādʀ/ **3** vt hear; (comprendre) understand; (vouloir dire) mean; **~ parler de** hear of; **~ dire que** hear that. ☐ **s'~** vpr (être d'accord) agree; **s'~ (bien)** get on (**avec** with); **cela s'entend** of course.

entendu, ~e /ātādy/ adj (convenu) agreed; (sourire, air) knowing; **bien ~** of course; **(c'est) ~!** all right!

entente /ātāt/ nf understanding; **bonne ~** good relationship.

enterrement /ātɛʀmã/ nm funeral.

enterrer /āteʀe/ **1** vt bury.

en-tête /ātɛt/ nm heading; **à ~** headed.

entêté, ~e /ātete/ adj stubborn. **entêtement** nm stubbornness. **entêter (s')** **1** vpr persist (**à, dans** in).

enthousiasme /ātuzjasm/ nm enthusiasm. **enthousiasmer** **1** vt fill with

enthusiasm. **enthousiaste** *adj* enthusiastic.

enticher (s') /(s)ɑ̃tiʃe/ **1** *vpr* **s'~ de**
become infatuated with.

entier, -ière /ɑ̃tje, -jɛʀ/ *adj* whole; (absolu) absolute; (entêté) unyielding.
● *nm* whole; **en ~** entirely.

entonnoir /ɑ̃tɔnwaʀ/ *nm* funnel;
(trou) crater.

entorse /ɑ̃tɔʀs/ *nf* sprain; (fig) **~ à**
(loi) infringement of.

entortiller /ɑ̃tɔʀtije/ **1** *vt* wind, wrap
(**autour** around); (duper **1**) get
round.

entourage /ɑ̃tuʀaʒ/ *nm* circle of family and friends; (bordure) surround.

entouré, ~e /ɑ̃tuʀe/ *adj* (personne)
supported.

entourer /ɑ̃tuʀe/ **1** *vt* surround (**de**
with); (réconforter) rally round; **~ qch
de mystère** shroud sth in mystery.

entracte /ɑ̃tʀakt/ *nm* interval.

entraide /ɑ̃tʀɛd/ *nf* mutual aid. **en-
traider (s')** **1** *vpr* help each other.

entrain /ɑ̃tʀɛ̃/ *nm* zest, spirit.

entraînement /ɑ̃tʀɛnmɑ̃/ *nm* (Sport)
training.

entraîner /ɑ̃tʀene/ **1** *vt* (emporter)
carry away; (provoquer) lead to;
(Sport) train; (actionner) drive. □ **s'~**
vpr train. **entraîneur** *nm* trainer.

entrave /ɑ̃tʀav/ *nf* hindrance. **entraver** **1** *vt* hinder.

entre /ɑ̃tʀ(ə)/ *prép* between; (parmi)
among(st); **~ autres** among other
things; **l'un d'~ nous/eux** one of
us/them.

entrebâillé, ~e /ɑ̃tʀəbaje/ *adj* ajar,
half-open.

entrechoquer (s') /(s)ɑ̃tʀəʃɔke/ **1**
vpr knock against each other.

entrecôte /ɑ̃tʀəkot/ *nf* rib steak.

entrecouper /ɑ̃tʀəkupe/ **1** *vt* **~ de**
intersperse with.

entrecroiser (s') /(s)ɑ̃tʀəkʀwaze/ **1**
vpr (routes) intertwine.

entrée /ɑ̃tʀe/ *nf* entrance; (vestibule)
hall; (accès) admission, entry; (billet)
ticket; (Culin) starter; (Ordinat) **tapez
sur E~** press Enter; **'~ interdite'** 'no
entry'.

entrejambes /ɑ̃tʀəʒɑ̃b/ *nm* crotch.

entremets /ɑ̃tʀəmɛ/ *nm* dessert.

entremise /ɑ̃tʀəmiz/ *nf* intervention;
par l'~ de through.

entreposer /ɑ̃tʀəpoze/ **1** *vt* store.

entrepôt /ɑ̃tʀəpo/ *nm* warehouse.

entreprenant, ~e /ɑ̃tʀəpʀənɑ̃, -t/ *adj*
(actif) enterprising; (séducteur)
forward.

entreprendre /ɑ̃tʀəpʀɑ̃dʀ/ **50** *vt* start
on, undertake; (personne) buttonhole;
~ de faire undertake to do.

entrepreneur /ɑ̃tʀəpʀənœʀ/ *nm* (de
bâtiment) contractor; (chef d'entreprise) firm manager.

entreprise /ɑ̃tʀəpʀiz/ *nf* (projet)
undertaking; (société) firm, business,
company.

entrer /ɑ̃tʀe/ **1** *vi* (aux être) go in,
enter; (venir) come in, enter; **~ dans**
go ou come into, enter; (club) join; **~
en collision** collide (**avec** with); **faire
~** (personne) show in; **laisser ~** let
in; **~ en guerre** go to war. ● *vt* (données) enter.

entre-temps /ɑ̃tʀətɑ̃/ *adv* meanwhile.

entretenir /ɑ̃tʀət(ə)niʀ/ **58** *vt* (appareil) maintain; (vêtement) look after;
(alimenter) (feu) keep going; (amitié)
keep alive; **~ qn de** converse with sb
about. □ **s'~** *vpr* speak (**de** about;
avec to). **entretien** *nm* maintenance;
(discussion) talk; (pour un emploi)
interview.

entrevoir /ɑ̃tʀəvwaʀ/ **63** *vt* make out;
(brièvement) glimpse.

entrevue /ɑ̃tʀəvy/ *nf* meeting.

entrouvert, ~e /ɑ̃tʀuvɛʀ, -t/ *adj* ajar,
half-open.

énumération /enymeʀasjɔ̃/ *nf* enu-
meration. **énumérer** **14** *vt* enumerate.

envahir /ɑ̃vaiʀ/ **2** *vt* invade, overrun;
(douleur, peur) overcome.

enveloppe /ɑ̃vlɔp/ *nf* envelope; (emballage) wrapping; **~ budgétaire**
budget. **envelopper** **1** *vt* wrap (up);
(fig) envelop.

envergure /ɑ̃vɛʀgyʀ/ *nf* wingspan;
(importance) scope; (qualité) calibre.

envers /ɑ̃vɛʀ/ *prép* toward(s), to. ● *nm*
(de tissu) wrong side; **à l'~** (tableau)
upside down; (devant derrière) back
to front; (chaussette) inside out.

envie /ɑ̃vi/ *nf* urge; (jalousie) envy;
avoir ~ de qch feel like sth; **avoir ~
de faire** want to do; (moins urgent)

e

feel like doing; **faire ∼ à qn** make sb envious.

envier /ãvje/ 45 *vt* envy. **envieux, -ieuse** *adj* envious.

environ /ãviʀɔ̃/ *adv* about.

environnant, ∼e /ãviʀɔnã, -t/ *adj* surrounding.

environnement /ãviʀɔnmã/ *nm* environment.

environs /ãviʀɔ̃/ *nmpl* vicinity; **aux ∼ de** (*lieu*) in the vicinity of; (*heure*) round about.

envisager /ãvizaʒe/ 40 *vt* consider; (*imaginer*) envisage; **∼ de faire** consider doing.

envoi /ãvwa/ *nm* dispatch; (*paquet*) consignment; **faire un ∼** send; **coup d'∼** (Sport) kick-off.

envoler (s') /(s)ãvɔle/ 1 *vpr* fly away; (*avion*) take off; (*papiers*) blow away.

envoyé, ∼e /ãvwaje/ *nm, f* envoy; **∼ spécial** special correspondent.

envoyer /ãvwaje/ 32 *vt* send; (*lancer*) throw.

éolienne /eɔljɛn/ *nf* windmill; **ferme d'∼s** wind farm.

épais, ∼se /epɛ, -s/ *adj* thick. **épaisseur** *nf* thickness.

épaissir /epesiʀ/ 2 *vt/i* thicken. □ **s'∼** *vpr* thicken; (*mystère*) deepen.

épanoui, ∼e /epanwi/ *adj* (*personne*) beaming, radiant.

épanouir (s') /(s)epanwiʀ/ 2 *vpr* (*fleur*) open out; (*visage*) beam; (*personne*) blossom. **épanouissement** *nm* (*éclat*) blossoming, full bloom.

épargne /epaʀɲ/ *nf* savings.

épargner /epaʀɲe/ 1 *vt/i* save; (ne pas tuer) spare; **∼ qch à qn** spare sb sth.

éparpiller /epaʀpije/ 1 *vt* scatter. □ **s'∼** *vpr* scatter; (*fig*) dissipate one's efforts.

épars, ∼e /epaʀ, -s/ *adj* scattered.

épatant, ∼e /epatã, -t/ *adj* 🅸 amazing.

épaule /epol/ *nf* shoulder.

épave /epav/ *nf* wreck.

épée /epe/ *nf* sword.

épeler /eple/ 6 *vt* spell.

éperdu, ∼e /epɛʀdy/ *adj* wild, frantic.

éperon /epʀɔ̃/ *nm* spur.

éphémère /efemɛʀ/ *adj* ephemeral.

épi /epi/ *nm* (de blé) ear; (mèche) tuft of hair; **∼ de maïs** corn cob.

épice /epis/ *nf* spice. **épicé, ∼e** *adj* spicy.

épicerie /episʀi/ *nf* grocery shop; (produits) groceries. **épicier, -ière** *nm, f* grocer.

épidémie /epidemi/ *nf* epidemic.

épiderme /epidɛʀm/ *nm* skin.

épier /epje/ 45 *vt* spy on.

épilepsie /epilɛpsi/ *nf* epilepsy. **épileptique** *adj & nmf* epileptic.

épiler /epile/ 1 *vt* remove unwanted hair from; (*sourcils*) pluck.

épilogue /epilɔg/ *nm* epilogue; (fig) outcome.

épinard /epinaʀ/ *nm* **∼s** spinach (+ *sg*).

épine /epin/ *nf* thorn, prickle; (d'animal) prickle, spine; **∼ dorsale** backbone. **épineux, -euse** *adj* thorny.

épingle /epɛ̃gl/ *nf* pin; **∼ de nourrice**, **∼ de sûreté** safety-pin.

épisode /epizɔd/ *nm* episode; **à ∼s** serialized.

épitaphe /epitaf/ *nf* epitaph.

épluche-légumes /eplyʃlegym/ *nm inv* (potato) peeler.

éplucher /eplyʃe/ 1 *vt* peel; (examiner: fig) scrutinize.

épluchure /eplyʃyʀ/ *nf* **∼s** peelings.

éponge /epɔ̃ʒ/ *nf* sponge. **éponger** 40 *vt* (*liquide*) mop up; (*surface, front*) mop; (*fig*) (*dettes*) wipe out.

épopée /epɔpe/ *nf* epic.

époque /epɔk/ *nf* time, period; **à l'∼** at the time; **d'∼** period.

épouse /epuz/ *nf* wife.

épouser /epuze/ 1 *vt* marry; (*forme, idée*) adopt.

épousseter /epuste/ 38 *vt* dust.

épouvantable /epuvãtabl/ *adj* appalling.

épouvantail /epuvãtaj/ *nm* scarecrow.

épouvante /epuvãt/ *nf* terror. **épouvanter** 1 *vt* terrify.

époux /epu/ *nm* husband; **les ∼** the married couple.

éprendre (s') /(s)epʀãdʀ/ 50 *vpr* **s'∼ de** fall in love with.

épreuve /epʀœv/ *nf* test; (Sport) event; (*malheur*) ordeal; (Photo, d'imprimerie) proof; **mettre à l'~** put to the test.

éprouver /epʀuve/ **1** vt (ressentir) experience; (affliger) distress; (tester) test.

éprouvette /epʀuvɛt/ nf test tube.

EPS abrév f (**éducation physique et sportive**) PE.

épuisé, ~e /epɥize/ adj exhausted; (livre) out of print. **épuisement** nm exhaustion.

épuiser /epɥize/ **1** vt (fatiguer, user) exhaust. □ **s'~** vpr become exhausted.

épuration /epyʀasjɔ̃/ nf purification; (Pol) purge. **épurer 1** vt purify; (Pol) purge.

équateur /ekwatœʀ/ nm equator.

équilibre /ekilibʀ/ nm balance; **être ou se tenir en ~** (personne) balance; (objet) be balanced. **équilibré, ~e** adj well-balanced.

équilibrer /ekilibʀe/ **1** vt balance. □ **s'~** vpr balance each other.

équilibriste /ekilibʀist/ nmf acrobat.

équipage /ekipaʒ/ nm crew.

équipe /ekip/ nf team; **~ de nuit/ jour** night/day shift.

équipé, ~e /ekipe/ adj equipped; **cuisine ~e** fitted kitchen.

équipement /ekipmɑ̃/ nm equipment; **~s** (installations) amenities, facilities.

équiper /ekipe/ **1** vt equip (**de** with). □ **s'~** vpr equip oneself.

équipier, -ière /ekipje, -jɛʀ/ nm, f team member.

équitable /ekitabl/ adj fair.

équitation /ekitasjɔ̃/ nf (horse-) riding.

équivalence /ekivalɑ̃s/ nf equivalence. **équivalent, ~e** adj equivalent.

équivaloir /ekivalwaʀ/ **60** vi **~ à** be equivalent to.

équivoque /ekivɔk/ adj equivocal; (louche) questionable. ● nf ambiguity.

érable /eʀabl/ nm maple.

érafler /eʀafle/ **1** vt scratch. **éraflure** nf scratch.

éraillé, ~e /eʀaje/ adj (voix) raucous.

ère /ɛʀ/ nf era.

éreintant, ~e /eʀɛ̃tɑ̃, -t/ adj exhausting. **éreinter (s')** **1** vpr wear oneself out.

ériger /eʀiʒe/ **40** vt erect. □ **s'~ en** vpr set (oneself) up as.

éroder /eʀɔde/ **1** vt erode. **érosion** nf erosion.

errer /eʀe/ **1** vi wander.

erreur /eʀœʀ/ nf mistake, error; **dans l'~** mistaken; **par ~** by mistake; **~ judiciaire** miscarriage of justice.

erroné, ~e /eʀɔne/ adj erroneous.

érudit, ~e /eʀydi, -t/ adj scholarly. ● nm, f scholar.

éruption /eʀypsjɔ̃/ nf eruption; (Méd) rash.

es /ɛ/ ➡ÊTRE **4**.

escabeau (pl **~x**) /ɛskabo/ nm stepladder.

escadron /ɛskadʀɔ̃/ nm (Mil) company.

escalade /ɛskalad/ nf climbing; (Pol, Comm) escalation. **escalader 1** vt climb.

escale /ɛskal/ nf (d'avion) stopover; (port) port of call; **faire ~ à** (avion, passager) stop over at; (navire, passager) put in at.

escalier /ɛskalje/ nm stairs (+ pl); **~ mécanique ou roulant** escalator.

escalope /ɛskalɔp/ nf escalope.

escargot /ɛskaʀgo/ nm snail.

escarpé, ~e /ɛskaʀpe/ adj steep.

escarpin /ɛskaʀpɛ̃/ nm court shoe; (US) pump.

escient: à bon ~ /abɔnesjɑ̃/ loc wisely.

esclandre /ɛsklɑ̃dʀ/ nm scene.

esclavage /ɛsklavaʒ/ nm slavery. **esclave** nmf slave.

escompte /ɛskɔ̃t/ nm discount. **escompter 1** vt expect; (Comm) discount.

escorte /ɛskɔʀt/ nf escort.

escrime /ɛskʀim/ nf fencing.

escroc /ɛskʀo/ nm swindler.

escroquer /ɛskʀɔke/ **1** vt swindle; **~ qch à qn** swindle sb out of sth. **escroquerie** nf swindle.

espace /ɛspas/ nm space; **~s verts** gardens and parks.

espacer /ɛspase/ **10** vt space out. □ **s'~** vpr become less frequent.

espadrille /ɛspadʀij/ nf rope sandal.

Espagne /ɛspaɲ/ nf Spain.

espagnol, ~e /ɛspaɲɔl/ *adj* Spanish.
● *nm* (Ling) Spanish. **E~,** ~**e** *nm, f*
Spaniard.

espèce /ɛspɛs/ *nf* kind, sort; (race) species; **en** ~**s** (*argent*) in cash; ~ **d'i-**
diot! 🖙 you idiot! 🖙.

espérance /ɛspeRɑ̃s/ *nf* hope.

espérer /ɛspeRe/ 🔢 *vt* hope for; ~
faire/que hope to do/that. ● *vi* hope.

espiègle /ɛspjɛgl/ *adj* mischievous.

espion, ~**ne** /ɛspjɔ̃, -ɔn/ *nm, f* spy. **es-**
pionnage *nm* espionage, spying. **es-**
pionner 🔢 *vt* spy (on).

espoir /ɛspwaR/ *nm* hope; **reprendre**
~ feel hopeful again.

esprit /ɛspRi/ *nm* (intellect) mind; (humour) wit; (fantôme) spirit; (ambiance) atmosphere; **perdre l'**~ lose
one's mind; **reprendre ses** ~**s** come
to; **faire de l'**~ try to be witty.

esquimau, ~**de** (*mpl* ~**x**) /ɛskimo,
-d/ *nm, f* Eskimo.

esquinter /ɛskɛ̃te/ 🔢 *vt* 🖙 ruin.

esquisse /ɛskis/ *nf* sketch; (fig)
outline.

esquiver /ɛskive/ 🔢 *vt* dodge. □ **s'**~
vpr slip away.

essai /esɛ/ *nm* (épreuve) test, trial;
(tentative) try; (article) essay; (au
rugby) try; ~**s** (Auto) qualifying round
(+ *sg*); **à l'**~ on trial.

essaim /esɛ̃/ *nm* swarm.

essayage /esɛjaʒ/ *nm* fitting; **salon**
d'~ fitting room.

essayer /eseje/ 🔢 *vt/i* try; (vêtement)
try (on); (voiture) try (out); ~ **de faire**
try to do.

essence /esɑ̃s/ *nf* (carburant) petrol;
(nature, extrait) essence; ~ **sans**
plomb unleaded petrol.

essentiel, ~**le** /esɑ̃sjɛl/ *adj* essential.
● *nm* **l'**~ the main thing; (quantité)
the main part.

essieu (*pl* ~**x**) /esjø/ *nm* axle.

essor /esɔR/ *nm* expansion; **prendre**
son ~ expand.

essorage /esɔRaʒ/ *nm* spin drying. **es-**
sorer 🔢 *vt* (linge) spin-dry; (en tor-
dant) wring.

essoreuse /esɔRøz/ *nf* spin-drier; ~ **à**
salade salad spinner.

essoufflé, ~**e** /ɛsufle/ *adj* out of
breath.

essuie-glace /esɥiglas/ *nm inv* windscreen wiper.

essuie-mains /esɥimɛ̃/ *nm inv* hand-
towel.

essuie-tout /esɥitu/ *nm inv* kitchen
paper.

essuyer /esɥije/ 🔢 *vt* wipe; (subir)
suffer. □ **s'**~ *vpr* dry *ou* wipe oneself.

est[1] /ɛ/ ➔**ÊTRE** 🔢.

est[2] /ɛst/ *nm* east. ● *adj inv* east; (partie) eastern; (direction) easterly.

estampe /ɛstɑ̃p/ *nf* print.

esthète /ɛstɛt/ *nmf* aesthete.

esthéticienne /ɛstetisjɛn/ *nf*
beautician.

esthétique /ɛstetik/ *adj* aesthetic.

estimation /ɛstimasjɔ̃/ *nf* (de coûts)
estimate; (valeur) valuation.

estime /ɛstim/ *nf* esteem.

estimer /ɛstime/ 🔢 *vt* (tableau) value;
(calculer) estimate; (respecter) esteem; (considérer) consider (**que** that).

estival, ~**e** (*mpl* **-aux**) /ɛstival, -o/ *adj*
summer. **estivant,** ~**e** *nm, f* summer
visitor.

estomac /ɛstɔma/ *nm* stomach.

estomaqué, ~**e** /ɛstɔmake/ *adj* 🖙
stunned.

Estonie /ɛstɔni/ *nf* Estonia.

estrade /ɛstRad/ *nf* platform.

estragon /ɛstRagɔ̃/ *nm* tarragon.

estropié, ~**e** /ɛstRɔpje/ *nm, f* cripple.
● *adj* crippled.

estuaire /ɛstɥɛR/ *nm* estuary.

et /e/ *conj* and; ~ **moi?** what about
me?; ~ **alors?** so what?

étable /etabl/ *nf* cow-shed.

établi, ~**e** /etabli/ *adj* established; **un**
fait bien ~ a well-established fact.
● *nm* work-bench.

établir /etabliR/ 🔢 *vt* establish; (liste,
facture) draw up; (personne, camp, record) set up. □ **s'**~ *vpr* (personne) settle; **s'**~ **à son compte** set up on
one's own.

établissement /etablismɑ̃/ *nm* (entreprise) organization; (institution) establishment; ~ **scolaire** school.

étage /etaʒ/ *nm* floor, storey; (de
fusée) stage; **à l'**~ upstairs; **au pre-**
mier ~ on the first floor.

étagère /etaʒɛR/ *nf* shelf; (meuble)
shelving unit.

étain /etɛ̃/ nm pewter.

étais, était /etɛ/ →ÊTRE **4**.

étalage /etalaʒ/ nm display; (vitrine) shop-window; **faire ~ de** flaunt. **étalagiste** nmf window-dresser.

étaler /etale/ **1** vt spread; (journal) spread (out); (pâte) roll out; (exposer) display; (richesse) flaunt. □ **s'~** vpr (prendre de la place) spread out; (tomber **1**) fall flat; **s'~ sur** (paiement) be spread over.

étalon /etalɔ̃/ nm (cheval) stallion; (modèle) standard.

étanche /etɑ̃ʃ/ adj watertight; (montre) waterproof.

étancher /etɑ̃ʃe/ **1** vt (soif) quench.

étang /etɑ̃/ nm pond.

étant /etɑ̃/ →ÊTRE **4**.

étape /etap/ nf stage; (lieu d'arrêt) stopover; (fig) stage.

état /eta/ nm state; (liste) statement; (métier) profession; **en bon/mauvais ~** in good/bad condition; **en ~ de** in a position to; **en ~ de marche** in working order; **faire ~ de** (citer) mention; **être dans tous ses ~s** be in a state; **~ civil** civil status; **~ des lieux** inventory of fixtures. **État** nm State.

état-major (pl **états-majors**) /etamaʒɔʀ/ nm (officiers) staff (+ pl).

États-Unis /etazyni/ nmpl **~ (d'Amérique)** United States (of America).

étau (pl **~x**) /eto/ nm vice.

étayer /eteje/ **31** vt prop up.

été¹ /ete/ →ÊTRE **4**.

été² /ete/ nm summer.

éteindre /etɛ̃dʀ/ **22** vt (feu) put out; (lumière, radio) turn off. □ **s'~** vpr (feu, lumière) go out; (appareil) go off; (mourir) die. **éteint, ~e** adj (feu) out; (volcan) extinct.

étendard /etɑ̃daʀ/ nm standard.

étendre /etɑ̃dʀ/ **3** vt (nappe) spread (out); (bras, jambes) stretch (out); (linge) hang out; (agrandir) extend. □ **s'~** vpr (s'allonger) lie down; (se propager) spread; (plaine) stretch; **s'~ sur** (sujet) dwell on.

étendu, ~e /etɑ̃dy/ adj extensive. **étendue** nf area; (d'eau) stretch; (importance) extent.

éternel, ~le /etɛʀnɛl/ adj (vie) eternal; (fig) endless.

éterniser (s') /(s)etɛʀnize/ **1** vpr (durer) drag on.

éternité /etɛʀnite/ nf eternity.

éternuement /etɛʀnymɑ̃/ nm sneeze. **éternuer** **1** vi sneeze.

êtes /ɛt/ →ÊTRE **4**.

éthique /etik/ adj ethical. ● nf ethics (+ sg).

ethnie /ɛtni/ nf ethnic group. **ethnique** adj ethnic.

étincelant, ~e /etɛ̃slɑ̃, -t/ adj sparkling. **étinceler** **38** vi sparkle. **étincelle** nf spark.

étiqueter /etikte/ **38** vt label. **étiquette** nf label; (protocole) etiquette.

étirer /etiʀe/ **1** vt stretch. □ **s'~** vpr stretch.

étoffe /etɔf/ nf fabric.

étoffer /etɔfe/ **1** vt expand. □ **s'~** vpr fill out.

étoile /etwal/ nf star; **à la belle ~** in the open; **~ filante** shooting star; **~ de mer** starfish.

étonnant, ~e /etɔnɑ̃, -t/ adj (curieux) surprising; (formidable) amazing. **étonnement** nm surprise; (plus fort) amazement.

étonner /etɔne/ **1** vt amaze. □ **s'~** vpr be amazed (de at).

étouffant, ~e /etufɑ̃, -t/ adj stifling.

étouffer /etufe/ **1** vt/i suffocate; (sentiment, révolte) stifle; (feu) smother; (bruit) muffle; **on étouffe** it is stifling. □ **s'~** vpr suffocate; (en mangeant) choke.

étourderie /etuʀdəʀi/ nf thoughtlessness; (acte) careless mistake.

étourdi, ~e /etuʀdi/ adj absent-minded. ● nm, f scatterbrain.

étourdir /etuʀdiʀ/ **2** vt stun; (fatiguer) make sb's head spin. **étourdissant, ~e** adj stunning.

étourneau (pl **~x**) /etuʀno/ nm starling.

étrange /etʀɑ̃ʒ/ adj strange.

étranger, -ère /etʀɑ̃ʒe, -ɛʀ/ adj (inconnu) strange, unfamiliar; (d'un autre pays) foreign. ● nm, f foreigner; (inconnu) stranger; **à l'~** abroad; **de l'~** from abroad.

étrangler /etʀɑ̃gle/ **1** vt strangle; (col) throttle. □ **s'~** vpr choke.

être /ɛtʀ/ **4**

● *verbe auxiliaire*

····▸ (du passé) have; **elle est partie/venue hier** she left/came yesterday.

····▸ (de la voix passive) be.

● *verbe intransitif (aux avoir)*

····▸ be; ~ **médecin** be a doctor; **je suis à vous** I'm all yours; **j'en suis à me demander si...** I'm beginning to wonder whether...; **qu'en est-il de...?** what's the news about...?

····▸ (appartenance) be, belong to.

····▸ (heure, date) be; **nous sommes le 3 mars** it's March 3.

····▸ (aller) be; **je n'y ai jamais été** I've never been; **il a été le voir** he went to see him.

····▸ **c'est** it is *or* it's; **c'est moi qui l'ai fait** I did it; **est-ce que tu veux du thé?** do you want some tea?

● *nom masculin*

····▸ being; ~ **humain** human being.

····▸ (personne) person; **un ~ cher** a loved one.

étreindre /etʀɛ̃dʀ/ **22** *vt* embrace. **étreinte** *nf* embrace.

étrennes /etʀɛn/ *nfpl* (New Year's) gift (+ *sg*); (argent) money.

étrier /etʀije/ *nm* stirrup.

étriqué, ~e /etʀike/ *adj* tight.

étroit, ~e /etʀwa, -t/ *adj* narrow; (vêtement) tight; (liens, surveillance) close; **à l'~** cramped. **étroitement** *adv* closely. **étroitesse** *nf* narrowness.

étude /etyd/ *nf* study; (enquête) survey; (bureau) office; **(salle d')~** (Scol) prep room; **à l'~** under consideration; **faire des ~s (de)** study; **il n'a pas fait d'~s** he didn't go to university; **~ de marché** market research.

étudiant, ~e /etydjã, -t/ *nm, f* student.

étudier /etydje/ **45** *vt/i* study.

étui /etɥi/ *nm* case.

étuve /etyv/ *nf* steam room.

eu, ~e /y/ →**AVOIR** **5**.

euro /øʀo/ *nm* euro.

Europe /øʀɔp/ *nf* Europe.

européen, ~ne /øʀɔpeɛ̃, -eɛn/ *adj* European. **E~, ~ne** *nm, f* European.

euthanasie /øtanazi/ *nf* euthanasia.

eux /ø/ *pron* they; (complément) them. **eux-mêmes** *pron* themselves.

évacuation /evakɥasjɔ̃/ *nf* evacuation; (d'eaux usées) discharge. **évacuer** **1** *vt* evacuate.

évadé, ~e /evade/ *adj* escaped. ● *nm, f* escaped prisoner. **évader (s')** **1** *vpr* escape.

évaluation /evalɥasjɔ̃/ *nf* assessment. **évaluer** **1** *vt* assess.

évangile /evãʒil/ *nm* gospel; **l'É~** the Gospel.

évanouir (s') /(s)evanwiʀ/ **2** *vpr* faint; (disparaître) vanish.

évaporation /evapɔʀasjɔ̃/ *nf* evaporation. **évaporer (s')** **1** *vpr* evaporate.

évasif, -ive /evazif, -v/ *adj* evasive.

évasion /evazjɔ̃/ *nf* escape.

éveil /evɛj/ *nm* awakening; **en ~** alert.

éveillé, ~e /eveje/ *adj* awake; (intelligent) alert.

éveiller /eveje/ **1** *vt* awake(n); (susciter) arouse. □ **s'~** *vpr* awake.

événement /evɛnmã/ *nm* event.

éventail /evãtaj/ *nm* fan; (gamme) range.

éventrer /evãtʀe/ **1** *vt* (sac) rip open.

éventualité /evãtɥalite/ *nf* possibility; **dans cette ~** in that event.

éventuel, ~le /evãtɥɛl/ *adj* possible. **éventuellement** *adv* possibly.

évêque /evɛk/ *nm* bishop.

évertuer (s') /(s)evɛʀtɥe/ **1** *vpr* **s'~ à** struggle hard to.

éviction /eviksjɔ̃/ *nf* eviction.

évidemment /evidamã/ *adv* obviously; (bien sûr) of course.

évidence /evidãs/ *nf* obviousness; (fait) obvious fact; **être en ~** be conspicuous; **mettre en ~** (fait) highlight. **évident, ~e** *adj* obvious, evident.

évier /evje/ *nm* sink.

évincer /evɛ̃se/ **10** *vt* oust.

éviter /evite/ **1** *vt* avoid (**de faire** doing); **~ qch à qn** (dérangement) save sb sth.

évocateur, -trice /evɔkatœʀ, -tʀis/ *adj* evocative. **évocation** *nf* evocation.

évolué, ~e /evɔlɥe/ adj highly developed.

évoluer /evɔlɥe/ **1** vi evolve; (situation) develop; (se déplacer) glide. **évolution** nf evolution; (d'une situation) development.

évoquer /evɔke/ **1** vt call to mind, evoke.

exacerber /ɛgzasɛʀbe/ **1** vt exacerbate.

exact, ~e /ɛgza(kt), -akt/ adj (précis) exact, accurate; (juste) correct; (personne) punctual. **exactement** adv exactly. **exactitude** nf exactness; punctuality.

ex æquo /ɛgzeko/ adv **être** ~ **tie** (**avec qn** with sb).

exagération /ɛgzaʒeʀasjɔ̃/ nf exaggeration. **exagéré,** ~e adj excessive.

exagérer /ɛgzaʒeʀe/ **14** vt/i exaggerate; (abuser) go too far.

exalté, ~e /ɛgzalte/ nm, f fanatic. **exalter** **1** vt excite; (glorifier) exalt.

examen /ɛgzamɛ̃/ nm examination; (Scol) exam. **examinateur, -trice** nm, f examiner. **examiner** **1** vt examine.

exaspération /ɛgzaspeʀasjɔ̃/ nf exasperation. **exaspérer** **14** vt exasperate.

exaucer /ɛgzose/ **10** vt grant; (personne) grant the wish(es) of.

excédent /ɛksedɑ̃/ nm surplus; ~ **de bagages** excess luggage; ~ **de la balance commerciale** trade surplus. **excédentaire** adj excess, surplus.

excéder /ɛksede/ **14** vt (dépasser) exceed; (agacer) irritate.

excellence /ɛksɛlɑ̃s/ nf excellence. **excellent,** ~e adj excellent. **exceller** **1** vi excel (**dans** in).

excentricité /ɛksɑ̃tʀisite/ nf eccentricity. **excentrique** adj & nmf eccentric.

excepté, ~e /ɛksɛpte/ adj & prép except.

excepter /ɛksɛpte/ **1** vt except.

exception /ɛksɛpsjɔ̃/ nf exception; **à l'**~ **de** except for; **d'**~ exceptional; **faire** ~ be an exception. **exceptionnel,** ~**le** adj exceptional. **exceptionnellement** adv exceptionally.

excès /ɛksɛ/ nm excess; ~ **de vitesse** speeding.

excessif, -ive /ɛksesif, -v/ adj excessive.

excitant, ~e /ɛksitɑ̃, -t/ adj stimulating; (palpitant) exciting. ● nm stimulant.

exciter /ɛksite/ **1** vt excite; (irriter) get excited. □ **s'**~ vpr get excited.

exclamer (s') /(s)ɛksklame/ **1** vpr exclaim.

exclure /ɛksklyʀ/ **16** vt exclude; (expulser) expel; (empêcher) preclude.

exclusif, -ive /ɛksklyzif, -v/ adj exclusive.

exclusion /ɛksklyzjɔ̃/ nf exclusion.

exclusivité /ɛkslyzivite/ nf (Comm) exclusive rights (+ pl); **projeter en** ~ show exclusively.

excursion /ɛkskyʀsjɔ̃/ nf excursion; (à pied) hike.

excuse /ɛkskyz/ nf excuse; ~**s** apology (+ sg); **faire des** ~**s** apologize.

excuser /ɛkskyze/ **1** vt excuse; **excusez-moi** excuse me. □ **s'**~ vpr apologize (**de** for).

exécrable /ɛgzekʀabl/ adj dreadful. **exécrer** **14** vt loathe.

exécuter /ɛgzekyte/ **1** vt carry out, execute; (Mus) perform; (tuer) execute.

exécutif, -ive /ɛgzekytif, -v/ adj & nm (Pol) executive.

exécution /ɛgzekysjɔ̃/ nf execution; (Mus) performance.

exemplaire /ɛgzɑ̃plɛʀ/ adj exemplary. ● nm copy.

exemple /ɛgzɑ̃pl/ nm example; **par** ~ for example; **donner l'**~ set an example.

exempt, ~e /ɛgzɑ̃, -t/ adj ~ **de** exempt (**de** from).

exempter /ɛgzɑ̃te/ **1** vt exempt (**de** from). **exemption** nf exemption.

exercer /ɛgzɛʀse/ **10** vt exercise; (influence, contrôle) exert; (former) train, exercise; ~ **un métier** have a job; ~ **le métier de...** work as a... □ **s'**~ vpr practise.

exercice /ɛgzɛʀsis/ nm exercise; (de métier) practice; **en** ~ in office; (médecin) in practice.

exhaler /ɛgzale/ **1** vt emit.

exhaustif, -ive /ɛgzostif, -v/ adj exhaustive.

exhiber /ɛgzibe/ **1** vt exhibit.

exhorter /ɛgzɔʀte/ **1** vt exhort (**à** to).

exigeant, ~e /ɛgziʒɑ̃, -t/ *adj* demanding; **être ~ avec qn** demand a lot of sb. **exigence** *nf* demand. **exiger** 40 *vt* demand.

exigu, ~ë /ɛgzigy/ *adj* tiny.

exil /ɛgzil/ *nm* exile. **exilé, ~e** *nm, f* exile.

exiler /ɛgzile/ 1 *vt* exile. □ **s'~** *vpr* go into exile.

existence /ɛgzistɑ̃s/ *nf* existence. **exister** 1 *vi* exist.

exode /ɛgzɔd/ *nm* exodus.

exonérer /ɛgzɔnere/ 14 *vt* exempt (**de** from).

exorbitant, ~e /ɛgzɔrbitɑ̃, -t/ *adj* exorbitant.

exorciser /ɛgzɔrsize/ 1 *vt* exorcize.

exotique /ɛgzɔtik/ *adj* exotic.

expansé, ~e /ɛkspɑ̃se/ *adj* (Tech) expanded.

expansif, -ive /ɛkspɑ̃sif, -v/ *adj* expansive. **expansion** *nf* expansion.

expatrié, ~e /ɛkspatrije/ *nm, f* expatriate.

expectative /ɛkspɛktativ/ *nf* **être dans l'~** wait and see.

expédient /ɛkspedjɑ̃/ *nm* expedient; **vivre d'~s** live by one's wits; **user d'~s** resort to expedients.

expédier /ɛkspedje/ 45 *vt* send, dispatch; (*tâche* 1) polish off. **expéditeur, -trice** *nm, f* sender.

expéditif, -ive /ɛkspeditif, -v/ *adj* quick.

expédition /ɛkspedisjɔ̃/ *nf* (envoi) dispatching; (voyage) expedition.

expérience /ɛksperjɑ̃s/ *nf* experience; (scientifique) experiment.

expérimental, ~e (*mpl* **-aux**) /ɛksperimɑ̃tal, o/ *adj* experimental. **expérimentation** *nf* experimentation. **expérimenté, ~e** *adj* experienced. **expérimenter** 1 *vt* test, experiment with.

expert, ~e /ɛkspɛr, -t/ *adj* expert. ● *nm* expert; (d'assurances) adjuster. **expert-comptable** (*pl* **experts-comptables**) *nm* accountant.

expertise /ɛkspɛrtiz/ *nf* valuation; (de dégâts) assessment. **expertiser** 1 *vt* value; (dégâts) assess.

expier /ɛkspje/ 45 *vt* atone for.

expiration /ɛkspirasjɔ̃/ *nf* expiry.

expirer /ɛkspire/ 1 *vi* breathe out; (finir, mourir) expire.

explicatif, -ive /ɛksplikatif, -v/ *adj* explanatory.

explication /ɛksplikasjɔ̃/ *nf* explanation; (fig) discussion; **~ de texte** (Scol) literary commentary.

explicite /ɛksplisit/ *adj* explicit.

expliquer /ɛksplike/ 1 *vt* explain. □ **s'~** *vpr* explain oneself; (discuter) discuss things; (être explicable) be understandable.

exploit /ɛksplwa/ *nm* exploit.

exploitant, ~e /ɛksplwatɑ̃, -t/ *nm, f* **~ (agricole)** farmer.

exploitation /ɛksplwatasjɔ̃/ *nf* exploitation; (d'entreprise) running; (ferme) farm.

exploiter /ɛksplwate/ 1 *vt* exploit; (*ferme*) run; (*mine*) work.

explorateur, -trice /ɛksplɔratœr, -tris/ *nm, f* explorer. **exploration** *nf* exploration. **explorer** 1 *vt* explore.

exploser /ɛksploze/ 1 *vi* explode; **faire ~** explode; (*bâtiment*) blow up.

explosif, -ive /ɛksplozif, -v/ *adj & nm* explosive. **explosion** *nf* explosion.

exportateur, -trice /ɛkspɔr- tatœr, -tris/ *nm, f* exporter. ● *adj* exporting. **exportation** *nf* export. **exporter** 1 *vt* export.

exposant, ~e /ɛkspozɑ̃, -t/ *nm, f* exhibitor.

exposé, ~e /ɛkspoze/ *nm* talk (**sur** on); (d'une action) account; **faire l'~ de la situation** give an account of the situation. ● *adj* **~ au nord** facing north.

exposer /ɛkspoze/ 1 *vt* display, show; (expliquer) explain; (soumettre, mettre en danger) expose (**à** to); (vie) endanger. □ **s'~ à** *vpr* expose oneself to.

exposition /ɛkspozisjɔ̃/ *nf* (d'art) exhibition; (de faits) exposition; (géographique) aspect.

exprès¹ /ɛksprɛ/ *adv* specially; (délibérément) on purpose.

exprès², -esse /ɛksprɛs/ *adj* express.

express /ɛksprɛs/ *adj & nm inv* (café) **~** espresso; (train) **~** fast train.

expressif, -ive /ɛkspresif, -v/ *adj* expressive. **expression** *nf* expression.

exprimer /ɛksprime/ 1 *vt* express. □ **s'~** *vpr* express oneself.

expulser /ɛkspylse/ **1** vt expel; (locataire) evict; (joueur) send off. **expulsion** nf (d'élève) expulsion; (de locataire) eviction; (d'immigré) deportation.

exquis, ~e /ɛkski, -z/ adj exquisite.

extase /ɛkstaz/ nf ecstasy.

extasier (s') /(s)ɛkstazje/ **45** vpr s'~ **sur** be ecstatic about.

extensible /ɛkstɑ̃sibl/ adj (tissu) stretch.

extension /ɛkstɑ̃sjɔ̃/ nf extension; (expansion) expansion.

exténuer /ɛkstenɥe/ **1** vt exhaust.

extérieur, ~e /ɛksteʀjœʀ/ adj outside; (signe, gaieté) outward; (politique) foreign. ● nm outside, exterior; (de personne) exterior; **à l'~ (de)** outside. **extérioriser** **1** vt show, externalize.

extermination /ɛkstɛʀminasjɔ̃/ nf extermination. **exterminer** **1** vt exterminate.

externe /ɛkstɛʀn/ adj external. ● nmf (Scol) day pupil.

extincteur /ɛkstɛ̃ktœʀ/ nm fire extinguisher.

extinction /ɛkstɛ̃ksjɔ̃/ nf extinction; **avoir une ~ de voix** have lost one's voice.

extorquer /ɛkstɔʀke/ **1** vt extort.

extra /ɛkstʀa/ adj inv first-rate. ● nm inv (repas) (special) treat.

extraction /ɛkstʀaksjɔ̃/ nf extraction.

extrader /ɛkstʀade/ **1** vt extradite.

extraire /ɛkstʀɛʀ/ **29** vt extract. **extrait** nm extract.

extraordinaire /ɛkstʀaɔʀdinɛʀ/ adj extraordinary.

extravagance /ɛkstʀavagɑ̃s/ nf extravagance. **extravagant, ~e** adj extravagant.

extraverti, ~e /ɛkstʀavɛʀti/ nm, f extrovert.

extrême /ɛkstʀɛm/ adj & nm extreme. **extrêmement** adv extremely.

Extrême-Orient /ɛkstʀɛmɔʀjɑ̃/ nm Far East.

extrémiste /ɛkstʀemist/ nmf extremist.

extrémité /ɛkstʀemite/ nf end; (mains, pieds) extremity.

exubérance /ɛgzybeʀɑ̃s/ nf exuberance. **exubérant, ~e** adj exuberant.

Ff

F abrév f (**franc, francs**) franc, francs.

fabricant, ~e /fabʀikɑ̃, -t/ nm, f manufacturer. **fabrication** nf making; manufacture.

fabrique /fabʀik/ nf factory. **fabriquer** **1** vt make; (industriellement) manufacture; (fig) make up.

fabuler /fabyle/ **1** vi fantasize.

fabuleux, -euse /fabylø, -z/ adj fabulous.

fac /fak/ nf **1** university.

façade /fasad/ nf front; (fig) façade.

face /fas/ nf face; (d'un objet) side; **en (~ de), d'en ~** opposite; **en ~ de** (fig) faced with; **~ à** facing; (fig) faced with; **faire ~ à** face. **face-à-face** nm inv (débat) one-to-one debate.

fâcher /faʃe/ **1** vt anger; **fâché** angry; (désolé) sorry. ◻ **se ~** vpr get angry; (se brouiller) fall out.

facile /fasil/ adj easy; (caractère) easygoing.

facilité /fasilite/ nf easiness; (aisance) ease; (aptitude) ability; **~s** (possibilités) facilities, opportunities; **~s d'importation** import opportunities; **~s de paiement** easy terms.

faciliter /fasilite/ **1** vt facilitate, make easier.

façon /fasɔ̃/ nf way; (de vêtement) cut; **de cette ~** in this way; **de ~ à** so as to; **de toute ~** anyway; **~s** (chichis) fuss; **faire des ~s** stand on ceremony; **sans ~s** (repas) informal; (personne) unpretentious. **façonner** **1** vt shape; (faire) make.

fac-similé (pl **~s**) /faksimile/ nm facsimile.

facteur, -trice /faktœʀ, -tʀis/ nm, f postman, postwoman. ● nm (élément) factor.

facture /faktyʀ/ nf bill; (Comm) invoice; **~ détaillée** itemized bill. **facturer** **1** vt invoice. **facturette** nf credit card slip.

facultatif, -ive /fakyltatif, -v/ adj optional.

faculté /fakylte/ nf faculty; (possibilité) power; (Univ) faculty.

fade /fad/ adj insipid.

faible /fɛbl/ adj weak; (espoir, quantité, écart) slight; (revenu, intensité) low; ~ d'esprit feeble-minded. ● nm (personne) weakling; (penchant) weakness. **faiblesse** nf weakness. **faiblir** ② vi weaken.

faïence /fajɑ̃s/ nf earthenware.

faillir /fajiʀ/ ② vi j'ai failli acheter I almost bought.

faillite /fajit/ nf bankruptcy; (fig) collapse.

faim /fɛ̃/ nf hunger; **avoir** ~ be hungry; **rester sur sa** ~ (fig) be left wanting more.

fainéant, ~e /feneɑ̃, -t/ adj idle. ● nm, f idler.

---

faire /fɛʀ/ ③③

➡ Pour les expressions comme **faire attention, faire la cuisine,** etc. ➡ **attention, cuisine** etc.

● verbe transitif

····➤ (préparer, créer) make; ~ **une tarte/une erreur** make a tart/a mistake.

····➤ (se livrer à une activité) do; ~ **du droit** do law; ~ **du foot/du violon** play football/the violin; **qu'est-ce qu'elle fait?** (dans la vie) what does she do?; (en ce moment précis) what is she doing?

····➤ (dans les calculs, mesures, etc.) **10 et 10 font 20** 10 and 10 make 20; **ça fait 25 euros** that's 25 euros; ~ **60 kilos** weigh 60 kilos; **il fait 1,75 m** he's 1.75 m tall.

····➤ (dans les expressions de temps) **ça fait une heure que j'attends** I have been waiting for an hour.

····➤ (imiter) ~ **le clown** act the clown; **faire le malade** pretend to be ill.

····➤ (parcourir) ~ **10 km** do ou cover 10 km; ~ **les musées** go round the museums.

····➤ (entraîner, causer) **ça ne fait**

rien it doesn't matter; **l'accident a fait 8 morts** 8 people died in the accident.

····➤ (dire) say; **'excusez-moi', fit-elle** 'excuse me', she said.

● verbe auxiliaire

····➤ (**faire** + infinitif + qn) make; ~ **pleurer qn** make sb cry.

····➤ (**faire** + infinitif + qch) have, get; ~ **réparer sa voiture** have ou get one's car mended.

····➤ (**ne faire que** + infinitif) (continuellement) **ne** ~ **que pleurer** do nothing but cry; (seulement) **je ne fais qu'obéir** I'm only following orders.

● verbe intransitif

····➤ (agir) do, act; ~ **vite** act quickly; **fais comme tu veux** do as you please; **fais comme chez toi** make yourself at home.

····➤ (paraître) look; ~ **joli** look pretty; **ça fait cher** it's expensive.

····➤ (en parlant du temps) **il fait chaud/gris** it's hot/overcast.

☐ **se faire** verbe pronominal

····➤ (obtenir, confectionner) make; **se** ~ **des amis** make friends; **se** ~ **un thé** make (oneself) a cup of tea.

····➤ (**se faire** + infinitif) **se** ~ **gronder** be scolded; **se** ~ **couper les cheveux** have one's hair cut.

····➤ (devenir) **il se fait tard** it's getting late.

····➤ (être d'usage) **ça ne se fait pas** it's not the done thing.

····➤ (emploi impersonnel) **comment se fait-il que tu sois ici?** how come you're here?

····➤ ☐ **se faire à** get used to; **je ne m'y fais pas** I can't get used to it.

····➤ ☐ **s'en faire** worry; **ne t'en fais pas** don't worry.

🖽 Lorsque **faire** remplace un verbe plus précis, on traduira quelquefois par ce dernier: **faire une visite** pay a visit, **faire un nid** build a nest.

---

faire-part /fɛʀpaʀ/ nm inv announcement.

fais /fɛ/ ➡**FAIRE** ③③.

faisan /fəzɑ̃/ nm pheasant.

faisceau (*pl* ~**x**) /fɛso/ *nm* (rayon) beam; (fagot) bundle.

fait, ~**e** /fɛ, fɛt/ *adj* done; (*fromage*) ripe; **tout** ~ ready made for; **tout** ~ ready made; **c'est bien** ~ **pour toi** it serves you right. ● *nm* fact; (événement) event; **au** ~ (**de**) informed (of); **de ce** ~ therefore; **du** ~ **de** on account of; ~ **divers** (trivial) news item; ~ **nouveau** new development; **prendre qn sur le** ~ catch sb in the act. ● →**FAIRE** 33.

faîte /fɛt/ *nm* top; (fig) peak.

faites /fɛt/ →**FAIRE** 33.

falaise /falɛz/ *nf* cliff.

falloir /falwaʀ/ 34 *vi* **il faut qch/qn** we/you *etc.* need sth/sb; **il faut du pain** he needs bread; **il faut rester** we/you *etc.* have to *ou* must stay; **il faut que j'y aille** I have to *ou* must go; **il faudrait que tu partes** you should leave; **il aurait fallu le faire** we/you *etc.* should have done it; **comme il faut** (*manger, se tenir*) properly; (*personne*) respectable, proper. □ **s'en** ~ *vpr* **il s'en est fallu de peu qu'il gagne** he nearly won; **il s'en faut de beaucoup que je sois** I am far from being.

falsifier /falsifje/ 45 *vt* falsify; (*signature, monnaie*) forge.

famé, ~**e** /fame/ *adj* **mal** ~ disreputable, seedy.

fameux, -euse /famø, -z/ *adj* famous; (excellent 1) first-rate.

familial, ~**e** (*mpl* -**iaux**) /familjal, -jo/ *adj* family.

familiale /familjal/ *nf* estate car; (US) station wagon.

familiariser /familjaʀize/ 1 *vt* familiarize (**avec** with). □ **se** ~ *vpr* familiarize oneself.

familier, -ière /familje, -jɛʀ/ *adj* familiar; (*amical*) informal.

famille /famij/ *nf* family; **en** ~ with one's family.

famine /famin/ *nf* famine.

fanatique /fanatik/ *adj* fanatical. ● *nmf* fanatic.

fanfare /fɑ̃faʀ/ *nf* brass band; (musique) fanfare.

fantaisie /fɑ̃tezi/ *nf* imagination, fantasy; (caprice) whim; (**de**) ~ (*boutons etc.*) fancy. **fantaisiste** *adj* unorthodox; (*personne*) eccentric.

fantasme /fɑ̃tasm/ *nm* fantasy.

fantastique /fɑ̃tastik/ *adj* fantastic.

fantôme /fɑ̃tom/ *nm* ghost; **cabinet(-)**~ (Pol) shadow cabinet.

faon /fɑ̃/ *nm* fawn.

FAQ *abrév f* (**Foire aux questions**) (Internet) FAQ, Frequently Asked Questions.

farce /faʀs/ *nf* (practical) joke; (Théât) farce; (hachis) stuffing.

farcir /faʀsiʀ/ 2 *vt* stuff.

fard /faʀ/ *nm* make-up; ~ **à paupières** eye-shadow; **piquer un** ~ blush.

fardeau (*pl* ~**x**) /faʀdo/ *nm* burden.

farfelu, ~**e** /faʀfəly/ *adj & nm,f* eccentric.

farine /faʀin/ *nf* flour. **farineux, -euse** *adj* floury. **farineux** *nmpl* starchy food.

farouche /faʀuʃ/ *adj* shy; (peu sociable) unsociable; (violent) fierce.

fascicule /fasikyl/ *nm* (brochure) booklet; (partie d'un ouvrage) fascicule.

fasciner /fasine/ 1 *vt* fascinate.

fascisme /faʃism/ *nm* fascism.

fasse /fas/ →**FAIRE** 33.

fast-food /fastfud/ *nm* fast-food place.

fastidieux, -ieuse /fastidjø, -z/ *adj* tedious.

fatal, ~**e** (*mpl* ~**s**) /fatal/ *adj* inevitable; (mortel) fatal. **fatalité** *nf* (destin) fate.

fatigant, ~**e** /fatigɑ̃, -t/ *adj* tiring; (ennuyeux) tiresome.

fatigue /fatig/ *nf* fatigue, tiredness.

fatigué, ~**e** /fatige/ *adj* tired.

fatiguer /fatige/ 1 *vt* tire; (*yeux, moteur*) strain. ● *vi* (moteur) labour. □ **se** ~ *vpr* get tired, tire (**de** of).

faubourg /fobuʀ/ *nm* suburb.

faucher /foʃe/ 1 *vt* (herbe) mow; (voler 1) pinch; ~ **qn** (véhicule, tir) mow sb down.

faucon /fokɔ̃/ *nm* falcon, hawk.

faudra, faudrait /fodʀa, fodʀɛ/ →**FALLOIR** 34.

faufiler (se) /(sə)fofile/ 1 *vpr* edge one's way, squeeze.

faune /fon/ *nf* wildlife, fauna.

faussaire /fosɛʀ/ *nmf* forger.

fausse /fos/ →**FAUX**².

fausser /fose/ **1** vt buckle; (fig) distort; ~ **compagnie à qn** give sb the slip.

faut /fo/ ➡**FALLOIR** 34.

faute /fot/ nf mistake; (responsabilité) fault; (délit) offence; (péché) sin; **en ~** at fault; **~ de** for want of; **~ de quoi** failing which; **sans ~** without fail; **~ de frappe** typing error; **~ de goût** bad taste; **~ professionnelle** professional misconduct.

fauteuil /fotœj/ nm armchair; (de président) chair; (Théât) seat; **~ roulant** wheelchair.

fautif, -ive /fotif, -v/ adj guilty; (faux) faulty. ● nm, f guilty party.

fauve /fov/ adj (couleur) fawn, tawny. ● nm wild cat.

faux¹ /fo/ nf scythe.

faux², **fausse** /fo, fos/ adj false; (falsifié) fake, forged; (numéro, calcul) wrong; (voix) out of tune; **c'est ~!** that is wrong!; **~ témoignage** perjury; **faire ~ bond à qn** stand sb up; **fausse couche** miscarriage; **~ frais** incidental expenses. ● adv (chanter) out of tune. ● nm forgery. **faux-filet** (pl **~s**) nm sirloin.

faveur /favœʀ/ nf favour; **de ~** (régime) preferential; **en ~ de** in favour of.

favorable /favɔʀabl/ adj favourable.

favori, ~te /favɔʀi, -t/ adj & nm,f favourite. **favoriser** **1** vt favour.

fax /faks/ nm fax. **faxer** **1** vt fax.

fébrile /febʀil/ adj feverish.

fécond, ~e /fekɔ̃, -d/ adj fertile. **féconder** **1** vt fertilize. **fécondité** nf fertility.

fédéral, ~e (mpl **-aux**) /federal, -o/ adj federal. **fédération** nf federation.

fée /fe/ nf fairy. **féerie** nf magical spectacle. **féerique** adj magical.

feindre /fɛ̃dʀ/ 22 vt feign; **~ de** pretend to.

fêler /fele/ **1** vt crack. □ **se ~** vpr crack.

félicitations /felisitasjɔ̃/ nfpl congratulations (**pour** on). **féliciter** **1** vt congratulate (**de** on).

félin, ~e /felɛ̃, -in/ adj & nm feline.

femelle /fəmɛl/ adj & nf female.

féminin, ~e /feminɛ̃, -in/ adj feminine; (sexe) female; (mode, équipe) women's. ● nm feminine. **féministe** nmf feminist.

femme /fam/ nf woman; (épouse) wife; **~ au foyer** housewife; **~ de chambre** chambermaid; **~ de ménage** cleaning lady.

fémur /femyʀ/ nm thigh-bone.

fendre /fɑ̃dʀ/ **3** vt (couper) split; (fissurer) crack. □ **se ~** vpr crack.

fenêtre /fənɛtʀ/ nf window.

fenouil /fənuj/ nm fennel.

fente /fɑ̃t/ nf (ouverture) slit, slot; (fissure) crack.

féodal, ~e (mpl **-aux**) /feɔdal, -o/ adj feudal.

fer /fɛʀ/ nm iron; **~ (à repasser)** iron; **~ à cheval** horseshoe; **~ de lance** spearhead; **~ forgé** wrought iron.

fera, ferait /fəʀa, fəʀɛ/ ➡**FAIRE** 33.

férié, ~e /feʀje/ adj **jour ~** public holiday.

ferme /fɛʀm/ nf farm; (maison) farm(house); **~ éolienne** wind farm. ● adj firm. ● adv (travailler) hard.

fermé, ~e /fɛʀme/ adj closed; (gaz, radio) off.

fermenter /fɛʀmɑ̃te/ **1** vi ferment.

fermer /fɛʀme/ **1** vt/i close, shut; (cesser d'exploiter) close ou shut down; (gaz, robinet) turn off. □ **se ~** vpr close, shut.

fermeté /fɛʀməte/ nf firmness.

fermeture /fɛʀmətyʀ/ nf closing; (dispositif) catch; **~ annuelle** annual closure; **~ éclair®** zip(-fastener); (US) zipper.

fermier, -ière /fɛʀmje, -jɛʀ/ adj farm. ● nm farmer. **fermière** nf farmer's wife.

féroce /feʀɔs/ adj ferocious.

ferraille /feʀɑj/ nf scrap-iron.

ferrer /feʀe/ **1** vt (cheval) shoe.

ferroviaire /feʀɔvjɛʀ/ adj rail(way).

ferry /feʀi/ nm ferry.

fertile /fɛʀtil/ adj fertile; **~ en** (fig) rich in. **fertiliser** **1** vt fertilize. **fertilité** nf fertility.

fervent, ~e /fɛʀvɑ̃, -t/ adj fervent. ● nm, f enthusiast (**de** of).

fesse /fɛs/ nf buttock. **fessée** nf spanking, smack.

festin /fɛstɛ̃/ nm feast.

festival (pl **~s**) /fɛstival/ nm festival.

fêtard, ~e /fɛtaʀ, -d/ *nm, f* ① party
animal.

fête /fɛt/ *nf* holiday; (religieuse) feast;
(du nom) name-day; (réception) party;
(en famille) celebration; (foire) fair;
(folklorique) festival; ~ **des Mères**
Mother's Day; ~ **foraine** fun-fair;
faire la ~ live it up; **les** ~**s (de fin
d'année)** the Christmas season. **fêter**
① *vt* celebrate; (*personne*) give a celebration for.

fétiche /fetiʃ/ *nm* fetish; (fig) mascot.

feu[1] (*pl* ~**x**) /fø/ *nm* fire; (lumière)
light; (de réchaud) burner; **à** ~ **doux/
vif** on a low/high heat; ~ **rouge/
vert/orange** red/green/amber light;
aux ~**x, tournez à droite** turn right
at the traffic lights; **avez-vous du** ~?
(pour cigarette) have you got a light?;
au ~! fire!; **mettre le** ~ **à** set fire to;
prendre ~ catch fire; **jouer avec le**
~ play with fire; **ne pas faire long** ~
not last; ~ **d'artifice** firework display;
~ **de joie** bonfire; ~ **de position**
sidelight.

feu[2] /fø/ *adj inv* (mort) late.

feuillage /fœjaʒ/ *nm* foliage.

feuille /fœj/ *nf* leaf; (de papier) sheet;
(formulaire) form; ~ **d'impôts** tax return; ~ **de paie** payslip.

feuilleté, ~e /fœjte/ *adj* **pâte** ~e puff
pastry. ● *nm* savoury pasty.

feuilleter /fœjte/ ① *vt* leaf through.

feuilleton /fœjtɔ̃/ *nm* (à suivre) serial;
(histoire complète) series.

feutre /føtʀ/ *nm* felt; (chapeau) felt
hat; (crayon) felt-tip (pen).

fève /fɛv/ *nf* broad bean.

février /fevʀije/ *nm* February.

fiable /fjabl/ *adj* reliable.

fiançailles /fjɑ̃saj/ *nfpl* engagement.

fiancé, ~e /fjɑ̃se/ *adj* engaged. ● *nm*
fiancé. **fiancée** *nf* fiancée. **fiancer (se)**
⑩ *vpr* become engaged (**avec** to).

fibre /fibʀ/ *nf* fibre; ~ **de verre**
fibreglass.

ficeler /fisle/ ㊳ *vt* tie up.

ficelle /fisɛl/ *nf* string.

fiche /fiʃ/ *nf* (index) card; (formulaire)
form, slip; (Électr) plug.

ficher[1] /fiʃe/ ① *vt* (enfoncer) drive
(**dans** into).

ficher[2] /fiʃe/ ① ① *vt* (faire) do; (donner) give; (mettre) put; ~ **le camp**

clear off. □ **se** ~ **de** *vpr* make fun of;
il s'en fiche he couldn't care less.

fichier /fiʃje/ *nm* file.

fichu, ~e /fiʃy/ *adj* ① (mauvais) rotten; (raté) done for; **mal** ~ terrible.

fictif, -ive /fiktif, -v/ *adj* fictitious. **fiction** *nf* fiction.

fidèle /fidɛl/ *adj* faithful. ● *nmf* (client)
regular; (Relig) believer; ~**s** (à l'église)
congregation. **fidélité** *nf* fidelity.

fier[1], **fière** /fjɛʀ/ *adj* proud (**de** of).

fier[2]**(se)** /(sə)fje/ ㊺ *vpr* **se** ~ **à** trust.

fierté /fjɛʀte/ *nf* pride.

fièvre /fjɛvʀ/ *nf* fever; **avoir de la** ~
have a temperature; ~ **aphteuse** foot-
and-mouth disease. **fiévreux, -euse**
adj feverish.

figer /fiʒe/ ㊵ *vi* (graisse) congeal;
(sang) clot; **figé sur place** frozen to
the spot. □ **se** ~ *vpr* (personne, sourire) freeze; (graisse) congeal;
(sang) clot.

figue /fig/ *nf* fig.

figurant, ~e /figyʀɑ̃, -t/ *nm, f* (au cinéma) extra.

figure /figyʀ/ *nf* face; (forme, personnage) figure; (illustration) picture.

figuré, ~e /figyʀe/ *adj* (sens) fig-
urative.

figurer /figyʀe/ ① *vi* appear. ● *vt* represent. □ **se** ~ *vpr* imagine.

fil /fil/ *nm* thread; (métallique, électrique) wire; (de couteau) edge; (à coudre) cotton; **au** ~ **de** with the passing
of; **au** ~ **de l'eau** with the current; ~
de fer wire; **au bout du** ~ ① on the
phone.

file /fil/ *nf* line; (voie: Auto) lane; ~
(d'attente) queue; (US) line; **en** ~ **indienne** in single file.

filer /file/ ① *vt* spin; (suivre) shadow;
~ **qch à qn** ① slip sb sth. ● *vi* (bas)
ladder, run; (liquide) run; (aller vite ①)
speed along, fly by; (partir ①) dash
off; (disparaître ①) ~ **entre les
mains** slip through one's fingers; ~
doux do as one's told.

filet /filɛ/ *nm* net; (d'eau) trickle; (de
viande) fillet; ~ **(à bagages)** (luggage) rack; ~ **à provisions** string bag
(for shopping).

filiale /filjal/ *nf* subsidiary (company).

filière /filjɛʀ/ *nf* (official) channels; (de
trafiquants) network; **passer par** *ou*

suivre la ~ (*employé*) work one's way up.

fille /fij/ *nf* girl; (opposé à fils) daughter. **fillette** *nf* little girl.

filleul /fijœl/ *nm* godson.

filleule /fijœl/ *nf* god-daughter.

film /film/ *nm* film; ~ **d'épouvante/ muet/parlant** horror/silent/talking film; ~ **dramatique** drama. **filmer** ① *vt* film.

filon /filõ/ *nm* (Géol) seam; (travail lucratif ①) money spinner; **avoir trouvé le bon** ~ be onto a good thing.

fils /fis/ *nm* son.

filtre /filtʀ/ *nm* filter. **filtrer** ① *vt/i* filter; (*personne*) screen.

fin[1] /fɛ̃/ *nf* end; **à la** ~ finally; **en** ~ **de compte** all things considered; ~ **de semaine** weekend; **mettre** ~ **à** put an end to; **prendre** ~ come to an end.

fin[2], ~**e** /fɛ̃, fin/ *adj* fine; (*tranche, couche*) thin; (*taille*) slim; (*plat*) exquisite; (*esprit, vue*) sharp; ~**es herbes** mixed herbs. ● *adv* (*couper*) finely.

final, ~e (*mpl* **-aux**) /final, -o/ *adj* final.

finale /final/ *nm* (Mus) finale. ● *nf* (Sport) final; (Gram) final syllable. **finalement** *adv* finally; (somme toute) after all. **finaliste** *nmf* finalist.

finance /finɑ̃s/ *nf* finance. **financer** ⑩ *vt* finance.

financier, -ière /finɑ̃sje, -jɛʀ/ *adj* financial. ● *nm* financier.

finesse /finɛs/ *nf* fineness; (de taille) slimness; (acuité) sharpness; ~**s** (de langue) niceties.

finir /finiʀ/ ② *vt/i* finish, end; (*arrêter*) stop; (*manger*) finish (up); **en** ~ **avec** have done with; ~ **par faire** end up doing; **ça va mal** ~ it will turn out badly.

finlandais, ~e /fɛ̃lɑ̃dɛ, -z/ *adj* Finnish. **F~, ~e** *nm, f* Finn.

Finlande /fɛ̃lɑ̃d/ *nf* Finland.

finnois, ~e /finwa/ *adj* Finnish. ● *nm* (Ling) Finnish.

firme /fiʀm/ *nf* firm.

fisc /fisk/ *nm* tax authorities. **fiscal, ~e** (*mpl* **-aux**) *adj* tax, fiscal. **fiscalité** *nf* tax system.

fissure /fisyʀ/ *nf* crack.

FIV *abrév f* (**fécondation in vitro**) IVF.

fixe /fiks/ *adj* fixed; (stable) steady; **à heure** ~ at a set time; **menu à prix** ~ set menu. ● *nm* basic pay.

fixer /fikse/ ① *vt* fix; ~ (**du regard**) stare at; **être fixé** (*personne*) have made up one's mind. □ **se** ~ *vpr* (s'attacher) be attached; (s'installer) settle down.

flacon /flakõ/ *nm* bottle.

flagrant, ~e /flagʀɑ̃, -t/ *adj* flagrant, blatant; **en** ~ **délit** in the act.

flair /flɛʀ/ *nm* (sense of) smell; (fig) intuition.

flamand, ~e /flamɑ̃, -d/ *adj* Flemish. ● *nm* (Ling) Flemish. **F~, ~e** *nm, f* Fleming.

flamant /flamɑ̃/ *nm* flamingo.

flambeau (*pl* ~**x**) /flɑ̃bo/ *nm* torch.

flambée /flɑ̃be/ *nf* blaze; (fig) explosion.

flamber /flɑ̃be/ ① *vi* blaze; (*prix*) shoot up. ● *vt* (*aiguille*) sterilize; (*volaille*) singe.

flamme /flam/ *nf* flame; (fig) ardour; **en** ~**s** ablaze.

flan /flɑ̃/ *nm* custard tart.

flanc /flɑ̃/ *nm* side; (d'animal, d'armée) flank.

flâner /flɑne/ ① *vi* stroll. **flânerie** *nf* stroll.

flanquer /flɑ̃ke/ ① *vt* flank; (jeter ①) chuck; (donner ①) give; ~ **à la porte** kick out.

flaque /flak/ *nf* (d'eau) puddle; (de sang) pool.

flash (*pl* ~**es**) /flaʃ/ *nm* (Photo) flash; (information) news flash; ~ **publicitaire** commercial.

flatter /flate/ ① *vt* flatter. □ **se** ~ **de** *vpr* pride oneself on.

flatteur, -euse /flatœʀ, -øz/ *adj* flattering. ● *nm, f* flatterer.

fléau (*pl* ~**x**) /fleo/ *nm* (désastre) scourge; (personne) pest.

flèche /flɛʃ/ *nf* arrow; (de clocher) spire; **monter en** ~ spiral; **partir en** ~ shoot off.

flécher /fleʃe/ ⑭ *vt* mark *ou* signpost (with arrows). **fléchette** *nf* dart.

fléchir /fleʃiʀ/ ② *vt* bend; (*personne*) move, sway. ● *vi* (faiblir) weaken; (*prix*) fall; (*poutre*) sag, bend.

flemme /flɛm/ *nf* ① laziness; **j'ai la** ~ **de faire** I can't be bothered doing.

flétrir (se) /(sə)fletʀiʀ/ 🔢 vpr (plante) wither; (fruit) shrivel; (beauté) fade.

fleur /flœʀ/ nf flower; **à ~ de terre/d'eau** just above the ground/water; **à ~s** flowery; **~ de l'âge** prime of life; **en ~s** in flower.

fleurir /flœʀiʀ/ 🔢 vi flower; (arbre) blossom; (fig) flourish. ● vt decorate with flowers. **fleuriste** nmf florist.

fleuve /flœv/ nm river.

flic /flik/ nm 🔢 cop.

flipper /flipœʀ/ nm pinball (machine).

flirter /flœʀte/ 🔢 vi flirt.

flocon /flɔkɔ̃/ nm flake.

flore /flɔʀ/ nf flora.

florissant, ~e /flɔʀisɑ̃, -t/ adj flourishing.

flot /flo/ nm flood, stream; **être à ~** be afloat; **les ~s** the waves.

flottant, ~e /flɔtɑ̃, -t/ adj (vêtement) loose; (indécis) indecisive.

flotte /flɔt/ nf fleet; (pluie 🔢) rain; (eau 🔢) water.

flottement /flɔtmɑ̃/ nm (incertitude) indecision.

flotter /flɔte/ 🔢 vi float; (drapeau) flutter; (nuage, parfum, pensées) drift; (pleuvoir 🔢) rain. **flotteur** nm float.

flou, ~e /flu/ adj out of focus; (fig) vague.

fluctuer /flyktɥe/ 🔢 vi fluctuate.

fluet, ~te /flyɛ, -t/ adj thin.

fluide /flɥid/ adj & nm fluid.

fluor /flyɔʀ/ nm (pour les dents) fluoride.

fluorescent, ~e /flyɔʀesɑ̃, -t/ adj fluorescent.

flûte /flyt/ nf flute; (verre) champagne glass.

fluvial, ~e (mpl **-iaux**) /flyvjal, -jo/ adj river.

flux /fly/ nm flow; **~ et reflux** ebb and flow.

FM abrév f (**frequency modulation**) FM.

fœtus /fetys/ nm foetus.

foi /fwa/ nf faith; **être de bonne/mauvaise ~** be acting in good/bad faith; **ma ~!** well (indeed)!

fole /fwa/ nm liver.

foin /fwɛ̃/ nm hay.

foire /fwaʀ/ nf fair; **faire la ~** 🔢 live it up.

fois /fwa/ nf time; **une ~** once; **deux ~** twice; **à la ~** at the same time; **des ~** (parfois) sometimes; **une ~ pour toutes** once and for all.

fol /fɔl/ ➡FOU.

folie /fɔli/ nf madness; (bêtise) foolish thing, folly; **faire une ~, faire des ~s** be extravagant.

folklore /fɔlklɔʀ/ nm folklore. **folklorique** adj folk; 🔢 eccentric.

folle /fɔl/ ➡FOU.

foncé, ~e /fɔ̃se/ adj dark.

foncer /fɔ̃se/ 🔢 vt darken. ● vi (s'assombrir) darken; (aller vite 🔢) dash along; **~ sur** 🔢 charge at.

foncier, -ière /fɔ̃sje, -jɛʀ/ adj fundamental; (Comm) real estate.

fonction /fɔ̃ksjɔ̃/ nf function; (emploi) position; **~s** (obligations) duties; **en ~ de** according to; **~ publique** civil service; **voiture de ~** company car. **fonctionnaire** nmf civil servant. **fonctionnement** nm working.

fonctionner /fɔ̃ksjɔne/ 🔢 vi work; **faire ~** work.

fond /fɔ̃/ nm bottom; (de salle, magasin, etc.) back; (essentiel) basis; (contenu) content; (plan) background; (Sport) long-distance running; **à ~** thoroughly; **au ~** basically; **de ~** (bruit) background; **de ~ en comble** from top to bottom; **au** ou **dans le ~** really; **~ de teint** foundation, make-up base.

fondamental, ~e (mpl **-aux**) /fɔ̃damɑ̃tal, -o/ adj fundamental.

fondateur, -trice /fɔ̃datœʀ, -tʀis/ nm, f founder. **fondation** nf foundation.

fonder /fɔ̃de/ 🔢 vt found; (baser) base (**sur** on); (**bien**) **fondé** wellfounded. ◻ **se ~ sur** vpr be guided by, be based on.

fonderie /fɔ̃dʀi/ nf foundry.

fondre /fɔ̃dʀ/ 🔢 vt/i melt; (dans l'eau) dissolve; (mélanger) merge; **faire ~** melt; dissolve; **~ en larmes** burst into tears; **~ sur** swoop on. ◻ **se ~** vpr merge.

fonds /fɔ̃/ nm fund; **~ de commerce** business. ● nmpl (capitaux) funds.

fondu, ~e /fɔ̃dy/ adj melted; (métal) molten.

font /fɔ̃/ ➡FAIRE 🔢.

fontaine /fɔ̃tɛn/ *nf* fountain; (*source*) spring.

fonte /fɔ̃t/ *nf* melting; (*fer*) cast iron; ~ **des neiges** thaw.

foot /fut/ *nm* 1 football.

football /futbol/ *nm* football.

footing /futiŋ/ *nm* jogging.

forain /fɔrɛ̃/ *nm* fairground entertainer; **marchand** ~ stallholder.

forçat /fɔrsa/ *nm* convict.

force /fɔrs/ *nf* force; (*physique*) strength; (*hydraulique etc.*) power; ~s (*physiques*) strength; **à** ~ **de** by sheer force of; **de** ~, **par la** ~ by force; ~ **de dissuasion** deterrent; ~ **de frappe** strike force, deterrent; ~ **de l'âge** prime of life; ~s **de l'ordre** police (force) ; ~s **de marché** market forces.

forcé, ~**e** /fɔrse/ *adj* forced; (*inévitable*) inevitable; **c'est** ~ **qu'il fasse** 1 he's bound to do. **forcément** *adv* necessarily; (*évidemment*) obviously.

forcené, ~**e** /fɔrsəne/ *adj* frenzied. ● *nm, f* maniac.

forcer /fɔrse/ 10 *vt* force (**à faire** to do); (*voix*) strain; ~ **la dose** 1 overdo it. ● *vi* force; (*exagérer*) overdo it. □ **se** ~ *vpr* force oneself.

forer /fɔre/ 1 *vt* drill.

forestier, -ière /fɔrɛstje, -jɛr/ *adj* forest. ● *nm, f* forestry worker.

forêt /fɔrɛ/ *nf* forest.

forfait /fɔrfɛ/ *nm* (Comm) (*prix fixe*) fixed price; (*offre promotionnelle*) package. **forfaitaire** *adj* (*prix*) fixed.

forger /fɔrʒe/ 40 *vt* forge; (*inventer*) make up.

forgeron /fɔrʒərɔ̃/ *nm* blacksmith.

formaliser (se) /(sə)fɔrmalize/ 1 *vpr* take offence (**de** at).

formalité /fɔrmalite/ *nf* formality.

format /fɔrma/ *nm* format. **formater** 1 *vt* (Ordinat) format.

formation /fɔrmasjɔ̃/ *nf* formation; (*professionnelle*) training; (*culture*) education; ~ **permanente** *ou* **continue** continuing education.

forme /fɔrm/ *nf* form; (*contour*) shape, form; ~s (*de femme*) figure; **être en** ~ be in good shape, be on form; **en** ~ **de** in the shape of; **en bonne et due** ~ in due form.

formel, ~**le** /fɔrmɛl/ *adj* formal; (*catégorique*) positive.

former /fɔrme/ 1 *vt* form; (*instruire*) train. □ **se** ~ *vpr* form.

formidable /fɔrmidabl/ *adj* fantastic.

formulaire /fɔrmylɛr/ *nm* form.

formule /fɔrmyl/ *nf* formula; (*expression*) expression; (*feuille*) form; ~ **de politesse** polite phrase, letter ending. **formuler** 1 *vt* formulate.

fort, ** ~e** /fɔr, -t/ *adj* strong; (*grand*) big; (*pluie*) heavy; (*bruit*) loud; (*pente*) steep; (*élève*) clever; **au plus** ~ **de** at the height of; **c'est une** ~**e tête** she/ he's headstrong. ● *adv* (*frapper*) hard; (*parler*) loud; (*très*) very; (*beaucoup*) very much. ● *nm* (*atout*) strong point; (Mil) fort.

fortifiant /fɔrtifjɑ̃/ *nm* tonic. **fortifier** 45 *vt* fortify.

fortune /fɔrtyn/ *nf* fortune; **de** ~ (*improvisé*) makeshift; **faire** ~ make one's fortune.

forum /fɔrɔm/ *nm* forum; ~ **de discussion** (Internet) newsgroup.

fosse /fos/ *nf* pit; (*tombe*) grave; ~ **d'orchestre** orchestra pit; ~ **septique** septic tank.

fossé /fose/ *nm* ditch; (*fig*) gulf; ~ **numérique** digital divide.

fossette /fosɛt/ *nf* dimple.

fossile /fosil/ *nm* fossil.

fou (**fol** *before vowel or mute h*) , **folle** /fu, fɔl/ *adj* mad; (*course, regard*) wild; (*énorme* 1) tremendous; ~ **de** crazy about; **le** ~ **rire** the giggles. ● *nm* madman; (*bouffon*) jester. **folle** *nf* madwoman.

foudre /fudr/ *nf* lightning.

foudroyant, ~**e** /fudrwajɑ̃, -t/ *adj* (*mort, maladie*) violent.

foudroyer /fudrwaje/ 31 *vt* (*orage*) strike; (*maladie etc.*) strike down; ~ **qn du regard** look daggers at sb.

fouet /fwɛ/ *nm* whip; (Culin) whisk.

fougère /fuʒɛr/ *nf* fern.

fougue /fug/ *nf* ardour. **fougueux, -euse** *adj* ardent.

fouille /fuj/ *nf* search; (Archéol) excavation.

fouiller /fuje/ 1 *vt/i* search; (*creuser*) dig; ~ **dans** (*tiroir*) rummage through.

fouillis /fuji/ *nm* jumble.

foulard /fular/ *nm* scarf.

foule /ful/ *nf* crowd; **une** ~ **de** (*fig*) a mass of.

foulée | frappé

foulée /fule/ *nf* stride; **il l'a fait dans la ~** he did it while he was at ou about it.

fouler /fule/ **1** *vt* (*raisin*) press; (*sol*) set foot on; **~ qch aux pieds** trample sth underfoot; (*fig*) ride roughshod over sth. □ **se ~** *vpr* **se ~ le poignet/le pied** sprain one's wrist/foot; **ne pas se ~** **1** not strain oneself.

four /fuʀ/ *nm* oven; (*de potier*) kiln; (*Théât*) flop; **~ à micro-ondes** microwave oven; **~ crématoire** crematorium.

fourbe /fuʀb/ *adj* deceitful.

fourche /fuʀʃ/ *nf* fork; (*à foin*) pitchfork. **fourchette** *nf* fork; (*Comm*) bracket, range.

fourgon /fuʀgɔ̃/ *nm* van.

fourmi /fuʀmi/ *nf* ant; **avoir des ~s** have pins and needles.

fourmiller /fuʀmije/ **1** *vi* swarm (**de** with).

fourneau (*pl* **~x**) /fuʀno/ *nm* stove.

fourni, ~e /fuʀni/ *adj* (*épais*) thick.

fournir /fuʀniʀ/ **2** *vt* supply, provide; (*client*) supply; (*effort*) put in; **~ à qn** supply sb with. □ **se ~ chez** *vpr* shop at.

fournisseur /fuʀnisœʀ/ *nm* supplier; **~ d'accès à l'Internet** Internet service provider.

fourniture /fuʀnityʀ/ *nf* supply.

fourrage /fuʀaʒ/ *nm* fodder.

fourré, ~e /fuʀe/ *adj* (*vêtement*) fur-lined; (*gâteau etc.*) filled (*with jam, cream, etc.*). ● *nm* thicket.

fourre-tout /fuʀtu/ *nm inv* (*sac*) holdall.

fourreur /fuʀœʀ/ *nm* furrier.

fourrière /fuʀjɛʀ/ *nf* (*lieu*) pound.

fourrure /fuʀyʀ/ *nf* fur.

foutre /futʀ/ **3** *vt* 🔲 = **ficher²** **1**.

foutu, ~e /futy/ *adj* 🔲 = **fichu**.

foyer /fwaje/ *nm* home; (*âtre*) hearth; (*club*) club; (*d'étudiants*) hostel; (*Théât*) foyer; (*Photo*) focus; (*centre*) centre.

fracas /fʀaka/ *nm* din; (*de train*) roar; (*d'objet qui tombe*) crash. **fracassant, ~e** *adj* (*bruyant*) deafening; (*violent*) shattering.

fraction /fʀaksjɔ̃/ *nf* fraction.

fracture /fʀaktyʀ/ *nf* fracture; **~ du poignet** fractured wrist.

fragile /fʀaʒil/ *adj* fragile; (*peau*) sensitive; (*cœur*) weak. **fragilité** *nf* fragility.

fragment /fʀagmɑ̃/ *nm* bit, fragment. **fragmenter** **1** *vt* split, fragment.

fraîchement /fʀɛʃmɑ̃/ *adv* (*récemment*) freshly; (*avec froideur*) coolly. **fraîcheur** *nf* coolness; (*nouveauté*) freshness. **fraîchir** **2** *vi* freshen, become colder.

frais¹, fraîche /fʀɛ, -ʃ/ *adj* fresh; (*temps, accueil*) cool; (*peinture*) wet; **~ et dispos** fresh; **il fait ~** it is cool. ● *adv* (*récemment*) newly, freshly. ● *nm* **mettre au ~** put in a cool place; **prendre le ~** get some fresh air.

frais² /fʀɛ/ *nmpl* expenses; (*droits*) fees; **aux ~ de** at the expense of; **faire des ~** spend a lot of money; **~ généraux** (*Comm*) overheads, running expenses; **~ de scolarité** school fees.

fraise /fʀɛz/ *nf* strawberry. **fraisier** *nm* strawberry plant; (*gâteau*) strawberry gateau.

framboise /fʀɑ̃bwaz/ *nf* raspberry. **framboisier** *nm* raspberry bush.

franc, franche /fʀɑ̃, -ʃ/ *adj* frank; (*regard*) frank, candid; (*cassure*) clean; (*net*) clear; (*libre*) free; (*véritable*) downright. ● *nm* franc.

français, ~e /fʀɑ̃sɛ, -z/ *adj* French. ● *nm* (*Ling*) French. **F~, ~e** *nm, f* Frenchman, Frenchwoman.

France /fʀɑ̃s/ *nf* France.

franchement /fʀɑ̃ʃmɑ̃/ *adv* frankly; (*nettement*) clearly; (*tout à fait*) really.

franchir /fʀɑ̃ʃiʀ/ **2** *vt* (*obstacle*) get over; (*distance*) cover; (*limite*) exceed; (*traverser*) cross.

franchise /fʀɑ̃ʃiz/ *nf* (*qualité*) frankness; (*Comm*) franchise; (*exemption*) exemption; **~ douanière** exemption from duties.

franc-maçon (*pl* **francs-maçons**) /fʀɑ̃masɔ̃/ *nm* Freemason. **franc-maçonnerie** *nf* Freemasonry.

franco /fʀɑ̃ko/ *adv* postage paid.

francophone /fʀɑ̃kɔfɔn/ *adj* French-speaking. ● *nmf* French speaker.

franc-parler /fʀɑ̃paʀle/ *nm inv* outspokenness.

frange /fʀɑ̃ʒ/ *nf* fringe.

frappe /fʀap/ *nf* (*de texte*) typing.

frappé, ~e /fʀape/ *adj* chilled.

frapper /fʀape/ **1** vt/i strike; (battre) hit, strike; (monnaie) mint; (à la porte) knock, bang; **frappé de panique** panic-stricken.

fraternel, ~le /fʀatɛʀnɛl/ adj brotherly. **fraternité** nf brotherhood.

fraude /fʀod/ nf fraud; (à un examen) cheating; **passer qch en ~** smuggle sth in. **frauder 1** vt/i cheat. **frauduleux, -euse** adj fraudulent.

frayer /fʀeje/ **31** vt open up. □ **se ~** vpr se ~ **un passage** force one's way (à travers, dans through).

frayeur /fʀejœʀ/ nf fright.

fredonner /fʀədɔne/ **1** vt hum.

free-lance /fʀilɑ̃s/ adj & nmf freelance.

freezer /fʀizœʀ/ nm freezer.

frein /fʀɛ̃/ nm brake; **mettre un ~ à** curb; **~ à main** hand brake.

freiner /fʀene/ **1** vt slow down; (modérer, enrayer) curb. ● vi (Auto) brake.

frêle /fʀɛl/ adj frail.

frelon /fʀəlɔ̃/ nm hornet.

frémir /fʀemiʀ/ **2** vi shudder, shake; (feuille, eau) quiver.

frêne /fʀɛn/ nm ash.

frénésie /fʀenezi/ nf frenzy. **frénétique** adj frenzied.

fréquemment /fʀekamɑ̃/ adv frequently. **fréquence** nf frequency. **fréquent, ~e** adj frequent. **fréquentation** nf frequenting.

fréquentations /fʀekɑ̃tasjɔ̃/ nfpl acquaintances; **avoir de mauvaises ~** keep bad company.

fréquenter /fʀekɑ̃te/ **1** vt frequent; (école) attend; (personne) see.

frère /fʀɛʀ/ nm brother.

fret /fʀɛt/ nm freight.

friand, ~e /fʀijɑ̃, -d/ adj **~ de** very fond of.

friandise /fʀijɑ̃diz/ nf sweet; (US) candy; (gâteau) cake.

fric /fʀik/ nm ⚀ money.

friction /fʀiksjɔ̃/ nf friction; (massage) rub-down.

frigidaire ® /fʀiʒidɛʀ/ nm refrigerator.

frigo /fʀigo/ nm ⚀ fridge. **frigorifique** adj (vitrine etc.) refrigerated.

frileux, -euse /fʀilø, -z/ adj sensitive to cold.

frime /fʀim/ nf ⚀ **c'est de la ~** it's all pretence; **pour la ~** for show.

frimousse /fʀimus/ nf face.

fringale /fʀɛ̃gal/ nf ⚀ ravenous appetite.

fringant, ~e /fʀɛ̃gɑ̃, -t/ adj dashing.

fringues /fʀɛ̃g/ nfpl ⚀ gear.

friper /fʀipe/ **1** vt crumple, crease. □ **se ~** vpr crumple, crease.

fripon, ~ne /fʀipɔ̃, -ɔn/ nm, f rascal. ● adj mischievous.

fripouille /fʀipuj/ nf rogue.

frire /fʀiʀ/ **58** vt/i fry; **faire ~** fry.

frise /fʀiz/ nf frieze.

friser /fʀize/ **1** vt/i (cheveux) curl; (personne) curl the hair of; **frisé** curly.

frisson /fʀisɔ̃/ nm (de froid) shiver; (de peur) shudder. **frissonner 1** vi shiver; shudder.

frit, ~e /fʀi, -t/ adj fried.

frite /fʀit/ nf chip; **avoir la ~** ⚀ feel good.

friteuse /fʀitøz/ nf chip pan; (électrique) (deep) fryer.

friture /fʀityʀ/ nf fried fish; (huile) (frying) oil ou fat.

frivole /fʀivɔl/ adj frivolous.

froid, ~e /fʀwa, -d/ adj & nm cold; **avoir/prendre ~** be/catch cold; **il fait ~** it is cold. **froidement** adv coldly; (calculer) coolly. **froideur** nf coldness.

froisser /fʀwase/ **1** vt crumple; (fig) offend. □ **se ~** vpr crumple; (fig) take offence; **se ~ un muscle** strain a muscle.

frôler /fʀole/ **1** vt brush against, skim; (fig) come close to.

fromage /fʀɔmaʒ/ nm cheese.

fromager, -ère /fʀɔmaʒe, -ɛʀ/ adj cheese. ● nm, f (fabricant) cheese-maker; (marchand) cheesemonger.

froment /fʀɔmɑ̃/ nm wheat.

froncer /fʀɔ̃se/ **10** vt gather; **~ les sourcils** frown.

front /fʀɔ̃/ nm forehead; (Mil, Pol) front; **de ~** at the same time; (de face) head-on; (côte à côte) abreast; **faire ~ à** face up to. **frontal, ~e** (mpl **-aux**) adj frontal; (Ordinat) front-end.

frontalier, -ière /fʀɔ̃talje, -jɛʀ/ adj border; **travailleur ~** commuter from across the border.

frontière /fʀɔ̃tjɛʀ/ nf border, frontier.

frottement /fʀɔtmã/ *nm* rubbing; (Tech) friction. **frotter 1** *vt/i* rub; (*allumette*) strike.

frottis /fʀɔti/ *nm* ~ **vaginal** cervical smear.

frousse /fʀus/ *nf* **1** fear; **avoir la** ~ **1** be scared.

fructifier /fʀyktifje/ **45** *vi* **faire** ~ put to work.

fructueux, -euse /fʀyktɥø, -z/ *adj* fruitful.

frugal, ~e (*mpl* **-aux**) /fʀygal, -o/ *adj* frugal.

fruit /fʀɥi/ *nm* fruit; **des** ~**s** (some) fruit; ~**s de mer** seafood. **fruité, ~e** *adj* fruity.

frustrant, ~e /fʀystʀã, -t/ *adj* frustrating. **frustrer 1** *vt* frustrate.

fuel /fjul/ *nm* fuel oil.

fugitif, -ive /fyʒitif, -v/ *adj* (*passager*) fleeting. ● *nm, f* fugitive.

fugue /fyg/ *nf* (Mus) fugue; **faire une** ~ run away.

fuir /fɥiʀ/ **35** *vi* flee, run away; (*eau, robinet, etc.*) leak. ● *vt* (quitter) flee; (éviter) shun.

fuite /fɥit/ *nf* flight; (de liquide, d'une nouvelle) leak; **en** ~ on the run; **mettre en** ~ put to flight; **prendre la** ~ take flight.

fulgurant, ~e /fylgyʀã, -t/ *adj* (*vitesse*) lightning.

fumé, ~e /fyme/ *adj* (*poisson, verre*) smoked.

fumée /fyme/ *nf* smoke; (vapeur) steam.

fumer /fyme/ **1** *vt/i* smoke.

fumeur, -euse /fymœʀ, -øz/ *nm, f* smoker; **zone non-~s** no smoking area.

fumier /fymje/ *nm* manure.

funambule /fynãbyl/ *nmf* tightrope walker.

funèbre /fynɛbʀ/ *adj* funeral; (fig) gloomy.

funérailles /fyneʀɑj/ *nfpl* funeral.

funéraire /fyneʀɛʀ/ *adj* funeral.

funeste /fynɛst/ *adj* fatal.

fur: au ~ **et à mesure** /ofyʀeaməzyʀ/ *loc* as one goes along, progressively; **au** ~ **et à mesure que** as.

furet /fyʀɛ/ *nm* ferret.

fureur /fyʀœʀ/ *nf* fury; (passion) passion; **avec** ~ furiously; passionately; **mettre en** ~ infuriate; **faire** ~ be all the rage.

furieux, -ieuse /fyʀjø, -z/ *adj* furious.

furoncle /fyʀõkl/ *nm* boil.

furtif, -ive /fyʀtif, -v/ *adj* furtive.

fuseau (*pl* ~**x**) /fyzo/ *nm* ski trousers; (pour filer) spindle; ~ **horaire** time zone.

fusée /fyze/ *nf* rocket.

fusible /fyzibl/ *nm* fuse.

fusil /fyzi/ *nm* rifle, gun; (de chasse) shotgun; ~ **mitrailleur** machine-gun.

fusion /fyzjõ/ *nf* fusion; (Comm) merger. **fusionner 1** *vt/i* merge.

fut /fy/ →ÊTRE **5**.

fût /fy/ *nm* (tonneau) barrel; (d'arbre) trunk.

futé, ~e /fyte/ *adj* cunning.

futile /fytil/ *adj* futile.

futur, ~e /fytyʀ/ *adj* future; ~**e femme/maman** wife-/mother-to-be. ● *nm* future.

fuyant, ~e /fɥijã, -t/ *adj* (front, ligne) receding; (personne) evasive.

fuyard, ~e /fɥijaʀ, -d/ *nm, f* runaway.

Gg

gabardine /gabaʀdin/ *nf* raincoat.

gabarit /gabaʀi/ *nm* size; (patron) template; (fig) calibre.

gâcher /gɑʃe/ **1** *vt* (gâter) spoil; (gaspiller) waste.

gâchette /gɑʃɛt/ *nf* trigger.

gâchis /gɑʃi/ *nm* waste.

gaffe /gaf/ *nf* **1** blunder; **faire** ~ be careful (à of).

gage /gaʒ/ *nm* security; (de bonne foi) pledge; (de jeu) forfeit; ~**s** (salaire) wages; **en** ~ **de** as a token of; **mettre en** ~ pawn; **tueur à** ~**s** hired killer.

gageure /gaʒyʀ/ *nf* challenge.

gagnant, ~e /gaɲã, -t/ *adj* winning. ● *nm, f* winner.

gagne-pain /gaɲpɛ̃/ *nm inv* job.

gagner /gaɲe/ **1** *vt* (match, prix) win; (argent, pain) earn; (terrain) gain;

gai, (*temps*) save; (atteindre) reach; (convaincre) win over; ~ **sa vie** earn one's living. ● *vi* win; (fig) gain.

gai, ~**e** /ge/ *adj* cheerful; (ivre) merry. **gaiement** *adv* cheerfully. **gaieté** *nf* cheerfulness.

gain /gɛ̃/ *nm* (salaire) earnings; (avantage) gain; (économie) saving; ~**s** (Comm) profits; (au jeu) winnings.

gaine /gɛn/ *nf* (corset) girdle; (étui) sheath.

galant, ~**e** /galɑ̃, -t/ *adj* courteous; (amoureux) romantic.

galaxie /galaksi/ *nf* galaxy.

gale /gal/ *nf* (de chat etc.) mange.

galère /galɛʀ/ *nf* (navire) galley; **c'est la** ~**!** 🚹 what an ordeal!

galérer /galeʀe/ 🚹 *vi* 🚹 (peiner) have a hard time.

galerie /galʀi/ *nf* gallery; (Théât) circle; (de voiture) roof-rack; ~ **marchande** shopping arcade.

galet /galɛ/ *nm* pebble.

galette /galɛt/ *nf* flat cake; ~ **des Rois** Twelfth Night cake.

Galles /gal/ *nfpl* **le pays de** ~ Wales.

gallois, ~**e** /galwa, -z/ *adj* Welsh. ● *nm* (Ling) Welsh. **G~**, ~**e** *nm, f* Welshman, Welshwoman.

galon /galɔ̃/ *nm* braid; (Mil) stripe; **prendre du** ~ be promoted.

galop /galo/ *nm* canter; **aller au** ~ canter; **grand** ~ gallop; ~ **d'essai** trial run. **galoper** 🚹 *vi* (cheval) canter; (au grand galop) gallop; (personne) run.

galopin /galɔpɛ̃/ *nm* 🚹 rascal.

gambader /gɑ̃bade/ 🚹 *vi* leap about.

gamelle /gamɛl/ *nf* (de soldat) mess kit; (d'ouvrier) lunch-box.

gamin, ~**e** /gamɛ̃, -in/ *adj* childish; (air) youthful. ● *nm, f* 🚹 kid.

gamme /gam/ *nf* (Mus) scale; (série) range; **haut de** ~ up-market, top of the range; **bas de** ~ down-market, bottom of the range.

gang /gɑ̃g/ *nm* 🚹 gang.

ganglion /gɑ̃glijɔ̃/ *nm* ganglion.

gangster /gɑ̃gstɛʀ/ *nm* gangster; (escroc) crook.

gant /gɑ̃/ *nm* glove; ~ **de ménage** rubber glove; ~ **de toilette** face- flannel, face-cloth.

garage /gaʀaʒ/ *nm* garage. **garagiste** *nmf* garage owner; (employé) car mechanic.

garant, ~**e** /gaʀɑ̃, -t/ *nm, f* guarantor. ● *adj* **se porter** ~ **de** vouch for.

garanti, ~**e** /gaʀɑ̃ti/ *adj* guaranteed.

garantie /gaʀɑ̃ti/ *nf* guarantee; ~**s** (de police d'assurance) cover. **garantir** 🔢 *vt* guarantee; (protéger) protect (de from).

garçon /gaʀsɔ̃/ *nm* boy; (jeune homme) young man; (célibataire) bachelor; ~ **(de café)** waiter; ~ **d'honneur** best man. **garçonnière** *nf* bachelor flat.

garde¹ /gaʀd/ *nf* guard; (d'enfants, de bagages) care; (service) guard (duty); (infirmière) nurse; **de** ~ on duty; ~ **à vue** (police) custody; **mettre en** ~ warn; **prendre** ~ be careful (à of); **(droit de)** ~ custody (de of).

garde² /gaʀd/ *nm* guard; (de propriété, parc) warden; ~ **champêtre** village policeman; ~ **du corps** bodyguard.

garde-à-vous /gaʀdavu/ *nm inv* (Mil) **se mettre au** ~ stand to attention.

garde-chasse (*pl* ~**s**) /gaʀdə- ʃas/ *nm* gamekeeper.

garde-manger /gaʀdmɑ̃ʒe/ *nm inv* meat safe; (placard) larder.

garder /gaʀde/ 🚹 *vt* (conserver, maintenir) keep; (vêtement) keep on; (surveiller) look after; (défendre) guard; ~ **le lit** stay in bed. □ **se** ~ *vpr* (denrée) keep; **se** ~ **de faire** be careful not to do.

garderie /gaʀdəʀi/ *nf* day nursery.

garde-robe (*pl* ~**s**) /gaʀdəʀɔb/ *nf* wardrobe.

gardien, ~**ne** /gaʀdjɛ̃, -ɛn/ *nm, f* (de locaux) security guard; (de prison, réserve) warden; (d'immeuble) caretaker; (de musée) attendant; (de zoo) keeper; (de traditions) guardian; ~ **de but** goalkeeper; ~ **de la paix** policeman; ~ **de nuit** night watchman; **gardienne d'enfants** childminder.

gare /gaʀ/ *nf* (Rail) station; ~ **routière** coach station; (US) bus station. ● *interj* ~ **(à toi)** watch out!

garer /gaʀe/ 🚹 *vt* park. □ **se** ~ *vpr* park; (s'écarter) move out of the way.

gargouille /gaʀguj/ *nf* waterspout; (sculptée) gargoyle. **gargouiller** 🚹 *vi* gurgle; (*stomach*) rumble.

garni, ~e /garni/ *adj* (*plat*) served with vegetables; **bien** ~ (rempli) well-filled.

garnir /garnir/ **2** *vt* (remplir) fill; (décorer) decorate; (couvrir) cover; (doubler) line; (Culin) garnish. **garniture** *nf* (légumes) vegetables; (ornement) trimming; (de voiture) trim.

gars /ga/ *nm* **1** lad; (adulte) guy, bloke.

gas-oil /gazwal/ *nm* diesel (oil).

gaspillage /gaspijaʒ/ *nm* waste. **gaspiller** **1** *vt* waste.

gastrique /gastrik/ *adj* gastric.

gastronome /gastronom/ *nmf* gourmet.

gâteau (*pl* ~x) /gato/ *nm* cake; ~ **sec** biscuit; (US) cookie; **un papa** ~ a doting dad.

gâter /gate/ **1** *vt* spoil. □ **se** ~ *vpr* (*viande*) go bad; (*dent*) rot; (*temps*) get worse.

gâterie /gatri/ *nf* little treat.

gâteux, -euse /gatø, -z/ *adj* senile.

gauche /goʃ/ *adj* left; (maladroit) awkward. ● *nf* left; **à** ~ on the left; (direction) (to the) left; **la** ~ the left (side); (Pol) the left (wing).

gaucher, -ère /goʃe, -ɛr/ *adj* left handed.

gaufre /gofr/ *nf* waffle. **gaufrette** *nf* wafer.

gaulois, ~e /golwa, -z/ *adj* Gallic; (fig) bawdy. **G**~, ~e *nm, f* Gaul.

gaver /gave/ **1** *vt* force-feed; (fig) cram. □ **se** ~ **de** *vpr* gorge oneself with; (fig) devour.

gaz /gaz/ *nm inv* gas; ~ **d'échappement** exhaust fumes; ~ **lacrymogène** tear-gas.

gaze /gaz/ *nf* gauze.

gazer /gaze/ **1** *vi* **1** **ça gaze?** how's things?

gazette /gazɛt/ *nf* newspaper.

gazeux, -euse /gazø, -z/ *adj* (boisson) fizzy; (*eau*) sparkling.

gazoduc /gazɔdyk/ *nm* gas pipeline.

gazon /gazɔ̃/ *nm* lawn, grass.

gazouiller /gazuje/ **1** *vi* (*oiseau*) chirp; (*bébé*) babble.

GDF *abrév m* (**Gaz de France**) French gas board.

géant, ~e /ʒeã, -t/ *adj* giant. ● *nm* giant. **géante** *nf* giantess.

geindre /ʒɛ̃dr/ **22** *vi* groan, moan.

gel /ʒɛl/ *nm* frost; (produit) gel; (Comm) freeze; ~ **coiffant** hair gel.

gelée /ʒ(ə)le/ *nf* frost; (Culin) jelly; ~ **blanche** hoarfrost.

geler /ʒəle/ **6** *vt/i* freeze; **on gèle** (on a froid) it's freezing; **il** *ou* **ça gèle** (il fait froid) it's freezing.

gélule /ʒelyl/ *nf* (Méd) capsule.

Gémeaux /ʒemo/ *nmpl* Gemini.

gémir /ʒemir/ **2** *vi* groan.

gênant, ~e /ʒɛnã, -t/ *adj* embarrassing; (irritant) annoying; (incommode) cumbersome.

gencive /ʒãsiv/ *nf* gum.

gendarme /ʒãdarm/ *nm* policeman, gendarme. **gendarmerie** *nf* police force; (local) police station.

Gendarmerie nationale ∧ section of the military, which provides the police service outside major towns.

---

gendre /ʒãdr/ *nm* son-in-law.

gène /ʒɛn/ *nm* gene.

gêne /ʒɛn/ *nf* discomfort; (confusion) embarrassment; (dérangement) trouble, inconvenience; (pauvreté) poverty.

gêné, ~e /ʒene/ *adj* embarrassed; (désargenté) short of money.

généalogie /ʒenealɔʒi/ *nf* genealogy.

gêner /ʒene/ **1** *vt* bother, disturb; (troubler) embarrass; (entraver) block; (faire mal) hurt.

général, ~e (*mpl* **-aux**) /ʒeneral, -o/ *adj* general; **en** ~ in general. ● *nm* (*pl* **-aux**) general.

généralement /ʒeneralmã/ *adv* generally.

généraliser /ʒeneralize/ **1** *vt* make general. ● *vi* generalize. □ **se** ~ *vpr* become widespread *ou* general.

généraliste /ʒeneralist/ *nmf* general practitioner, GP.

généralité /ʒeneralite/ *nf* general point.

génération /ʒenerasjɔ̃/ *nf* generation.

généreux, -euse /ʒenerø, -z/ *adj* generous.

g

générique /ʒeneʀik/ nm (au cinéma) credits. ● adj generic.

générosité /ʒeneʀozite/ nf generosity.

génétique /ʒenetik/ adj genetic. ● nf genetics.

Genève /ʒənɛv/ npr Geneva.

génial, ~e (mpl **-iaux**) /ʒenjal, -jo/ adj brilliant; (fantastique 🔟) fantastic.

génie /ʒeni/ nm genius; ~ **civil** civil engineering.

génital, ~e (mpl **-aux**) /ʒenital, -o/ adj genital.

génocide /ʒenɔsid/ nm genocide.

génoise /ʒenwaz/ nf sponge (cake).

génome /ʒenom/ nm genome.

génothèque /ʒenɔtɛk/ nf gene bank.

genou (pl ~**x**) /ʒənu/ nm knee; **être à ~x** be kneeling.

genre /ʒɑ̃ʀ/ nm sort, kind; (Gram) gender; (allure) **avoir bon/mauvais ~** to look nice/disreputable; (comportement) **c'est bien son ~** it's just like him/her.

gens /ʒɑ̃/ nmpl people.

gentil, ~le /ʒɑ̃ti, -j/ adj kind, nice; (sage) good. **gentillesse** nf kindness. **gentiment** adv kindly.

géographie /ʒeɔgʀafi/ nf geography.

geôlier, -ière /ʒolje, -jɛʀ/ nm, f gaoler, jailer.

géologie /ʒeɔlɔʒi/ nf geology.

géomètre /ʒeɔmɛtʀ/ nm surveyor.

géométrie /ʒeɔmetʀi/ nf geometry. **géométrique** adj geometric.

gérance /ʒeʀɑ̃s/ nf management.

gérant, ~e /ʒeʀɑ̃, -t/ nm, f manager, manageress; ~ **d'immeuble** landlord's agent.

gerbe /ʒɛʀb/ nf (de fleurs) bunch, bouquet; (d'eau) spray; (de blé) sheaf.

gercer /ʒɛʀse/ 🔟 vt chap; **avoir les lèvres gercées** have chapped lips. ● vi become chapped. **gerçure** nf crack, chap.

gérer /ʒeʀe/ 🔢 vt manage, run; (traiter: fig) (crise, situation) handle.

germe /ʒɛʀm/ nm germ; ~**s de soja** bean sprouts.

germer /ʒɛʀme/ 🔟 vi germinate.

gestation /ʒɛstasjɔ̃/ nf gestation.

geste /ʒɛst/ nm gesture.

gesticuler /ʒɛstikyle/ 🔟 vi gesticulate.

gestion /ʒɛstjɔ̃/ nf management. **gestionnaire** nmf administrator.

ghetto /gɛto/ nm ghetto.

gibier /ʒibje/ nm (animaux) game.

giboulée /ʒibule/ nf shower.

gicler /ʒikle/ 🔟 vi squirt; **faire ~** squirt.

gifle /ʒifl/ nf slap in the face. **gifler** 🔟 vt slap.

gigantesque /ʒigɑ̃tɛsk/ adj gigantic.

gigot /ʒigo/ nm leg (of lamb).

gigoter /ʒigɔte/ 🔟 vi wriggle; (nerveusement) fidget.

gilet /ʒilɛ/ nm waistcoat; (cardigan) cardigan; ~ **de sauvetage** life jacket.

gingembre /ʒɛ̃ʒɑ̃bʀ/ nm ginger.

girafe /ʒiʀaf/ nf giraffe.

giratoire /ʒiʀatwaʀ/ adj **sens ~** roundabout.

girofle /ʒiʀɔfl/ nm **clou de ~** clove.

girouette /ʒiʀwɛt/ nf weathercock, weathervane.

gisement /ʒizmɑ̃/ nm deposit.

gitan, ~e /ʒitɑ̃, -an/ nm, f gypsy.

gîte /ʒit/ nm (maison) home; (abri) shelter; ~ **rural** holiday cottage.

givre /ʒivʀ/ nm frost; (sur parebrise) ice.

givré, ~e /ʒivʀe/ adj 🔟 crazy.

glace /glas/ nf ice; (crème) icecream; (vitre) window; (miroir) mirror; (verre) glass.

glacé, ~e /glase/ adj (vent, accueil) icy; (hands) frozen; (gâteau) iced.

glacer /glase/ 🔟 vt freeze; (gâteau, boisson) chill; (pétrifier) chill. ▢ **se ~** vpr freeze.

glacier /glasje/ nm (Géog) glacier; (vendeur) ice-cream seller. **glacière** nf coolbox. **glaçon** nm ice-cube.

glaïeul /glajœl/ nm gladiolus.

glaise /glɛz/ nf clay.

gland /glɑ̃/ nm acorn; (ornement) tassel.

glande /glɑ̃d/ nf gland.

glander /glɑ̃de/ 🔟 vi 🔟 laze around.

glaner /glane/ 🔟 vt glean.

glauque /glok/ adj (fig) murky; (street) squalid.

glissade /glisad/ nf (jeu) slide; (dérapage) skid.

glissant, ~e /glisɑ̃, -t/ adj slippery.

glissement /glismɑ̃/ nm sliding; gliding; (fig) shift; ~ **de terrain** landslide.

glisser /glise/ **1** vi slide; (être glissant)
be slippery; (sur l'eau) glide; (déraper)
slip; (véhicule) skid. ● vt (objet) slip
(**dans** into); (remarque) slip in. □ **se ~**
vpr slip (**dans** into).

glissière /glisjɛʀ/ nf slide; **porte à ~**
sliding door; ~ **de sécurité** (Auto)
crash-barrier; **fermeture à ~** zip.

global, ~e (mpl **-aux**) /ɡlɔbal, -o/ adj
(entier, général) overall. **globalement**
adv as a whole.

globe /ɡlɔb/ nm globe; ~ **oculaire**
eyeball; ~ **terrestre** globe.

globule /ɡlɔbyl/ nm (du sang) corpuscle.

gloire /ɡlwaʀ/ nf glory, fame. **glorieux, -ieuse** adj glorious. **glorifier** **45**
vt glorify.

glose /ɡloz/ nf gloss.

glossaire /ɡlɔsɛʀ/ nm glossary.

gloussement /ɡlusmɑ̃/ nm chuckle;
(de poule) cluck.

glouton, ~ne /ɡlutɔ̃, -ɔn/ adj gluttonous. ● nm, f glutton.

gluant, ~e /ɡlyɑ̃, -t/ adj sticky.

glucose /ɡlykoz/ nm glucose.

glycérine /ɡliseʀin/ nf glycerin(e).

GO abrév fpl (**grandes ondes**)
long wave.

goal /ɡol/ nm **T** goalkeeper.

gobelet /ɡɔblɛ/ nm cup; (en verre)
tumbler.

gober /ɡɔbe/ **1** vt swallow (whole); **je
ne peux pas le ~ T** I can't
stand him.

goéland /ɡɔelɑ̃/ nm (sea)gull.

gogo: à ~ /aɡoɡo/ loc **T** galore, in
abundance.

goinfre /ɡwɛ̃fʀ/ nm (glouton **T**) pig.
goinfrer (se) **1** vpr **T** stuff oneself
(**de** with).

golf /ɡɔlf/ nm golf; (terrain) golf course.

golfe /ɡɔlf/ nm gulf.

gomme /ɡɔm/ nf rubber; (US) eraser;
(résine) gum. **gommer** **1** vt rub out.

gond /ɡɔ̃/ nm hinge; **sortir de ses ~s**
T go mad.

gondoler (se) /(sə)ɡɔ̃dɔle/ **1** vpr
(bois) warp; (métal) buckle.

gonflé, ~e /ɡɔ̃fle/ adj swollen; **il est
~ T** he's got a nerve.

gonflement /ɡɔ̃fləmɑ̃/ nm swelling.

gonfler /ɡɔ̃fle/ **1** vt (ballon, pneu)
pump up, blow up; (augmenter) increase; (exagérer) inflate. ● vi swell.

gorge /ɡɔʀʒ/ nf throat; (poitrine)
breast; (vallée) gorge.

gorgée /ɡɔʀʒe/ nf sip, gulp.

gorger /ɡɔʀʒe/ **40** vt fill (**de** with);
gorgé de full of. □ **se ~** vpr gorge
oneself (**de** with).

gorille /ɡɔʀij/ nm gorilla; (garde **T**)
bodyguard.

gosier /ɡozje/ nm throat.

gosse /ɡɔs/ nmf **T** kid.

gothique /ɡɔtik/ adj Gothic.

goudron /ɡudʀɔ̃/ nm tar. **goudronner**
1 vt tarmac.

gouffre /ɡufʀ/ nm abyss, gulf.

goujat /ɡuʒa/ nm lout, boor.

goulot /ɡulo/ nm neck; **boire au ~**
drink from the bottle.

goulu, ~e /ɡuly/ adj gluttonous. ● nm,
f glutton.

gourde /ɡuʀd/ nf (à eau) flask; (idiot
T) fool.

gourer (se) /(sə)ɡuʀe/ **1** vpr **T** make
a mistake.

gourmand, ~e /ɡuʀmɑ̃, -d/ adj
greedy. ● nm, f glutton.

gourmandise /ɡuʀmɑ̃diz/ nf greed;
~s sweets.

gourmet /ɡuʀmɛ/ nm gourmet.

gourmette /ɡuʀmɛt/ nf chain
bracelet.

gousse /ɡus/ nf ~ **d'ail** clove of garlic.

goût /ɡu/ nm taste; (gré) liking; **prendre ~ à** develop a taste for; **avoir
bon ~** (aliment) taste nice; (personne)
have good taste; **donner du ~ à** give
flavour.

goûter /ɡute/ **1** vt taste; (apprécier)
enjoy; ~ **à** ou **de** taste. ● vi have tea.
● nm tea, snack.

goutte /ɡut/ nf drop; (Méd) gout.
goutte-à-goutte nm inv drip. **goutter**
1 vi drip.

gouttière /ɡutjɛʀ/ nf gutter.

gouvernail /ɡuvɛʀnaj/ nm rudder;
(barre) helm.

gouvernement /ɡuvɛʀnəmɑ̃/ nm
government.

g

gouverner /guvɛʀne/ **1** vt/i govern; (dominer) control. **gouverneur** nm governor.

GPS abrév m (**global positioning system**) GPS.

grâce /gʀɑs/ nf (charme) grace; (faveur) favour; (volonté) grace; (Jur) pardon; (Relig) grace; ~ **à** thanks to; **rendre (~s) à** give thanks to.

gracier /gʀasje/ **45** vt pardon.

gracieusement /gʀasjøzmɑ̃/ adv gracefully; (gratuitement) free (of charge).

gracieux, -ieuse /gʀasjø, -z/ adj graceful.

grade /gʀad/ nm rank; **monter en ~** be promoted.

gradin /gʀadɛ̃/ nm tier, step; **en ~s** terraced; **les ~s** terraces.

gradué, ~e /gʀadɥe/ adj graded, graduated; **verre ~** measuring jug.

graffiti /gʀafiti/ nmpl graffiti.

grain /gʀɛ̃/ nm grain; (Naut) squall; ~ **de beauté** beauty spot; ~ **de café** coffee bean; ~ **de poivre** pepper corn; ~ **de raisin** grape.

graine /gʀɛn/ nf seed.

graisse /gʀɛs/ nf fat; (lubrifiant) grease. **graisser** **1** vt grease. **graisseux, -euse** adj greasy.

grammaire /gʀam(m)ɛʀ/ nf grammar.

gramme /gʀam/ nm gram.

grand, ~e /gʀɑ̃, -d/ adj big, large; (haut) tall; (intense, fort) great; (brillant) great; (principal) main; (plus âgé) big, elder; (adulte) grown-up; **au ~ air** in the open air; **au ~ jour** in broad daylight; (fig) in the open; **en ~e partie** largely; **~e banlieue** outer suburbs; ~ **ensemble** housing estate; **~es lignes** (Rail) main lines; ~ **magasin** department store; **~e personne** grown-up; ~ **public** general public; **~e surface** hypermarket; **~es vacances** summer holidays. ● adv (ouvrir) wide; ~ **ouvert** wide open; **voir** ~ think big. ● nm, f (adulte) grown-up; (enfant) big boy, big girl; (Scol) senior.

grand-chose /gʀɑ̃ʃoz/ pron **pas ~** not much, not a lot.

Grande-Bretagne /gʀɑ̃dbʀətaɲ/ nf Great Britain.

Grande école A prestigious *i* tertiary education institution to which admission is usually by competitive examination or *concours*. Places are much sought after as they generally guarantee more promising career prospects than the standard universities. Many *grandes écoles* specialize in particular disciplines or fields of study, e.g. *ENA* (public administration), *Sciences Po* (political science), etc.

grandeur /gʀɑ̃dœʀ/ nf greatness; (dimension) size; **folie des ~s** delusions of grandeur.

grandir /gʀɑ̃diʀ/ **2** vi grow; (bruit) grow louder. ● vt (talons) make taller; (loupe) magnify.

grand-mère (pl **grands-mères**) /gʀɑ̃mɛʀ/ nf grandmother.

grand-père (pl **grands-pères**) /gʀɑ̃pɛʀ/ nm grandfather.

grands-parents /gʀɑ̃paʀɑ̃/ nmpl grandparents.

grange /gʀɑ̃ʒ/ nf barn.

granulé /gʀanyle/ nm granule.

graphique /gʀafik/ adj graphic; (Ordinat) graphics; **informatique ~** computer graphics. ● nm graph.

graphologie /gʀafɔlɔʒi/ nf graphology.

grappe /gʀap/ nf cluster; ~ **de raisin** bunch of grapes.

gras, ~se /gʀɑ, -s/ adj (gros) fat; (aliment) fatty; (surface, peau, cheveux) greasy; (épais) thick; (caractères) bold; **faire la ~se matinée** sleep late. ● nm (Culin) fat.

gratifiant, ~e /gʀatifjɑ̃, -t/ adj gratifying; (travail) rewarding.

gratifier /gʀatifje/ **45** vt favour, reward (**de** with).

gratin /gʀatɛ̃/ nm gratin (baked dish with cheese topping); (élite **1**) upper crust.

gratis /gʀatis/ adv free.

gratitude /gʀatityd/ nf gratitude.

gratte-ciel /gʀatsjɛl/ nm inv skyscraper.

gratter /gʀate/ **1** vt/i scratch; (avec un outil) scrape; **ça me gratte** **1** it itches. □ **se ~** vpr scratch oneself; **se ~ la tête** scratch one's head.

gratuiciel /gratɥisjɛl/ nm (Internet) freeware.

gratuit, ~e /gratɥi, -t/ adj free; (acte) gratuitous. **gratuitement** adv free (of charge).

grave /grav/ adj (maladie, accident, problème) serious; (solennel) grave; (voix) deep; (accent) grave. **gravement** adv seriously; gravely.

graver /grave/ **1** vt engrave; (sur bois) carve; (Ordinat) burn.

graveur /gravœr/ nm (Ordinat) burner.

gravier /gravje/ nm du ~ gravel.

gravité /gravite/ nf gravity.

graviter /gravite/ **1** vi revolve.

gravure /gravyr/ nf engraving; (de tableau, photo) print, plate.

gré /gre/ nm (volonté) will; (goût) taste; **à son ~** (aglr) as one likes; **de bon ~** willingly; **bon ~ mal ~** like it or not; **je vous en saurais ~** I'd be grateful for that.

grec, ~que /grɛk/ adj Greek. ● nm (Ling) Greek. **G~, ~que** nm, f Greek.

Grèce nf /grɛs/ Greece.

greffe /grɛf/ nf graft; (d'organe) transplant. **greffer 1** vt graft; transplant.

greffier, -ière /grefje, -jɛr/ nm, f clerk of the court.

grêle /grɛl/ adj (maigre) spindly; (voix) shrill. ● nf hail.

grêler /grele/ **1** vi hail; **il grêle** it's hailing. **grêlon** nm hailstone.

grelot /grəlo/ nm (little) bell.

grelotter /grələte/ **1** vi shiver.

grenade /grənad/ nf (fruit) pomegranate; (explosif) grenade.

grenat /grəna/ adj inv dark red.

grenier /grənje/ nm attic; (pour grain) loft.

grenouille /grənuj/ nf frog.

grès /grɛ/ nm sandstone; (poterie) stoneware.

grésiller /grezije/ **1** vi sizzle; (radio) crackle.

grève /grɛv/ nf (rivage) shore; (cessation de travail) strike; **faire ~, être en ~** be on strike; **se mettre en ~** go on strike. **gréviste** nmf striker.

gribouiller /gribuje/ **1** vt/i scribble.

grief /grijɛf/ nm grievance.

grièvement /grijɛvmɑ̃/ adv seriously.

griffe /grif/ nf claw; (de couturier) label; **coup de ~** scratch.

griffé, ~e /grife/ adj (vêtement, article) designer.

griffer /grife/ **1** vt scratch, claw.

grignoter /griɲote/ **1** vt/i nibble.

gril /gril/ nm (de cuisinière) grill; (plaque) grill pan.

grillade /grijad/ nf (viande) grill.

grillage /grijaʒ/ nm wire netting.

grille /grij/ nf railings; (portail) (metal) gate; (de fenêtre) bars; (de cheminée) grate; (fig) grid. **grillepain** nm inv toaster.

griller /grije/ **1** vt (pain) toast; (viande) grill; (ampoule) blow; (feu rouge) go through; (appareil) burn out. ● vi (ampoule) blow; (Culin) **faire ~** (viande) grill; (pain) toast.

grillon /grijɔ̃/ nm cricket.

grimace /grimas/ nf (funny) face; (de douleur, dégoût) grimace; **faire des ~s** make faces; **faire la ~** pull a face, grimace.

grimper /grɛ̃pe/ **1** vt climb. ● vi climb; **~ sur** ou **dans un arbre** climb a tree.

grincement /grɛ̃smɑ̃/ nm creak- (ing).

grincer /grɛ̃se/ **10** vi creak; **~ des dents** grind one's teeth.

grincheux, -euse /grɛ̃ʃø, -z/ adj grumpy.

grippe /grip/ nf influenza, flu.

grippé, ~e /gripe/ adj être ~ have (the) flu; (mécanisme) be seized up ou jammed.

gris, ~e /gri, -z/ adj grey; (saoul) tipsy.

grivois, ~e /grivwa, -z/ adj bawdy.

grog /grɔg/ nm hot toddy.

grogner /grɔɲe/ **1** vi (animal) growl; (personne) grumble.

grognon /grɔɲɔ̃/ adj grumpy.

groin /grwɛ̃/ nm snout.

gronder /grɔ̃de/ **1** vi (tonnerre, volcan) rumble; (chien) growl; (conflit) be brewing. ● vt scold.

groom /grum/ nm bellboy.

gros, ~se /gro, -s/ adj big, large; (gras) fat; (important) big; (épais) thick;

g

(lourd) heavy; (buveur, fumeur) heavy; ~ **bonnet** 🔲 bigwig; ~ **lot** jackpot; ~ **mot** swear word; ~ **plan** close-up; ~**se caisse** bass drum; ~ **titre** headline. ● *nm, f* fat man, fat woman. ● *adv* (écrire) big; (risquer, gagner) a lot. ● *nm* **le ~ de** the bulk of; **de ~** (Comm) wholesale; **en ~** roughly; (Comm) wholesale.

groseille /ɡʀozɛj/ *nf* redcurrant; ~ **à maquereau** gooseberry.

grossesse /ɡʀosɛs/ *nf* pregnancy.

grosseur /ɡʀosœʀ/ *nf* (volume) size; (enflure) lump.

grossier, -ière /ɡʀosje, -jɛʀ/ *adj* (sans finesse) coarse, rough; (rudimentaire) crude; (vulgaire) coarse; (impoli) rude; (erreur) gross. **grossièrement** *adv* (sommairement) roughly; (vulgairement) coarsely. **grossièreté** *nf* coarseness; crudeness; rudeness; (mot) rude word.

grossir /ɡʀosiʀ/ 🔢 *vt* (faire augmenter) increase, boost; (agrandir) enlarge; (exagérer) exaggerate; ~ **les rangs** *ou* **la foule** swell the ranks. ● *vi* (personne) put on weight; (augmenter) grow.

grossiste /ɡʀosist/ *nmf* wholesaler.

grosso modo /ɡʀosomodo/ *adv* roughly.

grotesque /ɡʀotɛsk/ *adj* grotesque; (ridicule) ludicrous.

grotte /ɡʀot/ *nf* cave; grotto.

grouiller /ɡʀuje/ 🔢 *vi* swarm; ~ **de** be swarming with.

groupe /ɡʀup/ *nm* group; (Mus) group, band; ~ **électrogène** generating set; ~ **scolaire** school; ~ **de travail** working party.

groupement /ɡʀupmɑ̃/ *nm* grouping.

grouper /ɡʀupe/ 🔢 *vt* put together. □ **se ~** *vpr* group (together).

grue /ɡʀy/ *nf* (machine, oiseau) crane.

gruyère /ɡʀyjɛʀ/ *nm* gruyère (cheese).

gué /ɡe/ *nm* ford; **passer** *ou* **traverser à ~** ford.

guenon /ɡənɔ̃/ *nf* female monkey.

guépard /ɡepaʀ/ *nm* cheetah.

guêpe /ɡɛp/ *nf* wasp.

guère /ɡɛʀ/ *adv* **ne ~** hardly; **il n'y a ~ d'espoir** there is no hope; **elle n'a**

~ **dormi** she didn't sleep much, she hardly slept.

guérilla /ɡeʀija/ *nf* guerrilla warfare; (groupe) guerillas.

guérir /ɡeʀiʀ/ 🔢 *vt* (personne, maladie, mal) cure (de of); (plaie, membre) heal. ● *vi* get better; (blessure) heal; ~ **de** recover from. **guérison** *nf* curing; healing; (de personne) recovery.

guerre /ɡɛʀ/ *nf* war; **en ~** at war; **faire la ~** wage war (à against); ~ **civile** civil war; ~ **mondiale** world war.

guerrier, -ière /ɡeʀje, -jɛʀ/ *adj* warlike. ● *nm, f* warrior.

guet /ɡɛ/ *nm* watch; **faire le ~** be on the watch. **guet-apens** (*pl* **guets-apens**) *nm* ambush.

guetter /ɡete/ 🔢 *vt* watch; (attendre) watch out for.

gueule /ɡœl/ *nf* mouth; (figure 🔲) face; **ta ~!** shut up!; ~ **de bois** 🔲 hangover.

gueuleton /ɡœltɔ̃/ *nm* 🔲 blowout, slap-up meal.

gui /ɡi/ *nm* mistletoe.

guichet /ɡiʃɛ/ *nm* window, counter; (de gare) ticket-office; (Théât) box-office; **jouer à ~s fermés** (pièce) be sold out; ~ **automatique** cash dispenser.

guide /ɡid/ *nm* guide. ● *nf* (fille scout) girl guide.

guider /ɡide/ 🔢 *vt* guide.

guidon /ɡidɔ̃/ *nm* handlebars.

guignol /ɡiɲɔl/ *nm* puppet; (personne) clown; (spectacle) puppet-show.

guillemets /ɡijmɛ/ *nmpl* quotation marks, inverted commas; **entre ~** in inverted commas.

guillotine /ɡijɔtin/ *nf* guillotine.

guimauve /ɡimov/ *nf* marshmallow; **c'est de la ~** 🔲 it's slushy *ou* schmaltzy 🔲.

guindé, ~e /ɡɛ̃de/ *adj* stiff, formal; (style) stilted.

guirlande /ɡiʀlɑ̃d/ *nf* garland; tinsel.

guitare /ɡitaʀ/ *nf* guitar.

gym /ʒim/ *nf* gymnastics; (Scol) physical education, PE.

gymnase /ʒimnɑz/ *nm* gym(nasium). **gymnastique** *nf* gymnastics.

gynécologie /ʒinekɔlɔʒi/ *nf* gynaecology.

Hh

habile /abil/ adj skilful, clever.

habillé, ~e /abije/ adj (vêtement) smart; (soirée) formal.

habillement /abijmã/ nm clothing.

habiller /abije/ **1** vt dress (**de** in); (équiper) clothe; (recouvrir) cover (**de** with). □ **s'**~ vpr get dressed; (élégamment) dress up.

habit /abi/ nm (de personnage) outfit; (de cérémonie) tails; ~s clothes.

habitant, ~e /abitã, -t/ nm, f (de maison, quartier) resident; (de pays) inhabitant.

habitat /abita/ nm (mode de peuplement) settlement; (conditions) housing.

habitation /abitasjõ/ nf (logement) house.

habité, ~e /abite/ adj (terre) inhabited.

habiter /abite/ **1** vi live. ● vt live in.

habitude /abityd/ nf habit; **avoir l'**~ **de** be used to; **d'**~ usually; **comme d'**~ as usual.

habitué, ~e /abitɥe/ nm, f (client) regular.

habituel, ~le /abitɥɛl/ adj usual. **habituellement** adv usually.

habituer /abitɥe/ **1** vt ~ **qn à** get sb used to. □ **s'**~ **à** vpr get used to.

hache /'aʃ/ nf axe.

haché, ~e /'aʃe/ adj (viande) minced; (phrases) jerky.

hacher /'aʃe/ **1** vt mince; (au couteau) chop.

hachis /'aʃi/ nm minced meat; (US) ground meat; ~ **Parmentier** ≈ shepherd's pie.

hachisch /'aʃiʃ/ nm hashish.

hachoir /'aʃwaʀ/ nm (appareil) mincer; (couteau) chopper; (planche) chopping board.

haie /'ɛ/ nf hedge; **course de** ~s hurdle race.

haillon /'ajõ/ nm rag.

haine /'ɛn/ nf hatred.

haïr /'aiʀ/ **38** vt hate.

hâlé /'ale/ adj (sun-)tanned.

haleine /alɛn/ nf breath; **travail de longue** ~ long job.

haleter /'alte/ **6** vi pant.

hall /'ol/ nm hall; (de gare) concourse.

halle /'al/ nf market hall; ~s covered market.

halte /'alt/ nf stop; **faire** ~ stop. ● interj stop; (Mil) halt.

haltère /altɛʀ/ nm dumbbell; **faire des** ~s to do weightlifting.

hameau (pl ~x) /'amo/ nm hamlet.

hameçon /amsõ/ nm hook.

hanche /'ãʃ/ nf hip.

handicap /'ãdikap/ nm handicap. **handicapé,** ~e adj & nm, f disabled (person).

hangar /'ãgaʀ/ nm shed; (pour avions) hangar.

hanter /'ãte/ **1** vt haunt.

hantise /'ãtiz/ nf dread; **avoir la** ~ **de** dread.

haras /'aʀa/ nm stud-farm.

harasser /'aʀase/ **1** vt exhaust.

harcèlement /'aʀsɛlmã/ nm ~ **sexuel** sexual harassment.

harceler /'aʀsəle/ **6** vt harass.

hardi, ~e /'aʀdi/ adj bold.

hareng /'aʀã/ nm herring.

hargne /'aʀɲ/ nf (aggressive) bad temper.

haricot /'aʀiko/ nm bean; ~ **vert** French bean; (US) green bean.

harmonie /aʀmɔni/ nf harmony. **harmonieux, -ieuse** adj harmonious.

harmoniser /aʀmɔnize/ **1** vt harmonize. □ **s'**~ vpr harmonize.

harnacher /'aʀnaʃe/ **1** vt harness.

harnais /'aʀnɛ/ nm harness.

harpe /'aʀp/ nf harp.

harpon /'aʀpõ/ nm harpoon.

hasard /'azaʀ/ nm chance; (coïncidence) coincidence; **les** ~s **de** the fortunes of; **au** ~ (choisir etc.) at random; (flâner) aimlessly. **hasardeux, -euse** adj risky.

hasarder /'azaʀde/ **1** vt risk; (remarque) venture.

hâte /'at/ nf haste; **à la** ~, **en** ~ hurriedly; **avoir** ~ **de** look forward to.

hâter /'ate/ **1** vt hasten. □ **se** ~ vpr hurry (**de** to).

h

hâtif, -ive /'ɑtif, -v/ *adj* hasty; (précoce) early.

hausse /'os/ *nf* rise (**de** in); **~ des prix** price rise; **en ~** rising.

hausser /'ose/ **1** *vt* raise; (épaules) shrug.

haut, ~e /'o, 'ot/ *adj* high; (de taille) tall; **à voix ~e** aloud; **~ en couleur** colourful; **plus ~** higher up; (dans un texte) above; **en ~ lieu** in high places. ● *adv* high; **tout ~** out loud. ● *nm* top; **des ~s et des bas** ups and downs; **en ~** (regarder) up; (à l'étage) upstairs; **en ~ de)** ɑt the top (of).

hautbois /'obwa/ *nm* oboe.

haut-de-forme /'odfɔrm/ (*pl* **hauts-de-forme**) *nm* top hat.

hauteur /'otœr/ *nf* height; (colline) hill; (arrogance) haughtiness; **être à la ~** be up to it; **à la ~ de** (ville) near; **être à la ~ de la situation** be equal to the situation.

haut-le-cœur /'olkœr/ *nm inv* nausea.

haut-parleur (*pl* **~s**) /'oparlœr/ *nm* loudspeaker.

havre /'ɑvr/ *nm* haven (**de** of).

hayon /'ajɔ̃/ *nm* (Auto) hatchback.

hebdomadaire /ɛbdɔmadɛr/ *adj & nm* weekly.

hébergement /ebɛrʒəmɑ̃/ *nm* accommodation.

héberger /ebɛrʒe/ **40** *vt* (ami) put up; (réfugiés) take in.

hébreu (*pl* **~x**) /ebrø/ *am* Hebrew. ● *nm* (Ling) Hebrew; **c'est de l'~!** it's all Greek to me!

Hébreu (*pl* **~x**) /ebrø/ *nm* Hebrew; **les ~x** the Hebrews.

hécatombe /ekatɔ̃b/ *nf* slaughter.

hectare /ɛktar/ *nm* hectare (= 10,000 square metres).

hélas /'elɑs/ *interj* alas. ● *adv* sadly.

hélice /elis/ *nf* propeller.

hélicoptère /elikɔptɛr/ *nm* helicopter.

helvétique /ɛlvetik/ *adj* Swiss.

hématome /ematom/ *nm* bruise.

hémorragie /emɔraʒi/ *nf* haemorrhage.

hémorroïdes /emɔrɔid/ *nfpl* piles, haemorrhoids.

hennir /'enir/ **2** *vi* neigh.

hépatite /epatit/ *nf* hepatitis.

herbe /ɛrb/ *nf* grass; (Méd, Culin) herb; **en ~** in the blade; (fig) budding.

héréditaire /ereditɛr/ *adj* hereditary.

hérédité /eredite/ *nf* heredity.

hérisser /'erise/ **1** *vt* bristle; **~ qn** (fig) ruffle sb. □ **se ~** *vpr* bristle.

hérisson /'erisɔ̃/ *nm* hedgehog.

héritage /eritaʒ/ *nm* inheritance; (spirituel) heritage.

hériter /erite/ **1** *vt/i* inherit (**de** from); **~ de qch** inherit sth. **héritier, -ière** *nm, f* heir, heiress.

hermétique /ɛrmetik/ *adj* airtight; (fig) unfathomable.

hernie /'ɛrni/ *nf* hernia.

héroïne /erɔin/ *nf* (femme) heroine; (drogue) heroin.

héroïque /erɔik/ *adj* heroic.

héros /'ero/ *nm* hero.

hésiter /ezite/ **1** *vi* hesitate (**à** to); **j'hésite** I'm not sure.

hétérogène /eterɔʒɛn/ *adj* heterogeneous.

hétérosexuel, ~le /eterɔseksɥɛl/ *nm/ f & adj* heterosexual.

hêtre /'ɛtr/ *nm* beech.

heure /œr/ *nf* time; (soixante minutes) hour; **quelle ~ est-il?** what time is it?; **il est dix ~s** it is ten o'clock; **à l'~** (venir, être) on time; **d'~ en ~** by the hour; **toutes les deux ~s** every two hours; **~ de pointe** rush-hour; **~ de cours** (Scol) period; **~ indue** ungodly hour; **~s creuses** off peak periods; **~s supplémentaires** overtime.

heureusement /œrøzmɑ̃/ *adv* fortunately, luckily.

heureux, -euse /œrø, -z/ *adj* happy; (chanceux) lucky, fortunate.

heurt /'œr/ *nm* collision; (conflit) clash; **sans ~** smoothly.

heurter /'œrte/ **1** *vt* (cogner) hit; (mur) bump into, hit; (choquer) offend. □ **se ~ à** *vpr* bump into, hit; (fig) come up against.

hexagone /ɛgzagon/ *nm* hexagon; **l'~** France.

hiberner /ibɛrne/ **1** *vi* hibernate.

hibou (*pl* **~x**) /'ibu/ *nm* owl.

hier /jɛr/ *adv* yesterday; **~ soir** last night, yesterday evening.

hiérarchie /'jerarʃi/ *nf* hierarchy.

hilare /ilaʀ/ *adj* (*visage*) merry; **être ~** be laughing.

hindou, ~e /ɛ̃du/ *adj & nm, f* Hindu. **H~, ~e** *nm, f* Hindu.

hippique /ipik/ *adj* equestrian; **le concours ~** showjumping.

hippodrome /ipɔdʀom/ *nm* racecourse.

hippopotame /ipɔpɔtam/ *nm* hippopotamus.

hirondelle /iʀɔ̃dɛl/ *nf* swallow.

hisser /'ise/ **1** *vt* hoist, haul. □ **se ~** *vpr* heave oneself up.

histoire /istwaʀ/ *nf* (*récit*) story; (*étude*) history; (*affaire*) business; **~(s)** (*chichis*) fuss; (*ennuis*) trouble. **historique** *adj* historical.

hiver /ivɛʀ/ *nm* winter. **hivernal, ~e** (*mpl* **-aux**) *adj* winter; (*glacial*) wintry.

H.L.M. *abbrév m ou f* (**habitation à loyer modéré**) block of council flats; (US) low-rent apartment building.

hocher /'ɔʃe/ **1** *vt* **~ la tête** (*pour dire oui*) nod; (*pour dire non*) shake one's head.

hochet /'ɔʃɛ/ *nm* rattle.

hockey /'ɔkɛ/ *nm* hockey; **~ sur glace** ice hockey.

hollandais, ~e /'ɔlɑ̃dɛ, -z/ *adj* Dutch. ● *nm* (Ling) Dutch. **H~, ~e** *nm, f* Dutchman, Dutchwoman.

Hollande /'ɔlɑ̃d/ *nf* Holland.

homard /'ɔmaʀ/ *nm* lobster.

homéopathie /ɔmeɔpati/ *nf* homoeopathy.

homicide /ɔmisid/ *nm* homicide; **~ involontaire** manslaughter.

hommage /ɔmaʒ/ *nm* tribute; **~s** (*salutations*) respects; **rendre ~ à** pay tribute to.

homme /ɔm/ *nm* man; (*espèce*) man (kind); **~ d'affaires** businessman; **~ de la rue** man in the street; **~ d'État** statesman; **~ politique** politician.

homogène /ɔmɔʒɛn/ *adj* homogeneous.

homonyme /ɔmɔnim/ *nm* (*personne*) namesake.

homosexualité /ɔmɔsɛksɥalite/ *nf* homosexuality.

homosexuel, ~le /ɔmɔsɛksɥɛl/ *adj & nm, f* homosexual.

Hongrie /'ɔ̃gʀi/ *nf* Hungary.

hongrois, ~e /'ɔ̃gʀwa, -z/ *adj* Hungarian. ● *nm* (Ling) Hungarian. **H~, ~e** *nm, f* Hungarian.

honnête /ɔnɛt/ *adj* honest; (*juste*) fair. **honnêteté** *nf* honesty.

honneur /ɔnœʀ/ *nm* honour; (*mérite*) credit; **d'~** (*invité, place*) of honour; **en l'~ de** in honour of; **en quel ~?** ⓘ why?; **faire ~ à** (*équipe, famille*) bring credit to.

honorable /ɔnɔʀabl/ *adj* honourable; (*convenable*) respectable.

honoraire /ɔnɔʀɛʀ/ *adj* honorary. **honoraires** *nmpl* fees.

honorer /ɔnɔʀe/ **1** *vt* honour; (*faire honneur à*) do credit to.

honte /'ɔ̃t/ *nf* shame; **avoir ~** be ashamed (**de** of); **faire ~ à** make ashamed. **honteux, -euse** *adj* (*personne*) ashamed (**de** of): (*action*) shameful.

hôpital (*pl* **-aux**) /ɔpital, -o/ *nm* hospital.

hoquet /'ɔkɛ/ *nm* **le ~** (the) hiccups.

horaire /ɔʀɛʀ/ *adj* hourly. ● *nm* timetable; **~s libres** flexitime.

horizon /ɔʀizɔ̃/ *nm* horizon; (Fig) outlook.

horizontal, ~e (*mpl* **-aux**) /ɔʀizɔ̃tal, -o/ *adj* horizontal.

horloge /ɔʀlɔʒ/ *nf* clock.

hormis /'ɔʀmi/ *prép* save.

hormonal, ~e (*mpl* **-aux**) /ɔʀmɔnal, -o/ *adj* hormonal, hormone.

hormone /ɔʀmon/ *nf* hormone.

horreur /ɔʀœʀ/ *nf* horror; **avoir ~ de** hate.

horrible /ɔʀibl/ *adj* horrible.

horrifier /ɔʀifje/ **45** *vt* horrify.

hors /'ɔʀ/ *prép* **~ de** outside, (*avec mouvement*) out of; **~ d'atteinte** out of reach; **~ d'haleine** out of breath; **~ de prix** extremely expensive; **~ pair** outstanding; **~ de soi** beside oneself. **hors-bord** *nm inv* speedboat. **hors-d'œuvre** *nm inv* hors-d'œuvre. **hors-jeu** *adj inv* offside. **hors-la-loi** *nm inv* outlaw. **hors-piste** *nm* off-piste skiing. **hors-taxe** *adj inv* duty-free.

horticulteur, -trice /ɔʀtikyltœʀ, -tʀis/ *nm, f* horticulturist.

hospice /ɔspis/ *nm* home.

hospitalier, -ière /ɔspitalje, -jɛʀ/ *adj* hospitable; (Méd) hospital. **hospitali-**

h

ser **1** *vt* take to hospital. **hospitalité**
nf hospitality.

hostile /ɔstil/ *adj* hostile. **hostilité** *nf*
hostility.

hôte /ot/ *nm* (maître) host; (invité)
guest.

hôtel /otɛl/ *nm* hotel; ~ (**particulier**)
(private) mansion; ~ **de ville**
town hall.

hôtelier, -ière /otəlje, -jɛʀ/ *adj* hotel.
● *nm, f* hotel keeper. **hôtellerie** *nf*
hotel business.

hôtesse /otɛs/ *nf* hostess; ~ **de l'air**
stewardess.

hotte /'ɔt/ *nf* basket; ~ **aspirante** ex-
tractor (hood), (US) ventilator.

houblon /'ublɔ̃/ *nm* **le** ~ hops.

houille /'uj/ *nf* coal; ~ **blanche** hydroelectric power.

houle /'ul/ *nf* swell. **houleux, -euse** *adj*
(*mer*) rough; (*débat*) stormy.

housse /'us/ *nf* cover; ~ **de siège** seat
cover.

houx /'u/ *nm* holly.

huées /'ɥe/ *nfpl* boos. **huer** **1** *vt* boo.

huile /ɥil/ *nf* oil; (personne **1**) bigwig.
huiler **1** *vt* oil. **huileux, -euse**
adj oily.

huis /'ɥi/ *nm* **à** ~ **clos** in camera.

huissier /ɥisje/ *nm* (Jur) bailiff; (portier) usher.

huit /'ɥi(t)/ *adj* eight; ~ **jours** a week;
lundi en ~ a week on Monday. ● *nm*
eight. **huitième** *adj* & *nmf* eighth.

huître /ɥitʀ/ *nf* oyster.

humain, ~e /ymɛ̃, -ɛn/ *adj* human;
(compatissant) humane. **humanitaire**
adj humanitarian. **humanité** *nf* humanity.

humble /œ̃bl/ *adj* humble.

humeur /ymœʀ/ *nf* mood; (tempérament) temper; **de bonne/ mauvaise**
~ in a good/bad mood.

humide /ymid/ *adj* damp; (*chaleur, climat*) humid; (*lèvres, yeux*) moist. **humidité** *nf* humidity.

humilier /ymilje/ **45** *vt* humiliate.

humoristique /ymɔʀistik/ *adj* humorous.

humour /ymuʀ/ *nm* humour; **avoir de**
l'~ have a sense of humour.

hurlement /'yʀləmɑ̃/ *nm* howl (ing).
hurler **1** *vt/i* howl.

hutte /'yt/ *nf* hut.

hydratant, ~e /idʀatɑ̃, -t/ *adj* (*lotion*)
moisturizing.

hydravion /idʀavjɔ̃/ *nm* seaplane.

hydroélectrique /idʀoelɛktʀik/ *adj*
hydroelectric.

hydrogène /idʀɔʒɛn/ *nm* hydrogen.

hygiène /iʒjɛn/ *nf* hygiene. **hygiénique** *adj* hygienic.

hymne /imn/ *nm* hymn; ~ **national**
national anthem.

hyperlien /ipɛʀljɛ̃/ *nm* (Internet)
hyperlink.

hypermarché /ipɛʀmaʀʃe/ *nm* (supermarché) hypermarket.

hypertension /ipɛʀtɑ̃sjɔ̃/ *nf* high
blood-pressure.

hypertexte /ipɛʀtɛkst/ *nm* (Internet)
hypertext.

hypnotiser /ipnɔtize/ **1** *vt* hypnotize.

hypocrisie /ipɔkʀizi/ *nf* hypocrisy.

hypocrite /ipɔkʀit/ *adj* hypocritical.
● *nmf* hypocrite.

hypothèque /ipɔtɛk/ *nf* mortgage.

hypothèse /ipɔtɛz/ *nf* hypothesis.

hystérie /isteʀi/ *nf* hysteria.

. . . .

I i

. . . .

ici /isi/ *adv* (dans l'espace) here; (dans
le temps) now; **d'**~ **demain** by tomorrow; **d'**~ **là** in the meantime;
d'~ **peu** shortly; ~ **même** in this
very place; **jusqu'**~ until now; (dans
le passé) until then.

idéal, ~e (*mpl* ~**aux**) /ideal, -o/ *adj* &
nm ideal. **idéaliser** **1** *vt* idealize.

idée /ide/ *nf* idea; (esprit) mind; **avoir**
dans l'~ **de faire** plan to do; **il ne**
me viendrait jamais à l'~ **de faire** it
would never occur to me to do; ~
fixe obsession; ~ **reçue** conventional
opinion.

identification /idɑ̃tifikasjɔ̃/ *nf* identification. **identifier** **45** *vt*, **s'identifier**
vpr identify (**à** with).

identique /idɑ̃tik/ *adj* identical.

identité /idɑ̃tite/ *nf* identity.

idéologie /ideɔlɔʒi/ *nf* ideology.

idiome /idjom/ nm idiom.

idiot, ~e /idjo, -ɔt/ adj idiotic. ● nm, f idiot. **idiotie** nf idiocy; (acte, parole) idiotic thing.

idole /idɔl/ nf idol.

if /if/ nm yew.

ignare /iɲaʀ/ adj ignorant. ● nmf ignoramus.

ignoble /iɲɔbl/ adj vile.

ignorance /iɲɔʀɑ̃s/ nf ignorance.

ignorant, ~e /iɲɔʀɑ̃, -t/ adj ignorant. ● nm, f ignoramus.

ignorer /iɲɔʀe/ **1** vt not know; **je l'ignore** I don't know; (personne) ignore.

il /il/ pron (personne, animal familier) he; (chose, animal) it; (impersonnel) it; ~ **est vrai que** it is true that; ~ **neige/pleut** it is snowing/raining; ~ **y a** there is; (pluriel) there are; (temps) ago; (durée) for; ~ **y a 2 ans** 2 years ago; ~ **y a plus d'une heure que j'attends** I've been waiting for over an hour.

île /il/ nf island; ~ **déserte** desert island; ~**s anglo-normandes** Channel Islands; ~**s Britanniques** British Isles.

illégal, ~e (mpl ~aux) /ilegal, -o/ adj illegal.

illégitime /ileʒitim/ adj illegitimate.

illettré, ~e /iletʀe/ adj & nm, f illiterate.

illicite /ilisit/ adj illicit; (Jur) unlawful.

illimité, ~e /ilimite/ adj unlimited.

illisible /ilizibl/ adj illegible; (livre) unreadable.

illogique /ilɔʒik/ adj illogical.

illuminé, ~e /ilymine/ adj lit up; (monument) floodlit.

illusion /ilyzjɔ̃/ nf illusion; **se faire des** ~**s** delude oneself. **illusoire** adj illusory.

illustre /ilystʀ/ adj illustrious.

illustré, ~e /ilystʀe/ adj illustrated. ● nm comic.

illustrer /ilystʀe/ **1** vt illustrate. □ **s'**~ vpr become famous.

îlot /ilo/ nm islet; (de maisons) block.

ils /il/ pron they.

image /imaʒ/ nf picture; (métaphore) image; (reflet) reflection. **imagé,** ~e adj full of imagery.

imaginaire /imaʒinɛʀ/ adj imaginary. **imaginatif, -ive** adj imaginative. **imagination** nf imagination.

imaginer /imaʒine/ **1** vt imagine; (inventer) think up. □ **s'**~ vpr (se représenter) imagine (**que** that); (croire) think (**que** that).

imbécile /ɛ̃besil/ adj idiotic. ● nmf idiot.

imbiber /ɛ̃bibe/ **1** vt soak (**de** with). □ **s'**~ vpr become soaked (**de** with).

imbriqué, ~e /ɛ̃bʀike/ adj (lié) interlinked; (tuiles) overlapping.

imbu, ~e /ɛ̃by/ adj ~ **de** full of.

IMC abrév m (**indice de masse corporelle**) BMI.

imitateur, -trice /imitatœʀ, -tʀis/ nm, f imitator; (comédien) impersonator. **imiter** **1** vt imitate; (personnage) impersonate; (signature) forge; (faire comme) do the same as.

immatriculation /imatʀikylasjɔ̃/ nf registration.

immatriculer /imatʀikyle/ **1** vt register; **se faire** ~ register; **faire** ~ **une voiture** have a car registered.

immédiat, ~e /imedja, -t/ adj immediate. ● nm **dans l'**~ for the time being.

immense /imɑ̃s/ adj huge.

immerger /imɛʀʒe/ **40** vt immerse. □ **s'**~ vpr immerse oneself (**dans** in).

immeuble /imœbl/ nm block of flats, building; ~ **de bureaux** office building ou block.

immigrant, ~e /imigʀɑ̃, -t/ adj & nm, f immigrant. **immigration** nf immigration. **immigré,** ~e adj & nm, f immigrant. **immigrer** **1** vi immigrate.

imminent, ~e /iminɑ̃, -t/ adj imminent.

immobile /imɔbil/ adj still, motionless.

immobilier, -ière /imɔbilje, -jɛʀ/ adj property; **agence immobilière** estate agent's office; (US) real estate office; **agent** ~ estate agent; (US) real estate agent. ● nm **l'**~ property; (US) real estate.

immobiliser /imɔbilize/ **1** vt immobilize; (stopper) stop. □ **s'**~ vpr stop.

immonde /imɔ̃d/ adj filthy.

immoral, ~e (mpl **-aux**) /imɔʀal, -o/ adj immoral.

i

immortel, ~le /imɔʀtɛl/ adj immortal.

immuable /imɥabl/ adj unchanging.

immuniser /imynize/ 🔳 vt immunize; **immunisé contre** (à l'abri de) immune to. **immunité** nf immunity.

impact /ɛ̃pakt/ nm impact.

impair, ~e /ɛ̃pɛʀ/ adj (numéro) odd. ● nm blunder, faux pas.

imparfait, ~e /ɛ̃paʀfɛ, -t/ adj & nm imperfect.

impasse /ɛ̃pɑs/ nf (rue) dead end; (situation) deadlock.

impatient, ~e /ɛ̃pasjɑ̃, -t/ adj impatient.

impatienter /ɛ̃pasjɑ̃te/ 🔳 vt annoy. □ s'~ vpr get impatient (**contre qn** with sb).

impayé, ~e /ɛ̃peje/ adj unpaid.

impeccable /ɛ̃pekabl/ adj (propre) impeccable, spotless; (soigné) perfect.

impensable /ɛ̃pɑ̃sabl/ adj unthinkable.

impératif, -ive /ɛ̃peʀatif, -v/ adj imperative. ● nm (Gram) imperative; (contrainte) imperative; ~s (exigences) requirements, demands (**de** of).

impératrice /ɛ̃peʀatʀis/ nf empress.

impérial, ~e (mpl -iaux) /ɛ̃peʀjal, -jo/ adj imperial.

impérieux, -ieuse /ɛ̃peʀjø, -z/ adj imperious; (pressant) pressing.

imperméable /ɛ̃pɛʀmeabl/ adj impervious (**à** to); (manteau, tissu) waterproof. ● nm raincoat.

impersonnel, ~le /ɛ̃pɛʀsɔnɛl/ adj impersonal.

impertinent, ~e /ɛ̃pɛʀtinɑ̃, -t/ adj impertinent.

imperturbable /ɛ̃pɛʀtyʀbabl/ adj unshakeable, unruffled.

impétueux, -euse /ɛ̃petɥø, -z/ adj impetuous.

impitoyable /ɛ̃pitwajabl/ adj merciless.

implant /ɛ̃plɑ̃/ nm implant.

implanter /ɛ̃plɑ̃te/ 🔳 vt establish, set up. □ s'~ vpr become established.

implication /ɛ̃plikasjɔ̃/ nf (conséquence) implication; (participation) involvement.

impliquer /ɛ̃plike/ 🔳 vt (mêler) implicate (**dans** in); (signifier) imply, mean

(**que** that); (nécessiter) involve (**de faire** doing).

implorer /ɛ̃plɔʀe/ 🔳 vt implore, beg for.

impoli, ~e /ɛ̃pɔli/ adj impolite, rude.

importance /ɛ̃pɔʀtɑ̃s/ nf importance; (taille) size; (ampleur) extent; **sans** ~ unimportant.

important, ~e /ɛ̃pɔʀtɑ̃, -t/ adj important; (en quantité) considerable, sizeable, big; (air) self-important. ● nm **l'**~ the important thing.

importateur, -trice /ɛ̃pɔʀtatœʀ, -tʀis/ nm, f importer. ● adj importing. **importation** nf import.

importer /ɛ̃pɔʀte/ 🔳 vt (Comm) import. ● vi matter, be important (**à** to); **il importe que** it is important that; **n'importe**, **peu importe** it does not matter; **n'importe comment** anyhow; **n'importe où** anywhere; **n'importe qui** anybody; **n'importe quoi** anything.

importun, ~e /ɛ̃pɔʀtœ̃, -yn/ adj troublesome. ● nm, f nuisance.

imposer /ɛ̃poze/ 🔳 vt impose (**à on**); (taxer) tax; **en** ~ **à qn** impress sb. □ s'~ vpr (action) be essential; (se faire reconnaître) stand out; (s'astreindre à) **s'**~ **de faire** force oneself to do.

imposition /ɛ̃pozisjɔ̃/ nf taxation; ~ **des mains** laying-on of hands.

impossible /ɛ̃posibl/ adj impossible. ● nm **faire l'**~ do one's utmost.

impôt /ɛ̃po/ nm tax; ~s (contributions) tax(ation), taxes; ~ **sur le revenu** income tax.

impotent, ~e /ɛ̃pɔtɑ̃, -t/ adj disabled.

imprécis, ~e /ɛ̃pʀesi, -z/ adj imprecise.

imprégner /ɛ̃pʀeɲe/ 🔳 vt fill (**de** with); (imbiber) impregnate (**de** with). □ s'~ **de** vpr (fig) immerse oneself in.

impression /ɛ̃pʀesjɔ̃/ nf impression; (de livre) printing. **impressionnant**, ~e adj impressive; (choquant) disturbing. **impressionner** 🔳 vt impress; (choquer) disturb.

imprévisible /ɛ̃pʀeviziblˌ/ adj unpredictable.

imprévu, ~e /ɛ̃pʀevy/ adj unexpected. ● nm unexpected incident;

sauf ~ unless anything unexpected happens.

imprimante /ɛpʀimɑ̃t/ *nf* (Ordinat) printer; ~ **à jet d'encre** ink-jet printer; ~ **(à) laser** laser printer.

imprimé, ~e /ɛpʀime/ *adj* printed. ● *nm* printed form.

imprimer /ɛpʀime/ **1** *vt* print; (marquer) imprint. **imprimerie** *nf* (art) printing; (lieu) printing works. **imprimeur** *nm* printer.

improbable /ɛpʀɔbabl/ *adj* unlikely, improbable.

impropre /ɛpʀɔpʀ/ *adj* incorrect; ~ **à** unfit for.

improviste: à l'~ /alɛpʀɔvist/ *loc* unexpectedly.

imprudence /ɛpʀydɑ̃s/ *nf* carelessness; (acte) careless action.

imprudent, ~e /ɛpʀydɑ̃, -t/ *adj* careless; **il est ~ de** it is unwise to.

impudent, ~e /ɛpydɑ̃, -t/ *adj* impudent.

impuissant, ~e /ɛpɥisɑ̃, -t/ *adj* helpless; (Méd) impotent; ~ **à faire** powerless to do.

impulsif, -ive /ɛpylsif, -v/ *adj* impulsive. **impulsion** *nf* (poussée, influence) impetus; (instinct, mouvement) impulse.

impur, ~e /ɛpyʀ/ *adj* impure.

imputer /ɛpyte/ **1** *vt* ~ **à** attribute to, impute to.

inabordable /inabɔʀdabl/ *adj* (prix) prohibitive.

inacceptable /inaksɛptabl/ *adj* unacceptable.

inactif, -ive /inaktif, -v/ *adj* inactive.

inadapté, ~e /inadapte/ *adj* maladjusted. ● *nm, f* (Psych) maladjusted person.

inadmissible /inadmisibl/ *adj* unacceptable.

inadvertance /inadvɛʀtɑ̃s/ *nf* **par ~** by mistake.

inanimé, ~e /inanime/ *adj* (évanoui) unconscious; (mort) lifeless; (matière) inanimate.

inaperçu, ~e /inapɛʀsy/ *adj* unnoticed.

inapte /inapt/ *adj* unsuited (à to); ~ **à faire** incapable of doing; ~ **au service militaire** unfit for military service.

inattendu, ~e /inatɑ̃dy/ *adj* unexpected.

inaugurer /inogyʀe/ **1** *vt* inaugurate.

incapable /ɛkapabl/ *adj* incapable (**de** **qch** of sth); ~ **de faire** unable to do, incapable of doing. ● *nmf* incompetent.

incapacité /ɛkapasite/ *nf* inability, incapacity; **être dans l'~ de faire** be unable to do.

incarcérer /ɛkaʀseʀe/ **14** *vt* imprison, incarcerate.

incarnation /ɛkaʀnasjɔ̃/ *nf* embodiment, incarnation. **incarné, ~e** *adj* (ongle) ingrowing.

incassable /ɛkɑsabl/ *adj* unbreakable.

incendiaire /ɛsɑ̃djɛʀ/ *adj* incendiary; (propos) inflammatory. ● *nmf* arsonist.

incendie /ɛsɑ̃di/ *nm* fire; ~ **criminel** arson. **incendier** **45** *vt* set fire to.

incertain, ~e /ɛsɛʀtɛ̃, -ɛn/ *adj* uncertain; (contour) vague; (temps) unsettled. **incertitude** *nf* uncertainty.

inceste /ɛsɛst/ *nm* incest.

incidence /ɛsidɑ̃s/ *nf* effect.

incident /ɛsidɑ̃/ *nm* incident; ~ **technique** technical hitch.

incinérer /ɛsineʀe/ **14** *vt* incinerate; (mort) cremate.

inciser /ɛsize/ **1** *vt* make an incision in; (abcès) lance. **incisif, -ive** *adj* incisive. **incision** *nf* incision; (d'abcès) lancing.

incitation /ɛsitasjɔ̃/ *nf* (Jur) incitement (à to); (encouragement) incentive. **inciter** **1** *vt* incite (à to); (encourager) encourage.

inclinaison /ɛklinɛzɔ̃/ *nf* incline; (de la tête) tilt.

inclination /ɛklinasjɔ̃/ *nf* (penchant) inclination; (geste) (du buste) bow; (de la tête) nod.

incliner /ɛkline/ **1** *vt* tilt, lean; (courber) bend; (inciter) encourage (à to); ~ **la tête** (approuver) nod; (révérence) bow. ● *vi* ~ **à** be inclined to. □ **s'~** *vpr* lean forward; (se courber) bow down (**devant** before); (céder) give in, yield (**devant** to); (chemin) slope.

inclure /ɛklyʀ/ **16** *vt* include; (enfermer) enclose; **jusqu'au lundi inclus** up to and including Monday.

incohérence /ɛ̃kɔeʀɑ̃s/ nf incoherence; (contradiction) discrepancy. **incohérent, ~e** adj incoherent, inconsistent.

incolore /ɛ̃kɔlɔʀ/ adj colourless; (verre) clear.

incommoder /ɛ̃kɔmɔde/ **1** vt inconvenience, bother.

incompatible /ɛ̃kɔ̃patibl/ adj incompatible.

incompétent, ~e /ɛ̃kɔ̃petɑ̃, -t/ adj incompetent.

incomplet, -ète /ɛ̃kɔ̃plɛ, -t/ adj incomplete.

incompréhension /ɛ̃kɔ̃pʀeɑ̃sjɔ̃/ nf lack of understanding.

incompris, ~e /ɛ̃kɔ̃pʀi, -z/ adj misunderstood.

inconcevable /ɛ̃kɔ̃svabl/ adj inconceivable.

incongru, ~e /ɛ̃kɔ̃gʀy/ adj unseemly.

inconnu, ~e /ɛ̃kɔny/ adj unknown (à to). ● nm, f stranger. ● nm l'~ the unknown.

inconscience /ɛ̃kɔ̃sjɑ̃s/ nf unconsciousness; (folie) madness.

inconscient, ~e /ɛ̃kɔ̃sjɑ̃, -t/ adj unconscious (**de** of); (fou) mad. ● nm (Psych) subconscious.

incontestable /ɛ̃kɔ̃tɛstabl/ adj indisputable.

incontrôlable /ɛ̃kɔ̃tʀolabl/ adj unverifiable; (non maîtrisé) uncontrollable.

inconvenant, ~e /ɛ̃kɔ̃vnɑ̃, -t/ adj improper.

inconvénient /ɛ̃kɔ̃venjɑ̃/ nm disadvantage, drawback; (objection) objection.

incorporer /ɛ̃kɔʀpɔʀe/ **1** vt incorporate; (Culin) blend (**à** into); (Mil) enlist.

incorrect, ~e /ɛ̃kɔʀɛkt/ adj (faux) incorrect; (malséant) improper; (impoli) impolite; (déloyal) unfair.

incrédule /ɛ̃kʀedyl/ adj incredulous.

incriminer /ɛ̃kʀimine/ **1** vt (personne) incriminate; (conduite, action) attack.

incroyable /ɛ̃kʀwajabl/ adj incredible.

incruster /ɛ̃kʀyste/ **1** vt inlay (**de** with).

incubateur /ɛ̃kybatœʀ/ nm incubator.

inculpation /ɛ̃kylpasjɔ̃/ nf charge (**de**, **pour** of). **inculpé, ~e** nm, f accused.

inculper **1** vt charge (**de** with).

inculquer /ɛ̃kylke/ **1** vt instil (**à** into).

inculte /ɛ̃kylt/ adj uncultivated; (personne) uneducated.

incurver /ɛ̃kyʀve/ **1** vt curve, bend. □ **s'~** vpr curve, bend.

Inde /ɛ̃d/ nf India.

indécent, ~e /ɛ̃desɑ̃, -t/ adj indecent.

indécis, ~e /ɛ̃desi, -z/ adj (de nature) indecisive; (temporairement) undecided.

indéfini, ~e /ɛ̃defini/ adj (Gram) indefinite; (vague) undefined; (sans limites) indeterminate.

indemne /ɛ̃dɛmn/ adj unharmed.

indemniser /ɛ̃dɛmnize/ **1** vt compensate (**de** for).

indemnité /ɛ̃dɛmnite/ nf indemnity, compensation; (allocation) allowance; **~s de licenciement** redundancy payment.

indépendance /ɛ̃depɑ̃dɑ̃s/ nf independence. **indépendant, ~e** adj independent.

indéterminé, ~e /ɛ̃detɛʀmine/ adj unspecified.

index /ɛ̃dɛks/ nm forefinger; (liste) index.

indicateur, -trice /ɛ̃dikatœʀ, -tʀis/ nm, f (police) informer. ● nm (livre) guide; (Tech) indicator.

indicatif, -ve /ɛ̃dikatif, -v/ adj indicative (**de** of). ● nm (à la radio) signature tune; (téléphonique) dialling code; (Gram) indicative.

indication /ɛ̃dikasjɔ̃/ nf indication; (renseignement) information; (directive) instruction.

indice /ɛ̃dis/ nm sign; (dans une enquête) clue; (des prix) index; (évaluation) rating; **~ d'écoute** audience ratings.

indifférence /ɛ̃difeʀɑ̃s/ nf indifference.

indifférent, ~e /ɛ̃difeʀɑ̃, -t/ adj indifferent (**à** to); **ça m'est ~** it makes no difference to me.

indigène /ɛ̃diʒɛn/ adj & nmf native, indigenous; (du pays) local. ● nmf native.

indigent, ~e /ɛ̃diʒɑ̃, -t/ adj destitute.

indigeste /ɛ̃diʒɛst/ adj indigestible. **indigestion** nf indigestion.

indigne /ɛ̃diɲ/ *adj* unworthy (**de** of); (*acte*) vile. **indigner** (**s'**) **1** *vpr* become indignant (**de** at).

indiqué, **~e** /ɛ̃dike/ *adj* (*heure*) appointed; (*opportun*) appropriate; (*conseillé*) recommended.

indiquer /ɛ̃dike/ **1** *vt* (*montrer*) show, indicate; (*renseigner sur*) point out, tell; (*déterminer*) give, state, appoint; **~ du doigt** point to *ou* out *ou* at.

indirect, **~e** /ɛ̃diRɛkt/ *adj* indirect.

indiscipliné, **~e** /ɛ̃disipline/ *adj* unruly.

indiscret, **-ète** /ɛ̃diskRɛ, -t/ *adj* (*personne*) inquisitive; (*question*) indiscreet.

indiscutable /ɛ̃diskytabl/ *adj* unquestionable.

indispensable /ɛ̃dispɑ̃sabl/ *adj* indispensable; **il est ~ qu'il vienne** it is essential that he comes.

individu /ɛ̃dividy/ *nm* individual.

individuel, **~le** /ɛ̃dividɥɛl/ *adj* (pour une personne) individual; (qui concerne l'individu) personal; **chambre ~le** single room; **maison ~le** detached house.

indolore /ɛ̃dɔlɔR/ *adj* painless.

Indonésie /ɛ̃dɔnezi/ *nf* Indonesia.

indu, **~e** /ɛ̃dy/ *adj* **à une heure ~e** at some ungodly hour.

induire /ɛ̃dɥiR/ **17** *vt* infer (**de** from); (*inciter*) induce (**à faire** to do); **~ en erreur** mislead.

indulgence /ɛ̃dylʒɑ̃s/ *nf* indulgence; (de jury) leniency. **indulgent**, **~e** *adj* indulgent; (clément) lenient.

industrialisé, **~e** /ɛ̃dystRijalize/ *adj* industrialized.

industrie /ɛ̃dystRi/ *nf* industry.

industriel, **~le** /ɛ̃dystRijɛl/ *adj* industrial. ● *nm* industrialist.

inédit, **~e** /inedi, -t/ *adj* unpublished; (fig) original.

inefficace /inefikas/ *adj* (*remède, mesure*) ineffective; (*appareil, système*) inefficient.

inégal, **~e** (*mpl* **-aux**) /inegal, -o/ *adj* unequal; (irrégulier) uneven. **inégalable** *adj* matchless. **inégalité** *nf* (injustice) inequality; (irrégularité) unevenness; (disproportion) disparity.

inéluctable /inelyktabl/ *adj* inescapable.

inepte /inɛpt/ *adj* inept, absurd.

inerte /inɛRt/ *adj* inert; (immobile) lifeless; (sans énergie) apathetic. **inertie** *nf* inertia; (fig) apathy.

inespéré, **~e** /inɛspeRe/ *adj* unhoped for.

inestimable /inɛstimabl/ *adj* priceless; (aide) invaluable.

inexact, **~e** /inɛgza(kt) , -kt/ *adj* (imprécis) inaccurate; (incorrect) incorrect.

in extremis /inɛkstRemis/ *adv* (par nécessité) as a last resort; (au dernier moment) at the last minute. ● *adj* last-minute.

infaillible /ɛ̃fajibl/ *adj* infallible.

infâme /ɛ̃fɑm/ *adj* vile.

infantile /ɛ̃fɑ̃til/ *adj* (puéril) infantile; (maladie) childhood; (mortalité) infant.

infarctus /ɛ̃faRktys/ *nm* coronary, heart attack.

infatigable /ɛ̃fatigabl/ *adj* tireless.

infect, **~e** /ɛ̃fɛkt/ *adj* revolting.

infecter /ɛ̃fɛkte/ **1** *vt* infect. □ **s'~** *vpr* become infected. **infectieux**, **-ieuse** *adj* infectious. **infection** *nf* infection.

inférieur, **~e** /ɛ̃feRjœR/ *adj* (plus bas) lower; (moins bon) inferior (**à** to); **~ à** (plus petit que) smaller than; (plus bas que) lower than. ● *nm, f* Inferior. **infériorité** *nf* inferiority.

infernal, **~e** (*mpl* **-aux**) /ɛ̃fɛRnal, -o/ *adj* infernal.

infester /ɛ̃fɛste/ **1** *vt* infest.

infidèle /ɛ̃fidɛl/ *adj* unfaithful (**à** to). **infidélité** *nf* unfaithfulness; (acte) infidelity.

infiltrer (**s'**) /sɛ̃filtRe/ **1** *vpr* **s'~** (**dans**) (personnes, idées) infiltrate; (liquide) seep through.

infime /ɛ̃fim/ *adj* tiny, minute.

infini, **~e** /ɛ̃fini/ *adj* infinite. ● *nm* infinity; **à l'~** endlessly.

infinité /ɛ̃finite/ *nf* **l'~** infinity; **une ~ de** an endless number of.

infinitif /ɛ̃finitif/ *nm* infinitive.

infirme /ɛ̃fiRm/ *adj* disabled. ● *nmf* disabled person. **infirmerie** *nf* sickbay, infirmary. **infirmier** *nm* (male) nurse. **infirmière** *nf* nurse. **Infirmité** *nf* disability.

inflammable /ɛ̃flamabl/ *adj* inflammable.

inflation /ɛ̃flasjɔ̃/ *nf* inflation.

infliger /ɛ̃fliʒe/ **40** vt inflict; (*sanction*) impose.

influence /ɛ̃flyɑ̃s/ nf influence. **influencer** **10** vt influence. **influent, ~e** adj influential.

influer /ɛ̃flye/ **1** vi ~ **sur** influence.

informateur, -trice /ɛ̃fɔʀmatœʀ, -tʀis/ nm, f informant; (pour la police) informer.

informaticien, ~ne /ɛ̃fɔʀmatisjɛ̃, -ɛn/ nm, f computer scientist.

information /ɛ̃fɔʀmasjɔ̃/ nf information; (Jur) inquiry; **une ~** (some) information; (nouvelle) (some) news; **les ~s** the news.

informatique /ɛ̃fɔʀmatik/ nf computer science; (techniques) information technology. **informatiser** **1** vt computerize.

informer /ɛ̃fɔʀme/ **1** vt inform (**de** about, of). □ **s'~** vpr enquire (**de** about).

inforoute /ɛ̃fɔʀut/ nf (Ordinat) information highway.

infortune /ɛ̃fɔʀtyn/ nf misfortune.

infraction /ɛ̃fʀaksjɔ̃/ nf offence; ~ **à** (loi, règlement) breach of.

infrastructure /ɛ̃fʀastʀyktyʀ/ nf infrastructure; (équipements) facilities.

infructueux, -euse /ɛ̃fʀyktɥø, -z/ adj fruitless.

infuser /ɛ̃fyze/ **1** vt/i infuse, brew. **infusion** nf herbal tea, infusion.

ingénier (s') /(s)ɛ̃ʒenje/ **45** vpr **s'~ à** strive to.

ingénieur /ɛ̃ʒenjœʀ/ nm engineer.

ingénieux, -ieuse /ɛ̃ʒenjø, -z/ adj ingenious. **ingéniosité** nf ingenuity.

ingénu, ~e /ɛ̃ʒeny/ adj naïve.

ingérence /ɛ̃ʒerɑ̃s/ nf interference.

ingérer (s') /sɛ̃ʒere/ **14** vpr **s'~ dans** interfere in.

ingrat, ~e /ɛ̃gʀa, -t/ adj (personne) ungrateful; (travail) unrewarding, thankless; (visage) unattractive.

ingrédient /ɛ̃gʀedjɑ̃/ nm ingredient.

ingurgiter /ɛ̃gyʀʒite/ **1** vt swallow.

inhabité, ~e /inabite/ adj uninhabited.

inhabituel, ~le /inabitɥɛl/ adj unusual.

inhumain, ~e /inymɛ̃, -ɛn/ adj inhuman.

inhumation /inymasjɔ̃/ nf burial.

initial, ~e (mpl **-iaux**) /inisjal, -jo/ adj initial. **initiale** nf initial.

initialisation /inisjalizasjɔ̃/ nf (Ordinat) formatting. **initialiser** **1** vt format.

initiation /inisjasjɔ̃/ nf initiation; (formation) introduction (**à** to); **cours d'~** introductory course.

initiative /inisjativ/ nf initiative.

initier /inisje/ **45** vt initiate (**à** into); (faire découvrir) introduce (**à** to). □ **s'~** vpr **s'~ à qch** learn sth.

injecter /ɛ̃ʒɛkte/ **1** vt inject; **injecté de sang** bloodshot. **injection** nf injection.

injure /ɛ̃ʒyʀ/ nf insult. **injurier** **45** vt insult. **injurieux, -ieuse** adj insulting.

injuste /ɛ̃ʒyst/ adj unjust, unfair. **injustice** nf injustice.

inné, ~e /inne/ adj innate, inborn.

innocence /inɔsɑ̃s/ nf innocence. **innocent, ~e** adj & nm, f innocent. **innocenter** **1** vt clear, prove innocent.

innombrable /inɔ̃bʀabl/ adj countless.

innovateur, -trice /inɔvatœʀ, -tʀis/ nm, f innovator. **innovation** nf innovation. **innover** **1** vi innovate.

inodore /inɔdɔʀ/ adj odourless.

inoffensif, -ive /inɔfɑ̃sif, -v/ adj harmless.

inondation /inɔ̃dasjɔ̃/ nf flood; (action) flooding.

inonder /inɔ̃de/ **1** vt flood; (mouiller) soak; (envahir) inundate (**de** with); **inondé de soleil** bathed in sunlight.

inopiné, ~e /inɔpine/ adj unexpected; (mort) sudden.

inopportun, ~e /inɔpɔʀtœ̃, -yn/ adj inopportune, ill-timed.

inoubliable /inublijabl/ adj unforgettable.

inouï, ~e /inwi/ adj incredible; (événement) unprecedented.

inox® /inɔks/ nm stainless steel.

inoxydable /inɔksidabl/ adj **acier ~** stainless steel.

inqualifiable /ɛ̃kalifjabl/ adj unspeakable.

inquiet, -iète /ɛ̃kjɛ, -t/ adj worried. **inquiétant, ~e** adj worrying.

inquiéter /ɛ̃kjete/ **14** vt worry. □ s'~
vpr worry (**de** about). **inquiétude** nf
anxiety, worry.

insaisissable /ɛ̃sezizabl/ adj (personne) elusive; (nuance) indefinable.

insalubre /ɛ̃salybʀ/ adj unhealthy.

insatisfaisant, ~e /ɛ̃satisfəzɑ̃, -t/ adj
unsatisfactory. **insatisfait, ~e** adj
(mécontent) dissatisfied; (frustré) un-
fulfilled.

inscription /ɛ̃skʀipsjɔ̃/ nf inscription;
(immatriculation) enrolment.

inscrire /ɛ̃skʀiʀ/ **30** vt write (down);
(graver, tracer) inscribe; (personne)
enrol; (sur une liste) put down. □ s'~
vpr put one's name down; **s'~ à**
(école) enrol at; (club, parti) join; (examen) enter for.

insecte /ɛ̃sɛkt/ nm insect.

insécurité /ɛ̃sekyʀite/ nf insecurity.

insensé, ~e /ɛ̃sɑ̃se/ adj mad.

insensibilité /ɛ̃sɑ̃sibilite/ nf insensi-
tivity. **insensible** adj insensitive (à to);
(graduel) imperceptible.

insérer /ɛ̃seʀe/ **14** vt insert. □ s'~ vpr
be inserted; **s'~ dans** be part of.

insigne /ɛ̃siɲ/ nm badge; ~s (d'une
fonction) insignia.

insignifiant, ~e /ɛ̃siɲifjɑ̃, -t/ adj insignificant.

insinuation /ɛ̃sinɥasjɔ̃/ nf insinuation.

insinuer /ɛ̃sinɥe/ **1** vt insinuate.
□ s'~ vpr (socialement) ingratiate
oneself (**auprès de qn** with sb); **s'~
dans** (se glisser) slip into; (idée,
nuance) creep into.

insipide /ɛ̃sipid/ adj insipid.

insistance /ɛ̃sistɑ̃s/ nf insistence. **insistant, ~e** adj insistent.

insister /ɛ̃siste/ **1** vi insist (**pour faire**
on doing); ~ **sur** stress.

insolation /ɛ̃sɔlasjɔ̃/ nf (Méd) sun-
stroke.

insolent, ~e /ɛ̃sɔlɑ̃, -t/ adj insolent.

insolite /ɛ̃sɔlit/ adj unusual.

insolvable /ɛ̃sɔlvabl/ adj insolvent.

insomnie /ɛ̃sɔmni/ nf insomnia.

insonoriser /ɛ̃sɔnɔʀize/ **1** vt
soundproof.

insouciance /ɛ̃susjɑ̃s/ nf lack of concern. **insouciant, ~e** adj carefree.

insoutenable /ɛ̃sutnabl/ adj unbearable; (argument) untenable.

inspecter /ɛ̃spɛkte/ **1** vt inspect. **ins-
pecteur, -trice** nm, f inspector. **inspection** nf inspection.

inspiration /ɛ̃spiʀasjɔ̃/ nf inspiration;
(respiration) breath.

inspirer /ɛ̃spiʀe/ **1** vt inspire; ~ **la
méfiance à qn** inspire distrust in sb.
● vi breathe in. □ s'~ **de** vpr be in-
spired by.

instabilité /ɛ̃stabilite/ nf instability;
unsteadiness. **instable** adj unstable;
(temps) unsettled.

installation /ɛ̃stalasjɔ̃/ nf installation;
(de local) fitting out; (de locataire)
settling in. **installations** nfpl facilities.

installer /ɛ̃stale/ **1** vt install; (meuble)
put in; (étagère) put up; (gaz, téléphone) connect; (équiper) fit out.
□ s'~ vpr settle (down); (emménager)
settle in; **s'~ comme** set oneself
up as.

instance /ɛ̃stɑ̃s/ nf authority; (prière)
entreaty; **avec ~** with insistence; **en
~ pending; en ~ de** in the course of,
on the point of.

instant /ɛ̃stɑ̃/ nm moment, instant; **à
l'~** this instant.

instantané, ~e /ɛ̃stɑ̃tane/ adj instantaneous; (café) instant.

instar: à l'~ de /alɛ̃staʀdə/ loc like.

instaurer /ɛ̃stoʀe/ **1** vt institute.

instigateur, -trice /ɛ̃stigatœʀ, -tʀis/
nm, f instigator.

instinct /ɛ̃stɛ̃/ nm instinct; **d'~** in-
stinctively. **instinctif, -ive** adj instinctive.

instituer /ɛ̃stitɥe/ **1** vt establish.

institut /ɛ̃stity/ nm institute; ~ **de
beauté** beauty parlour.

instituteur, -trice /ɛ̃stitytœʀ, -tʀis/
nm, f primary-school teacher.

institution /ɛ̃stitysjɔ̃/ nf institution;
(école) private school.

instructif, -ive /ɛ̃stʀyktif, -v/ adj instructive.

instruction /ɛ̃stʀyksjɔ̃/ nf (formation)
education; (Mil) training; (document)
directive; ~s (ordres, mode d'emploi)
instructions; (Ordinat) (énoncé) instruction; (pas de séquence)
statement.

instruire /ɛ̃stʀɥiʀ/ **17** vt teach, educate; ~ **de** inform of. □ s'~ vpr learn,
educate oneself; **s'~ de** enquire

about. **instruit,** ∼e adj educated.

instrument /ɛ̃stʀymɑ̃/ nm instrument; (outil) tool; (moyen: fig) instrument; ∼ **de gestion** management tool; ∼s **de bord** (Aviat) controls.

insu: à l'∼ **de** /alɛ̃syda/ loc without the knowledge of.

insuffisance /ɛ̃syfizɑ̃s/ nf (pénurie) shortage; (médiocrité) inadequacy. **insuffisant,** ∼e adj inadequate; (en nombre) insufficient.

insulaire /ɛ̃sylɛʀ/ adj island. ● nmf islander.

insuline /ɛ̃sylin/ nf insulin.

insulte /ɛ̃sylt/ nf insult. **insulter** 1 vt insult.

insupportable /ɛ̃sypɔʀtabl/ adj unbearable.

insurger (s') /(s)ɛ̃syʀʒe/ 40 vpr rebel.

intact, ∼e /ɛ̃takt/ adj intact.

intangible /ɛ̃tɑ̃ʒibl/ adj intangible; (principe) inviolable.

intarissable /ɛ̃taʀisabl/ adj inexhaustible.

intégral, ∼e (mpl **-aux**) /ɛ̃tegʀal, -o/ adj complete; (texte, édition) unabridged; (paiement) full, in full. **intégralement** adv in full. **intégralité** nf whole.

intègre /ɛ̃tɛgʀ/ adj upright.

intégrer /ɛ̃tegʀe/ 14 vt integrate. □ **s'**∼ vpr (personne) integrate; (maison) fit in.

intégriste /ɛ̃tegʀist/ nmf fundamentalist.

intégrité /ɛ̃tegʀite/ nf integrity.

intellect /ɛ̃telɛkt/ nm intellect. **intellectuel,** ∼le adj & nm, f intellectual.

intelligence /ɛ̃teliʒɑ̃s/ nf intelligence; (compréhension) understanding; (complicité) agreement; **agir d'**∼ **avec qn** act in agreement with sb. **intelligent,** ∼e adj intelligent.

intempéries /ɛ̃tɑ̃peʀi/ nfpl severe weather.

intempestif, -ive /ɛ̃tɑ̃pɛstif, -v/ adj untimely.

intenable /ɛ̃tnabl/ adj unbearable; (enfant) impossible.

intendance /ɛ̃tɑ̃dɑ̃s/ nf (Scol) bursar's office.

intendant, ∼e /ɛ̃tɑ̃dɑ̃, -t/ nm (Mil) quartermaster. ● nm, f (Scol) bursar.

intense /ɛ̃tɑ̃s/ adj intense; (circulation) heavy. **intensif, -ive** adj intensive. **intensité** nf intensity.

intenter /ɛ̃tɑ̃te/ 1 vt ∼ **un procès** ou **une action** institute proceedings (**à**, **contre** against).

intention /ɛ̃tɑ̃sjɔ̃/ nf intention (**de faire** of doing); **à l'**∼ **de qn** for sb. **intentionnel,** ∼le adj intentional.

interactif, -ive /ɛ̃tɛʀaktif, -v/ adj (TV, vidéo) interactive.

interaction /ɛ̃tɛʀaksjɔ̃/ nf interaction.

intercaler /ɛ̃tɛʀkale/ 1 vt insert.

intercéder /ɛ̃tɛʀsede/ 14 vi intercede (**en faveur de** on behalf of).

intercepter /ɛ̃tɛʀsɛpte/ 1 vt intercept.

interdiction /ɛ̃tɛʀdiksjɔ̃/ nf ban; ∼ **de fumer** no smoking.

interdire /ɛ̃tɛʀdiʀ/ 37 vt forbid; (officiellement) ban, prohibit; ∼ **à qn de faire** forbid sb to do.

interdit, ∼e /ɛ̃tɛʀdi, -t/ adj prohibited, forbidden; (étonné) dumbfounded.

intéressant, ∼e /ɛ̃teʀesɑ̃, -t/ adj interesting; (avantageux) attractive.

intéressé, ∼e /ɛ̃teʀese/ adj (en cause) concerned; (pour profiter) self-interested. ● nm, f person concerned.

intéresser /ɛ̃teʀese/ 1 vt interest; (concerner) concern. □ **s'**∼ **à** vpr be interested in.

intérêt /ɛ̃teʀɛ/ nm interest; (égoïsme) self-interest; (∼s) (Comm) interest; **vous avez** ∼ **à** it is in your interest to.

interface /ɛ̃tɛʀfas/ nf (Ordinat) interface.

intérieur, ∼e /ɛ̃teʀjœʀ/ adj inner, inside; (mur, escalier) internal; (vol, politique) domestic; (vie, calme) inner. ● nm interior; (de boîte, tiroir) inside; **à l'**∼ **(de)** inside; (fig) within. **intérieurement** adv inwardly.

intérim /ɛ̃teʀim/ nm interim; **assurer l'**∼ deputize (**de** for); **par** ∼ on an interim basis; **président par** ∼ acting president; **faire de l'**∼ temp.

intérimaire /ɛ̃teʀimɛʀ/ adj temporary, interim. ● nmf (secrétaire) temp; (médecin) locum.

interjection /ɛ̃tɛʀʒɛksjɔ̃/ nf interjection.

i

interlocuteur, -trice /ɛ̃tɛʀlɔkytœʀ, -tʀis/ *nm, f* **son ~** the person one is speaking to.

interloqué, ~e /ɛ̃tɛʀlɔke/ *adj* **être ~** be taken aback.

intermède /ɛ̃tɛʀmɛd/ *nm* interlude.

intermédiaire /ɛ̃tɛʀmedjɛʀ/ *adj* intermediate. ● *nmf* intermediary. ● *nm* **sans ~** without an intermediary, direct; **par l'~ de** through.

interminable /ɛ̃tɛʀminabl/ *adj* endless.

intermittence /ɛ̃tɛʀmitɑ̃s/ *nf* **par ~** intermittently.

internat /ɛ̃tɛʀna/ *nm* boardingschool.

international, ~e (*mpl* **-aux**) /ɛ̃tɛʀnasjɔnal, -o/ *adj* international.

internaute /ɛ̃tɛʀnot/ *nmf* (Ordinat) Netsurfer, Internet user.

interne /ɛ̃tɛʀn/ *adj* internal; (*cours, formation*) in-house. ● *nmf* (Scol) boarder; (Méd) house officer; (US) intern.

internement /ɛ̃tɛʀnəmɑ̃/ *nm* (Pol) internment. **interner** ◨ *vt* (Pol) intern; (Méd) commit.

Internet /ɛ̃tɛʀnɛt/ *nm* Internet; **sur ~** on the Internet.

interpellation /ɛ̃tɛʀpelasjɔ̃/ *nf* (Pol) questioning. **interpeller** ◨ *vt* shout to; (*apostropher*) shout at; (*interroger*) question.

interphone /ɛ̃tɛʀfɔn/ *nm* intercom; (*d'immeuble*) entry phone.

interposer (s') /(s)ɛ̃tɛʀpoze/ ◨ *vpr* intervene.

interprétariat /ɛ̃tɛʀpretaʀja/ *nm* interpreting. **interprétation** *nf* interpretation; (*d'artiste*) performance. **interprète** *nmf* interpreter; (*artiste*) performer. **interpréter** ◳ *vt* interpret; (*jouer*) play; (*chanter*) sing.

interrogateur, -trice /ɛ̃tɛʀɔgatœʀ, -tʀis/ *adj* questioning. **interrogatif, -ive** *adj* interrogative. **interrogation** *nf* question; (*action*) questioning; (*épreuve*) test. **interrogatoire** *nm* interrogation. **interroger** ◳ *vt* question; (*élève*) test.

Interrompre /ɛ̃tɛʀɔ̃pʀ/ ◧ *vt* break off, interrupt; (*personne*) interrupt. ⎕ **s'~** *vpr* break off. **interrupteur** *nm* switch. **interruption** *nf* interruption; (*arrêt*) break.

interurbain, ~e /ɛ̃tɛʀyʀbɛ̃, -ɛn/ *adj* long distance, trunk.

intervalle /ɛ̃tɛʀval/ *nm* space; (*temps*) interval; **dans l'~** in the meantime.

intervenir /ɛ̃tɛʀvəniʀ/ ◵ *vi* (*agir*) intervene (**auprès de qn** with sb); (*survenir*) occur, take place; (Méd) operate. **intervention** *nf* intervention; (Méd) operation.

intervertir /ɛ̃tɛʀvɛʀtiʀ/ ◩ *vt* invert; (*rôles*) reverse.

interview /ɛ̃tɛʀvju/ *nf* interview. **interviewer** ◧ *vt* interview.

intestin /ɛ̃tɛstɛ̃/ *nm* intestine.

intime /ɛ̃tim/ *adj* intimate; (*fête, vie*) private; (*dîner*) quiet. ● *nmf* intimate friend.

intimider /ɛ̃timide/ ◧ *vt* intimidate.

intimité /ɛ̃timite/ *nf* intimacy; (*vie privée*) privacy.

intituler /ɛ̃tityle/ ◧ *vt* call, entitle. ⎕ **s'~** *vpr* be called *ou* entitled.

intolérable /ɛ̃tɔleʀabl/ *adj* intolerable. **intolérance** *nf* intolerance. **intolérant, ~e** *adj* intolerant.

intonation /ɛ̃tɔnasjɔ̃/ *nf* intonation.

intox /ɛ̃tɔks/ *nf* ◩ brainwashing.

intoxication /ɛ̃tɔksikasjɔ̃/ *nf* poisoning; (fig) brainwashing; **~ alimentaire** food poisoning. **intoxiquer** ◧ *vt* poison; (fig) brainwash.

intraitable /ɛ̃tʀɛtabl/ *adj* inflexible.

Intranet /ɛ̃tʀanɛt/ *nm* Intranet.

intransigeant, ~e /ɛ̃tʀɑ̃ziʒɑ̃, -t/ *adj* intransigent.

intransitif, -ive /ɛ̃tʀɑ̃zitif, -v/ *adj* intransitive.

intraveineux, -euse /ɛ̃tʀavɛnø, -z/ *adj* intravenous.

intrépide /ɛ̃tʀepid/ *adj* fearless.

intrigue /ɛ̃tʀig/ *nf* intrigue; (*scénario*) plot.

intrinsèque /ɛ̃tʀɛ̃sɛk/ *adj* intrinsic.

introduction /ɛ̃tʀɔdyksjɔ̃/ *nf* introduction; (*insertion*) insertion.

introduire /ɛ̃tʀɔdɥiʀ/ ◰ *vt* introduce, bring in; (*insérer*) put in, insert; **~ qn** show sb in. ⎕ **s'~** *vpr* get in; **s'~ dans** get into, enter.

introuvable /ɛ̃tʀuvabl/ *adj* that cannot be found.

introverti, ~e /ɛ̃tʀɔvɛʀti/ *nm, f* introvert. ● *adj* introverted.

intrus, ~e /ɛ̃tʁy, -z/ nm, f intruder. **intrusion** nf intrusion.

intuitif, -ive /ɛ̃tɥitif, -iv/ adj intuitive. **intuition** nf intuition.

inusable /inyzabl/ adj hardwearing.

inusité, ~e /inyzite/ adj little used.

inutile /inytil/ adj useless; (vain) needless. **inutilement** adv needlessly. **inutilisable** adj unusable.

invalide /ɛ̃valid/ adj & nmf disabled (person).

invariable /ɛ̃vaʁjabl/ adj invariable.

Invasion /ɛ̃vɑzjɔ̃/ nf invasion.

invectiver /ɛ̃vɛktive/ **1** vt abuse.

inventaire /ɛ̃vɑ̃tɛʁ/ nm inventory; (Comm) stocklist; **faire l'~** draw up an inventory; (Comm) do a stocktake.

inventer /ɛ̃vɑ̃te/ **1** vt invent. **inventeur, -trice** nm, f inventor. **inventif, -ive** adj inventive. **invention** nf invention.

inverse /ɛ̃vɛʁs/ adj opposite; (ordre) reverse; **en sens ~** in ou from the opposite direction. ● nm reverse; **c'est l'~** it's the other way round. **inversement** adv conversely. **inverser** **1** vt reverse, invert.

investir /ɛ̃vɛstiʁ/ **2** vt invest. **investissement** nm investment.

investiture /ɛ̃vɛstityʁ/ nf (de candidat) nomination; (de président) investiture.

invétéré, ~e /ɛ̃vetere/ adj inveterate; (menteur) compulsive; (enraciné) deep-rooted.

invisible /ɛ̃vizibl/ adj invisible.

invitation /ɛ̃vitasjɔ̃/ nf invitation. **invité**, ~e nm, f guest. **inviter** **1** vt invite (à to).

involontaire /ɛ̃vɔlɔ̃tɛʁ/ adj involuntary; (témoin, héros) unwitting.

invoquer /ɛ̃vɔke/ **1** vt call upon, invoke.

invraisemblable /ɛ̃vʁɛsɑ̃blabl/ adj improbable, unlikely; (incroyable) incredible. **invraisemblance** nf improbability.

iode /jɔd/ nm iodine.

ira, irait /iʁa, iʁɛ/ ➡ALLER **8**.

Irak /iʁak/ nm Iraq.

Iran /iʁɑ̃/ nm Iran.

iris /iʁis/ nm iris.

irlandais, ~e /iʁlɑ̃dɛ, -z/ adj Irish. **I~**, ~e nm, f Irishman, Irishwoman.

Irlande /iʁlɑ̃d/ nf Ireland.

IRM abrév m (imagerie par résonance magnétique) magnetic resonance imaging.

ironie /iʁɔni/ nf irony. **ironique** adj ironic.

irrationnel, ~le /iʁasjɔnɛl/ adj irrational.

irréalisable /iʁealizabl/ adj (idée, rêve) unachievable; (projet) unworkable.

irrécupérable /iʁekypeʁabl/ adj irretrievable; (capital) irrecoverable.

irréel, ~le /iʁeɛl/ adj unreal.

irréfléchi, ~e /iʁefleʃi/ adj thoughtless.

irrégulier, -ière /iʁegylje, -jɛʁ/ adj irregular.

irrémédiable /iʁemedjabl/ adj irreparable.

irremplaçable /iʁɑ̃plasabl/ adj irreplaceable.

irréparable /iʁepaʁabl/ adj (objet) beyond repair; (tort, dégâts) irreparable.

irréprochable /iʁepʁoʃabl/ adj flawless.

irrésistible /iʁezistibl/ adj irresistible; (drôle) hilarious.

irrésolu, ~e /iʁezɔly/ adj indecisive; (problème) unsolved.

irrespirable /iʁɛspiʁabl/ adj stifling.

irresponsable /iʁɛspɔ̃sabl/ adj irresponsible.

irrigation /iʁigasjɔ̃/ nf irrigation. **irriguer** **1** vt irrigate.

irritable /iʁitabl/ adj irritable.

irriter **1** /iʁite/ vt irritate. □ **s'~** vpr get annoyed (de at).

irruption /iʁypsjɔ̃/ nf faire ~ dans burst into.

Islam /islam/ nm Islam. **islamique** adj Islamic.

islamiste /islamist/ adj Islamist, Islamic; n m,f Islamist.

islandais, ~e /islɑ̃dɛ, -z/ adj Icelandic. ● nm (Ling) Icelandic. **I~**, ~e nm, f Icelander.

Islande /islɑ̃d/ nf Iceland.

isolant /izɔlɑ̃/ nm insulating material. **isolation** nf insulation.

isolé, ~e /izɔle/ adj isolated. **isolement** nm isolation.

isoler /izɔle/ **1** vt isolate; (Électr) insulate. □ **s'∼** vpr isolate oneself.

isoloir /izɔlwaʀ/ nm polling booth.

Isorel ® /izɔʀɛl/ nm hardboard.

Israël /isʀaɛl/ nm Israel. **israélien,**
∼ne adj Israeli.

israélite /isʀaelit/ adj Jewish.
● nmf Jew.

issu, ∼**e** /isy/ adj être ∼ de (*per-*
sonne) come from; (résulter de) result
ou stem from.

issue /isy/ nf (sortie) exit; (résultat)
outcome; (fig) solution; **à l'∼ de** at
the conclusion of; ∼ **de secours**
emergency exit; **rue** ou **voie sans** ∼
dead end.

Italie /itali/ nf Italy.

italien, ∼**ne** /italjɛ̃, -ɛn/ adj Italian.
● nm (Ling) Italian. **I∼,** ∼**ne** nm, f
Italian.

italique /italik/ nm italics.

itinéraire /itineʀɛʀ/ nm itinerary,
route.

I.U.T. abrév m (**Institut universitaire**
de technologie) university institute
of technology.

I.V.G. abrév f (**interruption volontaire**
de grossesse) abortion.

ivoire /ivwaʀ/ nm ivory.

ivre /ivʀ/ adj drunk. **ivresse** nf drunkenness; (fig) exhilaration. **ivrogne** nmf
drunk(ard).

• •

Jj

• •

j' /ʒ/ ➡JE.

jacinthe /ʒasɛ̃t/ nf hyacinth.

jadis /ʒadis/ adv long ago.

jaillir /ʒajiʀ/ **2** vi (*liquide*) spurt (out);
(*lumière*) stream out; (apparaître)
burst forth, spring out.

jalonner /ʒalɔne/ **1** vt mark (out).

jalousie /ʒaluzi/ nf jealousy; (store)
(venetian) blind. **jaloux, -ouse** adj
jealous.

jamais /ʒamɛ/ adv ever; **ne** ∼ never; **il**
ne boit ∼ he never drinks; **à** ∼ for
ever; **si** ∼ if ever.

jambe /ʒɑ̃b/ nf leg.

jambon /ʒɑ̃bɔ̃/ nm ham. **jambonneau**
(pl ∼**x**) nm knuckle of ham.

janvier /ʒɑ̃vje/ nm January.

Japon /ʒapɔ̃/ nm Japan.

japonais, ∼**e** /japɔnɛ, -z/ adj Japanese. ● nm (Ling) Japanese. **J∼,** ∼**e** nm,
f Japanese.

japper /ʒape/ **1** vi yap.

jaquette /ʒakɛt/ nf (de livre, femme)
jacket; (d'homme) morning coat.

jardin /ʒaʀdɛ̃/ nm garden; ∼ **d'enfants**
nursery (school); ∼ **public** public
park. **jardinage** nm gardening. **jardi-**
ner **1** vi do some gardening, garden.
jardinier, -ière nm, f gardener.

jardinière /ʒaʀdinjɛʀ/ nf (meuble)
plant-stand; ∼ **de légumes** mixed vegetables.

jarretelle /ʒaʀtɛl/ nf suspender; (US)
garter.

jarretière /ʒaʀtjɛʀ/ nf garter.

jatte /ʒat/ nf bowl.

jauge /ʒoʒ/ nf capacity; (de navire) ton-
nage; (compteur) gauge; ∼ **d'huile**
dipstick.

jaune /ʒon/ adj & nm yellow; (péj) scab;
∼ **d'œuf** (egg) yolk; **rire** ∼ give a
forced laugh. **jaunir** **2** vt/i turn yellow. **jaunisse** nf jaundice.

javelot /ʒavlo/ nm javelin.

jazz /dʒaz/ nm jazz.

J.C. abrév m (**Jésus-Christ**) 500 avant/
après ∼ 500 B.C./A.D.

je, j' /ʒə, ʒ/ pron I.

jean /dʒin/ nm jeans; **un** ∼ a pair of
jeans.

jet¹ /ʒɛ/ nm throw; (de liquide, vapeur)
jet; ∼ **d'eau** fountain.

jet² /dʒɛt/ nm (avion) jet.

jetable /ʒətabl/ adj disposable.

jetée /ʒəte/ nf pier.

jeter /ʒəte/ **38** vt throw; (au rebut)
throw away; (regard, ancre, lumière)
cast; (cri) utter; (bases) lay; ∼ **un**
coup d'œil have ou take a look (à at).
□ **se** ∼ vpr **se** ∼ **contre** crash ou bash
into; **se** ∼ **dans** (fleuve) flow into; **se**
∼ **sur** (se ruer sur) rush at.

jeton /ʒətɔ̃/ nm token; (pour compter)
counter; (au casino) chip.

jeu (pl ∼**x**) /ʒø/ nm game; (amusement) play; (au casino) gambling;
(Théât) acting; (série) set; (de lumière,

ressort) play; **en** ~ (*honneur*) at stake; (*forces*) at work; ~ **de cartes** (paquet) pack of cards; ~**d'échecs** (boîte) chess set; ~ **de mots** pun; ~ **télévisé** tv game show; ~ **vidéo** video game; ~**x de grattage** scratch cards; **les** ~**x olympiques/paralympiques** the Olympic Games/Paralympic Games.

jeudi /ʒødi/ *nm* Thursday.

jeun: à ~ /aʒœ̃/ *loc* on an empty stomach.

jeune /ʒœn/ *adj* young; ~ **fille** girl; ~ **pousse** (Comm) start-up; ~**s mariés** newlyweds. ● *nmf* young person; **les** ~**s** young people.

jeûne /ʒøn/ *nm* fast.

jeunesse /ʒœnɛs/ *nf* youth; (apparence) youthfulness; **la** ~ (jeunes) the young.

joaillerie /ʒɔajʀi/ *nf* jewellery; (magasin) jeweller's shop.

joie /ʒwa/ *nf* joy.

joindre /ʒwɛ̃dʀ/ 22 *vt* join (à to); (mains, pieds) put together; (efforts) combine; (contacter) contact; (dans une enveloppe) enclose. □ **se** ~ **à** *vpr* join.

joint, ~**e** /ʒwɛ̃, -t/ *adj* (efforts) joint; (pieds) together. ● *nm* joint; (de robinet) washer.

joli, ~**e** /ʒɔli/ *adj* pretty, nice; (somme, profit) nice; **c'est du** ~**!** (ironique) charming! **c'est bien** ~ **mais** that is all very well but.

joncher /ʒɔ̃ʃe/ 1 *vt* litter, be strewn over; **jonché de** littered with.

jonction /ʒɔ̃ksjɔ̃/ *nf* junction.

jongleur, -euse /ʒɔ̃glœʀ, øz/ *nm, f* juggler.

jonquille /ʒɔ̃kij/ *nf* daffodil.

joue /ʒu/ *nf* cheek.

jouer /ʒwe/ 1 *vt/i* play; (Théât) act; (au casino) gamble; (fonctionner) work; (film, pièce) put on; (cheval) back; (être important) count; ~ **à** (jeu, Sport) play; ~ **de** (Mus) play; ~ **la comédie** put on an act; **bien joué!** well done!

jouet /ʒwɛ/ *nm* toy; (personne: fig) plaything; (victime) victim.

joueur, -euse /ʒwœʀ, -øz/ *nm, f* player; (parieur) gambler.

joufflu, ~**e** /ʒufly/ *adj* chubby-cheeked; (visage) chubby.

jouir /ʒwiʀ/ 2 *vi* (sexe) come; ~ **de** (droit, avantage) enjoy; (bien, concession) enjoy the use of. **jouissance** *nf* pleasure; (usage) use (**de qch** of sth).

joujou (pl ~**x**) /ʒuʒu/ *nm* 1 toy.

jour /ʒuʀ/ *nm* day; (opposé à nuit) day (time); (lumière) daylight; (ouverture) gap; **de nos** ~**s** nowadays; **du** ~ **au lendemain** overnight; **il fait** ~ it is daylight; ~ **chômé** ou **férié** public holiday; ~ **de fête** holiday; ~ **ouvrable,** ~ **de travail** working day; **mettre à** ~ update; **mettre au** ~ uncover; **au grand** ~ in the open; **donner le** ~ give birth; **voir le** ~ be born; **vivre au** ~ **le jour** live from day to day.

journal (pl **-aux**) /ʒuʀnal, -o/ *nm* (news)paper; (spécialisé) journal; (intime) diary; (à la radio) news; ~ **de bord** log-book.

journalier, -ière /ʒuʀnalje, -jɛʀ/ *adj* daily.

journalisme /ʒuʀnalism/ *nm* journalism. **journaliste** *nmf* journalist.

journée /ʒuʀne/ *nf* day.

jovial, ~**e** (mpl **-iaux**) /ʒɔvjal, -jo/ *adj* jovial.

joyau (pl ~**x**) /ʒwajo/ *nm* gem.

joyeux, -euse /ʒwajø, -z/ *adj* merry, joyful; ~ **anniversaire** happy birthday.

jubiler /ʒybile/ 1 *vi* be jubilant.

jucher /ʒyʃe/ 1 *vt* perch. □ **se** ~ *vpr* perch.

judaïsme /ʒydaism/ *nm* Judaism.

judiciaire /ʒydisjɛʀ/ *adj* judicial.

judicieux, -ieuse /ʒydisjø, -z/ *adj* judicious.

judo /ʒydo/ *nm* judo.

juge /ʒyʒ/ *nm* judge; (arbitre) referee; ~ **de paix** Justice of the Peace; ~ **de touche** linesman.

jugé: au ~ /oʒyʒe/ *loc* by guesswork.

jugement /ʒyʒmɑ̃/ *nm* judgement; (criminel) sentence.

juger /ʒyʒe/ 40 *vt/i* judge; (estimer) consider (**que** that); ~ **de** judge.

juguler /ʒygyle/ 1 *vt* stamp out; curb.

juif, -ive /ʒɥif, -v/ *adj* Jewish. ● *nm, f* Jew.

juillet /ʒɥijɛ/ *nm* July.

juin /ʒɥɛ̃/ *nm* June.

jumeau, -elle (*mpl* ~x) /ʒymo, -ɛl/ *adj & nm, f* twin. **jumeler** 38 *vt* (*villes*) twin.

jumelles /ʒymɛl/ *nfpl* binoculars.

jument /ʒymɑ̃/ *nf* mare.

junior /ʒynjɔr/ *adj & nmf* junior.

jupe /ʒyp/ *nf* skirt.

jupon /ʒypɔ̃/ *nm* slip, petticoat.

juré, ~e /ʒyre/ *nm, f* juror. ● *adj* sworn.

jurer /ʒyre/ ❶ *vt* swear (**que** that). ● *vi* (pester) swear; (contraster) clash (**avec** with).

juridiction /ʒyridiksjɔ̃/ *nf* jurisdiction; (tribunal) court of law.

juridique /ʒyridik/ *adj* legal.

juriste /ʒyrist/ *nmf* legal expert.

juron /ʒyrɔ̃/ *nm* swearword.

jury /ʒyri/ *nm* (Jur) jury; (examinateurs) panel of judges.

jus /ʒy/ *nm* juice; (de viande) gravy; ~ **de fruit** fruit juice.

jusque /ʒysk(ə)/ *prép* **jusqu'à** (up) to, as far as; (temps) until, till; (limite) up to; (y compris) even; **jusqu'à ce que** until; **jusqu'à présent** until now; **jusqu'en** until; **jusqu'où?** how far?; ~ **dans**, ~ **sur** as far as.

juste /ʒyst/ *adj* fair, just; (légitime) just; (correct, exact) right; (vrai) true; (vêtement) tight; (quantité) on the short side; **le ~ milieu** the happy medium. ● *adv* rightly, correctly; (chanter) in tune; (seulement, exactement) just; (**un peu**) ~ (calculer, mesurer) a bit fine *ou* close; **au ~** exactly; **c'était ~** (presque raté) it was a close thing.

justement *adv* (précisément) precisely; (à l'instant) just; (avec justesse) correctly; (légitimement) justifiably.

justesse /ʒystɛs/ *nf* accuracy; **de ~** just, narrowly.

justice /ʒystis/ *nf* justice; (autorités) law; (tribunal) court.

justifier /ʒystifje/ 45 *vt* justify. ● *vi* ~ **de** prove. □ **se** ~ *vpr* justify oneself.

juteux, -euse /ʒytø, -z/ *adj* juicy.

juvénile /ʒyvenil/ *adj* youthful; (délinquance, mortalité) juvenile.

K k

kaki /kaki/ *adj inv & nm* khaki.

kangourou /kɑ̃guru/ *nm* kangaroo.

karaté /karate/ *nm* karate.

kart /kart/ *nm* go-cart.

kascher /kaʃɛr/ *adj inv* kosher.

kayak /kajak/ *nm* kayak.

képi /kepi/ *nm* kepi.

kermesse /kɛrmɛs/ *nf* fête.

kidnapper /kidnape/ ❶ *vt* kidnap.

kilo /kilo/ *nm* kilo.

kilogramme /kilɔɡram/ *nm* kilogram.

kilométrage /kilɔmetraʒ/ *nm* ≈ mileage. **kilomètre** *nm* kilometre.

kinésithérapeute /kineziterapø t/ *nmf* physiotherapist. **kinésithérapie** *nf* physiotherapy.

kiosque /kjɔsk/ *nm* kiosk; ~ **à musique** bandstand.

kit /kit/ *nm* kit; ~ **mains libres conducteur** hands-free kit.

klaxon® /klaksɔn/ *nm* (Auto) horn. **klaxonner** ❶ *vt* sound one's horn.

Ko *abrév m* (**kilo-octet**) (Ordinat) KB.

KO *abrév m* (**knock-out**) KO 🔟.

K-way® /kawɛ/ *nm inv* windcheater.

kyste /kist/ *nm* cyst.

L l

l', la /l, la/ ➡**le**.

---

là /la/

● *adverbe*

••••➤ (dans ce lieu) there; (ici) here; (chez soi) in; **c'est ~ que** this is where; ~ **où** where; **par ~** (dans cette direction) this way; (dans cette zone) around there; **de ~** hence.

••••➤ (à ce moment) then; **c'est ~ que** that's when.

j
k
l

····➤ **cet homme-~** that man; **ces maisons-~** those houses.

● *interjection*

····➤ **~** ① **c'est fini** there (now), it's all over!

là-bas /laba/ *adv* there; (à l'endroit que l'on indique) over there.

label /label/ *nm* seal, label.

laboratoire /labɔʀatwaʀ/ *nm* laboratory.

laborieux, -ieuse /labɔʀjø, -z/ *adj* laborious; (*personne*) industrious; **classes laborieuses** working classes.

labour /labuʀ/ *nm* ploughing; (US) plowing. **labourer** ① *vt* plough; (US) plow; (déchirer) rip at.

labyrinthe /labiʀɛ̃t/ *nm* maze, labyrinth.

lac /lak/ *nm* lake.

lacer /lase/ ⑩ *vt* lace up.

lacet /lasɛ/ *nm* (de chaussure) (shoe-)lace; (de route) sharp bend.

lâche /lɑʃ/ *adj* cowardly; (détendu) loose; (sans rigueur) lax. ● *nmf* coward.

lâcher /lɑʃe/ ① *vt* let go of; (laisser tomber) drop; (abandonner) give up; (laisser) leave; (libérer) release; (*flèche, balle*) fire; (*juron, phrase*) come out with; (desserrer) loosen; **~ prise** let go. ● *vi* give way.

lâcheté /lɑʃte/ *nf* cowardice.

lacrymogène /lakʀimɔʒɛn/ *adj* **gaz ~** tear gas.

lacune /lakyn/ *nf* gap.

là-dedans /lad(ə)dɑ̃/ *adv* (près) in here; (plus loin) in there.

là-dessous /lad(ə)su/ *adv* (près) under here; (plus loin) under there.

là-dessus /lad(ə)sy/ *adv* (sur une surface) on here; (plus loin) on there; (sur ce) with that; (quelque temps après) after that; **qu'avez-vous à dire ~?** what have you got to say about it?

ladite /ladit/ ➡**ledit.**

lagune /lagyn/ *nf* lagoon.

là-haut /lao/ *adv* (en hauteur) up here; (plus loin) up there; (à l'étage) upstairs.

laïc /laik/ *nm* layman.

laid, ~e /lɛ, lɛd/ *adj* ugly; (*action*) vile. **laideur** *nf* ugliness.

lainage /lɛnaʒ/ *nm* woollen garment.

laine /lɛn/ *nf* wool; **de ~** woollen.

laïque /laik/ *adj* (état, loi) secular; (habit, personne) lay; (école) nondenominational. ● *nmf* layman, laywoman.

laisse /lɛs/ *nf* lead, leash; **tenir en ~** keep on a lead.

laisser /lese/ ① *vt* (déposer) leave, drop off; (confier) leave (**à qn** with sb); (abandonner) leave; (rendre) **~ qn perplexe/froid** leave sb puzzled/cold; **~ qch à qn** (céder, prêter) let sb have sth; (donner) (choix, temps) give sb sth. □ **se ~** *vpr* **se ~ persuader/insulter** let oneself be persuaded/insulted; **elle ne se laisse pas faire** she won't be pushed around; **laisse-toi faire** leave it to me/him/her *etc.*; **se ~ aller** let oneself go. ● *v aux* **~ qn/qch faire** let sb/sth do; **laisse-moi faire** (ne m'aide pas) let me do it; (je m'en occupe) leave it to me; **laisse faire!** so what! **laisser-aller** *nm inv* carelessness; (dans la tenue) scruffiness. **laisser-passer** *nm inv* pass.

lait /lɛ/ *nm* milk; **~ longue conservation** long-life *ou* UHT milk; **frère/sœur de ~** foster-brother/-sister. **laitage** *nm* milk product. **laiterie** *nf* dairy. **laiteux, -euse** *adj* milky.

laitier, -ière /letje, -jɛʀ/ *adj* dairy. ● *nm, f* (livreur) milkman, milkwoman.

laiton /lɛtɔ̃/ *nm* brass.

laitue /lety/ *nf* lettuce.

lama /lama/ *nm* llama.

lambeau (*pl* **~x**) /lɑ̃bo/ *nm* shred; **en ~x** in shreds.

lame /lam/ *nf* blade; (lamelle) strip; (vague) wave; **~ de fond** ground swell; **~ de rasoir** razor blade.

lamentable /lamɑ̃tabl/ *adj* deplorable. **lamenter (se)** ① *vpr* moan (**sur** about, over).

lampadaire /lɑ̃padɛʀ/ *nm* standard lamp; (de rue) street lamp.

lampe /lɑ̃p/ *nf* lamp; (ampoule) bulb; (de radio) valve; **~ (de poche)** torch; (US) flashlight; **~ à souder** blowlamp; **~ de chevet** bedside lamp; **~ solaire, ~ à bronzer** sunlamp.

lance /lɑ̃s/ *nf* spear; (de tournoi) lance; (tuyau) hose; **~ d'incendie** fire hose.

lancement /lɑ̃smɑ̃/ *nm* throwing; (de navire, de missile, mise sur le marché) launch.

lance-missiles /lɑ̃smisil/ *nm inv* missile launcher.

lance-pierres /lɑ̃spjɛʀ/ *nm inv* catapult.

lancer /lɑ̃se/ **10** *vt* throw; (avec force) hurl; (*navire, idée, artiste*) launch; (*émettre*) give out; (*regard*) cast; (*moteur*) start. □ **se** ~ *vpr* (Sport) gain momentum; (se précipiter) rush; **se** ~ **dans** (*explication*) launch into; (*passe-temps*) take up. ● *nm* throw; (*action*) throwing.

lancinant, ~**e** /lɑ̃sinɑ̃, -t/ *adj* (*douleur*) shooting; (*problème*) nagging.

landau /lɑ̃do/ *nm* pram; (US) baby carriage.

lande /lɑ̃d/ *nf* heath, moor.

langage /lɑ̃gaʒ/ *nm* language; ~ **machine/de programmation** machine/programming language.

langouste /lɑ̃gust/ *nf* spiny lobster. **langoustine** *nf* Dublin Bay prawn.

langue /lɑ̃g/ *nf* (Anat) tongue; (Ling) language; **il m'a tiré la** ~ he stuck his tongue out at me; **de** ~ **anglaise** (*personne*) English-speaking; (*journal*) English-language; ~ **maternelle** mother tongue; ~ **vivante** modern language.

lanière /lanjɛʀ/ *nf* strap.

lanterne /lɑ̃tɛʀn/ *nf* lantern; (électrique) lamp; (de voiture) sidelight.

lapin /lapɛ̃/ *nm* rabbit; **poser un** ~ **à qn** **!** stand sb up; **le coup du** ~ rabbit punch; (en voiture) whiplash injury.

lapsus /lapsys/ *nm* slip (of the tongue).

laque /lak/ *nf* lacquer; (pour cheveux) hairspray; (peinture) gloss paint.

laquelle /lakɛl/ →LEQUEL.

lard /laʀ/ *nm* streaky bacon.

large /laʀʒ/ *adj* wide, broad; (grand) large; (généreux) generous; **avoir les idées** ~**s** be broad-minded; ~ **d'esprit** broad-minded. ● *adv* (calculer, mesurer) on the generous side; **voir** ~ think big. ● *nm* **faire 10 cm de** ~ **be** 10 cm wide; **le** ~ (mer) the open sea; **au** ~ **de** (Naut) off. **largement** *adv* widely; (ouvrir) wide; (amplement) amply; (généreusement) generously; (au moins) easily.

largesse /laʀʒɛs/ *nf* generous gift.

largeur /laʀʒœʀ/ *nf* width, breadth; ~ **d'esprit** broad-mindedness.

larguer /laʀge/ **1** *vt* drop; ~ **les amarres** cast off.

larme /laʀm/ *nf* tear; (goutte **!**) drop; **en** ~**s** in tears.

larmoyant, ~**e** /laʀmwajɑ̃, -t/ *adj* full of tears. **larmoyer** **31** *vi* (*yeux*) water; (pleurnicher) whine.

larynx /laʀɛ̃ks/ *nm* larynx.

las, ~**se** /lɑ, lɑs/ *adj* weary.

lasagnes /lazaɲ/ *nfpl* lasagna.

laser /lazɛʀ/ *nm* laser.

lasser /lɑse/ **1** *vt* weary. □ **se** ~ *vpr* grow tired, get weary (**de** of).

latéral, ~**e** (*mpl* -**aux**) /lateʀal, -o/ *adj* lateral.

latin, ~**e** /latɛ̃, -in/ *adj* Latin. ● *nm* (Ling) Latin.

latte /lat/ *nf* lath; (de plancher) board; (de siège) slat; (de mur, plafond) lath.

lauréat, ~**e** /lɔʀea, -t/ *adj* prizewinning. ● *nm, f* prize-winner.

laurier /lɔʀje/ *nm* (Bot) laurel; (Culin) bay-leaves.

lavable /lavabl/ *adj* washable.

lavabo /lavabo/ *nm* wash-basin; ~**s** toilet(s).

lavage /lavaʒ/ *nm* washing; ~ **de cerveau** brainwashing.

lavande /lavɑ̃d/ *nf* lavender.

lave /lav/ *nf* lava.

lave-glace (*pl* ~**s**) /lavglas/ *nm* windscreen washer.

lave-linge /lavlɛ̃ʒ/ *nm inv* washing machine.

laver /lave/ **1** *vt* wash; ~ **qn de** (fig) clear sb of. □ **se** ~ *vpr* wash (oneself); **se** ~ **les mains** wash one's hands.

laverie /lavʀi/ *nf* ~ (**automatique**) launderette; (US) laundromat.

lave-vaisselle /lavvɛsɛl/ *nm inv* dishwasher.

laxatif, -ive /laksatif, -v/ *adj & nm* laxative.

layette /lɛjɛt/ *nf* baby clothes.

---

le, la, l' (*pl* **les**) /lə, la, l, le/

    l' before vowel or mute h.

● *déterminant*
⋯➤ the.
⋯➤ (notion générale) **aimer la**

musique like music; **l'amour** love.

····▶ (possession) **avoir les yeux verts** have green eyes; **il s'est cassé la jambe** he broke his leg.

····▶ (prix) **10 euros ∼ kilo** 10 euros a kilo.

····▶ (temps) **∼ lundi** on Mondays; **tous les mardis** every Tuesday.

····▶ (avec nom propre) **les Dury** the Durys; **la reine Margot** Queen Margot; **la Belgique** Belgium.

····▶ (avec adjectif) the; **je veux la rouge** I want the red one; **les riches** the rich.

● *pronom*

····▶ (homme) him; (femme) her; (chose, animal) it; (au pluriel) them.

····▶ (remplaçant une phrase) **je te l'avais bien dit** I told you so; **je ∼ croyais aussi** I thought so too.

lécher /leʃe/ 🆔 *vt* lick; (*flamme*) lick; (*mer*) lap.

lèche-vitrines /lɛʃvitRin/ *nm inv* **faire du ∼** go window-shopping.

leçon /ləsɔ̃/ *nf* lesson; **faire la ∼ à** lecture sb; **∼ particulière** private lesson; **∼s de conduite** driving lessons.

lecteur, -trice /lɛktœR, -tRis/ *nm, f* reader; (Univ) foreign language assistant; **∼ de cassettes** cassette player; **∼ de disquettes** (disk) drive; **∼ laser** CD player; **∼ optique** optical scanner.

lecture /lɛktyR/ *nf* reading.

ledit, ladite (*pl* **lesdit(e)s**) /lədi, ladit, ledi(t)/ *adj* the aforementioned.

légal, ∼e (*mpl* **-aux**) /legal, -o/ *adj* legal. **légaliser** 🆔 *vt* legalize. **légalité** *nf* legality; (loi) law.

légendaire /leʒɑ̃dɛR/ *adj* legendary. **légende** *nf* (histoire, inscription) legend; (de carte) key; (d'illustration) caption.

léger, -ère /leʒe, -ɛR/ *adj* light; (*bruit, faute, maladie*) slight; (*café, argument*) weak; (imprudent) thoughtless; (frivole) fickle; **à la légère** thoughtlessly. **légèrement** *adv* lightly; (*agir*) thoughtlessly; (un peu) slightly. **légèreté** *nf* lightness; thoughtlessness.

légion /leʒjɔ̃/ *nf* legion.

Légion d'honneur The system of honours awarded by the state for meritorious achievement. The *Président de la République* is the *Grand maître*. The basic rank is *Chevalier*. Holders of the *Légion d'honneur* are entitled to wear *une rosette* (a small red lapel ribbon).

légionellose /leʒɔnɛloz/ *nf* (Méd) legionnaire's disease.

législatif, -ive /leʒislatif, -v/ *adj* legislative; **élections législatives** general election.

legislature /leʒislatyR/ *nf* term of office.

légitime /leʒitim/ *adj* (Jur) legitimate; (fig) rightful; **agir en état de ∼ défense** act in self-defence. **légitimité** *nf* legitimacy.

legs /lɛg/ *nm* legacy; (d'effets personnels) bequest.

léguer /lege/ 🆔 *vt* bequeath.

légume /legym/ *nm* vegetable.

lendemain /lɑ̃dmɛ̃/ *nm* **le ∼** the next day; (fig) the future; **le ∼ de** the day after; **le ∼ matin/soir** the next morning/evening; **du jour au ∼** from one day to the next.

lent, ∼e /lɑ̃, -t/ *adj* slow. **lentement** *adv* slowly. **lenteur** *nf* slowness.

lentille /lɑ̃tij/ *nf* (Culin) lentil; (verre) lens; **∼s de contact** contact lenses.

léopard /leɔpaR/ *nm* leopard.

lèpre /lɛpR/ *nf* leprosy.

lequel, laquelle (*pl* **les-quel(le)s), auquel, auquel(le)s**), **duquel** (*pl* **desquel(le)s**) /ləkɛl, lakɛl, lekɛl, ɔkɛl, dykɛl, dekɛl/

> à + lequel = auquel,
> à + lesquel(le)s = auxquel(le)s;
> de + lequel = duquel,
> de + lesquel(le)s = desquel(le)s

● *pronom*

····▶ (relatif) (personne) who; (complément indirect) whom; (autres cas) which; **l'ami auquel tu as écrit** the friend to whom you wrote; **les voisins chez lesquels Sophie est allée** the neighbours whose house Sophie went to.

····▶ (interrogatif) which; **∼ tu**

veux? which one do you want?
● *adjectif*
····➤ **auquel cas** In which case.

les /le/ →**le.**

lesbienne /lɛsbjɛn/ *nf* lesbian.

léser /leze/ **14** *vt* wrong.

lésiner /lezine/ **1** *vi* **ne pas ~ sur** not stint on.

lesquels, lesquelles /lekɛl/ →**lequel.**

lessive /lesiv/ *nf* (poudre) washing-powder; (liquide) washing liquid; (linge, action) washing.

leste /lɛst/ *adj* agile, nimble; (grivois) coarse.

Lettonie /letɔni/ *nf* Latvia.

lettre /lɛtʀ/ *nf* letter; **à la ~, au pied de la ~** literally; **en toutes ~s** in full; **les ~s** (Univ) (the) arts.

leucémie /løsemi/ *nf* leukaemia.

---

leur (*pl* **~s**) /lœʀ/
● *pronom personnel invariable*
····➤ them; **donne-le ~** give it to them; **je ~ fais confiance** I trust them.
● *adjectif possessif*
····➤ their; **~s enfants** their children; **à ~ arrivée** when they arrived.
● **le leur, la leur,** (*pl* **les leurs**) *pronom possessif*
····➤ theirs; **chacun le ~** one each; **je suis des ~s** I am one of them.

---

levain /ləvɛ̃/ *nm* leaven.

levé, ~e /ləve/ *adj* (debout) up.

levée /ləve/ *nf* (de peine, de sanctions) lifting; (de courrier) collection; (de troupes, d'impôts) levying.

lever /ləve/ **6** *vt* lift (up), raise; (interdiction) lift; (séance) close; (armée, impôts) levy. ● *vi* (pâte) rise. ☐ **se ~** *vpr* get up; (soleil, rideau) rise; (jour) break. ● *nm* **au ~** on getting up; **~ du jour** daybreak; **~ de rideau** (Théât) curtain (up); **~ du soleil** sunrise.

levier /ləvje/ *nm* lever; **~ de changement de vitesse** gear lever.

lèvre /lɛvʀ/ *nf* lip.

lévrier /levʀije/ *nm* greyhound.

levure /ləvyʀ/ *nf* yeast; **~ chimique** baking powder.

lexique /lɛksik/ *nm* vocabulary; (glossaire) lexicon.

lézard /lezaʀ/ *nm* lizard.

lézarde /lezaʀd/ *nf* crack.

liaison /ljɛzɔ̃/ *nf* connection; (transport, Ordinat) link; (contact) contact; (Gram, Mil) liaison; (amoureuse) affair; **être en ~ avec** be in contact with; **assurer la ~ entre** liaise between.

liane /ljan/ *nf* creeper.

Liban /libã/ *nm* Lebanon.

libeller /libele/ **1** *vt* (chèque) write; (contrat) draw up; **libellé à l'ordre de** made out to.

libellule /libelyl/ *nf* dragonfly.

libéral, ~e (*mpl* **-aux**) /liberal, -o/ *adj* liberal; **les professions ~es** the professions.

libérateur, -trice /liberatœʀ, -tʀis/ *adj* liberating. ● *nm, f* liberator. **libération** *nf* release; (de pays) liberation.

libérer /libere/ **14** *vt* (personne) free, release; (pays) liberate, free; (bureau, lieux) vacate; (gaz) release. ☐ **se ~** *vpr* free oneself.

liberté /libɛʀte/ *nf* freedom, liberty; (loisir) free time; **être/mettre en ~** be/set free; **~ conditionnelle** parole; **~ provisoire** provisional release (pending trial); **~ surveillée** probation; **~s publiques** civil liberties.

Libertel /libɛʀtɛl/ *nm* (Internet) Freenet.

libraire /libʀɛʀ/ *nmf* bookseller. **librairie** *nf* bookshop.

libre /libʀ/ *adj* free; (place, pièce) vacant, free; (passage) clear; (école) private (usually religious); **~ de qch/de faire** free from sth/to do. **libre-échange** *nm* free trade. **libre-service** (*pl* **libres-services**) *nm* (magasin) self-service shop; (restaurant) self-service restaurant.

licence /lisãs/ *nf* licence; (Univ) degree.

licencié, ~e /lisãsje/ *nm, f* graduate; **~ ès lettres/sciences** Bachelor of Arts/Science.

licenciements /lisãsimã/ *nm* redundancy; (pour faute) dismissal. **licencier** **45** *vt* make redundant; (pour faute) dismiss.

licorne /likɔʀn/ *nf* unicorn.

liège /ljɛʒ/ *nm* cork.

lien /ljɛ̃/ nm (rapport) link; (attache) bond, tie; (corde) rope; ~s affectifs/ de parenté emotional/family ties.

lier /lje/ [45] vt tie (up), bind; (relier) link; (engager, unir) bind; ~ conversation strike up a conversation; ils sont très liés they are very close. □ se ~ avec vpr make friends with.

lierre /ljɛʀ/ nm ivy.

lieu (pl ~x) /ljø/ nm place; ~x (locaux) premises; (d'un accident) scene; sur les ~x at the scene; au ~ de instead of; avoir ~ take place; donner ~ à give rise to; tenir ~ de serve as; s'il y a ~ if necessary; en premier ~ firstly; en dernier ~ lastly; ~ commun commonplace; ~ de rencontre meeting place.

lièvre /ljɛvʀ/ nm hare.

lifting /liftiŋ/ nm face-lift.

ligne /liɲ/ nf line; (trajet) route; (de métro, train) line; (formes) lines; (de femme) figure; en ~ (joueurs) lined up; (au téléphone) on the phone; (Ordinat) on line; ~ spécialisée (Internet) dedicated line.

ligoter /ligɔte/ [1] vt tie up.

ligue /lig/ nf league. **liguer (se)** [1] vpr join forces (contre against).

lilas /lila/ nm & a inv lilac.

limace /limas/ nf slug.

limande /limɑ̃d/ nf (poisson) dab.

lime /lim/ nf file; ~ à ongles nail file.

limitation /limitasjɔ̃/ nf limitation; ~ de vitesse speed limit.

limite /limit/ nf limit; (de jardin, champ) boundary; à la ~ de (fig) verging on, bordering on; à la ~ if it comes to it, at a pinch; dans une certaine ~ up to a point; dans la ~ du possible as far as possible. ● adj (vitesse, âge) maximum; cas ~ borderline case; date ~ deadline; date ~ de vente sell-by date.

limiter /limite/ [1] vt limit; (délimiter) form the border of. □ se ~ vpr limit oneself (à to).

limonade /limɔnad/ nf lemonade.

limpide /lɛ̃pid/ adj limpid, clear.

lin /lɛ̃/ nm (tissu) linen.

linge /lɛ̃ʒ/ nm linen; (lessive) washing; (torchon) cloth; ~ (de corps) underwear. **lingerie** nf underwear. **lingette** nf wipe.

lingot /lɛ̃go/ nm ingot.

linguistique /lɛ̃gɥistik/ adj linguistic. ● nf linguistics.

lion /ljɔ̃/ nm lion; le L~ Leo. **lionceau** (pl ~x) nm lion cub. **lionne** nf lioness.

liquidation /likidasjɔ̃/ nf liquidation; (vente) (clearance) sale; entrer en ~ go into liquidation.

liquide /likid/ adj liquid. ● nm (argent) ~ ready money; payer en ~ pay cash; ~ de frein brake fluid.

liquider /likide/ [1] vt liquidate; (vendre) sell.

lire /liʀ/ [39] vt/i read. ● nf lira.

lis¹ /li/ ➡LIRE [39].

lis² /lis/ nm (fleur) lily.

lisible /lizibl/ adj legible; (roman) readable.

lisière /lizjɛʀ/ nf edge.

lisse /lis/ adj smooth.

liste /list/ nf list; ~ d'attente waiting list; ~ électorale register of voters; être sur (la) ~ rouge be ex-directory.

listing /listiŋ/ nm printout.

lit /li/ nm bed; se mettre au ~ get into bed; ~ de camp camp-bed; ~ d'enfant cot; ~ d'une personne single bed; ~ de deux personnes, grand ~ double bed.

literie /litʀi/ nf bedding.

litière /litjɛʀ/ nf litter.

litige /litiʒ/ nm dispute.

litre /litʀ/ nm litre.

littéraire /liteʀɛʀ/ adj literary; (études, formation) arts.

littéral, ~e (mpl -aux) /liteʀal, -o/ adj literal.

littérature /liteʀatyʀ/ nf literature.

littoral (pl ~aux) /litɔʀal, -o/ nm coast.

Lituanie /litɥani/ nf Lithuania.

livide /livid/ adj deathly pale.

livraison /livʀɛzɔ̃/ nf delivery.

livre /livʀ/ nf (monnaie, poids) pound. ● nm book; ~ de bord log-book; ~ de compte books; ~ de poche paperback.

livrer /livʀe/ [1] vt (Comm) deliver; (abandonner) give over (à to); (remettre) (coupable, document) hand over (à to); livré à soi-même left to oneself. □ se ~ vpr (se rendre) give oneself up (à to); se ~ à (boisson, actes) indulge in; (ami) confide in.

livret /livʀɛ/ nm book; (Mus) libretto; ~ **de caisse d'épargne** savings book; ~ **scolaire** school report (book).

livreur, -euse /livʀœʀ, -øz/ nm, f delivery man, delivery woman.

local¹, ~**e** (mpl **-aux**) /lɔkal, -o/ adj local.

local² (pl **-aux**) /lɔkal, -o/ nm premises; **locaux** premises.

localement /lɔkalmã/ adv locally.

localisation /lɔkalizasjɔ̃/ nf localization.

localiser /lɔkalize/ ❶ vt (repérer) locate; (circonscrire) localize.

locataire /lɔkatɛʀ/ nmf tenant; (de chambre) lodger.

location /lɔkasjɔ̃/ nf (de maison) renting; (de voiture, de matériel) hire, rental; (de place) booking, reservation; (par propriétaire) renting out; hiring out; **en** ~ (voiture) on hire, rented; (habiter) in rented accommodation.

locomotive /lɔkɔmɔtiv/ nf engine, locomotive.

locution /lɔkysjɔ̃/ nf phrase.

loft /lɔft/ nm loft (apartment).

loge /lɔʒ/ nf (de concierge, de francmaçons) lodge; (d'acteur) dressing-room; (de spectateur) box.

logement /lɔʒmã/ nm accommodation; (appartement) flat; (habitat) housing.

loger /lɔʒe/ ❹ vt (réfugié, famille) house; (ami) put up; (client) accommodate. ● vi live. □ **se** ~ vpr live; **trouver à se** ~ find accommodation; **se** ~ **dans** (balle) lodge itself in.

logiciel /lɔʒisjɛl/ nm software; ~ **contributif** shareware; ~ **d'application** application software; ~ **de groupe** groupware; ~ **de jeux** games software; ~ **de navigation** browser; ~ **public** freeware.

logique /lɔʒik/ adj logical. ● nf logic.

logis /lɔʒi/ nm dwelling.

logistique /lɔʒistik/ nf logistics.

loi /lwa/ nf law.

loin /lwɛ̃/ adv far (away); **au** ~ far away; **de** ~ from far away; (de beaucoup) by far; ~ **de là** far from it; **plus** ~ further; **il revient de** ~ (fig) he had a close shave.

lointain, ~**e** /lwɛ̃tɛ̃, -ɛn/ adj distant. ● nm distance; **dans le** ~ in the distance.

loisir /lwaziʀ/ nm (spare) time; ~**s** (temps libre) leisure, spare time; (distractions) leisure activities; **à** ~ at one's leisure; **avoir le** ~ **de faire** have time to do.

londonien, ~**ne** /lɔ̃dɔnjɛ̃, -ɛn/ adj London. **L**~, ~**e** nm, f Londoner.

Londres /lɔ̃dʀ/ npr London.

long, longue /lɔ̃, lɔ̃g/ adj long; **à** ~ **terme** long-term; **être** ~ **à faire** be a long time doing. ● nm **de** ~ (mesure) long; **de** ~ **en large** back and forth; **(tout) le** ~ **de** (all) along. ● adv **en dire** ~ **sur qn/qch** say a lot about sb/sth; **en savoir plus** ~ **sur** know more about.

longer /lɔ̃ʒe/ ❹ vt go along; (limiter) border.

longitude /lɔ̃ʒityd/ nf longitude.

longtemps /lɔ̃tã/ adv a long time; **avant** ~ before long; **trop** ~ too long; **ça prendra** ~ it will take a long time; **prendre plus** ~ **que prévu** take longer than anticipated.

longuement /lɔ̃gmã/ adv (longtemps) for a long time; (en détail) at length.

longueur /lɔ̃gœʀ/ nf length; ~**s** (de texte) over-long parts; **à** ~ **de journée** all day long; **en** ~ lengthwise; ~ **d'onde** wavelength.

lopin /lɔpɛ̃/ nm ~ **de terre** patch of land.

loque /lɔk/ nf ~**s** rags; ~ **(humaine)** (human) wreck.

loquet /lɔkɛ/ nm latch.

lors de /lɔʀdə/ prép (au moment de) at the time of; (pendant) during.

lorsque /lɔʀsk(ə)/ conj when.

losange /lɔzãʒ/ nm diamond.

lot /lo/ nm (portion) share; (aux enchères) lot; (Ordinat) batch; (destin) lot; **gagner le gros** ~ hit the jackpot.

loterie /lɔtʀi/ nf lottery.

lotion /losjɔ̃/ nf lotion.

lotissement /lɔtismã/ nm (à construire) building plot; (construit) (housing) development.

louable /luabl/ adj praiseworthy.

louange nf praise.

louche /luʃ/ adj shady, dubious. ● nf ladle.

loucher /luʃe/ **1** vi squint.

louer /lwe/ **1** vt (approuver) praise (de for); (prendre en location) (maison) rent; (voiture, matériel) hire, rent; (place) book, reserve; (donner en location) (maison) rent out; (matériel) rent out, hire out; à ~ to let, for rent (US).

loufoque /lufɔk/ adj **1** crazy.

loup /lu/ nm wolf.

loupe /lup/ nf magnifying glass.

louper /lupe/ **1** vt **1** miss; (examen) flunk **1**.

lourd, ~e /luʀ, -ʀd/ adj heavy; (faute) serious; ~ de dangers fraught with danger; il fait ~ it's close ou muggy.

loutre /lutʀ/ nf otter.

louveteau (pl ~x) /luvto/ nm wolf cub; (scout) Cub (Scout).

loyal, ~e (mpl -aux) /lwajal, -o/ adj loyal, faithful; (honnête) fair. **loyauté** nf loyalty; fairness.

loyer /lwaje/ nm rent.

lu /ly/ →LIRE **39**.

lubrifiant /lybʀifjɑ̃/ nm lubricant.

lucide /lysid/ adj lucid. **lucidité** nf lucidity.

lucratif, -ive /lykʀatif, -v/ adj lucrative; à but non ~ non-profitmaking.

ludiciel /lydisjɛl/ nm (Ordinat) games software.

lueur /lɥœʀ/ nf (faint) light, glimmer; (fig) glimmer, gleam.

luge /lyʒ/ nf toboggan.

lugubre /lygybʀ/ adj gloomy.

---

lui /lɥi/

● pronom

····▶ (masculin) (sujet) he; ~, il est à l'étranger he's abroad; c'est ~! it's him!; (objet) him; (animal) it; c'est à ~ it's his; elle conduit mieux que ~ she's a better driver than he is.

····▶ (féminin) her; je ~ ai annoncé I told her.

····▶ (masculin/féminin) donne-le-~ give it to him/her.

---

lui-même /lɥimɛm/ pron himself; (animal) itself.

luire /lɥiʀ/ **17** vi shine; (reflet humide) glisten; (reflet chaud, faible) glow.

lumière /lymjɛʀ/ nf light; ~s (connaissances) knowledge; faire (toute) la ~ sur une affaire clear a matter up.

luminaire /lyminɛʀ/ nm lamp.

lumineux, -euse /lyminø, -z/ adj luminous; (éclairé) illuminated; (rayon) of light; (radieux) radiant; **source lumineuse** light source.

lunaire /lynɛʀ/ adj lunar.

lunatique /lynatik/ adj temperamental.

lunch /lœnʃ/ nm buffet lunch.

lundi /lœdi/ nm Monday.

lune /lyn/ nf moon; ~ de miel honeymoon.

lunettes /lynɛt/ nfpl glasses; (de protection) goggles; ~ de ski/natation ski/swimming goggles; ~ noires dark glasses; ~ de soleil sun-glasses.

lustre /lystʀ/ nm (éclat) lustre; (objet) chandelier.

lutin /lytɛ̃/ nm goblin.

lutte /lyt/ nf fight, struggle; (Sport) wrestling. **lutter** **1** vi fight, struggle; (Sport) wrestle. **lutteur, -euse** nm, f fighter; (Sport) wrestler.

luxe /lyks/ nm luxury; de ~ luxury; (produit) de luxe.

Luxembourg /lyksɑ̃buʀ/ nm Luxemburg.

luxer (se) /(sə)lykse/ **1** vpr se ~ le genou dislocate one's knee.

luxueux, -euse /lyksɥø, -z/ adj luxurious.

lycée /lise/ nm (secondary) school. **lycéen, ~ne** nm, f pupil (at secondary school).

lyophilisé, ~e /ljɔfilize/ adj freeze-dried.

lyrique /liʀik/ adj (poésie) lyric; (passionné) lyrical; **artiste/théâtre ~** opera singer/house.

lys /lis/ nm lily.

Mm

m' /m/ →ME.

ma /ma/ →MON.

macabre /makabʀ/ adj macabre.

macadam /makadam/ nm Tarmac®.

macaron /makaʀɔ̃/ nm (gâteau) macaroon; (insigne) badge.

macédoine /masedwan/ nf mixed diced vegetables; ~ **de fruits** fruit salad.

macérer /maseʀe/ **14** vt/i soak; (dans du vinaigre) pickle.

mâcher /maʃe/ **1** vt chew; **ne pas ~ ses mots** not mince one's words.

machin /maʃɛ̃/ nm **1** (chose) thing; (dont on ne trouve pas le nom) whatsit **1**.

machinal, ~e (mpl **-aux**) /maʃinal, -o/ adj automatic. **machinalement** adv mechanically, automatically.

machination /maʃinasjɔ̃/ nf plot; **des ~s** machinations.

machine /maʃin/ nf machine; (d'un train, navire) engine; ~ **à écrire** typewriter; ~ **à laver/coudre** washing-/sewing-machine; ~ **à sous** fruit machine; (US) slot machine. **machine-outil** (pl **machines-outils**) nf machine tool. **machinerie** nf machinery.

machiniste /maʃinist/ nm (Théât) stage-hand; (conducteur) driver.

mâchoire /maʃwaʀ/ nf jaw.

mâchonner /maʃɔne/ **1** vt chew.

maçon /masɔ̃/ nm (entrepreneur) builder; (poseur de briques) bricklayer; (qui construit en pierre) mason. **maçonnerie** nf (briques) brickwork; (pierres) stonework, masonry; (travaux) building.

madame (pl **mesdames**) /madam, medam/ nf (à une inconnue) (dans une lettre) M~ Dear Madam; **bonjour, ~** good morning; **mesdames et messieurs** ladies and gentlemen; (à une femme dont on connaît le nom) (dans une lettre) **Chère M~** Dear Mrs ou Ms X; **bonjour, ~** good morning Mrs ou Ms X; **oui M ~ le Ministre**

yes Minister; (formule de respect) **oui M~** yes madam.

mademoiselle (pl **mesdemoiselles**) /madmwazɛl, medmwazɛl/ nf (à une inconnue) (dans une lettre) M~ Dear Madam; **bonjour, ~** good morning; **entrez mesdemoiselles** come in (ladies); (à une jeune fille dont on connaît le nom) (dans une lettre) **Chère M~** Dear Ms ou Miss X; **bonjour, ~** good morning Miss ou Ms X.

magasin /magazɛ̃/ nm shop, store; (entrepôt) warehouse; (d'une arme) magazine; **en ~** in stock.

magazine /magazin/ nm magazine; (émission) programme.

Maghreb /magʀɛb/ nm North Africa.

magicien, ~ne /maʒisjɛ̃, -ɛn/ nm, f magician.

magie /maʒi/ nf magic. **magique** adj magic; (mystérieux) magical.

magistral, ~e (mpl **-aux**) /maʒistʀal, -o/ adj masterly; (grand: hum) tremendous; **cours ~** lecture.

magistrat /maʒistʀa/ nm magistrate.

magistrature /maʒistʀatyʀ/ nf judiciary; (fonction) public office.

magner (se) /(sə)maɲe/ **1** vpr **🅺** get a move on.

magnétique /maɲetik/ adj magnetic. **magnétiser 1** vt magnetize. **magnétisme** nm magnetism.

magnétophone /maɲetɔfɔn/ nm tape recorder; (à cassettes) cassette recorder.

magnétoscope /maɲetɔskɔp/ nm video recorder.

magnificence /maɲifisɑ̃s/ nf magnificence. **magnifique** adj magnificent.

magot /mago/ nm **1** hoard (of money).

magouille /maguj/ nf **1** scheming, skulduggery.

magret /magʀɛ/ nm ~ **de canard** duck breast.

mai /mɛ/ nm May.

maigre /mɛgʀ/ adj thin; (viande) lean; (yaourt) low-fat; (fig) poor, meagre; **faire ~** abstain from meat. **maigreur** nf thinness; leanness; (fig) meagreness.

maigrir /megʀiʀ/ **2** vi get thin(ner); (en suivant un régime) slim. ● vt make thin(ner).

m

maille /maj/ nf stitch; (de filet) mesh; ∼ **qui file** ladder, run; **avoir** ∼ **à partir avec qn** have a brush with sb.

maillet /majɛ/ nm mallet.

maillon /majɔ̃/ nm link.

maillot /majo/ nm (Sport) shirt, jersey; (∼ **de corps**) vest; (US) undershirt; (∼ **de bain**) (swimming) costume.

main /mɛ̃/ nf hand; **donner la** ∼ **à qn** hold sb's hand; **se donner la** ∼ hold hands; **en** ∼**s propres** in person; **en bonnes** ∼**s** in good hands; ∼ **courante** handrail; **se faire la** ∼ get the hang of it; **perdre la** ∼ lose one's touch; **sous la** ∼ to hand; **vol à** ∼ **armée** armed robbery; **fait (à la)** ∼ handmade; **haut les** ∼**s!** hands up! **main-d'œuvre** (pl **mains-d'œuvre**) nf labour; (ouvriers) labour force.

main-forte /mɛ̃fɔʀt/ nf inv **prêter** ∼ **à qn** come to sb's aid.

maint, ∼**e** /mɛ̃, mɛ̃t/ adj many a (+ sg); ∼**s** many; **à** ∼**es reprises** many times.

maintenant /mɛ̃t(ə)nɑ̃/ adv now; (de nos jours) nowadays; (l'époque actuelle) today.

maintenir /mɛ̃t(ə)niʀ/ [58] vt keep, maintain; (soutenir) support, hold up; (affirmer) maintain; (décision) stand by. □ **se** ∼ vpr (tendance) persist; (prix, malade) remain stable.

maintien /mɛ̃tjɛ̃/ nm (attitude) bearing; (conservation) maintenance.

maire /mɛʀ/ nm mayor.

mairie /meʀi/ nf town hall; (administration) town council.

mais /mɛ/ conj but; ∼ **oui** of course; ∼ **non** of course not.

maïs /mais/ nm maize, corn; (Culin) sweetcorn.

maison /mɛzɔ̃/ nf house; (foyer) home; (immeuble) building; (∼ **de commerce**) firm; **à la** ∼ at home; **rentrer** ou **aller à la** ∼ go home; ∼ **des jeunes (et de la culture)** youth club; ∼ **de repos** rest home; ∼ **de convalescence** convalescent home; ∼ **de retraite** old people's home; ∼ **mère** parent company. ● adj inv (Culin) home-made.

maître, -esse /mɛtʀ, -ɛs/ adj (qui contrôle) **être** ∼ **de soi** be one's own master; ∼ **de la situation** in control of the situation; (principal) (idée, qualité) key, main. ● nm, f (Scol) teacher; (d'animal) owner, master. ● nm (expert, guide) master; (dirigeant) leader; ∼ **de conférences** senior lecturer; ∼ **d'hôtel** head waiter; (domestique) butler. **maître-assistant,** ∼ **e** (pl **maîtres-assistants**) nm, f lecturer. **maître-chanteur** (pl **maîtres-chanteurs**) nm blackmailer. **maître-nageur** (pl **maîtres-nageurs**) nm swimming instructor. **maîtresse** nf (amante) mistress.

maîtrise /metʀiz/ nf mastery; (contrôle) control; (Mil) supremacy; (Univ) master's degree; (∼ **de soi**) self-control.

maîtriser /metʀize/ [1] vt (sujet, technique) master; (incendie, sentiment, personne) control. □ **se** ∼ vpr have self-control.

maïzena® /maizena/ nf cornflour.

majesté /maʒɛste/ nf majesty.

majestueux, -euse /maʒɛstɥø, z/ adj majestic.

majeur, ∼**e** /maʒœʀ/ adj major, main; (Jur) of age; **en** ∼**e partie** mostly; **la** ∼**e partie de** most of. ● nm middle finger.

majoration /maʒoʀasjɔ̃/ nf increase (de in). **majorer** [1] vt increase.

majoritaire /maʒoʀitɛʀ/ adj majority; **être** ∼ be in the majority. **majorité** nf majority; **en** ∼ chiefly.

Majorque /maʒoʀk/ nf Majorca.

majuscule /maʒyskyl/ adj capital. ● nf capital letter.

mal¹ /mal/ adv badly; (incorrectement) wrong(ly); **aller** ∼ (personne) be unwell; (affaires) go badly; ∼ **entendre/comprendre** not hear/understand properly; ∼ **en point** in a bad state; **pas** ∼ quite a lot. ● adj inv bad, wrong; **c'est ~ de** it is wrong ou bad to; **ce n'est pas ~** I it's not bad; **Nick n'est pas ~** I Nick is not bad-looking.

mal² (*pl* **maux**) /mal, mo/ *nm* evil; (douleur) pain, ache; (maladie) disease; (effort) trouble; (dommage) harm; (malheur) misfortune; **avoir ~ à la tête/à la gorge** have a headache/ a sore throat; **avoir le ~ de mer/du pays** be seasick/ homesick; **faire ~** hurt; **se faire ~** hurt oneself; **j'ai ~** it hurts; **faire du ~ à** hurt, harm; **se donner du ~ pour faire qch** go to a lot of trouble to do sth.

malade /malad/ *adj* sick, ill; (bras, œil) bad; (plante, poumons, côlon) diseased; **tomber ~** fall ill; (fou I) mad. ● *nmf* sick person; (d'un médecin) patient; **~ mental** mentally ill person.

maladie /maladi/ *nf* illness, disease; (manie I) mania.

maladif, -ive /maladif, -v/ *adj* sickly; (jalousie, peur) pathological.

maladresse /maladʀɛs/ *nf* clumsiness; (erreur) blunder.

maladroit, ~e /maladʀwa, -t/ *adj* clumsy; (sans tact) tactless.

malaise /malɛz/ *nm* feeling of faintness; (gêne) uneasiness; (état de crise) unrest.

malaisé, ~e /maleze/ *adj* difficult.

Malaisie /malezi/ *nf* Malaysia.

malaria /malaʀja/ *nf* malaria.

malaxer /malakse/ I *vt* (pétrir) knead; (mêler) mix.

malchance /malʃɑ̃s/ *nf* misfortune. **malchanceux, -euse** *adj* unlucky.

mâle /mɑl/ *adj* male; (viril) manly. ● *nm* male.

malédiction /malediksjɔ̃/ *nf* curse.

maléfice /malefis/ *nm* evil spell. **maléfique** *adj* evil.

malentendant, ~e /malɑ̃tɑ̃dɑ̃, -t/ *adj* hard of hearing.

malentendu /malɑ̃tɑ̃dy/ *nm* misunderstanding.

malfaçon /malfasɔ̃/ *nf* defect.

malfaisant, ~e /malfəzɑ̃, -t/ *adj* harmful; (personne) evil.

malfaiteur /malfɛtœʀ/ *nm* criminal.

malformation /malfɔʀmasjɔ̃/ *nf* malformation.

malgré /malgʀe/ *prép* in spite of, despite; **~ tout** nevertheless.

malheur /malœʀ/ *nm* misfortune; (accident) accident; **par ~** unfortunately; **faire un ~** I be a big hit; **porter ~** be ou bring bad luck.

malheureusement /malœ ʀøzmɑ̃/ *adv* unfortunately.

malheureux, -euse /malœʀø, -z/ *adj* unhappy; (regrettable) unfortunate; (sans succès) unlucky; (insignifiant) paltry, pathetic. ● *nm, f* (poor) wretch.

malhonnête /malɔnɛt/ *adj* dishonest. **malhonnêteté** *nf* dishonesty.

malice /malis/ *nf* mischief; **sans ~** harmless; **avec ~** mischievously. **malicieux, -ieuse** *adj* mischievous.

malignité /maliɲite/ *nf* malignancy. **malin, -igne** *adj* clever, smart; (méchant) malicious; (tumeur) malignant; (difficile I) difficult.

malingre /malɛ̃gʀ/ *adj* puny.

malle /mal/ *nf* (valise) trunk; (Auto) boot; (US) trunk.

mallette /malɛt/ *nf* (small) suitcase; (pour le bureau) briefcase.

malmener /malməne/ 6 *vt* manhandle; (fig) give a rough ride to.

malnutrition /malnytʀisjɔ̃/ *nf* malnutrition.

malodorant, ~e /malodoʀɑ̃, -t/ *adj* smelly, foul-smelling.

malpoli, ~e /malpoli/ *adj* rude, impolite.

malpropre /malpʀɔpʀ/ *adj* dirty.

malsain, ~e /malsɛ̃, -ɛn/ *adj* unhealthy.

malt /malt/ *nm* malt.

Malte /malt/ *nf* Malta.

maltraiter /maltʀete/ I *vt* illtreat.

malveillance /malvɛjɑ̃s/ *nf* malice. **malveillant, ~e** *adj* malicious.

maman /mamɑ̃/ *nf* mum(my), mother; (US) mom(my).

mamelle /mamɛl/ *nf* teat.

mamelon /mamlɔ̃/ *nm* (Anat) nipple; (colline) hillock.

mamie /mami/ *nf* I granny.

mammifère /mamifɛʀ/ *nm* mammal.

manche /mɑ̃ʃ/ *nf* sleeve; (Sport, Pol) round. ● *nm* (d'un instrument) handle; **~ à balai** broomstick; (Aviat) joystick. **M~** *nf* **la M~** the Channel; **le tunnel**

m

sous la M~ the Channel tunnel.

manchette /mɑ̃ʃɛt/ nf cuff; (de journal) headline.

manchot, ~te /mɑ̃ʃo, -ɔt/ nm, f one-armed person; (sans bras) armless person. ● nm (oiseau) penguin.

mandarine /mɑ̃daʀin/ nf tangerine, mandarin (orange).

mandat /mɑ̃da/ nm (postal) money order; (Pol) mandate; (procuration) proxy; (de police) warrant; ~ d'arrêt arrest warrant.

mandataire /mɑ̃datɛʀ/ nm representative; (Jul) proxy.

manège /manɛʒ/ nm riding school; (à la foire) merry-go-round; (manœuvre) trick, ploy.

manette /manɛt/ nf lever; (de jeu) joystick.

mangeable /mɑ̃ʒabl/ adj edible.

mangeoire /mɑ̃ʒwaʀ/ nf trough; (pour oiseaux) feeder.

manger /mɑ̃ʒe/ 🗓 vt eat; (fortune) go through; (profits) eat away at; (économies) use up; (ronger) eat into. ● vi eat; **donner à ~ à** feed. ● nm food.

mangue /mɑ̃g/ nf mango.

maniable /manjabl/ adj easy to handle.

maniaque /manjak/ adj fussy. ● nmf fusspot; (fou) maniac; (fanatique) fanatic; **un ~ de l'ordre** a stickler for tidiness.

manie /mani/ nf habit; (marotte) obsession.

maniement /manimɑ̃/ nm handling. **manier** 🗓 vt handle.

manière /manjɛʀ/ nf way, manner; ~s (politesse) manners; (chichis) fuss; **à la ~ de** in the style of; **de ~ à** so as to; **de toute ~** anyway, in any case.

maniéré, ~e /manjere/ adj affected.

manif /manif/ nf 🗓 demo.

manifestant, ~e /manifɛstɑ̃, -t/ nm, f demonstrator.

manifestation /manifɛstasjɔ̃/ nf expression, manifestation; (de maladie) phénomène) appearance; (Pol) demonstration; (événement) event; ~ **culturelle** cultural event.

manifeste /manifɛst/ adj obvious. ● nm manifesto.

manifester /manifɛste/ 🗓 vt show, manifest; (désir, crainte) express. ● vi

(Pol) demonstrate. □ **se ~** vpr (sentiment) show itself; (apparaître) appear; (répondre à un appel) come forward.

manigance /manigɑ̃s/ nf little plot. **manigancer** 🗓 vt plot.

manipulation /manipylasjɔ̃/ nf handling; (péj) manipulation.

manivelle /manivɛl/ nf handle, crank.

mannequin /mankɛ̃/ nm (personne) model; (statue) dummy.

manœuvrer /manœvʀe/ 🗓 vt manoeuvre; (machine) operate. ● vi manoeuvre.

manoir /manwaʀ/ nm manor.

manque /mɑ̃k/ nm lack (de of); (lacune) gap; ~ **à gagner** loss of earnings; **en (état de) ~** having withdrawal symptoms.

manqué, ~e /mɑ̃ke/ adj (écrivain) failed; **garçon ~** tomboy.

manquement /mɑ̃kmɑ̃/ nm ~ **à** breach of.

manquer /mɑ̃ke/ 🗓 vt miss; (gâcher) spoil; ~ **à** (devoir) fail in; ~ **de** be short of, lack; **il/ça lui manque** he misses him/it; ~ **(de) faire** (faillir) nearly do; **ne manquez pas de** be sure to; ~ **à sa parole** break one's word. ● vi be short ou lacking; (être absent) be absent; (en moins, disparu) be missing; **il me manque 20 euros** I'm 20 euros short.

mansarde /mɑ̃saʀd/ nf attic (room).

manteau (pl ~x) /mɑ̃to/ nm coat.

manucure /manykyʀ/ nmf manicurist. ● nf (soins) manicure.

manuel, ~le /manɥɛl/ adj manual. ● nm (livre) manual; (Scol) textbook.

manufacture /manyfaktyʀ/ nf factory; (fabrication) manufacture. **manufacturer** 🗓 vt manufacture.

manuscrit, ~e /manyskʀi, -t/ adj handwritten. ● nm manuscript.

mappemonde /mapmɔ̃d/ nf world map; (sphère) globe.

maquereau (pl ~x) /makʀo/ nm (poisson) mackerel; 🗓 pimp.

maquette /makɛt/ nf (scale) model; ~ **(de mise en page)** paste-up.

maquillage /makijaʒ/ nm make-up.

maquiller /makije/ 🗓 vt make up; (truquer) doctor, fake. □ **se ~** vpr make (oneself) up.

maquis /maki/ *nm* (paysage) scrub; (Mil) Maquis, underground.

maraîcher, -ère /maʀeʃe, -ɛʀ/ *nm, f* market gardener; (US) truck farmer.

marais /maʀɛ/ *nm* marsh.

marasme /maʀasm/ *nm* slump, stagnation; **dans le ~** in the doldrums.

marbre /maʀbʀ/ *nm* marble.

marc /maʀ/ *nm* (eau-de-vie) marc; **~ de café** coffee grounds.

marchand, ~e /maʀʃã, -d/ *adj* (valeur) market. ● *nm, f* trader; (de charbon, vins) merchant; **~ de couleurs** ironmonger; (US) hardware merchant; **~ de journaux** newsagent; **~ de légumes** greengrocer; **~ de poissons** fishmonger.

marchander /maʀʃãde/ 🔳 *vt* haggle over. ● *vi* haggle.

marchandise /maʀʃãdiz/ *nf* goods.

marche /maʀʃ/ *nf* (démarche, trajet) walk; (rythme) pace; (Mil, Mus, Pol) march; (d'escalier) step; (Sport) walking; (de machine) operation, working; (de véhicule) running; **en ~** (train) moving; (moteur, machine) running; **faire ~ arrière** (véhicule) reverse; **mettre en ~** start (up); **se mettre en ~** start moving.

marché /maʀʃe/ *nm* market; (contrat) deal; **faire son ~** do one's shopping; **~ aux puces** flea market; **~ noir** black market.

marchepied /maʀʃəpje/ *nm* (de train, camion) step.

marcher /maʀʃe/ 🔳 *vi* walk; (poser le pied) tread (**sur** on); (aller) go; (fonctionner) work, run; (prospérer) go well; (film, livre) do well; (consentir 🔳) agree; **faire ~ qn** 🔳 pull sb's leg.

mardi /maʀdi/ *nm* Tuesday; **M ~ gras** Shrove Tuesday.

mare /maʀ/ *nf* (étang) pond; (flaque) pool.

marécage /maʀekaʒ/ *nm* marsh; (sous les tropiques) swamp.

maréchal (*pl* **-aux**) /maʀeʃal, -o/ *nm* field marshal.

maréchal-ferrant (*pl* **-aux-ferrants** /maʀeʃalferã/ *nm* blacksmith.

marée /maʀe/ *nf* tide; (poissons) fresh fish; **~ haute/basse** high/low tide; **~ noire** oil slick.

marelle /maʀɛl/ *nf* hopscotch.

margarine /maʀgaʀin/ *nf* margarine.

marge /maʀʒ/ *nf* margin; **en ~ de** (à l'écart de) on the fringe(s) of; **~ bénéficiaire** profit margin.

marginal, ~e (*mpl* **-aux**) /maʀʒinal, -o/ *adj* marginal. ● *nm, f* drop-out.

marguerite /maʀgeʀit/ *nf* daisy; (qui imprime) daisy-wheel.

mari /maʀi/ *nm* husband.

mariage /maʀjaʒ/ *nm* marriage; (cérémonie) wedding.

marié, ~e /maʀje/ *adj* married. ● *nm, f* (bride) groom, bride; **les ~s** the bride and groom.

Marianne The symbolic female figure often used to represent the French Republic. There are statues of her in public places all over France, always wearing the Phrygian bonnet, a pointed cap which became a symbol of liberty as represented by the 1789 Revolution. She also appears on the standard French postage stamp.

marier /maʀje/ 45 *vt* marry. □ **se ~** *vpr* get married, marry; **se ~ avec** marry, get married to.

marin, ~e /maʀɛ̃, -in/ *adj* sea. ● *nm* sailor.

marine /maʀin/ *nf* navy; **~ marchande** merchant navy. ● *adj inv* navy (blue).

marionnette /maʀjɔnɛt/ *nf* puppet; (à fils) marionette.

maritalement /maʀitalmã/ *adv* (vivre) as husband and wife.

maritime /maʀitim/ *adj* maritime, coastal; (agent, compagnie) shipping.

marmaille /maʀmaj/ *nf* 🔳 brats.

marmelade /maʀməlad/ *nf* stewed fruit; **~ d'oranges** (orange) marmalade.

marmite /maʀmit/ *nf* (cooking-)pot.

marmonner /maʀmɔne/ 🔳 *vt* mumble.

marmot /maʀmo/ *nm* 🔳 kid.

Maroc /maʀɔk/ *nm* Morocco.

maroquinerie /maʀɔkinʀi/ *nf* (magasin) leather goods shop.

marquant, ~e /maʀkã, -t/ *adj* (remarquable) outstanding; (qu'on n'oublie pas) memorable.

m

marque /maʀk/ *nf* mark; (de produits) brand, make; (décompte) score; **à vos ~s!** (Sport) on your marks!; **de ~** (Comm) brand name; (fig) important; **~ de fabrique** trademark; **~ déposée** registered trademark.

marquer /maʀke/ **1** *vt* mark; (indiquer) show, say; (écrire) note down; (point, but) score; (joueur) mark; (influencer) leave its mark on; (exprimer) (volonté, sentiment) show. ● *vi* (laisser une trace) leave a mark; (événement) stand out; (Sport) score.

marquis, ~e /maʀki, -z/ *nm, f* marquis, marchioness.

marraine /maʀɛn/ *nf* godmother.

marrant, ~e /maʀɑ̃, -t/ *adj* **1** funny.

marre /maʀ/ *adv* **en avoir ~** **1** be fed up (de with).

marrer (se) /(sə)maʀe/ **1** *vpr* **1** laugh, have a (good) laugh.

marron /maʀɔ̃/ *nm* chestnut; (couleur) brown; (coup **1**) thump; **~ d'Inde** horse chestnut. ● *adj inv* brown.

mars /maʀs/ *nm* March.

> **Marseillaise, la** The popular name of the French national anthem, composed by Claude-Joseph Rouget de Lisle in 1792. It was adopted as a marching song by a group of Republican volunteers from Marseilles and became famous as they sang it on entering Paris.

---

marteau (*pl* **~x**) /maʀto/ *nm* hammer; **~ (de porte)** (door) knocker; **~ piqueur** *ou* **pneumatique** pneumatic drill; **être ~** **1** be mad.

marteler /maʀtəle/ **6** *vt* hammer; (poings, talons) pound; (scander) rap out.

martial, ~e (*mpl* **-iaux**) /maʀsjal, -jo/ *adj* military; (art) martial.

martien, ~ne /maʀsjɛ̃, -ɛn/ *adj & nm, f* Martian.

martyr, ~e /maʀtiʀ/ *nm, f* martyr. ● *adj* martyred; (enfant) battered.

martyre /maʀtiʀ/ *nm* (Relig) martyrdom; (fig) agony, suffering.

martyriser /maʀtiʀize/ **1** *vt* (Relig) martyr; (torturer) torture; (enfant) batter.

marxisme /maʀksism/ *nm* Marxism. **marxiste** *adj & nmf* Marxist.

masculin, ~e /maskylɛ̃, -in/ *adj* masculine; (sexe) male; (mode, équipe) men's. ● *nm* masculine.

masochisme /mazoʃism/ *nm* masochism.

masochiste /mazoʃist/ *nmf* masochist. ● *adj* masochistic.

masque /mask/ *nm* mask; **~ de beauté** face pack. **masquer** **1** *vt* (cacher) hide, conceal (à from); (lumière) block (off).

massacre /masakʀ/ *nm* massacre. **massacrer** **1** *vt* massacre; (abîmer **1**) ruin.

massage /masaʒ/ *nm* massage.

masse /mas/ *nf* (volume) mass; (gros morceau) lump, mass; (outil) sledgehammer; **en ~** (vendre) in bulk; (venir) in force; **produire en ~** mass-produce; **la ~** (foule) the masses; **une ~ de** **1** masses of; **la ~ de** the majority of.

masser /mase/ **1** *vt* (assembler) assemble; (pétrir) massage. □ **se ~** *vpr* (gens, foule) mass.

massif, -ive /masif, -v/ *adj* massive; (or, argent) solid. ● *nm* (de fleurs) clump; (parterre) bed; (Géog) massif. **massivement** *adv* (en masse) in large numbers.

massue /masy/ *nf* club, bludgeon.

mastic /mastik/ *nm* putty; (pour trous) filler.

mastiquer /mastike/ **1** *vt* (mâcher) chew.

mat /mat/ *adj* (couleur) matt; (bruit) dull; (teint) olive; **être ~** (aux échecs) be in checkmate.

mât /mɑ/ *nm* mast; (pylône) pole; **~ de drapeau** flagpole.

match /matʃ/ *nm* match; (US) game; **faire ~ nul** tie, draw; **~ aller** first leg; **~ retour** return match.

matelas /matla/ *nm* mattress; **~ pneumatique** air bed.

matelassé, ~e /matlase/ *adj* padded; (tissu) quilted.

matelot /matlo/ *nm* sailor.

mater /mate/ **1** *vt* (révolte) put down; (personne) bring into line.

matérialiser (se) /(sə)mateʀjalize/ **1** *vpr* materialize.

matérialiste /mateʀjalist/ *adj* materialistic. ● *nmf* materialist.

matériau (*pl* ~x) /mateʀjo/ *nm* material.

matériel, ~le /mateʀjɛl/ *adj* material. ● *nm* equipment, materials; ~ **informatique** hardware.

maternel, ~le /matɛʀnɛl/ *adj* maternal; (comme d'une mère) motherly. **maternelle** *nf* nursery school.

maternité /matɛʀnite/ *nf* maternity hospital; (état de mère) motherhood; **de** ~ maternity.

mathématicien, ~ne /matematisjɛ̃, -ɛn/ *nm, f* mathematician.

mathématique /matematik/ *adj* mathematical. **mathématiques** *nfpl* mathematics (+ *sg*).

maths /mat/ *nfpl* 🔢 maths (+ *sg*).

Matignon The *Hôtel Matignon* is the official residence and office of the French prime minister, situated in the *rue de Varenne*, Paris. The word *Matignon* is often used to refer to the prime minister's office. See ▷**ÉLYSÉE**

matière /matjɛʀ/ *nf* matter; (produit) material; (sujet) subject; **en** ~ **de** as regards; ~ **plastique** plastic; ~**s grasses** fat content; ~**s premières** raw materials.

matin /matɛ̃/ *nm* morning; **de bon** ~ early in the morning.

matinal, ~e (*mpl* -**aux**) /matinal, -o/ *adj* morning; (de bonne heure) early; **être** ~ be up early; (d'habitude) be an early riser.

matinée /matine/ *nf* morning; (spectacle) matinée.

matou /matu/ *nm* tomcat.

matraque /matʀak/ *nf* (de police) truncheon; (US) billy (club). **matraquer** 🔟 *vt* club, beat; (produit, chanson) plug.

matrimonial, ~e (*mpl* -**iaux**) /matʀimɔnjal, -jo/ *adj* matrimonial; **agence** ~e marriage bureau.

maturité /matyʀite/ *nf* maturity.

maudire /modiʀ/ 🔢 *vt* curse.

maudit, ~e /modi, -t/ *adj* 🔢 blasted, damned.

maugréer /mogʀee/ 🔢 *vi* grumble.

mausolée /mozɔle/ *nm* mausoleum.

maussade /mosad/ *adj* gloomy.

mauvais, ~e /movɛ, -z/ *adj* bad; (erroné) wrong; (malveillant) evil; (désagréable) nasty, bad; (mer) rough; **le** ~ **moment** the wrong time; ~e **herbe** weed; ~e **langue** gossip; ~e **passe** tight spot; ~ **traitements** ill-treatment. ● *adv* (sentir) bad; **il fait** ~ the weather is bad. ● *nm* **le bon et le** ~ the good and the bad.

mauve /mov/ *adj & nm* mauve.

mauviette /movjɛt/ *nf* weakling, wimp.

maux /mo/ →**MAL**².

maximal, ~e (*mpl* -**aux**) /maksimal, -o/ *adj* maximum.

maxime /maksim/ *nf* maxim.

maximum /maksimɔm/ *adj* maximum. ● *nm* maximum; **au** ~ as much as possible; (tout au plus) at most; **faire le** ~ do one's utmost.

mazout /mazut/ *nm* (fuel) oil.

me, m' /mə, m/ *pron* me; (indirect) (to) me; (réfléchi) myself.

méandre /meɑ̃dʀ/ *nm* meander.

mec /mek/ *nm* 🔢 bloke, guy.

mécanicien, ~ne /mekanisjɛ̃, -jɛn/ *nm, f* mechanic. ● *nm* train driver.

mécanique /mekanik/ *adj* mechanical; (jouet) clockwork; **problème** ~ engine trouble. ● *nf* mechanics (+ *sg*); (mécanisme) mechanism. **mécaniser** 🔟 *vt* mechanize.

mécanisme /mekanism/ *nm* mechanism.

méchamment /meʃamɑ̃/ *adv* spitefully. **méchanceté** *nf* nastiness; (action) wicked action.

méchant, ~e /meʃɑ̃, -t/ *adj* (cruel) wicked; (désagréable, grave) nasty; (enfant) naughty; (chien) vicious; (sensationnel 🔢) terrific. ● *nm, f* (enfant) naughty child.

mèche /mɛʃ/ *nf* (de cheveux) lock; (de bougie) wick; (d'explosif) fuse; (outil) drill bit; **de** ~ **avec** in league with.

méconnaissable /mekɔnɛsabl/ *adj* unrecognizable.

méconnaître /mekɔnɛtʀ/ 🔢 *vt* misunderstand, misread; (mésestimer) underestimate.

méconnu, ~e /mekɔny/ *adj* unrecognized; (artiste) neglected.

mécontent, ~e /mekɔ̃tɑ̃, -t/ *adj* dissatisfied (**de** with); (irrité) annoyed

m

(de at, with). **mécontentement** nm dissatisfaction; annoyance. **mécontenter** ◗ vt dissatisfy; (irriter) annoy.

médaille /medaj/ nf medal; (insigne) badge; (bijou) medallion. **médaillé, ~e** nm, f medallist.

médaillon /medajõ/ nm medallion; (bijou) locket.

médecin /mɛdsɛ̃/ nm doctor.

médecine /mɛdsin/ nf medicine.

média /medja/ nm medium; **les ~s** the media.

médiateur, -trice /medjatœʀ, -tʀis/ nm, f mediator.

médiatique /medjatik/ adj (événement, personnalité) media.

médical, ~e (mpl **-aux**) /medikal, -o/ adj medical.

médicament /medikamã/ nm medicine, drug.

médico-légal, ~e (mpl **-aux**) /medikɔlegal, -o/ adj forensic.

médiéval, ~e (mpl **-aux**) /medjeval, -o/ adj medieval.

médiocre /medjɔkʀ/ adj mediocre, poor. **médiocrité** nf mediocrity.

médire /mediʀ/ ◗ vi ~ **de** speak ill of, malign.

médisance /medizãs/ nf ~**(s)** malicious gossip.

méditer /medite/ ◗ vi meditate (**sur** on). ● vt contemplate; (paroles, conseils) mull over; ~ **de** plan to.

Méditerranée /mediteʀane/ nf **la ~** the Mediterranean.

méditerranéen, ~ne /mediteʀaneɛ̃, -ɛn/ adj Mediterranean.

médium /medjɔm/ nm (personne) medium.

méduse /medyz/ nf jellyfish.

meeting /mitiŋ/ nm meeting.

méfait /mefɛ/ nm misdeed; **les ~s de** (conséquences) the ravages of.

méfiance /mefjãs/ nf suspicion, distrust. **méfiant, ~e** adj suspicious, distrustful.

méfier (se) /(sə)mefje/ ◗ vpr be wary ou careful; **se ~ de** distrust, be wary of.

mégaoctet /megaɔktɛ/ nm (Ordinat) megabyte.

mégère /meʒɛʀ/ nf (femme) shrew.

mégot /mego/ nm cigarette end.

meilleur, ~e /mɛjœʀ/ adj (comparatif) better (**que** than); (superlatif) best; **le ~ livre** the best book; **mon ~ ami** my best friend; **~ marché** cheaper. ● nm, f **le ~, la ~e** the best (one). ● adv (sentir) better; **il fait ~** the weather is better.

mél /mel/ nm email; **envoyer un ~** send an email.

mélancolie /melãkɔli/ nf melancholy.

mélange /melãʒ/ nm mixture, blend.

mélanger /melãʒe/ ◗ vt mix; (thés, parfums) blend. ☐ **se ~** vpr mix; (thés, parfums) blend; (idées) get mixed up.

mélasse /melas/ nf black treacle; (US) molasses.

mêlée /mele/ nf free for all; (au rugby) scrum.

mêler /mele/ ◗ vt mix (**à** with); (qualités) combine; (embrouiller) mix up; ~ **qn à** (impliquer dans) involve sb in. ☐ **se ~** vpr mix; combine; **se ~ à** (se joindre à) mingle with; (participer à) join in; **se ~ de** meddle in; **mêle-toi de ce qui te regarde** mind your own business.

méli-mélo (pl **mélis-mélos**) /melimelo/ nm jumble.

mélo /melo/ ◗ nm melodrama. ● adj inv slushy, schmaltzy ◗.

mélodie /melɔdi/ nf melody. **mélodieux, -ieuse** adj melodious. **mélodique** adj melodic.

mélodramatique /melɔdʀamatik/ adj melodramatic. **mélodrame** nm melodrama.

mélomane /melɔman/ nmf music lover.

melon /məlõ/ nm melon; (**chapeau**) ~ bowler (hat).

membrane /mãbʀan/ nf membrane.

membre /mãbʀ/ nm (Anat) limb; (adhérent) member.

même /mɛm/ adj same; **ce livre ~** this very book; **la bonté ~** kindness itself; **en ~ temps** at the same time. ● pron **le ~, la ~** the same (one). ● adv even; **à ~** (sur) directly on; **à ~ de** in a position to; **de ~** (aussi) too; (de la même façon) likewise; **de ~ que** just as; **~ si** even if.

mémé /meme/ nf ◗ granny.

mémo /memo/ nm note, memo.

mémoire /memwaʀ/ *nm* (rapport) memorandum; (Univ) dissertation; ~s (souvenirs écrits) memoirs. ● *nf* memory; **à la ~ de** to the memory of; **de ~** from memory; ~ **morte/vive** (Ordinat) ROM/RAM.

mémorable /memɔʀabl/ *adj* memorable.

menace /mənas/ *nf* threat. **menacer** 🔟 *vt* threaten (**de faire** to do).

ménage /menaʒ/ *nm* (couple) couple; (travail) housework; (famille) household; **se mettre en ~** set up house.

ménagement /menaʒmɑ̃/ *nm* **avec ~s** gently; **sans ~s** (dire) bluntly; (jeter, pousser) roughly.

ménager¹, **-ère** /menaʒe, -ɛʀ/ *adj* household, domestic; **travaux ~s** housework.

ménager² /menaʒe/ 🔟 *vt* be gentle with, handle carefully; (utiliser) be careful with; (organiser) prepare (carefully); **ne pas ~ ses efforts** spare no effort.

ménagère /menaʒɛʀ/ *nf* housewife.

ménagerie /menaʒʀi/ *nf* menagerie.

mendiant, ~e /mɑ̃djɑ̃, -t/ *nm, f* beggar.

mendier /mɑ̃dje/ 🔟 *vt* beg for. ● *vi* beg.

mener /məne/ 🔟 *vt* lead; (entreprise, pays) run; (étude, enquête) carry out; (politique) pursue; ~ **à** (accompagner à) take to; (faire aboutir) lead to; ~ **à bien** see through. ● *vi* lead.

méningite /menɛ̃ʒit/ *nf* meningitis.

menotte /mənɔt/ *nf* 🔢 hand; ~s handcuffs.

mensonge /mɑ̃sɔ̃ʒ/ *nm* lie; (action) lying. **mensonger, -ère** *adj* untrue, false.

mensualité /mɑ̃sɥalite/ *nf* monthly payment.

mensuel, ~le /mɑ̃sɥɛl/ *adj* monthly. ● *nm* monthly (magazine). **mensuellement** *adv* monthly.

mensurations /mɑ̃syʀasjɔ̃/ *nfpl* measurements.

mental, ~e (*mpl* **-aux**) /mɑ̃tal, -o/ *adj* mental; **malade ~** mentally ill person; **handicapé ~** mentally handicapped person.

mentalité /mɑ̃talite/ *nf* mentality.

menteur, -euse /mɑ̃tœʀ, -øz/ *nm, f* liar. ● *adj* untruthful.

menthe /mɑ̃t/ *nf* mint.

mention /mɑ̃sjɔ̃/ *nf* mention; (annotation) note; (Scol) grade; **rayer la ~ inutile** delete as appropriate. **mentionner** 🔟 *vt* mention.

mentir /mɑ̃tiʀ/ 🔢 *vi* lie.

menton /mɑ̃tɔ̃/ *nm* chin.

menu, ~e /məny/ *adj* (petit) tiny; (fin) fine; (insignifiant) minor. ● *adv* (couper) fine. ● *nm* (carte) menu; (repas) meal; (Ordinat) menu; ~ **déroulant** pull-down menu.

menuiserie /mənɥizʀi/ *nf* carpentry, joinery. **menuisier** *nm* carpenter, joiner.

méprendre (se) /(sə)mepʀɑ̃dʀ/ 🔢 *vpr* **se ~ sur** be mistaken about.

mépris /mepʀi/ *nm* contempt, scorn (**de** for); **au ~ de** regardless of.

méprisable /mepʀizabl/ *adj* contemptible, despicable.

méprise /mepʀiz/ *nf* mistake.

méprisant, ~e /mepʀizɑ̃, -t/ *adj* scornful. **mépriser** 🔟 *vt* scorn, despise.

mer /mɛʀ/ *nf* sea; (marée) tide; **en pleine ~** out at sea.

mercenaire /mɛʀsənɛʀ/ *nm & a* mercenary.

mercerie /mɛʀs(ə)ʀi/ *nf* haberdashery; (US) notions store. **mercier, -ière** *nm, f* haberdasher; (US) notions seller.

merci /mɛʀsi/ *interj* thank you, thanks (**de, pour** for); ~ **beaucoup**, ~ **bien** thank you very much. ● *nm* thank you. ● *nf* mercy.

mercredi /mɛʀkʀədi/ *nm* Wednesday; ~ **des Cendres** Ash Wednesday.

merde /mɛʀd/ *nf* 🔳 shit 🔳.

mère /mɛʀ/ *nf* mother; ~ **de famille** mother.

méridional, ~e (*mpl* **-aux**) /meʀidjɔnal, -o/ *adj* southern. ● *nm, f* Southerner.

mérite /meʀit/ *nm* merit; **avoir du ~ à faire** deserve credit for doing.

mériter /meʀite/ 🔟 *vt* deserve; ~ **d'être lu** be worth reading.

méritoire /meʀitwaʀ/ *adj* commendable.

merlan /mɛʀlɑ̃/ *nm* whiting.

m

merle /mɛʀl/ *nm* blackbird.

merveille /mɛʀvɛj/ *nf* wonder, marvel; **à ∼** wonderfully; **faire des ∼s** work wonders.

merveilleux, -euse /mɛʀvɛjø, -z/ *adj* wonderful, marvellous.

mes /me/ ➡**MON**.

mésange /mezãʒ/ *nf* tit(mouse).

mésaventure /mezavãtyʀ/ *nf* misadventure; **par ∼** by some misfortune.

mesdames /medam/ ➡**MADAME**.

mesdemoiselles /medmwazɛl/ ➡**MADEMOISELLE**.

mésentente /mezãtãt/ *nf* disagreement.

mesquin, -e /mɛskɛ̃, -in/ *adj* meanminded, petty; (*chiche*) mean. **mesquinerie** *nf* meanness.

message /mesaʒ/ *nm* message; **un ∼ électronique** an email; **∼ texte** text message.

messager, -ère /mesaze, -ɛʀ/ *nm, f* messenger. ● *nm* **∼ de poche** pager.

messagerie /mesaʒʀi/ *nf* (*transports*) freight forwarding; (*télécommunications*) messaging; **∼ électronique** electronic mail; **∼ vocale** voice mail.

messe /mɛs/ *nf* (Relig) mass.

messieurs /mesjø/ ➡**MONSIEUR**.

mesure /məzyʀ/ *nf* measurement; (*quantité, unité*) measure; (*disposition*) measure, step; (*cadence*) time; **en ∼** in time; (*modération*) moderation; **à ∼ que** as; **dans la ∼ où** in so far as; **dans une certaine ∼** to some extent; **en ∼ de** in a position to; **sans ∼** to excess; (*fait*) **sur ∼** made-to-measure.

mesuré, ∼e /məzyʀe/ *adj* measured; (*atttitude*) moderate.

mesurer /məzyʀe/ **1** *vt* measure; (*juger*) assess; (*argent, temps*) ration. ● *vi* **∼ 15 mètres de long** be 15 metres long. □ **se ∼ avec** *vpr* pit oneself against.

met /me/ ➡**METTRE** 42.

métal (*pl* **-aux**) /metal, -o/ *nm* metal. **métallique** *adj* (*objet*) metal; (*éclat*) metallic.

métallurgie /metalyʀʒi/ *nf* (*industrie*) metalworking industry.

métamorphoser /metamɔʀfoze/ **1** *vt* transform. □ **se ∼** *vpr* be transformed; **se ∼ en** metamorphose into.

métaphore /metafɔʀ/ *nf* metaphor.

météo /meteo/ *nf* (*bulletin*) weather forecast.

météore /meteɔʀ/ *nm* meteor.

météorologie /meteɔʀɔlɔʒi/ *nf* meteorology.

météorologique /meteɔʀɔlɔʒik/ *adj* meteorological; **conditions ∼s** weather conditions.

méthode /metɔd/ *nf* method; (*ouvrage*) course, manual. **méthodique** *adj* methodical.

méticuleux, -euse /metikylø, -z/ *adj* meticulous.

métier /metje/ *nm* job; (*manuel*) trade; (*intellectuel*) profession; (*expérience*) experience, skill; **∼ (à tisser)** loom; **remettre qch sur le ∼** rework sth.

métis, ∼se /metis/ *adj* mixed race. ● *nm, f* person of mixed race.

métrage /metʀaʒ/ *nm* length; **court ∼** short (film); **long ∼** feature-length film.

mètre /mɛtʀ/ *nm* metre; (*règle*) rule; **∼ ruban** tape-measure.

métreur, -euse /metʀœʀ, -øz/ *nm, f* quantity surveyor.

métrique /metʀik/ *adj* metric.

métro /metʀo/ *nm* underground; (US) subway.

métropole /metʀopɔl/ *nf* metropolis; (*pays*) mother country. **métropolitain, ∼e** *adj* metropolitan.

mets /mɛ/ *nm* dish. ● ➡**METTRE** 42.

mettable /mɛtabl/ *adj* wearable.

metteur /mɛtœʀ/ *nm* **∼ en scène** director.

mettre /mɛtʀ/ 42 *vt* put; (*radio, chauffage*) put *ou* switch on; (*réveil*) set; (*installer*) put in; (*revêtir*) put on; (*porter habituellement*) (*vêtement, lunettes*) wear; (*prendre*) take; (*investir, dépenser*) put; (*écrire*) write, say; **elle a mis deux heures** it took her two hours; **∼ la table** lay the table; **∼ en question** question; **∼ en valeur** highlight; (*terrain*) develop; **mettons que** let's suppose that. ● *vi* **∼ bas** (*animal*) give birth. □ **se ∼** *vpr* (*vêtement, maquillage*) put on; (*se placer*) (*objet*) go; (*personne*) (*debout*) stand; (*assis*) sit; (*couché*) lie; **se ∼ en short** put shorts on; **se ∼ debout** stand up; **se ∼ au lit** go to bed; **se ∼ à table** sit down at table; **se ~ en ligne** line up; **se ~ du sable dans les yeux** get sand in one's eyes; **se ~ au chinois/ tennis** take up Chinese/tennis; **se ~ au travail** set to work; **se ~ à faire** start to do.

meuble /mœbl/ *nm* piece of furniture; **~s** furniture.

meublé /møble/ *nm* furnished flat.

meubler /møble/ **1** *vt* furnish; (fig) fill. □ **se ~** *vpr* buy furniture.

meugler /møgle/ **1** *vi* moo.

meule /møl/ *nf* millstone; **~ de foin** haystack.

meunier, -ière /mønje, -jɛʀ/ *nm, f* miller.

meurs, meurt /mœʀ/ →**MOURIR** **43**.

meurtre /mœʀtʀ/ *nm* murder.

meurtrier, -ière /mœʀtʀije, -jɛʀ/ *adj* deadly. ● *nm, f* murderer.

meurtrir /mœʀtʀiʀ/ **2** *vt* bruise.

meute /møt/ *nf* pack of hounds.

Mexique /mɛksik/ *nm* Mexico.

mi- /mi/ *préf* mid-, half-; **à mi-chemin** half-way; **à mi-pente** half-way up the hill; **à la mi-juin** in mid-June.

miauler /mjole/ **1** *vi* miaow.

micro /mikʀo/ *nm* microphone, mike; (Ordinat) micro.

microbe /mikʀɔb/ *nm* germ.

microfilm /mikʀɔfilm/ *nm* microfilm.

micro-onde /mikʀɔɔ̃d/ *nf* microwave; **un four à ~s** microwave (oven). **micro-ondes** *nm inv* microwave (oven).

micro-ordinateur (*pl* **~s**) /mikʀɔɔʀdinatœʀ/ *nm* personal computer.

microphone /mikʀɔfɔn/ *nm* microphone.

microprocesseur /mikʀɔpʀɔsɛsœʀ/ *nm* microprocessor.

microscope /mikʀɔskɔp/ *nm* microscope.

midi /midi/ *nm* twelve o'clock, midday, noon; (déjeuner) lunch-time; (sud) south. **Midi** *nm* **le M~** the South of France.

mie /mi/ *nf* soft part (of the loaf); **un pain de ~** a sandwich loaf.

miel /mjɛl/ *nm* honey.

mielleux, -euse /mjɛlø, -z/ *adj* unctuous.

mien, ~ne /mjɛ̃, -ɛn/ *pron* **le ~, la ~ne, les ~(ne)s** mine.

miette /mjɛt/ *nf* crumb; (fig) scrap; **en ~s** in pieces.

mieux /mjø/ *adj inv* better (**que** than); **le** *ou* **la** *ou* **les ~** (the) best. ● *nm* best; (progrès) improvement; **faire de son ~** do one's best; **le ~ serait de** the best thing would be to. ● *adv* better; **le** *ou* **la** *ou* **les ~** (**de deux**) the better; (de plusieurs) the best; **elle va ~** she is better; **j'aime ~ rester** I'd rather stay; **il vaudrait ~ partir** it would be best to leave; **tu ferais ~ de faire** you would be best to do.

mièvre /mjɛvʀ/ *adj* insipid.

mignon, ~ne /miɲɔ̃, -ɔn/ *adj* cute; (gentil) kind.

migraine /migʀɛn/ *nf* headache; (plus fort) migraine.

migrant /migʀɑ̃/ *nm, f* migrant.

migration /migʀasjɔ̃/ *nf* migration.

mijoter /miʒɔte/ **1** *vt/i* simmer; (tramer **1**) cook up.

mil /mil/ *nm* a thousand.

milice /milis/ *nf* militia.

milieu (*pl* **~x**) /miljø/ *nm* middle; (environnement) environment; (appartenance sociale) background; (groupe) circle; (voie) middle way; (criminel) underworld; **au ~ de** in the middle of; **en plein** *ou* **au beau ~ de** right in the middle (of).

militaire /militɛʀ/ *adj* military. ● *nm* soldier, serviceman.

militant, ~e /militɑ̃, -t/ *nm, f* militant.

militer /milite/ **1** *vi* be a militant; **~ pour** militate in favour of.

mille¹ /mil/ *adj & nm inv* a thousand; **deux ~** two thousand; **mettre dans le ~** (fig) hit the nail on the head.

mille² /mil/ *nm* **~ (marin)** (nautical) mile.

millénaire /milenɛʀ/ *nm* millennium. ● *adj* a thousand years old.

mille-pattes /milpat/ *nm inv* centipede.

millésime /milezim/ *nm* date; (de vin) vintage.

millet /mijɛ/ *nm* millet.

milliard /miljaʀ/ *nm* thousand million, billion. **milliardaire** *nmf* multimillionaire.

m

millième /miljɛm/ adj & nmf thousandth.

millier /milje/ nm thousand; **un ~ (de)** about a thousand.

millimètre /milimɛtr/ nm millimetre.

million /miljõ/ nm million; **deux ~s (de)** two million. **millionnaire** nmf millionaire.

mime /mim/ nmf mime-artist. ● nm (art) mime. **mimer** 1 vt mime; (imiter) mimic.

mimique /mimik/ nf expressions and gestures.

minable /minabl/ adj 1 (logement) shabby; (médiocre) pathetic, crummy.

minauder /minode/ 1 vi simper.

mince /mɛ̃s/ adj thin; (svelte) slim; (faible) (espoir, majorité) slim. ● interj 1 blast 1, darn it 1. **minceur** nf thinness; slimness.

mincir /mɛ̃sir/ 2 vi get slimmer; **ça te mincit** it makes you look slimmer.

mine /min/ nf expression; (allure) appearance; **avoir bonne ~** look well; **faire ~ de** make as if to; (exploitation, explosif) mine; (de crayon) lead; **~ de charbon** coalmine.

miner /mine/ 1 vt (saper) undermine; (garnir d'explosifs) mine.

minerai /minrɛ/ nm ore.

minéral, ~e /mineral, -o/ (mpl **-aux**) adj mineral. ● nm (pl **-aux**) mineral.

minéralogique /mineralɔʒik/ adj **plaque ~** numberplate; (US) license plate.

minet, ~te /minɛ, -t/ nm, f (chat 1) pussy(cat).

mineur, ~e /minœr/ adj minor; (Jur) under age. ● nm, f (Jur) minor. ● nm (ouvrier) miner.

miniature /minjatyr/ nf & adj miniature.

minier, -ière /minje, -jɛr/ adj mining.

minimal, ~e /minimal, o/ (mpl **-aux**) adj minimal, minimum.

minime /minim/ adj minimal, minor. ● nmf (Sport) junior.

minimum /minimɔm/ adj minimum. ● nm minimum; **au ~** (pour le moins) at the very least; **en faire un ~** do as little as possible.

ministère /ministɛr/ nm ministry; (gouvernement) government; **~ public** public prosecutor's office. **minis-**

tériel, ~le adj ministerial, government.

ministre /ministr/ nm minister; (au Royaume-Uni) Secretary of State; (US) Secretary.

Minitel® /minitɛl/ nm Minitel (telephone videotext system).

minorer /minɔre/ 1 vt reduce.

minoritaire /minɔritɛr/ adj minority; **être ~** be in the minority. **minorité** nf minority.

minuit /minɥi/ nm midnight.

minuscule /minyskyl/ adj minute. ● nf (lettre) lower case.

minute /minyt/ nf minute; **'talons ~'** 'heels repaired while you wait'.

minuterie /minytri/ nf time-switch.

minutie /minysi/ nf meticulousness.

minutieux, -ieuse /minysjø, -z/ adj meticulous.

mioche /mjɔʃ/ nm, f 1 kid.

mirabelle /mirabɛl/ nf (mirabelle) plum.

miracle /mirakl/ nm miracle; **par ~** miraculously.

miraculeux, -euse /mirakylø, -z/ adj miraculous.

mirage /miraʒ/ nm mirage.

mire /mir/ nf (fig) centre of attraction; (TV) test card.

mirobolant, ~e /mirɔbɔlɑ̃, -t/ adj 1 marvellous.

miroir /mirwar/ nm mirror.

miroiter /mirwate/ 1 vi shimmer, sparkle.

mis, ~e /mi, miz/ adj **bien ~** well-dressed. ● ➡METTRE 42.

mise /miz/ nf (argent) stake; (tenue) attire; **~ à feu** blast-off; **~ au point** adjustment; (fig) clarification; **~ de fonds** capital outlay; **~ en garde** warning; **~ en plis** set; **~ en scène** direction.

miser /mize/ 1 vt (argent) bet, stake (sur on). ● vi **~ sur** (parier) place a bet on; (compter sur) bank on.

misérable /mizerabl/ adj miserable, wretched; (indigent) destitute; (minable) seedy, squalid.

misère /mizɛr/ nf destitution; (malheur) trouble, woe. **miséreux, -euse** nm, f destitute person.

miséricorde /mizerikɔrd/ nf mercy.

missel /misɛl/ nm missal.

missile /misil/ nm missile.

mission /misjɔ̃/ nm mission. **mission-naire** nmf missionary.

missive /misiv/ nf missive.

mistral /mistral/ nm (vent) mistral.

mitaine /mitɛn/ nf fingerless mitt.

mite /mit/ nf (clothes-)moth.

mi-temps /mitɑ̃/ nf inv (arrêt) half-time; (période) half. ● nm inv part-time work; **à** ~ part-time.

miteux, -euse /mitø, -z/ adj shabby.

mitigé, ~**e** /mitiʒe/ adj (modéré) luke-warm; (succès) qualified.

mitonner /mitɔne/ **1** vt cook slowly with care; (fig) cook up.

mitoyen, ~**ne** /mitwajɛ̃, -ɛn/ adj **mur** ~ party wall.

mitrailler /mitrɑje/ **1** vt machine-gun; (fig) bombard.

mitraillette /mitrɑjɛt/ nf submachine gun. **mitrailleuse** nf machine gun.

mi-voix: à ~ /amivwa/ loc in a low voice.

mixeur /miksœr/ nm liquidizer, blender; (batteur) mixer.

mixte /mikst/ adj mixed; (commission) joint; (école) coeducational; (peau) combination.

mobile /mɔbil/ adj mobile; (pièce) moving; (feuillet) loose. ● nm (art) mobile; (raison) motive.

mobilier /mɔbilje/ nm furniture.

mobilisation /mɔbilizasjɔ̃/ nf mobil-ization. **mobiliser** **1** vt mobilize.

mobilité /mɔbilite/ nf mobility.

mobylette® /mɔbilɛt/ nf moped.

moche /mɔʃ/ adj **1** (laid) ugly; (mau-vais) lousy.

modalités /mɔdalite/ nfpl (conditions) terms; (façon de fonctionner) practical details.

mode /mɔd/ nf fashion; (coutume) cus-tom; **à la** ~ fashionable. ● nm method, mode; (genre) way; ~ **d'em-ploi** directions (for use).

modèle /mɔdɛl/ adj model. ● nm model; (exemple) example; (Comm) (type) model; (taille) size; (style) style; ~ **familial** family size; ~ **réduit** (small-scale) model.

modeler /mɔdle/ **6** vt model (**sur** on). ◻ **se** ~ **sur** vpr model oneself on.

modem /mɔdɛm/ nm modem.

modérateur, -trice /mɔderatœr, -tris/ adj moderating. **modération** nf moderation.

modéré, ~**e** /mɔdere/ adj & nm, f moderate.

modérer /mɔdere/ **14** vt (propos) moderate; (désirs, sentiments) curb. ◻ **se** ~ vpr restrain oneself.

moderne /mɔdɛrn/ adj modern. **mo-derniser** **1** vt modernize.

modeste /mɔdɛst/ adj modest. **mo-destie** nf modesty.

modification /mɔdifikasjɔ̃/ nf modifi-cation.

modifier /mɔdifje/ **45** vt change, mod-ify. ◻ **se** ~ vpr change, alter.

modique /mɔdik/ adj modest.

modiste /mɔdist/ nf milliner.

moduler /mɔdyle/ **1** vt modulate; (adapter) adjust.

moelle /mwal/ nf marrow; ~ **épinière** spinal cord; ~ **osseuse** bone marrow.

moelleux, -euse /mwalø, -z/ adj soft; (onctueux) smooth.

mœurs /mœr(s)/ nfpl (morale) morals; (usages) customs; (manières) habits, ways.

moi /mwa/ pron me; (indirect) (to) me; (sujet) I. ● nm self.

moignon /mwaɲɔ̃/ nm stump.

moi-même /mwamɛm/ pron myself.

moindre /mwɛ̃dr/ adj (moins grand) lesser; **le** ou **la** ~, **les** ~**s** the slight-est, the least.

moine /mwan/ nm monk.

moineau (pl ~**x**) /mwano/ nm sparrow.

moins /mwɛ̃/ prép minus; (pour dire l'heure) to; **une heure** ~ **dix** ten to one. ● adv less (**que** than); **le** ou **la** ou **les** ~ the least; **le** ~ **grand**/**haut** smallest/lowest; ~ **de** (avec un nom non dénombrable) less (**que** than); ~ **de dix euros** less than ten euros; ~ **de livres** fewer books; **au** ~, **du** ~ at least; **à** ~ **que** unless; **de** ~ less; **de** ~ **en** ~ less and less; **en** ~ less; (manquant) missing.

mois /mwa/ nm month.

moisi, ~**e** /mwazi/ adj mouldy. ● nm mould; **de** ~ (odeur) musty. **moisir** **2** vi go mouldy. **moisissure** nf mould.

moisson /mwasɔ̃/ nf harvest.

moissonner /mwasɔne/ **1** *vt* harvest, reap. **moissonneur, -euse** *nm, f* harvester.

moite /mwat/ *adj* sticky, clammy.

moitié /mwatje/ *nf* half; (milieu) halfway mark; **s'arrêter à la ~** stop halfway through; **à ~ vide** half empty; **à ~ prix** (at) half-price; **la ~ de** half (of). **moitié-moitié** *adv* half-and-half.

mol /mɔl/ →MOU.

molaire /mɔlɛʀ/ *nf* molar.

molécule /mɔlekyl/ *nf* molecule.

molester /mɔlɛste/ **1** *vt* manhandle, rough up.

molle /mɔl/ →MOU.

mollement /mɔlmɑ̃/ *adv* softly; (faiblement) feebly. **mollesse** *nf* softness; (faiblesse) feebleness; (apathie) listlessness.

mollet /mɔlɛ/ *nm* (de jambe) calf.

mollir /mɔliʀ/ **2** *vi* soften; (céder) yield.

môme /mom/ *nmf* **1** kid.

moment /mɔmɑ̃/ *nm* moment; (période) time; **(petit) ~** short while; **au ~ où** when; **par ~s** now and then; **du ~ où** *ou* **que** (pourvu que) as long as, provided that; (puisque) since; **en ce ~** at the moment.

momentané, ~e /mɔmɑ̃tane/ *adj* momentary. **momentanément** *adv* momentarily; (en ce moment) at present.

momie /mɔmi/ *nf* mummy.

mon, ma (**mon** *before vowel or mute h*) (*pl* **mes**) /mɔ̃, ma, mɔ̃n, me/ *adj* my.

Monaco /mɔnako/ *npr* Monaco.

monarchie /mɔnaʀʃi/ *nf* monarchy.

monarque /mɔnaʀk/ *nm* monarch.

monastère /mɔnastɛʀ/ *nm* monastery.

monceau (*pl* **~x**) /mɔ̃so/ *nm* heap, pile.

mondain, ~e /mɔ̃dɛ̃, -ɛn/ *adj* society, social.

monde /mɔ̃d/ *nm* world; **du ~** (a lot of) people; (quelqu'un) somebody; **le (grand) ~** (high) society; **se faire (tout) un ~ de qch** make a great deal of fuss about sth; **pas le moins du ~** not in the least.

mondial, ~e (*mpl* **-iaux**) /mɔ̃djal, -jo/ *adj* world; (influence) worldwide. **mondialement** *adv* the world over.

mondialisation /mɔ̃djalizasjɔ̃/ *nf* globalisation.

monétaire /mɔnetɛʀ/ *adj* monetary.

moniteur, -trice /mɔnitœʀ, -tʀis/ *nm, f* instructor; (de colonie de vacances) group leader; (US) (camp) counselor.

monnaie /mɔnɛ/ *nf* currency; (pièce) coin; (appoint) change; **faire la ~ de** get change for; **faire de la ~ à qn** give sb change; **menue** *ou* **petite ~** small change.

monnayer /mɔneje/ **31** *vt* convert into cash.

monologue /mɔnɔlɔg/ *nm* monologue.

monoparental, ~e /mɔnɔpaʀɑ̃tal/ *adj* **famille ~e** single-parent family.

monopole /mɔnɔpɔl/ *nm* monopoly. **monopoliser** **1** *vt* monopolize.

monospace /mɔnɔspas/ *nm* (Auto) people carrier.

monotone /mɔnɔtɔn/ *adj* monotonous. **monotonie** *nf* monotony.

Monseigneur (*pl* **Messeigneurs**) /mɔ̃sɛɲœʀ/ *nm* (à un duc, archevêque) Your Grace; (à un prince) Your Highness.

monsieur (*pl* **messieurs**) /məsjø, mesjø/ *nm* (à un inconnu) (dans une lettre) **M~** Dear Sir; **bonjour, ~** good morning; **mesdames et messieurs** ladies and gentlemen; (à un homme dont on connaît le nom) (dans une lettre) **Cher M~** Dear Mr X; **bonjour, ~** good morning Mr X; **M~ le curé** Father X; **oui M~ le ministre** yes Minister; (homme) man; (formule de respect) sir.

monstre /mɔ̃stʀ/ *nm* monster. ● *adj* **1** colossal.

monstrueux, -euse /mɔ̃stʀyø, -z/ *adj* monstrous. **monstruosité** *nf* monstrosity.

mont /mɔ̃/ *nm* mountain; **le ~ Everest** Mount Everest; **être toujours par ~s et par vaux** be always on the move.

montage /mɔ̃taʒ/ *nm* (assemblage) assembly; (au cinéma) editing.

montagne /mɔ̃taɲ/ *nf* mountain; (région) mountains; **~s russes** rollercoaster. **montagneux, -euse** *adj* mountainous.

montant, ~e /mɔ̃tɑ̃, -t/ *adj* rising; (col) high; (chemin) uphill. ● *nm*

amount; (pièce de bois) upright.
mont-de-piété (*pl* **monts-de-piété**)
/mɔ̃dpjete/ *nm* pawnshop.
monte-charge /mɔ̃tʃaʀʒ/ *nm inv*
goods lift.
montée /mɔ̃te/ *nf* ascent, climb; (de
prix) rise; (de coûts, risques) increase;
(côte) hill.
monter /mɔ̃te/ **1** *vt* (aux. avoir) take
up; (à l'étage) take upstairs; (escalier,
rue, pente) go up; (assembler) assemble; (tente, échafaudage) put up; (col,
manche) set in; (organiser) (pièce)
stage; (société) set up; (attaque, garde)
mount. ● *vi* (aux. être) go ou come
up; (à l'étage) go ou come upstairs;
(avion) climb; (route) go uphill, climb;
(augmenter) rise; (marée) come up; ~
sur (trottoir, toit) get up on; (cheval,
bicyclette) get on; ~ **à l'échelle/**
l'arbre climb the ladder/tree; ~ **dans**
(voiture) get in; (train, bus, avion) get
on; ~ **à bord** climb on board; ~ **(à**
cheval) ride; ~ **à bicyclette/moto**
ride a bike/motorbike.
monteur, -euse /mɔ̃tœʀ, -øz/ *nm, f*
(Tech) fitter; (au cinéma) editor.
montre /mɔ̃tʀ/ *nf* watch; **faire** ~
de show.
montrer /mɔ̃tʀe/ **1** *vt* show (à to); ~
du doigt point to. □ **se** ~ *vpr* show
oneself; (être) be; (s'avérer) prove
to be.
monture /mɔ̃tyʀ/ *nf* (cheval) mount;
(de lunettes) frames (+ pl); (de bijou)
setting.
monument /mɔnymɑ̃/ *nm* monument; ~ **aux morts** war memorial.
monumental (mpl **-aux**) *adj* monumental.
moquer (se) /(sə)mɔke/ **1** *vpr* **se** ~
de make fun of; **je m'en moque** 🔟 I
couldn't care less. **moquerie** *nf* mockery. **moqueur, -euse** *adj* mocking.
moquette /mɔkɛt/ *nf* fitted carpet;
(US) wall-to-wall carpeting.
moral, ~e (mpl **-aux**) /mɔʀal, -o/ *adj*
moral. ● *nm* (pl **-aux**) morale; **ne pas**
avoir le ~ feel down; **avoir le** ~ be
in good spirits; **ça m'a remonté le** ~
it gave me a boost.
morale /mɔʀal/ *nf* moral code;
(mœurs) morals; (de fable) moral;
faire la ~ **à** lecture. **moralité** *nf* (de
personne) morals (+ pl); (d'action,

œuvre) morality; (de fable) moral.
moralisateur, -trice /mɔʀalizatœʀ,
-tʀis/ *adj* moralizing.
morbide /mɔʀbid/ *adj* morbid.
morceau (pl ~**x**) /mɔʀso/ *nm* piece,
bit; (de sucre) lump; (de viande) cut;
(passage) passage; **manger un** ~ 🔟
have a bite to eat; **mettre en** ~**x**
smash ou tear to bits.
morceler /mɔʀsəle/ **6** *vt* divide up.
mordant, ~e /mɔʀdɑ̃, -t/ *adj* scathing;
(froid) biting. ● *nm* vigour, energy.
mordiller /mɔʀdije/ **1** *vt* nibble at.
mordre /mɔʀdʀ/ **3** *vi* bite (**dans** into);
~ **sur** (ligne) go over; (territoire) encroach on; ~ **à l'hameçon** bite.
● *vt* bite.
mordu, ~e /mɔʀdy/ 🔟 *nm, f* fan.
● *adj* smitten; ~ **de** crazy about.
morfondre (se) /(sə)mɔʀfɔ̃dʀ/ **3** *vpr*
wait anxiously; (languir) mope.
morgue /mɔʀg/ *nf* morgue, mortuary;
(attitude) arrogance.
moribond, ~e /mɔʀibɔ̃, -d/ *adj* dying.
morne /mɔʀn/ *adj* dull.
morphine /mɔʀfin/ *nf* morphine.
mors /mɔʀ/ *nm* (de cheval) bit.
morse /mɔʀs/ *nm* (animal) walrus;
(code) Morse code.
morsure /mɔʀsyʀ/ *nf* bite.
mort¹ /mɔʀ/ *nf* death.
mort², ~e /mɔʀ, -t/ *adj* dead; ~ **de**
fatigue dead tired. ● *nm, f* dead man,
dead woman; **les** ~**s** the dead.
mortalité /mɔʀtalite/ *nf* mortality;
(taux de) ~ death rate.
mortel, ~le /mɔʀtɛl/ *adj* mortal; (accident) fatal; (poison, silence) deadly.
● *nm, f* mortal. **mortellement** *adv*
mortally.
mortifié, ~e /mɔʀtifje/ *adj* mortified.
mort-né, ~e /mɔʀne/ *adj* stillborn.
mortuaire /mɔʀtɥeʀ/ *adj* (cérémonie)
funeral.
morue /mɔʀy/ *nf* cod.
mosaïque /mɔzaik/ *nf* mosaic.
mosquée /mɔske/ *nf* mosque.
mot /mo/ *nm* word; (lettre, message)
note; ~ **d'ordre** watchword; ~ **de**
passe password; ~**s croisés** crossword (puzzle).
motard /mɔtaʀ/ *nm* biker; (policier)
police motorcyclist.

m

moteur, -trice /mɔtœʀ, -tʀis/ *adj* (Méd) motor; (*force*) driving; **à 4 roues motrices** 4-wheel drive. ● *nm* engine, motor; **barque à ~** motor launch; **~ de recherche** (Internet) search engine.

motif /mɔtif/ *nm* (raisons) grounds (+ *pl*); (cause) reason; (Jur) motive; (dessin) pattern.

motion /mosjɔ̃/ *nf* motion.

motivation /mɔtivasjɔ̃/ *nf* motivation. **motiver 1** *vt* motivate.

moto /mɔto/ *nf* motor cycle. **motocycliste** *nmf* motorcyclist.

motorisé, ~e /mɔtɔʀize/ *adj* motorized.

motrice /mɔtʀis/ ➡**MOTEUR**.

motte /mɔt/ *nf* lump; (de beurre) slab; (de terre) clod; **~ de gazon** turf.

mou /mu/ (**mol** before vowel or mute *h*), **molle** /mu, mɔl/ *adj* soft; (ventre) flabby; (sans conviction) feeble; (apathique) sluggish, listless. ● *nm* slack; **avoir du ~** be slack.

mouchard, ~e /muʃaʀ, -d/ *nm, f* informer; (Scol) sneak.

mouche /muʃ/ *nf* fly; (de cible) bull's eye.

moucher (se) /(sə)muʃe/ **1** *vpr* blow one's nose.

moucheron /muʃʀɔ̃/ *nm* midge.

moucheté, ~e /muʃte/ *adj* speckled.

mouchoir /muʃwaʀ/ *nm* handkerchief, hanky; **~ en papier** tissue.

moue /mu/ *nf* pout; **faire la ~** pout.

mouette /mwɛt/ *nf* (sea)gull.

moufle /mufl/ *nf* (gant) mitten.

mouillé, ~e /muje/ *adj* wet.

mouiller /muje/ **1** *vt* wet, make wet; **~ l'ancre** drop anchor. □ **se ~** *vpr* get (oneself) wet.

moulage /mulaʒ/ *nm* cast.

moule /mul/ *nf* (coquillage) mussel. ● *nm* mould; **~ à gâteau** cake tin; **~ à tarte** flan dish. **mouler 1** *vt* mould; (statue) cast.

moulin /mulɛ̃/ *nm* mill; **~ à café** coffee grinder; **~ à poivre** pepper mill; **~ à vent** windmill.

moulinet /mulinɛ/ *nm* (de canne à pêche) reel; **faire des ~s avec qch** twirl sth around.

moulinette® /mulinɛt/ *nf* vegetable mill.

moulu, ~e /muly/ *adj* ground; (fatigué 1) worn out.

moulure /mulyʀ/ *nf* moulding.

mourant, ~e /muʀɑ̃, -t/ *adj* dying. ● *nm, f* dying person.

mourir /muʀiʀ/ **43** *vi* (aux. être) die; **~ d'envie de** be dying to; **~ de faim** be starving; **~ d'ennui** be dead bored.

mousquetaire /muskətɛʀ/ *nm* musketeer.

mousse /mus/ *nf* moss; (écume) froth, foam; (de savon) lather; (dessert) mousse; **~ à raser** shaving foam. ● *nm* ship's boy.

mousseline /muslin/ *nf* muslin; (de soie) chiffon.

mousser /muse/ **1** *vi* froth, foam; (savon) lather.

mousseux, -euse /musø, -z/ *adj* frothy. ● *nm* sparkling wine.

mousson /musɔ̃/ *nf* monsoon.

moustache /mustaʃ/ *nf* moustache; **~s** (d'animal) whiskers.

moustique /mustik/ *nm* mosquito.

moutarde /mutaʀd/ *nf* mustard.

mouton /mutɔ̃/ *nm* sheep; (peau) sheepskin; (viande) mutton.

mouvant, ~e /muvɑ̃, -t/ *adj* changing; (terrain) shifting, unstable.

mouvement /muvmɑ̃/ *nm* movement; (agitation) bustle; (en gymnastique) exercise; (impulsion) impulse; (tendance) tend, tendency; **en ~** in motion.

mouvementé, ~e /muvmɑ̃te/ *adj* eventful.

moyen, ~ne /mwajɛ̃, -ɛn/ *adj* average; (médiocre) poor; **de taille moyenne** medium-sized. ● *nm* means, way; **~s** means; (dons) ability; **au ~ de** by means of; **il n'y a pas ~ de** it is not possible to. **Moyen Âge** *nm* Middle Ages (+ *pl*).

moyennant /mwajɛnɑ̃/ *prép* (pour) for; (grâce à) with.

moyenne /mwajɛn/ *nf* average; (Scol) pass-mark; **en ~** on average; **~ d'âge** average age. **moyennement** *adv* moderately.

Moyen-Orient /mwajɛnɔʀjɑ̃/ *nm* Middle East.

m

153

moyeu (*pl* ~x) /mwajø/ *nm* hub.

mû, mue /my/ *adj* driven (**par** by).

mucoviscidose /mykɔvisidoz/ *nf* cystic fibrosis.

mue /my/ *nf* moulting; (de voix) breaking of the voice.

muer /mɥe/ **1** *vi* moult; (*voix*) break. □ **se** ~ **en** *vpr* change into.

muet, ~te /mɥɛ, -t/ *adj* (Méd) dumb; (fig) speechless (**de** with); (silencieux) silent. ● *nm, f* mute.

mufle /myfl/ *nm* nose, muzzle; (personne 🔢) boor, lout.

mugir /myʒiʀ/ **2** *vi* (*vache*) moo; (*bœuf*) bellow; (fig) howl.

muguet /mygɛ/ *nm* lily of the valley.

mule /myl/ *nf* (female) mule; (pantoufle) mule.

mulet /mylɛ/ *nm* (male) mule.

multicolore /myltikɔlɔʀ/ *adj* multicoloured.

multimédia /myltimedja/ *adj & nm* multimedia.

multinational, ~e (*mpl* **-aux**) /myltinasjɔnal, -o/ *adj* multinational. **multinationale** *nf* multinational (company).

multiple /myltipl/ *nm* multiple. ● *adj* numerous, many; (naissances) multiple.

multiplication /myltiplikasjɔ̃/ *nf* multiplication.

multiplicité /myltiplisite/ *nf* multiplicity.

multiplier /myltiplije/ **45** *vt* multiply; (*risques*) increase. □ **se** ~ *vpr* multiply; (*accidents*) be on the increase; (*difficultés*) increase.

multitude /myltityd/ *nf* multitude, mass.

municipal, ~e (*mpl* **-aux**) /mynisipal, -o/ *adj* municipal; **conseil** ~ town council. **municipalité** *nf* (ville) municipality; (conseil) town council.

munir /myniʀ/ **2** *vt* ~ **de** provide with. □ **se** ~ **de** *vpr* (apporter) bring; (emporter) take.

munitions /mynisjɔ̃/ *nfpl* ammunition.

mur /myʀ/ *nm* wall; ~ **du son** sound barrier.

mûr, ~e /myʀ/ *adj* ripe; (*personne*) mature.

muraille /myʀɑj/ *nf* (high) wall.

mural, ~e (*mpl* **-aux**) /myʀal, -o/ *adj* wall; **peinture** ~e mural.

mûre /myʀ/ *nf* blackberry.

mûrir /myʀiʀ/ **2** *vi* ripen; (*abcès*) come to a head; (*personne, projet*) mature. ● *vt* (*fruit*) ripen; (*personne*) mature.

murmure /myʀmyʀ/ *nm* murmur.

muscade /myskad/ *nf* **noix** ~ nutmeg.

muscle /myskl/ *nm* muscle. **musclé, ~e** *adj* muscular. **musculaire** *adj* muscular.

musculation /myskylasjɔ̃/ *nf* bodybuilding.

musculature /myskylatyʀ/ *nf* muscles (+ *pl*).

museau (*pl* ~x) /myzo/ *nm* muzzle; (de porc) snout.

musée /myze/ *nm* museum; (de peinture) art gallery.

muselière /myzəljɛʀ/ *nf* muzzle.

musette /myzɛt/ *nf* haversack.

muséum /myzeɔm/ *nm* natural history museum.

musical, ~e (*mpl* **-aux**) /myzikal, -o/ *adj* musical.

musicien, ~ne /myzisjɛ̃, -ɛn/ *adj* musical. ● *nm, f* musician.

musique /myzik/ *nf* music; (orchestre) band.

must /myst/ *nm* 🔢 must.

musulman, ~e /myzylmɑ̃, -an/ *adj & nm, f* Muslim.

mutation /mytasjɔ̃/ *nf* change; (biologique) mutation; (d'un employé) transfer.

muter /myte/ **1** *vt* transfer. ● *vi* mutate.

mutilation /mytilasjɔ̃/ *nf* mutilation. **mutiler** **1** *vt* mutilate. **mutilé, ~e** *nm, f* disabled person.

mutin, ~e /mytɛ̃, -in/ *adj* mischievous. ● *nm* mutineer; (prisonnier) rioter.

mutinerie /mytinʀi/ *nf* mutiny; (de prisonniers) riot.

mutisme /mytism/ *nm* silence.

mutuel, ~le /mytɥɛl/ *adj* mutual. **mutuelle** *nf* mutual insurance company. **mutuellement** *adv* mutually; (l'un l'autre) each other.

myope /mjɔp/ adj short-sighted. **myopie** nf short-sightedness.

myosotis /mjozɔtis/ nm forget-me-not.

myrtille /miʀtij/ nf bilberry, blueberry.

mystère /mistɛʀ/ nm mystery.

mystérieux, -ieuse /misteʀjø, -z/ adj mysterious.

mystification /mistifikasjɔ̃/ nf hoax.

mysticisme /mistisism/ nm mysticism.

mystique /mistik/ adj mystic(al). ● nmf mystic. ● nf mystique.

mythe /mit/ nm myth. **mythique** adj mythical.

mythologie /mitɔlɔʒi/ nf mythology.

Nn

n' /n/ →NE.

nacre /nakʀ/ nf mother-of-pearl.

nage /naʒ/ nf swimming; (manière) stroke; **traverser à la** ~ swim across; **en** ~ sweating.

nageoire /naʒwaʀ/ nf fin; (de mammifère) flipper.

nager /naʒe/ vt/i swim. **nageur, -euse** nm, f swimmer.

naguère /nagɛʀ/ adv (autrefois) formerly.

naïf, -ive /naif, -v/ adj naïve.

nain, ~e /nɛ̃, nɛn/ nm, f & adj dwarf.

naissance /nɛsɑ̃s/ nf birth; **donner** ~ **à** give birth to; (fig) give rise to.

naître /nɛtʀ/ vi be born; (résulter) arise (de from); **faire** ~ (susciter) give rise to.

naïveté /naivte/ nf naïvety.

nappe /nap/ nf tablecloth; (de pétrole, gaz) layer; ~ **phréatique** ground water.

napperon /napʀɔ̃/ nm (cloth) tablemat.

narco-dollars /naʀkodɔlaʀ/ nmpl drug money.

narcotique /naʀkɔtik/ adj & nm narcotic. **narco(-)trafiquant, ~e** (pl ~s) nm, f drug trafficker.

narguer /naʀge/ vt taunt; (autorité) flout.

narine /naʀin/ nf nostril.

nasal, ~e (mpl -aux) /nazal, -o/ adj nasal.

naseau (pl ~x) /nazo/ nm nostril.

natal, ~e (mpl ~s) /natal/ adj native.

natalité /natalite/ nf birth rate.

natation /natasjɔ̃/ nf swimming.

natif, -ive /natif, -v/ adj native.

nation /nasjɔ̃/ nf nation.

national, ~e (mpl -aux) /nasjɔnal, -o/ adj national. **nationale** nf A road; (US) highway. **nationaliser** vt nationalize.

nationalité /nasjɔnalite/ nf nationality.

natte /nat/ nf (de cheveux) plait; (US) braid; (tapis de paille) mat.

nature /natyʀ/ nf nature; ~ **morte** still life; **de** ~ **à** likely to; **payer en** ~ pay in kind. ● adj inv plain; (yaourt) natural; (thé) black.

naturel, ~le /natyʀɛl/ adj natural. ● nm nature; (simplicité) naturalness; (Culin) **au** ~ plain; (thon) in brine. **naturellement** adv naturally; (bien sûr) of course.

naufrage /nofʀaʒ/ nm shipwreck; **faire** ~ be shipwrecked; (bateau) be wrecked.

nauséabond, ~e /nozeabɔ̃, -d/ adj nauseating.

nausée /noze/ nf nausea.

nautique /notik/ adj nautical; **sports** ~s water sports.

naval, ~e (mpl ~s) /naval/ adj naval; **chantier** ~ shipyard.

navet /navɛ/ nm turnip; (film: péj) flop; (US) turkey.

navette /navɛt/ nf shuttle (service); **faire la** ~ shuttle back and forth.

navigateur, -trice /navigatœʀ, -tʀis/ nm, f sailor; (qui guide) navigator; (Internet) browser. **navigation** nf navigation; (trafic) shipping; (Internet) browsing.

naviguer /navige/ vi sail; (piloter) navigate; (Internet) browse; ~ **dans l'Internet** surf the Internet.

navire /naviʀ/ nm ship.

navré, ~e /navʀe/ adj sorry (de to).

ne, **n'** /nə, n/

n' before vowel or mute h.

● *adverbe*

••••▶ **je n'ai que 10 euros** I've only got 10 euros.

••••▶ **tu n'avais qu'à le dire!** you only had to say so!

••••▶ **je crains qu'il ~ parte** I am afraid he will leave.

➡ Pour les expressions comme **ne... guère, ne... jamais, ne... pas, ne... plus,** etc. **➡guère, jamais, pas, plus,** etc.

né, **~e** /ne/ *adj* born; **~e Martin** née Martin; (dans composés) **dernier-~** last-born. ● **➡NAÎTRE 44**

néanmoins /neɑ̃mwɛ̃/ *adv* nevertheless.

néant /neɑ̃/ *nm* nothingness; **réduire à ~** (*effet, efforts*) negate, nullify; (*espoir*) dash; **'revenus: ~'** 'income: nil'.

nécessaire /nesesɛʀ/ *adj* necessary. ● *nm* (sac) bag; (trousse) kit; **le ~** (l'indispensable) the necessities *ou* essentials; **faire le ~** do what is necessary.

nécessité /nesesite/ *nf* necessity; **de première ~** vital.

nécessiter /nesesite/ **1** *vt* necessitate.

néerlandais, **~e** /neɛʀlɑ̃dɛ, -z/ *adj* Dutch. ● *nm* (Ling) Dutch. **N~,** **~e** *nm, f* Dutchman, Dutchwoman.

néfaste /nefast/ *adj* harmful (à to).

négatif, **-ive** /negatif, -v/ *adj & nm* negative.

négligé, **~e** /negliʒe/ *adj* (*travail*) careless; (*tenue*) scruffy. ● *nm* (tenue) negligee.

négligent, **~e** /negliʒɑ̃, -t/ *adj* careless, negligent.

négliger /negliʒe/ **40** *vt* neglect; (ne pas tenir compte de) ignore, disregard; **~ de faire** fail to do. □ **se ~** *vpr* neglect oneself.

négoce /negɔs/ *nm* business, trade. **négociant,** **~e** *nm, f* merchant.

négociation /negɔsjasjɔ̃/ *nf* negotiation. **négocier** **45** *vt/i* negotiate.

nègre /nɛgʀ/ *adj* (*musique, art*) Negro. ● *nm* (écrivain) ghost writer.

neige /nɛʒ/ *nf* snow. **neiger 40** *vi* snow.

nénuphar /nenyfaʀ/ *nm* waterlily.

nerf /nɛʀ/ *nm* nerve; (vigueur) stamina; **être sur les ~s** be on edge.

nerveux, **-euse** /nɛʀvø, -z/ *adj* nervous; (irritable) nervy; (*centre, cellule*) nerve; (*voiture*) responsive. **nervosité** *nf* nervousness; (irritability) touchiness.

net, **~te** /nɛt/ *adj* (clair, distinct) clear; (propre) clean; (notable) marked; (soigné) neat; (*prix, poids*) net. ● **N~** *nm* (Ordinat) net. ● *adv* (s'arrêter) dead; (refuser) flatly; (parler) plainly; (se casser) cleanly; (tuer) outright. **nettement** *adv* (expliquer) clearly; (augmenter, se détériorer) markedly; (indiscutablement) distinctly, decidedly. **netteté** *nf* clearness.

netéconomie /netekɔnɔmi/ *nf* e-economy.

nétiquette /netikɛt/ *nf* netiquette.

nettoyage /netwajaʒ/ *nm* cleaning; **~ à sec** dry-cleaning; **produit de ~** cleaner; **~ ethnique** ethnic cleansing.

nettoyer /netwaje/ **31** *vt* clean.

neuf[1] /nœf/ (/nœv/ before vowels and mute h) *adj inv & nm* nine.

neuf[2], **-euve** /nœf, -v/ *adj* new; **tout ~** brand new. ● *nm* new; **remettre à ~** brighten up; **du ~** a new development; **quoi de ~?** what's new?

neutre /nøtʀ/ *adj* neutral; (Gram) neuter. ● *nm* (Gram) neuter.

neuve /nœv/ **➡NEUF**[2].

neuvième /nœvjɛm/ *adj & nm, f* ninth.

neveu (*pl* **~x**) /nəvø/ *nm* nephew.

névrose /nevʀoz/ *nf* neurosis. **névrosé,** **~e** *adj & nm, f* neurotic.

nez /ne/ *nm* nose; **~ à ~** face to face; **~ retroussé** turned-up nose.

ni /ni/ *conj* neither, nor; **~ grand ~ petit** neither big nor small; **~ l'un ~ l'autre ne fument** neither (one nor the other) smokes; **sortir sans manteau ~ chapeau** go without a coat or hat; **elle n'a dit ~ oui ~ non** she didn't say either yes or no.

niais, **~e** /njɛ, -z/ *adj* silly.

niche /niʃ/ *nf* (de chien) kennel; (cavité) niche.

nicher /niʃe/ **1** *vi* nest. □ **se ~** *vpr* nest; (se cacher) hide.

nicotine /nikɔtin/ *nf* nicotine.

n

nid /ni/ *nm* nest; **faire un ~** build a nest. **nid-de-poule** (*pl* **nids-de-poule**) *nm* pot-hole.

nièce /njɛs/ *nf* niece.

nier /nje/ 45 *vt* deny.

nigaud, ~e /nigo, -d/ *nm, f* fool.

nippon, ~ne /nipɔ̃, -ɔn/ *adj* Japanese. **N~, ~ne** *nm, f* Japanese.

niveau (*pl* **~x**) /nivo/ *nm* level; (compétence) standard; (étage) storey; (US) story; **au ~** up to standard; **mettre à ~** (Ordinat) upgrade; **~ à bulle** (d'air) spirit level; **~ de vie** standard of living.

niveler /nivle/ 6 *vt* level.

noble /nɔbl/ *adj* noble. ● *nm, f* nobleman, noblewoman. **noblesse** *nf* nobility.

noce /nɔs/ *nf* (fête 🔟) party; (invités) wedding guests; **~s** wedding; **faire la ~** 🔟 live it up.

nocif, -ive /nɔsif, -v/ *adj* harmful.

nocturne /nɔktyrn/ *adj* nocturnal. ● *nm* (Mus) nocturne. ● *nf* (Sport) evening fixture; (de magasin) late-night opening.

Noël /nɔɛl/ *nm* Christmas.

nœud /nø/ *nm* (Naut) knot; (pour lier) knot; (pour orner) bow; **~s** (fig) ties; **~ coulant** slipknot, noose; **~ papillon** bow-tie.

noir, ~e /nwar/ *adj* black; (obscur, sombre) dark; (triste) gloomy. ● *nm* black; (obscurité) dark; **travail au ~** moonlighting. ● *nm, f* (personne) Black.

noircir /nwarsir/ 2 *vt* blacken; **~ la situation** paint a black picture of the situation. ● *vi* (banane) go black; (mur) get dirty; (métal) tarnish. □ **se ~** *vpr* (ciel) darken.

noire /nwar/ *nf* (Mus) crotchet.

noisette /nwazɛt/ *nf* hazelnut; (de beurre) knob.

noix /nwa/ *nf* nut; (du noyer) walnut; (de beurre) knob; **~ de cajou** cashew nut; **~ de coco** coconut; **à la ~** 🔟 useless.

nom /nɔ̃/ *nm* name; (Gram) noun; **au ~ de** on behalf of; **~ et prénom** full name; **~ déposé** registered trademark; **~ de famille** surname; **~ de jeune fille** maiden name; **~ de plume** pen name; **~ propre** proper

noun; **~ d'utilisateur** username.

nomade /nɔmad/ *adj* nomadic; (worker) mobile. ● *nmf* nomad.

nombre /nɔ̃br/ *nm* number; **au ~ de** (parmi) among; (l'un de) one of; **en (grand) ~** in large numbers; **sans ~** countless.

nombreux, -euse /nɔ̃brø, -z/ *adj* (en grand nombre) many, numerous; (important) large; **de ~ enfants** many children; **nous étions très ~** there were a great many of us.

nombril /nɔ̃bril/ *nm* navel.

nomination /nɔminasjɔ̃/ *nf* appointment.

nommer /nɔme/ 1 *vt* name; (élire) (à un poste) appoint; (à un lieu) post. □ **se ~** *vpr* (s'appeler) be called.

non /nɔ̃/ *adv* no; (pas) not; **~ (pas) que** not that; **il vient, ~?** he is coming, isn't he?; **moi ~ plus** neither am/do/can/etc. I. ● *nm inv* no.

non- /nɔ̃/ *préf* non-; **~-fumeur** non-smoker.

nonante /nɔnɑ̃t/ *adj & nm* ninety.

non-sens /nɔ̃sɑ̃s/ *nm inv* absurdity.

nord /nɔr/ *adj inv* (façade, côte) north; (frontière, zone) northern. ● *nm* north; **le ~ de l'Europe** northern Europe; **vent de ~** northerly (wind); **aller vers le ~** go north; **le Nord** the North; **du Nord** northern. **nord-est** *nm* north-east.

nordique /nɔrdik/ *adj* Scandinavian.

nord-ouest /nɔrwɛst/ *nm* north-west.

normal, ~e (*mpl* **-aux**) /nɔrmal, -o/ *adj* normal. **normale** *nf* normality; (norme) norm; (moyenne) average.

normand, ~e /nɔrmɑ̃, -d/ *adj* Norman. **N~, ~e** *nm, f* Norman.

Normandie /nɔrmɑ̃di/ *nf* Normandy.

norme /nɔrm/ *nf* norm; (de production) standard; **~s de sécurité** safety standards.

Norvège /nɔrvɛʒ/ *nf* Norway.

norvégien, ~ne /nɔrveʒjɛ̃, -ɛn/ *adj* Norwegian. **N~, ~ne** *nm, f* Norwegian.

nos /no/ ➡NOTRE.

nostalgie /nɔstalʒi/ *nf* nostalgia; **avoir la ~ de son pays** be homesick. **nostalgique** *adj* nostalgic.

notaire /nɔtɛr/ *nm* notary public.

notamment /nɔtamɑ̃/ *adv* notably.

note /nɔt/ *nf* (remarque) note; (chiffrée) mark, grade; (facture) bill; (Mus) note; ~ **(de service)** memorandum.

noter /nɔte/ ▣ *vt* note, notice; (écrire) note (down); (devoir) mark; (US) grade; **bien/mal noté** (employé) highly/poorly rated.

notice /nɔtis/ *nf* note; (mode d'emploi) instructions, directions.

notifier /nɔtifje/ ▣ *vt* notify (à to).

notion /nɔsjɔ̃/ *nf* notion; **avoir des ~s de** have a basic knowledge of.

notoire /nɔtwaʀ/ *adj* well-known; (criminel) notorious.

notre (*pl* **nos**) /nɔtʀ, no/ *adj* our.

nôtre /notʀ/ *pron* **le** *ou* **la ~, les ~s** ours.

nouer /nwe/ ▣ *vt* tie, knot; (relations) strike up.

nouille /nuj/ *nf* (Culin) noodle; **des ~s** noodles, pasta; (idiot ▣) idiot.

nounours /nunuʀs/ *nm* ▣ teddy bear.

nourri, ~e /nuʀi/ *adj* **être logé ~** have bed and board; **~ au sein** breastfed.

nourrice /nuʀis/ *nf* childminder.

nourrir /nuʀiʀ/ ▣ *vt* feed; (espoir, crainte) harbour; (projet) nurture; (passion) fuel. ● *vi* be nourishing. □ **se ~** *vpr* eat; **se ~ de** feed on. **nourrissant, ~e** *adj* nourishing.

nourrisson /nuʀisɔ̃/ *nm* infant.

nourriture /nuʀityʀ/ *nf* food.

nous /nu/ *pron* (sujet) we; (complément) us; (indirect) (to) us; (réfléchi) ourselves; (l'un l'autre) each other; **la voiture est à ~** the car is ours. **nous-mêmes** *pron* ourselves.

nouveau (**nouvel** before vowel or mute h), **nouvelle** (*mpl* **~x**) /nuvo, nuvɛl/ *adj* new; **nouvel an** new year; **~x mariés** newly-weds; **~ venu, nouvelle venue** newcomer. ● *nm, f* (élève) new boy, new girl. ● *nm* **du ~** (fait nouveau) a new development; **de ~, à ~** again. **nouveau-né** (*pl* **~s**) *nm* newborn baby.

nouveauté /nuvote/ *nf* novelty; (chose) new thing; (livre) new publication; (disque) new release.

nouvelle /nuvɛl/ *nf* (piece of) news; (récit) short story; **~s** news.

Nouvelle-Zélande /nuvɛlzelɑ̃d/ *nf* New Zealand.

novembre /nɔvɑ̃bʀ/ *nm* November.

noyade /nwajad/ *nf* drowning.

noyau (*pl* **~x**) /nwajo/ *nm* (de fruit) stone; (US) pit; (de cellule) nucleus; (groupe) group; (centre: fig) core.

noyer /nwaje/ ▣ *vt* drown; (inonder) flood. □ **se ~** *vpr* drown; (volontairement) drown oneself; **se ~ dans un verre d'eau** make a mountain out of a molehill. ● *nm* walnut-tree.

nu, ~e /ny/ *adj* (corps, personne) naked; (mains, mur, fil) bare; **à l'œil ~** to the naked eye. ● *nm* nude; **mettre à ~** expose.

nuage /nɥaʒ/ *nm* cloud.

nuance /nɥɑ̃s/ *nf* shade; (de sens) nuance; (différence) difference. **nuancer** ▣ *vt* (opinion) qualify.

nucléaire /nykleɛʀ/ *adj* nuclear. ● *nm* **le ~** nuclear energy.

nudisme /nydism/ *nm* nudism.

nudité /nydite/ *nf* nudity; (de lieu) bareness.

nuée /nɥe/ *nf* swarm, host.

nues /ny/ *nfpl* **tomber des ~** be amazed; **porter qn aux ~** praise sb to the skies.

nuire /nɥiʀ/ ▣ *vi* **~ à** harm.

nuisible /nɥizibl/ *adj* harmful (à to).

nuit /nɥi/ *nf* night; **cette ~** tonight; (hier) last night; **il fait ~** it is dark; **~ blanche** sleepless night; **la ~, de ~** at night; **~ de noces** wedding night.

nul, ~le /nyl/ *adj* (aucun) no; (zéro) nil; (qui ne vaut rien) useless; (non valable) null; (contrat) void; (testament) invalid; **match ~** draw; **~ en sciences** no good at science; **nulle part** nowhere; **~ autre** no one else. ● *pron* no one. **nullement** *adv* not at all. **nullité** *nf* uselessness; (personne) nonentity.

numérique /nymeʀik/ *adj* numerical; (montre, horloge) digital.

numériser /nymeʀize/ *vt* digitize.

numéro /nymeʀo/ *nm* number; (de journal) issue; (spectacle) act; **~ de téléphone** telephone number; **~ vert** freephone number. **numéroter** ▣ *vt* number.

nuque /nyk/ *nf* nape (of the neck).

nurse /nœʀs/ *nf* nanny.

nutritif, -ive /nytʀitif, -v/ *adj* nutritious; (valeur) nutritional.

n

Oo

oasis /ɔazis/ nf oasis.
obéir /ɔbeiʀ/ **2** vt ~ à obey. ● vi
obey. **obéissance** nf obedience.
obéissant, ~e adj obedient.
obèse /ɔbɛz/ adj obese.
objecter /ɔbʒɛkte/ **1** vt object.
objectif, -ive /ɔbʒɛktif, -v/ adj objective. ● nm objective; (Photo) lens.
objection /ɔbʒɛksjɔ̃/ nf objection;
soulever des ~s raise objections.
objet /ɔbʒɛ/ nm (chose) object; (sujet)
subject; (but) purpose, object; **être** ou
faire l'~ de be the subject of; ~
d'art objet d'art; **~s trouvés** lost
property; (US) lost and found.
obligation /ɔbligasjɔ̃/ nf obligation;
(Comm) bond; **être dans l'~ de** be
under obligation to.
obligatoire /ɔbligatwaʀ/ adj compulsory. **obligatoirement** adv (par règlement) of necessity; (inévitablement)
inevitably.
obligeance /ɔbliʒɑ̃s/ nf **avoir l'~ de
faire** be kind enough to do.
obliger /ɔbliʒe/ **40** vt compel, force (à
faire to do); (aider) oblige; **être
obligé de** have to (**de** for).
oblique /ɔblik/ adj oblique; **regard ~**
sidelong glance; **en ~** at an angle.
oblitérer /ɔblitere/ **14** vt (timbre)
cancel.
obnubilé, ~e /ɔbnybile/ adj ob-
sessed.
obscène /ɔpsɛn/ adj obscene.
obscur, ~e /ɔpskyʀ/ adj dark; (confus,
humble) obscure; (vague) vague.
obscurcir /ɔpskyʀsiʀ/ **2** vt make
dark; (fig) obscure. □ **s'~** vpr (ciel)
darken.
obscurité /ɔpskyʀite/ nf dark-(ness);
(de passage, situation) obscurity.
obsédant, ~e /ɔpsedɑ̃, -t/ adj (problème) nagging; (musique, souvenir)
haunting.
obsédé, ~e /ɔpsede/ nm, f **(sexuel)**
sex maniac; ~ **du ski/jazz** ski/jazz
freak.
obséder /ɔpsede/ **14** vt obsess.

obsèques /ɔpsɛk/ nfpl funeral.
observateur, -trice /ɔpsɛʀ-vatœʀ,
-tʀis/ adj observant. ● nm, f observer.
observation /ɔpsɛʀvasjɔ̃/ nf observation; (remarque) remark, comment;
(reproche) criticism; (obéissance) observance; **en ~** under observation.
observer /ɔpsɛʀve/ **1** vt (regarder)
observe; (surveiller) watch, observe;
(remarquer) notice, observe; **faire ~
qch** point sth out (à to).
obsession /ɔpsesjɔ̃/ nf obsession.
obstacle /ɔpstakl/ nm obstacle; (pour
cheval) fence, jump; (pour athlète)
hurdle; **faire ~ à** stand in the way of,
obstruct.
obstétrique /ɔpstetʀik/ nf obstetrics
(+ sg).
obstiné, ~e /ɔpstine/ adj obstinate.
obstiner (s') /(s)ɔpstine/ **1** vpr persist (à in).
obstruction /ɔpstʀyksjɔ̃/ nf obstruction; (de conduit) blockage.
obstruer /ɔpstʀye/ **1** vt obstruct.
obtenir /ɔptəniʀ/ **58** vt get, obtain.
obtention nf obtaining.
obus /ɔby/ nm shell.
occasion /ɔkazjɔ̃/ nf opportunity (**de
faire** of doing); (circonstance) occasion; (achat) bargain; (article non
neuf) second-hand buy; **à l'~** sometimes; **d'~** second-hand. **occasion-
nel, ~le** adj occasional.
occasionner /ɔkazjɔne/ **1** vt cause.
occident /ɔksidɑ̃/ nm (direction) west;
l'O~ the West.
occidental, ~e (mpl **-aux**) /ɔksidɑ̃tal,
-o/ adj western. **O~, ~e** (mpl **-aux**)
nm, f westerner.
occulte /ɔkylt/ adj occult.
occupant, ~e /ɔkypɑ̃, -t/ nm, f occupant. ● nm (Mil) forces of occupation.
occupation /ɔkypasjɔ̃/ nf occupation.
occupé, ~e /ɔkype/ adj busy; (place,
pays) occupied; (téléphone) engaged,
busy; (toilettes) engaged.
occuper /ɔkype/ **1** vt occupy; (poste)
hold; (espace, temps) take up. □ **s'~**
vpr (s'affairer) keep busy (à **faire**
doing); **s'~ de** (personne, problème)
take care of; (bureau, firme) be in
charge of; (se mêler) **occupe-toi de
tes affaires** mind your own business.

occurrence: en l'~ /ɔ̃lɔkyʀɑ̃s/ *loc* in this case.

océan /ɔseɑ̃/ *nm* ocean.

Océanie /ɔseani/ *nf* Oceania.

ocre /ɔkʀ/ *adj inv* ochre.

octante /ɔktɑ̃t/ *adj* eighty.

octet /ɔktɛ/ *nm* byte.

octobre /ɔktɔbʀ/ *nm* October.

octogone /ɔktɔgɔn/ *nm* octagon.

octroyer /ɔktʀwaje/ **31** *vt* grant.

oculaire /ɔkylɛʀ/ *adj* **témoin ~** eye-witness; **troubles ~s** eye trouble.

oculiste /ɔkylist/ *nmf* ophthalmologist.

odeur /ɔdœʀ/ *nf* smell.

odieux, -ieuse /ɔdjø, -z/ *adj* odious.

odorant, ~e /ɔdɔʀɑ̃, -t/ *adj* sweet-smelling.

odorat /ɔdɔʀa/ *nm* sense of smell.

œil (*pl* **yeux**) /œj, jø/ *nm* eye; **à l'~** **1** for free; **à mes yeux** in my view; **faire de l'~ à** make eyes at; **faire les gros yeux à** glare at; **ouvrir l'~** keep one's eyes open; **~ poché** black eye; **fermer les yeux** shut one's eyes; (fig) turn a blind eye.

œillères /œjɛʀ/ *nfpl* blinkers.

œillet /œjɛ/ *nm* (plante) carnation; (trou) eyelet.

œuf (*pl* **~s**) /œf, ø/ *nm* egg; **~ à la coque/dur/sur le plat** boiled/ hard-boiled/fried egg.

œuvre /œvʀ/ *nf* (ouvrage, travail) work; **~ d'art** work of art; **(~ de bienfaisance)** charity; **être à l'~** be at work; **mettre en ~** (réforme, moyens) implement; **mise en ~** implementation. ● *nm* (ensemble spécifié) **l'~ entier de Beethoven** the complete works of Beethoven.

œuvrer /œvʀe/ **1** *vi* work.

offense /ɔfɑ̃s/ *nf* insult.

offenser /ɔfɑ̃se/ **1** *vt* offend. □ **s'~** *vpr* take offence (**de** at).

offensive /ɔfɑ̃siv/ *nf* offensive.

offert, ~e /ɔfɛʀ, -t/ →**OFFRIR 21**.

office /ɔfis/ *nm* office; (Relig) service; (de cuisine) pantry; **faire ~ de** act as; **d'~** without consultation, automatically; **~ du tourisme** tourist information office.

officiel, ~le /ɔfisjɛl/ *adj* official. ● *nm* official.

officier /ɔfisje/ **45** *vi* (Relig) officiate. ● *nm* officer.

officieux, -ieuse /ɔfisjø, -z/ *adj* unofficial.

offre /ɔfʀ/ *nf* offer; (aux enchères) bid; **l'~ et la demande** supply and demand; '**~s d'emploi**' 'situations vacant'.

offrir /ɔfʀiʀ/ **21** *vt* offer (**de faire** to do); (cadeau) give; (acheter) buy; **~ à boire** (chez soi) give a drink to; (au café) buy a drink for. □ **s'~** *vpr* (se proposer) offer oneself (**comme** as); (solution) present itself; (s'acheter) treat oneself to.

ogive /ɔʒiv/ *nf* **~ nucléaire** nuclear warhead.

OGM (organisation génétiquement modifié) genetically modified organism.

oie /wa/ *nf* goose.

oignon /ɔɲɔ̃/ *nm* (légume) onion; (de fleur) bulb.

oiseau (*pl* **~x**) /wazo/ *nm* bird.

oisif, -ive /wazif, -v/ *adj* idle.

olive /ɔliv/ *nf & adj inv* olive. **olivier** *nm* olive tree.

olympique /ɔlɛ̃pik/ *adj* Olympic.

ombrage /ɔ̃bʀaʒ/ *nm* shade; **prendre ~ de** take offence at. **ombragé, ~e** *adj* shady.

ombre /ɔ̃bʀ/ *nf* (pénombre) shade; (contour) shadow; (soupçon: fig) hint, shadow; **dans l'~** (agir, rester) behind the scenes; **faire de l'~ à qn** be in sb's light.

ombrelle /ɔ̃bʀɛl/ *nf* parasol.

omelette /ɔmlɛt/ *nf* omelette.

omettre /ɔmɛtʀ/ **42** *vt* omit, leave out.

omnibus /ɔmnibys/ *nm* stopping *ou* local train.

omoplate /ɔmɔplat/ *nf* shoulder blade.

on /ɔ̃/ *pron* (tu, vous) you; (nous) we; (ils, elles) they; (les gens) people, they; (quelqu'un) someone; (indéterminé) one, you; **~ dit** people say, they say, it is said; **~ m'a demandé mon avis** I was asked for my opinion.

oncle /ɔ̃kl/ *nm* uncle.

onctueux, -euse /ɔ̃ktɥø, -z/ *adj* smooth.

o

onde /ɔ̃d/ *nf* wave; ~**s courtes**/ **longues** short/long wave; **sur les** ~**s** on the air.

on-dit /ɔ̃di/ *nm inv* **les** ~ hearsay.

onduler /ɔ̃dyle/ **1** *vi* undulate; (*cheveux*) be wavy.

onéreux, -euse /ɔnerø, -z/ *adj* costly.

ONG *abrév f* (**organisation non gouvernmentale**) NGO, non-governmental organization.

ongle /ɔ̃gl/ *nm* (finger) nail; ~ **de pied** toenail; **se faire les** ~**s** do one's nails.

ont /ɔ̃/ →AVOIR **5**.

ONU *abrév f* (**Organisation des Nations unies**) UN.

onze /ɔ̃z/ *adj & nm* eleven. **onzième** *adj & nmf* eleventh.

OPA *abrév f* (**offre publique d'achat**) takeover bid.

opéra /ɔpera/ *nm* opera; (*édifice*) opera house. **opéra-comique** (*pl* **opéras-comiques**) *nm* light opera.

opérateur, -trice /ɔperatœr, -tris/ *nm, f* operator.

opération /ɔperasjɔ̃/ *nf* operation; (Comm) deal; (*calcul*) calculation; ~ **escargot** slow-moving protest convoy.

opératoire /ɔperatwar/ *adj* (Méd) surgical; **bloc** ~ operating suite.

opérer /ɔpere/ **14** *vt* (*personne*) operate on; (*exécuter*) carry out, make; ~ **qn d'une tumeur** operate on sb to remove a tumour; **se faire** ~ have surgery *ou* an operation. ● *vi* (Méd) operate; (*faire effet*) work. □ **s'**~ *vpr* (*se produire*) occur.

opiniâtre /ɔpinjɑtr/ *adj* tenacious.

opinion /ɔpinjɔ̃/ *nf* opinion.

opportuniste /ɔpɔrtynist/ *nmf* opportunist.

opposant, ~**e** /ɔpozɑ̃, -t/ *nm, f* opponent.

opposé, ~**e** /ɔpoze/ *adj* (*sens, angle, avis*) opposite; (*factions*) opposing; (*intérêts*) conflicting; **être** ~ **à** be opposed to. ● *nm* opposite; **à l'**~ **de** (*contrairement à*) contrary to, unlike.

opposer /ɔpoze/ **1** *vt* (*objets*) place opposite each other; (*personnes*) match, oppose; (*contraster*) contrast; (*résistance, argument*) put up. □ **s'**~ *vpr* (*personnes*) confront each other; (*styles*) contrast; **s'**~ **à** oppose.

opposition /ɔpozisjɔ̃/ *nf* opposition; **par** ~ **à** in contrast with; **entrer en** ~ **avec** come into conflict with; **faire** ~ **à un chèque** stop a cheque.

oppressant, ~**e** /ɔpresɑ̃, -t/ *adj* oppressive.

opprimer /ɔprime/ **1** *vt* oppress.

opter /ɔpte/ **1** *vi* ~ **pour** opt for.

opticien, ~**ne** /ɔptisjɛ̃, -ɛn/ *nm, f* optician.

optimisme /ɔptimism/ *nm* optimism.

optimiste /ɔptimist/ *nmf* optimist. ● *adj* optimistic.

option /ɔpsjɔ̃/ *nf* option.

optique /ɔptik/ *adj* (*verre*) optical. ● *nf* (*science*) optics (+ *sg*); (*perspective*) perspective.

or¹ /ɔr/ *nm* gold; **d'**~ golden; **en** ~ gold; (*occasion*) golden.

or² /ɔr/ *conj* now, well; (*indiquant une opposition*) and yet.

orage /ɔraʒ/ *nm* (thunder)storm. **orageux, -euse** *adj* stormy.

oral, ~**e** (*mpl* **-aux**) /ɔral, -o/ *adj* oral. ● *nm* (*pl* **-aux**) oral.

orange /ɔrɑ̃ʒ/ *adj inv* orange; (Aut) (*feu*) amber; (US) yellow. ● *nf* orange. **orangeade** *nf* orangeade. **oranger** *nm* orange tree.

orateur, -trice /ɔratœr, -tris/ *nm, f* speaker.

orbite /ɔrbit/ *nf* orbit; (*d'œil*) socket.

orchestre /ɔrkɛstr/ *nm* orchestra; (*de jazz*) band; (*parterre*) stalls.

ordinaire /ɔrdinɛr/ *adj* ordinary; (*habituel*) usual; (*qualité*) standard; (*médiocre*) very average. ● *nm* **l'**~ the ordinary; (*nourriture*) the standard fare; **d'**~, **à l'**~ usually. **ordinairement** *adv* usually.

ordinateur /ɔrdinatœr/ *nm* computer; ~ **personnel**/**de bureau** personal/desktop computer; ~ **portable** laptop (computer); ~ **hôte** (Internet) host.

ordonnance /ɔrdɔnɑ̃s/ *nf* (*ordre, décret*) order; (*de médecin*) prescription.

ordonné, ~**e** /ɔrdɔne/ *adj* tidy.

ordonner /ɔrdɔne/ **1** *vt* order (**à qn de** sb to); (*agencer*) arrange; (Méd) prescribe; (*prêtre*) ordain.

ordre /ɔrdr/ *nm* order; (*propreté*) tidiness; **aux** ~**s de qn** at sb's disposal; **avoir de l'**~ be tidy; **en** ~ tidy, in order; **de premier** ~ first-rate; **d'~ officiel** of an official nature; **l'~ du jour** (programme) agenda; **mettre de l'~** dans tidy up; **jusqu'à nouvel ~** until further notice; **un ~ de grandeur** an approximate idea.

ordure /ɔʀdyʀ/ nf filth; **~s** (détritus) rubbish; (US) garbage; **~s ménagères** household refuse.

oreille /ɔʀɛj/ nf ear.

oreiller /ɔʀeje/ nm pillow.

oreillons /ɔʀejɔ̃/ nmpl mumps.

orfèvre /ɔʀfɛvʀ/ nm goldsmith.

organe /ɔʀgan/ nm organ.

organigramme /ɔʀganigʀam/ nm organization chart; (Ordinat) flowchart.

organique /ɔʀganik/ adj organic.

organisateur, -trice /ɔʀganizatœʀ, -tʀis/ nm, f organizer.

organisation /ɔʀganizasjɔ̃/ nf organization.

organiser /ɔʀganize/ ❶ vt organize. □ **s'~** vpr organize oneself, get organized.

organisme /ɔʀganism/ nm body, organism.

orge /ɔʀʒ/ nf barley.

orgelet /ɔʀʒəlɛ/ nm sty.

orgue /ɔʀg/ nm organ; **~ de Barbarie** barrel-organ. **orgues** nfpl organ.

orgueil /ɔʀgœj/ nm pride. **or-gueilleux, -euse** adj proud.

orient /ɔʀjɑ̃/ nm (direction) east; **l'O~** the Orient.

oriental, ~e (mpl **-aux**) /ɔʀjɑ̃tal, -o/ adj eastern; (de l'Orient) oriental. **O~, ~e** (mpl **-aux**) nm, f Asian.

orientation /ɔʀjɑ̃tasjɔ̃/ nf direction; (tendance politique) leanings (+ pl); (de maison) aspect; (Sport) orienteering; **~ professionnelle** careers advice; **~ scolaire** curriculum counselling.

orienter /ɔʀjɑ̃te/ ❶ vt position; (personne) direct. □ **s'~** vpr (se repérer) find one's bearings; **s'~ vers** turn towards.

origan /ɔʀigɑ̃/ nm oregano.

originaire /ɔʀiʒinɛʀ/ adj **être ~ de** be a native of.

original, ~e (mpl **-aux**) /ɔʀiʒinal, -o/ adj original; (curieux) eccentric. ● nm (œuvre) original. ● nm, f eccentric. **originalité** nf originality; eccentricity.

origine /ɔʀiʒin/ nf origin; **à l'~** originally; **d'~** (pièce, pneu) original; **être d'~ noble** come from a noble background.

originel, ~le /ɔʀiʒinɛl/ adj original.

orme /ɔʀm/ nm elm.

ornement /ɔʀnəmɑ̃/ nm ornament.

orner /ɔʀne/ ❶ vt decorate.

orphelin, ~e /ɔʀfəlɛ̃, -in/ nm, f orphan. ● adj orphaned. **orphelinat** nm orphanage.

orteil /ɔʀtɛj/ nm toe.

orthodoxe /ɔʀtɔdɔks/ adj orthodox.

orthographe /ɔʀtɔgʀaf/ nf spelling.

ortie /ɔʀti/ nf nettle.

os /ɔs, o/ nm inv bone.

OS abrév m ➔**OUVRIER SPÉCIALISÉ.**

osciller /ɔsile/ ❶ vi sway; (Tech) oscillate; (hésiter) waver; (fluctuer) fluctuate.

osé, ~e /oze/ adj daring.

oseille /ozɛj/ nf (plante) sorrel.

oser /oze/ ❶ vi dare.

osier /ozje/ nm wicker.

ossature /ɔsatyʀ/ nf skeleton, frame.

ossements /ɔsmɑ̃/ nmpl bones, remains.

osseux, -euse /ɔsø, z/ adj bony; (Méd) bone.

otage /ɔtaʒ/ nm hostage.

OTAN /ɔtɑ̃/ abrév f (**Organisation du traité de l'Atlantique Nord**) NATO.

otarie /ɔtaʀi/ nf eared seal.

ôter /ote/ ❶ vt remove (**à qn** from sb); (déduire) take away.

otite /ɔtit/ nf ear infection.

ou /u/ conj or; **~ bien** or else; **~ (bien)... ~ (bien)...** either... or...; **vous ~ moi** either you or me.

où /u/ pron where; (dans lequel) in which; (sur lequel) on which; (auquel) at which; **d'~** from which; (pour cette raison) hence; **par ~** through which; **~ qu'il soit** wherever he may be; **juste au moment ~** just as; **le jour ~** the day when. ● adv where; **d'~?** where from?

ouate /wat/ nf cotton wool; (US) absorbent cotton.

oubli /ubli/ nm forgetfulness; (trou de mémoire) lapse of memory; (négligence) oversight; **tomber dans l'~** sink into oblivion.

O

oublier /ublije/ **45** vt forget; (omettre) leave out, forget. □ **s'~** vpr (chose) be forgotten.

ouest /wɛst/ adj inv (façade, côte) west; (frontière, zone) western. ● nm west; **l'~ de l'Europe** western Europe; **vent d'~** westerly (wind); **aller vers l'~** go west; **l'O~** the West; **de l'O~** western.

oui /wi/ adv & nm inv yes.

ouï-dire: par ~ /paRwidiR/ loc by hearsay.

ouïe /wi/ nf hearing; (de poisson) gill.

ouragan /uRagɑ̃/ nm hurricane.

ourlet /uRlɛ/ nm hem.

ours /uRs/ nm bear; **~ blanc** polar bear; **~ en peluche** teddy bear.

outil /uti/ nm tool. **outillage** nm tools (+ pl). **outiller** **1** vt equip.

outrage /utRaʒ/ nm (grave) insult.

outrance /utRɑ̃s/ nf **à ~** excessively. **outrancier, -ière** adj extreme.

outre /utR/ prép besides. ● adv passer **~** pay no heed; **~ mesure** unduly; **en ~** in addition. **outre-mer** adv overseas.

outrepasser /utRəpase/ **1** vt exceed.

outrer /utRe/ **1** vt exaggerate; (indigner) incense.

ouvert, ~e /uvɛR, -t/ adj open; (gaz, radio) on. ● **→OUVRIR** **21**.

ouverture /uvɛRtyR/ nf opening; (Mus) overture; (Photo) aperture; **~s** (offres) overtures; **~ d'esprit** open-mindedness.

ouvrable /uvRabl/ adj jour **~** working day; **aux heures ~s** during business hours.

ouvrage /uvRaʒ/ nm (travail, livre) work; (couture) (piece of) needlework.

ouvre-boîtes /uvRəbwat/ nm inv tin-opener.

ouvre-bouteilles /uvRəbutɛj/ nm inv bottle-opener.

ouvreur, -euse /uvRœR, -øz/ nm, f usherette.

ouvrier, -ière /uvRije, -jɛR/ nm, f worker; **~ qualifié/spécialisé** skilled/unskilled worker. ● adj working-class; (conflit) industrial; **syndicat ~** trade union.

ouvrir /uvRiR/ **21** vt open (up); (gaz, robinet) turn on. ● vi open (up). □ **s'~**

vpr open (up); **s'~ à qn** open one's heart to sb.

ovaire /ɔvɛR/ nm ovary.

ovale /ɔval/ adj & nm oval.

ovni /ɔvni/ abrév m (**objet volant non-identifié**) UFO.

ovule /ɔvyl/ nm (à féconder) ovum; (gynécologique) pessary.

oxygène /ɔksiʒɛn/ nm oxygen.

oxygéner (s') /(s)ɔksiʒene/ **14** vpr get some fresh air.

ozone /ozon/ nf ozone; **la couche d'~** the ozone layer.

....

Pp

....

pacifique /pasifik/ adj peaceful; (personne) peaceable; (Géog) Pacific. **P~** nm **le P~** the Pacific.

pacotille /pakɔtij/ nf junk, rubbish.

PACS abrév nm (**pacte de solidarité**) contract of civil union.

pacser (se) /səpakse/ **1** vpr sign a contract of civil union (PACS).

pagaie /pagɛ/ nf paddle.

pagaille /pagaj/ nf 🔟 mess, shambles (+ sg).

page /paʒ/ nf page; **mise en ~** layout; **tourner la ~** turn over a new leaf; **être à la ~** be up to date; **~ d'accueil** (Internet) home page.

paie /pɛ/ nf pay.

paiement /pɛmɑ̃/ nm payment.

païen, ~ne /pajɛ̃, -ɛn/ adj & nm, f pagan.

paillasson /pajasɔ̃/ nm doormat.

paille /paj/ nf straw. ● adj (cheveux) straw-coloured.

paillette /pajɛt/ nf (sur robe) sequin; (de savon) flake.

pain /pɛ̃/ nm bread; (miche) loaf (of bread); (de savon, cire) bar; **~ d'épices** gingerbread; **~ grillé** toast.

pair, ~e /pɛR/ adj (nombre) even. ● nm (personne) peer; **aller de ~** go together (**avec** with); **au ~** (jeune fille) au pair. **paire** nf pair.

paisible /pezibl/ adj peaceful.

paître /pɛtʀ/ 44 vi graze.

paix /pɛ/ nf peace; **fiche-moi la ~!** 🎧 leave me alone!

Pakistan /pakistã/ nm Pakistan.

palace /palas/ nm luxury hotel.

palais /palɛ/ nm palace; (Anat) palate; **~ de Justice** law courts; **~ des sports** sports stadium.

pâle /pɑl/ adj pale.

Palestine /palɛstin/ nf Palestine.

palier /palje/ nm (d'escalier) landing; (étape) stage.

pâlir /pɑliʀ/ 2 vt/i (turn) pale.

palissade /palisad/ nf fence.

pallier /palje/ 45 vt compensate for.

palmarès /palmaʀɛs/ nm list of prize-winners.

palme /palm/ nf palm leaf; (de nageur) flipper. **palmé, ~e** adj (patte) webbed.

palmier /palmje/ nm palm (tree).

palper /palpe/ 1 vt feel.

palpiter /palpite/ 1 vi (battre) pound; (frémir) quiver.

paludisme /palydism/ nm malaria.

pamplemousse /pɑpləmus/ nm grapefruit.

panaché, ~e /panaʃe/ adj (bariolé, mélangé) motley; **glace ~e** mixed-flavour ice cream. ● nm shandy.

pancarte /pɑkaʀt/ nf sign; (de manifestant) placard.

pané, ~e /pane/ adj breaded.

panier /panje/ nm basket; (de basket-ball) basket; **mettre au ~** 🎧 throw out; **~ à salade** salad shaker; (fourgon 🎧) police van.

panique /panik/ nf panic. **paniquer** 1 vi panic.

panne /pan/ nf breakdown; **être en ~** have broken down; **être en ~ sèche** have run out of petrol; **~ d'électricité** ou **de courant** power failure.

panneau (pl ~x) /pano/ nm sign; (publicitaire) hoarding; (de porte) panel; (**~ d'affichage**) notice board; (**~ de signalisation**) road sign.

panoplie /panɔpli/ nf (jouet) outfit; (gamme) range.

pansement /pɑsmã/ nm dressing; **~ adhésif** plaster. **panser** 1 vt (plaie) dress; (personne) dress the wound(s) of; (cheval) groom.

pantalon /pɑtalɔ/ nm trousers (+ pl).

panthère /pɑtɛʀ/ nf panther.

pantin /pɑtɛ/ nm puppet.

pantomime /pɑtɔmim/ nf mime; (spectacle) mime show.

pantoufle /pɑtufl/ nf slipper.

paon /pɑ/ nm peacock.

papa /papa/ nm dad(dy).

pape /pap/ nm pope.

paperasse /papʀas/ nf (péj) bumf.

papeterie /papɛtʀi/ nf (magasin) stationer's shop.

papier /papje/ nm paper; (formulaire) form; **~s (d'identité)** (identity) papers; **~ absorbant** kitchen paper; **~ aluminium** tin foil; **~ buvard** blotting paper; **~ cadeau** wrapping paper; **~ calque** tracing paper; **~ carbone** carbon paper; **~ collant** adhesive tape; **~ hygiénique** toilet paper; **~ journal** newspaper; **~ à lettres** writing paper; **~ mâché** papier mâché; **~ peint** wallpaper; **~ de verre** sandpaper.

papillon /papijɔ/ nm butterfly; (contravention 🎧) parking-ticket; **~ de nuit** moth.

papoter /papɔte/ 1 vi 🎧 chatter.

paquebot /pakbo/ nm liner.

pâquerette /pɑkʀɛt/ nf daisy.

Pâques /pɑk/ nfpl & nm Easter.

paquet /pakɛ/ nm packet; (de cartes) pack; (colis) parcel; **un ~ de** (beaucoup 🎧) a mass of.

par /paʀ/ prép by; (à travers) through; (motif) out of, from; (provenance) from; **commencer/finir ~ qch** begin/ end with sth; **commencer/finir ~ faire** begin by/ end up (by) doing; **~ an/mois** a ou per year/month; **~ jour** a day; **~ personne** each, per person; **~ avion** (lettre) (by) airmail; **~-ci, ~-là** here and there; **~ contre** on the other hand; **~ ici/là** this/that way.

parachute /paʀaʃyt/ nm parachute. **parachutiste** nmf parachutist; (Mil) paratrooper.

parader /paʀade/ 1 vi show off.

paradis /paʀadi/ nm (Relig) heaven; (lieu idéal) paradise; **~ fiscal** tax haven.

paradoxal, ~e (*mpl* **-aux**) /paʀadɔksal, -o/ *adj* paradoxical.

paraffine /paʀafin/ *nf* paraffin wax.

parages /paʀaʒ/ *nmpl* **dans les ~** around.

paragraphe /paʀagʀaf/ *nm* paragraph.

paraître /paʀɛtʀ/ 18 *vi* (se montrer) appear; (sembler) seem, appear; (ouvrage) be published, come out; **faire ~** (ouvrage) bring out; **il paraît qu'ils...** apparently they...; **oui, il paraît** so I hear.

parallèle /paʀalɛl/ *adj* parallel; (illégal) unofficial. ● *nm* parallel; **faire le ~** make a connection. ● *nf* parallel (line).

paralyser /paʀalize/ 1 *vt* paralyse. **paralysie** *nf* paralysis.

paramètre /paʀamɛtʀ/ *nm* parameter.

parapente /paʀapɑ̃t/ *nm* paraglider; (activité) paragliding.

parapharmacie /paʀafaʀmasi/ *nf* toiletries and vitamins (pl.)

parapher /paʀafe/ 1 *vi* initial; (signer) sign.

parapluie /paʀaplɥi/ *nm* umbrella.

parasite /paʀazit/ *nm* parasite; **~s** (radio) interference (+ sg).

parasol /paʀasɔl/ *nm* sunshade.

paratonnerre /paʀatɔnɛʀ/ *nm* lightning conductor ou rod.

paravent /paʀavɑ̃/ *nm* screen.

parc /paʀk/ *nm* park; (de bétail) pen; (de bébé) play-pen; (entrepôt) depot; **~ de loisirs** theme park; **~ relais** park and ride; **~ de stationnement** car park.

parce que /paʀsk(ə)/ *conj* because.

parchemin /paʀʃəmɛ̃/ *nm* parchment.

parcmètre /paʀkmɛtʀ/ *nm* parking meter.

parcourir /paʀkuʀiʀ/ 20 *vt* travel ou go through; (distance) travel; (des yeux) glance at ou over.

parcours /paʀkuʀ/ *nm* route; (voyage) journey.

par-delà /paʀdəla/ *prép* beyond.

par-derrière /paʀdɛʀjɛʀ/ *adv* (attaquer) from behind; (critiquer) behind sb's back.

par-dessous /paʀdəsu/ *prép & adv* under (neath).

pardessus /paʀdəsy/ *nm* overcoat.

par-dessus /paʀdəsy/ *prép & adv* over; **~ bord** overboard; **~ le marché** 1 into the bargain; **~ tout** above all.

par-devant /paʀdəvɑ̃/ *adv* (passer) by the front.

pardon /paʀdɔ̃/ *nm* forgiveness; **(je vous demande) ~!** (I am) sorry!; (pour demander qch) excuse me.

pardonner /paʀdɔne/ 1 *vt* forgive; **~ qch à qn** forgive sb for sth.

pare-brise /paʀbʀiz/ *nm inv* windscreen.

pare-chocs /paʀʃɔk/ *nm inv* bumper.

pareil, ~le /paʀɛj/ *adj* similar (à to); (tel) such (a); **c'est ~** it's the same; **ce n'est pas ~** it's not the same thing. ● *nm, f* equal. ● *adv* 1 the same.

parent, ~e /paʀɑ̃, -t/ *adj* related (de to). ● *nm, f* relative, relation; **~s** (père et mère) parents; **~ isolé** single parent; **réunion de ~s d'élèves** parents' evening.

parenté /paʀɑ̃te/ *nf* relationship.

parenthèse /paʀɑ̃tɛz/ *nf* bracket, parenthesis; (fig) digression.

parer /paʀe/ 1 *vt* (esquiver) parry; (orner) adorn. ● *vi* **~ à** deal with; **~ au plus pressé** tackle the most urgent things first.

paresse /paʀɛs/ *nf* laziness.

paresseux, -euse /paʀesø, -z/ *adj* lazy. ● *nm, f* lazy person.

parfait, ~e /paʀfɛ, -t/ *adj* perfect. **parfaitement** *adv* perfectly; (bien sûr) absolutely.

parfois /paʀfwa/ *adv* sometimes.

parfum /paʀfœ̃/ *nm* (senteur) scent; (substance) perfume, scent; (goût) flavour. **parfumé, ~e** *adj* fragrant; (savon) scented; (thé) flavoured.

parfumer /paʀfyme/ 1 *vt* (embaumer) scent; (gâteau) flavour. □ **se ~** *vpr* put on one's perfume. **parfumerie** *nf* (produits) perfumes; (boutique) perfume shop.

pari /paʀi/ *nm* bet.

Paris /paʀi/ *npr* Paris.

parisien, ~ne /paʀizjɛ̃, -ɛn/ *adj* Parisian; (banlieue) Paris. **P~, ~ne** *nm, f* Parisian.

parking /paʀkiŋ/ *nm* car park.

parlement /parləmɑ̃/ *nm* parliament.

parlementaire /parləmɑ̃tɛr/ *adj* parliamentary. ● *nmf* Member of Parliament.

parlementer /parləmɑ̃te/ **1** *vi* negotiate.

parler /parle/ **1** *vi* talk (à to); ∼ **de** talk about; **tu parles d'un avantage!** call that a benefit!; **de quoi ça parle?** what is it about? ● *vt* (*langue*) speak; (*politique, affaires*) talk. □ **se** ∼ *vpr* (*personnes*) talk (to each other); (*langue*) be spoken. ● *nm* speech; (dialecte) dialect.

parmi /parmi/ *prép* among(st).

paroi /parwa/ *nf* wall; ∼ **rocheuse** rock face.

paroisse /parwas/ *nf* parish.

parole /parɔl/ *nf* (*mot, promesse*) word; (*langage*) speech; **demander la** ∼ ask to speak; **prendre la** ∼ (begin to) speak; **tenir** ∼ keep one's word; **croire qn sur** ∼ take sb's word for it.

parquet /parkɛ/ *nm* (parquet) floor; **lame de** ∼ floorboard; **le** ∼ (Jur) prosecution.

parrain /parɛ̃/ *nm* godfather; (fig) sponsor.

parsemer /parsəme/ **6** *vt* strew (de with).

part /par/ *nf* share, part; **à** ∼ (de côté) aside; (séparément) separate; (excepté) apart from; **d'une** ∼ on the one hand; **d'autre** ∼ on the other hand; (de plus) moreover; **de la** ∼ **de** from; **de toutes** ∼s from all sides; **de** ∼ **et d'autre** on both sides; **faire** ∼ **à qn** inform sb (de of); **faire la** ∼ **des choses** make allowances for; **prendre** ∼ **à** take part in; (*joie, douleur*) share; **pour ma** ∼ as for me.

partage /partaʒ/ *nm* (division) dividing; (répartition) sharing out; **recevoir qch en** ∼ be left sth in a will.

partager /partaʒe/ **40** *vt* divide; (distribuer) share out; (avoir en commun) share. □ **se** ∼ **qch** *vpr* share sth.

partenaire /partənɛr/ *nmf* partner.

parterre /partɛr/ *nm* flower bed; (Théât) stalls.

parti /parti/ *nm* (Pol) party; (décision) decision; (en mariage) match; ∼ **pris** bias; **prendre** ∼ get involved; **pren-**

dre ∼ **pour qn** side with sb; **j'en ai pris mon** ∼ I've come to terms with that.

partial, ∼e (*mpl* **-iaux**) /parsjal, -jo/ *adj* biased.

participe /partisip/ *nm* (Gram) participle.

participant, ∼e /partisipɑ̃, -t/ *nm, f* participant (à in).

participation /partisipasjɔ̃/ *nf* participation; (financière) contribution; (d'un artiste) appearance.

participer /partisipe/ **1** *vi* ∼ **à** take part in, participate in; (*profits, frais*) share.

particule /partikyl/ *nf* particle.

particulier, -ière /partikylje, -jɛr/ *adj* (spécifique) particular; (bizarre) unusual; (privé) private; **rien de** ∼ nothing special. ● *nm* private individual; **en** ∼ in particular, particularly. **particulièrement** *adv* particularly.

partie /parti/ *nf* part; (cartes, Sport) game; (Jur) party; **une** ∼ **de pêche** a fishing trip; **en** ∼ partly, in part; **en grande** ∼ largely; **faire** ∼ **de** be part of; (adhérer à) be a member of; **faire** ∼ **intégrante de** be an integral part of.

partiel, ∼le /parsjɛl/ *adj* partial. ● *nm* (Univ) exam based on a module.

partir /partir/ **46** *vi* (aux être) go; (quitter un lieu) leave, go; (*tache*) come out; (*bouton*) come off; (*coup de feu*) go off; (commencer) start; ∼ **pour le Brésil** leave for Brazil; ∼ **du principe que** work on the assumption that; **à** ∼**de** from; **à** ∼ **de maintenant** from now on.

partisan, ∼e /partizɑ̃, -an/ *nm, f* supporter. ● *nm* (Mil) partisan; **être** ∼ **de** be in favour of.

partition /partisjɔ̃/ *nf* (Mus) score.

partout /partu/ *adv* everywhere; ∼ **où** wherever.

paru /pary/ ➡**PARAÎTRE 18**.

parure /paryr/ *nf* finery; (bijoux) set of jewels; (de draps) set.

parution /parysjɔ̃/ *nf* publication.

parvenir /parvənir/ **58** *vi* (aux être) ∼ **à** reach; ∼ **à faire** manage to do; **faire** ∼ send.

parvenu, ∼e /parvəny/ *nm, f* upstart.

p

pas | pâte

pas¹ /pɑ/

⟶ Pour les expressions comme **pas encore**, **pas mal**, etc. ⟶**encore**, **mal** etc.

● *adverbe*

····▶ not; **ne ~** not; **je ne sais ~** I don't know; **je ne pense ~** I don't think so; **il a aimé, moi ~** he liked it, I didn't; **~ cher/poli** cheap/impolite.

····▶ **~ du tout** not at all; **~ de chance!** tough luck!

····▶ **on a bien ri, ~ vrai?** 🔢 we had a good laugh, didn't we?

❗ In spoken colloquial French **ne... pas** is often shortened to **pas**. You will hear **j'ai pas compris** instead of **je n'ai pas compris** (*I didn't understand*). NB This is not correct written French.

pas² /pɑ/ *nm* step; (*bruit*) footstep; (*trace*) footprint; (*vitesse*) pace; **à deux ~ (de)** a step away (from); **marcher au ~** march; **rouler au ~** move very slowly; **à ~ de loup** stealthily; **faire les cent ~** walk up and down; **faire le premier ~** make the first move; **~ de porte** doorstep; **~ de vis** (Tech) thread.

passage /pɑsaʒ/ *nm* (*traversée*) crossing; (*visite*) visit; (*chemin*) way, passage; (*d'une œuvre*) passage; **de ~** (*voyageur*) visiting; (*amant*) casual; **la tempête a tout emporté sur son ~** the storm swept everything away; **~ clouté** pedestrian crossing; **~ interdit** (*panneau*) no thoroughfare; **~ à niveau** level crossing; **~ souterrain** subway.

passager, -ère /pɑsaʒe, -ɛʀ/ *adj* temporary. ● *nm, f* passenger; **~ clandestin** stowaway.

passant, ~e /pɑsɑ̃, -t/ *adj* (*rue*) busy. ● *nm, f* passer-by. ● *nm* (*anneau*) loop.

passe /pɑs/ *nf* pass; **bonne/mauvaise ~** good/bad patch; **en ~ de** on the road to.

passé, ~e /pɑse/ *adj* (*révolu*) past; (*dernier*) last; (*fané*) faded; **~ de mode** out of fashion. ● *nm* past. ● *prép* after.

passe-partout /pɑspaʀtu/ *nm inv* master-key. ● *adj inv* for all occasions.

passeport /pɑspɔʀ/ *nm* passport.

passer /pɑse/ 🔢 *vi* (*aux* être *ou* avoir) go past, pass; (*aller*) go; (*venir*) come; (*temps, douleur*) pass; (*film*) be on; (*couleur*) fade; **laisser ~** let through; (*occasion*) miss; (*en voiture*) drive past; **~ devant** (*à pied*) walk past; (*en voiture*) drive past; **~ par** go through; **où est-il passé?** where did he get to?; **~ outre** take no notice; **passons!** let's forget about it!; **passons aux choses sérieuses** let's turn to serious matters; **~ dans la classe supérieure** go up a year; **~ pour un idiot** look a fool. ● *vt* (*aux* avoir) (*franchir*) pass, cross; (*donner*) pass, hand; (*temps*) spend; (*enfiler*) slip on; (*vidéo, disque*) put on; (*examen*) take, sit; (*commande*) place; (*faire*) **~ le temps** while away the time; **~ l'aspirateur** hoover; **~ un coup de fil à qn** give sb a ring; **je vous passe Mme X** (*par le standard*) I'll put you through to Mrs X; (*en donnant l'appareil*) I'll pass you over to Mrs X; **~ qch en fraude** smuggle sth. □ **se ~** *vpr* happen, take place; (*s'écouler*) go by; **se ~ de** go *ou* do without.

passerelle /pɑsʀɛl/ *nf* footbridge; (*de navire*) gangway; (*d'avion*) (passenger) footbridge; (Internet) gateway.

passe-temps /pɑstɑ̃/ *nm inv* pastime.

passif, -ive /pɑsif, -v/ *adj* passive. ● *nm* (Comm) liabilities.

passion /pɑsjɔ̃/ *nf* passion. **passionnant, ~e** *adj* fascinating.

passionné, ~e /pɑsjɔne/ *adj* passionate; **être ~ de** have a passion for.

passionner /pɑsjɔne/ 🔢 *vt* fascinate. □ **se ~ pour** *vpr* have a passion for.

passoire /pɑswaʀ/ *nf* (à thé) strainer; (à légumes) colander.

pastèque /pɑstɛk/ *nf* watermelon.

pasteur /pɑstœʀ/ *nm* (Relig) minister.

pastille /pɑstij/ *nf* (*médicament*) pastille, lozenge.

patate /patat/ *nf* 🔢 spud; **~ (douce)** sweet potato.

patauger /patoʒe/ 🔢 *vi* splash about.

pâte /pɑt/ *nf* paste; (à gâteau) dough; (à tarte) pastry; (à frire) batter; **~s (alimentaires)** pasta (+ *sg.*) **~ à modeler** Plasticine®; **~ d'amandes** marzipan.

pâté /pate/ *nm* (Culin) pâté; (d'encre) blot; (de sable) sandpie; ~ **en croûte** ≈ pie; ~ **de maisons** block (of houses).

pâtée /pate/ *nf* feed, mash.

patente /patãt/ *nf* trade licence.

paternel, ~**le** /patɛʀnɛl/ *adj* paternal. **paternité** *nf* paternity.

pathétique /patetik/ *adj* moving.

patience /pasjãs/ *nf* patience. **patient,** ~**e** *adj & nm, f* patient. **patienter** 🔳 *vi* wait.

patin /patɛ̃/ *nm* skate; ~ **à roulettes** roller-skate.

patinage /patinaʒ/ *nm* skating. **patiner** 🔳 *vi* skate; (*roue*) spin. **patinoire** *nf* ice rink.

pâtisserie /patisʀi/ *nf* cake shop; (gâteau) pastry; (secteur) cake making. **pâtissier, -ière** *nm, f* confectioner, pastry-cook.

patrie /patʀi/ *nf* homeland.

patrimoine /patʀimwan/ *nm* heritage.

patriote /patʀijɔt/ *adj* patriotic. ● *nmf* patriot.

patron, ~**ne** /patʀɔ̃, -ɔn/ *nm, f* employer, boss; (propriétaire) owner, boss; (saint) patron saint. ● *nm* (couture) pattern. **patronal,** ~**e** (*mpl* **-aux**) *adj* employers'. **patronat** *nm* employers (+ *pl*).

patrouille /patʀuj/ *nf* patrol.

patte /pat/ *nf* leg; (pied) foot; (de chat) paw; ~**s** (favoris) sideburns; **marcher à quatre** ~**s** walk on all fours; (*bébé*) crawl; ~**s de derrière** hind legs.

paume /pom/ *nf* (de main) palm.

paumé, ~**e** /pome/ *nm, f* 🔳 misfit.

paupière /popjɛʀ/ *nf* eyelid.

pause /poz/ *nf* pause; (halte) break.

pauvre /povʀ/ *adj* poor. ● *nmf* poor man, poor woman. **pauvreté** *nf* poverty.

pavé /pave/ *nm* cobblestone.

pavillon /pavijɔ̃/ *nm* (maison) house; (drapeau) flag.

payant, ~**e** /pɛjã, -t/ *adj* (hôte) paying; **c'est** ~ you have to pay to get in.

payer /peje/ 🔳 *vt/i* pay; (*service, travail*) pay for; ~ **qch à qn** buy sb sth; **faire** ~ **qn** charge sb; **il me le paiera!** he'll pay for this. ☐ **se** ~ *vpr* **se** ~ **qch** buy oneself sth; **se** ~ **la tête de** make fun of.

pays /pei/ *nm* country; (région) region; **du** ~ local.

paysage /peizaʒ/ *nm* landscape.

paysan, ~**ne** /peizã, -an/ *nm, f* farmer, country person; (péj) peasant. ● *adj* (agricole) farming; (rural) country.

Pays-Bas /peiba/ *nmpl* **les** ~ the Netherlands.

PCV *abrév m* (**paiement contre vérification**) **téléphoner en** ~ reverse the charges.

PDG *abrév m* (**président-directeur général**) chairman and managing director.

péage /peaʒ/ *nm* toll; (lieu) tollgate.

peau (*pl* ~**x**) /po/ *nf* skin; (cuir) hide; ~ **de chamois** shammy (leather); ~**de mouton** sheepskin; **être bien/mal dans sa** ~ be/not be at ease with oneself.

pêche /pɛʃ/ *nf* (fruit) peach; (activité) fishing; (poissons) catch; ~ **à la ligne** angling.

péché /peʃe/ *nm* sin.

pêcher /peʃe/ *vt* (*poisson*) catch; (dénicher 🔳) dig up. ● *vi* fish. **pêcheur** *nm* fisherman; (à la ligne) angler.

pécuniaire /pekynjɛʀ/ *adj* financial.

pédagogie /pedagoʒi/ *nf* education.

pédale /pedal/ *nf* pedal.

pédalo ® /pedalo/ *nm* pedal boat.

pédant, ~**e** /pedã, -t/ *adj* pedantic.

pédestre /pedɛstʀ/ *adj* **faire de la randonnée** ~ go walking *ou* hiking.

pédiatre /pedjatʀ/ *nmf* paediatrician.

pédicure /pedikyʀ/ *nmf* chiropodist.

peigne /pɛɲ/ *nm* comb.

peigner /peɲe/ 🔳 *vt* comb; (*personne*) comb the hair of. ☐ **se** ~ *vpr* comb one's hair.

peignoir /pɛɲwaʀ/ *nm* dressing gown.

peindre /pɛ̃dʀ/ 🔳 *vt* paint.

peine /pɛn/ *nf* sadness, sorrow; (effort, difficulté) trouble; (Jur) sentence; **avoir de la** ~ feel sad; **faire de la** ~ **à** hurt; **ce n'est pas la** ~ **de sonner** you don't need to ring the bell; **j'ai de la** ~ **à le croire** I find it hard to believe; **se donner** *ou* **prendre la** ~ **de faire** go to the trouble of doing; ~ **de mort** death penalty. ● *adv* **à** ~ hardly.

peiner /pene/ 🔳 *vi* struggle. ● *vt* sadden.

p

peintre /pɛtʀ/ nm painter; ~ **en bâtiment** house painter.

peinture /pɛ̃tyʀ/ nf painting; (matière) paint; ~ **à l'huile** oil painting.

péjoratif, -ive /peʒɔʀatif, -v/ adj pejorative.

pelage /pəlaʒ/ nm coat, fur.

pêle-mêle /pɛlmɛl/ adv in a jumble.

peler /pəle/ **6** vt/i peel.

pèlerinage /pɛlʀinaʒ/ nm pilgrimage.

pelle /pɛl/ nf shovel; (d'enfant) spade.

pellicule /pelikyl/ nf film; ~s (cheveux) dandruff.

pelote /pəlɔt/ nf (of wool) ball.

peloton /p(ə)lɔtɔ̃/ nm platoon; (Sport) pack; ~ **d'exécution** firing squad.

pelotonner (se) /(sə)plɔtɔne/ **1** vpr curl up.

pelouse /p(ə)luz/ nf lawn.

peluche /p(ə)lyʃ/ nf (matière) plush; (jouet) cuddly toy; **en ~** (lapin, chien) fluffy.

pénal, ~e (mpl **-aux**) /penal, -o/ adj penal. **pénaliser** **1** vt penalize. **pénalité** nf penalty.

penchant /pɑ̃ʃɑ̃/ nm inclination; (goût) liking (**pour** for).

pencher /pɑ̃ʃe/ **1** vt tilt; ~ **pour** favour. ● vi lean (over), tilt. □ **se ~** vpr lean (forward); **se ~ sur** (problème) examine.

pendaison /pɑ̃dɛzɔ̃/ nf hanging.

pendant¹ /pɑ̃dɑ̃/ prép (au cours de) during; (durée) for; ~ **que** while.

pendant², ~e /pɑ̃dɑ̃, -t/ adj hanging; **jambes ~es** with one's legs dangling. ● nm (contrepartie) matching piece (**de** to); ~ **d'oreille** drop earring.

pendentif /pɑ̃dɑ̃tif/ nm pendant.

penderie /pɑ̃dʀi/ nf wardrobe.

pendre /pɑ̃dʀ/ **3** vt/i hang. □ **se ~** vpr hang (**à** from); (se tuer) hang oneself.

pendule /pɑ̃dyl/ nf clock. ● nm pendulum.

pénétrer /penetre/ **14** vi ~ **(dans)** enter; **faire ~ une crème** rub a cream in. ● vt penetrate.

pénible /penibl/ adj (travail) hard; (nouvelle) painful; (enfant) tiresome.

péniche /peniʃ/ nf barge.

pénitence /penitɑ̃s/ nf (Relig) penance; (punition) punishment; **faire ~** repent.

pénitentiaire /penitɑ̃sjɛʀ/ adj (établissement) penal.

pénombre /penɔ̃bʀ/ nf half-light.

pensée /pɑ̃se/ nf (idée) thought; (fleur) pansy.

penser /pɑ̃se/ **1** vt/i think; ~ **à** (réfléchir à) think about; (se souvenir de, prévoir) think of; ~ **faire** think of doing; **faire ~ à** remind one of.

pensif, -ive /pɑ̃sif, -v/ adj pensive.

pension /pɑ̃sjɔ̃/ nf (Scol) boarding school; (repas, somme) board; (allocation) pension; (~ **de famille**) guest house; ~ **alimentaire** (Jur) alimony. **pensionnaire** nmf (Scol) boarder; (d'hôtel) guest. **pensionnat** nm boarding school.

pente /pɑ̃t/ nf slope; **en ~** sloping.

Pentecôte /pɑ̃tkot/ nf **la ~** Whitsun.

pénurie /penyʀi/ nf shortage.

pépin /pepɛ̃/ nm (graine) pip; (ennui **1**) hitch.

pépinière /pepinjɛʀ/ nf (tree) nursery.

perçant, ~e /pɛʀsɑ̃, -t/ adj (cri) shrill; (regard) piercing.

perce-neige /pɛʀsənɛʒ/ nm or f inv snowdrop.

percepteur /pɛʀsɛptœʀ/ nm tax inspector.

percer /pɛʀse/ **10** vt pierce; (avec perceuse) drill; (mystère) penetrate. ● vi break through; (dent) come through. **perceuse** nf drill.

percevoir /pɛʀsəvwaʀ/ **52** vt perceive; (impôt) collect.

perche /pɛʀʃ/ nf (bâton) pole.

percher (se) /(sə)pɛʀʃe/ **1** vpr perch.

percolateur /pɛʀkɔlatœʀ/ nm coffee machine.

percuter /pɛʀkyte/ **1** vt (véhicule) crash into.

perdant, ~e /pɛʀdɑ̃, -t/ adj losing. ● nm, f loser.

perdre /pɛʀdʀ/ **3** vt/i lose; (gaspiller) waste; ~ **ses poils** (chat) moult. □ **se ~** vpr get lost; (rester inutilisé) go to waste.

perdrix /pɛʀdʀi/ nf partridge.

perdu, ~e /pɛʀdy/ adj lost; (endroit) isolated; (balle) stray; **c'est du temps ~** it's a waste of time.

père /pɛʀ/ nm father; ~ **de famille** father, family man; ~ **spirituel** father figure; **le ~ Noël** Santa Claus.

perfection /pɛʀfɛksjɔ̃/ *nf* perfection.

perfectionner /pɛʀfɛksjɔne/ **1** *vt* (*technique*) perfect; (*art*) refine. ◻ **se ~** *vpr* improve; **se ~ en anglais** improve one's English.

perforer /pɛʀfɔʀe/ **1** *vt* perforate; (*billet, bande*) punch.

performance /pɛʀfɔʀmɑ̃s/ *nf* performance.

perfusion /pɛʀfyzjɔ̃/ *nf* drip; **sous ~** on a drip.

péridurale /peʀidyʀal/ *nf* epidural.

péril /peʀil/ *nm* peril; **à tes risques et ~s** at your own risk.

périlleux, -euse /peʀijø, -z/ *adj* perilous.

périmé, ~e /peʀime/ *adj* (*produit*) past its use-by date; (*désuet*) outdated.

période /peʀjɔd/ *nf* period.

périodique /peʀjɔdik/ *adj* periodic(al). ● *nm* (*journal*) periodical.

péripétie /peʀipesi/ *nf* (unexpected) event, adventure.

périphérique /peʀifeʀik/ *adj* peripheral. ● *nm* (*boulevard*) ~ ring road.

périple /peʀipl/ *nm* journey.

périr /peʀiʀ/ **2** *vi* perish, die.

perle /pɛʀl/ *nf* (*d'huître*) pearl; (*de verre*) bead.

permanence /pɛʀmanɑ̃s/ *nf* permanence; (Scol) study room; **de ~** on duty; **en ~** permanently; **assurer une ~** keep the office open.

permanent, ~e /pɛʀmanɑ̃, -t/ *adj* permanent; (*constant*) constant; **formation ~e** continuous education. **permanente** *nf* (*coiffure*) perm.

permettre /pɛʀmɛtʀ/ **42** *vt* allow; **~ à qn de** allow sb to. ◻ **se ~** *vpr* (*achat*) afford; **se ~ de faire** take the liberty of doing.

permis, ~e /pɛʀmi, -z/ *adj* allowed. ● *nm* licence, permit; **~ (de conduire)** driving licence.

permission /pɛʀmisjɔ̃/ *nf* permission; **en ~** (Mil) on leave.

Pérou /peʀu/ *nm* Peru.

perpendiculaire /pɛʀpɑ̃dikylɛʀ/ *adj & nf* perpendicular.

perpétuité /pɛʀpetɥite/ *nf* **à ~** for life.

perplexe /pɛʀplɛks/ *adj* perplexed.

perquisition /pɛʀkizisjɔ̃/ *nf* (police) search.

perron /pɛʀɔ̃/ *nm* (front) steps.

perroquet /pɛʀɔkɛ/ *nm* parrot.

perruche /peʀyʃ/ *nf* budgerigar.

perruque /peʀyk/ *nf* wig.

persécuter /pɛʀsekyte/ **1** *vt* persecute.

persévérance /pɛʀseveʀɑ̃s/ *nf* perseverance. **persévérer** **14** *vi* persevere.

persienne /pɛʀsjɛn/ *nf* (outside) shutter.

persil /pɛʀsi/ *nm* parsley.

persistance /pɛʀsistɑ̃s/ *nf* persistence. **persistant, ~e** *adj* persistent; (*feuillage*) evergreen.

persister /pɛʀsiste/ **1** *vi* persist (**à faire** in doing).

personnage /pɛʀsɔnaʒ/ *nm* character; (*personne célèbre*) personality.

personnalité /pɛʀsɔnalite/ *nf* personality.

personne /pɛʀsɔn/ *nf* person; **~s** people. ● *pron* nobody, no-one; **je n'ai vu ~** I didn't see anybody.

personnel, ~le /pɛʀsɔnɛl/ *adj* personal; (*égoïste*) selfish. ● *nm* staff.

perspective /pɛʀspɛktiv/ *nf* (art, point de vue) perspective; (*vue*) view; (*éventualité*) prospect.

perspicace /pɛʀspikas/ *adj* shrewd. **perspicacité** *nf* shrewdness.

persuader /pɛʀsɥade/ **1** *vt* persuade (**de faire** to do).

persuasif, -ive /pɛʀsɥazif, -v/ *adj* persuasive.

perte /pɛʀt/ *nf* loss; (*ruine*) ruin; **à ~ de vue** as far as the eye can see; **~ de** (*temps, argent*) waste of; **~ sèche** total loss; **~s** (Méd) discharge.

pertinent, ~e /pɛʀtinɑ̃, -t/ *adj* pertinent.

perturbateur, -trice /pɛʀtyʀ-batœʀ, -tʀis/ *nm, f* disruptive element. **perturbation** *nf* disruption. **perturber** **1** *vt* disrupt; (*personne*) perturb.

pervers, ~e /pɛʀvɛʀ, -s/ *adj* (*dépravé*) perverted; (*méchant*) wicked.

pervertir /pɛʀvɛʀtiʀ/ **2** *vt* pervert.

pesant, ~e /pəzɑ̃, -t/ *adj* heavy.

pesanteur /pəzɑ̃tœʀ/ *nf* heaviness; **la ~** (force) gravity.

p

pesée /pəze/ nf weighing; (effort) pressure.

pèse-personne (pl ~s) /pɛzpɛʀ-sɔn/ nm (bathroom) scales.

peser /pəze/ 6 vt/i weigh; ~ **sur** bear upon.

pessimiste /pesimist/ adj pessimistic. ● nmf pessimist.

peste /pɛst/ nf plague; (personne 🗉) pest.

pet /pɛ/ nm 🗉 fart 🗉.

pétale /petal/ nm petal.

:::
Pétanque See ▷**BOULES.**   *i*
:::

pétard /petaʀ/ nm banger.

péter /pete/ 14 vi 🗉 fart 🗉, go bang; (casser) snap.

pétillant, ~e /petijã, -t/ adj (boisson) sparkling; (personne) bubbly.

pétiller /petije/ 1 vi (feu) crackle; (champagne, yeux) sparkle; ~ **d'intelligence** sparkle with intelligence.

petit, ~e /p(ə)ti, -t/ adj small; (avec nuance affective) little; (jeune) young, small; (défaut) minor; (mesquin) petty; **en ~** in miniature; ~ **à ~** little by little; **un ~ peu** a little bit; ~ **ami** boyfriend; **~e amie** girlfriend; **~es annonces** small ads; **~e cuillère** teaspoon; ~ **déjeuner** breakfast; ~ **pois** garden pea. ● nm, f little child; (Scol) junior; **~s** (de chat) kittens; (de chien) pups. **petite-fille** (pl **petites-filles**) nf granddaughter. **petit-fils** (pl **petits-fils**) nm grandson.

pétition /petisjɔ̃/ nf petition.

petits-enfants /pətizɑ̃fɑ̃/ nmpl grandchildren.

pétrin /petʀɛ̃/ nm **dans le ~** 🗉 in a fix 🗉.

pétrir /petʀiʀ/ 2 vt knead.

pétrole /petʀɔl/ nm oil; ~ **brut** crude oil.

pétrolier, -ière /petʀɔlje, -jɛʀ/ adj oil. ● nm (navire) oil-tanker.

peu /pø/ adv (~ **de**) (quantité) little, not much; (nombre) few, not many; ~ **intéressant** not very interesting; **il mange ~** he doesn't eat very much. ● pron few. ● nm little; **un ~ (de)** a little; **à ~ près** more or less; **de ~** only just; ~ **à ~** gradually; ~ **après/avant** shortly after/before; ~ **de**

chose not much; ~ **nombreux** few; ~ **souvent** seldom; **pour ~ que** if.

peuple /pœpl/ nm people. **peupler** 1 vt populate.

peuplier /pøplije/ nm poplar.

peur /pœʀ/ nf fear; **avoir ~** be afraid (**de** of); **de ~ de** for fear of; **faire ~ à** frighten. **peureux, -euse** adj fearful.

peut /pø/ ➡POUVOIR 49.

peut-être /pøtɛtʀ/ adv perhaps, maybe; ~ **qu'il viendra** he might come.

peux /pø/ ➡POUVOIR 49.

phare /faʀ/ nm (tour) lighthouse; (de véhicule) headlight; ~ **antibrouillard** fog lamp.

pharmacie /faʀmasi/ nf (magasin) chemist's (shop), pharmacy; (science) pharmacy; (armoire) medicine cabinet. **pharmacien, ~ne** nm, f chemist, pharmacist.

phénomène /fenɔmɛn/ nm phenomenon; (personne 🗉) eccentric.

philosophe /filɔzɔf/ nmf philosopher. ● adj philosophical. **philosophie** nf philosophy. **philosophique** adj philosophical.

phobie /fɔbi/ nf phobia.

phonétique /fɔnetik/ adj phonetic. ● nf phonetics.

phoque /fɔk/ nm (animal) seal.

photo /fɔto/ nf photo; (art) photography; **prendre en ~** take a photo of; ~ **d'identité** passport photograph.

photocopie /fɔtɔkɔpi/ nf photocopy. **photocopier** 45 vt photocopy.

photographe /fɔtɔgʀaf/ nmf photographer. **photographie** nf photograph; (art) photography. **photographier** 45 vt take a photo of.

phrase /fʀɑz/ nf sentence.

physicien, ~ne /fizisjɛ̃, -ɛn/ nm, f physicist.

physique /fizik/ adj physical. ● nm physique; **au ~** physically. ● nf physics (+ sg.)

piano /pjano/ nm piano.

pianoter /pjanɔte/ 1 vi tinkle; ~ **sur** (ordinateur) tap at.

PIB abrév m (**produit intérieur brut**) GDP.

pic /pik/ nm (outil) pickaxe; (sommet) peak; (oiseau) woodpecker; **à ~** (fa-

laise) sheer; (*couler*) straight to the bottom; **tomber à ~** 🎧 come just at the right time.

pichet /piʃɛ/ *nm* jug.

picorer /pikɔʀe/ **1** *vt/i* peck.

picotement /pikɔtmɑ̃/ *nm* tingling. **picoter** **1** *vt* sting; (*yeux*) sting.

pie /pi/ *nf* magpie.

pièce /pjɛs/ *nf* (d'habitation) room; (de monnaie) coin; (Théât) play; (pour raccommoder) patch; (écrit) document; (morceau) piece; (**~ de théâtre**) play; **dix euros (la ~)** ten euros each; **~ détachée** part; **~ d'identité** identity paper; **~s jointes** enclosures; (courrier électronique) attachments; **~s justificatives** written proof; **~ montée** tiered cake; **~ de rechange** spare part; **un deux- ~s** a tworoom flat.

pied /pje/ *nm* foot; (de meuble) leg; (de lampe) base; (de verre) stem; (d'appareil photo) stand; **être ~s nus** be barefoot; **à ~** on foot; **au ~ de la lettre** literally; **avoir ~** be able to touch the bottom; **jouer au tennis comme un ~** 🎧 be hopeless at tennis; **mettre sur ~** set up; **sur un ~ d'égalité** on an equal footing; **mettre les ~s dans le plat** 🎧 put one's foot in it; **c'est le ~** 🎧 it's great. **pied-bot** (*pl* **piedsbots**) *nm* club-foot.

piédestal /pjedɛstal/ *nm* pedestal.

piège /pjɛʒ/ *nm* trap.

piéger /pjeʒe/ **14** **40** *vt* trap; **lettre/ voiture piégée** letter/car bomb.

piercing /piʀsiŋ/ *nm* body piercing.

pierre /pjɛʀ/ *nf* stone; **~ précieuse** precious stone; **~ tombale** tombstone.

piétiner /pjetine/ **1** *vi* (avancer lentement) shuffle along; (fig) make no headway; **~ d'impatience** hop up and down with impatience. ● *vt* trample (on).

piéton /pjetɔ̃/ *nm* pedestrian.

pieu (*pl* **~x**) /pjø/ *nm* post, stake.

pieuvre /pjœvʀ/ *nf* octopus.

pieux, -ieuse /pjø, -z/ *adj* pious.

pigeon /piʒɔ̃/ *nm* pigeon.

piger /piʒe/ **40** *vt/i* 🎧 understand, get (it).

pile /pil/ *nf* (tas) pile; (Électr) battery; **~ ou face?** heads or tails? ● *adv* (s'ar-

rêter 🎧) dead; **à dix heures ~** 🎧 at ten on the dot.

pilier /pilje/ *nm* pillar.

pillage /pijaʒ/ *nm* looting. **pillard, ~e** *nm, f* looter. **piller** **1** *vt* loot.

pilote /pilɔt/ *nm* (Aviat, Naut) pilot; (Auto) driver. ● *adj* pilot. **piloter** **1** *vt* (Aviat, Naut) pilot; (Auto) drive.

pilule /pilyl/ *nf* pill; **la ~** the pill.

piment /pimɑ̃/ *nm* hot pepper; (fig) spice. **pimenté, ~e** *adj* spicy.

pin /pɛ̃/ *nm* pine.

pinard /pinaʀ/ *nm* 🎧 plonk 🎧, cheap wine.

pince /pɛ̃s/ *nf* (outil) pliers (+ *pl*); (levier) crowbar; (de crabe) pincer; (à sucre) tongs (+ *pl*); **~ à épiler** tweezers (+ *pl*); **~ à linge** clothes peg.

pinceau (*pl* **~x**) /pɛ̃so/ *nm* paintbrush.

pincée /pɛ̃se/ *nf* pinch (de of).

pincer /pɛ̃se/ **10** *vt* pinch; (attraper 🎧) catch. □ **se ~** *vpr* catch oneself; **se ~ le doigt** catch one's finger.

pince-sans-rire /pɛ̃sɑ̃ʀiʀ/ *nmf inv* **c'est un ~** he has a deadpan sense of humour.

pingouin /pɛ̃gwɛ̃/ *nm* penguin.

pingre /pɛ̃gʀ/ *adj* 🎧 stingy.

pintade /pɛ̃tad/ *nf* guinea fowl.

piocher /pjɔʃe/ **1** *vt/i* dig; (étudier 🎧) study hard, slog away (at).

pion /pjɔ̃/ *nm* (de jeu) counter; (aux échecs) pawn; (Scol 🎧) supervisor.

pipe /pip/ *nf* pipe; **fumer la ~** smoke a pipe.

piquant, ~e /pikɑ̃, -t/ *adj* (barbe) prickly; (goût) pungent; (remarque) cutting. ● *nm* prickle.

pique /pik/ *nm* (aux cartes) spades.

pique-nique (*pl* **~s**) /piknik/ *nm* picnic.

piquer /pike/ **1** *vt* (épine) prick; (épice) burn, sting; (abeille, ortie) sting; (serpent, moustique) bite; (enfoncer) stick; (coudre) (machine-) stitch; (curiosité) excite; (voler 🎧) pinch. ● *vi* (avion) dive; (goût) be hot. □ **se ~** *vpr* prick oneself.

piquet /pikɛ/ *nm* stake; (de tente) peg; (de parasol) pole; **~ de grève** (strike) picket.

piqûre /pikyʀ/ *nf* prick; (d'abeille) sting; (de serpent) bite; (point) stitch;

p

(Méd) injection, jab; **faire une ~ à qn** give sb an injection.

pirate /piʀat/ nm pirate; **~ informatique** computer hacker; **~ de l'air** hijacker.

pire /piʀ/ adj worse (**que** than); **les ~s mensonges** the most wicked lies. ● nm **le ~** the worst; **au ~** at worst.

pis /pi/ nm (de vache) udder. ● adj inv & adv worse; **aller de mal en ~** go from bad to worse.

piscine /pisin/ nf swimming pool; **~ couverte** indoor swimming-pool.

pissenlit /pisɑ̃li/ nm dandelion.

pistache /pistaʃ/ nf pistachio.

piste /pist/ nf track; (de personne, d'animal) track, trail; (Aviat) runway; (de cirque) ring; (de ski) slope; (de danse) floor; (Sport) racetrack; **~ cyclable** cycle lane.

pistolet /pistɔlɛ/ nm gun, pistol; (de peintre) spray-gun.

piteux, -euse /pitø, -z/ adj pitiful.

pitié /pitje/ nf pity; **il me fait ~** I feel sorry for him.

piton /pitɔ̃/ nm (à crochet) hook; (sommet pointu) peak.

pitoyable /pitwajabl/ adj pitiful.

pitre /pitʀ/ nm clown; **faire le ~** clown around.

pittoresque /pitɔʀɛsk/ adj picturesque.

pivot /pivo/ nm pivot. **pivoter** 🔟 vi revolve; (personne) swing round.

placard /plakaʀ/ nm cupboard; (affiche) poster. **placarder** 🔟 vt (affiche) post up; (mur) cover with posters.

place /plas/ nf place; (espace libre) room, space; (siège) seat, place; (prix d'un trajet) fare; (esplanade) square; (emploi) position; (de parking) space; **à la ~ de** instead of; **en ~, à sa ~** in its place; **faire ~ à** give way to; **sur ~** on the spot; **remettre qn à sa ~** put sb in his place; **ça prend de la ~** it takes up a lot of room; **se mettre à la ~ de qn** put oneself in sb's shoes ou place.

placement /plasmɑ̃/ nm (d'argent) investment.

placer /plase/ 🔟 vt place; (invité, spectateur) seat; (argent) invest. □ **se ~** vpr (personne) take up a position.

plafond /plafɔ̃/ nm ceiling.

plage /plaʒ/ nf beach; **~ horaire** time slot.

plagiat /plaʒja/ nm plagiarism.

plaider /plede/ 🔟 vt/i plead. **plaidoirie** nf (défense) speech. **plaidoyer** nm plea.

plaie /plɛ/ nf wound; (personne 🔟) nuisance.

plaignant, ~e /plɛɲɑ̃, -t/ nm, f plaintiff.

plaindre /plɛ̃dʀ/ 🗠 vt pity. □ **se ~** vpr complain (**de** about); **se ~ de** (souffrir de) complain of.

plaine /plɛn/ nf plain.

plainte /plɛ̃t/ nf complaint; (gémissement) groan. **plaintif, -ive** adj plaintive.

plaire /plɛʀ/ 🗠 vi **~ à** please; **ça lui plaît** he likes it; **elle lui plaît** he likes her; **ça me plaît de faire** I like ou enjoy doing; **s'il vous plaît** please. □ **se ~** vpr **il se plaît ici** he likes it here.

plaisance /plɛzɑ̃s/ nf **la (navigation de) ~** boating.

plaisant, ~e /plɛzɑ̃, -t/ adj pleasant; (drôle) amusing.

plaisanter /plɛzɑ̃te/ 🔟 vi joke. **plaisanterie** nf joke. **plaisantin** nm joker.

plaisir /plɛziʀ/ nm pleasure; **faire ~ à** please; **pour le ~** for fun ou pleasure.

plan /plɑ̃/ nm plan; (de ville) map; (de livre) outline; **~ d'eau** artificial lake; **~ social** planned redundancy programme; **premier ~** foreground.

planche /plɑ̃ʃ/ nf board, plank; (gravure) plate; **~ à repasser** ironing-board; **~ à voile** windsurfing board; (Sport) windsurfing.

plancher /plɑ̃ʃe/ nm floor.

planer /plane/ 🔟 vi glide; **~ sur** (mystère, danger) hang over.

planète /planɛt/ nf planet.

planeur /planœʀ/ nm glider.

planifier /planifje/ 🗠 vt plan.

plant /plɑ̃/ nm seedling; (de légumes) patch.

plante /plɑ̃t/ nf plant; **~ d'appartement** houseplant; **~ des pieds** sole (of the foot).

planter /plɑ̃te/ 🔟 vt (plante) plant; (enfoncer) drive in; (tente) put up; **res-**

ter **planté** 🔲 stand still.

plaque /plak/ *nf* plate; (de marbre)
slab; (insigne) badge; ~ **chauffante**
hotplate; ~ **commémorative** plaque;
~ **minéralogique** numberplate; ~ **de
verglas** patch of ice.

plaquer /plake/ 🔢 *vt* (bois) veneer;
(aplatir) flatten; (rugby) tackle; (abandonner 🔲) ditch 🔲; **tout** ~ chuck
it all.

plastique /plastik/ *adj & nm* plastic; **en**
~ plastic.

plastiquer /plastike/ 🔢 *vt* blow up.

plat, ~e /pla, -t/ *adj* flat. ● *nm* (Culin)
dish; (partie de repas) course; (de la
main) flat. ● **à plat** *adv* (poser) flat;
(batterie, pneu) flat; **à ~ ventre** flat on
one's face.

platane /platan/ *nm* plane tree.

plateau (*pl* ~**x**) /plato/ *nm* tray; (de
cinéma) set; (de balance) pan; (Géog)
plateau; ~ **de fromages** cheeseboard;
~ **de fruits de mer** seafood platter.
plate-bande (*pl* **plates-bandes**) *nf*
flower bed.

platine /platin/ *nm* platinum. ● *nf*
(tourne-disque) turntable; ~ **laser**
compact disc player.

plâtre /plɑtʀ/ *nm* plaster; (Méd) (plaster) cast.

plein, ~e /plɛ̃, -ɛn/ *adj* full (**de** of);
(total) complete. ● *nm* **faire le** ~
(d'essence) fill up (the tank); **à** ~
fully; **à ~ temps** full-time; **en ~ air**
in the open air; **en ~ milieu/ visage**
right in the middle/the face; **en ~e
nuit** in the middle of the night. ● *adv*
avoir des idées ~ la tête be full of
ideas. **pleinement** *adv* fully.

pleurer /plœʀe/ 🔢 *vi* cry, weep (**sur**
over); (yeux) water. ● *vt* mourn.

pleurnicher /plœʀniʃe/ 🔢 *vi* 🔲
snivel.

pleurs /plœʀ/ *nmpl* tears; **en ~** in
tears.

pleuvoir /pløvwaʀ/ 🔢 *vi* rain; (fig)
rain *ou* shower down; **il pleut** it is
raining; **il pleut à verse** *ou* **des
cordes** it is pouring.

pli /pli/ *nm* fold; (de jupe) pleat; (de
pantalon) crease; (lettre) letter; (habitude) habit; (faux ~) crease.

pliant, ~e /plijã, -t/ *adj* folding. ● *nm*
folding stool, camp-stool.

plier /plije/ 🔢 *vt* fold; (courber) bend;
(soumettre) submit (**à** to). ● *vi* bend.
□ **se ~** *vpr* fold; **se ~ à** submit to.

plinthe /plɛ̃t/ *nf* skirting-board.

plissé, ~e /plise/ *adj* (jupe) pleated.

plisser /plise/ 🔢 *vt* crease; (yeux)
screw up.

plomb /plɔ̃/ *nm* lead; (fusible) fuse; ~**s**
(de chasse) lead shot; **de** *ou* **en** ~
lead. **plombage** *nm* filling.

plomberie /plɔ̃bʀi/ *nf* plumbing.
plombier *nm* plumber.

plongée /plɔ̃ʒe/ *nf* diving; **en ~** (sous-
marin) submerged.

plongeoir /plɔ̃ʒwaʀ/ *nm* diving board.

plonger /plɔ̃ʒe/ 🔢 *vi* dive; (route)
plunge. ● *vt* plunge. □ **se ~** *vpr*
plunge into; **se ~ dans** (fig) (lecture)
bury oneself in. **plongeur, -euse** *nm, f*
diver; (de restaurant) dishwasher.

plu /ply/ **➙PLAIRE** 🔢, **PLEUVOIR** 🔢.

pluie /plɥi/ *nf* rain; (averse) shower; ~
battante/diluvienne driving/torren-
tial rain.

plume /plym/ *nf* feather; (pointe) nib.

plumeau (*pl* ~**x**) /plymo/ *nm* feather
duster.

plumier /plymje/ *nm* pencil box.

plupart: la ~ /laplypaʀ/ *loc* **la ~ des**
(gens, cas) most; **la ~ du temps** most
of the time; **pour la ~** for the
most part.

pluriel, ~le /plyʀjɛl/ *adj & nm* plural.

---

plus /ply, plys, plyz/

● *adverbe de comparaison*

····➤ more (**que** than); ~ **âgé/ tard**
older/later; ~ **beau** more beautiful; ~ **j'y pense...** the more I
think about it...; **deux fois** ~
twice as much; **deux fois ~ cher**
twice as expensive.

····➤ **le ~** the most; **le ~ grand**
the biggest; (de deux) the bigger.

····➤ ~ **de** (pain) more; (dix jours)
more than; **il est ~ de 8 heures**
it is after 8 o'clock.

····➤ **de ~** more (**que** than); (en
outre) moreover; **les enfants de
~ de 10 ans** children over 10
years old; **de ~ en ~** more
and more.

····➤ **en ~** on top of that; **c'est en**

p

~ it's extra; **en ~ de** in addition to.

····▶ **~ ou moins** more or less.

····▶ **au ~ tard** at the latest.

● *adverbe de négation*

····▶ **ne ~** (*temps*) no longer, not any more; **je n'y vais ~** I don't go there any longer *ou* any more.

····▶ **ne ~ de** (*quantité*) no more; **il n'y a ~ de pain** there is no more bread.

····▶ **~ que deux jours!** only two days left!

● *préposition & nom masculin*

····▶ (maths) plus.

plusieurs /plyzjœʀ/ *adj & pron* several.

plus-value (*pl* ~**s**) /plyvaly/ *nf* (bénéfice) profit.

plutôt /plyto/ *adv* rather (**que** than).

pluvieux, -ieuse /plyvjø, -z/ *adj* rainy.

PME *abrév f* (**petites et moyennes entreprises**) SME.

PNB *abrév m* (**produit national brut**) GNP.

pneu (*pl* ~**s**) /pnø/ *nm* tyre. **pneumatique** *adj* inflatable.

pneumonie /pnømɔni/ *nf* pneumonia; **~ atypique** severe acute respiratory syndrome.

poche /pɔʃ/ *nf* pocket; (sac) bag; ~**s** (sous les yeux) bags.

pocher /pɔʃe/ **1** *vt* (œuf) poach.

pochette /pɔʃɛt/ *nf* (de documents) folder; (sac) bag, pouch; (d'allumettes) book; (de disque) sleeve; (mouchoir) pocket handkerchief.

poêle /pwal/ *nf* (~ **à frire**) frying-pan. ● *nm* stove.

poème /pɔɛm/ *nm* poem. **poésie** *nf* poetry; (poème) poem. **poète** *nm* poet. **poétique** *adj* poetic.

poids /pwa/ *nm* weight; **~ coq/lourd/ plume** bantamweight/heavyweight/featherweight; **~ lourd** (camion) lorry, juggernaut; (US) truck.

poignard /pwaɲaʀ/ *nm* dagger. **poignarder** **1** *vt* stab.

poigne /pwaɲ/ *nf* **avoir de la ~** have a strong grip.

poignée /pwaɲe/ *nf* (de porte) handle; (quantité) handful; **~ de main** handshake.

poignet /pwaɲɛ/ *nm* wrist; (de chemise) cuff.

poil /pwal/ *nm* hair; (pelage) fur; (de brosse) bristle; ~**s** (de tapis) pile; **à ~** 🔄 naked; **à gratter** itching powder. **poilu, ~e** *adj* hairy.

poinçon /pwɛ̃sɔ̃/ *nm* awl; (marque) hallmark. **poinçonner** **1** *vt* (billet) punch.

poing /pwɛ̃/ *nm* fist.

point /pwɛ̃/ *nm* (endroit, Sport) point; (marque visible) spot, dot; (de couture) stitch; (pour évaluer) mark; **enlever un ~ par faute** take a mark off for each mistake; **à ~** (Culin) medium; (arriver) at the right time; **faire le ~** take stock; **mettre au ~** (*photo*) focus; (technique) develop; **mettre les choses au ~** get things clear; **Camille n'est pas encore au ~ pour ses examens** Camille is not ready for her exams; **sur le ~ de** about to; **au ~ que** to the extent that; (**~ final**) full stop, period; **deux ~s** colon; **~ d'interrogation/d'exclamation** question/exclamation mark; **~s de suspension** suspension points; **~ virgule** semicolon; **~ culminant** peak; **~ du jour** daybreak; **~ mort** (Auto) neutral; **~ de repère** landmark; **~ de suture** (Méd) stitch; **~ de vente** point of sale; **~ de vue** point of view. ● *adv* **(ne) ~** not.

pointe /pwɛ̃t/ *nf* point, tip; (clou) tack; (de grille) spike; (fig) touch (**de** of); **de ~** (industrie) high-tech; **en ~** pointed; **heure de ~** peak hour; **sur la ~ des pieds** on tiptoe.

pointer /pwɛ̃te/ **1** *vt* (cocher) tick off; (diriger) point, aim. ● *vi* (employé) (en arrivant) clock in; (en sortant) clock out. □ **se ~** *vpr* 🔄 turn up.

pointillé /pwɛ̃tije/ *nm* dotted line.

pointilleux, -euse /pwɛ̃tijø, -z/ *adj* fastidious, particular.

pointu, ~e /pwɛ̃ty/ *adj* pointed; (aiguisé) sharp.

pointure /pwɛ̃tyʀ/ *nf* size.

poire /pwaʀ/ *nf* pear.

poireau (*pl* ~**x**) /pwaʀo/ *nm* leek.

poirier /pwaʀje/ *nm* pear tree.

pois /pwa/ *nm* pea; (motif) dot; **robe à ~** polka dot dress.

poison /pwazɔ̃/ *nm* poison.

poisseux, -euse /pwasø, -z/ adj sticky.

poisson /pwasɔ̃/ nm fish; ~ **rouge** goldfish; ~ **d'avril** April fool; **les P~s** Pisces. **poissonnerie** nf fish shop. **poissonnier, -ière** nm, f fishmonger.

poitrine /pwatʀin/ nf chest; (seins) bosom.

poivre /pwavʀ/ nm pepper. **poivré, ~e** adj peppery. **poivrière** nf pepper-pot.

poivron /pwavʀɔ̃/ nm sweet pepper.

polaire /pɔlɛʀ/ adj polar. ● nf (veste) fleece.

pôle /pol/ nm pole.

polémique /pɔlemik/ nf debate. ● adj controversial.

poli, ~e /pɔli/ adj (personne) polite.

police /pɔlis/ nf (force) police (+ pl); (discipline) (law and) order; (d'assurance) policy.

policier, -ière /pɔlisje, -jɛʀ/ adj police; (roman) detective. ● nm policeman.

polir /pɔliʀ/ ② vt polish.

politesse /pɔlitɛs/ nf politeness; (parole) polite remark.

politicien, ~ne /pɔlitisjɛ̃, -ɛn/ nm, f (péj) politician.

politique /pɔlitik/ adj political; **homme ~** politician. ● nf politics; (ligne de conduite) policy.

pollen /pɔlɛn/ nm pollen.

polluant, ~e /pɔlɥɑ̃, -t/ adj polluting. ● nm pollutant.

polluer /pɔlɥe/ ① vt pollute. **pollution** nf pollution.

polo /pɔlo/ nm (Sport) polo; (vêtement) polo shirt.

Pologne /pɔlɔɲ/ nf Poland.

polonais, ~e /pɔlɔnɛ, -z/ adj Polish. ● nm (Ling) Polish. **P~, ~e** nm, f Pole.

poltron, ~ne /pɔltʀɔ̃, -ɔn/ adj cowardly. ● nm, f coward.

polygame /pɔligam/ nmf polygamist.

polyvalent, ~e /pɔlivalɑ̃, -t/ adj varied; (personne) versatile.

pommade /pɔmad/ nf ointment.

pomme /pɔm/ nf apple; (d'arrosoir) rose; ~ **d'Adam** Adam's apple; ~ **de pin** pine cone; ~ **de terre** potato; ~s **frites** chips; (US) French fries; **tomber dans les ~s** 🄸 pass out.

pommette /pɔmɛt/ nf cheekbone.

pommier /pɔmje/ nm apple tree.

pompe /pɔ̃p/ nf pump; (splendeur) pomp; ~ **à incendie** fire engine; ~s **funèbres** undertaker's (+ sg).

pomper /pɔ̃pe/ ① vt pump; (copier 🄸) copy, crib; ~ **l'air à qn** 🄸 get on sb's nerves.

pompier /pɔ̃pje/ nm fireman.

pomponner (se) /(sə)pɔ̃pɔne/ ① vpr get dolled up.

poncer /pɔ̃se/ 🄽 vt sand.

ponctuation /pɔ̃ktɥasjɔ̃/ nf punctuation.

ponctuel, ~le /pɔ̃ktɥɛl/ adj punctual.

pondre /pɔ̃dʀ/ 🄼 vt/i lay.

poney /pɔnɛ/ nm pony.

pont /pɔ̃/ nm bridge; (de navire) deck; (de graissage) ramp; **faire le ~** get an extended weekend; ~ **aérien** airlift. **pont-levis** (pl **ponts-levis**) nm drawbridge.

populaire /pɔpylɛʀ/ adj popular; (expression) colloquial; (quartier, origine) working-class. **popularité** nf popularity.

population /pɔpylasjɔ̃/ nf population.

porc /pɔʀ/ nm pig; (viande) pork.

porcelaine /pɔʀsəlɛn/ nf china, porcelain.

porc-épic (pl **porcs-épics**) /pɔʀkepik/ nm porcupine.

porcherie /pɔʀʃəʀi/ nf pigsty.

pornographie /pɔʀnɔgʀafi/ nf pornography.

port /pɔʀ/ nm port, harbour; **à bon ~** safely; ~ **maritime** seaport; (transport) carriage; (d'armes) carrying; (de barbe) wearing.

portable /pɔʀtabl/ nm (Ordinat) laptop (computer); (telephone) mobile (phone).

portail /pɔʀtaj/ nm gate.

portatif, -ive /pɔʀtatif, -v/ adj portable.

porte /pɔʀt/ nf door; (passage) doorway; (de jardin, d'embarquement) gate; **mettre à la ~** throw out; ~ **d'entrée** front door.

porté, ~e /pɔʀte/ adj ~ **à** inclined to; ~ **sur** keen on.

porte-avions /pɔʀtavjɔ̃/ nm inv aircraft carrier.

porte-bagages /pɔʀtbagaʒ/ nm inv (de vélo) carrier.

p

porte-bonheur /pɔʀtbɔnœʀ/ nm inv lucky charm.

porte-clefs /pɔʀtəkle/ nm inv key ring.

porte-documents /pɔʀtdɔkymã/ nm inv briefcase.

portée /pɔʀte/ nf (d'une arme) range; (de voûte) span; (d'animaux) litter; (impact) significance; (Mus) stave; **à ~ de (la) main** within (arm's) reach; **hors de ~ (de)** out of reach (of); **à la ~ de qn** at sb's level.

porte-fenêtre (pl **portes-fenêtres**) /pɔʀtfənɛtʀ/ nf French window.

portefeuille /pɔʀtəfœj/ nm wallet; (de ministre) portfolio.

porte-jarretelles /pɔʀtʒaʀtɛl/ nm inv suspender belt.

portemanteau (pl **~x**) /pɔʀtmãto/ nm coat ou hat stand.

porte-monnaie /pɔʀtmɔnɛ/ nm inv purse.

porte-parole /pɔʀtpaʀɔl/ nm inv spokesperson.

porter /pɔʀte/ **1** vt carry; (vêtement, bague) wear; (fruits, responsabilité, nom) bear; (coup) strike; (amener) bring; (inscrire) enter. ● vi (bruit) carry; (coup) hit home; **~ sur** rest on; (concerner) be about. □ **se ~** vpr **bien se ~** be ou feel well; **se ~ candidat** stand as a candidate.

porteur, -euse /pɔʀtœʀ, -øz/ nm, f (de nouvelles) bearer; (Méd) carrier. ● nm (Rail) porter.

portier /pɔʀtje/ nm doorman.

portière /pɔʀtjɛʀ/ nf door.

porto /pɔʀto/ nm port (wine).

portrait /pɔʀtʀɛ/ nm portrait. **portrait-robot** (pl **portraits-robots**) nm identikit®, photofit®.

portuaire /pɔʀtɥɛʀ/ adj port.

portugais, ~e /pɔʀtygɛ, -z/ adj Portuguese. ● nm (Ling) Portuguese. **P~, ~e** nm, f Portuguese.

Portugal /pɔʀtygal/ nm Portugal.

pose /poz/ nf installation; (attitude) pose; (Photo) exposure.

posé, ~e /poze/ adj calm, serious.

poser /poze/ **1** vt put (down); (installer) install, put in; (fondations) lay; (question) ask; (problème) pose; **~ sa candidature** apply (à for). ● vi (modèle) pose. □ **se ~** vpr (avion, oiseau) land; (regard) fall; (se présenter) arise.

positif, -ive /pozitif, -v/ adj positive.

position /pozisjõ/ nf position; **prendre ~** take a stand.

posologie /pozɔlɔʒi/ nf dosage.

posséder /pɔsede/ **14** vt (propriété) own, possess; (diplôme) have.

possessif, -ive /pɔsesif, -v/ adj possessive.

possession /pɔsesjõ/ nf possession; **prendre ~ de** take possession of.

possibilité /pɔsibilite/ nf possibility.

possible /pɔsibl/ adj possible; **dès que ~** as soon as possible; **le plus tard ~** as late as possible. ● nm **le ~** what is possible; **faire son ~** do one's utmost.

postal, ~e (mpl **-aux**) /pɔstal, -o/ adj postal.

poste /pɔst/ nf (service) post; (bureau) post office; **~ aérienne** airmail; **mettre à la ~** post; **~ restante** poste restante. ● nm (lieu, emploi) post; (de radio, télévision) set; (téléphone) extension (number); **~ d'essence** petrol station; **~ d'incendie** fire point; **~ de pilotage** cockpit; **~ de police** police station; **~ de secours** first-aid post.

poster¹ /pɔste/ **1** vt (lettre, personne) post.

poster² /pɔstɛʀ/ nm poster.

postérieur, ~e /pɔsteʀjœʀ/ adj later; (partie) back; **~ à** after. ● nm **1** posterior.

posthume /pɔstym/ adj posthumous.

postiche /pɔstiʃ/ adj false.

postier, -ière /pɔstje, -jɛʀ/ nm, f postal worker.

post-scriptum /pɔstskʀiptɔm/ nm inv postscript.

postuler /pɔstyle/ **1** vt/i apply (à for); (principe) postulate.

pot /po/ nm pot; (en plastique) carton; (en verre) jar; (chance **1**) luck; (boisson **1**) drink; **~ catalytique** catalytic converter; **~ d'échappement** exhaust pipe.

potable /pɔtabl/ adj eau **~** drinking water.

potage /pɔtaʒ/ nm soup.

potager, -ère /pɔtaʒe, -ɛʀ/ adj vegetable. ● nm vegetable garden.

pot-au-feu /pɔtofø/ nm inv (plat) stew.

pot-de-vin (pl **pots-de-vin**) /podvɛ̃/ nm bribe.

poteau (pl ~x) /pɔto/ nm post; (télé-graphique) pole; ~ **indicateur** signpost.

potelé, ~e /pɔtle/ adj plump.

potentiel, ~le /pɔtɑ̃sjɛl/ adj & nm potential.

poterie /pɔtʀi/ nf pottery; (objet) piece of pottery. **potier** nm potter.

potins /pɔtɛ̃/ nmpl gossip (+ sg).

potiron /pɔtiʀɔ̃/ nm pumpkin.

pou (pl ~x) /pu/ nm louse.

poubelle /pubɛl/ nf dustbin.

pouce /pus/ nm thumb; (de pied) big toe; (mesure) inch.

poudre /pudʀ/ nf powder; (~ à canon) gunpowder; **en** ~ (lait) powdered; (chocolat) drinking.

poudrier /pudʀije/ nm (powder) compact.

pouf /puf/ nm pouffe.

poulailler /pulaje/ nm henhouse.

poulain /pulɛ̃/ nm foal; (protégé) protégé.

poule /pul/ nf hen; (Culin) fowl; (femme 🖽) tart.

poulet /pulɛ/ nm chicken.

pouliche /puliʃ/ nf filly.

poulie /puli/ nf pulley.

pouls /pu/ nm pulse.

poumon /pumɔ̃/ nm lung.

poupe /pup/ nf stern.

poupée /pupe/ nf doll.

pour /puʀ/ prép for; (envers) to; (à la place de) on behalf of; (comme) as; ~ **cela** for that reason; ~ **cent** per cent; ~ **de bon** for good; ~ **faire** (in order to do; ~ **que** so that; ~ **moi** (à mon avis) as for me; **trop poli** ~ too polite to; ~ **ce qui est de** as for; **être** ~ be in favour. ● nm inv **le** ~ **et le contre** the pros and cons.

pourboire /puʀbwaʀ/ nm tip.

pourcentage /puʀsɑ̃taʒ/ nm percentage.

pourparlers /puʀpaʀle/ nmpl talks.

pourpre /puʀpʀ/ adj & nm crimson; (violet) purple.

pourquoi /puʀkwa/ conj & adv why. ● nm inv **le** ~ **et le comment** the why and the wherefore.

pourra, pourrait /puʀa, puʀɛ/ ➡POUVOIR 49.

pourri, ~e /puʀi/ adj rotten. **pourrir** 2 vt/i rot. **pourriture** nf rot.

poursuite /puʀsɥit/ nf pursuit (de of); ~**s** (Jur) legal action (+ sg).

poursuivre /puʀsɥivʀ/ 57 vt pursue; (continuer) continue (with); ~ **en justice)** take to court; (droit civil) sue. ● vi continue. □ **se** ~ vpr continue.

pourtant /puʀtɑ̃/ adv yet.

pourvoir /puʀvwaʀ/ 63 vi ~ **à** provide for; **pourvu de** supplied with.

pourvu que /puʀvyk(ə)/ conj (condition) provided (that); (souhait) let us hope (that).

pousse /pus/ nf growth; (bourgeon) shoot.

poussé, ~e /puse/ adj (études) advanced; (enquête) thorough.

poussée /puse/ nf pressure; (coup) push; (de prix) upsurge; (Méd) attack.

pousser /puse/ 1 vt push; (cri) let out; (soupir) heave; (continuer) continue; (exhorter) urge (à to); (forcer) drive (à to). ● vi push; (grandir) grow; **faire** ~ (cheveux) let grow; (plante) grow. □ **se** ~ vpr move over ou up; **pousse-toi!** move over!

poussette /pusɛt/ nf pushchair.

poussière /pusjɛʀ/ nf dust. **poussiéreux, -euse** adj dusty.

poussin /pusɛ̃/ nm chick.

poutre /putʀ/ nf beam; (en métal) girder.

pouvoir /puvwaʀ/ 49 v aux (possibilité) can, be able; (permission, éventualité) may, can; **il peut/pouvait/ pourrait venir** he can/could/might come; **je n'ai pas pu** I couldn't; **j'ai pu faire** (réussi à) I managed to do; **je n'en peux plus** I am exhausted; **il se peut que** it may be that. ● nm power; (gouvernement) government; **au** ~ in power; ~**s publics** authorities.

prairie /pʀeʀi/ nf meadow.

praticien, ~ne /pʀatisjɛ̃, -ɛn/ nm, f practitioner.

pratiquant, ~e /pʀatikɑ̃, -t/ adj practising. ● nm, f churchgoer.

pratique /pʀatik/ adj practical. ● nf practice; (expérience) experience; **la** ~ **du golf/du cheval** golfing/riding. **pratiquement** adv (en pratique) in practice; (presque) practically.

p

pratiquer /pʀatike/ **1** vt/i practise; (Sport) play; (faire) make.

pré /pʀe/ nm meadow.

pré-affranchi, ~e /pʀeafʀɑ̃ʃi/ adj postage-paid.

préalable /pʀealabl/ adj preliminary, prior. ● nm precondition; **au ~** first.

préambule /pʀeɑ̃byl/ nm preamble.

préavis /pʀeavi/ nm notice.

précaire /pʀekɛʀ/ adj precarious. **précarité** nf (d'emploi) insecurity.

précaution /pʀekosjɔ̃/ nf (mesure) precaution; (prudence) caution.

précédent, ~e /pʀesedɑ̃, -t/ adj previous. ● nm precedent.

précéder /pʀesede/ **14** vt/i precede.

précepteur, -trice /pʀesɛptœʀ, -tʀis/ nm, f (private) tutor.

prêcher /pʀeʃe/ **1** vt/i preach.

précieux, -ieuse /pʀesjø, -z/ adj precious.

précipitamment /pʀesipitamɑ̃/ adv hastily. **précipitation** nf haste.

précipiter /pʀesipite/ **1** vt throw, precipitate; (hâter) hasten. □ **se ~** vpr (se dépêcher) rush (**sur** at, on to); (se jeter) throw oneself; (s'accélérer) speed up.

précis, ~e /pʀesi, -z/ adj precise, specific; (mécanisme) accurate; **dix heures ~es** ten o'clock sharp. ● nm summary.

préciser /pʀesize/ **1** vt specify; **précisez votre pensée** could you be more specific. □ **se ~** vpr become clear(er). **précision** nf precision; (détail) detail.

précoce /pʀekos/ adj (enfant) precocious.

préconiser /pʀekonize/ **1** vt advocate.

précurseur /pʀekyʀsœʀ/ nm forerunner.

prédicateur /pʀedikatœʀ/ nm preacher.

prédilection /pʀedilɛksjɔ̃/ nf preference.

prédire /pʀediʀ/ **37** vt predict.

prédominer /pʀedomine/ **1** vi predominate.

préface /pʀefas/ nf preface.

préfecture /pʀefɛktyʀ/ nf prefecture; **~ de police** police headquarters.

préféré, ~e /pʀefeʀe/ adj & nm, f favourite.

préférence /pʀefeʀɑ̃s/ nf preference; **de ~** preferably.

préférentiel, ~le /pʀefeʀɑ̃sjɛl/ adj preferential.

préférer /pʀefeʀe/ **14** vt prefer (**à** to); **~ faire** prefer to do; **je ne préfère pas** I'd rather not; **j'aurais préféré ne pas savoir** I wish I hadn't found out.

préfet /pʀefɛ/ nm prefect; **~ de police** prefect ou chief of police.

préfixe /pʀefiks/ nm prefix.

préhistorique /pʀeistoʀik/ adj prehistoric.

préjudice /pʀeʒydis/ nm harm, prejudice; **porter ~ à** harm.

préjugé /pʀeʒyʒe/ nm prejudice; **être plein de ~s** be very prejudiced.

prélasser (se) /(sə)pʀelɑse/ **1** vpr loll (about).

prélèvement /pʀelɛvmɑ̃/ nm deduction; (de sang) sample. **prélever** **6** vt deduct (**sur** from); (sang) take.

préliminaire /pʀeliminɛʀ/ adj & nm preliminary; **~s** (sexuels) foreplay.

prématuré, ~e /pʀematyʀe/ adj premature. ● nm premature baby.

premier, -ière /pʀəmje, -jɛʀ/ adj first; (rang) front, first; (enfance) early; (nécessité, souci) prime; (qualité) top, prime; **de ~ ordre** first-rate; **~ ministre** Prime Minister. ● nm, f first (one). ● nm (date) first; (étage) first floor; **en ~** first. **première** nf (Rail) first class; (exploit jamais vu) first; (cinéma, Théât) première; (Aut) (vitesse) first (gear). **premièrement** adv firstly.

prémunir /pʀemyniʀ/ **2** vt protect (**contre** against).

prenant, ~e /pʀənɑ̃, -t/ adj (activité) engrossing; (enfant) demanding.

prénatal, ~e (mpl ~s) /pʀenatal/ adj antenatal.

prendre /pʀɑ̃dʀ/ **50** vt take; (attraper) catch, get; (acheter) get; (repas) have; (engager, adopter) take on; (poids) put on; (chercher) pick up; **qu'est-ce qui te prend?** what's the matter with you? ● vi (feu) catch; (vaccin) take. □ **se ~** vpr **se ~ pour** think one is; **s'en ~ à** attack; (rendre responsable) blame; **s'y ~** set about (it).

preneur, -euse /pʀənœʀ, -øz/ *nm, f* buyer; **être ~** be willing to buy; **trouver ~** find a buyer.

prénom /pʀenɔ̃/ *nm* first name.

prénommer /pʀenɔme/ **1** *vt* call. □ **se ~** *vpr* be called.

préoccupation /pʀeɔkypasjɔ̃/ *nf* (souci) worry; (idée fixe) preoccupation.

préoccuper /pʀeɔkype/ **1** *vt* worry; (absorber) preoccupy. □ **se ~ de** *vpr* think about.

préparation /pʀepaʀasjɔ̃/ *nf* preparation. **préparatoire** *adj* preparatory.

préparer /pʀepaʀe/ **1** *vt* prepare; (repas, café) make; **plats préparés** ready-cooked meals. □ **se ~** *vpr* prepare oneself (à for); (s'apprêter) get ready; (être proche) be brewing.

préposé, ~e /pʀepoze/ *nm, f* employee; (des postes) postman, postwoman.

préposition /pʀepozisjɔ̃/ *nf* preposition.

préretraite /pʀeʀətʀɛt/ *nf* early retirement.

près /pʀɛ/ *adv* near, close; **~ de** near (to), close to; (presque) nearly; **à cela ~ except** that; **de ~** closely.

présage /pʀezaʒ/ *nm* omen.

presbyte /pʀɛsbit/ *adj* longsighted, far-sighted.

prescrire /pʀɛskʀiʀ/ **30** *vt* prescribe.

préséance /pʀeseɑ̃s/ *nf* precedence.

présence /pʀezɑ̃s/ *nf* presence; (Scol) attendance.

présent, ~e /pʀezɑ̃, -t/ *adj* present. ● *nm* (temps, cadeau) present; **à ~** now.

présentateur, -trice /pʀezɑ̃ta-tœʀ, -tʀis/ *nm, f* presenter.

présentation /pʀezɑ̃tasjɔ̃/ *nf* (de personne) introduction; (exposé) presentation.

présenter /pʀezɑ̃te/ **1** *vt* present; (personne) introduce (à to); (montrer) show. ● *vi* **~ bien** have a pleasing appearance. □ **se ~** *vpr* introduce oneself (à to); (aller) go; (apparaître) appear; (candidat) come forward; (occasion) arise; **se ~ à** (examen) sit for; (élection) stand for; **se ~ bien** look good.

préservatif /pʀezɛʀvatif/ *nm* condom.

préserver /pʀezɛʀve/ **1** *vt* protect.

présidence /pʀezidɑ̃s/ *nf* (d'État) presidency; (de société) chairmanship.

président, ~e /pʀezidɑ̃, -t/ *nm, f* president; (de société, comité) chairman, chairwoman; **~-directeur général** managing director.

présidentiel, ~le /pʀezidɑ̃sjɛl/ *adj* presidential.

présider /pʀezide/ **1** *vt* preside.

présomptueux, -euse /pʀezɔ̃p-tɥø, -z/ *adj* presumptuous.

presque /pʀɛsk(ə)/ *adv* almost, nearly; **~ jamais** hardly ever; **~ rien** hardly anything; **~ pas (de)** hardly any.

presqu'île /pʀɛskil/ *nf* peninsula.

pressant, ~e /pʀesɑ̃, -t/ *adj* pressing, urgent.

presse /pʀɛs/ *nf* (journaux, appareil) press.

pressentiment /pʀesɑ̃timɑ̃/ *nm* premonition. **pressentir** **46** *vt* have a premonition of.

pressé, ~e /pʀese/ *adj* in a hurry; (orange, citron) freshly squeezed.

presser /pʀese/ **1** *vt* squeeze, press; (appuyer sur, harceler) press; (hâter) hasten; (inciter) urge (**de** to). ● *vi* (temps) press; (affaire) be pressing. □ **se ~** *vpr* (se hâter) hurry; (se grouper) crowd.

pressing /pʀesiŋ/ *nm* (teinturerie) dry-cleaner's.

pression /pʀesjɔ̃/ *nf* pressure; (bouton) press-stud.

prestance /pʀɛstɑ̃s/ *nf* (imposing) presence.

prestation /pʀɛstasjɔ̃/ *nf* allowance; (d'artiste) performance.

prestidigitation /pʀɛstidiʒita-sjɔ̃/ *nf* conjuring.

prestige /pʀɛstiʒ/ *nm* prestige. **prestigieux, -ieuse** *adj* prestigious.

présumé, e /pʀezyme/ *adj* alleged.

présumer /pʀezyme/ **1** *vt* presume; **~ que** assume that; **~ de** overrate.

prêt, ~e /pʀɛ, -t/ *adj* ready (**à qch** for sth, **à faire** to do). ● *nm* loan. **prêt-à-porter** *nm inv* ready-to-wear clothes.

prétendre /pʀetɑ̃dʀ/ **3** *vt* claim (**que** that); (vouloir) intend; **on le prétend riche** he is said to be very rich. **prétendu, ~e** *adj* so-called. **prétendument** *adv* supposedly, allegedly.

p

prétentieux, -ieuse /pʀetɑ̃sjø, -z/ adj pretentious.

prêter /pʀete/ **1** vt lend (à to); (attribuer) attribute; ~ **son aide à qn** give sb some help; ~ **attention** pay attention; ~ **serment** take an oath. ● vi ~ **à** lead to.

prêteur, -euse /pʀetœʀ, -øz/ nm, f (money-)lender; ~ **sur gages** pawnbroker.

prétexte /pʀetɛkst/ nm pretext, excuse.

prêtre /pʀɛtʀ/ nm priest.

preuve /pʀœv/ nf proof; **des** ~**s** evidence (+ sg); **faire** ~ **de** show; **faire ses** ~**s** prove oneself.

prévaloir /pʀevalwaʀ/ **60** vi prevail.

prévenant, ~**e** /pʀevnɑ̃, -t/ adj thoughtful.

prévenir /pʀevniʀ/ **58** vt (menacer) warn; (informer) tell; (médecin) call; (éviter, anticiper) prevent.

préventif, -ive /pʀevɑ̃tif, -v/ adj preventive.

prévention /pʀevɑ̃sjɔ̃/ nf prevention; **faire de la** ~ take preventive action; ~ **routière** road safety.

prévenu, ~**e** /pʀevny/ nm, f defendant.

prévisible /pʀevizibl/ adj predictable. **prévision** nf prediction; (météorologique) forecast.

prévoir /pʀevwaʀ/ **63** vt foresee; (temps) forecast; (organiser) plan (for), provide for; (envisager) allow (for); **prévu pour** (jouet) designed for; **comme prévu** as planned.

prévoyance /pʀevwajɑ̃s/ nf foresight. **prévoyant,** ~**e** adj farsighted.

prier /pʀije/ **45** vi pray. ● vt pray to; (demander à) ask (de to); **je vous en prie** please; (il n'y a pas de quoi) don't mention it.

prière /pʀijɛʀ/ nf prayer; (demande) request; ~ **de** (vous êtes prié de) will you please.

primaire /pʀimɛʀ/ adj primary.

prime /pʀim/ nf free gift; (d'employé) bonus; (subvention) subsidy; (d'assurance) premium.

primé, ~**e** /pʀime/ adj prizewinning.

primeurs /pʀimœʀ/ nfpl early fruit and vegetables.

primevère /pʀimvɛʀ/ nf primrose.

primitif, -ive /pʀimitif, -v/ adj primitive; (d'origine) original. ● nm, f primitive.

primordial, ~**e** (mpl **-iaux**) /pʀimɔʀdjal, -jo/ adj essential.

prince /pʀɛ̃s/ nm prince. **princesse** nf princess.

principal, ~**e** (mpl **-aux**) /pʀɛ̃sipal, -o/ adj main, principal. ● nm headmaster; (chose) main thing.

principe /pʀɛ̃sip/ nm principle; **en** ~ in theory; (d'habitude) as a rule.

printanier, -ière /pʀɛ̃tanje, -jɛʀ/ adj spring(-like).

printemps /pʀɛ̃tɑ̃/ nm spring.

prioritaire /pʀijɔʀitɛʀ/ adj priority; **être** ~ have priority. **priorité** nf priority; (Auto) right of way.

> **Priorité à droite** Except at roundabouts, and unless there are other indications or regulations in force, French drivers must always give way to traffic approaching from the right. ⓘ

pris, ~**e** /pʀi, -z/ adj (place) taken; (personne, journée) busy; (nez) stuffed up; ~ **de** (peur, fièvre) stricken with; ~ **de panique** panic-stricken. ● →**PRENDRE** **50**.

prise /pʀiz/ nf hold, grip; (animal attrapé) catch; (Mil) capture; (~ **de courant**) (mâle) plug; (femelle) socket; ~ **multiple** multiplug adapter; **avoir** ~ **sur qn** have a hold over sb; **aux** ~**s avec** to grapple with; ~ **de conscience** awareness; ~ **de contact** first contact, initial meeting; ~ **de position** stand; ~ **de sang** blood test.

prisé, ~**e** /pʀize/ adj popular.

prison /pʀizɔ̃/ nf prison, jail; (réclusion) imprisonment. **prisonnier, -ière** nm, f prisoner.

privation /pʀivasjɔ̃/ nf deprivation; (sacrifice) hardship.

privatiser /pʀivatize/ **1** vt privatize.

privé /pʀive/ adj private. ● nm (Comm) private sector; (Scol) private schools (+ pl); **en** ~ in private.

priver /pʀive/ **1** vt ~ **de** deprive of. □ **se** ~ (de) vpr go without.

privilège /pʀivilɛʒ/ nm privilege. **privilégié,** ~**e** nm, f privileged person.

prix /pʀi/ *nm* price; (récompense) prize; **à tout ~** at all costs; **au ~ de** (fig) at the expense of; **~ coûtant, ~ de revient** cost price; **à ~ fixe** set price.

probabilité /pʀɔbabilite/ *nf* probability. **probable** *adj* probable, likely. **probablement** *adv* probably.

probant, ~e /pʀɔbã, -t/ *adj* convincing, conclusive.

problème /pʀɔblɛm/ *nm* problem.

procédé /pʀɔsede/ *nm* process; (manière d'agir) practice.

procéder /pʀɔsede/ 14 *vi* proceed; **~ à** carry out.

procès /pʀɔsɛ/ *nm* (criminel) trial; (civil) lawsuit, proceedings (+ *pl*).

processus /pʀɔsesys/ *nm* process; **~ de paix** peace process.

procès-verbal (*pl* procèsverbaux) /pʀɔsɛvɛʀbal, -o/ *nm* minutes (+ *pl*); (contravention) ticket.

prochain, ~e /pʀɔʃɛ̃, -ɛn/ *adj* (suivant) next; (proche) imminent; (avenir) near. ● *nm* fellow man. **prochainement** *adv* soon.

proche /pʀɔʃ/ *adj* near, close; (avoisinant) neighbouring; (parent, ami) close; **~ de** close ou near to; **de ~ en ~** gradually; **dans un ~ avenir** in the near future; **être ~** (imminent) be approaching. ● *nm* close relative; (ami) close friend.

Proche-Orient /pʀɔʃɔʀjã/ *nm* Near East.

proclamation /pʀɔklamasjõ/ *nf* declaration, proclamation. **proclamer** 1 *vt* declare, proclaim.

procuration /pʀɔkyʀasjõ/ *nf* proxy.

procurer /pʀɔkyʀe/ 1 *vt* bring (à to). □ **se ~** *vpr* obtain.

procureur /pʀɔkyʀœʀ/ *nm* public prosecutor.

prodige /pʀɔdiʒ/ *nm* (fait) marvel; (personne) prodigy; **enfant/musicien ~** child/musical prodigy. **prodigieux, -ieuse** *adj* tremendous, prodigious.

prodigue /pʀɔdig/ *adj* wasteful; **fils ~** prodigal son.

producteur, -trice /pʀɔdyktœʀ, -tʀis/ *adj* producing. ● *nm, f* producer. **productif, -ive** *adj* productive. **production** *nf* production; (produit) product. **productivité** *nf* productivity.

produire /pʀɔdɥiʀ/ 17 *vt* produce. □ **se ~** *vpr* (survenir) happen; (acteur) perform.

produit /pʀɔdɥi/ *nm* product; **~s** (de la terre) produce (+ *sg*) ; **~ chimique** chemical; **~s alimentaires** foodstuffs; **~ de consommation** consumer goods; **~ intérieur brut** gross domestic product; **~ national brut** gross national product.

proéminent, ~e /pʀɔeminã, -t/ *adj* prominent.

profane /pʀɔfan/ *adj* secular. ● *nmf* lay person.

proférer /pʀɔfeʀe/ 14 *vt* utter.

professeur /pʀɔfɛsœʀ/ *nm* teacher; (Univ) lecturer; (avec chaire) professor.

profession /pʀɔfɛsjõ/ *nf* occupation; **~ libérale** profession.

professionnel, ~le /pʀɔfɛsjɔnɛl/ *adj* professional; (école) vocational. ● *nm, f* professional.

profil /pʀɔfil/ *nm* profile.

profit /pʀɔfi/ *nm* profit; **au ~ de** in aid of. **profitable** *adj* profitable.

profiter /pʀɔfite/ 1 *vi* **~ à** benefit; **~ de** take advantage of.

profond, ~e /pʀɔfõ, -d/ *adj* deep; (sentiment, intérêt) profound; (causes) underlying; **au plus ~ de** in the depths of. **profondément** *adv* deeply; (différent, triste) profoundly; (dormir) soundly. **profondeur** *nf* depth.

progéniture /pʀɔʒenityʀ/ *nf* offspring.

progiciel /pʀɔʒisjɛl/ *nm* (Ordinat) package.

programmation /pʀɔgʀamasjõ/ *nf* programming.

programme /pʀɔgʀam/ *nm* programme; (Scol) (d'une matière) syllabus; (général) curriculum; (Ordinat) program. **programmer** 1 *vt* (ordinateur, appareil) program; (émission) schedule. **programmeur, -euse** *nm, f* computer programmer.

progrès /pʀɔgʀɛ/ *nm & nmpl* progress; **faire des ~** make progress. **progresser** 1 *vi* progress. **progressif, -ive** *adj* progressive. **progression** *nf* progression.

prohibitif, -ive /pʀɔibitif, -v/ *adj* prohibitive.

p

proie /pʀwa/ *nf* prey; **en ~ à** tormented by.

projecteur /pʀɔʒɛktœʀ/ *nm* floodlight; (Mil) searchlight; (cinéma) projector.

projectile /pʀɔʒɛktil/ *nm* missile.

projection /pʀɔʒɛksjɔ̃/ *nf* projection; (séance) show.

projet /pʀɔʒɛ/ *nm* plan; (ébauche) draft; **~ de loi** bill.

projeter /pʀɔʒte/ 🖽 *vt* (prévoir) plan (**de** to); (*film*) project, show; (jeter) hurl, project.

prolétaire /pʀɔletɛʀ/ *nmf* proletarian.

prologue /pʀɔlɔg/ *nm* prologue.

prolongation /pʀɔlɔ̃gasjɔ̃/ *nf* extension; **~s** (football) extra time.

prolonger /pʀɔlɔ̃ʒe/ 🖽 *vt* extend. ☐ **se ~** *vpr* go on.

promenade /pʀɔmnad/ *nf* walk; (à bicyclette, à cheval) ride; (en auto) drive, ride; **faire une ~** go for a walk.

promener /pʀɔmne/ 🖽 *vt* take for a walk; **~ son regard sur** cast an eye over. ☐ **se ~** *vpr* walk; **(aller) se ~** go for a walk. **promeneur, -euse** *nm, f* walker.

promesse /pʀɔmɛs/ *nf* promise.

prometteur, -euse /pʀɔmɛtœʀ, -øz/ *adj* promising.

promettre /pʀɔmɛtʀ/ 🖽 *vt/i* promise. ● *vi* be promising. ☐ **se ~ de** *vpr* resolve to.

promoteur /pʀɔmɔtœʀ/ *nm* (immobilier) property developer.

promotion /pʀɔmɔsjɔ̃/ *nf* promotion; (Univ) year; (Comm) special offer.

prompt, ~e /pʀɔ̃, -t/ *adj* swift.

promu, ~e /pʀɔmy/ *adj* **être ~** be promoted.

prôner /pʀone/ 🖪 *vt* extol.

pronom /pʀɔnɔ̃/ *nm* pronoun. **pronominal, ~e** (*mpl* **-aux**) *adj* pronominal.

prononcé, ~e /pʀɔnɔ̃se/ *adj* strong.

prononcer /pʀɔnɔ̃se/ 🖽 *vt* pronounce; (*discours*) make. ☐ **se ~** *vpr* (*mot*) be pronounced; (*personne*) make a decision (**pour** in favour of). **prononciation** *nf* pronunciation.

pronostic /pʀɔnɔstik/ *nm* forecast; (Méd) prognosis.

propagande /pʀɔpagɑ̃d/ *nf* propaganda.

propager /pʀɔpaʒe/ 🖽 *vt* spread. ☐ **se ~** *vpr* spread.

prophète /pʀɔfɛt/ *nm* prophet. **prophétie** *nf* prophecy.

propice /pʀɔpis/ *adj* favourable.

proportion /pʀɔpɔʀsjɔ̃/ *nf* proportion; (en mathématiques) ratio; **toutes ~s gardées** relatively speaking. **proportionné, ~e** *adj* proportionate (**à** to). **proportionnel, ~le** *adj* proportional. **proportionnellement** *adv* proportionately.

propos /pʀɔpo/ *nm* intention; (sujet) subject; **à ~** at the right time; (dans un dialogue) by the way; **à ~ de** about; **à tout ~** at every possible occasion. ● *nmpl* (paroles) remarks.

proposer /pʀɔpoze/ 🖪 *vt* suggest, propose; (offrir) offer. ☐ **se ~** *vpr* volunteer (**pour** to). **proposition** *nf* proposal; (affirmation) proposition; (Gram) clause.

propre /pʀɔpʀ/ *adj* (non sali) clean; (soigné) neat; (honnête) decent; (à soi) own; (sens) literal; **~ à** (qui convient) suited to; (spécifique) particular to. ● *nm* **mettre au ~** write out again neatly; **c'est du ~!** (ironique) well done!

proprement /pʀɔpʀəmɑ̃/ *adv* (avec soin) neatly; (au sens strict) strictly; **le bureau ~ dit** the office itself.

propreté /pʀɔpʀəte/ *nf* cleanliness.

propriétaire /pʀɔpʀijetɛʀ/ *nmf* owner; (Comm) proprietor; (qui loue) landlord, landlady.

propriété /pʀɔpʀijete/ *nf* property; (droit) ownership.

propulser /pʀɔpylse/ 🖪 *vt* propel.

proroger /pʀɔʀɔʒe/ 🖽 *vt* (contrat) defer; (*passeport*) extend.

proscrire /pʀɔskʀiʀ/ 🖽 *vt* proscribe.

proscrit, ~e /pʀɔskʀi, -t/ *adj* proscribed. ● *nm, f* (exilé) exile.

prose /pʀoz/ *nf* prose.

prospectus /pʀɔspɛktys/ *nm* leaflet.

prospère /pʀɔspɛʀ/ *adj* flourishing, thriving. **prospérer** 🖽 *vi* thrive, prosper. **prospérité** *nf* prosperity.

prosterner (se) /(sə)pʀɔstɛʀne/ 🖪 *vpr* prostrate oneself; **prosterné devant** prostrate before.

prostituée /pʀɔstitɥe/ *nf* prostitute. **prostitution** *nf* prostitution.

protecteur, -trice /pʀɔtɛktœʀ, -tʀis/ *nm, f* protector. ● *adj* protective.

p

protection /pʀɔtɛksjɔ̃/ nf protection.
protégé, ∼e /pʀɔteʒe/ nm, f protégé.
protéger /pʀɔteʒe/ 40 vt protect. □ **se ∼** vpr protect oneself.
protéine /pʀɔtein/ nf protein.
protestant, ∼e /pʀɔtɛstɑ̃, -t/ adj & nm, f Protestant.
protestation /pʀɔtɛstasjɔ̃/ nf protest. **protester** 1 vt/i protest.
protocole /pʀɔtɔkɔl/ nm protocol.
protubérant, ∼e /pʀɔtybeʀɑ̃/ adj protruding.
proue /pʀu/ nf bow, prow.
prouesse /pʀuɛs/ nf feat, exploit.
prouver /pʀuve/ 1 vt prove.
provenance /pʀɔvnɑ̃s/ nf origin; **en ∼ de** from.
provençal, ∼e (mpl **-aux**) /pʀɔ-vɑ̃sal, -o/ adj & nm, f Provençal.
provenir /pʀɔvniʀ/ 58 vi **∼ de** come from.
proverbe /pʀɔvɛʀb/ nm proverb.
province /pʀɔvɛ̃s/ nf province; **de ∼** provincial; **la ∼** the provinces (+ pl). **provincial, ∼e** (mpl **-iaux**) adj & nm, f provincial.
proviseur /pʀɔvizœʀ/ nm headmaster, principal.
provision /pʀɔvizjɔ̃/ nf supply, store; (sur un compte) credit (balance); (acompte) deposit; **∼s** (vivres) food shopping.
provisoire /pʀɔvizwaʀ/ adj provisional.
provocant, ∼e /pʀɔvɔkɑ̃, -t/ adj provocative. **provocation** nf provocation. **provoquer** 1 vt cause; (sexuellement) arouse; (défier) provoke.
proxénète /pʀɔksenɛt/ nm pimp, procurer.
proximité /pʀɔksimite/ nf proximity; **à ∼ de** close to.
prude /pʀyd/ adj prudish.
prudemment /pʀydamɑ̃/ adv (conduire) carefully; (attendre) cautiously. **prudence** nf caution. **prudent, ∼e** adj (au volant) careful; (à agir) cautious; (sage) wise.
prune /pʀyn/ nf plum.
pruneau (pl **∼x**) /pʀyno/ nm prune.
prunelle /pʀynɛl/ nf (pupille) pupil; (fruit) sloe.
prunier /pʀynje/ nm plum tree.

psaume /psom/ nm psalm.
pseudonyme /psødɔnim/ nm pseudonym.
psychanalyse /psikanaliz/ nf psycho-analysis. **psychanalyste** nmf psycho-analyst.
psychiatre /psikjatʀ/ nmf psychiatrist. **psychiatrie** nf psychiatry. **psychiatrique** adj psychiatric.
psychique /psiʃik/ adj mental, psychological.
psychologie /psikɔlɔʒi/ nf psychology. **psychologique** adj psychological. **psychologue** nmf psychologist.
pu /py/ →POUVOIR 49.
puant, ∼e /pɥɑ̃, -t/ adj stinking.
pub /pyb/ nf 1 **la ∼** advertising; **une ∼** an advert.
puberté /pybɛʀte/ nf puberty.
public, -que /pyblik/ adj public. ● nm public; (assistance) audience; (Scol) state schools (+ pl); **en ∼** in public.
publication /pyblikasjɔ̃/ nf publication.
publicitaire /pyblisitɛʀ/ adj publicity. **publicité** nf publicity, advertising; (annonce) advertisement.
publier /pyblije/ 45 vt publish.
publiquement /pyblikmɑ̃/ adv publicly.
puce /pys/ nf flea; (électronique) chip; **marché aux ∼s** flea market.
pudeur /pydœʀ/ nf modesty.
pudibond, ∼e /pydibɔ̃, -d/ adj prudish.
pudique /pydik/ adj modest.
puer /pɥe/ 1 vi stink. ● vt stink of.
puéricultrice /pɥeʀikyltʀis/ nf pediatric nurse.
puéril, ∼e /pɥeʀil/ adj puerile.
puis /pɥi/ adv then.
puiser /pɥize/ 1 vt draw (**dans** from). ● vi **∼ dans qch** dip into sth.
puisque /pɥisk(ə)/ conj since, as.
puissance /pɥisɑ̃s/ nf power; **en ∼** potential.
puissant, ∼e /pɥisɑ̃, -t/ adj powerful.
puits /pɥi/ nm well; (de mine) shaft.
pull(-over) /pyl(ɔvɛʀ)/ nm pullover, jumper.
pulpe /pylp/ nf pulp.
pulsation /pylsasjɔ̃/ nf (heart-) beat.

p

pulvériser /pylveʀize/ 🛑 *vt* pulverize; (*liquide*) spray.

punaise /pynɛz/ *nf* (insecte) bug; (clou) drawing pin.

punch¹ /pɔ̃ʃ/ *nm* (boisson) punch.

punch² /pœnʃ/ *nm* **avoir du** ∼ have drive.

punir /pyniʀ/ 🛑 *vt* punish. **punition** *nf* punishment.

pupille /pypij/ *nf* (de l'œil) pupil.
● *nmf* (enfant) ward.

pupitre /pypitʀ/ *nm* (Scol) desk; ∼ **à musique** music stand.

pur /pyʀ/ *adj* pure; (whisky) neat.

purée /pyʀe/ *nf* purée; (de pommes de terre) mashed potatoes (+ *pl*).

pureté /pyʀte/ *nf* purity.

purgatoire /pyʀgatwaʀ/ *nm* purgatory.

purge /pyʀʒ/ *nf* purge. **purger** 🛑 *vt* (Pol, Méd) purge; (peine: Jur) serve.

purifier /pyʀifje/ 🛑 *vt* purify.

puritain, ∼e /pyʀitɛ̃, -ɛn/ *nm, f* puritan. ● *adj* puritanical.

pur-sang /pyʀsɑ̃/ *nm inv* (cheval) thoroughbred.

pus /py/ *nm* pus.

putain /pytɛ̃/ *nf* p whore.

puzzle /pœzl/ *nm* jigsaw (puzzle).

P-V *abrév m* (**procès-verbal**) ticket, traffic fine.

pyjama /piʒama/ *nm* pyjamas (+ *pl*); **un** ∼ a pair of pyjamas.

pylône /pilon/ *nm* pylon.

Pyrénées /piʀene/ *nfpl* **les** ∼ the Pyrenees.

pyromane /piʀɔman/ *nmf* arsonist.

Qq

QG *abrév m* (**quartier général**) HQ.

QI *abrév m* (**quotient intellectuel**) IQ.

qu' /k/ →QUE.

quadriller /kadʀije/ 🛑 *vt* (armée) take control of; (police) spread one's net over; **papier quadrillé** squared paper.

quadrupède /kadʀypɛd/ *nm* quadruped.

quadruple /kadʀypl/ *adj* quadruple. ● *nm* **le** ∼ **de** four times. **quadrupler** 🛑 *vt/i* quadruple.

quai /ke/ *nm* (de gare) platform; (de port) quay; (de rivière) bank.

qualification /kalifikasjɔ̃/ *nf* qualification; (compétence pratique) skills (+ *pl*).

qualifié, ∼e /kalifje/ *adj* (diplomé) qualified; (main-d'œuvre) skilled.

qualifier /kalifje/ 🛑 *vt* qualify; (décrire) describe (de as). ◻ **se** ∼ *vpr* qualify (**pour** for).

qualité /kalite/ *nf* quality; (titre) occupation; (fonction) position; **en sa** ∼ **de** in his ou her capacity as.

quand /kɑ̃/ *adv* when; ∼ **même** all the same. ● *conj* when; (toutes les fois que) whenever; ∼ **bien même** even if.

quant à /kɑ̃ta/ *prép* as for.

quantité /kɑ̃tite/ *nf* quantity; **une** ∼ **de** a lot of; **des** ∼**s (de)** masses ou lots (of).

quarantaine /kaʀɑ̃tɛn/ *nf* (Méd) quarantine; **une** ∼ **(de)** about forty; **avoir la** ∼ be in one's forties.

quarante /kaʀɑ̃t/ *adj & nm* forty.

quart /kaʀ/ *nm* quarter; (Naut) watch; **onze heures moins le** ∼ quarter to eleven; ∼ **(de litre)** quarter litre; ∼ **de finale** quarter- final; ∼ **d'heure** quarter of an hour; ∼ **de tour** ninety-degree turn.

quartier /kaʀtje/ *nm* area, district; (zone ethnique) quarter; (de lune, pomme, bœuf) quarter; (d'une orange) segment; ∼**s** (Mil) quarters; **de** ∼, **du** ∼ local; ∼ **général** headquarters; **avoir** ∼ **libre** be free.

quasiment /kazimɑ̃/ *adv* almost, practically.

quatorze /katɔʀz/ *adj & nm* fourteen.

quatre /katʀ(ə)/ *adj & nm* four. **quatre-vingt(s)** *adj & nm* eighty. **quatre-vingt-dix** *adj & nm* ninety.

quatre-quatre /katʀkatʀ/ *nm* four-wheel drive.

quatrième /katʀijɛm/ *adj & nmf* fourth. ● *nf* (Auto) fourth gear.

quatuor /kwatɥɔʀ/ *nm* quartet.

que, qu' /kə, k/

qu' before vowel or mute h.

● *conjonction*

····▸ that; **je crains ~...** I'm worried that...

····▸ (souhait, volonté) **je veux ~ tu viennes** I want you to come; **~ tu viennes ou non** whether you come or not; **qu'il entre** let him come in.

····▸ (comparaison) than; **plus grand ~ toi** taller than you.

● *pronom interrogatif*

····▸ what; **~ voulez-vous manger?** what would you like to eat?

● *pronom relatif*

····▸ (personne) whom, that; **l'homme ~ j'ai rencontré** the man (whom) I met.

····▸ (chose) that, which; **le cheval ~ Nick m'a offert** the horse (which) Nick gave me.

● *adverbe*

····▸ **que c'est joli!** it's so pretty!; **~ de monde!** what a lot of people!

Québec /kebɛk/ *nm* Quebec.

---

quel, quelle (*pl* **quel(le)s**) /kɛl/

● *adjectif interrogatif*

····▸ which, what; **~ auteur a écrit...?** which writer wrote...?; **~ jour sommes-nous?** what day is it today?

● *adjectif exclamatif*

····▸ what; **~ idiot!** what an idiot!; **quelle horreur!** that's horrible!

● *adjectif relatif*

····▸ **~ que soit son âge** whatever his age; **quelles que soient tes raisons** whatever your reasons; **~ que soit le gagnant** whoever the winner is.

quelconque /kɛlkɔ̃k/ *adj* any, some; (banal) ordinary; (médiocre) poor, second rate.

quelque /kɛlkə/ *adj* some; **~s** a few, some. ● *adv* (environ) about, some; **et ~ 1** and a bit; **~ chose** something; (dans les phrases interrogatives) anything; **~ part** somewhere; **~ peu** somewhat.

quelquefois /kɛlkəfwa/ *adv* sometimes.

quelques-uns, -unes /kɛlkəzœ̃, -yn/ *pron* some, a few.

quelqu'un /kɛlkœ̃/ *pron* someone, somebody; (dans les phrases interrogatives) anyone, anybody.

querelle /kəʀɛl/ *nf* quarrel. **quereller (se) 1** *vpr* quarrel. **querelleur, -euse** *adj* quarrelsome.

question /kɛstjɔ̃/ *nf* question; (affaire) matter, question; **poser une ~** ask a question; **en ~** in question; **il est ~ de** (cela concerne) it is about; (on parle de) there is talk of; **il n'en est pas ~** it is out of the question; **pas ~!** no way!

questionnaire /kɛstjɔnɛʀ/ *nm* questionnaire.

questionner /kɛstjɔne/ **1** *vt* question.

quête /kɛt/ *nf* (Relig) collection; (recherche) search; **en ~ de** in search of.

queue /kø/ *nf* tail; (de poêle) handle; (de fruit) stalk; (de fleur) stem; (file) queue; (US) line; (de train) rear; **faire la ~** queue (up); (US) line up; **~ de cheval** ponytail; **faire une ~ de poisson à qn** (Auto) cut in front of sb.

---

qui /ki/

● *pronom interrogatif*

····▸ (sujet) who; **~ a fait ça?** who did that?

····▸ (complément) whom; **à ~ est ce livre?** whose book is this?

● *pronom relatif*

····▸ (personne sujet) who; **c'est Isabelle qui vient d'appeler** it's Isabelle who's just called.

····▸ (autres cas) that, which; **qu'est-ce ~ te prend?** what is the matter with you?; **invite ~ tu veux** invite whoever you want; **~ que ce soit** whoever it is, anybody.

quiche /kiʃ/ *nf* quiche.

quiconque /kikɔ̃k/ *pron* whoever; (n'importe qui) anyone.

quille /kij/ *nf* (de bateau) keel; (jouet) skittle.

quincaillerie /kɛ̃kajʀi/ *nf* hardware; (magasin) hardware shop. **quincaillier, -ière** *nm, f* hardware dealer.

q

quintal /pl **-aux**/ /kɛ̃tal, -o/ nm quintal, one hundred kilos.

quinte /kɛ̃t/ nf ~ **de toux** coughing fit.

quintuple /kɛ̃typl/ adj quintuple. ● nm **le ~ de** five times. **quintupler 1** vt/i quintuple, increase fivefold.

quinzaine /kɛ̃zɛn/ nf **une ~ (de)** about fifteen.

quinze /kɛ̃z/ adj & nm inv fifteen; ~ **jours** two weeks.

quiproquo /kipʀoko/ nm misunderstanding.

quittance /kitɑ̃s/ nf receipt.

quitte /kit/ adj quits (**envers** with); ~ **à faire** even if it means doing.

quitter /kite/ **1** vt leave; (vêtement) take off; **ne quittez pas!** hold the line, please! □ **se ~** vpr part.

qui-vive /kiviv/ nm inv **être sur le ~** be alert.

quoi /kwa/ pron what; (après une préposition) which; **de ~ vivre** (assez) enough to live on; **de ~ écrire** something to write with; ~ **qu'il dise** whatever he says; ~ **que ce soit** anything; **il n'y a pas de ~** my pleasure; **il n'y a pas de ~ s'inquiéter** there's nothing to worry about.

quoique /kwak(ə)/ conj although, though.

quota /kota/ nm quota.

quote-part (pl **quotes-parts**) /kotpaʀ/ nf share.

quotidien, ~ne /kotidjɛ̃, -ɛn/ adj daily; (banal) everyday. ● nm daily (paper); (vie quotidienne) everyday life. **quotidiennement** adv daily.

. . . .

Rr

. . . .

rabâcher /ʀabɑʃe/ **1** vt keep repeating.

rabais /ʀabɛ/ nm reduction, discount. **rabaisser 1** vt (déprécier) belittle; (réduire) reduce.

rabat-joie /ʀabajwa/ nm inv killjoy.

rabattre /ʀabatʀ/ **1** vt (chapeau, visière) pull down; (refermer) shut; (diminuer) reduce; (déduire) take off; (col, drap) turn down. □ **se ~** vpr (se refermer) close; (véhicule) cut back in; **se ~ sur** make do with.

rabot /ʀabo/ nm plane.

rabougri, ~e /ʀabugʀi/ adj stunted.

racaille /ʀakɑj/ nf rabble.

raccommoder /ʀakomode/ **1** vt mend; (personnes **1**) reconcile.

raccompagner /ʀakɔ̃paɲe/ **1** vt see ou take back (home).

raccord /ʀakɔʀ/ nm link; (de papier peint) join; (retouche) touch-up. **raccorder 1** vt connect, join.

raccourci /ʀakuʀsi/ nm short cut; **en ~** in short.

raccourcir /ʀakuʀsiʀ/ **2** vt shorten. ● vi get shorter.

raccrocher /ʀakʀoʃe/ **1** vt hang back up; (passant) grab hold of; (relier) connect; ~ **le combiné** or **le téléphone** hang up. ● vi hang up. □ **se ~ à** vpr cling to; (se relier à) be connected to ou with.

race /ʀas/ nf race; (animale) breed; **de ~** (chien) pedigree; (cheval) thoroughbred.

racheter /ʀaʃte/ **6** vt buy (back); (acheter encore) buy more; (nouvel objet) buy another; (société) buy out; ~ **des chaussettes** buy new socks. □ **se ~** vpr make amends.

racial, ~e (mpl **-iaux**) /ʀasjal, -o/ adj racial.

racine /ʀasin/ nf root; ~ **carrée/cubique** square/cube root.

racisme /ʀasism/ nm racism. **raciste** adj & nmf racist.

racket /ʀakɛt/ nm racketeering.

raclée /ʀɑkle/ nf **1** thrashing.

racler /ʀɑkle/ **1** vt scrape. □ **se ~** vpr **se ~ la gorge** clear one's throat.

racolage /ʀakolaʒ/ nm soliciting.

raconter /ʀakɔ̃te/ **1** vt (histoire) tell; (vacances) tell about; (vie, épisode) describe; ~ **à qn que** tell sb that, say to sb that; **qu'est-ce que tu racontes?** what are you talking about?

radar /ʀadaʀ/ nm radar; (automatique) speed camera.

radeau (pl ~**x**) /ʀado/ nm raft.

radiateur /ʀadjatœʀ/ nm radiator; (électrique) heater.

radiation /ʀadjasjɔ̃/ nf radiation.

radical, ~e (*mpl* **-aux**) /ʀadikal, -o/ *adj* radical. ● *nm* (*pl* **-aux**) radical.

radieux, -ieuse /ʀadjø, -z/ *adj* radiant.

radin, ~e /ʀadɛ̃, -in/ *adj* 🔲 stingy 🔲.

radio /ʀadjo/ *nf* radio; **à la** ~ on the radio; (*radiographie*) X-ray.

radioactif, -ive /ʀadjoaktif, -v/ *adj* radioactive. **radioactivité** *nf* radioactivity.

radiocassette /ʀadjokasɛt/ *nf* radio cassette player.

radiodiffuser /ʀadjodifyze/ 🔳 *vt* broadcast.

radiographie /ʀadjoɡʀafi/ *nf* (*photographie*) X-ray.

radiomessageur /ʀadjomesa-ʒœʀ/ *nm* pager.

radis /ʀadi/ *nm* radish; **ne pas avoir un** ~ 🔲 be broke.

radoter /ʀadote/ 🔳 *vi* 🔲 talk drivel.

radoucir (se) /(sə)ʀadusiʀ/ 🔳 *vpr* (*humeur*) improve; (*temps*) become milder.

rafale /ʀafal/ *nf* (*de vent*) gust; (*de mitraillette*) burst.

raffermir /ʀafɛʀmiʀ/ 🔳 *vt* strengthen. □ **se** ~ *vpr* become stronger.

raffiné, ~e /ʀafine/ *adj* refined. **raffinement** *nm* refinement.

raffiner /ʀafine/ 🔳 *vt* refine. **raffinerie** *nf* refinery.

raffoler /ʀafole/ 🔳 *vt* 🔲 ~ **de** be crazy about.

raffut /ʀafy/ *nm* 🔲 din.

rafle /ʀafl/ *nf* (*police*) raid.

rafraîchir /ʀafʀeʃiʀ/ 🔳 *vt* cool (down); (*mur*) give a fresh coat of paint to; (*personne, mémoire*) refresh. □ **se** ~ *vpr* (*boire*) refresh oneself; (*temps*) get cooler. **rafraîchissant,** ~e *adj* refreshing.

rafraîchissement /ʀafʀeʃismɑ̃/ *nm* (*boisson*) cold drink; ~s refreshments.

ragaillardir /ʀaɡajaʀdiʀ/ 🔳 *vt* 🔲 cheer up.

rage /ʀaʒ/ *nf* rage; (*maladie*) rabies; **faire** ~ (*bataille, incendie*) rage; (*maladie*) be rife; ~ **de dents** raging toothache. **rageant,** ~e *adj* infuriating.

ragots /ʀaɡo/ *nmpl* 🔲 gossip.

ragoût /ʀaɡu/ *nm* stew.

raid /ʀɛd/ *nm* (Mil) raid; (Sport) trek.

raide /ʀɛd/ *adj* stiff; (*côte*) steep; (*corde*) tight; (*cheveux*) straight. ● *adv* (monter, descendre) steeply. **raideur** *nf* stiffness; steepness.

raidir /ʀediʀ/ 🔳 *vt* (*corps*) tense. □ **se** ~ *vpr* tense up; (*position*) harden; (*corde*) tighten.

raie /ʀɛ/ *nf* (*ligne*) line; (*bande*) strip; (*de cheveux*) parting; (*poisson*) skate.

raifort /ʀɛfoʀ/ *nm* horseradish.

rail /ʀɑj/ *nm* rail, track; **le** ~ (*transport*) rail.

raisin /ʀezɛ̃/ *nm* **le** ~ grapes; ~ **sec** raisin; **un grain de** ~ a grape.

raison /ʀezɔ̃/ *nf* reason; **à** ~ **de** at the rate of; **avec** ~ rightly; **avoir** ~ be right (**de faire** to do); **avoir** ~ **de qn** get the better of sb; **donner** ~ **à** prove right; **en** ~ **de** because of; ~ **de plus** all the more reason; **perdre la** ~ lose one's mind.

raisonnable /ʀezɔnabl/ *adj* reasonable, sensible.

raisonnement /ʀezɔnmɑ̃/ *nm* reasoning; (*propositions*) argument.

raisonner /ʀezɔne/ 🔳 *vi* think. ● *vt* (*personne*) reason with.

rajeunir /ʀaʒœniʀ/ 🔳 *vt* ~ **qn** make sb (look) younger; (*moderniser*) modernize; (Méd) rejuvenate. ● *vi* (*personne*) look younger.

rajuster /ʀaʒyste/ 🔳 *vt* straighten; (*salaires*) (re)adjust.

ralenti, ~e /ʀalɑ̃ti/ *adj* slow. ● *nm* (au cinéma) slow motion; **tourner au** ~ tick over, idle.

ralentir /ʀalɑ̃tiʀ/ 🔳 *vt/i* slow down. □ **se** ~ *vpr* slow down.

ralentisseur /ʀalɑ̃tisœʀ/ *nm* speed ramp.

râler /ʀale/ 🔳 *vi* groan; (*protester* 🔲) moan.

rallier /ʀalje/ 🔳 *vt* rally; (*rejoindre*) rejoin. □ **se** ~ *vpr* rally; **se** ~ **à** (*avis*) come round to; (*parti*) join.

rallonge /ʀalɔ̃ʒ/ *nf* (*de table*) leaf; (*de fil électrique*) extension lead. **rallonger** 🔳 *vt* lengthen; (*séjour, fil, table*) extend.

rallumer /ʀalyme/ 🔳 *vt* (*feu*) relight; (*lampe*) switch on again; (*ranimer*: fig) revive.

rallye /ʀali/ *nm* rally.

r

ramassage /ʀamasaʒ/ nm (cueillette) gathering; (d'ordures) collection; ~ **scolaire** school bus service.

ramasser /ʀamase/ ■ vt pick up; (récolter) gather; (recueillir, rassembler) collect. □ **se** ~ vpr huddle up, curl up.

rame /ʀam/ nf (aviron) oar; (train) train.

ramener /ʀamne/ ■ vt (rapporter, faire revenir) bring back; (reconduire) take back; ~ **à** (réduire à) reduce to. □ **se** ~ vpr ① turn up; **se** ~ **à** (problème) come down to.

ramer /ʀame/ ■ vi row.

ramollir /ʀamɔliʀ/ ② vt soften. □ **se** ~ vpr become soft.

ramoneur /ʀamɔnœʀ/ nm (chimney) sweep.

rampe /ʀɑ̃p/ nf banisters; (pente) ramp; ~ **d'accès** (Auto) slip road; ~ **de lancement** launching pad.

ramper /ʀɑ̃pe/ ■ vi crawl.

rancard /ʀɑ̃kaʀ/ nm ① date.

rancart /ʀɑ̃kaʀ/ nm **mettre** ou **jeter au** ~ ① scrap.

rance /ʀɑ̃s/ adj rancid.

rancœur /ʀɑ̃kœʀ/ nf resentment.

rançon /ʀɑ̃sɔ̃/ nf ransom. **rançonner** ■ vt rob, extort money from.

rancune /ʀɑ̃kyn/ nf grudge; **sans** ~! no hard feelings! **rancunier, -ière** adj vindictive.

randonnée /ʀɑ̃dɔne/ nf walk, ramble; **la** ~ **à cheval** pony trekking; **faire une** ~ go walking ou rambling.

rang /ʀɑ̃/ nm row; (hiérarchie, condition) rank; **se mettre en** ~ line up; **au premier** ~ in the first row; (fig) at the forefront; **de second** ~ (péj) second-rate.

rangée /ʀɑ̃ʒe/ nf row.

rangement /ʀɑ̃ʒmɑ̃/ nm (de pièce) tidying (up); (espace) storage space.

ranger /ʀɑ̃ʒe/ ⓰ vt put away; (chambre) tidy (up); (disposer) place. □ **se** ~ vpr (véhicule) park; (s'écarter) stand aside; (conducteur) pull over; (s'assagir) settle down; **se** ~ **à** (avis) accept.

ranimer /ʀanime/ ■ vt revive; (Méd) resuscitate. □ **se** ~ vpr come round.

rapace /ʀapas/ nm bird of prey. ● adj grasping.

rapatriement /ʀapatʀimɑ̃/ nm repatriation. **rapatrier** ㊺ vt repatriate.

rap /ʀap/ nm rap (music).

râpe /ʀɑp/ nf (Culin) grater; (lime) rasp.

râpé, ~e /ʀɑpe/ adj (vêtement) threadbare; (fromage) grated.

râper /ʀɑpe/ ■ vt grate; (bois) rasp.

rapide /ʀapid/ adj fast, rapid. ● nm (train) express (train); (cours d'eau) rapids (+ pl). **rapidement** adv fast, rapidly. **rapidité** nf speed.

rappel /ʀapɛl/ nm recall; (deuxième avis) reminder; (de salaire) back pay; (Méd) booster; (de diplomate) recall; (de réservistes) call-up; (Théât) curtain call.

rappeler /ʀaple/ ㊳ vt (par téléphone) call back; (réserviste) call up; (diplomate) recall; (évoquer) recall; ~ **qch à qn** remind sb of sth. □ **se** ~ vpr remember, recall.

rappeur, -euse /ʀapœːʀ, -øz/ nmf rapper.

rapport /ʀapɔʀ/ nm connection; (compte-rendu) report; (profit) yield; ~s (relations) relations; **en** ~ **avec** (accord) in keeping with; **mettre/se mettre en** ~ **avec** put/get in touch with; **par** ~ **à** (comparé à) compared with; (vis-à-vis de) with regard to; ~s (sexuels) intercourse.

rapporter /ʀapɔʀte/ ■ vt (ici) bring back; (là-bas) take back, return; (profit) bring in; (dire, répéter) report. ● vi (Comm) bring in a good return; (moucharder ①) tell tales. □ **se** ~ **à** vpr relate to.

rapporteur, -euse /ʀapɔʀtœʀ, -øz/ nm, f (mouchard) tell-tale. ● nm protractor.

rapprochement /ʀapʀɔʃmɑ̃/ nm reconciliation; (Pol) rapprochement; (rapport) connection; (comparaison) parallel.

rapprocher /ʀapʀɔʃe/ vt move closer (de to); (réconcilier) bring together; (comparer) compare; (date, rendezvous) bring forward. □ **se** ~ vpr get ou come closer (de to); (personnes, pays) come together; (s'apparenter) be close (de to).

rapt /ʀapt/ nm abduction.

raquette /ʀakɛt/ nf (de tennis) racket; (de ping-pong) bat.

rare /ʀaʀ/ adj rare; (insuffisant) scarce. **rarement** adv rarely, seldom. **rareté** nf rarity; scarcity.

ras, ~e /ʀɑ, ʀɑz/ adv **coupé** ~ cut short. ● adj (herbe, poil) short; **à** ~ **de terre** very close to the ground; **en avoir** ~ **le bol** 🔢 be really fed up; ~e **campagne** open country; **à** ~ **bord** to the brim.

raser /ʀɑze/ 🔢 vt shave; (cheveux, barbe) shave off; (frôler) skim; (abattre) raze. □ **se** ~ vpr shave.

rasoir /ʀɑzwaʀ/ nm razor. ● adj inv 🔢 boring.

rassasier /ʀɑsazje/ 🔢 vt satisfy, fill up; **être rassasié de** have had enough of.

rassemblement /ʀɑsɑ̃bləmɑ̃/ nm gathering; (manifestation) rally.

rassembler /ʀɑsɑ̃ble/ 🔢 vt gather; (forces, courage) summon up; (idées) collect. □ **se** ~ vpr gather.

rassis, ~e /ʀɑsi, -z/ adj (pain) stale.

rassurer /ʀɑsyʀe/ 🔢 vt reassure. □ **se** ~ vpr reassure oneself; **rassure-toi** don't worry.

rat /ʀɑ/ nm rat.

rate /ʀɑt/ nf spleen.

raté, ~e /ʀɑte/ nm, f (personne) failure. ● nm **avoir des** ~s (voiture) backfire.

râteau (pl ~x) /ʀɑto/ nm rake.

râtelier /ʀɑtəlje/ nm hayrack; (dentier 🔢) dentures.

rater /ʀɑte/ 🔢 vt (train, rendez-vous, cible) miss; (gâcher) make a mess of, spoil; (examen) fail. ● vi fail.

ratio /ʀɑsjo/ nm ratio.

rationaliser /ʀɑsjɔnalize/ 🔢 vt rationalize.

rationnel, ~le /ʀɑsjɔnɛl/ adj rational.

rationnement /ʀɑsjɔnmɑ̃/ nm rationing.

ratisser /ʀɑtise/ 🔢 vt rake; (fouiller) comb.

rattacher /ʀɑtaʃe/ 🔢 vt (lacets) tie up again; (ceinture de sécurité, collier) refasten; (relier) link; (incorporer) join.

rattrapage /ʀɑtʀɑpaʒ/ nm (Comm) adjustment; **cours de** ~ remedial lesson.

rattraper /ʀɑtʀɑpe/ 🔢 vt catch; (rejoindre) catch up with; (retard, erreur) make up for. □ **se** ~ vpr catch up; (se dédommager) make up for it; **se** ~ **à** catch hold of.

rature /ʀɑtyʀ/ nf deletion.

rauque /ʀok/ adj raucous, harsh.

ravager /ʀavaʒe/ 🔢 vt devastate, ravage.

ravages /ʀavaʒ/ nmpl **faire des** ~ wreak havoc.

ravaler /ʀavale/ 🔢 vt (façade) clean; (colère) swallow.

ravi, ~e /ʀavi/ adj delighted (**que** that).

ravin /ʀavɛ̃/ nm ravine.

ravir /ʀaviʀ/ 🔢 vt delight; ~ **qch à qn** rob sb of sth.

ravissant, ~e /ʀavisɑ̃, -t/ adj beautiful.

ravisseur, -euse /ʀavisœʀ, -øz/ nm, f kidnapper.

ravitaillement /ʀavitajmɑ̃/ nm provision of supplies (**de** to); (denrées) supplies; ~ **en essence** refuelling.

ravitailler /ʀavitaje/ 🔢 vt provide with supplies; (avion) refuel. □ **se** ~ vpr stock up.

raviver /ʀavive/ 🔢 vt revive; (feu, colère) rekindle.

rayé, ~e /ʀeje/ adj striped.

rayer /ʀeje/ 🔢 vt scratch; (biffer) cross out; '~ **la mention inutile'** 'delete as appropriate'.

rayon /ʀɛjɔ̃/ nm ray; (étagère) shelf; (de magasin) department; (de roue) spoke; (de cercle) radius; ~ **d'action** range; ~ **de miel** honeycomb; ~ **X** X-ray; **en connaître un** ~ 🔢 know one's stuff 🔢.

rayonnement /ʀɛjɔnmɑ̃/ nm (éclat) radiance; (influence) influence; (radiations) radiation. **rayonner** 🔢 vi radiate; (de joie) beam; (se déplacer) tour around (from a central point).

rayure /ʀɛjyʀ/ nf scratch; (dessin) stripe; **à** ~s striped.

raz-de-marée /ʀɑdmaʀe/ nm inv tidal wave; ~ **électoral** electoral landslide.

réacteur /ʀeaktœʀ/ nm jet engine; (nucléaire) reactor.

réaction /ʀeaksjɔ̃/ nf reaction; ~ **en chaîne** chain reaction; **moteur à** ~ jet engine.

réagir /ʀeaʒiʀ/ 🔢 vi react; ~ **sur** have an effect on.

réalisateur, -trice /ʀealizatœʀ, -tʀis/ nm, f (au cinéma) director; (TV) producer.

réalisation /ʀealizasjɔ̃/ nf (de rêve) fulfilment; (œuvre) achievement; (TV,

r

cinéma) production; **projet en ~** project in progress.

réaliser /ʀealize/ **1** vt carry out; (effort, bénéfice, achat) make; (rêve) fulfil; (film) direct; (capital) realize; (se rendre compte de) realize. □ **se ~** vpr be fulfilled.

réalisme /ʀealism/ nm realism.

réaliste /ʀealist/ adj realistic. ● nmf realist.

réalité /ʀealite/ nf reality.

réanimation /ʀeanimasjɔ̃/ nf resuscitation; **service de ~** intensive care. **réanimer** **1** vt resuscitate.

réarmement /ʀeaʀməmɑ̃/ nm rearmament.

rébarbatif, -ive /ʀebaʀbatif, -v/ adj forbidding, off-putting.

rebelle /ʀəbɛl/ adj rebellious; (soldat) rebel; **~ à** resistant to. ● nmf rebel.

rébellion /ʀebeljɔ̃/ nf rebellion.

rebondir /ʀəbɔ̃diʀ/ **2** vi bounce; rebound; (fig) get moving again.

rebondissement /ʀəbɔ̃dismɑ̃/ nm (new) development.

rebord /ʀəbɔʀ/ nm edge; **~ de la fenêtre** window ledge ou sill.

rebours: à ~ /aʀəbuʀ/ loc (compter, marcher) backwards.

rebrousse-poil: à ~ /aʀəbʀuspwal/ loc the wrong way; (fig) **prendre qn à ~** rub sb up the wrong way.

rebrousser /ʀəbʀuse/ **1** vt **~ chemin** turn back.

rebut /ʀəby/ nm **mettre** ou **jeter au ~** scrap.

rebutant, ~e /ʀəbytɑ̃, -t/ adj off-putting.

recaler /ʀəkale/ **1** vt **1** fail; **se faire ~, être recalé** fail.

recel /ʀəsɛl/ nm receiving. **receler** **6** vt (objet volé) receive; (cacher) conceal.

récemment /ʀesamɑ̃/ adv recently.

recensement /ʀəsɑ̃smɑ̃/ nm census; (inventaire) inventory. **recenser** **1** vt (population) take a census of; (objets) list.

récent, ~e /ʀesɑ̃, -t/ adj recent.

récépissé /ʀesepise/ nm receipt.

récepteur /ʀeseptœʀ/ nm receiver.

réception /ʀesepsjɔ̃/ nf reception; (de courrier) receipt. **réceptionniste** nmf receptionist.

récession /ʀesesjɔ̃/ nf recession.

recette /ʀəsɛt/ nf (Culin) recipe; (argent) takings; **~s** (Comm) receipts.

receveur, -euse /ʀəs(ə)vœʀ, -øz/ nm, f (de bus) conductor; **~ des contributions** tax collector.

recevoir /ʀəs(ə)vwaʀ/ **52** vt receive, get; (client, malade) see; (invités) welcome, receive; **être reçu à un examen** pass an exam.

rechange: de ~ /dəʀəʃɑ̃ʒ/ loc (roue, vêtements) spare; (solution) alternative.

réchapper /ʀeʃape/ **1** vt/i **~ de** come through, survive.

recharge /ʀəʃaʀʒ/ nf (de stylo) refill.

réchaud /ʀeʃo/ nm stove.

réchauffement /ʀeʃofmɑ̃/ nm (de température) rise (**de** in); **le ~ de la planète** global warming.

réchauffer /ʀeʃofe/ **1** vt warm up. □ **se ~** vpr warm oneself up; (temps) get warmer.

rêche /ʀɛʃ/ adj rough.

recherche /ʀəʃɛʀʃ/ nf search (**de** for); (raffinement) meticulousness; **~(s)** (Univ) research; **~s** (enquête) investigations; **~ d'emploi** jobhunting.

recherché, ~e /ʀəʃɛʀʃe/ adj in great demand; (style) original, recherché (péj); **~ pour meurtre** wanted for murder.

rechercher /ʀəʃɛʀʃe/ **1** vt search for.

rechute /ʀəʃyt/ nf (Méd) relapse; **faire une ~** have a relapse.

récidiver /ʀesidive/ **1** vi commit a second offence.

récif /ʀesif/ nm reef.

récipient /ʀesipjɑ̃/ nm container.

réciproque /ʀesipʀɔk/ adj mutual, reciprocal.

réciproquement /ʀesipʀɔkmɑ̃/ adv each other; **et ~** and vice versa.

récit /ʀesi/ nm (compte-rendu) account, story; (histoire) story.

réciter /ʀesite/ **1** vt recite.

réclamation /ʀeklamasjɔ̃/ nf complaint; (demande) claim.

réclame /ʀeklam/ nf advertisement; **faire de la ~** advertise; **en ~** on offer.

réclamer /ʀeklame/ **1** vt call for, demand. ● vi complain.

reclus, ~e /ʀəkly, -z/ nm, f recluse. ● adj reclusive.

réclusion /ʀeklyzjɔ̃/ *nf* imprisonment.

récolte /ʀekɔlt/ *nf* (action) harvest; (produits) crop, harvest; (fig) crop. **récolter** ◧ *vt* harvest, gather; (fig) collect, get.

recommandation /ʀəkɔmɑ̃dasjɔ̃/ *nf* recommendation.

recommandé *nm* registered letter; **envoyer en ~** send by registered post.

recommander /ʀəkɔmɑ̃de/ ◧ *vt* recommend.

recommencer /ʀəkɔmɑ̃se/ ◈ *vt* (reprendre) begin *ou* start again; (refaire) repeat. ● *vi* start *ou* begin again; **ne recommence pas** don't do it again.

récompense /ʀekɔ̃pɑ̃s/ *nf* reward; (prix) award. **récompenser** ◧ *vt* reward (**de** for).

réconcilier /ʀekɔ̃silje/ ◈ *vt* reconcile. □ **se ~** *vpr* become reconciled (**avec** with).

reconduire /ʀəkɔ̃dɥiʀ/ ◈ *vt* see home; (à la porte) show out; (renouveler) renew.

réconfort /ʀekɔ̃fɔʀ/ *nm* comfort.

reconnaissance /ʀəkɔnɛsɑ̃s/ *nf* gratitude; (fait de reconnaître) recognition; (Mil) reconnaissance. **reconnaissant, ~e** *adj* grateful (**de** for).

reconnaître /ʀəkɔnɛtʀ/ ◈ *vt* recognize; (admettre) admit (**que** that); (Mil) reconnoitre; (enfant, tort) acknowledge. □ **se ~** *vpr* (s'orienter) know where one is; (l'un l'autre) recognize each other.

reconstituer /ʀəkɔ̃stitɥe/ ◧ *vt* reconstitute; (crime) reconstruct; (époque) recreate.

reconversion /ʀəkɔ̃vɛʀsjɔ̃/ *nf* (de main-d'œuvre) redeployment.

recopier /ʀəkɔpje/ ◈ *vt* copy out.

record /ʀəkɔʀ/ *nm & a inv* record.

recouper /ʀəkupe/ ◧ *vt* confirm. □ **se ~** *vpr* check, tally, match up.

recourbé, ~e /ʀəkuʀbe/ *adj* curved; (nez) hooked.

recourir /ʀəkuʀiʀ/ ◈ *vi* **~ à** (expédient, violence) resort to; (remède, méthode) have recourse to.

recours /ʀəkuʀ/ *nm* resort; **avoir ~ à** have recourse to, resort to; **avoir ~ à qn** turn to sb.

recouvrer /ʀəkuvʀe/ ◧ *vt* recover.

recouvrir /ʀəkuvʀiʀ/ ◈ *vt* cover.

récréation /ʀekʀeasjɔ̃/ *nf* recreation; (Scol) break; (US) recess.

recroqueviller (se) /(sə)ʀəkʀɔkvije/ ◧ *vpr* curl up.

recrudescence /ʀəkʀydesɑ̃s/ *nf* new outbreak.

recrue /ʀəkʀy/ *nf* recruit.

recrutement /ʀəkʀytmɑ̃/ *nm* recruitment. **recruter** ◧ *vt* recruit.

rectangle /ʀɛktɑ̃gl/ *nm* rectangle. **rectangulaire** *adj* rectangular.

rectifier /ʀɛktifje/ ◈ *vt* correct, rectify.

recto /ʀɛkto/ *nm* **au ~** on the front of the page.

reçu, ~e /ʀəsy/ *adj* accepted; (candidat) successful. ● *nm* receipt. ● →**RECEVOIR** ◈.

recueil /ʀəkœj/ *nm* collection.

recueillement /ʀəkœjmɑ̃/ *nm* meditation.

recueillir /ʀəkœjiʀ/ ◈ *vt* collect; (prendre chez soi) take in. □ **se ~** *vpr* meditate.

recul /ʀəkyl/ *nm* retreat; (éloignement) distance; (déclin) decline; **avoir un mouvement de ~** recoil; **être en ~** be on the decline; **avec le ~** with hindsight.

reculé, ~e /ʀəkyle/ *adj* (région) remote.

reculer /ʀəkyle/ ◧ *vt* move back; (véhicule) reverse; (différer) postpone. ● *vi* move back; (voiture) reverse; (armée) retreat; (régresser) fall; (céder) back down; **~ devant** (fig) shrink from. □ **se ~** *vpr* move back.

récupération /ʀekypeʀasjɔ̃/ *nf* (de l'organisme, de dette) recovery; (d'objets) salvage.

récupérer /ʀekypeʀe/ ◈ *vt* recover; (vieux objets) salvage. ● *vi* recover.

récurer /ʀekyʀe/ ◧ *vt* scour; **poudre à ~** scouring powder.

récuser /ʀekyze/ ◧ *vt* challenge. □ **se ~** *vpr* state that one is not qualified to judge.

recyclage /ʀəsiklaʒ/ *nm* (de personnel) retraining; (de matériau) recycling.

recycler /ʀəsikle/ ◧ *vt* (personne) retrain; (chose) recycle. □ **se ~** *vpr* retrain.

rédacteur, -trice /ʀedaktœʀ, -tʀis/ nm, f author, writer; (de journal, magazine) editor.

rédaction /ʀedaksjɔ̃/ nf writing; (Scol) essay, composition; (personnel) editorial staff.

redevable /ʀədvabl/ adj être ∼ à qn de (argent) owe sb; (fig) be indebted to sb for.

redevance /ʀədvɑ̃s/ nf (de télévision) licence fee; (de téléphone) rental charge.

rédiger /ʀediʒe/ 40 vt write; (contrat) draw up.

redire /ʀədiʀ/ 27 vt repeat; **avoir** ou **trouver à ∼ à** find fault with.

redondant, ∼e /ʀədɔ̃dɑ̃, -t/ adj superfluous.

redonner /ʀədɔne/ 1 vt (rendre) give back; (donner davantage) give more; (donner de nouveau) give again.

redoubler /ʀəduble/ 1 vt increase; (classe) repeat; ∼ **de prudence** be even more careful. ● vi (Scol) repeat a year; (s'intensifier) intensify.

redoutable /ʀədutabl/ adj formidable.

redouter /ʀədute/ 1 vt dread.

redressement /ʀədʀɛsmɑ̃/ nm (reprise) recovery; ∼ **judiciaire** receivership.

redresser /ʀədʀese/ 1 vt straighten (out ou up); (situation) right, redress; (économie, entreprise) turn around. □ se ∼ vpr (personne) straighten (oneself) up; (se remettre debout) stand up; (pays, économie) recover.

réduction /ʀedyksjɔ̃/ nf reduction.

réduire /ʀeduiʀ/ 17 vt reduce (à to). □ se ∼ vpr be reduced ou cut; se ∼ à (revenir à) come down to.

réduit, ∼e /ʀedui, -t/ adj (objet) smallscale; (limité) limited. ● nm cubbyhole.

rééducation /ʀeedykasjɔ̃/ nf (de handicapé) rehabilitation; (Méd) physiotherapy. **rééduquer** 1 vt (personne) rehabilitate; (membre) restore normal movement to.

réel, ∼le /ʀeɛl/ adj real. ● nm reality. **réellement** adv really.

réexpédier /ʀeɛkspedje/ 45 vt forward; (retourner) send back.

refaire /ʀəfɛʀ/ 33 vt do again; (erreur, voyage) make again; (réparer) do up, redo.

réfectoire /ʀefɛktwaʀ/ nm refectory.

référence /ʀefeʀɑ̃s/ nf reference.

référendum /ʀefeʀɛ̃dɔm/ nm referendum.

référer /ʀefeʀe/ 14 vi **en ∼ à** consult. □ se ∼ à vpr refer to, consult.

refermer /ʀəfɛʀme/ 1 vt close (again). □ se ∼ vpr close (again).

réfléchi, ∼e /ʀefleʃi/ adj (personne) thoughtful; (verbe) reflexive.

réfléchir /ʀefleʃiʀ/ 2 vi think (à, sur about). ● vt reflect. □ se ∼ vpr be reflected.

reflet /ʀəflɛ/ nm reflection; (nuance) sheen.

refléter /ʀəflete/ 14 vt reflect. □ se ∼ vpr be reflected.

réflexe /ʀeflɛks/ adj reflex. ● nm reflex; (réaction) reaction.

réflexion /ʀeflɛksjɔ̃/ nf (pensée) thought, reflection; (remarque) remark, comment; **à la ∼** on second thoughts.

refluer /ʀəflye/ 1 vi flow back; (foule) retreat; (inflation) go down.

reflux /ʀəfly/ nm (marée) ebb, tide.

réforme /ʀefɔʀm/ nf reform. **réformer** 1 vt reform; (soldat) invalid out.

refouler /ʀəfule/ 1 vt (larmes) hold back; (désir) repress; (souvenir) suppress.

refrain /ʀəfʀɛ̃/ nm chorus; **le même ∼** the same old story.

refréner /ʀəfʀene/ 14 vt curb, check.

réfrigérateur /ʀefʀiʒeʀatœʀ/ nm refrigerator.

refroidir /ʀəfʀwadiʀ/ 2 vt/i cool (down). □ se ∼ vpr (personne, temps) get cold. **refroidissement** nm cooling; (rhume) chill.

refuge /ʀəfyʒ/ nm refuge; (chalet) mountain hut.

réfugié, ∼e /ʀefyʒje/ nm, f refugee. **réfugier (se)** 45 vpr take refuge.

refus /ʀəfy/ nm refusal; **ce n'est pas de ∼** 1 I wouldn't say no.

refuser /ʀəfyze/ 1 vt refuse (de to); (client, spectateur) turn away; (recaler) fail; (à un poste) turn down. □ se ∼ à vpr (évidence) reject; **se ∼ à faire** refuse to do.

regain /ʀəɡɛ̃/ nm ∼ **de** renewal ou revival of; (Comm) rise.

régal (pl ~s) /ʀegal/ nm treat, delight.

régaler /ʀegale/ **1** vt ~ qn de treat sb to. □ **se** ~ vpr (de nourriture) **je me régale** it's delicious.

regard /ʀəgaʀ/ nm (expression, coup d'œil) look; (vue) eye; (yeux) eyes; ~ **fixe** stare; **au** ~ **de** with regard to; **en** ~ **de** compared with.

regardant, ~e /ʀəgaʀdɑ̃, -t/ adj ~ **avec son argent** careful with money; **peu** ~ **(sur)** not fussy (about).

regarder /ʀəgaʀde/ **1** vt look at; (observer) watch; (considérer) consider; (concerner) concern; ~ **fixement** stare at; ~ **à** think about, pay attention to. ● vi look. □ **se** ~ vpr (soi-même) look at oneself; (personnes) look at each other.

régate /ʀegat/ nf regatta.

régie /ʀeʒi/ nf ~ **d'État** public corporation; (radio, TV) control room; (au cinéma) production; (Théât) stage management.

régime /ʀeʒim/ nm (organisation) system; (Pol) regime; (Méd) diet; (de moteur) speed; (de bananes) bunch; **se mettre au** ~ go on a diet; **à ce** ~ at this rate.

régiment /ʀeʒimɑ̃/ nm regiment.

région /ʀeʒjɔ̃/ nf region. **régional, ~e** (mpl **-aux**) adj regional.

> **Région** The largest administrative unit in France, consisting of a number of départements. Each has its own Conseil régional (regional council) which has responsibilities in education and economic planning. ▷ **DÉPARTEMENT**.   *i*

régir /ʀeʒiʀ/ **2** vt govern.

régisseur /ʀeʒisœʀ/ nm (Théât) stage manager; ~ **de plateau** (TV) floor manager; (au cinéma) studio manager.

registre /ʀeʒistʀ/ nm register.

réglage /ʀeglaʒ/ nm adjustment; (de moteur) tuning.

règle /ʀegl/ nf rule; (instrument) ruler; ~s (de femme) period; **en** ~ in order.

réglé, ~e /ʀegle/ adj (vie) ordered; (arrangé) settled; (papier) ruled.

règlement /ʀegləmɑ̃/ nm (règles) regulations; (solution) settlement; (paiement) payment. **réglementaire** adj (uniforme) regulation. **réglementa-**

tion nf regulation, rules. **réglementer** **1** vt regulate, control.

régler /ʀegle/ **14** vt settle; (machine) adjust; (programmer) set; (facture) settle; (personne) settle up with; ~ **son compte à** **1** settle a score with.

réglisse /ʀeglis/ nf liquorice.

règne /ʀɛɲ/ nm reign; (végétal, animal, minéral) kingdom.

regret /ʀəgʀɛ/ nm regret; **à** ~ with regret.

regretter /ʀəgʀete/ **1** vt regret; (personne) miss; (pour s'excuser) be sorry.

regrouper /ʀəgʀupe/ **1** vt group ou bring together. □ **se** ~ vpr gather ou group together.

régularité /ʀegylaʀite/ nf regularity; (de rythme, progrès) steadiness; (de surface, écriture) evenness.

régulier, -ière /ʀegylje, -jɛʀ/ adj regular; (qualité, vitesse) steady, even; (ligne, paysage) even; (légal) legal; (honnête) honest.

rehausser /ʀəose/ **1** vt raise; (faire valoir) enhance.

rein /ʀɛ̃/ nm kidney; ~s (dos) small of the back.

reine /ʀɛn/ nf queen.

réinsertion /ʀeɛ̃sɛʀsjɔ̃/ nf reintegration.

réintégrer /ʀeɛ̃tegʀe/ **14** vt (lieu) return to; (Jur) reinstate; (personne) reintegrate.

réitérer /ʀeiteʀe/ **14** vt repeat.

rejaillir /ʀəʒajiʀ/ **2** vi ~ **sur** splash back onto; ~ **sur qn** (succès) reflect on sb.

rejet /ʀəʒɛ/ nm rejection; ~s (déchets) waste.

rejeter /ʀəʒte/ **38** vt throw back; (refuser) reject; (déverser) discharge; ~ **une faute sur qn** shift the blame for a mistake onto sb.

rejoindre /ʀəʒwɛ̃dʀ/ **22** vt go back to, rejoin; (rattraper) catch up with; (rencontrer) join, meet up with. □ **se** ~ vpr (personnes) meet up; (routes) join, meet.

réjoui, ~e /ʀeʒwi/ adj joyful.

réjouir /ʀeʒwiʀ/ **2** vt delight. □ **se** ~ vpr be delighted (de at). **réjouissances** nfpl festivities. **réjouissant, ~e** adj cheering.

r

relâche /ʀəlɑʃ/ *nm* (repos) break, rest; **faire ~** (Théât) be closed.

relâcher /ʀəlɑʃe/ **1** *vt* slacken; (*personne*) release; (*discipline*) relax. □ **se ~** *vpr* slacken.

relais /ʀəlɛ/ *nm* (Sport) relay; (hôtel) hotel; (intermédiaire) intermediary; **prendre le ~ de** take over from.

relancer /ʀəlɑ̃se/ **10** *vt* boost, revive; (renvoyer) throw back.

relatif, -ive /ʀəlatif, -v/ *adj* relative; **~ à** relating to.

relation /ʀəlasjɔ̃/ *nf* relationship; (ami) acquaintance; (personne puissante) connection; **~s** relations; **~s extérieures** foreign affairs; **en ~ avec qn** in touch with sb.

relativement /ʀəlativmɑ̃/ *adv* relatively; **~ à** in relation to.

relativité /ʀəlativite/ *nf* relativity.

relax /ʀelaks/ *adj inv* **1** laid-back.

relaxer (se) /(sə)ʀəlakse/ **1** *vpr* relax.

relayer /ʀəleje/ **31** *vt* relieve; (émission) relay. □ **se ~** *vpr* take over from one another.

reléguer /ʀəlege/ **14** *vt* relegate.

relent /ʀəlɑ̃/ *nm* stink; (fig) whiff.

relève /ʀəlɛv/ *nf* relief; **prendre ou assurer la ~** take over (de from).

relevé, ~e /ʀəlve/ *adj* spicy. ● *nm* (de compteur) reading; (facture) bill; **~ bancaire, ~ de compte** bank statement; **faire le ~ de** list.

relever /ʀəlve/ **6** *vt* pick up; (personne tombée) help up; (remonter) raise; (col) turn up; (compteur) read; (défi) accept; (relayer) relieve; (remarquer, noter) note; (plat) spice up; (rebâtir) rebuild; **~ de** come within the competence of; (Méd) recover from. □ **se ~** *vpr* (personne) get up (again); (pays, économie) recover.

relief /ʀəljɛf/ *nm* relief; **mettre en ~** highlight.

relier /ʀəlje/ **45** *vt* link (up) (à to); (livre) bind.

religieux, -ieuse /ʀəliʒjø, -z/ *adj* religious. ● *nm, f* monk, nun.

religion /ʀəliʒjɔ̃/ *nf* religion.

reliure /ʀəljyʀ/ *nf* binding.

reluire /ʀəlɥiʀ/ **17** *vi* shine.

remaniement /ʀəmanimɑ̃/ *nm* revision; **~ ministériel** cabinet reshuffle.

remarquable /ʀəmaʀkabl/ *adj* remarkable.

remarque /ʀəmaʀk/ *nf* remark; (par écrit) comment.

remarquer /ʀəmaʀke/ **1** *vt* notice; (dire) say; **faire ~** point out (à to); **se faire ~** draw attention to oneself; **remarque(z)** mind you.

remblai /ʀɑ̃blɛ/ *nm* embankment.

remboursement /ʀɑ̃buʀsəmɑ̃/ *nm* (d'emprunt, dette) repayment; (Comm) refund.

rembourser /ʀɑ̃buʀse/ **1** *vt* (dette, emprunt) repay; (billet, frais) refund; (client) give a refund to; (ami) pay back.

remède /ʀəmɛd/ *nm* remedy; (médicament) medicine.

remédier /ʀəmedje/ **45** *vi* **~ à** remedy.

remerciements /ʀəmɛʀsimɑ̃/ *nmpl* thanks. **remercier** **45** *vt* thank (de for); (licencier) dismiss.

remettre /ʀəmɛtʀ/ **42** *vt* put back; (vêtement) put back on; (donner) hand over; (devoir, démission) hand in; (faire fonctionner) switch back on; (restituer) give back; (différer) put off; (ajouter) add; (se rappeler) remember; **~ en cause** ou **en question** call into question. □ **se ~** *vpr* (guérir) recover; **se ~ au tennis** take up tennis again; **se ~ au travail** get back to work; **se ~ à faire** start doing again; **s'en ~ à** leave it to.

remise /ʀəmiz/ *nf* (abri) shed; (rabais) discount; (transmission) handing over; (ajournement) postponement; **~ en cause** ou **en question** calling into question; **~ des prix** prizegiving; **~ des médailles** medals ceremony; **~ de peine** remission.

remontant /ʀəmɔ̃tɑ̃/ *nm* tonic.

remontée /ʀəmɔ̃te/ *nf* ascent; (d'eau, de prix) rise; **~ mécanique** ski lift.

remonte-pente (*pl* **~s**) /ʀəmɔ̃tpɑ̃t/ *nm* ski tow.

remonter /ʀəmɔ̃te/ **1** *vi* go ou come (back) up; (prix, niveau) rise (again); (revenir) go back (à to); **~ dans le temps** go back in time. ● *vt* (rue, escalier) go ou come (back) up; (relever) raise; (montre) wind up; (objet démonté) put together again; (personne) buck up.

r

remontoir /ʀəmɔ̃twaʀ/ *nm* winder.

remords /ʀəmɔʀ/ *nm* remorse; **avoir du** *or* **des** ~ feel remorse.

remorque /ʀəmɔʀk/ *nf* trailer; **en** ~ on tow. **remorquer** ◼ *vt* tow.

remous /ʀəmu/ *nm* eddy; (de bateau) backwash; (fig) turmoil.

rempart /ʀɑ̃paʀ/ *nm* rampart.

remplaçant, ~**e** /ʀɑ̃plasɑ̃, -t/ *nm, f* replacement; (joueur) reserve, substitute.

remplacement /ʀɑ̃plasmɑ̃/ *nm* replacement; **faire des** ~**s** do supply teaching. **remplacer** ◼ *vt* replace.

rempli, ~**e** /ʀɑ̃pli/ *adj* full (**de** of); (journée) busy.

remplir /ʀɑ̃pliʀ/ ◼ *vt* fill (up); (formulaire) fill in *ou* out; (condition) fulfil; (devoir, tâche, rôle) carry out. ◻ **se** ~ *vpr* fill (up). **remplissage** *nm* filling; (de texte) padding.

remporter /ʀɑ̃pɔʀte/ ◼ *vt* take back; (victoire) win.

remuant, ~**e** /ʀəmɥɑ̃, -t/ *adj* boisterous.

remue-ménage /ʀəmymenaʒ/ *nm inv* commotion, bustle.

remuer /ʀəmɥe/ ◼ *vt* move; (thé, café) stir; (passé) rake up. ◼ *vi* move; (gigoter) fidget. ◻ **se** ~ *vpr* move.

rémunération /ʀemyneʀasjɔ̃/ *nf* payment.

renaissance /ʀənɛsɑ̃s/ *nf* rebirth.

renard /ʀənaʀ/ *nm* fox.

renchérir /ʀɑ̃ʃeʀiʀ/ ◼ *vi* (dans une vente) raise the bidding; ~ **sur** go one better than. ◼ *vt* increase, put up.

rencontre /ʀɑ̃kɔ̃tʀ/ *nf* meeting; (de routes) junction; (Mil) encounter; (match) match; (US) game.

rencontrer /ʀɑ̃kɔ̃tʀe/ ◼ *vt* meet; (heurter) hit; (trouver) find. ◻ **se** ~ *vpr* meet.

rendement /ʀɑ̃dmɑ̃/ *nm* yield; (travail) output.

rendez-vous /ʀɑ̃devu/ *nm* appointment; (d'amoureux) date; (lieu) meeting-place; **prendre** ~ (**avec**) make an appointment (with).

rendormir (se) /(sə)ʀɑ̃dɔʀmiʀ/ ◼ *vpr* go back to sleep.

rendre /ʀɑ̃dʀ/ ◼ *vt* give back, return; (donner en retour) return; (monnaie) give; (justice) dispense; (jugement) pronounce; ~ **heureux/possible** make happy/possible; (vomir ◼) vomit; ~ **compte de** report on; ~ **service (à)** help; ~ **visite à** visit. ◼ *vi* (terres) yield; (activité) be profitable. ◻ **se** ~ *vpr* (capituler) surrender; (aller) go (**à** to); **se** ~ **utile** make oneself useful.

rêne /ʀɛn/ *nf* rein.

renfermé, ~**e** /ʀɑ̃fɛʀme/ *adj* withdrawn. ◼ *nm* **sentir le** ~ smell musty.

renflé, ~**e** /ʀɑ̃fle/ *adj* bulging.

renforcer /ʀɑ̃fɔʀse/ ◼ *vt* reinforce.

renfort /ʀɑ̃fɔʀ/ *nm* reinforcement; **à grand** ~ **de** with a great deal of.

renier /ʀənje/ ◼ *vt* (personne, œuvre) disown; (foi) renounce.

renifler /ʀənifle/ ◼ *vt/i* sniff.

renne /ʀɛn/ *nm* reindeer.

renom /ʀənɔ̃/ *nm* renown; (réputation) reputation. **renommé,** ~**e** *adj* famous. **renommée** *nf* (célébrité) fame; (réputation) reputation.

renoncement /ʀənɔ̃smɑ̃/ *nm* renunciation.

renoncer /ʀənɔ̃se/ ◼ *vi* ~ **à** (habitude, ami) give up, renounce; (projet) abandon; ~ **à faire** abandon the idea of doing.

renouer /ʀənwe/ ◼ *vt* tie up (again); (amitié) renew; ~ **avec qn** get back in touch with sb; (après une dispute) make up with sb.

renouveau (*pl* ~**x**) /ʀənuvo/ *nm* revival.

renouveler /ʀənuvle/ ◼ *vt* renew; (réitérer) repeat; (remplacer) replace. ◻ **se** ~ *vpr* be renewed; (incident) recur, happen again.

renouvellement /ʀənuvɛlmɑ̃/ *nm* renewal.

rénovation /ʀenɔvasjɔ̃/ *nf* (d'édi- fice) renovation; (d'institution) reform.

renseignement /ʀɑ̃sɛɲ(ə)mɑ̃/ *nm* ~(**s**) information; (**bureau des**) ~**s** information desk; (**service des**) ~**s téléphoniques** directory enquiries.

renseigner /ʀɑ̃seɲe/ ◼ *vt* inform, give information to. ◻ **se** ~ *vpr* enquire, make enquiries, find out.

rentabilité /ʀɑ̃tabilite/ *nf* profitability. **rentable** *adj* profitable.

rente /ʀɑ̃t/ *nf* (private) income; (pension) annuity. **rentier, -ière** *nm, f* person of private means.

rentrée /ʀɑ̃tʀe/ nf return; (revenu) income; **la ~ (des classes)** the start of the new school year; **faire sa ~** make a comeback.

> **Rentrée** The start of the new school year at the beginning of September, used as a major marketing opportunity by stores and supermarkets. The concept of the *rentrée* also extends to literary, political and other activities which resume after the holiday period. *La rentrée parlementaire*, for example, signals the return of Parliament after the summer recess.

rentrer /ʀɑ̃tʀe/ **1** vi (aux être) go ou come back home, return home; (entrer) go ou come in; (entrer à nouveau) go ou come back in; (revenu) come in; (élèves) go back (to school); **~ dans** (heurter) smash into; **tout est rentré dans l'ordre** everything is back to normal; **~ dans ses frais** break even. ● vt (aux avoir) bring in; (griffes) draw in; (vêtement) tuck in.

renverser /ʀɑ̃vɛʀse/ **1** vt knock over ou down; (piéton) knock down; (liquide) upset, spill; (mettre à l'envers) turn upside down; (gouvernement) overthrow; (inverser) reverse. □ **se ~** vpr (véhicule) overturn; (verre, vase) fall over.

renvoi /ʀɑ̃vwa/ nm return; (d'employé) dismissal; (d'élève) expulsion; (report) postponement; (dans un livre, fichier) cross-reference; (rot) burp.

renvoyer /ʀɑ̃vwaje/ **32** vt send back, return; (employé) dismiss; (élève) expel; (ajourner) postpone; (référer) refer; (réfléchir) reflect.

repaire /ʀəpɛʀ/ nm den.

répandre /ʀepɑ̃dʀ/ **3** vt (liquide) spill; (étendre, diffuser) spread; (odeur) give off. □ **se ~** vpr spread; (liquide) spill; **se ~ en injures** let out a stream of abuse.

répandu, -e /ʀepɑ̃dy/ adj widespread.

réparateur, -trice /ʀepaʀatœʀ, -tʀis/ nm engineer. **réparation** nf repair; (compensation) compensation. **réparer** **1** vt repair, mend; (faute) make amends for; (remédier à) put right.

repartie /ʀəpaʀti/ nf retort; **avoir de la ~** always have a ready reply.

repartir /ʀəpaʀtiʀ/ **46** vi start again; (voyageur) set off again; (s'en retourner) go back; (secteur économique) pick up again.

répartir /ʀepaʀtiʀ/ **2** vt distribute; (partager) share out; (étaler) spread. **répartition** nf distribution.

repas /ʀəpa/ nm meal.

repassage /ʀəpasaʒ/ nm ironing.

repasser /ʀəpase/ **1** vi come ou go back; **~ devant qch** go past sth again. ● vt (linge) iron; (examen) retake, resit; (film) show again.

repêcher /ʀəpeʃe/ **1** vt recover, fish out; (candidat) allow to pass.

repentir¹ /ʀəpɑ̃tiʀ/ nm repentance.

repentir² (se) /(sə)ʀəpɑ̃tiʀ/ **2** vpr (Relig) repent (**de** of); **se ~ de** (regretter) regret.

répercuter /ʀepɛʀkyte/ **1** vt (bruit) send back. □ **se ~** vpr echo; **se ~ sur** have repercussions on.

repère /ʀəpɛʀ/ nm mark; (jalon) marker; (événement) landmark; (référence) reference point.

repérer /ʀəpeʀe/ **14** vt locate, spot. □ **se ~** vpr get one's bearings.

répertoire /ʀepɛʀtwaʀ/ nm (artistique) repertoire; (liste) directory; **~ téléphonique** telephone directory; (personnel) telephone book. **répertorier** **45** vt index.

répéter /ʀepete/ **14** vt repeat; (Théât) rehearse. ● vi rehearse. □ **se ~** vpr be repeated; (personne) repeat oneself.

répétition /ʀepetisjɔ̃/ nf repetition; (Théât) rehearsal.

répit /ʀepi/ nm respite, break.

replier /ʀəplije/ **45** vt fold (up); (ailes, jambes) tuck in. □ **se ~** vpr withdraw (**sur soi-même** into oneself).

réplique /ʀeplik/ nf reply; (riposte) retort; (objection) objection; (Théât) line; (copie) replica. **répliquer** **1** vt/i reply; (riposter) retort; (objecter) answer back.

répondeur /ʀepɔ̃dœʀ/ nm answering machine.

répondre /ʀepɔ̃dʀ/ **3** vt (injure, bêtise) reply with; **~ que** answer ou reply that; **~ à** (être conforme à) answer; (affection, sourire) return; (avances, *appel, critique*) respond to; ~ **de** answer for. ● *vi* answer, reply; (être insolent) answer back; (réagir) respond (à to).

réponse /ʀepõs/ *nf* answer, reply; (fig) response.

report /ʀəpɔʀ/ *nm* (transcription) transfer; (renvoi) postponement.

reportage /ʀəpɔʀtaʒ/ *nm* report; (par écrit) article.

reporter¹ /ʀəpɔʀte/ ◫ *vt* take back; (ajourner) put off; (transcrire) transfer. ☐ **se ~ à** *vpr* refer to.

reporter² /ʀəpɔʀtɛʀ/ *nm* reporter.

repos /ʀəpo/ *nm* rest; (paix) peace. **reposant, ~e** *adj* restful.

reposer /ʀəpoze/ ◫ *vt* put down again; (délasser) rest. ● *vi* rest (**sur** on); **laisser ~** (*pâte*) leave to stand. ☐ **se ~** *vpr* rest; **se ~ sur** rely on.

repousser /ʀəpuse/ ◫ *vt* push back; (écarter) push away; (dégoûter) repel; (décliner) reject; (ajourner) postpone, put back. ● *vi* grow again.

reprendre /ʀəpʀɑ̃dʀ/ ◷ *vt* take back; (confiance, conscience) regain; (souffle) get back; (évadé) recapture; (recommencer) resume; (redire) repeat; (modifier) alter; (blâmer) reprimand; ~ **du pain** take some more bread; **on ne m'y reprendra pas** I won't be caught out again. ● *vi* (recommencer) resume; (affaires) pick up. ☐ **se ~** *vpr* (se ressaisir) pull oneself together; (se corriger) correct oneself.

représailles /ʀəpʀezaj/ *nfpl* reprisals.

représentant, ~e /ʀəpʀezɑ̃tɑ̃, -t/ *nm, f* representative.

représentation /ʀəpʀezɑ̃tasjõ/ *nf* representation; (Théât) performance.

représenter /ʀəpʀezɑ̃te/ ◫ *vt* represent; (figures) depict, show; (pièce de théâtre) perform. ☐ **se ~** *vpr* (s'imaginer) imagine.

répression /ʀepʀesjõ/ *nf* repression; (d'élan) suppression.

réprimande /ʀepʀimɑ̃d/ *nf* reprimand.

réprimer /ʀepʀime/ ◫ *vt* (peuple) repress; (sentiment) suppress; (fraude) crack down on.

reprise /ʀəpʀiz/ *nf* resumption; (Théât) revival; (TV) repeat; (de tissu) darn, mend; (essor) recovery; (Comm) part-

exchange, trade-in; **à plusieurs ~s** on several occasions.

repriser /ʀəpʀize/ ◫ *vt* darn, mend.

reproche /ʀəpʀɔʃ/ *nm* reproach; **faire des ~s à** find fault with.

reprocher /ʀəpʀɔʃe/ ◫ *vt* ~ **qch à qn** reproach *ou* criticize sb for sth.

reproducteur, -trice /ʀəpʀɔdyktœʀ, -tʀis/ *adj* reproductive.

reproduire /ʀəpʀɔdɥiʀ/ ◷ *vt* reproduce; (répéter) repeat. ☐ **se ~** *vpr* reproduce; (se répéter) recur.

reptile /ʀɛptil/ *nm* reptile.

repu, ~e /ʀəpy/ *adj* satiated, replete.

républicain, ~e /ʀepyblikɛ̃, -ɛn/ *adj & nm, f* republican.

république /ʀepyblik/ *nf* republic; ~ **populaire** people's republic.

répudier /ʀepydje/ ◳ *vt* repudiate; (droit) renounce.

répugnance /ʀepyɲɑ̃s/ *nf* repugnance; (hésitation) reluctance; **avoir de la ~ pour** loathe. **répugnant, ~e** *adj* repulsive.

répugner /ʀepyɲe/ ◫ *vt* be repugnant to, disgust; ~ **à** (effort, violence) be averse to; ~ **à faire** be reluctant to do.

répulsion /ʀepylsjõ/ *nf* repulsion.

réputation /ʀepytasjõ/ *nf* reputation.

réputé, ~e /ʀepyte/ *adj* renowned (**pour** for); (école, compagnie) reputable; ~ **pour être** reputed to be.

requérir /ʀɔkeʀiʀ/ ◷ *vt* require, demand.

requête /ʀɔkɛt/ *nf* request; (Jur) petition.

requin /ʀɔkɛ̃/ *nm* shark.

requis, ~e /ʀɔki, -z/ *adj* (exigé) required; (nécessaire) necessary.

RER *abrév m* (**réseau express régional**) *Parisian rapid transit rail system.*

rescapé, ~e /ʀɛskape/ *nm, f* survivor. ● *adj* surviving.

rescousse /ʀɛskus/ *nf* **à la ~** to the rescue.

réseau (*pl ~x*) /ʀezo/ *nm* network; ~ **local** local area network, LAN; **le ~ des ~x** (Ordinat) Internet.

réservation /ʀezɛʀvasjõ/ *nf* reservation, booking.

réserve /ʀezɛʀv/ *nf* reserve; (restriction) reservation, reserve; (indienne)

r

reservation; (entrepôt) store-room; **en ~** in reserve; **les ~s** (Mil) the reserves.

réserver /Rezɛʀve/ **1** vt reserve; (place) book, reserve. □ **se ~** vpr **~ qch** save sth for oneself; **se ~ pour** save oneself for; **se ~ le droit de** reserve the right to.

réservoir /Rezɛʀvwaʀ/ nm tank; (lac) reservoir.

résidence /Rezidɑ̃s/ nf residence; **~ secondaire** second home; **~ universitaire** hall of residence.

résident, ~e /Rezidɑ̃, -t/ nm, f resident; (étranger) foreign resident.

résider /Rezide/ **1** vi reside; **~ dans qch** (difficulté) lie in.

résigner (se) /(sə)Rezine/ **1** vpr **se ~ à faire** resign oneself to doing.

résilier /Rezilje/ **45** vt terminate.

résine /Rezin/ nf resin.

résistance /Rezistɑ̃s/ nf resistance; (fil électrique) element. **résistant, ~e** adj tough.

résister /Reziste/ **1** vi resist; **~ à** (agresseur, assaut, influence, tentation) resist; (corrosion, chaleur) withstand.

résolu, ~e /Rezɔly/ adj resolute; **~ à faire** determined to do. ● →**RÉSOUDRE 53**.

résolution /Rezɔlysjɔ̃/ nf (fermeté) resolution; (d'un problème) solving.

résonner /Rezɔne/ **1** vi resound.

résorber /RezɔRbe/ **1** vt reduce. □ **se ~** vpr be reduced.

résoudre /RezudR/ **53** vt solve; (crise, conflit) resolve. □ **se ~ à** vpr (se décider) resolve to; (se résigner) resign oneself to.

respect /Rɛspɛ/ nm respect. **respectabilité** nf respectability.

respecter /Rɛspɛkte/ **1** vt respect; **faire ~** (loi, décision) enforce.

respectueux, -euse /Rɛspɛktɥø, -z/ adj respectful; **~ de l'environnement** environmentally friendly.

respiration /RɛspiRasjɔ̃/ nf breathing; (haleine) breath. **respiratoire** adj respiratory, breathing.

respirer /RɛspiRe/ **1** vi breathe; (se reposer) catch one's breath. ● vt breathe (in); (exprimer) radiate.

resplendir /Rɛsplɑ̃diR/ **2** vi shine (**de** with). **resplendissant, ~e** adj brilliant, radiant.

responsabilité /Rɛspɔ̃sabilite/ nf responsibility; (légale) liability.

responsable /Rɛspɔ̃sabl/ adj responsible (**de** for); **~ de** (chargé de) in charge of. ● nmf person in charge; (coupable) person responsible.

resquiller /Rɛskije/ **1** vi **1** (dans le train) fare-dodge; (au spectacle) get in without paying; (dans la queue) jump the queue.

ressaisir (se) /(sə)RəseziR/ **2** vpr pull oneself together; (équipe sportive, valeurs boursières) make a recovery.

ressemblance /Rəsɑ̃blɑ̃s/ nf resemblance.

ressemblant, ~e /Rəsɑ̃blɑ̃, -t/ adj **être ~** (portrait) be a good likeness.

ressembler /Rəsɑ̃ble/ **1** vi **~ à** resemble, look like. □ **se ~** vpr be alike; (physiquement) look alike.

ressentiment /Rəsɑ̃timɑ̃/ nm resentment.

ressentir /Rəsɑ̃tiR/ **46** vt feel. □ **se ~ de** vpr feel the effects of.

resserrer /RəseRe/ **1** vt tighten; (contracter) compress; (vêtement) take in. □ **se ~** vpr tighten; (route) narrow; (se regrouper) move closer together.

ressort /RəsɔR/ nm (objet) spring; (fig) energy; **être du ~ de** be the province of; (Jur) be within the jurisdiction of; **en dernier ~** as a last resort.

ressortir /RəsɔRtiR/ **46** vi go ou come back out; (se voir) stand out; (film, disque) be re-released; **faire ~** bring out; **il ressort que** it emerges that. ● vt take out again; (redire) come out with again; (disque, film) re-release.

ressortissant, ~e /RəsɔRtisɑ̃, -t/ nm, f national.

ressource /RəsuRs/ nf resource; **~s** resources; **à bout de ~** at one's wits' end.

ressusciter /Resysite/ **1** vi come back to life. ● vt bring back to life; (fig) revive.

restant, ~e /Rɛstɑ̃, -t/ adj remaining. ● nm remainder.

restaurant /RɛstɔRɑ̃/ nm restaurant.

restauration /RɛstɔRasjɔ̃/ nf restoration; (hôtellerie) catering.

r

restaurer /ʀɛstɔʀe/ **1** vt restore. □ se ~ vpr eat.

reste /ʀɛst/ nm rest; (d'une soustraction) remainder; ~s remains (de of); (nourriture) leftovers; un ~ de poulet some left-over chicken; au ~, du ~ moreover, besides.

rester /ʀɛste/ **1** vi (aux être) stay, remain; (subsister) be left, remain; **il reste du pain** there is some bread left (over); **il me reste du pain** I have some bread left (over); **il me reste à** it remains for me to; **en ~ à** go no further than; **en ~ là** stop there.

restituer /ʀɛstitɥe/ **1** vt (rendre) return; (recréer) reproduce; (rétablir) reconstruct.

restreindre /ʀɛstʀɛ̃dʀ/ **22** vt restrict. □ se ~ vpr (dans les dépenses) cut back.

restriction /ʀɛstʀiksjɔ̃/ nf restriction.

résultat /ʀezylta/ nm result.

résulter /ʀezylte/ **1** vi ~ de result from, be the result of.

résumé /ʀezyme/ nm summary; **en ~** in short; (pour finir) to sum up. **résumer** **1** vt summarize.

résurrection /ʀezyʀɛksjɔ̃/ nf resurrection; (renouveau) revival.

rétablir /ʀetabliʀ/ **2** vt restore; (personne) restore to health. □ se ~ vpr (ordre, silence) be restored; (guérir) recover. **rétablissement** nm restoration; (de malade, monnaie) recovery.

retard /ʀətaʀ/ nm lateness; (sur un programme) delay; (infériorité) backwardness; **avoir du ~** be late; (montre) be slow; **en ~** be late; (retardé) behind; **en ~ sur l'emploi du temps** behind schedule; **rattraper** ou **combler son ~** catch up; **prendre du ~** fall behind.

retardataire /ʀətaʀdatɛʀ/ nmf latecomer. ● adj late.

retarder /ʀətaʀde/ **1** vt ~ **qn/ qch** delay sb/sth, hold sb/sth up; (par rapport à une heure convenue) make sb/sth late; (montre) put back. ● vi (montre) be slow; (personne) be out of touch.

retenir /ʀətniʀ/ **58** vt hold back; (souffle, attention, prisonnier) hold; (eau, chaleur) retain, hold; (larmes) hold back; (garder) keep; (retarder) detain, hold up; (réserver) book; (se rappeler)

remember; (déduire) deduct; (accepter) accept. □ se ~ vpr (se contenir) restrain oneself; **se ~ à** hold on to; **se ~ de faire** stop oneself from doing.

rétention /ʀetɑ̃sjɔ̃/ nf retention.

retentir /ʀətɑ̃tiʀ/ **2** vi ring out, resound; **~ sur** have an impact on. **retentissant, ~e** adj resounding. **retentissement** nm (effet) effect.

retenue /ʀətny/ nf restraint; (somme) deduction; (Scol) detention.

réticent, ~e /ʀetisɑ̃, -t/ adj (hésitant) hesitant; (qui rechigne) reluctant; (réservé) reticent.

rétine /ʀetin/ nf retina.

retiré, ~e /ʀətiʀe/ adj (vie) secluded; (lieu) remote.

retirer /ʀətiʀe/ **1** vt (sortir) take out; (ôter) take off; (argent, offre, candidature) withdraw; (écarter) (main, pied) withdraw; (billet, bagages) collect, pick up; (avantage) derive; **~ à qn** take away from sb. □ se ~ vpr withdraw, retire.

retombées /ʀətɔ̃be/ nfpl (conséquences) effects; **~ radioactives** nuclear fall-out.

retomber /ʀətɔ̃be/ **1** vi (faire une chute) fall again; (retourner au sol) land, come down; **~ dans** (erreur) fall back into.

retouche /ʀətuʃ/ nf alteration; (de photo, tableau) retouch.

retour /ʀətuʀ/ nm return; **être de ~** be back (de from); **~ en arrière** flashback; **par ~ du courrier** by return of post; **en ~** in return.

retourner /ʀətuʀne/ **1** vt (aux avoir) turn over; (vêtement) turn inside out; (maison) turn upside down; (lettre, compliment) return; (émouvoir **1**) shake, upset. ● vi (aux être) go back, return. □ se ~ vpr turn round; (dans son lit) twist and turn; **s'en ~** go back; **se ~ contre** turn against.

retrait /ʀətʀɛ/ nm withdrawal; (des eaux) receding; **être (situé) en ~ (de)** be set back (from).

retraite /ʀətʀɛt/ nf retirement; (pension) (retirement) pension; (fuite, refuge) retreat; **mettre à la ~** pension off; **prendre sa ~** retire.

retraité, ~e /ʀətʀete/ adj retired. ● nm, f (old-age) pensioner.

r

retrancher /ʀətʀɑ̃ʃe/ **1** vt remove; (soustraire) deduct, subtract. □ **se** ~ vpr (Mil) entrench oneself; **se** ~ **derrière** take refuge behind.

retransmettre /ʀətʀɑ̃smɛtʀ/ **42** vt broadcast.

rétrécir /ʀetʀesiʀ/ **2** vt make narrower; (vêtement) take in. ● vi (tissu) shrink. □ **se** ~ vpr (rue) narrow.

rétribution /ʀetʀibysjɔ̃/ nf payment.

rétroactif, -ive /ʀetʀɔaktif, -v/ adj retrospective; **augmentation à effet** ~ backdated pay rise.

retrousser /ʀətʀuse/ **1** vt pull up; (manche) roll up.

retrouvailles /ʀətʀuvɑj/ nfpl reunion.

retrouver /ʀətʀuve/ **1** vt find (again); (rejoindre) meet (again); (forces, calme) regain; (lieu) be back in; (se rappeler) remember. □ **se** ~ vpr find oneself (back); (se réunir) meet (again); (être présent) be found; **s'y** ~ (s'orienter, comprendre) find one's way; (rentrer dans ses frais □) break even.

rétroviseur /ʀetʀɔvizœʀ/ nm (Auto) (rear-view) mirror.

réunion /ʀeynjɔ̃/ nf meeting; (rencontre) gathering; (après une séparation) réunion; (d'objets) collection.

réunir /ʀeyniʀ/ **2** vt gather, collect; (rapprocher) bring together; (convoquer) call together; (raccorder) join; (qualités) combine. □ **se** ~ vpr meet.

réussi, ~e /ʀeysi/ adj successful.

réussir /ʀeysiʀ/ **2** vi succeed, be successful; ~ **à faire** succeed in doing, manage to do; ~ **à un examen** pass an exam; ~ **à qn** (méthode) work well for sb; (climat, mode de vie) agree with sb. ● vt (vie) make a success of.

réussite /ʀeysit/ nf success; (jeu) patience.

revaloir /ʀəvalwaʀ/ **60** vt **je vous revaudrai cela** (en mal) I'll pay you back for this; (en bien) I'll repay you some day.

revanche /ʀəvɑ̃ʃ/ nf revenge; (Sport) return ou revenge match; **en** ~ on the other hand.

rêvasser /ʀɛvase/ **1** vi daydream.

rêve /ʀɛv/ nm dream; **faire un** ~ have a dream.

réveil /ʀevɛj/ nm waking up, (fig) awakening; (pendule) alarm clock.

réveillé, ~e /ʀeveje/ adj awake.

réveille-matin /ʀevɛjmatɛ̃/ nm inv alarm clock.

réveiller /ʀeveje/ **1** vt wake (up); (sentiment, souvenir) awaken; (curiosité) arouse. □ **se** ~ vpr wake up.

réveillon /ʀevɛjɔ̃/ nm (Noël) Christmas Eve; (nouvel an) New Year's Eve. **réveillonner** **1** vi see Christmas ou New Year in.

révéler /ʀevele/ **14** vt reveal. □ **se** ~ vpr be revealed; **se** ~ **facile** turn out to be easy, prove easy.

revendeur, -euse /ʀəvɑ̃dœʀ, -øz/ nm, f dealer, stockist; ~ **de drogue** drug dealer.

revendication /ʀəvɑ̃dikasjɔ̃/ nf claim. **revendiquer** **1** vt claim.

revendre /ʀəvɑ̃dʀ/ **3** vt sell (again); **avoir de l'énergie à** ~ have energy to spare.

revenir /ʀəvniʀ/ **58** vi (aux être) come back, return (à to); ~ **à** (activité) go back to; (se résumer à) come down to; (échoir à) fall to; ~ **à 100 euros** cost 100 euros; ~ **de** (maladie, surprise) get over; ~ **sur ses pas** retrace one's steps; **faire** ~ (Culin) brown; **ça me revient!** now I remember!; **je n'en reviens pas!** □ I can't get over it!

revenu /ʀəvny/ nm income; (de l'État) revenue.

rêver /ʀeve/ **1** vt/i dream (à of; **de faire** of doing).

réverbère /ʀevɛʀbɛʀ/ nm street lamp.

révérence /ʀeveʀɑ̃s/ nf reverence; (salut d'homme) bow; (salut de femme) curtsy.

rêverie /ʀɛvʀi/ nf daydream; (activité) daydreaming.

revers /ʀəvɛʀ/ nm reverse; (de main) back; (d'étoffe) wrong side; (de veste) lapel; (de pantalon) turn-up; (de manche) cuff; (tennis) backhand; (fig) set-back.

revêtement /ʀəvɛtmɑ̃/ nm covering; (de route) surface; ~ **de sol** floor covering. **revêtir** **61** vt cover; (habit) put on; (prendre, avoir) assume.

rêveur, -euse /ʀɛvœʀ, -øz/ adj dreamy. ● nm, f dreamer.

réviser /ʀevize/ **1** vt revise; (*machine, véhicule*) service. **révision** nf revision; service.

revivre /ʀəvivʀ/ **62** vi come alive again. ● vt relive.

révocation /ʀevɔkasjɔ̃/ nf repeal; (d'un fonctionnaire) dismissal.

revoir¹ /ʀəvwaʀ/ **63** vt see (again); (réviser) revise.

revoir² /ʀəvwaʀ/ nm au ~ goodbye.

révolte /ʀevɔlt/ nf revolt. **révolté, ~e** nm, f rebel.

révolter /ʀevɔlte/ **1** vt appal, revolt. □ **se ~** vpr revolt.

révolu, ~e /ʀevɔly/ adj past; **avoir 21 ans ~s** be over 21 years of age.

révolution /ʀevɔlysjɔ̃/ nf revolution. **révolutionnaire** adj & nmf revolutionary. **révolutionner** **1** vt revolutionize.

revolver /ʀevɔlvɛʀ/ nm revolver, gun.

révoquer /ʀevɔke/ **1** vt repeal; (fonctionnaire) dismiss.

revue /ʀəvy/ nf (examen, défilé) review; (magazine) magazine; (spectacle) variety show.

rez-de-chaussée /ʀedʃose/ nm inv ground floor; (US) first floor.

RF abrév f (**République Française**) French Republic.

rhinocéros /ʀinɔseʀɔs/ nm rhinoceros.

rhubarbe /ʀybaʀb/ nf rhubarb.

rhum /ʀɔm/ nm rum.

rhumatisme /ʀymatism/ nm rheumatism.

rhume /ʀym/ nm cold; ~ **des foins** hay fever.

ri /ʀi/ →**RIRE** **54**.

ricaner /ʀikane/ **1** vi snigger.

riche /ʀiʃ/ adj rich (**en** in). ● nmf rich man, rich woman.

richesse /ʀiʃɛs/ nf wealth; (de sol, décor) richness; ~**s** wealth; (ressources) resources.

ride /ʀid/ nf wrinkle; (sur l'eau) ripple.

rideau (pl ~**x**) /ʀido/ nm curtain; (métallique) shutter; (fig) screen.

ridicule /ʀidikyl/ adj ridiculous. ● nm (d'une situation) absurdity; (le grotesque) **le ~** ridicule. **ridiculiser** **1** vt ridicule.

rien /ʀjɛ̃/ pron nothing; (quoi que ce soit) anything; **de ~!** don't mention it!; ~ **de bon** nothing good; **elle n'a**

~ **dit** she didn't say anything; ~ **d'autre/de plus** nothing else/more; ~ **du tout** nothing at all; ~ **que** (seulement) just, only; **trois fois** ~ next to nothing; **il n'y est pour** ~ he has nothing to do with it; ~ **à faire!** (c'est impossible) it's no good!; (refus) no way! **1**. ● nm **un** ~ **de** a touch of; **être puni pour un** ~ be punished for the slightest thing; **se disputer pour un** ~ fight over nothing; **en un** ~ **de temps** in next to no time.

rieur, -euse /ʀijœʀ, -øz/ adj cheerful; (yeux) laughing.

rigide /ʀiʒid/ adj rigid.

rigolade /ʀigɔlad/ nf fun.

rigoler /ʀigɔle/ **1** vi laugh; (s'amuser) have some fun; (plaisanter) joke.

rigolo, ~te /ʀigɔlo, -ɔt/ adj **1** funny. ● nm, f **1** joker.

rigoureux, -euse /ʀiguʀø, -z/ adj rigorous; (hiver) harsh; (sévère) strict; (travail, recherches) meticulous.

rigueur /ʀigœʀ/ nf rigour; **à la** ~ at a pinch; **être de** ~ be obligatory; **tenir** ~ **à qn de qch** bear sb a grudge for sth.

rime /ʀim/ nf rhyme.

rimer /ʀime/ **1** vi rhyme (**avec** with); **cela ne rime à rien** it makes no sense.

rinçage /ʀɛ̃saʒ/ nm rinse; (action) rinsing.

rincer /ʀɛ̃se/ **10** vt rinse.

riposte /ʀipɔst/ nf retort.

riposter /ʀipɔste/ **1** vi retaliate; ~ **à** (attaque) counter; (insulte) reply to. ● vt retort (**que** that).

rire /ʀiʀ/ **54** vi laugh (**de** at); (plaisanter) joke; (s'amuser) have fun; **c'était pour** ~ it was a joke. ● nm laugh; **des** ~**s** laughter.

risée /ʀize/ nf **la** ~ **de** the laughing stock of.

risque /ʀisk/ nm risk. **risqué, ~e** adj risky; (osé) daring.

risquer /ʀiske/ **1** vt risk (**de faire** of doing); (être passible de) face; **il risque de pleuvoir** it might rain; **tu risques de te faire mal** you might hurt yourself. □ **se ~ à/ dans** vpr venture to/into.

ristourne /ʀistuʀn/ nf discount.

r

rite /ʀit/ nm rite; (habitude) ritual. **rituel, ∼le** adj & nm ritual.

rivage /ʀivaʒ/ nm shore.

rival, ∼e (mpl **-aux**) /ʀival, -o/ adj & nm, f rival. **rivaliser 1** vi compete (avec with). **rivalité** nf rivalry.

rive /ʀiv/ nf (de fleuve) bank; (de lac) shore.

riverain, ∼e /ʀivʀɛ̃, -ɛn/ adj riverside. ● nm, f riverside resident; (d'une rue) resident.

rivière /ʀivjɛʀ/ nf river.

riz /ʀi/ nm rice. **rizière** nf paddy field.

robe /ʀɔb/ nf (de femme) dress; (de juge) robe; (de cheval) coat; ∼ **de chambre** dressing-gown.

robinet /ʀɔbinɛ/ nm tap; (US) faucet.

robot /ʀɔbo/ nm robot; ∼ **ménager** food processor.

robuste /ʀɔbyst/ adj robust.

roche /ʀɔʃ/ nf rock.

rocher /ʀɔʃe/ nm rock.

rock /ʀɔk/ nm (Mus) rock.

rodage /ʀɔdaʒ/ nm en ∼ (Auto) running in.

roder /ʀɔde/ **1** vt (Auto) run in; **être rodé** (personne) have got the hang of things.

rôder /ʀode/ **1** vi roam; (suspect) prowl.

rogne /ʀɔɲ/ nf 1 anger; **en** ∼ in a temper.

rogner /ʀɔɲe/ **1** vt trim; ∼ **sur** cut down on.

rognon /ʀɔɲɔ̃/ nm (Culin) kidney.

roi /ʀwa/ nm king; **les R** ∼ **mages** the Magi; **la fête des R**∼ Twelfth Night.

rôle /ʀol/ nm role, part.

roller /ʀɔlɛʀ/ nm (patin) rollerblade®; (activité) rollerblading.

romain, ∼e /ʀɔmɛ̃, -ɛn/ adj Roman. **R**∼, **∼e** nm, f Roman. **romaine** nf (laitue) cos.

roman /ʀɔmɑ̃/ nm novel; (genre) fiction.

romance /ʀɔmɑ̃s/ nf ballad.

romancier, -ière /ʀɔmɑ̃sje, -jɛʀ/ nm, f novelist.

romanesque /ʀɔmanɛsk/ adj romantic; (fantastique) fantastic; (récit) fictional; **œuvres** ∼**s** novels, fiction.

romantique /ʀɔmɑ̃tik/ adj & nmf romantic. **romantisme** nm romanticism.

rompre /ʀɔ̃pʀ/ **3** vt break; (relations) break off. ● vi (se séparer) break up; ∼ **avec** (fiancé) break up with; (parti) break away from; (tradition) break with. □ **se** ∼ vpr break.

ronce /ʀɔ̃s/ nf bramble.

rond, ∼e /ʀɔ̃, -d/ adj round; (gras) plump; (ivre 1) drunk. ● nm (cercle) ring; (tranche) slice; **en** ∼ in a circle; **il n'a pas un** ∼ 1 he hasn't got a penny.

ronde /ʀɔ̃d/ nf (de policier) beat; (de soldat, gardien) watch; (Mus) semibreve.

rondelle /ʀɔ̃dɛl/ nf (Tech) washer; (tranche) slice.

rondement /ʀɔ̃dmɑ̃/ adv promptly; (franchement) frankly.

rondeur /ʀɔ̃dœʀ/ nf roundness; (franchise) frankness; (embonpoint) plumpness.

rondin /ʀɔ̃dɛ̃/ nm log.

rond-point (pl **ronds-points**) /ʀɔ̃pwɛ̃/ nm roundabout; (US) traffic circle.

ronfler /ʀɔ̃fle/ **1** vi snore; (moteur) purr.

ronger /ʀɔ̃ʒe/ **40** vt gnaw (at); (vers, acide) eat into. □ **se** ∼ vpr se ∼ **les ongles** bite one's nails.

rongeur /ʀɔ̃ʒœʀ/ nm rodent.

ronronner /ʀɔ̃ʀɔne/ **1** vi purr.

rosbif /ʀɔsbif/ nm roast beef.

rose /ʀoz/ nf rose. ● adj & nm pink.

rosé, ∼e /ʀoze/ adj pinkish. ● nm rosé.

roseau (pl ∼**x**) /ʀozo/ nm reed.

rosée /ʀoze/ nf dew.

rosier /ʀozje/ nm rose bush.

rossignol /ʀɔsiɲɔl/ nm nightingale.

rotatif, -ive /ʀɔtatif, -v/ adj rotary.

roter /ʀɔte/ **1** vi 1 burp.

rôti /ʀoti/ nm joint; (cuit) roast; ∼ **de porc** roast pork.

rotin /ʀɔtɛ̃/ nm (rattan) cane.

rôtir /ʀotiʀ/ **2** vt roast.

rôtissoire /ʀotiswaʀ/ nf roasting spit.

rotule /ʀɔtyl/ nf kneecap.

rouage /ʀwaʒ/ nm (Tech) wheel; **les** ∼**s** the works; (d'une organisation: fig) wheels.

roucouler /ʀukule/ **1** vi coo.

roue /ʀu/ nf wheel; ∼ **dentée** cog (wheel); ∼ **de secours** spare wheel.

rouer /Rwe/ **1** vt ~ **de coups** thrash.

rouge /Ruʒ/ adj red; (fer) red-hot. ● nm red; (vin) red wine; (fard) blusher; ~ **à lèvres** lipstick. ● nmf (Pol) red. **rouge-gorge** (pl **rouges-gorges**) nm robin.

rougeole /Ruʒɔl/ nf measles (+ sg). **rouget** /Ruʒɛ/ nm red mullet.

rougeur /RuʒœR/ nf redness; (tache) red blotch.

rougir /RuʒiR/ **2** vi turn red; (de honte) blush.

rouille /Ruj/ nf rust. **rouillé, ~e** adj rusty.

rouiller /Ruje/ **1** vi rust. □ **se ~** vpr get rusty.

rouleau (pl ~**x**) /Rulo/ nm roll; (outil, vague) roller; ~ **à pâtisserie** rolling pin; ~ **compresseur** steamroller.

roulement /Rulmã/ nm rotation; (bruit) rumble; (alternance) rotation; (de tambour) roll; ~ **à billes** ball-bearing; **travailler par** ~ work in shifts.

rouler /Rule/ **1** vt roll; (ficelle, manches) roll up; (pâte) roll out; (duper **1**) cheat. ● vi (véhicule, train) go, travel; (conducteur) drive. □ **se ~ dans** vpr (herbe) roll in; (couverture) roll oneself up in.

roulette /Rulɛt/ nf (de meuble) castor; (de dentiste) drill; (jeu) roulette; **comme sur des** ~**s** very smoothly.

roulotte /Rulɔt/ nf caravan.

roumain, ~e /Rumɛ̃, -ɛn/ adj Romanian. R~, ~e nm, f Romanian.

Roumanie /Rumani/ nf Romania.

rouquin, ~e /Rukɛ̃, -in/ **1** adj red-haired. ● nm, f redhead.

rouspéter /Ruspete/ **14** vi **1** grumble, moan.

rousse /Rus/ ➡ROUX.

roussir /RusiR/ **2** vt scorch. ● vi turn brown.

route /Rut/ nf road; (Naut, Aviat) route; (direction) way; (voyage) journey; (chemin: fig) path; **en** ~ on the way; **en** ~! let's go!; **mettre en** ~ start; ~ **nationale** trunk road, main road; **se mettre en** ~ set out.

routier, -ière /Rutje, -jɛR/ adj road. ● nm long-distance lorry ou truck driver; (restaurant) transport café; (US) truck stop.

routine /Rutin/ nf routine.

roux, rousse /Ru, Rus/ adj red, russet; (personne) red-haired; (chat) ginger. ● nm, f redhead.

royal, ~e (mpl -**aux**) /Rwajal, -jo/ adj royal; (cadeau) fit for a king.

royaume /Rwajom/ nm kingdom.

Royaume-Uni /Rwajomyni/ nm United Kingdom.

royauté /Rwajote/ nf royalty.

RTT abrév f (**réduction du temps de travail**) reduction in working hours.

ruban /Rybã/ nm ribbon; (de chapeau) band; ~ **adhésif** sticky tape; ~ **magnétique** magnetic tape.

rubéole /Rybeɔl/ nf German measles (+ sg).

rubis /Rybi/ nm ruby.

rubrique /RybRik/ nf heading; (article) column.

ruche /Ryʃ/ nf beehive.

rude /Ryd/ adj (au toucher) rough; (pénible) tough; (grossier) coarse; (fameux **1**) tremendous.

rudement /Rydmã/ adv (frapper) hard; (traiter) harshly; (très **1**) really.

rudimentaire /RydimãtɛR/ adj rudimentary.

rue /Ry/ nf street.

ruée /Rɥe/ nf rush.

ruer /Rɥe/ **1** vi (cheval) buck. □ **se ~** vpr rush (**dans** into; **vers** towards); **se** ~ **sur** pounce on.

rugby /Rygbi/ nm rugby.

rugir /RyʒiR/ **2** vi roar.

rugueux, -euse /Rygø, -z/ adj rough.

ruine /Rɥin/ nf ruin; **en** (~**s**) in ruins. **ruiner** **1** vt ruin.

ruisseau (pl ~**x**) /Rɥiso/ nm stream; (rigole) gutter.

rumeur /RymœR/ nf (nouvelle) rumour; (son) murmur, hum.

ruminer /Rymine/ **1** vi (animal) ruminate; (méditer) meditate.

rupture /RyptyR/ nf break; (action) breaking; (de contrat) breach; (de pourparlers) breakdown; (de relations) breaking off; (de couple, coalition) break-up.

rural, ~e (mpl -**aux**) /RyRal, -o/ adj rural.

ruse /Ryz/ nf cunning; **une** ~ a trick, a ruse. **rusé, ~e** adj cunning.

r

russe /ʀys/ *adj* Russian. ● *nm* (Ling) Russian. **R∼** *nmf* Russian.

Russie /ʀysi/ *nf* Russia.

rustique /ʀystik/ *adj* rustic.

rythme /ʀitm/ *nm* rhythm; (vitesse) rate; (de la vie) pace. **rythmique** *adj* rhythmical.

•••••••••••••••••••••••••••••

Ss

•••••••••••••••••••••••••••••

s' /s/ ➡SE.

sa /sa/ ➡SON¹.

SA *abrév f* (**société anonyme**) PLC.

sabbatique /sabatik/ *adj* (année) sabbatical year.

sable /sɑbl/ *nm* sand; **∼s mouvants** quicksands. **sabler** *vt* 🔟 grit.

sablier /sablije/ *nm* (Culin) eggtimer.

sablonneux, -euse /sablɔnø, -z/ *adj* sandy.

sabot /sabo/ *nm* (de cheval) hoof; (chaussure) clog; (de frein) shoe; **∼ de Denver®** (wheel) clamp.

saboter /sabɔte/ 🔟 *vt* sabotage; (bâcler) botch.

sac /sak/ *nm* bag; (grand, en toile) sack; **mettre à ∼** (maison) ransack; (ville) sack; **∼ à dos** rucksack; **∼ à main** handbag; **∼ de couchage** sleeping-bag; **mettre dans le même ∼** lump together.

saccadé, ∼e /sakade/ *adj* jerky.

saccager /sakaʒe/ 🔠 *vt* (abîmer) wreck; (maison) ransack; (ville, pays) sack.

saccharine /sakaʀin/ *nf* saccharin.

sachet /saʃɛ/ *nm* (small) bag; (d'aromates) sachet; **∼ de thé** teabag.

sacoche /sakɔʃ/ *nf* bag; (de vélo) saddlebag.

sacre /sakʀ/ *nm* (de roi) coronation; (d'évêque) consecration. **sacré, ∼e** *adj* sacred; (maudit 🔟) damned. **sacrement** *nm* sacrament. **sacrer** 🔟 *vt* crown; consecrate.

sacrifice /sakʀifis/ *nm* sacrifice.

sacrifier /sakʀifje/ 🔠 *vt* sacrifice; **∼ à** conform to. □ **se ∼** *vpr* sacrifice oneself.

sacrilège /sakʀilɛʒ/ *nm* sacrilege. ● *adj* sacrilegious.

sadique /sadik/ *adj* sadistic. ● *nmf* sadist.

sage /saʒ/ *adj* wise; (docile) good, well behaved. ● *nm* wise man.

sage-femme (*pl* **sages-femmes**) /saʒfam/ *nf* midwife.

sagesse /saʒɛs/ *nf* wisdom.

Sagittaire /saʒitɛʀ/ *nm* **le ∼** Sagittarius.

saignant, ∼e /sɛɲɑ̃, -t/ *adj* (Culin) rare.

saigner /seɲe/ 🔟 *vt/i* bleed; **∼ du nez** have a nosebleed.

saillant, ∼e /sajɑ̃, -t/ *adj* prominent.

sain, ∼e /sɛ̃, sɛn/ *adj* healthy; (moralement) sane; **∼ et sauf** safe and sound.

saindoux /sɛ̃du/ *nm* lard.

saint, ∼e /sɛ̃, -t/ *adj* holy; (bon, juste) saintly. ● *nm, f* saint. **Saint- Esprit** *nm* Holy Spirit. **sainteté** *nf* holiness; (d'un lieu) sanctity. **Sainte Vierge** *nf* Blessed Virgin. **Saint-Sylvestre** *nf* New Year's Eve.

sais /sɛ/ ➡SAVOIR 🔢.

saisie /sezi/ *nf* (Jur) seizure; (Comput) keyboarding; **∼ de données** data capture.

saisir /seziʀ/ 🔢 *vt* grab (hold of); (proie) seize; (occasion, biens) seize; (comprendre) grasp; (frapper) strike; (Ordinat) keyboard, capture; **saisi de** (peur) stricken by, overcome by. □ **se ∼ de** *vpr* seize. **saisissant, ∼e** *adj* (spectacle) gripping.

saison /sezɔ̃/ *nf* season; **la morte ∼** the off season. **saisonnier, -ière** *adj* seasonal.

sait /sɛ/ ➡SAVOIR 🔢.

salade /salad/ *nf* (plat) salad; (plante) lettuce. **saladier** *nm* salad bowl.

salaire /salɛʀ/ *nm* wages (+ *pl*), salary.

salarié, ∼e /salaʀje/ *adj* wageearning. ● *nm, f* wage earner.

sale /sal/ *adj* dirty; (mauvais) nasty.

salé, ∼e /sale/ *adj* (goût) salty; (plat) salted; (opposé à sucré) savoury; (grivois 🔟) spicy; (excessif 🔟) steep. **saler** 🔟 *vt* salt.

saleté /salte/ *nf* dirtiness; (crasse) dirt; (obscénité) obscenity; **∼(s)** (camelote) rubbish; (détritus) mess.

salir /saliʀ/ **2** *vt* (make) dirty; (*réputation*) tarnish. □ **se** ~ *vpr* get dirty. **salissant**, ~**e** *adj* dirty; (*étoffe*) easily dirtied.

salive /saliv/ *nf* saliva.

salle /sal/ *nf* room; (grande, publique) hall; (de restaurant) dining room; (Théât, cinéma) auditorium; **cinéma à trois** ~**s** three-screen cinema; ~ **à manger** dining room; ~ **d'attente** waiting room; ~ **de bains** bathroom; ~ **de causette** chatroom. ~ **de séjour** living room; ~ **de classe** classroom; ~ **d'embarquement** departure lounge; ~ **d'opération** operating theatre; ~ **des ventes** saleroom.

salon /salɔ̃/ *nm* lounge; (de coiffure, beauté) salon; (exposition) show; ~ **de thé** tea-room; ~ **virtuel** chatroom.

salopette /salɔpɛt/ *nf* dungarees (+ *pl*); (d'ouvrier) overalls (+ *pl*).

saltimbanque /saltɛ̃bãk/ *nmf* (street) acrobat.

salubre /salybʀ/ *adj* healthy.

saluer /salɥe/ **1** *vt* greet; (en partant) take one's leave of; (de la tête) nod to; (de la main) wave to; (Mil) salute; (accueillir favorablement) welcome.

salut /saly/ *nm* greeting; (de la tête) nod; (de la main) wave; (Mil) salute; (rachat) salvation. ● *interj* (bonjour 🔟) hello; (au revoir 🔟) bye.

salutation /salytasjɔ̃/ *nf* greeting.

samedi /samdi/ *nm* Saturday.

SAMU /samy/ *abrév m* (**Service d'assistance médicale d'urgence**) ≈ mobile accident unit.

---
i   **SAMU** A twenty-four hour service coordinated by each *département* to send mobile medical services and staff, ambulances and helicopters to scenes of accidents and other emergencies.
---

sanction /sãksjɔ̃/ *nf* sanction. **sanctionner** **1** *vt* sanction; (punir) punish.

sandale /sãdal/ *nf* sandal.

sang /sã/ *nm* blood; **se faire du mauvais** ~ **ou un** ~ **d'encre** be worried stiff. **sang-froid** *nm inv* self-control. **sanglant**, ~**e** *adj* bloody.

sangle /sãgl/ *nf* strap.

sanglier /sãglije/ *nm* wild boar.

sanglot /sãglo/ *nm* sob. **sangloter** **1** *vi* sob.

sanguin, ~**e** /sãgɛ̃, -in/ *adj* (groupe) blood.

sanguinaire /sãginɛʀ/ *adj* bloodthirsty.

sanitaire /sanitɛʀ/ *adj* (directives) health; (conditions) sanitary; (appareils, installations) bathroom, sanitary. **sanitaires** *nmpl* bathroom.

sans /sã/ *prép* without; ~ **ça**, ~ **quoi** otherwise; ~ **arrêt** nonstop; ~ **encombre/faute/tarder** without incident/fail/delay; ~ **fin/goût/limite** endless/tasteless/limitless; ~ **importance/pareil/précédent/travail** unimportant/unparalleled/ unprecedented/unemployed; **j'ai aimé mais** ~ **plus** it was good, it wasn't great.

sans-abri /sãzabʀi/ *nmf inv* homeless person.

sans-gêne /sãʒɛn/ *adj inv* inconsiderate, thoughtless. ● *nm inv* thoughtlessness.

sans-papiers /sãpapje/ *nm inv* illegal immigrant.

santé /sãte/ *nf* health; **à ta** *ou* **votre** ~**!** cheers!

saoul, ~**e** /su, sul/ ➡ SOUL.

sapin /sapɛ̃/ *nm* fir (tree); ~ **de Noël** Christmas tree.

sarcasme /saʀkasm/ *nm* sarcasm. **sarcastique** *adj* sarcastic.

sardine /saʀdin/ *nf* sardine.

sas /sɑs/ *nm* (Naut, Aviat) airlock.

satané, ~**e** /satane/ *adj* 🔟 damned.

satellite /satelit/ *nm* satellite.

satin /satɛ̃/ *nm* satin.

satire /satiʀ/ *nf* satire.

satisfaction /satisfaksjɔ̃/ *nf* satisfaction.

satisfaire /satisfɛʀ/ **33** *vt* satisfy. ● *vi* ~ **à** fulfil. **satisfaisant**, ~**e** *adj* (acceptable) satisfactory. **satisfait**, ~**e** *adj* satisfied (**de** with).

saturer /satyʀe/ **1** *vt* saturate.

sauce /sos/ *nf* sauce; ~ **tartare** tartar sauce. **saucière** *nf* sauceboat.

saucisse /sosis/ *nf* sausage.

saucisson /sosisɔ̃/ *nm* (slicing) sausage.

sauf¹ /sof/ *prép* except; ~ **erreur** if I'm not mistaken; ~ **imprévu** unless any-

S

thing unforeseen happens; ~ **avis contraire** unless otherwise stated.

sauf², **-ve** /sof, sov/ adj safe, unharmed.

sauge /soʒ/ nf (Culin) sage.

saule /sol/ nm willow; ~ **pleureur** weeping willow.

saumon /somɔ̃/ nm salmon. ● adj inv salmon-(pink).

sauna /sona/ nm sauna.

saupoudrer /sopudʀe/ **1** vt sprinkle (**de** with).

saut /so/ nm jump; **faire un** ~ **chez qn** pop round to sb's (place); **le** ~ (Sport) jumping; ~ **en hauteur/longueur** high/long jump; ~ **périlleux** somersault; **au** ~ **du lit** on getting up.

sauté, ~**e** /sote/ adj & nm (Culin) sauté.

saute-mouton /sotmutɔ̃/ nm inv leap-frog.

sauter /sote/ **1** vi jump; (exploser) blow up; (fusible) blow; (se détacher) come off; **faire** ~ (détruire) blow up; (fusible) blow; (casser) break; ~ **à la corde** skip; ~ **aux yeux** be obvious; ~ **au cou de qn** fling one's arms round sb; ~ **sur une occasion** jump at an opportunity. ● vt jump (over); (page, classe) skip.

sauterelle /sotʀɛl/ nf grasshopper.

sautiller /sotije/ **1** vi hop.

sauvage /sovaʒ/ adj wild; (primitif, cruel) savage; (farouche) unsociable; (illégal) unauthorized. ● nmf unsociable person; (brute) savage.

S **sauve** /sov/ →**SAUF.²**

sauvegarder /sovgaʀde/ **1** vt safeguard; (Ordinat) back up.

sauver /sove/ **1** vt save; (d'un danger) rescue, save; (matériel) salvage. □ **se** ~ vpr (fuir) run away; (partir **1**) be off. **sauvetage** nm rescue. **sauveteur** nm rescuer. **sauveur** nm saviour.

savant, ~**e** /savã, -t/ adj learned; (habile) skilful. ● nm scientist.

saveur /savœʀ/ nf flavour; (fig) savour.

savoir /savwaʀ/ **55** vt know; **elle sait conduire/nager** she can drive/ swim; **faire** ~ **à qn que** inform sb that; **(pas) que je sache** (not) as far as I know; **à** ~ namely. ● nm learning.

savon /savɔ̃/ nm soap; **passer un** ~ **à qn 1** give sb a telling-off. **savonnette** nf bar of soap.

savourer /savuʀe/ **1** vt savour. **savoureux**, **-euse** adj tasty; (fig) spicy.

scandale /skɑ̃dal/ nm scandal; (tapage) uproar; (en public) noisy scene; **faire** ~ shock people; **faire un** ~ make a scene. **scandaleux**, **-euse** adj scandalous. **scandaliser 1** vt scandalize, shock.

scander /skɑ̃de/ **1** vt (vers) scan; (slogan) chant.

scandinave /skɑ̃dinav/ adj Scandinavian. **S**~ nmf Scandinavian.

Scandinavie /skɑ̃dinavi/ nf Scandinavia.

scarabée /skaʀabe/ nm beetle.

sceau (pl ~**x**) /so/ nm seal.

scélérat /seleʀa/ nm scoundrel.

sceller /sele/ **1** vt seal.

scène /sɛn/ nf scene; (estrade, art dramatique) stage; **mettre en** ~ (pièce) stage; (film) direct; **mise en** ~ direction; ~ **de ménage** domestic dispute.

scepticisme /sɛptisism/ nm scepticism.

sceptique /sɛptik/ adj sceptical. ● nmf sceptic.

schéma /ʃema/ nm diagram. **schématique** adj schematic; (sommaire) sketchy. **schématiser 1** vt simplify.

schizophrène /skizofʀɛn/ adj & nmf schizophrenic.

sciatique /sjatik/ adj (nerf) sciatic. ● nf sciatica.

scie /si/ nf saw.

sciemment /sjamã/ adv knowingly.

science /sjɑ̃s/ nf science; (savoir) knowledge.

science-fiction /sjɑ̃sfiksjɔ̃/ nf science fiction.

scientifique /sjɑ̃tifik/ adj scientific. ● nmf scientist.

scier /sje/ **45** vt saw.

scintiller /sɛ̃tije/ **1** vi glitter; (étoile) twinkle.

scission /sisjɔ̃/ nf split.

sclérose /skleʀoz/ nf sclerosis; ~ **en plaques** multiple sclerosis.

scolaire /skɔlɛʀ/ adj school. **scolarisé**, ~**e** adj going to school. **scolarité** nf schooling.

score /skɔʀ/ nm score.

scorpion /skɔʀpjõ/ nm scorpion; **le S~** Scorpio.

scotch /skɔtʃ/ nm (boisson) Scotch (whisky); (ruban adhésif)® Sellotape®.

scout, ~e /skut/ nm & adj scout.

scrupule /skʀypyl/ nm scruple. **scrupuleux, -euse** adj scrupulous.

scruter /skʀyte/ 1 vt examine, scrutinize.

scrutin /skʀytɛ̃/ nm (vote) ballot; (élections) polls (+ pl).

sculpter /skylte/ 1 vt sculpt, carve. **sculpteur** nm sculptor. **sculpture** nf sculpture.

SDF abrév m (**sans domicile fixe**) homeless person.

se, s' /sə, s/

s' before vowel or mute h.

● pronom
····▸ himself, (féminin) herself; (indéfini) oneself; (non humain) itself; (au pluriel) themselves; **~ laver les mains** wash one's hands; (réciproque) each other, one another; **ils se détestent** they hate each other.

! The translation of **se** will vary according to which verb it is associated with. You should therefore refer to the verb to find it. For example, **se promener**, **se taire** will be treated respectively under **promener** and **taire**.

séance /seãs/ nf session; (Théât, cinéma) show; **~ de pose** sitting; **~ tenante** forthwith.

seau (pl **~x**) /so/ nm bucket, pail.

sec, sèche /sɛk, sɛʃ/ adj dry; (fruits) dried; (coup, bruit) sharp; (cœur) hard; (whisky) neat. ● nm **à ~** (sans eau) dry; (sans argent) broke; **au ~** in a dry place.

sèche-cheveux /sɛʃʃəvø/ nm inv hairdrier.

sèchement /sɛʃmã/ adv drily.

sécher /seʃe/ 14 vt/i dry; (cours: 1) skip; (ne pas savoir 1) be stumped. □ **se ~** vpr dry oneself. **sécheresse** nf (de climat) dryness; (temps sec) drought. **séchoir** nm drier.

second, ~e /səgõ, -d/ adj & nm, f second. ● nm (adjoint) second in command; (étage) second floor. **secondaire** adj secondary. **seconde** nf (instant) second; (vitesse) second gear.

seconder /səgõde/ 1 vt assist.

secouer /səkwe/ 1 vt shake; (poussière, torpeur) shake off. □ **se ~** vpr 1 (se dépêcher) get a move on; (réagir) shake oneself up.

secourir /səkuʀiʀ/ 20 vt assist, help. **secouriste** nmf first-aid worker.

secours /səkuʀ/ nm assistance, help; **au ~!** help!; **de ~** (sortie) emergency; (équipe, opération) rescue. ● nmpl (Méd) first aid.

secousse /səkus/ nf jolt, jerk; (séisme) tremor.

secret, -ète /səkʀɛ, -t/ adj secret. ● nm secret; (discrétion) secrecy; **le ~ professionnel** professional confidentiality; **~ de Polichinelle** open secret; **en ~** in secret, secretly.

secrétaire /səkʀeteʀ/ nmf secretary; **~ de direction** personal assistant. ● nm (meuble) writing desk; **~ d'État** junior minister.

secrétariat /səkʀetaʀja/ nm secretarial work; (bureau) secretariat.

sectaire /sɛktɛʀ/ adj sectarian.

secte /sɛkt/ nf sect.

secteur /sɛktœʀ/ nm area; (Comm) sector; (circuit: Électr) mains (+ pl).

section /sɛksjõ/ nf section; (Scol) stream; (Mil) platoon. **sectionner** 1 vt sever.

sécuriser /sekyʀize/ 1 vt reassure.

sécurisé, e /sekyʀize/ adj (Ordinat) secure; **une ligne ~e** a secure line.

sécurité /sekyʀite/ nf security; (absence de danger) safety; **en ~** safe, secure; **Sécurité sociale** nf social services, social security services; **~ des frontières** homeland security.

sédatif /sedatif/ nm sedative.

sédentaire /sedãtɛʀ/ adj sedentary.

séducteur, -trice /sedyktœʀ, -tʀis/ adj seductive. ● nm, f seducer. **séduction** nf seduction; (charme) charm.

séduire /sedɥiʀ/ 17 vt charm; (plaire à) appeal to; (sexuellement) seduce. **séduisant, ~e** adj attractive.

ségrégation /segʀegasjõ/ nf segregation.

S

seigle /sɛgl/ *nm* rye.

seigneur /sɛɲœʀ/ *nm* lord; **le S~** the Lord.

sein /sɛ̃/ *nm* breast; **au ~ de** within.

séisme /seism/ *nm* earthquake.

seize /sɛz/ *adj & nm* sixteen.

séjour /seʒuʀ/ *nm* stay; (pièce) living room. **séjourner** ◨ *vi* stay.

sel /sɛl/ *nm* salt; (piquant) spice.

sélectif, -ive /selɛktif, -v/ *adj* selective.

sélection /selɛksjɔ̃/ *nf* selection. **sélectionner** ◨ *vt* select.

selle /sɛl/ *nf* saddle; **~s** (Méd) stools.

sellette /selɛt/ *nf* **sur la ~** (personne) in the hot seat.

selon /səlɔ̃/ *prép* according to; **~ que** depending on whether.

semaine /səmɛn/ *nf* week; **en ~** during the week.

sémantique /semɑ̃tik/ *adj* semantic. ● *nf* semantics.

semblable /sɑ̃blabl/ *adj* similar (à to). ● *nm* fellow (creature).

semblant /sɑ̃blɑ̃/ *nm* **faire ~ de** pretend to; **un ~ de** a semblance of.

sembler /sɑ̃ble/ ◨ *vi* seem (à to; que that); **il me semble que** it seems to me that.

semelle /səmɛl/ *nf* sole; **~ compensée** wedge heel.

semence /s(ə)mɑ̃s/ *nf* seed.

semer /s(ə)me/ ⑥ *vt* (graine, doute) sow; (jeter, parsemer) strew; (personne ᴵ) lose; **~ la panique** spread panic.

semestre /səmɛstʀ/ *nm* half year; (Univ) semester. **semestriel, ~le** *adj* (revue) biannual; (examen) end-of-semester.

séminaire /seminɛʀ/ *nm* (Relig) seminary; (Univ) seminar.

semi-remorque /s(ə)miʀ(ə)mɔʀk/ *nm* articulated lorry.

semis /s(ə)mi/ *nm* seedling.

semoule /s(ə)mul/ *nf* semolina.

sénat /sena/ *nm* senate. **sénateur** *nm* senator.

sénile /senil/ *adj* senile.

senior /senjɔʀ/ *adj* (âgé) senior; (mode, publication) for senior citizens. ● *nmf* senior citizen.

sens /sɑ̃s/ *nm* (Méd) sense; (signification) meaning, sense; (direction) direction; **à mon ~** to my mind; **à ~**

unique (rue) one-way; **ça n'a pas de ~** it doesn't make sense; **~ commun** common sense; **~ giratoire** roundabout; **~ interdit** no-entry sign; (rue) one-way street; **dans le ~ des aiguilles d'une montre** clockwise; **dans le ~ inverse des aiguilles d'une montre** anticlockwise; **~ dessus dessous** upside down; **~ devant derrière** back to front.

sensation /sɑ̃sasjɔ̃/ *nf* feeling, sensation; **faire ~** create a sensation. **sensationnel, ~le** *adj* sensational.

sensé, ~e /sɑ̃se/ *adj* sensible.

sensibiliser /sɑ̃sibilize/ ◨ *vt* **~ l'opinion** increase people's awareness (**à qch** to sth).

sensibilité /sɑ̃sibilite/ *nf* sensitivity. **sensible** *adj* sensitive (à to); (appréciable) noticeable. **sensiblement** *adv* noticeably.

sensoriel, ~le /sɑ̃sɔʀjɛl/ *adj* sensory.

sensualité /sɑ̃sɥalite/ *nf* sensuousness; sensuality. **sensuel, ~le** *adj* sensual.

sentence /sɑ̃tɑ̃s/ *nf* sentence.

senteur /sɑ̃tœʀ/ *nf* scent.

sentier /sɑ̃tje/ *nm* path.

sentiment /sɑ̃timɑ̃/ *nm* feeling; **faire du ~** sentimentalize; **j'ai le ~ que...** I get the feeling that... **sentimental, ~e** (*mpl* **-aux**) *adj* sentimental.

sentir /sɑ̃tiʀ/ ⑯ *vt* feel; (odeur) smell; (pressentir) sense; **~ la lavande** smell of lavender; **je ne peux pas le ~** ᴵ I can't stand him. ● *vi* smell. ◻ **se ~** *vpr* **se ~ fier/mieux** feel proud/better.

séparation /separasjɔ̃/ *nf* separation.

séparatiste /separatist/ *adj & nmf* separatist.

séparé, ~e /separe/ *adj* separate; (conjoints) separated.

séparer /separe/ ◨ *vt* separate; (en deux) split. ◻ **se ~** *vpr* separate, part (**de** from); (se détacher) split; **se ~ de** (se défaire de) part with.

sept /sɛt/ *adj & nm* seven.

septante /sɛptɑ̃t/ *adj & nm* seventy.

septembre /sɛptɑ̃bʀ/ *nm* September.

septentrional, ~e (*mpl* **-aux**) /sɛptɑ̃tʀijonal, -o/ *adj* northern.

septième /sɛtjɛm/ *adj & nmf* seventh.

sépulture /sepyltyʀ/ *nf* burial; (lieu) burial place.

séquelles /sekɛl/ *nfpl* (maladie) after-effects; (fig) aftermath.

séquence /sekɑ̃s/ *nf* sequence.

séquestrer /sekɛstʀe/ **1** *vt* confine (illegally).

sera, serait /sɔʀa, sɔʀɛ/ →**ÊTRE 4**.

serbe /sɛʀb/ *adj* Serbian. **S~** *nmf* Serbian.

Serbie /sɛʀbi/ *nf* Serbia.

serein, ~e /sɔʀɛ̃, -ɛn/ *adj* serene.

sérénité /seʀenite/ *nf* serenity.

sergent /sɛʀʒɑ̃/ *nm* sergeant.

série /seʀi/ *nf* series (+ *sg*) ; (d'objets) set; **de ~** (*véhicule etc.*) standard; **fabrication** *ou* **production en ~** mass production.

sérieusement /seʀjøzmɑ̃/ *adv* seriously.

sérieux, -ieuse /seʀjø, -z/ *adj* serious; (digne de confiance) reliable; (*chances, raison*) good. ● *nm* seriousness; **garder son ~** keep a straight face; **prendre au ~** take seriously.

serin /sɔʀɛ̃/ *nm* canary.

seringue /sɔʀɛ̃g/ *nf* syringe.

serment /sɛʀmɑ̃/ *nm* oath; (promesse) vow.

sermon /sɛʀmɔ̃/ *nm* sermon. **sermonner 1** *vt* lecture.

séropositif, -ive /seʀɔpɔzitif, -v/ *adj* HIV positive.

serpent /sɛʀpɑ̃/ *nm* snake; **~ à sonnettes** rattlesnake.

serpillière /sɛʀpijɛʀ/ *nf* floorcloth.

serre /sɛʀ/ *nf* (de jardin) greenhouse; (griffe) claw.

serré, ~e /seʀe/ *adj* (habit, nœud, écrou) tight; (personnes) packed, crowded; (lutte, mailles) close; (écriture) cramped; (cœur) heavy.

serrer /seʀe/ **1** *vt* (saisir) grip; (presser) squeeze; (vis, corde, ceinture) tighten; (poing, dents) clench; **~ qn dans ses bras** hug sb; **~ les rangs** close ranks; **~ qn** (vêtement) be tight on sb; **~ qn de près** follow sb closely; **~ la main à** shake hands with. ● *vi* **~ à droite** keep over to the right. □ **se ~** *vpr* (se rapprocher) squeeze (up).

serrure /seʀyʀ/ *nf* lock. **serrurier** *nm* locksmith.

servante /sɛʀvɑ̃t/ *nf* (maid) servant.

serveur, -euse /sɛʀvœʀ, -øz/ *nm, f* (homme) waiter; (femme) waitress.

● *nm* (Ordinat.) server.

serviable /sɛʀvjabl/ *adj* helpful.

service /sɛʀvis/ *nm* service; (fonction, temps de travail) duty; (pourboire) service (charge); (dans une société) department; (**~ non**) **compris** service (not) included; **être de ~** be on duty; **pendant le ~** (when) on duty; **rendre ~ à qn** be a help to sb; **~ à thé** tea set; **~ d'ordre** stewards (+ *pl*); **~ aprèsvente** after-sales service; **~ militaire** military service; **les ~s secrets** the secret service (+ *sg*).

serviette /sɛʀvjɛt/ *nf* (de toilette) towel; (cartable) briefcase; (**~ de table**) serviette, napkin; **~ hygiénique** sanitary towel.

servir /sɛʀviʀ/ **46** *vt/i* serve; (être utile) be of use, serve; **~ qn (à table)** wait on sb; **ça sert à** (outil, récipient) it is used for; **ça me sert à/de** I use it to/as; **ça ne sert à rien** (action) it's pointless; **~ de** serve as, be used as; **~ à qn de guide** act as a guide for sb. □ **se ~** *vpr* (à table) help oneself (de to); **se ~ de** use. **serviteur** *nm* servant.

ses /se/ →**SON**[1].

session /sesjɔ̃/ *nf* session.

seuil /sœj/ *nm* doorstep; (entrée) doorway; (fig) threshold.

seul, ~e /sœl/ *adj* alone, on one's own; (unique) only; **un ~ exemple** only one example; **pas un ~ ami** not a single friend; **lui ~ le sait** only he knows; **dans le ~ but de** with the sole aim of; **parler tout ~** talk to oneself; **faire qch tout ~** do sth on one's own. ● *nm, f* **le ~ la ~e** the only one. **seulement** *adv* only.

sève /sɛv/ *nf* sap.

sévère /sevɛʀ/ *adj* severe. **sévérité** *nf* severity.

sévices /sevis/ *nmpl* physical abuse.

sévir /seviʀ/ **2** *vi* (fléau) rage; **~ contre** punish.

sevrer /sɔvʀe/ **6** *vt* wean.

sexe /sɛks/ *nm* sex; (organes) genitals (+ *pl*). **sexiste** *adj* sexist. **sexualité** *nf* sexuality. **sexuel, ~le** *adj* sexual.

shampooing /ʃɑ̃pwɛ̃/ *nm* shampoo.

shérif /ʃeʀif/ *nm* sheriff.

short /ʃɔʀt/ *nm* shorts (+ *pl*).

S

si (**s'** *before il, ils*) /si, s/ *conj* if; (interrogation indirecte) if, whether; ~ **on allait se promener?** what about a walk?; **s'il vous** *ou* **te plaît** please; ~ **oui** if so; ~ **seulement** if only. ● *adv* (tellement) so; (oui) yes; **un ~ bon repas** such a good meal; ~ **habile qu'il soit** however skilful he may be; ~ **bien que** with the result that.

sida /sida/ *nm* (Méd) Aids.

sidérurgie /sideʀyʀʒi/ *nf* steel industry.

siècle /sjɛkl/ *nm* century; (époque) age.

siège /sjɛʒ/ *nm* seat; (Mil) siege; ~ **éjectable** ejector seat; ~ **social** head office, headquarters (+ *pl*). **siéger** 14 40 *vi* (assemblée) sit.

sien, ~**ne** /sjɛ̃, -ɛn/ *pron* **le** ~, **la** ~**ne**, **les** (~**ne**)**s** (homme) his; (femme) hers; (chose) its; **les** ~**s** (famille) one's family.

sieste /sjɛst/ *nf* nap, siesta.

sifflement /sifləmɑ̃/ *nm* whistling; **un** ~ a whistle.

siffler /sifle/ 1 *vi* whistle; (avec un sifflet) blow one's whistle; (serpent, gaz) hiss. ● *vt* (air) whistle; (chien) whistle to *ou* for; (acteur) hiss.

sifflet /siflɛ/ *nm* whistle; ~**s** (huées) boos.

sigle /sigl/ *nm* acronym.

signal (*pl* -**aux**) /siɲal, -o/ *nm* signal; ~ **sonore** (de répondeur) tone.

signalement /siɲalmɑ̃/ *nm* description.

signaler /siɲale/ 1 *vt* indicate; (par une sonnerie, un écriteau) signal; (dénoncer, mentionner) report; (faire remarquer) point out.

signalisation /siɲalizasjɔ̃/ *nf* signalling, signposting; (signaux) signals (+ *pl*).

signataire /siɲatɛʀ/ *nmf* signatory.

signature /siɲatyʀ/ *nf* signature; (action) signing; ~ **électronique** digital signature.

signe /siɲ/ *nm* sign; (de ponctuation) mark; **faire** ~ **à qn** wave at sb; (contacter) contact; **faire** ~ **à qn de** beckon sb to; **faire** ~ **que non** shake one's head; **faire** ~ **que oui** nod.

signer /siɲe/ 1 *vt* sign. □ **se** ~ *vpr* (Relig) cross oneself.

signet /siɲɛ/ *nm* (pour livre, Internet) bookmark; ~**s favoris** (Internet) hotlist.

significatif, -ive /siɲifikatif, -v/ *adj* significant.

signification /siɲifikasjɔ̃/ *nf* meaning. **signifier** 45 *vt* mean, signify; (faire connaître) make known (**à** to).

silence /silɑ̃s/ *nm* silence; (Mus) rest; **garder le** ~ keep silent.

silencieux, -ieuse /silɑ̃sjø, -z/ *adj* silent. ● *nm* silencer.

silex /silɛks/ *nm inv* flint.

silhouette /silwɛt/ *nf* outline, silhouette.

sillon /sijɔ̃/ *nm* furrow; (de disque) groove.

sillonner /sijɔne/ 1 *vt* crisscross.

similaire /similɛʀ/ *adj* similar. **similitude** *nf* similarity.

simple /sɛ̃pl/ *adj* simple; (non double) single. ● *nm* ~ **dames/messieurs** ladies'/men's singles (+ *pl*). **simple d'esprit** *nmf* simpleton. **simplement** *adv* simply. **simplicité** *nf* simplicity; (naïveté) simpleness.

simplification /sɛ̃plifikasjɔ̃/ *nf* simplification. **simplifier** 45 *vt* simplify.

simpliste /sɛ̃plist/ *adj* simplistic.

simulacre /simylakʀ/ *nm* pretence, sham.

simulation /simylasjɔ̃/ *nf* simulation. **simuler** 1 *vt* simulate.

simultané, ~**e** /simyltane/ *adj* simultaneous.

sincère /sɛ̃sɛʀ/ *adj* sincere. **sincérité** *nf* sincerity.

singe /sɛ̃ʒ/ *nm* monkey; (grand) ape. **singer** 40 *vt* mimic, ape.

singulier, -ière /sɛ̃gylje, -jɛʀ/ *adj* peculiar, remarkable; (Gram) singular. ● *nm* (Gram) singular.

sinistre /sinistʀ/ *adj* sinister. ● *nm* disaster; (incendie) blaze; (dommages) damage.

sinistré, ~**e** /sinistʀe/ *adj* stricken. ● *nm, f* disaster victim.

sinon /sinɔ̃/ *conj* (autrement) otherwise; (sauf) except (**que** that); **difficile** ~ **impossible** difficult if not impossible.

sinueux, -euse /sinɥø, -z/ *adj* winding; (fig) tortuous.

sirène /siʀɛn/ *nf* (appareil) siren; (femme) mermaid.

sirop /siʀo/ *nm* (de fruits, Méd) syrup; (boisson) cordial.

sismique /sismik/ *adj* seismic.

site /sit/ *nm* site; ~ **touristique** place of interest; ~ **Internet** *or* **Web** Web site.

sitôt /sito/ *adv* ~ **entré** immediately after coming in; ~ **que** as soon as; **pas de** ~ not for a while.

situation /sitɥasjɔ̃/ *nf* situation; (emploi) job, position; ~ **de famille** marital status.

situé, ~**e** /sitɥe/ *adj* situated.

situer /sitɥe/ **1** *vt* situate, locate. □ **se** ~ *vpr* (se trouver) be situated.

six /sis/ (/si/ before consonant, /siz/ before vowel) *adj & nm* six. **sixième** *adj & nmf* sixth.

sketch (*pl* ~**es**) /skɛtʃ/ *nm* (Théât) sketch.

ski /ski/ *nm* (matériel) ski; (Sport) skiing; **faire du** ~ ski; ~ **de fond** cross-country skiing; ~ **nautique** water skiing. **skier** 45 *vi* ski.

slave /slav/ *adj* Slav; (Ling) Slavonic.

slip /slip/ *nm* (d'homme) underpants (+ *pl*); (de femme) knickers (+ *pl*); ~ **de bain** (swimming) trunks (+ *pl*); (du bikini) bikini bottom.

slogan /slɔgɑ̃/ *nm* slogan.

Slovaquie /slɔvaki/ *nf* Slovakia.

Slovénie /slɔveni/ *nf* Slovenia.

smoking /smɔkiŋ/ *nm* dinner jacket.

SNCF *abrév f* (**Société nationale des Chemins de fer français**) *French national railway company.*

snob /snɔb/ *nmf* snob. ● *adj* snobbish. **snobisme** *nm* snobbery.

sobre /sɔbʀ/ *adj* sober.

social, ~**e** (*mpl* -**iaux**) /sɔsjal, -jo/ *adj* social.

socialisme /sɔsjalism/ *nm* socialism. **socialiste** *nmf & a* socialist.

société /sɔsjete/ *nf* society; (entreprise) company; ~ **point com** dot-com.

socle /sɔkl/ *nm* (de colonne, statue) plinth; (de lampe) base.

socquette /sɔkɛt/ *nf* ankle sock.

soda /sɔda/ *nm* fizzy drink.

sœur /sœʀ/ *nf* sister.

soi /swa/ *pron* oneself; **derrière** ~ behind one; **en** ~ in itself; **aller de** ~ be obvious.

soi-disant /swadizɑ̃/ *adj inv* so-called. ● *adv* supposedly.

soie /swa/ *nf* silk.

soif /swaf/ *nf* thirst; **avoir** ~ be thirsty; **donner** ~ make one thirsty.

soigné, ~**e** /swaɲe/ *adj* (apparence) tidy, neat; (travail) carefully done.

soigner /swaɲe/ **1** *vt* (s'occuper de) look after, take care of; (tenue, style) take care over; (maladie) treat. □ **se** ~ *vpr* look after oneself.

soigneusement /swaɲøzmɑ̃/ *adv* carefully. **soigneux**, -**euse** *adj* careful (de about); (ordonné) tidy.

soi-même /swamɛm/ *pron* oneself.

soin /swɛ̃/ *nm* care; (ordre) tidiness; ~**s** care; (Méd) treatment; **avec** ~ carefully; **avoir** *ou* **prendre** ~ **de qn/de faire** take care of sb/to do; **premiers** ~**s** first aid (+ *sg*).

soir /swaʀ/ *nm* evening; **à ce** ~ see you tonight.

soirée /swaʀe/ *nf* evening; (réception) party.

soit /swa/ *conj* (à savoir) that is to say; ~... ~ either... or. ● →**ÊTRE** 4.

soixante /swasɑ̃t/ *adj & nm* sixty. **soixante-dix** *adj & nm* seventy.

soja /sɔʒa/ *nm* (graines) soya beans (+ *pl*); (plante) soya.

sol /sɔl/ *nm* ground; (de maison) floor; (terrain agricole) soil.

solaire /sɔlɛʀ/ *adj* solar; (huile, filtre) sun.

soldat /sɔlda/ *nm* soldier.

solde[1] /sɔld/ *nf* (salaire) pay.

solde[2] /sɔld/ *nm* (Comm) balance; **les** ~**s** the sales; ~**s** (écrit en vitrine) sale; **en** ~ (acheter) at sale price.

solder /sɔlde/ **1** *vt* sell off at sale price; (compte) settle. □ **se** ~ **par** *vpr* (aboutir à) end in.

sole /sɔl/ *nf* (poisson) sole.

soleil /sɔlɛj/ *nm* sun; (fleur) sunflower; **il y a du** ~ it's sunny.

solennel, ~**le** /sɔlanɛl/ *adj* solemn.

solfège /sɔlfɛʒ/ *nm* musical theory.

solidaire /sɔlidɛʀ/ *adj* (mécanismes) interdependent; (collègues) (mutually) supportive; **être** ~ **de qn** support sb.

S

solidarité *nf* solidarity.

solide /sɔlid/ *adj* solid; (*personne*) strong. ● *nm* solid.

solidifier /sɔlidifje/ 45 *vt* solidify. □ **se ~** *vpr* solidify.

solitaire /sɔlitɛʀ/ *adj* solitary. ● *nmf* (*personne*) loner. **solitude** *nf* solitude.

solliciter /sɔlisite/ 1 *vt* seek; (faire appel à) call upon; **être très sollicité** be very much in demand.

sollicitude /sɔlisityd/ *nf* concern.

solo /sɔlo/ *nm & a inv* (Mus) solo.

solution /sɔlysjɔ̃/ *nf* solution.

solvable /sɔlvabl/ *adj* solvent.

solvant /sɔlvɑ̃/ *nm* solvent.

sombre /sɔ̃bʀ/ *adj* dark; (triste) sombre.

sombrer /sɔ̃bʀe/ 1 *vi* sink (**dans** into).

sommaire /sɔmɛʀ/ *adj* (exécution) summary; (description) rough. ● *nm* contents (+ *pl*); **au ~** on the programme.

sommation /sɔmasjɔ̃/ *nf* (Mil) warning; (Jur) notice.

somme /sɔm/ *nf* sum; **en ~**, **~ toute** in short; **faire la ~ de** add (up), total (up). ● *nm* nap.

sommeil /sɔmɛj/ *nm* sleep; **avoir ~** be ou feel sleepy; **en ~** (projet) put on ice. **sommeiller** 1 *vi* doze; (fig) lie dormant.

sommelier /sɔməlje/ *nm* wine steward.

sommer /sɔme/ 1 *vt* summon.

sommes /sɔm/ ➡ÊTRE 4.

sommet /sɔmɛ/ *nm* top; (de montagne) summit; (de triangle) apex; (gloire) height.

sommier /sɔmje/ *nm* bed base.

somnambule /sɔmnɑ̃byl/ *nm* sleepwalker.

somnifère /sɔmnifɛʀ/ *nm* sleeping pill.

somnolent, **~e** /sɔmnɔlɑ̃, -t/ *adj* drowsy. **somnoler** 1 *vi* doze.

somptueux, **-euse** /sɔ̃ptɥø, -z/ *adj* sumptuous.

son¹, **sa** (**son** *before vowel or mute h*) (*pl* **ses**) /sɔ̃, sa, sɔ̃, se/ *adj* (homme) his; (femme) her; (chose) its; (indéfini) one's.

son² /sɔ̃/ *nm* (bruit) sound; (de blé) bran; **baisser le ~** turn the volume down.

sondage /sɔ̃daʒ/ *nm* **~ (d'opinion)** (opinion) poll.

sonde /sɔ̃d/ *nf* (de forage) drill; (Méd) (d'évacuation) catheter; (d'examen) probe.

sonder /sɔ̃de/ 1 *vt* (population) poll; (explorer) sound; (terrain) drill; (intentions) sound out.

songe /sɔ̃ʒ/ *nm* dream.

songer /sɔ̃ʒe/ 40 *vt* **~ que** think that; **~ à** think about. **songeur**, **-euse** *adj* pensive.

sonné, **~e** /sɔne/ *adj* (étourdi) groggy; I crazy.

sonner /sɔne/ 1 *vt/i* ring; (clairon, glas) sound; (heure) strike; (domestique) ring for; **midi sonné** well past noon; **~ de** (clairon) sound, blow.

sonnerie /sɔnʀi/ *nf* ringing; (de clairon) sounding; (sonnette) bell; (téléphone portable) ringtone.

sonnette /sɔnɛt/ *nf* bell.

sonore /sɔnɔʀ/ *adj* resonant; (onde, effets) sound; (rire) resounding.

sonorisation /sɔnɔʀizasjɔ̃/ *nf* (matériel) public address system.

sonorité /sɔnɔʀite/ *nf* resonance; (d'un instrument) tone.

sont /sɔ̃/ ➡ÊTRE 4.

sophistiqué, **~e** /sɔfistike/ *adj* sophisticated.

sorcellerie /sɔʀsɛlʀi/ *nf* witchcraft. **sorcier** *nm* (guérisseur) witch doctor; (maléfique) sorcerer. **sorcière** *nf* witch.

sordide /sɔʀdid/ *adj* sordid; (lieu) squalid.

sort /sɔʀ/ *nm* (destin, hasard) fate; (condition) lot; (maléfice) spell; **tirer (qch) au ~** draw lots (for sth).

sortant, **~e** /sɔʀtɑ̃, -t/ *adj* (président etc.) outgoing.

sorte /sɔʀt/ *nf* sort, kind; **de ~ que** so that; **en quelque ~** in a way; **de la ~** in this way; **faire en ~ que** make sure that.

sortie /sɔʀti/ *nf* exit; (promenade, dîner) outing; (déclaration I) remark; (parution) publication; (de disque, film) release; (d'un ordinateur) output; **~s** (argent) outgoings.

sortilège /sɔʀtilɛʒ/ *nm* (magic) spell.

sortir /sɔʀtiʀ/ 46 *vi* (*aux être*) go out, leave; (venir) come out; (aller au spectacle) go out; (*livre, film*) come out; (*plante*) come up; **~ de** (*pièce*) leave; (*milieu social*) come from; (*limites*) go beyond; **~ du commun** *ou* **de l'ordinaire** be out of the ordinary. ● *vt* (*aux avoir*) take out; (*livre, modèle*) bring out; (dire 🔟) come out with; **~ qn de** get sb out of; **être sorti d'affaire** be in the clear. ☐ **s'en ~** *vpr* cope, manage.

sosie /sɔzi/ *nm* double.

sot, ~te /so, sɔt/ *adj* silly.

sottise /sɔtiz/ *nf* silliness; (action, remarque) foolish thing; **faire des ~s** be naughty.

sou /su/ *nm* 🔟 **~s** money; **sans le ~** without a penny; **près de ses ~s** tight-fisted.

soubresaut /subʀəso/ *nm* (sudden) start.

souche /suʃ/ *nf* (d'arbre) stump; (de famille) stock; (de carnet) counterfoil.

souci /susi/ *nm* (inquiétude) worry; (préoccupation) concern; (plante) marigold; **se faire du ~** worry.

soucier (se) /(sə)susje/ 45 *vpr* **se ~ de** care about. **soucieux, -ieuse** *adj* concerned (**de** about).

soucoupe /sukup/ *nf* saucer; **~ volante** flying saucer.

soudain, ~e /sudɛ̃, -ɛn/ *adj* sudden. ● *adv* suddenly.

soude /sud/ *nf* soda.

souder /sude/ 🔟 *vt* weld, solder; **famille très soudée** close-knit family. ☐ **se ~** *vpr* (os) knit (together).

soudoyer /sudwaje/ 31 *vt* bribe.

souffle /sufl/ *nm* (haleine) breath; (respiration) breathing; (explosion) blast; (vent) breath of air; **le ~ coupé** out of breath; **à couper le ~** breathtaking.

souffler /sufle/ 🔟 *vi* blow; (haleter) puff. ● *vt* (bougie) blow out; (poussière, fumée) blow; (verre) blow; (par explosion) destroy; (chuchoter) whisper; **~ la réplique à** prompt. **souffleur, -euse** *nm, f* (Théât) prompter.

souffrance /sufʀɑ̃s/ *nf* suffering; **en ~** (affaire) pending. **souffrant, ~e** *adj* unwell.

souffrir /sufʀiʀ/ 21 *vi* suffer (**de** from). ● *vt* (endurer) suffer; **il ne peut pas le ~** he cannot stand *ou* bear him.

soufre /sufʀ/ *nm* sulphur.

souhait /swɛ/ *nm* wish; **à tes ~s!** bless you!; **paisible à ~** incredibly peaceful. **souhaitable** *adj* desirable.

souhaiter /swete/ 🔟 *vt* **~ qch à qn** wish sb sth; **~ que/faire** hope that/to do; **~ la bienvenue à qn** welcome sb.

soûl, ~e /su, sul/ *adj* drunk. ● *nm* **tout son ~** as much as one can.

soulagement /sulaʒmɑ̃/ *nm* relief. **soulager** 40 *vt* relieve.

soûler /sule/ 🔟 *vt* make drunk. ☐ **se ~** *vpr* get drunk.

soulèvement /sulɛvmɑ̃/ *nm* uprising.

soulever /sulve/ 6 *vt* lift, raise; (question, poussière) raise; (enthousiasme) arouse; (foule) stir up. ☐ **se ~** *vpr* lift *ou* raise oneself up; (se révolter) rise up.

soulier /sulje/ *nm* shoe.

souligner /suliɲe/ 🔟 *vt* underline; (yeux) outline; (taille) emphasize.

soumettre /sumɛtʀ/ 42 *vt* (assujettir) subject (**à** to); (présenter) submit (**à** to). ☐ **se ~** *vpr* submit (**à** to). **soumis, ~e** *adj* submissive. **soumission** *nf* submission.

soupape /supap/ *nf* valve.

soupçon /supsɔ̃/ *nm* suspicion; **un ~ de** (un peu de) a touch of. **soupçonner** 🔟 *vt* suspect. **soupçonneux, -euse** *adj* suspicious.

soupe /sup/ *nf* soup.

souper /supe/ 6 *vi* have supper. ● *nm* supper.

soupeser /supəze/ 🔟 *vt* judge the weight of; (fig) weigh up.

soupière /supjɛʀ/ *nf* (soup) tureen.

soupir /supiʀ/ *nm* sigh; **pousser un ~** heave a sigh.

soupirer /supiʀe/ 🔟 *vi* sigh.

souple /supl/ *adj* supple; (règlement, caractère) flexible. **souplesse** *nf* suppleness; (de règlement) flexibility.

source /suʀs/ *nf* (de rivière, origine) source; (eau) spring; **prendre sa ~ à** rise in; **de ~ sûre** from a reliable source; **~ thermale** hot spring.

sourcil /suʀsi/ *nm* eyebrow.

sourciller /suʀsije/ 🔟 *vi* **sans ~** without batting an eyelid.

S

sourd, ~e /suʀ, -d/ *adj* deaf; (*bruit, douleur*) dull; **faire la ~e oreille** turn a deaf ear. ● *nm, f* deaf person.

sourd-muet (*pl* **sourds-muets**), **sourde-muette** (*pl* **sourdes-muettes**) /suʀmɥɛ, suʀdmɥɛt/ *adj* deaf and dumb. ● *nm, f* deafmute.

souricière /suʀisjɛʀ/ *nf* mousetrap; (fig) trap.

sourire /suʀiʀ/ **54** *vi* smile (à at); **~ à** (*fortune*) smile on. ● *nm* smile; **garder le ~** keep smiling.

souris /suʀi/ *nf* mouse; **des ~** mice.

sournois, ~e /suʀnwa, -z/ *adj* sly, underhand.

sous /su/ *prép* under, beneath; **~ la main** handy; **~ la pluie** in the rain; **~ peu** shortly; **~ terre** underground.

sous-alimenté, ~e /suzalimɑ̃te/ *adj* undernourished.

souscription /suskʀipsjɔ̃/ *nf* subscription. **souscrire** **30** *vi* **~ à** subscribe to.

sous-entendre /suzɑ̃tɑ̃dʀ/ **3** *vt* imply. **sous-entendu** *nm* innuendo, insinuation.

sous-estimer /suzɛstime/ **1** *vt* underestimate.

sous-jacent, ~e /suʒasɑ̃, -t/ *adj* underlying.

sous-marin, ~e /sumaʀɛ̃, -in/ *adj* underwater; (*plongée*) deep-sea. ● *nm* submarine.

soussigné, ~e /susiɲe/ *adj & nm, f* undersigned.

sous-sol /susɔl/ *nm* (cave) basement.

sous-titre /sutitʀ/ *nm* subtitle.

soustraction /sustʀaksjɔ̃/ *nf* (déduction) subtraction.

soustraire /sustʀɛʀ/ **29** *vt* (déduire) subtract; (retirer) take away (à from). □ **se ~ à** *vpr* escape from.

sous-traitant /sutʀɛtɑ̃/ *nm* subcontractor.

sous-verre /suvɛʀ/ *nm inv* glass mount.

sous-vêtement /suvɛtmɑ̃/ *nm* underwear.

soute /sut/ *nf* (de bateau) hold; **~ à charbon** coal-bunker.

soutenir /sutniʀ/ **59** *vt* support; (*effort, rythme*) sustain; (résister à) withstand; **~ que** maintain that.

soutenu, ~e /sutny/ *adj* (constant) sustained; (style) formal.

souterrain, ~e /sutɛʀɛ̃, -ɛn/ *adj* underground. ● *nm* underground passage.

soutien /sutjɛ̃/ *nm* support.

soutien-gorge (*pl* **soutiensgorge**) /sutjɛ̃gɔʀʒ/ *nm* bra.

soutirer /sutiʀe/ **1** *vt* **~ à qn** extract from sb.

souvenir¹ /suvniʀ/ *nm* memory, recollection; (objet) memento; (cadeau) souvenir; **en ~ de** in memory of.

souvenir² (**se**) /(sə)suvniʀ/ **59** *vpr* **se ~ de** remember; **se ~ que** remember that.

souvent /suvɑ̃/ *adv* often.

souverain, ~e /suvʀɛ̃, -ɛn/ *adj* sovereign. ● *nm, f* sovereign.

soviétique /sɔvjetik/ *adj* Soviet.

soyeux, -euse /swajø, -z/ *adj* silky.

spacieux, -ieuse /spasjø, -z/ *adj* spacious.

sparadrap /spaʀadʀa/ *nm* (sticking) plaster.

spatial, ~e (*mpl* **-iaux**) /spasjal, -jo/ *adj* space.

speaker, ~ine /spikœʀ, -kʀin/ *nm, f* announcer.

spécial, ~e (*mpl* **-iaux**) /spesjal, -jo/ *adj* special; (bizarre) odd. **spécialement** *adv* (exprès) specially; (très) especially.

spécialiser (**se**) /səspesjalize/ **1** *vpr* specialize (dans in). **spécialiste** *nmf* specialist. **spécialité** *nf* speciality; (US) specialty.

spécifier /spesifje/ **45** *vt* specify.

spécifique /spesifik/ *adj* specific.

spécimen /spesimɛn/ *nm* specimen.

spectacle /spɛktakl/ *nm* show; (vue) sight, spectacle.

spectaculaire /spɛktakylɛʀ/ *adj* spectacular.

spectateur, -trice /spɛktatœʀ, -tʀis/ *nm, f* (Sport) spectator; (témoin oculaire) onlooker; **les ~s** (Théât) the audience (+ sg).

spectre /spɛktʀ/ *nm* (revenant) spectre; (images) spectrum.

spéculateur, -trice /spekylatœʀ, -tʀis/ *nm, f* speculator. **spéculation** *nf* speculation. **spéculer** **1** *vi* speculate.

spéléologie /speleɔlɔʒi/ *nf* cave exploration, pot-holing.

spermatozoïde /spɛʁmatɔzɔid/ *nm* spermatozoon. **sperme** *nm* sperm.

sphère /sfɛʁ/ *nf* sphere.

spirale /spiʁal/ *nf* spiral.

spirituel, ~le /spiʁitɥɛl/ *adj* spiritual; (*amusant*) witty.

spiritueux /spiʁitɥø/ *nm* (*alcool*) spirit.

splendeur /splɑ̃dœʁ/ *nf* splendour. **splendide** *adj* splendid.

sponsoriser /spɔ̃sɔʁize/ **1** *vt* sponsor.

spontané, ~e /spɔ̃tane/ *adj* spontaneous. **spontanéité** *nf* spontaneity.

sport /spɔʁ/ *adj inv* (*vêtements*) casual. ● *nm* sport; **veste/voiture de ~** sports jacket/car.

sportif, -ive /spɔʁtif, -v/ *adj* (*personne*) sporty; (*physique*) athletic; (*résultats*) sports. ● *nm, f* sportsman, sportswoman.

spot /spɔt/ *nm* spotlight; (**~ publicitaire**) ad.

square /skwaʁ/ *nm* small public garden.

squatter /skwate/ **1** *vt* squat in.

squelette /skəlɛt/ *nm* skeleton. **squelettique** *adj* skeletal.

SRAS *abrév m* (**syndrome respiratoire aigu sévère**) SARS.

SSII *abrév f* (**société de services et d'ingénierie informatiques**) computer services company

stabiliser /stabilize/ **1** *vt* stabilize. **stable** *adj* stable.

stade /stad/ *nm* (Sport) stadium; (*phase*) stage.

stage /staʒ/ *nm* (*cours*) course; (*professionnel*) placement. **stagiaire** *nmf* course member; (*apprenti*) trainee.

stagner /stagne/ **1** *vi* stagnate.

stand /stɑ̃d/ *nm* stand; (de fête foraine) stall.

standard /stɑ̃daʁ/ *nm* switchboard. ● *adj inv* standard. **standardiser** **1** *vt* standardize.

standardiste /stɑ̃daʁdist/ *nmf* switchboard operator.

standing /stɑ̃diŋ/ *nm* status, standing; **de ~** (*hôtel*) luxury.

starter /staʁtɛʁ/ *nm* (Auto) choke.

station /stasjɔ̃/ *nf* station; (halte) stop; **~ debout** standing position; **~ de taxis** taxi rank; **~ balnéaire/ de ski**

seaside/ski resort; **~ thermale** spa.

stationnaire /stasjɔnɛʁ/ *adj* stationary.

stationnement /stasjɔnmɑ̃/ *nm* parking. **stationner** **1** *vi* park.

station-service (*pl* **stations-service**) /stasjɔ̃sɛʁvis/ *nf* service station.

statique /statik/ *adj* static.

statistique /statistik/ *nf* statistic; (science) statistics (+ *sg.*) ● *adj* statistical.

statue /staty/ *nf* statue.

statuer /statɥe/ **1** *vi* **~ sur** give a ruling on.

statut /staty/ *nm* status. **statutaire** *adj* statutory.

sténo /steno/ *nf* (sténographie) shorthand. **sténodactylo** *nf* shorthand typist. **sténographie** *nf* shorthand.

stéréo /steʁeo/ *nf & adj inv* stereo.

stéréotype /steʁeɔtip/ *nm* stereotype.

stérile /steʁil/ *adj* sterile.

stérilet /steʁilɛ/ *nm* coil, IUD.

stérilisation /steʁilizasjɔ̃/ *nf* sterilization. **stériliser** **1** *vt* sterilize.

stéroïde /steʁɔid/ *adj & nm* steroid.

stimulant /stimylɑ̃/ *nm* stimulus; (*médicament*) stimulant.

stimulateur /stimylatœʁ/ *nm* **~ cardiaque** (Méd) pacemaker.

stimuler /stimyle/ **1** *vt* stimulate.

stipuler /stipyle/ **1** *vt* stipulate.

stock /stɔk/ *nm* stock. **stocker** **1** *vt* stock.

stoïque /stɔik/ *adj* stoical. ● *nmf* stoic.

stop /stɔp/ *interj* stop. ● *nm* stop sign; (feu arrière) brake light; **faire du ~** **1** hitch-hike. **stopper** **1** *vt/i* stop.

store /stɔʁ/ *nm* blind; (de magasin) awning.

strapontin /stʁapɔ̃tɛ̃/ *nm* folding seat, jump seat.

stratégie /stʁateʒi/ *nf* strategy. **stratégique** *adj* strategic.

stress /stʁɛs/ *nm* stress. **stressant, ~e** *adj* stressful. **stressé, ~e** *adj* stressed. **stresser** **1** *vt* put under stress.

strict /stʁikt/ *adj* strict; (tenue, vérité) plain; **le ~ minimum** the bare minimum. **strictement** *adv* strictly.

strident, ~e /stʁidɑ̃, -t/ *adj* shrill.

strophe /stʁɔf/ *nf* stanza, verse.

structure /stʀyktyʀ/ *nf* structure.

studieux, -ieuse /stydjø, -z/ *adj* studious.

studio /stydjo/ *nm* (d'artiste, de télévision) studio; (logement) studio flat.

stupéfaction /stypefaksjɔ̃/ *nf* amazement. **stupéfait, ∼e** *adj* amazed.

stupéfiant, ∼e /stypefjɑ̃, -t/ *adj* astounding. ● *nm* drug, narcotic.

stupéfier /stypefje/ **45** *vt* amaze.

stupeur /stypœʀ/ *nf* amazement; (Méd) stupor.

stupide /stypid/ *adj* stupid. **stupidité** *nf* stupidity.

style /stil/ *nm* style.

styliste /stilist/ *nmf* fashion designer.

stylo /stilo/ *nm* pen; ∼ **(à) bille** ball-point pen; ∼ **(à) encre** fountain pen.

su /sy/ →SAVOIR **55**.

suave /sɥav/ *adj* sweet.

subalterne /sybaltɛʀn/ *adj & nmf* subordinate.

subconscient /sypkɔ̃sjɑ̃/ *nm* subconscious.

subir /sybiʀ/ **2** *vt* be subjected to; (traitement, expériences) undergo.

subit, ∼e /sybi, -t/ *adj* sudden.

subjectif, -ive /sybʒɛktif, -v/ *adj* subjective.

subjonctif /sybʒɔ̃ktif/ *nm* subjunctive.

subjuguer /sybʒyge/ **1** *vt* (charmer) captivate.

sublime /syblim/ *adj* sublime.

submerger /sybmɛʀʒe/ **40** *vt* submerge; (fig) overwhelm.

subordonné, ∼e /sybɔʀdɔne/ *adj & nm, f* subordinate.

subside /sybzid/ *nm* grant.

subsidiaire /sybzidjɛʀ/ *adj* subsidiary; **question** ∼ tiebreaker.

subsistance /sybzistɑ̃s/ *nf* subsistence. **subsister** **1** *vi* subsist; (durer, persister) exist.

substance /sypstɑ̃s/ *nf* substance.

substantiel, ∼le /sypstɑ̃sjɛl/ *adj* substantial.

substantif /sypstɑ̃tif/ *nm* noun.

substituer /sypstitɥe/ **1** *vt* substitute (à for). □ **se** ∼ **à** *vpr* (remplacer) substitute for. **substitut** *nm* substitute; (Jur) deputy public prosecutor.

subtil, ∼e /syptil/ *adj* subtle.

subtiliser /syptilize/ **1** *vt* ∼ **qch (à qn)** steal sth (from sb).

subvenir /sybvəniʀ/ **59** *vi* ∼ **à** provide for.

subvention /sybvɑ̃sjɔ̃/ *nf* subsidy. **subventionner** **1** *vt* subsidize.

subversif, -ive /sybvɛʀsif, -v/ *adj* subversive.

suc /syk/ *nm* juice.

succédané /syksedane/ *nm* substitute (**de** for).

succéder /syksede/ **14** *vi* ∼ **à** succeed. □ **se** ∼ *vpr* succeed one another.

succès /syksɛ/ *nm* success; **à** ∼ (film, livre) successful; **avoir du** ∼ be a success.

successeur /syksesœʀ/ *nm* successor. **successif, -ive** *adj* successive. **succession** *nf* succession; (Jur) inheritance.

succinct, ∼e /syksɛ̃, -t/ *adj* succinct.

succomber /sykɔ̃be/ **1** *vi* die; ∼ **à** succumb to.

succulent, ∼e /sykylɑ̃, -t/ *adj* delicious.

succursale /sykyʀsal/ *nf* (Comm) branch.

sucer /syse/ **10** *vt* suck.

sucette /sysɛt/ *nf* (bonbon) lollipop; (tétine) dummy; (US) pacifier.

sucre /sykʀ/ *nm* sugar; ∼ **d'orge** barley sugar; ∼ **en poudre** caster sugar; ∼ **glace** icing sugar; ∼ **roux** brown sugar.

sucré /sykʀe/ *adj* sweet; (additionné de sucre) sweetened. **sucrer** **1** *vt* sugar, sweeten. **sucreries** *nfpl* sweets.

sucrier, -ière /sykʀije, -jɛʀ/ *adj* sugar. ● *nm* (récipient) sugar-bowl.

sud /syd/ *nm* south. ● *adj inv* south; (partie) southern.

sud-est /sydɛst/ *nm* south-east.

sud-ouest /sydwɛst/ *nm* southwest.

Suède /sɥɛd/ *nf* Sweden.

suédois, ∼e /sɥedwa, -z/ *adj* Swedish. ● *nm* (Ling) Swedish. **S∼, ∼e** *nm, f* Swede.

suer /sɥe/ **1** *vt/i* sweat; **faire** ∼ **qn** **1** get on sb's nerves.

sueur /sɥœʀ/ *nf* sweat; **en** ∼ covered in sweat.

suffire /syfiʀ/ **57** *vi* be enough (**à qn** for sb); **il suffit de compter** all you have to do is count; **une goutte suffit** a drop is enough; ~ **à** (besoin) satisfy. □ **se ~** vpr **se ~ à soi-même** be self-sufficient.

suffisamment /syfizamɑ̃/ adv sufficiently; ~ **de qch** enough of sth. **suffisance** nf (vanité) conceit. **suffisant, ~e** adj sufficient; (vaniteux) conceited.

suffixe /syfiks/ nm suffix.

suffoquer /syfɔke/ **1** vt/i choke, suffocate.

suffrage /syfʀaʒ/ nm (voix: Pol) vote; (système) suffrage.

suggérer /sygʒeʀe/ **14** vt suggest. **suggestion** nf suggestion.

suicidaire /sɥisidɛʀ/ adj suicidal. **suicide** nm suicide. **suicider (se)** **1** vpr commit suicide.

suinter /sɥɛ̃te/ **1** vi ooze.

suis /sɥi/ →ÊTRE **4**, →SUIVRE **57**.

Suisse /sɥis/ nf Switzerland. ● nmf Swiss. **suisse** adj Swiss.

suite /sɥit/ nf continuation, rest; (d'un film) sequel; (série) series; (appartement, escorte) suite; (résultat) consequence; **à la ~, de ~** (successivement) in a row; **à la ~ de** (derrière) behind; **à la ~ de, par ~ de** (en conséquence) as a result of; **faire ~ (à)** follow; **par la ~** afterwards; **~ à votre lettre du** further to your letter of the; **des ~s de** as a result of.

suivant¹, ~e /sɥivɑ̃, -t/ adj following, next. ● nm, f following ou next person.

suivant² /sɥivɑ̃/ prép (selon) according to.

suivi, ~e /sɥivi/ adj (effort) steady, sustained; (cohérent) consistent; **peu/très ~** (cours) poorly/well attended.

suivre /sɥivʀ/ **57** vt/i follow; (comprendre) follow; **faire ~** (courrier) forward. □ **se ~** vpr follow each other.

sujet, ~te /syʒɛ, -t/ adj **~ à** liable ou subject to. ● nm (d'un royaume) subject; (question) subject; (motif) cause; (Gram) subject; **au ~ de** about.

super /sypɛʀ/ nm (essence) fourstar. ● adj inv **1** (très) great. ● adv **1** ultra, really.

superbe /sypɛʀb/ adj superb.

supérette /sypeʀɛt/ nf minimarket.

superficie /sypɛʀfisi/ nf area.

superficiel, ~le /sypɛʀfisjɛl/ adj superficial.

superflu /sypɛʀfly/ adj superfluous. ● nm (excédent) surplus.

supérieur, ~e /sypeʀjœʀ/ adj (plus haut) upper; (quantité, nombre) greater (à than); (études, principe) higher (à than); (meilleur, hautain) superior (à to). ● nm, f superior. **supériorité** nf superiority.

superlatif, -ive /sypɛʀlatif, -v/ adj & nm superlative.

supermarché /sypɛʀmaʀʃe/ nm supermarket.

superposer /sypɛʀpoze/ **1** vt superimpose; **lits superposés** bunk beds.

superproduction /sypɛʀpʀɔdyksjɔ̃/ nf (film) blockbuster.

superpuissance /sypɛʀpɥisɑ̃s/ nf superpower.

superstitieux, -ieuse /sypɛʀstisjø, -z/ adj superstitious.

superviser /sypɛʀvize/ **1** vt supervise.

suppléant, ~e /sypleɑ̃, -t/ nmf & adj (professeur ~) supply teacher; (juge) ~ deputy (judge).

suppléer /syplee/ **15** vt (remplacer) fill in for. ● vi ~ **à** (compenser) make up for.

supplément /syplemɑ̃/ nm (argent) extra charge; (de frites, légumes) extra portion; **en ~** extra; **un ~ de** (travail) additional; **payer un ~** pay a supplement. **supplémentaire** adj extra, additional.

supplice /syplis/ nm torture.

supplier /syplije/ **45** vt beg, beseech (de to).

support /sypɔʀ/ nm support; (Ordinat) medium.

supportable /sypɔʀtabl/ adj bearable.

supporter¹ /sypɔʀte/ **1** vt (privations) bear; (personne) put up with; (structure: Ordinat) support; **il ne supporte pas les enfants/de perdre** he can't stand children/losing.

supporter² /sypɔʀtɛʀ/ nm (Sport) supporter.

supposer /sypoze/ **1** vt suppose; (impliquer) imply; **à ~ que** supposing that.

suppression /sypʀesjɔ̃/ nf (de taxe) abolition; (de sanction) lifting; (de mot) deletion. **supprimer** **1** vt (allocation) withdraw; (contrôle) lift; (train)

S

cancel; (*preuve*) suppress.

suprématie /sypʀemasi/ *nf* supremacy.

suprême /sypʀɛm/ *adj* supreme.

sur /syʀ/ *prép* on, upon; (*pardessus*) over; (au sujet de) about, on; (proportion) out of; (mesure) by; ∼ **la photo** in the photograph; **mettre/ jeter** ∼ put/throw on to; ∼ **mesure** made to measure; ∼ **place** on the spot; ∼ **ce, je pars** with that, I must go; ∼ **le moment** at the time.

sûr /syʀ/ *adj* certain, sure; (sans danger) safe; (digne de confiance) reliable; (*main*) steady; (*jugement*) sound; **être** ∼ **de soi** be self-confident; **j'en étais** ∼**!** I knew it!

surabondance /syʀabɔ̃dɑ̃s/ *nf* over-abundance.

surcharge /syʀʃaʀʒ/ *nf* overloading; (poids) excess load. **surcharger** ◻ *vt* overload; (*texte*) alter.

surchauffer /syʀʃofe/ ◻ *vt* overheat.

surcroît /syʀkʀwa/ *nm* increase (**de** in); **de** ∼ in addition.

surdité /syʀdite/ *nf* deafness.

surélever /syʀelve/ ◻ *vt* raise.

sûrement /syʀmɑ̃/ *adv* certainly; (sans danger) safely; **il a** ∼ **oublié** he must have forgotten.

surenchère /syʀɑ̃ʃɛʀ/ *nf* higher bid. **surenchérir** ◻ *vi* bid higher (**sur** than).

surestimer /syʀɛstime/ ◻ *vt* over-estimate.

sûreté /syʀte/ *nf* safety; (de pays) security; (d'un geste) steadiness; **être en** ∼ be safe; **S**∼ **(nationale)** police (+ *pl*).

surexcité, ∼**e** /syʀɛksite/ *adj* very excited.

surf /sœʀf/ *nm* surfing.

surface /syʀfas/ *nf* surface; **faire** ∼ (*sous-marin,* fig) surface; **en** ∼ on the surface.

surfait, ∼**e** /syʀfɛ, -t/ *adj* overrated.

surfer /sœʀfe/ ◻ *vi* go surfing; ∼ **sur l'Internet** surf the Internet.

surgelé, ∼**e** /syʀʒəle/ *adj* (deep-)frozen; **aliments** ∼**s** frozen food.

surgir /syʀʒiʀ/ ◻ *vi* appear (suddenly); (*difficulté*) crop up.

sur-le-champ /syʀləʃɑ̃/ *adv* right away.

surlendemain /syʀlɑ̃dmɛ̃/ *nm* **le** ∼ two days later; **le** ∼ **de** two days after.

surligneur /syʀliɲœʀ/ *nm* highlighter (pen).

surmenage /syʀmənaʒ/ *nm* overwork.

surmonter /syʀmɔ̃te/ ◻ *vt* (vaincre) overcome, surmount; (être au-dessus de) surmount, top.

surnaturel, ∼**le** /syʀnatyʀɛl/ *adj* supernatural.

surnom /syʀnɔ̃/ *nm* nickname. **surnommer** ◻ *vt* nickname.

surpeuplé, ∼**e** /syʀpœple/ *adj* over-populated.

surplomber /syʀplɔ̃be/ ◻ *vt/i* overhang.

surplus /syʀply/ *nm* surplus.

suprenant, ∼**e** /syʀpʀənɑ̃, -t/ *adj* surprising. **surprendre** ◻ *vt* (étonner) surprise; (prendre au dépourvu) catch, surprise; (entendre) overhear. **surpris,** ∼**e** *adj* surprised (**de** at).

surprise /syʀpʀiz/ *nf* surprise.

surréaliste /syʀealist/ *adj & nmf* surrealist.

sursaut /syʀso/ *nm* start, jump; **en** ∼ with a start; ∼ **de** (regain) burst of. **sursauter** ◻ *vi* start, jump.

sursis /syʀsi/ *nm* reprieve; (Mil) deferment; **deux ans (de prison) avec** ∼ a two-year suspended sentence.

surtaxe /syʀtaks/ *nf* surcharge.

surtout /syʀtu/ *adv* especially; (avant tout) above all; ∼ **pas** certainly not.

surveillance /syʀvejɑ̃s/ *nf* watch; (d'examen) supervision; (de la police) surveillance. **surveillant,** ∼**e** *nm, f* (de prison) warder; (au lycée) supervisor (in charge of discipline). **surveiller** ◻ *vt* watch; (*travaux, élèves*) supervise.

survenir /syʀvəniʀ/ ◻ *vi* occur, take place; (*personne*) turn up.

survêtement /syʀvɛtmɑ̃/ *nm* (Sport) tracksuit.

survie /syʀvi/ *nf* survival.

survivant, ∼**e** /syʀvivɑ̃, -t/ *adj* surviving. ● *nm, f* survivor.

survivre /syʀvivʀ/ ◻ *vi* survive; ∼ **à** (*conflit*) survive; (*personne*) outlive.

survoler /syʀvɔle/ ◻ *vt* fly over; (*livre*) skim through.

sus: en ∼ /ɑ̃sys/ *loc* in addition.

susceptible /sysɛptibl/ adj touchy; ~ **de faire** likely to do.

susciter /sysite/ **1** vt (éveiller) arouse; (occasionner) create.

suspect, ~e /syspɛ, -ɛkt/ adj (individu, faits) suspicious; (témoignage) suspect; ~ **de** suspected of. ● nm, f suspect. **suspecter 1** vt suspect.

suspendre /syspɑ̃dʀ/ **3** vt (accrocher) hang (up); (interrompre, destituer) suspend; **suspendu à** hanging from. □ **se ~ à** vpr hang from.

suspens: en ~ /ɑ̃syspɑ̃/ loc (affaire) outstanding; (dans l'indécision) in suspense.

suspense /syspɛns/ nm suspense.

suture /sytyʀ/ nf **point de ~** stitch.

svelte /svɛlt/ adj slender.

S.V.P. abrév (**s'il vous plaît**) please.

syllabe /silab/ nf syllable.

symbole /sɛ̃bɔl/ nm symbol. **symboliser 1** vt symbolize.

symétrie /simetʀi/ nf symmetry.

sympa /sɛ̃pa/ adj inv **1** nice; **sois ~** be a pal.

sympathie /sɛ̃pati/ nf (goût) liking; (compassion) sympathy; **avoir de la ~ pour** like. **sympathique** adj nice, pleasant. **sympathisant, ~e** nm, f sympathizer. **sympathiser 1** vi get on well (**avec** with).

symphonie /sɛ̃fɔni/ nf symphony.

symptôme /sɛ̃ptom/ nm symptom.

synagogue /sinagɔg/ nf synagogue.

synchroniser /sɛ̃kʀɔnize/ **1** vt synchronize.

syncope /sɛ̃kɔp/ nf (Méd) blackout.

syndic /sɛ̃dik/ nm ~ (**d'immeuble**) property manager.

syndicaliste /sɛ̃dikalist/ nmf (trade-)unionist. ● adj (trade-) union.

syndicat /sɛ̃dika/ nm (trade) union; ~ **d'initiative** tourist office.

syndiqué, ~e /sɛ̃dike/ adj **être ~** be a (trade-)union member.

synonyme /sinɔnim/ adj synonymous. ● nm synonym.

syntaxe /sɛ̃taks/ nf syntax.

synthèse /sɛ̃tɛz/ nf synthesis. **synthétique** adj synthetic.

synthé(tiseur) /sɛ̃te(tizœʀ)/ nm synthesizer.

systématique /sistematik/ adj systematic.

système /sistɛm/ nm system; **le ~ D** **1** resourcefulness.

Tt

t' /t/ ➡TE.

ta /ta/ ➡TON[1].

tabac /taba/ nm tobacco; (magasin) tobacconist's shop.

table /tabl/ nf table; **à ~!** dinner is ready!; ~ **de nuit** bedside table; ~ **des matières** table of contents; ~ **à repasser** ironing board; ~ **roulante** (tea-)trolley; (US) (serving) cart.

tableau (pl ~**x**) /tablo/ nm picture; (peinture) painting; (panneau) board; (graphique) chart; (Scol) blackboard; ~ **d'affichage** notice-board; ~ **de bord** dashboard.

tablette /tablɛt/ nf shelf; ~ **de chocolat** bar of chocolate.

tableur /tablœʀ/ nm spreadsheet.

tablier /tablije/ nm apron; (de pont) platform; (de magasin) shutter.

tabou /tabu/ nm & adj taboo.

tabouret /tabuʀɛ/ nm stool.

tache /taʃ/ nf mark, spot; (salissure) stain; **faire ~ d'huile** spread; ~ **de rousseur** freckle.

tâche /taʃ/ nf task, job.

tacher /taʃe/ **1** vt stain. □ **se ~** vpr (personne) get oneself dirty.

tâcher /taʃe/ **1** vi ~ **de faire** try to do.

tacheté, ~e /taʃte/ adj spotted.

tact /takt/ nm tact.

tactique /taktik/ adj tactical. ● nf (Mil) tactics; **une ~** a tactic.

taie /tɛ/ nf ~ (**d'oreiller**) pillowcase.

taille /taj/ nf (milieu du corps) waist; (hauteur) height; (grandeur) size; **de ~** sizeable; **être de ~ à faire** be up to doing.

taille-crayons /tajkʀɛjɔ̃/ nm inv pencil-sharpener.

tailler /taje/ **1** vt cut; (arbre) prune; (crayon) sharpen; (vêtement) cut out.

s

t

□ **se ~** vpr 🔲 clear off.

tailleur /tajœʀ/ nm (costume) woman's suit; (couturier) tailor; **en ~** cross-legged; **~ de pierre** stonecutter.

taire /tɛʀ/ 🔢 vt not to reveal; **faire ~** silence. □ **se ~** vpr be silent ou quiet; (devenir silencieux) fall silent.

talc /talk/ nm talcum powder.

talent /talɑ̃/ nm talent. **talentueux, -euse** adj talented, gifted.

talon /talɔ̃/ nm heel; (de chèque) stub.

tambour /tɑ̃buʀ/ nm drum, (d'église) vestibule.

Tamise /tamiz/ nf Thames.

tampon /tɑ̃pɔ̃/ nm (de bureau) stamp; (ouate) wad, pad; (**~ hygiénique**) tampon.

tamponner /tɑ̃pɔne/ 🔢 vt (document) stamp; (véhicule) crash into; (plaie) swab.

tandem /tɑ̃dɛm/ nm (vélo) tandem; (personnes) fig) duo.

tandis que /tɑ̃di(ə)/ conj while.

tanière /tanjɛʀ/ nf den.

tant /tɑ̃/ adv (travailler, manger) so much; **~ de** (quantité) so much; (nombre) so many; **~ que** as long as; **en ~ que** as; **~ mieux!** all the better!; **~ pis!** too bad!

tante /tɑ̃t/ nf aunt.

tantôt /tɑ̃to/ adv sometimes.

tapage /tapaʒ/ nm din.

tape /tap/ nf slap. **tape-à-l'œil** adj inv flashy, tawdry.

taper /tape/ 🔢 vt hit; (prendre 🔲) scrounge; **~ (à la machine)** type. ● vi (cogner) bang; (soleil) beat down; **~ dans** (puiser dans) dig into; **~ sur** hit; **~ sur l'épaule de qn** tap sb on the shoulder. □ **se ~** vpr (corvée 🔲) get stuck with 🔲.

tapis /tapi/ nm carpet; (petit) rug; **~ de bain** bathmat; **~ roulant** (pour objets) conveyor belt; (pour piétons) moving walkway.

tapisser /tapise/ 🔢 vt (wall) paper; (fig) cover (**de** with). **tapisserie** nf tapestry; (papier peint) wallpaper.

taquin, ~e /takɛ̃, -in/ adj fond of teasing. ● nm, f tease(r).

tard /taʀ/ adv late; **au plus ~** at the latest; **plus ~** later; **sur le ~** late in life.

tarder /taʀde/ 🔢 vi (être lent à venir) be a long time coming; **~ (à faire)** take a long time (doing), delay (doing); **sans (plus) ~** without (further) delay; **il me tarde de** I'm longing to.

tardif, -ive /taʀdif, -v/ adj late.

tare /taʀ/ nf (défaut) defect.

tarif /taʀif/ nm rate; (de train, taxi) fare; **plein ~** full price.

tarir /taʀiʀ/ 🔢 vt/i dry up. □ **se ~** vpr dry up.

tarte /taʀt/ nf tart. ● adj inv (ridicule 🔲) ridiculous.

tartine /taʀtin/ nf slice of bread; **~ de beurre** slice of bread and butter. **tartiner** 🔢 vt spread.

tartre /taʀtʀ/ nm (de bouilloire) fur, scale; (sur les dents) tartar.

tas /tɑ/ nm pile, heap; **un** ou **des ~ de** 🔲 lots of.

tasse /tɑs/ nf cup; **~ à thé** teacup.

tasser /tɑse/ 🔢 vt pack, squeeze; (terre) pack (down). □ **se ~** vpr (terrain) sink; (se serrer) squeeze up.

tâter /tɑte/ 🔢 vt feel; (opinion: fig) sound out. ● vi **~ de** try out.

tatillon, ~ne /tatijɔ̃, -jɔn/ adj finicky.

tâtonnements /tɑtɔnmɑ̃/ nmpl (essais) trial and error (+ sg). **tâtons: à ~** /atɑtɔ̃/ loc **avancer à ~** grope one's way along.

tatouage /tatwaʒ/ nm (dessin) tattoo.

taupe /top/ nf mole.

taureau (pl **~x**) /tɔʀo/ nm bull; **le T~** Taurus.

taux /to/ nm rate.

taxe /taks/ nf tax.

taxi /taksi/ nm taxi(-cab); (personne 🔲) taxi driver.

taxiphone ® /taksifɔn/ nm pay phone.

Tchécoslovaquie /tʃekɔslɔvaki/ nf Czechoslovakia.

tchèque /tʃɛk/ adj Czech; **République ~** Czech Republic. **T~** nmf Czech.

te, t' /tə, t/ pron you; (indirect) (to) you; (réfléchi) yourself.

technicien, ~ne /tɛknisjɛ̃, -ɛn/ nm, f technician.

technique /tɛknik/ adj technical. ● nf technique.

techno /tɛkno/ nf (Mus) techno.

technologie /tɛknɔlɔʒi/ nf technology.

teindre /tɛ̃dʀ/ 22 vt dye. □ se ~ les cheveux dye one's hair.

teint /tɛ̃/ nm complexion.

teinte /tɛ̃t/ nf shade. **teinter** 1 vt (verre) tint; (bois) stain.

teinture /tɛ̃tyʀ/ nf (produit) dye.

teinturier, -ière /tɛ̃tyʀje, -jɛʀ/ nm, f dry-cleaner.

tel, ~le /tɛl/ adj such; **un ~ livre** such a book; **~ que** such as, like; (ainsi que) (just) as; **~ ou ~** such-and-such; **~ quel** (just) as it is.

télé /tele/ nf 🔟 TV; **~ réalité** nf reality TV.

télécharger /teleʃaʀʒe/ 40 vt (Ordinat) download.

télécommande /telekɔmɑ̃d/ nf remote control.

télécommunications /telekɔmynikasjɔ̃/ nfpl telecommunications.

téléconférence /telekɔ̃feʀɑ̃s/ nf teleconferencing.

télécopie /telekɔpi/ nf fax. **télécopieur** nm fax machine.

téléfilm /telefilm/ nm TV film.

télégramme /telegʀam/ nm telegram.

télégraphier /telegʀafje/ 45 vt/i ~ (à) cable.

téléguidé, ~e /telegide/ adj radio-controlled.

télématique /telematik/ nf telematics (+ sg).

téléphérique /telefeʀik/ nm cable car.

téléphone /telefɔn/ nm (tele-) phone; **~ à carte** cardphone. **téléphoner** 1 vt/i ~ (à) (tele)phone.

téléphonie /telefɔni/ nf telephony; **~ mobile** mobile telephony. **téléphonique** adj (tele)phone.

télé-réalité /teleʀealite/ nf reality TV.

téléserveur /teleseʀvœʀ/ nm (Internet) remote server.

télésiège /telesjɛʒ/ nm chairlift.

téléski /teleski/ nm ski tow.

téléspectateur, -trice /tele spɛktatœʀ, -tʀis/ nm, f (tv) viewer.

télévente /televɑ̃t/ nf telesales (+ pl).

télévisé, ~e /televize/ adj (débat) televised; **émission ~e** television pro-

gramme. **télévision** nf television.

télex /telɛks/ nm telex.

tellement /tɛlmɑ̃/ adv (tant) so much; (si) so; **~ de** (quantité) so much; (nombre) so many.

téméraire /temeʀɛʀ/ adj (personne) reckless.

témoignage /temwaɲaʒ/ nm testimony, evidence; (récit) account; **~ de** (marque) token of.

témoigner /temwaɲe/ 1 vi testify (de to). ● vt (montrer) show; **~ que** testify that.

témoin /temwɛ̃/ nm witness; (Sport) baton; **être ~ de** witness; **~ oculaire** eyewitness.

tempe /tɑ̃p/ nf (Anat) temple.

tempérament /tɑ̃peʀamɑ̃/ nm temperament, disposition.

température /tɑ̃peʀatyʀ/ nf temperature.

tempête /tɑ̃pɛt/ nf storm; **~ de neige** snowstorm.

temple /tɑ̃pl/ nm temple; (protestant) church.

temporaire /tɑ̃pɔʀɛʀ/ adj temporary.

temps /tɑ̃/ nm (notion) time; (Gram) tense; (étape) stage; **à ~ partiel/plein** part-/full-time; **ces derniers ~** lately; **dans le ~** at one time; **dans quelque ~** in a while; **de ~ en ~** from time to time; **~ d'arrêt** pause; **avoir tout son ~** have plenty of time; (météo) weather; **~ de chien** filthy weather; **quel ~ fait-il?** what's the weather like?

tenace /tənas/ adj stubborn.

tenaille /tənaj/ nf pincers (+ pl).

tendance /tɑ̃dɑ̃s/ nf tendency; (évolution) trend; **avoir ~ à** tend to.

tendon /tɑ̃dɔ̃/ nm tendon.

tendre¹ /tɑ̃dʀ/ 3 vt stretch; (piège) set; (bras) stretch out; (main) hold out; (cou) crane; **~ qch à qn** hold sth out to sb; **~ l'oreille** prick up one's ears. ● vi ~ à tend to.

tendre² /tɑ̃dʀ/ adj tender; (couleur, bois) soft. **tendresse** nf tenderness.

tendu, ~e /tɑ̃dy/ adj (corde) tight; (personne, situation) tense.

ténèbres /tenɛbʀ/ nfpl darkness.

teneur /tənœʀ/ nf content.

tenir /təniʀ/ 59 vt hold; (pari, promesse, hôtel) keep; (place) take up;

t

(*propos*) utter; (*rôle*) play; ~ **de** (avoir reçu de) have got from; ~ **pour** regard as; ~ **chaud** keep warm; ~ **compte de** take into account; ~ **le coup** hold out; ~ **tête à** stand up to. ● *vi* hold; ~ **à** be attached to; ~ **à faire** be anxious to do; ~ **bon** stand firm; ~ **dans** fit into; ~ **de qn** take after sb; **tiens!** (surprise) hey! □ **se** ~ *vpr* (debout) stand; (avoir lieu) be held; **se** ~ **à** hold on to; **s'en** ~ **à** (se limiter à) confine oneself to.

tennis /tenis/ *nm* tennis; ~ **de table** table tennis. ● *nmpl* (chaussures) sneakers.

ténor /tenɔR/ *nm* tenor.

tension /tɑ̃sjɔ̃/ *nf* tension; **avoir de la** ~ have high blood pressure.

tentation /tɑ̃tasjɔ̃/ *nf* temptation.

tentative /tɑ̃tativ/ *nf* attempt.

tente /tɑ̃t/ *nf* tent.

tenter /tɑ̃te/ **1** *vt* (allécher) tempt; (essayer) try (**de faire** to do).

tenture /tɑ̃tyR/ *nf* curtain; ~**s** draperies.

tenu, ~e /təny/ *adj* **bien** ~ well kept; ~ **de** required. ● **→TENIR** 58.

tenue /təny/ *nf* (habillement) dress; (de maison) upkeep; (conduite) (good) behaviour; (maintien) posture; ~ **de soirée** evening dress.

Tergal ® /tɛRgal/ *nm* Terylene®.

terme /tɛRm/ *nm* (mot) term; (date limite) time-limit; (fin) end; **né avant** ~ premature; **à long/court** ~ long-/short-term; **en bons** ~**s** on good terms (**avec** with).

terminaison /tɛRminɛzɔ̃/ *nf* (Gram) ending.

terminal, ~e (*mpl* **-aux**) /tɛRmi- nal, -o/ *adj* terminal. ● *nm* terminal. **terminale** *nf* (Scol) ≈ sixth form; (US) twelfth grade.

terminer /tɛRmine/ **1** *vt/i* finish; (*discours*) end, finish. □ **se** ~ *vpr* end (**par** with).

terne /tɛRn/ *adj* dull, drab.

ternir /tɛRniR/ **2** *vt/i* tarnish. □ **se** ~ *vpr* tarnish.

terrain /tɛRɛ̃/ *nm* ground; (parcelle) piece of land; (à bâtir) plot; ~ **d'aviation** airfield; ~ **de camping** campsite; ~ **de golf** golf course; ~ **de jeu** playground; ~ **vague** waste ground.

terrasse /tɛRas/ *nf* terrace; **à la** ~ (d'un café) outside (a café).

terrasser /tɛRase/ **1** *vt* (*adversaire*) knock down; (*maladie*) strike down.

terre /tɛR/ *nf* (planète, matière) earth; (étendue, pays) land; (sol) ground; **à** ~ (Naut) ashore; **par** ~ (dehors) on the ground; (dedans) on the floor; ~ (**cuite**) terracotta; **la** ~ **ferme** dry land; ~ **glaise** clay. **terreau** (*pl* ~**x**) *nm* compost. **terre-plein** (*pl* **terres-pleins**) *nm* platform; (de route) central reservation.

terrestre /tɛRɛstR/ *adj* (*animaux*) land; (de notre planète) of the Earth.

terreur /tɛRœR/ *nf* terror.

terrible /tɛRibl/ *adj* terrible; (formidable 1) terrific.

terrier /tɛRje/ *nm* (trou) burrow; (chien) terrier.

terrifier /tɛRifje/ 45 *vt* terrify.

territoire /tɛRitwaR/ *nm* territory.

terroir /tɛRwaR/ *nm* land; **du** ~ local.

terroriser /tɛRɔRize/ **1** *vt* terrorize.

terrorisme /tɛRɔRism/ *nm* terrorism. **terroriste** *nmf* terrorist.

tertiaire /tɛRsjɛR/ *adj* (*secteur*) service.

tes /te/ **→TON¹**.

test /tɛst/ *nm* test.

testament /tɛstamɑ̃/ *nm* (Jur) will; (politique, artistique) testament; **Ancien/Nouveau T**~ Old/New Testament.

tétanos /tetanos/ *nm* tetanus.

têtard /tɛtaR/ *nm* tadpole.

tête /tɛt/ *nf* head; (visage) face; (cheveux) hair; **à la** ~ **de** at the head of; **à** ~ **reposée** at one's leisure; **de** ~ (*calculer*) in one's head; **faire la** ~ sulk; **tenir** ~ **à qn** stand up to sb; **il n'en fait qu'à sa** ~ he does just as he pleases; **en** ~ (Sport) in the lead; **faire une** ~ (au football) head the ball; **une forte** ~ a rebel; **la** ~ **la première** head first; **de la** ~ **aux pieds** from head to toe.

tête-à-tête /tɛtatɛt/ *nm inv* tête-à-tête; **en** ~ in private.

tétée /tete/ *nf* feed.

tétine /tetin/ *nf* (de biberon) teat; (sucette) dummy; (US) pacifier.

têtu, ~e /tety/ *adj* stubborn.

texte /tɛkst/ *nm* text; (de leçon) subject; (morceau choisi) passage.

texteur /tɛkstœʀ/ nm (Ordinat) word-processor.

textile /tɛkstil/ nm & adj textile.

texto /tɛksto/ nm 🄸 text message.

TGV abrév m (**train à grande vitesse**) TGV, high-speed train.

> *i* **TGV** Abbreviation of *Train à grande vitesse*, the high-speed electric passenger train operated by the SNCF. It runs on special track and can reach speeds of up to 300 km/h (180 mph). Marseilles, for example, is now only three hours from Paris by *TGV*.

thé /te/ nm tea.

théâtre /teɑtʀ/ nm theatre; (d'un crime) scene; **faire du ~** act.

théière /tejɛʀ/ nf teapot.

thème /tɛm/ nm theme; (traduction: Scol) prose.

théorie /teɔʀi/ nf theory. **théorique** adj theoretical.

thérapie /teʀapi/ nf therapy.

thermique /tɛʀmik/ adj thermal.

thermomètre /tɛʀmɔmɛtʀ/ nm thermometer.

thermos® /tɛʀmos/ nm ou f Thermos® (flask).

thermostat /tɛʀmɔsta/ nm thermostat.

thèse /tɛz/ nf thesis.

thon /tɔ̃/ nm tuna.

thym /tɛ̃/ nm thyme.

tibia /tibja/ nm shinbone.

tic /tik/ nm (contraction) tic, twitch; (manie) habit.

ticket /tikɛ/ nm ticket.

tiède /tjɛd/ adj lukewarm; (nuit) warm.

tiédir /tjediʀ/ 🄸 vt/i (faire) **~** warm up.

tien, ~ne /tjɛ̃, -ɛn/ pron **le ~, la ~ne, les ~(ne)s** yours; **à la ~ne!** cheers!

tiens, tient /tjɛ̃/ ➞TENIR 🄸🄸.

tiercé /tjɛʀse/ nm place-betting.

tiers, tierce /tjɛʀ, tjɛʀs/ adj third. ● nm (fraction) third; (personne) third party. **tiers-monde** nm Third World.

tige /tiʒ/ nf (Bot) stem, stalk; (en métal) shaft, rod.

tigre /tigʀ/ nm tiger.

tigresse /tigʀɛs/ nf tigress.

tilleul /tijœl/ nm lime tree.

timbre /tɛ̃bʀ/ nm stamp; (sonnette) bell; (de voix) tone. **~ poste** (pl **~s poste**) nm postage stamp. **timbrer** 🄸 vt stamp.

timide /timid/ adj shy, timid. **timidité** nf shyness.

timoré, ~e /timɔʀe/ adj timorous.

tintement /tɛ̃tmɑ̃/ nm (de sonnette) ringing; (de clés) jingling.

tique /tik/ nf tick.

tir /tiʀ/ nm (Sport) shooting; (action de tirer) firing; (feu, rafale) fire; **~ à l'arc** archery; **~ au pigeon** clay pigeon shooting.

tirage /tiʀaʒ/ nm (de photo) printing; (de journal) circulation; (de livre) edition; (Ordinat) hard copy; (de cheminée) draught; **~ au sort** draw.

tire-bouchon (pl **~s**) /tiʀbuʃɔ̃/ nm corkscrew.

tirelire /tiʀliʀ/ nf piggy bank.

tirer /tiʀe/ 🄸 vt pull; (langue) stick out; (conclusion, trait, rideaux) draw; (coup de feu) fire; (gibier) shoot; (photo) print; **~ de** (sortir) take ou get out of; (extraire) extract from; (plaisir, nom) derive from; **~ parti de** take advantage of; **~ profit de** profit from; **se faire ~ l'oreille** get told off. ● vi shoot, fire (sur at); **~ sur** (corde) pull at; (couleur) verge on; **~ à sa fin** be drawing to a close; **~ au clair** clarify; **~ au sort** draw lots (for). □ **se ~** vpr 🄸 clear off; **se ~ de** get out of; **s'en ~** (en réchapper) pull through; (réussir 🄸) cope.

tiret /tiʀɛ/ nm dash.

tireur /tiʀœʀ/ nm gunman; **~ d'élite** marksman; **~ isolé** sniper.

tiroir /tiʀwaʀ/ nm drawer. **tiroircaisse** (pl **tiroirs-caisses**) nm till, cash register.

tisane /tizan/ nf herbal tea.

tissage /tisaʒ/ nm weaving. **tisser** 🄸 vt weave. **tisserand** nm weaver.

tissu /tisy/ nm fabric, material; (biologique) tissue; **un ~ de mensonges** (fig) a pack of lies. **tissu-éponge** (pl **tissus-éponge**) nm towelling.

titre /titʀ/ nm title; (diplôme) qualification; (Comm) bond; **~s** (droits) claims; **(gros) ~s** headlines; **à ~ d'exemple** as an example; **à juste ~**

rightly; **à ~ privé** in a private capacity; **à double ~** on two accounts; **~ de propriété** title deed.

tituber /titybe/ **1** *vi* stagger.

titulaire /titylɛʀ/ *adj* **être ~** be a permanent staff member; **être ~ de** hold. ● *nmf* (de permis) holder. **titulariser** **1** *vt* give permanent status to.

toast /tost/ *nm* (pain) piece of toast; (canapé, allocution) toast.

toboggan /tɔbɔgɑ̃/ *nm* (de jeu) slide; (Auto) flyover.

toi /twa/ *pron* you; (réfléchi) yourself; **dépêche-~** hurry up.

toile /twal/ *nf* cloth; (tableau) canvas; **~ d'araignée** cobweb; **~ de fond** (fig) backdrop; **la ~** (Internet) the Web.

toilette /twalɛt/ *nf* (habillement) outfit; **~s** (cabinets) toilet(s); **de ~** (articles, savon) toilet; **faire sa ~** have a wash.

toi-même /twamɛm/ *pron* yourself.

toit /twa/ *nm* roof; **~ ouvrant** (Auto) sunroof.

toiture /twatyʀ/ *nf* roof.

tôle /tol/ *nf* (plaque) iron sheet; **~ ondulée** corrugated iron.

tolérant, ~e /tɔleʀɑ̃, -t/ *adj* tolerant. **tolérer** **14** *vt* tolerate.

tomate /tɔmat/ *nf* tomato.

tombe /tɔ̃b/ *nf* grave; (pierre) gravestone.

tombeau (*pl* **~x**) /tɔ̃bo/ *nm* tomb.

tomber /tɔ̃be/ **1** *vi* (aux être) fall; (fièvre, vent) drop; **faire ~** knock over; (gouvernement) bring down; **laisser ~** (objet, amoureux) drop; (collègue) let down; (activité) give up; **laisse ~!** **1** forget it!; **~ à l'eau** (projet) fall through; **~ bien** ou **à point** come at the right time; **~ en panne** break down; **~ en syncope** faint; **~ sur** (trouver) run across.

tombola /tɔ̃bɔla/ *nf* tombola; (US) lottery.

tome /tɔm/ *nm* volume.

ton¹, ta (**ton** before vowel or mute h) (*pl* **tes**) /tɔ̃, ta, tɔ̃, te/ *adj* your.

ton² /tɔ̃/ *nm* (hauteur de voix) pitch; **d'un ~ sec** drily; **de bon ~** in good taste.

tonalité /tɔnalite/ *nf* (Mus) key; (de téléphone) dialling tone; (US) dial tone.

tondeuse /tɔ̃døz/ *nf* (à moutons) shears (+ *pl*); (à cheveux) clippers (+ *pl*); **~ à gazon** lawn-mower. **tondre** **3** *vt* (herbe) mow; (mouton) shear; (cheveux) clip.

tonne /tɔn/ *nf* tonne.

tonneau (*pl* **~x**) /tɔno/ *nm* barrel; (en voiture) somersault.

tonnerre /tɔnɛʀ/ *nm* thunder.

tonton /tɔ̃tɔ̃/ *nm* **1** uncle.

tonus /tɔnys/ *nm* energy.

torche /tɔʀʃ/ *nf* torch.

torchon /tɔʀʃɔ̃/ *nm* (pour la vaisselle) tea towel.

tordre /tɔʀdʀ/ **3** *vt* twist. □ **se ~** *vpr* **se ~ la cheville** twist one's ankle; **se ~ de douleur** writhe in pain; **se ~ (de rire)** split one's sides.

tordu, ~e /tɔʀdy/ *adj* twisted, bent; (esprit) warped, twisted.

torpille /tɔʀpij/ *nf* torpedo.

torrent /tɔʀɑ̃/ *nm* torrent.

torride /tɔʀid/ *adj* torrid; (chaleur) scorching.

torse /tɔʀs/ *nm* chest; (Anat) torso.

tort /tɔʀ/ *nm* wrong; **avoir ~** be wrong (**de faire** to do); **donner ~ à** prove wrong; **être dans son ~** be in the wrong; **faire (du) ~ à** harm; **à ~** wrongly; **à ~ et à travers** without thinking.

torticolis /tɔʀtikɔli/ *nm* stiff neck.

tortiller /tɔʀtije/ **1** *vt* twist, twirl. □ **se ~** *vpr* wriggle.

tortionnaire /tɔʀsjɔnɛʀ/ *nm* torturer.

tortue /tɔʀty/ *nf* tortoise; (d'eau) turtle.

tortueux, -euse /tɔʀtɥø, -z/ *adj* (chemin) twisting; (explication) tortuous.

torture /tɔʀtyʀ/ *nf* torture. **torturer** **1** *vt* torture.

tôt /to/ *adv* early; **au plus ~** at the earliest; **le plus ~ possible** as soon as possible; **~ ou tard** sooner or later; **ce n'est pas trop ~!** it's about time!

total, ~e (*mpl* **-aux**) /tɔtal, -o/ *adj* total. ● *nm* (*pl* **-aux**) total; **au ~** all in all. **totalement** *adv* totally. **totaliser** **1** *vt* total. **totalitaire** *adj* totalitarian.

totalité /tɔtalite/ *nf* **la** ~ **de** all of.

touche /tuʃ/ *nf* (de piano) key; (de peinture) touch; **(ligne de)** ~ (Sport) touchline.

toucher /tuʃe/ **1** *vt* touch; (émouvoir) move, touch; (contacter) get in touch with; (cible) hit; (argent) draw; (chèque) cash; (concerner) affect. ● *vi* ~ **à** touch; (question) touch on; (fin, but) approach; **je vais lui en** ~ **deux mots** I'll talk to him about it. ☐ **se** ~ *vpr* (lignes) touch. ● *nm* (sens) touch.

touffe /tuf/ *nf* (de poils, d'herbe) tuft; (de plantes) clump.

toujours /tuʒuʀ/ *adv* always; (encore) still; (de toute façon) anyway; **pour** ~ for ever; ~ **est-il que** the fact remains that.

toupet /tupɛ/ *nm* (culot 🖫) cheek, nerve.

tour /tuʀ/ *nf* tower; (immeuble) tower block; (échecs) rook; ~ **de contrôle** control tower. ● *nm* (mouvement, succession, tournure) turn; (excursion) trip; (à pied) walk; (en auto) drive; (artifice) trick; (circonférence) circumference; (Tech) lathe; ~ **(de piste)** lap; **à** ~ **de rôle** in turn; **à mon** ~ when it is my turn; **c'est mon** ~ **de** it is my turn to; **faire le** ~ **de** go round; (question) survey; ~ **d'horizon** overview; ~ **de potier** potter's wheel; ~ **de taille** waist measurement; (ligne) waistline.

> **Tour de France** The race for professional cyclists held annually in July since 1903, when it was created by Henri Desgrange (1865-1940). Renowned for its mountain stages, it covers approximately 4,800 km (3,000 miles) over a three-week period, finishing triumphantly on the *Champs Élysées*. Throughout the *Tour*, the previous day's leader wears the coveted *maillot jaune* (yellow jersey).   *i*

tourbillon /tuʀbijɔ̃/ *nm* whirlwind; (d'eau) whirlpool; (fig) swirl.

tourisme /tuʀism/ *nm* tourism; **faire du** ~ do some sightseeing.

touriste /tuʀist/ *nmf* tourist. **touristique** *adj* tourist; (route) scenic.

tourmenter /tuʀmɑ̃te/ *vt* torment. ☐ **se** ~ *vpr* worry.

tournant, ~**e** /tuʀnɑ̃, -t/ *adj* (qui pivote) revolving. ● *nm* bend; (fig) turning-point.

tourne-disque (*pl* ~**s**) /tuʀnədisk/ *nm* record-player.

tournée /tuʀne/ *nf* (de facteur, au café) round; **c'est ma** ~ I'll buy this round; (d'artiste) tour.

tourner /tuʀne/ **1** *vt* turn; (film) shoot, make; ~ **le dos à** turn one's back on; ~ **en dérision** mock. ● *vi* turn; (toupie, tête) spin; (moteur, usine) run; ~ **autour de** go round; (personne, maison) hang around; (terre) revolve round; (question) centre on; ~ **de l'œil** 🖫 faint; **mal** ~ (affaire) turn out badly. ☐ **se** ~ *vpr* turn.

tournesol /tuʀnəsɔl/ *nm* sunflower.

tournevis /tuʀnəvis/ *nm* screwdriver.

tournoi /tuʀnwa/ *nm* tournament.

tourte /tuʀt/ *nf* pie.

tourterelle /tuʀtəʀɛl/ *nf* turtle dove.

Toussaint /tusɛ̃/ *nf* **la** ~ All Saints' Day.

tousser /tuse/ **1** *vi* cough.

tout, ~**e** (*pl* **tous, toutes**) /tu, tut/ *nm* (ensemble) whole; **en** ~ in all; **pas du** ~**!** not at all! ● *adj* all; (n'importe quel) any; ~ **le pays** the whole country, all the country; ~**e la nuit/journée** the whole night/day; ~ **un paquet** a whole pack; **tous les jours** every day; **tous les deux ans** every two years; ~ **le monde** everyone; **tous les deux, toutes les deux** both of them; **tous les trois** all three (of them). ● *pron* everything; all; anything; **tous** /tus/, **toutes** all; **tous ensemble** all together; **prends** ~ take everything; ~ **ce que tu veux** everything you want. ● *adv* (très) very; (entièrement) all; ~ **au bout/début** right at the end/beginning; ~ **en marchant** while walking; ~ **à coup** all of a sudden; ~ **à l'heure** in a moment; (passé) a moment ago; ~ **au ou le long de** throughout; ~ **au plus/moins** at most/least; ~ **de même** all the same; ~ **de suite** straight away; ~ **entier** whole; ~ **neuf** brand new; ~ **nu** stark naked. **tout-à-l'égout** *nm inv* main drainage.

toutefois /tutfwa/ *adv* however.

tout(-)terrain /tuteʀɛ̃/ adj inv all terrain.

toux /tu/ nf cough.

toxicomane /tɔksikɔman/ nmf drug addict.

toxique /tɔksik/ adj toxic.

trac /tʀak/ nm **le ~** nerves; (Théât) stage fright.

tracas /tʀaka/ nm worry.

trace /tʀas/ nf (traînée, piste) trail; (d'animal, de pneu) tracks; **~s de pas** footprints.

tracer /tʀase/ 🔟 vt draw; (écrire) write; (route) open up.

trachée-artère /tʀaʃeaʀtɛʀ/ nf windpipe.

tracteur /tʀaktœʀ/ nm tractor.

tradition /tʀadisjɔ̃/ nf tradition. **traditionnel, ~le** adj traditional.

traducteur, -trice /tʀadyktœʀ, -tʀis/ nm, f translator. **traduction** nf translation.

traduire /tʀadɥiʀ/ 🔟 vt translate; **~ en justice** take to court.

trafic /tʀafik/ nm (commerce, circulation) traffic.

trafiquant, ~e /tʀafikɑ̃, -t/ nm, f trafficker; (d'armes, de drogues) dealer.

trafiquer /tʀafike/ 🔟 vi traffic. ● vt 🔟 (moteur) fiddle with.

tragédie /tʀaʒedi/ nf tragedy. **tragique** adj tragic.

trahir /tʀaiʀ/ 🔟 vt betray. **trahison** nf betrayal; (Mil) treason.

train /tʀɛ̃/ nm (Rail) train; (allure) pace; **aller bon ~** walk briskly; **en ~ de faire** (busy) doing; **~ d'atterrissage** undercarriage; **~ électrique** (jouet) electric train set; **~ de vie** lifestyle.

traîne /tʀɛn/ nf (de robe) train; **à la ~** lagging behind.

traîneau (pl **~x**) /tʀɛno/ nm sleigh.

traînée /tʀɛne/ nf (trace) trail; (longue) streak; (femme: péj) slut.

traîner /tʀɛne/ 🔟 vt drag (along); **~ les pieds** drag one's feet. ● vi (pendre) trail; (rester en arrière) trail behind; (flâner) hang about; (papiers, affaires) lie around; **~ (en longueur)** drag on. ▢ **se ~** vpr (par terre) crawl.

traire /tʀɛʀ/ 🔟 vt milk.

trait /tʀɛ/ nm line; (en dessinant) stroke; (caractéristique) feature, trait;

~s (du visage) features; **avoir ~ à** relate to; **d'un ~** (boire) in one gulp; **~ d'union** hyphen; (fig) link.

traite /tʀɛt/ nf (de vache) milking; (Comm) draft; **d'une (seule) ~** in one go, at a stretch.

traité /tʀete/ nm (pacte) treaty; (ouvrage) treatise.

traitement /tʀɛtmɑ̃/ nm treatment; (salaire) salary; **~ de données** data processing; **~ de texte** word processing.

traiter /tʀete/ 🔟 vt treat; (affaire) deal with; (données, produit) process; **~ qn de lâche** call sb a coward. ● vi deal (avec with); **~ de** (sujet) deal with.

traiteur /tʀɛtœʀ/ nm caterer; (boutique) delicatessen.

traître, -esse /tʀɛtʀ, -ɛs/ adj treacherous. ● nm, f traitor.

trajectoire /tʀaʒɛktwaʀ/ nf path.

trajet /tʀaʒe/ nm (voyage) journey; (itinéraire) route.

trame /tʀam/ nf (de tissu) weft.

tramway /tʀamwɛ/ nm tram; (US) streetcar.

tranchant, ~e /tʀɑ̃ʃɑ̃, -t/ adj sharp; (fig) cutting. ● nm cutting edge; **à double ~** two-edged.

tranche /tʀɑ̃ʃ/ nf (rondelle) slice; (bord) edge; (d'âge, de revenu) bracket.

tranchée /tʀɑ̃ʃe/ nf trench.

trancher /tʀɑ̃ʃe/ 🔟 vt cut; (question) decide; (contraster) contrast (sur with).

tranquille /tʀɑ̃kil/ adj quiet; (esprit) at rest; (conscience) clear; **être/laisser ~** be/leave in peace; **tiens-toi ~!** be quiet! **tranquillisant** nm tranquillizer. **tranquilliser** 🔟 vt reassure. **tranquillité** nf (peace and) quiet; (d'esprit) peace of mind.

transcription /tʀɑ̃skʀipsjɔ̃/ nf transcription; (copie) transcript. **transcrire** 🔟 vt transcribe.

transe /tʀɑ̃s/ nf **en ~** in a trance.

transférer /tʀɑ̃sfeʀe/ 🔟 vt transfer.

transfert /tʀɑ̃sfɛʀ/ nm transfer; **~ d'appel** (au téléphone) call diversion.

transformation /tʀɑ̃sfɔʀmasjɔ̃/ nf change; transformation.

transformer /tʀɑ̃sfɔʀme/ 🔟 vt change; (radicalement) transform; (vê-

tement) alter. □ **se** ~ *vpr* change; (radicalement) be transformed; **(se)** ~ **en** turn into.

transgénique /tʀɑ̃sʒenik/ *adj* genetically modified.

transiger /tʀɑ̃siʒe/ **40** *vi* compromise.

transiter /tʀɑ̃zite/ **1** *vt/i* ~ **par** pass through.

transitif, -ive /tʀɑ̃zitif, -v/ *adj* transitive.

translucide /tʀɑ̃slysid/ *adj* translucent.

transmettre /tʀɑ̃smɛtʀ/ **42** *vt* (*savoir, maladie*) pass on; (*ondes*) transmit; (à la radio) broadcast. **transmission** *nf* transmission; (*radio*) broadcasting.

transparence /tʀɑ̃spaʀɑ̃s/ *nf* transparency. **transparent, ~e** *adj* transparent.

transpercer /tʀɑ̃spɛʀse/ **10** *vt* pierce.

transpiration /tʀɑ̃spiʀasjɔ̃/ *nf* perspiration. **transpirer** **1** *vi* perspire.

transplanter /tʀɑ̃splɑ̃te/ **1** *vt* (Bot, Méd) transplant.

transport /tʀɑ̃spɔʀ/ *nm* transport(ation); **durant le** ~ in transit; **les** ~**s** transport (+ *sg*); **les** ~**s en commun** public transport (+ *sg*). **transporter** /tʀɑ̃spɔʀte/ **1** *vt* transport; (à la main) carry. **transporteur** *nm* haulier; (US) trucker.

transversal, ~e (*mpl* **-aux**) /tʀɑ̃svɛʀsal, -o/ *adj* cross, transverse.

trapu, ~e /tʀapy/ *adj* stocky.

traumatisant, ~e /tʀomatizɑ̃, -t/ *adj* traumatic. **traumatiser** *vt* **1** traumatize. **traumatisme** *nm* trauma.

travail (*pl* **-aux**) /tʀavaj, -o/ *nm* work; (emploi, tâche) job; (façonnage) working; **travaux** work (+ *sg*); (routiers) roadworks; ~ **à la chaîne** production line work; **travaux dirigés** (Scol) practical; **travaux forcés** hard labour; **travaux manuels** handicrafts; **travaux ménagers** housework.

travailler /tʀavaje/ **1** *vi* work; (se déformer) warp. ● *vt* (façonner) work; (étudier) work at ou on.

travailleur, -euse /tʀavajœʀ, -øz/ *nm, f* worker. ● *adj* hardworking.

travailliste /tʀavajist/ *adj* Labour. ● *nmf* Labour party member.

travers /tʀavɛʀ/ *nm* (défaut) failing; ~ through; **au** ~ **(de)** through; **de** ~

(*chapeau, nez*) crooked; (*regarder*) askance; **j'ai avalé de** ~ it went down the wrong way; **en** ~ **(de)** across.

traversée /tʀavɛʀse/ *nf* crossing.

traverser /tʀavɛʀse/ **1** *vt* cross; (transpercer) go (right) through; (période, forêt) go ou pass through.

traversin /tʀavɛʀsɛ̃/ *nm* bolster.

travesti /tʀavɛsti/ *nm* transvestite.

trébucher /tʀebyʃe/ **1** *vi* stumble, trip (over); **faire** ~ trip (up).

trèfle /tʀɛfl/ *nm* (plante) clover; (cartes) clubs.

treillis /tʀeji/ *nm* trellis; (en métal) wire mesh; (tenue militaire) combat uniform.

treize /tʀɛz/ *adj & nm* thirteen.

> **Treizième mois** An addition to an employee's salary, equal to his/her usual monthly payment, which some employees receive at the end of the calendar year.   *i*

tréma /tʀema/ *nm* diaeresis.

tremblement /tʀɑ̃bləmɑ̃/ *nm* shaking; ~ **de terre** earthquake. **trembler** **1** *vi* shake, tremble; (lumière, voix) quiver.

tremper /tʀɑ̃pe/ **1** *vt/i* soak; (plonger) dip; (acier) temper; **faire** ~ soak; ~ **dans** (fig) be mixed up. □ **se** ~ *vpr* (se baigner) have a dip.

tremplin /tʀɑ̃plɛ̃/ *nm* springboard.

trente /tʀɑ̃t/ *adj & nm* thirty; **se mettre sur son** ~ **et un** dress up; **tous les** ~**-six du mois** once in a blue moon.

trépied /tʀepje/ *nm* tripod.

très /tʀɛ/ *adv* very; ~ **aimé/estimé** much liked/esteemed.

trésor /tʀezɔʀ/ *nm* treasure; **le T** ~ **public** the revenue department.

trésorerie /tʀezɔʀʀi/ *nf* (bureaux) accounts department; (du Trésor public) revenue office; (argent) funds (+ *pl*); (gestion) accounts (+ *pl*). **trésorier, -ière** *nm, f* treasurer.

tressaillement /tʀesajmɑ̃/ *nm* quiver; start.

tresse /tʀɛs/ *nf* braid, plait.

trêve /tʀɛv/ *nf* truce; (fig) respite; ~ **de plaisanteries** that's enough joking.

tri /tʀi/ *nm* (classement) sorting; (sélection) selection; **faire le** ~ **de** (classer)

    t

sort; (choisir) select; **centre de ~** sorting office.

triangle /tʀijɑ̃gl/ nm triangle.

tribal, ~e (mpl **-aux**) /tʀibal, -o/ adj tribal.

tribord /tʀibɔʀ/ nm starboard.

tribu /tʀiby/ nf tribe.

tribunal (mpl **-aux**) /tʀibynal, -o/ nm court.

tribune /tʀibyn/ nf (de stade) grandstand; (d'orateur) rostrum; (débat) forum; (d'église) gallery.

tribut /tʀiby/ nm tribute.

tributaire /tʀibytɛʀ/ adj **~ de** dependent on.

tricher /tʀiʃe/ **1** vi cheat. **tricheur, -euse** nm, f cheat.

tricolore /tʀikɔlɔʀ/ adj three-coloured; (écharpe) red, white and blue; (équipe) French.

tricot /tʀiko/ nm (activité) knitting; (pull) sweater; **en ~** knitted; **~ de corps** vest; (US) undershirt. **tricoter 1** vt/i knit.

trier /tʀije/ **45** vt (classer) sort; (choisir) select.

trimestre /tʀimɛstʀ/ nm quarter; (Scol) term. **trimestriel, ~le** adj quarterly; (bulletin) end-of-term.

tringle /tʀɛ̃gl/ nf rail.

trinquer /tʀɛ̃ke/ **1** vi clink glasses.

triomphant, ~e /tʀijɔ̃fɑ̃, -t/ adj triumphant. **triomphe** nm triumph. **triompher 1** vi triumph (**de** over); (jubiler) be triumphant.

tripes /tʀip/ nfpl (mets) tripe (+ sg); (entrailles **1**) guts.

triple /tʀipl/ adj triple, treble. ● nm **le ~** three times as much (**de** as). **triplés, -es** nm, fpl triplets.

tripot /tʀipo/ nm gambling den.

tripoter /tʀipɔte/ **1** vt **1** (personne) grope; (objet) fiddle with.

trisomique /tʀizɔmik/ adj **être ~** have Down's syndrome.

triste /tʀist/ adj sad; (rue, temps, couleur) dreary; (lamentable) dreadful. **tristesse** nf sadness; dreariness.

trivial, ~e (mpl **-iaux**) /tʀivjal, -jo/ adj coarse.

troc /tʀɔk/ nm exchange; (Comm) barter.

trognon /tʀɔɲɔ̃/ nm (de fruit) core.

trois /tʀwɑ/ adj & nm three; **hôtel ~ étoiles** three-star hotel. **troisième** adj & nmf third.

trombone /tʀɔ̃bɔn/ nm (Mus) trombone; (agrafe) paperclip.

trompe /tʀɔ̃p/ nf (d'éléphant) trunk; (Mus) horn.

tromper /tʀɔ̃pe/ **1** vt deceive, mislead; (déjouer) elude. □ **se ~** vpr be mistaken; **se ~ de route/d'heure** take the wrong road/get the time wrong.

trompette /tʀɔ̃pɛt/ nf trumpet.

trompeur, -euse /tʀɔ̃pœʀ, -øz/ adj (apparence) deceptive.

tronc /tʀɔ̃/ nm trunk; (boîte) collection box.

tronçon /tʀɔ̃sɔ̃/ nm section.

tronçonneuse /tʀɔ̃sɔnøz/ nf chain saw.

trône /tʀon/ nm throne. **trôner 1** vi (vase) have pride of place (**sur** on).

trop /tʀo/ adv (grand, loin) too; (boire, marcher) too much; **~ (de)** quantité) too much; (nombre) too many; **ce serait ~ beau** one should be so lucky; **de ~ en ~** too much; too many; **il a bu un verre de ~** he's had one too many; **se sentir de ~** feel one is in the way.

trophée /tʀɔfe/ nm trophy.

tropical, ~e (mpl **-aux**) /tʀɔpikal, -o/ adj tropical. **tropique** nm tropic.

trop-plein (pl **~s**) /tʀoplɛ̃/ nm excess; (dispositif) overflow.

troquer /tʀɔke/ **1** vt exchange; (Comm) barter (**contre** for).

trot /tʀo/ nm trot; **aller au ~** trot. **trotter 1** vi trot.

trotteuse /tʀɔtøz/ nf (de montre) second hand.

trottoir /tʀɔtwaʀ/ nm pavement; (US) sidewalk; **~ roulant** moving walkway.

trou /tʀu/ nm hole; (moment) gap; (lieu: péj) dump; **~ (de mémoire)** memory lapse; **~ de serrure** keyhole; **faire son ~** carve one's niche.

trouble /tʀubl/ adj (eau, image) unclear; (louche) shady. ● nm (émoi) emotion; **~s** (Pol) disturbances; (Méd) disorder (+ sg). **troubler** /tʀuble/ **1** vt disturb; (eau) make cloudy; (inquiéter) trouble. □ **se ~** vpr (personne) become flustered.

trouer /tʀue/ **1** vt make a hole ou holes in; **mes chaussures sont trouées** my shoes have got holes in them.

troupe /tʀup/ nf troop; (d'acteurs) company.

troupeau (pl ~x) /tʀupo/ nm herd; (de moutons) flock.

trousse /tʀus/ nf case, bag; **aux ~s de** hot on sb's heels; **~ de toilette** toilet bag.

trousseau (pl ~x) /tʀuso/ nm (de clefs) bunch; (de mariée) trousseau.

trouver /tʀuve/ **1** vt find; (penser) think; **il est venu me ~** he came to see me. □ **se ~** vpr (être) be; (se sentir) feel; **il se trouve que** it happens that; **si ça se trouve** maybe; **se ~ mal** faint.

truand /tʀyɑ̃/ nm gangster.

truc /tʀyk/ nm (moyen) way; (artifice) trick; (chose **1**) thing. **trucage** nm (cinéma) special effect.

truffe /tʀyf/ nf (champignon, chocolat) truffle; (de chien) nose.

truffer /tʀyfe/ **1** vt (fig) fill, pack (**de** with).

truie /tʀɥi/ nf (animal) sow.

truite /tʀɥit/ nf trout.

truquer /tʀyke/ **1** vt fix, rig; (photo) fake; (résultats) fiddle.

tsar /tsaʀ/ nm tsar, czar.

tu /ty/ pron (parent, ami, enfant) you. **→TAIRE 47**.

tuba /tyba/ nm (Mus) tuba; (Sport) snorkel.

tube /tyb/ nm tube.

tuberculose /tybɛʀkyloz/ nf tuberculosis.

tuer /tɥe/ **1** vt kill; (d'une balle) shoot, kill; (épuiser) exhaust; **~ par balles** shoot dead. □ **se ~** vpr kill oneself; (accident) be killed.

tuerie /tyʀi/ nf killing.

tue-tête: **à ~** /atytɛt/ loc at the top of one's voice.

tuile /tɥil/ nf tile; (malchance **1**) (stroke of) bad luck.

tulipe /tylip/ nf tulip.

tumeur /tymœʀ/ nf tumour.

tumulte /tymylt/ nm commotion; (désordre) turmoil.

tunique /tynik/ nf tunic.

Tunisie /tynizi/ nf Tunisia.

tunnel /tynɛl/ nm tunnel.

turbo /tyʀbɔ/ adj turbo. ● nf (voiture) turbo.

turbulent, ~e /tyʀbulɑ̃, -t/ adj boisterous, turbulent.

turc, -que /tyʀk/ adj Turkish. ● nm (Ling) Turkish. **T~, -que** Turk.

turfiste /tyʀfist/ nmf racegoer.

Turquie /tyʀki/ nf Turkey.

tutelle /tytɛl/ nf (Jur) guardianship; (fig) protection.

tuteur, -trice /tytœʀ, -tʀis/ nm, f (Jur) guardian. ● nm (bâton) stake.

tutoiement /tytwamɑ̃/ nm use of the 'tu' form. **tutoyer 31** vt address using the 'tu' form.

tuyau (pl ~x) /tɥijo/ nm pipe; (conseil **1**) tip; **~ d'arrosage** hosepipe.

TVA abrév f (**taxe à la valeur ajoutée**) VAT.

tympan /tɛ̃pɑ̃/ nm ear-drum.

type /tip/ nm (genre, traits) type; (individu **1**) bloke, guy; **le ~ même de** a classic example of. ● adj inv typical.

typique /tipik/ adj typical.

tyran /tiʀɑ̃/ nm tyrant. **tyrannie** nf tyranny. **tyranniser 1** vt oppress, tyrannize.

Uu

UE abrév f (**Union européenne**) European Union.

Ukraine /ykʀɛn/ nf Ukraine.

ulcère /ylsɛʀ/ nm (Méd) ulcer.

ULM abrév m (**ultraléger motorisé**) microlight.

ultérieur, ~e /ylteʀjœʀ/ adj later. **ultérieurement** adv later.

ultime /yltim/ adj final.

un, une /œ̃, yn/
● déterminant
····➤ a; (devant voyelle) an; **~ animal** an animal; **~ jour** one day; **pas ~arbre** not a single tree; **il fait ~ froid!** it's so cold!

● *pronom*
····▸ one; **l'~ d'entre nous** one of us; **les ~s croient que...** some believe...
····▸ **la une** the front page.
····▸ **j'en veux une** I want one.
● *adjectif*
····▸ one, a, an; **j'ai ~ garçon et deux filles** I have a *ou* one boy and two girls; **il est une heure** it is one o'clock.
● *nom masculin & féminin*
····▸ **~ par ~** one by one.

unanime /ynanim/ *adj* unanimous.

unanimité /ynanimite/ *nf* unanimity; **à l'~** unanimously.

uni, ~e /yni/ *adj* united; (*couple*) close; (*surface*) smooth; (*tissu*) plain.

unième /ynjɛm/ *adj* -first; **vingt et ~** twenty-first; **cent ~** one hundred and first.

unifier /ynifje/ 45 *vt* unify.

uniforme /ynifɔrm/ *nm* uniform. ● *adj* uniform. **uniformiser** 1 *vt* standardize. **uniformité** *nf* uniformity.

unilatéral, ~e (*mpl* -**aux**) /ynilateral, -o/ *adj* unilateral.

union /ynjɔ̃/ *nf* union; **l'U ~ européenne** the European Union.

unique /ynik/ *adj* (*seul*) only; (*prix, voie*) one; (*incomparable*) unique; **enfant ~** only child; **sens ~** oneway street. **uniquement** *adv* only, solely.

unir /ynir/ 2 *vt* unite. □ **s'~** *vpr* unite, join.

unité /ynite/ *nf* unit; (*harmonie*) unity; **~ centrale** (Ordinat) processor.

univers /ynivɛr/ *nm* universe.

universel, ~le /ynivɛrsɛl/ *adj* universal.

universitaire /ynivɛrsitɛr/ *adj* (*résidence*) university; (*niveau*) academic. ● *nmf* academic.

université /ynivɛrsite/ *nf* university.

uranium /yranjɔm/ *nm* uranium.

urbain, ~e /yrbɛ̃, -ɛn/ *adj* urban. **urbanisme** *nm* town planning.

urgence /yrʒɑ̃s/ *nf* (*cas*) emergency; (*de situation, tâche*) urgency; **d'~** (*mesure*) emergency; (*transporter*) urgently; **les ~s** casualty (+ *sg*). **urgent, ~e** *adj* urgent.

urine /yrin/ *nf* urine. **urinoir** *nm* urinal.

urne /yrn/ *nf* (*électorale*) ballot box; (*vase*) urn; **aller aux ~s** go to the polls.

urticaire /yrtikɛr/ *nf* hives (+ *pl*), urticar.

us /ys/ *nmpl* **les ~ et coutumes** habits and customs.

usage /yzaʒ/ *nm* use; (*coutume*) custom; (*de langage*) usage; **à l'~ de** for; **d'~** (*habituel*) customary; **faire ~ de** make use of.

usagé, ~e /yzaʒe/ *adj* worn.

usager /yzaʒe/ *nm* user.

usé, ~e /yze/ *adj* worn (out); (*banal*) trite.

user /yze/ 1 *vt* wear (out). ● *vi* **~ de** use. □ **s'~** *vpr* (*tissu*) wear (out).

usine /yzin/ *nf* factory, plant; **~ sidérurgique** ironworks (+ *pl*).

usité, ~e /yzite/ *adj* common.

ustensile /ystɑ̃sil/ *nm* utensil.

usuel, ~le /yzɥɛl/ *adj* ordinary, everyday.

usure /yzyr/ *nf* (*détérioration*) wear (and tear).

utérus /yterys/ *nm* womb, uterus.

utile /ytil/ *adj* useful.

utilisable /ytilizabl/ *adj* usable. **utilisation** *nf* use. **utiliser** 1 *vt* use.

utopie /ytɔpi/ *nf* Utopia; (*idée*) Utopian idea. **utopique** *adj* Utopian.

UV¹ *abrév f* (**unité de valeur**) course unit.

UV² *abrév mpl* (**ultraviolets**) ultraviolet rays; **faire des ~** use a sunbed.

················

Vv

················

va /va/ ➡ALLER 8.

vacance /vakɑ̃s/ *nf* (*poste*) vacancy.

vacances /vakɑ̃s/ *nfpl* holiday(s); (US) vacation; **en ~** on holiday; **~ d'été, grandes ~** summer holidays. **vacancier, -ière** *nm, f* holidaymaker; (US) vacationer.

vacant, ~e /vakɑ̃, -t/ *adj* vacant.

vacarme /vakarm/ *nm* din.

vaccin /vaksɛ̃/ *nm* vaccine. **vacciner** 1 *vt* vaccinate.

vache /vaʃ/ *nf* cow. ● *adj* (méchant 🔲) nasty.

vaciller /vasije/ **1** *vi* sway, wobble; (*lumière*) flicker; (*hésiter*) falter; (*santé, mémoire*) fail.

vadrouiller /vadʁuje/ **1** *vi* 🔲 wander about.

va-et-vient /vaevjɛ̃/ *nm inv* toing and froing; (*de personnes*) comings and goings; **faire le ∼** go to and fro; (*interrupteur*) two-way switch.

vagabond, ∼e /vagabɔ̃, -d/ *nm, f* vagrant.

vagin /vaʒɛ̃/ *nm* vagina.

vague /vag/ *adj* vague. ● *nm* **regarder dans le ∼** stare into space; **il est resté dans le ∼** he was vague about it. ● *nf* wave; **∼ de fond** ground swell; **∼ de froid** cold spell; **∼ de chaleur** heatwave.

vaillant, ∼e /vajɑ̃, -t/ *adj* brave; (*vigoureux*) strong.

vaille /vaj/ →VALOIR 60.

vain, ∼e /vɛ̃, vɛn/ *adj* vain, futile; **en ∼** in vain.

vaincre /vɛ̃kʁ/ 59 *vt* defeat; (*surmonter*) overcome. **vaincu, ∼e** *nm, f* (Sport) loser. **vainqueur** *nm* victor; (Sport) winner.

vals /vɛ/ →ALLER 8.

vaisseau (*pl* ∼x) /vɛso/ *nm* ship; (*veine*) vessel; **∼ spatial** spaceship.

vaisselle /vɛsɛl/ *nf* crockery; (à laver) dishes; **faire la ∼** do the washing-up, wash the dishes; **liquide ∼** washing-up liquid.

valable /valabl/ *adj* valid; (*de qualité*) worthwhile.

valet /valɛ/ *nm* (aux cartes) jack; (**∼ de chambre**) manservant.

valeur /valœʁ/ *nf* value; (*mérite*) worth, value; **∼s** (Comm) stocks and shares; **avoir de la ∼** be valuable; **prendre/perdre de la ∼** go up/down in value; **objets de ∼** valuables; **sans ∼** worthless.

valide /valid/ *adj* (*personne*) fit; (*billet*) valid. **valider** **1** *vt* validate.

valise /valiz/ *nf* (suit) case; **faire ses ∼s** pack (one's bags).

vallée /vale/ *nf* valley.

valoir /valwaʁ/ 60 *vi* (*mériter*) be worth; (*égaler*) be as good as; (*être valable*) (*règle*) apply; **faire ∼** (*mérite, qualité*) emphasize; (*terrain*) cultivate; (*droit*) assert; **se faire ∼** put oneself forward; **∼ cher/100 euros** be worth a lot/100 euros; **que vaut ce vin?** what's this wine like?; **ne rien ∼** be useless *ou* no good; **ça ne me dit rien qui vaille** I don't like the sound of that; **∼ la peine** *or* **le coup** 🔲 be worth it; **il vaut/vaudrait mieux faire** it is/would be better to do. ● *vt* **∼ qch à qn** (*éloges, critiques*) earn sb sth; (*admiration*) win sb sth. □ **se ∼** *vpr* (*être équivalents*) be as good as each other; **ça se vaut** it's all the same.

valoriser /valɔʁize/ **1** *vt* add value to; (*produit*) promote; (*profession*) make attractive; (*région, ressources*) develop.

valse /vals/ *nf* waltz.

vandale /vɑ̃dal/ *nmf* vandal.

vanille /vanij/ *nf* vanilla.

vanité /vanite/ *nf* vanity. **vaniteux, -euse** *adj* vain, conceited.

vanne /van/ *nf* (*d'écluse*) sluicegate; (*propos* 🔲) dig 🔲

vantard, ∼e /vɑ̃taʁ, -d/ *adj* boastful. ● *nm, f* boaster.

vanter /vɑ̃te/ **1** *vt* praise. □ **se ∼** *vpr* boast (**de** about); **se ∼ de faire** pride oneself on doing.

vapeur /vapœʁ/ *nf* (*eau*) steam; (*brume, émanation*) vapour; **∼s** fumes; **à ∼** (*bateau, locomotive*) steam; **faire cuire à la ∼** steam.

vaporisateur /vapɔʁizatœʁ/ *nm* spray, atomizer. **vaporiser** **1** *vt* spray.

varappe /vaʁap/ *nf* rock-climbing.

variable /vaʁjabl/ *adj* variable; (*temps*) changeable.

varicelle /vaʁisɛl/ *nf* chickenpox.

varié, ∼e /vaʁje/ *adj* (*non monotone, étendu*) varied; (*divers*) various; **sandwichs ∼s** a selection of sandwiches.

varier /vaʁje/ 45 *vt/i* vary.

variété /vaʁjete/ *nf* variety; **spectacle de ∼s** variety show.

vase /vɑz/ *nm* vase. ● *nf* silt, mud.

vaseux, -euse /vɑzø, -z/ *adj* (*confus* 🔲) woolly, hazy.

vaste /vast/ *adj* vast, huge.

vaurien, ∼ne /voʁjɛ̃, -ɛn/ *nm, f* good-for-nothing.

vautour /votuʁ/ *nm* vulture.

V

vautrer (se) /(sə)votʀe/ **1** *vpr* sprawl; **se ~ dans** (*vice*, *boue*) wallow in.

veau (*pl* **~x**) /vo/ *nm* calf; (*viande*) veal; (*cuir*) calfskin.

vécu, **~e** /veky/ *adj* (*réel*) true, real.
→VIVRE **62**.

vedette /vədɛt/ *nf* (*artiste*) star; **en ~** (*objet*) in a prominent position; (*personne*) in the limelight; **joueur ~** star player; (*bateau*) launch.

végétal (*mpl* **-aux**) /veʒetal, -o/ *adj* plant. ● *nm* (*pl* **-aux**) plant.

végétalien, **~ne** /veʒetaljɛ̃, ɛn/ *adj & nm, f* vegan.

végétarien, **~ne** /veʒetaʀjɛ̃, -ɛn/ *adj & nm, f* vegetarian.

végétation /veʒetasjɔ̃/ *nf* vegetation; **~s** (Méd) adenoids.

véhicule /veikyl/ *nm* vehicle.

veille /vɛj/ *nf* (*état*) wakefulness; (*jour précédent*) **la ~ (de)** the day before; **la ~ de Noël** Christmas Eve; **à la ~ de** on the eve of; **la ~ au soir** the previous evening.

veillée /veje/ *nf* evening (gathering).

veiller /veje/ **1** *vi* stay up; (*monter la garde*) be on watch. ● *vt* (*malade*) watch over; **~ à** attend to; **~ sur** watch over.

veilleur /vɛjœʀ/ *nm* **~ de nuit** night-watchman.

veilleuse /vɛjøz/ *nf* night light; (*de véhicule*) sidelight; (*de réchaud*) pilot light; **mettre qch en ~** put sth on the back burner.

veine /vɛn/ *nf* (Anat) vein; (*nervure*, *filon*) vein; (*chance* **1**) luck; **avoir de la ~** **1** be lucky.

véliplanchiste /veliplɑ̃ʃist/ *nmf* wind-surfer.

vélo /velo/ *nm* bike; (*activité*) cycling; **faire du ~** go cycling; **~ tout terrain** mountain bike.

vélomoteur /velomotœʀ/ *nm* moped.

velours /v(ə)luʀ/ *nm* velvet; **~ côtelé** corduroy.

velouté, **~e** /vəlute/ *adj* smooth. ● *nm* (Culin) **~ d'asperges** cream of asparagus soup.

vendanges /vɑ̃dɑ̃ʒ/ *nfpl* grape harvest.

vendeur, **-euse** /vɑ̃dœʀ, -øz/ *nm, f* shop assistant; (*marchand*) salesman, saleswoman; (Jur) vendor, seller.

vendre /vɑ̃dʀ/ **3** *vt* sell; **à ~** for sale. □ **se ~** *vpr* (*être vendu*) be sold; (*trouver acquéreur*) sell; **se ~ bien** sell well.

vendredi /vɑ̃dʀədi/ *nm* Friday; **V~ saint** Good Friday.

vénéneux, **-euse** /venenø, -z/ *adj* poisonous.

vénérer /venere/ **14** *vt* revere.

vénérien, **~ne** /veneʀjɛ̃, -ɛn/ *adj* **maladie ~ne** venereal disease.

vengeance /vɑ̃ʒɑ̃s/ *nf* revenge, vengeance.

venger /vɑ̃ʒe/ **40** *vt* avenge. □ **se ~** *vpr* take ou get one's revenge (**de qch** for sth; **de qn** on sb).

vengeur, **-eresse** /vɑ̃ʒœʀ, -əʀɛs/ *adj* vengeful. ● *nm, f* avenger.

venimeux, **-euse** /vənimø, -z/ *adj* poisonous, venomous.

venin /vənɛ̃/ *nm* venom.

venir /vəniʀ/ **58** *vi* (*aux être*) come (**de** from); **faire ~ qn** send for sb, call sb; **en ~ à** come to; **en ~ aux mains** come to blows; **où veut-elle en ~?** what is she driving at?; **il m'est venu à l'esprit** *or* **à l'idée que** it occurred to me that; **s'il venait à pleuvoir** if it should rain; **dans les jours à ~** in the next few days. ● *v aux* **~ de faire** have just done; **il vient/venait d'arriver** he has/had just arrived; **~ faire** come to do; **viens voir** come and see.

vent /vɑ̃/ *nm* wind; **il fait du ~** it is windy; **être dans le ~** **1** be trendy.

vente /vɑ̃t/ *nf* sale; **~ (aux enchères)** auction; **en ~** on ou for sale; **mettre qch en ~** put sth up for sale; **~ de charité** (charity) bazaar; **~ au détail/en gros** retailing/wholesaling; **équipe de ~** sales team.

ventilateur /vɑ̃tilatœʀ/ *nm* fan, ventilator. **ventiler** **1** *vt* ventilate.

ventouse /vɑ̃tuz/ *nf* suction pad; (*pour déboucher*) plunger.

ventre /vɑ̃tʀ/ *nm* stomach; (*d'animal*) belly; (*utérus*) womb; **avoir du ~** have a paunch.

venu, **~e** /vəny/ *adj* **bien ~** (à propos) apt, timely; **mal ~** badly timed; **il serait mal ~ de faire** it wouldn't be a good idea to do. ● →VENIR **59**

venue /vəny/ *nf* coming.

ver /vɛʀ/ *nm* worm; (dans la nourriture) maggot; (du bois) woodworm; ∼ **luisant** glow-worm; ∼ **à soie** silkworm; ∼ **solitaire** tapeworm; ∼ **de terre** earthworm.

verbal, ∼e (*mpl* **-aux**) /vɛʀbal, -o/ *adj* verbal.

verbe /vɛʀb/ *nm* verb.

verdir /vɛʀdiʀ/ **2** *vi* turn green.

véreux, -euse /veʀø, -z/ *adj* wormy; (malhonnête) shady.

verger /vɛʀʒe/ *nm* orchard.

verglas /vɛʀɡla/ *nm* black ice.

véridique /veʀidik/ *adj* true.

vérification /veʀifikasjɔ̃/ *nf* check-(ing), verification.

vérifier /veʀifje/ **45** *vt* check, verify; (confirmer) confirm.

véritable /veʀitabl/ *adj* true, real; (authentique) real.

vérité /veʀite/ *nf* truth; (de tableau, roman) realism; **en** ∼ in fact, actually.

> **Verlan** A form of French slang which reverses the order of syllables in many common words. The term itself is derived from the word *l'envers* the syllables of which are reversed to create *vers-l'en* (*verlan*). Single syllable words are also converted so *femme* becomes *meuf*, *mec* becomes *keum*, etc.

i

vermine /vɛʀmin/ *nf* vermin.

verni, ∼e /vɛʀni/ *adj* (chaussures) patent (leather); (chanceux **1**) lucky.

vernir /vɛʀniʀ/ **2** *vt* varnish. □ **se** ∼ *vpr* se ∼ **les ongles** apply nail polish.

vernis /vɛʀni/ *nm* varnish; (de poterie) glaze; ∼ **à ongles** nail polish.

verra, verrait /vɛʀa, vɛʀɛ/ ➡**VOIR 64**.

verre /vɛʀ/ *nm* glass; (de lunettes) lens; ∼ **à vin** wine glass; **prendre** *ou* **boire** **un** ∼ have a drink; ∼ **de contact** contact lens; ∼ **dépoli** frosted glass.

verrière /vɛʀjɛʀ/ *nf* (toit) glass roof; (paroi) glass wall.

verrou /vɛʀu/ *nm* bolt; **sous les** ∼**s** behind bars.

verrouillage /vɛʀujaz/ *nm* ∼ **central** *or* **centralisé (des portes)** central locking.

verrue /vɛʀy/ *nf* wart; ∼ **plantaire** verruca.

vers¹ /vɛʀ/ *prép* towards; (aux environs de) (temps) about; (lieu) near, around; (période) towards; ∼ **le soir** towards evening.

vers² /vɛʀ/ *nm* (poésie) line of verse.

versatile /vɛʀsatil/ *adj* unpredictable, volatile.

verse: à ∼ /avɛʀs/ *loc* in torrents.

Verseau /vɛʀso/ *nm* **le** ∼ Aquarius.

versement /vɛʀsəmɑ̃/ *nm* payment; (échelonné) instalment.

verser /vɛʀse/ **1** *vt/i* pour; (larmes, sang) shed; (payer) pay. ● *vi* pour; (voiture) overturn; ∼ **dans** (fig) lapse into.

version /vɛʀsjɔ̃/ *nf* version; (traduction) translation.

verso /vɛʀso/ *nm* back (of the page); **voir au** ∼ see overleaf.

vert, ∼e /vɛʀ, -t/ *adj* green; (vieillard) sprightly. ● *nm* green; **les** ∼**s** the Greens.

vertèbre /vɛʀtɛbʀ/ *nf* vertebra; **se déplacer une** ∼ slip a disc.

vertical, ∼e (*mpl* **-aux**) /vɛʀtikal, -o/ *adj* vertical.

vertige /vɛʀtiʒ/ *nm* dizziness; ∼**s** dizzy spells; **avoir le** ∼ feel dizzy. **vertigineux, -euse** *adj* dizzy; (très grand) staggering.

vertu /vɛʀty/ *nf* virtue; **en** ∼ **de** in accordance with. **vertueux, -euse** *adj* virtuous.

verveine /vɛʀvɛn/ *nf* verbena.

vessie /vesi/ *nf* bladder.

veste /vɛst/ *nf* jacket.

vestiaire /vɛstjɛʀ/ *nm* cloakroom; (Sport) changing-room; (US) locker-room.

vestibule /vɛstibyl/ *nm* hall; (Théât, d'hôtel) foyer.

vestige /vɛstiʒ/ *nm* (objet) relic; (trace) vestige.

veston /vɛstɔ̃/ *nm* jacket.

vêtement /vɛtmɑ̃/ *nm* article of clothing; ∼**s** clothes, clothing.

vétéran /veteʀɑ̃/ *nm* veteran.

vétérinaire /veteʀinɛʀ/ *nmf* vet, veterinary surgeon, (US) veterinarian.

vêtir /vetiʀ/ **61** *vt* dress. □ **se** ∼ *vpr* dress.

        V

veto /veto/ *nm inv* veto.

vêtu, **~e** /vety/ *adj* dressed (**de** in).

veuf, **veuve** /vœf, -œv/ *adj* widowed. ● *nm, f* widower, widow.

veuille /vœj/ ➡**VOULOIR** 64.

veut, **veux** /vø/ ➡**VOULOIR** 64.

vexation /vɛksasjɔ̃/ *nf* humiliation.

vexer /vɛkse/ 1 *vt* upset, hurt. □ **se ~** *vpr* be upset, be hurt.

viable /vjabl/ *adj* viable; (*projet*) feasible.

viande /vjɑ̃d/ *nf* meat.

vibrer /vibʀe/ 1 *vi* vibrate; **faire ~** (*âme, foules*) stir.

vicaire /vikɛʀ/ *nm* curate.

vice /vis/ *nm* (moral) vice; (physique) defect.

vicier /visje/ 45 *vt* contaminate; (*air*) pollute.

vicieux, **-ieuse** /visjø, -z/ *adj* depraved. ● *nm, f* pervert.

victime /viktim/ *nf* victim; (d'un accident) casualty.

victoire /viktwaʀ/ *nf* victory; (Sport) win. **victorieux**, **-ieuse** *adj* victorious; (*équipe*) winning.

vidange /vidɑ̃ʒ/ *nf* emptying; (Auto) oil change; (tuyau) waste pipe *ou* outlet.

vide /vid/ *adj* empty. ● *nm* (absence, manque) vacuum, void; (espace) space; (trou) gap; (sans air) vacuum; **à ~** empty; **emballé sous ~** vacuum packed; **suspendu dans le ~** dangling in space.

vide-greniers /vidgʀənje/ *nm inv* bric-a-brac sale.

vidéo /video/ *adj inv* video; **jeu ~** video game. ● *nf* video.

vidéocassette *nf* video (tape).

vidéoclip *nm* music video.

vidéoconférence *nf* videoconferencing; (séance) videoconference. **vidéodisque** *nm* videodisc. **vidéophone** *nm* videophone.

vide-ordures /vidɔʀdyʀ/ *nm inv* rubbish chute.

vidéothèque /videotɛk/ *nf* video library.

vider /vide/ 1 *vt* empty; (*poisson*) gut; (expulser 1) throw out. □ **se ~** *vpr* empty.

vie /vi/ *nf* life; (durée) lifetime; **à ~**, **pour la ~** for life; **donner la ~ à** give birth to; **en ~** alive; **la ~ est chère** the cost of living is high.

vieil /vjɛj/ ➡**VIEUX**.

vieillard /vjɛjaʀ/ *nm* old man.

vieille /vjɛj/ ➡**VIEUX**.

vieillesse /vjɛjɛs/ *nf* old age.

vieillir /vjɛjiʀ/ 2 *vi* grow old, age; (*mot, idée*) become old-fashioned. ● *vt* age. **vieillissement** *nm* ageing.

viens, **vient** /vjɛ̃/ ➡**VENIR** 59.

vierge /vjɛʀʒ/ *nf* virgin; **la V~** Virgo. ● *adj* virgin; (*feuille, cassette*) blank; (*cahier, pellicule*) unused, new.

vieux (**vieil** before vowel or mute h) , **vieille** (*mpl* **vieux**) /vjø, vjɛj/ *adj* old. ● *nm, f* old man, old woman; **petit ~** little old man; **les ~** old people; **vieille fille** (péj) spinster; **~ garçon** old bachelor. **vieux jeu** *adj inv* old-fashioned.

vif, **vive** /vif, viv/ *adj* (animé) lively; (*émotion, vent*) keen; (*froid*) biting; (*lumière*) bright; (*douleur, contraste, parole*) sharp; (*souvenir, style, teint*) vivid; (*succès, impatience*) great; **brûler/enterrer ~** burn/bury alive; **de vive voix** personally. ● *nm* **à ~** (*plaie*) open; **avoir les nerfs à ~** be on edge; **blessé au ~** cut to the quick.

vigie /viʒi/ *nf* lookout.

vigilant, **~e** /viʒilɑ̃, -t/ *adj* vigilant.

Vigipirate /viʒipiʀat/ *nm* government public security measures.

vigne /viɲ/ *nf* (plante) vine; (vignoble) vineyard. **vigneron**, **~ne** *nm, f* wine-grower.

vignette /viɲɛt/ *nf* (étiquette) label; (Auto) road tax disc.

vignoble /viɲɔbl/ *nm* vineyard.

vigoureux, **-euse** /viguʀø, -z/ *adj* vigorous, sturdy.

vigueur /viguœʀ/ *nf* vigour; **être/entrer en ~** (*loi*) be/come into force; **en ~** current.

VIH *abrév m* (**virus immunodéficitaire humain**) HIV.

vilain, **~e** /vilɛ̃, -ɛn/ *adj* (mauvais) nasty; (laid) ugly. ● *nm, f* naughty boy, naughty girl.

villa /villa/ *nf* detached house.

village /vilaʒ/ *nm* village.

villageois, ~e /vilaʒwa, -z/ adj village. ● nm, f villager.

ville /vil/ nf town; (importante) city; ~ **d'eaux** spa.

vin /vɛ̃/ nm wine; ~ **d'honneur** reception.

vinaigre /vinɛgʀ/ nm vinegar. **vinaigrette** nf oil and vinegar dressing, vinaigrette.

vingt /vɛ̃/ (/vɛ̃t/ before vowel and in numbers 22-29) adj & nm twenty.

vingtaine /vɛ̃tɛn/ nf une ~ (de) about twenty.

vingtième /vɛ̃tjɛm/ adj & nmf twentieth.

vinicole /vinikɔl/ adj wine(-producing).

viol /vjɔl/ nm (de femme) rape; (de lieu, loi) violation.

violemment /vjɔlamɑ̃/ adv violently.

violence /vjɔlɑ̃s/ nf violence; (acte) act of violence. **violent, ~e** adj violent.

violer /vjɔle/ ◆ vt rape; (lieu, loi) violate.

violet, ~te /vjɔlɛ, -t/ adj purple. ● nm purple. **violette** nf violet.

violon /vjɔlɔ̃/ nm violin; ~ **d'Ingres** hobby.

violoncelle /vjɔlɔ̃sɛl/ nm cello.

vipère /vipɛʀ/ nf viper, adder.

virage /viʀaʒ/ nm bend; (en ski) turn; (changement d'attitude: fig) change of course.

virée /viʀe/ nf ◆ trip, tour; (en voiture) drive; (à vélo) ride.

virement /viʀmɑ̃/ nm (Comm) (credit) transfer; ~ **automatique** standing order.

virer /viʀe/ ◆ vi turn; ~ **de bord** tack; (fig) do a U-turn; ~ **au rouge** turn red. ● vt (argent) transfer; (expulser ◆) throw out; (élève) expel; (licencier ◆) fire.

virgule /viʀgyl/ nf comma; (dans un nombre) (decimal) point.

viril, ~e /viʀil/ adj virile.

virtuel, ~le /viʀtɥɛl/ adj (potentiel) potential; (mémoire, réalité) virtual.

virulent, ~e /viʀylɑ̃, -t/ adj virulent.

virus /viʀys/ nm virus.

vis¹ /vi/ →VIVRE ◆, →VOIR ◆.

vis² /vis/ nf screw.

visa /viza/ nm visa.

visage /vizaʒ/ nm face.

vis-à-vis /vizavi/ prép ~ **de** (en face de) opposite; (à l'égard de) in relation to; (comparé à) compared to, beside. ● nm inv (personne) person opposite; **en** ~ opposite each other.

visée /vize/ nf aim; **avoir des** ~s **sur** have designs on.

viser /vize/ ◆ vt (cible, centre) aim at; (poste, résultats) aim for; (concerner) be aimed at; (document) stamp; ~ **à** aim at; (mesure, propos) be aimed at; ~ **à faire** aim to do. ● vi aim.

viseur /vizœʀ/ nm (d'arme) sights (+ pl); (Photo) viewfinder.

visière /vizjɛʀ/ nf (de casquette) peak; (de casque) visor.

vision /vizjɔ̃/ nf vision.

visite /vizit/ nf visit; (pour inspecter) inspection; (personne) visitor; **heures de** ~ visiting hours; ~ **guidée** guided tour; ~ **médicale** medical; **rendre** ~ **à, faire une** ~ **à** pay a visit; **être en** ~ **(chez qn)** be visiting (sb); **avoir de la** ~ have visitors.

visiter /vizite/ ◆ vt visit; (appartement) view. **visiteur, -euse** nm, f visitor.

visser /vise/ vt screw (on).

visuel, ~le /vizɥɛl/ adj visual. ● nm (Ordinat) visual display unit, VDU.

vit /vi/ →VIVRE ◆, →VOIR ◆.

vital, ~e (mpl **-aux**) /vital, -o/ adj vital.

vitamine /vitamin/ nf vitamin.

vite /vit/ adv fast, quickly; (tôt) soon; ~**!** quick!; **faire** ~ be quick; **au plus** ~, **le plus** ~ **possible** as quickly as possible.

vitesse /vitɛs/ nf speed; (régime: Auto) gear; **à toute** ~ at top speed; **en** ~ in a hurry, quickly; **boîte à cinq** ~s five-speed gearbox.

viticole /vitikɔl/ adj (industrie) wine; (région) wine-producing. **viticulteur** nm wine-grower.

vitrage /vitʀaʒ/ nm (vitres) windows; **double** ~ double glazing.

vitrail (pl **-aux**) /vitʀaj, -o/ nm stained-glass window.

vitre /vitʀ/ nf (window) pane; (de véhicule) window.

vitrine /vitʀin/ nf (shop) window; (meuble) display cabinet.

V

vivace /vivas/ adj (plante) perennial; (durable) enduring.

vivacité /vivasite/ nf liveliness; (agilité) quickness; (d'émotion, d'intelligence) keenness; (de souvenir, style, teint) vividness.

vivant, ~e /vivã, -t/ adj (example, symbole) living; (en vie) alive, living; (actif, vif) lively. ● nm un bon ~ a bon viveur; **de son ~** in his lifetime; **les ~s** the living.

vive¹ /viv/ →VIF.

vive² /viv/ interj ~ **le roi!** long live the king!

vivement /vivmã/ adv (fortement) strongly; (vite, sèchement) sharply; (avec éclat) vividly; (beaucoup) greatly; ~ **la fin!** I'll be glad when it's the end!

vivier /vivje/ nm fish pond; (arti- ficiel) fish tank.

vivifier /vivifje/ [45] vt invigorate.

vivre /vivʀ/ [63] vi live; ~ **de** (nourriture) live on; ~ **encore** be still alive; **faire** ~ (famille) support. ● vt (vie) live; (période, aventure) live through.

vivres /vivʀ/ nmpl supplies.

VO abrév f (**version originale**) **en** ~ in the original language.

vocabulaire /vɔkabylɛʀ/ nm vocabulary.

vocal, ~e (mpl **-aux**) /vɔkal, -o/ adj vocal.

vœu (pl ~x) /vø/ nm (souhait) wish; (promesse) vow; **meilleurs ~x** best wishes.

vogue /vɔg/ nf fashion, vogue; **en** ~ in fashion ou vogue.

voguer /vɔge/ [1] vi sail.

voici /vwasi/ prép here is, this is; (au pluriel) here are, these are; **me** ~ here I am; ~ **un an** (temps passé) a year ago; ~ **un an que** it is a year since.

voie /vwa/ nf (route) road; (partie de route) lane; (chemin) way; (moyen) means, way; (rails) track; (quai) platform; **en** ~ **de** in the process of; **en** ~ **de développement** (pays) developing; **espèce en** ~ **de disparition** endangered species; **par la** ~ **des airs** by air; **par** ~ **orale** orally; **sur la bonne/mauvaise** ~ (fig) on the right/wrong track; **montrer la** ~ lead the

way; ~ **de dégagement** slip-road; ~ **ferrée** railway; (US) railroad; **V** ~ **lactée** Milky Way; ~ **navigable** waterway; ~ **publique** public highway; ~ **sans issue** (sur panneau) no through road; (fig) dead end.

voilà /vwala/ prép there is, that is; (au pluriel) there are, those are; (voici) here is, here are; **le** ~ there he is; ~**!** right!; (en offrant qch) there you are!; ~ **un an** (temps passé) a year ago; ~ **un an que** it is a year since; **tu en veux?** en ~ do you want some? here you are; **en** ~ **des histoires!** what a fuss!; **et** ~ **que** and then.

voilage /vwalaʒ/ nm net curtain.

voile /vwal/ nf (de bateau) sail; (Sport) sailing. ● nm veil; (tissu léger) net.

voilé, ~e /vwale/ adj (allusion, femme) veiled; (flou) hazy.

voiler /vwale/ [1] vt (dissimuler) veil; (déformer) buckle. □ **se** ~ vpr (devenir flou) become hazy; (se déformer) (roue) buckle.

voilier /vwalje/ nm sailing ship.

voir /vwaʀ/ [64] vt see; **faire** ~ **qch à qn** show sth to sb; **laisser** ~ show; **avoir quelque chose à** ~ **avec** have something to do with; **ça n'a rien à** ~ that's got nothing to do with it; **je ne peux pas le** ~ [1] I can't stand him. ● vi **y** ~ be able to see; **je n'y vois rien** I cannot see; ~ **trouble** have blurred vision; **voyons** let's see now; **voyons, soyez sages!** come on now, behave yourselves! □ **se** ~ vpr (dans la glace) see oneself; (être visible) show; (se produire) be seen; (se trouver) find oneself; (se fréquenter, se rencontrer) see each other; (être vu) be seen.

voire /vwaʀ/ adv or even, not to say.

voirie /vwaʀi/ nf (service) highway maintenance.

voisin, ~e /vwazɛ̃, -in/ adj (de voisinage) neighbouring; (proche) nearby; (adjacent) next (**de** to); (semblable) similar (**de** to). ● nm, f neighbour; **le** ~ the man next door, the neighbour.
voisinage nm neighbourhood; (proximité) proximity.

voiture /vwatyʀ/ nf (motor) car; (wagon) coach, carriage; **en** ~**!** all aboard!; ~ **bélier** ramraiding car; ~ **à cheval** horse-drawn carriage; ~ **de**

course racing car; ~ **école** driving school car; ~ **d'enfant** pram; (US) baby carriage; ~ **de tourisme** saloon car.

voix /vwa/ nf voice; (suffrage) vote; **à ~ basse** in a whisper.

vol /vɔl/ nm (d'avion, d'oiseau) flight; (groupe d'oiseaux) flock, flight; (délit) theft; (hold-up) robbery; ~ **à l'étalage** shoplifting; ~ **à la tire** pickpocketing; **à ~ d'oiseau** as the crow flies; **de haut ~** high-ranking; ~ **libre** hang-gliding; ~ **à voile** gliding.

volaille /vɔlaj/ nf **la ~** (poules) poultry; **une ~** a fowl.

volant /vɔlɑ̃/ nm (steering-)wheel; (de jupe) flounce; (de badminton) shuttlecock; **donner un coup de ~** turn the wheel sharply.

volcan /vɔlkɑ̃/ nm volcano.

volée /vɔle/ nf flight; (oiseaux) flight, flock; (de coups, d'obus, au tennis) volley; **à toute ~** hard; **à la ~** in flight, in mid-air.

voler /vɔle/ **1** vi (oiseau) fly; (dérober) steal (à from). ● vt steal; ~ **qn** rob sb; **il ne l'a pas volé** he deserved it.

volet /vɔlɛ/ nm (de fenêtre) shutter; (de document) (folded ou tear-off) section; **trié sur le ~** hand-picked.

voleur, -euse /vɔlœr, -øz/ nm, f thief; **au ~!** stop thief! ● adj thieving.

volley-ball /vɔlebol/ nm volleyball.

volontaire /vɔlɔ̃tɛr/ adj (délibéré) voluntary; (opiniâtre) determined. ● nmf volunteer. **volontairement** adv voluntarily; (exprès) intentionally.

volonté /vɔlɔ̃te/ nf (faculté, intention) will; (souhait) wish; (énergie) willpower; **à ~** (comme on veut) as required; **du vin à ~** unlimited wine; **bonne ~** goodwill; **mauvaise ~** ill will.

volontiers /vɔlɔ̃tje/ adv (de bon gré) with pleasure, willingly, gladly; (admettre) readily.

volt /vɔlt/ nm volt.

volte-face /vɔltəfas/ nf inv (fig) U-turn; **faire ~** do a U-turn.

voltige /vɔltiʒ/ nf acrobatics (+ pl).

volume /vɔlym/ nm volume.

volumineux, -euse /vɔlyminø, -z/ adj bulky; (livre, dossier) thick.

volupté /vɔlypte/ nf voluptuousness.

vomi /vɔmi/ nm vomit.

vomir /vɔmir/ **2** vt vomit; (fig) belch out. ● vi be sick, vomit.

vomissement /vɔmismɑ̃/ nm vomiting; **~s du matin** morning sickness.

vont /vɔ̃/ →ALLER **8**.

vorace /vɔras/ adj voracious.

vos /vo/ →VOTRE.

votant, -e /vɔtɑ̃, -t/ nm, f voter.

vote /vɔt/ nm (action) voting; (suffrage) vote; ~ **d'une loi** passing of a bill; ~ **par correspondance/procuration** postal/proxy vote.

voter /vɔte/ **1** vi vote. ● vt vote for; (adopter) pass; (crédits) vote.

votre (pl **vos**) /vɔtr, vo/ adj your.

vôtre /votr/ pron **le** ou **la ~**, **les ~s** yours.

vouer /vwe/ **1** vt (vie, temps) dedicate (à to); **voué à l'échec** doomed to failure.

vouloir /vulwar/ **64** vt (exiger) want (**faire** to do); (souhaiter) want; **que veux-tu boire?** what would you like to drink?; **je voudrais bien y aller** I'd really like to go; **je veux bien venir** I'm happy to come; **comme tu voudras** as you wish; (accepter) **veuillez vous asseoir** please sit down; **veuillez patienter** (au téléphone) please hold the line; (signifier) ~ **dire** mean; **qu'est-ce que cela veut dire?** what does that mean?; **en ~ à qn** bear a grudge against sb. □ **s'en ~** vpr regret; **je m'en veux de lui avoir dit** I really regret having told her.

voulu, ~e /vuly/ adj (délibéré) intentional; (requis) required.

vous /vu/ pron (sujet, complément) you; (indirect) (to) you; (réfléchi) yourself; (pluriel) yourselves; (l'un l'autre) each other. **vous-même** pron yourself. **vous-mêmes** pron yourselves.

voûte /vut/ nf (plafond) vault; (porche) archway.

vouvoiement /vuvwamɑ̃/ nm use of the 'vous' form. **vouvoyer** **31** vt address using the 'vous' form.

voyage /vwajaʒ/ nm trip; (déplacement) journey; (par mer) voyage; **~(s)** (action) travelling; ~ **d'affaires** business trip; ~ **d'études** study trip; ~ **de noces** honeymoon; ~ **organisé** (package) tour.

V

voyager /vwajaʒe/ 40 vi travel.

voyageur, -euse /vwajaʒœʀ, -øz/ nm, f traveller; (passager) passenger; ~ **de commerce** travelling salesman.

voyant, ~e /vwajã, -t/ adj gaudy. ● nm (signal) (warning) light.

voyelle /vwajɛl/ nf vowel.

voyou /vwaju/ nm hooligan.

vrac: en ~ /ãvʀak/ loc (pêle-mêle) haphazardly; (sans emballage) loose; (en gros) in bulk.

vrai, ~e /vʀɛ/ adj true; (authentique) real. ● nm truth; **à ~ dire** to tell the truth; **pour de ~** for real. **vraiment** adv really.

vraisemblable /vʀɛsãblabl/ adj (probable) likely; (excuse, histoire) plausible. **vraisemblablement** adv probably. **vraisemblance** nf likelihood, plausibility.

vrombir /vʀɔ̃biʀ/ 2 vi roar.

VRP abrév m (**voyageur représentant placier**) rep, representative.

VTC abrév m (**vélo tous chemins**) hybrid bike.

VTT abrév m (**vélo tout terrain**) mountain bike.

vu, ~e /vy/ adj **bien ~** well thought of; **ce serait plutôt mal ~** it wouldn't go down well; **bien ~!** good point! ● prép in view of; **~ que** seeing that. ● ➡VOIR 64.

vue /vy/ nf (spectacle) sight; (vision) (eye) sight; (panorama, idée, image, photo) view; **avoir en ~** have in mind; **à ~** (tirer) on sight; (payable) at sight; **de ~** by sight; **perdre de ~** lose sight of; **en ~** (proche) in sight; (célèbre) in the public eye; **en ~ de faire** with a view to doing; **à ~ d'œil** visibly; **avoir des ~s sur** have designs on.

vulgaire /vylgɛʀ/ adj (grossier) vulgar; (ordinaire) common.

vulnérable /vylneʀabl/ adj vulnerable.

Ww

wagon /vagɔ̃/ nm (de voyageurs) carriage; (de marchandises) wagon. **wagon-lit** (pl **wagons-lits**) nm sleeper. **wagon-restaurant** (pl **wagons-restaurants**) nm restaurant car.

walkman® /wokman/ nm personal stereo, walkman®.

> **Wallon** A regional Romance *i*
> language spoken in southern
> Belgium (*Wallonie*) by approximately
> 600,000 *Wallons*. It belongs to the
> same linguistic family as the French
> language, and is sometimes con-
> sidered a French dialect. *Wallon*
> should not be confused with Belgian
> French, which differs from the
> French of France in pronunciation
> and vocabulary only.

waters /watɛʀ/ nmpl toilets.

watt /wat/ nm watt.

wc /(dubla)vese/ nmpl toilet (+ sg).

Web /wɛb/ nm Web; **un site ~** a website; **une page ~** web page.

webcam /wɛbkam/ nf webcam.

webmestre /wɛbmɛstʀ/ nm webmaster.

week-end /wikɛnd/ nm weekend.

whisky (pl **-ies**) /wiski/ nm whisky.

Xx

xénophobe /gzenɔfɔb/ adj xenophobic. ● nmf xenophobe.

xérès /gzeʀɛs/ nm sherry.

xylophone /ksilɔfon/ nm xylophone.

Yy

Zz

y /i/
● *adverbe*
····▸ there; (dessus) on it; (pluriel)
on them; (dedans) in it; (pluriel)
in them; **j'∼ vais** I'm on my way;
n'∼ va pas don't go; **du lait? il
n'∼ en a pas** milk? there's none;
tu n'∼ arriveras jamais you'll
never manage it.
● *pronom*
····▸ **s'∼ habituer** get used to it.
····▸ **s'∼ attendre** expect it.
····▸ **∼ penser** think about it.
····▸ **∼ être pour qch** have sth to
do with it.

yaourt /'jauʀ(t) / *nm* yoghurt. **yaour-
tière** *nf* yoghurt-maker.
yard /'jaʀd/ *nm* yard (= 91,44 cm).
yen /'jɛn/ *nm* yen.
yeux /jø/ →**ŒIL.**
yoga /'jɔga/ *nm* yoga.
yougoslave /'jugɔslav/ *adj* Yugoslav.
Y∼ *nmf* Yugoslav.
Yougoslavie /'jugɔslavi/ *nf* Yugoslavia.
yo-yo® /'jojo/ *nm inv* yo-yo®.

zapper /zape/ **1** *vi* (à la télévision)
channel-hop.
zèbre /zɛbʀ/ *nm* zebra.
zèle /zɛl/ *nm* zeal.
zéro /zeʀo/ *nm* nought, zero; (température) zero; (Sport) nil; (tennis) love;
(personne) nonentity; **partir de ∼**
start from scratch; **repartir à ∼** start
all over again.
zeste /zɛst/ *nm* peel; **un ∼ de** (fig) a
touch of.
zézayer /zezeje/ **31** *vi* lisp.
zigzag /zigzag/ *nm* zigzag; **en ∼**
winding.
zinc /zɛ̃g/ *nm* (métal) zinc; (comptoir
1) bar.
zizanie /zizani/ *nf* discord; **semer la ∼**
put the cat among the pigeons.
zizi /zizi/ *nm* **1** willy.
zodiaque /zɔdjak/ *nm* zodiac.
zona /zona/ *nm* (Méd) shingles (+ *sg*).
zone /zon/ *nf* zone, area; (banlieue
pauvre) slums; **∼ bleue** restricted
parking zone; **∼ euro** eurozone; **∼ de
saisie** input box.
zoo /zo(o) / *nm* zoo.
zoom /zum/ *nm* zoom lens.
zut /zyt/ *interj* **1** damn **1**.

a /eɪ, ə/ *determiner*

an avant voyelle ou h muet.

➡️ For expressions such as **make a noise, make a fortune** ➡️**noise, fortune.**

····➤ un/une. ∼ **tree** un arbre; ∼ **chair** une chaise.

····➤ (per) **two euros** ∼ **kilo** deux euros le kilo; **three times** ∼ **day** trois fois par jour.

❗ When talking about what people do or are, **a** is not translated into French: **she's a teacher** *elle est professeur;* **he's a widower** *il est veuf.*

aback /ə'bæk/ *adv* **taken** ∼ déconcerté.

abandon /ə'bændən/ *vt* abandonner. ● *n* abandon *m*.

abate /ə'beɪt/ *vi* (*flood, fever*) baisser; (*storm*) se calmer. ● *vt* diminuer.

abbey /'æbɪ/ *n* abbaye *f*

abbot /'æbət/ *n* abbé *m*.

abbreviate /ə'briːvɪeɪt/ *vt* abréger. **abbreviation** *n* abréviation *f*.

abdicate /'æbdɪkeɪt/ *vt*/*i* abdiquer.

abdomen /'æbdəmən/ *n* abdomen *m*.

abduct /əb'dʌkt/ *vt* enlever. **abductor** *n* ravisseur/-euse *m*/*f*.

abhor /əb'hɔː(r)/ *vt* (*pt* **abhorred**) exécrer.

abide /ə'baɪd/ *vt* supporter; ∼ **by** respecter.

ability /ə'bɪlətɪ/ *n* capacité *f* (**to do** à faire); (*talent*) talent *m*.

abject /'æbdʒekt/ *adj* (*state*) misérable; (*coward*) abject.

ablaze /ə'bleɪz/ *adj* en feu.

able /'eɪbl/ *adj* (*skilled*) compétent; **be** ∼ **to do** pouvoir faire; (*know how to*) savoir faire. **ably** *adv* avec compétence.

abnormal /æb'nɔːml/ *adj* anormal. **abnormality** *n* anomalie *f*.

aboard /ə'bɔːd/ *adv* à bord. ● *prep* à bord de.

abode /ə'bəʊd/ *n* demeure *f*; **of no fixed** ∼ sans domicile fixe.

abolish /ə'bɒlɪʃ/ *vt* abolir.

Aborigine /æbə'rɪdʒənɪ/ *n* aborigène *mf* (d'Australie).

abort /ə'bɔːt/ *vt* faire avorter; (Comput) abandonner. ● *vi* avorter.

abortion /ə'bɔːʃn/ *n* avortement *m*; **have an** ∼ se faire avorter.

abortive /ə'bɔːtɪv/ *adj* (*attempt*) avorté; (*coup*) manqué.

about /ə'baʊt/ *adv* (approximately) environ; ∼ **the same** à peu près pareil; **there was no-one** ∼ il n'y avait personne. ● *prep* **it's** ∼ **...** il s'agit de ...; **what I like** ∼ **her is** ce que j'aime chez elle c'est; **to wander** ∼ **the streets** errer dans les rues; **how/what** ∼ **some tea?** et si on prenait un thé?; **what** ∼ **you?** et toi? ● *adj* **be** ∼ **to do** être sur le point de faire; **be up and** ∼ être debout. ∼**-face**, ∼**-turn** *n* (fig) volte-face *f inv.*

above /ə'bʌv/ *prep* au-dessus de; **he is not** ∼ **lying** Il n'est pas incapable de mentir; ∼ **all** surtout. ● *adv* **the apartment** ∼ l'appartement du dessus; **see** ∼ voir ci-dessus. ∼**-board** *adj* honnête. ∼**-mentioned** *adj* susmentionné.

abrasive /ə'breɪsɪv/ *adj* abrasif; (*manner*) mordant. ● *n* abrasif *m*.

abreast /ə'brest/ *adv* de front; **keep** ∼ **of** se tenir au courant de.

abroad /ə'brɔːd/ *adv* à l'étranger.

abrupt /ə'brʌpt/ *adj* (sudden, curt) brusque; (steep) abrupt. **abruptly** *adv* (suddenly) brusquement; (curtly) avec brusquerie.

abscess /'æbses/ *n* abcès *m*.

abseil /'æbseɪl/ *vi* descendre en rappel.

absence /'æbsəns/ *n* absence *f*; (lack) manque *m*; **in the** ∼ **of** faute de.

absent /'æbsənt/ *adj* absent.

absentee /æbsən'tiː/ *n* absent/-e *m*/*f*.

absent-minded *adj* distrait.

absolute /'æbsəluːt/ *adj* (*monarch, majority*) absolu; (*chaos, idiot*) véritable. **absolutely** *adv* absolument.

a

absolve /əb'zɒlv/ vt ~ sb of sth décharger qn de qch.

absorb /əb'zɔːb/ vt absorber.

abstain /əb'steɪn/ vi s'abstenir (**from** de).

abstract[1] /'æbstrækt/ adj abstrait. ● n (summary) résumé m; **in the** ~ dans l'abstrait.

abstract[2] /əb'strækt/ vt tirer.

absurd /əb'sɜːd/ adj absurde.

abundance /ə'bʌndəns/ n abondance f. **abundant** adj abondant. **abundantly** adv (entirely) tout à fait.

abuse[1] /ə'bjuːz/ vt (position) abuser de; (person) maltraiter; (insult) injurier.

abuse[2] /ə'bjuːs/ n (misuse) abus m (**of** de); (cruelty) mauvais traitement m; (insults) injures fpl.

abusive /ə'bjuːsɪv/ adj (person) grossier; (language) injurieux.

abysmal /ə'bɪzml/ adj épouvantable.

abyss /ə'bɪs/ n abîme m.

academic /ækə'demɪk/ adj (career) universitaire; (year) académique; (scholarly) intellectuel; (theoretical) théorique. ● n universitaire mf.

academy /ə'kædəmɪ/ n (school) école f; (society) académie f.

accelerate /ək'seləreɪt/ vi (speed up) s'accélérer; (Auto) accélérer. **accelerator** n accélérateur m.

accent[1] /'æksent/ n accent m.

accent[2] /æk'sent/ vt accentuer.

accept /ək'sept/ vt accepter. **acceptable** adj acceptable. **acceptance** n (of offer) acceptation f; (of proposal) approbation f.

access /'ækses/ n accès m. **accessible** adj accessible.

accessory /ək'sesərɪ/ adj accessoire. ● n (Jur) complice mf (**to** de).

accident /'æksɪdənt/ n accident m; (chance) hasard m; **by** ~ par hasard. **accidental** adj (death) accidentel; (meeting) fortuit. **accidentally** adv accidentellement; (by chance) par hasard.

acclaim /ə'kleɪm/ vt applaudir. ● n louanges fpl.

acclimatize /ə'klaɪmətaɪz/ vt/i (s')acclimater (**to** à).

accommodate /ə'kɒmədeɪt/ vt loger; (adapt to) s'adapter à; (satisfy) satisfaire. **accommodating** adj accommodant. **accommodation** n logement m.

accompaniment /ə'kʌmpənɪmənt/ n accompagnement m. **accompany** vt accompagner.

accomplice /ə'kʌmplɪs/ n complice mf (**in, to** de).

accomplish /ə'kʌmplɪʃ/ vt accomplir; (objective) réaliser. **accomplished** adj très compétent. **accomplishment** n (feat) réussite f; (talent) talent m.

accord /ə'kɔːd/ vi concorder (**with** avec). ● vt accorder (**sb sth** qch à qn). ● n accord m; **of my own** ~ de moi-même.

accordance /ə'kɔːdəns/ n **in** ~ **with** conformément à.

according /ə'kɔːdɪŋ/ adv ~ **to** (principle, law) selon; (person, book) d'après. **accordingly** adv en conséquence.

accordion /ə'kɔːdɪən/ n accordéon m.

accost /ə'kɒst/ vt aborder.

account /ə'kaʊnt/ n (Comm) compte m; (description) compte-rendu m; **on** ~ **of** à cause de; **on no** ~ en aucun cas; **take into** ~ tenir compte de; **it's of no** ~ peu importe. □ ~ **for** (explain) expliquer; (represent) représenter. **accountability** n responsabilité f. **accountable** adj responsable (**for** de; **to** envers).

accountancy /ə'kaʊntənsɪ/ n comptabilité f. **accountant** n comptable mf. **accounts** npl comptabilité f, comptes mpl.

accumulate /ə'kjuːmjʊleɪt/ vt/i (s')accumuler.

accuracy /'ækjərəsɪ/ n (of figures) justesse f; (of aim) précision f; (of forecast) exactitude f. **accurate** adj juste, précis. **accurately** adv exactement, précisément.

accusation /ækjuː'zeɪʃn/ n accusation f.

accuse /ə'kjuːz/ vt accuser; **the** ~**d** l'accusé/-e m/f.

accustomed /ə'kʌstəmd/ adj accoutumé; **become** ~ **to** s'accoutumer à.

ace /eɪs/ n (card, person) as m.

ache /eɪk/ n douleur f. ● vi (person) avoir mal; **my leg** ~**s** ma jambe me fait mal.

achieve /ə'tʃiːv/ vt (aim) atteindre; (result) obtenir; (ambition) réaliser.

achievement n (feat) réussite f; (fulfilment) réalisation f (**of** de).

acid /'æsɪd/ adj & n acide (m). **acidity** n acidité f. ~ **rain** n pluies fpl acides.

acknowledge /ək'nɒlɪdʒ/ vt (error, authority) reconnaître. (letter) accuser réception de. **acknowledgement** n reconnaissance f.

acne /'æknɪ/ n acné f.

acorn /'eɪkɔːn/ n (Bot) gland m.

acoustic /ə'kuːstɪk/ adj acoustique. **acoustics** npl acoustique f.

acquaint /ə'kweɪnt/ vt ~ **sb with sth** mettre qn au courant de qch; **be** ~**ed with** (person) connaître. (fact) savoir. **acquaintance** n connaissance f.

acquire /ə'kwaɪə(r)/ vt acquérir; (habit) prendre.

acquit /ə'kwɪt/ vt (pt **acquitted**) (Jur) acquitter. **acquittal** n acquittement m.

acre /'eɪkə(r)/ n acre f, ≈ demi-hectare m.

acrid /'ækrɪd/ adj âcre.

acrimonious /ækrɪ'məʊnɪəs/ adj acrimonieux.

acrobat /'ækrəbæt/ n acrobate mf. **acrobatics** npl acrobaties fpl.

acronym /'ækrənɪm/ n acronyme m.

across /ə'krɒs/ adv & prep (side to side) d'un côté à l'autre (de); (on other side) de l'autre côté (**from** de); **go or walk** ~ traverser; **lie** ~ **the bed** se coucher en travers du lit; ~ **the world** partout dans le monde.

act /ækt/ n acte m; (Jur, Pol) loi f; **put on an** ~ jouer la comédie. ● vi agir; (Theat) jouer; ~ **as** servir de. ● vt (part, role) jouer.

acting /'æktɪŋ/ n (Theat) jeu m. ● adj (temporary) intérimaire.

action /'ækʃn/ n action f; (Mil) combat m; **out of** ~ hors service; **take** ~ agir.

activate /'æktɪveɪt/ vt (machine) faire démarrer; (alarm) déclencher.

active /'æktɪv/ adj actif; (volcano) en activité; **take an** ~ **interest in** s'intéresser activement à. **activist** n activiste mf. **activity** n activité f.

actor /'æktə(r)/ n acteur m. **actress** n actrice f.

actual /'æktʃʊəl/ adj réel; **the** ~ **words** les mots exacts; **in the** ~ **house** (the house itself) dans la maison elle-même. **actuality** n réalité f.

actually adv (in fact) en fait; (really) vraiment.

acute /ə'kjuːt/ adj (anxiety) vif; (illness) aigu; (shortage) grave; (mind) pénétrant.

ad /æd/ n (TV) pub f 🄸; **small** ~ petite annonce f.

AD abbr (**Anno Domini**) ap. J.-C.

adamant /'ædəmənt/ adj catégorique.

adapt /ə'dæpt/ vt/i (s')adapter (**to** à). **adaptability** n adaptabilité f. **adaptable** adj souple. **adaptation** n adaptation f. **adaptor** n (Electr) adaptateur m.

add /æd/ vt/i ajouter (**to** à); (in maths) additionner. □ ~ **up** (facts, figures) s'accorder; ~ **sth up** additionner qch; ~ **up to** s'élever à.

adder /'ædə(r)/ n vipère f.

addict /'ædɪkt/ n toxicomane mf; (fig) accro mf 🄸.

addicted /ə'dɪktɪd/ adj **be** ~ avoir une dépendance (**to** à); (fig) être accro 🄸 (**to** à). **addiction** n (Med) dépendance f (**to** à); passion f (**to** pour). **addictive** adj qui crée une dépendance.

addition /ə'dɪʃn/ n (item) ajout m; (in maths) addition f; **in** ~ en plus. **additional** adj supplémentaire.

additive /'ædɪtɪv/ n additif m.

address /ə'dres/ n adresse f; (speech) discours m. ● vt (letter) mettre l'adresse sur; (crowd) s'adresser à; ~ **sth to** adresser qch à. **addressee** n destinataire mf.

adequate /'ædɪkwət/ adj suffisant; (satisfactory) satisfaisant.

adhere /əd'hɪə(r)/ vi (lit, fig) adhérer (**to** à); ~ **to** (policy) observer.

adjacent /ə'dʒeɪsnt/ adj contigu; ~ **to** attenant à.

adjective /'ædʒɪktɪv/ n adjectif m.

adjoin /ə'dʒɔɪn/ vt être contigu à. **adjoining** adj (room) voisin.

adjourn /ə'dʒɜːn/ vt (trial) ajourner; **the session was** ~**ed** la séance a été levée. ● vi s'arrêter; (Parliament) lever la séance; ~ **to** passer à.

adjust /ə'dʒʌst/ vt (level, speed) régler; (price) ajuster; (clothes) rajuster. ● vt/i ~ **(oneself) to** s'adapter à. **adjustable** adj réglable. **adjustment** n (of rates) rajustement m; (of control) réglage m; (of person) adaptation f.

ad lib /ˌæd ˈlɪb/ vt/i (pt **ad libbed**) improviser.

administer /ədˈmɪnɪstə(r)/ vt administrer.

administration /ədmɪnɪˈstreɪʃn/ n administration f. **administrative** adj administratif. **administrator** n administrateur/-trice m/f.

admiral /ˈædmərəl/ n amiral m.

admiration /ædməˈreɪʃn/ n admiration f. **admire** vt admirer. **admirer** n admirateur/-trice m/f.

admission /ədˈmɪʃn/ n (to a place) entrée f; (confession) aveu m.

admit /ədˈmɪt/ vt (pt **admitted**) (acknowledge) reconnaître, admettre. (crime) avouer; (new member) admettre; ~ **to** reconnaître. **admittance** n entrée f. **admittedly** adv il est vrai.

ado /əˈduː/ n without more ~ sans plus de cérémonie.

adolescence /ædəˈlesns/ n adolescence f. **adolescent** n & a adolescent/-e m/f.

adopt /əˈdɒpt/ vt adopter. **adopted** adj (child) adoptif. **adoption** n adoption f. **adoptive** adj adoptif.

adorable /əˈdɔːrəbl/ adj adorable. **adoration** n adoration f. **adore** vt adorer.

adorn /əˈdɔːn/ vt orner.

adrift /əˈdrɪft/ adj & adv à la dérive.

adult /ˈædʌlt/ adj & n adulte (mf).

adultery /əˈdʌltərɪ/ n adultère m.

adulthood /ˈædʌlthʊd/ n âge m adulte.

advance /ədˈvɑːns/ vt (sum) avancer; (tape, career) faire avancer; (interests) servir. ● vi (lit) avancer; (progress) progresser. ● n avance f; (progress) progrès m; in~ à l'avance. **advanced** adj avancé; (studies) supérieur.

advantage /ədˈvɑːntɪdʒ/ n avantage m; **take** ~ **of** profiter de; (person) exploiter. **advantageous** adj avantageux.

adventure /ədˈventʃə(r)/ n aventure f. **adventurer** /ədˈventʃərə(r)/ n aventurier-ière m/f. **adventurous** adj aventureux.

adverb /ˈædvɜːb/ n adverbe m.

adverse /ˈædvɜːs/ adj défavorable.

advert /ˈædvɜːt/ n annonce f; (TV) pub f 🔲.

advertise /ˈædvətaɪz/ vt faire de la publicité pour; (car, house, job) mettre une annonce pour. ● vi faire de la publicité; (for staff) passer une annonce. **advertisement** n publicité f; (in newspaper) annonce f. **advertiser** n annonceur m. **advertising** n publicité f.

advice /ədˈvaɪs/ n conseils mpl; some ~, **a piece of** ~ un conseil.

advise /ədˈvaɪz/ vt conseiller; (inform) aviser; ~ **against** déconseiller. **adviser** n conseiller/-ère m/f. **advisory** adj consultatif.

advocate¹ /ˈædvəkət/ n (Jur) avocat m; (supporter) partisan m.

advocate² /ˈædvəkeɪt/ vt recommander.

aerial /ˈeərɪəl/ adj aérien. ● n antenne f.

aerobics /eəˈrəʊbɪks/ n aérobic m.

aeroplane /ˈeərəpleɪn/ n avion m.

aerosol /ˈeərəsɒl/ n bombe f aérosol.

aesthetic /iːsˈθetɪk/ adj esthétique.

afar /əˈfɑː(r)/ adv from ~ de loin.

affair /əˈfeə(r)/ n (matter) affaire f; (romance) liaison f.

affect /əˈfekt/ vt affecter.

affection /əˈfekʃn/ n affection f. **affectionate** adj affectueux.

affinity /əˈfɪnətɪ/ n affinité f.

afflict /əˈflɪkt/ vt affliger.

affluence /ˈæflʊəns/ n richesse f.

afford /əˈfɔːd/ vt avoir les moyens d'acheter; (provide) fournir; **can you** ~ **the time?** avez-vous le temps?

afloat /əˈfləʊt/ adj & adv (boat) à flot.

afoot /əˈfʊt/ adv sth is ~ il se prépare qch.

afraid /əˈfreɪd/ adj be ~ (frightened) avoir peur (**of, to** de; **that** que); (worried) craindre (**that** que); **I'm** ~ **I can't come** je suis désolé mais je ne peux pas venir.

Africa /ˈæfrɪkə/ n Afrique f.

African /ˈæfrɪkən/ n Africain/-e m/f. ● adj africain.

after /ˈɑːftə(r)/ adv & prep après; **soon** ~ peu après; **be** ~ **sth** rechercher qch; ~ **all** après tout. ● conj après que; ~ **doing** après avoir fait.

aftermath /ˈɑːftəmæθ/ n conséquences fpl (**of** de).

afternoon /ɑːftəˈnuːn/ n après-midi m or f inv; **in the** ~ (dans) l'après-midi.

after: ~ **shave** n après-rasage m. ~ **thought** n pensée f après coup.

afterwards /'ɑːftəwədz/ *adv* après, par la suite.

again /ə'geɪn/ *adv* encore; ~ **and** ~ à plusieurs reprises; **start** ~ recommencer; **she never saw him** ~ elle ne l'a jamais revu.

against /ə'geɪnst/ *prep* contre; ~ **the law** illégal.

age /eɪdʒ/ *n* âge *m*; (era) ère *f*, époque *f*; **I've been waiting for** ~**s** j'attends depuis des heures. ● *vt/i* (*pres p* **ageing**) vieillir.

aged[1] /'eɪdʒd/ *adj* ~ **six** âgé de six ans.

aged[2] /'eɪdʒɪd/ *adj* âgé.

ageism /'eɪdʒɪzəm/ *n* discrimination *f* en raison de l'âge.

agency /'eɪdʒɪnsɪ/ *n* agence *f*.

agenda /ə'dʒendə/ *n* ordre *m* du jour; (fig) programme *m*.

agent /'eɪdʒənt/ *n* agent *m*.

aggravate /'ægrəveɪt/ *vt* (make worse) aggraver; (annoy) exaspérer. **aggravation** *n* (worsening) aggravation *f*; (annoyance) ennuis *mpl*.

aggression /ə'greʃn/ *n* agression *f*. **aggressive** *adj* agressif. **aggressiveness** *n* agressivité *f*. **aggressor** *n* agresseur *m*.

agitate /'ædʒɪteɪt/ *vt* agiter.

ago /ə'gəʊ/ *adv* il y a; **a month** ~ il y a un mois; **long** ~ il y a longtemps; **how long** ~? il y a combien de temps?

agonize /'ægənaɪz/ *vi* se tourmenter (over à propos de). **agonized** *adj* angoissé. **agonizing** *adj* déchirant. **agony** *n* douleur *f* atroce; (mental) angoisse *f*.

agree /ə'griː/ *vi* être d'accord (on sur; with avec); ~ **to** consentir à; ~ **with** (approve of) approuver. ● *vt* être d'accord (**that** sur le fait que); (admit) convenir (**that** que); (date, solution) se mettre d'accord sur.

agreeable /ə'griːəbl/ *adj* agréable; **be** ~ (willing) être d'accord.

agreed /ə'griːd/ *adj* (time, place) convenu; **we're** ~ nous sommes d'accord.

agreement /ə'griːmənt/ *n* accord *m*; **in** ~ d'accord.

agricultural /ægrɪ'kʌltʃərəl/ *adj* agricole. **agriculture** *n* agriculture *f*.

aground /ə'graʊnd/ *adv* **run** ~ (ship) s'échouer.

ahead /ə'hed/ *adv* (in front) en avant, devant; (in advance) à l'avance; **be 10 points** ~ avoir 10 points d'avance; ~ **of time** en avance; **go** ~! allez-y!

aid /eɪd/ *vt* aider. ● *n* aide *f*; **in** ~ **of** au profit de.

aide /eɪd/ *n* aide *mf*.

Aids /eɪdz/ *n* (Med) sida *m*.

aim /eɪm/ *vt* (gun) braquer (at sur); **be** ~**ed at sb** (campaign, remark) viser qn. ● *vi* ~ **for/at sth** viser qch; ~ **to do** avoir l'intention de faire. ● *n* but *m*; **take** ~ viser. **aimless** *adj* sans but.

air /eə(r)/ *n* air *m*; **by** ~ par avion; **on the** ~ à l'antenne. ● *vt* aérer; (views) exprimer. ● *adj* (base, disaster) aérien; (pollution, pressure) atmosphérique. ~ **bed** *n* matelas *m* pneumatique. ~**conditioning** *n* climatisation *f*. ~**craft** *n inv* avion *m*. ~**craft carrier** *n* porte-avions *m inv*. ~**field** *n* terrain *m* d'aviation. ~ **force** *n* armée *f* de l'air. ~ **freshener** *n* désodorisant *m* d'atmosphère. ~ **hostess** *n* hôtesse *f* de l'air. ~**lift** *vt* transporter par pont aérien. ~**line** *n* compagnie *f* aérienne. ~**liner** *n* avion *m* de ligne. ~**lock** *n* (in pipe) bulle *f* d'air; (chamber) sas *m*. ~**mail** *n* (by) ~**mail** par avion. ~**plane** *n* (US) avion *m*. ~**port** *n* aéroport *m*. ~ **raid** *n* attaque *f* aérienne. ~-**tight** *adj* hermétique. ~ **traffic controller** *n* contrôleur/-euse *m/f* aérien/-ne. ~**waves** *npl* ondes *fpl*.

airy /'eərɪ/ *adj* (-ier, -iest) (room) clair et spacieux.

aisle /aɪl/ *n* (of church) allée *f* centrale; (in train) couloir *m*.

ajar /ə'dʒɑː(r)/ *adv & adj* entrouvert.

akin /ə'kɪn/ *adj* ~ **to** semblable à.

alarm /ə'lɑːm/ *n* alarme *f*; (clock) réveil *m*; (feeling) frayeur *f*. ● *vt* inquiéter. ~ **clock** *n* réveil *m*.

alas /ə'læs/ *interj* hélas.

Albania /æl'beɪnɪə/ *n* Albanie *f*.

album /'ælbəm/ *n* album *m*.

alcohol /'ælkəhɒl/ *n* alcool *m*.

alcoholic /ælkə'hɒlɪk/ *adj* alcoolique; (drink) alcoolisé. ● *n* alcoolique *mf*.

ale /eɪl/ *n* bière *f*.

alert /ə'lɜːt/ *adj* alerte; (watchful) vigilant. ● *n* alerte *f*; **on the** ~ sur le qui-

a

vive. ● vt alerter; ~ sb to prévenir qn de. **alertness** n vivacité f; vigilance f.

A-level /'eɪlevl/ n ≈ baccalauréat m

algebra /'ældʒɪbrə/ n algèbre f.

Algeria /æl'dʒɪərɪə/ n Algérie f.

alias /'eɪlɪəs/ n (pl ~es) faux nom m. ● prep alias.

alibi /'ælɪbaɪ/ n alibi m.

alien /'eɪlɪən/ n & a étranger/-ère (m/f) (to à).

alienate /'eɪlɪəneɪt/ vt éloigner.

alight /ə'laɪt/ adj en feu, allumé.

alike /ə'laɪk/ adj semblable. ● adv de la même façon; **look** ~ se ressembler.

alive /ə'laɪv/ adj vivant; ~ **to** conscient de; ~ **with** grouillant de.

---

all /ɔ:l/

● pronoun

····▸ (everything) tout; **is that** ~? c'est tout?; **that was** ~ **(that) he said** c'est tout ce qu'il a dit; **I ate it** ~ j'ai tout mangé.

! Use the translation **tous** for a group of masculine or mixed gender people or objects and **toutes** for a group of feminine gender: **we were all delighted** nous étions tous ravis; **'where are the cups?'—'they're all in the kitchen'** 'où sont les tasses?'-'elles sont toutes dans la cuisine'.

● determiner

····▸ tout/toute/tous/toutes; ~ **the time** tout le temps; ~ **his life** toute sa vie; ~ **of us** nous tous; ~ **(the) women** toutes les femmes.

● adverb

····▸ (completely) tout; **they were** ~ **alone** ils étaient tous seuls; **tell me** ~ **about it** raconte-moi tout; ~ **for** tout à fait pour; **not** ~ **that well** pas si bien que ça; ~ **too** bien trop.

! When the adjective that follows is in the feminine and begins with a consonant, the translation is toute/toutes: **she was all alone** elle était toute seule.

---

allege /ə'ledʒ/ vt prétendre. ~**d** adj présumé; **allegedly** adv prétendument.

allergic /ə'lɜ:dʒɪk/ adj allergique (**to** à). **allergy** n allergie f.

alleviate /ə'li:vɪeɪt/ vt alléger.

alley /'ælɪ/ n (street) ruelle f.

alliance /ə'laɪəns/ n alliance f.

allied /'ælaɪd/ adj allié.

alligator /'ælɪgeɪtə(r)/ n alligator m.

allocate /'æləkeɪt/ vt (funds) affecter; (time) accorder; (task) assigner.

allot /ə'lɒt/ vt (pt **allotted**) (money) attribuer; (task) assigner. **allotment** n attribution f; (land) parcelle f de terre.

all-out /'ɔ:laʊt/ adj (effort) acharné; (strike) total.

allow /ə'laʊ/ vt (authorize) autoriser à; (let) laisser; (enable) permettre; (concede) accorder; ~ **for** tenir compte de.

allowance /ə'laʊəns/ n allocation f; **make** ~s **for sth** tenir compte de qch; **make** ~s **for sb** essayer de comprendre qn.

alloy /'ælɔɪ/ n alliage m.

all right /ɔ:l'raɪt/ adj (not bad) pas mal; **are you** ~? ça va?; **is it** ~ **if ...?** est-ce que ça va si ...? ● adv (see) bien; (function) comme il faut. ● interj d'accord.

ally¹ /'ælaɪ/ n allié/-e m/f.

ally² /ə'laɪ/ vt allier; ~ **oneself with** s'allier avec.

almighty /ɔ:l'maɪtɪ/ adj tout-puissant; (very great) formidable.

almond /'ɑ:mənd/ n amande f. ~ **tree** n amandier m.

almost /'ɔ:lməʊst/ adv presque; **he** ~ **died** il a failli mourir.

alone /ə'ləʊn/ adj & adv seul.

along /ə'lɒŋ/ prep le long de; **walk** ~ **the beach** marcher sur la plage. ● adv **come** ~ venir; **walk** ~ marcher; **push/pull sth** ~ pousser/tirer qch; **all** ~ (time) depuis le début; ~ **with** avec.

alongside /ə'lɒŋsaɪd/ adv à côté; **come** ~ (Naut) accoster. ● prep (next to) à côté de; (all along) le long de.

aloof /ə'lu:f/ adj distant.

aloud /ə'laʊd/ adv à haute voix.

alphabet /'ælfəbet/ n alphabet m. **alphabetical** adj alphabétique.

alpine /ˈælpaɪn/ adj (landscape) alpestre; (climate) alpin.

already /ɔːlˈredɪ/ adv déjà.

alright /ɔːlˈraɪt/ a & adv ➡ALL RIGHT.

Alsatian /ælˈseɪʃn/ n (dog) berger m allemand.

also /ˈɔːlsəʊ/ adv aussi.

altar /ˈɔːltə(r)/ n autel m.

alter /ˈɔːltə(r)/ vt/i changer; (building) transformer; (garment) retoucher. **alteration** n changement m; (to building) transformation f; (to garment) retouche f.

alternate[1] /ˈɔːltəneɪt/ vt/i alterner.

alternate[2] /ɔːlˈtɜːnət/ adj en alternance; **on ~ days** un jour sur deux. **alternately** adv alternativement.

alternative /ɔːlˈtɜːnətɪv/ adj autre; (solution) de rechange. ● n (specified option) alternative f; (possible option) choix m. **alternatively** adv sinon.

alternator /ˈɔːltəneɪtə(r)/ n alternateur m.

although /ɔːlˈðəʊ/ conj bien que.

altitude /ˈæltɪtjuːd/ n altitude f.

altogether /ɔːltəˈɡeðə(r)/ adv (completely) tout à fait; (on the whole) tout compte fait.

aluminium /æljʊˈmɪnjəm/ n aluminium m.

always /ˈɔːlweɪz/ adv toujours.

am /æm/ ➡BE.

a.m. /eɪem/ adv du matin.

amalgamate /əˈmælɡəmeɪt/ vt/i (merge) fusionner; (metals) (s')amalgamer.

amateur /ˈæmətə(r)/ n & adj amateur (m).

amaze /əˈmeɪz/ vt stupéfaire. **amazed** adj stupéfait. **amazement** n stupéfaction f. **amazing** adj stupéfiant; (great) exceptionnel.

ambassador /æmˈbæsədə(r)/ n ambassadeur m.

amber /ˈæmbə(r)/ n ambre m; (Auto) orange m.

ambiguity /æmbɪˈɡjuːətɪ/ n ambiguïté f.

ambiguous /æmˈbɪɡjʊəs/ adj ambigu.

ambition /æmˈbɪʃn/ n ambition f. **ambitious** adj ambitieux.

ambulance /ˈæmbjʊləns/ n ambulance f.

ambush /ˈæmbʊʃ/ n embuscade f. ● vt tendre une embuscade à.

amenable /əˈmiːnəbl/ adj obligeant; **~ to** (responsive) sensible à.

amend /əˈmend/ vt modifier. **amendment** n (to rule) amendement m.

amends /əˈmendz/ npl **make ~** réparer son erreur.

amenities /əˈmiːnətɪz/ npl équipements mpl.

America /əˈmerɪkə/ n Amérique f.

American /əˈmerɪkən/ n Américain/-e m/f. ● adj américain.

American dream Cette expression désigne un principe américain selon lequel la réussite, en particulier financière et sociale, est accessible à quiconque travaille avec acharnement. Pour les immigrants, s'y ajoute le rêve de liberté et d'égalité.

amiable /ˈeɪmɪəbl/ adj aimable.

amicable /ˈæmɪkəbl/ adj amical.

amid(st) /əˈmɪd(st)/ prep au milieu de.

amiss /əˈmɪs/ adj **there is something ~** il y a quelque chose qui ne va pas.

ammonia /əˈməʊnɪə/ n (gas) ammoniac m; (solution) ammoniaque f.

ammunition /æmjʊˈnɪʃn/ n munitions fpl.

amnesty /ˈæmnəstɪ/ n amnistie f.

among(st) /əˈmʌŋ(st)/ prep parmi; (affecting a group) chez; **be ~ the poorest** être un des plus pauvres; **be ~ the first** être dans les premiers.

amorous /ˈæmərəs/ adj amoureux.

amount /əˈmaʊnt/ n quantité f; (total) montant m; (sum of money) somme f. ● vi **~ to** (add up to) s'élever à; (be equivalent to) revenir à.

amp /æmp/ n ampère m.

amphibian /æmˈfɪbɪən/ n amphibie m.

ample /ˈæmpl/ adj (resources) largement suffisant; (proportions) généreux.

amplifier /ˈæmplɪfaɪə(r)/ n amplificateur m.

amputate /ˈæmpjʊteɪt/ vt amputer.

amuse /əˈmjuːz/ vt amuser.

amusement /əˈmjuːzmənt/ n (mirth) amusement m; (diversion) distraction f. **~ arcade** n salle f de jeux.

an /æn, ən/ ➡A.

a

anaemia /əˈniːmɪə/ n anémie f.

anaesthetic /ænɪsˈθetɪk/ n anesthésique m.

analyse /ˈænəlaɪz/ vt analyser. **analysis** n (pl **-yses**) analyse f. **analyst** n analyste mf.

anarchist /ˈænəkɪst/ n anarchiste mf.

anatomical /ænəˈtɒmɪkl/ adj anatomique. **anatomy** n anatomie f.

ancestor /ˈænsestə(r)/ n ancêtre m.

anchor /ˈæŋkə(r)/ n ancre f. ● vt mettre à l'ancre. ● vi jeter l'ancre.

anchovy /ˈæntʃəvɪ/ n anchois m.

ancient /ˈeɪnʃənt/ adj ancien.

ancillary /ænˈsɪlərɪ/ adj auxiliaire.

and /ænd, ənd/ conj et; **two hundred ~ sixty** deux cent soixante; **go ~ see him** allez le voir; **richer ~ richer** de plus en plus riche.

anew /əˈnjuː/ adv (once more) encore, de nouveau; (in a new way) à nouveau.

angel /ˈeɪndʒl/ n ange m.

anger /ˈæŋgə(r)/ n colère f. ● vt mettre en colère, fâcher.

angle /ˈæŋgl/ n angle m. ● vi pêcher (à la ligne); **~ for** (fig) quêter. **angler** n pêcheur/-euse m/f.

Anglo-Saxon /æŋgləʊˈsæksn/ adj anglo-saxon. ● n Anglo-Saxon/-ne m/f.

angry /ˈæŋgrɪ/ adj (**-ier, -iest**) fâché, en colère; **get ~** se fâcher, se mettre en colère (**with** contre); **make sb ~** mettre qn en colère.

anguish /ˈæŋgwɪʃ/ n angoisse f.

animal /ˈænɪml/ n & adj animal (m).

animate¹ /ˈænɪmət/ adj (person) vivant; (object) animé.

animate² /ˈænɪmeɪt/ vt animer.

aniseed /ˈænɪsiːd/ n anis m.

ankle /ˈæŋkl/ n cheville f. **~ sock** n socquette f.

annex /əˈneks/ vt annexer.

anniversary /ænɪˈvɜːsərɪ/ n anniversaire m.

announce /əˈnaʊns/ vt annoncer (**that** que). **announcement** n (spoken) annonce f; (written) avis m. **announcer** n (radio, TV) speaker/-ine m/f.

annoy /əˈnɔɪ/ vt agacer, ennuyer. **annoyance** n contrariété f. **annoyed** adj fâché (**with** contre); **get ~ed** se fâcher. **annoying** adj ennuyeux.

annual /ˈænjʊəl/ adj annuel. ● n publication f annuelle. **annually** adv (earn, produce) par an; (do, inspect) tous les ans.

annul /əˈnʌl/ vt (pt **annulled**) annuler.

anonymity /ænəˈnɪmətɪ/ n anonymat m. **anonymous** adj anonyme.

anorak /ˈænəræk/ n anorak m.

another /əˈnʌðə(r)/ det & pron un/-e autre; **~ coffee** (one more) encore un café; **~ ten minutes** encore dix minutes, dix minutes de plus; **can I have ~?** est-ce que je peux en avoir un autre?

answer /ˈɑːnsə(r)/ n réponse f; (solution) solution f; (phone) **there's no ~** ça ne répond pas. ● vt répondre à; (prayer) exaucer; **~ the door** ouvrir la porte. ● vi répondre. □ **~ back** répondre; **~ for** répondre de; **~ to** (superior) dépendre de; (description) répondre à. **answerable** adj responsable (**for** de; **to** devant). **answering machine** n répondeur m.

ant /ænt/ n fourmi f.

antagonism /ænˈtægənɪzəm/ n antagonisme m. **antagonize** vt provoquer l'hostilité de.

Antarctic /ænˈtɑːktɪk/ n **the ~** l'Antarctique m. ● adj antarctique.

antenatal /æntɪˈneɪtl/ adj prénatal.

antenna /ænˈtenə/ n (pl **-ae**) (of insect) antenne f; (pl **-as**; aerial: US) antenne f.

anthem /ˈænθəm/ n (Relig) motet m; (of country) hymne m national.

anthrax /ˈænθræks/ n charbon m.

antibiotic /æntɪbaɪˈɒtɪk/ n & adj antibiotique (m).

antibody /ˈæntɪbɒdɪ/ n anticorps m.

anticipate /ænˈtɪsɪpeɪt/ vt (foresee, expect) prévoir, s'attendre à.

anticipation /æntɪsɪˈpeɪʃn/ n attente f; **in ~ of** en prévision or attente de.

anticlimax /æntɪˈklaɪmæks/ n (letdown) déception f.

anticlockwise /æntɪˈklɒkwaɪz/ adv & adj dans le sens inverse des aiguilles d'une montre.

antics /ˈæntɪks/ npl pitreries fpl.

antifreeze /ˈæntɪfriːz/ n antigel m.

antiquated /ˈæntɪkweɪtɪd/ adj (idea) archaïque; (building) vétuste.

antique /æn'tiːk/ *adj* (old) ancien; (old-style) à l'ancienne. ● *n* objet *m* ancien, antiquité *f.* ~ **dealer** *n* antiquaire *mf.* ~ **shop** *n* magasin *m* d'antiquités.

anti-Semitic /æntɪsɪ'mɪtɪk/ *adj* anti-sémite.

antiseptic /æntɪ'septɪk/ *adj & n* anti-septique (*m*).

antisocial /æntɪ'səʊʃl/ *adj* asocial, antisocial; (reclusive) sauvage.

antlers /'æntləz/ *npl* bois *mpl.*

anxiety /æŋ'zaɪətɪ/ *n* (worry) anxiété *f;* (eagerness) impatience *f.*

anxious /'æŋkʃəs/ *adj* (troubled) anxieux; (eager) impatient (**to** de).

any /'enɪ/ *det* (some) du, de l', de la, des; (after negative) de, d'; (every) tout; (no matter which) n'importe quel; **at** ~ **moment** à tout moment; **have you** ~ **water?** avez-vous de l'eau? ● *pron* (no matter which one) n'importe lequel; (any amount of it or them) en; **I do not have** ~ je n'en ai pas; **did you see** ~ **of them?** en avez-vous vu? ● *adv* (a little) un peu; **do you have** ~ **more?** en avez-vous encore?; **do you have** ~ **more tea?** avez-vous encore du thé?; **I don't do it** ~ **more** je ne le fais plus.

anybody /'enɪbɒdɪ/ *pron* (no matter who) n'importe qui; (somebody) quelqu'un; (after negative) personne; **he did not see** ~ il n'a vu personne.

anyhow /'enɪhaʊ/ *adv* (anyway) de toute façon; (carelessly) n'importe comment.

anyone /'enɪwʌn/ *pron* ➡ANYBODY.

anything /'enɪθɪŋ/ *pron* (no matter what) n'importe quoi; (something) quelque chose; (after negative) rien; **he did not see** ~ il n'a rien vu; ~ **but** nullement; ~ **you do** tout ce que tu fais.

anyway /'enɪweɪ/ *adv* de toute façon.

anywhere /'enɪweə(r)/ *adv* (no matter where) n'importe où; (somewhere) quelque part; (after negative) nulle part; **he does not go** ~ il ne va nulle part; ~ **you go** partout où tu vas, où que tu ailles; ~ **else** partout ailleurs.

apart /ə'pɑːt/ *adv* (on or to one side) à part; (separated) séparé; (into pieces) en pièces; ~ **from** à part, excepté; **ten metres** ~ à dix mètres l'un de l'autre; **come** ~ (break) tomber en morceaux; (machine) se démonter; **legs** ~ les jambes écartées; **keep** ~ séparer; **take** ~ démonter.

apartment /ə'pɑːtmənt/ *n* (US) appartement *m.*

ape /eɪp/ *n* singe *m.* ● *vt* singer.

aperitif /ə'perətɪf/ *n* apéritif *m.*

apex /'eɪpeks/ *n* sommet *m.*

apologetic /əpɒlə'dʒetɪk/ *adj* (tone) d'excuse; **be** ~ s'excuser. **apologetically** *adv* en s'excusant.

apologize /ə'pɒlədʒaɪz/ *vi* s'excuser (**for** de; **to** auprès de).

apology /ə'pɒlədʒɪ/ *n* excuses *fpl.*

apostrophe /ə'pɒstrəfɪ/ *n* apostrophe *f.*

appal /ə'pɔːl/ *vt* (*pt* **appalled**) horrifier. **appalling** *adj* épouvantable.

apparatus /æpə'reɪtəs/ *n* appareil *m.*

apparent /ə'pærənt/ *adj* apparent. **apparently** *adv* apparemment.

appeal /ə'piːl/ *n* appel *m;* (attractiveness) attrait *m,* charme *m.* ● *vi* (Jur) faire appel; ~ **to sb** (beg) faire appel à qn; (attract) plaire à qn; ~ **to sb for sth** demander qch à qn. **appealing** *adj* (attractive) attirant.

appear /ə'pɪə(r)/ *vi* apparaître. (arrive) se présenter; (seem, be published) paraître. (Theat) jouer; ~ **on TV** passer à la télé. **appearance** *n* apparition *f;* (aspect) apparence *f.*

appease /ə'piːz/ *vt* apaiser.

appendix /ə'pendɪks/ *n* (*pl* **-ices**) appendice *m.*

appetite /'æpɪtaɪt/ *n* appétit *m.*

appetizer /'æpɪtaɪzə(r)/ *n* (snack) amuse-gueule *m inv;* (drink) apéritif *m.*

appetizing /'æpɪtaɪzɪŋ/ *adj* appétissant.

applaud /ə'plɔːd/ *vt/i* applaudir; (decision) applaudir à. **applause** *n* applaudissements *mpl.*

apple /'æpl/ *n* pomme *f;* ~-**tree** *n* pommier *m.*

appliance /ə'plaɪəns/ *n* appareil *m.*

applicable /'æplɪkəbl/ *adj* valable; **if** ~ le cas échéant.

applicant /'æplɪkənt/ *n* candidat/-e *m/f* (**for** à).

application /æplɪ'keɪʃn/ *n* application *f;* (request, form) demande *f;* (for job) candidature *f.*

a

apply /əˈplaɪ/ vt appliquer. ● vi ~ **to** (refer) s'appliquer à; (ask) s'adresser à; ~ **for** (job) postuler pour; (grant) demander; ~ **oneself to** s'appliquer à.

appoint /əˈpɔɪnt/ vt (to post) nommer; (fix) désigner; **well-~ed** bien équipé.

appointment /əˈpɔɪntmənt/ n nomination f; (meeting) rendez-vous m inv; (job) poste m; **make an ~** prendre rendez-vous (**with** avec).

appraisal /əˈpreɪzl/ n évaluation f. **appraise** vt évaluer.

appreciate /əˈpriːʃɪeɪt/ vt (like) apprécier; (understand) comprendre; (be grateful for) être reconnaissant de. ● vi prendre de la valeur. **appreciation** n appréciation f; (gratitude) reconnaissance f; (rise) augmentation f. **appreciative** adj reconnaissant; (audience) enthousiaste.

apprehend /æprɪˈhend/ vt (arrest) appréhender; (understand) comprendre. **apprehension** n (arrest) appréhension f; (fear) crainte f.

apprehensive /æprɪˈhensɪv/ adj inquiet; **be ~ of** craindre.

apprentice /əˈprentɪs/ n apprenti m. ● vt mettre en apprentissage.

approach /əˈprəʊtʃ/ vt (s')approcher de; (accost) aborder; (with request) s'adresser à. ● vi (s')approcher. ● n approche f; **an ~ to** (problem) une façon d'aborder; (person) une démarche auprès de. **approachable** adj abordable.

appropriate[1] /əˈprəʊprɪeɪt/ vt s'approprier.

appropriate[2] /əˈprəʊprɪət/ adj approprié, propre. **appropriately** adv à propos.

approval /əˈpruːvl/ n approbation f; **on ~** à or sous condition.

approve /əˈpruːv/ vt approuver. ● vi ~ **of** approuver. **approving** adj approbateur.

approximate[1] /əˈprɒksɪmeɪt/ vi ~ **to** se rapprocher de.

approximate[2] /əˈprɒksɪmət/ adj approximatif. **approximately** adv environ. **approximation** n approximation f.

apricot /ˈeɪprɪkɒt/ n abricot m.

April /ˈeɪprɪl/ n avril m. ~ **Fools Day** n le premier avril.

apron /ˈeɪprən/ n tablier m.

apt /æpt/ adj (suitable) approprié; **be ~ to** avoir tendance à.

aptitude /ˈæptɪtjuːd/ n aptitude f.

aptly /ˈæptlɪ/ adv à propos.

Aquarius /əˈkweərɪəs/ n Verseau m.

aquatic /əˈkwætɪk/ adj aquatique; (Sport) nautique.

Arab /ˈærəb/ n Arabe mf. ● adj arabe.

Arabian /əˈreɪbɪən/ adj d'Arabie.

Arabic /ˈærəbɪk/ adj & n (Ling) arabe (m).

arbitrary /ˈɑːbɪtrərɪ/ adj arbitraire.

arbitrate /ˈɑːbɪtreɪt/ vi arbitrer. **arbitration** n arbitrage m. **arbitrator** n médiateur/-trice m/f.

arcade /ɑːˈkeɪd/ n (shops) galerie f; (arches) arcades fpl.

arch /ɑːtʃ/ n arche f; (of foot) voûte f plantaire. ● vt/i (s')arquer. ● adj (playful) malicieux.

archaeological /ɑːkɪəˈlɒdʒɪkl/ adj archéologique. **archaeologist** n archéologue mf. **archaeology** n archéologie f.

archbishop /ɑːtʃˈbɪʃəp/ n archevêque m.

archery /ˈɑːtʃərɪ/ n tir m à l'arc.

architect /ˈɑːkɪtekt/ n architecte mf; (of plan) artisan m. **architectural** adj architectural. **architecture** n architecture f.

archives /ˈɑːkaɪvz/ npl archives fpl.

archway /ˈɑːtʃweɪ/ n voûte f.

Arctic /ˈɑːktɪk/ n **the ~** l'Arctique m. ● adj (climate) arctique; (expedition) polaire; (conditions) glacial.

ardent /ˈɑːdnt/ adj ardent.

are /ɑː(r)/ ➡BE.

area /ˈeərɪə/ n (region) région f; (district) quartier m; (fig) domaine m; (in geometry) aire f; **parking/picnic ~** aire f de parking/de pique-nique.

arena /əˈriːnə/ n arène f.

aren't /ɑː(r)nt/ ➡ARE NOT.

Argentina /ɑːdʒənˈtiːnə/ n Argentine f.

arguable /ˈɑːɡjʊəbl/ adj discutable. **arguably** adv selon certains.

argue /ˈɑːɡjuː/ vi (quarrel) se disputer; (reason) argumenter. ● vt (debate) discuter; ~ **that** alléguer que.

argument /ˈɑːɡjʊmənt/ n dispute f; (reasoning) argument m; (discussion) débat m. **argumentative** adj ergoteur.

Aries /ˈeərɪːz/ n Bélier m.

arise /əˈraɪz/ vi (pt **arose**; pp **arisen**) (*problem*) survenir; (*question*) se poser; ∼ **from** résulter de.

aristocrat /ˈærɪstəkræt/ n aristocrate *mf*.

arithmetic /əˈrɪθmətɪk/ n arithmétique *f*.

ark /ɑːk/ n (Relig) arche *f*.

arm /ɑːm/ n bras *m*; ∼ **in arm** bras dessus bras dessous. ● vt armer; ∼**ed robbery** vol *m* à main armée.

armament /ˈɑːməmənt/ n armement *m*.

arm: /ɑːm/ ∼**-band** n brassard *m*. ∼**chair** n fauteuil *m*.

armour /ˈɑːmə(r)/ n armure *f*. **armoured** adj blindé. **armoury** n arsenal *m*.

armpit /ˈɑːmpɪt/ n aisselle *f*.

arms /ɑːmz/ npl (weapons) armes *fpl*. ∼ **dealer** n trafiquant *m* d'armes.

army /ˈɑːmɪ/ n armée *f*.

aroma /əˈrəʊmə/ n arôme *m*. **aromatic** adj aromatique.

arose /əˈrəʊz/ ➡**ARISE**.

around /əˈraʊnd/ adv (tout) autour; (here and there) çà et là. ● prep autour de; ∼ **here** par ici.

arouse /əˈraʊz/ vt (awaken, cause) éveiller; (excite) exciter.

arrange /əˈreɪndʒ/ vt arranger; (time, date) fixer; ∼ **to** s'arranger pour.

arrangement /əˈreɪndʒmənt/ n arrangement *m*; (agreement) entente *f*; **make** ∼**s** prendre des dispositions.

array /əˈreɪ/ n **an** ∼ **of** (display) un étalage impressionnant de.

arrears /əˈrɪəz/ npl arriéré *m*; **in** ∼ (rent) arriéré; **he is in** ∼ il a des retards dans ses paiements.

arrest /əˈrest/ vt arrêter; (attention) retenir. ● n arrestation *f*; **under** ∼ en état d'arrestation.

arrival /əˈraɪvl/ n arrivée *f*; **new** ∼ nouveau venu *m*, nouvelle venue *f*.

arrive /əˈraɪv/ vi arriver; ∼ **at** (destination) arriver à; (decision) parvenir à.

arrogance /ˈærəgəns/ n arrogance *f*.

arrow /ˈærəʊ/ n flèche *f*.

arse /ɑːs/ n 🖾 cul *m* 🖾.

arson /ˈɑːsn/ n incendie *m* criminel. **arsonist** n incendiaire *mf*.

art /ɑːt/ n art *m*; (fine arts) beaux-arts *mpl*.

artery /ˈɑːtərɪ/ n artère *f*.

art gallery n (public) musée *m* (d'art); (private) galerie *f* (d'art).

arthritis /ɑːˈθraɪtɪs/ n arthrite *f*.

artichoke /ˈɑːtɪtʃəʊk/ n artichaut *m*.

article /ˈɑːtɪkl/ n article *m*; ∼ **of clothing** vêtement *m*.

articulate /ɑːˈtɪkjʊlət/ adj (person) capable de s'exprimer clairement; (speech) distinct.

articulated lorry n semiremorque *m*.

artificial /ɑːtɪˈfɪʃl/ adj artificiel.

artist /ˈɑːtɪst/ n artiste *mf*.

arts /ɑːts/ npl **the** ∼ les arts *mpl*; (Univ) lettres *fpl*.

artwork /ˈɑːtwɜːk/ n (of book) illustrations *fpl*.

as /æz/, /əz/ conj comme; (while) pendant que; (over gradual period of time) au fur et à mesure que; ∼ **she grew older** au fur et à mesure qu'elle vieillissait; **do** ∼ **I say** fais ce que je dis; ∼ **usual** comme d'habitude.
● prep ∼ **a mother** en tant que mère; ∼ **a gift** en cadeau; ∼ **from Monday** à partir de lundi; ∼ **for,** ∼ **to** quant à; ∼ **if** comme si; **you look** ∼ **if you're tired** vous avez l'air (d'être) fatigué. ● adv ∼ **tall** ∼ aussi grand que; ∼ **much** ∼, ∼ **many** ∼ autant que; ∼ **soon** ∼ aussitôt que; **you look** ∼ **well** ∼ aussi bien que; ∼ **wide** ∼ **possible** aussi large que possible.

asbestos /æzˈbestɒs/ n amiante *f*.

ascend /əˈsend/ vt gravir. ● vi monter.

ascertain /æsəˈteɪn/ vt établir (that que).

ash /æʃ/ n cendre *f*; ∼(**-tree**) frêne *m*.

ashamed /əˈʃeɪmd/ adj **be** ∼ avoir honte (of de).

ashore /əˈʃɔː(r)/ adv à terre.

ashtray /ˈæʃtreɪ/ n cendrier *m*.

Asia /ˈeɪʃə/ n Asie *f*.

Asian /ˈeɪʃn/ n Asiatique *mf*. ● adj asiatique.

aside /əˈsaɪd/ adv de côté; ∼ **from** à part. ● n aparté *m*.

ask /ɑːsk/ vt/i demander; (a question) poser; (invite) inviter; ∼ **sb sth** demander qch à qn; ∼ **sb to do** demander à qn de faire; ∼ **about** (thing) se

a

renseigner sur; (*person*) demander des nouvelles de; ~ **for** demander.

asleep /ə'sli:p/ *adj* endormi; (numb) engourdi. ● *adv* **fall** ~ s'endormir.

asparagus /ə'spærəgəs/ *n*(plant) asperge *f*; (Culin) asperges *fpl*.

aspect /'æspekt/ *n* aspect *m*; (direction) orientation *f*.

asphyxiate /əs'fıksıeıt/ *vt/i* (s')asphyxier.

aspire /ə'spaıə(r)/ *vi* aspirer (**to** à; **to do** à faire).

aspirin /'æspərın/ *n* aspirine® *f*.

ass /æs/ *n* âne *m*; (person 🔢) idiot/-e *m/f*.

assail /ə'seıl/ *vt* attaquer. **assailant** *n* agresseur *m*.

assassin /ə'sæsın/ *n* assassin *m*. **assassinate** *vt* assassiner. **assassination** *n* assassinat *m*.

assault /ə'sɔ:lt/ *n* (Mil) assaut *m*; (Jur) agression *f*. ● *vt* (*person*: Jur) agresser.

assemble /ə'sembl/ *vt*(construct) assembler; (gather) rassembler. ● *vi* se rassembler.

assembly /ə'semblı/ *n* assemblée *f*. ~ **line** *n* chaîne *f* de montage.

assent /ə'sent/ *n* assentiment *m*. ● *vi* consentir.

assert /ə'sɜ:t/ *vt* affirmer; (*rights*) revendiquer. **assertion** *n* affirmation *f*. **assertive** *adj* assuré.

assess /ə'ses/ *vt* évaluer; (*payment*) déterminer le montant de. **assessment** *n* évaluation *f*. **assessor** *n* (valuer) expert *m*.

asset /'æset/ *n* (advantage) atout *m*; (financial) bien *m*; ~ **s** (Comm) actif *m*.

assign /ə'saın/ *vt* (allot) assigner; ~ **sb to** (appoint) affecter qn à.

assignment /ə'saınmənt/ *n* (task) mission *f*; (diplomatic) poste *m*; (academic) devoir *m*.

assist /ə'sıst/ *vt/i* aider. **assistance** *n* aide *f*.

assistant /ə'sıstənt/ *n* aide *mf*; (in shop) vendeur/-euse *m/f*. ● *adj* (manager) adjoint.

associate[1] /ə'səʊʃıət/ *n & adj* associé/-e (*m/f*).

associate[2] /ə'səʊʃıeıt/ *vt* associer. ● *vi* ~ **with** fréquenter. **association** *n* association *f*.

assorted /ə'sɔ:tıd/ *adj* divers; (*foods*) assorti.

assortment /ə'sɔ:tmənt/ *n* assortiment *m*; (of people) mélange *m*.

assume /ə'sju:m/ *vt* supposer; (*power, attitude*) prendre; (*role, burden*) assumer.

assurance /ə'ʃɔ:rəns/ *n* assurance *f*.

assure /ə'ʃɔ:(r)/ *vt* assurer.

asterisk /'æstərısk/ *n* astérisque *m*.

asthma /'æsmə/ *n* asthme *m*.

astonish /ə'stɒnıʃ/ *vt* étonner.

astound /ə'staʊnd/ *vt* stupéfier.

astray /ə'streı/ *adv* **go** ~ s'égarer; **lead** ~ égarer.

astride /ə'straıd/ *adv & prep* à califourchon (sur).

astrologer /ə'strɒlədʒə(r)/ *n* astrologue *mf*. **astrology** *n* astrologie *f*.

astronaut /'æstrənɔ:t/ *n* astronaute *mf*.

astronomer /ə'strɒnəmə(r)/ *n* astronome *mf*.

asylum /ə'saıləm/ *n* asile *m*.

---

at /æt, ət/

● *preposition*

➡️ For expressions such as **laugh at, look at,** look at →**laugh, look.**

····➤ (in position or place) à; **he's ~ his desk** il est à son bureau; **she's ~ work/school** elle est au travail/à l'école.

····➤ (at someone's house or business) chez; ~**Mary's/the dentist's** chez Mary/le dentiste.

····➤ (in times, ages) à; ~ **four o'clock** à quatre heures; ~ **two years of age** à l'âge de deux ans.

····➤ (in email addresses) arobase *f*

---

ate &/eıt/ →**EAT.**

atheist /'eıθııst/ *n* athée *mf*.

athlete /'æθli:t/ *n* athlète *mf*. **athletic** *adj* athlétique. **athletics** *npl* athlétisme *m*; (US) sports *mpl*.

Atlantic /ət'læntık/ *adj* atlantique. ● *n* **the** ~ **(Ocean)** l'Atlantique *m*.

atlas /'ætləs/ *n* atlas *m*.

atmosphere /'ætməsfıə(r)/ *n* (air) atmosphère *f*; (mood) ambiance *f*. **at-**

mospheric *adj* atmosphérique; d'ambiance.

atom /ˈætəm/ *n* atome *m*.

atrocious /əˈtrəʊʃəs/ *adj* atroce.

atrocity /əˈtrɒsətɪ/ *n* atrocité *f*.

attach /əˈtætʃ/ *vt/i* (s')attacher; (*letter*) joindre (**to** à).

attaché /əˈtæʃeɪ/ *n* (Pol) attaché/-e *m/f*. ∼ **case** *n* attaché-case *m*.

attached /əˈtætʃt/ *adj* be ∼ **to** (like) être attaché à; **the** ∼ **letter** la lettre ci-jointe.

attachment /əˈtætʃmənt/ *n* (accessory) accessoire *m*; (affection) attachement *m*; (e-mail) pièces *fpl* jointes.

attack /əˈtæk/ *n* attaque *f*; (Med) crise *f*. ● *vt* attaquer.

attain /əˈteɪn/ *vt* atteindre (à); (gain) acquérir.

attempt /əˈtempt/ *vt* tenter. ● *n* tentative *f*; **an** ∼ **on sb's life** un attentat contre qn.

attend /əˈtend/ *vt* assister à; (*class*) suivre; (*school, church*) aller à. ● *vi* assister; ∼ **(to)** (look after) s'occuper de. **attendance** *n* présence *f*; (people) assistance *f*.

attendant /əˈtendənt/ *n* employé/-e *m/f*. ● *adj* associé.

attention /əˈtenʃn/ *n* attention *f*; ∼**!** (Mil) garde-à-vous! **pay** ∼ faire *or* prêter attention (**to** à).

attentive /əˈtentɪv/ *adj* attentif; (considerate) attentionné. **attentively** *adv* attentivement. **attentiveness** *n* attention *f*.

attest /əˈtest/ *vt/i* ∼ **(to)** attester.

attic /ˈætɪk/ *n* grenier *m*.

attitude /ˈætɪtjuːd/ *n* attitude *f*.

attorney /əˈtɜːnɪ/ *n* (US) avocat/-e *m/f*.

attract /əˈtrækt/ *vt* attirer. **attraction** *n* attraction *f*; (charm) attrait *m*.

attractive /əˈtræktɪv/ *adj* attrayant, séduisant. **attractively** *adv* agréablement. **attractiveness** *n* attrait *m*, beauté *f*.

attribute[1] /əˈtrɪbjuːt/ *vt* ∼ **to** attribuer à.

attribute[2] /ˈætrɪbjuːt/ *n* attribut *m*.

aubergine /ˈəʊbəʒiːn/ *n* aubergine *f*.

auction /ˈɔːkʃn/ *n* vente *f* aux enchères. ● *vt* vendre aux enchères. **auctioneer** *n* commissaire priseur *m*.

audacious /ɔːˈdeɪʃəs/ *adj* audacieux.

audience /ˈɔːdɪəns/ *n* (theatre, radio) public *m*; (interview) audience *f*.

audiovisual /ɔːdɪəʊˈvɪʒʊəl/ *adj* audiovisuel.

audit /ˈɔːdɪt/ *n* vérification *f* des comptes. ● *vt* vérifier.

audition /ɔːˈdɪʃn/ *n* audition *f*. ● *vt/i* auditionner (**for** pour).

auditor /ˈɔːdɪtə(r)/ *n* commissaire *m* aux comptes.

August /ˈɔːgəst/ *n* août *m*.

aunt /ɑːnt/ *n* tante *f*.

auspicious /ɔːˈspɪʃəs/ *adj* favorable.

Australia /ɒˈstreɪlɪə/ *n* Australie *f*.

Australian /ɒˈstreɪlɪən/ *n* Australien/-ne *m/f*. ● *adj* australien.

Austria /ˈɒstrɪə/ *n* Autriche *f*.

Austrian /ˈɒstrɪən/ *n* Autrichien/-ne *m/f*. ● *adj* autrichien.

authentic /ɔːˈθentɪk/ *adj* authentique.

author /ˈɔːθə(r)/ *n* auteur *m*.

authoritarian /ɔːθɒrɪˈteərɪən/ *adj* autoritaire.

authoritative /ɔːˈθɒrətətɪv/ *adj* (credible) qui fait autorité; (manner) autoritaire.

authority /ɔːˈθɒrətɪ/ *n* autorité *f*; (permission) autorisation *f*.

authorization /ɔːθəraɪˈzeɪʃn/ *n* autorisation *f*. **authorize** *vt* autoriser.

autistic /ɔːˈtɪstɪk/ *adj* (person) autiste; (response) autistique.

autograph /ˈɔːtəgrɑːf/ *n* autographe *m*. ● *vt* signer, dédicacer.

automate /ˈɔːtəmeɪt/ *vt* automatiser.

automatic /ɔːtəˈmætɪk/ *adj* automatique. ● *n* (Auto) voiture *f* automatique.

automobile /ˈɔːtəməbiːl/ *n* (US) auto(mobile) *f*.

autonomous /ɔːˈtɒnəməs/ *adj* autonome.

autumn /ˈɔːtəm/ *n* automne *m*.

auxiliary /ɔːgˈzɪlɪərɪ/ *adj & n* auxiliaire (*mf*); ∼ **(verb)** auxiliaire *m*.

avail /əˈveɪl/ *vt* ∼ **oneself of** profiter de. ● *n* of no ∼ inutile; **to no** ∼ sans résultat.

availability /əveɪləˈbɪlətɪ/ *n* disponibilité *f*. **available** *adj* disponible.

avenge /əˈvendʒ/ *vt* venger; ∼ **oneself** se venger (**on** de).

avenue /ˈævənjuː/ n avenue f; (line of approach:fig) voie f.

average /ˈævərɪdʒ/ n moyenne f; **on ~** en moyenne. ● adj moyen. ● vt faire la moyenne de; (produce, do) faire en moyenne.

aviary /ˈeɪvɪərɪ/ n volière f.

avocado /ævəˈkɑːdəʊ/ n avocat m.

avoid /əˈvɔɪd/ vt éviter. **avoidance** n (of injuries) prévention f; (of responsibility) refus m.

await /əˈweɪt/ vt attendre.

awake /əˈweɪk/ vt/i (pt **awoke**; pp **awoken**) (s')éveiller. ● adj be ~ ne pas dormir, être (r)éveillé.

award /əˈwɔːd/ vt (grant) attribuer; (prize) décerner; (points) accorder. ● n récompense f,prix m; (scholarship) bourse f; **pay ~** augmentation f (de salaire).

aware /əˈweə(r)/ adj (well-informed) averti; **be ~ of** (danger) être conscient de; (fact) savoir; **become ~ of** prendre conscience de. **awareness** n conscience f.

away /əˈweɪ/ adv (far) (au) loin; (absent) absent, parti; **~ from** loin de; **move ~** s'écarter; (to new home) déménager; **six kilometres ~** à six kilomètres (de distance); **take ~** emporter; **he was snoring ~** il ronflait. ● adj & n **~ (match)** match m à l'extérieur.

awe /ɔː/ n crainte f (révérencielle).

awe-inspiring /ˈɔːɪnspaɪərɪŋ/ adj impressionnant.

awesome /ˈɔːsəm/ adj redoutable.

awful /ˈɔːfl/ adj affreux. **awfully** adv (badly) affreusement; (very 🄸) rudement.

awkward /ˈɔːkwəd/ adj difficile; (inconvenient) inopportun; (clumsy) maladroit; (embarrassing) gênant; (embarrassed) gêné. **awkwardly** adv maladroitement; avec gêne. **awkwardness** n maladresse f; (discomfort) gêne f.

awning /ˈɔːnɪŋ/ n auvent m; (of shop) store m.

awoke, awoken →AWAKE.

axe /æks/ n hache f. ● vt (pres p **axing**) réduire; (eliminate) supprimer; (employee) renvoyer.

axis /ˈæksɪs/ n (pl **axes**) axe m.

axle /ˈæksl/ n essieu m.

Bb

BA abbr →BACHELOR OF ARTS.

babble /ˈbæbl/ vi babiller; (stream) gazouiller. ● n babillage m.

baby /ˈbeɪbɪ/ n bébé m. **~ carriage** n (US) voiture f d'enfant. **~-sit** vi faire du babysitting, garder des enfants. **~-sitter** n baby-sitter mf.

bachelor /ˈbætʃələ(r)/ n célibataire m. **B~ of Arts** licencié/-e m/f ès lettres.

back /bæk/ n (of person, hand, page, etc.) dos m; (of house) derrière m; (of vehicle) arrière m; (of room) fond m; (of chair) dossier m; (in football) arrière m; **at the ~ of the book** à la fin du livre; **in ~ of** (US) derrière. ● adj (leg, wheel) arrière inv; (door, gate) de derrière; (taxes) arriéré. ● adv en arrière; (returned) de retour, rentré; **come ~** revenir; **give ~** rendre; **take ~ reprendre; I want it ~** je veux le récupérer. ● vt (support) appuyer; (bet on) miser sur; (vehicle) faire reculer. ● vi (of person, vehicle) reculer. **~ down** céder; **~out** se désister; (Auto) sortir en marche arrière; **~ up** (support) appuyer. **~ache** n mal m de dos. **~-bencher** n (Pol) député m. **~bone** n colonne f vertébrale. **~date** vt antidater. **~fire** vi (Auto) pétarader; (fig) mal tourner. **~gammon** n trictrac m.

background /ˈbækgraʊnd/ n fond m, arrièreplan m; (context) contexte m; (environment) milieu m; (experience) formation f. ● adj (music, noise) de fond.

backhand /ˈbækhænd/ n revers m. **backhander** n (bribe) pot-de-vin m.

backing /ˈbækɪŋ/ n soutien m.

back: ~lash n retour m de bâton; (reaction f violente (**against** contre). **~log** n retard m. **~ number** n vieux numéro m. **~pack** n sac m à dos. **~side** n (buttocks 🄸) derrière m. **~stage** adj & adv dans les coulisses. **~stroke** n dos m crawlé. **~track** vi rebrousser chemin; (change one's opinion) faire marche arrière.

backup /'bækʌp/ n soutien m; (Comput) sauvegarde f ● adj de secours; (Comput) de sauvegarde.

backward /'bækwəd/ adj (step etc.) en arrière; (retarded) arriéré.

backwards /'bækwəd/ adv en arrière; (walk) à reculons; (read) à l'envers; **go ∼ and forwards** aller et venir.

bacon /'beɪkən/ n lard m; (in rashers) bacon m.

bacteria /bæk'tɪərɪə/ npl bactéries fpl.

bad /bæd/ adj (**worse**, **worst**) mauvais; (wicked) méchant; (ill) malade; (accident) grave; (food) gâté; **feel ∼ se** sentir mal; **go ∼** se gâter; **∼ language** gros mots mpl; **too ∼!** tant pis!; (I'm sorry) dommage!

badge /bædʒ/ n badge m; (coat of arms) insigne m.

badger /'bædʒə(r)/ n blaireau m. ● vt harceler.

badly /'bædlɪ/ adv mal; (hurt) gravement; **want ∼** avoir grande envie de.

badminton /'bædmɪntn/ n badminton m.

bad-tempered adj irritable.

baffle /'bæfl/ vt déconcerter.

bag /bæg/ n sac m; **∼ s** (luggage) bagages mpl; (under eyes 🇬🇧) valises fpl; **∼s of** plein de.

baggage /'bægɪdʒ/ n bagages mpl; **∼ reclaim** réception f des bagages.

baggy /'bægɪ/ adj large.

bagpipes /'bægpaɪps/ npl cornemuse f.

bail /beɪl/ n caution f; **on ∼** sous caution; (cricket) bâtonnet m. ● vt mettre en liberté provisoire.

bailiff /'beɪlɪf/ n huissier m.

bait /beɪt/ n appât m. ● vt appâter; (fig) tourmenter.

bake /beɪk/ vt faire cuire au four; **∼ a cake** faire un gâteau. ● vi cuire; (person) faire du pain. **baked beans** npl haricots mpl blancs à la tomate. **baked potato** n pomme f de terre en robe des champs. **baker** n boulanger/-ère m/f. **bakery** n boulangerie f.

balance /'bæləns/ n équilibre m; (scales) balance f; (outstanding sum: Comm) solde m; (of payments, of trade) balance f; (remainder) restant m. ● vt mettre en équilibre; (weigh up also Comm) balancer; (budget) équilibrer; (to compensate) contrebalancer.

● vi être en équilibre.

balcony /'bælkənɪ/ n balcon m.

bald /bɔːld/ adj chauve; (tyre) lisse; (fig) simple.

balk /bɔːk/ vt contrecarrer. ● vi **∼ at** reculer devant.

ball /bɔːl/ n (golf, tennis, etc.) balle f; (football) ballon m; (billiards) bille f; (of wool) pelote f; (sphere) boule f; (dance) bal m.

ballet /'bæleɪ/ n ballet m.

balloon /bə'luːn/ n ballon m.

ballot /'bælət/ n scrutin m. ● vt consulter par vote (**on** sur). **∼ box** n urne f. **∼ paper** n bulletin m de vote.

ballpoint pen n stylo m (à) bille.

ban /bæn/ vt (pt **banned**) interdire; **∼ sb from** exclure qn de; **∼ sb from doing** interdire à qn de faire. ● n interdiction f (**on** de).

banal /bə'nɑːl/ adj banal.

banana /bə'nɑːnə/ n banane f.

band /bænd/ n (strip, group of people) bande f; (pop group) groupe m; (brass band) fanfare f. ● vi **∼ together** se réunir.

bandage /'bændɪdʒ/ n bandage m. ● vt bander.

B and B abbr ➡BED AND BREAKFAST.

bandit /'bændɪt/ n bandit m.

bandstand /'bændstænd/ n kiosque m à musique.

bang /bæŋ/ n (blow, noise) coup m; (explosion) détonation f; (of door) claquement m. ● vt/i taper; (door) claquer; **∼ one's head** se cogner la tête. ● interj vlan. ● adv 🇬🇧 **∼ in the middle** en plein milieu; **∼ on time** à l'heure pile.

banger /'bæŋə(r)/ n (firework) pétard m; (Culin) saucisse f; (old) **∼** (car 🇬🇧) guimbarde f.

banish /'bænɪʃ/ vt bannir.

banister /'bænɪstə(r)/ n rampe f d'escalier.

bank /bæŋk/ n (Comm) banque f; (of river) rive f; (of sand) banc m. ● vt mettre en banque. ● vi (Aviat) virer; **∼ with** avoir un compte à; **∼ on** compter sur. **∼ account** n compte m en banque. **∼ card** n carte f bancaire. **∼ holiday** n jour m férié.

banking /'bæŋkɪŋ/ n opérations fpl bancaires; (as career) la banque.

b

Bank holiday Jour chômé où *i*
les banques sont fermées au
Royaume-Uni, en général à l'occasion d'une fête religieuse ou civile
(*Christmas Day, Easter Monday, May
Day*, etc.). La plupart tombe un
lundi: par exemple, le *spring bank
holiday*, qui coïncide avec la Pentecôte, tombe le dernier lundi de mai
ou le premier lundi de juin.

---

banknote /'bæŋknəʊt/ *n* billet *m* de
banque.

bankrupt /'bæŋkrʌpt/ *adj* **be ~** être
en faillite; **go ~** faire faillite. ● *n*
failli/-e *m/f*. ● *vt* mettre en faillite.
bankruptcy *n* faillite *f*.

bank statement *n* relevé *m* de
compte.

banner /'bænə(r)/ *n* bannière *f*.

baptism /'bæptizəm/ *n* baptême *m*.
baptize *vt* baptiser.

bar /bɑː(r)/ *n* (of metal) barre *f*; (on
window, cage) barreau *m*; (of chocolate) tablette *f*; (pub) bar *m*;
(counter) comptoir *m*; (Mus) mesure *f*;
(fig) obstacle *m*; **~ of soap** savonnette *f*; **the ~** (Jur) le barreau. ● *vt* (*pt*
barred) (obstruct) barrer; (prohibit)
interdire; (exclude) exclure.
● *prep* sauf.

barbecue /'bɑːbɪkjuː/ *n* barbecue *m*.
● *vt* faire au barbecue.

barbed wire *n* fil *m* de fer barbelé.

barber /'bɑːbə(r)/ *n* coiffeur *m* (*pour
hommes*).

bar code *n* code *m* (à) barres.

bare /beə(r)/ *adj* nu; (*cupboard*) vide.
● *vt* mettre à nu. **~foot** *adj* nu-pieds
inv, pieds nus. **barely** *adv* à peine.

bargain /'bɑːgɪn/ *n* (deal) marché *m*;
(cheap thing) occasion *f*. ● *vi* négocier;
(haggle) marchander; **not ~ for** ne
pas s'attendre à.

barge /bɑːdʒ/ *n* péniche *f*. ● *vi* **~ in** interrompre; (into room) faire irruption.

bark /bɑːk/ *n* (of tree) écorce *f*; (of
dog) aboiement *m*. ● *vi* aboyer.

barley /'bɑːlɪ/ *n* orge *f*.

bar: ~maid *n* serveuse *f*. **~man** *n* (*pl*
-men) barman *m*.

barn /bɑːn/ *n* grange *f*.

barracks /'bærəks/ *npl* caserne *f*.

barrel /'bærəl/ *n* tonneau *m*; (of oil)
baril *m*; (of gun) canon *m*.

barren /'bærən/ *adj* stérile.

barricade /bærɪ'keɪd/ *n* barricade *f*.
● *vt* barricader.

barrier /'bærɪə(r)/ *n* barrière *f*; **ticket
~** guichet *m*.

barrister /'bærɪstə(r)/ *n* avocat *m*.

bartender /'bɑːtendə(r)/ *n* (US) barman *m*.

barter /'bɑːtə(r)/ *n* troc *m*. ● *vt* troquer
(**for** contre).

base /beɪs/ *n* base *f*. ● *vt* baser (**on** sur;
in à). ● *adj* ignoble. **baseball** *n* baseball *m*.

basement /'beɪsmənt/ *n* sous-sol *m*.

bash /bæʃ/ 🔲 *vt* cogner; **~ed in** en-
foncé. ● *n* coup *m* violent; **have a ~
at** s'essayer à.

basic /'beɪsɪk/ *adj* fondamental, élémentaire; **the ~s** l'essentiel *m*. **basically** *adv* au fond.

basil /'bæzl/ *n* basilic *m*.

basin /'beɪsn/ *n* (for liquids) cuvette *f*;
(for food) bol *m*; (for washing) lavabo
m; (of river) bassin *m*.

basis /'beɪsɪs/ *n* (*pl* **bases**) base *f*.

bask /bɑːsk/ *vi* se prélasser (**in** à).

basket /'bɑːskɪt/ *n* corbeille *f*; (with
handle) panier *m*. **basketball** *n*
basket(- ball) *m*.

Basque /bæsk/ *n* (person) Basque *mf*;
(Ling) basque *m*. ● *adj* basque.

bass¹ /beɪs/ *adj* (*voice, part*) de basse;
(*sound, note*) grave. ● *n* (*pl* **basses**)
basse *f*.

bass² /bæs/ *n inv* (freshwater fish) perche *f*; (sea) bar *m*.

bassoon /bə'suːn/ *n* basson *m*.

bastard /'bɑːstəd/ *n* (illegitimate)
bâtard/-e *m/f*; (insult 🔳) salaud *m* 🔳.

bat /bæt/ *n* (cricket etc.) batte *f*; (table
tennis) raquette *f*; (animal) chauve-souris *f*. ● *vt* (*pt* **batted**) (ball) frapper;
not ~ an eyelid ne pas sourciller.

batch /bætʃ/ *n* (of cakes, people) four-
née *f*; (of goods, text *also* Comput)
lot *m*.

bath /bɑːθ/ *n* (*pl* **-s**) bain *m*; (tub) baignoire *f*; **have a ~** prendre un bain;
(swimming) **~s** piscine *f*. ● *vt* donner
un bain à.

bathe /beɪð/ *vt* baigner. ● *vi* se baigner;
(US) prendre un bain.

bathing /'beɪðɪŋ/ n baignade f. ∼-**costume** n maillot m de bain.

bath: ∼**robe** n (US) robe f de chambre. ∼**room** n salle f de bains.

baton /'bætn/ n (policeman's) matraque f; (Mus) baguette f.

batter /'bætə(r)/ vt battre. ● n (Culin) pâte f (à frire).

battery /'bætərɪ/ n (Mil, Auto) batterie f; (of torch, radio) pile f.

battle /'bætl/ n bataille f; (fig) lutte f. ● vi se battre. ∼**field** n champ m de bataille.

baulk /bɔ:k/ vt/i ➙BALK.

bay /beɪ/ n (Bot) laurier m; (Geog, Archit) baie f; (area) aire f; (bark) aboiement m; **keep** or **hold at** ∼ tenir à distance. ● vi aboyer. ∼-**leaf** n feuille f de laurier. ∼ **window** n fenêtre f en saillie.

bazaar /bə'zɑ:(r)/ n (shop, market) bazar m; (sale) vente f.

BC abbr (**before Christ**) avant J.-C.

BBS abbr (**Bulletin Board System**) (Internet) babillard m électronique, BBS m.

---

be /bi:/

present **am, is, are**; past **was, were**; past participle **been**.

● intransitive verb

⋯➤ être; **I am tired** je suis fatigué; **it's me** c'est moi.

⋯➤ (feelings) avoir; **I am hot** j'ai chaud; **he is hungry/thirsty** il a faim/soif; **her hands are cold** elle a froid aux mains.

⋯➤ (age) avoir; **I am 15** j'ai 15 ans.

⋯➤ (weather) faire; **it's warm** il fait chaud; **it's 25°** il fait 25°.

⋯➤ (health) aller; **how are you?** comment allez-vous or comment vas-tu?

⋯➤ (visit) aller; **I've never been to Italy** je ne suis jamais allé en Italie.

● auxiliary verb

⋯➤ (in tenses) **I am working** je travaille; **he was writing to his mother** il écrivait à sa mère; **she is to do it at once** (obligation) elle doit le faire tout de suite.

⋯➤ (in passives) **he was killed** il a été tué; **the window has been fixed** on a réparé la fenêtre.

⋯➤ (in tag questions) **their house is lovely, isn't it?** leur maison est très jolie, n'est-ce pas?

⋯➤ (in short answers) **'I am a painter'—'are you?'** 'je suis peintre'—'ah oui?'; **'are you a doctor?'—'yes, I am'** 'êtes-vous médecin?'—'oui'; **'you're not going out'—'yes I am'** 'tu ne sors pas'—'si'.

---

beach /bi:tʃ/ n plage f.

beacon /'bi:kən/ n (lighthouse) phare m; (marker) balise f.

bead /bi:d/ n perle f.

beak /bi:k/ n bec m.

beaker /'bi:kə(r)/ n gobelet m.

beam /bi:m/ n (timber) poutre f; (of light) rayon m; (of torch) faisceau m. ● vi rayonner. ● vt (broadcast) transmettre.

bean /bi:n/ n haricot m.

bear /beə(r)/ n ours m. ● vt (pt **bore**; pp **borne**) (carry, show, feel) porter; (endure, sustain) supporter; (child) mettre au monde. ● vi ∼ **left** (go) prendre à gauche; ∼ **in mind** tenir compte de. ∼ **out** confirmer; ∼ **up** tenir le coup. **bearable** adj supportable.

beard /bɪəd/ n barbe f.

bearer /'beərə(r)/ n porteur/-euse m/f.

bearing /'beərɪŋ/ n (behaviour) maintien m; (relevance) rapport m; **get one's** ∼**s** s'orienter.

beast /bi:st/ n bête f; (person) brute f.

beat /bi:t/ vt/i (pt **beat**; pp **beaten**) battre; ∼ **a retreat** battre en retraite; ∼ **it!** dégage! ⓘ; **it** ∼**s me** ⓘ ça me dépasse. ● n (of drum, heart) battement m; (Mus) mesure f; (of policeman) ronde f. ∼ **off** repousser; ∼ **up** tabasser. **beating** n raclée f.

beautiful /'bju:tɪfl/ adj beau.

beauty /'bju:tɪ/ n beauté f. ∼**parlour** n institut m de beauté. ∼**spot** n grain m de beauté; (place) site m pittoresque.

beaver /'bi:və(r)/ n castor m.

became /bɪ'keɪm/ ➙BECOME.

b

because /bɪˈkɒz/ conj parce que; ~ **of** à cause de.

become /bɪˈkʌm/ vt/i (pt **became**; pp **become**) devenir; (befit) convenir à; **what has** ~ **of her?** qu'est-ce qu'elle est devenue?

bed /bed/ n lit m; (layer) couche f; (of sea) fond m; (of flowers) parterre m; **go to** ~ (aller) se coucher. ● vi (pt **bedded**) ~ **down** se coucher. **bed and breakfast** n chambre f avec petit déjeuner, chambre f d'hôte. ~ **bug** n punaise f. ~**clothes** npl couvertures fpl.

bedding /ˈbedɪŋ/ n literie f.

bed: ~**ridden** adj cloué au lit. ~**room** n chambre f (à coucher). ~**side** n chevet m. ~**sit**, ~**sitter** n chambre f meublée, studio m. ~**spread** n dessus m de lit. ~**time** n heure f du coucher.

bee /biː/ n abeille f; **make a** ~-**line for** aller tout droit vers.

beech /biːtʃ/ n hêtre m.

beef /biːf/ n bœuf m. ~**burger** n hamburger m.

beehive /ˈbiːhaɪv/ n ruche f.

been /biːn/ →BE.

beer /bɪə(r)/ n bière f.

beetle /ˈbiːtl/ n scarabée m.

beetroot /ˈbiːtruːt/ n inv betterave f.

before /bɪˈfɔː(r)/ prep (time) avant; (place) devant; **the day** ~ **yesterday** avant-hier. ● adv avant; (already) déjà; **the day** ~ la veille. ● conj ~ **leaving** avant de partir; ~ **I forget** avant que j'oublie. **beforehand** adv à l'avance.

beg /beg/ vt (pt **begged**) (food, money, favour) demander (**from** à); ~ **sb to do** supplier qn de faire. ● vi mendier; **it is going** ~**ging** personne n'en veut.

began /bɪˈgæn/ →BEGIN.

beggar /ˈbegə(r)/ n mendiant/-e m/f.

begin /bɪˈgɪn/ vt/i (pt **began**, pp **begun**, pres p **beginning**) commencer (**to do** à faire). **beginner** n débutant/-e m/f. **beginning** n commencement m, début m.

begun /bɪˈgʌn/ →BEGIN.

behalf /bɪˈhɑːf/ n **on** ~ **of** (act, speak, campaign) pour; (phone, write) de la part de.

behave /bɪˈheɪv/ vi se conduire; (oneself) se conduire bien.

behaviour /bɪˈheɪvjə(r)/, (US) **behavior** n comportement m (**towards** envers).

behead /bɪˈhed/ vt décapiter.

behind /bɪˈhaɪnd/ prep derrière; (in time) en retard sur. ● adv derrière; (late) en retard; **leave** ~ oublier. ● n (buttocks 🔢) derrière m 🔢.

beige /beɪʒ/ adj & n beige (m).

being /ˈbiːɪŋ/ n (person) être m.

belch /beltʃ/ vi avoir un renvoi. ● vt ~ **out** (smoke) s'échapper. ● n renvoi m.

Belgian /ˈbeldʒən/ n Belge mf. ● adj belge. **Belgium** n Belgique f.

belief /bɪˈliːf/ n conviction f; (trust) confiance f; (faith: Relig) foi f.

believe /bɪˈliːv/ vt/i croire; ~ **in** croire à; (deity) croire en. **believer** n croyant/-e m/f.

bell /bel/ n cloche f; (small) clochette f; (on door) sonnette f.

belly /ˈbeli/ n ventre m. ~ **button** n nombril m.

belong /bɪˈlɒŋ/ vi ~ **to** appartenir à; (club) être membre de.

belongings /bɪˈlɒŋɪŋz/ npl affaires fpl.

beloved /bɪˈlʌvɪd/ adj & n bien-aimé/-e (m/f).

below /bɪˈləʊ/ prep sous, au-dessous de; (fig) indigne de. ● adv en dessous; (on page) ci-dessous.

belt /belt/ n ceinture f; (Tech) courroie f; (fig) zone f. ● vt (hit 🔢) rosser. ● vi (rush 🔢) ~ **in/out** entrer/sortir à toute vitesse.

beltway /ˈbeltweɪ/ n (US) périphérique m.

bemused /bɪˈmjuːzd/ adj perplexe.

bench /bentʃ/ n banc m; **the** ~ (Jur) la magistrature (assise).

bend /bend/ vt (pt **bent**) (knee, arm, wire) plier; (head, back) courber. ● vi (road) tourner; (person) ~ **down/over** se pencher. ● n courbe f; (in road) virage m; (of arm, knee) pli m.

beneath /bɪˈniːθ/ prep sous, au-dessous de; (fig) indigne de. ● adv en dessous.

benefactor /ˈbenɪfæktə(r)/ n bienfaiteur/-trice m/f.

beneficial /benɪˈfɪʃl/ adj bénéfique.

benefit /ˈbenɪfɪt/ n avantage m; (allowance) allocation f. ● vt (be useful to) profiter à; (do good to) faire du bien à. ● *vi* profiter; ∼ **from** tirer profit de.

benign /bɪ'naɪn/ *adj* (kindly) bienveillant; (Med) bénin.

bent /bent/ →**BEND**. ● *n* (talent) aptitude *f*; (inclination) penchant *m*. ● *adj* tordu; ⊠ corrompu; ∼ **on doing** décidé à faire.

bequest /bɪ'kwest/ *n* legs *m*.

bereaved /bɪ'riːvd/ *adj* endeuillé; **the** ∼ la famille endeuillée. **bereavement** *n* deuil *m*.

berry /'berɪ/ *n* baie *f*.

berserk /bə'sɜːk/ *adj* fou furieux.

berth /bɜːθ/ *n* (in train, ship) couchette *f*; (anchorage) mouillage *m*; **give a wide** ∼ **to** éviter. ● *vi* mouiller.

beside /bɪ'saɪd/ *prep* à côté de; ∼ **one-self** hors de soi; ∼ **the point** sans rapport.

besides /bɪ'saɪdz/ *prep* en plus de. ● *adv* en plus.

beslege /bɪ'siːdʒ/ *vt* assiéger.

best /best/ *adj* meilleur; **the** ∼ **book** le meilleur livre; **the** ∼ **part of** la plus grande partie de; **the** ∼ **thing is to** le mieux est de. ● *adv* (**the**) ∼ (*behave, play*) le mieux. ● *n* **the** ∼ le meilleur, la meilleure; **do one's** ∼ faire de son mieux; **make the** ∼ **of** s'accommoder de. ∼ **man** *n* témoin. ∼**-seller** *n* best-seller *m*, livre *m* à succès.

bet /bet/ *n* pari *m*. ● *vt/i* (*pt* **bet** or **betted**, *pres p* **betting**) parier (**on** sur).

betray /bɪ'treɪ/ *vt* trahir.

better /'betə(r)/ *adj* meilleur; **the** ∼ **part of** la plus grande partie de; **get** ∼ s'améliorer; (recover) se remettre. ● *adv* mieux; **I had** ∼ **go** je ferais mieux de partir. ● *vt* (improve) améliorer; (do better than) surpasser. ● *n* **get the** ∼ **of** l'emporter sur; **so much the** ∼ tant mieux. ∼ **off** *adj* (richer) plus riche; **he is/would be** ∼ **off at home** il est/serait mieux chez lui.

betting shop *n* bureau *m* du PMU.

between /bɪ'twiːn/ *prep* entre. ● *adv* **in** ∼ au milieu.

beverage /'bevərɪdʒ/ *n* boisson *f*.

beware /bɪ'weə(r)/ *vi* prendre garde (**of** à).

bewilder /bɪ'wɪldə(r)/ *vt* déconcerter.

beyond /bɪ'jɒnd/ *prep* au-delà de; (control, reach) hors de; (besides) ex-cepté. ● *adv* au-delà; **it is** ∼ **me** ça me dépasse.

bias /'baɪəs/ *n* (inclination) tendance *f*; (prejudice) parti *m* pris. ● *vt* (*pt* **biased**) influer sur. **biased** *adj* partial.

bib /bɪb/ *n* bavoir *m*.

Bible /'baɪbl/ *n* Bible *f*.

biceps /'baɪseps/ *n* biceps *m*.

bicycle /'baɪsɪkl/ *n* vélo *m*, bicyclette *f*. ● *adj* (bell, chain) de vélo; (pump, clip) à vélo.

bid /bɪd/ *n* (at auction) enchère *f*; (attempt) tentative *f*. ● *vt/i* (*pt* **bade**, *pp* **bidden** or **bid**, *pres p* **bidding**) (offer) offrir, mettre une enchère (de) (**for** pour); ∼ **sb good morning** dire bonjour à qn; ∼ **sb farewell** faire ses adieux à qn.

bidding /'bɪdɪŋ/ *n* (at auction) enchères *fpl*; **he did my** ∼ il a fait ce que je lui ai dit.

bifocals /baɪ'fəʊklz/ *npl* verres *mpl* à double foyer.

big /bɪg/ *adj* (**bigger**, **biggest**) grand; (in bulk) gros.

bike /baɪk/ *n* vélo *m*.

bikini /bɪ'kiːnɪ/ *n* bikini *m*.

bilberry /'bɪlbrɪ/ *n* myrtille *f*.

bilingual /baɪ'lɪŋgwəl/ *adj* bilingue.

bill /bɪl/ *n* (invoice) facture *f*; (in hotel, for gas) note *f*; (in restaurant) addition *f*; (of sale) acte *m*; (Pol) projet *m* de loi; (banknote: US) billet *m* de banque; (Theat) **on the** ∼ à l'affiche; (of bird) bec *m*. ● *vt* (person: Comm) envoyer la facture à. ∼**board** *n* panneau *m* d'affichage.

billet /'bɪlɪt/ *n* cantonnement *m*. ● *vt* (*pt* **billeted**) cantonner (**on** chez).

billiards /'bɪljədz/ *n* billard *m*.

billion /'bɪlɪən/ *n* billion *m*; (US) milliard *m*.

bin /bɪn/ *n* (for rubbish) poubelle *f*; (for storage) casier *m*.

bind /baɪnd/ *vt* (*pt* **bound**) attacher; (book) relier; **be bound by** être tenu par. ● *n* (bore) corvée *f*.

binding /'baɪndɪŋ/ *n* reliure *f*. ● *adj* (agreement, contract) qui lie.

binge /bɪndʒ/ *n* (drinking) beuverie *f*; (eating) gueuleton *m*.

binoculars /bɪ'nɒkjʊləz/ *npl* jumelles *fpl*.

b

b

biochemistry /baɪəʊˈkemɪstrɪ/ n biochimie f.

biodegradable /baɪəʊdɪˈɡreɪdəbl/ adj biodégradable.

biographer /baɪˈɒɡrəfə(r)/ n biographe mf. **biography** n biographie f.

biological /baɪəˈlɒdʒɪkl/ adj biologique.

biologist /baɪˈɒlədʒɪst/ n biologiste mf.

biology /baɪˈɒlədʒɪ/ n biologie f.

bioterrorism /baɪəˈterərɪzm/ n bioterrorisme m.

birch /bɜːtʃ/ n (tree) bouleau m; (whip) fouet m.

bird /bɜːd/ n oiseau m; (girl 🔲) nana f.

Biro® /ˈbaɪrəʊ/ n stylo m à bille, bic® m.

birth /bɜːθ/ n naissance f; give ~ accoucher. ~ **certificate** n acte m de naissance. ~-**control** n contraception f. ~**day** n anniversaire m. ~**mark** n tache f de naissance. ~-**rate** n taux m de natalité.

biscuit /ˈbɪskɪt/ n biscuit m; (US) petit pain m (au lait).

bishop /ˈbɪʃəp/ n évêque m.

bit /bɪt/ →BITE. ● n morceau m; (of horse) mors m; (of tool) mèche f; **a ~** (a little) un peu; (Comput) bit m.

bitch /bɪtʃ/ n chienne f; (woman 🔲) garce f 🔲. ● vi dire du mal (**about** de).

bite /baɪt/ vt/i (pt **bit**; pp **bitten**) mordre; ~ **one's nails** se ronger les ongles. ● n morsure f; (by insect) piqûre f; (mouthful) bouchée f; **have a ~** manger un morceau.

bitter /ˈbɪtə(r)/ adj amer; (weather) glacial. ● n bière f. **bitterly** adv amèrement; **it is ~ly cold** il fait un temps glacial.

bizarre /bɪˈzɑː(r)/ adj bizarre.

black /blæk/ adj noir; ~ **and blue** couvert de bleus. ● n (colour) noir m; B~ (person) Noir/-e mf. ● vt noircir; (goods) boycotter. ~**berry** n mûre f. ~**bird** n merle m. ~**board** n tableau m noir. ~**currant** n cassis m.

blacken /ˈblækən/ vt/i noircir.

black: ~ **eye** n œil m poché. ~**head** n point m noir. ~ **ice** n verglas m. ~**leg** n jaune m.

blacklist /ˈblæklɪst/ n liste f noire. ● vt mettre à l'index.

blackmail /ˈblækmeɪl/ n chantage m. ● vt faire chanter. **blackmailer** n maître-chanteur m.

black: ~ **market** n marché m noir. ~**out** n panne f de courant; (Med) syncope f. ~ **pudding** n boudin m. ~ **sheep** n brebis f galeuse. ~**smith** n forgeron m. ~ **spot** n point m noir.

bladder /ˈblædə(r)/ n vessie f.

blade /bleɪd/ n (of knife) lame f; (of propeller, oar) pale f; ~ **of grass** brin m d'herbe.

blame /bleɪm/ vt accuser; ~ **sb for sth** reprocher qch à qn; **he is to ~** il est responsable (**for** de). ● n responsabilité f (**for** de).

bland /blænd/ adj (insipid) fade.

blank /blæŋk/ adj (page) blanc; (screen) vide; (cheque) en blanc; **to look ~** avoir l'air ébahi. ● n blanc m; ~ (**cartridge**) cartouche f à blanc.

blanket /ˈblæŋkɪt/ n couverture f; (layer) couche f.

blasphemous /ˈblæsfəməs/ adj blasphématoire; (person) blasphémateur.

blast /blɑːst/ n explosion f; (wave of air) souffle m; (of wind) rafale f; (noise from siren etc.) coup m. ● vt (blow up) faire sauter. ~ **off** décoller. ~ **furnace** n haut-fourneau m. ~ **off** n lancement m.

blatant /ˈbleɪtnt/ adj (obvious) flagrant; (shameless) éhonté.

blaze /bleɪz/ n feu m; (accident) incendie m. ● vt ~ **a trail** faire œuvre de pionnier. ● vi (fire) brûler; (sky, eyes) flamboyer.

bleach /bliːtʃ/ n (for cleaning) eau f de Javel; (for hair, fabric) décolorant m. ● vt/i blanchir; (hair) décolorer.

bleak /bliːk/ adj (landscape) désolé; (outlook, future) sombre.

bleed /bliːd/ vt/i (pt **bled**) saigner.

bleep /bliːp/ n bip m.

blemish /ˈblemɪʃ/ n imperfection f; (on fruit, reputation) tache f. ● vt entacher.

blend /blend/ vt mélanger. ● vi se fondre ensemble; **to ~ with** se marier à. ● n mélange m. **blender** n mixeur n, mixer n.

bless /bles/ vt bénir; **be ~ed with** jouir de; ~ **you!** à vos souhaits! **blessed** adj (holy) saint; (damned 🔲) sacré. **blessing** n bénédiction f; (benefit) avantage *m;* (stroke of luck) chance *f.*

blew /bluː/ →BLOW.

blight /blaɪt/ *n* (disease: Bot) rouille *f;* (fig) plaie *f.*

blind /blaɪnd/ *adj* aveugle (**to** à;) (corner, bend) sans visibilité. ● *vt* aveugler. ● *n* (on window) store *m;* **the** ~ les aveugles *mpl.*

blindfold /ˈblaɪndfəʊld/ *adj* **be** ~ avoir les yeux bandés. ● *adv* les yeux bandés. ● *n* bandeau *m.* ● *vt* bander les yeux à.

blindness /ˈblaɪndnɪs/ *n* (Med) cécité *f;* (fig) aveuglement *m.*

blind spot *n* (Auto) angle *m* mort.

blink /blɪŋk/ *vi* cligner des yeux; (light) clignoter.

bliss /blɪs/ *n* délice *m.* **blissful** *adj* délicieux.

blister /ˈblɪstə(r)/ *n* ampoule *f;* (on paint) cloque *f.* ● *vi* cloquer.

blitz /blɪts/ *n* (Aviat) raid *m* éclair. ● *vt* bombarder.

blob /blɒb/ *n* (drop) (grosse) goutte *f;* (stain) tache *f.*

block /blɒk/ *n* bloc *m;* (buildings) pâté *m* de maisons; (in pipe) obstruction *f;* ~ **(of flats)** immeuble *m;* ~ **letters** majuscules *fpl.* ● *vt* bloquer.

blockade /blɒˈkeɪd/ *n* blocus *m.* ● *vt* bloquer.

blockage /ˈblɒkɪdʒ/ *n* obstruction *f.*

blockbuster *n* gros succès *m.*

bloke /bləʊk/ *n* 🔲 type *m.*

blond /blɒnd/ *adj & n* blond (*m*).

blonde /blɒnd/ *adj & n* blonde (*f*).

blood /blʌd/ *n* sang *m.* ● *adj* (donor, bath) de sang; (bank, poisoning) du sang; (group, vessel) sanguin. ~**-pressure** *n* tension *f* artérielle. ~**shed** *n* effusion *f* de sang. ~**shot** *adj* injecté de sang. ~**stream** *n* sang *m.* ~ **test** *n* prise *f* de sang.

bloody /ˈblʌdɪ/ *adj* (**-ier, -iest**) sanglant; 🔲 sacré. ● *adv* 🔲 vachement 🔲. ~**-minded** *adj* 🔲 hargneux, obstiné.

bloom /bluːm/ *n* fleur *f.* ● *vi* fleurir; (person) s'épanouir.

blossom /ˈblɒsəm/ *n* fleur(s) *f* (*pl*). ● *vi* fleurir; (person) s'épanouir.

blot /blɒt/ *n* tache *f.* ● *vt* (*pt* **blotted**) tacher; (dry) sécher; ~ **out** effacer.

blotch /blɒtʃ/ *n* tache *f.*

blouse /blaʊz/ *n* chemisier *m.*

blow /bləʊ/ *vt/i* (*pt* **blew**; *pp* **blown**) souffler; (fuse) (faire) sauter; (squander 🔲) claquer; (opportunity) rater; ~ **one's nose** se moucher; ~ **a whistle** siffler. ● *n* coup *m.* □ ~ **away** or **off** emporter; ~ **out** souffler; ~ **over** passer; ~ **up** (faire) sauter; (tyre) gonfler; (Photo) agrandir.

blow-dry *n* brushing *m.* ● *vt* faire un brushing à.

blown /bləʊn/ →BLOW.

bludgeon /ˈblʌdʒən/ *n* matraque *f.* ● *vt* matraquer.

blue /bluː/ *adj* bleu; (movie) porno. ● *n* bleu *m;* **come out of the** ~ être inattendu; **have the** ~**s** avoir le cafard. ~**bell** *n* jacinthe *f* des bois. ~**print** *n* projet *m.*

bluff /blʌf/ *vt/i* bluffer. ● *n* bluff *m;* **call sb's** ~ dire chiche à qn. ● *adj* (person) carré.

blunder /ˈblʌndə(r)/ *vi* faire une bourde; (move) avancer à tâtons. ● *n* gaffe *f.*

blunt /blʌnt/ *adj* (knife) émoussé; (person) brusque. ● *vt* émousser. **bluntly** *adv* carrément.

blur /blɜː(r)/ *n* image *f* floue. ● *vt* (*pt* **blurred**) brouiller.

blurb /blɜːb/ *n* résumé *m* publicitaire.

blush /blʌʃ/ *vi* rougir. ● *n* rougeur *f.* **blusher** *n* fard *m* à joues.

blustery /ˈblʌstərɪ/ *adj* ~ **wind** bourrasque *f.*

BMI *abbr* (**body mass index**) IMC *m.*

boar /bɔː(r)/ *n* sanglier *m.*

board /bɔːd/ *n* planche *f;* (for notices) tableau *m;* (food) pension *f;* **full** ~ pension *f* complète; **half** ~ demipension *f;* (committee) conseil *m;* ~ **of directors** conseil *m* d'administration; **go by the** ~ tomber à l'eau; **on** ~ à bord. ● *vt/i* (bus, train) monter dans; (Naut) monter à bord (de); ~ **with** être en pension chez.

boarding-school *n* école *f* privée avec internat.

boast /bəʊst/ *vi* se vanter (**about** de). ● *vt* s'enorgueillir de. ● *n* vantardise *f.*

boat /bəʊt/ *n* bateau *m;* (small) canot *m;* **in the same** ~ logé à la même enseigne.

bode /bəʊd/ vi ~ **well**/**ill** être de bon/ mauvais augure.

bodily /'bɒdɪlɪ/ adj (need, well-being) physique; (injury) corporel. ● adv physiquement; (in person) en personne.

body /'bɒdɪ/ n corps m; (mass) masse f; (organization) organisme m; ~ **part** n partie f de corps; ~**(work)** (Auto) carrosserie f; **the main ~ of** le gros de. ~**-building** n culturisme m. ~**guard** n garde m du corps.

bog /bɒg/ n marais m. ● vt (pt **bogged**) **get ~ged down** s'enliser dans.

bogus /'bəʊgəs/ adj faux.

boil /bɔɪl/ n furoncle m; **bring to the ~** porter à ébullition. ● vt/i bouillir. ~ **down to** se ramener à; ~ **over** déborder. **boiled** adj (egg) à la coque; (potatoes) à l'eau.

boiler /'bɔɪlə(r)/ n chaudière f; ~ **suit** bleu m (de travail).

boisterous /'bɔɪstərəs/ adj tapageur; (child) turbulent.

bold /bəʊld/ adj hardi; (cheeky) effronté; (type) gras.

Bolivia /bə'lɪvɪə/ n Bolivie f.

bollard /'bɒlɑːd/ n (on road) balise f.

bolt /bəʊlt/ n (on door) verrou m; (for nut) boulon m; (lightning) éclair m. ● vt (door) verrouiller; (food) engouffrer. ● vi s'emballer.

bomb /bɒm/ n bombe f; ~ **scare** alerte f à la bombe. ● vt bombarder.

bomber /'bɒmə(r)/ n (aircraft) bombardier m; (person) plastiqueur m.

bond /bɒnd/ n (agreement) engagement m; (link) lien m; (Comm) obligation f, bon m; **in ~** (entreposé) en douane.

bone /bəʊn/ n os m; (of fish) arête f. ● vt désosser. ~**-dry** adj tout à fait sec.

bonfire /'bɒnfaɪə(r)/ n feu m; (for celebration) feu m de joie.

bonnet /'bɒnɪt/ n (hat) bonnet m; (of vehicle) capot m.

bonus /'bəʊnəs/ n prime f.

bony /'bəʊnɪ/ adj (-ier, -iest) (thin) osseux; (fish) plein d'arêtes.

boo /buː/ interj hou. ● vt/i huer. ● n huée f.

booby trap /'buːbɪtræp/ n mécanisme m piégé. ● vt (pt **-trapped**) piéger.

book /bʊk/ n livre m; (exercise) cahier m; (of tickets etc.) carnet m; ~**s** (Comm) comptes mpl. ● vt (reserve) réserver; (driver) dresser un PV à; (player) prendre le nom de; (write down) inscrire. ● vi retenir des places; **(fully) ~ed** complet. ~**case** n bibliothèque f. **booking-office** n guichet m. ~**keeping** n comptabilité f. **booklet** n brochure f. ~**maker** n bookmaker m. ~**mark** n (for book, Internet) signet m. ~**seller** n libraire mf. ~**shop** n librairie f. ~**stall** n kiosque m (à journaux).

boom /buːm/ vi (gun, wind, etc.) gronder; (trade) prospérer. ● n grondement m; (Comm) boom m, prospérité f.

boost /buːst/ vt stimuler; (morale) remonter; (price) augmenter; (publicize) faire de la réclame pour.

boot /buːt/ n (knee-length) botte f; (anklelength) chaussure f (montante); (for walking) chaussure f de marche; (Sport) chaussure f de sport; (of vehicle) coffre m; **get the ~** 🗙 se faire virer. ● vt/i ~ **up** (Comput) amorcer.

booth /buːð/ n (for telephone) cabine f; (at fair) baraque f.

booze /buːz/ vi 🗓 boire (beaucoup). ● n 🗓 alcool m.

border /'bɔːdə(r)/ n (edge) bord m; (frontier) frontière f; (in garden) bordure f. ● vi ~ **on** être voisin de, avoisiner.

bore /bɔː(r)/ vt ennuyer; **be ~d** s'ennuyer; ➡BEAR. ● vi (Tech) forer. ● n raseur/-euse m/f; (thing) ennui m. **boredom** n ennui m. **boring** adj ennuyeux.

born /bɔːn/ adj né; **be ~** naître.

borne /bɔːn/ ➡BEAR.

borough /'bʌrə/ n municipalité f.

borrow /'bɒrəʊ/ vt emprunter **(from** à).

Bosnia /'bɒznɪə/ n Bosnie f.

Bosnian /'bɒznɪən/ adj bosniaque. ● n Bosniaque.

bosom /'bʊzəm/ n poitrine f; ~ **friend** ami/-e m/f intime.

boss /bɒs/ n 🗓 patron/-ne m/f. ● vt ~ **(about)** 🗓 mener par le bout du nez.

bossy /'bɒsɪ/ adj autoritaire.

botch /bɒtʃ/ vt bâcler, saboter.

both /bəʊθ/ *det* les deux; ~ **the books** les deux livres. ● *pron* tous/toutes (les) deux, l'un/-e et l'autre; **we ~ agree** nous sommes tous les deux d'accord; **I bought ~ (of them)** j'ai acheté les deux; **I saw ~ of you** je vous ai vus tous les deux; ~ **Paul and Anne** (et) Paul et Anne. ● *adv* à la fois.

bother /'bɒðə(r)/ *vt* (annoy, worry) ennuyer; (disturb) déranger. ● *vi* se déranger; **don't ~ (calling)** ce n'est pas la peine (d'appeler); **don't ~ about us** ne t'inquiète pas pour nous; **I can't be ~ed** j'ai la flemme 🔲. ● *n* ennui *m;* (effort) peine *f;* **it's no ~** ce n'est rien.

bottle /'bɒtl/ *n* bouteille *f;* (for baby) biberon *m.* ● *vt* mettre en bouteille. ~ **up** contenir. ~ **bank** *n* collecteur *m* (de verre usagé). ~**neck** *n* (traffic jam) embouteillage *m.* ~**-opener** *n* ouvre-bouteilles *m inv.*

bottom /'bɒtəm/ *n* fond *m;* (of hill, page, etc.) bas *m;* (buttocks) derrière *m* 🔲. ● *adj* inférieur, du bas.

bought /bɔːt/ →**BUY.**

bounce /baʊns/ *vi* rebondir; (person) faire des bonds, bondir; (cheques 🔲) être refusé. ● *vt* faire rebondir. ● *n* rebond *m.*

bound /baʊnd/ *vi* (leap) bondir; ~**ed by** limité par. ● *n* bond *m.* →**BIND.** ● *adj* **be ~ for** être en route pour, aller vers; ~ **to** (obliged) obligé de; (certain) sûr de.

boundary /'baʊndrɪ/ *n* limite *f.*

bounds /baʊndz/ *npl* limites *fpl;* **out of ~** être interdit d'accès.

bout /baʊt/ *n* période *f;* (Med) accès *m;* (boxing) combat *m.*

bow¹ /bəʊ/ *n* (weapon) arc *m;* (of violin) archet *m;* (knot) nœud *m.*

bow² /baʊ/ *n* salut *m;* (of ship) proue *f.* ● *vt/i* (s')incliner.

bowels /'baʊəlz/ *npl* intestins *mpl;* (fig) profondeurs *fpl.*

bowl /bəʊl/ *n* (for washing) cuvette *f;* (for food) bol *m;* (for soup) assiette *f* creuse. ● *vt/i* (cricket) lancer; ~ **over** bouleverser.

bowler /'bəʊlə(r)/ *n* (cricket) lanceur *m;* ~ **(hat)** (chapeau) melon *m.*

bowling /'bəʊlɪŋ/ *n* (ten-pin) bowling *m;* (on grass) jeu *m* de boules. ~**-alley** *n* bowling *m.*

bow tie *n* nœud *m* papillon.

box /bɒks/ *n* boîte *f;* (cardboard) carton *m;* (Theat) loge *f;* **the ~** 🔲 la télé. ● *vt* mettre en boîte; (Sport) boxer; ~ **sb's ears** gifler qn; ~ **in** enfermer.

boxing /'bɒksɪŋ/ *n* boxe *f.* ● *adj* de boxe. **B~ Day** *n* le lendemain de Noël.

box office *n* guichet *m.*

boy /bɔɪ/ *n* garçon *m;* ~ **band** boys band *m.*

boycott /'bɔɪkɒt/ *vt* boycotter. ● *n* boycottage *m.*

boyfriend /'bɔɪfrend/ *n* (petit) ami *m.*

bra /brɑː/ *n* soutien-gorge *m.*

brace /breɪs/ *n* (fastener) attache *f;* (dental) appareil *m;* (tool) vilbrequin *m;* ~**s** (for trousers) bretelles *fpl.* ● *vt* soutenir; ~ **oneself** rassembler ses forces.

bracket /'brækɪt/ *n* (for shelf etc.) tasseau *m,* support *m;* (group) tranche *f;* **in ~s** entre parenthèses. ● *vt* mettre entre parenthèses ou crochets.

braid /breɪd/ *n* (trimming) galon *m;* (hair) tresse *f.*

brain /breɪn/ *n* cerveau *m;* ~**s** (fig) intelligence *f.* ● *vt* assommer. **brainless** *adj* stupide. ~**wash** *vt* faire subir un lavage de cerveau à. ~**wave** *n* idée *f* géniale, trouvaille *f.* **brainy** *adj* (-**ier**, -**iest**) doué.

brake /breɪk/ *n* (Auto *also* fig) frein *m.* ● *vt/i* freiner. ~ **light** *n* feu *m* stop.

bran /bræn/ *n* son *m.*

branch /brɑːntʃ/ *n* (of tree) branche *f;* (of road) embranchement *m;* (Comm) succursale *f;* (of bank) agence *f.* ● *vi* ~ **(off)** bifurquer.

brand /brænd/ *n* marque *f.* ● *vt* ~ **sb as sth** désigner qn comme qch.

brand-new /brænd'njuː/ *adj* tout neuf.

brandy /'brændɪ/ *n* cognac *m.*

brass /brɑːs/ *n* cuivre *m;* **get down to ~ tacks** en venir aux choses sérieuses; **the ~** (Mus) les cuivres *mpl;* **top ~** 🔲 galonnés *mpl.*

brat /bræt/ *n* 🔲 môme *mf* 🔲.

brave /breɪv/ *adj* courageux; (smile) brave. ● *n* (American Indian) brave *m.* ● *vt* braver. **bravery** *n* courage *m.*

brawl /brɔːl/ *n* bagarre *f.* ● *vi* se bagarrer.

Brazil /brə'zɪl/ *n* Brésil *m.*

b

breach /briːtʃ/ n (of copyright, privilege) violation f; (in relationship) rupture f; (gap) brèche f. ● vt ouvrir une brèche dans.

bread /bred/ n pain m; ~ **and butter** tartine f. ~**-bin**, (US) ~**-box** n boîte f à pain. ~**crumbs** npl chapelure f.

breadth /bretθ/ n largeur f.

bread-winner /'bredwɪnə(r)/ n soutien m de famille.

break /breɪk/ vt (pt **broke**, pp **broken**) casser; (smash into pieces) briser; (vow, silence, rank, etc.) rompre; (law) violer; (a record) battre; (news) révéler; (journey) interrompre; (heart, strike, ice) briser; ~ **one's arm** se casser le bras. ● vi (se) casser; se briser. ● n cassure f, rupture f; (in relationship, continuity) rupture f; (interval) interruption f; (at school) récréation f, récré f; (for coffee) pause f; (luck Ⅰ) chance f. ~ **away from** se détacher; ~ **down** vi (collapse) s'effondrer; (negotiations) échouer; (machine) tomber en panne; vt (door) enfoncer; (analyse) analyser; ~ **even** rentrer dans ses frais; ~ **into** cambrioler; ~ **off** (se) détacher; (suspend) rompre; (stop talking) s'interrompre; ~ **out** (fire, war, etc.) éclater; ~ **up** (end) (faire) cesser; (couple) rompre; (marriage) (se) briser; (crowd) (se) disperser; (schools) être en vacances. **breakable** adj fragile. **breakage** n casse f.

breakdown /'breɪkdaʊn/ n (Tech) panne f; (Med) dépression f; (of figures) analyse f. ● adj (Auto) de dépannage.

breakfast /'brekfəst/ n petit déjeuner m.

break /breɪk/ n: ~**-in** n cambriolage m. ~**through** n percée f.

breast /brest/ n sein m; (chest) poitrine f. ~**-feed** vt (pt **-fed**) allaiter. ~**-stroke** n brasse f.

breath /breθ/ n souffle m, haleine f; **out of** ~ à bout de souffle; **under one's** ~ tout bas.

breathalyser® /'breθəlaɪzə(r)/ n alcootest m.

breathe /briːð/ vt/i respirer. ~ **in** inspirer; ~ **out** expirer.

breathless /'breθlɪs/ adj à bout de souffle.

breathtaking /'breθteɪkɪŋ/ adj à vous couper le souffle.

bred /bred/ →BREED.

breed /briːd/ vt (pt **bred**) élever; (give rise to) engendrer. ● vi se reproduire. ● n race f.

breeze /briːz/ n brise f.

brew /bruː/ vt (beer) brasser; (tea) faire infuser. ● vi (beer) fermenter; (tea) infuser; (fig) se préparer. ● n décoction f. **brewer** n brasseur m. **brewery** n brasserie f.

bribe /braɪb/ n pot-de-vin m. ● vt soudoyer. **bribery** n corruption f.

brick /brɪk/ n brique f. ~**layer** n maçon m.

bridal /'braɪdl/ adj (dress) de mariée; (car, chamber) des mariés.

bride /braɪd/ n mariée f. ~**groom** n marié m. ~**smaid** n demoiselle f d'honneur.

bridge /brɪdʒ/ n pont m; (Naut) passerelle f; (of nose) arête f; (card game) bridge m. ● vt ~ **a gap** combler une lacune.

bridle /'braɪdl/ n bride f. ● vt brider. ~**-path** n piste f cavalière.

brief /briːf/ adj bref. ● n instructions fpl; (Jur) dossier m. ● vt donner des instructions à.

briefcase /'briːfkeɪs/ n serviette f.

briefs /briːfs/ npl slip m.

bright /braɪt/ adj brillant, vif; (day, room) clair; (cheerful) gai; (clever) intelligent.

brighten /'braɪtn/ vt égayer. ● vi (weather) s'éclaircir; (face) s'éclairer.

brilliant /'brɪlɪənt/ adj (student, career) brillant; (light) éclatant; (very good Ⅰ) super.

brim /brɪm/ n bord m. ● vi (pt **brimmed**); ~ **over** déborder (**with** de).

bring /brɪŋ/ vt (pt **brought**) (thing) apporter; (person, vehicle) amener; ~ **to bear** (pressure etc.) exercer. ~ **about** provoquer; ~ **back** (return with) rapporter; (colour, shine) redonner; ~ **down** faire tomber; (shoot down, knock down) abattre; ~ **forward** avancer; ~ **off** réussir; ~ **out** (take out) sortir; (show) faire ressortir; (book) publier; ~ **round** faire revenir à soi; **~ up** (*child*) élever; (Med) vomir; (*question*) aborder.

brink /brɪŋk/ n bord m.

brisk /brɪsk/ adj vif.

bristle /ˈbrɪsl/ n poil m. ● vi se hérisser; **bristling with** hérissé de.

Britain /ˈbrɪtn/ n Grande-Bretagne f.

British /ˈbrɪtɪʃ/ adj britannique; **the ~** les Britanniques mpl.

Briton /ˈbrɪtn/ n Britannique mf.

Brittany /ˈbrɪtəni/ n Bretagne f.

brittle /ˈbrɪtl/ adj fragile.

broad /brɔːd/ adj large; (*choice, range*) grand. **~ bean** n fève f.

broadband /ˈbrɔːdbænd/ adj à haut débit. ● n ADSL m haut débit m.

broadcast /ˈbrɔːdkɑːst/ vt/i (pl **broadcast**) diffuser; (person) parler à la television or à la radio. ● n émission f.

broadly /ˈbrɔːdli/ adv en gros.

broad-minded /brɔːdˈmaɪndɪd/ adj large d'esprit.

broccoli /ˈbrɒkəli/ n inv brocoli m.

brochure /ˈbrəʊʃə(r)/ n brochure f.

broke /brəʊk/ →BREAK. ● adj (penniless 🔢) fauché.

broken /ˈbrəʊkən/ →BREAK. ● adj **~ English** mauvais anglais m.

bronchitis /brɒŋˈkaɪtɪs/ n bronchite f.

bronze /brɒnz/ n bronze m.

brooch /brəʊtʃ/ n broche f.

brood /bruːd/ n nichée f, couvée f. ● vi méditer tristement.

broom /bruːm/ n balai m.

broth /brɒθ/ n bouillon m.

brothel /ˈbrɒθl/ n maison f close.

brother /ˈbrʌðə(r)/ n frère m. **~hood** n fraternité f. **~-in-law** n (pl **~s-in-law**) beau-frère m.

brought /brɔːt/ →BRING.

brow /braʊ/ n front m; (of hill) sommet m.

brown /braʊn/ adj (object) marron; (hair) brun; **~ bread** pain m complet; **~ sugar** sucre m roux. ● n marron m; brun m. ● vt/i brunir; (Culin) (faire) dorer.

Brownie /ˈbraʊni/ n jeannette f.

browse /braʊz/ vi flâner; (animal) brouter. ● vt (Comput) naviguer.

browser n (Comput) navigateur m.

bruise /bruːz/ n bleu m. ● vt (knee, arm etc.) faire un bleu à; (fruit) abîmer.

brush /brʌʃ/ n brosse f; (skirmish) accrochage m; (bushes) broussailles fpl. ● vt brosser. **~ against** frôler; **~ aside** (dismiss) repousser; (move) écarter; **~ up (on)** se remettre à.

Brussels /ˈbrʌslz/ n Bruxelles. **~ sprouts** npl choux mpl de Bruxelles.

brutal /ˈbruːtl/ adj brutal.

brute /bruːt/ n brute f; **by ~ force** par la force.

BSE abbr (Bovine Spongiform Encephalopathy) encephalopathie f spongiforme bovine, ESB f.

bubble /ˈbʌbl/ n bulle f; **blow ~s** faire des bulles. ● vi bouillonner; **~ over** déborder. **~ bath** n bain m moussant.

buck /bʌk/ n mâle m; (US, 🔢) dollar m; **pass the ~** rejeter la responsabilité (**to** sur). ● vi (horse) ruer; **~ up** 🔢 prendre courage; (hurry 🔢) se grouiller 🔢.

bucket /ˈbʌkɪt/ n seau m (**of** de).

buckle /ˈbʌkl/ n boucle f. ● vt/i (fasten) (se) boucler; (bend) voiler.

bud /bʌd/ n bourgeon m. ● vi (pt **budded**) bourgeonner.

Buddhism /ˈbʊdɪzəm/ n bouddhisme m.

budding /ˈbʌdɪŋ/ adj (talent) naissant; (athlete) en herbe.

budge /bʌdʒ/ vt/i (faire) bouger.

budgerigar /ˈbʌdʒərɪgɑː(r)/ n perruche f.

budget /ˈbʌdʒɪt/ n budget m. ● vi **~ for** prévoir (dans son budget).

buff /bʌf/ n (colour) chamois m; 🔢 fanatique mf.

buffalo /ˈbʌfələʊ/ n (pl **-oes** or **-o** buffle m; (US) bison m.

buffer /ˈbʌfə(r)/ n tampon m; **~ zone** zone f tampon.

buffet¹ /ˈbʊfeɪ/ n (meal, counter) buffet m; **~ car** buffet m.

buffet² /ˈbʌfɪt/ n (blow) soufflet m. ● vt (pt **buffeted**) souffleter.

bug /bʌg/ n (bedbug) punaise f; (any small insect) bestiole f; (germ) microbe m; (stomachache 🔢) ennuis mpl

b

gastriques; (device) micro *m;* (defect) défaut *m;* (Comput) bogue *f,* bug *m.* ● *vt* (*pt* **bugged**) mettre des micros dans; 🅇 embêter.

buggy /'bʌgɪ/ *n* poussette *f.*

build /bɪld/ *vt/i* (*pt* **built**) bâtir, construire. ● *n* carrure *f.* ~ **up** (increase) augmenter, monter; (accumulate) (s')accumuler. **builder** *n* entrepreneur *m* en bâtiment; (workman) ouvrier *m* du bâtiment.

building /'bɪldɪŋ/ *n* (structure) bâtiment *m;* (dwelling) immeuble *m.* ~ **society** *n* caisse *f* d'épargne.

build-up /'bɪldʌp/ *n* accumulation *f;* (fig) publicité *f.*

built /bɪlt/ ➡BUILD.

built-in /bɪlt'ɪn/ *adj* encastré.

built-up area *n* agglomération *f,* zone *f* urbanisée.

bulb /bʌlb/ *n* (Bot) bulbe *m;* (Electr) ampoule *f.*

Bulgaria /bʌl'geərɪə/ *n* Bulgarie *f.*

Bulgarian /bʌl'geərɪən/ *n* (person) Bulgare *mf;* (Ling) bulgare *m.* ● *adj* bulgare.

bulge /bʌldʒ/ *n* renflement *m.* ● *vi* se renfler, être renflé; **be bulging with** être gonflé *or* bourré de.

bulimia /bju:'lɪmɪə/ *n* boulimie *f.*

bulk /bʌlk/ *n* volume *f;* **in** ~ (buy, sell) en gros; (transport) en vrac; **the** ~ **of** la majeure partie de.

bull /bʊl/ *n* taureau *m.* ~**dog** *n* bouledogue *m.* ~**doze** *vt* raser au bulldozer.

bullet /'bʊlɪt/ *n* balle *f.*

bulletin /'bʊlətɪn/ *n* bulletin *m.*

bullet-proof /'bʊlɪtpru:f/ *adj* (vest) pare-balles *inv;* (vehicle) blindé.

bullfight /'bʊlfaɪt/ *n* corrida *f.*

bullion /'bʊlɪən/ *n* or *m or* argent *m* en lingots.

bullring /'bʊlrɪŋ/ *n* arène *f.*

bull's-eye /'bʊlzaɪ/ *n* mille *m.*

bully /'bʊlɪ/ *n* (child) petite brute *f;* (adult) tyran *m.* ● *vt* maltraiter.

bum /bʌm/ *n* 🅇 derrière *m* 🅣; (US, 🅇) vagabond/-e *m/f.*

bumble-bee /'bʌmblbi:/ *n* bourdon *m.*

bump /bʌmp/ *n* (swelling) bosse *f;* (on road) bosse *f.* ● *vt/i* cogner, heurter. ~

along cahoter; ~ **into** (hit) rentrer dans; (meet) tomber sur.

bumper /'bʌmpə(r)/ *n* pare-chocs *m inv.* ● *adj* exceptionnel.

bumpy /'bʌmpɪ/ *adj* (road) accidenté.

bun /bʌn/ *n* (cake) petit pain *m;* (hair) chignon *m.*

bunch /bʌntʃ/ *n* (of flowers) bouquet *m;* (of keys) trousseau *m;* (of people) groupe *m;* (of bananas) régime *m;* ~ **of grapes** grappe *f* de raisin.

bundle /'bʌndl/ *n* paquet *m.* ● *vt* mettre en paquet; (push) fourrer.

bung /bʌŋ/ *n* bouchon *m.* ● *vt* (stop up) boucher; (throw 🅇) flanquer 🅣.

bunion /'bʌnjən/ *n* (Med) oignon *m.*

bunk /bʌŋk/ *n* (on ship, train) couchette *f.* ~**-beds** *npl* lits *mpl* superposés.

buoy /bɔɪ/ *n* bouée *f.* ● *vt* ~ **up** (hearten) soutenir, encourager.

buoyancy /'bɔɪənsɪ/ *n* (of floating object) flottabilité *f;* (cheerfulness) gaieté *f.*

burden /'bɜ:dn/ *n* fardeau *m.* ● *vt* ennuyer (**with** de).

bureau /'bjʊərəʊ/ *n* (*pl* **-eaux**) bureau *m.*

bureaucracy /bjʊə'rɒkrəsɪ/ *n* bureaucratie *f.*

burglar /'bɜ:glə(r)/ *n* cambrioleur *m;* ~ **alarm** alarme *f.* **burglarize** *vt* (US) cambrioler. **burglary** *n* cambriolage *m.* **burgle** *vt* cambrioler.

Burgundy /'bɜ:gəndɪ/ *n* (wine) bourgogne *m.*

burial /'berɪəl/ *n* enterrement *m.*

burn /bɜ:n/ *vt/i* (*pt* **burned** *or* **burnt**) brûler. ● *n* brûlure *f.* ~ **down** être réduit en cendres. **burner** *n* (on cooker) brûleur *m;* (on computer) graveur *m.* **burning** *adj* en flammes; (fig) brûlant.

burnt /bɜ:nt/ ➡BURN.

burp /bɜ:p/ *n* 🅣 rot *m.* ● *vi* 🅣 roter.

burrow /'bʌrəʊ/ *n* terrier *m.* ● *vt* creuser.

bursar /'bɜ:sə(r)/ *n* intendant/-e *m/f.* **bursary** *n* bourse *f.*

burst /bɜ:st/ *vt/i* (*pt* **burst**) (balloon, bubble) crever; (pipe) (faire) éclater. ● *n* explosion *f;* (of laughter) éclat *m;* (surge) élan *m.* ~ **into** (room) faire interruption dans; ~ **into tears** fondre en larmes; ~ **out** ~ **out laughing** éclater de rire; ~ **with be** ~**ing with** déborder de.

bury /'berɪ/ vt (person etc.) enterrer; (hide, cover) enfouir; (engross, thrust) plonger.

bus /bʌs/ n (pl **buses**) (auto)bus m. ● vt transporter en bus. ● vi (pt **bussed**) prendre l'autobus.

bush /bʊʃ/ n (shrub) buisson m; (land) brousse f.

business /'bɪznɪs/ n (task, concern) affaire f; (commerce) affaires fpl; (line of work) métier m; (shop) commerce m; **he has no** ~ **to** il n'a pas le droit de; **mean** ~ être sérieux; **that's none of your** ~! ça ne vous regarde pas! ~**like** adj sérieux. ~**man** n homme m d'affaires.

busker /'bʌskə(r)/ n musicien/-ne m/f des rues.

bus-stop n arrêt m d'autobus.

bust /bʌst/ n (statue) buste m; (bosom) poitrine f. ● vt/i (pt **busted** or **bust**) (burst 🅻) crever; (break 🅻) (se) casser. ● adj (broken, finished 🅻) fichu; **go** ~ 🅻 faire faillite.

bustle /'bʌsl/ vi s'affairer. ● n affairement m, remue-ménage m.

busy /'bɪzɪ/ adj (**-ier, -iest**) (person) occupé; (street) animé; (day) chargé. ● vt ~ **oneself with** s'occuper à.

but /bʌt/ conj mais. ● prep sauf; ~ **for** sans; **nobody** ~ personne d'autre que; **nothing** ~ rien que. ● adv (only) seulement.

butcher /'bʊtʃə(r)/ n boucher m. ● vt massacrer.

butler /'bʌtlə(r)/ n maître m d'hôtel.

butt /bʌt/ n (of gun) crosse f; (of cigarette) mégot m; (of joke) cible f; (barrel) tonneau m; (US, 🅻) derrière m 🅻. ● vi ~ **in** interrompre.

butter /'bʌtə(r)/ n beurre m. ● vt beurrer. ~**-bean** n haricot m blanc. ~**cup** n bouton-d'or m.

butterfly /'bʌtəflaɪ/ n papillon m.

buttock /'bʌtək/ n fesse f.

button /'bʌtn/ n bouton m. ● vt/i ~ (**up**) (se) boutonner.

buttonhole /'bʌtnhəʊl/ n boutonnière f. ● vt accrocher.

buy /baɪ/ vt (pt **bought**) acheter (**from** à); ~ **sth for sb** acheter qch à qn, prendre qch pour qn; (believe 🅻) croire, avaler.

buzz /bʌz/ n bourdonnement m. ● vi bourdonner. **buzzer** n sonnerie f.

by /baɪ/ prep par, de; (near) à côté de; (before) avant; (means) en, à, par; ~ **bike** à vélo; ~ **car** en auto; ~ **day** de jour; ~ **the kilo** au kilo; ~ **running** en courant; ~ **sea** par mer; ~ **that time** à ce moment-là; ~ **the way** à propos; ~ **oneself** tout seul. ● adv **close** ~ tout près; ~ **and large** dans l'ensemble.

bye(-bye) /'baɪbaɪ/ interj 🅻 au revoir, salut 🅻.

by-election n élection f partielle.

Byelorussia /bjeləʊ'rʊʃə/ n Biélorussie f.

by-law /'baɪlɔː/ n arrêté m municipal.

bypass /'baɪpɑːs/ n (Auto) rocade f; (Med) pontage m. ● vt contourner.

by-product n dérivé m; (fig) conséquence f.

byte /baɪt/ n octet m.

Cc

cab /kæb/ n taxi m; (of lorry, train) cabine f.

cabbage /'kæbɪdʒ/ n chou m.

cabin /'kæbɪn/ n (hut) cabane f; (in ship, aircraft) cabine f.

cabinet /'kæbɪnɪt/ n petit placard m; (glassfronted) vitrine f; (Pol) cabinet m.

cable /'keɪbl/ n câble m. ● vt câbler. ~**-car** n téléphérique m. ~ **television** n télévision f par câble.

cache /kæʃ/ n (hoard) cache f; (place) cachette f.

cackle /'kækl/ n (of hen) caquet m; (laugh) ricanement m. ● vi caqueter; (laugh) ricaner.

cactus /'kæktəs/ n (pl **-ti** or ~**es**) cactus m.

cadet /kə'det/ n élève m officier.

Caesarean /sɪ'zeərɪən/ adj ~ (**section**) césarienne f.

b

c

café /'kæfeɪ/ n café m, snack-bar m.

caffeine /'kæfi:n/ n caféine f.

cage /keɪdʒ/ n cage f. ● vt mettre en cage.

cagey /'keɪdʒɪ/ adj réticent.

cagoule /kə'dʒu:l/ n K-way® m.

cajole /kə'dʒəʊl/ vt ~ sb into doing sth amener qn à faire qch par la cajolerie.

cake /keɪk/ n gâteau m; (of soap) pain m. ● vi former une croûte (on sur).

calculate /'kælkjʊleɪt/ vt calculer; (estimate) évaluer. **calculated** adj délibéré; (risk) calculé. **calculating** adj calculateur. **calculation** n calcul m. **calculator** n calculatrice f.

calculus /'kælkjʊləs/ n (pl -li or ~es) calcul m.

calendar /'kælɪndə(r)/ n calendrier m.

calf /kɑ:f/ n (pl **calves**) (young cow or bull) veau m; (of leg) mollet m.

calibre /'kælɪbə(r)/ n calibre m.

call /kɔ:l/ vt/i appeler; (loudly) crier; **he's ~ed John** il s'appelle John; ~ **sb stupid** traiter qn d'imbécile. ● n appel m; (of bird) cri m; (visit) visite f; **make/ pay a ~ on** rendre visite à; **be on ~** être de garde; ~ **box** cabine f téléphonique. ~ **centre** n centre m d'appels. ~ **back** rappeler; (visit) repasser; ~ **for** (help) appeler à; (demand) demander; (require) exiger; (collect) passer prendre; ~ **in** passer. ~ **off** annuler. ~ **on** (visit) rendre visite à; (urge) demander à (**to do** de faire). ~ **out (to)** appeler. ~ **round** venir. ~ **up** appeler.

calling /'kɔ:lɪŋ/ n vocation f.

callous /'kæləs/ adj inhumain.

calm /kɑ:m/ adj calme. ● n calme m. ● vt/i ~ **(down)** (se) calmer.

calorie /'kælərɪ/ n calorie f.

camcorder /'kæmkɔ:də(r)/ n caméscope® m.

came /keɪm/ ➡COME.

camel /'kæml/ n chameau m.

camera /'kæmərə/ n appareil(-photo) m; (TV, cinema) caméra f; **in ~** à huis clos. ~**man** n (pl -**men**) cadreur m, cameraman m.

camouflage /'kæməflɑ:ʒ/ n camouflage m. ● vt camoufler.

camp /kæmp/ n camp m. ● vi camper.

campaign /kæm'peɪn/ n campagne f. ● vi faire campagne.

camper /'kæmpə(r)/ n campeur/-euse m/f. ~ **(-van)** n camping-car m.

camping /'kæmpɪŋ/ n camping m; **go ~** faire du camping.

campsite /'kæmpsaɪt/ n camping m.

campus /'kæmpəsɪz/ n (pl ~**es**) campus m.

---

can¹ /kæn, kən/

> *infinitive* **be able to**; *present* **can**; *present negative* **can't, cannot** (*formal*); *past* **could**; *past participle* **been able to**

● *auxiliary verb*

····▸ pouvoir; **where ~ I buy stamps?** où est-ce que je peux acheter des timbres?; **she can't come** elle ne peut pas venir.

····▸ (be allowed to) pouvoir; ~ **I smoke?** est-ce que je peux fumer?

····▸ (know how to) savoir; **she ~ swim** elle sait nager; **he can't drive** il ne sait pas conduire.

····▸ (with verbs of perception) **I ~ hear you** je t'entends; ~ **they see us?** est-ce qu'ils nous voient?

---

can² /kæn/ n (for food) boîte f; (of petrol) bidon m. ● vt (pt **canned**) mettre en conserve.

Canada /'kænədə/ n Canada m.

Canadian /kə'neɪdɪən/ n Canadien/-ne m/f. ● adj canadien.

canal /kə'næl/ n canal m.

canary /kə'neərɪ/ n canari m.

cancel /'kænsl/ vt/i (pt **cancelled**) (call off, revoke) annuler; (cross out) barrer; (a stamp) oblitérer; ~ **out** (se) neutraliser. **cancellation** n annulation f.

cancer /'kænsə(r)/ n cancer m; **have ~** avoir un cancer.

Cancer /'kænsə(r)/ n Cancer m.

cancerous /'kænsərəs/ adj cancéreux.

candid /'kændɪd/ adj franc.

candidate /'kændɪdət/ n candidat/-e m/f.

candle /'kændl/ n bougie f; (in church) cierge m. ~**stick** n bougeoir m.

candy /'kændɪ/ *n* (US) bonbon(s) *m(pl)*. **~-floss** *n* barbe *f* à papa.

cane /keɪn/ *n* canne *f*; (for baskets) rotin *m*; (for punishment) badine *f*. ● *vt* donner des coups de badine à.

canister /'kænɪstə(r)/ *n* boîte *f*.

cannabis /'kænəbɪs/ *n* cannabis *m*.

cannibal /'kænɪbl/ *n* cannibale *mf*.

cannon /'kænən/ *n* (*pl* ~ *or* ~**s**) canon *m*. **~-ball** *n* boulet *m* de canon.

cannot ➡**CAN NOT**.

canoe /kə'nuː/ *n* canoë *m*. ● *vi* faire du canoë. **canoeist** *n* canoéiste *mf*.

canon /'kænən/ *n* (clergyman) chanoine *m*; (rule) canon *m*.

can-opener *n* ouvre-boîtes *m inv*.

canopy /'kænəpɪ/ *n* dais *m*; (for bed) baldaquin *m*.

can't ➡**CAN NOT**.

canteen /kæn'tiːn/ *n* (restaurant) cantine *f*; (flask) bidon *m*.

canter /'kæntə(r)/ *n* petit galop *m*. ● *vi* aller au petit galop.

canvas /'kænvəs/ *n* toile *f*.

canvass /'kænvəs/ *vt/i* (Comm, Pol) faire du démarchage (auprès de); ~ **opinion** sonder l'opinion.

canyon /'kænjən/ *n* cañon *m*.

cap /kæp/ *n* (hat) casquette *f*; (of bottle, tube) bouchon *m*; (of beer or milk bottle) capsule *f*; (of pen) capuchon *m*; (for toy gun) amorce *f*. ● *vt* (*pt* **capped**) couronner.

capability /keɪpə'bɪlətɪ/ *n* capacité *f*.

capable /'keɪpəbl/ *adj* (person) compétent; ~ **of doing** capable de faire.

capacity /kə'pæsətɪ/ *n* capacité *f*; **in my ~ as a doctor** en ma qualité de médecin.

cape /keɪp/ *n* (cloak) cape *f*; (Geog) cap *m*.

caper /'keɪpə(r)/ *vi* gambader. ● *n* (leap) cabriole *f*; (funny film) comédie *f*; (Culin) câpre *f*.

capital /'kæpɪtl/ *adj* (letter) majuscule; (offence) capital. ● *n* (town) capitale *f*; (money) capital *m*; ~ **(letter)** majuscule *f*.

capitalism /'kæpɪtəlɪzəm/ *n* capitalisme *m*.

capitalize /'kæpɪtəlaɪz/ *vi* ~ **on** tirer parti de.

Capitol Hill Ce quartier historique de Washington D.C. abrite le bâtiment du Capitole, dans lequel se réunit le Congrès depuis 1800, la cour suprême fédérale, plus haute instance judiciaire des États-Unis, et la bibliothèque du Congrès, l'une des plus grandes au monde. Par métonymie, *the Capitol* ou *the Hill* font référence au Congrès. ▷**CONGRESS**

capitulate /kə'pɪtʃʊleɪt/ *vi* capituler.

Capricorn /'kæprɪkɔːn/ *n* Capricorne *m*.

capsize /kæp'saɪz/ *vt/i* (faire) chavirer.

capsule /'kæpsjuːl/ *n* capsule *f*.

captain /'kæptɪn/ *n* capitaine *m*.

caption /'kæpʃn/ *n* (under photo) légende *f*; (subtitle) sous-titre *m*.

captivate /'kæptɪveɪt/ *vt* captiver.

captive /'kæptɪv/ *adj* & *n* captif/-ive (*m/f*). **captivity** *n* captivité *f*.

capture /'kæptʃə(r)/ *vt* (person, animal) capturer; (moment, likeness) saisir. ● *n* capture *f*.

car /kɑː(r)/ *n* voiture *f*. ● *adj* (industry) automobile; (accident) de voiture; (journey) en voiture.

caravan /'kærəvæn/ *n* caravane *f*.

carbohydrate /kɑːbə'haɪdreɪt/ *n* hydrate *m* de carbone.

carbon /'kɑːbən/ *n* carbone *m*. ~ **footprint** empreinte *f* écologique.

carburettor /'kɑːrbəreɪtər/ *n* carburateur *m*.

card /kɑːd/ *n* carte *f*.

cardboard /'kɑːdbɔːd/ *n* carton *m*.

cardiac /'kɑːdɪæk/ *adj* cardiaque; ~ **arrest** arrêt *m* du cœur.

cardigan /'kɑːdɪɡən/ *n* cardigan *m*.

carer /'keərə(r)/ *n* (relative) *personne ayant un parent handicapé ou un malade à charge*; (professional) aide *f* à la domicile.

cardinal /'keərə(r)/ *adj* (sin) capital; (rule) fondamental; (number) cardinal. ● *n* cardinal *m*.

card index *n* fichier *m*.

care /keə(r)/ *n* (attention) soin *m*, attention *f*; (worry) souci *m*; (looking after) soins *mpl*; **take ~ of** (deal with) s'occuper de; (be careful with) prendre soin de; **take ~ to do sth** faire

bien attention à faire qch. ● *vi* ~
about s'intéresser à; ~ **for** s'occuper
de; (*invalid*) soigner; ~ **to do** vouloir
faire; **I don't** ~ ça m'est égal.

career /kə'rɪə(r)/ *n* carrière *f*. ● *vi* ~
in/out entrer/sortir à toute vitesse.

carefree /'keəfri:/ *adj* insouciant.

careful /'keəfl/ *adj* prudent; (*research,
study*) méticuleux; **(be)** ~**!** (fais) attention! **carefully** *adv* avec soin; (*cautiously*) prudemment.

careless /'keəlɪs/ *adj* négligent; (*work*)
bâclé.

caress /kə'res/ *n* caresse *f*. ● *vt* caresser.

caretaker /'keəteɪkə(r)/ *n* concierge
mf. ● *adj* (*president*) par intérim.

car ferry *n* ferry *m*.

cargo /'kɑːɡəʊ/ *n* (*pl* ~**es**) chargement
m; (Naut) cargaison *f*.

Caribbean /kærɪ'biːən/ *adj* des Caraïbes, des Antilles. ● *n* **the** ~ (*sea*) la
mer des Antilles; (*islands*) les Antilles *fpl*.

caring /'keərɪŋ/ *adj* affectueux.

carnation /kɑː'neɪʃn/ *n* œillet *m*.

carnival /'kɑːnɪvl/ *n* carnaval *m*.

carol /'kærəl/ *n* chant *m* de Noël.

carp /kɑːp/ *n inv* carpe *f*. ● *vi* maugréer.

car-park *n* parc *m* de stationnement,
parking *m*.

carpenter /'kɑːpəntə(r)/ *n* (*joiner*) menuisier *m*; (*builder*) charpentier *m*. **carpentry** *n* menuiserie *f*; (*structural*)
charpenterie *f*.

carpet /'kɑːpɪt/ *n* (*fitted*) moquette *f*;
(*loose*) tapis *m*. ● *vt* (*pt* **carpeted**)
mettre de la moquette dans.

carriage /'kærɪdʒ/ *n* (*rail*) wagon *m*;
(*ceremonial*) carrosse *m*; (*of goods*)
transport *m*; (*cost*) port *m*.

carriageway /'kærɪdʒweɪ/ *n*
chaussée *f*.

carrier /'kærɪə(r)/ *n* transporteur *m*;
(Med) porteur/-euse *m/f*; ~ **(bag)** sac
m en plastique.

carrot /'kærət/ *n* carotte *f*.

carry /'kærɪ/ *vt/i* porter; (*goods*) transporter; (*involve*) comporter; (*motion*)
voter; **be carried away** s'emballer.
□ ~ **off** emporter; (*prize*) remporter;
~ **on** (*continue*) continuer; (*business*)
conduire; (*conversation*) mener; ~ **out**
(*order, plan*) exécuter; (*duty*) remplir;

(*experiment, operation, repair*) effectuer. ~**-cot** *n* portebébé *m*.

car sharing *n* covoiturage *m*.

cart /kɑːt/ *n* charrette *f*. ● *vt* (*heavy bag*
🔢) trimballer 🔢.

carton /'kɑːtn/ *n* (*box*) boîte *f*; (*of yoghurt, cream*) pot *m*; (*of cigarettes*) cartouche *f*.

cartoon /kɑː'tuːn/ *n* dessin *m* humoristique; (*cinema*) dessin *m* animé; (*strip
cartoon*) bande *f* dessinée.

cartridge /'kɑːtrɪdʒ/ *n* cartouche *f*.

carve /kɑːv/ *vt* tailler; (*meat*) découper.

car-wash *n* lavage *m* automatique.

cascade /kæ'skeɪd/ *n* cascade *f*. ● *vi*
tomber en cascade.

case /keɪs/ *n* cas *m*; (Jur) affaire *f*; (*suitcase*) valise *f*; (*crate*) caisse *f*; (*for spectacles*) étui *m*; (*just*) **in** ~ au cas où;
in ~ **he comes** au cas où il viendrait;
in ~ **of fire** en cas d'incendie; **in any**
~ de toute façon; **the** ~ **for sth** les
arguments *mpl* en faveur de qch; **the**
~ **for the defence** la défense.

cash /kæʃ/ *n* espèces *fpl*, argent *m*; **in**
~ en espèces. ● *adj* (*price*) comptant.
● *vt* encaisser; ~ **in (on)** profiter (de).
~**-back** *n* retrait *m* d'argent à la
caisse. ~ **desk** *n* caisse *f*. ~ **dispenser** *n* distributeur *m* de billets.

cashew /'kæʃuː/ *n* cajou *m*.

cash flow *n* marge *f* brute d'auto-
financement.

cashier /kæ'ʃɪə(r)/ *n* caissier/-ière *m/f*.

cashmere /kæʃ'mɪə(r)/ *n* cache-
mire *m*.

cash: ~**point** *n* distributeur *m* de
billets. ~ **point card** *n* carte *f* de retrait. ~ **register** *n* caisse *f* enregistreuse.

casino /kə'siːnəʊ/ *n* casino *m*.

casket /'kɑːskɪt/ *n* (*box*) coffret *m*;
(*coffin*) cercueil *m*.

casserole /'kæsərəʊl/ *n* (*pan*) daubière
f; (*food*) ragoût *m*.

cassette /kə'set/ *n* cassette *f*.

cast /kɑːst/ *vt* (*pt* **cast**) (*object, glance*)
jeter; (*shadow*) projeter; (*metal*) cou-
ler; ~ **(off)** (*shed*) se dépouiller de; ~
one's vote voter; ~ **iron** fonte *f*. ● *n*
(*cinema, Theat, TV*) distribution *f*;
(*Med*) plâtre *m*.

castaway /'kɑːstəweɪ/ *n* naufragé/-
e *m/f*.

cast-iron *adj* de fonte; (fig) en béton.

castle /'kɑːsl/ *n* château *m*; (chess) tour *f*.

cast-offs *npl* vieux vêtements *mpl*.

castor /'kɑːstə(r)/ *n* (wheel) roulette *f*.

castrate /kæ'streɪt/ *vt* châtrer.

casual /'kæʒʊəl/ *adj* (informal) décontracté; (*remark*) désinvolte; (*acquaintance*) de passage; (*work*) temporaire. **casually** *adv* d'un air détaché; (*dress*) simplement.

casualty /'kæʒʊəltɪ/ *n* victime *f*; (part of hospital) urgences *fpl*.

cat /kæt/ *n* chat *m*; (feline) félin *m*.

catalogue /'kætəlɒg/ *n* catalogue *m*. ● *vt* dresser un catalogue de.

catalyst /'kætəlɪst/ *n* catalyseur *m*.

catalytic /kætə'lɪtɪk/ *adj* ∼ **converter** pot *m* catalytique.

catapult /'kætəpʌlt/ *n* lance-pierres *m inv*. ● *vt* projeter.

cataract /'kætərækt/ *n* (Med, Geog) cataracte *f*.

catarrh /kə'tɑː(r)/ *n* catarrhe *m*.

catastrophe /kə'tæstrəfɪ/ *n* catastrophe *f*.

catch /kætʃ/ *vt* (*pt* **caught**) attraper; (*bus, plane*) prendre; (understand) saisir; ∼ **sb doing** surprendre qn en train de faire; ∼ **fire** prendre feu; ∼ **sight of** apercevoir; ∼ **sb's attention/eye** attirer l'attention de qn. ● *vi* (get stuck) se prendre (**in** dans); (start to burn) prendre. ● *n* (fastening) fermeture *f*; (drawback) piège *m*; (in sport) prise *f*. ∼ **on** devenir populaire. ∼ **out** prendre de court. ∼ **up** rattraper son retard; ∼ **up with sb** rattraper qn.

catching /'kætʃɪŋ/ *adj* contagieux.

catchment /'kætʃmənt/ *n* ∼ **area** (School) secteur *m*.

catch-phrase *n* formule *f* favorite.

catchy /'kætʃɪ/ *adj* entraînant.

category /'kætəgərɪ/ *n* catégorie *f*.

cater /'keɪtə(r)/ *vi* organiser des réceptions; ∼ **for/to** (*guests*) accueillir; (*needs*) pourvoir à; (*reader*) s'adresser à. **caterer** *n* traiteur *m*.

caterpillar /'kætəpɪlə(r)/ *n* chenille *f*.

cathedral /kə'θiːdrəl/ *n* cathédrale *f*.

catholic /'kæθəlɪk/ *adj* éclectique. **Catholic** *adj* & *n* catholique (*mf*). **Cath-**

olicism *n* catholicisme *m*.

Catseye® *n* plot *m* rétroréfléchissant.

cattle /'kætl/ *npl* bétail *m*.

caught /kɔːt/ →CATCH.

cauliflower /'kɒlɪflaʊə(r)/ *n* chou-fleur *m*.

cause /kɔːz/ *n* cause *f*; (reason) raison *f*, motif *m*. ● *vt* causer; ∼ **sth to grow/move** faire pousser/bouger qch.

causeway /'kɔːzweɪ/ *n* chaussée *f*.

caution /'kɔːʃn/ *n* prudence *f*; (warning) avertissement *m*. ● *vt* avertir. **cautious** *adj* prudent. **cautiously** *adv* prudemment.

cave /keɪv/ *n* grotte *f*. ● *vi* ∼ **in** s'effondrer; (agree) céder. ∼**man** *n* (*pl* -**men**) homme *m* des cavernes.

cavern /'kævən/ *n* caverne *f*.

caviare /'kævɪɑː(r)/ *n* caviar *m*.

caving /'keɪvɪŋ/ *n* spéléologie *f*.

CCTV *abbr* (closed circuit television) télévision *f* en circuit fermé.

CD *abbr* (**compact disc**) disque *m* compact, CD *m*.

CD-ROM /siːdiː'rɒm/ *n* disque *m* optique compact, CD-ROM *m*.

cease /siːs/ *vt/i* cesser. ∼-**fire** *n* cessez-le-feu *m inv*.

cedar /'siːdə(r)/ *n* cèdre *m*.

cedilla /sɪ'dɪlə/ *n* cédille *f*.

ceiling /'siːlɪŋ/ *n* plafond *m*.

celebrate /'selɪbreɪt/ *vt* (occasion) fêter; (Easter, mass) célébrer. ● *vi* faire la fête. **celebrated** *adj* célèbre. **celebration** *n* fête *f*.

celebrity /sɪ'lebrətɪ/ *n* célébrité *f*.

celery /'selərɪ/ *n* céleri *m*.

cell /sel/ *n* cellule *f*; (Electr) élément *m*.

cellar /'selə(r)/ *n* cave *f*.

cellist /'tʃelɪst/ *n* violoncelliste *mf*. **cello** *n* violoncelle *m*.

cellphone /'selfəʊn/ *n* (téléphone *m*) portable.

Celt /kelt/ *n* Celte *mf*.

cement /sɪ'ment/ *n* ciment *m*. ● *vt* cimenter. ∼-**mixer** *n* bétonnière *f*.

cemetery /'semətrɪ/ *n* cimetière *m*.

censor /'sensə(r)/ *n* censeur *m*. ● *vt* censurer.

censure /'senʃə(r)/ *n* censure *f*. ● *vt* critiquer.

census /'sensəs/ *n* recensement *m*.

cent /sent/ *n* cent *m*.

C

centenary /sen'ti:nərı/ n centenaire m.

centigrade /'sentıgreıd/ adj centigrade.

centilitre, (US) **centiliter** /'sentıli:tə(r)/ n centilitre m.

centimetre, (US) **centimeter** /'sentımi:tə(r)/ n centimètre m.

centipede /'sentıpi:d/ n millepattes m inv.

central /'sentrəl/ adj central; ~ **heating** chauffage m central; ~ **locking** fermeture f centralisée des portes. **centralize** vt centraliser. **centrally** adv (situated) au centre.

centre /'sentə(r)/, (US) **center** n centre m. ● vt (pt **centred**) centrer. ● vi ~ **on** tourner autour de.

century /'sentʃərı/ n siècle m.

ceramic /sı'ræmık/ adj (art) céramique; (object) en céramique.

cereal /'sıərıəl/ n céréale f.

ceremonial /serı'məunıəl/ adj (dress) de cérémonie. ● n cérémonial m. **ceremony** n cérémonie f.

certain /'sз:tn/ adj certain; for ~ avec certitude; **make** ~ **of** s'assurer de. **certainly** adv certainement. **certainty** n certitude f.

certificate /sə'tıfıkət/ n certificat m.

certify /'sз:tıfaı/ vt certifier.

cesspit, cesspool /'sespıt, 'sespu:l/ n fosse f d'aisances.

chafe /tʃeıf/ vt/i frotter (contre).

chagrin /'ʃægrın/ n dépit m.

chain /tʃeın/ n chaîne f; ~ **reaction** réaction f en chaîne; ~ **store** magasin m à succursales multiples. ● vt enchaîner. ~**-smoke** vi fumer sans arrêt.

chair /tʃeə(r)/ n chaise f; (armchair) fauteuil m; (Univ) chaire f; (chairperson) président/-e m/f. ● vt (preside over) présider. ~**man** n (pl **-men**) président/-e m/f. ~**woman** n (pl **-women**) présidente f.

chalk /tʃɔ:k/ n craie f.

challenge /'tʃælındʒ/ n défi m; (opportunity) challenge m. ● vt (summon) défier (**to do** de faire); (question truth of) contester. **challenger** n (Sport) challenger m. **challenging** adj stimulant.

chamber /'tʃeımbə(r)/ n (old use) chambre f. ~**maid** n femme f de chambre. ~ **music** n musique f de chambre. ~**-pot** n pot m de chambre.

champagne /ʃæm'peın/ n champagne m.

champion /'tʃæmpıən/ n champion/-ne m/f. ● vt défendre. **championship** n championnat m.

chance /tʃɑ:ns/ n (luck) hasard m; (opportunity) occasion f; (likelihood) chances fpl; (risk) risque m; **by** ~ par hasard; **by any** ~ par hasard; ~**s are that** il est probable que. ● adj fortuit. ● vt ~ **doing** prendre le risque de faire; ~ **it** tenter sa chance.

chancellor /'tʃɑ:nsələ(r)/ n chancelier m; C~ **of the Exchequer** Chancelier de l'échiquier.

chandelier /ʃændə'lıə(r)/ n lustre m.

change /tʃeındʒ/ vt (alter) changer; (exchange) échanger (**for** contre). (money) changer; ~ **trains/one's dress** changer de train/de robe; ~ **one's mind** changer d'avis. ● vi changer; (change clothes) se changer; ~ **into** se transformer en; ~ **over** passer (**to** à). ● n changement m; (money) monnaie f; **a** ~ **for the better** une amélioration; **a** ~ **for the worse** un changement en pire; **a** ~ **of clothes** des vêtements de rechange; **for a** ~ pour changer. **changeable** adj changeant. **changing room** n (in shop) cabine f d'essayage; (Sport) vestiaire m.

channel /'tʃænl/ n (for liquid, information) canal m; (TV) chaîne f; (groove) rainure f. ● vt (pt **channelled**) canaliser. C~ **the (English)** C~ la Manche; **the** C~ **tunnel** le tunnel sous la Manche; **the** C~ **Islands** les îles fpl Anglo-Normandes

chant /tʃɑ:nt/ n (Relig) mélopée f; (of demonstrators) chant m scandé. ● vt/i scander; (Relig) psalmodier.

chaos /'keıɒs/ n chaos m.

chap /tʃæp/ n (man 🆒) type m 🆒

chapel /'tʃæpl/ n chapelle f.

chaplain /'tʃæplın/ n aumônier m.

chapped /tʃæpt/ adj gercé.

chapter /'tʃæptə(r)/ n chapitre m.

char /tʃɑ:(r)/ vt (pt **charred**) carboniser.

character /'kærəktə(r)/ n caractère m; (in novel, play) personnage m; **of good** ~ de bonne réputation.

characteristic /kærəktəˈrɪstɪk/ *adj* & *n* caractéristique (*f*).

charcoal /ˈtʃɑːkəʊl/ *n* charbon *m* de bois; (art) fusain *m*.

charge /tʃɑːdʒ/ *n* (fee) frais *mpl*; (Mil) charge *f*; (Jur) inculpation *f*; (task, custody) charge *f*; **in ~ of** responsable de; **take ~ of** prendre en charge, se charger de. ● *vt* (customer) faire payer; (enemy, gun) charger; (Jur) inculper (**with** de); **~ £20 an hour** prendre 20 livres de l'heure; **~ card** carte *f* d'achat. ● *vi* faire payer; (bull) foncer; (person) se précipiter.

charisma /kəˈrɪzmə/ *n* charisme *m*. **charismatic** *adj* charismatique.

charitable /ˈtʃærɪtəbl/ *adj* charitable. **charity** *n* charité *f*; (organization) organisation *f* caritative.

charm /tʃɑːm/ *n* charme *m*; (trinket) amulette *f*. ● *vt* charmer. **charming** *adj* charmant.

chart /tʃɑːt/ *n* (graph) graphique *m*; (table) tableau *m*; (map) carte *f*. ● *vt* (route) porter sur la carte.

charter /ˈtʃɑːtə(r)/ *n* charte *f*; **~ (flight)** charter *m*. ● *vt* affréter; **~ed accountant** expert-comptable *m*.

chase /tʃeɪs/ *vt* poursuivre; **~ away** or **off** chasser. ● *vi* courir (**after** après). ● *n* chasse *f*.

chassis /ˈʃæsɪ/ *n* châssis *m*.

chastise /tʃæˈstaɪz/ *vt* châtier.

chat /tʃæt/ *n* conversation *f*; (on Internet) causette *f*, bavardage *m*; **have a ~** bavarder; **~ show** talk-show *m*. **~room** *n* salle *f* de causette, salle *f* de bavardage. ● *vi* (*pt* **chatted**) bavarder. **~ up** 🔲 draguer 🔲.

chatter /ˈtʃætə(r)/ *n* bavardage *m*. ● *vi* bavarder; **his teeth are ~ing** il claque des dents. **~box** *n* bavard/-e *m/f*.

chatty /ˈtʃætɪ/ *adj* bavard.

chauffeur /ˈʃəʊfə(r)/ *n* chauffeur *m*.

chauvinist /ˈʃəʊvɪnɪst/ *n* chauvin/-e *m/f*. **macho** *m*.

cheap /tʃiːp/ *adj* bon marché *inv*; (fare, rate) réduit; (joke, gimmick) facile; **~er** meilleur marché *inv*. **cheapen** *vt* déprécier. **cheaply** *adv* à bas prix.

cheat /tʃiːt/ *vi* tricher. ● *vt* tromper. ● *n* tricheur/-euse *m/f*.

check /tʃek/ *vt/i* vérifier; (tickets, rises, inflation) contrôler; (stop) arrêter; (tick

off: US) cocher. ● *n* contrôle *m*; (curb) frein *m*; (chess) échec *m*; (pattern) carreaux *mpl*; (bill: US) addition *f*; (cheque: US) chèque *m*. **~ in** remplir la fiche; (at airport) enregistrer; **~ out** partir; **~ sth out** vérifier qch. **~ up** vérifier. **~ up on** (story) vérifier; (person) faire une enquête sur.

check: ~-in *n* enregistrement *m*. **checking account** *n* (US) compte *m* courant. **~-list** *n* liste *f* de contrôle. **~mate** *n* échec *m* et mat. **~-out** *n* caisse *f*. **~-point** *n* contrôle *m*. **~-up** *n* examen *m* médical.

cheek /tʃiːk/ *n* joue *f*; (impudence) culot *m* 🔲. **cheeky** *adj* effronté.

cheer /tʃɪə(r)/ *n* gaieté *f*; **~s** acclamations *fpl*; (when drinking) à la vôtre. ● *vt/i* applaudir; **~ sb (up)** (gladden) remonter le moral à qn; **~ up** prendre courage. **cheerful** *adj* joyeux. **cheerfulness** *n* gaieté *f*.

cheerio /tʃɪərɪˈəʊ/ *interj* 🔲 salut 🔲.

cheese /tʃiːz/ *n* fromage *m*.

cheetah /ˈtʃiːtə/ *n* guépard *m*.

chef /ʃef/ *n* chef *m*.

chemical /ˈkemɪkl/ *adj* chimique. ● *n* produit *m* chimique.

chemist /ˈkemɪst/ *n* pharmacien/-ne *m/f*; (scientist) chimiste *mf*; **~'s (shop)** pharmacie *f*. **chemistry** *n* chimie *f*.

cheque /tʃek/ *n* chèque *m*. **~-book** *n* chéquier *m*. **~ card** *n* carte *f* bancaire.

chequered /ˈtʃekəd/ *adj* (pattern) à damiers; (fig) en dents de scie.

cherish /ˈtʃerɪʃ/ *vt* chérir; (hope) caresser.

cherry /ˈtʃerɪ/ *n* cerise *f*; (tree, wood) cerisier *m*.

chess /tʃes/ *n* échecs *mpl*. **~-board** *n* échiquier *m*.

chest /tʃest/ *n* (Anat) poitrine *f*; (box) coffre *m*; **~ of drawers** commode *f*.

chestnut /ˈtʃesnʌt/ *n* (nut) marron *m*, châtaigne *f*; (tree) marronnier *m*; (sweet) châtaignier *m*.

chew /tʃuː/ *vt* mâcher.

chic /ʃiːk/ *adj* chic *inv*.

chick /tʃɪk/ *n* poussin *m*.

chicken /ˈtʃɪkɪn/ *n* poulet *m*. ● *adj* 🔲 froussard. ● *vi* **~ out** 🔲 se dégonfler. **~-pox** *n* varicelle *f*.

chick-pea /ˈtʃɪkpiː/*n* pois *m* chiche.

chicory /'tʃɪkərɪ/ n (for salad) endive f; (in coffee) chicorée f.

chief /tʃi:f/ n chef m. ● adj principal. **chiefly** adv principalement.

chilblain /'tʃɪlbleɪn/ n engelure f.

child /tʃaɪld/ n (pl **children**) enfant mf. **~birth** n accouchement m. **childhood** n enfance f. **childish** adj puéril. **childless** adj sans enfants. **childlike** adj enfantin. **~-minder** n nourrice f.

Chile /'tʃɪlɪən/ n Chili m.

chill /tʃɪl/ n froid m; (Med) refroidissement m. ● adj froid. ● vt (person) faire frissonner; (wine) rafraîchir; (food) mettre à refroidir.

chilli /'tʃɪlɪ/ n (pl **~es**) piment m.

chilly /'tʃɪlɪ/ adj froid; **it's ~** il fait froid.

chime /tʃaɪm/ n carillon m. ● vt/i carillonner.

chimney /'tʃɪmnɪ/ n cheminée f. **~-sweep** n ramoneur m.

chimpanzee /tʃɪmpən'zi:/ n chimpanzé m.

chin /tʃɪn/ n menton m.

china /'tʃaɪnə/ n porcelaine f.

China /'tʃaɪnə/ n Chine f.

Chinese /tʃaɪ'ni:z/ n (person) Chinois/-e m/f; (Ling) chinois m. ● adj chinois.

chip /tʃɪp/ n (on plate) ébréchure f; (piece) éclat m; (of wood) copeau m; (Culin) frite f; (Comput) puce f; (**potato**) **~s** (US) chips fpl. ● vt/i (pt **chipped**) (s')ébrécher; **~ in** 🔲 dire son mot; (with money) contribuer.

chiropodist /kɪ'rɒpədɪst/ n pédicure mf.

chirp /tʃɜ:p/ n pépiement m. ● vi pépier. **chirpy** adj gai.

chisel /'tʃɪzl/ n ciseau m. ● vt (pt **chiselled**) ciseler.

chit /tʃɪt/ n note f; (voucher) bon m.

chitchat /'tʃɪttʃæt/ n 🔲 bavardage m.

chivalrous /'ʃɪvəlrəs/ adj galant.

chives /tʃaɪvz/ npl ciboulette f.

chlorine /'klɔ:ri:n/ n chlore m.

choc ice /'tʃɒkaɪs/ n esquimau m.

chock-a-block /tʃɒkə'blɒk/ adj plein à craquer.

chocolate /'tʃɒklət/ n chocolat m.

choice /tʃɔɪs/ n choix m. ● adj de choix.

choir /'kwaɪə(r)/ n chœur m. **~boy** n jeune choriste m.

choke /tʃəʊk/ vt/i (s')étrangler; **~ (up)** boucher. ● n starter m.

cholesterol /kə'lestərɒl/ n cholestérol m.

choose /tʃu:z/ vt/i (pt **chose**. pp **chosen**) choisir; **~ to do** décider de faire. **choosy** adj difficile.

chop /tʃɒp/ vt/i (pt **chopped**) (wood) couper; (food) hacher; **chopping board** planche f à découper; **~ down** abattre. ● n (meat) côtelette f. **chopper** n hachoir m. 🔲 hélico m 🔲.

choppy /'tʃɒpɪ/ adj (sea) agité.

chopstick /'tʃɒpstɪk/ n baguette f (chinoise).

chord /kɔ:d/ n (Mus) accord m.

chore /tʃɔ:(r)/ n (routine) tâche f; (unpleasant) corvée f.

chortle /'tʃɔ:tl/ n gloussement m. ● vi glousser.

chorus /'kɔ:rəs/ n chœur m; (of song) refrain m.

chose, chosen /tʃəʊz, 'tʃəʊzən/ **⟹CHOOSE.**

Christ /kraɪst/ n le Christ.

christen /'krɪsn/ vt baptiser. **christening** n baptême m.

Christian /'krɪstʃən/ adj & n chrétien/-ne (m/f). **~ name** nom m de baptême. **Christianity** n christianisme m.

Christmas /'krɪsməs/ n Noël m; **~ Day/Eve** le jour/la veille de Noël. ● adj (card, tree) de Noël.

chronic /'krɒnɪk/ adj (situation, disease) chronique; (bad 🔲) nul.

chronicle /'krɒnɪkl/ n chronique f.

chronological /krɒnə'lɒdʒɪkl/ adj chronologique.

chrysanthemum /krɪ'sænθəməm/ n chrysanthème m.

chubby /'tʃʌbɪ/ adj (**-ier, -iest**) potelé.

chuck /tʃʌk/ vt 🔲 lancer; **~ away** or **out** 🔲 balancer.

chuckle /'tʃʌkl/ n gloussement m. ● vi glousser.

chuffed /tʃʌft/ adj 🔲 vachement content 🔲.

chunk /tʃʌŋk/ n morceau m. **chunky** adj (sweater, jewellery) gros; (person) costaud.

church /tʃɜ:tʃ/ n église f. **~ goer** n pratiquant/-e m/f. **~yard** n cimetière m.

churn /tʃɜːn/ n baratte f; (milk-can) bidon m. ● vt baratter; ~ **out** produire en série.

chute /ʃuːt/ n toboggan m; (for rubbish) vide-ordures m inv.

chutney /ˈtʃʌtnɪ/ n condiment m aigredoux.

cider /ˈsaɪdə(r)/ n cidre m.

cigar /sɪˈgɑː(r)/ n cigare m.

cigarette /sɪgəˈret/ n cigarette f; ~ **end** mégot m.

cinder /ˈsɪndə(r)/ n cendre f.

cinema /ˈsɪnəmə/ n cinéma m.

cinnamon /ˈsɪnəmən/ n cannelle f.

circle /ˈsɜːkl/ n cercle m; (Theat) balcon m. ● vt (go round) tourner autour de; (word, error) encercler. ● vi tourner en rond.

circuit /ˈsɜːkɪt/ n circuit m. ~ **board** n carte f de circuit imprimé. ~**-breaker** n disjoncteur m.

circuitous /sɜːˈkjuːɪtəs/ adj indirect.

circular /ˈsɜːkjʊlə(r)/ adj & n circulaire (f).

circulate /ˈsɜːkjʊleɪt/ vt/i (faire) circuler. **circulation** n circulation f; (of newspaper) tirage m.

circumcise /ˈsɜːkəmsaɪz/ vt circoncire.

circumference /səˈkʌmfərəns/ n circonférence f.

circumflex /ˈsɜːkəmfleks/ n circonflexe m.

circumstance /ˈsɜːkəmstəns/ n circonstance f; ~s (financial) situation f; **under no** ~s en aucun cas.

circus /ˈsɜːkəs/ n cirque m.

cistern /ˈsɪstən/ n réservoir m.

citizen /ˈsɪtɪzn/ n citoyen/-ne m/f; (of town) habitant/-e m/f. **citizenship** n nationalité f.

citrus /ˈsɪtrəs/ adj ~ **fruit(s)** agrumes mpl; ~ **tree** citrus m.

city /ˈsɪtɪ/ n (grande) ville f.

The City Quartier londonien des affaires et de la finance, la *City* est le siège des grandes banques, des compagnies d'assurance et de la plupart des sociétés d'agents de change. 500 000 personnes viennent y travailler chaque jour.   *i*

---

civic /ˈsɪvɪk/ adj (official) municipal; (pride, duty) civique.

civil /ˈsɪvl/ adj civil. ~ **disobedience** n résistance f passive. ~ **engineer** n ingénieur m des travaux publics.

civilian /sɪˈvɪlɪən/ adj & n civil/-e (m/f).

civilization /sɪvəlaɪˈzeɪʃn/ n civilisation f. **civilize** vt civiliser.

civil: ~ **law** n droit m civil. ~ **liberties** npl libertés fpl individuelles. ~ **rights** npl droits mpl civils. ~ **servant** n fonctionnaire mf. ~ **service** n fonction f publique. ~ **war** n guerre f civile.

claim /kleɪm/ vt (demand) revendiquer; (assert) prétendre. ● n revendication f; (assertion) affirmation f; (for insurance) réclamation f; (right) droit m. **claimant** n (of benefits) demandeur/-euse m/f.

clairvoyant /kleəˈvɔɪənt/ n voyant/-e m/f.

clam /klæm/ n palourde f.

clamber /ˈklæmbə(r)/ vi grimper.

clammy /ˈklæmɪ/ adj (-ier, -iest) moite.

clamour /ˈklæmə(r)/ n clameur f. ● vi ~ **for** réclamer.

clamp /klæmp/ n valet m; (Med) pince f; (wheel) ~ sabot m de Denver. ● vt cramponner; (jaw) serrer; (car) mettre un sabot de Denver à; ~ **down on** faire de la répression contre.

clan /klæn/ n clan m.

clang /ˈklæŋ/ n son m métallique.

clap /klæp/ vt/i (pt **clapped**) applaudir; (put forcibly) mettre; ~ **one's hands** frapper dans ses mains. ● n applaudissement m; (of thunder) coup m.

claret /ˈklærət/ n bordeaux m rouge.

clarification /klærɪfɪˈkeɪʃn/ n clarification f. **clarify** vt/i (se) clarifier.

clarinet /klærəˈnet/ n clarinette f.

clarity /ˈklærətɪ/ n clarté f.

clash /klæʃ/ n choc m; (fig) conflit m. ● vi (metal objects) s'entrechoquer; (armies) s'affronter; (meetings) avoir lieu en même temps; (colours) jurer.

clasp /klɑːsp/ n (fastener) fermoir m. ● vt serrer.

class /klɑːs/ n classe f. ● vt classer; ~ **sb/sth as** assimiler qn/qch à.

classic /ˈklæsɪk/ adj & n classique (m). ~**s** (Univ) lettres fpl classiques. **classical** adj classique.

classified /ˈklæsɪfaɪd/ adj (information) secret; ~ **(ad)** petite annonce f.

classroom /'klɑːsrʊm/ n salle f de classe.

clatter /'klætə(r)/ n cliquetis m. ● vi cliqueter.

clause /klɔːz/ n clause f; (Gram) proposition f.

claw /klɔː/ n (of animal, small bird) griffe f; (of bird of prey) serre f; (of lobster) pince f. ● vt griffer.

clay /kleɪ/ n argile f.

clean /kliːn/ adj propre; (shape, stroke) net. ● adv complètement. ● vt nettoyer; ~ **one's teeth** se brosser les dents. ● vi ~ **up** faire le nettoyage. **cleaner** n (at home) femme f de ménage; (industrial) agent m de nettoyage; (of clothes) teinturier/-ière m/f. **cleanliness** n propreté f. **cleanly** adv proprement; (sharply) nettement.

cleanse /klenz/ vt nettoyer; (fig) purifier.

clean-shaven adj glabre.

clear /klɪə(r)/ adj (explanation) clair; (need, sign) évident; (glass) transparent; (profit) net; (road) dégagé; **make sth ~** être très clair sur qch; ~ **of** (away from) à l'écart de. ● adv complètement; **stand ~ of** s'éloigner de. ● vt (free) dégager (**of** de). (table) débarrasser; (building) évacuer; (cheque) compenser; (jump over) franchir; (debt) liquider; (Jur) disculper. ● vi (fog) se dissiper; (cheque) être compensé. ~ **away** or **off** (remove) enlever. ~ **off** or **out** 🅸 décamper. ~ **out** (clean) nettoyer. ~ **up** (tidy) ranger; (weather) s'éclaircir.

clearance /'klɪərəns/ n (permission) autorisation f; (space) espace m; ~ **sale** liquidation f.

clear-cut adj net.

clearing /'klɪərɪŋ/ n clairière f.

clearly /'klɪəlɪ/ adv clairement.

clef /klef/ n (Mus) clé f.

cleft /kleft/ n fissure f.

clench /klentʃ/ vt serrer.

clergy /'klɜːdʒɪ/ n clergé m. **~man** n (pl **-men**) ecclésiastique m.

cleric /'klerɪk/ n clerc m. **clerical** adj (Relig) clérical; (staff, work) de bureau.

clerk /klɑːk/ n employé/-e m/f de bureau; (US) (sales) ~ vendeur/-euse m/f.

clever /'klevə(r)/ adj intelligent; (skilful) habile.

click /klɪk/ n déclic m; (Comput) clic m. ● vi faire un déclic; (people 🅸) sympathiser; (Comput) cliquer (**on** sur.) ● vt (heels, tongue) faire claquer.

client /'klaɪənt/ n client/-e m/f.

clientele /kliːən'tel/ n clientèle f.

cliff /klɪf/ n falaise f.

climate /'klaɪmɪt/ n climat m. ~ **change** changement m climatique.

climax /'klaɪmæks/ n (of story, contest) point m culminant; (sexual) orgasme m.

climb /klaɪm/ vt grimper; (steps) monter; (tree, ladder) grimper à; (mountain) faire l'ascension de. ● vi grimper; ~ **into** (car) monter dans; ~ **into bed** se mettre au lit. ● n (of mountain) escalade f; (steep hill, rise) montée f. ~ **down** (fig) reculer. **climber** n (Sport) alpiniste mf.

clinch /klɪntʃ/ vt (deal) conclure; (victory, order) décrocher.

cling /klɪŋ/ vi (pt **clung**) se cramponner (**to** à.) (stick) coller. **~-film** n scellofrais® m.

clinic /'klɪnɪk/ n centre m médical; (private) clinique f. **clinical** adj clinique.

clink /klɪŋk/ n tintement m. ● vt/i (faire) tinter.

clip /klɪp/ n (for paper) trombone m; (for hair) barrette f; (for tube) collier m; (of film) extrait m. ● vt (pt **clipped**) (fasten) attacher (**to** à). cut) couper.

clippers /'klɪpəz/ npl tondeuse f; (for nails) coupe-ongles m inv.

clipping /'klɪpɪŋ/ n (from press) coupure f de presse.

cloak /kləʊk/ n cape f; (man's) houppelande f. **~room** n vestiaire m; (toilet) toilettes fpl.

clobber /'klɒbə(r)/ n 🅸 attirail m. ● vt (hit 🅸) tabasser 🅸.

clock /klɒk/ n pendule f; (large) horloge f. ● vi ~ **on/in** or **off/out** pointer; ~ **up** (miles) faire. **~-tower** n beffroi m. **~wise** adj & adv dans le sens des aiguilles d'une montre.

clockwork /'klɒkwɜːk/ n mécanisme m. ● adj mécanique.

clog /klɒg/ n sabot m. ● vt/i (pt **clogged**) (se) boucher.

cloister /'klɔɪstə(r)/ n cloître m.

clone /kləʊn/ n clone m. ● vt cloner.

close¹ /kləʊs/ adj (friend) proche (**to** de). (link) étroit; (examination) minutieux; (match) serré; (weather) lourd; ~ **together** (crowded) serrés; ~ **by**, ~ **at hand** tout près; **have a** ~ **shave** l'échapper belle; **keep a** ~ **watch on** surveiller de près. ● adv près. ● n (street) impasse f.

close² /kləʊz/ vt fermer; (meeting, case) mettre fin à. ● vi se fermer; (shop) fermer; (meeting, play) prendre fin. ● n fin f.

closely /'kləʊslɪ/ adv (follow) de près. **closeness** n proximité f.

closet /'klɒzɪt/ n (US) placard m.

close-up n gros plan m.

closure /'kləʊʒə(r)/ n fermeture f.

clot /klɒt/ n (of blood) caillot m; (in sauce) grumeau m. ● vt/i (pt **clotted**) (se) coaguler.

cloth /klɒθ/ n (fabric) tissu m; (duster) chiffon m; (table-cloth) nappe f.

clothe /kləʊð/ vt vêtir.

clothes /kləʊðz/ npl vêtements mpl. ~**-hanger** n cintre m. ~**-line** n corde f à linge.

clothing /'kləʊðɪŋ/ n vêtements mpl.

cloud /klaʊd/ n nuage m. ● vi ~ **over** se couvrir (de nuages); (face) s'assombrir. **cloudy** adj (sky) couvert; (liquid) trouble.

clout /klaʊt/ n (blow) coup m de poing; (power) influence f. ● vt frapper.

clove /kləʊv/ n clou m de girofle; ~ **of garlic** gousse f d'ail.

clover /'kləʊvə(r)/ n trèfle m.

clown /klaʊn/ n clown m. ● vi faire le clown.

club /klʌb/ n (group) club m; (weapon) massue f; **(golf)** ~ club m (de golf); ~**s** (cards) trèfle m. ● vt/i (pt **clubbed**) matraquer. ~ **together** cotiser.

cluck /klʌk/ vi glousser.

clue /kluː/ n indice m; (in crossword) définition f; **I haven't a** ~ 🄸 je n'en ai pas la moindre idée.

clump /klʌmp/ n massif m.

clumsy /'klʌmzɪ/ adj (**-ier, -iest**) maladroit; (tool) peu commode.

clung /klʌŋ/ ➡**CLING**.

cluster /'klʌstə(r)/ n (of people, islands) groupe m; (of flowers, berries) grappe f. ● vi se grouper.

clutch /klʌtʃ/ vt (hold) serrer fort; (grasp) saisir. ● vi ~ **at** (try to grasp) essayer de saisir. ● n (Auto) embrayage m; (of eggs) couvée f; (of people) groupe m.

clutter /'klʌtə(r)/ n désordre m. ● vt ~ **(up)** encombrer.

coach /kəʊtʃ/ n autocar m; (of train) wagon m; (horse-drawn) carrosse m; (Sport) entraîneur/-euse m/f. ● vt (team) entraîner; (pupil) donner des leçons particulières à.

coal /kəʊl/ n charbon m. ~**field** n bassin m houiller. ~**-mine** n mine f de charbon.

coarse /kɔːs/ adj grossier.

coast /kəʊst/ n côte f. ● vi (car, bicycle) descendre en roue libre. **coastal** adj côtier.

coast: ~**guard** n (person) gardecôte m; (organization) gendarmerie f maritime. ~**line** n littoral m.

coat /kəʊt/ n manteau m; (of animal) pelage m; (of paint) couche f; ~ **of arms** armoiries fpl. ● vt enduire, couvrir; (with chocolate) enrober (**with** de). **coating** n couche f.

coax /kəʊks/ vt cajoler.

cob /kɒb/ n (of corn) épi m.

cobbler /'kɒblə(r)/ n cordonnier m.

cobblestones /'kɒblstəʊnz/ npl pavés mpl.

cobweb /'kɒbweb/ n toile f d'araignée.

cocaine /kəʊ'keɪn/ n cocaïne f.

cock /kɒk/ n (rooster) coq m. (oiseau) mâle m. ● vt (gun) armer; (ears) dresser.

cockerel /'kɒkrəl/ n jeune coq m.

cockle /'kɒkl/ n (Culin) coque f.

cock: ~**pit** n poste m de pilotage. ~**roach** n cafard m. ~**tail** n cocktail m.

cocky /'kɒkɪ/ adj (**-ier, -iest**) trop sûr de soi.

cocoa /'kəʊkəʊ/ n cacao m.

coconut /'kəʊkənʌt/ n noix f de coco.

COD abbr (**cash on delivery**) envoi m contre remboursement.

cod /'kɒd/ n inv morue f; ~**-liver oil** huile f de foie de morue.

code /kəʊd/ n code m. ● vt coder.

coerce /kəʊ'ɜːs/ vt contraindre.

coexist /kəʊɪg'zɪst/ vi coexister.

coffee /'kɒfɪ/ n café m. ~ **bar** n café m. ~ **bean** n grain m de café. ~-**pot** n cafetière f. ~-**table** n table f basse.

coffin /'kɒfɪn/ n cercueil m.

cog /kɒg/ n pignon m; (fig) rouage m.

cognac /'kɒnjæk/ n cognac m.

coil /kɔɪl/ vt/i (s')enrouler. ● n (of rope) rouleau m; (of snake) anneau m; (contraceptive) stérilet m.

coin /kɔɪn/ n pièce f (de monnaie). ● vt (word) inventer.

coincide /kəʊɪn'saɪd/ vi coïncider. **coincidence** n coïncidence f. **coincidental** adj dû à une coïncidence.

colander /'kʌləndə(r)/ n passoire f.

cold /kəʊld/ adj froid; (person) **be** or **feel** ~ avoir froid; **it is** ~ il fait froid; **get** ~ **feet** avoir les jetons 🅣; ~-**blooded** (lit) à sang froid; (fig) sans pitié. ● n froid m; (Med) rhume m; ~ **sore** bouton m de fièvre. **coldness** n froideur f.

coleslaw /'kəʊlslɔː/ n salade f de chou cru.

colic /'kɒlɪk/ n coliques fpl.

collaborate /kə'læbəreɪt/ vi collaborer.

collapse /kə'læps/ vi s'effondrer; (person) s'écrouler; (fold) se plier. ● n effondrement m.

collar /'kɒlə(r)/ n col m; (of dog) collier m. ~-**bone** n clavicule f.

collateral /kə'lætərəl/ n nantissement m.

colleague /'kɒliːg/ n collègue mf.

collect /kə'lekt/ vt rassembler; (pick up) ramasser; (call for) passer prendre; (money, fare) encaisser; (taxes, rent) percevoir; (as hobby) collectionner. ● vi se rassembler; (dust) s'amasser. ● adv **call** ~ (US) appeler en PCV. **collection** n collection f; (of money) collecte f; (in church) quête f; (of mail) levée f.

collective /kə'lektɪv/ adj collectif.

collector /kə'lektə(r)/ n (as hobby) collectionneur/-euse m/f; (of taxes) percepteur m; (of rent, debt) encaisseur m.

college /'kɒlɪdʒ/ n (for higher education) établissement m d'enseignement supérieur; (within university) collège

m; **be at** ~ faire des études supérieures.

collide /kə'laɪd/ vi entrer en collision (with avec).

colliery /'kɒlɪərɪ/ n houillère f.

collision /kə'lɪʒn/ n collision f.

colloquial /kə'ləʊkwɪəl/ adj familier. **colloquialism** n expression f familière.

Colombia /kə'lɒmbɪə/ n Colombie f.

colon /'kəʊlən/ n (Gram) deux-points m inv; (Anat) côlon m.

colonel /'kɜːnl/ n colonel m.

colonial /kə'ləʊnɪəl/ adj & n colonial/-e (m/f).

colour, (US) **color** /'kʌlə(r)/ n couleur f; ~-**blind** daltonien. ● adj (photo) en couleur; (TV set) couleur inv. ● vt colorer; (with crayon) colorier. **coloured** adj de couleur. **colourful** adj aux couleurs vives; (fig) haut en couleur. **colouring** n (of skin) teint m; (in food) colorant m.

colt /kəʊlt/ n poulain m.

column /'kɒləm/ n colonne f.

coma /'kəʊmə/ n coma m.

comb /kəʊm/ n peigne m. ● vt peigner; ~ **one's hair** se peigner; ~ **a place** passer un lieu au peigne fin.

combat /'kɒmbæt/ n combat m. ● vt (pt **combated**) combattre.

combination /kɒmbɪ'neɪʃn/ n combinaison f.

combine¹ /kəm'baɪn/ vt/i (se) combiner, (s')unir.

combine² /'kɒmbaɪn/ n (Comm) groupe m; ~ **harvester** moissonneuse-batteuse f.

come /kʌm/ vi (pt **came**, pp **come**) venir; (bus, letter) arriver; (postman) passer; ~ **and look!** viens voir!; ~ **in** (size, colour) exister en; **when it** ~**s to** lorsqu'il s'agit de. ~ **about** survenir. ~ **across** (meaning) passer; ~ **across sth** tomber sur qch. ~ **away** (leave) partir; (come off) se détacher. ~ **back** revenir. ~ **by** obtenir. ~ **down** descendre; (price) baisser; ~ **forward** se présenter. ~ **in** entrer; ~ **in useful** être utile. ~ **in for** recevoir. ~ **into** (money) hériter de. ~ **off** (succeed) réussir; (fare) s'en tirer; (detach) se détacher. ~ **on** (actor) entrer en scène; (light) s'allumer; (improve) faire des progrès; ~ **on!** allez!. ~ **out** sortir. ~ **round** reprendre connaissance; (change mind) changer d'avis; ~ **through** s'en tirer. ~ **to** reprendre connaissance; ~ **to sth** (amount) revenir à qch; (decision, conclusion) arriver à qch. ~ **up** (problem) être soulevé; (opportunity) se présenter; (sun) se lever; ~ **up against** se heurter à. ~ **up with** trouver.

comedian /kə'miːdɪən/ n comique m.

comedy /'kɒmədɪ/ n comédie f.

comfort /'kʌmfət/ n confort m; (consolation) réconfort m. ● vt consoler. **comfortable** adj (chair, car) confortable; (person) à l'aise; (wealthy) aisé.

comfortably /'kʌmftəblɪ/ adv confortablement; ~ **off** aisé.

comfy /'kʌmfɪ/ adj 🗉 ➡**COMFORTABLE**.

comic /'kɒmɪk/ adj comique. ● n (person) comique m; ~ **(book)**, ~ **strip** bande f dessinée.

coming /'kʌmɪŋ/ n arrivée f; ~**s and goings** allées et venues fpl. ● adj à venir.

comma /'kɒmə/ n virgule f.

command /kə'mɑːnd/ n (authority) commandement m; (order) ordre m; (mastery) maîtrise f. ● vt ordonner à **(to do** de faire); (be able to use) disposer de; (respect) inspirer. **commandeer** vt réquisitionner. **commander** n commandant m. **commanding** adj imposant. **commandment** n commandement m.

commando /kə'mɑːndəʊ/ n commando m.

commemorate /kə'meməreɪt/ vt commémorer.

commence /kə'mens/ vt/i commencer.

commend /kə'mend/ vt (praise) louer; (entrust) confier.

commensurate /kə'menʃərət/ adj proportionné.

comment /'kɒment/ n commentaire m. ● vi faire des commentaires; ~ **on** commenter. **commentary** n commentaire m; (radio, TV) reportage m. **commentate** vi faire un reportage. **commentator** n commentateur/-trice m/f.

commerce /'kɒmɜːs/ n commerce m.

commercial /kə'mɜːʃl/ adj commercial; (traveller) de commerce. ● n publicité f.

commiserate /kə'mɪzəreɪt/ vi compatir (with avec).

commission /kə'mɪʃn/ n commission f; (order for work) commande f; **out of** ~ hors service. ● vt (order) commander; (Mil) nommer officier; ~ **to do** charger de faire. **commissioner** n préfet m (de police); (in EU) membre m de la Commission européenne.

commit /kə'mɪt/ vt (pt **committed**) commettre; (entrust) confier; ~ **oneself** s'engager; ~ **perjury** se parjurer; ~ **suicide** se suicider; ~ **to memory** apprendre par cœur. **commitment** n engagement m.

committee /kə'mɪtɪ/ n comité m.

commodity /kə'mɒdətɪ/ n article m.

common /'kɒmən/ adj (shared by all) commun (**to** à); (usual) courant; (vulgar) vulgaire, commun; **in** ~ en commun; ~ **people** le peuple; ~ **sense** bon sens m. ● n terrain m communal; **the C**~**s** Chambre f des Communes.

commoner /'kɒmənə(r)/ n roturier/-ière m/f.

common law n droit m coutumier.

commonly /'kɒmənlɪ/ adv communément.

commonplace /'kɒmənpleɪs/ adj banal. ● n banalité f.

common-room n salle f de détente.

Commonwealth /'kɒmənwelθ/ n **the** ~ le Commonwealth m.

Commonwealth of Nations Association de nations ayant pour la plupart fait partie de l'empire britannique et qui maintiennent une coopération avec la Grande-Bretagne en matière d'économie, de culture et d'éducation. Des championnats d'athlétisme, les *Commonwealth Games* ont lieu tous les quatre ans. Le mot *Commonwealth* figure dans le nom officiel de quelques États américains (*Kentucky, Virginia, Pennsylvania, Massachusetts*).

commotion /kə'məʊʃn/ n (noise) vacarme m; (disturbance) agitation f.

communal /'kɒmjʊnl/ adj (shared) commun; (life) collectif.

commune /'kɒmjuːn/ n (group) communauté f.

communicate /kə'mju:nɪkeɪt/ *vt/i* communiquer. **communication** *n* communication *f*. **communicative** *adj* communicatif.

communion /kə'mju:nɪən/ *n* communion *f*.

Communism /'kɒmjʊnɪzəm/ *n* communisme *m*. **Communist** *adj & n* communiste (*mf*).

community /kə'mju:nətɪ/ *n* communauté *f*.

commute /kə'mju:t/ *vi* faire la navette. ● *vt* (Jur) commuer. **commuter** *n* navetteur/-euse *m/f*.

compact /kəm'pækt/ *adj* compact; (lady's case) poudrier *m*.

compact disc *n* disque *m* compact. ~ **player** *n* platine *f* laser.

companion /kəm'pænɪən/ *n* compagnon/-agne *m/f*. **companionship** *n* camaraderie *f*.

company /'kʌmpənɪ/ *n* (companionship, firm) compagnie *f*; (guests) invités/-es *m/fpl*.

comparative /kəm'pærətɪv/ *adj* (study, form) comparatif; (comfort) relatif.

compare /kəm'peə(r)/ *vt* comparer (with, to à). ~**d with** par rapport à. ● *vi* être comparable. **comparison** *n* comparaison *f*.

compartment /kəm'pɑ:tmənt/ *n* compartiment *m*.

compass /'kʌmpəs/ *n* (for direction) boussole *f*; (scope) portée *f*; **a pair of** ~**es** un compas.

compassionate /kəm'pæʃənət/ *adj* compatissant.

compatible /kəm'pætəbl/ *adj* compatible.

compel /kəm'pel/ *vt* (*pt* **compelled**) contraindre. **compelling** *adj* irrésistible.

compensate /'kɒmpenseɪt/ *vt/i* (financially) dédommager (for de). ~ **for sth** compenser qch. **compensation** *n* compensation *f*; (financial) dédommagement *m*.

compete /kəm'pi:t/ *vi* concourir; ~ **with** rivaliser avec.

competent /'kɒmpɪtənt/ *adj* compétent.

competition /kɒmpə'tɪʃn/ *n* (contest) concours *m*; (Sport) compétition *f*;

(Comm) concurrence *f*.

competitive /kəm'petɪtɪv/ *adj* (prices) compétitif; (person) qui a l'esprit de compétition.

competitor /kəm'petɪtə(r)/ *n* concurrent/-e *m/f*.

compile /kəm'paɪl/ *vt* (list) dresser; (book) rédiger.

complacency /kəm'pleɪsnsɪ/ *n* suffisance *f*.

complain /kəm'pleɪn/ *vi* se plaindre (**about, of** de). **complaint** *n* plainte *f*; (official) réclamation *f*; (illness) maladie *f*.

complement /'kɒmplɪmənt/ *n* complément *m*. ● *vt* compléter. **complementary** *adj* complémentaire.

complete /kəm'pli:t/ *adj* complet; (finished) achevé; (downright) parfait. ● *vt* achever; (a form) remplir. **completely** *adv* complètement. **completion** *n* achèvement *m*.

complex /'kɒmpleks/ *adj* complexe. ● *n* (Psych) complexe *m*.

complexion /kəm'plekʃn/ *n* (of face) teint *m*; (fig) caractère *m*.

compliance /kəm'plaɪəns/ *n* (agreement) conformité *f*.

complicate /'kɒmplɪkeɪt/ *vt* compliquer. **complicated** *adj* compliqué. **complication** *n* complication *f*.

compliment /'kɒmplɪmənt/ *n* compliment *m*. ● *vt* complimenter. **complimentary** *adj* (offert) à titre gracieux; (praising) flatteur.

comply /kəm'plaɪ/ *vi* ~ **with** se conformer à, obéir à.

component /kəm'pəʊnənt/ *n* (of machine) pièce *f*; (chemical substance) composant *m*; (element: fig) composante *f*. ● *adj* constituant.

compose /kəm'pəʊz/ *vt* composer; ~ **oneself** se calmer. **composed** *adj* calme. **composer** *n* (Mus) compositeur *m*. **composition** *n* composition *f*.

composure /kəm'pəʊʒə(r)/ *n* calme *m*.

compound /'kɒmpaʊnd/ *n* (substance, word) composé *m*; (enclosure) enclos *m*. ● *adj* composé.

comprehend /kɒmprɪ'hend/ *vt* comprendre. **comprehension** *n* compréhension *f*.

comprehensive /kɒmprɪ'hensɪv/ adj étendu, complet; (*insurance*) tous risques *inv.* ~ **school** n collège m d'enseignement secondaire.

compress /kəm'pres/ vt comprimer.

comprise /kəm'praɪz/ vt comprendre, inclure.

compromise /'kɒmprəmaɪz/ n compromis m. ● vt compromettre. ● vi transiger, arriver à un compromis.

compulsive /kəm'pʌlsɪv/ adj (Psych) compulsif; (*liar, smoker*) invétéré.

compulsory /kəm'pʌlsərɪ/ adj obligatoire.

compute /kəm'pjuːt/ vt calculer.

computer /kəm'pjuːt/ n ordinateur m; ~ **science** informatique f. **computerize** vt informatiser.

comrade /'kɒmreɪd/ n camarade mf.

con¹ /kɒn/ vt (pt **conned** 🔀) rouler 🔀, escroquer (**out of** de.) ● n 🔀 escroquerie f.

con² /kɒn/ →PRO.

conceal /kən'siːl/ vt dissimuler (**from** à.)

concede /kən'siːd/ vt concéder. ● vi céder.

conceited /kən'siːtɪd/ adj vaniteux.

conceive /kən'siːv/ vt/i concevoir; ~ **of** concevoir.

concentrate /'kɒnsntreɪt/ vt/i (se) concentrer. **concentration** n concentration f.

concept /'kɒnsept/ n concept m.

conception /kən'sepʃn/ n conception f.

concern /kən'sɜːn/ n (interest, business) affaire f; (worry) inquiétude f; (firm: Comm) entreprise f, affaire f. ● vt concerner; ~ **oneself with, be** ~**ed with** s'occuper de. **concerned** adj inquiet. **concerning** prep en ce qui concerne.

concert /'kɒnsət/ n concert m.

concession /kən'seʃn/ n concession f.

conciliation /kənsɪlɪ'eɪʃn/ n conciliation f.

concise /kən'saɪs/ adj concis.

conclude /kən'kluːd/ vt conclure. ● vi se terminer. **conclusion** n conclusion f. **conclusive** adj concluant.

concoct /kən'kɒkt/ vt confectionner; (invent: fig) fabriquer. **concoction** n mélange m.

concourse /'kɒŋkɔːs/ n (Rail) hall m.

concrete /'kɒŋkriːt/ n béton m. ● adj de béton; (fig) concret. ● vt bétonner.

concur /kən'kɜː(r)/ vi (pt **concurred**) être d'accord.

concurrently /kən'kʌrəntlɪ/ adv simultanément.

concussion /kən'kʌʃn/ n commotion f (cérébrale).

condemn /kən'dem/ vt condamner.

condensation /kɒnden'seɪʃn/ n (on walls) condensation f; (on windows) buée f. **condense** vt/i (se) condenser.

condition /kən'dɪʃn/ n condition f; **on** ~ **that** à condition que. ● vt conditionner. **conditional** adj conditionnel.

conditioner /kən'dɪʃənə(r)/ n après-shampooing m.

condolences /kən'dəʊlənsɪz/ npl condoléances fpl.

condom /'kɒndɒm/ n préservatif m.

condone /kən'dəʊn/ vt pardonner, fermer les yeux sur.

conducive /kən'djuːsɪv/ adj ~ **to** favorable à.

conduct¹ /'kɒndʌkt/ n conduite f.

conduct² /kən'dʌkt/ vt conduire; (orchestra) diriger. **conductor** n chef m d'orchestre; (of bus) receveur m; (on train: US) chef m de train; (Electr) conducteur m. **conductress** n receveuse f.

cone /kəʊn/ n cône m. (of ice-cream) cornet m.

confectioner /kən'fekʃənə(r)/ n confiseur/-euse m/f. **confectionery** n confiserie f.

confer /kən'fɜː(r)/ vt/i (pt **conferred**) conférer.

conference /'kɒnfərəns/ n conférence f.

confess /kən'fes/ vt/i avouer; (Relig) (se) confesser. **confession** n confession f; (of crime) aveu m.

confide /kən'faɪd/ vt confier. ● vi ~ **in** se confier à.

confidence /'kɒnfɪdəns/ n (trust) confiance f. (boldness) confiance f en soi; (secret) confidence f; **in** ~ en confidence. **confident** adj sûr.

confidential /kɒnfr'denʃl/ adj confidentiel.

configuration /kənfɪgə'reɪʃn/ n configuration f. ● **configure** vt configurer.

confine /kən'faɪn/ vt enfermer; (limit) limiter; ~d space espace m réduit; ~d to limité à.

confirm /kən'fɜ:m/ vt confirmer. **confirmed** adj (bachelor) endurci; (smoker) invétéré.

confiscate /'kɒnfɪskeɪt/ vt confisquer.

conflict[1] /'kɒnflɪkt/ n conflit m.

conflict[2] /kən'flɪkt/ vi (statements, views) être en contradiction (**with** avec.) (appointments) tomber en même temps (**with** que). **conflicting** adj contradictoire.

conform /kən'fɔ:m/ vt/i (se) conformer.

confound /kən'faʊnd/ vt confondre.

confront /kən'frʌnt/ vt affronter; ~ **with** confronter avec.

confuse /kən'fju:z/ vt (bewilder) troubler; (mistake, confound) confondre; **become** ~d s'embrouiller; **I am** ~d je m'y perds. **confusing** adj déroutant. **confusion** n confusion f.

congeal /kən'dʒi:l/ vt/i (se) figer.

congested /kən'dʒestɪd/ adj (road) embouteillé; (passage) encombré; (Med) congestionné. **congestion** n (traffic) encombrement(s) m(pl); (Med) congestion f.

congratulate /kən'grætʃʊleɪt/ vt féliciter (**on** de). **congratulations** npl félicitations fpl.

congregate /'kɒŋgrɪgeɪt/ vi se rassembler. **congregation** n assemblée f.

congress /'kɒŋgres/ n congrès m. **C** ~ (US) le Congrès.

> **Congress** Le Congrès est le corps législatif des États-Unis composé de la Chambre des représentants (House of Representatives) qui compte 435 membres, et du Sénat (Senate) qui compte 100 sénateurs, deux par État. Pour devenir loi, un projet de loi doit être approuvé par les deux chambres, et ratifié par le président. ▷**CAPITOL**.

---

conjugate /'kɒndʒʊgeɪt/ vt conjuguer. **conjugation** n conjugaison f.

conjunction /kən'dʒʌŋkʃn/ n (Ling) conjonction f. **in** ~**with** conjointement avec.

conjunctivitis /kəndʒʌŋktɪ'vaɪtɪs/ n conjonctivite f.

conjure /kʌn'dʒə(r)/ vi faire des tours de passe-passe. ● vt ~ **up** faire apparaître. **conjuror** n prestidigitateur/-trice m/f.

con man n ⊠ escroc m.

connect /kə'nekt/ vt/i (se) relier; (in mind) faire le rapport entre; (install, wire up to mains) brancher; ~ **with** (of train) assurer la correspondance avec; ~**ed** (idea, event) lié; **be** ~**ed with** avoir rapport à.

connection /kə'nekʃn/ n rapport m. (Rail) correspondance f; (phone call) communication f; (Electr) contact m; (joining piece) raccord m; ~**s** (Comm) relations fpl.

connive /kə'naɪv/ vi ~ **at** se faire le complice de.

conquer /'kɒŋkə(r)/ vt vaincre; (country) conquérir. **conqueror** n conquérant m.

conquest /'kɒŋkwest/ n conquête f.

conscience /'kɒnʃəns/ n conscience f. **conscientious** adj consciencieux.

conscious /'kɒnʃəs/ adj conscient; (deliberate) voulu. **consciously** adv consciemment. **consciousness** n conscience f; (Med) connaissance f.

conscript /'kɒnskrɪpt/ n appelé m.

consecutive /kən'sekjʊtɪv/ adj consécutif.

consensus /kən'sensəs/ n consensus m.

consent /kən'sent/ vi consentir (**to** à). ● n consentement m.

consequence /'kɒnsɪkwəns/ n conséquence f. **consequently** adv par conséquent.

conservation /kɒnsə'veɪʃn/ n préservation f. ~ **area** zone f protégée. **conservationist** n défenseur m de l'environnement.

conservative /kən'sɜ:vətɪv/ adj conservateur; (estimate) minimal.

Conservative Party n parti m conservateur.

conservatory /kən'sɜ:vətrɪ/ n (greenhouse) serre f; (room) véranda f.

conserve /kən'sɜ:v/ vt conserver; (energy) économiser.

consider /kən'sɪdə(r)/ vt considérer; (allow for) tenir compte de; (possibility) envisager (**doing** de faire).

considerable /kən'sɪdərəbl/ adj considérable; (much) beaucoup de.

considerate /kən'sɪdərət/ adj prévenant, attentionné. **consideration** n considération f. (respect) égard(s) m(pl).

considering /kən'sɪdərɪŋ/ prep compte tenu de.

consignment /kən'saɪnmənt/ n envoi m.

consist /kən'sɪst/ vi consister (of en; in doing à faire).

consistency /kən'sɪstənsɪ/ n (of liquids) consistance f. (of argument) cohérence f.

consistent /kən'sɪstənt/ adj cohérent; ~ with conforme à.

consolation /kɒnsə'leɪʃn/ n consolation f.

consolidate /kən'sɒlɪdeɪt/ vt/i (se) consolider.

consonant /'kɒnsənənt/ n consonne f.

conspicuous /kən'spɪkjʊəs/ adj (easily seen) en évidence; (showy) voyant; (noteworthy) remarquable.

conspiracy /kən'spɪrəsɪ/ n conspiration f.

constable /'kʌnstəbl/ n agent m de police, gendarme m.

constant /'kɒnstənt/ adj (questions) incessant; (unchanging) constant; (friend) fidèle. ● n constante f. **constantly** adv constamment.

constellation /kɒnstə'leɪʃn/ n constellation f.

constipation /kɒnstɪ'peɪʃn/ n constipation f.

constituency /kən'stɪtjʊənsɪ/ n circonscription f électorale.

constituent /kən'stɪtjʊənt/ adj constitutif. ● n élément m constitutif; (Pol) électeur/-trice m/f.

constitution /kɒnstɪ'tjuːʃn/ n constitution f.

constrain /kən'streɪn/ vt contraindre. **constraint** n contrainte f.

constrict /kən'strɪkt/ vt (flow) comprimer; (movement) gêner.

construct /kən'strʌkt/ vt construire. **construction** n construction f. **constructive** adj constructif.

consulate /'kɒnsjʊlət/ n consulat m.

consult /kən'sʌlt/ vt consulter. ● vi ~ with conférer avec. **consultant** n

conseiller/-ère m/f. (Med) spécialiste m/f. **consultation** n consultation f.

consume /kən'sjuːm/ vt consommer; (destroy) consumer. **consumer** n consommateur/-trice m/f.

consummate /'kɒnsəmeɪt/ vt consommer.

consumption /kən'sʌmpʃn/ n consommation f; (Med) phtisie f.

contact /'kɒntækt/ n contact m; (person) relation f. ● vt contacter. ~ **lenses** npl lentilles fpl (de contact).

contagious /kən'teɪdʒəs/ adj contagieux.

contain /kən'teɪn/ vt contenir; ~ oneself se contenir. **container** n récipient m. (for transport) container m.

contaminate /kən'tæmɪneɪt/ vt contaminer.

contemplate /'kɒntəmpleɪt/ vt (gaze at) contempler; (think about) envisager.

contemporary /kən'temprərɪ/ adj & n contemporain/-e (m/f).

contempt /kən'tempt/ n mépris m. **contemptible** adj méprisable. **contemptuous** adj méprisant.

contend /kən'tend/ vt soutenir. ● vi ~ with (compete) rivaliser avec; (face) faire face à. **contender** n adversaire mf.

content¹ /'kɒntent/ n (of letter) contenu m. (amount) teneur f; ~s contenu m.

content² /kən'tent/ adj satisfait. ● vt contenter. **contented** adj satisfait. **contentment** n contentement m.

contest¹ /'kɒntest/ n (competition) concours m. (struggle) lutte f.

contest² /kən'test/ vt contester; (compete for or in) disputer. **contestant** n concurrent/-e m/f.

context /'kɒntekst/ n contexte m.

continent /'kɒntɪnənt/ n continent m; **the C** ~ l'Europe f (continentale). **continental** adj continental, européen. **continental quilt** n couette f.

contingency /kən'tɪndʒənsɪ/ n éventualité f. ~ **plan** plan m d'urgence.

continual /kən'tɪnjʊəl/ adj continuel.

continuation /kəntɪnjʊ'eɪʃn/ n continuation f. (after interruption) reprise f; (new episode) suite f.

continue /kən'tɪnjuː/ vt/i continuer; (resume) reprendre. **continued** adj continu.

continuous /kən'tɪnjʊəs/ adj continu. **continuously** adv (without a break) sans interruption; (repeatedly) continuellement.

contort /kən'tɔːt/ vt tordre; ~ **oneself** se contorsionner.

contour /'kɒntʊə(r)/ n contour m.

contraband /'kɒntrəbænd/ n contrebande f.

contraception /kɒntrə'sepʃn/ n contraception f. **contraceptive** adj & n contraceptif (m).

contract¹ /'kɒntrækt/ n contrat m.

contract² /kən'trækt/ vt/i (se) contracter. **contraction** n contraction f.

contractor /kən'træktə(r)/ n entrepreneur/-euse m/f.

contradict /kɒntrə'dɪkt/ vt contredire. **contradictory** adj contradictoire.

contrary¹ /'kɒntrərɪ/ adj contraire (to à). ● n contraire m. **on the** ~ au contraire. ● adv ~ to contrairement à.

contrary² /kən'treərɪ/ adj entêté.

contrast¹ /'kɒntrɑːst/ n contraste m.

contrast² /kən'trɑːst/ vt/i contraster.

contravention /kɒntrə'venʃn/ n infraction f.

contribute /kən'trɪbjuːt/ vt donner. ● vi ~ **to** contribuer à; (take part) participer à; (newspaper) collaborer à. **contribution** n contribution f. **contributor** n collaborateur/-trice m/f.

contrive /kən'traɪv/ vt imaginer; ~ **to do** trouver moyen de faire.

control /kən'trəʊl/ vt (pt **controlled**) (firm) diriger; (check) contrôler; (restrain) maîtriser. ● n contrôle m. (mastery) maîtrise f. ~**s** commandes fpl. (knobs) boutons mpl; **have under** ~ (event) avoir en main; **in** ~ **of** maître de. ~ **tower** n tour f de contrôle.

controversial /kɒntrə'vɜːʃl/ adj discutable, discuté. **controversy** n controverse f.

conurbation /kɒnɜː'beɪʃn/ n agglomération f, conurbation f.

convalesce /kɒnvə'les/ vi être en convalescence.

convene /kən'viːn/ vt convoquer. ● vi se réunir.

convenience /kən'viːnɪəns/ n commodité f. ~**s** toilettes fpl. **all modern** ~**s** tout le confort moderne; **at your** ~ quand cela vous conviendra, à votre convenance. ~ **foods** npl plats mpl tout préparés.

convenient /kən'viːnɪənt/ adj commode, pratique; (time) bien choisi; **be** ~ **for** convenir à.

convent /'kɒnvənt/ n couvent m.

convention /kən'venʃn/ n (assembly, agreement) convention f. (custom) usage m. **conventional** adj conventionnel.

conversation /kɒnvə'seɪʃn/ n conversation f. **conversational** adj (tone) de la conversation; (French) de tous les jours.

converse¹ /kən'vɜːs/ vi s'entretenir, converser (**with** avec).

converse² /'kɒnvɜːs/ adj & n inverse (m). **conversely** adv inversement.

conversion /kən'vɜːʃn/ n conversion f.

convert¹ /kən'vɜːt/ vt convertir; (house) aménager. ● vi ~ **into** se transformer en.

convert² /'kɒnvɜːt/ n converti/-e m/f.

convertible /kən'vɜːtəbl/ adj convertible. ● n (car) décapotable f.

convey /kən'veɪ/ vt (wishes, order) transmettre; (goods, people) transporter; (idea, feeling) communiquer. **conveyor belt** n tapis m roulant.

convict¹ /kən'vɪkt/ vt déclarer coupable.

convict² /'kɒnvɪkt/ n prisonnier/-ière m/f.

conviction /kən'vɪkʃn/ n (Jur) condamnation f. (opinion) conviction f.

convince /kən'vɪns/ vt convaincre.

convoke /kən'vəʊk/ vt convoquer.

convoy /'kɒnvɔɪ/ n convoi m.

convulse /kən'vʌls/ vt convulser; (fig) bouleverser; **be** ~**d with laughter** se tordre de rire.

cook /kʊk/ vt/i (faire) cuire; (of person) faire la cuisine; ~ **up** 🔲 fabriquer. ● n cuisinier/-ière m/f. **cooker** n (stove) cuisinière f. **cookery** n cuisine f.

cookie /'kʊkɪ/ n (US) biscuit m.

cooking /'kʊkɪŋ/ n cuisine f. ● adj de cuisine.

cool /kuːl/ adj frais; (calm) calme; (unfriendly) froid. ● n fraîcheur f. (calm-

ness ☒) sang-froid *m*; **in the** ∼ au frais. ● *vt/i* rafraîchir. ∼ **box** *n* glacière *f*.

coolly /ˈkuːllɪ/ *adv* calmement, froidement.

coop /kuːp/ *n* poulailler *m*. ● *vt* ∼ **up** enfermer.

cooperate /kəʊˈɒpəreɪt/ *vi* coopérer. **co-operation** *n* coopération *f*.

cooperative /kəʊˈɒpərətɪv/ *adj* coopératif. ● *n* coopérative *f*.

coordinate /kəʊˈɔːdɪnət/ *vt* coordonner.

cop /kɒp/ *vt* (*pt* **copped**) ☒ piquer. ● *n* (*policeman*) ☒ flic *m*. ∼ **out** ☒ se dérober.

cope /kəʊp/ *vi* s'en sortir ☒, se débrouiller; ∼ **with** (*problem*) faire face à.

copper /ˈkɒpə(r)/ *n* cuivre *m*. (*coin*) sou *m*; ☒ flic *m*. ● *adj* de cuivre.

copulate /ˈkɒpjʊleɪt/ *vi* s'accoupler.

copy /ˈkɒpɪ/ *n* copie *f*. (*of book, newspaper*) exemplaire *m*; (*print: Photo*) épreuve *f*. ● *vt/i* copier.

copyright /ˈkɒpɪraɪt/ *n* droit *m* d'auteur, copyright *m*.

copy-writer *n* rédacteur-concepteur *m*, rédactrice-conceptrice *f*.

cord /kɔːd/ *n* (petite) corde *f*; (*of curtain, pyjamas*) cordon *m*; (*Electr*) cordon *m* électrique; (*fabric*) velours *m* côtelé.

cordial /ˈkɔːdɪəl/ *adj* cordial. ● *n* (*drink*) sirop *m*.

corduroy /ˈkɔːdərɔɪ/ *n* velours *m* côtelé.

core /kɔː(r)/ *n* (*of apple*) trognon *m*; (*of problem*) cœur *m*; (*Tech*) noyau *m*. ● *vt* (*apple*) évider.

cork /kɔːk/ *n* liège *m*. (*for bottle*) bouchon *m*. ● *vt* boucher. **corkscrew** *n* tire-bouchon *m*.

corn /kɔːn/ *n* blé *m*. (maize: US) maïs *m*; (*seed*) grain *m*; (*hard skin*) cor *m*.

cornea /ˈkɔːnɪə/ *n* cornée *f*.

corner /ˈkɔːnə(r)/ *n* coin *m*; (bend in road) virage *m*; (football) corner *m*. ● *vt* coincer, acculer; (*market*) accaparer. ● *vi* prendre un virage.

cornflour /ˈkɔːnflaʊə(r)/ *n* farine *f* de maïs.

cornice /ˈkɔːnɪs/ *n* corniche *f*.

corny /ˈkɔːnɪ/ *adj* (**-ier, -iest**) (*joke*) éculé.

corollary /kəˈrɒlərɪ/ *n* corollaire *m*.

coronary /ˈkɒrənrɪ/ *n* infarctus *m*.

coronation /kɒrəˈneɪʃn/ *n* couronnement *m*.

corporal /ˈkɔːpərəl/ *n* caporal *m*. ∼**punishment** *n* châtiment *m* corporel.

corporate /ˈkɔːpərət/ *adj* (*ownership*) en commun; (*body*) constitué.

corporation /kɔːpəˈreɪʃn/ *n* (Comm) société *f*.

corpse /kɔːps/ *n* cadavre *m*.

corpuscle /ˈkɔːpʌsl/ *n* globule *m*.

correct /kəˈrekt/ *adj* (right) exact, juste, correct; (proper) correct; **you are** ∼ vous avez raison. ● *vt* corriger.

correction /kəˈrekʃn/ *n* correction *f*.

correlate /ˈkɒrəleɪt/ *vt/i* (faire) correspondre.

correspond /kɒrɪˈspɒnd/ *vi* correspondre. **correspondence** *n* correspondance *f*.

corridor /ˈkɒrɪdɔː(r)/ *n* couloir *m*.

corrode /kəˈrəʊd/ *vt/i* (se) corroder.

corrugated /ˈkɒrəgeɪtɪd/ *adj* ondulé; ∼ **iron** tôle *f* ondulée.

corrupt /kəˈrʌpt/ *adj* corrompu. ● *vt* corrompre. **corruption** *n* corruption *f*.

Corsica /ˈkɔːsɪkə/ *n* Corse *f*.

cosh /kɒʃ/ *n* matraque *f*. ● *vt* matraquer.

cosmetic /kɒzˈmetɪk/ *n* produit *m* de beauté. ● *adj* cosmétique; (fig, pej) superficiel. ∼ **surgery** *n* chirurgie *f* esthétique

cosmopolitan /kɒzməˈpɒlɪtn/ *adj* & *n* cosmopolite (*mf*).

cosmos /ˈkɒzmɒs/ *n* cosmos *m*.

cost /kɒst/ *vt* (*pt* **cost**) coûter. (*pt* **costed**) établir le prix de. ● *n* coût *m*. ∼**s** (Jur) dépens *mpl*. **at all** ∼**s** à tout prix; **to one's** ∼ à ses dépens; ∼ **price** prix *m* de revient; ∼ **of living** coût *m* de la vie. ∼**-effective** *adj* rentable.

costly /ˈkɒstlɪ/ *adj* (**-ier, -iest**) coûteux; (valuable) précieux.

costume /ˈkɒstjuːm/ *n* costume *m*. (for swimming) maillot *m*. ∼ **jewellery** *npl* bijoux *mpl* de fantaisie.

cosy /ˈkəʊzɪ/ *adj* (**-ier, -iest**) confortable, intime.

cot /kɒt/ n lit m d'enfant; (camp-bed: US) lit m de camp.

cottage /'kɒtɪdʒ/ n petite maison f de campagne; (thatched) chaumière f. ~ **pie** n hachis m Parmentier.

cotton /'kɒtn/ n coton m. (for sewing) fil m (à coudre). ● vi ~ **on** 🅇 piger. ~ **wool** n coton m hydrophile.

couch /kaʊtʃ/ n canapé m. ● vt (express) formuler.

cough /kɒf/ vi tousser. ● n toux f. ~ **up** 🅇 cracher, payer.

could /kʊd/ ➡CAN¹.

couldn't ➡COULD NOT.

council /'kaʊnsl/ n conseil m. ~ **house** n maison f louée par la municipalité, ≈ H.L.M. m or f.

councillor /'kaʊnsələ(r)/ n conseiller/-ère m/f municipal/-e.

counsel /'kaʊnsl/ n conseil m. ● n inv (Jur) avocat/-e m/f. **counsellor** n conseiller/-ère m/f.

count /kaʊnt/ vt/i compter. ● n (numerical record) décompte m. (nobleman) comte m. ~ **on** compter sur.

counter /'kaʊntə(r)/ n comptoir m. (in bank) guichet m; (token) jeton m. ● adv ~ **to** à l'encontre de. ● adj opposé. ● vt opposer; (blow) parer. ● vi riposter.

counteract /kaʊntə'rækt/ vt neutraliser.

counterbalance /'kaʊntəbæləns/ n contrepoids m. ● vt contrebalancer.

counterfeit /'kaʊntəfɪt/ adj & n faux (m). ● vt contrefaire.

counterfoil /'kaʊntəfɔɪl/ n souche f.

counter-productive /kaʊntəprə'dʌktɪv/ adj qui produit l'effet contraire.

countess /'kaʊntɪs/ n comtesse f.

countless /'kaʊntlɪs/ adj innombrable.

country /'kʌntrɪ/ n (land, region) pays m. (homeland) patrie f; (countryside) campagne f.

countryman /'kʌntrɪmən/ n (pl -men) campagnard m; (fellow citizen) compatriote m.

countryside /'kʌntrɪsaɪd/ n campagne f.

county /'kaʊntɪ/ n comté m.

coup /kuː/ n (achievement) joli coup m. (Pol) coup m d'état.

couple /'kʌpl/ n (people, animals) couple m. **a** ~ **of** (two or three) deux ou trois. ● vt/i (s')accoupler.

coupon /'kuːpɒn/ n coupon m; (for shopping) bon m or coupon m de réduction.

courage /'kʌrɪdʒ/ n courage m.

courgette /kʊə'ʒet/ n courgette f.

courier /'kʊrɪə(r)/ n messager/-ère m/f; (for tourists) guide m.

course /kɔːs/ n cours m; (for training) stage m; (series) série f; (Culin) plat m; (for golf) terrain m; (at sea) itinéraire m. **change** ~ changer de cap; ~ **(of action)** façon f de faire; **during the** ~ **of** pendant; **in due** ~ en temps utile; **of** ~ bien sûr.

court /kɔːt/ n cour f; (tennis) court m; **go to** ~aller devant les tribunaux. ● vt faire la cour à; (danger) rechercher.

courteous /'kɜːtɪəs/ adj courtois.

courtesy /'kɜːtəsɪ/ n courtoisie f; **by** ~ **of** avec la permission de.

courthouse /'kɔːthaʊs/ n (US) palais m de justice.

court-martial vt (pt -martialled) faire passer en conseil de guerre. ● n cour f martiale.

court: ~**room** n salle f de tribunal. ~**shoe** n escarpin m. ~**yard** n cour f.

cousin /'kʌzn/ n cousin/-e m/f. **first** ~ cousin/-e m/f germain/-e.

cove /kəʊv/ n anse f, crique f.

covenant /'kʌvənənt/ n convention f.

cover /'kʌvə(r)/ vt couvrir. ● n (for bed, book) couverture f. (lid) couvercle m; (for furniture) housse f; (shelter) abri m; **take** ~ se mettre à l'abri. ~ **up** cacher; (crime) couvrir; ~**up for** couvrir.

coverage /'kʌvərɪdʒ/ n reportage m.

covering /'kʌvərɪŋ/ n enveloppe f. ~ **letter** lettre f d'accompagnement.

covert /'kʌvət/ adj (activity) secret; (threat) voilé; (look) dérobé.

cover-up n opération f de camouflage.

cow /kaʊ/ n vache f.

coward /'kaʊəd/ n lâche mf.

cowboy /'kaʊbɔɪ/ n cow-boy m.

cowshed /'kaʊʃed/ n étable f.

coy /kɔɪ/ adj (faussement) timide, qui fait le or la timide.

cozy US →COSY.

crab /kræb/ n crabe m. ∼**-apple** n pomme f sauvage.

crack /kræk/ n fente f; (in glass) fêlure f; (noise) craquement m; (joke 🗷) plaisanterie f. ● adj 🗓 d'élite. ● vt/i (break partially) (se) fêler; (split) (se) fendre; (nut) casser; (joke) raconter; (problem) résoudre; **get** ∼**ing** 🗓 s'y mettre. ∼ **down on** 🗓 sévir contre. ∼ **up** 🗓 craquer.

cracker /'krækə(r)/ n (Culin) biscuit m (salé); (for Christmas) diablotin f.

crackle /'krækl/ vi crépiter. ● n crépitement m.

cradle /'kreɪdl/ n berceau m. ● vt bercer.

craft /krɑːft/ n métier m artisanal; (technique) art m; (boat) bateau m. **craftsman** n (pl **-men**) artisan m. **craftsmanship** n art m.

crafty /'krɑːftɪ/ adj (**-ier, -iest**) rusé.

crag /kræg/ n rocher m à pic.

cram /kræm/ vt/i (pt **crammed**). (for an exam) bachoter (**for** pour;) ∼ **into** (pack) (s')entasser dans; ∼ **with** (fill) bourrer de.

cramp /kræmp/ n crampe f.

cramped /kræmpt/ adj à l'étroit.

cranberry /'krænbərɪ/ n canneberge f.

crane /kreɪn/ n grue f. ● vt (neck) tendre.

crank /kræŋk/ n excentrique mf. (Tech) manivelle f.

crap /kræp/ n (nonsense 🗷) conneries fpl 🗷; (faeces 🗷) merde f 🗷.

crash /kræʃ/ n accident m; (noise) fracas m; (of thunder) coup m; (of firm) faillite f. ● vt/i avoir un accident (avec); (of plane) s'écraser; (two vehicles) se percuter; ∼ **into** rentrer dans. ∼ **course** n cours m intensif. ∼**-helmet** n casque m (anti-choc). ∼**-land** vi atterrir en catastrophe.

crate /kreɪt/ n cageot m.

cravat /krə'væt/ n foulard m.

crave /kreɪv/ vt/i ∼ **for** désirer ardemment. **craving** n envie f irrésistible.

crawl /krɔːl/ vi (insect) ramper; (vehicle) se traîner; **be** ∼**ing with** grouiller de. ● n (pace) pas m. (swimming) crawl m.

crayfish /'kreɪfɪʃ/ n inv écrevisse f.

crayon /'kreɪən/ n craie f grasse.

craze /kreɪz/ n engouement m.

crazy /'kreɪzɪ/ adj (**-ier, -iest**) fou; ∼ **about** (person) fou de; (thing) fana or fou de.

creak /kriːk/ n grincement m. ● vi grincer.

cream /kriːm/ n crème f. ● adj crème inv. ● vt écrémer.

crease /kriːs/ n pli m. ● vt/i (se) froisser.

create /kriːˈeɪt/ vt créer. **creation** n création f. **creative** adj (person) créatif; (process) créateur. **creator** n créateur/-trice m/f.

creature /'kriːtʃə(r)/ n créature f.

crèche /kreʃ/ n garderie f.

credentials /krɪˈdenʃlz/ npl (identity) pièces fpl d'identité; (competence) références fpl.

credibility /kredəˈbɪlətɪ/ n crédibilité f

credit /'kredɪt/ n (credence) crédit m. (honour) honneur m; **in** ∼ créditeur; ∼**s** (cinema) générique m. ● adj (balance) créditeur. ● vt croire; (Comm) créditer; ∼ **sb with** attribuer à qn. ∼ **card** n carte f de crédit. ∼ **note** n avoir m.

creditor /'kredɪtə(r)/ n créancier/-ière m/f.

creditworthy /'kredɪtwɜːðɪ/ adj solvable.

creed /kriːd/ n credo m.

creek /kriːk/ n (US) ruisseau m. **up the** ∼ 🗷 dans le pétrin 🗷.

creep /kriːp/ vi (pt **crept**) (insect, cat) ramper; (fig) se glisser. ● n (person 🗷) pauvre type m 🗓. **give sb the** ∼**s** faire frissonner qn. **creeper** n liane f.

cremate /krɪˈmeɪt/ vt incinérer. **cremation** n incinération f. **crematorium** n (pl **-ia**) crématorium m.

crêpe /kreɪp/ n crêpe m. ∼ **paper** n papier m crêpon.

crept /krept/ →CREEP.

crescent /'kresnt/ n croissant m; (of houses) rue f en demi-lune.

cress /kres/ n cresson m.

crest /krest/ n crête f. (coat of arms) armoiries fpl.

cretin /'kretɪn/ n crétin/-e m/f.

crevice /'krevɪs/ n fente f.

crew /kruː/ n (of plane, ship) équipage m; (gang) équipe f. ~ **cut** n coupe f en brosse. ~ **neck** n (col) ras du cou m.

crib /krɪb/ n lit m d'enfant. ● vt/i (pt **cribbed**) copier.

cricket /'krɪkɪt/ n (Sport) cricket m. (insect) grillon m.

crime /kraɪm/ n crime m; (minor) délit m; (acts) criminalité f.

criminal /'krɪmɪnl/ adj & n criminel/-le (m/f).

crimson /'krɪmzn/ adj & n cramoisi (m).

cringe /krɪndʒ/ vi reculer; (fig) s'humilier.

crinkle /'krɪŋkl/ vt/i (cloth) (se) froisser. ● n pli m.

cripple /'krɪpl/ n infirme mf. ● vt estropier; (fig) paralyser.

crisis /'kraɪsɪs/ n (pl **crises**) crise f.

crisp /krɪsp/ adj (Culin) croquant; (air, reply) vif. **crisps** npl chips fpl.

criss-cross /'krɪskrɒs/ adj entrecroisé. ● vt/i (s')entrecroiser.

criterion /kraɪ'tɪərɪən/ n (pl **-ia**) critère m.

critic /'krɪtɪk/ n critique m. **critical** adj critique. **critically** adv d'une manière critique; (ill) gravement.

criticism /'krɪtɪsɪzəm/ n critique f.

criticize /'krɪtɪsaɪz/ vt/i critiquer.

croak /krəʊk/ n (bird) croassement m; (frog) coassement m. ● vi croasser; coasser.

Croatia /krəʊ'eɪʃə/ n Croatie f.

Croatian /krəʊ'eɪʃn/ n Croate mf. ● adj Croate.

crochet /'krəʊʃeɪ/ n crochet m. ● vt faire du crochet.

crockery /'krɒkərɪ/ n vaisselle f.

crocodile /'krɒkədaɪl/ n crocodile m.

crook /krʊk/ n (criminal 🄵) escroc m; (stick) houlette f.

crooked /'krʊkɪd/ adj tordu; (winding) tortueux; (askew) de travers; (dishonest: fig) malhonnête.

crop /krɒp/ n récolte f; (fig) quantité f. ● vt (pt **cropped**) couper. ● vi ~ **up** se présenter.

cross /krɒs/ n croix f; (hybrid) hybride m. ● vt/i traverser; (legs, animals) croiser; (cheque) barrer; (paths) se croiser; ~ **sb's mind** venir à l'esprit de qn.

● adj en colère, fâché (**with** contre). **talk at** ~ **purposes** parler sans se comprendre. □ ● **off** or **out** rayer. ~**-check** vt vérifier (pour confirmer). ~**-country (running)** n cross m. ~**-examine** vt faire subir un contre-interrogatoire à. ~**-eyed** adj **be** ~**-eyed** loucher. ~**fire** n feux mpl croisés.

crossing /'krɒsɪŋ/ n (by boat) traversée f; (on road) passage m clouté.

crossly /'krɒslɪ/ adv avec colère.

cross: ~**-reference** n renvoi m. ~**roads** n carrefour m. ~**word** n mots mpl croisés.

crotch /krɒtʃ/ n (of garment) entre-jambes m inv.

crouch /kraʊtʃ/ vi s'accroupir.

crow /krəʊ/ n corbeau m; **as the** ~ **flies** à vol d'oiseau. ● vi (of cock) chanter; (fig) jubiler. ~**bar** n pied-de-biche m.

crowd /kraʊd/ n foule f. **crowded** adj plein.

crown /kraʊn/ n couronne f; (top part) sommet m. ● vt couronner.

Crown Court n Cour f d'assises.

crucial /'kruːʃl/ adj crucial.

crucifix /'kruːsɪfɪks/ n crucifix m.

crucify /'kruːsɪfaɪ/ vt crucifier.

crude /kruːd/ adj (raw) brut; (rough, vulgar) grossier.

cruel /krʊəl/ adj (**crueller, cruellest**) cruel.

cruise /kruːz/ n croisière f. ● vi (ship) croiser; (tourists) faire une croisière; (vehicle) rouler; **cruising speed** vitesse f de croisière.

crumb /krʌm/ n miette f.

crumble /'krʌmbl/ vt/i (s')effriter; (bread) (s')émietter; (collapse) s'écrouler.

crumple /'krʌmpl/ vt/i (se) froisser.

crunch /krʌntʃ/ vt croquer. ● n (event) moment m critique; **when it comes to the** ~ quand ça devient sérieux.

crusade /kruː'seɪd/ n croisade f. **crusader** n (knight) croisé m; (fig) militant/-e m/f.

crush /krʌʃ/ vt écraser; (clothes) froisser. ● n (crowd) presse f; **a** ~ **on** 🄸 le béguin pour.

crust /krʌst/ n croûte f. **crusty** adj croustillant.

crutch /krʌtʃ/ n béquille f; (crotch) entrejambes m inv.

crux /krʌks/ n **the ~ of** (problem) le point crucial de.

cry /kraɪ/ n cri m. ● vi (weep) pleurer; (call out) crier. □ **~ off** se décommander.

crying /'kraɪɪŋ/ adj (need) urgent; **a ~ shame** une vraie honte. ● n pleurs mpl.

cryptic /'krɪptɪk/ adj énigmatique.

crystal /'krɪstl/ n cristal m. **~-clear** adj parfaitement clair.

cub /kʌb/ n petit m; **Cub (Scout)** louveteau m.

Cuba /'kju:bə/ n Cuba f.

cube /kju:b/ n cube m. **cubic** adj cubique; (metre) cube.

cubicle /'kju:bɪkl/ n (in room, hospital) box m; (at swimming-pool) cabine f.

cuckoo /'kʊku:/ n coucou m.

cucumber /'kju:kʌmbə(r)/ n concombre m.

cuddle /'kʌdl/ vt câliner. ● vi (**kiss and**) **~** s'embrasser. ● n caresse f. **cuddly** adj câlin; **cuddly toy** peluche f.

cue /kju:/ n signal m; (Theat) réplique f; (billiards) queue f.

cuff /kʌf/ n manchette f; (US: on trousers) revers m; **off the ~** impromptu. ● vt gifler. **~-link** n bouton m de manchette.

cul-de-sac /'kʌldəsæk/ n (pl **culs-de-sac**) impasse f.

cull /kʌl/ vt (select) choisir; (kill) massacrer.

culminate /'kʌlmmeɪt/ vi **~ in** se terminer par. **culmination** n point m culminant.

culprit /'kʌlprɪt/ n coupable mf.

cult /kʌlt/ n culte m.

cultivate /'kʌltɪveɪt/ vt cultiver. **cultivation** n culture f.

cultural /'kʌltʃərəl/ adj culturel.

culture /'kʌltʃə(r)/ n culture f. **cultured** adj cultivé.

cumbersome /'kʌmbəsəm/ adj encombrant.

cunning /'kʌnɪŋ/ adj rusé. ● n astuce f, ruse f.

cup /kʌp/ n tasse f; (prize) coupe f; **Cup final** finale f de la coupe.

cupboard /'kʌbəd/ n placard m.

cup-tie n match m de coupe.

curate /'kjʊərət/ n vicaire m.

curator /kjʊə'reɪtə(r)/ n (of museum) conservateur m.

curb /kɜ:b/ n (restraint) frein m; (of path) (US) bord m du trottoir. ● vt (desires) refréner; (price increase) freiner.

cure /'kjʊə(r)/ vt guérir; (fig) éliminer; (Culin) fumer; (in brine) saler. ● n (recovery) guérison f; (remedy) remède m.

curfew /'kɜ:fju:/ n couvre-feu m.

curiosity /kjʊərɪ'ɒsətɪ/ n curiosité f. **curious** adj curieux.

curl /kɜ:l/ vt/i (hair) boucler. ● n boucle f. □ **~up** se pelotonner; (shrivel) se racornir.

curler /'kɜ:lə(r)/ n bigoudi m.

curly /'kɜ:lɪ/ adj (**-ier, -iest**) bouclé.

currant /'kʌrənt/ n raisin m de Corinthe.

currency /'kʌrənsɪ/ n (money) monnaie f; (of word) fréquence f; **foreign ~** devises fpl étrangères.

current /'kʌrənt/ adj (term, word) usité; (topical) actuel; (year) en cours. ● n courant m. **~ account** n compte m courant. **~ events** npl l'actualité f.

currently /'kʌrəntlɪ/ adv actuellement.

curriculum /kə'rɪkjʊləm/ n (pl **-la**) programme m scolaire. **~ vitae** n curriculum vitae m.

curry /'kʌrɪ/ n curry m. ● vt **~ favour with** chercher les bonnes grâces de.

curse /kɜ:s/ n (spell) malédiction f; (swearword) juron m. ● vt maudire. ● vi (swear) jurer.

cursor /'kɜ:sə(r)/ n curseur m.

curt /kɜ:t/ adj brusque.

curtain /'kɜ:tn/ n rideau m.

curve /kɜ:v/ n courbe f. ● vi (line) s'incurver; (edge) se recourber; (road) faire une courbe. ● vt courber.

cushion /'kʊʃn/ n coussin m. ● vt (a blow) amortir; (fig) protéger.

custard /'kʌstəd/ n crème f anglaise; (set) flan m.

custody /'kʌstədɪ/ n (of child) garde f; (Jur) détention f préventive.

custom /'kʌstəm/ n coutume f; (patronage: Comm) clientèle f. **customary** adj habituel.

customer /'kʌstəmə(r)/ n client/-e m/f; (person 🔢) type m.

customize /'kʌstəmaɪz/ vt personnaliser.

custom-made adj fait sur mesure.

customs /'kʌstəmz/ npl douane f. ● adj douanier. ~ **officer** n douanier m.

cut /kʌt/ vt/i (pt cut. pres p cutting) vt couper; (hedge) tailler; (prices) réduire. ● vi couper. ● n (wound) coupure f; (of clothes) coupe f; (in surgery) incision f; (share) part f; (in prices) réduction f. □ ~ **back** vi faire des économies. vt réduire. ~ **down (on)** réduire. ~ **in** (in conversation) intervenir. ~ **off** couper; (tide, army) isoler; ~ **out** vt découper; (leave out) supprimer; vi (engine) s'arrêter. ~ **short** (visit) écourter. ~ **up** couper; (carve) découper.

cutback /'kʌtbæk/ n réduction f.

cute /kjuːt/ adj 🔢 mignon.

cutlery /'kʌtlərɪ/ n couverts mpl.

cutlet /'kʌtlɪt/ n côtelette f.

cut-price adj à prix réduit.

cutting /'kʌtɪŋ/ adj cinglant. ● n (from newspaper) coupure f; (plant) bouture f.

CV abbr →CURRICULUM VITAE.

cyanide /'saɪənaɪd/ n cyanure m.

cyberspace /'saɪbəspeɪs/ n cyberspace m.

cycle /'saɪbəspeɪs/ n cycle m; (bicycle) vélo m. ● vi aller à vélo.

cycling /'saɪklɪŋ/ n cyclisme m. ~ **shorts** npl cycliste m.

cyclist /'saɪklɪst/ n cycliste mf.

cylinder /'sɪlɪndə(r)/ n cylindre m.

cymbal /'sɪmbl/ n cymbale f.

cynic /'sɪnɪk/ n cynique mf. **cynical** adj cynique. **cynicism** n cynisme m.

cypress /'saɪprəs/ n cyprès m.

Cypriot /'sɪprɪət/ n Chypriote mf. ● adj cypriote.

Cyprus /'saɪprəs/ n Chypre f.

cyst /sɪst/ n kyste m.

czar /zɑː(r)/ n tsar m.

Czech /tʃek/ n (person) Tchèque mf; (Ling) tchèque m. ~ **Republic** n République f tchèque.

Dd

dab /dæb/ vt (pt dabbed) tamponner; ~ **sth on** appliquer qch par petites touches. ● n touche f.

dabble /'dæbl/ vi ~ **in sth** faire qch en amateur.

dad /dæd/ n 🔢 papa m. **daddy** n 🔢 papa m.

daffodil /'dæfədɪl/ n jonquille f.

daft /dɑːft/ adj bête.

dagger /'dægə(r)/ n poignard m.

Dáil Éireann Ces mots de gaélique irlandais, que l'on prononce /dɔɪl 'ɜː(ə)n/ désignent la Chambre des représentants au parlement de la République d'Irlande. Les 166 députés qui la composent représentent 42 circonscriptions électorales et sont élus par un système de scrutin à la représentation proportionnelle pour cinq ans.

---

daily /'deɪlɪ/ adj quotidien. ● adv tous les jours. ● n (newspaper) quotidien m.

dainty /'deɪntɪ/ adj (-ier, -iest) (lace, food) délicat; (shoe, hand) mignon.

dairy /'deərɪ/ n (on farm) laiterie f; (shop) crémerie f. ● adj (farm, cow, product) laitier; (butter) fermier.

daisy /'deɪzɪ/ n pâquerette f.

dam /dæm/ n barrage m.

damage /'dæmɪdʒ/ n (to property) dégâts mpl; (Med) lésions fpl; **to do sth** ~ (cause, trade) porter atteinte à; ~**s** (Jur) dommages-intérêts mpl. ● vt (property) endommager; (health) nuire à; (reputation) porter atteinte à. **damaging** adj (to health) nuisible; (to reputation) préjudiciable.

damn /dæm/ vt (Relig) damner; (condemn: fig) condamner. ● interj 🔢 zut 🔢, merde ⊠. ● n **not give/care a** ~ **about** se ficher de 🔢. ● adj fichu 🔢. ● adv franchement.

damp /dæmp/ n humidité f. ● adj humide. **dampen** vt (lit) humecter; (fig) refroidir. **dampness** n humidité f.

dance /dɑːns/ vt/i danser. ● n danse f; (gathering) bal m; ~ **hall** dancing m.

dancer n danseur/-euse m/f.

dandelion /'dændɪlaɪən/ n pissenlit m.

dandruff /'dændrʌf/ n pellicules fpl.

Dane /deɪn/ n Danois/-e m/f.

danger /'deɪndʒə(r)/ n danger m; (risk) risque m; **be in ∼ of** risquer de. **dangerous** adj dangereux.

dangle /'dæŋgl/ vt (object) balancer; (legs) laisser pendre. ● vi (object) se balancer (**from** à).

Danish /'deɪnɪʃ/ n (Ling) danois m.
● adj danois.

dare /deə(r)/ vt oser ((**to**) **do** faire). ∼ **sb to do** défier qn de faire. ● n défi m. **daring** adj audacieux.

dark /dɑːk/ adj (day, colour, suit, mood, warning) sombre; (hair, eyes, skin) brun; (secret, thought) noir. ● n noir m; (nightfall) tombée f de la nuit; **in the ∼** (fig) dans le noir. **darken** vt/i (sky) (s')obscurcir; (mood) (s')assombrir. **darkness** n obscurité f. ∼**-room** n chambre f noire.

darling /'dɑːlɪŋ/ adj & n chéri/-e (m/f).

dart /dɑːt/ n fléchette f; ∼**s** (game) fléchettes fpl. ● vi ∼ **in/away** entrer/filer comme une flèche.

dash /dæʃ/ vi se précipiter; ∼ **off** se sauver. ● vt (hope) anéantir; ∼ **sth against** projeter qch contre. ● n course f folle; (of liquid) goutte f; (of colour) touche f; (in punctuation) tiret m.

dashboard /'dæʃbɔːd/ n tableau m de bord.

data /'deɪtə/ npl données fpl. ∼**base** n base f de données. ∼ **capture** n saisie f de données. ∼ **processing** n traitement m des données. ∼ **protection** n protection f de l'information.

date /deɪt/ n date f; (meeting) rendez-vous m; (fruit) datte f; **out of ∼** (old-fashioned) démodé; (passport) périmé; **to ∼** à ce jour; **up to ∼** (modern) moderne; (list) à jour. ● vt/i dater; (go out with) sortir avec; ∼ **from** dater de. **dated** adj démodé.

daughter /'dɔːtə(r)/ n fille f. ∼**-in-law** n (pl ∼**s-in-law**) belle-fille f.

daunt /dɔːnt/ vt décourager.

dawdle /'dɔːdl/ vi flâner, traînasser Ⅱ.

dawn /dɔːn/ n aube f. ● vi (day) se lever; **it** ∼**ed on me that** je me suis rendu compte que.

day /deɪ/ n jour m; (whole day) journée f; (period) époque f; **the ∼ before** la veille; **the following** or **next ∼** le lendemain. ∼**break** n aube f.

daydream /'deɪdriːm/ n rêves mpl. ● vi rêvasser (**about** de).

day: ∼**light** n jour m. ∼**time** n journée f. ∼ **trader** spéculateur m à la journée, scalpeur m.

daze /deɪz/ n **in a ∼** (from blow) étourdi; (from drug) hébété. **dazed** adj (by blow) abasourdi; (by news) ahuri.

dazzle /'dæzl/ vt éblouir.

dead /ded/ adj mort; (numb) engourdi.
● adv complètement; **in ∼ centre** au beau milieu; **stop ∼** s'arrêter net. ● n **in the ∼ of** au cœur de; **the ∼** les morts. **deaden** vt (sound, blow) amortir; (pain) calmer. ∼ **end** n impasse f. ∼**line** n date f limite. ∼**lock** n impasse f.

deadly /'dedlɪ/ adj (**-ier, -iest**) mortel; (weapon) meurtrier.

deaf /def/ adj sourd. **deafen** vt assourdir. **deafness** n surdité f.

deal /diːl/ vt (pt **dealt**) donner; (blow) porter. ● vi (trade) être en activité; ∼ **in** être dans le commerce de. ● n affaire f; (cards) donne f; **a great** or **good ∼** beaucoup (**of** de). □ ∼ **with** (handle, manage) s'occuper de; (be about) traiter de. **dealer** n marchand/-e m/f; (agent) concessionnaire mf. **dealings** npl relations fpl.

dear /dɪə(r)/ adj cher; (in letter) **Dear Sir/Madam** Monsieur/Madame. ● n (my) ∼ mon chéri/ma chérie m/f. ● adv cher. ● interj **oh** ∼**!** oh mon Dieu!

death /deθ/ n mort f; ∼ **penalty** peine f de mort.

debatable /dɪ'beɪtəbl/ adj discutable.

debate /dɪ'beɪt/ n (formal) débat m; (informal) discussion f. ● vt (formally) débattre de; (informally) discuter.

debit /'debɪt/ n débit m. ● adj (balance) débiteur. ● vt (pt **debited**) débiter.

debris /'debriː/ n débris mpl; (rubbish) déchets mpl.

debt /det/ n dette f; **be in ∼** avoir des dettes.

debug /diː'bʌg/ vt (Comput) déboguer.

decade /'dekeɪd/ n décennie f.

decadent /'dekədənt/ adj décadent.

d

decaffeinated /diːˈkæfɪneɪtɪd/ adj décaféiné.

decay /dɪˈkeɪ/ vi (vegetation) pourrir; (tooth) se carier; (fig) décliner. ● n pourriture f; (of tooth) carie f; (fig) déclin m.

deceased /dɪˈsiːst/ adj décédé. ● n défunt/-e m/f.

deceit /dɪˈsiːt/ n tromperie f. **deceitful** adj trompeur.

deceive /dɪˈsiːv/ vt tromper.

December /dɪˈsembə(r)/ n décembre m.

decent /ˈdiːsnt/ adj (respectable) comme il faut; (adequate) convenable; (good) bon; (kind) gentil; (not indecent) décent. **decently** adv convenablement.

deception /dɪˈsepʃn/ n tromperie f. **deceptive** adj trompeur.

decide /dɪˈsaɪd/ vt/i décider (**to do** de faire); (question) régler; ~ **on** se décider pour. **decided** adj (firm) résolu; (clear) net. **decidedly** adv nettement.

decimal /ˈdesɪml/ adj décimal. ● n décimale f; ~ **point** virgule f.

decipher /dɪˈsaɪfə(r)/ vt déchiffrer.

decision /dɪˈsɪʒn/ n décision f.

decisive /dɪˈsaɪsɪv/ adj (conclusive) décisif; (firm) décidé.

deck /dek/ n pont m; (of cards: US) jeu m; (of bus) étage m. ~**-chair** n chaise f longue.

declaration /deklǝˈreɪʃn/ n déclaration f. **declare** vt déclarer.

decline /dɪˈklaɪn/ vt/i refuser; (fall) baisser. ● n (waning) déclin m; (drop) baisse f; **in** ~ sur le déclin.

decode /diːˈkǝʊd/ vt décoder.

decommission /diːkǝˈmɪʃn/vt (arms) mettre hors service; (reactor) démanteler.

decompose /diːkǝmˈpǝʊz/ vt/i (se) décomposer.

decor /ˈdeɪkɔː(r)/ n décor m.

decorate /ˈdekǝreɪt/ vt décorer; (room) refaire, peindre. **decoration** n décoration f. **decorative** adj décoratif.

decorator /ˈdekǝreɪtǝ(r)/ n peintre m; (**interior**) ~ décorateur/-trice m/f.

decoy /ˈdiːkɔɪ/ n (person, vehicle) leurre m; (for hunting) appeau m.

decrease¹ /dɪˈkriːs/ vt/i diminuer.

decrease² /ˈdiːkriːs/ n diminution f.

decree /dɪˈkriː/ n (Pol, Relig) décret m; (Jur) jugement m. ● vt (pt **decreed**) décréter.

decrepit /dɪˈkrepɪt/ adj (building) délabré; (person) décrépit.

dedicate /ˈdedɪkeɪt/ vt dédier; ~ **oneself to** se consacrer à.

dedicated /ˈdedɪkeɪtɪd/ adj dévoué; ~ **line** (Internet) ligne f spécialisée.

dedication /dedɪˈkeɪʃn/ n dévouement m; (in book) dédicace f.

deduce /dɪˈdjuːs/ vt déduire.

deduct /dɪˈdʌkt/ vt déduire; (from wages) retenir.

deed /diːd/ n acte m.

deem /diːm/ vt considérer.

deep /diːp/ adj profond; (mud, carpet) épais. ● adv profondément; ~ **in thought** absorbé dans ses pensées. **deepen** vt/i (admiration, concern) augmenter.

deep-freeze n congélateur m. ● vt congeler.

deep vein thrombosis n thrombose f veineuse profonde.

deer /dɪǝ(r)/ n inv cerf m; (doe) biche f.

deface /dɪˈfeɪs/ vt dégrader.

default /dɪˈfɔːlt/ vi (Jur) ~ (**on payments**) ne pas régler ses échéances. ● n (on payments) non-remboursement m; **by** ~ par défaut; **win by** ~ gagner par forfait. ● adj (Comput) par défaut.

defeat /dɪˈfiːt/ vt vaincre; (thwart) faire échouer. ● n défaite f.

defect¹ /ˈdiːfekt/ n défaut m.

defect² /dɪˈfekt/ vi faire défection; ~ **to** passer à.

defective /dɪˈfektɪv/ adj défectueux.

defector /dɪˈfektǝ(r)/ n transfuge mf.

defence /dɪˈfens/ n défense f.

defend /dɪˈfend/ vt défendre. **defendant** n (Jur) accusé/-e m/f. **defender** n défenseur m.

defensive /dɪˈfensɪv/ adj défensif. ● n défensive f.

defer /dɪˈfɜː(r)/ vt (pt **deferred**) (postpone) reporter; (judgement) suspendre; (payment) différer.

deference /ˈdefǝrǝns/ n déférence f. **deferential** adj déférent.

defiance /dɪˈfaɪəns/ *n* défi *m*; **in ~ of** contre. **defiant** *adj* rebelle. **defiantly** *adv* avec défi.

deficiency /dɪˈfɪʃənsɪ/ *n* insuffisance *f*; (fault) défaut *m*.

deficient /dɪˈfɪʃnt/ *adj* insuffisant; **be ~ in** manquer de.

deficit /ˈdefɪsɪt/ *n* déficit *m*.

define /dɪˈfaɪn/ *vt* définir.

definite /ˈdefɪnɪt/ *adj* (exact) précis; (obvious) net; (firm) ferme; (certain) certain. **definitely** *adv* certainement; (clearly) nettement.

definition /defɪˈnɪʃn/ *n* définition *f*.

deflate /dɪˈfleɪt/ *vt* dégonfler.

deflect /dɪˈflekt/ *vt* (missile) dévier; (criticism) détourner.

deforestation /diːfɒrɪˈsteɪʃn/ *n* déforestation *f*.

deform /dɪˈfɔːm/ *vt* déformer.

defraud /dɪˈfrɔːd/ *vt* (client, employer) escroquer; (state, customs) frauder; **~ sb of sth** escroquer qch à qn.

defrost /diːˈfrɒst/ *vt* dégivrer.

deft /deft/ *adj* adroit.

defunct /dɪˈfʌŋkt/ *adj* défunt.

defuse /diːˈfjuːz/ *vt* désamorcer.

defy /dɪˈfaɪ/ *vt* défier; (attempts) résister à.

degenerate[1] /dɪˈdʒenəreɪt/ *vi* dégénérer (**into** en).

degenerate[2] /dɪˈdʒenərət/ *adj* & *n* dégénéré/-e (*m/f*).

degrade /dɪˈɡreɪd/ *vt* (humiliate) humilier; (damage) dégrader.

degree /dɪˈɡriː/ *n* degré *m*; (Univ) diplôme *m* universitaire; (Bachelor's degree) licence *f*; **to such a ~ that** à tel point que.

dehydrate /diːˈhaɪdreɪt/ *vt/i* (se) déshydrater.

deign /deɪn/ *vt* **~ to do** daigner faire.

dejected /dɪˈdʒektɪd/ *adj* découragé.

delay /dɪˈleɪ/ *vt* (flight) retarder; (decision) différer; **~ doing** attendre pour faire. ● *n* (of plane, post) retard *m*; (time lapse) délai *m*.

delegate[1] /ˈdelɪɡət/ *n* délégué/-e *m/f*.

delegate[2] /ˈdelɪɡeɪt/ *vt* déléguer. **delegation** *n* délégation *f*.

delete /dɪˈliːt/ *vt* supprimer; (Comput) effacer; (with pen) barrer. **deletion** *n* suppression *f*; (with line) rature *f*.

deliberate[1] /dɪˈlɪbəreɪt/ *vi* délibérer.

deliberate[2] /dɪˈlɪbərət/ *adj* délibéré; (steps, manner) mesuré. **deliberately** *adv* (do, say) exprès; (sarcastically, provocatively) délibérément.

delicacy /ˈdelɪkəsɪ/ *n* délicatesse *f*; (food) mets *m* raffiné.

delicate /ˈdelɪkət/ *adj* délicat.

delicatessen /delɪkəˈtesn/ *n* épicerie *f* fine.

delicious /dɪˈlɪʃəs/ *adj* délicieux.

delight /dɪˈlaɪt/ *n* joie *f*, plaisir *m*. ● *vt* ravir. ● *vi* **~ in** prendre plaisir à. **delighted** *adj* ravi. **delightful** *adj* charmant/-e.

delinquent /dɪˈlɪŋkwənt/ *adj* & *n* délinquant/-e (*m/f*).

delirious /dɪˈlɪrɪəs/ *adj* délirant.

deliver /dɪˈlɪvə(r)/ *vt* (message) remettre; (goods) livrer; (speech) faire; (baby) mettre au monde; (rescue) délivrer. **delivery** *n* (of goods) livraison *f*; (of mail) distribution *f*; (of baby) accouchement *m*.

delude /dɪˈluːd/ *vt* tromper; **~ oneself** se faire des illusions.

deluge /ˈdeljuːdʒ/ *n* déluge *m*. ● *vt* submerger (**with** de).

delusion /dɪˈluːʒn/ *n* illusion *f*.

delve /delv/ *vi* fouiller.

demand /dɪˈmɑːnd/ *vt* (request, require) demander; (forcefully) exiger. ● *n* (request) demande *f*; (pressure) exigence *f*; **in ~** très demandé; **on ~** à la demande. **demanding** *adj* exigeant.

demean /dɪˈmiːn/ *vt* **~ oneself** s'abaisser.

demeanour, (US)**demeanor** /dɪˈmiːnə(r)/ *n* comportement *m*.

demented /dɪˈmentɪd/ *adj* fou.

demise /dɪˈmaɪz/ *n* disparition *f*.

demo /ˈdeməʊ/ *n* (demonstration Ⅰ) manif *f* Ⅰ.

democracy /dɪˈmɒkrəsɪ/ *n* démocratie *f*.

democrat /ˈdeməkræt/ *n* démocrate *mf*. **democratic** *adj* démocratique.

demolish /dɪˈmɒlɪʃ/ *vt* démolir.

demon /ˈdiːmən/ *n* démon *m*.

demonstrate /ˈdemənstreɪt/ *vt* démontrer; (concern, skill) manifester. ● *vi* (Pol) manifester. **demonstration**

d

n démonstration f; (Pol) manifestation f. **demonstrative** adj démonstratif.

demonstrator n manifestant/-e m/f.

demoralize /dɪ'mɒrəlaɪz/ vt démoraliser.

demote /diː'məʊt/ vt rétrograder.

den /den/ n (of lion) antre m; (room) tanière f.

denial /dɪ'naɪəl/ n (of rumour) démenti m; (of rights) négation f; (of request) rejet m.

denim /'denɪm/ n jean m; ~s (jeans) jean m.

Denmark /'denmɑːk/ n Danemark m.

denomination /dɪnɒmɪ'neɪʃn/ n (Relig) confession f; (money) valeur f.

denounce /dɪ'naʊns/ vt dénoncer.

dense /dens/ adj dense. **densely** adv (packed) très. **density** n densité f.

dent /dent/ n bosse f. ● vt cabosser.

dental /'dentl/ adj dentaire; ~ floss fil m dentaire; ~ surgeon chirurgien-dentiste m.

dentist /'dentɪst/ n dentiste mf. **dentistry** n médecine f dentaire.

dentures /'dentʃəz/ npl dentier m.

deny /dɪ'naɪ/ vt nier (that que); (rumour) démentir; ~ sb sth refuser qch à qn.

deodorant /diː'əʊdərənt/ n déodorant m.

depart /dɪ'pɑːt/ vi partir; ~ from (deviate) s'éloigner de.

department /dɪ'pɑːtmənt/ n (in shop) rayon m; (in hospital, office) service m; (Univ) département m; D~ of Health ministère m de la Santé; ~ store grand magasin m.

departure /dɪ'pɑːtʃə(r)/ n départ m; a ~ from (custom, truth) une entorse à.

depend /dɪ'pend/ vi dépendre (on de). ~ on (rely on) compter sur; **it (all)** ~s ça dépend; ~ing on the season suivant la saison. **dependable** adj (person) digne de confiance. **dependant** n personne f à charge. **dependence** n dépendance f.

dependent /dɪ'pendənt/ adj dépendant; be ~ on dépendre de.

depict /dɪ'pɪkt/ vt (describe) dépeindre; (in picture) représenter.

deplete /dɪ'pliːt/ vt réduire.

deport /dɪ'pɔːt/ vt expulser.

depose /dɪ'pəʊz/ vt déposer.

deposit /dɪ'pɒzɪt/ vt (pt **deposited**) déposer. ● n (in bank) dépôt m; (on house) versement m initial; (on holiday) acompte m; (against damage) caution f; (on bottle) consigne f; (of mineral) gisement m; ~ account compte m de dépôt. **depositor** n (Comm) déposant/-e m/f.

depot /'depəʊ/ n dépôt m; (US) gare f.

depreciate /dɪ'priːʃɪeɪt/ vt/i (se) déprécier.

depress /dɪ'pres/ vt déprimer. **depressing** adj déprimant. **depression** n dépression f; (Econ) récession f.

deprivation /deprɪ'veɪʃn/ n privation f.

deprive /dɪ'praɪv/ vt ~ of priver de. **deprived** adj démuni.

depth /depθ/ n profondeur f; (of knowledge, ignorance) étendue f; (of colour, emotion) intensité f.

deputize /'depjʊtaɪz/ vi ~ for remplacer.

deputy /'depjʊtɪ/ n adjoint/-e m/f. ● adj adjoint; ~ chairman vice-président m.

derail /dɪ'reɪl/ vt faire dérailler. **derailment** n déraillement m.

deranged /dɪ'reɪndʒd/ adj dérangé.

derelict /'derəlɪkt/ adj abandonné.

deride /dɪ'raɪd/ vt ridiculiser. **derision** n moqueries fpl. **derisory** adj dérisoire.

derivative /də'rɪvətɪv/ adj & n dérivé (m).

derive /dɪ'raɪv/ vt ~ sth from tirer qch de. ● vi ~ from découler de.

derogatory /dɪ'rɒgətrɪ/ adj (word) péjoratif; (remark) désobligeant.

descend /dɪ'send/ vt/i descendre; be ~ed from descendre de. **descendant** n descendant/-e m/f. **descent** n descente f; (lineage) origine f.

describe /dɪ'skraɪb/ vt décrire; ~ sb as sth qualifier qn de qch. **description** n description f. **descriptive** adj descriptif.

desert[1] /'dezət/ n désert m.

desert[2] /dɪ'zɜːt/ vt/i abandonner; (cause) déserter. **deserted** adj désert. **deserter** n déserteur m.

deserts /dɪ'zɜːts/ npl get one's ~ avoir ce qu'on mérite.

deserve /dɪ'zɜːv/ vt mériter (to de). **deservedly** adv à juste titre. **deserv-**

ing adj (person) méritant; (action) louable.

design /dɪ'zaɪn/ n (sketch) plan m; (idea) conception f; (pattern) motif m; (art of designing) design m; (aim) dessein m. ● vt (sketch) dessiner; (devise, intend) concevoir.

designate /'dezɪɡneɪt/ vt désigner.

designer /dɪ'zaɪnə(r)/ n concepteur/-trice m/f; (of fashion, furniture) créateur/-trice m/f. ● adj (clothes) de haute couture; (sunglasses, drink) de dernière mode.

desirable /dɪ'zaɪərəbl/ adj (outcome) souhaitable; (person) désirable.

desire /dɪ'zaɪə(r)/ n désir m. ● vt désirer.

desk /desk/ n bureau m; (of pupil) pupitre m; (in hotel) réception f; (in bank) caisse f.

desolate /'desələt/ adj (place) désolé; (person) affligé.

despair /dɪ'speə(r)/ n désespoir m. ● vi désespérer (of de).

desperate /'despərət/ adj désespéré; (criminal) prêt à tout; be ~ for avoir désespérément besoin de. **desperately** adv désespérément; (worried) terriblement; (ill) gravement.

desperation /despə'reɪʃn/ n désespoir m; in ~ en désespoir de cause.

despicable /dɪ'spɪkəbl/ adj méprisable.

despise /dɪ'spaɪz/ vt mépriser.

despite /dɪ'spaɪt/ prep malgré.

despondent /dɪ'spɒndənt/ adj découragé.

dessert /dɪ'zɜːt/ n dessert m. ~**spoon** n cuillère f à dessert.

destination /destɪ'neɪʃn/ n destination f.

destiny /'destɪnɪ/ n destin m.

destitute /'destɪtjuːt/ adj sans ressources.

destroy /dɪ'strɔɪ/ vt détruire; (animal) abattre. **destroyer** n (warship) contre-torpilleur m.

destruction /dɪ'strʌkʃn/ n destruction f. **destructive** adj destructeur.

detach /dɪ'tætʃ/ vt détacher; ~**ed house** maison f (individuelle).

detail /'diːteɪl/ n détail m; go into ~ entrer dans les détails. ● vt (plans) exposer en détail.

detain /dɪ'teɪn/ vt retenir; (in prison) placer en détention. **detainee** n détenu/-e m/f.

detect /dɪ'tekt/ vt (error, trace) déceler; (crime, mine, sound) détecter. **detection** n détection f. **detective** n inspecteur/-trice m/f; (private) détective m.

detention /dɪ'tenʃn/ n détention f; (School) retenue f.

deter /dɪ'tɜː(r)/ vt (pt deterred) dissuader (from de).

detergent /dɪ'tɜːdʒənt/ adj & n détergent (m).

deteriorate /dɪ'tɪərɪəreɪt/ vi se détériorer.

determine /dɪ'tɜːmɪn/ vt déterminer; ~ to do résoudre de faire. **determined** adj (person) décidé; (air) résolu.

deterrent /dɪ'terənt/ n moyen m de dissuasion. ● adj (effect) dissuasif.

detest /dɪ'test/ vt détester.

detonate /'detəneɪt/ vt/i (faire) détoner. **detonation** n détonation f. **detonator** n détonateur m.

detour /'diːtʊə(r)/ n détour m.

detract /dɪ'trækt/ vi ~ from (success, value) porter atteinte à; (pleasure) diminuer.

detriment /'detrɪmənt/ n to the ~ of au détriment de. **detrimental** adj nuisible (to à).

devalue /diː'væljuː/ vt dévaluer.

devastate /'devəsteɪt/ vt (place) ravager; (person) accabler.

develop /dɪ'veləp/ vt (plan) élaborer; (mind, body) développer; (land) mettre en valeur; (illness) attraper; (habit) prendre. ● vi (child, country, plot, business) se développer; (hole, crack) se former.

development /dɪ'veləpmənt/ n développement m; (housing) ~ lotissement m; (new) ~ fait m nouveau.

deviate /'diːvɪeɪt/ vi dévier; ~ from (norm) s'écarter de.

device /dɪ'vaɪs/ n appareil m; (means) moyen m; (bomb) engin m explosif.

devil /'devl/ n diable m.

devious /'diːvɪəs/ adj (person) retors.

devise /dɪ'vaɪz/ vt (scheme) concevoir; (product) inventer.

devoid /dɪ'vɔɪd/ adj ~ of dépourvu de.

devolution /diːvəˈluːʃn/ n (Pol) régionalisation f.

devote /dɪˈvəʊt/ vt consacrer (**to** à). **devoted** adj dévoué. **devotion** n dévouement m; (Relig) dévotion f.

devour /dɪˈvaʊə(r)/ vt dévorer.

devout /dɪˈvaʊt/ adj fervent.

dew /djuː/ n rosée f.

diabetes /daɪəˈbiːtiːz/ n diabète m.

diabolical /daɪəˈbɒlɪkl/ adj diabolique; (bad 🔲) atroce.

diagnose /ˈdaɪəgnəʊz/ vt diagnostiquer. **diagnosis** n (pl **-oses**) diagnostic m.

diagonal /daɪˈægənl/ adj diagonal. ● n diagonale f.

diagram /ˈdaɪəgræm/ n schéma m.

dial /ˈdaɪəl/ n cadran m. ● vt (pt **dialled**) (number) faire; (person) appeler; **dialling code** indicatif m; **dialling tone** tonalité f.

dialect /ˈdaɪəlekt/ n dialecte m.

dialogue /ˈdaɪəlɒg/ n dialogue m.

diameter /daɪˈæmɪtə(r)/ n diamètre m.

diamond /ˈdaɪəmənd/ n diamant m; (shape) losange m; (baseball) terrain m; ∼s (cards) carreau m.

diaper /ˈdaɪəpə(r)/ n (US) couche f.

diaphragm /ˈdaɪəfræm/ n diaphragme m.

diarrhoea, (US) **diarrhea** /daɪəˈrɪə/ n diarrhée f.

diary /ˈdaɪərɪ/ n (for appointments) agenda m; (journal) journal m intime.

dice /daɪs/ n inv dé m. ● vt (food) couper en dés.

dictate /dɪkˈteɪt/ vt/i dicter.

dictation /dɪkˈteɪʃn/ n dictée f.

dictator /dɪkˈteɪtə(r)/ n dictateur m. **dictatorship** n dictature f.

dictionary /ˈdɪkʃənrɪ/ n dictionnaire m.

did /dɪd/ →DO.

didn't →DID NOT.

die /daɪ/ vi (pres p **dying**) mourir; (plant) crever; **be dying to do** mourir d'envie de faire. □ ∼ **down** diminuer. ∼ **out** disparaître.

diesel /ˈdiːzl/ n gazole m; ∼ **engine** moteur m diesel.

diet /ˈdaɪət/ n (usual food) alimentation f; (restricted) régime m. ● vi être au régime. **dietary** adj alimentaire. **diet-**

ician n diététicien/-ne m/f.

differ /ˈdɪfə(r)/ vi différer (**from** de).

difference /ˈdɪfrəns/ n différence f; (disagreement) différend m. **different** adj différent (**from**, **to** de).

differentiate /dɪfəˈrenʃɪeɪt/ vt différencier. ● vi faire la différence (**between** entre).

differently /ˈdɪfrəntlɪ/ adv différemment (**from** de).

difficult /ˈdɪfɪkəlt/ adj difficile. **difficulty** n difficulté f.

diffuse¹ /dɪˈfjuːs/ adj diffus.

diffuse² /dɪˈfjuːz/ vt diffuser.

dig /dɪg/ vt/i (pt **dug**; pres p **digging**) (excavate) creuser; (in garden) bêcher. ● n (poke) coup m de coude; (remark) pique f 🔲; (Archeol) fouilles fpl. □ ∼ **up** déterrer.

digest /daɪˈdʒest/ vt/i digérer. **digestible** adj digestible. **digestion** n digestion f.

digger /ˈdɪgə(r)/ n excavateur m.

digit /ˈdɪdʒɪt/ n chiffre m. ● **digitize** vt numériser.

digital /ˈdɪdʒɪtl/ adj (clock) à affichage numérique; (display, recording) numérique. ∼ **audio tape** n cassette f audionumérique. ∼ **camera** n appareil m photo numérique.

dignified /ˈdɪgnɪfaɪd/ adj digne.

dignitary /ˈdɪgnɪtərɪ/ n dignitaire m.

dignity /ˈdɪgnətɪ/ n dignité f.

digress /daɪˈgres/ vi faire une digression.

dilapidated /dɪˈlæpɪdeɪtɪd/ adj délabré.

dilate /daɪˈleɪt/ vt/i (se) dilater.

dilemma /daɪˈlemə/ n dilemme m.

diligent /ˈdɪlɪdʒənt/ adj appliqué.

dilute /daɪˈljuːt/ vt diluer.

dim /dɪm/ adj (**dimmer, dimmest**) (weak) faible; (dark) sombre; (indistinct) vague; 🔲 stupide. ● vt/i (pt **dimmed**) (light) baisser.

dime /daɪm/ n (US) (pièce f de) dix cents.

dimension /dɪˈmenʃn/ n dimension f.

diminish /dɪˈmɪnɪʃ/ vt/i diminuer.

dimple /ˈdɪmpl/ n fossette f.

din /dɪn/ n vacarme m.

dine /daɪn/ vi dîner. **diner** n dîneur/-euse m/f; (US) restaurant m à service rapide.

dinghy /'dɪŋgɪ/ n dériveur m.

dingy /'dɪndʒɪ/ adj (**-ier, -iest**) minable.

dining room /'daɪnɪŋrʊm/n salle f à manger.

dinner /'dɪnə(r)/ n (evening meal) dîner m; (lunch) déjeuner m; **have** ~ dîner. ~**jacket** n smoking m. ~ **party** n dîner m.

dinosaur /'daɪnəsɔ:(r)/ n dinosaure m.

dip /dɪp/ vt/i (pt **dipped**) plonger; ~ **into** (book) feuilleter; (savings) puiser dans; ~ **one's headlights** se mettre en code. ● n (slope) déclivité f; (in sea) bain m rapide.

diploma /dɪ'pləʊmə/ n diplôme m (**in** en).

diplomacy /dɪp'ləʊməsɪ/ n diplomatie f. **diplomat** n diplomate mf. **diplomatic** adj (Pol) diplomatique; (tactful) diplomate.

dire /'daɪə(r)/ adj affreux; (need, poverty) extrême.

direct /daɪ'rekt/ adj direct. ● adv directement. ● vt diriger; (letter, remark) adresser; (a play) mettre en scène; ~ **sb to** indiquer à qn le chemin de; (order) signifier à qn de.

direction /daɪ'rekʃn/ n direction f; (Theat) mise f en scène; ~**s** indications fpl; **ask** ~**s** demander le chemin; ~**s for use** mode m d'emploi.

directly /daɪ'rektlɪ/ adv directement; (at once) tout de suite. ● conj dès que.

director /daɪ'rektə(r)/ n directeur/-trice m/f; (Theat) metteur m en scène.

directory /daɪ'rektərɪ/ n (phone book) annuaire m. ~ **enquiries** npl renseignements mpl téléphoniques.

dirt /dɜ:t/ n saleté f; (earth) terre f; ~ **cheap** ☒ très bon marché inv. ~**-track** n (Sport) cendrée f.

dirty /dɜ:tɪ/ adj (**-ier, -iest**) sale; (word) grossier; **get** ~ se salir. ● vt/i (se) salir.

disability /dɪsə'bɪlətɪ/ n handicap m.

disable /dɪs'eɪbl/ vt rendre infirme. **disabled** adj handicapé.

disadvantage /dɪsəd'vɑ:ntɪdʒ/ n désavantage m. **disadvantaged** adj défavorisé.

disagree /dɪsə'gri:/ vi ne pas être d'accord (**with** avec). ~ **with sb** (food, climate) ne pas convenir à qn. **disagreement** n désaccord m; (quarrel) différend m.

disappear /dɪsə'pɪə(r)/ vi disparaître. **disappearance** n disparition f (**of** de).

disappoint /dɪsə'pɔɪnt/ vt décevoir. **disappointment** n déception f.

disapproval /dɪsə'pru:vl/ n désapprobation f (**of** de).

disapprove /dɪsə'pru:v/ vi ~ (**of**) désapprouver.

disarm /dɪs'ɑ:m/ vt/i désarmer. **disarmament** n désarmement m.

disarray /dɪsə'reɪ/ n désordre m.

disaster /dɪ'zɑ:stə(r)/ n désastre m. **disastrous** adj désastreux.

disband /dɪs'bænd/ vi disperser. ● vt dissoudre.

disbelief /dɪsbɪ'li:f/ n incrédulité f.

disc /dɪsk/ n disque m; (Comput) →DISK.

discard /dɪs'kɑ:d/ vt se débarrasser de; (beliefs) abandonner.

discharge /dɪs'tʃɑ:dʒ/ vt (unload) décharger; (liquid) déverser; (duty) remplir; (dismiss) renvoyer; (prisoner) libérer. ● vi (of pus) s'écouler.

disciple /dɪ'saɪpl/ n disciple m.

disciplinary /'dɪsɪplɪnərɪ/ adj disciplinaire.

discipline /'dɪsɪplɪn/ n discipline f. ● vt discipliner; (punish) punir.

disc jockey n disc-jockey m, animateur m.

disclaimer /dɪs'kleɪmə(r)/ n démenti m.

disclose /dɪs'kləʊz/ vt révéler. **disclosure** n révélation f (**of** de).

disco /'dɪskəʊ/ n (club ⊞) discothèque f; (event) soirée f disco.

discolour /dɪs'kʌlə(r)/ vt/i (se) décolorer.

discomfort /dɪs'kʌmfət/ n gêne f.

disconcert /dɪskən'sɜ:t/ vt déconcerter.

disconnect /dɪskə'nekt/ vt détacher; (unplug) débrancher; (cut off) couper.

discontent /dɪskən'tent/ n mécontentement m.

discontinue /dɪskən'tɪnju:/ vt (service) supprimer; (production) arrêter.

discord /'dɪskɔːd/ n discorde f; (Mus) discordance f.

discount¹ /'dɪskaʊnt/ n remise f; (on minor purchase) rabais m.

discount² /dɪsˈkaʊnt/ vt (advice) ne pas tenir compte de; (possibility) écarter.

discourage /dɪˈskʌrɪdʒ/ vt décourager.

discourse /'dɪskɔːs/ n discours m.

discourteous /dɪsˈkɜːtɪəs/ adj peu courtois.

discover /dɪsˈkʌvə(r)/ vt découvrir. **discovery** n découverte f.

discreet /dɪˈskriːt/ adj discret.

discrepancy /dɪsˈkrepənsɪ/ n divergence f.

discretion /dɪˈskreʃn/ n discrétion f.

discriminate /dɪˈskrɪmɪneɪt/ vt/i distinguer; ~ against faire de la discrimination contre. **discriminating** adj qui a du discernement. **discrimination** n discernement m; (bias) discrimination f.

discus /'dɪskəs/ n disque m.

discuss /dɪˈskʌs/ vt (talk about) discuter de; (in writing) examiner. **discussion** n discussion f.

disdain /dɪsˈdeɪn/ n dédain m.

disease /dɪˈziːz/ n maladie f.

disembark /dɪsɪmˈbɑːk/ vt/i débarquer.

disenchanted /dɪsɪnˈtʃɑːntɪd/ adj désabusé.

disentangle /dɪsɪnˈtæŋgl/ vt démêler.

disfigure /dɪsˈfɪgə(r)/ vt défigurer.

disgrace /dɪsˈgreɪs/ n (shame) honte f; (disfavour) disgrâce f. ● vt déshonorer. **disgraced** adj (in disfavour) disgracié. **disgraceful** adj honteux.

disgruntled /dɪsˈgrʌntld/ adj mécontent.

disguise /dɪsˈgaɪz/ vt déguiser. ● n déguisement m; in ~ déguisé.

disgust /dɪsˈgʌst/ n dégoût m. ● vt dégoûter.

dish /dɪʃ/ n plat m; the ~es (crockery) la vaisselle. ● vt ~ out distribuer; ~ up servir.

dishcloth /'dɪʃklɒθ/ n lavette f; (for drying) torchon m.

dishearten /dɪsˈhɑːtn/ vt décourager.

dishevelled /dɪˈʃevld/ adj échevelé.

dishonest /dɪsˈɒnɪst/ adj malhonnête.

dishonour, (US) **dishonor** /dɪsˈɒnə(r)/ n déshonneur m.

dishwasher /'dɪʃwɒʃə(r)/ n lave-vaisselle m inv.

disillusion /dɪsɪˈluːʒn/ vt désabuser. **disillusionment** n désillusion f.

disincentive /dɪsɪnˈsentɪv/ n be a ~ to décourager.

disinclined /dɪsɪnˈklaɪnd/ adj ~ to peu disposé à.

disinfect /dɪsɪnˈfekt/ vt désinfecter. **disinfectant** n désinfectant m.

disintegrate /dɪsˈɪntɪgreɪt/ vt/i (se) désintégrer.

disinterested /dɪsˈɪntrəstɪd/ adj désintéressé.

disjointed /dɪsˈdʒɔɪntɪd/ adj (talk) décousu.

disk /dɪsk/ n (US) ➡DISC; (Comput) disque m. ~ drive n drive m, lecteur m de disquettes.

diskette /dɪˈsket/ n disquette f.

dislike /dɪsˈlaɪk/ n aversion f. ● vt ne pas aimer.

dislocate /'dɪsləkeɪt/ vt (limb) disloquer.

dislodge /dɪsˈlɒdʒ/ vt (move) déplacer; (drive out) déloger.

disloyal /dɪsˈlɔɪəl/ adj déloyal (to envers).

dismal /'dɪzməl/ adj morne, triste.

dismantle /dɪsˈmæntl/ vt démonter, défaire.

dismay /dɪsˈmeɪ/ n consternation f (at devant). ● vt consterner.

dismiss /dɪsˈmɪs/ vt renvoyer; (appeal) rejeter; (from mind) écarter. **dismissal** n renvoi m.

dismount /dɪsˈmaʊnt/ vi descendre, mettre pied à terre.

disobedient /dɪsəˈbiːdɪənt/ adj désobéissant.

disobey /dɪsəˈbeɪ/ vt désobéir à. ● vi désobéir.

disorder /dɪsˈɔːdə(r)/ n désordre m; (ailment) trouble(s) m(pl). **disorderly** adj désordonné.

disorganized /dɪsˈɔːgənaɪzd/ adj désorganisé.

disown /dɪsˈəʊn/ vt renier.

disparaging /dɪˈspærɪdʒɪŋ/ adj désobligeant.

dispassionate /dɪˈspæʃənət/ adj impartial; (unemotional) calme.

dispatch /dɪˈspætʃ/ vt (send, complete) expédier; (troops) envoyer. ● n expédition f. envoi m; (report) dépêche f.

dispel /dɪˈspel/ vt (pt **dispelled**) dissiper.

dispensary /dɪˈspensərɪ/ n (in hospital) pharmacie f; (in pharmacy) officine f.

dispense /dɪˈspens/ vt distribuer; (medicine) préparer. ● vi ~ **with** se passer de. **dispenser** n (container) distributeur m.

disperse /dɪˈspɜːs/ vt/i (se) disperser.

display /dɪˈspleɪ/ vt montrer, exposer; (feelings) manifester. ● n exposition f; manifestation f; (Comm) étalage m; (of computer) visuel m.

displeased /dɪsˈpliːzd/ adj mécontent (**with** de).

disposable /dɪˈspəʊzəbl/ adj jetable.

disposal /dɪˈspəʊzl/ n (of waste) évacuation f; **at sb's** ~ à la disposition de qn.

dispose /dɪˈspəʊz/ vt disposer. ● vi ~ **of** se débarrasser de; **well** ~**d to** bien disposé envers.

disposition /dɪspəˈzɪʃn/ n disposition f; (character) naturel m.

disprove /dɪsˈpruːv/ vt réfuter.

dispute /dɪˈspjuːt/ vt contester. ● n discussion f; (Pol) conflit m; **in** ~ contesté.

disqualify /dɪsˈkwɒlɪfaɪ/ vt rendre inapte; (Sport) disqualifier; ~ **from driving** retirer le permis à.

disquiet /dɪsˈkwaɪət/ n inquiétude f. **disquieting** adj inquiétant.

disregard /dɪsrɪˈgɑːd/ vt ne pas tenir compte de. ● n indifférence f (**for** à).

disrepair /dɪsrɪˈpeə(r)/ n délabrement m.

disreputable /dɪsˈrepjʊtəbl/ adj peu recommandable.

disrepute /dɪsrɪˈpjuːt/ n discrédit m.

disrespect /dɪsrɪˈspekt/ n manque m de respect. **disrespectful** adj irrespectueux.

disrupt /dɪsˈrʌpt/ vt (disturb, break up) perturber; (plans) déranger. **disruption** n perturbation f. **disruptive** adj perturbateur.

dissatisfied /dɪˈsætɪsfaɪd/ adj mécontent.

dissect /dɪˈsekt/ vt disséquer.

disseminate /dɪˈsemɪneɪt/ vt diffuser.

dissent /dɪˈsent/ vi différer (**from** de). ● n dissentiment m.

dissertation /dɪsəˈteɪʃn/ n mémoire m.

disservice /dɪsˈsɜːvɪs/ n **do a** ~ **to sb** rendre un mauvais service à qn.

dissident /ˈdɪsɪdənt/ adj & n dissident/-e (m/f).

dissimilar /dɪˈsɪmɪlə(r)/ adj dissemblable, différent.

dissipate /ˈdɪsɪpeɪt/ vt/i (se) dissiper. **dissipated** adj (person) dissolu.

dissolve /dɪˈzɒlv/ vt/i (se) dissoudre.

dissuade /dɪˈsweɪd/ vt dissuader.

distance /ˈdɪstəns/ n distance f; **from a** ~ de loin; **in the** ~ au loin. **distant** adj éloigné, lointain; (relative) éloigné; (aloof) distant.

distaste /dɪsˈteɪst/ n dégoût m. **distasteful** adj désagréable.

distil /dɪˈstɪl/ vt (pt **distilled**) distiller.

distinct /dɪˈstɪŋkt/ adj distinct; (definite) net; **as** ~ **from** par opposition à. **distinction** n distinction f; (in exam) mention f très bien. **distinctive** adj distinctif.

distinguish /dɪˈstɪŋgwɪʃ/ vt/i distinguer.

distort /dɪˈstɔːt/ vt déformer. **distortion** n distorsion f; (of facts) déformation f.

distract /dɪˈstrækt/ vt distraire. **distracted** adj (distraught) éperdu. **distracting** adj gênant. **distraction** n (lack of attention, entertainment) distraction f.

distraught /dɪˈstrɔːt/ adj éperdu.

distress /dɪˈstres/ n douleur f; (poverty, danger) détresse f. ● vt peiner. **distressing** adj pénible.

distribute /dɪˈstrɪbjuːt/ vt distribuer.

district /ˈdɪstrɪkt/ n région f; (of town) quartier m.

distrust /dɪsˈtrʌst/ n méfiance f. ● vt se méfier de.

disturb /dɪˈstɜːb/ vt déranger; (alarm, worry) troubler. **disturbance** n dérangement m (**of** de); (noise) tapage m. **disturbances** npl (Pol) troubles mpl.

disturbed adj troublé; (psychologically) perturbé. **disturbing** adj troublant.

disused /dɪs'juːzd/ adj désaffecté.

ditch /dɪtʃ/ n fossé m. ● vt ✖ abandonner.

ditto /'dɪtəʊ/ adv idem.

dive /daɪv/ vi plonger; (rush) se précipiter. ● n plongeon m; (of plane) piqué m; (place ✖) bouge m. **diver** n plongeur/-euse m/f.

diverge /daɪ'vɜːdʒ/ vi diverger. **divergent** adj divergent.

diverse /daɪ'vɜːs/ adj divers.

diversion /daɪ'vɜːʃn/ n détournement m; (distraction) diversion f; (of traffic) déviation f. **divert** vt détourner; (traffic) dévier.

divide /dɪ'vaɪd/ vt/i (se) diviser.

dividend /'dɪvɪdend/ n dividende m.

divine /dɪ'vaɪn/ adj divin.

diving: ~**-board** n plongeoir m. ~**-suit** n scaphandre m.

division /dɪ'vɪʒn/ n division f.

divorce /dɪ'vɔːs/ n divorce m (from avec). ● vt/i divorcer (d'avec).

divulge /daɪ'vʌldʒ/ vt divulguer.

DIY abbr ➡DO-IT-YOURSELF.

dizziness /'dɪzɪnɪs/ n vertige m.

dizzy /'dɪzɪ/ adj (**-ier, -iest**) vertigineux; **be** or **feel** ~ avoir le vertige.

---

do /duː/

present **do, does**; present negative **don't, do not**; past **did**; past participle **done**

● transitive and intransitive verb

····➤ faire; **she is doing her homework** elle fait ses devoirs.

····➤ (progress, be suitable) aller; **how are you doing?** comment ça va?

····➤ (be enough) suffire; **will five dollars** ~? cinq dollars, ça suffira?

● auxiliary verb

····➤ (in questions) ~ **you like Mozart?** aimes-tu Mozart?, est-ce que tu aimes Mozart?; **did your sister phone?** est-ce que ta sœur a téléphoné?, ta sœur a-t-elle téléphoné?

····➤ (in negatives) **I don't like Mozart** je n'aime pas Mozart.

····➤ (emphatic uses) **I** ~ **like your dress** j'aime beaucoup ta robe; **I** ~ **think you should go** je pense vraiment que tu devrais y aller.

····➤ (referring back to another verb) **I live in Orford and so does Lily** j'habite à Orford et Lily aussi; **she gets paid more than I** ~ elle est payée plus que moi; **'I don't like carrots'—'neither** ~ **I'** 'je n'aime pas les carottes'—'moi non plus'.

····➤ (imperatives) **don't shut the door** ne ferme pas la porte; ~ **be quiet** tais-toi!

····➤ (short questions and answers) **you like fish, don't you?** tu aimes le poisson, n'est-ce pas?; **Lola didn't phone, did she?** Lola n'a pas téléphoné par hasard?; **'does he play tennis?'—'no he doesn't/yes he does'** 'est-ce qu'il joue au tennis?'—'non/oui'; **'Marion didn't say that'—'yes she did'** 'Marion n'a pas dit ça'—'si'.

□ **do away with** supprimer. **do up** (fasten) fermer; (house) refaire; **do with it's to** ~ **with** c'est à propos de; **it's nothing to** ~ **with** ça n'a rien à voir avec. **do without** se passer de.

---

docile /'dəʊsaɪl/ adj docile.

dock /dɒk/ n (Jur) banc m des accusés; dock m. ● vi arriver au port. ● vt mettre à quai; (wages) faire une retenue sur.

doctor /'dɒktə(r)/ n médecin m, docteur m; (Univ) docteur m. ● vt (cat) châtrer; (fig) altérer.

doctorate /'dɒktərət/ n doctorat m.

document /'dɒkjʊmənt/ n document m. **documentary** adj & n documentaire (m). **documentation** n documentation f.

dodge /dɒdʒ/ vt esquiver. ● vi faire un saut de côté. ● n mouvement m de côté.

dodgems /'dɒdʒəmz/ npl autos fpl tamponneuses.

dodgy /'dɒdʒɪ/ adj (**-ier, -iest**) (🇬🇧: difficult) épineux, délicat; (untrustworthy) louche 🇬🇧.

doe /dəʊ/ n (deer) biche f.

does /dʌz/ ➡DO.

doesn't ➡DOES NOT.

dog /dɒg/ n chien m. ● vt (pt **dogged**) poursuivre. ~**-collar** n col m romain. ~**-eared** adj écorné.

dogged /'dɒgɪd/ adj obstiné.

dogma /'dɒgmə/ n dogme m. **dogmatic** adj dogmatique.

dogsbody /'dɒgzbɒdi/ n bonne f à tout faire.

do-it-yourself /duːɪtjɔː'self/ n bricolage m.

doldrums /'dɒldrəmz/ npl be in the ~ (person) avoir le cafard.

dole /dəʊl/ vt ~ out distribuer. ● n Ⓘ indemnité f de chômage; **on the** ~ Ⓘ au chômage.

doll /'dɒl/ n poupée f. ● vt ~ up Ⓘ bichonner.

dollar /'dɒlə(r)/ n dollar m.

dollop /'dɒləp/ n (of food Ⓘ) gros morceau m.

dolphin /'dɒlfɪn/ n dauphin m.

domain /dəʊ'meɪn/ n domaine m.

dome /dəʊm/ n dôme m.

domestic /də'mestɪk/ adj familial; (trade, flights) intérieur; (animal) domestique. **domesticated** adj (animal) domestiqué.

domestic science n arts mpl ménagers.

dominant /'dɒmɪnənt/ adj dominant.

dominate /'dɒmɪneɪt/ vt/i dominer. **domination** n domination f.

domineering /dɒmɪ'nɪərɪŋ/ adj dominateur.

domino /'dɒmɪnəʊ/ n (pl ~es) domino m; ~es (game) dominos mpl.

donate /dəʊ'neɪt/ vt faire don de. **donation** n don m.

done /dʌn/ ➡DO.

donkey /'dɒŋki/ n âne m. ~ **work** n travail m pénible.

donor /'dəʊnə(r)/ n donateur/-trice m/f; (of blood) donneur/-euse m/f.

don't ➡DO NOT.

doodle /'duːdl/ vi griffonner.

doom /duːm/ n (ruin) ruine f; (fate) destin m. ● vt be ~ed to être destiné or condamné à; ~ed (to failure) voué à l'échec.

door /dɔː(r)/ n porte f; (of vehicle) portière f, porte f. ~**bell** n sonnette f. ~**man** n (pl **-men**) portier m. ~**mat** n paillasson m. ~**step** n pas m de (la) porte, seuil m. ~**way** n porte f.

dope /dəʊp/ n Ⓘ cannabis m; (idiot ☒) imbécile mf. ● vt doper. **dopey** adj (foolish ☒) imbécile.

dormant /'dɔːmənt/ adj en sommeil.

dormitory /'dɔːmɪtrɪ/ n dortoir m; (Univ, US) résidence f.

dosage /'dəʊsɪdʒ/ n dose f; (on label) posologie f.

dose /dəʊs/ n dose f.

dot /dɒt/ n point m; **on the** ~ Ⓘ à l'heure pile.

dot-com /dɒt'kɒm/ n (société) point com f; ~ **millionaire** n millionaire mf de l'Internet. ~ **shares** npl actions fpl des sociétés point com.

dote /dəʊt/ vi ~ **on** adorer.

dotted /'dɒtɪd/ adj (fabric) à pois; ~ **line** pointillé m; ~ **with** parsemé de.

double /'dʌbl/ adj double; (room, bed) pour deux personnes; ~ **the size** deux fois plus grand. ● adv deux fois; **pay** ~ payer le double. ● n double m; (stuntman) doublure f; ~**s** (tennis) double m; **at** or **on the** ~ au pas de course. ● vt/i doubler; (fold) plier en deux. ~**-bass** n (Mus) contrebasse f. ~**-check** vt revérifier. ~ **chin** n double menton m. ~**-cross** vt tromper. ~**-decker** n autobus m à impériale.

doubt /daʊt/ n doute m. ● vt douter de; ~ **if** or **that** douter que. **doubtful** adj incertain, douteux; (person) qui a des doutes. **doubtless** adv sans doute.

dough /dəʊ/ n pâte f; (money ☒) fric m Ⓘ.

doughnut /'dəʊnʌt/ n beignet m.

douse /daʊs/ vt arroser; (light, fire) éteindre.

dove /dʌv/ n colombe f.

Dover /'dəʊvə(r)/ n Douvres.

dowdy /'daʊdi/ adj (**-ier, -iest**) (clothes) sans chic, monotone; (person) sans élégance.

down /daʊn/ adv en bas; (of sun) couché; (lower) plus bas; **come** or **go** ~ descendre; **go** ~ **to the post office** aller à la poste; ~ **under** aux antipodes; ~ **with** à bas. ● prep en bas de; (along) le long de. ● vt (knock down,

d

shoot down) abattre; (drink) vider. ● n (fluff) duvet m.

down: ~-**and-out** n clochard/-e m/f. ~**cast** adj démoralisé. ~**fall** n chute f. ~**grade** vt déclasser. ~-**hearted** adj découragé.

downhill /daʊn'hɪl/ adv go ~ descendre; (pej) baisser.

down: ~**load** n (Comput) télécharger. ~-**market** adj bas de gamme. ~ **payment** n acompte m. ~**pour** n grosse averse f.

downright /'daʊnraɪt/ adj (utter) véritable; (honest) franc. ● adv carrément.

downstairs /daʊn'steəz/ adv en bas. ● adj d'en bas.

down: ~**stream** adv en aval. ~-**to-earth** adj pratique.

> **Downing Street** Célèbre rue de Londres où se trouvent la résidence officielle du Premier ministre au n°10 et celle du Chancelier de l'Échiquier au n°11. Les médias emploient souvent *Number 10 Downing Street* ou *Downing Street* pour désigner le Premier ministre ou le gouvernement britannique.

downtown /'daʊntaʊn/ adj (US) du centre-ville; ~ **Boston** le centre de Boston.

downward /'daʊnwəd/ adj & adv, **downwards** adv vers le bas.

doze /dəʊz/ vi somnoler; ~ **off** s'assoupir. ● n somme m.

dozen /'dʌzn/ n douzaine f; **a** ~ **eggs** une douzaine d'œufs; ~**s of** 🔢 des dizaines de.

Dr abbr (**Doctor**) Docteur.

drab /dræb/ adj terne.

draft /drɑːft/ n (outline) brouillon m; (Comm) traite f; **the** ~ (Mil, US) la conscription; **a** ~ **treaty** un projet de traité; (US) ➡DRAUGHT. ● vt faire le brouillon de; (draw up) rédiger.

drag /dræg/ vt/i (pt **dragged**) traîner; (river) draguer; (pull away) arracher; ~ **on** s'éterniser. ● n (task 🔢) corvée f; (person 🔢) raseur/-euse m/f; **in** ~ en travesti.

dragon /'drægən/ n dragon m.

drain /dreɪn/ vt (land) drainer; (vegetables) égoutter; (tank, glass) vider;

(use up) épuiser; ~ **(off)** (liquid) faire écouler. ● vi ~ **(off)** (of liquid) s'écouler. ● n (sewer) égout m; ~**(-pipe)** tuyau m d'écoulement; **a** ~ **on** une ponction sur. **draining-board** n égouttoir m.

drama /'drɑːmə/ n art m dramatique, théâtre m; (play, event) drame m. **dramatic** adj (situation) dramatique; (increase) spectaculaire. **dramatist** n dramaturge m. **dramatize** vt adapter pour la scène; (fig) dramatiser.

drank /dræŋk/ ➡DRINK.

drape /dreɪp/ vt draper. **drapes** npl (US) rideaux mpl.

drastic /'dræstɪk/ adj sévère.

draught /drɑːft/ n courant m d'air; ~**s** (game) dames fpl. ~ **beer** n bière f pression.

draughty /'drɑːftɪ/ adj plein de courants d'air.

draw /drɔː/ vt (pt **drew**; pp **drawn**) (picture) dessiner; (line) tracer; (pull) tirer; (attract) attirer. ● vi dessiner; (Sport) faire match nul; (come, move) venir. ● n (Sport) match m nul; (in lottery) tirage m au sort. □ ~ **back** reculer. ~ **near** (s')approcher (**to** de). ~ **out** (money) retirer. ~ **up** vi (stop) s'arrêter; vt (document) dresser; (chair) approcher.

drawback /'drɔːbæk/ n inconvénient m.

drawbridge /'drɔːbrɪdʒ/ n pont-levis m.

drawer /'drɔː(r)/ n tiroir m.

drawing /'drɔːɪŋ/ n dessin m. ~-**board** n planche f à dessin. ~-**pin** n punaise f. ~-**room** n salon m.

drawl /drɔːl/ n voix f traînante.

drawn /drɔːn/ ➡DRAW. ● adj (features) tiré; (match) nul.

dread /dred/ n terreur f, crainte f. ● vt redouter. **dreadful** adj épouvantable, affreux. **dreadfully** adv terriblement.

dream /driːm/ n rêve m. ● vt/i (pt **dreamed** or **dreamt**) rêver; ~ **up** imaginer. ● adj (ideal) de ses rêves.

dreary /'drɪərɪ/ adj (-**ier**, -**iest**) triste; (boring) monotone.

dredge /dredʒ/ vt (river) draguer; ~ **sth up** (fig) exhumer.

dregs /dregz/ npl lie f.

drench /drentʃ/ vt tremper.

dress /dres/ n robe f; (clothing) tenue f. ● vt/i (s')habiller; (food) assaisonner; (wound) panser; ~ **up as** se déguiser en; **get ~ed** s'habiller. ~ **circle** n premier balcon m.

dresser /'dresə(r)/ n (furniture) buffet m; **be a stylish** ~ s'habiller avec chic.

dressing /'dresɪŋ/ n (sauce) assaisonnement m; (bandage) pansement m. ~**-gown** n robe f de chambre. ~**-room** n (Sport) vestiaire m; (Theat) loge f. ~**-table** f coiffeuse f.

dressmaker /'dresmeɪkə(r)/ n couturière f. **dressmaking** n couture f.

dress rehearsal n répétition f générale.

dressy /'dresɪ/ adj (-ier, -iest) chic inv.

drew /druː/ ⇒DRAW .

dribble /'drɪbl/ vi (liquid) dégoulIner; (person) baver; (football) dribbler.

dried /draɪd/ adj (fruit) sec.

drier /'draɪə(r)/ n séchoir m.

drift /drɪft/ vi aller à la dérive; (pile up) s'amonceler; ~ **towards** glisser vers. ● n dérive f. amoncellement m; (of events) tournure f; (meaning) sens m; **snow** ~ congère f. **driftwood** n bois m flotté.

drill /drɪl/ n (tool) perceuse f; (for teeth) roulette f; (training) exercice m; (procedure 🔲) marche f à suivre; (**pneumatic**) ~ marteau m piqueur. ● vt percer; (train) entraîner. ● vi être à l'exercice.

drink /drɪŋk/ vt/i (pt **drank**; pp **drunk**) boire. ● n (liquid) boisson f; (glass of alcohol) verre m; **a** ~ **of water** un verre d'eau. **drinking water** n eau f potable.

drip /drɪp/ vi (pt **dripped**) (é)goutter; (washing) s'égoutter. ● n goutte f; (person 🔲) lavette f.

drip-dry vt laisser égoutter. ● adj sans essorage.

drive /draɪv/ vt (pt **drove**; pp **driven**) (vehicle) conduire; (sb somewhere) chasser, pousser; (machine) actionner; ~ **mad** rendre fou. ● vi conduire. ● n promenade f en voiture; (private road) allée f; (fig) énergie f; (Psych) instinct m; (Pol) campagne f; (Auto) traction f; (golf, Comput) drive m; **it's a two-**

hour ~ il y a deux heures de route; **lefthand** ~ conduite f à gauche. ▫ ~ **at** en venir à.

drivel /'drɪvl/ n bêtises fpl.

driver /'draɪvə(r)/ n conducteur/-trice m/f, chauffeur m. ~**'s license** n (US) permis m de conduire.

driving /'draɪvɪŋ/ n conduite f; **take one's** ~ **test** passer son permis. ● adj (rain) battant; (wind) cinglant. ~ **licence** n permis m de conduire. ~ **school** n auto-école f.

drizzle /'drɪzl/ n bruine f. ● vi bruiner.

drone /drəʊn/ n (of engine) ronronnement m; (of insects) bourdonnement m. ● vi ronronner; bourdonner.

drool /druːl/ vi baver (**over** sur).

droop /druːp/ vi pencher, tomber.

drop /drɒp/ n goutte f; (fall, lowering) chute f. ● vt/i (pt **dropped**) (laisser) tomber; (decrease, lower) baisser; ~ (**off**) (person from car) déposer; ~ **a line** écrire un mot (**to** à). ▫ ~ **in** passer (**on** chez). ~ **off** (doze) s'assoupir. ~ **out** se retirer (**of** de); (of student) abandonner.

dropout /'drɒpaʊt/ n marginal/-e m/f, raté/-e m/f.

droppings /'drɒpɪŋz/ npl crottes fpl.

drought /draʊt/ n sécheresse f.

drove /drəʊv/ ⇒DRIVE.

droves /drəʊvz/ npl foules fpl.

drown /draʊn/ vt/i (se) noyer.

drowsy /'draʊzɪ/ adj somnolent; **be** or **feel** ~ avoir envie de dormir.

drug /drʌg/ n drogue f; (Med) médicament m. ● vt (pt **drugged**) droguer. ~ **addict** n drogué/-e m/f. **drugstore** n (US) drugstore m.

drum /drʌm/ n tambour m; (for oil) bidon m; ~**s** batterie f. ● vi (pt **drummed**) tambouriner. ● vt ~ **into** sb répéter sans cesse à qn; ~ **up** (support) susciter; (business) créer. **drummer** n tambour m; (in pop group) batteur m.

drumstick /'drʌmstɪk/ n baguette f de tambour; (of chicken) pilon m.

drunk /drʌŋk/ ⇒DRINK. ● adj ivre; **get** ~ s'enivrer. ● n ivrogne/-esse m/f. **drunkard** n ivrogne/-esse m/f. **drunken** adj ivre. **drunkenness** n ivresse f.

d

dry /draɪ/ adj (**drier, driest**) sec; (day) sans pluie; **be** or **feel ~** avoir soif. ● vt/i (faire) sécher; **~ up** (dry dishes) essuyer la vaisselle; (of supplies) (se) tarir; (be silent 🔲) se taire. **~-clean** vt nettoyer à sec. **~-cleaner** n teinturier m. **~ run** n galop m d'essai.

DTD abbr (Document Type Definition) DTD f.

dual /'dju:əl/ adj double. **~ carriageway** n route f à quatre voies. **~-purpose** adj qui fait double emploi.

dub /dʌb/ vt (pt **dubbed**) (film) doubler (**into** en); (nickname) surnommer.

dubious /'dju:bɪəs/ adj (pej) douteux; **be ~ about** avoir des doutes sur.

duck /dʌk/ n canard m. ● vi se baisser subitement. ● vt (head) baisser; (person) plonger dans l'eau.

duct /'dʌkt/ n conduit m.

dud /dʌd/ adj (tool 🔲) mal fichu; (coin 🔲) faux; (cheque 🔲) sans provision. ● n be a ~ (not work 🔲) ne pas marcher.

due /dju:/ adj (owing) dû; (expected) attendu; (proper) qui convient; **~ to** à cause de; (caused by) dû à; **she's ~ to leave now** il est prévu qu'elle parte maintenant; **in ~ course** (at the right time) en temps voulu; (later) plus tard. ● adv **~ east** droit vers l'est. ● n dû m; **~s** droits mpl; (of club) cotisation f.

duel /'dju:əl/ n duel m.

duet /dju:'et/ n duo m.

dug /dʌg/ →DIG.

duke /dju:k/ n duc m.

dull /dʌl/ adj ennuyeux; (colour) terne; (weather) maussade; (sound) sourd. ● vt (pain) atténuer; (shine) ternir.

duly /'dju:lɪ/ adv comme il convient; (as expected) comme prévu.

dumb /dʌm/ adj muet; (stupid 🔲) bête. □ **~ down** (course, TV coverage) baisser le niveau intellectuel de.

dumbfound /dʌm'faʊnd/ vt sidérer, ahurir.

dummy /'dʌmɪ/ n (of tailor) mannequin m; (of baby) sucette f. ● adj factice. **~ run** n galop m d'essai.

dump /dʌmp/ vt déposer; (get rid of 🔲) se débarrasser de. ● n tas m d'ordures; (refuse tip) décharge f; (Mil) dépôt m; (dull place 🔲) trou m 🔲; **be**

in the ~s 🔲 avoir le cafard.

dune /dju:n/ n dune f.

dung /dʌŋ/ n (excrement) bouse f, crotte f; (manure) fumier m.

dungarees /dʌŋgə'ri:z/ npl salopette f.

dungeon /'dʌndʒən/ n cachot m.

duplicate[1] /'dju:plɪkət/ n double m. ● adj identique.

duplicate[2] /'dju:plɪkeɪt/ vt faire un double de; (on machine) polycopier.

durable /'djʊərəbl/ adj (tough) résistant; (enduring) durable.

duration /djʊ'reɪʃn/ n durée f.

during /'djʊərɪŋ/ prep pendant.

dusk /dʌsk/ n crépuscule m.

dusky /'dʌskɪ/ adj (-ier, -iest) foncé.

dust /dʌst/ n poussière f. ● vt/i épousseter; (sprinkle) saupoudrer (**with** de). **~bin** n poubelle f.

duster /'dʌstə(r)/ n chiffon m.

dust: ~man n (pl **-men**) éboueur m. **~pan** n pelle f (à poussière).

dusty /'dʌstɪ/ adj (-ier, -iest) poussiéreux.

Dutch /dʌtʃ/ adj néerlandais; **go ~** partager les frais. ● n (Ling) néerlandais m. **~man** n Néerlandais m. **~woman** n Néerlandaise f.

dutiful /'dju:tɪfl/ adj obéissant.

duty /'dju:tɪ/ n devoir m; (tax) droit m; (of official) fonction f; **on ~** de service. **~-free** adj hors-taxe.

duvet /'du:veɪ/ n couette f.

DVD abbr (**digital versatile disc**) DVD m.

dwarf /dwɔ:f/ n nain/-e m/f. ● vt rapetisser.

dwell /dwel/ vi (pt **dwelt**) demeurer; **~ on** s'étendre sur. **dweller** n habitant/-e m/f. **dwelling** n habitation f.

dwindle /'dwɪndl/ vi diminuer.

dye /daɪ/ vt teindre. ● n teinture f.

dying /'daɪɪŋ/ adj mourant; (art) qui se perd.

dynamic /daɪ'næmɪk/ adj dynamique.

dynamite /'daɪnəmaɪt/ n dynamite f.

dysentery /'dɪsəntrɪ/ n dysenterie f.

dyslexia /dɪs'leksɪə/ n dyslexie f. **dyslexic** adj & n dyslexique (mf).

Ee

each /iːtʃ/ *det* chaque *inv*; ∼ **one** chacun/-e *m/f.* ● *pron* chacun/-e *m/f*; **oranges at 30p** ∼ des oranges à 30 pence pièce.

each other *pron* l'un/l'une l'autre, les uns/les unes les autres; **know** ∼ se connaître; **love** ∼ s'aimer.

eager /'iːɡə(r)/ *adj* impatient (**to** de); (*person, acceptance*) enthousiaste; ∼ **for** avide de.

eagle /'iːɡl/ *n* aigle *m*.

ear /ɪə(r)/ *n* oreille *f*; (of corn) épi *m*. ∼**ache** *n* mal *m* à l'oreille. ∼**-drum** *n* tympan *m*.

earl /ɜːl/ *n* comte *m*.

early /'ɜːlɪ/ (**-ier, -iest**) *adv* tôt, de bonne heure; (ahead of time) en avance; **as I said earlier** comme je l'ai déjà dit. ● *adj* (attempt, years) premier; (hour) matinal; (fruit) précoce; (retirement) anticipé; **have an** ∼ **dinner** dîner tôt; **in** ∼ **summer** au début de l'été; **at the earliest** au plus tôt.

earmark /'ɪəmɑːk/ *vt* désigner (**for** pour).

earn /ɜːn/ *vt* gagner; (interest: Comm) rapporter.

earnest /'ɜːnɪst/ *adj* sérieux; **in** ∼ sérieusement.

earnings /'ɜːnɪŋz/ *npl* salaire *m*; (profits) gains *mpl*.

ear: ∼**phones** *npl* casque *m*. ∼**-ring** *n* boucle *f* d'oreille. ∼**shot** *n* **within/in** ∼**shot** à portée de voix.

earth /ɜːθ/ *n* terre *f*; **why/how/where on** ∼**...?** pourquoi/comment/où diable...? ● *vt* (Electr) mettre à la terre. **earthenware** *n* faïence *f*. ∼**quake** *n* tremblement *m* de terre.

ease /iːz/ *n* facilité *f*; (comfort) bien-être *m*; **at** ∼ à l'aise; (Mil) au repos; **with** ∼ facilement. ● *vt* (pain, pressure) atténuer; (congestion) réduire; (transition) faciliter. ● *vi* (pain, pressure) s'atténuer; (congestion, rain) diminuer.

easel /'iːzl/ *n* chevalet *m*.

east /iːst/ *n* est *m*; **the E**∼ (Orient) l'Orient *m*. ● *adj* (side, coast) est; (wind) d'est. ● *adv* à l'est.

Easter /'iːstə(r)/ *n* Pâques *m*; ∼ **egg** œuf *m* de Pâques.

easterly /'iːstəlɪ/ *adj* (wind) d'est; (direction) de l'est.

eastern de l'est; ∼ **France** l'est de la France.

eastward /'iːstwəd/ *adj* (side) est *inv*; (journey) vers l'est.

easy /'iːzɪ/ *adj* (**-ier, -iest**) facile; **go** ∼ **with** ⊡ y aller doucement avec; **take it** ∼ ne te fatigue pas. ∼**going** *adj* accommodant.

eat /iːt/ *vt/i* (*pt* **ate**; *pp* **eaten**) manger; ∼ **into** ronger.

eavesdrop /'iːvzdrɒp/ *vi* (*pt* **-dropped**) écouter aux portes.

ebb /eb/ *n* reflux *m*. ● *vi* descendre; (fig) décliner.

EC *abbr* (**European Commission**) CE *f*.

eccentric /ɪk'sentrɪk/ *adj & n* excentrique (*mf*).

echo /'ekəʊ/ *n* (*pl* **-oes**) écho *m*. ● *vt* répercuter; (idea, opinion) reprendre. ● *vi* retentir, résonner (**to, with** de).

eclipse /ɪ'klɪps/ *n* éclipse *f*. ● *vt* éclipser.

ecological /iːkə'lɒdʒɪkl/ *adj* écologique.

ecology /ɪ'kɒlədʒɪ/ *n* écologie *f*.

e-commerce /'iːkɒmɜːs/ *n* commerce *m* électronique, commerce *m* en ligne.

economic /iːkə'nɒmɪk/ *adj* économique; (profitable) rentable; ∼ **refugee** réfugié/-e *m/f* économique. **economical** *adj* économique; (person) économe. **economics** *n* économie *f*, sciences *fpl* économiques. **economist** *n* économiste *mf*.

economize /ɪ'kɒnəmaɪz/ *vi* ∼ (**on**) économiser.

economy /ɪ'kɒnəmɪ/ *n* économie *f*. ∼**-class syndrome** *n* syndrome *m* de la classe économique.

ecosystem /'iːkəʊsɪstəm/ *n* écosystème *m*.

ecstasy /'ekstəsɪ/ *n* extase *f*; (drug) ecstasy *m*.

edge /edʒ/ *n* bord *m*; (of town) abords *mpl*; (of knife) tranchant *m*; **have the** ∼ **on** ⊡ l'emporter sur; **on** ∼ énervé. ● *vt* (trim) border. ● *vi* ∼ **forward**

avancer doucement.

edgeways /ˈedʒweɪz/ *adv* I can't get a word in ~ je n'arrive pas à placer un mot.

edible /ˈedɪbl/ *adj* comestible.

Edinburgh Festival Festival international des Arts qui se déroule tous les étés à Édimbourg (Écosse) depuis 1947. Pendant trois semaines, au programme du festival institutionnel et du festival parallèle (*Fringe festival*), se côtoient les plus grands noms de la musique, de la danse, du théâtre, les artistes d'avant-garde et les nouveaux talents.

---

edit /ˈedɪt/ *vt* (*pt* **edited**) (*newspaper, page*) être le rédacteur/la rédactrice de; (*check*) réviser; (*cut*) couper; (*TV, cinema*) monter.

edition /ɪˈdɪʃn/ *n* édition *f.*

editor /ˈedɪtə(r)/ *n* (*writer*) rédacteur/-trice *m/f*; (*of works, anthology*) éditeur/-trice *m/f*; (*TV, cinema*) monteur/-teuse *m/f*; the ~ (**in chief**) le rédacteur en chef.

editorial /edɪˈtɔːrɪəl/ *adj* de la rédaction. ● *n* éditorial *m.*

educate /ˈedʒʊkeɪt/ *vt* instruire; (*mind*) éduquer. **educated** *adj* instruit. **education** *n* éducation *f*; (*schooling*) études *fpl.* **educational** *adj* éducatif; (*method*) d'enseignement.

eel /iːl/ *n* anguille *f.*

eerie /ˈɪərɪ/ *adj* (**-ier, -iest**) sinistre.

effect /ɪˈfekt/ *n* effet *m*; **come into ~** entrer en vigueur; **in ~** effectivement; **take ~** agir. ● *vt* effectuer.

effective /ɪˈfektɪv/ *adj* efficace; (*actual*) effectif. **effectively** *adv* efficacement; (*in effect*) en réalité. **effectiveness** *n* efficacité *f.*

effeminate /ɪˈfemɪnət/ *adj* efféminé.

effervescent /efəˈvesnt/ *adj* effervescent.

efficiency /ɪˈfɪʃnsɪ/ *n* efficacité *f*; (*of machine*) rendement *m.* **efficient** *adj* efficace. **efficiently** *adv* efficacement.

effort /ˈefət/ *n* efforts *mpl*; **make an ~** faire un effort; **be worth the ~** en valoir la peine. **effortless** *adj* facile.

effusive /ɪˈfjuːsɪv/ *adj* expansif.

e.g. /iːˈdʒiː/ *abbr* par ex.

egg /eg/ *n* œuf *m.* ● *vt* ~ **on** pousser. ~**-cup** *n* coquetier *m.* ~**-plant** *n* (US) aubergine *f.* ~**shell** *n* coquille *f* d'œuf.

ego /ˈiːgəʊ/ *n* amour-propre *m*; (*Psych*) moi *m.* **egotism** *n* égotisme *m.* **egotist** *n* égotiste *mf.*

Egypt /ˈiːdʒɪpt/ *n* Égypte *f.*

EHIC *abbr* (**European Health Insurance Card**) CEAM *f.*

eiderdown /ˈaɪdədaʊn/ *n* édredon *m.*

eight /eɪt/ *adj & n* huit (*m*). **eighteen** *adj & n* dix-huit (*m*). **eighth** *adj & n* huitième (*mf*). **eighty** *adj & n* quatre-vingts (*m*).

either /ˈaɪðə(r)/ *det & pron* l'un/une ou l'autre; (*with negative*) ni l'un/une ni l'autre; **you can take ~** tu peux prendre n'importe lequel/laquelle. ● *adv* non plus. ● *conj* ~**...or** ou (bien)...ou (bien); (*with negative*) ni...ni.

eject /ɪˈdʒekt/ *vt* (*troublemaker*) expulser; (*waste*) rejeter.

elaborate[1] /ɪˈlæbərət/ *adj* compliqué.

elaborate[2] /ɪˈlæbəreɪt/ *vt* élaborer. ● *vi* préciser; ~ **on** s'étendre sur.

elastic /ɪˈlæstɪk/ *adj & n* élastique (*m*); ~ **band** élastique *m.* **elasticity** *n* élasticité *f.*

elated /ɪˈleɪtɪd/ *adj* transporté de joie.

elbow /ˈelbəʊ/ *n* coude *m*; ~ **room** espace *m* vital.

elder /ˈeldə(r)/ *adj & n* aîné/-e (*m/f*); (*tree*) sureau *m.*

elderly /ˈeldəlɪ/ *adj* âgé; **the ~** les personnes *fpl* âgées.

eldest /ˈeldɪst/ *adj & n* aîné/-e (*m/f*).

elect /ɪˈlekt/ *vt* élire; ~ **to do** choisir de faire. ● *adj* (*president etc.*) futur. **election** *n* élection *f.* **elector** *n* électeur/-trice *m/f.* **electoral** *adj* électoral. **electorate** *n* électorat *m.*

electric /ɪˈlektrɪk/ *adj* électrique; ~ **blanket** couverture *f* chauffante. **electrical** *adj* électrique. **electrician** *n* électricien/-ne *m/f.* **electricity** *n* électricité *f.* **electrify** *vt* électrifier; (*excite*) électriser. **electrocute** *vt* électrocuter.

electronic /ɪlekˈtrɒnɪk/ *adj* électronique. ~ **publishing** *n* édition *f.* **electronics** *n* électronique *f.*

elegance /ˈelɪgəns/ *n* élégance *f.*

element /ˈelɪmənt/ *n* élément *m*; (*of heater etc.*) résistance *f.* **elementary** *adj* élémentaire.

elephant /'elɪfənt/ n éléphant m.

elevate /'elɪveɪt/ vt élever. **elevation** n élévation f. **elevator** n (US) ascenseur m.

eleven /ɪ'levn/ adj & n onze (m). **eleventh** adj & n onzième (mf).

elicit /ɪ'lɪsɪt/ vt obtenir (**from** de).

eligible /'elɪdʒəbl/ adj admissible (**for** à); **be ~ for** (entitled to) avoir droit à.

eliminate /ɪ'lɪmɪneɪt/ vt éliminer.

elm /elm/ n orme m.

elongate /'iːlɒŋɡeɪt/ vt allonger.

elope /ɪ'ləʊp/ vi s'enfuir (**with** avec). **elopement** n fugue f (amoureuse).

eloquence /'eləkwəns/ n éloquence f.

else /els/ adv d'autre; **somebody/nothing ~** quelqu'un/rien d'autre; **everybody ~** tous les autres; **somewhere/ something ~** autre part/chose; **or ~** ou bien. **elsewhere** adv ailleurs.

elude /ɪ'luːd/ vt échapper à.

elusive /ɪ'luːsɪv/ adj insaisissable.

email /'iːmeɪl/ n (medium) courrier m électronique; (item) e-mail m, mél m; **~ sb** envoyer un e-mail à qn; **~ sth** envoyer qch par courrier électronique.

emancipate /ɪ'mænsɪpeɪt/ vt émanciper.

embankment /ɪm'bæŋkmənt/ n (of river) quai m; (of railway) remblai m.

embark /ɪm'bɑːk/ vt embarquer. ● vi (Naut) embarquer; **~ on** (journey) entreprendre; (campaign, career) se lancer dans.

embarrass /ɪm'bærəs/ vt plonger dans l'embarras; **be/feel ~ed** être/se sentir gêné. **embarrassment** n confusion f, gêne f.

embassy /'embəsɪ/ n ambassade f.

embed /ɪm'bed/ vt (pt **embedded**) enfoncer (**in** dans).

embellish /ɪm'belɪʃ/ vt embellir.

embers /'embəz/ npl braises fpl.

embezzle /ɪm'bezl/ vt détourner (**from** de). **embezzlement** n détournement m de fonds.

emblem /'embləm/ n emblème m.

embodiment /ɪm'bɒdɪmənt/ n incarnation f. **embody** vt incarner; (legally) incorporer.

emboss /ɪm'bɒs/ vt (metal) repousser; (paper) gaufrer.

embrace /ɪm'breɪs/ vt (person) étreindre; (religion) embrasser; (include) comprendre. ● n étreinte f.

embroider /ɪm'brɔɪdə(r)/ vt broder. **embroidery** n broderie f.

embryo /'embrɪəʊ/ n embryon m.

emerald /'emərəld/ n émeraude f.

emerge /ɪ'mɜːdʒ/ vi (person) sortir (**from** de); **it ~d that** il est apparu que. **emergence** n apparition f.

emergency /ɪ'mɜːdʒənsɪ/ n (crisis) crise f; (urgent case: Med) urgence f; **in an ~** en cas d'urgence. ● adj d'urgence. **~ exit** n sortie f de secours; **~ landing** n atterrissage m forcé. **~ room** (US) salle f des urgences.

emigrant /'emɪɡrənt/ n émigrant/-e m/f. **emigrate** vi émigrer.

eminence /'emɪnəns/ n éminence f. **eminent** adj éminent.

emission /ɪ'mɪʃn/ n émission f.

emit /ɪ'mɪt/ vt (pt **emitted**) émettre.

emotion /ɪ'məʊʃn/ n émotion f. **emotional** adj (development) émotif; (reaction) émotionel; (film, scene) émouvant.

emotive /ɪ'məʊtɪv/ adj qui soulève les passions.

emperor /'empərə(r)/ n empereur m.

emphasis /'emfəsɪs/ n accent m; **lay ~ on** mettre l'accent sur. **emphasize** vt mettre l'accent sur. **emphatic** adj catégorique; (manner) énergique.

empire /'empaɪə(r)/ n empire m.

employ /ɪm'plɔɪ/ vt employer. **employee** n employé/-e m/f. **employer** n employeur/-euse m/f.

employment /ɪm'plɔɪmənt/ n emploi m; **find ~** trouver du travail.

empower /ɪm'paʊə(r)/ vt autoriser (**to do** à faire).

empty /'emptɪ/ adj (**-ier, -iest**) vide; (street) désert; (promise) vain; **on an ~ stomach** à jeun. ● vt/i (se) vider. **~-handed** adj les mains vides.

emulate /'emjʊleɪt/ vt imiter.

enable /ɪ'neɪbl/ vt **~ sb to** permettre à qn de.

enamel /ɪ'næml/ n émail m. ● vt (pt **enamelled**) émailler.

encase /ɪn'keɪs/ vt revêtir, recouvrir (**in** de).

enchant /ɪn'tʃɑːnt/ vt enchanter.

enclose /ɪnˈkləʊz/ vt entourer; (land) clôturer; (with letter) joindre. **enclosed** adj (space) clos; (with letter) ci-joint. **enclosure** n enceinte f; (with letter) pièce f jointe.

encompass /ɪnˈkʌmpəs/ vt inclure.

encore /ˈɒŋkɔː(r)/ interj & n bis (m).

encounter /ɪnˈkaʊntə(r)/ vt rencontrer. ● n rencontre f.

encourage /ɪnˈkʌrɪdʒ/ vt encourager.

encroach /ɪnˈkrəʊtʃ/ vi ~ upon empiéter sur.

encyclopedia /ɪnsaɪkləˈpiːdɪə/ n encyclopédie f. **encyclopaedic** adj encyclopédique.

end /end/ n fin f; (farthest part) bout m; **come to an** ~ prendre fin; ~-**product** produit m fini; **in the** ~ finalement; **no** ~ **of** ⓘ énormément de; **on** ~ (upright) debout; (in a row) de suite; **put an** ~**to** mettre fin à. ● vt (marriage) mettre fin à; ~ **one's days** finir ses jours. ● vi se terminer; ~ **up doing** finir par faire.

endanger /ɪnˈdeɪndʒə(r)/ vt mettre en danger.

endearing /ɪnˈdɪərɪŋ/ adj attachant.

endeavour, (US) **endeavor** /ɪnˈdevə(r)/ n (attempt) tentative f; (hard work) effort m. ● vi faire tout son possible (**to do** pour faire).

ending /ˈendɪŋ/ n fin f.

endive /ˈendɪv/ n chicorée f.

endless /ˈendlɪs/ adj interminable; (supply) inépuisable; (patience) infini.

endorse /ɪnˈdɔːs/ vt (candidate, decision) appuyer; (product, claim) approuver; (cheque) endosser.

endurance /ɪnˈdjʊərəns/ n endurance f.

endure /ɪnˈdjʊə(r)/ vt supporter. ● vi durer. **enduring** adj durable.

enemy /ˈenəmɪ/ n & adj ennemi/-e (m/f).

energetic /enəˈdʒetɪk/ adj énergique. **energy** n énergie f.

enforce /ɪnˈfɔːs/ vt (rule, law) appliquer, faire respecter; (silence, discipline) imposer (**on** à); ~**d** forcé.

engage /ɪnˈgeɪdʒ/ vt (staff) engager; (attention) retenir; **be** ~**d in** se livrer à. ● vi ~ **in** se livrer à. **engaged** adj fiancé; (busy) occupé; **get** ~**d** se fiancer. **engagement** n fiançailles fpl;

(meeting) rendezvous m; (undertaking) engagement m.

engaging /ɪnˈgeɪdʒɪŋ/ adj attachant, engageant.

engine /ˈendʒɪn/ n moteur m; (of train) locomotive f; (of ship) machines fpl. ~-**driver** n mécanicien m.

engineer /endʒɪˈnɪə(r)/ n ingénieur m; (repairman) technicien m; (on ship) mécanicien m. ● vt (contrive) manigancer.

engineering /endʒɪˈnɪərɪŋ/ n ingénierie f; (industry) mécanique f; **civil** ~ génie m civil

England /ˈɪŋglənd/ n Angleterre f.

English /ˈɪŋglɪʃ/ adj anglais. ● n (Ling) anglais m; **the** ~ les Anglais mpl. ~**man** n Anglais m. ~-**speaking** adj anglophone. ~**woman** n Anglaise f.

engrave /ɪnˈgreɪv/ vt graver.

engrossed /ɪnˈgrəʊst/ adj absorbé (**in** dans).

engulf /ɪnˈgʌlf/ vt engouffrer.

enhance /ɪnˈhɑːns/ vt (prospects, status) améliorer; (price, value) augmenter.

enjoy /ɪnˈdʒɔɪ/ vt aimer (**doing** faire); (benefit from) jouir de; ~ **oneself** s'amuser; ~ **your meal!** bon appétit! **enjoyable** adj agréable. **enjoyment** n plaisir m.

enlarge /ɪnˈlɑːdʒ/ vt agrandir. ● vi s'agrandir; (pupil) se dilater; ~ **on** s'étendre sur. **enlargement** n agrandissement m.

enlighten /ɪnˈlaɪtn/ vt éclairer (**on** sur). **enlightenment** n instruction f; (information) éclaircissement m.

enlist /ɪnˈlɪst/ vt (person) recruter; (fig) obtenir. ● vi s'engager.

enmity /ˈenmətɪ/ n inimitié f.

enormous /ɪˈnɔːməs/ adj énorme. **enormously** adv énormément.

enough /ɪˈnʌf/ adv & n assez; **have** ~ **of** en avoir assez de. ● det assez de; ~ **glasses/time** assez de verres/de temps.

enquire →INQUIRE. **enquiry** →INQUIRY.

enrage /ɪnˈreɪdʒ/ vt mettre en rage, rendre furieux.

enrol /ɪnˈrəʊl/ vt/i (pt **enrolled**) (s')inscrire. **enrolment** n inscription f.

ensure /ɪnˈʃɔː(r)/ vt garantir; ~ **that** (ascertain) s'assurer que.

entail /ɪnˈteɪl/ vt entraîner.

entangle /ɪnˈtæŋgl/ vt emmêler.

enter /ˈentə(r)/ vt (room, club, phase) entrer dans; (note down, register) inscrire; (data) entrer, saisir. ● vi entrer (into dans); ~ **for** s'inscrire à.

enterprise /ˈentəpraɪz/ n entreprise f; (boldness) initiative f. **enterprising** adj entreprenant.

entertain /entəˈteɪn/ vt amuser, divertir; (guests) recevoir; (ideas) considérer. **entertainer** n artiste mf. **entertaining** adj divertissant. **entertainment** n divertissement m; (performance) spectacle m.

enthral /ɪnˈθrɔːl/ vt (pt **enthralled**) captiver.

enthusiasm /ɪnˈθjuːzɪæzəm/ n enthousiasme m (for pour).

enthusiast /ɪnˈθjuːzɪæst/ n passionné/-e mf (for de). **enthusiastic** adj (supporter) enthousiaste; **be** ~**ic about** être enthousiasmé par. **enthusiastically** adv avec enthousiasme.

entice /ɪnˈtaɪs/ vt attirer; ~ **sb to do** entraîner qn à faire.

entire /ɪnˈtaɪə(r)/ adj entier. **entirely** adv entièrement. **entirety** n **in its** ~**ty** en entier.

entitle /ɪnˈtaɪtl/ vt donner droit à (to sth à qch; to do de faire); ~**d** (book) intitulé; **be** ~**d to sth** avoir droit à qch.

entrance[1] /ˈentrəns/ n (entering, way in) entrée f (to de); (right to enter) admission f. ● adj (charge, exam) d'entrée.

entrance[2] /ɪnˈtrɑːns/ vt transporter.

entrant /ˈentrənt/ n (Sport) concurrent/-e mf; (in exam) candidat/-e mf.

entrenched /ɪnˈtrentʃt/ adj (opinion) inébranlable; (Mil) retranché.

entrepreneur /ɒntrəprəˈnɜː(r)/ n entrepreneur/-euse mf.

entrust /ɪnˈtrʌst/ vt confier; ~ **sb with sth** confier qch à qn.

entry /ˈentrɪ/ n entrée f; ~**form** fiche f d'inscription.

envelop /ɪnˈveləp/ vt (pt **enveloped**) envelopper.

envelope /ˈenvələup/ n enveloppe f.

envious /ˈenvɪəs/ adj envieux (of de).

environment /ɪnˈvaɪərənmənt/ n (ecological) environnement m; (social) milieu m. **environmental** adj du milieu; de l'environnement. **environmentalist** n écologiste mf.

envisage /ɪnˈvɪzɪdʒ/ vt prévoir (doing de faire).

envoy /ˈenvɔɪ/ n envoyé/-e mf.

envy /ˈenvɪ/ n envie f. ● vt envier; ~ **sb sth** envier qch à qn.

epic /ˈepɪk/ n épopée f. ● adj épique.

epidemic /epɪˈdemɪk/ n épidémie f.

epilepsy /ˈepɪlepsɪ/ n épilepsie f.

episode /ˈepɪsəud/ n épisode m.

epitome /ɪˈpɪtəmɪ/ n modèle m. **epitomize** vt incarner.

equal /ˈiːkwəl/ adj & n égal/-e (m/f); ~ **opportunities/rights** égalité f des chances/droits; ~ **to** (task) à la hauteur de. ● vt (pt **equalled**) égaler. **equality** n égalité f. **equalize** vt/i égaliser. **equalizer** n (goal) but m égalisateur. **equally** adv (divide) en parts égales; (just as) tout aussi.

equanimity /ekwəˈnɪmətɪ/ n sérénité f.

equate /ɪˈkweɪt/ vt assimiler (with à). **equation** n équation f.

equator /ɪˈkweɪtə(r)/ n équateur m.

equilibrium /iːkwɪˈlɪbrɪəm/ n équilibre m.

equip /ɪˈkwɪp/ vt (pt **equipped**) équiper (with de). **equipment** n équipement m.

equity /ˈekwətɪ/ n équité f.

equivalence /ɪˈkwɪvələns/ n équivalence f.

era /ˈɪərə/ n ère f, époque f.

eradicate /ɪˈrædɪkeɪt/ vt éliminer; (disease) éradiquer.

erase /ɪˈreɪz/ vt effacer. **eraser** n (rubber) gomme f.

erect /ɪˈrekt/ adj droit. ● vt ériger. **erection** n érection f.

erode /ɪˈrəud/ vt éroder; (fig) saper. **erosion** n érosion f.

erotic /ɪˈrɒtɪk/ adj érotique.

errand /ˈerənd/ n commission f, course f.

erratic /ɪˈrætɪk/ adj (behaviour, person) imprévisible; (performance) inégal.

error /ˈerə(r)/ n erreur f.

erupt /ɪ'rʌpt/ vi (volcano) entrer en éruption; (fig) éclater.

escalate /'eskəleɪt/ vt intensifier. ● vi (conflict) s'intensifier. **escalation** n intensification f. **escalator** n escalier m mécanique, escalator® m.

escapade /'eskəpeɪd/ n frasque f.

escape /ɪ'skeɪp/ vt échapper à. ● vi s'enfuir, s'évader; (gas) fuir. ● n fuite f, évasion f; (of gas etc.) fuite f; **have a lucky** or **narrow ~** l'échapper belle.

escapism /ɪ'skeɪpɪzəm/ n évasion f (du réel).

escort[1] /'eskɔːt/ n (guard) escorte f; (companion) compagnon/ compagne m/f.

escort[2] /ɪ'skɔːt/ vt escorter.

Eskimo /'eskɪməʊ/ n Esquimau/-de m/f.

especially /ɪ'speʃəlɪ/ adv en particulier.

espionage /'espɪənɑːʒ/ n espionnage m.

espresso /e'spresəʊ/ n (café) express m.

essay /'eseɪ/ n (in literature) essai m; (School) rédaction f; (Univ) dissertation f.

essence /'esns/ n essence f.

essential /ɪ'senʃl/ adj essentiel; **the ~s** l'essentiel m. **essentially** adv essentiellement.

establish /ɪ'stæblɪʃ/ vt établir; (business) fonder.

establishment /ɪ'stæblɪʃmənt/ n (process) instauration f; (institution) établissement m; **the E~** l'ordre m établi.

estate /ɪ'steɪt/ n (house and land) domaine m; (possessions) biens mpl; (housing estate) cité f; **~ agent** n agent m immobilier. **~ car** n break m.

esteem /ɪ'stiːm/ n estime f.

esthetic /es'θetɪk/ adj (US) ➡**AES-THETIC.**

estimate[1] /'estɪmət/ n (calculation) estimation f; (Comm) devis m.

estimate[2] /'estɪmeɪt/ vt évaluer; **~ that** estimer que. **estimation** n (esteem) estime f; (judgment) opinion f.

Estonia /ɪ'stəʊnɪə/ n Estonie f.

estuary /'estʃʊərɪ/ n estuaire m.

eternal /ɪ'tɜːnl/ adj éternel.

eternity /ɪ'tɜːnətɪ/ n éternité f.

ethic /'eθɪk/ n éthique f; **~s** moralité f. **ethical** adj éthique.

ethnic /'eθnɪk/ adj ethnique. **~ cleansing** nettoyage m ethnique.

EU abbr **European Union** UE f, Union f européenne.

euphoria /juː'fɔːrɪə/ n euphorie f.

euro /'jʊərəʊ/ n euro m. **~ zone** zone f euro.

Europe /'jʊərəp/ n Europe f.

European /jʊərə'pɪən/ adj & n européen/-ne (m/f); **~ Community** Communauté f européenne.

eurosceptic /'jʊərəʊskeptɪk/ n eurosceptique mf.

euthanasia /'jʊərəʊskeptɪk/ n euthanasie f.

evacuate /ɪ'vækjʊeɪt/ vt évacuer.

evade /ɪ'veɪd/ vt (blow) esquiver; (question) éluder.

evaluation /ɪvæljʊ'eɪʃn/ n évaluation f.

evaporate /ɪvæljʊ'eɪʃn/ vi s'évaporer; **~d milk** lait m condensé.

evasion /ɪ'veɪʒn/ n fuite f (of devant); (excuse) faux-fuyant m; **tax ~** évasion f fiscale. **evasive** adj évasif.

eve /iːv/ n veille f (of de).

even /'iːvn/ adj (surface, voice, contest) égal; (teeth, hem) régulier; (number) pair; **get ~with** se venger de. ● adv même; **~ better**/etc. (still) encore mieux/etc.; **~ so** quand même. □ **~ out** (differences) s'atténuer; **~ sth out** (inequalities) réduire qch; **~ up** équilibrer.

evening /'iːvnɪŋ/ n soir m; (whole evening, event) soirée f.

evenly /'iːvnlɪ/ adv (spread, apply) uniformément; (breathe) régulièrement; (equally) en parts égales.

event /ɪ'vent/ n événement m; (Sport) épreuve f; **in the ~ of** en cas de. **eventful** adj mouvementé.

eventual /ɪ'ventʃʊəl/ adj (outcome, decision) final; (aim) à long terme. **eventuality** n éventualité f. **eventually** adv finalement; (in future) un jour ou l'autre.

ever /'evə(r)/ adv jamais; (at all times) toujours.

evergreen /'evəgriːn/ n arbre m à feuilles persistantes.

everlasting /evə'lɑːstɪŋ/ adj éternel.

ever since *prep & adv* depuis.

every /'evrɪ/ *adj* ~ **house/window** toutes les maisons/les fenêtres; ~ **time/minute** chaque fois/minute; ~ **day** tous les jours; ~ **other day** tous les deux jours. **everybody** *pron* tout le monde. **everyday** *adj* quotidien. **everyone** *pron* tout le monde. **everything** *pron* tout. **everywhere** *adv* partout; ~**where he goes** partout où il va.

evict /ɪ'vɪkt/ *vt* expulser (**from** de).

evidence /'evɪdəns/ *n* (proof) preuves *fpl* (**that** que; **of, for** de); (testimony) témoignage *m*; (traces) trace *f* (**of** de); **give** ~ témoigner; **be in** ~ être visible. **evident** *adj* manifeste. **evidently** *adv* (apparently) apparemment; (obviously) manifestement.

evil /'iːvl/ *adj* malfaisant. ● *n* mal *m*.

evoke /ɪ'vəʊk/ *vt* évoquer.

evolution /iːvə'luːʃn/ *n* évolution *f.*

evolve /ɪ'vɒlv/ *vi* évoluer. ● *vt* élaborer.

ewe /juː/ *n* brebis *f.*

ex- /eks/ *pref* ex-, ancien.

exact /ɪg'zækt/ *adj* exact; **the** ~ **opposite** exactement le contraire. ● *vt* exiger (**from** de). **exactly** *adv* exactement.

exaggerate /ɪg'zædʒəreɪt/ *vt/i* exagérer.

exalted /ɪg'zɔːltɪd/ *adj* élevé.

exam /ɪg'zæm/ *n* ✗ examen *m.*

examination /ɪgzæmɪ'neɪʃn/ *n* examen *m.*

examine /ɪg'zæmɪn/ *vt* examiner; (witness) interroger. **examiner** *n* examinateur/-trice *m/f.*

example /ɪg'zɑːmpl/ *n* exemple *m*; **for** ~ par exemple; **make an** ~ **of** punir pour l'exemple.

exasperate /ɪg'zæspəreɪt/ *vt* exaspérer.

excavate /'ekskəveɪt/ *vt* fouiller. **excavations** *npl* fouilles *fpl.*

exceed /ɪk'siːd/ *vt* dépasser. **exceedingly** *adv* extrêmement.

excel /ɪk'sel/ *vi* (*pt* **excelled**) exceller (**at, in** en; **at doing** à faire). ● *vt* surpasser.

excellence /'eksələns/ *n* excellence *f.* **excellent** *adj* excellent.

except /ɪk'sept/ *prep* sauf, excepté; ~ **for** à part. ● *vt* excepter. **excepting** *prep* sauf, excepté.

exception /ɪk'sepʃn/ *n* exception *f*; **take** ~ **to** s'offusquer de. **exceptional** *adj* exceptionnel.

excerpt /'eksɜːpt/ *n* extrait *m.*

excess¹ /ɪk'ses/ *n* excès *m.*

excess² /'ekses/ *adj* ~ **weight** excès *m* de poids; ~ **baggage** excédent *m* de bagages.

excessive /ɪk'sesɪv/ *adj* excessif.

exchange /ɪks'tʃeɪndʒ/ *vt* échanger (**for** contre). ● *n* échange *m*; (between currencies) change *m*; ~ **rate** taux *m* de change; **telephone** ~ central *m* téléphonique.

Exchequer /ɪks'tʃekə(r)/ *n* (Pol) ministère *m* britannique des finances.

excise /'eksaɪz/ *n* excise *f*, taxe *f.*

excite /ɪk'saɪt/ *vt* exciter; (enthuse) enthousiasmer. **excited** *adj* excité; **get** ~**d** s'exciter. **excitement** *n* excitation *f.* **exciting** *adj* passionnant.

exclaim /ɪk'skleɪm/ *vt* s'exclamer.

exclamation /eksklə'meɪʃn/ *n* exclamation *f*; ~ **mark** or **point** (US) point *m* d'exclamation.

exclude /ɪk'skluːd/ *vt* exclure.

exclusive /ɪk'skluːsɪv/ *adj* (club) fermé; (rights) exclusif; (news item) en exclusivité; ~ **of meals** repas non compris. **exclusively** *adv* exclusivement.

excruciating /ɪk'skruːʃɪeɪtɪŋ/ *adj* atroce.

excursion /ɪk'skɜːʃn/ *n* excursion *f.*

excuse¹ /ɪk'skjuːz/ *vt* excuser; ~ **from** (exempt) dispenser de; ~ **me!** excusez-moi!, pardon!

excuse² /ɪk'skjuːs/ *n* (reason) excuse *f*; (pretext) prétexte *m* (**for sth** à qch; **for doing** pour faire).

ex-directory /eksdaɪ'rektərɪ/ *adj* sur liste rouge.

execute /'eksɪkjuːt/ *vt* exécuter. **executioner** *n* bourreau *m.*

executive /ɪg'zekjʊtɪv/ *n* (person) cadre *m*; (committee) exécutif *m.* ● *adj* exécutif.

exemplary /ɪg'zemplərɪ/ *adj* exemplaire.

exemplify /ɪg'zemplɪfaɪ/ *vt* illustrer.

exempt /ɪg'zempt/ adj exempt (**from** de). ● vt exempter.

exercise /'eksəsaɪz/ n exercice m; ~ **book** cahier m. ● vt exercer; (restraint, patience) faire preuve de. ● vi faire de l'exercice.

exert /ɪg'zɜːt/ vt exercer; ~ **oneself** se fatiguer. **exertion** n effort m.

exhaust /ɪg'zɔːst/ vt épuiser. ● n (Auto) pot m d'échappement.

exhaustive /ɪg'zɔːstɪv/ adj exhaustif.

exhibit /ɪg'zɪbɪt/ vt exposer; (fig) manifester. ● n objet m exposé.

exhibition /eksɪ'bɪʃn/ n exposition f; (of skill) démonstration f. **exhibitionist** n exhibitionniste mf.

exhibitor /ɪg'zɪbɪtə(r)/ n exposant/-e m/f.

exhilarate /ɪg'zɪləreɪt/ vt griser.

exile /'eksaɪl/ n exil m; (person) exilé/-e m/f. ● vt exiler.

exist /ɪg'zɪst/ vi exister. **existence** n existence f; **be in** ~**ence** exister. **existing** adj actuel.

exit /'eksɪt/ n sortie f. ● vt/i (also Comput) sortir (de).

exodus /'eksədəs/ n exode m.

exonerate /ɪg'zɒnəreɪt/ vt disculper.

exotic /ɪg'zɒtɪk/ adj exotique.

expand /ɪk'spænd/ vt développer; (workforce) accroître. ● vi se développer; (population) s'accroître; (metal) se dilater.

expanse /ɪk'spæns/ n étendue f.

expansion /ɪk'spænʃn/ n développement m; (Pol, Comm) expansion f.

expatriate /eks'pætrɪət/ adj & n expatrié/-e (m/f).

expect /ɪk'spekt/ vt s'attendre à; (suppose) supposer; (demand) exiger; (baby) attendre.

expectancy /ɪk'spektənsɪ/ n attente f.

expectant /ɪk'spektənt/ adj ~ **mother** future maman f.

expectation /ekspek'teɪʃn/ n (assumption) prévision f; (hope) aspiration f; (demand) exigence f.

expedient /ɪk'spiːdɪənt/ adj opportun. ● n expédient m.

expedition /ekspɪ'dɪʃn/ n expédition f.

expel /ɪk'spel/ vt (pt **expelled**) expulser; (pupil) renvoyer.

expend /ɪk'spend/ vt consacrer.

expenditure /ɪk'spendɪtʃə(r)/ n dépenses fpl.

expense /ɪk'spens/ n frais mpl; **at sb's** ~ aux frais de qn; ~ **account** frais mpl de représentation. **expensive** adj cher; (tastes) de luxe. **expensively** adv luxueusement.

experience /ɪk'spɪərɪəns/ n expérience f. ● vt (undergo) connaître; (feel) éprouver; ~**d** expérimenté.

experiment /ɪk'sperɪmənt/ n expérience f. ● vi expérimenter, faire des essais.

expert /'ekspɜːt/ n spécialiste mf. ● adj spécialisé, expert. **expertise** n compétence f. **expertly** adv de manière experte.

expire /ɪk'spaɪə(r)/ vi expirer; ~**d** périmé. **expiry** n expiration f.

explain /ɪk'spleɪn/ vt expliquer. **explanation** n explication f. **explanatory** adj explicatif.

explicit /ɪk'splɪsɪt/ adj explicite.

explode /ɪk'spləʊd/ vt/i (faire) exploser.

exploit¹ /'eksplɔɪt/ n exploit m.

exploit² /ɪk'splɔɪt/ vt exploiter.

exploration /eksplə'reɪʃn/ n exploration f. **exploratory** adj (talks) exploratoire. **explore** vt explorer; (fig) étudier. **explorer** n explorateur/-trice m/f.

explosion /ɪk'spləʊʒn/ n explosion f. **explosive** adj & n explosif (m).

exponent /ɪk'spəʊnənt/ n avocat/-e m/f (**of** de).

export¹ /ɪk'spɔːt/ vt exporter.

export² /'ekspɔːt/ n (process) exportation f; (product) produit m d'exportation.

expose /ɪk'spəʊz/ vt exposer; (disclose) révéler.

exposure /ɪk'spəʊʒə(r)/ n révélation f; (Photo) pose f; **die of** ~ mourir de froid.

express /ɪk'spres/ vt exprimer. ● adj exprès. ● adv **send sth** ~ envoyer qch en exprès. ● n (train) rapide m. **expression** n expression f. **expressive** adj expressif. **expressly** adv expressément.

exquisite /'ekskwɪzɪt/ adj exquis.

extend /ɪk'stend/ vt (visit) prolonger; (house) agrandir; (range) élargir; (arm, leg) étendre. ● vi (stretch) s'étendre;

(in time) se prolonger. **extension** n (of line, road) prolongement m; (of visa, loan) prorogation f; (building) addition f; (phone number) poste m; (cable) rallonge f.

extensive /ɪk'stensɪv/ adj vaste; (study) approfondi; (damage) considérable. **extensively** adv (much) beaucoup; (very) très.

extent /ɪk'stent/ n (size, scope) étendue f; (degree) mesure f; **to some ~** dans une certaine mesure; **to such an ~ that** à tel point que.

extenuating /ɪk'stenjʊeɪtɪŋ/ adj atténuant.

exterior /ɪk'stɪərɪə(r)/ adj & n extérieur (m).

exterminate /ɪk'stɜːmɪneɪt/ vt exterminer.

external /ɪk'stɜːnl/ adj extérieur; (cause, medical use) externe.

extinct /ɪk'stɪŋkt/ adj (species) disparu; (volcano, passion) éteint.

extinguish /ɪk'stɪŋgwɪʃ/ vt éteindre. **extinguisher** n extincteur m.

extol /ɪk'stəʊl/ vt (pt **extolled**) louer, chanter les louanges de.

extort /ɪk'stɔːt/ vt extorquer (**from** à). **extortion** n (Jur) extorsion f. **extortionate** adj exorbitant.

extra /'ekstrə/ adj supplémentaire; ~ **charge** supplément m; ~ **time** (football) prolongation f; ~ **strong** extrafort. ● adv encore; plus. ● n supplément m; (cinema) figurant/-e m/f.

extract[1] /ɪk'strækt/ vt sortir (**from** de); (tooth) extraire; (promise) arracher.

extract[2] /'ekstrækt/ n extrait m.

extra-curricular /ekstrəkə'rɪkjʊlə(r)/ adj parascolaire.

extradite /'ekstrədaɪt/ vt extrader.

extramarital /ekstrə'mærɪtl/ adj extraconjugal.

extramural /ekstrə'mjʊərəl/ adj (Univ) hors faculté.

extraordinary /ɪk'strɔːdnrɪ/ adj extraordinaire.

extravagance /ɪk'strævəgəns/ n prodigalité f. **extravagant** adj (person) dépensier; (claim) extravagant.

extreme /ɪk'striːm/ adj & n extrême (m). **extremely** adv extrêmement. **ex-**

tremist n extrémiste mf. **extremity** n extrémité f.

extricate /'ekstrɪkeɪt/ vt dégager.

extrovert /'ekstrəvɜːt/ n extraverti/-e m/f.

exuberance /ɪg'zjuːbərəns/ n exubérance f.

exude /ɪg'zjuːd/ vt (charm) respirer; (smell) exhaler.

eye /aɪ/ n œil m (pl yeux); **keep an ~ on** surveiller. ● vt (pt **eyed**; pres p **eyeing**) regarder. **~ball** n globe m oculaire. **~brow** n sourcil m. **~catching** adj attrayant. **~lash** n cil m. **~lid** n paupière f. **~-opener** n révélation f. **~-shadow** n ombre f à paupières. **~sight** n vue f. **~sore** n horreur f. **~witness** n témoin m oculaire.

e

f

Ff

fable /'feɪbl/ n fable f.

fabric /'fæbrɪk/ n (cloth) tissu m.

fabulous /'fæbjʊləs/ adj fabuleux; (marvellous 🔝) formidable.

face /feɪs/ n visage m, figure f; (expression) air m; (appearance, dignity) face f; (of clock) cadran m; (Geol) face f; (of rock) paroi f; **in the ~ of** face à; **make a (funny) ~** faire la grimace; ~ **to ~** face à face. ● vt être en face de; (risk) devoir affronter; (confront) faire face à; (deal with) **I can't ~ him** je n'ai pas le courage de le voir. ● vi (person) regarder; (chair) être tourné vers; (window) donner sur; ~ **up to** faire face à; **~d with** face à.

facelift /'feɪslɪft/ n lifting m; **give a ~ to** donner un coup de neuf à.

face value n valeur f nominale; **take sth at~** prendre qch au pied de la lettre.

facial /'feɪʃl/ adj (hair) du visage; (injury) au visage. ● n soin m du visage.

facility /fə'sɪlətɪ/ n (building) complexe m; (feature) fonction f; **facilities** (equipment) équipements mpl.

facsimile /fæk'sɪməlɪ/ n fac-similé m.

fact /fækt/ n fait m; **as a matter of ~**, **in ~** en fait; **know for a ~ that** savoir de source sûre que; **owing/due to the ~ that** étant donné que.

factor /'fæktə(r)/ n facteur m.

factory /'fæktərɪ/ n usine f.

factual /'fæktʃʊəl/ adj (account, description) basé sur les faits; (evidence) factuel.

faculty /'fækltɪ/ n faculté f.

fade /feɪd/ vi (sound) s'affaiblir; (memory) s'effacer; (flower) se faner; (material) se décolorer; (colour) passer.

fail /feɪl/ vi échouer; (grow weak) (s'af-)faiblir; (run short) manquer; (engine) tomber en panne. ● vt (exam) échouer à; **~ to do** (not do) ne pas faire; (not be able) ne pas réussir à faire; **without ~** à coup sûr.

failing /'feɪlɪŋ/ n défaut m; **~ that/this** sinon.

failure /'feɪljə(r)/ n échec m; (person) raté/-e m/f; (breakdown) panne f; **~ to do** (inability) incapacité f de faire.

faint /feɪnt/ adj léger, faible; **feel ~** (ill) se sentir mal; **I haven't the ~est idea** je n'en ai pas la moindre idée. ● vi s'évanouir. ● n évanouissement m; **~-hearted** adj timide.

fair /feə(r)/ n foire f. ● adj (hair) blond; (skin) clair; (weather) beau; (amount) raisonnable; (just) juste, équitable. ● adv (play) loyalement. **~ trade** commerce m équitable.

fairground n champ m de foire.

fairly /'feəlɪ/ adv (justly) équitablement; (rather) assez.

fairness /'feənɪs/ n justice f.

fairy /'feərɪ/ n fée f. **~ story, ~-tale** n conte m de fées.

faith /feɪθ/ n (belief) foi f; (confidence) confiance f.

faithful /'feɪθfl/ adj fidèle.

fake /feɪk/ n (forgery) faux m; (person) imposteur m; **it is a ~** c'est un faux. ● adj faux. ● vt (signature) contrefaire; (results) falsifier; (illness) feindre.

falcon /'fɔːlkən/ n faucon m.

fall /fɔːl/ vi (pt **fell**; pp **fallen**) tomber; **~ short** être insuffisant. ● n chute f; (autumn: US) automne m; **Niagara F~s** chutes fpl du Niagara. □ **~ back on** se rabattre sur. **~ behind** prendre du retard. **~ down** or **off** tomber. **~ for** (person 🔲) tomber amoureux de; (a trick 🔲) se laisser prendre à. **~ in**

(Mil) se mettre en rangs. **~ off** (decrease) diminuer. **~ out** se brouiller (**with** avec). **~ over** tomber (par terre). **~ through** (plans) tomber à l'eau.

fallacy /'fæləsɪ/ n erreur f.

false /fɔːls/ adj faux. **~ teeth** npl dentier m.

falter /'fɔːltə(r)/ vi (courage) faiblir; (when speaking) bafouiller 🔲.

fame /feɪm/ n renommée f. **famed** adj célèbre (**for** pour).

familiar /fə'mɪlɪə(r)/ adj familier; **be ~ with** connaître.

family /'fæməlɪ/ n famille f.

famine /'fæmɪn/ n famine f.

famished /'fæmɪʃt/ adj affamé.

famous /'feɪməs/ adj célèbre (**for** pour).

fan /fæn/ n (mechanical) ventilateur m; (hand-held) éventail m; (of person) fan mf 🔲, admirateur/-trice m/f; (enthusiast) fervent/-e m/f, passionné/-e m/f. ● vt (pt **fanned**) (face) éventer; (fig) attiser. ● vi **~ out** se déployer en éventail.

fanatic /fə'nætɪk/ n fanatique mf.

fan belt n courroie f de ventilateur.

fancy /'fænsɪ/ n (whim, fantasy) fantaisie f; **take a ~to sb** se prendre d'affection pour qn; **it took my ~** ça m'a plu. ● adj (buttons etc.) fantaisie inv; (prices) extravagant; (impressive) impressionnant. ● vt s'imaginer; (want 🔲) avoir envie de; (like 🔲) aimer. **~ dress** n déguisement m.

fang /fæŋ/ n (of dog) croc m; (of snake) crochet m.

fantasize /'fæntəsaɪz/ vi fantasmer.

fantastic /fæn'tæstɪk/ adj fantastique.

fantasy /'fæntəsɪ/ n fantaisie f; (daydream) fantasme m.

fanzine /'fænziːn/ n magazine m des fans, fanzine m.

FAQ abbr (**Frequently Asked Questions**) (Internet) FAQ f, foire f aux questions.

far /fɑː(r)/ adv loin; (much) beaucoup; (very) très; **~ away, ~ off** au loin; **as ~ as** (up to) jusqu'à; **as ~as I know** autant que je sache; **by ~** de loin; **~ from** loin de. ● adj lointain; (end, side) autre. **~away** adj lointain.

farce /fɑːs/ n farce f.

fare /feə(r)/ n (prix du) billet m; (food) nourriture f. ● vi (progress) aller; (manage) se débrouiller.

Far East n Extrême-Orient m.

farewell /feəˈwel/ interj & n adieu (m).

farm /fɑːm/ n ferme f. ● vt cultiver. **~ out** céder en sous-traitance. ● vi être fermier. **farmer** n fermier m. **~house** n ferme f. **farming** n agriculture f. **~yard** n basse-cour f.

fart /fɑːt/ 🔲 vi péter 🔲. ● n pet m 🔲.

farther /ˈfɑːðə(r)/ adv plus loin. ● adj plus éloigné.

farthest /ˈfɑːðɪst/ adv le plus loin. ● adj le plus éloigné.

fascinate /ˈfæsɪneɪt/ vt fasciner.

Fascism /ˈfæʃɪzəm/ n fascisme m.

fashion /ˈfæʃn/ n (current style) mode f; (manner) façon f; **in ~** à la mode; **out of ~** démodé. ● vt façonner. **fashionable** adj à la mode.

fast /fɑːst/ adj rapide; (colour) grand teint inv; (firm) fixe, solide; **be ~** (of a clock) avancer. ● adv vite; (firmly) ferme; **be ~ asleep** dormir d'un sommeil profond. ● vi jeûner. ● n jeûne m.

fasten /ˈfɑːsn/ vt/i (s')attacher. **fastener, fastening** n attache f, fermeture f.

fast food n fast-food m. restauration f rapide.

fat /fæt/ n graisse f; (on meat) gras m. ● adj (**fatter, fattest**) gros, gras; (meat) gras; (profit) gros; **a ~ lot** 🔲 bien peu (of de).

fatal /ˈfeɪtl/ adj mortel; (fateful, disastrous) fatal. **fatality** n mort m. **fatally** adv mortellement.

fate /feɪt/ n sort m. **fateful** adj fatidique.

father /ˈfɑːðə(r)/ n père m. **~hood** n paternité f. **~-in-law** n (pl **~s-inlaw**) beau-père m.

fathom /ˈfæðəm/ n brasse f (= 1.8 m). ● vt **~(out)** comprendre.

fatigue /fəˈtiːg/ n épuisement m; (Tech) fatigue f. ● vt fatiguer.

fatten /ˈfætn/ vt/i engraisser. **fattening** adj qui fait grossir.

fatty /ˈfætɪ/ adj (food) gras; (tissue) adipeux.

faucet /ˈfɔːsɪt/ n (US) robinet m.

fault /fɔːlt/ n (defect, failing) défaut m; (blame) faute f; (Geol) faille f; **at ~** fautif; **find ~ with** critiquer. ● vt **~ sth/sb** prendre en défaut qn/qch. **faulty** adj défectueux.

favour, (US) **favor** /ˈfeɪvə(r)/ n faveur f; **do sb a ~** rendre service à qn; **in ~ of** pour. ● vt favoriser; (support) être en faveur de; (prefer) préférer. **favourable** adj favorable.

favourite /ˈfeɪvərɪt/ adj & n favori/-te (m/f).

fawn /fɔːn/ n (animal) faon m; (colour) beige m foncé. ● vi **~ on** flagorner.

fax /fæks/ n fax m, télécopie f. ● vt faxer, envoyer par télécopie. **~ machine** n fax m. télécopieur m; (for public use) Publifax® m.

FBI abbr (**Federal Bureau of Investigation**) (US) Police f judiciaire fédérale.

fear /fɪə(r)/ n crainte f, peur f; (fig) risque m; **for ~ of/that** de peur de/que. ● vt craindre.

feasible /ˈfiːzəbl/ adj faisable; (likely) plausible.

feast /fiːst/ n festin m; (Relig) fête f. ● vi festoyer. ● vt régaler (**on** de).

feat /fiːt/ n exploit m.

feather /ˈfeðə(r)/ n plume f. ● vt **~ one's nest** s'enrichir.

feature /ˈfiːtʃə(r)/ n caractéristique f; (of person, face) trait m; (film) long métrage m; (article) article m de fond. ● vt (advert) représenter; (give prominence to) mettre en vedette. ● vi figurer (**in** dans).

February /ˈfebrʊərɪ/ n février m.

fed /fed/ →FEED. ● adj **be ~ up** 🔲 en avoir marre 🔲 (**with** de).

federal /ˈfedərəl/ adj fédéral.

fee /fiː/ n (for entrance) prix m; **~(s)** (of doctor) honoraires mpl; (of actor, artist) cachet m; (for tuition) frais mpl; (for enrolment) droits mpl.

feeble /ˈfiːbl/ adj faible.

feed /fiːd/ vt (pt **fed**) nourrir, donner à manger à; (suckle) allaiter; (supply) alimenter. ● vi se nourrir (**on** de). **~ in information** rentrer des données. ● n nourriture f; (of baby) tétée f.

feedback /ˈfiːdbæk/ n réaction (s) f(pl); (Med, Tech) feed-back m.

feel /fiːl/ vt (pt **felt**) (touch) tâter; (be conscious of) sentir; (emotion) ressentir; (experience) éprouver; (think) estimer. ● vi (tired, lonely) se sentir; **~**

hot/thirsty avoir chaud/soif; ~ **as if** avoir l'impression que; ~ **awful** (ill) se sentir malade; ~ **like** (want 🔲) avoir envie de.

feeler /'fiːlə(r)/ n antenne f; **put out** ~**s** tâter le terrain.

feeling /'fiːlɪŋ/ n (emotion) sentiment m; (physical) sensation f; (impression) impression f.

feet /fiːt/ →FOOT.

feign /feɪn/ vt feindre.

fell /fel/ →FALL. ● vt (cut down) abattre

fellow /'feləʊ/ n compagnon m, camarade m; (of society) membre m; (man 🔲) type m 🔲. ~**-countryman** n compatriote m. ~**-passenger** n compagnon m de voyage.

fellowship /'feləʊʃɪp/ n camaraderie f; (group) association f.

felony /'feləni/ n crime m.

felt /felt/ →FEEL. ● n feutre m. ~**-tip** n feutre m.

female /'fiːmeɪl/ adj (animal) femelle; (voice, sex) féminin. ● n femme f; (animal) femelle f.

feminine /'femənɪn/ adj & n féminin (m). **femininity** n féminité f. **feminist** n féministe mf.

fence /fens/ n barrière f; **sit on the** ~ ne pas prendre position. ● vt ~ **(in)** clôturer. ● vi (Sport) faire de l'escrime. **fencing** n escrime f.

fend /fend/ vi ~ **for oneself** se débrouiller tout seul. ● vt ~ **off** (blow, attack) parer.

fender /'fendə(r)/ n (for fireplace) garde-cendre m; (mudguard: US) garde-boue m inv.

ferment[1] /'fɜːment/ n ferment m; (excitement: fig) agitation f.

ferment[2] /fə'ment/ vt/i (faire) fermenter.

fern /fɜːn/ n fougère f.

ferocious /fə'rəʊʃəs/ adj féroce.

ferret /'ferɪt/ n (animal) furet m. ● vi ~ **about** fureter. ● vt ~ **out** dénicher.

ferry /'feri/ n (long-distance) ferry m; (short-distance) bac m. ● vt transporter.

fertile /'fɜːtaɪl/ adj fertile; (person, animal) fécond. **fertilizer** n engrais m.

festival /'festɪvl/ n festival m; (Relig) fête f.

festive /'festɪv/ adj de fête, gai; ~ **season** période f des fêtes. **festivity** n réjouissances fpl.

fetch /fetʃ/ vt (go for) aller chercher; (bring person) amener; (bring thing) apporter; (be sold for) rapporter.

fête /feɪt/ n fête f; (church) kermesse f. ● vt fêter.

fetish /'fetɪʃ/ n (object) fétiche m; (Psych) obsession f.

feud /fjuːd/ n querelle f.

fever /'fiːvə(r)/ n fièvre f. **feverish** adj fiévreux.

few /fjuː/ det peu de; **a** ~ **houses** quelques maisons; **quite a** ~ **people** un bon nombre de personnes. ● pron quelques-uns/quelques-unes.

fewer /'fjuːə(r)/ det moins de; **be** ~ être moins nombreux (**than** que). **fewest** det le moins de.

fiancé /fɪ'ɒnseɪ/ n fiancé m. **fiancée** n fiancée f.

fibre, (US) **fiber** /'faɪbə(r)/ n fibre f. ~**glass** n fibre f de verre.

fiction /'fɪkʃn/ n fiction f; (works of) ~ romans mpl. **fictional** adj fictif.

fiddle /'fɪdl/ n 🔲 violon m; (swindle 🔲) combine f. ● vi 🔀 frauder. ● vt 🔲 falsifier; ~ **with** 🔲 tripoter 🔲.

fidget /'fɪdʒɪt/ vi gigoter sans cesse.

field /fiːld/ n champ m; (Sport) terrain m; (fig) domaine m. ● vt (ball: cricket) bloquer.

fierce /fɪəs/ adj féroce; (storm, attack) violent.

fiery /'faɪərɪ/ adj (**-ier, -iest**) (hot) ardent; (spirited) fougueux.

fifteen /fɪf'tiːn/ adj & n quinze (m).

fifth /fɪfθ/ adj & n cinquième (mf).

fifty /'fɪftɪ/ adj & n cinquante (m).

fig /fɪg/ n figue f.

fight /faɪt/ vi (pt **fought**) se battre; (struggle: fig) lutter; (quarrel) se disputer. ● vt se battre avec; (evil: fig) lutter contre. ● n (struggle) lutte f; (quarrel) dispute f; (brawl) bagarre f; (Mil) combat m. □ ~ **back** se défendre (**against** contre). ~**off** surmonter. ~**over** se disputer qch. **fighter** n (determined person) lutteur/-euse m/f; (plane) avion m de chasse. **fighting** n combats mpl.

figment /'fɪgmənt/ n **a** ~ **of the imagination** un produit de l'imagination.

figure /'fɪgə(r)/ n (number) chiffre m; (diagram) figure f; (shape) forme f; (body) ligne f, ∼**s** arithmétique f. ● vt s'imaginer. ● vi (appear) figurer; **that** ∼**s** (US, Ⅱ) c'est logique; ∼ **out** comprendre; ∼ **of speech** n façon f de parler.

file /faɪl/ n (tool) lime f. dossier m, classeur m; (Comput) fichier m; (row) file f. ● vt limer; (papers) classer; (Jur) déposer. ▫ ∼ **in** entrer en file. ∼ **past** défiler devant.

filing cabinet n classeur m.

fill /fɪl/ vt/i (se) remplir. ● n have had **one's** ∼ en avoir assez. ▫ ∼ **in** (form) remplir. ∼ **out** prendre du poids. ∼ **up** (Auto) faire le plein (de carburant); (bath, theatre) (se) remplir.

fillet /'fɪlɪt/ n filet m. ● vt découper en filets.

filling /'fɪlɪŋ/ n (of tooth) plombage m; (of sandwich) garniture f. ∼ **station** n station-service f.

film /fɪlm/ n film m; (Photo) pellicule f. ● vt filmer. ∼**-goer** n cinéphile mf. ∼**star** n vedette f de cinéma.

filter /'fɪltə(r)/ n filtre m; (traffic signal) flèche f. ● vt/i filtrer; (of traffic) suivre la flèche. ∼ **coffee** n café m filtre.

filth /fɪlθ/ n crasse f. **filthy** adj crasseux.

fin /fɪn/ n (of fish, seal) nageoire f; (of shark) aileron m.

final /'faɪnl/ adj dernier; (conclusive) définitif. ● n (Sport) finale f.

finale /fɪ'nɑːlɪ/ n (Mus) finale m.

finalize /'faɪnəlaɪz/ vt mettre au point, fixer.

finally /'faɪnəlɪ/ adv (lastly, at last) enfin, finalement; (once and for all) définitivement.

finance /'faɪnæns/ n finance f. ● adj financier. ● vt financer. **financial** adj financier.

find /faɪnd/ vt (pt **found**) trouver; (sth lost) retrouver. ● n trouvaille f; ∼ **out** vt découvrir; vi se renseigner (**about** sur). **findings** npl conclusions fpl.

fine /faɪn/ adj fin; (excellent) beau; ∼ **arts** beaux-arts mpl. ● n amende f. ● vt condamner à une amende.

finger /'fɪŋgə(r)/ n doigt m. ● vt palper. ∼**-nail** n ongle m. ∼**print** n empreinte f digitale. ∼**tip** n bout m du doigt.

finish /'fɪnɪʃ/ vt/i finir; ∼ **doing** finir de faire; ∼ **up doing** finir par faire; ∼ **up in** se retrouver à. ● n fin f; (of race) arrivée f; (appearance) finition f.

finite /'faɪnaɪt/ adj fini.

Finland /'fɪnlənd/ n Finlande f. **Finn** n Finlandais/-e m/f.

Finnish /'fɪnɪʃ/ adj finlandais. ● n (Ling) finnois m.

fir /fɜː(r)/ n sapin m.

fire /'faɪə(r)/ n (element) feu m; (blaze) incendie m; (heater) radiateur m; **set** ∼ **to** mettre le feu à. ● vt (bullet) tirer; (dismiss) renvoyer; (fig) enflammer. ● vi tirer (**at** sur). ∼ **a gun** tirer un coup de revolver/de fusil. ∼ **alarm** n alarme f incendie. ∼**arm** n arme f à feu. ∼ **brigade** n pompiers mpl. ∼ **engine** n voiture f de pompiers. ∼ **escape** n escalier m de secours. ∼ **extinguisher** n extincteur m. ∼ **man** n (pl **-men**) pompier m. ∼**place** n cheminée f. ∼ **station** n caserne f de pompiers. ∼**wall** n mur m coupe-feu; (Internet) pare-feu m inv. ∼**wood** n bois m de chauffage. ∼**work** n feu m d'artifice.

firing squad n peloton m d'exécution.

firm /fɜːm/ n entreprise f, société f. ● adj ferme; (belief) solide.

first /fɜːst/ adj premier; **at** ∼ **hand** de première main; **at** ∼ **sight** à première vue; ∼ **of all** tout d'abord. ● n premier/-ière m/f. ● adv d'abord, premièrement; (arrive) le premier, la première; **at** ∼ d'abord. ∼ **aid** n premiers soins mpl. ∼**-class** adj de première classe. ∼ **floor** n premier étage m; (US) rez-de-chaussée m inv. ∼ **gear** n première (vitesse) f. **F∼ Lady** n (US) épouse f du Président.

firstly /'fɜːstlɪ/ adv premièrement.

first name n prénom m.

fish /fɪʃ/ n poisson m; ∼ **shop** poissonnerie f. ● vi pêcher; ∼ **for** (cod) pêcher; ∼ **out** (from water) repêcher; (take out Ⅱ) sortir. **fisherman** n (pl **-men**) n pêcheur m.

fishing /'fɪʃɪŋ/ n pêche f; **go** ∼ aller à la pêche. ∼ **rod** n canne f à pêche.

fishmonger /'fɪʃmʌŋgə(r)/ n poissonnier/-ière m/f.

fist /fɪst/ n poing m.

fit /fɪt/ n accès m, crise f; **be a good** ∼ (dress) être à la bonne taille. ● adj (**fit-**

ter, **fittest**) en bonne santé; (proper) convenable; (good enough) bon; (able) capable; **in no ~ state to do** pas en état de faire. ● vt/i (pt **fitted**) (into space) aller; (install) poser. **~ in** vt caser; vi (newcomer) s'intégrer. **~ out, ~ up** équiper.

fitness /'fɪtnɪs/ n forme f; (of remark) justesse f.

fitted /'fɪtɪd/ adj (wardrobe) encastré. **~ carpet** n moquette f.

fitting /'fɪtɪŋ/ adj approprié. ● n essayage m. **~ room** n cabine f d'essayage.

five /faɪv/ adj & n cinq (m).

fix /fɪks/ vt (make firm, attach, decide) fixer; (mend) réparer; (deal with) arranger; **~ sb up with sth** trouver qch à qn.

fixture /'fɪkstʃə(r)/ n (Sport) match m; **~s** (in house) installations fpl.

fizz /fɪz/ vi pétiller. ● n pétillement m. **fizzy** adj gazeux.

flabbergast /'flæbəgɑːst/ vt sidérer.

flabby /'flæbɪ/ adj flasque.

flag /flæg/ n drapeau m; (Naut) pavillon m. ● vt (pt **flagged**) **~ (down)** faire signe de s'arrêter à. ● vi (weaken) faiblir; (sick person) s'affaiblir. **~-pole** n mât m. **~stone** n dalle f.

flake /fleɪk/ n flocon m; (of paint, metal) écaille f. ● vi s'écailler.

flamboyant /flæm'bɔɪənt/ adj (colour) éclatant; (manner) extravagant.

flame /fleɪm/ n flamme f; **burst into ~s** exploser; **go up in ~s** brûler. ● vi flamber.

flamingo /flə'mɪŋɡəʊ/ n flamant m (rose).

flammable /'flæməbl/ adj inflammable.

flan /flæn/ n tarte f; (custard tart) flan m.

flank /flæŋk/ n flanc m. ● vt flanquer.

flannel /'flænl/ n (material) flannelle f; (for face) gant m de toilette.

flap /flæp/ vi (pt **flapped**) battre. ● vt **~ its wings** battre des ailes. ● n (of pocket) rabat m; (of table) abattant m.

flare /fleə(r)/ vi **~ up** (fighting) éclater. ● n flamboiement m; (Mil) fusée f éclairante; (in skirt) évasement m. **flared** adj évasé.

flash /flæʃ/ vi briller; (on and off) clignoter; **~ past** passer à toute vitesse. ● vt faire briller; (aim torch) diriger (at sur); (flaunt) étaler; **~ one's headlights** faire un appel de phares. ● n (of news, camera) flash m; **in a ~** en un éclair. **~back** n retour m en arrière. **~light** n lampe f de poche.

flask /flɑːsk/ n (for chemicals) flacon m; (for drinks) thermos® m or f inv.

flat /flæt/ adj (**flatter**, **flattest**) plat; (tyre) à plat; (refusal) catégorique. (fare, rate) fixe. ● adv (say) carrément. ● n (rooms) appartement m; (tyre 🔟) crevaison f; (Mus) bémol m.

flat out adv (drive) à toute vitesse; (work) d'arrache-pied.

flatten /'flætn/ vt/i (s')aplatir.

flatter /'flætə(r)/ vt flatter.

flaunt /flɔːnt/ vt étaler, afficher.

flavour, (US) **flavor** /'fleɪvə(r)/ n goût m; (of ice-cream) parfum m. ● vt parfumer (**with** à), assaisonner (**with** de). **flavouring** n arôme m artificiel.

flaw /flɔː/ n défaut m.

flea /fliː/ n puce f. **~ market** n marché m aux puces.

fleck /flek/ n petite tache f.

fled /fled/ **→FLEE.**

flee /fliː/ vt/i (pt **fled**) fuir.

fleece /fliːs/ n toison f; (garment) polaire f. ● vt plumer.

fleet /fliːt/ n (Naut, Aviat) flotte f; **a ~ of vehicles** (in reserve) parc m; (on road) convoi m.

fleeting /'fliːtɪŋ/ adj très bref.

Flemish /'flemɪʃ/ adj flamand. ● n (Ling) flamand m.

flesh /fleʃ/ n chair f; **one's (own) ~ and blood** la chair de sa chair.

flew /fluː/ **→FLY.**

flex /fleks/ vt (knee) fléchir; (muscle) faire jouer. ● n (Electr) fil m.

flexible /'fleksəbl/ adj flexible.

flexitime /'fleksɪtaɪm/ n horaire m variable.

flick /flɪk/ n petit coup m. ● vt donner un petit coup à; **~ through** feuilleter.

flight /flaɪt/ n (of bird, plane) vol m; **~ of stairs** escalier m; (fleeing) fuite f; **take ~** prendre la fuite. **~-deck** n poste m de pilotage.

flimsy /'flɪmzɪ/ adj (**-ier, -iest**) (pej) mince, peu solide.

flinch /flɪntʃ/ vi (wince) broncher; (draw back) reculer.

fling /flɪŋ/ vt (pt **flung**) jeter.

flint /flɪnt/ n (rock) silex m.

flip /flɪp/ vt (pt **flipped**) donner un petit coup à; ~ **through** feuilleter. ● n chiquenaude f.

flippant /'flɪpənt/ adj désinvolte.

flipper /'flɪpə(r)/ n (of seal) nageoire f; (of swimmer) palme f.

flirt /flɜːt/ vi flirter. ● n flirteur/-euse m/f.

float /fləʊt/ vt/i (faire) flotter. ● n flotteur m; (cart) char m.

flock /flɒk/ n (of sheep) troupeau m; (of people) foule f. ● vi affluer.

flog /flɒg/ vt (pt **flogged**) (beat) fouetter; (sell 🇬🇧) vendre.

flood /flʌd/ n inondation f; (fig) flot m. ● vt inonder. ● vi (building) être inondé; (river) déborder; (people: fig) affluer.

floodlight /'flʌdlaɪt/ n projecteur m. ● vt (pt **floodlit**) illuminer.

floor /flɔː(r)/ n sol m, plancher m; (for dancing) piste f; (storey) étage m. ● vt (knock down) terrasser; (baffle) stupéfier. ~-**board** n planche f.

flop /flɒp/ vi (pt **flopped**) (drop) s'affaler; (fail 🇬🇧) échouer; (head) tomber. ● n 🇬🇧 échec m, fiasco m.

floppy /'flɒpɪ/ adj lâche, flasque. ~ **(disk)** n disquette f.

florist /'flɒrɪst/ n fleuriste mf.

flounder /'flaʊndə(r)/ vi (animal, person) se débattre (**in** dans); (economy) stagner. ● n flet m; (US) poisson m plat.

flour /'flaʊə(r)/ n farine f.

flourish /'flʌrɪʃ/ vi prospérer. ● vt brandir. ● n geste m élégant.

flout /flaʊt/ vt se moquer de.

flow /fləʊ/ vi couler; (circulate) circuler; (traffic) s'écouler; (hang loosely) flotter; ~ **in** affluer; ~ **into** (of river) se jeter dans. ● n (of liquid, traffic) écoulement m; (of tide) flux m; (of orders, words: fig) flot m. ~ **chart** n organigramme m.

flower /'flaʊə(r)/ n fleur f. ● vi fleurir.

flown /fləʊn/ ➞FLY.

flu /fluː/ n grippe f.

fluctuate /'flʌktjʊeɪt/ vi varier.

fluent /'fluːənt/ adj (style) aisé; **be** ~ **(in a language)** parler (une langue) couramment.

fluff /flʌf/ n peluche(s) f(pl). (down) duvet m.

fluid /'fluːɪd/ adj & n fluide (m).

fluke /fluːk/ n coup m de chance.

flung /flʌŋ/ ➞FLING.

fluoride /'flɔːraɪd/ n fluor m.

flush /flʌʃ/ vi rougir. ● vt nettoyer à grande eau; ~ **the toilet** tirer la chasse d'eau. ● n (blush) rougeur f; (fig) excitation f. ● adj ~ **with** (level with) au ras de. □ ~ **out** chasser.

fluster /'flʌstə(r)/ vt énerver.

flute /fluːt/ n flûte f.

flutter /'flʌtə(r)/ vi voleter; (of wings) battre. ● n (wings) battement m; (fig) agitation f; (bet 🇬🇧) pari m.

flux /flʌks/ n changement m continuel.

fly /flaɪ/ n mouche f; (of trousers) braguette f. ● vi (pt **flew**; pp **flown**) voler; (passengers) voyager en avion; (flag) flotter; (rush) filer. ● vt (aircraft) piloter; (passengers, goods) transporter par avion; (flag) arborer. □ ~ **off** s'envoler.

flyer /'flaɪə(r)/ n (person) aviateur m; (circular) prospectus m.

flying /'flaɪɪŋ/ adj (saucer) volant; **with** ~ **colours** haut la main; ~ **start** excellent départ m; ~ **visit** visite f éclair (adj inv). ● n (activity) aviation f.

flyover /'flaɪəʊvə(r)/ n pont m (routier).

foal /fəʊl/ n poulain m.

foam /fəʊm/ n écume f, mousse f; ~ **(rubber)** caoutchouc m mousse. ● vi écumer, mousser.

focus /'fəʊkəs/ n (pl ~**es** or **-ci**) foyer m; (fig) centre m; **be in/out of** ~être/ ne pas être au point. ● vt/i (faire) converger; (instrument) mettre au point; (with camera) faire la mise au point (**on** sur); (fig) (se) concentrer. ~ **group** groupe m de discussion.

fodder /'fɒdə(r)/ n fourrage m.

foe /fəʊ/ n ennemi/-e m/f.

foetus /'fiːtəs/ n fœtus m.

fog /fɒg/ n brouillard m. ● vt/i (pt **fogged**) (window) (s')embuer.

foggy /'fɒgɪ/ adj brumeux; **it is ~** il fait du brouillard.

foil /fɔɪl/ n (tin foil) papier m d'aluminium; (deterrent) repoussoir m. ● vt (thwart) déjouer.

fold /fəʊld/ vt/i (paper, clothes) (se) plier; (arms) croiser; (fail) s'effondrer. ● n pli m; (for sheep) parc m à moutons; (Relig) bercail m. **folder** n (file) chemise f; (leaflet) dépliant m. **folding** adj pliant.

foliage /'fəʊlɪɪdʒ/ n feuillage m.

folk /fəʊk/ n gens mpl; **~s** parents mpl. ● adj (dance) folklorique; (music) folk.

folklore /'fəʊklɔː(r)/ n folklore m.

follow /'fɒləʊ/ vt/i suivre; **it ~s that** il s'ensuit que; **~ suit** en faire autant; **~ up** (letter) donner suite à. **follower** n partisan m.

following /'fɒləʊwɪŋ/ n partisans mpl. ● adj suivant; **~ day** lendemain. ● prep à la suite de.

fond /fɒnd/ adj (loving) affectueux; (hope) cher; **be ~ of** aimer.

fondle /'fɒndl/ vt caresser.

fondness /'fɒndnɪs/ n affection f; (for things) attachement m.

food /fuːd/ n nourriture f; **French ~** la cuisine française. ● adj alimentaire. **~ processor** n robot m (ménager).

fool /fuːl/ n idiot/-e m/f. ● vt duper. ● vi **~ around** faire l'idiot; **foolish** adj idiot.

foot /fʊt/ n (pl **feet**) pied m; (measure) pied m (=30.48 cm); (of stairs, page) bas m; **on** or **to one's feet** debout; **under sb's feet** dans les jambes de qn. ● vt (bill) payer.

foot-and-mouth disease n fièvre f aphteuse.

football /'fʊtbɔːl/ n (ball) ballon m; (game) football m. **footballer** n footballeur m.

foot: **~-bridge** n passerelle f; **~hold** n prise f.

footing /'fʊtɪŋ/ n **on an equal ~** sur un pied d'égalité; **be on a friendly ~ with sb** avoir des rapports amicaux avec qn; **lose one's ~** perdre pied.

foot: **~note** n note f (en bas de la page). **~path** n (in countryside) sentier m; (in town) chemin m. **~print** n empreinte f (de pied). **~step** n pas m. **~wear** n chaussures fpl.

for /fɔː(r)/

● preposition

····▸ pour; **~ me** pour moi; **music ~ dancing** de la musique pour danser; **what is it ~?** ça sert à quoi?

····▸ (with a time period that is still continuing) depuis; **I've been waiting ~ two hours** j'attends depuis deux heures; **I haven't seen him ~ ten years** je ne l'ai pas vu depuis dix ans.

····▸ (with a time period that has ended) pendant; **I waited ~ two hours** j'ai attendu pendant deux heures.

····▸ (with a future time period) pour; **I'm going to Paris ~ six weeks** je vais à Paris pour six semaines.

····▸ (with distances) pendant; **I drove ~ 50 kilometres** j'ai roulé pendant 50 kilomètres.

forbid /fə'bɪd/ vt (pt **forbade**. pp **forbidden**) interdire, défendre (**sb to do** à qn de faire). **~ sb sth** interdire or défendre qch à qn; **you are forbidden to leave** il vous est interdit de partir. **forbidding** adj menaçant.

force /fɔːs/ n force f; **come into ~** entrer en vigueur; **the ~s** les forces fpl armées. ● vt forcer. □ **~ into** faire entrer de force. **~ on** imposer à. **forced** adj forcé.

force-feed vt (pt **-fed**) (person) nourrir de force; (animal) gaver.

forceful /'fɔːsfl/ adj énergique.

ford /fɔːd/ n gué m. ● vt passer à gué.

forearm /'fɔːrɑːm/ n avant-bras m inv.

forecast /'fɔːkɑːst/ vt (pt **forecast**) prévoir. ● n weather **~** météo f.

forecourt /'fɔːkɔːt/ n (of garage) devant m; (of station) cour f.

forefinger /'fɔːfɪŋgə(r)/ n index m.

forefront /'fɔːfrʌnt/ n **at/in the ~ of** à la pointe de.

foregone /'fɔːgɒn/ adj **it's a ~ conclusion** c'est couru d'avance.

foreground /'fɔːgraʊnd/ n premier plan m.

forehead /'fɒrɪd/ n front m.

foreign /'fɒrən/ adj étranger; (trade) extérieur; (travel) à l'étranger. **for-**

eigner n étranger/-ère m/f.

foreman /'fɔːmən/ n (pl **-men**) contre-maître m.

foremost /'fɔːməʊst/ adj le plus émi-nent. ● adv **first and ~** tout d'abord.

forensic /fə'rensɪk/ adj médico-légal; **~ medicine** médecine f légale.

foresee /fɔː'siː/ vt (pt **-saw**, pp **-seen**) prévoir.

forest /'fɒrɪst/ n forêt f. **forestry** n syl-viculture f.

foretaste /'fɔːteɪst/ n avant-goût m.

forever /fə'revə(r)/ adv toujours.

foreword /'fɔːwɜːd/ n avant-propos m inv.

forfeit /'fɔːfɪt/ n (penalty) peine f; (in game) gage m. ● vt perdre.

forgave /fə'geɪv/ ➡FORGIVE.

forge /fɔːdʒ/ n forge f. ● vt (metal, friendship) forger; (copy) contrefaire, falsifier. ● vi **~ ahead** aller de l'avant, avancer. **forger** n faussaire m. **forgery** n faux m, contrefaçon f.

forget /fə'get/ vt/i (pt **forgot**. pp **for-gotten**) oublier; **~ oneself** s'oublier. **forgetful** adj distrait. **~-me-not** n myosotis m.

forgive /fə'gɪv/ vt (pt **forgave**. pp **for-given**) pardonner (**sb for sth** qch à qn).

fork /fɔːk/ n fourchette f; (for digging) fourche f; (in road) bifurcation f. ● vi (road) bifurquer; **~ out** 🅸 payer. **forked** adj fourchu. **~-lift truck** n chariot m élévateur.

form /fɔːm/ n forme f; (document) for-mulaire m; (School) classe f; **on ~** en forme. ● vt/i (se) former.

formal /'fɔːml/ adj officiel, en bonne et due forme; (person) compassé, céré-monieux; (dress) de cérémonie; (denial, grammar) formel; (language) soutenu. **formality** n cérémonial m; (require-ment) formalité f.

format /'fɔːmæt/ n format m. ● vt (pt **formatted**) (disk) formater.

former /'fɔːmə(r)/ adj ancien; (first of two) premier; **the ~** celui-là, celle-là. **formerly** adv autrefois.

formula /'fɔːmjʊlə/ n (pl **-ae** or **-as**) formule f. **formulate** vt formuler.

fort /fɔːt/ n (Mil) fort m; **to hold the ~** s'occuper de tout.

forth /fɔːθ/ adv **from this day ~** à par-tir d'aujourd'hui; **and so ~** et ainsi de suite; **go back and ~** aller et venir.

forthcoming /fɔːθ'kʌmɪŋ/ adj à venir, prochain; (sociable 🅸) communicatif.

forthright /'fɔːθraɪt/ adj direct.

forthwith /fɔːθ'wɪθ/ adv sur-le-champ.

fortnight /'fɔːtnaɪt/ n quinze jours mpl, quinzaine f.

fortnightly /'fɔːtnaɪtlɪ/ adj bimensuel. ● adv tous les quinze jours.

fortunate /'fɔːtʃənət/ adj heureux; **be ~** avoir de la chance. **fortunately** adv heureusement.

fortune /'fɔːtʃuːn/ n fortune f; **make a ~** faire fortune; **have the good ~ to** avoir la chance de. **~-teller** n diseur/-euse m/f de bonne aventure.

forty /'fɔːtɪ/ adj & n quarante (m). **~ winks** un petit somme.

forward /'fɔːwəd/ adj en avant; (ad-vanced) précoce; (bold) effronté. ● n (Sport) avant m. ● adv en avant; **come ~** se présenter; **go ~** avancer. ● vt (letter, e-mail) faire suivre; (goods) ex-pédier; (fig) favoriser. **forwardness** n précocité f. **forwards** adv en avant.

fossil /'fɒsl/ n & adj fossile (m).

foster /'fɒstə(r)/ vt (promote) encoura-ger; (child) élever. ● adj (child, parent) adoptif; (family, home) de placement.

fought /fɔːt/ ➡FIGHT.

foul /faʊl/ adj (smell, weather) infect; (place, action) immonde; (language) ordurier. ● n (football) faute f. ● vt souiller, encrasser; **~ up** 🅸 gâcher. **~-mouthed** adj grossier.

found /faʊnd/ ➡FIND. ● vt fonder. **foundation** n fondation f; (basis) fon-dement m; (make-up) fond m de teint. **founder** n fondateur/-trice m/f.

fountain /'faʊntɪn/ n fontaine f; **~-pen** n stylo m à encre.

four /fɔː(r)/ adj & n quatre (m).

fourteen /fɔː'tiːn/ adj & n quatorze (m).

fourth /fɔːθ/ adj & n quatrième (mf).

four-wheel drive n (car) quatre-quatre m.

fowl /faʊl/ n (one bird) poulet m; (group) volaille f.

fox /fɒks/ n renard m. ● vt (baffle) mys-tifier; (deceive) tromper.

fraction /'frækʃn/ n fraction f.

f

fracture /'fræktʃə(r)/ n fracture f. • vt/i (se) fracturer.

fragile /'frædʒaɪl/ adj fragile.

fragment /'frægmənt/ n fragment m.

fragrance /'freɪgrəns/ n parfum m.

frail /freɪl/ adj frêle.

frame /freɪm/ n (of building, boat) charpente f; (of picture) cadre m; (of window) châssis m; (of spectacles) monture f; ~ **of mind** humeur f. • vt encadrer; (fig) formuler; (Jur, ▣) monter un coup contre. ~**work** n structure f; (context) cadre m.

France /frɑːns/ n France f.

franchise /'fræntʃaɪz/ n (Pol) droit m de vote; (Comm) franchise f.

frank /fræŋk/ adj franc. • vt affranchir. **frankly** adv franchement.

frantic /'fræntɪk/ adj frénétique. ~ **with** fou de.

fraternity /frə'tɜːnətɪ/ n (bond) fraternité f; (group, club) confrérie f.

fraud /frɔːd/ n (deception) fraude f; (person) imposteur m. **fraudulent** adj frauduleux.

fray /freɪ/ n **the** ~ la bataille. • vt/i (s')effilocher.

freckle /'frekl/ n tache f de rousseur.

free /friː/ adj libre; (gratis) gratuit; (lavish) généreux; ~ **(of charge)** gratuit(ement); **a** ~ **hand** carte f blanche. • vt (pt **freed**) libérer; (clear) dégager.

freedom /'friːdəm/ n liberté f.

free: ~ **enterprise** n la libre entreprise. ~ **kick** n coup m franc. ~**lance** adj & n free-lance (mf), indépendant/-e (m/f).

freely /'friːlɪ/ adv librement.

Freemason /'friːmeɪsn/ n franc-maçon m.

Freenet /'friːnet/ n (Comput) Libertel m.

free: ~**phone,** ~ **number** n numéro m vert. ~**-range** adj (eggs) de ferme.

Freeware /'friːweə(r)/ n (Comput) Gratuiciel m.

freeway /'friːweɪ/ n (US) autoroute f.

freeze /friːz/ vt/i (pt **froze**, pp **frozen**) geler; (Culin) (se) congeler; (wages) bloquer. • n gel m. blocage m; ~**-dried** adj lyophilisé.

freezer /'friːzə(r)/ n congélateur m.

freezing /'friːzɪŋ/ adj glacial; **below** ~ au-dessous de zéro.

freight /freɪt/ n fret m.

French /frentʃ/ adj français. • n (Ling) français m; **the** ~ les Français mpl; ~ **bean** n haricot m vert; ~ **fries** npl frites fpl; ~**man** n Français m; ~**-speaking** adj francophone; ~ **window** n porte-fenêtre f; ~**woman** n Française f.

frenzied /'frenzɪd/ adj frénétique.

frenzy n frénésie f.

frequent[1] /'friːkwənt/ adj fréquent.

frequent[2] /frɪ'kwent/ vt fréquenter.

fresco /'freskəʊ/ n fresque f.

fresh /freʃ/ adj frais; (different, additional) nouveau; (cheeky ▣) culotté.

freshen /'freʃn/ vi (weather) fraîchir. ~ **up** (person) se rafraîchir.

freshly /'freʃlɪ/ adv nouvellement.

freshness /'freʃnɪs/ n fraîcheur f.

freshwater /'freʃwɔːtə(r)/ adj d'eau douce.

friction /'frɪkʃn/ n friction f.

Friday /'fraɪdɪ/ n vendredi m.

fridge /frɪdʒ/ n frigo m.

fried /fraɪd/ ➡**FRY.** • adj frit; ~ **eggs** œufs mpl sur le plat.

friend /frend/ n ami/-e m/f. **friendly** adj (**-ier, -iest**) amical, gentil. **friendship** n amitié f.

frieze /friːz/ n frise f.

fright /fraɪt/ n peur f; (person, thing) horreur f.

frighten /'fraɪtn/ vt effrayer; ~ **off** faire fuir. **frightened** adj effrayé; **be** ~**ed** avoir peur (**of** de). **frightening** adj effrayant.

frill /frɪl/ n (trimming) fanfreluche f; **with no** ~**s** très simple.

fringe /frɪndʒ/ n (edging, hair) frange f; (of area) bordure f; (of society) marge f. ~ **benefits** npl avantages mpl sociaux.

frisk /frɪsk/ vt (search) fouiller.

fritter /'frɪtə(r)/ n beignet m. • vt ~ **away** gaspiller.

frivolity /frɪ'vɒlətɪ/ n frivolité f.

frizzy /'frɪzɪ/ adj crépu.

fro ➡**TO AND FRO.**

frog /frɒg/ n grenouille f; **a** ~ **in one's throat** un chat dans la gorge.

frolic /'frɒlɪk/ vi (pt **frolicked**) s'ébattre. • n ébats mpl.

from /frɒm/ prep de; (with time, prices) à partir de, de; (habit, conviction) par; (according to) d'après; **take ~ sb** prendre à qn; **take ~ one's pocket** prendre dans sa poche.

front /frʌnt/ n (of car, train) avant m; (of garment, building) devant m; (Mil, Pol) front m; (of book, pamphlet) début m; (appearance: fig) façade f. ● adj de devant, avant inv; (first) premier; **~ door** porte f d'entrée; **in ~ (of)** devant. **frontage** n façade f.

frontier /'frʌntɪə(r)/ n frontière f.

frost /frɒst/ n gel m, gelée f; (on glass) givre m. ● vt/i (se) givrer. **~-bite** n gelure f.

frosty /'frɒstɪ/ adj (weather, welcome) glacial; (window) givré.

froth /frɒθ/ n (on beer) mousse f; (on water) écume f. ● vi mousser, écumer.

frown /fraʊn/ vi froncer les sourcils; **~ on** désapprouver. ● n froncement m de sourcils.

froze /frəʊz/ ➡FREEZE.

frozen /'frəʊzn/ ➡FREEZE. ● adj congelé.

fruit /fruːt/ n fruit m; (collectively) fruits mpl. **fruitful** adj (discussions) fructueux. **~ machine** n machine f à sous.

frustrate /frʌ'streɪt/ vt (plan) faire échouer; (person: Psych) frustrer; (upset 🔢) exaspérer. **frustration** n (Psych) frustration f; (disappointment) déception f.

fry /fraɪ/ vt/i (pt **fried**) (faire) frire. **frying-pan** n poêle f (à frire).

FTP abbr (**File Transfer Protocol**) (Internet) protocole m FTP.

fudge /fʌdʒ/ n caramel m mou. ● vt (issue) esquiver.

fuel /'fjuːəl/ n combustible m; (for car engine) carburant m. ● vt (pt **fuelled**) alimenter en combustible.

fugitive /'fjuːdʒətɪv/ n & a fugitif/-ive (m/f).

fulfil /fʊl'fɪl/ vt (pt **fulfilled**) accomplir, réaliser; (condition) remplir; **~ oneself** s'épanouir. **fulfilling** adj satisfaisant. **fulfilment** n réalisation f. épanouissement m.

full /fʊl/ adj plein (**of** de); (bus, hotel) complet; (programme) chargé; (skirt) ample; **be ~ (up)** n'avoir plus faim; **at ~ speed** à toute vitesse. ● n in ~ intégralement; **to the ~** complètement. **~ back** n (Sport) arrière m. **~ moon** n pleine lune f. **~ name** n nom m et prénom m. **~-scale** adj (drawing etc.) grandeur nature inv; (fig) de grande envergure. **~ stop** n point m. **~-time** adj & adv à plein temps.

fully /'fʊlɪ/ adv complètement; **~ fledged** (member, citizen) à part entière.

fume /fjuːm/ vi rager. **fumes** npl émanations fpl, vapeurs fpl.

fun /fʌn/ n amusement m; **be ~** être chouette; **for ~** pour rire; **make ~ of** se moquer de.

function /'fʌŋkʃn/ n (purpose, duty) fonction f; (event) réception f. ● vi fonctionner.

fund /fʌnd/ n fonds m. ● vt fournir les fonds pour.

fundamental /fʌndə'mentl/ adj fondamental. **fundamentalist** n intégriste mf.

funeral /'fjuːnərəl/ n enterrement m. ● adj funèbre.

funfair /'fʌnfeə(r)/ n fête f foraine.

fungus /'fʌŋgəs/ n (pl -gi) (plant) champignon m; (mould) moisissure f.

funnel /'fʌnl/ n (for pouring) entonnoir m; (of ship) cheminée f.

funny /'fʌnɪ/ adj (-ier, -iest) drôle; (odd) bizarre.

fur /fɜː(r)/ n (for garment) fourrure f; (on animal) poils mpl; (in kettle) tartre m.

furious /'fjʊərɪəs/ adj furieux.

furnace /'fɜːnɪs/ n fourneau m.

furnish /'fɜːnɪʃ/ vt (room) meubler; (supply) fournir. **furnishings** npl ameublement m.

furniture /'fɜːnɪtʃə(r)/ n meubles mpl, mobilier m.

furry /'fɜːrɪ/ adj (animal) à fourrure; (toy) en peluche.

further /'fɜːðə(r)/ adj plus éloigné; (additional) supplémentaire. ● adv plus loin; (more) davantage. ● vt avancer. **~ education** n formation f continue.

furthermore /fɜːðə'mɔː(r)/ adv en outre, de plus.

furthest /'fɜːðɪst/ adj le plus éloigné. ● adv le plus loin.

fury /'fjʊərɪ/ n fureur f.

fuse /fjuːz/ vt/i (melt) fondre; (unite: fig) fusionner; ~ **the lights** faire sauter les plombs. ● n (of plug) fusible m; (of bomb) amorce f.

fuss /fʌs/ n (when upset) histoire(s) f(pl); (when excited) agitation f; **make a** ~ faire des histoires. s'agiter; (about food) faire des chichis; **make a** ~ **of** faire grand cas de. ● vi s'agiter. **fussy** adj (finicky) tatillon; (hard to please) difficile.

future /'fjuːtʃə(r)/ adj futur. ● n avenir m; (Gram) futur m; **in** ~ à l'avenir.

fuzzy /'fʌzɪ/ adj (hair) crépu; (photograph) flou; (person 🛈) à l'esprit confus.

Gg

Gaelic /'geɪlɪk/ n gaélique m.

gag /gæg/ n (on mouth) bâillon m; (joke) blague f. ● vt (pt **gagged**) bâillonner.

gain /geɪn/ vt (respect, support) gagner; (speed, weight) prendre. ● vi (of clock) avancer. ● n (increase) augmentation f (in de); (profit) gain m.

galaxy /'gæləksɪ/ n galaxie f.

gale /geɪl/ n tempête f.

gallery /'gælərɪ/ n galerie f; **(art)** ~ musée m.

Gallic /'gælɪk/ adj français.

gallon /'gælən/ n gallon m (imperial = 4.546 litres; Amer. = 3.785 litres).

gallop /'gæləp/ n galop m. ● vi (pt **galloped**) galoper.

galore /gə'lɔː(r)/ adv (prizes, bargains) en abondance; (drinks, sandwiches) à gogo 🛈.

gamble /'gæmbl/ vt/i jouer. ~ **on** miser sur. ● n (venture) entreprise f risquée; (bet) pari m; (risk) risque m. **gambling** n jeu m.

game /geɪm/ n jeu m; (football) match m; (tennis) partie f; (animals, birds) gibier m. ● adj (brave) courageux. ~ **for** prêt à. ~**keeper** n gardechasse m.

gammon /'gæmən/ n jambon m.

gang /gæŋ/ n (of youths) bande f; (of workmen) équipe f. ● vi ~ **up** se liguer (**on**, **against** contre).

gangmaster n gangmaster m, chef m d'équipe (d'ouvriers saisonniers).

gangway /'gæŋweɪ/ n passage m; (aisle) allée f; (of ship) passerelle f.

gaol /dʒeɪl/ n & vt ➡**JAIL**.

Gap Year La prise d'une année sabbatique est une pratique répandue chez les jeunes britanniques avant d'entrer à l'université. Certains trouvent un stage dans une entreprise et en profitent pour mettre de l'argent de côté pour leurs études, mais beaucoup partent travailler ou étudier à l'étranger ou faire le tour du monde.

gap /gæp/ n trou m, vide m; (in time) intervalle m; (in education) lacune f; (difference) écart m.

gape /geɪp/ vi rester bouche bée. **gaping** adj béant.

garage /'gærɑːʒ/ n garage m. ● vt mettre au garage.

garbage /'gɑːbɪdʒ/ n (US) ordures fpl.

garden /'gɑːdn/ n jardin m. ● vi jardiner. **gardener** n jardinier/-ière m/f. **gardening** n jardinage m.

gargle /'gɑːgl/ vi se gargariser.

garish /'geərɪʃ/ adj (clothes) tape-à-l'œil.

garland /'gɑːlənd/ n guirlande f.

garlic /'gɑːlɪk/ n ail m.

garment /'gɑːmənt/ n vêtement m.

garnish /'gɑːnɪʃ/ vt garnir (**with** de). ● n garniture f.

garter /'gɑːtə(r)/ n jarretière f.

gas /gæs/ n (pl ~**es**) gaz m; (Med) anesthésie m; (petrol: US) essence f. ● adj (mask, pipe) à gaz. ● vt asphyxier; (Mil) gazer.

gash /gæʃ/ n entaille f. ● vt entailler.

gasoline /'gæsəliːn/ n (petrol: US) essence f.

gasp /gɑːsp/ vi haleter; (in surprise: fig) avoir le souffle coupé. ● n halètement m.

gate /geɪt/ n (in garden, airport) porte f; (of field, level crossing) barrière f. ~**way** n porte f; (Internet) passerelle f.

gather /'gæðə(r)/ vt (people, objects) rassembler; (pick up) ramasser; (flowers) cueillir; (fig) comprendre; ~

speed prendre de la vitesse; (sewing) froncer. ● vi (*people*) se rassembler; (pile up) s'accumuler. **gathering** n réunion m.

gauge /geɪdʒ/ n jauge f, indicateur m. ● vt (*speed*, *distance*) jauger; (*reaction*, *mood*) évaluer.

gaunt /gɔːnt/ adj décharné.

gauze /gɔːz/ n gaze f.

gave /geɪv/ →GIVE.

gay /geɪ/ adj (joyful) gai; (homosexual) gay inv. ● n gay mf.

gaze /geɪz/ vi ~ (**at**) regarder (fixement). ● n regard m (fixe).

GB abbr →GREAT BRITAIN.

gear /gɪə(r)/ n (equipment) matériel m; (Tech) engrenage m; (Auto) vitesse f; **in** ~ en prise. **out of** ~ au point mort. ● vt **to be geared to** s'adresser à. ~**box** n (Auto) boîte f de vitesses. ~**-lever**, (US) ~**-shift** n levier m de vitesse.

geese /giːs/ →GOOSE.

gel /dʒel/ n (for hair) gel m.

gem /dʒem/ n pierre f précieuse.

Gemini /'dʒemɪnaɪ/ n Gémeaux mpl.

gender /'dʒendə(r)/ n (Ling) genre m; (of person) sexe m.

gene /dʒiːn/ n gène m. ~ **library** n génothèque f.

general /'dʒenrəl/ adj général. ● n général m; **in** ~ en général.

general election n élections fpl législatives.

generalization /dʒenrəlaɪ'zeɪʃn/ n généralisation f. **generalize** vt/i généraliser.

general practitioner n (Med) généraliste m.

generate /'dʒenəreɪt/ vt produire.

generation /dʒenə'reɪʃn/ n génération f.

generator /'dʒenəreɪtə(r)/ n (Electr) groupe m électrogène.

generosity /dʒenə'rɒsətɪ/ n générosité f. **generous** adj généreux; (plentiful) copieux.

genetics /dʒɪ'netɪks/ n génétique f.

Geneva /dʒɪ'niːvə/ n Genève f.

genial /'dʒiːnɪəl/ adj affable, sympathique.

genitals /'dʒenɪtlz/ npl organes mpl génitaux.

genius /'dʒiːnɪəs/ n (pl ~es) génie m.

genome /'dʒiːnəʊm/ n génome m.

gentle /'dʒentl/ adj (mild, kind) doux; (*pressure*, *breeze*) léger; (*reminder*, *hint*) discret.

gentleman /'dʒentlmən/ n (pl -men) (man) monsieur m; (well-bred) gentleman m.

gently /'dʒentlɪ/ adv doucement.

gents /dʒents/ npl (toilets) toilettes fpl; (on sign) 'Messieurs'.

genuine /'dʒenjuːm/ adj (*reason*, *motive*) vrai; (*jewel*, *substance*) véritable; (*person*, *belief*) sincère.

geography /dʒɪ'ɒgrəfɪ/ n géographie f.

geology /dʒɪ'ɒlədʒɪ/ n géologie f.

geometry /dʒɪ'ɒmətrɪ/ n géométrie f.

geriatric /dʒerɪ'ætrɪk/ adj gériatrique.

germ /dʒɜːm/ n (Med) microbe m.

German /'dʒɜːmən/ n (person) Allemand/-e m/f; (Ling) allemand m. ● adj allemand.

German measles n rubéole f.

Germany /'dʒɜːmənɪ/ n Allemagne f.

gesture /'dʒestʃə(r)/ n geste m.

---

get /get/

past **got**; past participle **got**, **gotten** (US); present participle **getting**

● *transitive verb*

⋯▸ recevoir. **we got a letter** nous avons reçu une lettre.

⋯▸ (obtain) **I got a job in Paris** j'ai trouvé un travail à Paris. **I'll ~ sth to eat at the airport** je mangerai qch à l'aéroport.

⋯▸ (buy) acheter. ~ **sb a present** acheter un cadeau à qn.

⋯▸ (achieve) obtenir. **he got it right** il a obtenu le bon résultat. ~ **good grades** avoir de bonnes notes.

⋯▸ (fetch) chercher. **go and ~ a chair** va chercher une chaise.

⋯▸ (transport) prendre. **we can ~ the bus** on peut prendre le bus.

⋯▸ (understand Ⅰ) comprendre. **now let me ~ this right** alors si je comprends bien…

g

····➤ (experience) ~ **a surprise** être surpris. ~ **a shock** avoir un choc.

····➤ (illness) ~ **measles** attraper la rougeole. ~ **a cold** s'enrhumer.

····➤ (ask or persuade) ~ **him to call me** dis-lui de m'appeler. **I'll ~ her to help me** je lui demanderai de m'aider.

····➤ (cause to be done) ~ **a TV repaired** faire réparer une télévision. ~ **one's hair cut** se faire couper les cheveux.

● *intransitive verb*

····➤ devenir. **he's getting old** il vieillit; **it's getting late** il se fait tard.

····➤ (in passives) ~ **married** se marier. ~ **hurt** être blessé.

····➤ (arrive) arriver. ~ **to the airport** arriver à l'aéroport. □ ~ **about** (*person*) se déplacer. ~ **along** (manage) se débrouiller; (progress) avancer. ~ **along with** s'entendre avec. ~ **at** (reach) atteindre; (imply) vouloir dire. ~ **away** partir; (escape) s'échapper. ~ **back** *vi* revenir. ● *vt* récupérer. ~ **by** *vi* (manage) se débrouiller. ● *vt* (pass) passer. ~ **down** *vt/i* descendre. ● *vt* (depress) déprimer. ~ **in** entrer. ~ **into** (*car*) monter dans; (*dress*) mettre. ~ **off** *vt* (*bus*) descendre; (remove) enlever. ● *vi* (from bus) descendre; (leave) partir; (Jur) être acquitté. ~ **on** *vi* (to bus) monter; (succeed) réussir. ● *vt* (*bus*) monter. ~ **on with** (*person*) s'entendre avec; (*job*) attaquer. ~ **out** sortir. ~ **out of** (fig) se soustraire. ~ **over** (*illness*) se remettre de. ~ **round** (*rule*) contourner; (*person*) entortiller. ~ **through** *vi* passer; (on phone) ~ **through to sb** avoir qn. ● *vt* traverser. ~ **up** se lever. ~ **up to** faire.

getaway /'getəweɪ/ *n* fuite *f*.

ghastly /'gɑːstlɪ/ *adj* (**-ier, -iest**) affreux.

gherkin /'gɜːkɪn/ *n* cornichon *m*.

ghetto /'getəʊ/ *n* ghetto *m*.

ghost /gəʊst/ *n* fantôme *m*.

giant /'dʒaɪənt/ *n & adj* géant (*m*).

gibberish /'dʒɪbərɪʃ/ *n* baragouin *m*, charabia *m*.

giblets /'dʒɪblɪts/ *npl* abats *mpl*.

giddy /'gɪdɪ/ *adj* (**-ier, -iest**) vertigineux. **be** *or* **feel** ~ avoir le vertige.

gift /gɪft/ *n* (present) cadeau *m*; (ability) don *m*.

gifted /'gɪftɪd/ *adj* doué.

gift wrap *n* papier *m* cadeau.

gigantic /dʒaɪ'gæntɪk/ *adj* gigantesque.

giggle /'gɪgl/ *vi* ricaner (sottement), glousser. ● *n* ricanement *m*; **the ~s** le fou rire.

gimmick /'gɪmɪk/ *n* truc *m*.

gin /dʒɪn/ *n* gin *m*.

ginger /'dʒɪndʒə(r)/ *n* gingembre *m*. ● *adj* (*hair*) roux. ~ **beer** *n* boisson *f* gazeuse au gingembre. ~**bread** *n* pain *m* d'épices.

gingerly /'dʒɪndʒəlɪ/ *adv* avec précaution.

giraffe /dʒɪ'rɑːf/ *n* girafe *f*.

girl /gɜːl/ *n* (child) (petite) fille *f*; (young woman) (jeune) fille *f*. ~ **band** *n* girls band *m*. ~**friend** *n* amie *f*; (of boy) petite amie *f*.

giro /'dʒaɪrəʊ/ *n* virement *m* bancaire; (cheque) mandat *m*.

gist /dʒɪst/ *n* essentiel *m*.

give /gɪv/ *vt* (*pt* **gave**; *pp* **given**) donner; (gesture) faire; (*laugh, sigh*) pousser; ~ **sb sth** donner qch à qn. ● *vi* donner; (yield) céder; (stretch) se détendre. ● *n* élasticité *f*. □ ~ **away** donner; (secret) trahir; ~ **back** rendre. ~ **in** (yield) céder (**to** à). ~ **off** (*heat, fumes*) dégager; (*signal, scent*) émettre. ~ **out** *vt* distribuer. ~ **over** (devote) consacrer; (stop 🔢) cesser; ~ **up** *vt/i* (renounce) renoncer (à); (yield) céder. ~ **oneself up** se rendre. ~ **way** céder; (collapse) s'effondrer.

given /'gɪvn/ ➡GIVE. ● *adj* donné. ~ **name** *n* prénom *m*.

glad /glæd/ *adj* content. **gladly** *adv* avec plaisir.

glamorous /'glæmərəs/ *adj* séduisant, ensorcelant.

glamour, (US) **glamor** /'glæmə(r)/ *n* enchantement *m*, séduction *f*.

glance /glɑːns/ *n* coup *m* d'œil. ● *vi* ~ **at** jeter un coup d'œil à.

gland /glænd/ *n* glande *f*.

glare /gleə(r)/ vi briller très fort. ~ **at** regarder d'un air furieux. ● n (of lights) éclat m (aveuglant); (stare: fig) regard m furieux. **glaring** adj (dazzling) éblouissant; (obvious) flagrant.

glass /glɑːs/ n verre m. **glasses** npl (spectacles) lunettes fpl.

glaze /gleɪz/ vt (door) vitrer; (pottery) vernisser. ● n vernis m.

gleam /gliːm/ n lueur f. ● vi luire.

glide /glaɪd/ vi glisser; (of plane) planer. **glider** n planeur m.

glimpse /glɪmps/ n (insight) aperçu m; **catch a ~ of** entrevoir.

glitter /ˈglɪtə(r)/ vi scintiller. ● n scintillement m.

global /ˈgləʊbl/ adj (world-wide) mondial; (allembracing) global. ~ **warming** n réchauffement m de la planète.

globalization /gləʊbəlaɪˈzeɪʃən/ n globalisation f.

globe /gləʊbəlaɪˈzeɪʃən/ n globe m.

gloom /gluːm/ n obscurité f; (sadness: fig) tristesse f. **gloomy** adj triste; (pessimistic) pessimiste.

glorious /ˈglɔːrɪəs/ adj splendide; (deed, hero) glorieux.

glory /ˈglɔːrɪ/ n gloire f; (beauty) splendeur f. ● vi ~ **in** être très fier de.

gloss /glɒs/ n lustre m, brillant m. ● adj brillant. ● vi ~ **over** (make light of) glisser sur; (cover up) dissimuler.

glossary /ˈglɒsərɪ/ n glossaire m.

glossy /ˈglɒsɪ/ adj brillant.

glove /glʌv/ n gant m. ~ **compartment** n (Auto) boîte f à gants.

glow /gləʊ/ vi (fire) rougeoyer; (person, eyes) rayonner. ● n rougeoiement m, éclat m. **glowing** adj (report) enthousiaste.

glucose /ˈgluːkəʊs/ n glucose m.

glue /gluː/ n colle f. ● vt (pres p **gluing**) coller.

GM abbr (genetically modified) transgénique.

gnaw /glɪf/ vt/i ronger.

GNP abbr (**Gross National Product**) produit m national brut, PNB m.

---

go /gəʊ/

present **go**, **goes**; past **went**; past participle **gone**

● intransitive verb

····➤ aller; ~ **to school/town/market** aller à l'école/en ville/au marché. ~ **for a swim/walk** aller nager/se promener.

····➤ (leave) s'en aller. **I must be ~ing** il faut que je m'en aille.

····➤ (vanish) **the money's gone** il n'y a plus d'argent. **my bike's gone** mon vélo n'est plus là.

····➤ (work, function) marcher. **is the car ~ing?** est-ce que la voiture marche?

····➤ (become) devenir. ~ **blind** devenir aveugle. ~ **pale/red** pâlir/rougir.

····➤ (turn out, progress) aller. **how's it going?** comment ça va? **how did the exam ~ ?** comment s'est passé l'examen?

····➤ (in future tenses) be ~**ing to do** aller faire.

● noun

····➤ (turn) tour m; (try) essai m; **have a ~!** essaie!; **full of ~** ⓘ dynamique.

□ **go across** traverser. **go after** poursuivre. **go away** partir. ~ **away!** va-t'en!, allez-vous-en! **go back** retourner. ~ **back** in rentrer. ~ **back to work** reprendre le travail. **go down** (quality, price) baisser; (person) descendre; (sun) se coucher. **go in** entrer. **go in for** (exam) se présenter à. **go off** (leave) partir; (bomb) exploser; (alarm clock) sonner; (milk) tourner; (light) s'éteindre. **go on** (continue) continuer; (light) s'allumer. ~ **on doing** continuer à faire. **what's ~ing on?** qu'est-ce qui se passe? **go out** sortir; (light, fire) s'éteindre. **go over** vérifier. **go round** (be enough) être assez. ~ **round to see sb** passer voir qn. **go through** (check) examiner; (search) fouiller; ~ **through a difficult time** traverser une période difficile. **go together** aller ensemble. **go under** (sink) couler; (fail) échouer. **go up** (person) monter; (price, salary) augmenter. **go without** se passer de.

go-ahead /ˈɡəʊəhed/ n feu m vert. ● adj dynamique.

goal /ɡəʊl/ n but m. ~keeper n gardien m de but. ~-post n poteau m de but.

goat /ɡəʊt/ n chèvre f.

gobble /ˈɡɒbl/ vt engouffrer.

go-between /ˈɡəʊbɪtwiːn/ n intermédiaire mf.

god /ɡɒd/ n dieu m. ~child n (pl -children) filleul/-e m/f. ~daughter n filleule f.

goddess /ˈɡɒdɪs/ n déesse f.

god: ~father n parrain m. ~mother n marraine f. ~send n aubaine f. ~son n filleul m.

goggles /ˈɡɒɡlz/ npl lunettes fpl (protectrices).

going /ˈɡəʊɪŋ/ n it is slow/hard ~ c'est lent/difficile. ● adj (price, rate) actuel.

go-kart /ˈɡəʊkɑːt/ n kart m.

gold /ɡəʊld/ n or m. ● adj en or, d'or.

golden /ˈɡəʊldən/ adj en or, d'or; (in colour) doré; (opportunity) unique.

gold: ~fish n poisson m rouge. ~-plated adj plaqué or. ~smith n orfèvre m.

golf /ɡɒlf/ n golf m. ~-course n terrain m de golf.

gone /ɡɒn/ →GO. ● adj parti. ~ six o'clock six heures passées. the butter's all ~ il n'y a plus de beurre.

good /ɡʊd/ adj (better, best) bon; (weather) beau; (well-behaved) sage; as ~ as (almost) pratiquement. that's ~ of you c'est gentil (de ta part). be ~ with savoir s'y prendre avec. feel ~ se sentir bien. it is ~ for you ça vous fait du bien. ● n bien m; do ~ faire du bien. is it any ~? est-ce que c'est bien?. it's no ~ ça ne vaut rien. it is no ~ shouting ça ne sert à rien de crier. for ~ pour toujours. ~ afternoon interj bonjour. ~bye interj & n au revoir (m inv). ~ evening interj bonsoir. G~ Friday n Vendredi m saint. ~-looking adj beau. ~ morning interj bonjour. ~-natured adj gentil.

goodness /ˈɡʊdnɪs/ n bonté f; my ~! mon Dieu!

goodnight interj bonsoir, bonne nuit.

goods /ɡʊdz/ npl marchandises fpl.

goodwill /ɡʊdˈwɪl/ n bonne volonté f.

google® /ˈɡuːɡl/vt/i chercher sur (le moteur de recherche) Google®, googler.

goose /ɡuːs/ n (pl geese) oie f. gooseberry n groseille f à maquereau. ~-pimples npl chair f de poule.

gorge /ɡɔːdʒ/ n (Geog) gorge f. ● vt ~ oneself se gaver (on de).

gorgeous /ˈɡɔːdʒəs/ adj magnifique, splendide, formidable.

gorilla /ɡəˈrɪlə/ n gorille m.

gory /ˈɡɔːrɪ/ adj (-ier, -iest) sanglant; (horrific: fig) horrible.

gospel /ˈɡɒspl/ n évangile m; the G~ l'Évangile m.

gossip /ˈɡɒsɪp/ n bavardages mpl, commérages mpl; (person) bavard/-e m/f. ● vi bavarder.

got /ɡɒt/ →GET. ● have ~ avoir. have ~ to do devoir faire.

govern /ˈɡʌvn/ vt/i gouverner. **governess** n gouvernante f. **government** n gouvernement m. **governor** n gouverneur m.

gown /ɡaʊn/ n robe f; (of judge, teacher) toge f.

GP abbr →GENERAL PRACTITIONER.

GPS abbr (Global Positioning System) GPS m.

grab /ɡræb/ vt (pt grabbed) saisir.

grace /ɡreɪs/ n grâce f. ● vt (honour) honorer; (adorn) orner. **graceful** adj gracieux.

gracious /ˈɡreɪʃəs/ adj (kind) bienveillant; (elegant) élégant.

grade /ɡreɪd/ n catégorie f; (of goods) qualité f; (on scale) grade m; (school mark) note f; (class: US) classe f. ● vt classer; (school work) noter. ~ school n (US) école f primaire.

gradual /ˈɡrædʒʊəl/ adj progressif, graduel. **gradually** adv progressivement, peu à peu.

graduate¹ /ˈɡrædʒʊət/ n (Univ) diplômé/-e m/f.

graduate² /ˈɡrædjʊeɪt/ vi obtenir son diplôme. ● vt graduer. **graduation** n remise f des diplômes.

graffiti /ɡrəˈfiːtɪ/ npl graffiti mpl.

graft /ɡrɑːft/ n (Med, Bot) greffe f; (work) boulot m. ● vt greffer (on to sur); (work) trimer.

grain /greɪn/ n (seed, quantity, texture) grain m; (in wood) fibre f.

gram /græm/ n gramme m.

grammar /'græmə(r)/ n grammaire f.

grand /grænd/ adj magnifique; (duke, chorus) grand.

grandad /'grændæd/ n 🔲 papy m.

grand: ~child n (girl) petite-fille f; (boy) petit-fils m; her ~children ses petits-enfants mpl. ~daughter n petite-fille f. ~father n grand-père m. ~ma →GRANNY. ~mother n grandmère f. ~parents npl grandsparents mpl. ~piano n piano m à queue. ~son n petit-fils m. ~stand n tribune f.

granny /'grænɪ/ n 🔲mémé f, mamie f.

grant /grɑːnt/ vt (permission) accorder; (request) accéder à; (admit) admettre (that que); take sth for ~ed considérer qch comme une chose acquise. ● n subvention f; (Univ) bourse f.

granule /'grænjuːl/ n (of sugar, salt) grain m; (of coffee) granulé m.

grape /greɪp/ n grain m de raisin. ~s raisin(s) m (pl).

grapefruit /'greɪpfruːt/ n inv pamplemousse m.

graph /grɑːf/ n graphique m.

graphic /'græfɪk/ adj (arts) graphique; (fig) vivant, explicite. **graphics** npl (Comput) graphiques mpl.

grasp /grɑːsp/ vt saisir. ● n (hold) prise f; (strength of hand) poigne f; (reach) portée f; (fig) compréhension f.

grass /grɑːs/ n herbe f. ~hopper n sauterelle f. ~land n prairie f.

grass roots npl peuple m. ● adj (movement) populaire; (support) de base.

grate /greɪt/ n (hearth) âtre m; (fire basket) grille f. ● vt râper. ● vi grincer.

grateful /'greɪtfl/ adj reconnaissant.

grater /'greɪtə(r)/ n râpe f.

gratified /'grætɪfaɪd/ adj très heureux. **gratify** vt faire plaisir à.

grating /'greɪtɪŋ/ n (bars) grille f; (noise) grincement m.

gratitude /'grætɪtjuːd/ n reconnaissance f.

gratuity /grə'tjuːətɪ/ n (tip) pourboire m; (bounty: Mil) prime f.

grave[1] /greɪv/ n tombe f. ● adj (serious) grave.

grave[2] /grɑːv/ adj ~ accent accent m grave.

gravel /'grævl/ n graviers mpl.

grave: ~stone n pierre f tombale. ~yard n cimetière m.

gravity /'grævətɪ/ n (seriousness) gravité f; (force) pesanteur f.

gravy /'greɪvɪ/ n jus m (de viande).

gray /greɪ/ (US) adj & n →GREY.

graze /greɪz/ vi (eat) paître. ● vt (touch) frôler; (scrape) écorcher. ● n écorchure f.

grease /griːs/ n graisse f. ● vt graisser. **greasy** adj graisseux.

great /greɪt/ adj grand; (very good 🔲) génial 🔲, formidable 🔲, (grandfather, grandmother) arrière-.

Great Britain n Grande-Bretagne f.

greatly /'greɪtlɪ/ adv (very) très; (much) beaucoup.

Greece /griːs/ n Grèce f.

greed /griːd/ n avidité f; (for food) gourmandise f. **greedy** adj avide; gourmand.

Greek /griːk/ n (person) Grec/-que m/f; (Ling) grec m. ● adj grec.

green /griːn/ adj vert; (fig) naïf. ● n vert m; (grass) pelouse f; (golf) green m; ~s légumes mpl verts. ~ grocer n marchand/-e m/f de fruits et légumes.

> **Green Card** Document qui ⓘ permet à un étranger de vivre et de travailler aux États-Unis, et qui lui donne les mêmes droits que ceux d'un citoyen américain, à l'exception du droit de vote. Les services d'immigration américains distribuent 50 000 green cards par an au moyen d'une loterie à laquelle participent des millions de candidats.

greenhouse n serre f; ~ effect effet m de serre.

greet /griːt/ vt (welcome) accueillir; (address politely) saluer. **greeting** n accueil m.

greetings /'griːtɪŋz/ interj salutations 🔲 ● npl (Christmas) vœux mpl. ~ card n carte f de vœux.

grew /gruː/ →GROW.

grey /greɪ/ adj gris; (fig) triste; go ~ (hair, person) grisonner. ● n gris m. ~hound n lévrier m.

grid /grɪd/ n grille f; (network: Electr) réseau m.

grief /griːf/ n chagrin m; **come to ~** (person) avoir un malheur; (fail) tourner mal.

grievance /'griːvns/ n griefs mpl.

grieve /griːv/ vt/i (s')affliger; **~ for** pleurer.

grill /grɪl/ n (cooking device) gril m; (food) grillade f; (Auto) calandre f. ● vt/i (faire) griller; (interrogate) mettre sur la sellette.

grim /grɪm/ adj sinistre.

grimace /grɪ'meɪs/ n grimace f. ● vi grimacer.

grime /graɪm/ n crasse f.

grin /grɪn/ vi (pt grinned) sourire. ● n (large) sourire m.

grind /graɪnd/ vt (pt ground) (grain) écraser; (coffee) moudre; (sharpen) aiguiser; **~ one's teeth** grincer des dents. ● vi **~ to a halt** s'immobiliser. ● n corvée f.

grip /grɪp/ vt (pt gripped) saisir; (interest) passionner. ● n prise f; (strength of hand) poigne f; **come to ~s with** en venir aux prises avec.

grisly /'grɪzlɪ/ adj (-ier, -iest) (remains) macabre; (sight) horrible.

gristle /'grɪsl/ n cartilage m.

grit /grɪt/ n (for roads) sable m; (fig) courage m. ● vt (pt gritted) (road) sabler; (teeth) serrer.

groan /grəʊn/ vi gémir. ● n gémissement m.

grocer /'grəʊsə(r)/ n (person) épicier/-ière m/f; (shop) épicerie f. **groceries** npl (shopping) courses fpl; (goods) épicerie f. **grocery** n (shop) épicerie f.

groin /grɔɪn/ n aine f.

groom /gruːm/ n marié m; (for horses) palefrenier/-ière m/f. ● vt (horse) panser; (fig) préparer.

groove /gruːv/ n (for door etc.) rainure f; (in record) sillon m.

grope /grəʊp/ vi tâtonner. **~ for** chercher à tâtons.

gross /grəʊs/ adj (behaviour) vulgaire; (Comm) brut. ● n inv grosse f.

grotto /'grɒtəʊ/ n (pl **~es**) grotte f.

grouch /graʊtʃ/ vi (grumble 🎧) rouspéter, râler.

ground¹ /graʊnd/ n terre f, sol m; (area) terrain m; (reason) raison f; (Electr, US) masse f; **~s** terres fpl, parc m; (of coffee) marc m; **on the ~** par terre. **lose ~** perdre du terrain. ● vt (Naut) échouer; (aircraft) retenir au sol.

ground² /graʊnd/ ➡GRIND. ● adj **~ beef** (US) bifteck m haché.

ground: ~ floor n rez-de-chaussée m inv. **~work** n travail m préparatoire.

group /gruːp/ n groupe m. ● vt/i (se) grouper. **~ware** n (Comput) logiciel m de groupe.

grovel /'grɒvl/ vi (pt grovelled) ramper.

grow /grəʊ/ vi (pt grew; pp grown) (person) grandir; (plant) pousser; (become) devenir; (crime) augmenter. ● vt cultiver. **~ up** devenir adulte, grandir. **grower** n cultivateur/-trice m/f.

growl /graʊl/ vi (dog) gronder; (person) grogner. ● n grognement m.

grown /grəʊn/ ➡GROW. ● adj adulte. **~-up** adj & n adulte (mf).

growth /grəʊθ/ n (of person, plant) croissance f; (in numbers) accroissement m; (of hair, tooth) pousse f; (Med) grosseur f, tumeur f.

grudge /grʌdʒ/ vt **~ doing** faire à contrecœur. **~ sb sth** (success, wealth) en vouloir à qn de qch. ● n rancune f; **have a ~ against** en vouloir à.

grumble /'grʌmbl/ vi ronchonner, grogner (at après).

grumpy /'grʌmpɪ/ adj (-ier, -iest) grincheux, grognon.

grunt /grʌnt/ vi grogner. ● n grognement m.

guarantee /gærən'tiː/ n garantie f. ● vt garantir.

guard /gɑːd/ vt protéger; (watch) surveiller. ● vi **~ against** se protéger contre. ● n (Mil) garde f; (person) garde m; (on train) chef m de train.

guardian /'gɑːdɪən/ n gardien/-ne m/f; (of orphan) tuteur/-trice m/f.

guess /ges/ vt/i deviner; (suppose) penser. ● n conjecture f.

guest /gest/ n invité/-e m/f; (in hotel) client/-e m/f. **~-house** n pension f. **~-room** n chambre f d'amis.

guidance /'gaɪdns/ n (advice) conseils mpl; (information) information f.

guide /gaɪd/ n (person, book) guide m; (girl) guide f. ● vt guider. **~book** n guide m. **~ dog** n chien m d'aveugle. **~line** n indication f; (advice) conseils mpl.

guillotine /'gɪləti:n/ n (for execution) guillotine f; (for paper) massicot m.

guilt /gɪlt/ n culpabilité f. **guilty** adj coupable.

guinea-pig /'gɪnɪpɪg/ n (animal) cochon m d'Inde; (fig) cobaye m.

guitar /gɪ'tɑ:(r)/ n guitare f.

gulf /gʌlf/ n (part of sea) golfe m; (hollow) gouffre m.

gull /gʌl/ n mouette f, (larger) goéland m.

gullible /'gʌləbl/ adj crédule.

gully /'gʌlɪ/ n (ravine) ravin m; (drain) rigole f.

gulp /gʌlp/ vt **~ (down)** avaler en vitesse. ● vi (from fear etc.) avoir la gorge serrée. ● n gorgée f.

gum /gʌm/ n (Anat) gencive f; (glue) colle f; (for chewing) chewing-gum m. ● vt (pt **gummed**) gommer.

gun /gʌn/ n (pistol) revolver m; (rifle) fusil m; (large) canon m. ● vt (pt **gunned**) **~ down** abattre. **~ fire** n fusillade f. **~powder** n poudre f à canon. **~shot** n coup m de feu.

gurgle /'gɜ:gl/ n (of water) gargouillement m; (of baby) gazouillis m. ● vi (water) gargouiller; (baby) gazouiller.

gush /gʌʃ/ vi **~ (out)** jaillir. ● n jaillissement m.

gust /gʌst/ n rafale f; (of smoke) bouffée f.

gut /gʌt/ n (belly 🄳) ventre m. ● vt (pt **gutted**) (fish) vider; (of fire) dévaster. **gutted** adj 🄳 abattu.

guts /gʌts/ npl 🄳 (insides of human) tripes fpl 🄳; (insides of animal, building) entrailles fpl; (courage) cran m 🄳.

gutter /'gʌtə(r)/ n (on roof) gouttière f; (in street) caniveau m.

guy /gaɪ/ n (man 🄳) type m.

gym /dʒɪm/ n (place) gymnase m; (activity) gym(nastique) f.

gymnasium /dʒɪm'neɪzɪəm/ n gymnase m.

gymnastics /dʒɪm'næstɪks/ npl gymnastique f.

gynaecologist /gaɪnə'kɒlədʒɪst/ n gynécologue mf.

gypsy /'dʒɪpsɪ/ n bohémien/-ne m/f.

Hh

habit /'hæbɪt/ n habitude f; (costume: Relig) habit m; **be in/get into the ~ of** avoir/prendre l'habitude de.

habitual /hə'bɪtʃʊəl/ adj (usual) habituel; (smoker, liar) invétéré.

hack /hæk/ n (writer) écrivaillon m. ● vi (Comput) pirater; **~ into** s'introduire dans. ● vt tailler. **hacker** n (Comput) pirate m informatique.

hackneyed /'hæknɪd/ adj rebattu.

had /hæd/ →HAVE.

haddock /'hædək/ n inv églefin m.

haemorrhage /'hemərɪdʒ/ n hémorragie f.

haggard /'hægəd/ adj (person) exténué; (face, look) défait.

haggle /'hægl/ vi marchander; **~ over** sth discuter du prix de qch.

hail /heɪl/ n grêle f. ● vt (greet) saluer; (taxi) héler. ● vi grêler; **~ from** venir de. **~stone** n grêlon m.

hair /heə(r)/ n (on head) cheveux mpl; (on body, of animal) poils mpl; (single strand on head) cheveu m; (on body) poil m. **~brush** n brosse f à cheveux. **~cut** n coupe f de cheveux. **~do** n 🄳 coiffure f. **~dresser** n coiffeur/-euse m/f. **~drier** n séchoir m (à cheveux). **~pin** n épingle f à cheveux. **~ remover** n dépilatoire m. **~-style** n coiffure f.

hairy /'heərɪ/ adj (-ier, -iest) poilu; (terrifying) 🄳 horrifiant.

half /hɑ:f/ n (pl halves) (part) moitié f; (fraction) demi m; **~ a dozen** une demi-douzaine; **~ an hour** une demi-heure; **four and a ~** quatre et demi; **an hour and a ~** une heure et demie; **~ and half** moitié moitié; **in ~** en deux. ● adj demi; **~ price** à moitié prix. ● adv à moitié. **~-back** n (Sport) demi m. **~-hearted** adj tiède.

~-mast *n* at ~-mast en berne. ~-**term** *n* vacances *fpl* de demi-trimestre. ~-**time** *n* mi-temps *f.* ~**way** *adv* à mi-chemin. ~**wit** *n* imbécile *mf.*

hall /hɔːl/ *n* (in house) entrée *f;* (corridor) couloir *m;* (in airport) hall *m;* (for events) salle *f;* ~ **of residence** résidence *f* universitaire.

hallmark /'hɔːlmɑːk/ *n* (on gold) poinçon *m;* (fig) caractéristique *f.*

hallo →**HELLO.**

Hallowe'en /hæləʊ'iːn/ *n* la veille de la Toussaint.

halt /hɔːlt/ *n* arrêt *m;* (temporary) suspension *f;* (Mil) halte *f.* ● *vt* (proceedings) interrompre; (arms sales, experiments) mettre fin à. ● *vi* (vehicle) s'arrêter; (army) faire halte.

halve /hɑːv/ *vt* (time) réduire de moitié; (fruit) couper en deux.

ham /hæm/ *n* jambon *m.*

hamburger /'hæmbɜːgə(r)/ *n* hamburger *m.*

hammer /'hæmə(r)/ *n* marteau *m.* ● *vt/i* marteler; ~ **sth into sth** enfoncer qch dans qch; ~ **sth out** (agreement) parvenir à qch.

hammock /'hæmək/ *n* hamac *m.*

hamper /'hæmpə(r)/ *n* panier *m.* ● *vt* gêner.

hamster /'hæmstə(r)/ *n* hamster *m.*

hand /hænd/ *n* main *f;* (of clock) aiguille *f;* (writing) écriture *f;* (worker) ouvrier/-ière *m/f;* (cards) jeu *m;* **give sb a** ~ donner un coup de main à qn; **at** ~ proche; **on** ~ disponible; **on the one** ~...**on the other** ~ d'une part ...d'autre part; **to** ~ à portée de la main. ● *vt* ~ **sb sth,** ~**sth to sb** donner qch à qn. □ ~**in** or **over** remettre; ~ **out** distribuer. ~**bag** *n* sac *m* à main. ~-**baggage** *n* bagages *mpl* à main. ~**book** *n* manuel *m.* ~**brake** *n* frein *m* à main. ~**cuffs** *npl* menottes *fpl.*

handicap /'hændɪkæp/ *n* handicap *m.* ● *vt* (pt **handicapped**) handicaper.

handkerchief /'hæŋkətʃɪf/ *n* (pl ~**s**) mouchoir *m.*

handle /'hændl/ *n* (of door, bag) poignée *f;* (of implement) manche *m;* (of cup, bucket) anse *f;* (of frying pan)

queue *f.* ● *vt* (manage) manier; (deal with) traiter; (touch) manipuler.

handout /'hændaʊt/ *n* document *m;* (leaflet) prospectus *m;* (money) aumône *f.*

hands-free kit *n* kit *m* mains libres conducteur.

handshake /'hændʃeɪk/ *n* poignée *f* de main.

handsome /'hænsəm/ *adj* (good looking) beau; (generous) généreux.

handwriting /'hændraɪtɪŋ/ *n* écriture *f.*

handy /'hændɪ/ *adj* (-ier, -iest) (book, skill) utile; (size, shape, tool) pratique; (person) doué. ~**man** *n* (pl -men) bricoleur *m.*

hang /hæŋ/ *vt* (pt **hung**) (from hook, hanger) accrocher; (from rope) suspendre; (pt **hanged**) (person) pendre. ● *vi* (from hook) être accroché; (from rope) être suspendu; (person) être pendu. ● *n* **get the** ~ **of doing** 🔲 piger comment faire 🔲. □ ~ **about** traîner; ~ **on** 🔲 hold out) tenir; (wait) attendre; ~ **on to sth** s'agripper à qch; ~ **out** *vi* 🔲 (live) crécher 🔲; (spend time) passer son temps; *vt* (washing) étendre; ~ **up** (telephone) raccrocher.

hanger /'hæŋə(r)/ *n* (for clothes) cintre *m.*

hang-gliding /'hæŋglaɪdɪŋ/ *n* vol *m* libre.

hangover /'hæŋəʊvə(r)/ *n* gueule *f* de bois 🔲.

hang-up /'hæŋʌp/ *n* 🔲 complexe *m.*

haphazard /hæp'hæzəd/ *adj* peu méthodique.

happen /'hæpən/ *vi* arriver, se passer; ~ **to sb** arriver à qn; **it so** ~**s that** il se trouve que.

happily /'hæpɪlɪ/ *adv* joyeusement; (fortunately) heureusement.

happiness /'hæpɪnɪs/ *n* bonheur *m.*

happy /'hæpɪ/ *adj* (-ier, -iest) heureux; **I'm not** ~ **about it** je ne suis pas content; ~ **with sth** satisfait de qch; ~ **medium** juste milieu *m.*

harass /'hærəs/ *vt* harceler. **harassment** *n* harcèlement *m.*

harbour, (US) **harbor** /'hɑːbə(r)/ *n* port *m.* ● *vt* (shelter) héberger.

hard /hɑːd/ adj dur; (difficult) difficile, dur; (evidence, fact) solide; **find it ~to do** avoir du mal à faire; **~ on sb** dur envers qn. ● adv (work) dur; (pull, hit, cry) fort; (think, study) sérieusement. **~board** n aggloméré m. **~ copy** n (Comput) tirage m. **~ disk** n disque m dur.

hardly /'hɑːdlɪ/ adv à peine; (expect, hope) difficilement; **~ ever** presque jamais.

hardship /'hɑːdʃɪp/ n (poverty) privations fpl; (ordeal) épreuve f.

hard: ~ shoulder n bande f d'arrêt d'urgence. **~ up** adj 🄁 fauché 🄁. **~ware** n (Comput) matériel m, hardware m; (goods) quincaillerie f. **~-working** adj travailleur.

hardy /'hɑːdɪ/ adj (-ier, -iest) résistant.

hare /heə(r)/ n lièvre m.

harm /hɑːm/ n mal m; **there is no ~ in** il n'y a pas de mal à. ● vt (person) faire du mal à; (object) endommager. **harmful** adj nuisible. **harmless** adj inoffensif.

harmony /'hɑːmənɪ/ n harmonie f.

harness /'hɑːnɪs/ n harnais m. ● vt (horse) harnacher; (use) exploiter.

harp /hɑːp/ n harpe f. ● vi **~ on (about)** rabâcher.

harrowing /'hærəʊɪŋ/ adj (experience) atroce; (story) déchirant.

harsh /hɑːʃ/ adj (punishment) sévère; (person) dur; (light) cru; (voice) rude; (chemical) corrosif. **harshness** n dureté f.

harvest /'hɑːvɪst/ n récolte f; **the wine ~** les vendanges fpl. ● vt (corn) moissonner; (vegetables) récolter.

has /hæz/ ➡HAVE.

hassle /'hæsl/ n complications fpl. ● vt 🄁 talonner (about à propos de); (worry) stresser.

haste /heɪst/ n hâte f; **in ~** à la hâte; **make ~** se dépêcher.

hasty /'heɪstɪ/ adj (-ier, -iest) précipité.

hat /hæt/ n chapeau m.

hatch /hætʃ/ n (Aviat) panneau m mobile; (Naut) écoutille f; (for food) passeplats m inv. ● vt/i (eggs) (faire) éclore.

hate /heɪt/ n haine f. ● vt détester; (violently) haïr; (sport, food) avoir horreur de.

hatred /'heɪtrɪd/ n haine f.

haughty /'hɔːtɪ/ adj (-ier, -iest) hautain.

haul /hɔːl/ vt tirer. ● n (by thieves) butin m; (by customs) saisie f; **it will be a long ~** l'étape sera longue; **long/short ~** (transport) long/court courrier m. **haulage** n transport m routier. **haulier** n (firm) société f de transports routiers.

haunt /hɔːnt/ vt hanter. ● n lieu m de prédilection.

have /hæv/

● present **have, has**;
● past **had**;
● past participle **had**

● transitive verb
····▶ (possess) avoir; **I ~ (got) a car** j'ai une voiture; **they ~ (got) problems** ils ont des problèmes.

····▶ (do sth) **~ a try** essayer; **~ a bath** prendre un bain.

····▶ **~ sth done** faire faire qch; **~ your hair cut** se faire couper les cheveux.

● auxiliary verb
····▶ (in perfect tenses) avoir; être; **I ~ seen him** je l'ai vu; **she had fallen** elle était tombée.

····▶ (in tag questions) **you've seen her, haven't you?** tu l'as vue, n'est-ce pas?; **you haven't seen her, ~you?** tu ne l'as pas vue, par hasard?

····▶ (in short answers) **'you've never met him'—'yes I ~'** 'tu ne l'as jamais rencontré'—'mais si!'

····▶ (must) **~ to** devoir; **I ~ to go** je dois partir; **you don't ~ to do it** tu n'es pas obligé de le faire.

➡ For expressions such as **have a walk, have dinner** ➡**walk, dinner.**

haven /'heɪvn/ n refuge m; (fig) havre m.

havoc /'hævək/ n dévastation f.

hawk /hɔːk/ n faucon m.

hay /heɪ/ n foin m; **~ fever** rhume m des foins.

h

haywire /'heɪwaɪə(r)/ adj go ~ (plans) dérailler; (machine) se détraquer.

hazard /'hæzəd/ n risque m; ~ **(warning) lights** feux mpl de détresse. ● vt hasarder.

haze /heɪz/ n brume f.

hazel /'heɪzl/ n (bush) noisetier m. ~**nut** n noisette f.

hazy /'heɪzɪ/ adj (-ier, -iest) (misty) brumeux; (fig) vague.

he /hiː/ pron il; (emphatic) lui; **here ~ is** le voici.

head /hed/ n tête f; (leader) chef m; (of beer) mousse f; ~**s or tails?** pile ou face? ● vt (list) être en tête de; (team) être à la tête de; (chapter) intituler; ~ **the ball** faire une tête. ● vi ~ **for** se diriger vers.

headache /'hedeɪk/ n mal m de tête; **have a ~** avoir mal à la tête.

heading /'hedɪŋ/ n titre m; (subject category) rubrique f.

head: ~**lamp**, ~**light** n phare m. ~**line** n gros titre m. ~**master** n directeur m. ~**mistress** n directrice f. ~ **office** n siège m social. ~-**on** adj & adv de front. ~**phones** npl casque m. ~**quarters** npl siège m social; (Mil) quartier m général. ~ **rest** n (Auto) repose-tête m inv. ~**strong** adj têtu.

heal /hiːl/ vt/i guérir.

health /helθ/ n santé f. ~ **centre** n centre m médico-social. ~ **food** n produits mpl diététiques. ~ **insurance** n assurance f maladie.

healthy /'helθɪ/ adj (person, plant, skin, diet) sain; (air) salutaire.

heap /hiːp/ n tas m; ~**s of** ① un tas de. ● vt ~ **(up)** entasser.

hear /hɪə(r)/ vt (pt **heard**) entendre; (news, rumour) apprendre; (lecture, broadcast) écouter. ● vi entendre; ~ **from** recevoir des nouvelles de; ~ **of** or **about** entendre parler de.

hearing /'hɪərɪŋ/ n ouïe f; (of case) audience f; **give sb a ~** écouter qn. ~-**aid** n prothèse f auditive.

hearse /hɜːs/ n corbillard m.

heart /hɑːt/ n cœur m; ~**s** (cards) cœur m; **at ~** au fond; **by ~** par cœur; **be ~-broken** avoir le cœur brisé; **lose ~** perdre courage. ~ **attack** n crise f cardiaque. ~**burn** n brû-

lures fpl d'estomac. ~**felt** adj sincère.

hearth /hɑːθ/ n foyer m.

heartily /'hɑːtɪlɪ/ adv (greet) chaleureusement; (laugh, eat) de bon cœur.

hearty /'hɑːtɪ/ adj (-ier, -iest) (sincere) chaleureux; (meal) solide.

heat /hiːt/ n chaleur f; (contest) épreuve f éliminatoire. ● vt (house) chauffer; ~ **(up)** (food) faire chauffer; (reheat) réchauffer. **heated** adj (fig) passionné; (lit) (pool) chauffé. **heater** n appareil m de chauffage.

heather /'heðə(r)/ n bruyère f.

heating /'hiːtɪŋ/ n chauffage m.

heave /hiːv/ vt (lift) hisser; (pull) traîner péniblement; ~ **a sigh** pousser un soupir. ● vi (pull) tirer de toutes ses forces; (retch) avoir un haut-le-cœur.

heaven /'hevn/ n ciel m.

heavily /'hevɪlɪ/ adv lourdement; (smoke, drink) beaucoup.

heavy /'hevɪ/ adj (-ier, -iest) lourd; (cold, work) gros; (traffic) dense. ~ **goods vehicle** n poids m lourd. ~-**handed** adj maladroit. ~**weight** n poids m lourd.

Hebrew /'hiːbruː/ n (person) Hébreu m; (Ling) hébreu m. ● adj hébreu; (Ling) hébraïque.

hectic /'hektɪk/ adj (activity) intense; (period, day) mouvementé.

hedge /hedʒ/ n haie f. ● vi (in answering) se dérober.

hedgehog /'hedʒhɒg/ n hérisson m.

heel /hiːl/ n talon m.

hefty /'heftɪ/ adj (-ier, -iest) (person) costaud ①; (object) pesant.

height /haɪt/ n hauteur f; (of person) taille f; (of plane, mountain) altitude f; (of fame, glory) apogée m; (of joy, folly, pain) comble m.

heir /eə(r)/ n héritier/-ière m/f. **heiress** n héritière f. **heirloom** n objet m de famille.

held /held/ →HOLD.

helicopter /'helɪkɒptə(r)/ n hélicoptère m.

hell /hel/ n enfer m.

hello /hə'ləʊ/ interj bonjour!; (on phone) allô!

helmet /'helmɪt/ n casque m.

help /help/ vt/i aider (to do à faire); ~ **(sb) with a bag/the housework** aider qn à porter un sac/à faire le ménage; ~ **oneself** se servir; **he can't ~ it** ce n'est pas de sa faute. ● *n* aide *f*. ● *interj* au secours! **helper** *n* aide *mf*. **helpful** *adj* utile; (*person*) serviable. **helping** *n* portion *f*. **helpless** *adj* impuissant.

hem /hem/ *n* ourlet *m*. ● *vt* (*pt* **hemmed**) faire un ourlet à; ~ **in** cerner.

hen /hen/ *n* poule *f*.

hence /hens/ *adv* (for this reason) d'où; (from now) d'ici. **henceforth** *adv* désormais.

hepatitis /hepə'taɪtɪs/ *n* hépatite *f*.

her /hɜː(r)/ *pron* la, l'; (indirect object) lui; **it's ~** c'est elle; **for ~** pour elle. ● *adj* son, sa; *pl* ses.

herb /hɜːb/ *n* herbe *f*; ~**s** (Culin) fines herbes *fpl*.

herd /hɜːd/ *n* troupeau *m*.

here /hɪə(r)/ *adv* ici; ~**!** (take this) tiens!; tenez!; ~ **is**, ~ **are** voici; **I'm** ~ je suis là. **hereabouts** *adv* par ici. **hereafter** *adv* après; (in book) ci-après. **hereby** *adv* par le présent acte; (in letter) par la présente.

herewith /hɪə'wɪð/ *adv* ci-joint.

heritage /'herɪtɪdʒ/ *n* patrimoine *m*. ~ **tourism** *n* tourisme *m* culturel.

hernia /'hɜːnɪə/ *n* hernie *f*.

hero /'hɪərəʊ/ *n* (*pl* ~**es**) héros *m*.

heroic /hɪ'rəʊɪk/ *adj* héroïque.

heroin /'herəʊɪn/ *n* héroïne *f*.

heroine /'herəʊɪn/ *n* héroïne *f*.

heron /'herən/ *n* héron *m*.

herring /'herɪŋ/ *n* hareng *m*.

hers /hɜːz/ *pron* le sien, la sienne, les sien(ne)s; **it is ~** c'est à elle *or* le sien *or* la sienne.

herself /hə'self/ *pron* (emphatic) elle-même; (reflexive) se; **proud of ~** fière d'elle; **by ~** toute seule.

hesitate /'hezɪteɪt/ *vi* hésiter. **hesitation** *n* hésitation *f*.

heterosexual /hetərə'sekʃʊəl/ *adj* & *n* hétérosexuel/-le (*m/f*).

hexagon /'heksəgən/ *n* hexagone *m*.

heyday /'heɪdeɪ/ *n* apogée *m*.

HGV *abbr* ➡HEAVY GOODS VEHICLE.

hi /haɪ/ *interj* 🔊 salut! 🔊.

hiccup /'hɪkʌp/ *n* hoquet *m*; **(the)** ~**s** le hoquet. ● *vi* hoqueter.

hide /haɪd/ *vt* (*pt* **hid**; *pp* **hidden**) cacher (**from** à). ● *vi* se cacher (**from** de); **go into hiding** se cacher. ● *n* (skin) peau *f*.

hideous /'hɪdɪəs/ *adj* (*monster, object*) hideux; (*noise*) affreux.

hiding /'haɪdɪŋ/ *n* **go into** ~ se cacher; **give sb a ~** administrer une correction à qn.

hierarchy /'haɪərɑːkɪ/ *n* hiérarchie *f*.

hi-fi /'haɪfaɪ/ *n* (chaîne *f*) hi-fi *f* *inv*.

high /haɪ/ *adj* haut; (*price, number*) élevé; (*priest, speed*) grand; (*voice*) aigu; **in the ~ season** en pleine saison. ● *n* **a (new)** ~ un niveau record. ● *adv* haut. **adj** & *n* intellectuel/-le (*m/f*). ~ **brow** *n* chaise *f* haute. ~ **court** *n* cour *f* suprême. **higher education** *n* enseignement *m* supérieur. ~**-jump** *n* saut *m* en hauteur. ~**-level** *adj* à haut niveau.

highlight /'haɪlaɪt/ *n* (best moment) point *m* fort; ~**s** (in hair) reflet *m*; (artificial) mèches *fpl*; (Sport) résumé *m*. ● *vt* (emphasize) souligner.

highly /'haɪlɪ/ *adv* extrêmement; (paid) très bien; **speak/think ~ of** dire/penser beaucoup de bien de.

Highness /'haɪnɪs/ *n* Altesse *f*.

high: ~**-rise (building)** *n* tour *f*. ~ **school** *n* lycée *m*. ~**-speed** *adj* (*train*) à grande vitesse; (*film*) ultrarapide. ~ **street** *n* rue *f* principale. ~**-tech** *adj* de pointe.

High School Établissement d'enseignement secondaire aux États-Unis, souvent subdivisé en *Junior high school* (12-14 ans) et *Senior high school* (15-17 ans) où les élèves passent un examen pour être admis dans un *College* (établissement d'enseignement supérieur).

---

highway /'haɪweɪ/ *n* route *f* nationale; (US) autoroute *f*; ~ **code** code *m* de la route.

hijack /'haɪdʒæk/ *vt* détourner. ● *n* détournement *m*. **hijacker** *n* pirate *m* (de l'air).

hike /haɪk/ *n* randonnée *f*; **price** ~ hausse *f* de prix. ● *vi* faire de la randonnée.

hilarious /hɪˈleərɪəs/ adj désopilant.

hill /hɪl/ n colline f; (slope) côte f. **hilly** adj vallonné.

him /hɪm/ pron le, l'; (indirect object) lui; **it's ~** c'est lui; **for ~** pour lui.

himself /hɪmˈself/ pron (emphatic) lui-même; (reflexive) se; **proud of ~** fier de lui; **by ~** tout seul.

hind /haɪnd/ adj de derrière.

hinder /ˈhɪndə(r)/ vt (hamper) gêner; (prevent) empêcher. **hindrance** n obstacle m, gêne f.

hindsight /ˈhaɪndsaɪt/ n **with ~** rétrospectivement.

Hindu /hɪnˈduː/ n Hindou/-e m/f. ● adj hindou.

hinge /hɪndʒ/ n charnière f. ● vi **~ on** dépendre de.

hint /hɪnt/ n allusion f; (of spice, accent) pointe f; (of colour) touche f; (advice) conseil m. ● vt laisser entendre. ● vi **~ at** faire allusion à.

hip /hɪp/ n hanche f.

hippopotamus /hɪpəˈpɒtəməs/ n (pl **~es**) hippopotame m.

hire /ˈhaɪə(r)/ vt (thing) louer; (person) engager. ● n location f. **~-car** n voiture f de location. **~-purchase** n achat m à crédit.

his /hɪz/ adj son, sa, pl ses. ● pron le sien, la sienne, les sien(ne)s; **it is ~** c'est à lui or le sien or la sienne.

hiss /hɪs/ n sifflement m. ● vt/i siffler.

history /ˈhɪstrɪ/ n histoire f; **make ~** entrer dans l'histoire.

hit /hɪt/ vt (pt **hit**; pres p **hitting**) frapper; (collide with) heurter; (find) trouver; (affect, reach) toucher. ● vi **~ on** (find) tomber sur; **~ it off** s'entendre bien (**with** avec). ● n (blow) coup m; (fig) succès m; (song) tube m 🔲; (on Internet) (visit) visite f, accès m; (result) page f trouvée, résultat m.

hitch /hɪtʃ/ vt (fasten) accrocher; **~ up** remonter. ● n (snag) anicroche f. **~-hike** vi faire du stop 🔲. **~-hiker** n auto-stoppeur/-euse m/f.

hi-tech /ˈhɪtʃhaɪk/ adj de pointe.

HIV abbr (**human immunodeficiency virus**) VIH m.

hive /haɪv/ n ruche f. ● vt **~ off** séparer; (industry) céder.

HIV-positive adj séropositif.

hoard /hɔːd/ vt amasser; (supplies) stocker. ● n trésor m; (of provisions) provisions fpl.

hoarse /hɔːs/ adj enroué.

hoax /həʊks/ n canular m.

hobby /ˈhɒbɪ/ n passe-temps m inv.

hockey /ˈhɒkɪ/ n hockey m.

hog /hɒg/ n cochon m. ● vt (pt **hogged**) 🔲 monopoliser.

hold /həʊld/ vt (pt **held**) tenir; (contain) contenir; (conversation, opinion) avoir; (shares, record, person) détenir; **~ (the line), please** ne quittez pas. ● vi (rope, weather) tenir. ● n prise f; **get ~ of** attraper; (ticket) se procurer; (person) (by phone) joindre; **on ~** en attente. □ **~ back** (contain) retenir; (hide) cacher; **~ down** (job) garder; (person) tenir; (costs) limiter; **~ on** (stand firm) tenir bon; (wait) attendre; **~ on to** (keep) garder; (cling to) se cramponner à; **~ out** (offer) offrir; vi (resist) tenir le coup; **~ up** (support) soutenir; (delay) retarder; (rob) attaquer.

holder /ˈhəʊldə(r)/ n détenteur/-trice m/f; (of passport, post) titulaire mf; (for object) support m.

holding /ˈhəʊldɪŋ/ n participation f.

hold-up /ˈhəʊldɪŋ/ n retard m; (of traffic) embouteillage m; (robbery) hold-up m inv.

hole /həʊl/ n trou m.

holiday /ˈhɒlədeɪ/ n vacances fpl; (public) jour m férié; (time off) congé m. ● vi passer ses vacances. ● adj de vacances. **~-maker** n vacancier/-ière m/f.

Holland /ˈhɒlənd/ n Hollande f.

hollow /ˈhɒləʊ/ adj creux; (fig) faux. ● n creux m. ● vt creuser.

holly /ˈhɒlɪ/ n houx m.

holy /ˈhəʊlɪ/ adj (**-ier, -iest**) saint; (water) bénit; **H~ Ghost, H~ Spirit** Saint-Esprit m.

homage /ˈhɒmɪdʒ/ n hommage m.

home /həʊm/ n (place to live) logement m; maison f; (institution) maison f; (family base) foyer m; (country) pays m. ● adj de la maison, du foyer; (of family) de famille; (Pol) intérieur; (match, visit) à domicile. ● adv (at) **~** à la maison, chez soi; **come** or **go ~** rentrer; (from abroad) rentrer dans son pays; **feel at ~ with** être à l'aise avec. **~ computer** n ordinateur m, PC m.

homeland /ˈhəʊmlənd/n patrief; **~ security** n sécurité f des frontières.

homeless /ˈhəʊmlɪs/ adj sans abri. ● n **the ~** les sans-abri mpl.

homely /ˈhəʊmlɪ/ adj (-ier, -iest) (cosy) accueillant; (simple) sans prétention; (person: US) sans attraits.

home: **~-made** adj (fait) maison. **H~ Office** n ministère m de l'Intérieur. **~ page** n (Internet) page f d'accueil. **H~ Secretary** n Ministre m de l'Intérieur. **~sick** adj be **~sick** avoir le mal du pays. **~work** n devoirs mpl.

homosexual /hɒməˈsekʃʊəl/ adj & n homosexuel/-le (m/f).

honest /ˈɒnɪst/ adj (truthful) intègre; (trustworthy) honnête; (sincere) franc. **honestly** adv honnêtement; franchement. **honesty** n honnêteté f.

honey /ˈhʌnɪ/ n miel m; (person 🔁) chéri-e m/f. **~moon** n voyage m de noces; (fig) lune f de miel.

honk /hɒŋk/ vi klaxonner.

honorary /ˈɒnərərɪ/ adj (person) honoraire; (degree) honorifique.

honour, (US) **honor** /ˈɒnə(r)/ n honneur m. ● vt honorer.

hood /hʊd/ n capuchon m; (on car, pram) capote f; (car engine cover: US) capot m.

hoof /huːf/ n (pl ~s) sabot m.

hook /hʊk/ n crochet m; (on garment) agrafe f; (for fishing) hameçon m; **off the ~** tiré d'affaire; (phone) décroché. ● vt accrocher.

hoot /huːt/ n (of owl) (h)ululement m; (of car) coup m de klaxon. ● vi (owl) (h)ululer; (car) klaxonner; (jeer) huer.

hoover /ˈhuːvə(r)/ vt **~ a room** passer l'aspirateur dans une pièce.

Hoover® /ˈhuːvə(r)/ n aspirateur m.

hop /hɒp/ vi (pt hopped) sauter (à cloche-pied); **~ in!** 🔁 vas-y, monte! ● n bond m; **~s** houblon m.

hope /həʊp/ n espoir m. ● vt/i espérer; **~ for** espérer avoir; **I ~ so** je l'espère.

hopeful /ˈhəʊpfl/ adj (news, sign) encourageant; (person) plein d'espoir; (mood) optimiste. **hopefully** adv (with luck) avec un peu de chance; (with hope) avec optimisme.

hopeless /ˈhəʊplɪs/ adj désespéré; (useless: fig) nul 🔁.

horizon /həˈraɪzn/ n horizon m.

horizontal /hɒrɪˈzɒntl/ adj horizontal.

hormone /ˈhɔːməʊn/ n hormone f.

horn /hɔːn/ n corne f; (of car) klaxon® m; (Mus) cor m.

horoscope /ˈhɒrəskəʊp/ n horoscope m.

horrible /ˈhɒrɪbl/ adj horrible.

horrid /ˈhɒrɪd/ adj horrible.

horrific /həˈrɪfɪk/ adj horrifiant.

horrify /ˈhɒrɪfaɪ/ vt horrifier.

horror /ˈhɒrə(r)/ n horreur f. ● adj (film, story) d'épouvante.

horse /hɔːs/ n cheval m. **~back** n on **~back** à cheval. **~-chestnut** n marron m (d'Inde). **~man** n (pl -men) cavalier m. **~power** n puissance f (en chevaux). **~-race** n course f de chevaux. **~-radish** n raifort m. **~-shoe** n fer m à cheval. **~ show** n concours m hippique.

hose /həʊz/ n tuyau m. ● vt arroser. **~-pipe** n tuyau m.

hospitable /hɒˈspɪtəbl/ adj hospitalier.

hospital /ˈhɒspɪtl/ n hôpital m.

host /həʊst/ n (to guests) hôte m; (on TV) animateur m; (Internet) ordinateur m hôte; **a ~ of** une foule de; (Relig) hostie f.

hostage /ˈhɒstɪdʒ/ n otage m; **hold sb ~** garder qn en otage.

hostel /ˈhɒstl/ n foyer m; (youth) **~** auberge f (de jeunesse).

hostess /ˈhəʊstɪs/ n hôtesse f.

hostile /ˈhɒstaɪl/ adj hostile.

hot /hɒt/ adj (hotter, hottest) chaud; (Culin) épicé; **be** or **feel ~** avoir chaud; **it is ~** il fait chaud; **in ~ water** 🔁 dans le pétrin. ● vt/i (pt hotted) **~ up** 🔁 chauffer. **~ air balloon** n montgolfière f. **~ dog** n hot-dog m.

hotel /həʊˈtel/ n hôtel m.

hot: **~headed** adj impétueux. **~ list** n (Internet) signets mpl favoris. **~plate** n plaque f chauffante. **~ water bottle** n bouillotte f.

hound /haʊnd/ n chien m de chasse. ● vt poursuivre.

h

hour /avə(r)/ n heure f.

hourly /'avəlɪ/ adj horaire; **on an ~ basis** à l'heure. ● adv toutes les heures.

house[1] /haʊs/ n maison f; (Pol) Chambre f; **on the ~** aux frais de la maison.

house[2] /haʊz/ vt loger; (of building) abriter.

household /'haʊshəʊld/ n (house, family) ménage m. ● adj ménager.

house: **~keeper** n gouvernante f. **~-proud** adj méticuleux. **~-warming** n pendaison f de crémaillère. **~wife** n (pl **-wives**) ménagère f. **~work** n travaux mpl ménagers.

housing /'haʊzɪŋ/ n logement m; **~ association** service m de logement; **~ development** cité f; (smaller) lotissement m.

hover /'hɒvə(r)/ vi (bird) voleter; (vacillate) vaciller. **hovercraft** n aéroglisseur m.

how /haʊ/ adv comment; **~ are you?** comment allez-vous?; **~ long/tall is...?** quelle est la longueur/hauteur de...?; **~ many?**, **~ much?** combien?; **~ pretty!** comme or que c'est joli!; **~ about a walk?** si on faisait une promenade?; **~ do you do?** (greeting) enchanté.

however /haʊ'evə(r)/ adv (nevertheless) cependant; **~ hard I try** j'ai beau essayer; **~ much it costs** quel que soit le prix; **~ young/poor he is** si jeune/pauvre soit-il; **~ you like** comme tu veux.

howl /haʊl/ n hurlement m. ● vi hurler.

HP abbr ➡HIRE-PURCHASE.

hp abbr ➡HORSEPOWER.

HQ abbr ➡HEADQUARTERS.

hub /hʌb/ n moyeu m; (fig) centre m.

hug /hʌg/ vt (pt **hugged**) serrer dans ses bras. ● n étreinte f; **give sb a ~** serrer qn dans ses bras.

huge /hju:dʒ/ adj énorme.

hull /hʌl/ n (of ship) coque f.

hum /hʌm/ vt/i (pt **hummed**) (person) fredonner; (insect) bourdonner; (engine) ronronner. ● n bourdonnement m; ronronnement m.

human /'hju:mən/ adj humain. ● n humain m. **~ being** n être m humain.

humane /hju:'meɪn/ adj (person) humain; (act) d'humanité; (killing) sans cruauté.

humanitarian /hju:mænɪ'teərɪən/ adj humanitaire.

humanity /hju:'mænətɪ/ n humanité f.

humble /'hʌmbl/ adj humble.

humid /'hju:mɪd/ adj humide.

humiliate /hju:'mɪlɪeɪt/ vt humilier.

humorous /'hju:mərəs/ adj humoristique; (person) plein d'humour.

humour, (US) **humor** /'hju:mə(r)/ n humour m; (mood) humeur f. ● vt amadouer.

hump /hʌmp/ n bosse f. ● vt 🔢 porter.

hunchback /'hʌntʃbæk/ n bossu/-e m/f.

hundred /'hʌndrəd/ adj & n cent (m); **two ~ and one** deux cent un; **~s of** des centaines de. **hundredth** adj & n centième (mf).

hung /hʌŋ/ ➡HANG.

Hungarian /hʌŋ'geərɪən/ n (person) Hongrois/-e m/f; (Ling) hongrois m. ● adj hongrois. **Hungary** n Hongrie f.

hunger /'hʌŋgə(r)/ n faim f. ● vi **~ for** avoir faim de.

hungry /'hʌŋgrɪ/ adj (**-ier**, **-iest**) affamé; **be ~** avoir faim.

hunt /hʌnt/ vt/i chasser; **~ for** chercher. ● n chasse f. **hunter** n chasseur m. **hunting** n chasse f.

hurdle /'hɜ:dl/ n (Sport) haie f; (fig) obstacle m.

hurricane /'hʌrɪkən/ n ouragan m.

hurry /'hʌrɪ/ vi se dépêcher; **~ out** sortir précipitamment. ● vt (work) terminer à la hâte; (person) bousculer. ● n hâte f; **in a ~** pressé.

hurt /hɜ:t/ vt/i (pt **hurt**) faire mal (à); (injure, offend) blesser. ● adj blessé. ● n blessure f.

hurtle /'hɜ:tl/ vi **~ down** dévaler; **~ along a road** foncer sur une route.

husband /'hʌzbənd/ n mari m.

hush /hʌʃ/ vt faire taire; **~ up** (news) étouffer. ● n silence m. ● interj chut!

husky /'hʌskɪ/ adj (**-ier**, **-iest**) enroué. ● n husky m.

hustle /'hʌsl/ vt (push, rush) bousculer. ● vi (hurry) se dépêcher; (work: US) se démener. ● n **~ and bustle** agitation f.

hut /hʌt/ n cabane f.

hyacinth /'haɪəsɪnθ/ n jacinthe f.

hydrant /'haɪdrənt/ n **(fire)** ~ bouche f d'incendie.

hydraulic /haɪ'drɔːlɪk/ adj hydraulique.

hydroelectric /haɪdrəʊɪ'lektrɪk/ adj hydroélectrique.

hydrogen /'haɪdrədʒən/ n hydrogène m; ~ **bomb** bombe f à hydrogène.

hyena /haɪ'iːnə/ n hyène f.

hygiene /'haɪdʒiːn/ n hygiène f. **hygienic** adj hygiénique.

hymn /hɪm/ n cantique m; (fig) hymne m.

hype /haɪp/ n Ⓘ battage m publicitaire. ● vt ~ **(up)** (film, book) faire du battage pour.

hyperactive /haɪpər'æktɪv/ adj hyperactif.

hyperlink /'haɪpəlɪŋk/ n hyperlien m.

hypermarket /'haɪpəmɑːkɪt/ n hypermarché m.

hypertext /'haɪpətekst/ n hypertexte m.

hyphen /'haɪfn/ n trait m d'union.

hypnosis /hɪp'nəʊsɪs/ n hypnose f.

hypocrisy /hɪ'pɒkrəsɪ/ n hypocrisie f. **hypocrite** n hypocrite mf. **hypocritical** adj hypocrite.

hypothesis /haɪ'pɒθəsɪs/ n (pl -ses) hypothèse f.

hysteria /hɪ'stɪərɪə/ n hystérie f. **hysterical** adj hystérique.

hysterics /hɪ'sterɪks/ npl crise f de nerfs; **be in** ~ rire aux larmes.

．．．．．．．．．．．．．．．．．．．．．．．．．．．．

I i

．．．．．．．．．．．．．．．．．．．．．．．．．．．．

I /aɪ/ pron je, j'; (stressed) moi.

ice /aɪs/ n glace f; (on road) verglas m. ● vt (cake) glacer. ● vi ~ **(up)** (window) se givrer; (river) geler. ~**box** n (US) réfrigérateur m. ~**-cream** n glace f. ~**-cube** n glaçon m. ~ **hockey** n hockey m sur glace.

Iceland /'aɪslənd/ n Islande f. **Icelander** n Islandais/-e m/f. **Icelandic** adj & n islandais (m).

ice: ~ **lolly** n glace f (sur bâtonnet). ~ **rink** n patinoire f. ~ **skate** n patin m à glace.

icicle /'aɪsɪkl/ n stalactite f (de glace).

icing /'aɪsɪŋ/ n (sugar) glaçage m.

icy /'aɪsɪ/ adj (-ier, -iest) (hands, wind) glacé; (road) verglacé; (manner, welcome) glacial.

ID /ɪd/ n pièce f d'identité; ~ **card** carte f d'identité.

idea /aɪ'dɪə/ n idée f.

ideal /aɪ'diːəl/ adj idéal. ● n idéal m.

identical /aɪ'dentɪkl/ adj identique.

identification /aɪdentɪfɪ'keɪʃn/ n identification f; (papers) pièce f d'identité.

identify /aɪ'dentɪfaɪ/ vt identifier. ● vi ~ **with** s'identifier à.

identikit /aɪ'dentɪkɪt/ n ~ **picture** portraitrobot m.

identity /aɪ'dentətɪ/ n identité f; ~ **theft** vol m d'identité.

ideological /aɪdɪə'lɒdʒɪkl/ adj idéologique.

idiom /'ɪdɪəm/ n (phrase) idiome m; (language) parler m, langue f. **idiomatic** adj idiomatique.

idiosyncrasy /ɪdɪə'sɪŋkrəsɪ/ n particularité f.

idiot /'ɪdɪət/ n idiot/-e m/f. **idiotic** adj idiot.

idle /'aɪdl/ adj (lazy) paresseux; (doing nothing) oisif; (boast, threat) vain. ● vi (engine) tourner au ralenti. ● vt ~ **away** gaspiller.

idol /'aɪdl/ n idole f. **idolize** vt idolâtrer.

idyllic /ɪ'dɪlɪk/ adj idyllique.

i.e. abbr c-à-d, c'est-à-dire.

if /ɪf/ conj si.

ignite /ɪg'naɪt/ vt/i (s')enflammer.

ignition /ɪg'nɪʃn/ n (Auto) allumage m; ~ **(switch)** contact m; ~ **key** clé f de contact.

ignorance /'ɪgnərəns/ n ignorance f. **ignorant** adj ignorant (**of** de). **ignorantly** adv par ignorance.

ignore /ɪg'nɔː(r)/ vt (person) ignorer; (mistake, remark) ne pas relever; (feeling, fact) ne pas tenir compte de.

ill /ɪl/ adj malade. ● adv mal. ● n mal m. ~**-advised** adj malavisé. ~ **at ease** adj mal à l'aise. ~**-bred** adj mal élevé.

illegal /ɪ'liːgl/ adj illégal.

h

i

illegible /ɪ'ledʒəbl/ *adj* illisible.

illegitimate /ɪlɪ'dʒɪtɪmət/ *adj* illégitime.

ill: ~**-fated** *adj* malheureux. ~ **feeling** *n* ressentiment *m*.

illiterate /ɪ'lɪtərət/ *adj & n* analphabète (*mf*).

illness /'ɪlnɪs/ *n* maladie *f*.

ill-treat *vt* maltraiter.

illuminate /ɪ'lu:mɪneɪt/ *vt* éclairer; (decorate with lights) illuminer. **illumination** *n* éclairage *m*. illumination *f*.

illusion /ɪ'lu:ʒn/ *n* illusion *f*.

illustrate /'ɪləstreɪt/ *vt* illustrer. **illustration** *n* illustration *f*. **illustrative** *adj* qui illustre.

image /'ɪmɪdʒ/ *n* image *f*; (of firm, person) image *f* de marque. **imagery** *n* images *fpl*.

imaginable /ɪ'mædʒɪnəbl/ *adj* imaginable. **imaginary** *adj* imaginaire. **imagination** *n* imagination *f*. **imaginative** *adj* plein d'imagination.

imagine /ɪ'mædʒɪn/ *vt* (s')imaginer (that que); ~ **being rich** s'imaginer riche.

imbalance /ɪm'bæləns/ *n* déséquilibre *m*.

imitate /'ɪmɪteɪt/ *vt* imiter.

immaculate /ɪ'mækjʊlət/ *adj* impeccable.

immaterial /ɪmə'tɪərɪəl/ *adj* sans importance (**to** pour; **that** que).

immature /ɪmə'tjʊə(r)/ *adj* (*person*) immature; (*plant*) qui n'est pas arrivé à maturité.

immediate /ɪ'mi:dɪət/ *adj* immédiat.

immediately /ɪ'mi:dɪətlɪ/ *adv* immédiatement. ● *conj* dès que.

immense /ɪ'mens/ *adj* immense. **immensely** *adv* extrêmement, immensément. **immensity** *n* immensité *f*.

immerse /ɪ'mɜ:s/ *vt* plonger (**in** dans). **immersion** *n* immersion *f*; **immersion heater** chauffe-eau *m inv* électrique.

immigrant /'ɪmɪgrənt/ *n & adj* immigré/-e (*m/f*). (newly-arrived) immigrant/-e (*m/f*). **immigrate** *vi* immigrer. **immigration** *n* immigration *f*.

imminent /'ɪmɪnənt/ *adj* imminent.

immobilizer /ɪ'məʊbɪlaɪzə(r)/ *n* système *m* antidémarrage.

immoral /ɪ'məʊbɪlaɪzə(r)/ *adj* immoral.

immortal /ɪ'mɔ:tl/ *adj* immortel.

immune /ɪ'mju:n/ *adj* immunisé (**from, to** contre); (*reaction, system*) immunitaire. **immunity** *n* immunité *f*. **immunization** *n* immunisation *f*. **immunize** *vt* immuniser.

impact /'ɪmpækt/ *n* impact *m*.

impair /ɪm'peə(r)/ *vt* (*performance*) affecter; (*ability*) affaiblir.

impart /ɪm'pɑ:t/ *vt* communiquer, transmettre.

impartial /ɪm'pɑ:ʃl/ *adj* impartial.

impassable /ɪm'pɑ:səbl/ *adj* (*barrier*) infranchissable; (*road*) impraticable.

impassive /ɪm'pæsɪv/ *adj* impassible.

impatience /ɪm'peɪʃns/ *n* impatience *f*. **impatient** *adj* impatient; **get impatient** s'impatienter. **impatiently** *adv* impatiemment.

impeccable /ɪm'pekəbl/ *adj* impeccable.

impede /ɪm'pi:d/ *vt* entraver.

impediment /ɪm'pedɪmənt/ *n* entrave *f*; **speech** ~ défaut *m* d'élocution.

impending /ɪm'pendɪŋ/ *adj* imminent.

imperative /ɪm'perətɪv/ *adj* urgent. ● *n* impératif *m*.

imperfect /ɪm'pɜ:fɪkt/ *adj* incomplet; (faulty) défectueux. ● *n* (Gram) imparfait *m*. **imperfection** *n* imperfection *f*.

imperial /ɪm'pɪərɪəl/ *adj* impérial; (measure) conforme aux normes britanniques. **imperialism** *n* impérialisme *m*.

impersonal /ɪm'pɜ:sənl/ *adj* impersonnel.

impersonate /ɪm'pɜ:səneɪt/ *vt* se faire passer pour; (mimic) imiter.

impertinent /ɪm'pɜ:tɪnənt/ *adj* impertinent.

impervious /ɪm'pɜ:vɪəs/ *adj* imperméable (**to** à).

impetuous /ɪm'petʃʊəs/ *adj* impétueux.

impetus /'ɪmpɪtəs/ *n* impulsion *f*.

impinge /ɪm'pɪndʒ/ *vi* ~ **on** affecter; (encroach) empiéter sur.

implement /'ɪmplɪmənt/ *n* instrument *m*; (tool) outil *m*. ● *vt* exécuter, mettre en application; (software) implanter. **implementation** *n* mise *f* en application.

implicit /ɪm'plɪsɪt/ *adj* (implied) implicite (**in** dans); (unquestioning) absolu.

imply /ɪmˈplaɪ/ vt (assume, mean) impliquer; (insinuate) laisser entendre.

impolite /ɪmpəˈlaɪt/ adj impoli.

import¹ /ɪmˈpɔːt/ vt importer.

import² /ˈɪmpɔːt/ n (article) importation f; (meaning) signification f.

importance /ɪmˈpɔːtns/ n importance f. **important** adj important.

impose /ɪmˈpəʊz/ vt imposer (on sb à qn; on sth sur qch). ● vi s'imposer; on sb abuser de la bienveillance de qn. **imposing** adj imposant.

impossible /ɪmˈpɒsəbl/ adj impossible. ● n the ~ l'impossible m.

impotent /ˈɪmpətənt/ adj impuissant.

impound /ɪmˈpaʊnd/ vt confisquer, saisir.

impoverish /ɪmˈpɒvərɪʃ/ vt appauvrir.

impractical /ɪmˈpræktɪkl/ adj peu réaliste.

impregnable /ɪmˈpregnəbl/ adj imprenable.

impress /ɪmˈpres/ vt impressionner; ~ sth on sb faire bien comprendre qch à qn. **impression** n impression f. **impressionable** adj impressionnable. **impressive** adj impressionnant.

imprint¹ /ˈɪmprɪnt/ n empreinte f.

imprint² /ɪmˈprɪnt/ vt (fix) graver (on dans); (print) imprimer.

imprison /ɪmˈprɪzn/ vt emprisonner.

improbable /ɪmˈprɒbəbl/ adj (not likely) improbable; (incredible) invraisemblable.

improper /ɪmˈprɒpə(r)/ adj (unseemly) malséant; (dishonest) irrégulier.

improve /ɪmˈpruːv/ vt/i (s')améliorer. **improvement** n amélioration f.

improvise /ˈɪmprəvaɪz/ vt/i improviser.

impudent /ˈɪmpjʊdənt/ adj impudent.

impulse /ˈɪmpʌls/ n impulsion f; on ~ sur un coup de tête. **impulsive** adj impulsif. **impulsively** adv par impulsion.

impurity /ɪmˈpjʊərətɪ/ n impureté f.

in /ɪn/ prep (inside, within) dans; (expressing place, position) à, en; (expressing time) en, dans; ~ **the box/ garden** dans la boîte/le jardin; ~ **Paris/school** à Paris/l'école; ~ **town** en ville; ~ **the country** à la campagne; ~ **English** en anglais; ~ **India**

en Inde; ~ **Japan** au Japon; ~ **winter** en hiver; ~ **spring** au printemps; ~ **an hour** (at end of) au bout d'une heure; ~ **an hour('s time)** dans une heure; ~ **(the space of) an hour** en une heure; ~ **doing** en faisant; ~ **the evening** le soir; **one** ~ **ten** un sur dix; ~ **between** entre les deux; (time) entretemps; ~ **a firm voice** d'une voix ferme; ~ **blue** en bleu; ~ **ink** à l'encre; ~ **uniform** en uniforme; ~ **a skirt** en jupe; ~ **a whisper** en chuchotant; ~ **a loud voice** d'une voix forte; **the best** ~ le meilleur de; **we are** ~ **for** on va avoir; **have it** ~ **for sb** 🄸 avoir qn dans le collimateur. ● adv (inside) dedans; (at home) là, à la maison; (in fashion) à la mode; **come** ~ entrer; **run** ~ entrer en courant.

inability /ɪnəˈbɪlətɪ/ n incapacité f (to do de faire).

inaccessible /ɪnækˈsesəbl/ adj inaccessible.

inaccurate /ɪnˈækjʊrət/ adj inexact.

inactive /ɪnˈæktɪv/ adj inactif. **inactivity** n inaction f.

inadequate /ɪnˈædɪkwət/ adj insuffisant.

inadvertently /ɪnədˈvɜːtntlɪ/ adv par mégarde.

inadvisable /ɪnədˈvaɪzəbl/ adj inopportun, à déconseiller.

inane /ɪˈneɪn/ adj idiot, débile.

inanimate /ɪnˈænɪmət/ adj inanimé.

inappropriate /ɪnəˈprəʊprɪət/ adj inopportun; (term) inapproprié.

inarticulate /ɪnɑːˈtɪkjʊlət/ adj qui a du mal à s'exprimer.

inasmuch as /ɪnəzˈmʌtʃəz/ adv dans la mesure où; (because) vu que.

inaugurate /ɪˈnɔːgjʊreɪt/ vt (open, begin) inaugurer; (person) investir.

inborn /ˈɪnbɔːn/ adj inné.

inbred /ɪnˈbred/ adj (inborn) inné.

Inc. abbr (**incorporated**) S.A.

incapable /ɪnˈkeɪpəbl/ adj incapable (of doing de faire).

incapacitate /ɪnkəˈpæsɪteɪt/ vt immobiliser.

incense¹ /ˈɪnsens/ n encens m.

incense² /ɪnˈsens/ vt mettre en fureur.

incentive /ɪnˈsentɪv/ n motivation f; (payment) prime f.

incessant /ɪnˈsesnt/ adj incessant. **incessantly** adv sans cesse.

incest /ˈɪnsest/ n inceste m. **incestuous** adj incestueux.

inch /ɪntʃ/ n pouce m (=2.54 cm.). ● vi ~ **towards** se diriger petit à petit vers.

incidence /ˈɪnsɪdəns/ n fréquence f.

incident /ˈɪnsɪdənt/ n incident m. **incidental** adj secondaire. **incidentally** adv à propos; (by chance) par la même occasion.

incinerate /ɪnˈsɪnəreɪt/ vt incinérer. **incinerator** n incinérateur m.

incite /ɪnˈsaɪt/ vt inciter, pousser.

inclination /ɪnklɪˈneɪʃn/ n (tendency) tendance f; (desire) envie f.

incline¹ /ɪnˈklaɪn/ vt/i (s')incliner; be ~d to avoir tendance à.

incline² /ˈɪnklaɪn/ n pente f.

include /ɪnˈkluːd/ vt comprendre, inclure. **including** prep (y) compris. **inclusion** n inclusion f.

inclusive /ɪnˈkluːsɪv/ adj & adv inclus; ~ **of delivery** livraison comprise.

income /ˈɪnkʌm/ n revenus mpl; ~ **tax** impôt m sur le revenu.

incoming /ˈɪnkʌmɪŋ/ adj (tide) montant; (tenant, government) nouveau; (call) qui vient de l'extérieur.

incompatible /ɪnkəmˈpætɪbl/ adj incompatible.

incompetent /ɪnˈkɒmpɪtənt/ adj incompétent.

incomplete /ɪnkəmˈpliːt/ adj incomplet.

incomprehensible /ɪnkɒmprɪˈhensəbl/ adj incompréhensible.

inconceivable /ɪnkənˈsiːvəbl/ adj inconcevable.

inconclusive /ɪnkənˈkluːsɪv/ adj peu concluant.

incongruous /ɪnˈkɒŋgrʊəs/ adj déconcertant, surprenant.

inconsiderate /ɪnkənˈsɪdərət/ adj (person) peu attentif à autrui; (act) maladroit.

inconsistent /ɪnkənˈsɪstənt/ adj (argument) incohérent; (performance) inégal; (behaviour) changeant; ~ **with** en contradiction avec.

inconspicuous /ɪnkənˈspɪkjʊəs/ adj qui passe inaperçu.

incontinent /ɪnˈkɒntɪnənt/ adj incontinent.

inconvenience /ɪnkənˈviːnɪəns/ n dérangement m; (drawback) inconvénient m. ● vt déranger. **inconvenient** adj incommode; **if it's not inconvenient for you** si cela ne vous dérange pas.

incorporate /ɪnˈkɔːpəreɪt/ vt incorporer (into dans); (contain) comporter.

incorrect /ɪnkəˈrekt/ adj incorrect.

increase¹ /ˈɪnkriːs/ n augmentation f (in, of de). **be on the** ~ être en progression.

increase² /ɪnˈkriːs/ vt/i augmenter. **increasing** adj croissant. **increasingly** adv de plus en plus.

incredible /ɪnˈkredəbl/ adj incroyable.

incriminate /ɪnˈkrɪmɪneɪt/ vt incriminer. **incriminating** adj compromettant.

incubate /ˈɪnkjʊbeɪt/ vt (eggs) couver. **incubation** n incubation f. **incubator** n couveuse f.

incur /ɪnˈkɜː(r)/ vt (pt incurred) (penalty, anger) encourir; (debts) contracter.

indebted /ɪnˈdetɪd/ adj ~ **to sb** redevable à qn (for de); (grateful) reconnaissant à qn.

indecent /ɪnˈdiːsnt/ adj indécent.

indecisive /ɪndɪˈsaɪsɪv/ adj indécis; (ending) peu concluant.

indeed /ɪnˈdiːd/ adv en effet; (emphatic) vraiment.

indefinite /ɪnˈdefɪnət/ adj vague; (period, delay) illimité. **indefinitely** adv indéfiniment.

indelible /ɪnˈdeləbl/ adj indélébile.

indemnity /ɪnˈdemnətɪ/ n (protection) assurance f; (payment) indemnité f.

indent /ɪnˈdent/ vt (text) renfoncer. **indentation** n (dent) marque f.

independence /ɪndɪˈpendəns/ n indépendance f. **independent** adj indépendant. **independently** adv de façon indépendante; **independently of** indépendamment de.

index /ˈɪndeks/ n (pl ~es) (in book) index m; (in library) catalogue m; (in economy) indice m; ~ **card** fiche f; ~ **(finger)** index m. ● vt classer. ~**-linked** adj indexé.

India /ˈɪndɪə/ n Inde f.

Indian /'ɪndɪən/ n Indien/-ne m/f. ● adj indien.

indicate /'ɪndɪkeɪt/ vt indiquer. **indication** n indication f.

indicative /ɪn'dɪkətɪv/ adj & n indicatif (m).

indicator /'ɪndɪkeɪtə(r)/ n (pointer) aiguille f; (on vehicle) clignotant m; (board) tableau m.

indict /ɪn'daɪt/ vt inculper. **indictment** n accusation f.

indifferent /ɪn'dɪfrənt/ adj indifférent; (not good) médiocre.

indigenous /ɪn'dɪdʒɪnəs/ adj indigène.

indigestible /ɪndɪ'dʒestəbl/ adj indigeste. **indigestion** n indigestion f.

indignant /ɪn'dɪgnənt/ adj indigné.

indirect /ɪndɪ'rekt/ adj indirect. **indirectly** adv indirectement.

indiscreet /ɪndɪ'skriːt/ adj indiscret. **Indiscretion** n indiscrétion f.

indiscriminate /ɪndɪ'skrɪmɪnət/ adj sans distinction. **indiscriminately** adv sans distinction.

indisputable /ɪndɪ'spjuːtəbl/ adj indiscutable.

individual /ɪndɪ'vɪdʒʊəl/ adj individuel; (tuition) particulier. ● n individu m. **individualist** n individualiste mf. **individuality** n individualité f. **individually** adv individuellement.

indoctrinate /ɪn'dɒktrɪneɪt/ vt endoctriner. **indoctrination** n endoctrinement m.

indolent /'ɪndələnt/ adj indolent.

Indonesia /ɪndəʊ'niːzjə/ n Indonésie f.

indoor /'ɪndɔː(r)/ adj (clothes) d'intérieur; (pool, court) couvert. **indoors** adv à l'intérieur.

induce /ɪn'djuːs/ vt (influence) persuader; (stronger) inciter (**to do** à faire). **inducement** n (financial) récompense f; (incentive) motivation f.

induction /ɪn'dʌkʃn/ n (Electr) induction f; (inauguration) installation f.

indulge /ɪn'dʌldʒ/ vt (person, whim) céder à; (child) gâter. ● vi ~ **in** se livrer à. **indulgence** n indulgence f; (treat) plaisir m. **indulgent** adj indulgent.

industrial /ɪn'dʌstrɪəl/ adj industriel; (accident) du travail; ~ **action** grève f; ~ **dispute** conflit m social. **industrialist** n industriel/-le m/f. **industrialized** adj industrialisé.

industrious /ɪn'dʌstrɪəs/ adj diligent.

industry /'ɪndəstrɪ/ n industrie f; (zeal) zèle m.

inebriated /ɪ'niːbrɪeɪtɪd/ adj ivre.

inedible /ɪn'edɪbl/ adj immangeable.

ineffective /ɪnɪ'fektɪv/ adj inefficace.

inefficient /ɪnɪ'fɪʃnt/ adj inefficace; (person) incompétent.

ineligible /ɪn'elɪdʒəbl/ adj inéligible; **be** ~ **for** ne pas avoir droit à.

inept /ɪ'nept/ adj incompétent; (tactless) maladroit.

inequality /ɪnɪ'kwɒlətɪ/ n inégalité f.

inescapable /ɪnɪ'skeɪpəbl/ adj indéniable.

inevitable /ɪn'evɪtəbl/ adj inévitable.

inexcusable /ɪnɪk'skjuːzəbl/ adj inexcusable.

inexhaustible /ɪnɪg'zɔːstəbl/ adj inépuisable.

inexpensive /ɪnɪk'spensɪv/ adj pas cher.

inexperience /ɪnɪk'spɪərɪəns/ n inexpérience f. **inexperienced** adj inexpérimenté.

infallible /ɪn'fæləbl/ adj infaillible.

infamous /'ɪnfəməs/ adj (person) tristement célèbre; (deed) infâme.

infancy /'ɪnfənsɪ/ n petite enfance f; **in its** ~ (fig) à ses débuts mpl. **infant** n (baby) bébé m; (at school) enfant m. **infantile** adj infantile.

infatuated /ɪn'fætʃʊeɪtɪd/ adj ~ **with** entiché de. **infatuation** n engouement m.

infect /ɪn'fekt/ vt contaminer; ~ **sb with sth** transmettre qch à qn. **infection** n infection f. **infectious** adj contagieux.

infer /ɪn'fɜː(r)/ vt (pt **inferred**) (deduce) déduire.

inferior /ɪn'fɪərɪə(r)/ adj inférieur (**to** à). (work, product) de qualité inférieure. ● n inférieur/-e m/f. **inferiority** n infériorité f.

inferno /ɪn'fɜːnəʊ/ n (hell) enfer m; (blaze) brasier m.

Infertile /ɪn'fɜːtaɪl/ adj infertile.

infest /ɪn'fest/ vt infester (**with** de).

infidelity /ɪnfɪ'delətɪ/ n infidélité f.

infighting /'ɪnfaɪtɪŋ/ n conflits mpl internes.

infinite /'ɪnfɪnət/ adj infini. **infinitely** adv infiniment. **infinitive** n infinitif m. **infinity** n infinité f.

infirm /ɪn'fɜːm/ adj infirme. **infirmary** n hôpital m; (sick-bay) infirmerie f. **infirmity** n infirmité f.

inflame /ɪn'fleɪm/ vt enflammer. **inflammable** adj inflammable. **inflammation** n inflammation f. **inflammatory** adj incendiaire.

inflatable /ɪn'fleɪtəbl/ adj gonflable. **inflate** vt (lit, fig) gonfler.

inflation /ɪn'fleɪʃn/ n inflation f.

inflection /ɪn'flekʃn/ n (of word root) flexion f; (of vowel, voice) inflexion f.

inflict /ɪn'flɪkt/ vt infliger (**on** à).

influence /'ɪnfluəns/ n influence f; **under the** ~ (drunk Ⓘ) éméché. ● vt (person) influencer; (choice) influer sur. **influential** adj (powerful) influent; (theory, artist) très suivi.

influenza /ɪnflʊ'enzə/ n grippe f.

influx /'ɪnflʌks/ n afflux m.

inform /ɪn'fɔːm/ vt informer (**of** de). **keep** ~**ed** tenir au courant.

informal /ɪn'fɔːml/ adj (simple) simple, sans façons; (unofficial) officieux; (colloquial) familier. **informality** n simplicité f. **informally** adv (dress) en tenue décontractée; (speak) en toute simplicité.

informant /ɪn'fɔːmənt/ n indicateur/-trice m/f.

information /ɪnfə'meɪʃn/ n renseignements mpl, informations fpl; **some** ~ un renseignement. ~ **superhighway** n autoroute f de l'information. ~ **technology** n informatique f.

informative /ɪn'fɔːmətɪv/ adj (book) riche en renseignements; (visit) instructif.

informer /ɪn'fɔːmə(r)/ n indicateur/-trice m/f.

infrequent /ɪn'friːkwənt/ adj rare.

infringe /ɪn'frɪndʒ/ vt (rule) enfreindre; (rights) ne pas respecter. **infringement** n infraction f.

infuriate /ɪn'fjʊərɪeɪt/ vt exaspérer.

ingenuity /ɪndʒɪ'njuːətɪ/ n ingéniosité f.

ingot /'ɪŋgət/ n lingot m.

ingrained /ɪn'greɪnd/ adj (hatred) enraciné; (dirt) bien incrusté.

ingratiate /ɪn'greɪʃɪeɪt/ vt ~ **oneself with** se faire bien voir de.

ingredient /ɪn'griːdɪənt/ n ingrédient m.

inhabit /ɪn'hæbɪt/ vt habiter. **inhabitable** adj habitable. **inhabitant** n habitant/-e m/f.

inhale /ɪn'heɪl/ vt inhaler; (smoke) avaler. **inhaler** n inhalateur m.

inherent /ɪn'hɪərənt/ adj inhérent (**in** à). **inherently** adv en soi, par sa nature.

inherit /ɪn'herɪt/ vt hériter de; ~ **sth from sb** hériter qch de qn. **inheritance** n héritage m.

inhibit /ɪn'hɪbɪt/ vt (restrain) inhiber; (prevent) entraver.

inhospitable /ɪnhɒ'spɪtəbl/ adj inhospitalier.

inhuman /ɪn'hjuːmən/ adj inhumain.

initial /ɪ'nɪʃl/ n initiale f. ● vt (pt **initialled**) parapher. ● adj initial.

initiate /ɪ'nɪʃɪeɪt/ vt (project) mettre en œuvre; (talks) amorcer; (person) initier (**into** à). **initiation** n initiation f; (start) amorce f.

initiative /ɪ'nɪʃətɪv/ n initiative f.

inject /ɪn'dʒekt/ vt injecter (**into** dans). (new element: fig) insuffler (**into** à). **injection** n injection f, piqûre f.

injure /'ɪndʒə(r)/ vt blesser; (damage) nuire à. **injury** n blessure f.

injustice /ɪn'dʒʌstɪs/ n injustice f.

ink /ɪŋk/ n encre f.

inkling /'ɪŋklɪŋ/ n petite idée f.

inland /'ɪnlənd/ adj intérieur; **I~ Revenue** service m des impôts britannique.

in-laws /'ɪnlɔːz/ npl (parents) beaux-parents mpl; (family) belle-famille f.

inlay[1] /ɪn'leɪ/ vt (pt **inlaid**) incruster (**with** de); (on wood) marqueter.

inlay[2] /'ɪnleɪ/ n incrustation f; (on wood) marqueterie f.

inlet /'ɪnlet/ n bras m de mer; (Tech) arrivée f.

inmate /'ɪnmeɪt/ n (of asylum) interné/-e m/f; (of prison) détenu/-e m/f.

inn /ɪn/ n auberge f.

innate /ɪ'neɪt/ adj inné.

inner /'mə(r)/ adj intérieur; ~ **city** quartiers mpl déshérités; ~ **tube** chambre f à air.

innocent /'məsnt/ adj & n innocent/-e (m/f).

innocuous /ɪ'nɒkjʊəs/ adj Inoffensif.

innovate /'məveɪt/ vi innover.

innuendo /ɪnjuː'endəʊ/ n (pl ~**es**) insinuations fpl; (sexual) allusions fpl grivoises.

innumerable /ɪ'njuːmərəbl/ adj innombrable.

inoculate /ɪ'nɒkjʊleɪt/ vt vacciner (**against** contre).

inopportune /ɪn'ɒpətjuːn/ adj inopportun.

in-patient /'ɪnpeɪʃnt/ n malade mf hospitalisé/-e.

input /'ɪnpʊt/ n (of energy) alimentation f (**of** en); (contribution) contribution f; (data) données fpl; (computer process) saisie f des données. ● vt (data) saisir.

inquest /'ɪŋkwest/ n enquête f.

inquire /ɪn'kwaɪə(r)/ vi se renseigner (**about, into** sur). ● vt demander.

inquiry /ɪn'kwaɪərɪ/ n demande f de renseignements; (inquest) enquête f.

inquisitive /ɪn'kwɪzətɪv/ adj curieux.

inroad /'ɪnrəʊd/ n make ~s into faire une avancée sur.

insane /ɪn'seɪn/ adj fou; (Jur) aliéné. **insanity** n folie f; (Jur) aliénation f mentale.

inscribe /ɪn'skraɪb/ vt inscrire. **inscription** n inscription f.

inscrutable /ɪn'skruːtəbl/ adj énigmatique.

insect /'ɪnsekt/ n Insecte m. **insecticide** n insecticide m.

insecure /ɪnsɪ'kjʊə(r)/ adj (person) qui manque d'assurance; (job) précaire; (lock, property) peu sûr. **insecurity** n (of person) manque m d'assurance; (of situation) insécurité f.

insensitive /ɪn'sensətɪv/ adj insensible; (remark) indélicat.

inseparable /ɪn'seprəbl/ adj inséparable (**from** de).

insert /ɪn'sɜːt/ vt insérer (**in** dans).

in-service /'ɪnsɜːvɪs/ adj (training) continu.

inshore /ɪn'ʃɔː(r)/ adj côtier.

inside /ɪn'saɪd/ n intérieur m; ~**s** ⚑ entrailles fpl. ● adj intérieur. ● adv à l'intérieur; **go** ~ entrer. ● prep à l'intérieur de; (of time) en moins de; ~ **out** à l'envers; (thoroughly) à fond.

insight /'ɪnsaɪt/ n (perception) perspicacité f; (idea) aperçu m.

insignia /ɪn'sɪgnɪə/ npl insigne m.

insignificant /ɪnsɪg'nɪfɪkənt/ adj (cost, difference) négligeable; (person) insignifiant.

insincere /ɪnsɪn'sɪə(r)/ adj peu sincère.

insinuate /ɪn'sɪnjʊeɪt/ vt insinuer.

insist /ɪn'sɪst/ vt/i insister (**that** pour que). ~ **on** exiger; ~ **on doing** vouloir à tout prix faire. **insistence** n insistance f. **insistent** adj insistant. **insistently** adv avec insistance.

insofar as /ɪnsəʊ'fɑːəz/ adv dans la mesure où.

insolent /'ɪnsələnt/ adj insolent.

insolvent /ɪn'sɒlvənt/ adj insolvable.

insomnia /ɪn'sɒmnɪə/ n insomnie f. **insomniac** n insomniaque mf.

inspect /ɪn'spekt/ vt (school, machinery) inspecter; (tickets) contrôler. **inspection** n inspection f; (of passport, ticket) contrôle m. **inspector** n inspecteur/-trice m/f; (on bus) contrôleur/-euse m/f.

inspiration /ɪnspə'reɪʃn/ n inspiration f. **inspire** vt inspirer.

install /ɪn'stɔːl/ vt installer.

instalment /ɪn'stɔːlmənt/ n (payment) versement m; (of serial) épisode m.

instance /'ɪnstəns/ n exemple m; (case) cas m; **for** ~ par exemple; **in the first** ~ en premier lieu.

instant /'ɪnstənt/ adj immédiat; (food) instantané. ● n instant m. **instantaneous** adj instantané. **instantly** adv immédiatement.

instead /ɪn'sted/ adv plutôt; ~ **of doing** au lieu de faire; ~ **of sb** à la place de qn.

instep /'ɪnstep/ n cou-de-pied m.

instigate /'ɪnstɪgeɪt/ vt (attack) lancer; (proceedings) engager.

instil /ɪn'stɪl/ vt (pt **instilled**) inculquer; (fear) insuffler.

instinct /'ɪnstɪŋkt/ n instinct m. **instinctive** adj instinctif.

institute /'ɪnstɪtjuːt/ n institut m. ● vt instituer; (proceedings) engager. **insti-**

i

tution n institution f; (school, hospital) établissement m.

instruct /ɪnˈstrʌkt/ vt (teach) instruire; (order) ordonner; ~ **sb in sth** enseigner qch à qn; ~ **sb to do** donner l'ordre à qn de faire. **instruction** n instruction f. **instructions** npl (for use) mode m d'emploi. **instructive** adj instructif. **instructor** n (skiing, driving) moniteur/-trice m/f.

instrument /ˈɪnstrʊmənt/ n instrument m.

instrumental /ɪnstrʊˈmentl/ adj instrumental; **be** ~ **in** contribuer à. **instrumentalist** n instrumentaliste mf.

insubordinate /ɪnsəˈbɔːdɪnət/ adj insubordonné.

insufficient /ɪnsəˈfɪʃnt/ adj insuffisant.

insular /ˈɪnsjʊlə(r)/ adj (Geog) insulaire; (mind, person: fig) borné.

insulate /ˈɪnsjʊleɪt/ vt (room, wire) isoler.

insulin /ˈɪnsjʊlɪn/ n insuline f.

insult¹ /ɪnˈsʌlt/ vt insulter.

insult² /ˈɪnsʌlt/ n insulte f.

insurance /ɪnˈʃɔːrəns/ n assurance f (against contre).

insure /ɪnˈʃɔː(r)/ vt assurer; ~ **that** (US) s'assurer que.

intact /ɪnˈtækt/ adj intact.

intake /ˈɪnteɪk/ n (of food) consommation f; (School, Univ) admissions fpl.

integral /ˈɪntɪɡrəl/ adj intégral (to à).

integrate /ˈɪntɪɡreɪt/ vt/i (s')intégrer (with à; into dans).

integrity /ɪnˈteɡrəti/ n intégrité f.

intellect /ˈɪntəlekt/ n intelligence f. **intellectual** adj & n intellectuel/-le (m/f).

intelligence /ɪnˈtelɪdʒəns/ n intelligence f; (Mil) renseignements mpl. **intelligent** adj intelligent. **intelligently** adv intelligemment.

intend /ɪnˈtend/ vt (outcome) vouloir; ~ **to do** avoir l'intention de faire. **intended** adj (result) voulu; (visit) projeté.

intense /ɪnˈtens/ adj intense; (person) sérieux. **intensely** adv (very) extrêmement.

intensify /ɪnˈtensɪfaɪ/ vt/i (s')intensifier.

intensive /ɪnˈtensɪv/ adj intensif; **in** ~ **care** en réanimation.

intent /ɪnˈtent/ n intention f. ● adj absorbé; ~ **on doing** résolu à faire.

intention /ɪnˈtenʃn/ n intention f. **intentional** adj intentionnel.

intently /ɪnˈtentlɪ/ adv attentivement.

interact /ɪntərˈækt/ vi (factors) agir l'un sur l'autre; (people) communiquer. **interactive** adj (TV, video) interactif.

intercept /ɪntəˈsept/ vt intercepter.

interchange /ˈɪntətʃeɪndʒ/ n (road junction) échangeur m; (exchange) échange m.

interchangeable /ɪntəˈtʃeɪndʒəbl/ adj interchangeable.

intercom /ˈɪntəkɒm/ n interphone® m.

interconnected /ɪntəkəˈnektɪd/ adj (parts) raccordé; (problems) lié.

intercourse /ˈɪntəkɔːs/ n rapports mpl.

interest /ˈɪntrəst/ n intérêt m; ~ **rate** taux m d'intérêt. ● vt intéresser (in à). **interested** adj intéressé; **be** ~**ed in** s'intéresser à. **interesting** adj intéressant.

interface /ˈɪntəfeɪs/ n interface f.

interfere /ɪntəˈfɪə(r)/ vi se mêler des affaires des autres; ~ **in** se mêler de; ~ **with** (freedom) empiéter sur; (tamper with) toucher. **interference** n ingérence f; (sound, light waves) brouillage m; (radio) parasites mpl.

interim /ˈɪntərɪm/ n **in the** ~ entretemps. ● adj (government) provisoire; (payment) intermédiaire.

interior /ɪnˈtɪərɪə(r)/ n intérieur m. ● adj intérieur.

interjection /ɪntəˈdʒekʃn/ n interjection f.

interlock /ɪntəˈlɒk/ vt/i (Tech) (s')emboîter, (s')enclencher.

interlude /ˈɪntəluːd/ n intervalle m; (Theat, Mus) intermède m.

intermediary /ɪntəˈmiːdɪərɪ/ adj & n intermédiaire (mf).

intermediate /ɪntəˈmiːdɪət/ adj intermédiaire; (exam, level) moyen.

intermission /ɪntəˈmɪʃn/ n (Theat) entracte m.

intermittent /ɪntəˈmɪtənt/ adj intermittent.

intern¹ /ɪnˈtɜːn/ vt interner.

intern² /ˈɪntɜːn/ n (US) stagiaire mf; (Med) interne mf.

internal /ɪnˈtɜːnl/ *adj* interne; (domestic: Pol) intérieur; **I∼ Revenue** (US) service *m* des impôts américain.

international /ɪntəˈnæʃnəl/ *adj* international.

Internet /ˈɪntənet/ *n* Internet *m*; **on the ∼** sur Internet; **∼ access** accès à Internet; **∼ service provider** fournisseur *m* d'accès Internet.

interpret /ɪnˈtɜːprɪt/ *vt* interpréter (**as** comme). ● *vi* faire l'interprète. **interpretation** *n* interprétation *f.* **interpreter** *n* interprète *mf.*

interrelated /ɪntərɪˈleɪtɪd/ *adj* interdépendant, lié.

interrogate /ɪnˈterəgeɪt/ *vt* interroger. **interrogative** *adj & n* (Ling) interrogatif (*m*).

interrupt /ɪntəˈrʌpt/ *vt/i* interrompre. **interruption** *n* interruption *f.*

intersect /ɪntəˈsekt/ *vt/i* (lines, roads) (se) croiser. **intersection** *n* intersection *f.*

interspersed /ɪntəˈspɜːst/ *adj* parsemé (**with** de).

intertwine /ɪntəˈtwaɪn/ *vt/i* (s')entrelacer.

interval /ˈɪntəvl/ *n* intervalle *m*; (Theat) entracte *m*.

intervene /ɪntəˈviːn/ *vi* intervenir; (of time) s'écouler (**between** entre); (happen) arriver.

interview /ˈɪntəvjuː/ *n* (for job) entretien *m*; (by a journalist) interview *f.* ● *vt* (candidate) faire passer un entretien à; (celebrity) interviewer.

intestine /ɪnˈtestɪn/ *n* intestin *m*.

intimacy /ˈɪntɪməsɪ/ *n* intimité *f.*

intimate¹ /ˈɪntɪmeɪt/ *vt* (state) annoncer; (hint) laisser entendre.

intimate² /ˈɪntɪmət/ *adj* intime. **intimately** *adv* intimement.

intimidate /ɪnˈtɪmɪdeɪt/ *vt* intimider.

into /ˈɪntuː/, /ˈɪntə/ *prep* (put, go, fall) dans; (divide, translate, change) en; **be ∼ jazz** être fana du jazz 🔳; **8 ∼ 24 is 3** 24 divisé par 8 égale 3.

intolerant /ɪnˈtɒlərənt/ *adj* intolérant.

intonation /ɪntəˈneɪʃn/ *n* intonation *f.*

intoxicate /ɪnˈtɒksɪkeɪt/ *vt* enivrer. **intoxicated** *adj* ivre. **intoxication** *n* ivresse *f.*

intractable /ɪnˈtræktəbl/ *adj* (person) intraitable; (problem) rebelle.

intranet /ˈɪntrənet/ *n* (Comput) intranet *m*.

intransitive /ɪnˈtrænsətɪv/ *adj* intransitif.

intravenous /ɪntrəˈviːnəs/ *adj* (Med) intraveineux.

intricate /ˈɪntrɪkət/ *adj* complexe.

intrigue /ɪnˈtriːg/ *vt* intriguer. ● *n* intrigue *f.* **intriguing** *adj* fascinant; (curious) curieux.

intrinsic /ɪnˈtrɪnzɪk/ *adj* intrinsèque (**to** à).

introduce /ɪntrəˈdjuːs/ *vt* (person, idea, programme) présenter; (object, law) introduire (**into** dans). **introduction** *n* introduction *f*; (of person) présentation *f.* **introductory** *adj* (words) préliminaire.

introvert /ˈɪntrəvɜːt/ *n* introverti/-e *m/f.*

intrude /ɪnˈtruːd/ *vi* (person) s'imposer (**on sb** à qn), déranger. **intruder** *n* intrus/-e *m/f.* **intrusion** *n* intrusion *f.*

intuition /ɪntjuːˈɪʃn/ *n* intuition *f.* **intuitive** *adj* intuitif.

inundate /ˈɪnʌndeɪt/ *vt* inonder (**with** de).

invade /ɪnˈveɪd/ *vt* envahir.

invalid¹ /ˈɪnvəliːd/ *n* malade *mf*; (disabled) infirme *mf.*

invalid² /ɪnˈvælɪd/ *adj* (passport) pas valable; (claim) sans fondement. **invalidate** *vt* (argument) infirmer; (claim) annuler.

invaluable /ɪnˈvæljʊəbl/ *adj* inestimable.

invariable /ɪnˈveərɪəbl/ *adj* invariable. **invariably** *adv* invariablement.

invasion /ɪnˈveɪʒn/ *n* invasion *f.*

invent /ɪnˈvent/ *vt* inventer. **invention** *n* invention *f.* **inventive** *adj* inventif. **inventor** *n* inventeur/-trice *m/f.*

inventory /ˈɪnvəntrɪ/ *n* inventaire *m.*

invert /ɪnˈvɜːt/ *vt* (order) intervertir; (image, values) renverser; **∼ed commas** guillemets *mpl.*

invest /ɪnˈvest/ *vt* investir; (time, effort) consacrer. ● *vi* faire un investissement; **∼ in** (buy) s'acheter.

investigate /ɪnˈvestɪgeɪt/ *vt* examiner; (crime) enquêter sur. **investigation** *n* investigation *f.* **investigator** *n* (police) enquêteur/-euse *m/f.*

investment /ɪn'vestmənt/ n investissement m; **emotional ~** engagement m personnel. **investor** n investisseur/-euse m/f; (in shares) actionnaire mf.

invigilate /ɪn'vɪdʒɪleɪt/ vi (exam) surveiller. **invigilator** n surveillant/-e m/f.

invigorate /ɪn'vɪgəreɪt/ vt revigorer.

invisible /ɪn'vɪzəbl/ adj invisible.

invitation /ɪnvɪ'teɪʃn/ n invitation f. **invite** vt inviter; (ask for) demander. **inviting** adj engageant.

invoice /'ɪnvɔɪs/ n facture f. ● vt facturer.

involuntary /ɪn'vɒləntrɪ/ adj involontaire.

involve /ɪn'vɒlv/ vt impliquer; (person) faire participer (in à). **involved** adj (complex) compliqué; (at stake) en jeu; **be ~d in** (work) participer à; (crime) être mêlé à. **involvement** n participation f (in à).

inward /'ɪnwəd/ adj (feeling) intérieur. **inwardly** adv intérieurement. **inwards** adv vers l'intérieur.

iodine /'aɪədiːn/ n iode m; (antiseptic) teinture f d'iode.

iota /aɪ'əʊtə/ n iota m; **not one ~** pas un grain de.

IOU abbr (**I owe you**) reconnaissance f de dette.

IQ abbr (**intelligence quotient**) QI m.

Iran /ɪ'rɑːn/ n Iran m.

Iraq /ɪ'rɑːk/ n Irak m.

irate /aɪ'reɪt/ adj furieux.

IRC abbrev (**Internet Relay Chat**) (Internet) conversation f IRC.

Ireland /'aɪələnd/ n Irlande f.

Irish /'aɪərɪʃ/ n & adj irlandais (m). **~man** n Irlandais m. **~woman** n Irlandaise f.

iron /'aɪən/ n fer m; (appliance) fer m (à repasser). ● adj (will) de fer; (bar) en fer. ● vt repasser.

ironic /aɪ'rɒnɪk/ adj ironique.

iron: ironing-board n planche f à repasser. **~monger** n quincaillier m.

irony /'aɪərənɪ/ n ironie f.

irrational /ɪ'ræʃənl/ adj irrationnel; (person) pas raisonnable.

irregular /ɪ'regjʊlə(r)/ adj irrégulier.

irrelevant /ɪ'reləvnt/ adj hors de propos.

irreplaceable /ɪrɪ'pleɪsəbl/ adj irremplaçable.

irresistible /ɪrɪ'zɪstəbl/ adj irrésistible.

irrespective /ɪrɪ'spektɪv/ adj **~ of** sans tenir compte de.

irresponsible /ɪrɪ'spɒnsəbl/ adj irresponsable.

irreverent /ɪ'revərənt/ adj irrévérencieux.

irrigate /'ɪrɪgeɪt/ vt irriguer.

irritable /'ɪrɪtəbl/ adj irritable.

irritate /'ɪrɪteɪt/ vt irriter. **irritating** adj irritant.

is /ɪz/ ➔BE.

ISDN abbr (integrated services digital network) RNIS n, réseau m numérique à intégration de services.

Islam /ɪz'lɑːm/ n (faith) islam m; (Muslims) Islam m. **Islamic** adj islamique.

island /'aɪlənd/ n île f.

isle /aɪl/ n île f.

isolate /'aɪsəleɪt/ vt isoler. **isolation** n isolement m.

Israel /'ɪzreɪl/ n Israël m.

Israeli /ɪz'reɪlɪ/ n Israélien/-ne m/f. ● adj israélien.

issue /'ɪsjuː/ n question f; (outcome) résultat m; (of magazine) numéro m; (of stamps) émission f; (offspring) descendance f; **at ~** en cause. ● vt distribuer; (stamps) émettre; (book) publier; (order) délivrer. ● vi **~ from** provenir de.

---

it /ɪt/

● pronoun

····➤ (subject) il, elle; **'where's the book/chair?'— '~'s in the kitchen'** 'où est le livre/la chaise?'—'il/elle est dans la cuisine'.

····➤ (object) le, la, l'; **~'s my book and I want ~** c'est mon livre et je le veux; **I liked his shirt, did you notice ~?** sa chemise m'a plu, l'as-tu remarquée?; **give ~ to me** donne-le-moi.

····➤ (with preposition) **we talked a lot about ~** on en a beaucoup parlé; **Elliott went to ~** Elliott y est allé.

····➤ (impersonal) il; **~'s raining** il pleut; **~ will snow** il va neiger.

IT abbr ➞INFORMATION TECHNOLOGY.

Italian /ɪˈtæljən/ n (person) Italien/-ne m/f; (Ling) italien m. ● adj italien.

italics /ɪˈtælɪks/ npl italique m.

Italy /ˈɪtəlɪ/ n Italie f.

itch /ɪtʃ/ n démangeaison f. ● vi démanger; **my arm ~es** j'ai le bras qui me démange; **be ~ing to do** mourir d'envie de faire.

item /ˈaɪtəm/ n article m; (on agenda) point m.

itemize /ˈaɪtəmaɪz/ vt détailler; **~d bill** facture f détaillée.

itinerary /aɪˈtɪnərərɪ/ n itinéraire m.

its /ɪts/ det son, sa; pl ses.

it's ➞IT IS, IT HAS.

itself /ɪtˈself/ pron lui-même, elle-même; (reflexive) se.

ivory /ˈaɪvərɪ/ n ivoire m; **~ tower** tour f d'ivoire.

ivy /ˈaɪvɪ/ n lierre m.

The Ivy League Ce terme désigne les huit universités les plus prestigieuses de la côte est des États-Unis (Harvard, Yale, Columbia, Cornell, Dartmouth, Brown, Princeton, Pennsylvania). Elles doivent ce nom au lierre qui pousse sur les bâtiments des plus anciennes d'entre elles. Ces universités sont réputées tant dans les domaines académiques que sportifs.

Jj

jab /dʒæb/ vt (pt **jabbed**) **~ sth into sth** planter qch dans qch. ● n coup m; (injection) piqûre f.

jack /dʒæk/ n (Auto) cric m; (cards) valet m; (Electr) jack m. ● vt **~ up** soulever avec un cric.

jacket /ˈdʒækɪt/ n veste f, veston m; (of book) jaquette f.

jackknife /ˈdʒæknaɪf/ n couteau m pliant. ● vi (lorry) se mettre en portefeuille.

jackpot /ˈdʒækpɒt/ n gros lot m; **hit the ~** gagner le gros lot.

jade /dʒeɪd/ n (stone) jade m.

jaded /ˈdʒeɪdɪd/ adj (tired) fatigué; (bored) blasé.

jagged /ˈdʒægɪd/ adj (rock) déchiqueté; (knife) dentelé.

jail /dʒeɪl/ n prison f. ● vt mettre en prison.

jam /dʒæm/ n confiture f; **(traffic) ~** embouteillage m. ● vt/i (pt **jammed**) (wedge) (se) coincer; (cram) (s')entasser; (street) encombrer; (radio) brouiller.

Jamaica /dʒəˈmeɪkə/ n Jamaïque f.

jam-packed adj Ⅰ bondé; **~ with** bourré de.

jangle /ˈdʒæŋgl/ n tintement m. ● vt/i (faire) tinter.

janitor /ˈdʒænɪtə(r)/ n (US) gardien m.

January /ˈdʒænjʊərɪ/ n janvier m.

Japan /dʒəˈpæn/ n Japon m.

Japanese /dʒæpəˈniːz/ n (person) Japonais/-e m/f; (Ling) japonais m. ● adj japonais.

jar /dʒɑː(r)/ n pot m, bocal m. ● vi (pt **jarred**) rendre un son discordant; (colours) détonner. ● vt ébranler.

jargon /ˈdʒɑːgən/ n jargon m.

jaundice /ˈdʒɔːndɪs/ n jaunisse f.

javelin /ˈdʒævlɪn/ n javelot m.

jaw /dʒɔː/ n mâchoire f.

jay /dʒeɪ/ n geai m.

jazz /dʒæz/ n jazz m. ● vt **~ up** (dress) rajeunir; (event) ranimer.

jealous /ˈdʒeləs/ adj jaloux. **jealousy** n jalousie f.

jeans /dʒiːnz/ npl jean m.

jeer /dʒɪə(r)/ vt/i **~ (at)** huer. ● n huée f.

jelly /ˈdʒelɪ/ n gelée f. **~fish** n méduse f.

jeopardize /ˈdʒepədaɪz/ vt (career, chance) compromettre; (lives) mettre en péril.

jerk /dʒɜːk/ n secousse f; (fool ✖) crétin m Ⅰ. ● vt tirer brusquement. ● vi tressaillir. **jerky** adj saccadé.

jersey /ˈdʒɜːzɪ/ n (garment) pull-over m; (fabric) jersey m.

jet /dʒet/ n (plane, stream) jet m; (mineral) jais m; **~ lag** décalage m horaire.

jettison /ˈdʒetɪsn/ vt jeter par-dessus bord; (Aviat) larguer; (fig) rejeter.

jetty /ˈdʒetɪ/ n jetée f.

Jew /dʒuː/ n juif/juive m/f.

jewel /'dʒuːəl/ n bijou m. **jeweller** n bijoutier/-ière m/f. **jeweller('s)** n (shop) bijouterie f. **jewellery** n bijoux mpl.

Jewish /'dʒuːɪʃ/ adj juif.

jibe /dʒaɪb/ n moquerie f.

jigsaw /'dʒɪgsɔː/ n puzzle m.

jingle /'dʒɪŋgl/ vt/i (faire) tinter. ● n tintement m; (advertising) refrain m publicitaire, sonal m.

jinx /dʒɪŋks/ n (person) porte-malheur m inv; (curse) sort m.

jitters /'dʒɪtəz/ npl have the ~ 𝕀 être nerveux. **jittery** adj nerveux.

job /dʒɒb/ n emploi m; (post) poste m; out of a ~ sans emploi; it is a good ~ that heureusement que; just the ~ tout à fait ce qu'il faut. ~ centre n bureau m des services nationaux de l'emploi. **jobless** adj sans emploi.

jockey /'dʒɒkɪ/ n jockey m.

jog /dʒɒg/ n go for a ~ aller faire un jogging. ● vt (pt **jogged**) heurter; (memory) rafraîchir. ● vi faire du jogging. **jogging** n jogging m.

join /dʒɔɪn/ vt (attach) réunir, joindre; (club) devenir membre de; (company) entrer dans; (army) s'engager dans; (queue) se mettre dans; ~ sb (in activity) se joindre à qn; (meet) rejoindre qn. ● vi (become member) adhérer; (pieces) se joindre; (roads) se rejoindre. ● n raccord m. □ ~ in participer; ~ in sth participer à qch; ~ up (Mil) s'engager; ~ sth up relier qch. **joiner** n menuisier/-ière m/f.

joint /dʒɔɪnt/ adj (action) collectif; (measures, venture) commun; (winner) ex aequo inv; (account) joint; ~ author coauteur m. ● n (join) joint m; (Anat) articulation f; (Culin) rôti m; out of ~ déboîté.

joke /dʒəʊk/ n plaisanterie f; (trick) farce f; it's no ~ ce n'est pas drôle. ● vi plaisanter. **joker** n blagueur/-euse m/f; (cards) joker m.

jolly /'dʒɒlɪ/ adj (-ier, -iest) (person) enjoué; (tune) joyeux. ● adv 𝕀 drôlement.

jolt /dʒəʊlt/ vt secouer. ● vi cahoter. ● n secousse f; (shock) choc m.

jostle /'dʒɒsl/ vt/i (se) bousculer.

jot /dʒɒt/ vt (pt **jotted**) ~ (down) noter.

journal /'dʒɜːnl/ n journal m. **journalism** n journalisme m. **journalist** n journaliste mf.

journey /'dʒɜːnɪ/ n (trip) voyage m; (short or habitual) trajet m. ● vi voyager.

joy /dʒɔɪ/ n joie f. **joyful** adj joyeux.

joy: ~riding n rodéo m à la voiture volée. ~stick n (Comput) manette f; (Aviat) manche m à balai.

jubilant /'dʒuːbɪlənt/ adj (person) exultant; (mood) réjoui.

Judaism /'dʒuːdeɪɪzəm/ n judaïsme m.

judge /dʒʌdʒ/ n juge m. ● vt juger; (distance) estimer; **judging by/from** à en juger par. **judg(e)ment** n jugement m.

judicial /dʒuːˈdɪʃl/ adj judiciaire. **judiciary** n magistrature f.

judo /'dʒuːdəʊ/ n judo m.

jug /dʒʌg/ n (glass) carafe f; (pottery) pichet m.

juggernaut /'dʒʌgənɔːt/ n (lorry) poids m lourd.

juggle /'dʒʌgl/ vt/i jongler (avec). **juggler** n jongleur/-euse m/f.

juice /dʒuːs/ n jus m. **juicy** adj juteux; (details 𝕀) croustillant.

jukebox /'dʒuːkbɒks/ n juke-box m.

July /dʒuːˈlaɪ/ n juillet m.

jumble /'dʒʌmbl/ vt mélanger. ● n (of objects) tas m; (of ideas) fouillis m; ~ sale vente f de charité.

jumbo /'dʒʌmbəʊ/ n (also ~ **jet**) gros-porteur m.

jump /dʒʌmp/ vt sauter; ~ the lights passer au feu rouge; ~ the queue passer devant tout le monde. ● vi sauter; (in surprise) sursauter; (price) monter en flèche; ~ at (opportunity) sauter sur. ● n saut m, bond m; (increase) bond m.

jumper /'dʒʌmpə(r)/ n pull(-over) m; (dress: US) robe f chasuble.

jump-leads npl câbles mpl de démarrage.

jumpy /'dʒʌmpɪ/ adj nerveux.

junction /'dʒʌŋkʃn/ n (of roads) carrefour m; (on motorway) échangeur m.

June /dʒuːn/ n juin m.

jungle /'dʒʌŋgl/ n jungle f.

junior /'dʒuːnɪə(r)/ adj (young) jeune; (in rank) subalterne; (school) primaire.

● *n* cadet/-te *m/f;* (School) élève *mf* du primaire.

junk /dʒʌŋk/ *n* bric-à-brac *m inv;* (poor quality) camelote *f;* ~ **food** nourriture *f* industrielle.

junkie /'dʒʌŋkɪ/ *n* 🔀 drogué/-e *m/f.*

junk: ~ **mail** *n* prospectus *mpl.*
~**-shop** *n* boutique *f* de bric-à-brac.

jurisdiction /dʒʊərɪs'dɪkʃn/ *n* compétence *f;* (Jur) juridiction *f.*

juror /'dʒʊərə(r)/ *n* juré *m.*

jury /'dʒʊərɪ/ *n* jury *m.*

just /dʒʌst/ *adj* (fair) juste. ● *adv* (immediately, slightly) juste; (simply) tout simplement; (exactly) exactement; **he has/had** ~ **left** il vient/venait de partir; **have** ~ **missed** avoir manqué de peu; **I'm** ~ **leaving** je suis sur le point de partir; **it's** ~ **a cold** ce n'est qu'un rhume; ~ **as tall/well as** tout aussi grand/bien que; ~ **listen!** écoutez donc!; **it's** ~ **ridiculous** c'est vraiment ridicule.

justice /'dʒʌstɪs/ *n* justice *f;* **J**~ **of the Peace** juge *m* de paix.

justification /dʒʌstɪfɪ'keɪʃn/ *n* justification *f.* **justify** *vt* justifier.

jut /dʒʌt/ *vi* (*pt* **jutted**) ~ **(out)** s'avancer en saillie.

juvenile /'dʒuːvənaɪl/ *adj* (childish) puéril; (*offender*) mineur; (*delinquent*) jeune. ● *n* jeune *mf;* (Jur) mineur/-e *m/f.*

juxtapose /dʒʌkstə'pəʊz/ *vt* juxtaposer.

Kk

kangaroo /kæŋgə'ruː/ *n* kangourou *m.*

karate /kə'rɑːtɪ/ *n* karaté *m.*

kebab /kɪ'bæb/ *n* brochette *f.*

keel /kiːl/ *n* (of ship) quille *f.* ● *vi* ~ **over** (*bateau*) chavirer; (*person*) s'écrouler.

keen /kiːn/ *adj* (*interest, wind, feeling*) vif; (*mind, analysis*) pénétrant; (*edge, appetite*) aiguisé; (eager) enthousiaste; **be** ~ **on** être passionné de; **be** ~ **to do** *or* **on doing** tenir beaucoup à

faire. **keenly** *adv* vivement. **keenness** *n* enthousiasme *m.*

keep /kiːp/ *vt* (*pt* **kept**) garder; (*promise, shop, diary*) tenir; (*family*) faire vivre; (*animals*) élever; (*rule*) respecter; (celebrate) célébrer; (delay) retenir; ~ **sth clean/warm** garder qch propre/au chaud; ~ **sb in/out** empêcher qn de sortir/d'entrer; ~ **sb from doing** empêcher qn de faire. ● *vi* (*food*) se conserver; ~ **(on)** continuer (**doing à** faire). ● *n* pension *f;* (of castle) donjon *m.* ☐ ~ **down** rester allongé; ~ **sth down** limiter qch; ~ **your voice down!** baisse la voix!; ~ **to** (*road*) ne pas s'écarter de; (*rules*) respecter; ~ **up** (*car, runner*) suivre; (*rain*) continuer; ~ **up with sb** (in speed) aller aussi vite que; (*class, inflation, fashion, news*) suivre.

keeper /'kiːpə(r)/ *n* gardien/-ne *m/f.*

keepsake /'kiːpseɪk/ *n* souvenir *m.*

kennel /'kenl/ *n* niche *f.*

kept /kept/ ➡**KEEP.**

kerb /kɜːb/ *n* bord *m* du trottoir.

kernel /'kɜːnl/ *n* amande *f;* ~ **of truth** fond *m* de vérité.

kettle /'ketl/ *n* bouilloire *f.*

key /kiː/ *n* clé *f;* (of computer, piano) touche *f.* ● *adj* (*industry, figure*) clé (*inv*). ● *vt* ~ **(in)** saisir. ~**board** *n* clavier *m.* ~**hole** *n* trou *m* de serrure. ~**-pad** *n* (of telephone) clavier *m* numérique. ~**-ring** *n* porte-clés *m inv.* ~**stroke** *n* (Comput) frappe *f.*

khaki /'kɑːkɪ/ *adj* kaki *inv.*

kick /kɪk/ *vt/i* donner un coup de pied (à); (*horse*) botter. ● *n* coup *m* de pied; (of gun) recul *m;* **get a** ~ **out of doing** 🔀 prendre plaisir à faire. ☐ ~ **out** 🔀 virer 🔀.

kick-off *n* coup *m* d'envoi.

kid /kɪd/ *n* (goat, leather) chevreau *m;* (child 🔀) gosse *mf* 🔀. ● *vt/i* (*pt* **kidded**) blaguer.

kidnap /'kɪdnæp/ *vt* (*pt* **kidnapped**) enlever. **kidnapping** *n* enlèvement *m.*

kidney /'kɪdnɪ/ *n* rein *m;* (Culin) rognon *m.*

kill /kɪl/ *vt* tuer; (*rumour:* fig) arrêter. ● *n* mise *f* à mort. **killer** *n* tueur/-euse *m/f.* **killing** *n* meurtre *m.*

kiln /kɪln/ *n* four *m.*

kilo /'kiːləʊ/ *n* kilo *m.*

kilobyte /'kɪləbaɪt/ n kilo-octet m.

kilogram /'kɪləgræm/ n kilo-gramme m.

kilometre, (US) **kilometer** /'kɪləmiːtə(r)/ n kilomètre m.

kilowatt /'kɪləwɒt/ n kilowatt m.

kin /kɪn/ n parents mpl.

kind /kaɪnd/ n genre m, sorte f; **in ~** en nature; **~ of** (somewhat ⊞) assez. ● adj gentil, bon.

kindergarten /'kɪndəgɑːtn/ n jardin m d'enfants.

kindle /'kɪndl/ vt/i (s')allumer.

kindly /'kaɪndlɪ/ adj (**-ier, -iest**) (person) gentil; (interest) bienveillant. ● adv avec gentillesse; **would you ~ do** auriez-vous l'amabilité de faire.

kindness /'kaɪndnɪs/ n bonté f.

king /kɪŋ/ n roi m. **kingdom** n royaume m; (Bot) règne m. **~fisher** n martin-pêcheur m. **~-size(d)** adj géant.

kiosk /'kiːɒsk/ n kiosque m; **telephone ~** cabine f téléphonique; (Internet) borne f interactive, kiosque m.

kiss /kɪs/ n baiser m. ● vt/i (s')embrasser.

kit /kɪt/ n (clothing) affaires fpl; (set of tools) trousse f; (for assembly) kit m. ● vt (pt **kitted**) **~ out** équiper.

kitchen /'kɪtʃɪn/ n cuisine f.

kite /kaɪt/ n (toy) cerf-volant m; (bird) milan m.

kitten /'kɪtn/ n chaton m.

kitty /'kɪtɪ/ n (fund) cagnotte f.

knack /næk/ n tour m de main (**of doing** pour faire).

knead /niːd/ vt pétrir.

knee /niː/ n genou m. **~cap** n rotule f.

kneel /niːl/ vi (pt **knelt**) **~ (down)** se mettre à genoux; (in prayer) s'agenouiller.

knew /njuː/ ➡KNOW.

knickers /'nɪkəz/ npl petite culotte f, slip m.

knife /naɪf/ n (pl **knives**) couteau m. ● vt poignarder.

knight /naɪt/ n chevalier m; (chess) cavalier m. ● vt anoblir. **~hood** n titre m de chevalier.

knit /nɪt/ vt/i (pt **knitted** or **knit**) tricoter; (bones) (se) souder. **knitting** n tricot m. **knitwear** n tricots mpl.

knob /nɒb/ n bouton m.

knock /nɒk/ vt/i cogner; (criticize ⊞) critiquer; **~ sth off/out** faire tomber qch. ● n coup m. □ **~ down** (chair, pedestrian) renverser; (demolish) abattre; (reduce) baisser; **~ off** (stop work ⊞) arrêter de travailler; **~ £ 10 off** faire une réduction de 10 livres; **~ it off!** ⊞ ça suffit!; **~ out** assommer; **~ over** renverser; **~ up** (meal) préparer en vitesse.

knockout /'nɒkaʊt/ n (boxing) knock-out m.

knot /nɒt/ n nœud m. ● vt (pt **knotted**) nouer.

know /nəʊ/ vt/i (pt **knew**; pp **known**) (answer, reason, language) savoir (**that** que); (person, place, name, rule, situation) connaître; (recognize) reconnaître; **~ how to do** savoir faire; **~ about** (event) être au courant de; (subject) s'y connaître en; **~ of** (from experience) connaître; (from information) avoir entendu parler de. **~-how** n savoir-faire m inv.

knowingly /'nəʊɪŋlɪ/ adv (intentionally) délibérément; (meaningfully) d'un air entendu.

knowledge /'nɒlɪdʒ/ n connaissance f; (learning) connaissances fpl. **knowledgeable** adj savant.

knuckle /'nʌkl/ n jointure f, articulation f.

Koran /kə'rɑːn/ n Coran m.

Korea /kə'rɪə/ n Corée f.

kosher /'kəʊʃə(r)/ adj casher inv.

L l

lab /læb/ n ⊞ labo m.

label /'leɪbl/ n étiquette f. ● vt (pt **labelled**) étiqueter.

laboratory /lə'bɒrətrɪ/ n laboratoire m.

laborious /lə'bɔːrɪəs/ adj laborieux.

labour, (US) **labor** /'leɪbə(r)/ n travail m; (workers) main-d'œuvre f; **in ~** en train d'accoucher. ● vi peiner (**to do** faire). ● vt trop insister sur.

k
l

Labour /ˈleɪbə(r)/ n le parti travailliste.
● adj travailliste.

laboured /ˈleɪbəd/ adj laborieux.

labourer /ˈleɪbərə(r)/ n ouvrier/-ière
m/f; (on farm) ouvrier/-ière m/f
agricole.

lace /leɪs/ n dentelle f; (of shoe) lacet
m. ● vt (shoe) lacer; (drink) arroser.

lacerate /ˈlæsəreɪt/ vt lacérer.

lack /læk/ n manque m; **for ~ of** faute
de. ● vt manquer de; **be ~ing** manquer (**in** de).

lad /læd/ n garçon m, gars m.

ladder /ˈlædə(r)/ n échelle f; (in stocking) maille f filée. ● vt/i (stocking) filer.

laden /ˈleɪdn/ adj chargé (**with** de).

ladle /ˈleɪdl/ n louche f.

lady /ˈleɪdɪ/ n (pl **ladies**) dame f; **ladies
and gentlemen** mesdames et mes-
sieurs; **young ~** jeune femme or fille
f. **~bird** n coccinelle f.

ladylike /ˈleɪdɪlaɪk/ adj distingué.

lag /læg/ vi (pt **lagged**) traîner. ● vt
(pipes) calorifuger. ● n (interval) décalage m.

lager /ˈlɑːgə(r)/ n bière f blonde.

lagoon /ləˈguːn/ n lagune f.

laid /leɪd/ →LAY¹, **~ back** adj décontracté.

lain /leɪn/ →LIE².

lake /leɪk/ n lac m.

lamb /læm/ n agneau m; **leg of ~**
gigot m d'agneau.

lame /leɪm/ adj boiteux.

lament /ləˈment/ n lamentation f. ● vt/i
se lamenter (sur).

laminated /ˈlæmɪneɪtɪd/ adj laminé.

lamp /læmp/ n lampe f. **~post** n réverbère m. **~shade** n abat-jour m inv.

lance /lɑːns/ vt (Med) inciser.

land /lænd/ n terre f; (plot) terrain m;
(country) pays m. ● adj terrestre; (policy, reform) agraire. ● vt/i débarquer;
(aircraft) (se) poser, (faire) atterrir;
(fall) tomber; (obtain) décrocher; (a
blow) porter; **~ up** se retrouver.

landing /ˈlændɪŋ/ n débarquement m;
(Aviat) atterrissage m; (top of stairs)
palier m. **~stage** n débarcadère m.

land: ~lady n propriétaire f; (of pub)
patronne f. **~lord** n propriétaire m; (of
pub) patron m. **~mark** n (point de)
repère m. **~mine** n mine f terrestre.

landscape /ˈlænskeɪp/ n paysage m.
● vt aménager.

landslide /ˈlænslaɪd/ n glissement m
de terrain; (Pol) raz-de-marée m inv
(électoral).

lane /leɪn/ n (path, road) chemin m;
(strip of road) voie f; (of traffic) file f;
(Aviat) couloir m.

language /ˈlæŋgwɪdʒ/ n langue f;
(speech, style) langage m. **~ engineering** n ingénierie f des langues. **~
laboratory** n laboratoire m de langue.

lank /læŋk/ adj (hair) plat.

lanky /ˈlæŋkɪ/ adj (**-ier, -iest**) grand et
maigre.

lantern /ˈlæntən/ n lanterne f.

lap /læp/ n genoux mpl; (Sport) tour m
(de piste). ● vi (pt **lapped**) (waves)
clapoter. □ **~ up** laper.

lapel /ləˈpel/ n revers m.

lapse /læps/ vi (decline) se dégrader;
(expire) se périmer; **~ into** retomber
dans. ● n défaillance f, erreur f; (of
time) intervalle m.

laptop /ˈlæptɒp/ n (Comput) portable m.

lard /lɑːd/ n saindoux m.

larder /ˈlɑːdə(r)/ n garde-manger m inv.

large /lɑːdʒ/ adj grand, gros; **at ~** en
liberté; **by and ~** en général. **largely**
adv en grande mesure.

lark /lɑːk/ n (bird) alouette f; (bit of fun
🔲) rigolade f. ● vi 🔲 rigoler.

larva /ˈlɑːvə/ n (pl **-vae**) larve f.

laryngitis /lærɪnˈdʒaɪtɪs/ n laryngite f.

laser /ˈleɪzə(r)/ n laser m. **~ printer** n
imprimante f laser. **~ treatment** n
(Med) laserothérapie f.

lash /læʃ/ vt fouetter. ● n coup m de
fouet; (eyelash) cil m. □ **~ out**
(spend) dépenser follement; **~ out
against** attaquer.

lass /læs/ n jeune fille f.

lasso /læˈsuː/ n lasso m.

last /lɑːst/ adj dernier; **the ~ straw** le
comble; **the ~ word** le mot de la fin;
on its ~ legs sur le point de rendre
l'âme; **~ night** hier soir. ● adv en dernier; (most recently) la dernière fois.
● n dernier/-ière m/f; (remainder) reste
m; **at (long) ~** enfin. ● vi durer.
~-ditch adj ultime. **lasting** adj durable. **lastly** adv en dernier lieu.
~-minute adj de dernière minute.

latch /lætʃ/ n loquet m.

late /leɪt/ adj (not on time) en retard; (former) ancien; (hour, fruit) tardif; **the ~ Mrs X** feu Mme X. ● adv (not early) tard; (not on time) en retard; **in ~ July** fin juillet; **of ~** dernièrement. **lately** adv dernièrement. **latest** adj →LATE; (last) dernier.

lathe /leɪð/ n tour m.

lather /ˈlɑːðə(r)/ n mousse f. ● vt savonner. ● vi mousser.

Latin /ˈlætɪn/ n (Ling) latin m. ● adj latin. **~ America** n Amérique f latine.

latitude /ˈlætɪtjuːd/ n latitude f.

latter /ˈlætə(r)/ adj dernier. ● n **the ~** celui-ci, celle-ci.

Latvia /ˈlætvɪə/ n Lettonie f.

laudable /ˈlɔːdəbl/ adj louable.

laugh /lɑːf/ vi rire (**at** de). ● n rire m. **laughable** adj ridicule.

laughing stock n risée f.

laughter /ˈlɑːftə(r)/ n (act) rire m; (sound of laughs) rires mpl.

launch /lɔːntʃ/ vt (rocket) lancer; (boat) mettre à l'eau; **~ (out) into** se lancer dans. ● n lancement m; (boat) vedette f. **launching pad** n aire f de lancement.

launderette /lɔːndrəmæt/ n laverie f automatique.

laundry /ˈlɔːndrɪ/ n (place) blanchisserie f; (clothes) linge m.

laurel /ˈlɒrəl/ n laurier m.

lava /ˈlɑːvə/ n lave f.

lavatory /ˈlævətrɪ/ n toilettes fpl.

lavender /ˈlævəndə(r)/ n lavande f.

lavish /ˈlævɪʃ/ adj (person) généreux; (lush) somptueux. ● vt prodiguer (**on** à). **lavishly** adv luxueusement.

law /lɔː/ n loi f; (profession, subject of study) droit m; **~ and order** l'ordre public. **~-abiding** adj respectueux des lois. **~court** n tribunal m.

lawful /ˈlɔːfl/ adj légal.

lawn /lɔːn/ n pelouse f, gazon m. **~-mower** n tondeuse f à gazon.

lawsuit /ˈlɔːsuːt/ n procès m.

lawyer /ˈlɔːjə(r)/ n avocat m.

lax /læks/ adj (government) laxiste; (security) relâché.

laxative /ˈlæksətɪv/ n laxatif m.

lay¹ /leɪ/ adj (non-clerical) laïque; (worker) non-initié. ● vt (pt **laid**) poser; mettre; (trap) tendre; (table) mettre; (plan) former; (eggs) pondre. ● vi pondre; **~ waste** ravager. □ **~ aside** mettre de côté; **~ down** (dé)poser; (condition) (im-) poser; **~ off** vt (worker) licencier; vi 🔢 arrêter; **~ on** (provide) fournir; **~ out** (design) dessiner; (display) disposer; (money) dépenser.

lay² /leɪ/ →LIE².

lay-by /ˈleɪbaɪ/ n (pl **~s**) aire f de repos.

layer /ˈleɪə(r)/ n couche f.

layman /ˈleɪmən/ n (pl **-men**) profane m.

layout /ˈleɪaʊt/ n disposition f.

laze /leɪz/ vi paresser. **laziness** n paresse f. **lazy** adj (**-ier, -iest**) paresseux.

lead¹ /liːd/ vt/i (pt **led**) mener; (team) diriger; (life) mener; (induce) amener; **~ to** conduire à, mener à. ● n avance f; (clue) indice m; (leash) laisse f; (Theat) premier rôle m; (wire) fil m; **in the ~** en tête. □ **~ away** emmener; **~ up to** (come to) en venir à; (precede) précéder.

lead² /led/ n plomb m; (of pencil) mine f.

leader /ˈliːdə(r)/ n chef m; (of country, club) dirigeant/-e m/f; (leading article) éditorial m. **leadership** n direction f.

lead-free adj (petrol) sans plomb.

leading /ˈliːdɪŋ/ adj principal.

leaf /liːf/ n (pl **leaves**) feuille f; (of table) rallonge f. ● vi **~ through** feuilleter.

leaflet /ˈliːflɪt/ n prospectus m.

leafy /ˈliːfɪ/ adj feuillu.

league /liːg/ n ligue f; (Sport) championnat m; **in ~ with** de mèche avec.

leak /liːk/ n fuite f. ● vi fuir; (news: fig) s'ébruiter. ● vt répandre; (fig) divulguer.

lean¹ /liːn/ adj maigre. ● n (of meat) maigre m.

lean² /liːn/ vt/i (pt **leaned** or **leant**) (rest) (s')appuyer; (slope) pencher. □ **~ out** se pencher à l'extérieur; **~ over** (of person) se pencher.

leaning /ˈliːnɪŋ/ adj penché. ● n tendance f.

leap /liːp/ vi (pt **leaped** or **leapt**) bondir. ● n bond m. **~ year** n année f bissextile.

learn /lɜːn/ vt/i (pt **learned** or **learnt**) apprendre (**to do** à faire). **learned** adj érudit. **learner** n débutant/-e m/f. **learning curve** n courbe f d'apprentissage.

lease /liːs/ n bail m. ● vt louer à bail.

leash /liːʃ/ n laisse f.

least /liːst/ adj the ~ (smallest amount of) le moins de; (slightest) le or la moindre. ● n le moins. ● adv le moins; (with adjective) le or la moins; **at** ~ au moins.

leather /ˈleðə(r)/ n cuir m.

leave /liːv/ vt (pt **left**) laisser; (depart from) quitter; (person) laisser tranquille; **be left (over)** rester. ● n (holiday) congé m; (consent) permission f; **take one's** ~ prendre congé (**of** de); **on** ~ (Mil) en permission. □ ~ **alone** (thing) ne pas toucher; (person) laisser tranquille; ~ **behind** laisser; ~ **out** omettre.

Lebanon /ˈlebənən/ n Liban m.

lecture /ˈlektʃə(r)/ n cours m, conférence f; (rebuke) réprimande f. ● vt/i faire un cours or une conférence (à); (rebuke) réprimander. **lecturer** n conférencier/-ière m/f; (Univ) enseignant/-e m/f.

led /led/ →**LEAD**[1].

ledge /ledʒ/ n (window) rebord m; (rock) saillie f.

ledger /ˈledʒə(r)/ n grand livre m.

leech /liːtʃ/ n sangsue f.

leek /liːk/ n poireau m.

leer /lɪə(r)/ vi ~ **(at)** lorgner. ● n regard m sournois.

leeway /ˈliːweɪ/ n (fig) liberté f d'action; (Naut) dérive f.

left /left/ →**LEAVE**. ● adj gauche. ● adv à gauche. ● n gauche f. ~**-hand** adj à or de gauche. ~**-handed** adj gaucher.

left luggage (office) n consigne f.

left-overs npl restes mpl.

left-wing adj de gauche.

leg /leg/ n jambe f; (of animal) patte f; (of table) pied m; (of chicken) cuisse f; (of lamb) gigot m; (of journey) étape f.

legacy /ˈlegəsɪ/ n legs m.

legal /ˈliːgl/ adj légal; (affairs) juridique.

legend /ˈledʒənd/ n légende f.

leggings /ˈlegɪŋz/ npl (for woman) caleçon m.

legible /ˈledʒəbl/ adj lisible.

legionnaire /liːdʒəˈneə(r)/ n légionnaire m.

legislation /ledʒɪsˈleɪʃn/ n (body of laws) législation f; (law) loi f. **legislature** n corps m législatif.

legitimate /lɪˈdʒɪtɪmət/ adj légitime.

leisure /ˈleʒə(r)/ n loisirs mpl; **at one's** ~ à tête reposée. ● adj (centre) de loisirs.

leisurely /ˈleʒəlɪ/ adj lent. ● adv sans se presser.

lemon /ˈlemən/ n citron m.

lemonade /leməˈneɪd/ n (fizzy) limonade f; (still) citronnade f.

lend /lend/ vt (pt **lent**) prêter; (credibility) conférer; ~ **itself to** se prêter à.

length /leŋθ/ n longueur f; (in time) durée f; (section) morceau m; **at** ~ (at last) enfin; **at (great)** ~ longuement.

lengthen /ˈleŋθən/ vt/i (s')allonger.

lengthways /ˈleŋθweɪz/ adv dans le sens de la longueur.

lengthy /ˈleŋθɪ/ adj long.

lenient /ˈliːnɪənt/ adj indulgent.

lens /lenz/ n lentille f; (of spectacles) verre m; (Photo) objectif m.

lent /lent/ →**LEND**.

Lent /lent/ n Carême m.

lentil /ˈlentl/ n lentille f.

Leo /ˈliːəʊ/ n Lion m.

leopard /ˈlepəd/ n léopard m.

leotard /ˈliːətɑːd/ n body m.

leprosy /ˈleprəsɪ/ n lèpre f.

lesbian /ˈlezbɪən/ n lesbienne f. ● adj lesbien.

less /les/ adj (in quantity) moins de (**than** que). ● adv, n & prep moins; ~ **than** (with numbers) moins de; **work** ~ **than** travailler moins que; **ten pounds** ~ dix livres de moins; ~ **and** ~ de moins en moins. **lessen** vt/i diminuer. **lesser** adj moindre.

lesson /ˈlesn/ n leçon f.

let /let/ vt (pt **let**; pres p **letting**) laisser; (lease) louer. ● v aux ~ **us do**, ~'**s do** faisons; ~ **him do** qu'il fasse; ~ **me know the results** informe-moi des résultats. ● n location f. □ ~ **down** baisser; (deflate) dégonfler; (fig) décevoir; ~ **go** vt lâcher; vi lâcher prise; ~ **sb in/out** laisser or faire entrer/sortir qn; ~ **a dress out** élargir une robe; ~

oneself in for (*task*) s'engager à; (*trouble*) s'attirer; ~ **off** (explode, fire) faire éclater *or* partir; (excuse) dispenser; (not punish) ne pas punir; ~ **up** ⊡ s'arrêter.

let-down *n* déception *f*.

lethal /'li:θl/ *adj* mortel; (weapon) meurtrier.

letter /'letə(r)/ *n* lettre *f*. ~**-bomb** *n* lettre *f* piégée. ~**-box** *n* boîte *f* à *or* aux lettres.

lettering /'letərɪŋ/ *n* (letters) caractères *mpl*.

lettuce /'letɪs/ *n* laitue *f*, salade *f*.

let-up /'letʌp/ *n* répit *m*.

leukaemia /lu:'ki:mɪə/ *n* leucémie *f*.

level /'levl/ *adj* plat, uni; (on surface) horizontal; (in height) au même niveau (**with** que); (in score) à égalité. ● *n* niveau *m*; (spirit) ~ niveau *m* à bulle; **be on the** ~ ⊡ être franc. ● *vt* (*pt* **levelled**) niveler; (aim) diriger. ~ **crossing** *n* passage *m* à niveau. ~**-headed** *adj* équilibré.

lever /'li:və(r)/ *n* levier *m*. ● *vt* soulever au moyen d'un levier.

leverage /'li:vərɪdʒ/ *n* influence *f*.

levy /'levɪ/ *vt* (tax) prélever. ● *n* impôt *m*.

lexicon /'leksɪkən/ *n* lexique *m*.

liability /laɪə'bɪlətɪ/ *n* responsabilité *f*; ⊡ handicap *m*; **liabilities** (debts) dettes *fpl*.

liable /'laɪəbl/ *adj* be ~ **to do** avoir tendance à faire, pouvoir faire; ~ **to** (illness) sujet à; (fine) passible de; ~ **for** responsable de.

liaise /lɪ'eɪz/ *vi* ⊡ faire la liaison. **liaison** *n* liaison *f*.

liar /'laɪə(r)/ *n* menteur/-euse *m/f*.

libel /'laɪbl/ *n* diffamation *f*. ● *vt* (*pt* **libelled**) diffamer.

liberal /'lɪbərəl/ *adj* libéral; (generous) généreux, libéral.

Liberal /'lɪbərəl/ *adj & n* (Pol) libéral/-e (*m/f*).

liberate /'lɪbəreɪt/ *vt* libérer.

liberty /'lɪbətɪ/ *n* liberté *f*; **at** ~ **to** libre de; **take liberties** prendre des libertés.

Libra /'li:brə/ *n* Balance *f*.

librarian /laɪ'breərɪən/ *n* bibliothécaire *mf*.

library /'laɪbrərɪ/ *n* bibliothèque *f*.

libretto /lɪ'bretəʊ/ *n* livret *m*.

lice /laɪs/ ➡LOUSE.

licence, (US) **license** /'laɪsns/ *n* permis *m*; (for television) redevance *f*; (Comm) licence *f*; (liberty: fig) licence *f*. ~ **plate** *n* plaque *f* minéralogique.

license /'laɪsns/ *vt* accorder un permis à, autoriser.

lick /lɪk/ *vt* lécher; (defeat ⊡) rosser; (fig) **a** ~ **of paint** un petit coup de peinture. ● *n* coup *m* de langue.

lid /lɪd/ *n* couvercle *m*.

lie¹ /laɪ/ *n* mensonge *m*. ● *vi* (*pt* **lied**; *pres p* **lying**) (tell lies) mentir.

lie² /laɪ/ *vi* (*pt* **lay**; *pp* **lain**; *pres p* **lying**) s'allonger; (remain) rester; (be) se trouver, être; (in grave) reposer; **be lying** être allongé. □ ~ **down** s'allonger; ~ **in** faire la grasse matinée; ~ **low** se cacher.

lieutenant /lef'tenənt/ *n* lieutenant *m*.

life /laɪf/ *n* (*pl* **lives**) vie *f*. ~**-belt** *n* bouée *f* de sauvetage. ~**boat** *n* canot *m* de sauvetage. ~**buoy** *n* bouée *f* de sauvetage. ~ **coach** *n* conseiller/ère *m/f* en développement personnel. ~ **cycle** *n* cycle *m* de vie. ~**-guard** *n* sauveteur *m*. ~ **insurance** *n* assurance-vie *f*. ~**-jacket** *n* gilet *m* de sauvetage.

lifeless /'laɪflɪs/ *adj* inanimé.

lifelike /'laɪflaɪk/ *adj* très ressemblant.

life: ~**long** *adj* de toute la vie. ~ **sentence** *n* condamnation *f* à perpétuité. ~**-size(d)** *adj* grandeur nature *inv*. ~ **story** *n* vie *f*. ~**-style** *n* style *m* de vie. ~ **support machine** *n* appareil *m* de respiration artificielle.

lifetime /'laɪftaɪm/ *n* vie *f*; **in one's** ~ de son vivant.

lift /lɪft/ *vt* lever; (steal ⊡) voler. ● *vi* (of fog) se lever. ● *n* (in building) ascenseur *m*; **give a** ~ **to** emmener (en voiture). ~**-off** *n* (Aviat) décollage *m*.

light /laɪt/ *n* lumière *f*; (lamp) lampe *f*; (for fire, on vehicle) feu *m*; (headlight) phare *m*; **bring to** ~ révéler; **come to** ~ être révélé; **have you got a** ~? vous avez du feu? ● *adj* (not dark) clair; (not heavy) léger. ● *vt* (*pt* **lit** *or* **lighted**) allumer; (room) éclairer; (match) frotter. □ ~ **up** *vi* s'allumer; *vt* (room) éclairer. ~ **bulb** *n* ampoule *f*.

lighten /'laɪtn/ vt (give light to) éclairer; (make brighter) éclaircir; (make less heavy) alléger.

lighter /'laɪtə(r)/ n briquet m; (for stove) allume-gaz m inv.

light: ~**-headed** adj (dizzy) qui a un vertige; (frivolous) étourdi. ~**-hearted** adj gai. ~**house** f phare m.

lighting /'laɪtɪŋ/ n éclairage m.

lightly /'laɪtlɪ/ adv légèrement.

lightning /'laɪtnɪŋ/ n éclair m, foudre f. ● adj (visit) éclair inv.

lightweight /'laɪtweɪt/ adj léger. ● n (boxing) poids m léger.

light year n année f lumière.

like¹ /laɪk/ adj semblable, pareil; be ~**-minded** avoir les mêmes sentiments. ● prep comme. ● conj [T] comme. ● n pareil m; **the ~s of you** les gens comme vous.

like² /laɪk/ vt aimer (bien); **I should ~** je voudrais, j'aimerais; **would you ~?** voudriez-vous?, voudrais-tu?; ~**s** goûts mpl. **likeable** adj sympathique.

likelihood /'laɪklɪhʊd/ n probabilité f.

likely /'laɪklɪ/ adj (**-ier, -iest**) probable. ● adv probablement; **he is ~ to do it** fera probablement; **not ~!** [T] pas question!

likeness /'laɪknɪs/ n ressemblance f.

likewise /'laɪkwaɪz/ adv également.

liking /'laɪkɪŋ/ n (for thing) penchant m; (for person) affection f.

lilac /'laɪlək/ n lilas m. ● adj lilas inv.

Lilo® /'laɪləʊ/ n matelas m pneumatique.

lily /'lɪlɪ/ n lis m, lys m.

limb /lɪm/ n membre m.

limber /'lɪmbə(r)/ vi ~ **up** faire des exercices d'assouplissement.

limbo /'lɪmbəʊ/ n **be in ~** (forgotten) être tombé dans l'oubli.

lime /laɪm/ n (fruit) citron m vert; ~**(-tree)** tilleul m.

limelight /'laɪmlaɪt/ n **in the ~** en vedette.

limestone /'laɪmstəʊn/ n calcaire m.

limit /'lɪmɪt/ n limite f. ● vt limiter.

limited company n société f anonyme.

limp /lɪmp/ vi boiter. ● n **have a ~** boiter. ● adj mou.

line /laɪn/ n ligne f; (track) voie f; (wrinkle) ride f; (row) rangée f, file f; (of poem) vers m; (rope) corde f; (of goods) gamme f; (queue: US) queue f; **be in ~ for** avoir de bonnes chances de; **hold the ~** ne quittez pas; **in ~ with** en accord avec; **stand in ~** faire la queue. ● vt (paper) régler; (streets) border; (garment) doubler; (fill) remplir, garnir. □ ~ **up** (s')aligner; (in queue) faire la queue; ~ **sth up** prévoir qch. ~ **dancing** danse f en ligne.

linen /'lɪnɪn/ n (sheets) linge m; (material) lin m.

liner /'laɪnə(r)/ n paquebot m.

linesman /'laɪnzmən/ n (football) juge m de touche; (tennis) juge m de ligne.

linger /'lɪŋɡə(r)/ vi s'attarder; (smells) persister.

linguist /'lɪŋɡwɪst/ n linguiste mf. **linguistics** n linguistique f.

lining /'laɪnɪŋ/ n doublure f.

link /lɪŋk/ n lien m; (of chain) maillon m. ● vt relier; (relate) (re)lier; ~ **up** (of roads) se rejoindre. **linkage** n lien m. **links** n inv terrain m de golf. ~**-up** n liaison f.

lino /'laɪnəʊ/ n lino m.

lion /'laɪən/ n lion m. **lioness** n lionne f.

lip /lɪp/ n lèvre f; (edge) rebord m; **pay** ~**-service to** n'approuver que pour la forme. ~**-read** vt/i lire sur les lèvres. ~**salve** n baume m pour les lèvres. ~**stick** n rouge m (à lèvres).

liquid /'lɪkwɪd/ n & adj liquide (m).

liquidation /lɪkwɪ'deɪʃn/ n liquidation f; **go into ~** déposer son bilan.

liquidize /'lɪkwɪdaɪz/ vt passer au mixeur. **liquidizer** n mixeur m.

liquor /'lɪkə(r)/ n alcool m.

liquorice /'lɪkərɪs/ n réglisse f.

lisp /lɪsp/ n zézaiement m; **with a ~** en zézayant. ● vi zézayer.

list /lɪst/ n liste f. ● vt dresser la liste de. ● vi (ship) gîter.

listen /'lɪsn/ vi écouter; ~ **to, ~ in (to)** écouter. **listener** n auditeur/-trice m/f.

listless /'lɪstlɪs/ adj apathique.

lit /lɪt/ ➡LIGHT.

liter ➡LITRE.

literal /'lɪtərəl/ adj (meaning) littéral; (translation) mot à mot. **literally** adv littéralement; mot à mot.

literary /'lɪtərərɪ/ adj littéraire.

literate /'lɪtərət/ adj qui sait lire et écrire.

literature /'lɪtrətʃə(r)/ n littérature f; (brochures) documentation f.

Lithuania /lɪθju:'eɪnɪə/ n Lituanie f.

litigation /lɪtɪ'geɪʃn/ n litiges mpl.

litre, (US) **liter** /'li:tə(r)/ n litre m.

litter /'lɪtə(r)/ n (rubbish) détritus mpl, papiers mpl; (animals) portée f. ● vt éparpiller; (make untidy) laisser des détritus dans; ~**ed with** jonché de. ~**-bin** n poubelle f.

little /'lɪtl/ adj petit; (not much) peu de. ● n peu m; **a** ~ un peu (de). ● adv peu.

live¹ /laɪv/ adj vivant; (wire) sous tension; (broadcast) en direct; **be a** ~ **wire** être très dynamique.

live² /lɪv/ vt/i vivre; (reside) habiter, vivre; ~ **it up** mener la belle vie. □ ~ **down** faire oublier; ~ **on** (feed oneself on) vivre de; (continue) survivre; ~ **up to** se montrer à la hauteur de.

livelihood /'laɪvlɪhʊd/ n moyens mpl d'existence.

lively /'laɪvlɪ/ adj (-ier, -iest) vif, vivant.

liven /'laɪvn/ vt/i ~ **up** (s')animer; (cheer up) (s')égayer.

liver /'lɪvə(r)/ n foie m.

livestock /'laɪvstɒk/ n bétail m.

livid /'lɪvɪd/ adj livide; (angry) furieux.

living /'lɪvɪŋ/ adj vivant. ● n vie f; **make a** ~ gagner sa vie; ~ **conditions** conditions fpl de vie. ~**-room** n salle f de séjour.

lizard /'lɪzəd/ n lézard m.

load /ləʊd/ n charge f; (loaded goods) chargement m, charge f; (weight, strain) poids m; ~**s of** 🇬🇧 des tas de 🇬🇧. ● vt charger.

loaf /ləʊf/ n (pl **loaves**) pain m. ● vi ~ (**about**) fainéanter.

loan /ləʊn/ n prêt m; (money borrowed) emprunt m. ● vt prêter.

loathe /ləʊð/ vt détester (**doing** faire). **loathing** n dégoût m.

lobby /'lɒbɪ/ n entrée f, vestibule m; (Pol) lobby m, groupe m de pression. ● vt faire pression sur.

lobster /'lɒbstə(r)/ n homard m.

local /'ləʊkl/ adj local; (shops) du quartier; ~ **government** administration f

locale. ● n personne f du coin; (pub 🇬🇧) pub m du coin.

localization /ləʊklaɪ'zeɪʃn/ n localisation f.

locally /'ləʊklɪ/ adv localement; (nearby) dans les environs.

locate /ləʊ'keɪt/ vt (situate) situer; (find) repérer.

location /ləʊ'keɪʃn/ n emplacement m; **on** ~ (cinema) en extérieur.

lock /lɒk/ n (of door) serrure f; (on canal) écluse f; (of hair) mèche f. ● vt/i fermer à clef; (wheels: Auto) (se) bloquer. □ ~ **in** or **up** (person) enfermer; ~ **out** (by mistake) enfermer dehors.

locker /'lɒkə(r)/ n casier m.

locket /'lɒkɪt/ n médaillon m.

locksmith /'lɒksmɪθ/ n serrurier m.

locum /'ləʊkəm/ n (doctor) remplaçant/-e m/f.

lodge /lɒdʒ/ n (house) pavillon m (de gardien or de chasse); (of porter) loge f. ● vt (accommodate) loger; (money, complaint) déposer. ● vi être logé (**with** chez); (become fixed) se loger. **lodger** n locataire mf, pensionnaire mf. **lodgings** n logement m.

loft /lɒft/ n grenier m.

lofty /'lɒftɪ/ adj (-ier, -iest) (tall, noble) élevé; (haughty) hautain.

log /lɒg/ n (of wood) bûche f; ~ (~**book**) (Naut) journal m de bord; (Auto) ≈ carte f grise. ● vt (pt **logged**) noter; (distance) parcourir. □ ~ **on** (Comput) se connecter; ~ **off** (Comput) se déconnecter.

logic /'lɒdʒɪk/ adj logique. **logical** adj logique.

logistics /lə'dʒɪstɪks/ n logistique f.

loin /lɔɪn/ n (Culin) filet m; ~**s** reins mpl.

loiter /'lɔɪtə(r)/ vi traîner.

loll /lɒl/ vi se prélasser.

lollipop /'lɒlɪpɒp/ n sucette f.

London /'lʌndən/ n Londres. **Londoner** n Londonien/-ne m/f.

lone /ləʊn/ adj solitaire.

lonely (-ier, -iest) solitaire; (person) seul, solitaire.

long /lɒŋ/ adj long; **how** ~ **is?** quelle est la longueur de?; (in time) quelle est la durée de?; **how** ~? combien de temps?; **a** ~ **time** longtemps. ● adv longtemps; **he will not be** ~ il n'en a pas pour longtemps; **as** or **so ~ as** pourvu que; **before ~** avant peu; **I no ~er do** je ne fais plus. ● vi avoir bien or très envie (**for, to** de); **~ for sb** (pine for) se languir de qn. **~-distance** adj (flight) sur long parcours; (phone call) interurbain; (runner) de fond. **~ face** n grimace f. **~hand** n écriture f courante.

longing /'lɒŋɪŋ/ n envie f (**for** de); (nostalgia) nostalgie f (**for** de).

longitude /'lɒndʒɪtjuːd/ n longitude f.

long: ~ **jump** n saut m en longueur. **~-range** adj (missile) à longue portée; (forecast) à long terme. **~-sighted** adj presbyte. **~-standing** adj de longue date. **~-term** adj à long terme. **~ wave** n grandes ondes fpl. **~-winded** adj verbeux.

loo /luː/ n 🇬🇧 toilettes fpl.

look /lʊk/ vi regarder; (seem) avoir l'air; **~ like** ressembler à, avoir l'air de. ● n regard m; (appearance) air m, aspect m; (good) **~s** beauté f. ▢ **~ after** s'occuper de, soigner; **~ at** regarder; **~ back on** repenser à; **~ down on** mépriser; **~ for** chercher; **~ forward to** attendre avec impatience; **~ in on** passer voir; **~ into** examiner; **~ out** faire attention; **~ out for** (person) guetter; (symptoms) guetter l'apparition de; **~ round** se retourner; **~ up** (word) chercher; (visit) passer voir; **~ up to** respecter.

lookout /'lʊkaʊt/ n (Mil) poste m de guet; (person) guetteur m; **be on the ~ for** rechercher.

loom /luːm/ vi surgir; (war) menacer; (interview) être imminent. ● n métier m à tisser.

loony /'luːnɪ/ n & adj 🇬🇧 fou, folle (mf).

loop /luːp/ n boucle f. ● vt boucler. **~hole** n lacune f.

loose /luːs/ adj (knot) desserré; (page) détaché; (clothes) ample, lâche; (tooth) qui bouge; (lax) relâché; (not packed) en vrac; (inexact) vague; (pej) immoral; **at a ~ end** désœuvré; **come ~** bouger. **loosely** adv sans serrer; (roughly) vaguement. **loosen** vt (slacken) desserrer; (untie) défaire.

loot /luːt/ n butin m. ● vt piller.

lord /lɔːd/ n seigneur m; (British title) lord m; **the L~** le Seigneur; **(good) L~!** mon Dieu!

lorry /'lɒrɪ/ n camion m.

lose /luːz/ vt/i (pt **lost**) perdre; **get lost** se perdre. **loser** n perdant/-e m/f.

loss /lɒs/ n perte f; **be at a ~** être perplexe; **be at a ~ to** être incapable de; **heat ~** déperdition f de chaleur.

lost /lɒst/ →LOSE. ● adj perdu. **~ property** n objets mpl trouvés.

lot /lɒt/ n **the ~** (le) tout; (people) tous mpl, toutes fpl; **a ~ (of)**, **~s (of)** 🇬🇧 beaucoup (de); **quite a ~ (of)** 🇬🇧 pas mal (de); (fate) sort m; (at auction) lot m; (land) lotissement m.

lotion /'ləʊʃn/ n lotion f.

lottery /'lɒtərɪ/ n loterie f.

loud /laʊd/ adj bruyant, fort. ● adv fort; **out ~** tout haut. **loudly** adv fort. **~speaker** n haut-parleur m.

lounge /laʊndʒ/ vi paresser. ● n salon m.

louse /laʊs/ n (pl **lice**) pou m.

lousy /'laʊzɪ/ adj (**-ier, -iest**) 🇬🇧 infect.

lout /laʊt/ n rustre m.

lovable /'lʌvəbl/ adj adorable.

love /lʌv/ n amour m; (tennis) zéro m; **in ~** amoureux (**with** de); **make ~** faire l'amour. ● vt (person) aimer; (like greatly) aimer (beaucoup) (**to do** faire). **~ affair** n liaison f amoureuse. **~ life** n vie f amoureuse.

lovely /'lʌvlɪ/ adj (**-ier, -iest**) joli; (delightful 🇬🇧) très agréable.

lover /'lʌvə(r)/ n (male) amant m; (female) maîtresse f; (devotee) amateur m (**of** de).

loving /'lʌvɪŋ/ adj affectueux.

low /ləʊ/ adj & adv bas; **~ in sth** à faible teneur en qch. ● n (low pressure) dépression f; **reach a (new) ~** atteindre son niveau le plus bas. ● vi meugler. **~-calorie** adj basses-calories. **~-cut** adj décolleté.

lower /'ləʊə(r)/ adj & adv →LOW. ● vt baisser; **~ oneself** s'abaisser.

low: **~-fat** adj (diet) sans matières grasses; (cheese) allégé. **~-key** adj modéré; (discreet) discret. **~lands** npl plaine(s) f(pl). **~-lying** adj à faible altitude.

loyal /'lɔɪəl/ adj loyal (**to** envers).

loyalty /'lɔɪəltɪ/ n fidélité f. **~ card** n carte f de fidélité.

lozenge /'lɒzəndʒ/ n (shape) losange m; (tablet) pastille f.

LP *n* (disque *m*) 33 tours *m*.

Ltd. *abbr* (**Limited**) SA.

lubricant /'lu:brɪkənt/ *n* lubrifiant *m*.

lubricate *vt* lubrifier.

luck /lʌk/ *n* chance *f*; **bad** ∼ malchance *f*; **good** ∼**!** bonne chance!

luckily /'lʌkɪlɪ/ *adv* heureusement.

lucky /'lʌkɪ/ *adj* (**-ier, -iest**) qui a de la chance, heureux; (event) heureux; (number) qui porte bonheur; **it's** ∼ **that** heureusement que.

ludicrous /'lu:dɪkrəs/ *adj* ridicule.

lug /lʌg/ *vt* (*pt* **lugged**) traîner.

luggage /'lʌgɪdʒ/ *n* bagages *mpl*. ∼**-rack** *n* porte-bagages *m inv*.

lukewarm /lu:k'wɔ:m/ *adj* tiède.

lull /lʌl/ *vt* **he** ∼**ed them into thinking that** il leur a fait croire que. ● *n* accalmie *f*.

lullaby /'lʌləbaɪ/ *n* berceuse *f*.

lumber /'lʌmbə(r)/ *n* bois *m* de charpente. ● *vt* 🇬🇧 ∼ **sb with** (*chore*) coller à qn 🇬🇧. ∼**jack** *n* bûcheron *m*.

luminous /'lu:mɪnəs/ *adj* lumineux.

lump /lʌmp/ *n* morceau *m*; (swelling on body) grosseur *f*; (in liquid) grumeau *m*. ● *vt* ∼ **together** réunir. ∼ **sum** *n* somme *f* globale.

lunacy /'lu:nəsɪ/ *n* folie *f*.

lunar /'lu:nə(r)/ *adj* lunaire.

lunatic /'lu:nətɪk/ *n* fou/folle *m/f*.

lunch /lʌntʃ/ *n* déjeuner *m*. ● *vi* déjeuner.

luncheon /'lʌntʃən/ *n* déjeuner *m*. ∼ **voucher** *n* chèque-repas *m*.

lung /lʌŋ/ *n* poumon *m*.

lunge /lʌndʒ/ *vi* bondir (**at** sur; **forward** en avant).

lurch /lɜ:tʃ/ *n* **leave in the** ∼ planter là, laisser en plan. ● *vi* (*person*) tituber.

lure /lʊə(r)/ *vt* appâter, attirer. ● *n* (attraction) attrait *m*, appât *m*.

lurid /'lʊərɪd/ *adj* choquant, affreux; (gaudy) voyant.

lurk /lɜ:k/ *vi* se cacher; (in ambush) s'embusquer; (prowl) rôder; (*suspicion, danger*) menacer.

luscious /'lʌʃəs/ *adj* appétissant.

lush /lʌʃ/ *adj* luxuriant.

lust /lʌst/ *n* luxure *f*.

Luxemburg /'lʌksəmbɜːg/ *n* Luxembourg *m*.

luxurious /lʌg'zjʊərɪəs/ *adj* luxueux.

luxury /'lʌkʃərɪ/ *n* luxe *m*. ● *adj* de luxe.

lying /'laɪɪŋ/ ➡LIE[1], ➡LIE[2]. ● *n* mensonges *mpl*.

lyric /'lɪrɪk/ *adj* lyrique. **lyrical** *adj* lyrique. **lyrics** *npl* paroles *fpl*.

Mm

MA *abbr* ➡MASTER OF ARTS.

mac /mæk/ *n* 🇬🇧 imper *m*.

machine /mə'ʃi:n/ *n* machine *f*. ● *vt* (sew) coudre à la machine; (Tech) usiner. ∼**gun** *n* mitrailleuse *f*.

mackerel /'mækrəl/ *n inv* maquereau *m*.

mackintosh /'mækɪntɒʃ/ *n* imperméable *m*.

mad /mæd/ *adj* (**madder, maddest**) fou; (foolish) insensé; (*dog*) enragé; (angry 🇬🇧) furieux; **be** ∼ **about** se passionner pour; (*person*) être fou de; **drive sb** ∼ exaspérer qn; **like** ∼ comme un fou. ∼ **cow disease** *n* maladie *f* de la vache folle.

madam /'mædəm/ *n* madame *f*; (unmarried) mademoiselle *f*.

made /meɪd/ ➡MAKE.

madly /'mædlɪ/ *adv* (interested, in love) follement; (frantically) comme un fou.

madman /'mædmən/ *n* (*pl* **-men**) fou *m*.

madness /'mædnɪs/ *n* folie *f*.

magazine /mægə'zi:n/ *n* revue *f*, magazine *m*; (of gun) magasin *m*.

maggot /'mægət/ *n* (in fruit) ver *m*, (for fishing) asticot *m*.

magic /'mædʒɪk/ *n* magie *f*. ● *adj* magique.

magician /mə'dʒɪʃn/ *n* magicien/-ne *m/f*.

magistrate /'mædʒɪstreɪt/ *n* magistrat *m*.

magnet /'mægnɪt/ *n* aimant *m*. **magnetic** *adj* magnétique.

magnificent /mæg'nɪfɪsnt/ adj magnifique.

magnify /'mægnɪfaɪ/ vt grossir; (sound) amplifier; (fig) exagérer. **magnifying glass** n loupe f.

magpie /'mægpaɪ/ n pie f.

mahogany /mə'hɒgənɪ/ n acajou m.

maid /meɪd/ n (servant) bonne f; (in hotel) femme f de chambre.

maiden /'meɪdn/ n (old use) jeune fille f. ● adj (aunt) célibataire; (voyage) premier. ~ **name** n nom m de jeune fille.

mail /meɪl/ n (postal service) poste f; (letters) courrier m; (armour) cotte f de mailles. ● adj (bag, van) postal. ● vt envoyer par la poste. ~ **box** n boîte f aux lettres; (Comput) boîte f aux lettres électronique. **mailing list** n liste f d'adresses. ~**man** n (pl **-men**) (US) facteur m. ~ **order** n vente f par correspondance. ~ **shot** n publipostage m.

main /meɪn/ adj principal; a ~ **road** une grande route. ● n (water/gas) ~ conduite f d'eau/de gaz; **the** ~**s** (Electr) le secteur; **in the** ~ en général. ~**frame** n unité f centrale. ~**land** n continent m. ~**stream** n tendance f principale, ligne f.

maintain /meɪn'teɪn/ vt (continue, keep, assert) maintenir; (house, machine, family) entretenir; (rights) soutenir.

maintenance /'meɪntənəns/ n (care) entretien m; (continuation) maintien m; (allowance) pension f alimentaire.

maisonette /meɪzə'net/ n duplex m.

maize /meɪz/ n maïs m.

majestic /mə'dʒestɪk/ adj majestueux.

majesty /'mædʒəstɪ/ n majesté f.

major /'meɪdʒə(r)/ adj majeur. ● n commandant m. ● vi ~ **in** (Univ, US) se spécialiser en.

majority /mə'dʒɒrətɪ/ n majorité f; **the** ~ **of people** la plupart des gens. ● adj majoritaire.

make /meɪk/ vt/i (pt **made**) faire; (manufacture) fabriquer; (friends) se faire; (money) gagner; (decision) prendre; (place, position) arriver à; (cause to be) rendre; ~ **sb do sth** faire faire qch à qn; (force) obliger qn à faire qch; **be made of** être fait de; ~ **one-**

self **at home** se mettre à l'aise; ~ **sb happy** rendre qn heureux; ~ **it** arriver; (succeed) réussir; **I** ~ **it two o'clock** j'ai deux heures; **I** ~ **it 150** d'après moi, ça fait 150; **I cannot** ~ **anything of it** je n'y comprends rien; **can you** ~ **Friday?** vendredi, c'est possible?; ~ **as if to** faire mine de. ● n (brand) marque f. □ ~ **do** (manage) se débrouiller (**with** avec); ~ **for** se diriger vers; (cause) tendre à créer; ~ **good** vi réussir; vt compenser; (repair) réparer; ~ **off** filer (**with** avec); ~ **out** distinguer; (understand) comprendre; (draw up) faire; (assert) prétendre; ~ **up** vt faire, former; (story) inventer; (deficit) combler; vi se réconcilier; ~ **up for** compenser; (time) rattraper; ~ **up one's mind** se décider.

make-believe adj feint, illusoire. ● n fantaisie f.

maker /'meɪkə(r)/ n fabricant m.

makeshift /'meɪkʃɪft/ adj improvisé.

make-up /'meɪkʌp/ n maquillage m; (of object) constitution f; (Psych) caractère m.

malaria /mə'leərɪə/ n paludisme m.

Malaysia /mə'leɪzɪə/ n Malaisie f.

male /meɪl/ adj (voice, sex) masculin; (Bot, Tech) mâle. ● n mâle m.

malfunction /mæl'fʌŋkʃn/ n mauvais fonctionnement m. ● vi mal fonctionner.

malice /'mælɪs/ n méchanceté f. **malicious** adj méchant.

malignant /mə'lɪgnənt/ adj malveillant; (tumour) malin.

mall /mɔːl/ n (shopping) ~ (in suburbs) centre m commercial; (in town) galerie f marchande.

malnutrition /mælnjuː'trɪʃn/ n sous-alimentation f.

Malta /'mɔːltə/ n Malte f.

mammal /'mæml/ n mammifère m.

mammoth /'mæməθ/ n mammouth m. ● adj (task) gigantesque; (organization) géant.

man /mæn/ n (pl **men**) homme m; (in sports team) joueur m; (chess) pièce f; ~ **to man** d'homme à homme. ● vt (pt **manned**) (desk) tenir; (ship) armer; (guns) servir; (be on duty at) être de service à.

m

manage /'mænɪdʒ/ vt (project, organization) diriger; (shop, affairs) gérer; (handle) manier; **I could ~ another drink** 🖭 je prendrais bien encore un verre; **can you ~ Friday?** vendredi, c'est possible? ● vi se débrouiller; **~ to do** réussir à faire. **manageable** adj (tool, size, person) maniable; (job) faisable.

management /'mænɪdʒmənt/ n (managers) direction f; (of shop) gestion f.

manager /'mænɪdʒə(r)/ n directeur/-trice m/f; (of shop) gérant/-e m/f; (of actor) impresario m.

mandate /'mændeɪt/ n mandat m.

mandatory /'mændətərɪ/ adj obligatoire.

mane /meɪn/ n crinière f.

mango /'mæŋɡəʊ/ n (pl ~es) mangue f.

manhandle /'mænhændl/ vt maltraiter, malmener.

man: **~hole** n regard m. **~hood** n âge m d'homme; (quality) virilité f.

maniac /'meɪnɪæk/ n maniaque mf, fou m, folle f.

manicure /'mænɪkjʊə(r)/ n manucure f. ● vt soigner, manucurer.

manifest /'mænɪfest/ adj manifeste. ● vt manifester.

manipulate /mə'nɪpjʊleɪt/ vt (tool, person) manipuler.

mankind /mæn'kaɪnd/ n genre m humain.

manly /'mænlɪ/ adj viril.

man-made adj (fibre) synthétique; (pond) artificiel; (disaster) d'origine humaine.

manned // adj (spacecraft) habité.

manner /'mænə(r)/ n manière f; (attitude) attitude f; (kind) sorte f; **~s** (social behaviour) manières fpl.

mannerism /'mænərɪzəm/ n particularité f; (quirk) manie f.

manoeuvre /mə'nuːvə(r)/ n manœuvre f. ● vt/i manœuvrer.

manor /'mænə(r)/ n manoir m.

manpower /'mænpaʊə(r)/ n main-d'œuvre f.

mansion /'mænʃn/ n (in countryside) demeure f; (in town) hôtel m particulier.

manslaughter /'mænslɔːtə(r)/ n homicide m involontaire.

mantelpiece /'mæntlʃelf/ n (manteau m de) cheminée.

manual /'mænjʊəl/ adj (labour) manuel; (typewriter) mécanique. ● n (handbook) manuel m.

manufacture /mænjʊ'fæktʃə(r)/ vt fabriquer. ● n fabrication f.

manure /mə'njʊə(r)/ n fumier m.

many /'menɪ/ adj & n beaucoup (de); **a great** or **good ~** un grand nombre (de); **~ a** bien des.

map /mæp/ n carte f; (of streets) plan m. ● vt (pt **mapped**) faire la carte de; **~ out** (route) tracer; (arrange) organiser.

mar /mɑː(r)/ vt (pt **marred**) gâcher.

marble /'mɑːbl/ n marbre m; (for game) bille f.

March /mɑːtʃ/ n mars m.

march /mɑːtʃ/ vi (Mil) marcher (au pas). ● vt **~ off** (lead away) emmener. ● n marche f.

margin /'mɑːdʒɪn/ n marge f.

marginal /'mɑːdʒɪnl/ adj marginal; (increase) léger, faible; (seat: Pol) disputé.

marinate /'mærɪneɪt/ vt faire mariner (in dans).

marine /mə'riːn/ adj marin. ● n (shipping) marine f; (sailor) fusilier m marin.

marital /'mærɪtl/ adj conjugal. **~ status** n situation f de famille.

mark /mɑːk/ n (currency) mark m; (stain) tache f; (trace) marque f; (School) note f; (target) but m. ● vt marquer; (exam) corriger; **~ out** délimiter; (person) désigner; **~ time** marquer le pas.

marker /'mɑːkə(r)/ n (pen) marqueur m; (tag) repère m; (School, Univ) examinateur/-trice m/f.

market /'mɑːkɪt/ n marché m; **on the ~** en vente. ● vt (sell) vendre; (launch) commercialiser. **~ research** n étude f de marché.

marmalade /'mɑːməleɪd/ n confiture f d'oranges.

maroon /mə'ruːn/ n bordeaux m inv. ● adj bordeaux inv.

marooned /mə'ruːnd/ adj abandonné; (snowbound) bloqué.

marquee /mɑːˈkiː/ n grande tente f; (of circus) chapiteau m; (awning: US) auvent m.

marriage /ˈmærɪdʒ/ n mariage m (**to** avec).

married /ˈmærɪd/ adj marié (**to** à); (life) conjugal; **get ~** se marier (**to** avec).

marrow /ˈmærəʊ/ n (of bone) moelle f; (vegetable) courge f.

marry /ˈmærɪ/ vt épouser; (give or unite in marriage) marier. ● vi se marier.

marsh /mɑːʃ/ n marais m.

marshal /ˈmɑːʃl/ n maréchal m; (at event) membre m du service d'ordre. ● vt (pt **marshalled**) rassembler.

martyr /ˈmɑːtə(r)/ n martyr/-e m/f. ● vt martyriser.

marvel /ˈmɑːvl/ n merveille f. ● vi (pt **marvelled**) s'émerveiller (**at** de).

marvellous /ˈmɑːvələs/ adj merveilleux.

marzipan /ˈmɑːzɪpæn/ n pâte f d'amandes.

masculine /ˈmæskjʊlɪn/ adj & n masculin (m).

mash /mæʃ/ n (potatoes 🇬🇧) purée f. ● vt écraser. **mashed potatoes** npl purée f (de pommes de terre).

mask /mɑːsk/ n masque m. ● vt masquer.

Mason /ˈmeɪsn/ n franc-maçon m.

masonry /ˈmeɪsənrɪ/ n maçonnerie f.

mass /mæs/ n (Relig) messe f; masse f; **the ~es** les masses fpl. ● vt/i (se) masser.

massacre /ˈmæsəkə(r)/ n massacre m. ● vt massacrer.

massage /ˈmæsɑːʒ/ n massage m. ● vt masser.

massive /ˈmæsɪv/ adj (large) énorme; (heavy) massif.

mass media n médias mpl.

mass-produce vt fabriquer en série.

mast /mɑːst/ n (on ship) mât m; (for radio, TV) pylône m.

master /ˈmɑːstə(r)/ n maître m; (in secondary school) professeur m; **M~ of Arts** titulaire mf d'une maîtrise ès lettres. ● vt maîtriser.

masterpiece /ˈmɑːstəpiːs/ n chef-d'œuvre m.

mastery /ˈmɑːstərɪ/ n maîtrise f.

mat /mæt/ n (petit) tapis m; (at door) paillasson m.

match /mætʃ/ n (for lighting fire) allumette f; (Sport) match m; (equal) égal/-e m/f; (marriage) mariage m; (sb to marry) parti m; **be a ~ for** pouvoir tenir tête à. ● vt opposer; (go with) aller avec; (cups) assortir; (equal) égaler. ● vi (be alike) être assorti. **matchbox** n boîte f à allumettes.

matching /ˈmætʃɪŋ/ adj assorti.

mate /meɪt/ n camarade mf; (of animal) compagnon m, compagne f; (assistant) aide mf; (chess) mat m. ● vt/i (s')accoupler (**with** avec).

material /məˈtɪərɪəl/ n matière f; (fabric) tissu m; (documents, for building) matériau(x) m(pl); **~s** (equipment) matériel m. ● adj matériel; (fig) important. **materialistic** adj matérialiste.

materialize /məˈtɪərɪəlaɪz/ vi se matérialiser, se réaliser.

maternal /məˈtɜːnl/ adj maternel.

maternity /məˈtɜːnətɪ/ n maternité f. ● adj (clothes) de grossesse. **~ hospital** n maternité f. **~ leave** n congé m maternité.

mathematics /mæθəˈmætɪks/ n & npl mathématiques fpl.

maths, (US) **math** /mæθs/ n maths fpl.

mating /ˈmeɪtɪŋ/ n accouplement m.

matrimony /ˈmætrɪmənɪ/ n mariage m.

matron /ˈmeɪtrən/ n (married, elderly) dame f âgée; (in hospital) infirmière f en chef.

matt /mæt/ adj mat.

matter /ˈmætə(r)/ n (substance) matière f; (affair) affaire f; **as a ~ of fact** en fait; **what is the ~?** qu'est-ce qu'il y a? ● vi importer; **it does not ~** ça ne fait rien; **no ~ what happens** quoi qu'il arrive.

mattress /ˈmætrɪs/ n matelas m.

mature /məˈtjʊə(r)/ adj (psychologically) mûr; (plant) adulte. ● vt/i (se) mûrir. **maturity** n maturité f.

mauve /məʊv/ adj & n mauve (m).

maverick /ˈmævərɪk/ n non-conformiste mf.

maximize /ˈmæksɪmaɪz/ vt porter au maximum.

m

maximum /'mæksɪməm/ adj & n (pl **-ima**) maximum (m).

---
may /meɪ/

past **might**

● auxiliary verb

····▸ (possibility) they ∼ be able to come ils pourront peut-être venir; she ∼ not have seen him elle ne l'a peut-être pas vu; it ∼rain il risque de pleuvoir; 'will you come?'—'I might' 'tu viendras?'—'peut-être'.

····▸ (permission) you ∼ leave vous pouvez partir; ∼ I smoke? puis-je fumer?

····▸ (wish) ∼ he be happy qu'il soit heureux.

May /meɪ/ n mai m.

maybe /'meɪbi:/ adv peut-être.

mayhem /'meɪhem/ n (havoc) ravages mpl.

mayonnaise /meɪə'neɪz/ n mayonnaise f.

mayor /meə(r)/ n maire m.

maze /meɪz/ n labyrinthe m.

Mb abbr (**megabyte**) (Comput) Mo.

me /mi:/ pron me, m'; (after prep.) moi; (indirect object) me, m'; he knows ∼ il me connaît.

meadow /'medəʊ/ n pré m.

meagre /'mi:gə(r)/ adj maigre.

meal /mi:l/ n repas m; (grain) farine f.

mean /mi:n/ adj (poor) misérable; (miserly) avare; (unkind) méchant; (average) moyen. ● n milieu m; (average) moyenne f; in the ∼-time en attendant. ● vt (pt **meant**) vouloir dire, signifier; (involve) entraîner; I ∼ that! je suis sérieux; be meant for être destiné à; ∼ to do avoir l'intention de faire.

meaning /'mi:nɪŋ/ n sens m, signification f. **meaningful** adj significatif. **meaningless** adj dénué de sens.

means /mi:nz/ n moyen(s) m (pl;) by ∼ of sth au moyen de qch. ● npl (wealth) moyens mpl financiers; by all ∼ certainement; by no ∼ nullement.

meant /ment/ ➡MEAN.

meantime /'mi:ntaɪm/, **meanwhile** adv en attendant.

measles /'mi:zlz/ n rougeole f.

measure /'meʒə(r)/ n mesure f; (ruler) règle f. ● vt/i mesurer; ∼up to être à la hauteur de. **measurement** n mesures fpl.

meat /mi:t/ n viande f. **meaty** adj de viande; (fig) substantiel.

mechanic /mɪ'kænɪk/ n mécanicien/-ne m/f.

mechanical /mɪ'kænɪkl/ adj mécanique.

mechanism /'mekənɪzəm/ n mécanisme m.

medal /'medl/ n médaille f.

meddle /'medl/ vi (interfere) se mêler (in de); (tinker) toucher (with à).

media /'mi:dɪə/ n ➡MEDIUM. ● npl the∼ les média mpl; talk to the ∼ parler à la presse.

median /'mi:dɪən/ adj médian. ● n médiane f.

mediate /'mi:dɪeɪt/ vi servir d'intermédiaire.

medical /'medɪkl/ adj médical; (student) en médecine. ● n visite f médicale.

medication /medɪ'keɪʃn/ n médicaments mpl.

medicine /'medsn/ n (science) médecine f; (substance) médicament m.

medieval /medɪ'i:vl/ adj médiéval.

mediocre /mi:dɪ'əʊkə(r)/ adj médiocre.

meditate /'medɪteɪt/ vt/i méditer.

Mediterranean /medɪtə'reɪnɪən/ adj méditerranéen. ● n the ∼ la Méditerranée f.

medium /'mi:dɪəm/ n (pl media) (mid-point) milieu m; (for transmitting data) support m; (pl **mediums**) (person) médium m. ● adj moyen.

medley /'medlɪ/ n mélange m; (Mus) potpourri m.

meet /mi:t/ vt (pt met) rencontrer; (see again) retrouver; (be introduced to) faire la connaissance de; (face) faire face à; (requirement) satisfaire. ● vi se rencontrer; (see each other again) se retrouver; (in session) se réunir.

meeting /'mi:tɪŋ/ n réunion f; (between two people) rencontre f.

megabyte /'megəbaɪt/ n (Comput) mégaoctet m.

m

melancholy /'melənkəlɪ/ n mélancolie f. ● adj mélancolique.

mellow /'meləʊ/ adj (fruit) mûr; (sound, colour) moelleux, doux; (person) mûri. ● vt/i (mature) mûrir; (soften) (s')adoucir.

melody /'melədɪ/ n mélodie f.

melon /'melən/ n melon m.

melt /melt/ vt/i (faire) fondre.

member /'membə(r)/ n membre m. **M~ of Parliament** n député m. **membership** n adhésion f; (members) membres mpl; (fee) cotisation f.

memento /mɪ'mentəʊ/ n (pl ~es) (object) souvenir m.

memo /'meməʊ/ n note f.

memoir /'memwɑ:(r)/ n (record, essay) mémoire m.

memorandum /memə'rændəm/ n note f.

memorial /mə'mɔ:rɪəl/ n monument m. ● adj commémoratif.

memorize /'meməraɪz/ vt apprendre par cœur.

memory /'memərɪ/ n (mind, in computer) mémoire f; (thing remembered) souvenir m; **from ~** de mémoire; **in ~ of** à la mémoire de.

men /men/ →MAN.

menace /'menəs/ n menace f; (nuisance) peste f. ● vt menacer.

mend /mend/ vt réparer; (darn) raccommoder; **~ one's ways** s'amender. ● n raccommodage m; **on the ~** en voie de guérison.

meningitis /menɪn'dʒaɪtɪs/ n méningite f.

menopause /'menəpɔ:z/ n ménopause f.

mental /'mentl/ adj mental; (hospital) psychiatrique.

mentality /men'tælətɪ/ n mentalité f.

mention /'menʃn/ vt mentionner; **don't ~it!** il n'y a pas de quoi!, je vous en prie! ● n mention f.

menu /'menju:/ n (food, on computer) menu m; (list) carte f.

MEP abbr (**Member of the European Parliament**) député m au Parlement européen.

mercenary /'mɜ:sɪnərɪ/ adj & n mercenaire (m.)

merchandise /'mɜ:tʃəndaɪz/ n marchandises fpl.

merchant /'mɜ:tʃənt/ n marchand m. ● adj (ship, navy) marchand. **~ bank** n banque f de commerce.

merciful /'mɜ:sɪfl/ adj miséricordieux.

mercury /'mɜ:kjʊrɪ/ n mercure m.

mercy /'mɜ:sɪ/ n pitié f; **at the ~ of** à la merci de.

mere /mɪə(r)/ adj simple. **merest** adj moindre.

merge /mɜ:dʒ/ vt/i (se) mêler (**with** à) (companies: Comm) fusionner. **merger** n fusion f.

mermaid /'mɜ:meɪd/ n sirène f.

merrily /'merɪlɪ/ adv (happily) joyeusement; (unconcernedly) avec insouciance.

merry /'merɪ/ adj (**-ier, -iest**) gai; **make ~** faire la fête. **~-go-round** n manège m.

mesh /meʃ/ n maille f; (fabric) tissu m à mailles; (network) réseau m.

mesmerize /'mezməraɪz/ vt hypnotiser.

mess /mes/ n désordre m, gâchis m; (dirt) saleté f; (Mil) mess m; **make a ~ of** gâcher. ● vt **~ up** gâcher.; vi **~ about** s'amuser; (dawdle) traîner; **~ with** (tinker with) tripoter.

message /'mesɪdʒ/ n message m.

messenger /'mesɪndʒə(r)/ n messager/-ère m/f.

messy /'mesɪ/ adj (**-ier, -iest**) en désordre; (dirty) sale.

met /met/ →MEET.

metal /'metl/ n métal m. ● adj de métal. **metallic** adj métallique; (paint, colour) métallisé.

metallurgy /mɪ'tælədʒɪ/ n métallurgie f.

metaphor /'metəfɔ:(r)/ n métaphore f.

meteor /'mi:tɪə(r)/ n météore m.

meteorite /'mi:tɪəraɪt/ n météorite m.

meteorology /mi:tɪə'rɒlədʒɪ/ n météorologie f.

meter /'mi:tə(r)/ n compteur m; (US) →METRE.

method /'meθəd/ n méthode f.

methylated spirit(s) /'meθəleɪtɪd 'spɪrɪt(s)/ n alcool m à brûler.

meticulous /mɪ'tɪkjʊləs/ adj méticuleux.

metre, (US) **meter** /'mi:tə(r)/ n mètre m.

m

metric /'metrɪk/ adj métrique.

metropolis /mə'trɒpəlɪs/ n métropole f. **metropolitan** adj métropolitain.

mew /mju:/ n miaulement m. ● vi miauler.

mews /mju:z/ npl appartements mpl chic aménagés dans d'anciennes écuries.

Mexico /'meksɪkəʊ/ n Mexique m.

miaow /mi:'aʊ/ n & vi ➡MEW.

mice /maɪs/ ➡MOUSE.

mickey /'mɪkɪ/ n take the ~ out of 🔢 se moquer de.

microchip /'maɪkrəʊtʃɪp/ n puce f; circuit m intégré.

microlight /'maɪkrəʊlaɪt/ n ULM m.

microprocessor /'maɪkrəʊprəʊsesə(r)/ n microprocesseur m.

microscope /'maɪkrəskəʊp/ n microscope m.

microwave /'maɪkrəweɪv/ n microonde f; ~ **(oven)** four m à microondes. ● vt passer au four à microondes.

mid /mɪd/ adj in ~ **air** en plein ciel; in ~ **March** à la mi-mars; ~ **afternoon** milieu m de l'après-midi; **he's in his ~ twenties** il a environ vingt-cinq ans.

midday /mɪd'deɪ/ n midi m.

middle /'mɪdl/ adj (door, shelf) du milieu; (size) moyen. ● n milieu m; in the ~ of au milieu de. ~-**aged** adj d'âge mûr. **M~ Ages** n Moyen âge m. ~ **class** n classe f moyenne. **M~ East** n Moyen-Orient m.

midge /mɪdʒ/ n moucheron m.

midget /'mɪdʒɪt/ n nain/-e m/f. ● adj minuscule.

midnight /'mɪdnaɪt/ n minuit f; **it's ~** il est minuit.

midst /mɪdst/ n in the ~ of au beau milieu de; **in our ~** parmi nous.

midsummer /mɪd'sʌmə(r)/ n milieu m de l'été; (solstice) solstice m d'été.

midway /mɪd'weɪ/ adv ~ **between/ along** à mi-chemin entre/le long de.

midwife /'mɪdwaɪf/ n (pl -**wives**) sagefemme f.

might[1] /maɪt/ v aux I ~ **have been killed!** j'aurais pu être tué; **you ~ try doing sth** vous pourriez faire qch; ➡MAY.

might[2] /maɪt/ n puissance f.

mighty /'maɪtɪ/ adj puissant; (huge 🔢) énorme. ● adv 🔢 vachement 🔢.

migrant /'maɪgrənt/ adj & n (bird) migrateur (m); (worker) migrant/-e (m/f).

migrate /maɪ'greɪt/ vi émigrer. **migration** n migration f.

mild /maɪld/ adj (surprise, taste, tobacco, attack) léger; (weather, cheese, soap, person) doux; (case, infection) bénin.

mile /maɪl/ n mile m (= 1,6 km); **walk for ~s** marcher pendant des kilomètres; ~s **better** 🔢 bien meilleur. **mileage** n nombre m de miles, kilométrage m.

milestone /'maɪlstəʊn/ n (lit) borne f; (fig) étape f importante.

military /'mɪlɪtrɪ/ adj militaire.

militia /mɪ'lɪʃə/ n milice f.

milk /mɪlk/ n lait m. ● vt (cow) traire; (fig) pomper.

milkman /'mɪlkmən/ n (pl -**men**) laitier m.

milky /'mɪlkɪ/ adj (skin, colour) laiteux; (tea) au lait; **M~ Way** Voie f lactée.

mill /mɪl/ n moulin m; (factory) usine f. ● vt moudre. ● vi ~ **around** grouiller.

millennium /mɪ'lenɪəm/ n (pl -**s**) millénaire m.

millimetre, (US) **millimeter** /'mɪlɪmi:tə(r)/ n millimètre m.

million /'mɪljən/ n million m; **a ~ pounds** un million de livres. **millionaire** n millionnaire m.

millstone /'mɪlstəʊn/ n meule f; (fig) boulet m.

mime /maɪm/ n (actor) mime mf; (art) mime m. ● vt/i mimer.

mimic /'mɪmɪk/ vt (pt mimicked) imiter. ● n imitateur/-trice m/f.

mince /mɪns/ vt hacher; **not to ~ matters** ne pas mâcher ses mots. ● n viande f hachée.

mind /maɪnd/ n esprit m; (sanity) raison f; (opinion) avis m; **be on sb's ~** préoccuper qn; **bear that in ~** ne l'oubliez pas; **change one's ~** changer d'avis; **make up one's ~** se décider (**to** à). ● vt (have charge of) s'occuper de; (heed) faire attention à; **I do not ~ the noise** le bruit ne me dérange pas; **I don't** ~ ça m'est égal; **would you** ~ **checking?** je peux vous demander de vérifier?

minder /'maɪndə(r)/ n (bodyguard) garde m de corps; **(child)** ~ nourrice f.

mindless /'maɪndlɪs/ adj (programme) bête; (work) abrutissant; (vandalism) gratuit.

mine /maɪn/ n mine f. ● vt extraire; (Mil) miner. ● pron le mien, la mienne, les mien(ne)s; **the blue car is** ~ la voiture bleue est la mienne or à moi.

minefield /'maɪnfi:ld/ n (lit) champ m de mines; (fig) terrain m miné.

miner /'maɪnə(r)/ n mineur m.

mineral /'mɪnərəl/ n & adj minéral (m); ~ **water** eau f minérale.

minesweeper /'maɪnswi:pə(r)/ n (ship) dragueur m de mines.

mingle /'mɪŋgl/ vt/i (se) mêler (with à).

minibus /'mɪnɪbʌs/ n minibus m.

minicab /'mɪnɪkæb/ n taxi m (non agréé).

minimal /'mɪnɪml/ adj minimal.

minimize /'mɪnɪmaɪz/ vt minimiser; (Comput) réduire.

minimum /'mɪnɪməm/ adj & n (pl) **-ima** minimum (m),

minister /'mɪnɪstə(r)/ n ministre m. **ministerial** adj ministériel. **ministry** n ministère m.

mink /mɪŋk/ n vison m.

minor /'maɪnə(r)/ adj (change, surgery) mineur; (injury, burn) léger; (road) secondaire. ● n (Jur) mineur/-e m/f.

minority /maɪ'nɒrəti/ n minorité f; **in the** ~ en minorité. ● adj minoritaire.

mint /mɪnt/ n (Bot, Culin) menthe f; (sweet) bonbon m à la menthe; (fortune 🔢) fortune f. ● vt frapper; **in** ~ **condition** à l'état neuf.

minus /'maɪnəs/ prep moins; (without 🔢) sans. ● n moins m; (drawback) inconvénient m.

minute¹ /'mɪnɪt/ n minute f; ~**s** (of meeting) compte-rendu m.

minute² /maɪ'nju:t/ adj (object) minuscule; (risk, variation) minime.

miracle /'mɪrəkl/ n miracle m.

mirror /'mɪrə(r)/ n miroir m, glace f; (Auto) rétroviseur m. ● vt refléter.

misbehave /mɪsbɪ'heɪv/ vi se conduire mal.

miscalculation /mɪskælkjʊ'leɪʃn/ n (lit) erreur f de calcul; (fig) mauvais calcul m.

miscarriage /'mɪskærɪdʒ/ n fausse couche f; ~ **of justice** erreur f judiciaire.

miscellaneous /mɪsə'leɪnɪəs/ adj divers.

mischief /'mɪstʃɪf/ n (playfulness) espièglerie f; (by children) bêtises fpl.
mischievous adj espiègle; (malicious) méchant.

misconduct /mɪs'kɒndʌkt/ n mauvaise conduite f.

misconstrue /mɪskən'stru:/ vt mal interpréter.

misdemeanour, (US) **misdemeanor** /mɪsdɪ'mi:nə(r)/ n (Jur) délit m.

miser /'maɪzə(r)/ n avare mf.

miserable /'mɪzrəbl/ adj (sad) malheureux; (wretched) misérable; (performance, result) lamentable.

misery /'mɪzəri/ n (unhappiness) souffrance f; (misfortune) misère f; (person 🔢) rabat-joie mf inv.

misfit /'mɪsfɪt/ n inadapté/-e m/f.

misfortune /mɪs'fɔːtʃuːn/ n malheur m.

misgiving /mɪs'gɪvɪŋ/ n (doubt) doute m; (apprehension) crainte f.

misguided /mɪs'gaɪdɪd/ adj (foolish) imprudent; (mistaken) erroné; **be** ~ (person) se tromper.

mishap /'mɪshæp/ n incident m.

misjudge /mɪs'dʒʌdʒ/ vt (distance, speed) mal évaluer; (person) mal juger.

mislay /mɪs'leɪ/ vt (pt **mislaid**) égarer.

mislead /mɪs'liːd/ vt (pt) **misled** tromper. **misleading** adj trompeur.

misplace /mɪs'pleɪs/ vt mal ranger; (lose) égarer. **misplaced** adj (fear, criticism) déplacé.

misprint /'mɪsprɪnt/ n coquille f, faute f typographique.

misread /mɪs'riːd/ vt (pt) **misread** mal lire; (intentions) mal interpréter.

miss /mɪs/ vt/i manquer; (bus) rater; **he** ~**es her/Paris** elle/Paris lui manque; **you're** ~**ing the point** tu n'as rien compris; ~ **sth out** omettre qch; ~ **out on sth** laisser passer qch. ● n

m

coup *m* manqué; **it was a near ~ on** l'a échappé belle.

Miss /mɪs/ *n* Mademoiselle *f*; **~ Smith** (written) Mlle Smith.

misshapen /mɪsˈʃeɪpən/ *adj* difforme.

missile /ˈmɪsaɪl/ *n* (Mil) missile *m*; (thrown) projectile *m*.

mission /ˈmɪʃn/ *n* mission *f*. **missionary** *n* missionnaire *mf*.

misspell /mɪsˈspel/ *vt* (*pt* **misspelt** or **misspelled**) mal écrire.

mist /mɪst/ *n* brume *f*; (on window) buée *f*. ● *vt/i* (s')embuer.

mistake /mɪˈsteɪk/ *n* erreur *f*; **by ~** par erreur; **make a ~** faire une erreur. ● *vt* (*pt* **mistook**, *pp* **mistaken**) (*meaning*) mal interpréter; **~ for** prendre pour.

mistaken /mɪˈsteɪkən/ *adj* (*enthusiasm*) mal placé; **be ~** avoir tort.

mistletoe /ˈmɪsltəʊ/ *n* gui *m*.

mistreat /mɪsˈtriːt/ *vt* maltraiter.

mistress /ˈmɪstrɪs/ *n* maîtresse *f*.

misty /ˈmɪstɪ/ *adj* (**-ier, -iest**) brumeux; (*window*) embué.

misunderstanding /mɪsʌndəˈstændɪŋ/ *n* malentendu *m*.

misuse /mɪsˈjuːz/ *vt* (*word*) mal employer; (*power*) abuser de; (*equipment*) faire mauvais usage de.

mitten /ˈmɪtn/ *n* moufle *f*.

mix /mɪks/ *n* mélange *m*. ● *vt* mélanger; (*drink*) préparer; (*cement*) malaxer. ● *vi* se mélanger (**with** avec, à); (socially) être sociable; **~ with sb** fréquenter qn. □ **~ up** (confuse) confondre; (jumble up) mélanger; **get ~ed up in** se trouver mêlé à.

mixed /mɪkst/ *adj* (*school*) mixte; (*collection, diet*) varié; (*nuts, sweets*) assorti.

mixer /ˈmɪksə(r)/ *n* (Culin) batteur *m* électrique; **be a good ~** être sociable; **~ tap** mélangeur *m*.

mixture /ˈmɪkstʃə(r)/ *n* mélange *m*.

mix-up /ˈmɪksʌp/ *n* confusion *f* (**over** sur).

moan /məʊn/ *n* gémissement *m*. ● *vi* gémir; (complain 🔳) râler 🔳.

mob /mɒb/ *n* (crowd) foule *f*; (gang) gang *m*; **the M~** la Mafia. ● *vt* (*pt* **mobbed**) assaillir.

mobile /ˈməʊbaɪl/ *adj* mobile; **~ phone** téléphone *m* portable. ● *n* mobile *m*.

mobilize /ˈməʊbɪlaɪz/ *vt/i* mobiliser.

mock /mɒk/ *vt/i* se moquer (de). ● *adj* faux.

mockery /ˈmɒkərɪ/ *n* moquerie *f*; **a ~ of** une parodie de.

mock-up *n* maquette *f*.

mode /məʊd/ *n* mode *m*.

model /ˈmɒdl/ *n* (Comput, Auto) modèle *m*; (scale representation) maquette *f*; (person showing clothes) mannequin *m*. ● *adj* modèle; (*car*) modèle réduit *inv*; (*railway*) miniature. ● *vt* (*pt* **modelled**) modeler; (*clothes*) présenter. ● *vi* être mannequin; (pose) poser. **modelling** *n* métier *m* de mannequin.

modem /ˈməʊdem/ *n* modem *m*.

moderate /ˈmɒdərət/ *adj & n* modéré/-e (*m/f*).

moderation /mɒdəˈreɪʃn/ *n* modération *f*; **in ~** avec modération.

modern /ˈmɒdn/ *adj* moderne; **~ languages** langues *fpl* vivantes. **modernize** *vt* moderniser.

modest /ˈmɒdɪst/ *adj* modeste. **modesty** *n* modestie *f*.

modification /mɒdɪfɪˈkeɪʃn/ *n* modification *f*. **modify** *vt* modifier.

module /ˈmɒdjuːl/ *n* module *m*.

moist /mɔɪst/ *adj* (*soil*) humide; (*skin, palms*) moite; (*cake*) moelleux. **moisten** *vt* humecter. **moisture** *n* humidité *f*. **moisturizer** *n* crème *f* hydratante.

molar /ˈməʊlə(r)/ *n* molaire *f*.

mold (US) →**MOULD.**

mole /məʊl/ *n* grain *m* de beauté; (animal) taupe *f*.

molecule /ˈmɒlɪkjuːl/ *n* molécule *f*.

molest /məˈlest/ *vt* (pester) importuner; (sexually) agresser sexuellement.

moment /ˈməʊmənt/ *n* (short time) instant *m*; (point in time) moment *m*. **momentarily** *adv* momentanément; (soon: US) très bientôt. **momentary** *adj* momentané.

momentum /məˈmentəm/ *n* élan *m*.

monarch /ˈmɒnək/ *n* monarque *m*. **monarchy** *n* monarchie *f*.

Monday /ˈmʌndeɪ/ *n* lundi *m*.

monetary /ˈmʌnɪtrɪ/ *adj* monétaire.

money /'mʌnɪ/ n argent m; **make ~** (person) gagner de l'argent; (business) rapporter de l'argent. **~box** n tirelire f. **~ order** n mandat m postal.

monitor /'mɒnɪtə(r)/ n dispositif m de surveillance; (Comput) moniteur m. ● vt surveiller; (broadcast) être à l'écoute de.

monk /mʌŋk/ n moine m.

monkey /'mʌŋkɪ/ n singe m.

monopolize /mə'nɒpəlaɪz/ vt monopoliser. **monopoly** n monopole m.

monotonous /mə'nɒtənəs/ adj monotone. **monotony** n monotonie f.

monsoon /mɒn'suːn/ n mousson f.

monster /'mɒnstə(r)/ n monstre m. **monstrous** adj monstrueux.

month /mʌnθ/ n mois m.

monthly /'mʌnθlɪ/ adj mensuel. ● adv (pay) au mois; (publish) tous les mois. ● n (periodical) mensuel m.

monument /'mɒnjʊmənt/ n monument m.

moo /muː/ vi meugler.

mood /muːd/ n humeur f; **in a good/ bad ~** de bonne/mauvaise humeur. **moody** adj d'humeur changeante.

moon /muːn/ n lune f.

moonlight /'muːnlaɪt/ n clair m de lune. **moonlighting** n 🆒 travail m au noir.

moor /mɔː(r)/ n lande f. ● vt amarrer.

mop /mɒp/ n balai m à franges; **~ of hair** crinière f 🆒. ● vt (pt mopped) **~ (up)** éponger.

moped /'məʊped/ n vélomoteur m.

moral /'mɒrəl/ adj moral. ● n morale f; **~s** moralité f.

morale /mə'rɑːl/ n moral m.

morbid /'mɔːbɪd/ adj morbide.

more /mɔː(r)/ adv plus; **~ serious** plus sérieux; **work ~** travailler plus; **sleep ~ and ~** dormir de plus en plus; **once ~** une fois de plus; **I don't go there any ~** je n'y vais plus; **~ or less** plus ou moins. ● det plus de; **a little ~ wine** un peu plus de vin; **~ bread** encore un peu de pain; **there's no ~ bread** il n'y a plus de pain; **nothing ~** rien de plus. ● pron plus; **cost ~ than** coûter plus cher que; **I need ~ of it** il m'en faut davantage.

moreover /mɔː'rəʊvə(r)/ adv de plus.

morning /'mɔːnɪŋ/ n matin m; (whole morning) matinée f.

Morocco /mə'rɒkəʊ/ n Maroc m.

morsel /'mɔːsl/ n morceau m.

mortal /'mɔːtl/ adj & n mortel/-le (m/f).

mortgage /'mɔːgɪdʒ/ n empruntlogement m. ● vt hypothéquer.

mortuary /'mɔːtʃərɪ/ n morgue f.

mosaic /məʊ'zeɪɪk/ n mosaïque f.

mosque /mɒsk/ n mosquée f.

mosquito /məs'kiːtəʊ/ n (pl ~es) moustique m.

moss /mɒs/ n mousse f.

most /məʊst/ det (nearly all) la plupart de; **~ people** la plupart des gens; **the ~ votes/money** le plus de voix/ d'argent. ● n le plus. ● pron la plupart; **~ of us** la plupart d'entre nous; **~ of the money** la plus grande partie de l'argent; **the ~ I can do is ...** tout ce que je peux faire c'est ... ● adv **the ~ beautiful house/hotel in Oxford** la maison la plus belle/l'hôtel le plus beau d'Oxford; **~ interesting** très intéressant; **what I like ~ (of all) is** ce que j'aime le plus c'est. **mostly** adv surtout.

moth /mɒθ/ n papillon m de nuit; (in cloth) mite f.

mother /'mʌðə(r)/ n mère f. ● vt (lit) materner; (fig) dorloter. **motherhood** n maternité f. **~-in-law** n (pl ~s-in-law) belle-mère f. **~-of-pearl** n nacre f. **M~'s Day** n la fête des mères. **~-to-be** n future maman f. **~ tongue** n langue f maternelle.

motion /'məʊʃn/ n mouvement m; (proposal) motion f; **~ picture** (US) film m. ● vt/i **~ (to) sb** to faire signe à qn de. **motionless** adj immobile.

motivate /'məʊtɪveɪt/ vt motiver.

motive /'məʊtɪv/ n motif m; (Jur) mobile m.

motor /'məʊtə(r)/ n moteur m; (car) auto f. ● adj (industry, insurance, vehicle) automobile; (activity, disorder: Med) moteur. **~bike** n moto f. **~ car** n auto f. **~-cyclist** n motocycliste mf. **~ home** n autocaravane f.

motorist /'məʊtərɪst/ n automobiliste mf.

motorway /'məʊtəweɪ/ n autoroute f.

mottled /'mɒtld/ adj tacheté.

motto /'mɒtəʊ/ n (pl ~es) devise f.

m

mould /məʊld/ n (shape) moule m; (fungus) moisissure f. ● vt mouler; (influence) former. **moulding** n moulure f. **mouldy** adj moisi.

mount /maʊnt/ n (hill) mont m; (horse) monture f. ● vt (stairs) gravir; (platform, horse, bike) monter sur; (jewel, picture, campaign, exhibit) monter. ● vi monter; (number, toll) augmenter; (concern) grandir.

mountain /ˈmaʊntɪn/ n montagne f; ∼ **bike** (vélo) tout terrain m, VTT m. **mountaineer** n alpiniste mf.

mourn /mɔːn/ vt/i ∼ **(for)** pleurer. **mournful** adj mélancolique. **mourning** n deuil m.

mouse /maʊs/ n (pl **mice**) souris f. ∼**trap** n souricière f.

mouth /maʊθ/ n bouche f; (of dog, cat) gueule f; (of cave, tunnel) entrée f. **mouthful** n bouchée f. ∼**wash** n eau f dentifrice. ∼**watering** adj appétissant.

move /muːv/ vt (object) déplacer; (limb, head) bouger; (emotionally) émouvoir; ∼ **house** déménager. ● vi bouger; (vehicle) rouler; (change address) déménager; (act) agir. ● n mouvement m; (in game) coup m; (player's turn) tour m; (step, act) manœuvre f; (house change) déménagement m; **on the** ∼ en mouvement. □ ∼ **back** reculer; ∼ **in** emménager; ∼ **in with** s'installer avec; ∼ **on** (person) se mettre en route; (vehicle) repartir; (time) passer; ∼ **sth on** faire avancer qch; ∼ **sb on** faire circuler qn; ∼ **over** or **up** se pousser.

movement /ˈmuːvmənt/ n mouvement m.

movie /ˈmuːvɪ/ n (US) film m; **the** ∼**s** le cinéma.

moving /ˈmuːvɪŋ/ adj (vehicle) en marche; (part, target) mobile; (staircase) roulant; (touching) émouvant.

mow /məʊ/ vt (pp **mowed** or **mown**) (lawn) tondre; (hay) couper; ∼ **down** faucher. **mower** n tondeuse f.

MP abbr ➡**MEMBER OF PARLIAMENT**.

Mr /ˈmɪstə(r)/ n (pl **Messrs**) ∼ **Smith** Monsieur or M. Smith; ∼ **President** Monsieur le Président.

Mrs /ˈmɪsɪz/ n (pl **Mrs**) ∼ **Smith** Madame or Mme Smith.

Ms /məz/ n Mme.

much /mʌtʃ/ adv beaucoup; **too** ∼ trop; **very** ∼ beaucoup; **I like them as** ∼ **as you (do)** je les aime autant que toi. ● pron beaucoup; **not** ∼ pas grand-chose; **he didn't say** ∼ il n'a pas dit grand-chose; **I ate so** ∼ **that** j'ai tellement mangé que. ● det beaucoup de; **too** ∼ **money** trop d'argent; **how** ∼ **time is left?** combien de temps reste-t-il?

muck /mʌk/ n saletés fpl; (manure) fumier m. □ ∼ **about** 🅣 faire l'imbécile. **mucky** adj sale.

mud /mʌd/ n boue f.

muddle /ˈmʌdl/ n (mix-up) malentendu m; (mess) pagaille f 🅣; **get into a** ∼ s'embrouiller. □ ∼ **through** se débrouiller; ∼ **up** embrouiller.

muddy /ˈmʌdɪ/ adj couvert de boue.

muffle /ˈmʌfl/ vt emmitoufler; (bell) assourdir; (voice) étouffer.

mug /mʌg/ n grande tasse f; (for beer) chope f; (face 🅣) gueule f 🅧; (fool 🅣) poire f 🅣. ● vt (pt **mugged**) agresser. **mugger** n agresseur m.

muggy /ˈmʌgɪ/ adj lourd.

mule /mjuːl/ n mulet m.

multicoloured /mʌltɪˈkʌləd/ adj multicolore.

multiple /ˈmʌltɪpl/ adj & n multiple (m); ∼ **sclerosis** sclérose f en plaques.

multiplication /mʌltɪplɪˈkeɪʃn/ n multiplication f. **multiply** vt/i (se) multiplier.

multistorey /mʌltɪˈstɔːrɪ/ adj (car park) à niveaux multiples.

mum /mʌm/ n 🅣 maman f.

mumble /ˈmʌmbl/ vt/i marmonner.

mummy /ˈmʌmɪ/ n (mother 🅣) maman f; (embalmed body) momie f.

mumps /mʌmps/ n oreillons mpl.

munch /mʌntʃ/ vt mâcher.

mundane /mʌnˈdeɪn/ adj terre-à-terre.

municipal /mjuːˈnɪsɪpl/ adj municipal.

mural /ˈmjʊərəl/ adj mural. ● n peinture f murale.

murder /ˈmɜːdə(r)/ n meurtre m. ● vt assassiner. **murderer** n meurtrier m, assassin m.

murky /ˈmɜːkɪ/ adj (**-ier**, **-iest**) (water) glauque; (past) trouble.

murmur /'mɜːmə(r)/ n murmure m.
● vt/i murmurer.

muscle /'mʌsl/ n muscle m. ● vi ~ **in**
Ⓘ s'imposer (**on** dans).

muscular /'mʌskjʊlə(r)/ adj (tissue,
disease) musculaire; (body, person)
musclé.

museum /mjuːˈzɪəm/ n musée m.

mushroom /'mʌʃrʊm/ n champignon
m. ● vi (town) proliférer; (demand)
s'accroître rapidement.

music /'mjuːzɪk/ n musique f.

musical /'mjuːzɪkl/ adj (person) musicien; (voice) mélodieux; (accompaniment) musical; (instrument) de musique. ● n comédie f musicale.

musician /mjuːˈzɪʃn/ n musicien/-
ne m/f.

Muslim /'mʊzlɪm/ n Musulman/-e m/f.
● adj musulman.

mussel /'mʌsl/ n moule f.

must /mʌst/ v aux devoir; **you** ~ **go**
vous devez partir, il faut que vous par-
tiez; **she** ~ **be consulted** il faut la
consulter; **he** ~ **be old** il doit être
vieux; **I** ~ **have done it** j'ai dû le
faire. ● n **be a** ~ Ⓘ être indispensable.

mustard /'mʌstəd/ n moutarde f.

musty /'mʌstɪ/ adj (-ier, -iest) (room)
qui sent le renfermé; (smell) de moisi.

mute /mjuːt/ adj & n muet/-te (m/f).
muted adj (colour) sourd; (response)
tiède; (celebration) mitigé.

mutilate /'mjuːtɪleɪt/ vt mutiler.

mutter /'mʌtə(r)/ vt/i marmonner.

mutton /'mʌtn/ n mouton m.

mutual /'mjuːtʃʊəl/ adj (reciprocal) réciproque; (common) commun; (con-
sent) mutuel. **mutually** adv mutuellement.

muzzle /'mʌzl/ n (snout) museau m;
(device) muselière f; (of gun) canon m.
● vt museler.

my /maɪ/ adj mon, ma, pl mes.

myself /maɪˈself/ pron (reflexive) me,
m'; **I've hurt** ~ je me suis fait mal;
(emphatic) moi-même; **I did it** ~ je
l'ai fait moi-même; (after preposition)
moi, moi-même; **I am proud of** ~ je
suis fier de moi.

mysterious /mɪˈstɪərɪəs/ adj mystérieux.

mystery /'mɪstərɪ/ n mystère m.

mystic /'mɪstɪk/ adj & n mystique (mf).
mystical adj mystique.

myth /mɪθ/ n mythe m. **mythical** adj
mythique. **mythology** n mythologie f.

Nn

nag /næg/ vt/i (pt **nagged**) critiquer;
(pester) harceler. **nagging** adj persistant.

nail /neɪl/ n clou m; (of finger, toe)
ongle m; **on the** ~ sans tarder, tout
de suite. ● vt clouer. ~ **polish** n vernis m à ongles.

naïve /naɪˈiːv/ adj naïf.

naked /'neɪkɪd/ adj nu; **to the** ~ **eye** à
l'œil nu.

name /neɪm/ n nom m; (fig) réputation
f. ● vt nommer; (terms) fixer; **be** ~d
after porter le nom de.

namely /'neɪmlɪ/ adv à savoir.

nanny /'nænɪ/ n nurse f.

nap /næp/ n somme m.

nape /neɪp/ n nuque f.

napkin /'næpkɪn/ n serviette f.

nappy /'næpɪ/ n couche f.

narcotic /nɑːˈkɒtɪk/ adj & n narcotique (m).

narrative /'nærətɪv/ n récit m. **narra-
tor** n narrateur/-trice m/f.

narrow /'nærəʊ/ adj étroit. ● vt/i (se)
rétrécir; (limit) (se) limiter; ~ **down**
the choices limiter les choix.
~**-minded** adj à l'esprit étroit; (ideas)
étroit.

nasal /'neɪzl/ adj nasal.

nasty /'nɑːstɪ/ adj (-ier, -iest) mauvais,
désagréable; (malicious) méchant.

nation /'neɪʃn/ n nation f.

national /'næʃənl/ adj national. ● n
ressortissant/-e m/f.

nationality /næʃəˈnælɪtɪ/ n nationalité f.

nationalize /'næʃnəlaɪz/ vt nationaliser.

nationally /'næʃnəlɪ/ adv à l'échelle
nationale.

m

n

National Trust Association caritative britannique fondée en 1895 pour assurer la protection de certains édifices ou parties de littoral menacés par l'industrialisation. Cette association est aujourd'hui le premier propriétaire foncier britannique car elle a acquis ou reçu en dons depuis sa création de nombreux sites et bâtiments; la plupart sont ouverts au public.

native /'neɪtɪv/ n (local inhabitant) autochtone mf; (non-European) indigène mf; **be a ~ of** être originaire de. ● adj indigène, (country) natal; (inborn) inné; **~ language** langue f maternelle; **~ speaker of French** personne f de langue maternelle française.

natural /'nætʃrəl/ adj naturel.

naturally /'nætʃrəlɪ/ adv (normally, of course) naturellement; (by nature) de nature.

nature /'neɪtʃə(r)/ n nature f.

naughty /'nɔːtɪ/ adj (-ier, -iest) vilain, méchant; (indecent) grivois.

nausea /'nɔːsɪə/ n nausée f. **nauseous** adj (smell) écœurant.

nautical /'nɔːtɪkl/ adj nautique.

naval /'neɪvl/ adj (battle) naval; (officer) de marine.

navel /'neɪvl/ n nombril m.

navigate /'nævɪgeɪt/ vt (sea) naviguer sur; (ship) piloter. ● vi naviguer. **navigation** n navigation f.

navy /'neɪvɪ/ n marine f. ● adj ~ **(blue)** bleu inv marine.

near /nɪə(r)/ adv près; **draw ~** (s')approcher (to de). ● prep près de. ● adj proche; **~ to** près de. ● vt approcher de.

nearby /nɪə'baɪ/ adj proche. ● adv à proximité.

nearly /'nɪəlɪ/ adv presque; **I ~ forgot** j'ai failli oublier; **not ~ as pretty as** loin d'être aussi joli que.

nearness /'nɪənɪs/ n proximité f.

nearside /'nɪəsaɪd/ adj (Auto) du côté du passager.

neat /niːt/ adj soigné, net; (room) bien rangé; (clever) habile; (drink) sec. **neatly** adv avec soin; habilement.

necessarily /nesə'serəlɪ/ adv nécessairement.

necessary /'nesəsərɪ/ adj nécessaire.

necessitate /nɪ'sesɪteɪt/ vt nécessiter.

necessity /nɪ'sesɪtɪ/ n nécessité f; (thing) chose f indispensable.

neck /nek/ n cou m; (of dress) encolure f. **~ and neck** adj à égalité. **~lace** n collier m. **~line** n encolure f. **~tie** n cravate f.

nectarine /'nektərɪn/ n brugnon m, nectarine f.

need /niːd/ n besoin m. ● vt avoir besoin de; (demand) demander; **you ~ not come** vous n'êtes pas obligé de venir.

needle /'niːdl/ n aiguille f.

needless /'niːdlɪs/ adj inutile.

needlework /'niːdlwɜːk/ n couture f; (object) ouvrage m (à l'aiguille).

needy /'niːdɪ/ adj (-ier, -iest) nécessiteux. ● n the ~ les indigents.

negative /'negətɪv/ adj négatif. ● n (of photograph) négatif m; (word: Gram) négation f; **in the ~** (answer) par la négative; (Gram) à la forme négative.

neglect /nɪ'glekt/ vt négliger, laisser à l'abandon; **~ to do** négliger de faire. ● n manque m de soins; **(state of) ~** abandon m.

negligent /'neglɪdʒənt/ adj négligent.

negotiate /nɪ'gəʊʃɪeɪt/ vt/i négocier. **negotiation** n négociation f.

neigh /neɪ/ n hennissement m. ● vi hennir.

neighbour, (US) **neighbor** /'neɪbə(r)/ n voisin/-e m/f. **neighbourhood** n voisinage m, quartier m; **in the ~hood of** aux alentours de. **neighbouring** adj voisin. **neighbourly** adj amical.

neither /'naɪðə(r)/ adj & pron aucun/-e des deux, ni l'un/-e ni l'autre. ● adv ni; **~ big nor small** ni grand ni petit. ● conj (ne) non plus; **~ am I coming** je ne viendrai pas non plus.

nephew /'nefjuː/ n neveu m.

nerve /nɜːv/ n nerf m; (courage) courage m; (calm) sang-froid m; (impudence 🖪) culot m; **~s** (before exams) trac m. **~-racking** adj éprouvant.

nervous /'nɜːvəs/ adj nerveux; **be or feel ~** (afraid) avoir peur; **~ breakdown** dépression f nerveuse. **nervousness** n nervosité f; (fear) crainte f.

nest /nest/ n nid m. ● vi nicher. **~-egg** n pécule m.

n

nestle /'nesl/ *vi* se blottir.

net /net/ *n* filet *m*; (Comput) net *m*, Internet *m*. ● *vt* (*pt* **netted**) prendre au filet. ● *adj* (weight) net. ~**ball** *n* netball *m*.

Netherlands /'neðələndz/ *n* **the** ~ les Pays-Bas *mpl*.

netiquette /'netiket/ *n* nétiquette *f*.

Netsurfer /'netiket/ *n* Internaute *mf*.

nettle /'netl/ *n* ortie *f*.

network /'netwɜ:k/ *n* réseau *m*.

neurotic /njʊə'rɒtik/ *adj* & *n* névrosé/-e (*m/f*).

neuter /'nju:tə(r)/ *adj* & *n* neutre (*m*). ● *vt* (castrate) castrer.

neutral /'nju:trəl/ *adj* neutre; ~ **(gear)** (Auto) point *m* mort.

never /'nevə(r)/ *adv* (ne) jamais; **he** ~ **refuses** il ne refuse jamais; **I** ~ **saw him** 🔲 je ne l'ai pas vu; ~ **again** plus jamais; ~ **mind** (don't worry) ne vous en faites pas; (it doesn't matter) peu importe.

nevertheless /nevəðə'les/ *adv* néanmoins, toutefois.

new /nju:/ *adj* nouveau; (brand-new) neuf. ~**-born** *adj* nouveau-né. ~**comer** *n* nouveau venu *m*, nouvelle venue *f*.

newly /'nju:li/ *adv* nouvellement. ~**-weds** *npl* jeunes mariés *mpl*.

news /nju:z/ *n* nouvelle(s) *f(pl)*; (radio, press) informations *fpl*; (TV) actualités *fpl*, informations *fpl*. ~ **agency** *n* agence *f* de presse. ~**agent** *n* marchand/-e *m/f* de journaux. ~**caster** *n* présentateur/-trice *m/f*. ~**group** *n* (Internet) forum *m* de discussion. ~**letter** *n* bulletin *m*. ~**paper** *n* journal *m*.

new year *n* nouvel an *m*. **New Year's Day** *n* le jour de l'an. **New Year's Eve** *n* la Saint-Sylvestre.

New Zealand /nju:'zi:lənd/ *n* Nouvelle-Zélande *f*.

next /nekst/ *adj* prochain; (adjoining) voisin; (following) suivant; ~ **to** à côté de; ~ **door** à côté (**to** de). ● *adv* la prochaine fois; (afterwards) ensuite. ● *n* suivant/-e *m/f*. (e-mail) message *m* suivant. ~**door** *adj* d'à côté. ~ **of kin** *n* parent *m* le plus proche.

nib /nib/ *n* plume *f*.

nibble /'nibl/ *vt/i* grignoter.

nice /nais/ *adj* agréable, bon; (kind) gentil; (pretty) joli; (respectable) bien *inv*; (subtle) délicat. **nicely** *adv* agréablement; gentiment; (well) bien.

nicety /'naisəti/ *n* subtilité *f*.

niche /ni:ʃ/ *n* (recess) niche *f*; (fig) place *f*, situation *f*.

nick /nik/ *n* petite entaille *f*; **be in good/bad** ~ 🔲 être en bon/mauvais état. ● *vt* (steal, arrest 🔲) piquer.

nickel /'nikl/ *n* (metal) nickel *m*; (US) pièce *f* de cinq cents.

nickname /'nikneim/ *n* surnom *m*. ● *vt* surnommer.

nicotine /'nikəti:n/ *n* nicotine *f*.

niece /ni:s/ *n* nièce *f*.

niggling /'niglin/ *adj* (person) tatillon; (detail) insignifiant.

night /nait/ *n* nuit *f*; (evening) soir *m*. ● *adj* de nuit. ~**-cap** *n* boisson *f* (avant d'aller se coucher). ~**-club** *n* boîte *f* de nuit. ~**-dress** *n* chemise *f* de nuit. ~**fall** *n* tombée *f* de la nuit. **nightie** *n* chemise *f* de nuit.

nightingale /'naitingeil/ *n* rossignol *m*.

nightly /'naitli/ *adj* & *adv* (de) chaque nuit *or* soir.

night /nait/: ~**mare** *n* cauchemar *m*. ~**-time** *n* nuit *f*.

nil /nil/ *n* (Sport) zéro *m*. ● *adj* (chances, risk) nul.

nimble /'nimbl/ *adj* agile.

nine /nain/ *adj* & *n* neuf (*m*).

nineteen /nain'ti:n/ *adj* & *n* dix-neuf (*m*).

ninety /'nainti/ *adj* & *n* quatre-vingt-dix (*m*).

ninth /nainθ/ *adj* & *n* neuvième (*mf*).

nip /nip/ *vt/i* (*pt* **nipped**) (pinch) pincer; (rush 🔲) courir; ~ **out/back** sortir/rentrer rapidement. ● *n* pincement *m*.

nipple /'nipl/ *n* mamelon *m*; (of baby's bottle) tétine *f*.

nippy /'nipi/ *adj* (**-ier, -iest**) (air) piquant; (car) rapide.

nitrogen /'naitrədʒən/ *n* azote *m*.

no /nəʊ/ *det* aucun/-e; pas de; ~ **man** aucun homme; ~ **money/time** pas d'argent/de temps; ~ **one** →**NOBODY**; ~ **smoking/entry** défense de fumer/d'entrer; ~ **way!** 🔲 pas question! ● *adv* non. ● *n* (*pl* **noes**) non *m inv*.

n

nobility /nəʊˈbɪləti/ n noblesse f.

noble /ˈnəʊbl/ adj noble. ~**man** n (pl -men) noble m.

nobody /ˈnəʊbədi/ pron (ne) personne; **he knows** ~ il ne connaît personne. ● n nullité f.

nocturnal /nɒkˈtɜːnl/ adj nocturne.

nod /nɒd/ vt/i (pt nodded); ~ (one's head) faire un signe de tête; ~ off s'endormir. ● n signe m de tête.

noise /nɔɪz/ n bruit m; **make a** ~ faire du bruit. **noisily** adv bruyamment. **noisy** adj (-ier, -iest) bruyant.

no man's land n no man's land m.

nominal /ˈnɒmɪnl/ adj symbolique, nominal; (value) nominal.

nominate /ˈnɒmɪneɪt/ vt nommer; (put forward) proposer.

none /nʌn/ pron aucun/-e; ~ **of us** aucun/-e de nous; **I have** ~ je n'en ai pas.

non-existent /nɒnɪgˈzɪstənt/ adj inexistant.

nonplussed /nɒnˈplʌst/ adj perplexe.

nonsense /ˈnɒnsns/ n absurdités fpl.

non-smoker /nɒnˈsməʊkə(r)/ n non-fumeur m.

non-stick adj antiadhésif.

non-stop /nɒnˈstɒp/ adj (train, flight) direct. ● adv sans arrêt.

noodles /ˈnuːdlz/ npl nouilles fpl.

noon /nuːn/ n midi m.

nor /nɔː(r)/ adv ni. ● conj (ne) non plus; ~ **shall I come** je ne viendrai pas non plus.

norm /nɔːm/ n norme f.

normal /ˈnɔːml/ adj normal.

Norman /ˈnɔːmən/ n Normand/-e m/f. ● adj (village) normand; (arch) roman.

north /nɔːθ/ n nord m. ● adj nord inv, du nord. ● adv vers le nord.

North America n Amérique f du Nord.

north-east /nɔːθˈiːst/ n nord-est m.

northerly /ˈnɔːðəli/ adj (wind, area) du nord; (point) au nord.

northern /ˈnɔːðən/ adj (accent) du nord; (coast) nord. **northerner** n habitant/-e m/f du nord.

northward /ˈnɔːθwəd/ adj (side) nord inv; (journey) vers le nord.

north-west /nɔːθˈwest/ n nord-ouest m.

Norway /ˈnɔːweɪ/ n Norvège f.

Norwegian /nɔːˈwiːdʒən/ n (person) Norvégien/-ne m/f; (language) norvégien m. ● adj norvégien.

nose /nəʊz/ n nez m. ● vi ~ **about** fouiner.

nosedive /ˈnəʊzdaɪv/ n piqué m. ● vi descendre en piqué.

nostalgia /nɒˈstældʒə/ n nostalgie f.

nostril /ˈnɒstrɪl/ n narine f; (of horse) naseau m.

nosy /ˈnəʊzi/ adj (-ier, -iest) 🚹 curieux, indiscret.

not /nɒt/ adv (ne) pas; **I do** ~ **know** je ne sais pas; ~ **at all** pas du tout; ~ **yet** pas encore; **I suppose** ~ je suppose que non.

notably /ˈnəʊtəbli/ adv notamment.

notch /nɒtʃ/ n entaille f. ● vt ~ **up** (score) marquer.

note /nəʊt/ n note f; (banknote) billet m; (short letter) mot m. ● vt noter; (notice) remarquer. ~**book** n carnet m.

nothing /ˈnʌθɪŋ/ pron (ne) rien; **he eats** ~ il ne mange rien; ~ **else** rien d'autre; ~ **much** pas grand-chose; **for** ~ pour rien, gratis. ● n rien m; (person) nullité f. ● adv nullement.

notice /ˈnəʊtɪs/ n avis m, annonce f; (poster) affiche f; (advance) ~ préavis m; **at short** ~ dans des délais très brefs; **give in one's** ~ donner sa démission; **take** ~ faire attention (of à). ● vt remarquer, observer. **noticeable** adj visible. ~-**board** n tableau m d'affichage.

notify /ˈnəʊtɪfaɪ/ vt (inform) aviser; (make known) notifier.

notion /ˈnəʊʃn/ n idée f, notion f.

notorious /nəʊˈtɔːrɪəs/ adj (criminal) notoire; (district) mal famé; (case) tristement célèbre.

notwithstanding /nɒtwɪθˈstændɪŋ/ prep malgré. ● adv néanmoins.

nought /nɔːt/ n zéro m.

noun /naʊn/ n nom m.

nourish /ˈnʌrɪʃ/ vt nourrir. **nourishing** adj nourrissant. **nourishment** n nourriture f.

novel /'nɒvl/ n roman m. ● adj nouveau. **novelist** n romancier/ ière m/f. **novelty** n nouveauté f.

November /nə'vembə(r)/ n novembre m.

now /naʊ/ adv maintenant. ● conj maintenant que; **just ~** maintenant; (a moment ago) tout à l'heure; **~ and again, ~ and then** de temps à autre.

nowadays /'naʊədeɪz/ adv de nos jours.

nowhere /'nəʊweə(r)/ adv nulle part.

nozzle /'nɒzl/ n (tip) embout m; (of hose) jet m.

nuclear /'nju:klɪə(r)/ adj nucléaire.

nude /nju:d/ adj nu. ● n nu/-e m/f; **in the ~** tout nu.

nudge /nʌdʒ/ vt pousser du coude. ● n coup m de coude.

nudism /'nju:dɪzəm/ n nudisme m. **nudity** n nudité f.

nuisance /'nju:sns/ n (thing, event) ennui m; (person) peste f; **be a ~** être embêtant.

null /nʌl/ adj nul.

numb /nʌm/ adj engourdi (**with** par). ● vt engourdir.

number /'nʌmbə(r)/ n nombre m; (of ticket, house, page) numéro m; (written figure) chiffre m; **a ~ of people** plusieurs personnes. ● vt numéroter; (count, include) compter. **~-plate** n plaque f d'immatriculation.

numeral /'nju:mərəl/ n chiffre m.

numerate /'nju:mərət/ adj qui sait compter.

numerical /nju:'merɪkl/ adj numérique.

numerous /'nju:mərəs/ adj nombreux.

nun /nʌn/ n religieuse f.

nurse /nɜ:s/ n infirmier/-ière m/f; (nanny) nurse f. ● vt soigner; (hope) nourrir.

nursery /'nɜ:sərɪ/ n (room) chambre f d'enfants; (for plants) pépinière f; **(day) ~** crèche f. **~ rhyme** n comptine f. **~ school** n (école) maternelle f.

nursing home n maison f de retraite.

nut /nʌt/ n (walnut, Brazil nut) noix f; (hazelnut) noisette f; (peanut) cacahuète f; (Tech) écrou m. **~crackers** npl casse-noix m inv.

nutmeg /'nʌtmeg/ n muscade f.

nutrient /'nju:trɪənt/ n substance f nutritive.

nutritious /nju:'trɪʃəs/ adj nutritif.

nuts /nʌts/ adj (crazy 🅸) cinglé.

nutshell /'nʌtʃel/ n coquille f de noix; **in a ~** en un mot.

nylon /'naɪlɒn/ n nylon m.

· ·

Oo

· ·

oak /əʊk/ n chêne m.

OAP abbr **old-age pensioner** retraité/-e m/f.

oar /ɔ:(r)/ n rame f.

oath /əʊθ/ n (promise) serment m; (swearword) juron m.

oats /əʊts/ npl avoine f.

obedience /ə'bi:dɪəns/ n obéissance f. **obedient** adj obéissant. **obediently** adv docilement.

obese /əʊ'bi:s/ adj obèse.

obey /ə'beɪ/ vt/i obéir (à).

object¹ /'ɒbdʒɪkt/ n (thing) objet m; (aim) but m; (Gram) complément m d'objet; **money is no ~** l'argent n'est pas un problème.

object² /əb'dʒekt/ vi protester. ● vt **~ that** objecter que; **~ to** (behaviour) désapprouver; (plan) protester contre. **objection** n objection f; (drawback) inconvénient m.

objective /əb'dʒektɪv/ adj & n objectif (m).

obligation /ɒblɪ'geɪʃn/ n devoir m.

obligatory /ə'blɪgətrɪ/ adj obligatoire.

oblige /ə'blaɪdʒ/ vt obliger (**to do** à faire).

oblivion /ə'blɪvɪən/ n oubli m. **oblivious** adj inconscient (**to, of** de).

oblong /'ɒblɒŋ/ adj oblong. ● n rectangle m.

obnoxious /əb'nɒkʃəs/ adj odieux.

oboe /'əʊbəʊ/ n hautbois m.

obscene /əb'si:n/ adj obscène.

obscure /əb'skjʊə(r)/ adj obscur. ● vt obscurcir; (conceal) cacher.

n

o

observance /əbˈzɜːvəns/ n (of law) respect m; (of sabbath) observance f. **observant** adj observateur.

observation /ɒbzəˈveɪʃn/ n observation f.

observe /əbˈzɜːv/ vt observer; (remark) remarquer.

obsess /əbˈses/ vt obséder. **obsession** n obsession f. **obsessive** adj (person) maniaque; (thought) obsédant; (illness) obsessionnel.

obsolete /ˈɒbsəliːt/ adj dépassé.

obstacle /ˈɒbstəkl/ n obstacle m.

obstinate /ˈɒbstənət/ adj obstiné.

obstruct /əbˈstrʌkt/ vt (road) bloquer; (view) cacher; (progress) gêner. **obstruction** n (act) obstruction f; (thing) obstacle m; (in traffic) encombrement m.

obtain /əbˈteɪn/ vt obtenir. ● vi avoir cours. **obtainable** adj disponible.

obvious /ˈɒbvɪəs/ adj évident. **obviously** adv manifestement.

occasion /əˈkeɪʒn/ n occasion f; (big event) événement m; **on ∼** à l'occasion.

occasional /əˈkeɪʒənl/ adj (event) qui a lieu de temps en temps; **the ∼ letter** une lettre de temps en temps. **occasionally** adv de temps à autre.

occupation /ɒkjʊˈpeɪʃn/ n (activity) occupation f; (job) métier m, profession f. **occupational therapy** n ergothérapie f.

occupier /ˈɒkjʊpaɪə(r)/ n occupant/-e m/f.

occupy /ˈɒkjʊpaɪ/ vi occuper.

occur /əˈkɜː(r)/ vi (pt **occurred**) se produire; (arise) se présenter; **∼ to sb** venir à l'esprit de qn.

occurrence /əˈkʌrəns/ n (event) fait m; (instance) occurrence f.

ocean /ˈəʊʃn/ n océan m.

Oceania /əʊʃɪˈeɪnɪə/ n Océanie f.

o'clock /əˈklɒk/ adv it is six **∼** il est six heures; **at one ∼** à une heure.

October /ɒkˈtəʊbə(r)/ n octobre m.

octopus /ˈɒktəpəs/ n (pl) **∼es** pieuvre f.

odd /ɒd/ adj bizarre; (number) impair; (left over) qui reste; (sock) dépareillé; **write the ∼ article** écrire un article de temps en temps; **∼ jobs** menus travaux mpl; **twenty ∼** vingt et quelques. **oddity** n bizarrerie f.

odds /ɒdz/ npl chances fpl; (in betting) cote f (on de); **it makes no ∼** ça ne fait rien; **∼ and ends** des petites choses.

odour, (US) **odor** /ˈəʊdə(r)/ n odeur f. **odourless** adj inodore.

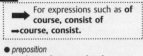

of /ɒv/

⟹ For expressions such as **of course**, **consist of** ⟹**course**, **consist**.

● preposition

⟶ de; **a photo ∼ the dog** une photo du chien; **the king ∼ the beasts** le roi des animaux; **(made) ∼ gold** en or; **it's kind ∼ you** c'est très gentil de votre part; **some ∼ us** quelques-uns d'entre nous; **∼ it/them** en; **have you heard ∼ it?** est-ce que tu en as entendu parler?

off /ɒf/ adv be **∼** partir, s'en aller; **I'm ∼** je m'en vais; **30 metres ∼** à 30 mètres; **a month ∼** dans un mois. ● adj (gas, water) coupé; (tap) fermé; (light, TV) éteint; (party, match) annulé; (bad) tourné; **Friday is my day ∼** je ne travaille pas le vendredi; **25% ∼** 25% de remise. ● prep **3 metres ∼ the ground** 3 mètres (au-dessus) du sol; **just ∼ the kitchen** juste à côté de la cuisine; **that is ∼ the point** là n'est pas la question.

offal /ˈɒfl/ n abats mpl.

offence /əˈfens/ n (Jur) infraction f; **give ∼ to** offenser; **take ∼** s'offenser (at de).

offend /əˈfend/ vt offenser; **be ∼ed** s'offenser (at de). ● vi (Jur) commettre une infraction. **offender** n délinquant/-e m/f.

offensive /əˈfensɪv/ adj (remark) injurieux; (language) grossier; (smell) repoussant; (weapon) offensif. ● n offensive f.

offer /ˈɒfə(r)/ vt (pt **offered**) offrir. ● n offre f; **on ∼** en promotion.

offhand /ɒfˈhænd/ adj désinvolte. ● adv à l'improviste.

office /ˈɒfɪs/ n bureau m; (duty) fonction f; **in ~** au pouvoir. ● adj de
bureau.

officer /ˈɒfɪsə(r)/ n (army) officier m;
(**police ~**) policier m; (**government
~**) fonctionnaire mf.

official /əˈfɪʃl/ adj officiel. ● n (civil servant) fonctionnaire mf; (of party,
union) officiel/-le m/f; (of police, customs) agent m.

off: ~-licence n magasin m de vins et
spiritueux. **~-line** adj autonome;
(switched off) déconnecté; (Comput)
hors connexion. **~-load** vt (stock)
écouler; (Comput) décharger. **~-peak**
adj (call) au tarif réduit; (travel) en période creuse. **~-putting** adj rebutant.
~-set vt (pt **-set**. pres p **-setting**)
compenser. **~-shore** adj (out to sea) au
large, en mer; (towards the sea) de
terre; **an ~ breeze** une brise de terre.
● adv (funds) hors-lieu inv. **~-side** adj
(Sport) hors jeu inv; (Auto) du côté du
conducteur. **~-spring** n inv progéniture f.

> **Off-licence** On trouve ces
> magasins de vins et spiritueux 🛈
> dans tous les quartiers commerçants
> des villes britanniques. Les gens y
> achètent surtout de l'alcool à em-
> porter, mais on y vend aussi des
> boissons non alcoolisées, des frian-
> dises ou du tabac et on peut même
> y louer des verres pour une
> fête. ▷**PUB.**

often /ˈɒfn/ adv souvent; **how ~ do
you meet?** vous vous voyez tous les
combien?; **every so ~** de temps en
temps.

oil /ɔɪl/ n (for lubrication, cooking) huile
f; (for fuel) pétrole m; (for heating)
mazout m. ● vt huiler. **~ field** n gisement m pétrolifère. **~-painting** n
peinture f à l'huile. **~ skins** npl ciré m.
~-tanker n pétrolier m.

oily /ˈɔɪlɪ/ adj graisseux.

ointment /ˈɔɪntmənt/ n pommade f.

OK, okay /əʊˈkeɪ/ adj d'accord; **is it ~
if…?** ça va si…?; **feel ~** aller bien.

old /əʊld/ adj vieux; (person) vieux, âgé;
(former) ancien; **how ~ Is he?** quel
âge a-t-il?; **he is eight years ~** il a
huit ans; **~er, ~est** aîné. **~ age** n
vieillesse f. **~-age pensioner** n

retraité/-e m/f. **~-fashioned** adj démodé; (person) vieux jeu inv. **~ man** n
vieillard m, vieux m. **~ woman** n
vieille f.

olive /ˈɒlɪv/ n olive f; **~ oil** huile f d'o-
live. ● adj olive inv.

Olympic /əˈlɪmpɪk/ adj olympique. **~
Games** npl Jeux mpl olympiques.

omelette /ˈɒmlɪt/ n omelette f.

omen /ˈəʊmən/ n augure m.

ominous /ˈɒmɪnəs/ adj (presence,
cloud) menaçant; (sign) de mauvais
augure.

omission /əˈmɪʃn/ n omission f. **omit**
vt (pt **omitted**) omettre.

on /ɒn/ prep sur; **~ the table** sur la
table; **put the key ~ it** mets la clé
dessus; **~ 22 March** le 22 mars; **~
Monday** lundi; **~ TV** à la télé; **~
video** en vidéo; **be ~ steroids** prendre des stéroïdes; **~ arriving** en arrivant. ● adj (TV, oven, light) allumé;
(dishwasher, radio) en marche; (tap)
ouvert; (lid) mis; **the match is still ~**
le match aura lieu quand même; **the
news is ~ in 10 minutes** les informations sont dans 10 minutes. ● adv
have sth ~ porter qch; **20 years ~**
20 ans plus tard; **from that day ~** à
partir de ce jour-là; **further ~** plus
loin; **~ and off** (occasionally) de
temps en temps; **go ~ and ~** (person) parler pendant des heures.

once /wʌns/ adv une fois; (formerly)
autrefois. ● conj une fois que; **all at ~**
tout d'un coup.

oncoming /ˈɒnkʌmɪŋ/ adj (vehicle) qui
approche.

one /wʌn/ det & n un/-e (m/f). ● pron
un/-e m/f; (impersonal) on; **~ (and
only)** seul (et unique); **a big ~** un
grand/une grande; **this/that ~** celui-
ci/-là, celle-ci/-là; **~ another** l'un/-e
l'autre. **~-off** adj 🇬🇧 unique, exceptionnel. **~ self** pron soi-même; (reflexive) se. **~-way** adj (street) à sens unique; (ticket) simple.

ongoing /ˈɒngəʊɪŋ/ adj (process) continu; **be ~** être en cours.

onion /ˈʌnɪən/ n oignon m.

on-line /ɒnˈlaɪn/ adj & adv en ligne.

onlooker /ˈɒnlʊkə(r)/ n spectateur/-
trice m/f.

only /ˈəʊnlɪ/ adj seul; **~ son** fils unique. ● adv & conj seulement; **he is ~**

O

six il n'a que six ans.

onset /'ɒnset/ n début m.

onward(s) /'ɒnwəd(z)/ adv en avant.

open /'əʊpən/ adj ouvert; (view) dégagé; (free to all) public; (undisguised) manifeste; (question) en attente; **in the ~ air** en plein air. ● vt/i (door) (s')ouvrir; (shop, play) ouvrir; **~ out** or **up** (s')ouvrir. **~-ended** adj (stay) de durée indéterminée; (debate, question) ouvert. **~-heart** adj (surgery) à cœur ouvert.

opening /'əʊpnɪŋ/ n (of book) début m; (of exhibition, shop) ouverture f; (of film) première f; (in market) débouché m; (job) poste m (disponible).

open: **~-minded** adj be **~-minded** avoir l'esprit ouvert. **~-plan** adj paysagé.

Open University Organisme britannique d'enseignement universitaire à distance. Les étudiants de tous âges travaillent chez eux et suivent les cours à la télévision ou sur Internet; ils envoient leurs travaux à leur directeur d'études (tutor) qu'ils peuvent rencontrer lors de stages en été. Les diplômes obtenus ont la même valeur que ceux délivrés par les universités traditionnelles.

opera /'ɒprə/ n opéra m.

operate /'ɒpəreɪt/ vt/i opérer; (Tech) (faire) fonctionner; **~ on** (Med) opérer; **operating theatre** salle f d'opération.

operation /ɒpə'reɪʃn/ n opération f; **have an ~** se faire opérer; **in ~** (plan) en vigueur; (mine) en service.

operative /'ɒpərətɪv/ n employé/-e m/f. ● adj (law) en vigueur.

operator /'ɒpəreɪtə(r)/ n opérateur/-trice m/f; (telephonist) standardiste mf.

opinion /ə'pɪnɪən/ n opinion f, avis m. **opinionated** adj qui a des avis sur tout.

opponent /ə'pəʊnənt/ n adversaire mf.

opportunity /ɒpə'tjuːnətɪ/ n occasion f (**to do** de faire).

oppose /ə'pəʊz/ vt s'opposer à; **as ~d to** par opposition à. **opposing** adj opposé.

opposite /'ɒpəzɪt/ adj (direction, side) opposé; (building) d'en face. ● n contraire m. ● adv en face. ● prep **~ (to)** en face de.

opposition /ɒpə'zɪʃn/ n opposition f.

oppress /ə'pres/ vt opprimer. **oppressive** adj (cruel) oppressif; (heat) oppressant.

opt /ɒpt/ vi **~ for** opter pour; **~ out** refuser de participer (**of** à); **~ to do** choisir de faire.

optical /'ɒptɪkl/ adj optique. **~ illusion** n illusion f d'optique. **~ scanner** n lecteur m optique.

optician /ɒp'tɪʃn/ n opticien/-ne m/f.

optimism /'ɒptɪmɪzəm/ n optimisme m. **optimist** n optimiste mf. **optimistic** adj optimiste.

option /'ɒpʃn/ n option f; (choice) choix m.

optional /'ɒpʃənl/ adj facultatif; **~ extras** accessoires mpl en option.

or /ɔː(r)/ conj ou; (with negative) ni.

oral /'ɔːrəl/ n & adj oral (m).

orange /'ɒrɪndʒ/ n (fruit) orange f; (colour) orange m. ● adj (colour) orange inv.

orbit /'ɔːbɪt/ n orbite f. ● vt décrire une orbite autour de.

orchard /'ɔːtʃəd/ n verger m.

orchestra /'ɔːkɪstrə/ n orchestre m.

orchid /'ɔːkɪd/ n orchidée f.

ordeal /ɔː'diːl/ n épreuve f.

order /'ɔːdə(r)/ n ordre m; (Comm) commande f; **in ~** (tidy) en ordre; (document) en règle; **in ~ that** pour que; **in ~ to** pour. ● vt ordonner; (goods) commander; **~ sb to** ordonner à qn de.

orderly /'ɔːdəlɪ/ adj (tidy) ordonné; (not unruly) discipliné. ● n (Mil) planton m; (Med) aide-soignant/-e m/f.

ordinary /'ɔːdənrɪ/ adj (usual) ordinaire; (average) moyen.

ore /ɔː(r)/ n minerai m.

organ /'ɔːgən/ n organe m; (Mus) orgue m.

organic /ɔː'gænɪk/ adj organique; (produce) biologique.

organization /ɔːgənaɪ'zeɪʃn/ n organisation f.

organize /'ɔːgənaɪz/ vt organiser.

organizer /'ɔːgənaɪzə(r)/ n organisateur/-trice m/f; **electronic ~**

agenda *m* électronique.

orgasm /ˈɔːgæzəm/ *n* orgasme *m*.

Orient /ˈɔːrɪənt/ *n* the ~ l'Orient *m*. **oriental** *adj* oriental.

origin /ˈɒrɪdʒɪn/ *n* origine *f*.

original /əˈrɪdʒənl/ *adj* original; (*inhabitant*) premier; (*member*) originaire. **originality** *n* originalité *f*. **originally** *adv* (at the outset) à l'origine.

originate /əˈrɪdʒɪmeɪt/ *vi* (plan) prendre naissance; ~ **from** provenir de; (person) venir de. ● *vt* être l'auteur de. **originator** *n* (of idea) auteur *m*; (of invention) créateur/-trice *m/f*.

ornament /ˈɔːnəmənt/ *n* (decoration) ornement *m*; (object) objet *m* décoratif.

orphan /ˈɔːfn/ *n* orphelin/-e *m/f*. ● *vt* rendre orphelin. **orphanage** *n* orphelinat *m*.

orthopaedic /ɔːθəˈpiːdɪk/ *adj* orthopédique.

ostentatious /ɒstenˈteɪʃəs/ *adj* tape-à-l'œil *inv*.

osteopath /ˈɒstɪəpæθ/ *n* ostéopathe *mf*.

ostrich /ˈɒstrɪtʃ/ *n* autruche *f*.

other /ˈʌðə(r)/ *adj* autre; the ~ one l'autre *mf*. ● *n & pron* autre *mf*; (some) ~s d'autres. ● *adv* ~ **than** (apart from) à part; (otherwise than) autrement que. **otherwise** *adv* autrement.

otter /ˈɒtə(r)/ *n* loutre *f*.

ouch /aʊtʃ/ *interj* aïe!

ought /ɔːt/ *v aux* devoir; **you** ~ **to stay** vous devriez rester; **he** ~ **to succeed** il devrait réussir; **I** ~ **to have done it** j'aurais dû le faire.

ounce /aʊns/ *n* once *f* (= 28.35 g).

our /ˈaʊə(r)/ *adj* notre, *pl* nos.

ours /ˈaʊəz/ *poss* le *or* la nôtre, les nôtres.

ourselves /aʊəˈselvz/ *pron* (reflexive) nous; (emphatic) nous-mêmes; (after preposition) **for** ~ pour nous, pour nous-mêmes.

out /aʊt/ *adv* dehors; **he's** ~ il est sorti; **further** ~ plus loin; **be** ~ (book) être publié; (light) être éteint; (sun) briller; (flower) être épanoui; (tide) être bas; (player) être éliminé; ~ **of hors de**; **go/walk/get** ~ **of** sortir de; ~ **of pity** par pitié; **made** ~ **of** fait de; **5** ~ **of 6** 5 sur 6. ~**break** *n*

(of war) déclenchement *m*; (of violence, boils) éruption *f*. ~**burst** *n* explosion *f*. ~**cast** *n* paria *m*. ~**class** *vt* surclasser. ~**come** *n* résultat *m*. ~**cry** *n* tollé *m*. ~**dated** *adj* démodé. ~**door** *adj* (activity) de plein air; (pool) en plein air. ~**doors** *adv* dehors.

outer /ˈaʊtə(r)/ *adj* extérieur; ~ **space** espace *m* extra-atmosphérique.

outfit /ˈaʊtfɪt/ *n* (clothes) tenue *f*.

outgoing /ˈaʊtgəʊɪŋ/ *adj* (minister, tenant) sortant; (sociable) ouvert. **outgoings** *npl* dépenses *fpl*.

outgrow /aʊtˈgrəʊ/ *vt* (*pt* -**grew**. *pp* -**grown**) (clothes) devenir trop grand pour; (habit) dépasser.

outing /ˈaʊtɪŋ/ *n* sortie *f*.

outlaw /ˈaʊtlɔː/ *n* hors-la-loi *m inv*. ● *vt* déclarer illégal.

outlet /ˈaʊtlet/ *n* (for water, gas) tuyau *m* de sortie; (for goods) débouché *m*; (for feelings) exutoire *m*.

outline /ˈaʊtlaɪn/ *n* contour *m*; (of plan) grandes lignes *fpl*; (of essay) plan *m*. ● *vt* tracer le contour de; (summarize) exposer brièvement.

out: ~**live** *vt* survivre à. ~**look** *n* perspective *f*. ~**number** *vt* surpasser en nombre. ~ **of date** *adj* démodé; (expired) périmé. ~ **of hand** *adj* incontrôlable. ~ **of order** *adj* en panne. ~ **of work** *adj* sans travail. ~**patient** *n* malade *mf* externe.

output /ˈaʊtpʊt/ *n* rendement *m*; (Comput) sortie *f*. ● *vt/i* (Comput) sortir.

outrage /ˈaʊtreɪdʒ/ *n* (anger) indignation *f*; (atrocity) attentat *m*; (scandal) outrage *m*. ● *vt* (morals) outrager; (person) scandaliser. **outrageous** *adj* scandaleux.

outright /ˈaʊtraɪt/ *adv* (completely) catégoriquement; (killed) sur le coup. ● *adj* (majority) absolu; (ban) catégorique; (hostility) pur et simple.

outset /ˈaʊtset/ *n* début *m*.

outside /aʊtˈsaɪd/ *n* extérieur *m*. ● *adv* dehors. ● *prep* en dehors de; (in front of) devant. ● *adj* extérieur. **outsider** *n* étranger/-ère *m/f*; (Sport) outsider *m*.

out: ~ **skirts** *npl* périphérie *f*. ~**spoken** *adj* franc. ~**standing** *adj* exceptionnel; (not settled) en suspens.

outward /'aʊtwəd/ adj & adv vers l'extérieur; (sign) extérieur. (journey) d'aller. **outwards** adv vers l'extérieur.

oval /'əʊvl/ n & adj ovale (m).

Oval Office Symbole même de la présidence américaine, le bureau ovale du président des États-Unis est situé dans l'aile ouest de la Maison-Blanche et a été inauguré en 1909. Le goût des pièces de forme ovale remonte à la présidence de George Washington (1789-1797) qui donnait des réceptions à son domicile de Philadelphie dans un salon ovale.

ovary /'əʊvərɪ/ n ovaire m.

oven /'ʌvn/ n four m.

over /'əʊvə(r)/ prep (across) par-dessus; (above) au-dessus de; (covering) sur; (more than) plus de; **it's ~ the road** c'est de l'autre côté de la rue; **~ here/there** par ici/là; **children ~ six** les enfants de plus de six ans; **~ the weekend** pendant le weekend; **all ~ the house** partout dans la maison. ● adj, adv (term) terminé; (war) fini; **get sth ~ with** en finir avec qch; **ask sb ~** inviter qn; **~ and ~ (again)** à plusieurs reprises; **five times ~** cinq fois de suite.

overall /əʊvər'ɔːl/ adj global, d'ensemble; (length) total. ● adv globalement.

overalls /'əʊvərɔːls/ npl combinaison f.

over /'əʊvə(r)/ **~board** adv par-dessus bord. **~cast** adj couvert. **~charge** vt faire payer trop cher à. **~coat** n pardessus m.

overcome /əʊvə'kʌm/ vt (pt **-came**. pp **-come**) (enemy) vaincre; (difficulty, fear) surmonter; **~by** accablé de.

overcrowded /əʊvə'kraʊdɪd/ adj bondé; (country) surpeuplé.

overdo /əʊvə'duː/ vt (pt **-did**. pp **-done**) (Culin) trop cuire; **~ it** (overwork) en faire trop.

over: **~dose** n surdose f, overdose f. **~ draft** n découvert m. **~ draw** vt (pt **-drew**. pp **-drawn**) faire un découvert sur. **~ due** adj en retard; (bill) impayé.

overflow¹ /əʊvə'fləʊ/ vi déborder.

overflow² /'əʊvəfləʊ/ n (outlet) tropplein m. **~ car park** n parking m de délestage.

overhaul /əʊvə'hɔːl/ vt réviser.

overhead¹ /əʊvə'hed/ adv au-dessus; (in sky) dans le ciel.

overhead² /'əʊvəhed/ adj aérien; **~ projector** rétroprojecteur m. **overheads** npl frais mpl généraux.

over: **~hear** vt (pt **-heard**) entendre par hasard. **~lap** vt/i (pt **-lapped**) (se) chevaucher. **~leaf** adv au verso. **~load** vt surcharger. **~look** vt (window) donner sur; (miss) ne pas voir.

overnight¹ /əʊvə'naɪt/ adv dans la nuit; (instantly: fig) du jour au lendemain.

overnight² /'əʊvənaɪt/ adj (train) de nuit; (stay) d'une nuit; (fig) soudain.

over: **~power** vt (thief) maîtriser; (army) vaincre; (fig) accabler. **~-priced** adj trop cher. **~rate** vt surestimer. **~react** vi réagir de façon excessive. **~riding** adj (consideration) numéro un; (importance) primordial. **~rule** vt (decision) annuler.

overrun /əʊvə'rʌn/ vt (pt **-ran**. pp **-run**; pres p **-running**) (country) envahir; (budget) dépasser. ● vi (meeting) durer plus longtemps que prévu.

overseas /əʊvə'siːz/ adj étranger. ● adv outre-mer, à l'étranger.

over: **~see** vt (pt **-saw**. pp **-seen**) surveiller. **~sight** n omission f. **~sleep** vi (pt **-slept**) se réveiller trop tard. **~take** vt/i (pt **-took**. pp **-taken**) dépasser; (fig) frapper. **~time** n heures fpl supplémentaires. **~turn** vt/i (se) renverser. **~weight** adj trop gros.

overwhelm /əʊvə'welm/ vt (enemy) écraser; (shame) accabler. **overwhelmed** adj (with offers, calls) submergé (**with, by** de); (with shame, work) accablé; (by sight) ébloui. **overwhelming** adj (heat, grief) accablant; (defeat, victory) écrasant; (urge) irrésistible.

overwork /əʊvə'wɜːk/ vt/i (se) surmener. ● n surmenage m.

owe /əʊ/ vt devoir. **owing** adj dû; **owing to** en raison de.

owl /aʊl/ n hibou m.

own /əʊn/ adj propre. ● pron **my ~** le mien, la mienne; **a house of one's ~** sa propre maison; **on one's ~** tout seul. ● vt posséder; **~ up (to)** 🔲 avouer. **owner** n propriétaire mf. **own-**

ership n propriété f; (of land) possession f.

Oxbridge Formé de la combinaison de Oxford et Cam-
bridge, ce mot-valise est fréquemment employé pour désigner les
universités de ces deux villes, en
particulier quand on veut les distinguer des autres universités britanniques, car ce sont les plus prestigieuses.

oxygen /'ɒksɪdʒən/ n oxygène m.
oyster /'ɔɪstə(r)/ n huître f.
ozone /'əʊzəʊn/ n ozone m; ~ **layer**
couche f d'ozone.

Pp

PA abbr ➡PERSONAL ASSISTANT.
pace /peɪs/ n pas m; (speed) allure f;
keep ~ with suivre. ● vt (room) arpenter. ● vi ~ **(up and down)** faire
les cent pas.
Pacific /pə'sɪfɪk/ n ~ **(Ocean)** océan m
Pacifique.
pack /pæk/ n paquet m; (Mil) sac m; (of
hounds) meute f; (of thieves) bande f;
(of lies) tissu m. ● vt (into case) mettre
dans une valise; (into box, crate) emballer; (for sale) conditionner; (crowd)
remplir complètement; ~ **one's suitcase** faire sa valise. ● vi faire ses valises; ~ **into** (cram) s'entasser dans; ~
off expédier; **send ~ing** envoyer
promener.
package /'pækɪdʒ/ n paquet m;
(Comput) progiciel m; ~ **deal** offre f
globale; ~ **holiday** voyage m organisé. ● vt empaqueter.
packed /pækt/ adj (crowded) bondé;
~ **lunch** repas m froid.
packet /'pækɪt/ n paquet m.
packing /'pækɪŋ/ n (action, material)
emballage m.
pad /pæd/ n (of paper) bloc m; (to protect) protection f; (for ink) tampon m;
(launch) ~ rampe f de lancement. ●
vt (pt **padded**) rembourrer; (text: fig)
délayer. ● vi (pt **padded**) (walk) mar-

cher à pas feutrés. **padding** n rembourrage m.
paddle /'pædl/ n pagaie f. ● vt ~ **a
canoe** pagayer. ● vi patauger.
padlock /'pædlɒk/ n cadenas m. ● vt
cadenasser.
paediatrician /piːdjə'trɪʃən/ n pédiatre mf.
pagan /'peɪgən/ adj & n païen/-ne
(m/f).
page /peɪdʒ/ n (of book) page f. ● vt
(on pager) rechercher; (over speaker)
faire appeler. **pager** n radiomessageur m.
pain /peɪn/ n douleur f; ~s efforts mpl;
be in ~ souffrir; **take ~s to** se donner du mal pour. ● vt (grieve) peiner.
painful adj douloureux; (laborious) pénible. ~**killer** n analgésique m. **painless** adj (operation) indolore; (death)
sans souffrance; (trouble-free) sans
peine. **painstaking** adj minutieux.
paint /peɪnt/ n peinture f; ~s (in tube,
box) couleurs fpl. ● vt/i peindre. ~
brush n pinceau m. **painter** n peintre
m. **painting** n peinture f. ~**work** n
peintures fpl.
pair /peə(r)/ n paire f; (of people) couple m; **a ~ of trousers** un pantalon.
● vi ~ **off** former un couple.
pajamas /pə'dʒɑːməz/ npl (US)
➡PYJAMAS.
Pakistan /pɑːkɪ'stɑːn/ n Pakistan m.
palace /'pælɪs/ n palais m.
palatable /'pælətəbl/ adj (food) savoureux; (solution) acceptable. **palate** n
palais m.
pale /peɪl/ adj pâle. ● vi pâlir.
Palestine /'pæləstaɪn/ n Palestine f.
pallid /'pælɪd/ adj pâle.
palm /pɑːm/ n (of hand) paume f;
(tree) palmier m; (symbol) palme f.
□ ~ **off** ① ~ **sth off as** faire passer
qch pour; ~ **sth off on sb** refiler qch
à qn ①.
palpitate /'pælpɪteɪt/ vi palpiter.
paltry /'pɔːltrɪ/ adj (-ier, -iest) dérisoire, piètre.
pamper /'pæmpə(r)/ vt choyer.
pamphlet /'pæmflɪt/ n brochure f.
pan /pæn/ n casserole f; (for frying)
poêle f.
pancake /'pæŋkeɪk/ n crêpe f.

o
p

pandemonium /pændɪ'məʊnɪəm/ n tohu-bohu m.

pander /'pændə(r)/ vi ~ **to** (person, taste) flatter bassement.

pane /peɪn/ n carreau m, vitre f.

panel /'pænl/ n (of door) panneau m; (of experts, judges) commission f; (on discussion programme) invités mpl; **(instrument)** ~ tableau m de bord.

pang /pæŋ/ n serrement m au cœur; ~**s of conscience** remords mpl.

panic /'pænɪk/ n panique f. ● vt/i (pt **panicked**) (s')affoler. ~-**stricken** adj pris de panique, affolé.

pansy /'pænzɪ/ n (Bot) pensée f.

pant /pænt/ vi haleter.

panther /'pænθə(r)/ n panthère f.

pantomime /'pæntəmaɪm/ n (show) spectacle m de Noël; (mime) mime m.

pantry /'pæntrɪ/ n garde-manger m inv.

pants /pænts/ npl (underwear) slip m; (trousers: US) pantalon m.

paper /'peɪpə(r)/ n papier m; (newspaper) journal m; (exam) épreuve f; (essay) exposé m; (wallpaper) papier m peint; (identity) ~**s** papiers mpl (d'identité); **on** ~ par écrit. ● vt (room) tapisser. ~**back** n livre m de poche. ~-**clip** n trombone m. ~ **feed tray** n (Comput) bac m d'alimentation en papier. ~ **work** n (work) travail m administratif; (documentation) documents mpl.

par /pɑː(r)/ n **be below** ~ ne pas être en forme; **on a** ~ **with** (performance) comparable à; (person) l'égal de; (golf) par m.

parachute /'pærəʃuːt/ n parachute m. ● vi descendre en parachute.

parade /pə'reɪd/ n (procession) parade f; (Mil) défilé m. ● vi défiler. ● vt faire étalage de.

paradise /'pærədaɪs/ n paradis m.

paradox /'pærədɒks/ n paradoxe m.

paraffin /'pærəfɪn/ n pétrole m (lampant); (wax) paraffine f.

paragliding /'pærəglaɪdɪŋ/ n parapente m.

paragon /'pærəgən/ n modèle m.

paragraph /'pærəgrɑːf/ n paragraphe m.

parallel /'pærəlel/ adj parallèle. ● n parallèle m; (maths) parallèle f.

Paralympics /pærə'lɪmpɪks/ npl **the** ~ les jeux paralympiques.

paralyse /pærə'laɪz/ vt paralyser. **paralysis** n paralysie f.

paramedic /pærə'medɪk/ n auxiliaire mf médical/-e.

parameter /pə'ræmɪtə(r)/ n paramètre m.

paramount /'pærəmaʊnt/ adj suprême.

paranoia /pærə'nɔɪə/ n paranoïa f. **paranoid** adj paranoïaque; (Psych) paranoïde.

paraphernalia /pærəfə'neɪlɪə/ n attirail m.

parasol /'pærəsɒl/ n ombrelle f; (on table, at beach) parasol m.

paratrooper /'pærətruːpə(r)/ n (Mil) parachutiste mf.

parcel /'pɑːsl/ n paquet m.

parchment /'pɑːtʃmənt/ n parchemin m.

pardon /'pɑːdn/ n pardon m; (Jur) grâce f; **I beg your** ~ je vous demande pardon. ● vt (pt **pardoned**) pardonner (**sb for sth** qch à qn); (Jur) gracier.

parent /'peərənt/ n parent m.

parenthesis /pə'renθəsɪs/ n (pl -**theses**) parenthèse f.

parenthood /'peərənthʊd/ n (fatherhood) paternité f; (motherhood) maternité f.

Paris /'pærɪs/ n Paris.

parish /'pærɪʃ/ n (Relig) paroisse f; (municipal) commune f.

park /pɑːk/ n parc m. ● vt/i (se) garer; (remain parked) stationner. ~ **and ride** n parc m relais.

parking /'pɑːkɪŋ/ n stationnement m; **no** ~ stationnement interdit. ~ **lot** n (US) parking m. ~ **meter** n parcmètre m. ~ **ticket** n (fine) contravention f, PV m🛈.

parliament /'pɑːləmənt/ n parlement m. **parliamentary** adj parlementaire.

Parliament Corps législatif britannique composé de la Chambre des communes (House of Commons) et de la Chambre des lords (House of Lords) qui siègent au Palais de Westminster. Le souverain convoque et dissout le Parlement,

p

parlour | patch

ouvre chaque session parlementaire et signe les textes de lois. ▷**Scot-tish Parliament**, ▷**Welsh Assem-bly**, ▷**Dáil**

parlour, (US) **parlor** /'pɑːlə(r)/ n salon m.

parody /'pærədɪ/ n parodie f. ● vt parodier.

parole /pə'rəʊl/ n **on ~** en liberté conditionnelle.

parrot /'pærət/ n perroquet m.

parry /'pærɪ/ vt (Sport) parer; (question) éluder. ● n parade f.

parsley /'pɑːslɪ/ n persil m.

parsnip /'pɑːsnɪp/ n panais m.

part /pɑːt/ n partie f; (of serial) épisode m; (of machine) pièce f; (Theat) rôle m; (side in dispute) parti m; **in ~** en partie; **on the ~ of** de la part de; **take ~ in** participer à. ● adj partiel. ● adv en partie. ● vt/i (separate) (se) séparer, ~ **with** se séparer de.

part-exchange n reprise f; **take sth in ~** reprendre qch.

partial /'pɑːʃl/ adj partiel; (biased) partial; **be ~ to** avoir un faible pour.

participant /pɑː'tɪsɪpənt/ n participant/-e m/f. **participate** vi participer (**in** à). **participation** n participation f.

participle /'pɑːtɪsɪpl/ n participe m.

particular /pə'tɪkjʊlə(r)/ n détail m; **~s** détails mpl; **in ~** en particulier. ● adj particulier; (fussy) difficile; (careful) méticuleux; **that ~ man** cet homme-là. **particularly** adv particulièrement.

parting /'pɑːtɪŋ/ n séparation f; (in hair) raie f. ● adj d'adieu.

partition /pɑː'tɪʃn/ n (of room) cloison f; (Pol) partition f. ● vt (room) cloisonner; (country) partager.

partly /'pɑːtlɪ/ adv en partie.

partner /'pɑːtnə(r)/ n (professional) associé/-e m/f; (economic, sporting) partenaire mf; (spouse) époux/-se m/f; (unmarried) partenaire mf. **partnership** n association f.

partridge /'pɑːtrɪdʒ/ n perdrix f.

part-time adj & adv à temps partiel.

party /'pɑːtɪ/ n fête f; (formal) réception f; (group) groupe m; (Pol) parti m; (Jur) partie f.

pass /pɑːs/ vt/i (pt **passed**) passer; (overtake) dépasser; (in exam) réussir; (approve) (candidate) admettre; (invoice) approuver; (remark) faire; (judgement) prononcer; (law, bill) adopter; **~ (by)** (building) passer devant; (person) croiser. ● n (permit) laisser-passer m inv; (ticket) carte f d'abonnement; (Geog) col m; (Sport) passe f; **~ (mark)** (in exam) moyenne f. □ **~ away** mourir; **~ out** (faint) s'évanouir; **~ sth out** distribuer qch; **~ over** (overlook) délaisser; **~ up** (forego) laisser passer.

passage /'pæsɪdʒ/ n (way through, text) passage m; (of voyage) traversée f; (corridor) couloir m.

passenger /'pæsɪndʒə(r)/ n (in car, plane, ship) passager/-ère m/f; (in train, bus, tube) voyageur/-euse m/f.

passer-by /pɑːsə'baɪ/ n (pl **passers-by**) passant/-e m/f.

passing /'pɑːsɪŋ/ adj (motorist) qui passe; (whim) passager; (reference) en passant.

passion /'pæʃn/ n passion f. **passionate** adj passionné.

passive /'pæsɪv/ adj passif.

passport /'pɑːspɔːt/ n passeport m.

password /'pɑːswɜːd/ n mot m de passe.

past /pɑːst/ adj (times, problems) passé; (president) ancien; **the ~ months** ces derniers mois. ● n passé m. ● prep (beyond) après; **walk/go ~ sth** passer devant qch; **10 ~ 6** six heures dix; **it's ~ 11** il est 11 heures passées. ● adv **go/walk ~** passer.

pasta /'pæstə/ n pâtes fpl (alimentaires).

paste /peɪst/ n (glue) colle f; (dough) pâte f; (of fish, meat) pâté m; (jewellery) strass m. ● vt coller.

pasteurize /'pɑːstʃəraɪz/ vt pasteuriser.

pastime /'pɑːstaɪm/ n passe-temps m inv.

pastry /'peɪstrɪ/ n (dough) pâte f; (tart) pâtisserie f.

pat /pæt/ vt (pt **patted**) tapoter. ● n petite tape f.

patch /pætʃ/ n pièce f; (over eye) bandeau m; (spot) tache f; (of snow, ice) plaque f; (of vegetables) carré m; **bad**

p

~ période *f* difficile. □ ~ **up** (*trousers*) rapiécer; (*quarrel*) résoudre.

patent /'pætnt/ *adj* (*obvious*) manifeste; (*patented*) breveté; ~ **leather** cuir *m* verni. ● *n* brevet *m*. ● *vt* faire breveter.

path /pɑːθ/ *n* (*pl* -**s**) sentier *m*, chemin *m*; (*in park*) allée *f*; (*of rocket*) trajectoire *f*.

pathetic /pə'θetɪk/ *adj* misérable; (*bad* 🔲) lamentable.

patience /'peɪʃns/ *n* patience *f*.

patient /'peɪʃnt/ *adj* patient. ● *n* patient/-e *m/f*. **patiently** *adv* patiemment.

patriotic /pætrɪ'ɒtɪk/ *adj* patriotique; (*person*) patriote.

patrol /pə'trəʊl/ *n* patrouille *f*; ~ **car** voiture *f* de police. ● *vt/i* patrouiller (*dans*).

patron /'peɪtrən/ *n* (*of the arts*) mécène *m*; (*customer*) client/-e *m/f*. **patronage** *n* clientèle *f*; (*support*) patronage *m*. **patronize** *vt* (*person*) traiter avec condescendance; (*establishment*) fréquenter.

patter /'pætə(r)/ *n* (*of steps*) bruit *m*; (*of rain*) crépitement *m*.

pattern /'pætn/ *n* motif *m*, dessin *m*; (*for sewing*) patron *m*; (*for knitting*) modèle *m*.

paunch /pɔːntʃ/ *n* ventre *m*.

pause /pɔːz/ *n* pause *f*. ● *vi* faire une pause; (*hesitate*) hésiter.

pave /peɪv/ *vt* paver; ~ **the way** ouvrir la voie (**for** à).

pavement /'peɪvmənt/ *n* trottoir *m*; (*US*) chaussée *f*.

paving stone *n* pavé *m*.

paw /pɔː/ *n* patte *f*. ● *vt* (*animal*) donner des coups de patte à; (*touch* 🔲) peloter 🔲.

pawn /pɔːn/ *n* pion *m*. ● *vt* mettre en gage. ~**broker** *n* prêteur/-euse *m/f* sur gages. ~-**shop** *n* mont-de-piété *m*.

pay /peɪ/ *vt* (*pt* **paid**) payer; (*interest*) rapporter; (*compliment, attention*) faire; (*visit, homage*) rendre. ● *vi* payer; (*business*) rapporter; ~ **for sth** payer qch. ● *n* salaire *m*; ~ **rise** augmentation *f* (*de salaire*). ~ **back** rembourser; ~ **in** déposer; ~ **off** (*loan*) rembourser; (*worker*) congédier; (*succeed*) être payant; ~ **out** payer, débourser.

payable /'peɪəbl/ *adj* payable; ~ **to** (*cheque*) à l'ordre de.

payment /'peɪmənt/ *n* paiement *m*; (*regular*) versement *m*; (*reward*) récompense *f*.

payroll /'peɪrəʊl/ *n* fichier *m* des salaires; **be on the** ~ **of** être employé par.

PC *abbr* ➡**PERSONAL COMPUTER.**

PDA *abbr* (personal digital assistant) assistant *m* personnel numérique.

PE *abbr* (**physical education**) éducation *f* physique, EPS *f*.

pea /piː/ *n* (petit) pois *m*

peace /piːs/ *n* paix *f*; ~ **of mind** tranquillité *f* d'esprit. **peaceful** *adj* (*tranquil*) paisible; (*peaceable*) pacifique.

peach /piːtʃ/ *n* pêche *f*.

peacock /'piːkɒk/ *n* paon *m*.

peak /piːk/ *n* (*of mountain*) pic *m*; (*of cap*) visière *f*; (*maximum*) maximum *m*; (*on graph*) sommet *m*; (*of career*) apogée *m*; (*of fitness*) meilleur *m*; ~ **hours** heures *fpl* de pointe.

peal /piːl/ *n* (*of bells*) carillon *m*; (*of laughter*) éclat *m*.

peanut /'piːnʌt/ *n* cacahuète *f*; ~s (*money*) 🔲 clopinettes *fpl* 🔲.

pear /peə(r)/ *n* poire *f*.

pearl /pɜːl/ *n* perle *f*.

peasant /'peznt/ *n* paysan/-ne *m/f*.

peat /piːt/ *n* tourbe *f*.

pebble /'pebl/ *n* caillou *m*; (*on beach*) galet *m*.

peck /pek/ *vt/i* (*food*) picorer; (*attack*) donner des coups de bec (à). ● *n* coup *m* de bec; **a** ~ **on the cheek** une bise.

peckish /'pekɪʃ/ *adj* **be** ~ 🔲 avoir faim.

peculiar /pɪ'kjuːlɪə(r)/ *adj* (*odd*) bizarre; (*special*) particulier (**to** à). **peculiarity** *n* bizarrerie *f*.

pedal /'pedl/ *n* pédale *f*. ● *vi* pédaler.

pedantic /pɪ'dæntɪk/ *adj* pédant.

peddle /'pedl/ *vt* colporter; (*drugs*) faire du trafic de.

pedestrian /pɪ'destrɪən/ *n* piéton *m*. ● *adj* (*precinct, street*) piétonnier; (*fig*) prosaïque; ~ **crossing** passage *m* pour piétons.

pedigree /'pedɪgriː/ *n* (*of animal*) pedigree *m*; (*of person*) ascendance *f*. ● *adj* (*dog*) de pure race.

pee /piː/ *vi* 🔲 faire pipi 🔲.

peek /piːk/ *vi & n* ➡**PEEP**.

peel /piːl/ *n* (*on fruit*) peau *m*; (*removed*) épluchures *fpl*. ● *vt* (*fruit, vegetables*) éplucher; (*prawn*) décortiquer. ● *vi* (*of skin*) peler; (*of paint*) s'écailler.

peep /piːp/ *vi* jeter un coup d'œil (furtif) (**at** à). ● *n* coup *m* d'œil (furtif). **∼hole** *n* judas *m*.

peer /pɪə(r)/ *vi* ∼ (**at**) regarder fixement. ● *n* (*equal, noble*) pair *m*. **peerage** *n* pairie *f*.

peg /peg/ *n* (*for clothes*) pince *f* à linge; (*to hang coats*) patère *f*; (*for tent*) piquet *m*. ● *vt* (*pt* **pegged**) (*clothes*) accrocher avec des pinces; (*prices*) indexer.

pejorative /prˈdʒɒrətɪv/ *adj* péjoratif.

pelican /ˈpelɪkən/ *n* pélican *m*; ∼ **crossing** *passage m* pour piétons.

pellet /ˈpelɪt/ *n* (*round mass*) boulette *f*; (*for gun*) plomb *m*.

pelt /pelt/ *vt* bombarder (**with** de). ● *n* (*skin*) peau *f*.

pelvis /ˈpelvɪs/ *n* (*Anat*) bassin *m*.

pen /pen/ *n* stylo *m*; (*for sheep*) enclos *m*; (*for baby, cattle*) parc *m*.

penal /ˈpiːnl/ *adj* pénal. **penalize** *vt* pénaliser.

penalty /ˈpenltɪ/ *n* peine *f*; (*fine*) amende *f*; (*in football*) penalty *m*.

penance /ˈpenəns/ *n* pénitence *f*.

pence /pens/ ➡**PENNY**.

pencil /ˈpensl/ *n* crayon *m*. ● *vt* (*pt* **pencilled**) crayonner; ∼ **in** noter provisoirement. **∼-sharpener** *n* taille-crayons *m inv*.

pending /ˈpendɪŋ/ *adj* (*matter*) en souffrance; (*Jur*) en instance. ● *prep* (*until*) en attendant.

penetrate /ˈpenɪtreɪt/ *vt* pénétrer; (*silence, defences*) percer; (*organization*) infiltrer. ● *vi* pénétrer. **penetrating** *adj* pénétrant.

pen-friend *n* correspondant/-e *m/f*.

penguin /ˈpeŋgwɪn/ *n* manchot *m*, pingouin *m*.

pen: **∼knife** *n* (*pl* **-knives**) canif *m*. **∼-name** *n* pseudonyme *m*.

penniless /ˈpenɪlɪs/ *adj* sans le sou.

penny /ˈpenɪ/ *n* (*pl* **pennies** or **pence**) (*unit of currency*) penny *m*; (*small*

amount) centime *m*.

pension /ˈpenʃn/ *n* (*from state*) pension *f*; (*from employer*) retraite *f*; ∼ **scheme** plan *m* de retraite. ● *vt* ∼ **off** mettre à la retraite. **pensioner** *n* retraité/-e *m/f*.

pensive /ˈpensɪv/ *adj* songeur.

penthouse /ˈpenthaʊs/ *n* appartement *m* de luxe (*au dernier étage*).

penultimate /penˈʌltɪmət/ *adj* avant-dernier.

people /ˈpiːpl/ *npl* gens *mpl*, personnes *fpl*; **English** ∼ les Anglais *mpl*; ∼ **say** on dit. ● *n* peuple *m*. ● *vt* peupler. ∼ **carrier** *n* monospace *m*.

pepper /ˈpepə(r)/ *n* poivre *m*; (*vegetable*) poivron *m*. ● *vt* (*Culin*) poivrer.

peppermint /ˈpepəmɪnt/ *n* (*plant*) menthe *f* poivrée; (*sweet*) bonbon *m* à la menthe.

per /pɜː(r)/ *prep* par; ∼ **annum** par an; ∼ **cent** pour cent; ∼ **kilo** le kilo; **ten km** ∼ **hour** dix km à l'heure.

percentage /pəˈsentɪdʒ/ *n* pourcentage *m*.

perception /pəˈsepʃn/ *n* perception *f*. **perceptive** *adj* perspicace.

perch /pɜːtʃ/ *n* (*of bird*) perchoir *m*. ● *vi* (se) percher.

perennial /pəˈrenɪəl/ *adj* perpétuel; (*plant*) vivace.

perfect[1] /pəˈfekt/ *vt* perfectionner.

perfect[2] /ˈpɜːfɪkt/ *adj* parfait. ● *n* (Ling) parfait *m*. **perfectly** *adv* parfaitement.

perfection /pəˈfekʃn/ *n* perfection *f*; **to** ∼ à la perfection.

perforate /ˈpɜːfəreɪt/ *vt* perforer.

perform /pəˈfɔːm/ *vt* (*task*) exécuter; (*function*) remplir; (*operation*) procéder à; (*play*) jouer; (*song*) chanter. ● *vi* (*actor, musician, team*) jouer; ∼ **well/ badly** (*candidate, business*) avoir de bons/de mauvais résultats. **performance** *n* interprétation *f*; (*of car, team*) performance *f*; (*show*) représentation *f*; (*fuss*) histoire *f*. **performer** *n* artiste *mf*.

perfume /ˈpɜːfjuːm/ *n* parfum *m*.

perhaps /pəˈhæps/ *adv* peut-être.

peril /ˈperəl/ *n* péril *m*. **perilous** *adj* périlleux.

perimeter /pəˈrɪmɪtə(r)/ *n* périmètre *m*.

p

period /'pɪərɪəd/ n période f; (era) époque f; (lesson) cours m; (Gram) point m; (Med) règles fpl. ● adj d'époque. **periodical** n périodique m.

peripheral /pə'rɪfərəl/ adj (vision, suburb) périphérique; (issue) annexe. ● n (Comput) périphérique m.

perish /'perɪʃ/ vi périr; (rubber) se détériorer.

perjury /'pɜːdʒərɪ/ n faux témoignage m.

perk /pɜːk/ n ① avantage m. ● vt/i ~ **up** ① (se) remonter. **perky** adj ① gai.

perm /pɜːm/ n permanente f. ● vt **have one's hair ~ed** se faire faire une permanente.

permanent /'pɜːmənənt/ adj permanent. **permanently** adv (happy) en permanence; (employed) de façon permanente.

permissible /pə'mɪsɪbl/ adj permis.

permission /pə'mɪʃn/ n permission f.

permissive /pə'mɪsɪv/ adj libéral; (pej) permissif.

permit[1] /pə'mɪt/ vt (pt **permitted**) permettre (**sb to** à qn de), autoriser (**sb to** qn à).

permit[2] /'pɜːmɪt/ n permis m.

perpendicular /pɜːpən'dɪkjʊlə(r)/ adj perpendiculaire.

perpetrator /'pɜːpɪtreɪtə(r)/ n auteur m.

perpetuate /pə'petjʊeɪt/ vt perpétuer.

perplexed /pə'plekst/ adj perplexe.

persecute /'pɜːsɪkjuːt/ vt persécuter.

perseverance /pɜːsɪ'vɪərəns/ n persévérance f. **persevere** vi persévérer.

persist /pə'sɪst/ vi persister (**in doing** à faire). **persistence** n persistance f. **persistent** adj (cough, snow) persistant; (obstinate) obstiné; (noise, pressure) continuel.

person /'pɜːsn/ n personne f; **in** ~ en personne.

personal /'pɜːsənl/ adj (life, problem, opinion) personnel; (safety, freedom, insurance) individuel. ~ **ad** n petite annonce f. ~ **assistant** n secrétaire mf de direction. ~ **computer** n ordinateur m (personnel), microordinateur m.

personality /pɜːsə'nælətɪ/ n personnalité f; (star) vedette f.

personal: ~ **organizer** n agenda m. ~ **stereo** n baladeur m.

personnel /pɜːsə'nel/ n personnel m.

perspiration /pɜːspɪ'reɪʃn/ n (sweat) sueur f; (sweating) transpiration f. **perspire** vi transpirer.

persuade /pə'sweɪd/ vt persuader (**to** de). **persuasion** n persuasion f. **persuasive** adj persuasif.

pertinent /'pɜːtɪnənt/ adj pertinent.

perturb /pə'tɜːb/ vt troubler.

Peru /pə'ruː/ n Pérou m.

pervasive /pə'veɪsɪv/ adj (smell) pénétrant; (feeling) envahissant.

perverse /pə'vɜːs/ adj (desire) pervers; (refusal, attitude) illogique. **perversion** n perversion f.

pervert[1] /pə'vɜːt/ vt (truth) travestir; (values) fausser; (justice) entraver.

pervert[2] /'pɜːvɜːt/ n pervers/-e m/f.

pessimist /'pesɪmɪst/ n pessimiste mf. **pessimistic** adj pessimiste.

pest /pest/ n (insect) insecte m nuisible; (animal) animal m nuisible; (person ①) enquiquineur/-euse m/f ①.

pester /'pestə(r)/ vt harceler.

pet /pet/ n animal m de compagnie; (favourite) chouchou/-te m/f. ● adj (theory, charity) favori; ~ **hate** bête f noire; ~ **name** petit nom m. ● vt (pt **petted**) caresser; (spoil) chouchouter ①.

petal /'petl/ n pétale m.

peter /'piːtə(r)/ vi ~ **out** (conversation) tarir; (supplies) s'épuiser.

petite /pə'tiːt/ adj (woman) menue.

petition /pə'tɪʃn/ n pétition f. ● vt adresser une pétition à.

petrol /'petrəl/ n essence f. ~ **bomb** n cocktail m molotov. ~ **station** n station-service f. ~ **tank** n réservoir m d'essence.

petticoat /'petɪkəʊt/ n jupon m.

petty /'petɪ/ adj (-ier, -iest) (minor) petit; (mean) mesquin; ~ **cash** petite caisse f.

pew /pjuː/ n banc m (d'église).

pharmacist /'fɑːməsɪst/ n pharmacien/-ne m/f. **pharmacy** n pharmacie f.

phase /feɪz/ n phase f. ● vt ~ **in/out** introduire/supprimer peu à peu.

PhD abbr (**Doctor of Philosophy**) doctorat m.

pheasant /'feznt/ n faisan/-e m/f.

phenomenon /fə'nɒmɪnən/ n (pl **-ena**) phénomène m.

phew /fju:/ interj ouf.

philosopher /fɪ'lɒsəfə(r)/ n philosophe mf. **philosophical** adj philosophique; (resigned) philosophe. **philosophy** n philosophie f.

phlegm /flem/ n (Med) mucosité f.

phobia /'fəʊbɪə/ n phobie f.

phone /fəʊn/ n téléphone m; **on the ~** au téléphone. ● vt (person) téléphoner à; **~ England** téléphoner en Angleterre. ● vi téléphoner; **~ back** rappeler. **~ book** n annuaire m. **~ booth**, **~ box** n cabine f téléphonique. **~ call** n coup m de fil 🔒. **~ card** n télécarte f. **~-in** n émission f à ligne ouverte. **~ number** n numéro m de téléphone.

phonetic /fə'netɪk/ adj phonétique.

phoney /'fəʊnɪ/ adj (**-ier, -iest**) 🔒 faux. ● n (person) charlatan m; **it's a ~** c'est un faux.

photocopier /'fəʊtəʊkɒpɪə(r)/ n photocopieuse f.

photocopy /'fəʊtəʊkɒpɪ/ n photocopie f. ● vt photocopier.

photograph /'fəʊtəgrɑːf/ n photographie f. ● vt photographier. **photographer** n photographe mf.

phrase /freɪz/ n expression f; (idiom) locution f. ● vt exprimer, formuler. **~-book** n guide m de conversation.

physical /'fɪzɪkl/ adj physique.

physicist /'fɪzɪsɪst/ n physicien/-ne m/f.

physics /'fɪzɪks/ n physique f.

physiotherapist /fɪzɪəʊ'θerəpɪst/ n kinésithérapeute mf. **physiotherapy** n kinésithérapie f.

physique /fɪ'ziːk/ n physique m.

piano /pɪ'ænəʊ/ n piano m.

pick /pɪk/ n choix m; (best) meilleur/-e m/f; (tool) pioche f. ● vt choisir; (flower) cueillir; (lock) crocheter; **~ a quarrel with** chercher querelle à; **~ one's nose** se curer le nez. □ **~ on** harceler; **~ out** vt choisir; (identify) distinguer; **~ up** vt ramasser; (sth fallen) relever; (weight) soulever; (habit, passenger, speed) prendre; (learn) apprendre; vi s'améliorer.

pickaxe /'pɪkæks/ n pioche f.

picket /'pɪkɪt/ n (striker) gréviste mf; (stake) piquet m; **~ (line)** piquet m de grève. ● vt (pt **picketed**) installer un piquet de grève devant.

pickle /'pɪkl/ n conserves fpl au vinaigre; (gherkin) cornichon m. ● vt conserver dans du vinaigre.

pick-up /'pɪkʌp/ n (stylus-holder) lecteur m; (on guitar) capteur m; (collection) ramassage m; (improvement) reprise f.

picnic /'pɪknɪk/ n pique-nique m. ● vi (pt **picnicked**) pique-niquer.

pictorial /pɪk'tɔːrɪəl/ adj (magazine) illustré; (record) graphique.

picture /'pɪktʃə(r)/ n image f; (painting) tableau m; (photograph) photo f; (drawing) dessin m; (film) film m; (fig) description f; **the ~s** le cinéma. ● vt s'imaginer; **be ~d** (shown) être représenté.

picturesque /pɪktʃə'resk/ adj pittoresque.

pie /paɪ/ n (sweet) tarte f; (savoury) tourte f.

piece /piːs/ n morceau m; (of string, ribbon) bout m; (of currency, machine) pièce f; **a ~ of advice/furniture** un conseil/meuble; **go to ~s** (fig) s'effondrer; **take to ~s** démonter.

pier /pɪə(r)/ n jetée f.

pierce /pɪəs/ vt percer.

pig /pɪg/ n porc m, cochon m.

pigeon /'pɪdʒɪn/ n pigeon m. **~-hole** n casier m.

pig-headed adj entêté.

pigsty /'pɪgstaɪ/ n porcherie f.

pigtail /'pɪgteɪl/ n natte f.

pike /paɪk/ n inv (fish) brochet m.

pile /paɪl/ n (heap) tas m; (stack) pile f; (of carpet) poil m; **~s of** 🔒 un tas de 🔒. ● vt **~ (up)** entasser. ● vi **~ into** s'engouffrer dans; **~ up** (snow, leaves) s'entasser; (debts, work) s'accumuler. **~-up** n (Auto) carambolage m.

pilgrim /'pɪlgrɪm/ n pèlerin m. **pilgrimage** n pèlerinage m.

pill /pɪl/ n pilule f.

pillar /'pɪlə(r)/ n pilier m. **~-box** n boîte f aux lettres.

pillion /'pɪlɪən/ n siège m de passager; **ride ~** monter en croupe.

pillow /'pɪləʊ/ n oreiller m. **~case** n taie f d'oreiller.

p

pilot /'paɪlət/ n pilote m. ● adj pilote.
● vt (pt **piloted**) piloter. ~**-light** n
veilleuse f.

pimple /'pɪmpl/ n bouton m.

pin /pɪn/ n épingle f; (of plug) fiche f;
(for wood, metal) goujon m; (in surgery) broche f; **have ~s and needles**
avoir des fourmis. ● vt (pt **pinned**)
épingler, attacher; (trap) coincer; ~
sb down (fig) forcer qn à se décider;
~ **up** accrocher.

pinafore /'pɪnəfɔː(r)/ n tablier m.

pincers /'pɪnsəz/ npl tenailles fpl.

pinch /pɪntʃ/ vt pincer; (steal 🛈) piquer. ● vi (be too tight) serrer. ● n
(mark) pinçon m; (of salt) pincée f; **at
a** ~ à la rigueur.

pine /paɪn/ n (tree) pin m. ● vi ~
(away) dépérir; ~ **for** languir après.

pineapple /'paɪnæpl/ n ananas m.

pinecone /'paɪnkəʊn/ n pomme f
de pin.

pink /pɪŋk/ adj & n rose (m).

pinpoint /'pɪnpɔɪnt/ vt (problem,
cause, location) indiquer; (time) déterminer.

pint /paɪnt/ n pinte f (GB = 0.57 litre;
US = 0.47 litre).

pin-up /'pɪnʌp/ n pin-up f inv. 🛈

pioneer /paɪə'nɪə(r)/ n pionnier m. ● vt
~ **the use of** être le premier à
utiliser.

pious /'paɪəs/ adj pieux.

pip /pɪp/ n (seed) pépin m; (sound)
top m.

pipe /paɪp/ n tuyau m; (to smoke) pipe
f; (Mus) chalumeau m; ~**s** cornemuse
f. ● vt transporter par tuyau. □ ~
down se taire.

pipeline /'paɪplaɪn/ n oléoduc m; **in
the** ~ en cours.

piping /'paɪpɪŋ/ n tuyauterie f; ~ **hot**
fumant.

pirate /'paɪərət/ n pirate m. ● vt pirater.

Pisces /'paɪsiːz/ n Poissons mpl.

pistol /'pɪstl/ n pistolet m.

pit /pɪt/ n fosse f; (mine) puits m;
(quarry) carrière f; (for orchestra) fosse
f; (of stomach) creux m; (of cherry: US)
noyau m. ● vt (pt **pitted**) marquer;
(fig) opposer; ~ **oneself against** se
mesurer à.

pitch /pɪtʃ/ n (Sport) terrain m; (of
voice, note) hauteur f; (degree) degré

m; (Mus) ton m; (tar) brai m. ● vt jeter;
(tent) planter. ● vi (ship) tanguer. □ ~
in 🛈 contribuer.

pitfall /'pɪtfɔːl/ n écueil m.

pitiful /'pɪtɪfl/ adj pitoyable. **pitiless** adj
impitoyable.

pit stop n arrêt m mécanique.

pittance /'pɪtns/ n **earn a** ~ gagner
trois fois rien.

pity /'pɪtɪ/ n pitié f; (regrettable fact)
dommage m; **take** ~ **on** avoir pitié
de; **what a** ~**!** quel dommage! ● vt
avoir pitié de.

pivot /'pɪvət/ n pivot m. ● vi (pt
pivoted) pivoter.

placard /'plækɑːd/ n affiche f.

place /pleɪs/ n endroit m, lieu m;
(house) maison f; (seat, rank) place f;
at or **to my** ~ chez moi; **change** ~**s**
changer de place; **in the first** ~ d'a-
bord; **out of** ~ déplacé; **take** ~ avoir
lieu. ● vt placer; (order) passer; (remember) situer; **be** ~**d** (in race) se
placer. ~**-mat** n set m.

placid /'plæsɪd/ adj placide.

plagiarism /'pleɪdʒərɪzəm/ n plagiat
m. **plagiarize** vt/i plagier.

plague /pleɪg/ n (bubonic) peste f;
(epidemic) épidémie f; (of ants, lo-
custs) invasion f. ● vt harceler.

plaice /pleɪs/ n inv carrelet m.

plain /pleɪn/ adj (obvious) clair; (candid) franc; (simple) simple; (not
pretty) sans beauté; (not patterned)
uni; ~ **chocolate** chocolat m noir; **in**
~ **clothes** en civil. ● adv franchement.
● n plaine f. **plainly** adv clairement;
franchement; simplement.

plaintiff /'pleɪntɪf/ n (Jur) plaignant/-
e m/f.

plaintive /'pleɪntɪv/ adj plaintif.

plait /plæt/ vt tresser. ● n natte f.

plan /plæn/ n projet m, plan m; (diagram) plan m. ● vt (pt **planned**) projeter (**to do** de faire); (timetable, day)
organiser; (economy, work) planifier.
● vi prévoir; ~ **to** s'attendre à.

plane /pleɪn/ n (level) plan m; (aeroplane) avion m; (tool) rabot m. ● adj
plan. ● vt raboter.

planet /'plænɪt/ n planète f.

plank /plæŋk/ n planche f.

planning /'plænɪŋ/ n (of economy,
work) planification f; (of holiday, party)

organisation *f*; (of town) urbanisme *m*; **family** ~ planning *m* familial; ~ **permission** permis *m* de construire.

plant /plɑːnt/ *n* plante *f*; (Tech) matériel *m*; (factory) usine *f*. ● *vt* planter; (bomb) placer.

plaster /'plɑːstə(r)/ *n* plâtre *m*; (adhesive) sparadrap *m*. ● *vt* plâtrer; (cover) couvrir (**with** de).

plastic /'plæstɪk/ *adj* en plastique; (art, substance) plastique; ~ **surgery** chirurgie *f* esthétique. ● *n* plastique *m*.

plate /pleɪt/ *n* assiette *f*; (of metal) plaque *f*; (silverware) argenterie *f*; (in book) gravure *f*. ● *vt* (metal) plaquer.

plateau /'plætəʊ/ *n* (pl ~x) plateau *m*; (fig) palier *m*.

platform /'plætfɔːm/ *n* (stage) estrade *f*; (for speaking) tribune *f*; (Rail) quai *m*; (Pol) plate-forme *f*.

platoon /plə'tuːn/ *n* (Mil) section *f*.

play /pleɪ/ *vt/i* jouer; (instrument) jouer de; (record) mettre; (game) jouer à; (opponent) jouer contre; (match) disputer; ~ **safe** ne pas prendre de risques. ● *n* jeu *m*; (Theat) pièce *f*. □ ~ **down** minimiser; ~**on** (fears) exploiter; ~ **up** 🄸 commencer à faire de siennes 🄸; ~ **up sth** mettre l'accent sur qch.

playful /'pleɪfl/ *adj* (remark) taquin; (child) joueur.

play: ~**ground** *n* cour *f* de récréation. ~**group**, ~**school** *n* garderie *f*.

playing /'pleɪɪŋ/ *n* (Sport) jeu *m*; (Theat) interprétation *f*. ~**card** *n* carte *f* à jouer. ~**field** *n* terrain *m* de sport.

play: ~**pen** *n* parc *m* (pour bébé). ~**wright** *n* auteur *m* dramatique.

plc *abbr* (**public limited company**) SA.

plea /pliː/ *n* (for mercy, tolerance) appel *m*; (for food, money) demande *f*; (reason) excuse *f*; **make a** ~ **of guilty** plaider coupable.

plead /pliːd/ *vt/i* supplier; (Jur) plaider.

pleasant /'pleznt/ *adj* agréable.

please /pliːz/ *vt/i* plaire (à), faire plaisir (à); ~ **oneself, do as one** ~**s** faire ce qu'on veut. ● *adv* s'il vous *or* te plaît. **pleased** *adj* content (**with** de). **pleasing** *adj* agréable.

pleasure /'pleʒə(r)/ *n* plaisir *m*; **with** ~ avec plaisir; **my** ~ je vous en prie.

pleat /pliːt/ *n* pli *m*. ● *vt* plisser.

pledge /pledʒ/ *n* (token) gage *m*; (promise) promesse *f*. ● *vt* promettre; (pawn) mettre en gage.

plentiful /'plentɪfl/ *adj* abondant.

plenty /'plentɪ/ *n* abondance *f*; ~ **(of)** (a great deal) beaucoup (de); (enough) assez (de).

pliers /'plaɪəz/ *npl* pinces *fpl*.

plight /plaɪt/ *n* détresse *f*.

plinth /plɪnθ/ *n* socle *m*.

plod /plɒd/ *vi* (pt **plodded**) avancer péniblement.

plonk /plɒŋk/ *n* 🄸 pinard *m* 🄸.

plot /plɒt/ *n* (conspiracy) complot *m*; (of novel) intrigue *f*; ~ **(of land)** terrain *m*. ● *vt/i* (pt **plotted**) (plan) comploter; (mark out) tracer.

plough /plaʊ/ *n* charrue *f*. ● *vt/i* labourer. □ ~ **back** réinvestir; ~ **through** avancer péniblement dans.

plow /plaʊ/ *n & vt* (US) ➞PLOUGH.

ploy /plɔɪ/ *n* stratagème *m*.

pluck /plʌk/ *vt* (flower, fruit) cueillir; (bird) plumer; (eyebrows) épiler; (strings: Mus) pincer; ~ **up courage** prendre son courage à deux mains. **plucky** *adj* courageux.

plug /plʌg/ *n* (for sink) bonde *f*; (Electr) fiche *f*, prise *f*. ● *vt* (pt **plugged**) (hole) boucher; (publicize 🄸) faire du battage autour de. □ ~ **in** brancher. ~**-hole** *n* bonde *f*.

plum /plʌm/ *n* prune *f*; ~ **pudding** (plum-)pudding *m*.

plumber /'plʌmə(r)/ *n* plombier *m*.

plume /pluːm/ *n* (of feathers) panache *m*.

plummet /'plʌmɪt/ *vi* tomber, plonger.

plump /plʌmp/ *adj* potelé, dodu.

plunge /plʌndʒ/ *vt/i* (dive, thrust) plonger; (fall) tomber. ● *n* plongeon *m*; (fall) chute *f*; **take the** ~ se jeter à l'eau. **plunger** *n* (for sink) ventouse *f*.

plural /'plʊərəl/ *adj* pluriel; (noun) au pluriel; (ending) du pluriel. ● *n* pluriel *m*.

plus /plʌs/ *prep* plus; **ten** ~ plus de dix. ● *adj* (Electr & fig) positif. ● *n* signe *m* plus; (fig) atout *m*.

ply /plaɪ/ *vt* (tool) manier; (trade) exercer. ● *vi* faire la navette; ~ **sb with drink** offrir continuellement à boire à qn.

plywood /'plaɪwʊd/ *n* contreplaqué *m*.

p

p.m. /piːˈem/ adv de l'après-midi or du soir.

pneumatic drill /njuːˈmætɪk drɪl/ n marteaupiqueur m.

pneumonia /njuːˈməʊnɪə/ n pneumonie f.

PO abbr ➡POST OFFICE.

poach /pəʊtʃ/ vt/i (game) braconner; (staff) débaucher; (Culin) pocher.

PO Box n boîte f postale.

pocket /ˈpɒkɪt/ n poche f; **be out of ~** avoir perdu de l'argent. ● vt empocher. ● adj de poche. **~-book** n (notebook) carnet m; (wallet: US) portefeuille m; (handbag: US) sac m à main. **~-money** n argent m de poche.

pod /pɒd/ n (peas) cosse f; (vanilla) gousse f.

podgy /ˈpɒdʒɪ/ adj (**-ier, -iest**) dodu.

poem /ˈpəʊɪm/ n poème m. **poet** n poète m. **poetic** adj poétique. **poetry** n poésie f.

point /pɔɪnt/ n (position) point m; (tip) pointe f; (decimal point) virgule f; (remark) remarque f; **good ~s** qualités fpl; **on the ~ of** sur le point de; **~ in time** moment m; **~ of view** point m de vue; **to the ~** pertinent; **what is the ~?** à quoi bon? ● vt (aim) braquer; (show) indiquer; **~ out** signaler. ● vi indiquer du doigt; **~ out that, make the ~ that** faire remarquer que. **~-blank** adj & adv à bout portant.

pointed /ˈpɔɪntɪd/ adj (sharp) pointu; (window) en pointe; (remark) lourd de sens.

pointless /ˈpɔɪntlɪs/ adj inutile.

poise /pɔɪz/ n (confidence) assurance f; (physical elegance) aisance f.

poison /ˈpɔɪzn/ n poison m. ● vt empoisonner. **poisonous** adj (substance) toxique; (plant) vénéneux; (snake) venimeux.

poke /pəʊk/ vt/i (push) pousser; (fire) tisonner; (thrust) fourrer; **~ fun at** se moquer de. ● n (petit) coup m. □ **~out** (head) sortir.

poker /ˈpəʊkə(r)/ n (for fire) tisonnier m; (cards) poker m.

Poland /ˈpəʊlənd/ n Pologne f.

polar /ˈpəʊlə(r)/ adj polaire.

pole /pəʊl/ n (stick) perche f; (for flag) mât m; (Geog) pôle m.

Pole /pəʊl/ n Polonais/-e m/f.

pole-vault n saut m à la perche.

police /pəˈliːs/ n police f. ● vt faire la police dans. **~ constable** n agent m de police. **~man** n (pl **-men**) agent m de police. **~ station** n commissariat m de police. **~woman** n (pl **-women**) femme-agent f.

policy /ˈpɒləsɪ/ n politique f; (insurance) police f (d'assurance).

polish /ˈpɒlɪʃ/ vt polir; (shoes, floor) cirer. ● n (for shoes) cirage m; (for floor) encaustique f; (for nails) vernis m; (shine) poli m; (fig) raffinement m. □ **~ off** finir en vitesse; **~ up** (language) perfectionner.

Polish /ˈpəʊlɪʃ/ adj polonais. ● n (Ling) polonais m.

polished /ˈpɒlɪʃt/ adj raffiné.

polite /pəˈlaɪt/ adj poli.

political /pəˈlɪtɪkl/ adj politique.

politician /pɒlɪˈtɪʃn/ n homme m politique, femme f politique.

politics /ˈpɒlətɪks/ n politique f.

poll /pəʊl/ n (vote casting) scrutin m; (survey) sondage m; **go to the ~s** aller aux urnes. ● vt (votes) obtenir.

pollen /ˈpɒlən/ n pollen m.

polling booth n isoloir m.

polling station n bureau m de vote.

pollution /pəˈluːʃn/ n pollution f.

polo /ˈpəʊləʊ/ n polo m. **~ neck** n col m roulé.

pomegranate /ˈpɒmɪɡrænɪt/ n grenade f.

pomp /pɒmp/ n pompe f.

pompous /ˈpɒmpəs/ adj pompeux.

pond /pɒnd/ n étang m; (artificial) bassin m; (stagnant) mare f.

ponder /ˈpɒndə(r)/ vt/i réfléchir (à), méditer (sur).

pong /pɒŋ/ n (stink 🔢) puanteur f. ● vi 🔢 puer.

pony /ˈpəʊnɪ/ n poney m. **~tail** n queue f de cheval.

poodle /ˈpuːdl/ n caniche m.

pool /puːl/ n (puddle) flaque f; (pond) étang m; (of blood) mare f; (for swimming) piscine f; (fund) fonds m commun; (of ideas) réservoir m; (snooker) billard m américain; **~s** pari m mutuel sur le football. ● vt mettre en commun.

poor /pɔː(r)/ adj (not wealthy) pauvre; (not good) médiocre, mauvais.

poorly /ˈpɔːlɪ/ adj malade. ● adv mal.

pop /pɒp/ n (noise) pan m; (music) pop m. ● adj pop inv. ● vt/i (pt **popped**) (burst) crever; (put) mettre; ~ **in/out/off** entrer/sortir/partir. □ ~ **up** surgir. ~**-up** fenêtre f pop-up.

pope /pəʊp/ n pape m.

poppy /ˈpɒpɪ/ n pavot m; (wild) coquelicot m.

popular /ˈpɒpjʊlə(r)/ adj populaire; (in fashion) en vogue; **be** ~ **with** plaire à.

population /pɒpjʊˈleɪʃn/ n population f.

porcelain /ˈpɔːsəlɪn/ n porcelaine f.

porcupine /ˈpɔːkjʊpaɪn/ n porc-épic m.

pork /pɔːk/ n porc m.

pornography /pɔːˈnɒɡrəfɪ/ n pornographie f.

port /pɔːt/ n (harbour) port m; (left: Naut) bâbord m; ~ **of call** escale f; (wine) porto m.

portable /ˈpɔːtəbl/ adj portable.

porter /ˈpɔːtə(r)/ n (carrier) porteur m; (doorkeeper) portier m.

portfolio /pɔːtˈfəʊlɪəʊ/ n (Pol, Comm) portefeuille m.

portion /ˈpɔːʃn/ n (at meal) portion f; (part) partie f.

portrait /ˈpɔːtreɪt/ n portrait m.

portray /pɔːˈtreɪ/ vt représenter.

Portugal /ˈpɔːtʃʊɡl/ n Portugal m.

Portuguese /pɔːtʃʊˈɡiːz/ n (Ling) portugais m; (person) Portugais/-e m/f. ● adj portugais.

pose /pəʊz/ vt/i poser; ~ **as** (expert) se poser en. ● n pose f.

poser /ˈpəʊzə(r)/ n (person) frimeur/-euse m/f; (puzzle) colle f.

posh /pɒʃ/ adj 🔲 chic inv.

position /pəˈzɪʃn/ n position f; (job, state) situation f. ● vt placer.

positive /ˈpɒzətɪv/ adj positif; (sure) sûr, certain; (real) réel, vrai.

possess /pəˈzes/ vt posséder.

possession /pəˈzeʃn/ n possession f; **take** ~ **of** prendre possession de.

possessive /pəˈzesɪv/ adj possessif.

possible /ˈpɒsəbl/ adj possible.

possibly /ˈpɒsəblɪ/ adv peut-être; **if I** ~ **can** si cela m'est possible; **I cannot**

~ **leave** il m'est impossible de partir.

post /pəʊst/ n (pole) poteau m; (station, job) poste m; (mail service) poste f; (letters) courrier m. ● adj postal. ● vt (letter) poster; **keep** ~**ed** tenir au courant; ~ **(up)** (a notice) afficher; (appoint) affecter.

postage /ˈpəʊstɪdʒ/ n affranchissement m; **tarif** m postal.

postal /ˈpəʊstl/ adj postal. ~ **order** n mandat m.

post: ~**box** n boîte f aux lettres. ~**card** n carte f postale. ~ **code** n code m postal.

poster /ˈpəʊstə(r)/ n (for information) affiche f; (for decoration) poster m.

postgraduate /pəʊstˈɡrædʒʊət/ n étudiant/-e m/f de troisième cycle.

posthumous /ˈpɒstjʊməs/ adj posthume.

post: ~**man** n (pl -**men**) facteur m. ~**mark** n cachet m de la poste.

post-mortem /pəʊstˈmɔːtəm/ n autopsie f.

post office n poste f.

postpone /pəˈspəʊn/ vt remettre.

postscript /ˈpəʊsskrɪpt/ n (to letter) postscriptum m inv.

posture /ˈpɒstʃə(r)/ n posture f. ● vi prendre des poses.

pot /pɒt/ n pot m; (drug 🔲) hasch m; **go to** ~ 🔲 aller à la ruine; **take** ~ **luck** tenter sa chance. ● vt (plants) mettre en pot.

potato /pəˈteɪtəʊ/ n (pl ~**es**) pomme f de terre.

pot-belly n bedaine f.

potential /pəˈtenʃl/ adj & n potentiel (m).

pothole /ˈpɒthəʊl/ n (in rock) caverne f; (in road) nid m de poule. **pot-holing** n spéléologie f.

potter /ˈpɒtə(r)/ n potier m. ● vi bricoler. **pottery** n (art) poterie f; (objects) poteries fpl.

potty /ˈpɒtɪ/ adj (-**ier, -iest**) (crazy 🔲) toqué. ● n pot m.

pouch /paʊtʃ/ n poche f; (for tobacco) blague f.

poultry /ˈpəʊltrɪ/ n volailles fpl.

pounce /paʊns/ vi bondir (**on** sur). ● n bond m.

pound /paʊnd/ n (weight) livre f (= 454 g); (money) livre f; (for dogs, cars)

p

fourrière f. ● vt (crush) piler; (bombard) pilonner. ● vi frapper fort; (of heart) battre fort; (walk) marcher à pas lourds.

pour /pɔː(r)/ vt verser. ● vi couler, ruisseler (**from** de); (rain) pleuvoir à torrents. □ ~ **in/out** (people) arriver/ sortir en masse; ~ **off** or **out** vider. **pouring rain** n pluie f torrentielle.

pout /paʊt/ vi faire la moue.

poverty /'pɒvəti/ n misère f, pauvreté f.

powder /'paʊdə(r)/ n poudre f. ● vt poudrer.

power /'paʊə(r)/ n (strength) puissance f; (control) pouvoir m; (energy) énergie f; (Electr) courant m. ● vt (engine) faire marcher; (plane) propulser; ~**ed by** (engine) propulsé par; (generator) alimenté par. ~ **cut** n coupure f de courant.

powerful /'paʊəfl/ adj puissant.

powerless /'paʊəlɪs/ adj impuissant.

power: ~**point** n prise f de courant. ~**station** n centrale f électrique.

practical /'præktɪkl/ adj pratique. ~ **joke** n farce f.

practice /'præktɪs/ n (procedure) pratique f; (of profession) exercice m; (Sport) entraînement m; **in** ~ (in fact) en pratique; (well-trained) en forme; **out of** ~ rouillé; **put into** ~ mettre en pratique.

practise /'præktɪs/ vt/i (musician, typist) s'exercer (à); (Sport) s'entraîner (à); (put into practice) pratiquer; (profession) exercer.

practitioner /præk'tɪʃənə(r)/ n praticien/-ienne m/f; **dental** ~ dentiste mf.

praise /preɪz/ vt faire l'éloge de; (God) louer. ● n éloges mpl, louanges fpl.

pram /præm/ n landau m.

prance /prɑːns/ vi caracoler.

prawn /prɔːn/ n crevette f rose.

pray /preɪ/ vi prier. **prayer** n prière f.

preach /priːtʃ/ vt/i prêcher; ~ **at** or **to** prêcher.

precarious /prɪ'keərɪəs/ adj précaire.

precaution /prɪ'kɔːʃn/ n précaution f.

precede /prɪ'siːd/ vt précéder.

precedence /'presɪdəns/ n (in importance) priorité f; (in rank) préséance f.

precedent /'presɪdənt/ n précédent m.

precinct /'priːsɪŋkt/ n quartier m commerçant; (pedestrian area) zone f piétonne; (district: US) circonscription f.

precious /'preʃəs/ adj précieux.

precipitate /prɪ'sɪpɪteɪt/ vt (person, event, chemical) précipiter.

précis /'preɪsiː/ n résumé m.

precise /prɪ'saɪs/ adj précis; (careful) méticuleux. **precision** n précision f.

precocious /prɪ'kəʊʃəs/ adj précoce.

preconceived /priːkən'siːvd/ adj préconçu.

predator /'predətə(r)/ n prédateur m.

predicament /prɪ'dɪkəmənt/ n situation f difficile.

predict /prɪ'dɪkt/ vt prédire. **predictable** adj prévisible. **prediction** n prédiction f.

predispose /priːdɪ'spəʊz/ vt prédisposer **to do** à faire).

predominant /prɪ'dɒmɪnənt/ adj prédominant.

pre-empt /priː'empt/ vt (anticipate) anticiper; (person) devancer.

preface /'prefɪs/ n (to book) préface f; (to speech) préambule m.

prefect /'priːfekt/ n (pupil) élève m/f chargé/-e de la discipline; (official) préfet m.

prefer /prɪ'fɜː(r)/ vt (pt **preferred**) préférer (**to do** faire). **preferably** adv de préférence. **preference** n préférence f. **preferential** adj préférentiel.

prefix /'priːfɪks/ n préfixe m.

pregnancy /'pregnənsɪ/ n grossesse f. **pregnant** adj (woman) enceinte; (animal) pleine; (pause) éloquent.

prehistoric /priːhɪ'stɒrɪk/ adj préhistorique.

prejudge /priː'dʒʌdʒ/ vt (issue) préjuger de; (person) juger d'avance.

prejudice /'predʒʊdɪs/ n préjugé(s) m(pl); (harm) préjudice m. ● vt (claim) porter préjudice à; (person) léser. **prejudiced** adj partial; (person) qui a des préjugés.

premature /'premətjʊə(r)/ adj prématuré.

premeditated /priː'medɪteɪtɪd/ adj prémédité.

premises /'premɪsɪz/ npl locaux mpl; **on the** ~ sur les lieux.

premium /'priːmɪəm/ n (insurance) prime f; **be at a** ~ être précieux.

p

preoccupied /priːˈɒkjʊpaɪd/ adj préoccupé.

preparation /prepəˈreɪʃn/ n préparation f; ~s préparatifs mpl.

preparatory /prɪˈpærətrɪ/ adj préparatoire. ~ **school** n école f primaire privée; (US) école f secondaire privée.

prepare /prɪˈpeə(r)/ vt/i (se) préparer (**for** à); **be** ~**d for** (expect) s'attendre à; ~**d to** prêt à.

preposition /prepəˈzɪʃn/ n préposition f.

preposterous /prɪˈpɒstərəs/ adj absurde, ridicule.

prep school n →PREPARATORY SCHOOL.

prerequisite /priːˈrekwɪzɪt/ n condition f préalable.

prescribe /prɪˈskraɪb/ vt prescrire.

prescription /prɪˈskrɪpʃn/ n (Med) ordonnance f.

presence /ˈprezns/ n présence f; ~ **of mind** présence f d'esprit.

present[1] /ˈpreznt/ adj présent. ● n présent m; (gift) cadeau m; **at** ~ à présent; **for the** ~ pour le moment.

present[2] /prɪˈzent/ vt présenter; (film, concert) donner; ~ **sb with** offrir à qn. **presentation** n présentation f. **presenter** n présentateur/-trice m/f.

preservation /prezəˈveɪʃn/ n (of food) conservation f; (of wildlife) préservation f.

preservative /prɪˈzɜːvətɪv/ n (Culin) agent m de conservation.

preserve /prɪˈzɜːv/ vt préserver; (Culin) conserver. ● n réserve f; (fig) domaine m; (jam) confiture f.

presidency /ˈprezɪdənsɪ/ n présidence f.

president /ˈprezɪdənt/ n président/-e m/f.

press /pres/ vt/i (button) appuyer (sur); (squeeze) presser; (iron) repasser; (pursue) poursuivre; **be** ~**ed for** (time) manquer de; ~ **for sth** faire pression pour avoir qch; ~ **sb to do sth** pousser qn à faire qch; ~ **on** continuer (**with sth** qch). ● n (newspapers, machine) presse f; (for wine) pressoir m. ~ **cutting** n coupure f de presse.

pressing /ˈpresɪŋ/ adj pressant.

press: ~ **release** n communiqué m de presse. ~-**stud** n bouton-pression m. ~-**up** n pompe f.

pressure /ˈpreʃə(r)/ n pression f. ● vt faire pression sur. ~-**cooker** n cocotte-minute f. ~ **group** n groupe m de pression.

pressurize /ˈpreʃəraɪz/ vt (cabin) pressuriser; (person) faire pression sur.

prestige /preˈstiːʒ/ n prestige m.

presumably /prɪˈzjuːməblɪ/ adv vraisemblablement.

presume /prɪˈzjuːm/ vt (suppose) présumer.

pretence, (US) **pretense** /prɪˈtens/ n feinte f, simulation f; (claim) prétention f; (pretext) prétexte m.

pretend /prɪˈtend/ vt/i faire semblant (**to do** de faire); ~ **to** (lay claim to) prétendre à.

pretentious /prɪˈtenʃəs/ adj prétentieux.

pretext /ˈpriːtekst/ n prétexte m.

pretty /ˈprɪtɪ/ adj (-ier, -iest) joli. ● adv assez; ~ **much** presque.

prevail /prɪˈveɪl/ vi (be usual) prédominer; (win) prévaloir; ~ **on** persuader (**to do** de faire). **prevailing** adj actuel; (wind) dominant.

prevalent /ˈprevələnt/ adj répandu.

prevent /prɪˈvent/ vt empêcher (**from doing** de faire). **prevention** n prévention f. **preventive** adj préventif.

preview /ˈpriːvjuː/ n avant-première f; (fig) aperçu m.

previous /ˈpriːvɪəs/ adj précédent, antérieur; ~ **to** avant. **previously** adv auparavant.

prey /preɪ/ n proie f; **bird of** ~ rapace m. ● vi ~ **on** faire sa proie de; (worry) préoccuper.

price /praɪs/ n prix m. ● vt fixer le prix de. **priceless** adj inestimable; (amusing 🇬🇧) impayable 🇬🇧.

prick /prɪk/ vt (with pin) piquer; ~ **up one's ears** dresser l'oreille. ● n piqûre f.

prickle /ˈprɪkl/ n piquant m.

pride /praɪd/ n orgueil m; (satisfaction) fierté f; ~ **of place** place f d'honneur. ● vpr ~ **oneself on** s'enorgueillir de.

priest /priːst/ n prêtre m.

prim /prɪm/ adj (**primmer, primmest**) guindé, méticuleux.

p

primarily /'praɪmərəlɪ/ adv essentiellement.

primary /'praɪmərɪ/ adj (school, elections) primaire; (chief, basic) premier, fondamental. ● n (Pol: US) primaire f.

prime /praɪm/ adj principal, premier; (first-rate) excellent. ● vt (pump, gun) amorcer; (surface) apprêter. **P~ Minister** n Premier Ministre m.

primitive /'prɪmɪtɪv/ adj primitif.

primrose /'prɪmrəʊz/ n primevère f (jaune).

prince /prɪns/ n prince m. **princess** n princesse f.

principal /'prɪnsəpl/ adj principal. ● n (of school) directeur/-trice m/f.

principle /'prɪnsəpl/ n principe m; **in/on ~** en/par principe.

print /prɪnt/ vt imprimer; (write in capitals) écrire en majuscules; **~ed matter** imprimés mpl. ● n (of foot) empreinte f; (letters) caractères mpl; (photograph) épreuve f; (engraving) gravure f; **in ~** disponible; **out of ~** épuisé. **printer** n (person) imprimeur m; (Comput) imprimante f.

prion /'priːɒn/ n prion m.

prior /'praɪə(r)/ adj précédent. ● n (Relig) prieur m. **~ to** prep avant (de).

priority /praɪ'ɒrɪtɪ/ n priorité f; **take ~** avoir la priorité (**over** sur).

prise /praɪz/ vt forcer; **~ open** ouvrir en forçant.

prison /'prɪzn/ n prison f. **prisoner** n prisonnier/-ière m/f. **~ officer** n gardien/-ne m/f de prison.

pristine /'prɪstiːn/ adj **be in ~ condition** être comme neuf.

privacy /'prɪvəsɪ/ n intimité f, solitude f.

private /'praɪvɪt/ adj privé; (confidential) personnel; (lessons, house) particulier; (ceremony) intime; **in ~** en privé; (of ceremony) dans l'intimité. ● n (soldier) simple soldat m. **privately** adv en privé; dans l'intimité; (inwardly) intérieurement.

privilege /'prɪvəlɪdʒ/ n privilège m. **privileged** adj privilégié; **be ~d to** avoir le privilège de.

prize /praɪz/ n prix m. ● vt (value) priser.

pro /prəʊ/ n **the ~s and cons** le pour et le contre.

probable /'prɒbəbl/ adj probable. **probably** adv probablement.

probation /prə'beɪʃn/ n (testing) essai m; (Jur) liberté f surveillée.

probe /prəʊb/ n (device) sonde f; (fig) enquête f. ● vt sonder. ● vi **~ into** sonder.

problem /'prɒbləm/ n problème m. ● adj difficile. **problematic** adj problématique.

procedure /prə'siːdʒə(r)/ n procédure f; (way of doing sth) démarche f à suivre.

proceed /prə'siːd/ vi (go) aller, avancer; (pass) passer (**to** à); (act) procéder; **~ (with)** continuer; **~ to do** se mettre à faire.

proceedings /prə'siːdɪŋz/ npl (discussions) débats mpl; (meeting) réunion f; (report) actes mpl; (Jur) poursuites fpl.

proceeds /'prəʊsiːdz/ npl (profits) produit m, bénéfices mpl.

process /'prəʊses/ n processus m; (method) procédé m; **in ~** en cours; **in the ~ of doing** en train de faire. **~or** n (Culin) robot m (ménager); (Comput) unité f centrale. ● vt (material, data) traiter.

procession /prə'seʃn/ n défilé m.

procrastinate /prəʊ'kræstɪneɪt/ vi différer, tergiverser.

procure /prə'kjʊə(r)/ vt obtenir.

prod /prɒd/ vt/i (pt **prodded**) pousser doucement. ● n petit coup m.

prodigy /'prɒdɪdʒɪ/ n prodige m.

produce[1] /'prɒdjuːs/ n produits mpl.

produce[2] /prə'djuːs/ vt/i produire; (bring out) sortir; (show) présenter; (cause) provoquer; (Theat, TV), mettre en scène; (radio) réaliser; (cinema) produire. **producer** n metteur m en scène; réalisateur m; producteur m.

product /'prɒdʌkt/ n produit m.

production /prə'dʌkʃn/ n production f; (Theat, TV) mise f en scène; (radio) réalisation f.

productive /prə'dʌktɪv/ adj productif. **productivity** n productivité f.

profession /prə'feʃn/ n profession f.

professional /prə'feʃənl/ adj professionnel; (of high quality) de professionnel; (person) qui exerce une profession libérale. ● *n* professionnel/-le *m/f.*

professor /prə'fesə(r)/ *n* professeur *m* (*titulaire d'une chaire*).

proficient /prə'fɪʃnt/ *adj* compétent.

profile /'prəʊfaɪl/ *n* (of face) profil *m;* (of body, mountain) silhouette *f;* (by journalist) portrait *m.*

profit /'prɒfɪt/ *n* profit *m,* bénéfice *m.* ● *vi* ~ **by** tirer profit de. **profitable** *adj* rentable.

profound /prə'faʊnd/ *adj* profond.

profusely /prə'fjuːslɪ/ *adv* (*bleed*) abondamment; (*apologize*) avec effusion. **profusion** *n* profusion *f.*

program /'prəʊɡræm/ *n* (US) **➡PRO-GRAMME; (computer)** ~ programme *m.* ● *vt* (*pt* **programmed**) programmer.

programme /'prəʊɡræm/ *n* programme *m;* (broadcast) émission *f.*

programmer /'prəʊɡræmə(r)/ *n* programmeur/-euse *m/f.*

programming /'prəʊɡræmɪŋ/ *n* (Comput) programmation *f.*

progress¹ /'prəʊɡres/ *n* progrès *m* (*pl*) (in ~) en cours; **make** ~ faire des progrès; ~ **report** compte-rendu *m.*

progress² /prə'ɡres/ *vi* (advance, improve) progresser.

progressive /prə'ɡresɪv/ *adj* progressif; (reforming) progressiste.

prohibit /prə'hɪbɪt/ *vt* interdire (**sb from doing** à qn de faire).

project¹ /prə'dʒekt/ *vt* projeter. ● *vi* (jut out) être en saillie.

project² /'prɒdʒekt/ *n* (plan) projet *m;* (undertaking) entreprise *f;* (School) dossier *m.*

projection /prə'dʒekʃn/ *n* projection *f* ; saillie *f;* (estimate) prévision *f.*

projector /prə'dʒektə(r)/ *n* projecteur *m.*

proliferate /prə'lɪfəreɪt/ *vi* proliférer.

prolong /prə'lɒŋ/ *vt* prolonger.

prominent /'prɒmɪnənt/ *adj* (projecting) proéminent; (conspicuous) bien en vue; (fig) important.

promiscuous /prə'mɪskjʊəs/ *adj* de mœurs faciles.

promise /'prɒmɪs/ *n* promesse *f.* ● *vt/i* promettre. **promising** *adj* prometteur;

(*person*) qui promet.

promote /prə'məʊt/ *vt* promouvoir; (advertise) faire la promotion de. **promotion** *n* promotion *f.*

prompt /prɒmpt/ *adj* rapide; (punctual) à l'heure, ponctuel. ● *adv* (on the dot) pile. ● *vt* inciter; (cause) provoquer; (Theat) souffler à. ● *n* (Comput) message *m* guide-opérateur. **prompter** *n* souffleur/-euse *m/f.* **promptly** *adv* rapidement; ponctuellement.

Proms Festival annuel de musique classique qui se déroule au Royal Albert Hall à Londres. *Proms* est l'abréviation de *promenade concerts*, car une partie des auditeurs reste debout. Aux États-Unis, *prom* (*night*) est un bal très habillé qui marque la fin des études secondaires.

prone /prəʊn/ *adj* ~ **to** sujet à.

pronoun /'prəʊnaʊn/ *n* pronom *m.*

pronounce /prə'naʊns/ *vt* prononcer. **pronunciation** *n* prononciation *f.*

proof /pruːf/ *n* (evidence) preuve *f;* (test, trial copy) épreuve *f;* (of alcohol) teneur *f* en alcool. ● *adj* ~ **against** à l'épreuve de.

prop /prɒp/ *n* support *m;* (Theat) accessoire *m.* ● *vt* (*pt* **propped**) ~ **(up)** (support) étayer; (lean) appuyer.

propaganda /prɒpə'ɡændə/ *n* propagande *f.*

propel /prə'pel/ *vt* (*pt* **propelled**) (*vehicle, ship*) propulser; (*person*) pousser.

propeller /prə'pelə(r)/ *n* hélice *f.*

proper /'prɒpə(r)/ *adj* correct, bon; (adequate) convenable; (real) vrai; (thorough 🄸) parfait. **properly** *adv* correctement, comme il faut; (adequately) convenablement.

proper noun *n* nom *m* propre.

property /'prɒpətɪ/ *n* (house) propriété *f;* (things owned) biens *mpl,* propriété *f.* ● *adj* immobilier, foncier.

prophecy /'prɒfəsɪ/ *n* prophétie *f.*

prophet /'prɒfɪt/ *n* prophète *m.*

proportion /prə'pɔːʃn/ *n* (ratio, dimension) proportion *f;* (amount) partie *f.*

proposal /prə'pəʊzl/ *n* proposition *f;* (of marriage) demande *f* en mariage.

p

propose /prə'pəʊz/ vt proposer. ● vi faire une demande en mariage; ~ **to do** se proposer de faire.

proposition /prɒpə'zɪʃn/ n proposition f; (matter 🇮) affaire f. ● vt 🇮 faire des propositions malhonnêtes à.

proprietor /prə'praɪətə(r)/ n propriétaire m.

propriety /prə'praɪətɪ/ n (correct behaviour) bienséance f.

prose /prəʊz/ n prose f; (translation) thème m.

prosecute /'prɒsɪkjuːt/ vt poursuivre en justice. **prosecution** n poursuites fpl. **prosecutor** n procureur m.

prospect[1] /'prɒspekt/ n (outlook) perspective f; (chance) espoir m.

prospect[2] /prə'spekt/ vt/i prospecter.

prospective /prə'spektɪv/ adj (future) futur; (possible) éventuel.

prospectus /prə'spektəs/ n brochure f; (Univ) livret m de l'étudiant.

prosperity /prɒ'sperətɪ/ n prospérité f. **prosperous** adj prospère.

prostitute /'prɒstɪtjuːt/ n prostituée f.

prostrate /'prɒstreɪt/ adj (prone) à plat ventre; (exhausted) prostré.

protect /prə'tekt/ vt protéger. **protection** n protection f. **protective** adj protecteur; (clothes) de protection.

protein /'prəʊtiːn/ n protéine f.

protest[1] /'prəʊtest/ n protestation f; **under~** en protestant.

protest[2] /prə'test/ vt/i protester.

Protestant /'prɒtɪstənt/ adj & n protestant/-e (m/f).

protester /prə'testə(r)/ n manifestant/-e m/f.

protocol /'prəʊtəkɒl/ n protocole m.

protrude /prə'truːd/ vi dépasser.

proud /praʊd/ adj fier, orgueilleux.

prove /pruːv/ vt prouver. ● vi (~ **to be**) **easy** se révéler facile; ~ **oneself** faire ses preuves. **proven** adj éprouvé.

proverb /'prɒvɜːb/ n proverbe m.

provide /prə'vaɪd/ vt fournir (**sb with sth** qch à qn). ● vi ~ **for** (allow for) prévoir; (guard against) parer à; (person) pourvoir aux besoins de.

provided /prə'vaɪdɪd/ conj ~ **that** à condition que.

providing /prə'vaɪdɪŋ/ conj
➡PROVIDED.

province /'prɒvɪns/ n province f; (fig) compétence f.

provision /prə'vɪʒn/ n (stock) provision f; (supplying) fourniture f; (stipulation) dispositions fpl; ~**s** (food) provisions fpl.

provisional /prə'vɪʒənl/ adj provisoire.

provocative /prə'vɒkətɪv/ adj provocant.

provoke /prə'vəʊk/ vt provoquer.

prow /praʊ/ n proue f.

prowess /'praʊɪs/ n prouesses fpl.

prowl /praʊl/ vi rôder.

proxy /'prɒksɪ/ n **by** ~ par procuration.

prudish /'pruːdɪʃ/ adj pudibond, prude.

prune /pruːn/ n pruneau m. ● vt (cut) tailler.

pry /praɪ/ vi ~ **into** mettre son nez dans.

psalm /sɑːm/ n psaume m.

pseudonym /'sjuːdənɪm/ n pseudonyme m.

psychiatric /saɪkɪ'ætrɪk/ adj psychiatrique. **psychiatrist** n psychiatre mf. **psychiatry** n psychiatrie f.

psychic /'saɪkɪk/ adj (phenomenon) métapsychique; (person) doué de télépathie.

psychoanalyse /saɪkəʊ'ænəlaɪz/ vt psychanalyser.

psychological /saɪkə'lɒdʒɪkl/ adj psychologique. **psychologist** n psychologue mf. **psychology** n psychologie f.

PTO abbr (**please turn over**) TSVP.

pub /pʌb/ n pub m.

> **Pub** Au Royaume-Uni, établissement où l'on sert des boissons (alcoolisées ou non) et parfois des repas légers. Certains appartiennent à une marque de bière alors que les *free houses* sont indépendants. C'est un lieu convivial où l'on vient passer un bon moment (fléchettes, billard, jeux de groupes). Aujourd'hui, la loi leur permet d'ouvrir de 11h à 23h.

puberty /'pjuːbətɪ/ n puberté f.

public /ˈpʌblɪk/ adj public; (*library*) municipal; **in ~** en public.

publican /ˈpʌblɪkən/ n patron/-ne m/f de pub.

publication /pʌblɪˈkeɪʃn/ n publication f.

public house n pub m.

publicity /pʌbˈlɪsətɪ/ n publicité f.

publicize /ˈpʌblɪsaɪz/ vt faire connaître au public.

public: ~ relations n relations fpl publiques. **~ school** n école f privée; (US) école f publique. **~ transport** n transports mpl en commun.

> **Public schools** Mis à part l'É- *i*
> cosse où ce terme désigne
> souvent une école publique, les *pub-*
> *lic schools* britanniques sont en réa-
> lité des écoles privées qui fonction-
> nent souvent sur le mode de
> l'internat et dont les frais de scola-
> rité sont très élevés. Ces écoles ac-
> cordent cependant des bourses aux
> élèves brillants mais peu fortunés.
> Les *public schools* américaines sont
> des écoles publiques et la scolarité y
> est gratuite.▸ STATE SCHOOL.

publish /ˈpʌblɪʃ/ vt publier. **publisher** n éditeur m. **publishing** n édition f.

pudding /ˈpʊdɪŋ/ n dessert m; (steamed) pudding m.

puddle /ˈpʌdl/ n flaque f d'eau.

puff /pʌf/ n (of smoke) bouffée f; (of breath) souffle m. ● vt/i souffler. **~ at** (cigar) tirer sur. **~ out** (swell) (se) gonfler.

pull /pʊl/ vt/i tirer; (muscle) se froisser; **~ a face** faire une grimace; **~ one's weight** faire sa part du travail; **~ sb's leg** faire marcher qn. ● n traction f; (fig) attraction f; (influence) influence f; **give a ~** tirer. **~ away** (Auto) démarrer; **~ back or out** (withdraw) (se) retirer; **~ down** (building) démolir; **~ in** (enter) entrer; (stop) s'arrêter; **~ off** enlever; (fig) réussir; **~ out** (from bag) sortir; (extract) arracher; (Auto) déboîter; **~ over** (Auto) se ranger (sur le côté); **~ through** s'en tirer; **~ oneself together** se ressaisir.

pull-down menu n (Comput) menu m déroulant.

pulley /ˈpʊlɪ/ n poulie f.

pullover /ˈpʊləʊvə(r)/ n pull(-over) m.

pulp /pʌlp/ n (of fruit) pulpe f; (for paper) pâte f à papier.

pulpit /ˈpʊlpɪt/ n chaire f.

pulsate /pʌlˈseɪt/ vi battre.

pulse /pʌls/ n (Med) pouls m.

pump /pʌmp/ n pompe f; (plimsoll) chaussure f de sport. ● vt/i pomper; (person) soutirer des renseignements à; **~ up** gonfler.

pumpkin /ˈpʌmpkɪn/ n citrouille f.

pun /pʌn/ n jeu m de mots.

punch /pʌntʃ/ vt donner un coup de poing à; (ticket) poinçonner. ● n coup m de poing; (vigour 🄸) punch m; (device) poinçonneuse f; (drink) punch m. **~-line** n chute f.

punctual /ˈpʌŋktʃʊəl/ adj à l'heure; (habitually) ponctuel.

punctuation /pʌŋktʃʊˈeɪʃn/ n ponctuation f.

puncture /ˈpʌŋktʃə(r)/ n crevaison f. ● vt/i crever.

pungent /ˈpʌndʒənt/ adj âcre.

punish /ˈpʌnɪʃ/ vt punir (**for sth** de qch). **punishment** n punition f.

punk /pʌŋk/ n (music, fan) punk m; (US: 🄸) voyou m.

punt /pʌnt/ n (boat) barque f; (Hist) (Irish pound) livre f irlandaise.

puny /ˈpjuːnɪ/ adj **-ier, -iest** chétif.

pupil /ˈpjuːpɪl/ n (person) élève mf; (of eye) pupille f.

puppet /ˈpʌpɪt/ n marionnette f.

puppy /ˈpʌpɪ/ n chiot m.

purchase /ˈpɜːtʃəs/ vt acheter (**from sb** à qn). ● n achat m.

pure /pjʊə(r)/ adj pur.

purgatory /ˈpɜːgətrɪ/ n purgatoire m.

purge /pɜːdʒ/ vt purger (**of** de). ● n purge f.

purification /pjʊərɪfɪˈkeɪʃn/ n (of water, air) épuration f; (Relig) purification f. **purify** vt épurer; purifier.

puritan /ˈpjʊərɪtən/ n puritain/-e m/f.

purity /ˈpjʊərətɪ/ n pureté f.

purple /ˈpɜːpl/ adj & n violet (m).

purpose /ˈpɜːpəs/ n but m; (determination) résolution f; **on ~** exprès; **to no ~** sans résultat.

purr /pɜː(r)/ n ronronnement m. ● vi ronronner.

p

purse /pɜːs/ n porte-monnaie m inv; (handbag: US) sac m à main. ● vt (lips) pincer.

pursue /pəˈsjuː/ vt poursuivre.

pursuit /pəˈsjuːt/ n poursuite f; (hobby) activité f, occupation f.

pus /pʌs/ n pus m.

push /pʊʃ/ vt/i pousser; (button) appuyer sur; (thrust) enfoncer; (recommend 🅘) proposer avec insistance; be ~ed for (time) manquer de; be ~ing thirty 🅘 friser la trentaine; ~ sb around bousculer qn ● n poussée f; (effort) gros effort m; (drive) dynamisme m; give the ~ to 🅘 flanquer à la porte 🅘. □ ~ in resquiller; ~ on continuer; ~ up (lift) relever; (prices) faire monter.

pushchair /ˈpʊʃtʃeə(r)/ n poussette f.

pusher /ˈpʊʃə(r)/ n revendeur/-euse m/f (de drogue).

push-up n pompe f.

put /pʊt/ vt/i (pt put; pres p putting) mettre, placer, poser; (question) poser; ~ the damage at a million estimer les dégâts à un million; ~ sth tactfully dire qch avec tact. □ ~ across communiquer; ~ away ranger; (in hospital, prison) enfermer; ~ back (postpone) remettre; (delay) retarder; ~ down (dé)poser; (write) inscrire; (pay) verser; (suppress) réprimer; ~ forward (plan) soumettre; ~ in (insert) introduire; (fix) installer; (submit) soumettre; ~ in for faire une demande de; ~ off (postpone) renvoyer à plus tard; (disconcert) déconcerter; (displease) rebuter; ~ sb off sth dégoûter qn de qch; ~ on (clothes, radio) mettre; (light) allumer; (accent, weight) prendre; ~ out sortir; (stretch) (é)tendre; (extinguish) éteindre; (disconcert) déconcerter; (inconvenience) déranger; ~ up lever, remonter; (building) construire; (notice) mettre; (price) augmenter; (guest) héberger; (offer) offrir; ~ up with supporter.

putt /pʌt/ vi putter. ● n putt m.

putty /ˈpʌt/ n mastic m.

puzzle /ˈpʌzl/ n énigme f; (game) casse-tête m inv; (jigsaw) puzzle m. ● vt rendre perplexe. ● vi se creuser la tête.

pyjamas /pəˈdʒɑːməz/ npl pyjama m.

pylon /ˈpaɪlən/ n pylône m.

Qq

quack /kwæk/ n (of duck) coin-coin m inv; (doctor) charlatan m.

quadrangle /ˈkwɒdræŋgl/ (of college) n cour f.

quadruple /ˈkwɒdrʊpl/ adj & n quadruple (m). ● vt/i quadrupler.

quail /kweɪl/ n (bird) caille f.

quaint /kweɪnt/ adj pittoresque; (old) vieillot; (odd) bizarre.

qualification /kwɒlɪfɪˈkeɪʃn/ n diplôme m; (ability) compétence f; (fig) réserve f, restriction f.

qualified /ˈkwɒlɪfaɪd/ adj diplômé; (able) qualifié (to do pour faire); (fig) conditionnel.

qualify /ˈkwɒlɪfaɪ/ vt qualifier; (modify) mettre des réserves à; (statement) nuancer. ● vi obtenir son diplôme (as de); (Sport) se qualifier; ~ for remplir les conditions requises pour.

quality /ˈkwɒlətɪ/ n qualité f.

qualm /kwɑːm/ n scrupule m.

quantity /ˈkwɒntətɪ/ n quantité f.

quarantine /ˈkwɒrəntiːn/ n quarantaine f.

quarrel /ˈkwɒrəl/ n dispute f, querelle f. ● vi (pt quarrelled) se disputer.

quarry /ˈkwɒrɪ/ n (excavation) carrière f; (prey) proie f. ● vt extraire.

quart /kwɔːt/ n ≈ litre m.

quarter /ˈkwɔːtə(r)/ n quart m; (of year) trimestre m; (25 cents: US) quart m de dollar; (district) quartier m; ~s logement m; from all ~s de toutes parts. ● vt diviser en quatre; (troops) cantonner.

quarterly /ˈkwɔːtəlɪ/ adj trimestriel. ● adv tous les trois mois.

quartet /kwɔːˈtet/ n quatuor m.

quartz /kwɔːts/ n quartz m. ● adj (watch) à quartz.

quash /kwɒʃ/ vt (suppress) étouffer; (Jur) annuler.

quaver /ˈkweɪvə(r)/ vi trembler, chevroter. ● n (Mus) croche f.

quay /kiː/ n (Naut) quai m.

queasy /'kwiːzɪ/ adj **feel ~** avoir mal au cœur.

queen /kwiːn/ n reine f; (cards) dame f.

queer /kwɪə(r)/ adj étrange; (dubious) louche; 🔞 homosexuel.

quench /kwentʃ/ vt éteindre; (thirst) étancher; (desire) étouffer.

query /'kwɪərɪ/ n question f. ● vt mettre en question.

quest /kwest/ n recherche f.

question /'kwestʃən/ n question f; **in ~** en question; **out of the ~** hors de question. ● vt interroger; (doubt) mettre en question, douter de. **~ mark** n point m d'interrogation.

questionnaire /kwestʃə'neə(r)/ n questionnaire m.

queue /kjuː/ n queue f. ● vi (pres p **queuing**) faire la queue.

quibble /'kwɪbl/ vi ergoter.

quick /kwɪk/ adj rapide; (clever) vif/vive; **be ~** (hurry) se dépêcher. ● adv vite. ● n **cut to the~** piquer au vif. **quicken** vt/i (s')accélérer. **quickly** adv rapidement, vite. **~sand** n sables mpl mouvants.

quid /kwɪd/ n inv 🔞 livre f sterling.

quiet /'kwaɪət/ adj (calm, still) tranquille; (silent) silencieux; (gentle) doux; (discreet) discret; **keep ~** se taire. ● n tranquillité f; **on the ~** en cachette. **quieten** vt/i (se) calmer. **quietly** adv (speak) doucement; (sit) en silence.

quilt /kwɪlt/ n édredon m; **(continental) ~** couette f.

quirk /kwɜːk/ n bizarrerie f.

quit /kwɪt/ vt (pt **quitted**) quitter; (smoking) arrêter de. ● vi abandonner; (resign) démissionner; **~ doing** (US) cesser de faire.

quite /kwaɪt/ adv tout à fait, vraiment; (rather) assez; **~ a few** un bon nombre (de).

quits /kwɪts/ adj quitte (**with** envers); **call it ~** en rester là.

quiver /'kwɪvə(r)/ vi trembler.

quiz /kwɪz/ n (pl **quizzes**) test m; (game) jeu-concours m. ● vt (pt **quizzed**) questionner.

quotation /kwəʊ'teɪʃn/ n citation f; (price) devis m; (stock exchange) cotation f; **~ marks** guillemets mpl.

quote /kwəʊt/ vt citer; (reference, number) rappeler; (price) indiquer; (share price) coter. ● vi **~ for** faire un devis pour; **~ from** citer. ● n (quotation) citation f; (estimate) devis m; **in ~s** 🔞 entre guillemets.

Rr

rabbi /'ræbaɪ/ n rabbin m.

rabbit /'ræbɪt/ n lapin m.

rabies /'reɪbiːz/ n (disease) rage f.

race /reɪs/ n (contest) course f; (group) race f. ● adj racial; **~ relations** relations fpl inter-raciales. ● vt (compete with) faire la course avec; (horse) faire courir. ● vi courir; (pulse) battre précipitamment; (engine) s'emballer. **~course** n champ m de courses. **~horse** n cheval m de course. **~-track** n piste f; (for horses) champ m de courses.

racing /'reɪsɪŋ/ n courses fpl; **~ car** voiture f de course.

racism /'reɪsɪzəm/ n racisme m. **racist** adj & n raciste (mf).

rack /ræk/ n (shelf) étagère f; (for clothes) portant m; (for luggage) compartiment m à bagages; (for dishes) égouttoir m. ● vt **~ one's brains** se creuser la cervelle.

racket /'rækɪt/ n (Sport) raquette f; (noise) vacarme m; (swindle) escroquerie f; (crime) trafic m.

radar /'reɪdɑː(r)/ n & adj radar (m).

radial /'reɪdɪəl/ n **~ (tyre)** pneu m radial.

radiate /'reɪdɪeɪt/ vt (happiness) rayonner de; (heat) émettre. ● vi rayonner (**from** de). **radiation** n (radioactivity) radiation f. **radiator** n radiateur m.

radical /'rædɪkl/ n & a radical/-e (m/f).

radio /'reɪdɪəʊ/ n radio f; **on the ~** à la radio. ● vt (message) envoyer par radio; (person) appeler par radio.

radioactive /reɪdɪəʊ'æktɪv/ adj radioactif.

radiographer /reɪdɪ'ɒgrəfə(r)/ n manipulateur/-trice m/f radiographe.

radish /'rædɪʃ/ n radis m.

q

r

radius /'reɪdɪəs/ n (pl **-dii**) rayon m.

raffle /'ræfl/ n tombola f.

rag /ræg/ n chiffon m; ∼s loques fpl.

rage /reɪdʒ/ n rage f, colère f; **be all the** ∼ faire fureur. ● vi (person) tempêter; (storm, battle) faire rage.

ragged /'rægɪd/ adj (clothes) en loques; (person) dépenaillé.

raid /reɪd/ n (Mil, on stock market) raid m; (by police) rafle f; (by criminals) hold-up m inv. ● vt faire un raid or une rafle or un hold-up dans. **raider** n (thief) pillard m; (Mil) commando m; (corporate) raider m.

rail /reɪl/ n (on balcony) balustrade f; (stairs) rampe f; (for train) rail m; (for curtain) tringle f; **by** ∼ par chemin de fer.

railing /'reɪlɪŋ/ n (also ∼s) grille f.

railway, (US) **railroad** n chemin m de fer. ∼ **line** n voie f ferrée. ∼ **station** n gare f.

rain /reɪn/ n pluie f. ● vi pleuvoir. ∼**bow** n arc-en-ciel m. ∼**coat** n imperméable m. ∼**fall** n précipitation f. ∼ **forest** n forêt f tropicale.

rainy /'reɪnɪ/ adj (**-ier, -iest**) pluvieux; (season) des pluies.

raise /reɪz/ vt (barrier, curtain) lever; (child, cattle) élever; (question) soulever; (price, salary) augmenter. ● n (US) augmentation f.

raisin /'reɪzn/ n raisin m sec.

rake /reɪk/ n râteau m. ● vt (garden) ratisser; (search) fouiller dans. □ ∼ **in** (money) amasser; ∼ **up** (past) remuer.

rally /'rælɪ/ vt/i (se) rallier; (strength) reprendre; (after illness) aller mieux; ∼ **round** venir en aide. ● n rassemblement m; (Auto) rallye m; (tennis) échange m.

ram /ræm/ n bélier m. ● vt (pt **rammed**) (thrust) enfoncer; (crash into) rentrer dans.

RAM abbr (**random access memory**) RAM f.

ramble /'ræmbl/ n randonnée f. ● vi faire une randonnée. □ ∼ **on** discourir.

ramp /ræmp/ n (slope) rampe f; (in garage) pont m de graissage.

rampage¹ /ræm'peɪdʒ/ vi se déchaîner (**through** dans).

rampage² /'ræmpeɪdʒ/ n **go on the** ∼ tout saccager.

ran /ræn/ ➡RUN.

rancid /'rænsɪd/ adj rance.

random /'rændəm/ adj (fait) au hasard. ● n **at** ∼ au hasard.

rang /ræŋ/ ➡RING².

range /reɪndʒ/ n (of prices, products) gamme f; (of people, beliefs) variété f; (of radar, weapon) portée f; (of aircraft) autonomie f; (of mountains) chaîne f. ● vi aller; (vary) varier.

rank /ræŋk/ n rang m; (Mil) grade m. ● vt/i ∼ **among** (se) classer parmi.

ransack /'rænsæk/ vt (search) fouiller; (pillage) mettre à sac.

ransom /'rænsəm/ n rançon f.

rap /ræp/ n coup m sec; (Mus) rap m. ● vi (pt **rapped**) donner des coups secs (**on** sur).

rape /reɪp/ vt violer. ● n viol m.

rapid /'ræpɪd/ adj rapide.

rapist /'reɪpɪst/ n violeur m.

rapturous /'ræptʃərəs/ adj (delight) extasié; (welcome) enthousiaste.

rare /reə(r)/ adj rare; (Culin) saignant. **rarely** adv rarement.

rascal /'rɑːskl/ n coquin/-e m/f.

rash /ræʃ/ n (Med) rougeurs fpl. ● adj irréfléchi.

raspberry /'rɑːzbrɪ/ n framboise f.

rat /ræt/ n rat m. ● vi (pt **ratted**) ∼ **on** (desert) lâcher; (inform on) dénoncer.

rate /reɪt/ n (ratio, level) taux m; (speed) rythme m; (price) tarif m; (of exchange) taux m; **at any** ∼ en tout cas. ● vt (value) estimer; (deserve) mériter; ∼ **sth highly** admirer beaucoup qch. ● vi ∼ **as** être considéré comme.

rather /'rɑːðə(r)/ adv (by preference) plutôt; (fairly) assez, plutôt; (a little) un peu; **I would** ∼ **go** j'aimerais mieux partir; ∼ **than go** plutôt que de partir.

rating /'reɪtɪŋ/ n (score, value) cote f; **the** ∼s (TV) l'indice m d'écoute, l'audimat® m.

ratio /'reɪʃɪəʊ/ n proportion f.

ration /'ræʃn/ n ration f. ● vt rationner.

rational /'ræʃənl/ adj rationnel; (person) sensé.

rationalize /'ræʃnəlaɪz/ vt justifier; (organize) rationaliser.

r

rattle /'rætl/ vi (bottles, chains) s'entre-choquer; (window) vibrer. ● vt (bottles, chains) faire s'entrechoquer; (fig, ▯) énerver. ● n cliquetis m; (toy) hochet m. ~**snake** n serpent m à sonnette, crotale m.

rave /reɪv/ vi (enthuse) s'emballer; (in fever) délirer; (in anger) tempêter.

raven /'reɪvn/ n corbeau m.

ravenous /'rævənəs/ adj **be** ~ avoir une faim de loup.

ravine /rə'viːn/ n ravin m.

raving /'reɪvɪŋ/ adj ~ **lunatic** fou m furieux, folle f furieuse.

ravishing /'rævɪʃɪŋ/ adj ravissant.

raw /rɔː/ adj cru; (not processed) brut; (wound) à vif; (immature) inexpéri-menté; **get a** ~ **deal** être mal traité; ~ **material** matière f première.

ray /reɪ/ n (of light) rayon m; ~ **of hope** lueur f d'espoir.

razor /'reɪzə(r)/ n rasoir m. ~-**blade** n lame f de rasoir.

re /riː/ prep au sujet de; (at top of letter) objet.

reach /riːtʃ/ vt (place, level) atteindre; (decision) arriver à; (contact) joindre; (audience, market) toucher. ● vi ~ **up/down** lever/baisser le bras; ~ **across** étendre le bras. ● n portée f; **within** ~ **of** à portée de; (close to) à proximité de.

react /rɪ'ækt/ vi réagir. **reaction** n réaction f. **reactor** n réacteur m.

read /riːd/ vt/i (pt **read**) lire; (study) étudier; (instrument) indiquer; ~ **about sb** lire quelque chose sur qn; ~ **out** lire à haute voix. **reader** n lecteur/-trice m/f. **reading** n lecture f; (measurement) indication f; (interpret-ation) interprétation f.

readjust /riːə'dʒʌst/ vt rajuster. ● vi se réadapter (**to** à).

read-only memory, ROM n mé-moire f morte.

ready /'redɪ/ adj (-**ier, -iest**) prêt; (quick) prompt. ~-**made** adj tout fait. ~-**to-wear** adj prêt-à-porter.

real /rɪəl/ adj (not imaginary) véritable, réel; (not artificial) vrai; **it's a** ~ **shame** c'est vraiment dommage. ~ **estate** n biens mpl immobiliers.

realism /'riːəlɪzəm/ n réalisme m. **real-istic** adj réaliste.

reality /rɪ'ælətɪ/ n réalité f. ~ **TV** n télé-réalité f.

reasonable /'riːznəbl/ adj raisonnable.

realize /'rɪəlaɪz/ vt se rendre compte de, comprendre; (fulfil, turn into cash) réaliser; (price) atteindre.

really /'rɪəlɪ/ adv vraiment.

reap /riːp/ vt (crop) recueillir; (benefits) récolter.

reappear /riːə'pɪə(r)/ vi reparaître.

rear /rɪə(r)/ n arrière m; (of person) derrière m. ▯ ● adj (seat) arrière inv; (entrance) de derrière. ● vt élever. ● vi (horse) se cabrer. ~-**view mirror** n rétroviseur m.

reason /'riːzn/ n raison f (**to do, for doing** de faire); **within** ~ dans la li-mite du raisonnable.

reassurance /riːə'ʃɔːrəns/ n réconfort m. **reassure** vt rassurer.

rebate /'riːbeɪt/ n (refund) rembourse-ment m; (discount) remise f.

rebel[1] /'rebl/ n & adj rebelle (mf).

rebel[2] /rɪ'bel/ vi (pt **rebelled**) se rebel-ler. **rebellion** n rébellion f.

rebound[1] /rɪ'baʊnd/ vi rebondir; ~ **on** (backfire) se retourner contre.

rebound[2] /'riːbaʊnd/ n rebond m.

rebuke /rɪ'bjuːk/ vt réprimander. ● n réprimande f.

recall /rɪ'kɔːl/ vt (remember) se souve-nir de; (call back) rappeler. ● n (mem-ory) mémoire f; (Comput, Mil) rappel m.

recap /riː'kæp/ vt/i (pt **recapped**) réca-pituler. ● n récapitulation f.

recede /rɪ'siːd/ vi s'éloigner; **his hair is receding** son front se dégarnit.

receipt /rɪ'siːt/ n (written) reçu m; (of letter) réception f; ~**s** (Comm) recet-tes fpl.

receive /rɪ'siːv/ vt recevoir; (stolen goods) receler. **receiver** n (telephone) combiné m; (TV) récepteur m.

recent /'riːsnt/ adj récent. **recently** adv récemment.

receptacle /rɪ'septəkl/ n récipient m.

reception /rɪ'sepʃn/ n réception f; **give sb a warm** ~ donner un accueil chaleureux à qn.

recess /rɪ'ses/ n (alcove) alcôve m; (for door) embrasure f; (Jur, Pol) vacances fpl; (School, US) récréation f.

r

recession /rɪ'seʃn/ n récession f.

recharge /riː'tʃɑːdʒ/ vt recharger.

recipe /'resəpɪ/ n recette f.

recipient /rɪ'sɪpɪənt/ n (of honour) récipiendaire mf; (of letter) destinataire mf.

reciprocate /rɪ'sɪprəkeɪt/ vt (compliment) retourner; (kindness) payer de retour. ● vi en faire autant.

recite /rɪ'saɪt/ vi réciter.

reckless /'reklɪs/ adj imprudent.

reckon /'rekən/ vt/i calculer; (judge) considérer; (think) penser; ∼ on/with compter sur/avec. **reckoning** n (guess) estimation f; (calculation) calculs mpl.

reclaim /rɪ'kleɪm/ vt récupérer; (flooded land) assécher.

recline /rɪ'klaɪn/ vi s'allonger; (seat) s'incliner.

recluse /rɪ'kluːs/ n reclus/-e m/f.

recognition /rekəg'nɪʃn/ n reconnaissance f; **beyond** ∼ méconnaissable; **gain** ∼ être reconnu.

recognize /'rekəgnaɪz/ vt reconnaître.

recollect /rekə'lekt/ vt se souvenir de, se rappeler. **recollection** n souvenir m.

recommend /rekə'mend/ vt recommander. **recommendation** n recommandation f.

reconcile /'rekənsaɪl/ vt (people) réconcilier; (facts) concilier; ∼ oneself to se résigner à.

recondition /riːkən'dɪʃn/ vt remettre à neuf.

reconsider /riːkən'sɪdə(r)/ vt réexaminer. ● vi réfléchir.

reconstruct /riːkən'strʌkt/ vt reconstruire; (crime) faire une reconstitution de.

record¹ /rɪ'kɔːd/ vt/i (in register, on tape) enregistrer; (in diary) noter; ∼that rapporter que.

record² /'rekɔːd/ n (of events) compterendu m; (official) procès-verbal m; (personal, administrative) dossier m; (historical) archives fpl; (past history) réputation f; (Mus) disque m; (Sport) record m; (criminal) ∼ casier m judiciaire; **off the** ∼ officieusement. ● adj record inv.

recorder /rɪ'kɔːdə(r)/ n (Mus) flûte f à bec.

recording /rɪ'kɔːdɪŋ/ n enregistrement m.

record-player n tourne-disque m.

recover /rɪ'kʌvə(r)/ vt récupérer. ● vi se remettre; (economy) se redresser. **recovery** n (Med) rétablissement m; (of economy) relance f.

recreation /rekrɪ'eɪʃn/ n récréation f.

recruit /rɪ'kruːt/ n recrue f. ● vt recruter. **recruitment** n recrutement m.

rectangle /'rektæŋgl/ n rectangle m.

rectify /'rektɪfaɪ/ vt rectifier.

recuperate /rɪ'kuːpəreɪt/ vt récupérer. ● vi se rétablir.

recur /rɪ'kɜː(r)/ vi (pt recurred) se reproduire.

recycle /riː'saɪkl/ vt recycler.

red /red/ adj (**redder, reddest**) rouge; (hair) roux. ● n rouge m; **in the** ∼ en déficit. **R∼ Cross** n Croix- Rouge f. **∼currant** n groseille f.

redecorate /riː'dekəreɪt/ vt repeindre, refaire.

redeploy /riːdɪ'plɔɪ/ vt réorganiser; (troops) répartir.

red: ∼**-handed** adj en flagrant délit. ∼**-hot** adj brûlant.

redirect /riːdɪ'rekt/ vt (traffic) dévier; (letter) faire suivre.

redness /'rednɪs/ n rougeur f.

redo /riː'duː/ vt (pt -did; pp -done) refaire.

redress /rɪ'dres/ vt (wrong) redresser; (balance) rétablir. ● n réparation f.

reduce /rɪ'djuːs/ vt réduire; (temperature) faire baisser. **reduction** n réduction f.

redundancy /rɪ'dʌndənsɪ/ n licenciement m.

redundant /rɪ'dʌndənt/ adj superflu; (worker) licencié; **make** ∼ licencier.

reed /riːd/ n (plant) roseau m.

reef /riːf/ n récif m, écueil m.

reel /riːl/ n (of thread) bobine f; (of film) bande f; (winding device) dévidoir m. ● vi chanceler. ● vt ∼ off réciter.

refectory /rɪ'fektrɪ/ n réfectoire m.

refer /rɪ'fɜː(r)/ vt/i (pt referred) ∼ to (allude to) faire allusion à; (concern) s'appliquer à; (consult) consulter; (direct) renvoyer à.

r

referee /refə'ri:/ n (Sport) arbitre m.
● vt (pt **refereed**) arbitrer.

reference /'refərəns/ n référence f;
(mention) allusion f; (person) personne
f pouvant fournir des références; **in** or
with ∼ to en ce qui concerne;
(Comm) suite à.

referendum /refə'rendəm/ n (pl ∼s)
référendum m.

refill[1] /ri:'fil/ vt (glass) remplir à nouveau; (pen) recharger.

refill[2] /'ri:fil/ n recharge f.

refine /rɪ'faɪn/ vt raffiner.

reflect /rɪ'flekt/ vt refléter; (heat, light)
renvoyer. ● vi réfléchir (**on** à); **∼ well**/
badly on sb faire honneur/du tort
à qn.

reflection /rɪ'flekʃn/ n réflexion f;
(image) reflet m; **on ∼** à la réflexion.

reflective /rɪ'flektɪv/ adj (surface) ré-
fléchissant; (person) réfléchi.

reflector /rɪ'flektə(r)/ n (on car) cata-
dioptre m.

reflex /'ri:fleks/ adj & n réflexe (m).

reflexive /rɪ'fleksɪv/ adj (Gram) réfléchi.

reform /rɪ'fɔ:m/ vt réformer. ● vi (person) s'amender. ● n réforme f.

refrain /rɪ'freɪn/ n refrain m. ● vi s'abstenir (**from** de).

refresh /rɪ'freʃ/ vt (drink) rafraîchir;
(rest) reposer. **refreshments** npl rafraî-
chissements mpl.

refrigerate /rɪ'frɪdʒəreɪt/ vt réfrigérer.
refrigerator n réfrigérateur m.

refuel /ri:'fjʊəl/ vt/i (pt **refuelled**) (se)
ravitailler.

refuge /'refju:dʒ/ n refuge m; **take ∼**
se réfugier. **refugee** n réfugié/-e m/f.

refund[1] /ri:'fʌnd/ vt rembourser.

refund[2] /'ri:fʌnd/ n remboursement m.

refurbish /ri:'fɜ:bɪʃ/ vt remettre
à neuf.

refuse[1] /rɪ'fju:z/ vt/i refuser.

refuse[2] /'refju:s/ n ordures fpl.

regain /rɪ'geɪn/ vt retrouver; (lost
ground) regagner.

regard /rɪ'gɑ:d/ vt considérer; **as ∼s**
en ce qui concerne. ● n égard m, estime f; **in this ∼** à cet égard; **∼s** amitiés fpl. **regarding** prep en ce qui
concerne.

regardless /rɪ'gɑ:dlɪs/ adv malgré
tout; **∼ of** sans tenir compte de.

regime /'reʒi:m/ n régime m.

regiment /'redʒɪmənt/ n régiment m.

region /'ri:dʒən/ n région f; **in the ∼
of** environ.

register /'redʒɪstə(r)/ n registre m. ● vt
(record) enregistrer; (vehicle) faire immatriculer; (birth) déclarer; (letter) recommander; (indicate) indiquer; (express) exprimer. ● vi (enrol) s'inscrire;
(at hotel) se présenter; (fig) être
compris.

registrar /redʒɪs'trɑ:(r)/ n officier m
de l'état civil; (Univ) responsable m du
bureau de la scolarité.

registration /redʒɪ'streɪʃn/ n (of
voter, student) inscription f; (of birth)
déclaration f; **∼ (number)** (Auto) numéro m d'immatriculation.

registry office n bureau m de l'état
civil.

regret /rɪ'gret/ n regret m. ● vt (pt **re-
gretted**) regretter (**to do** de faire).
regretfully adv à regret.

regular /'regjʊlə(r)/ adj régulier;
(usual) habituel. ● n habitué/-e m/f.
regularity n régularité f. **regularly**
adv régulièrement.

regulate /'regjʊleɪt/ vt régler. **regulation** n (rule) règlement m; (process)
réglementation f.

rehabilitate /ri:ə'bɪlɪteɪt/ vt (in public
esteem) réhabiliter; (prisoner) ré-
insérer.

rehearsal /rɪ'hɜ:sl/ n répétition f. **rehearse** vt/i répéter.

reign /reɪn/ n règne m. ● vi régner
(**over** sur).

reimburse /ri:ɪm'bɜ:s/ vt rembourser.

reindeer /'reɪndɪə(r)/ n inv renne m.

reinforce /ri:ɪn'fɔ:s/ vt renforcer. **reinforcement** n renforcement m; **∼s**
renforts mpl.

reinstate /ri:ɪn'steɪt/ vt (person) réintégrer; (law) rétablir.

reject[1] /'ri:dʒekt/ n marchandise f de
deuxième choix.

reject[2] /rɪ'dʒekt/ vt (offer, plea) rejeter;
(goods) refuser. **rejection** n (personal)
rejet m; (of candidate, work) refus m.

rejoice /rɪ'dʒɔɪs/ vi se réjouir.

relapse /'ri:læps/ n rechute f. ● vi re-
chuter; **∼ into** retomber dans.

relate /rɪ'leɪt/ vt raconter; (associate)
associer. ● vi **∼ to** se rapporter à; (get

r

on with) s'entendre avec. **related** adj (ideas) lié; **we are ~d** nous sommes parents.

relation /rɪ'leɪʃn/ n rapport m; (person) parent/-e m/f. **relationship** n relations fpl; (link) rapport m.

relative /'relətɪv/ n parent/-e m/f. ● adj relatif; (respective) respectif.

relax /rɪ'læks/ vt (grip) relâcher; (muscle) décontracter; (discipline) assouplir. ● vi (person) se détendre; (grip) se relâcher. **relaxation** n détente f. **relaxing** adj délassant.

relay[1] /'ri:leɪ/ n (also ~ **race**) course f de relais.

relay[2] /ri:'leɪ/ vt relayer.

release /rɪ'li:s/ vt (prisoner) libérer; (fastening) faire jouer; (object, hand) lâcher; (film) faire sortir; (news) publier. ● n libération f; (of film) sortie f; (new record, film) nouveauté f.

relevance /'reləvəns/ n pertinence f, intérêt m.

relevant /'reləvənt/ adj pertinent; **be ~ to** avoir rapport à.

reliability /rɪlaɪə'bɪləti/ n (of firm) sérieux m; (of car) fiabilité f; (of person) honnêteté f. **reliable** adj (firm) sérieux; (person, machine) fiable.

reliance /rɪ'laɪəns/ n dépendance f.

relic /'relɪk/ n vestige m; (object) relique f.

relief /rɪ'li:f/ n soulagement m (**from** à); (assistance) secours m; (outline) relief m; ~ **road** route f de délestage.

relieve /rɪ'li:v/ vt soulager; (help) secourir; (take over from) relayer.

religion /rɪ'lɪdʒən/ n religion f. **religious** adj religieux.

relish /'relɪʃ/ n plaisir m; (Culin) condiment m. ● vt (food) savourer; (idea) se réjouir de.

relocate /ri:ləʊ'keɪt/ vt muter. ● vi (company) déménager; (worker) être muté. **relocation** n délocalisation f.

reluctance /rɪ'lʌktəns/ n répugnance f.

reluctant /rɪ'lʌktənt/ adj (person) peu enthousiaste; (consent) accordé à contrecœur; ~ **to** peu disposé à. **reluctantly** adv à contrecœur.

rely /rɪ'laɪ/ vi ~ **on** (count) compter sur; (be dependent) dépendre de.

remain /rɪ'meɪn/ vi rester. **remainder** n reste m.

remand /rɪ'mɑːnd/ vt mettre en détention provisoire. ● n **on ~** en détention provisoire.

remark /rɪ'mɑːk/ n remarque f. ● vt remarquer. ● vi ~ **on** faire des remarques sur. **remarkable** adj remarquable.

remedy /'remədɪ/ n remède m. ● vt remédier à.

remember /rɪ'membə(r)/ vt se souvenir de, se rappeler; ~ **to do** ne pas oublier de faire. **remembrance** n souvenir m.

remind /rɪ'maɪnd/ vt rappeler (**sb of sth** qch à qn); ~ **sb to do** rappeler à qn de faire. **reminder** n rappel m.

reminisce /remɪ'nɪs/ vi évoquer ses souvenirs.

remission /rɪ'mɪʃn/ n (Med) rémission f; (Jur) remise f.

remnant /'remnənt/ n reste m; (trace) vestige m; (of cloth) coupon m.

remodel /ri:'mɒdl/ vt (pt **remodelled**) remodeler.

remorse /rɪ'mɔːs/ n remords m.

remote /rɪ'məʊt/ adj (place, time) lointain; (person) distant; (slight) vague; ~ **control** télécommande f.

removable /rɪ'muːvəbl/ adj amovible.

removal /rɪ'muːvl/ n (of employee) renvoi m; (of threat) suppression f; (of troops) retrait m; (of stain) détachage m; (from house) déménagement m; ~ **men** déménageurs mpl.

remove /rɪ'muːv/ vt enlever; (dismiss) renvoyer; (do away with) supprimer; (Comput) effacer.

remunerate /rɪ'mjuːnəreɪt/ vt rémunérer. **remuneration** n rémunération f.

render /'rendə(r)/ vt rendre.

renegade /'renɪgeɪd/ n renégat/-e m/f.

renew /rɪ'njuː/ vt renouveler; (resume) reprendre. **renewable** adj renouvelable.

renounce /rɪ'naʊns/ vt renoncer à; (disown) renier.

renovate /'renəveɪt/ vt rénover.

renown /rɪ'naʊn/ n renommée f.

rent /rent/ n loyer m. ● vt louer; **for ~** à louer. **rental** n prix m de location.

reopen /riː'əʊpən/ vt/i rouvrir.

reorganize /riːˈɔːɡənaɪz/ vt réorganiser.

rep /rep/ n (Comm) représentant/-e m/f.

repair /rɪˈpeə(r)/ vt réparer. ● n réparation f; **in good/bad ~** en bon/mauvais état.

repatriate /riːˈpætrɪeɪt/ vt rapatrier. **repatriation** n rapatriement m.

repay /rɪˈpeɪ/ vt (pt **repaid**) rembourser; (reward) récompenser. **repayment** n remboursement m.

repeal /rɪˈpiːl/ vt abroger. ● n abrogation f.

repeat /rɪˈpiːt/ vt/i répéter; (renew) renouveler; **~ itself, ~ oneself** se répéter. ● n répétition f; (broadcast) reprise f.

repel /rɪˈpel/ vt (pt **repelled**) repousser.

repent /rɪˈpent/ vi se repentir (**of** de).

repercussion /riːpəˈkʌʃn/ n répercussion f.

repetition /repɪˈtɪʃn/ n répétition f.

replace /rɪˈpleɪs/ vt (put back) remettre; (take the place of) remplacer. **replacement** n remplacement m (**of** de); (person) remplaçant/-e m/f; (new part) pièce f de rechange.

replay /ˈriːpleɪ/ n (Sport) match m rejoué; (recording) répétition f immédiate.

replenish /rɪˈplenɪʃ/ vt (refill) remplir; (renew) renouveler.

replica /ˈreplɪkə/ n copie f exacte.

reply /rɪˈplaɪ/ vt/i répondre. ● n réponse f.

report /rɪˈpɔːt/ vt rapporter, annoncer (**that** que); (notify) signaler; (denounce) dénoncer. ● vi faire un rapport; **~ (on)** (news item) faire un reportage sur; **~ to** (go) se présenter chez. ● n rapport m; (in press) reportage m; (School) bulletin m. **reporter** n reporter m.

repossess /riːpəˈzes/ vt reprendre.

represent /reprɪˈzent/ vt représenter.

representation /reprɪzenˈteɪʃn/ n représentation f; **make ~s to** protester auprès de.

representative /reprɪˈzentətɪv/ adj représentatif, typique (**of** de). ● n représentant/-e m/f.

repress /rɪˈpres/ vt réprimer.

reprieve /rɪˈpriːv/ n (delay) sursis m; (pardon) grâce f. ● vt accorder un sursis à; gracier.

reprimand /ˈreprɪmɑːnd/ vt réprimander. ● n réprimande f.

reprisals /rɪˈpraɪzlz/ npl représailles fpl.

reproach /rɪˈprəʊtʃ/ vt reprocher (**sb for sth** qch à qn). ● n reproche m.

reproduce /riːprəˈdjuːs/ vt/i (se) reproduire. **reproduction** n reproduction f. **reproductive** adj reproducteur.

reptile /ˈreptaɪl/ n reptile m.

republic /rɪˈpʌblɪk/ n république f. **republican** adj & n républicain/-e (m/f).

repudiate /rɪˈpjuːdɪeɪt/ vt répudier; (contract) refuser d'honorer.

reputable /ˈrepjʊtəbl/ adj honorable, de bonne réputation.

reputation /repjʊˈteɪʃn/ n réputation f.

repute /rɪˈpjuːt/ n réputation f.

request /rɪˈkwest/ n demande f. ● vt demander (**of, from** à).

require /rɪˈkwaɪə(r)/ vt (of thing) demander; (of person) avoir besoin de; (demand, order) exiger. **required** adj requis. **requirement** n exigence f; (condition) condition f (requise).

rescue /ˈreskjuː/ vt sauver. ● n sauvetage m (**of** de); (help) secours m.

research /rɪˈsɜːtʃ/ n recherche(s) f(pl). ● vt/i faire des recherches (sur). **researcher** n chercheur/-euse m/f.

resemblance /rɪˈzembləns/ n ressemblance f. **resemble** vt ressembler à.

resent /rɪˈzent/ vt être indigné de, s'offenser de. **resentment** n ressentiment m.

reservation /rezəˈveɪʃn/ n (doubt) réserve f; (booking) réservation f; (US) réserve f (indienne); **make a ~** réserver.

reserve /rɪˈzɜːv/ vt réserver. ● n (stock, land) réserve f; (Sport) remplaçant/-e m/f; **in ~** en réserve; **the ~s** (Mil) les réserves fpl. **reserved** adj (person, room) réservé.

reshuffle /riːˈʃʌfl/ vt (Pol) remanier. ● n (Pol) remaniement m (ministériel).

residence /ˈrezɪdəns/ n résidence f; (of students) foyer m; **in ~** (doctor) résidant.

resident /ˈrezɪdənt/ adj résidant; **be ~** résider. ● n habitant/-e m/f; (foreigner)

r

résident/-e *m/f*; (in hotel) pensionnaire *mf*. **residential** *adj* résidentiel.

resign /rɪ'zaɪn/ *vt* abandonner; (*job*) démissionner de. ● *vi* démissionner; ~ **oneself to** se résigner à. **resignation** *n* résignation *f*; (from job) démission *f*. **resigned** *adj* résigné.

resilience /rɪ'zɪlɪəns/ *n* élasticité *f*; ressort *m*.

resin /'rezɪn/ *n* résine *f*.

resist /rɪ'zɪst/ *vt/i* résister (à). **resistance** *n* résistance *f*. **resistant** *adj* (Med) rebelle; (*metal*) résistant.

resolution /rezə'luːʃn/ *n* résolution *f*.

resolve /rɪ'zɒlv/ *vt* résoudre (**to do** de faire). ● *n* résolution *f*.

resort /rɪ'zɔːt/ *vi* ~ **to** avoir recours à. ● *n* (recourse) recours *m*; (place) station *f*; **in the last** ~ en dernier ressort.

resource /rɪ'sɔːs/ *n* ressource *f*; ~**s** (wealth) ressources *fpl*. **resourceful** *adj* ingénieux.

respect /rɪ'spekt/ *n* respect *m*; (aspect) égard *m*; **with** ~ **to** à l'égard de, relativement à. ● *vt* respecter.

respectability /rɪspektə'bɪlətɪ/ *n* respectabilité *f*. **respectable** *adj* respectable.

respectful /rɪ'spektfl/ *adj* respectueux.

respective /rɪ'spektɪv/ *adj* respectif.

respite /'respaɪt/ *n* répit *m*.

respond /rɪ'spɒnd/ *vi* répondre (**to** à); ~ **to** (react to) réagir à. **response** *n* réponse *f*.

responsibility /rɪspɒnsə'bɪlətɪ/ *n* responsabilité *f*. **responsible** *adj* responsable; (*job*) qui comporte des responsabilités.

responsive /rɪ'spɒnsɪv/ *adj* réceptif.

rest /rest/ *vt/i* (se) reposer; (lean) (s')appuyer (**on** sur); (be buried, lie) reposer; (remain) demeurer. ● *n* repos *m*; (support) support *m*; **have a** ~ se reposer; **the** ~ (remainder) le reste (**of** de); (other people) les autres.

restaurant /'restrɒnt/ *n* restaurant *m*.

restless /'restlɪs/ *adj* agité.

restoration /restə'reɪʃn/ *n* rétablissement *m*; restauration *f*.

restore /rɪ'stɔː(r)/ *vt* rétablir; (*building*) restaurer; ~ **sth to sb** restituer qch à qn.

restrain /rɪ'streɪn/ *vt* contenir; ~ **sb from** retenir qn de. **restrained** *adj* (moderate) mesuré; (in control of self) maître de soi.

restrict /rɪ'strɪkt/ *vt* restreindre. **restriction** *n* restriction *f*.

rest room *n* (US) toilettes *fpl*.

result /rɪ'zʌlt/ *n* résultat *m*. ● *vi* résulter; ~ **in** aboutir à.

resume /rɪ'zjuːm/ *vt/i* reprendre.

résumé /'rezjuːmeɪ/ *n* résumé *m*; (of career: US) CV *m*, curriculum vitae *m*.

resurrect /rezə'rekt/ *vt* ressusciter.

resuscitate /rɪ'sʌsɪteɪt/ *vt* réanimer.

retail /'riːteɪl/ *n* détail *m*. ● *adj & adv* au détail. ● *vt/i* (se) vendre (au détail). **retailer** *n* détaillant/-e *m/f*.

retain /rɪ'teɪn/ *vt* (hold back, remember) retenir; (keep) conserver.

retaliate /rɪ'tælɪeɪt/ *vi* riposter. **retaliation** *n* représailles *fpl*.

retch /retʃ/ *vi* avoir un haut-le-cœur.

retire /rɪ'taɪə(r)/ *vi* (from work) prendre sa retraite; (withdraw) se retirer; (go to bed) se coucher. **retired** *adj* retraité. **retirement** *n* retraite *f*.

retort /rɪ'tɔːt/ *vt/i* répliquer. ● *n* réplique *f*.

retrace /riː'treɪs/ *vt* ~ **one's steps** revenir sur ses pas.

retract /rɪ'trækt/ *vt/i* (se) rétracter.

retrain /riː'treɪn/ *vt/i* (se) recycler.

retreat /rɪ'triːt/ *vi* (Mil) battre en retraite. ● *n* retraite *f*.

retrieval /rɪ'triːvl/ *n* (Comput) extraction *f*. **retrieve** *vt* (*object*) récupérer; (*situation*) redresser; (*data*) extraire.

retrospect /'retrəʊspekt/ *n* **in** ~ rétrospectivement.

return /rɪ'tɜːn/ *vi* (come back) revenir; (go back) retourner; (go home) rentrer. ● *vt* (give back) rendre; (bring back) rapporter; (send back) renvoyer; (put back) remettre. ● *n* retour *m*; (yield) rapport *m*; ~**s** (Comm) bénéfices *mpl*; **in** ~ **for** en échange de. ~ **ticket** *n* allerretour *m*.

reunion /riː'juːnɪən/ *n* réunion *f*.

reunite /riːjuː'naɪt/ *vt* réunir.

rev /rev/ *n* (Auto 🔲) tour *m*. ● *vt/i* (*pt* **revved**) ~ **(up)** (engine 🔲) (s')emballer.

reveal /rɪ'viːl/ *vt* révéler; (allow to appear) laisser voir.

revelation /revə'leɪʃn/ n révélation f.

revenge /rɪ'vendʒ/ n vengeance f. ● vt venger.

revenue /'revənju:/ n revenu m.

reverberate /rɪ'vɜːbəreɪt/ vi (sound, light) se répercuter.

reverend /'revərənd/ adj révérend.

reversal /rɪ'vɜːsl/ n renversement m; (of view) revirement m.

reverse /rɪ'vɜːs/ adj contraire, inverse. ● n contraire m; (back) revers m, envers m; (gear) marche f arrière. ● vt (situation, bracket) renverser; (order) inverser; (decision) annuler; ● **the charges** appeler en PCV. ● vi (Auto) faire marche arrière.

review /rɪ'vju:/ n (inspection, magazine) revue f; (of book) critique f. ● vt passer en revue; (situation) réexaminer; faire la critique de. **reviewer** n critique m.

revise /rɪ'vaɪz/ vt réviser; (text) revoir. **revision** n révision f.

revival /rɪ'vaɪvl/ n (of economy) reprise f; (of interest) regain m.

revive /rɪ'vaɪv/ vt (person, hopes) ranimer; (custom) rétablir. ● vi se ranimer.

revoke /rɪ'vəʊk/ vt révoquer.

revolt /rɪ'vəʊlt/ vt/i (se) révolter. ● n révolte f. **revolting** adj dégoûtant.

revolution /revə'lu:ʃn/ n révolution f.

revolve /rɪ'vɒlv/ vi tourner.

revolver /rɪ'vɒlvə(r)/ n revolver m.

revolving door n porte f à tambour.

reward /rɪ'wɔːd/ n récompense f. ● vt récompenser (**for** de). **rewarding** adj rémunérateur; (worthwhile) qui (en) vaut la peine.

rewind /riː'waɪnd/ vt (pt **rewound**) rembobiner.

rewire /riː'waɪə(r)/ vt refaire l'installation électrique de.

rhetorical /rɪ'tɒrɪkl/ adj (de) rhétorique; (question) de pure forme.

rheumatism /'ruːmətɪzəm/ n rhumatisme m.

rhinoceros /raɪ'nɒsərəs/ n (pl ~ **es**) rhinocéros m.

rhubarb /'ruːbɑːb/ n rhubarbe f.

rhyme /raɪm/ n rime f; (poem) vers mpl. ● vt/i (faire) rimer.

rhythm /'rɪðəm/ n rythme m. **rhythmic-(al)** adj rythmique.

rib /rɪb/ n côte f.

ribbon /'rɪbən/ n ruban m; **in ~s** en lambeaux.

rice /raɪs/ n riz m. **~ pudding** n riz m au lait.

rich /rɪtʃ/ adj riche.

rid /rɪd/ vt (pt **rid**; pres p **ridding**) débarrasser (**of** de); **get ~ of** se débarrasser de.

ridden /'rɪdn/ ➡RIDE.

riddle /'rɪdl/ n énigme f. ● vt ~ **with** (bullets) cribler de; (mistakes) bourrer de.

ride /raɪd/ vi (pt **rode**; pp **ridden**) aller (à bicyclette, à cheval); (in car) rouler; (on a horse as sport) monter à cheval. ● vt (a particular horse) monter; (distance) parcourir. ● n promenade f, tour m; (distance) trajet m; **give sb a ~** (US) prendre qn en voiture; **go for a ~** aller faire un tour (à bicyclette, à cheval). **rider** n cavalier/-ière m/f; (In horse race) jockey m; (cyclist) cycliste mf; (motorcyclist) motocycliste mf.

ridge /rɪdʒ/ n arête f, crête f.

ridiculous /rɪ'dɪkjʊləs/ adj ridicule.

riding /'raɪdɪŋ/ n équitation f.

rifle /'raɪfl/ n fusil m. ● vt (rob) dévaliser.

rift /rɪft/ n (crack) fissure f; (between people) désaccord m.

rig /rɪg/ vt (pt **rigged**) (equip) équiper; (election, match) truquer. ● n (for oil) derrick m. □ ~ **out** habiller; ~ **up** (arrange) arranger.

right /raɪt/ adj (morally) bon; (fair) juste; (best) bon, qu'il faut; (not left) droit; **be ~** (person) avoir raison (**to** de); (calculation, watch) être exact; **put ~** arranger, rectifier. ● n (entitlement) droit m; (not left) droite f; (not evil) le bien; **be in the ~** avoir raison; **on the ~** à droite. ● vt (a wrong, sth fallen) redresser. ● adv (not left) à droite; (directly) tout droit; (exactly) bien, juste; (completely) tout (à fait); ~ **away** tout de suite; ~ **now** (at once) tout de suite; (at present) en ce moment.

righteous /'raɪtʃəs/ adj vertueux.

rightful /'raɪtfl/ adj légitime.

right-handed adj droitier.

rightly /'raɪtlɪ/ adv correctement; (with reason) à juste titre.

r

right of way n (Auto) priorité f.
right wing adj de droite.
rigid /'rɪdʒɪd/ adj rigide.
rigorous /'rɪgərəs/ adj rigoureux.
rim /rɪm/ n bord m.
rind /raɪnd/ n (on cheese) croûte f; (on bacon) couenne f; (on fruit) écorce f.
ring[1] /rɪŋ/ n (hoop) anneau m; (jewellery) bague f; (circle) cercle m; (boxing) ring m; **(wedding)** ~ alliance f. ● vt entourer; (word in text) entourer d'un cercle.
ring[2] /rɪŋ/ vt/i (pt **rang**; pp **rung**) sonner; (of words) retentir; ~ **the bell** sonner. ● n sonnerie f; **give sb a** ~ donner un coup de fil à qn. □ ~ **back** rappeler; ~ **off** raccrocher; ~ **up** téléphoner (à). ~**tone** sonnerie f.
ring road n périphérique m.
rink /rɪŋk/ n patinoire f.
rinse /rɪns/ vt rincer; ~ **out** rincer. ● n rinçage m.
riot /'raɪət/ n émeute f; (of colours) profusion f; **run** ~ se déchaîner. ● vi faire une émeute.
rip /rɪp/ vt/i (pt **ripped**) (se) déchirer; **let** ~ (not check) laisser courir; ~ **off** ⊠ rouler. ● n déchirure f.
ripe /raɪp/ adj mûr. **ripen** vt/i mûrir.
rip-off n ⊡ vol m; arnaque f ⊡.
ripple /'rɪpl/ n ride f, ondulation f. ● vt/i (water) (se) rider.
rise /raɪz/ vi (pt **rose**; pp **risen**) (increase) monter, s'élever; (stand up, get up) se lever; (rebel) se soulever; (sun) se lever; (water) monter; ~ **up** se soulever. ● n (slope) pente f; (increase) hausse f; (in pay) augmentation f; (progress, boom) essor m; **give** ~ **to** donner lieu à.
risk /rɪsk/ n risque m; **at** ~ menacé. ● vt risquer; ~ **doing** (venture) se risquer à faire. **risky** adj risqué.
rite /raɪt/ n rite m; **last** ~s derniers sacrements mpl.
rival /'raɪvl/ n rival/-e m/f. ● adj rival; (claim) opposé. ● vt (pt **rivalled**) rivaliser avec.
river /'rɪvə(r)/ n rivière f; (flowing into sea) fleuve m. ● adj (fishing, traffic) fluvial.
rivet /'rɪvɪt/ n (bolt) rivet m. ● vt (pt **riveted**) river, riveter.

Riviera /rɪvɪ'eərə/ n **the (French)** ~ la Côte d'Azur.
road /rəʊd/ n route f; (in town) rue f; (small) chemin m; **the** ~ **to** (glory: fig) le chemin de. ● adj (sign, safety) routier. ~-**map** n carte f routière. ~ **rage** n violence f au volant. ~**worthy** adj en état de marche.
roam /rəʊm/ vi errer. ● vt (streets, seas) parcourir.
roar /rɔː(r)/ n hurlement m; (of lion, wind) rugissement m; (of lorry, thunder) grondement m. ● vt/i hurler; (lion, wind) rugir; (lorry, thunder) gronder; ~ **with laughter** rire aux éclats.
roast /rəʊst/ vt/i rôtir. ● n (meat) rôti m. ● adj rôti. ~ **beef** n rôti m de bœuf.
rob /rɒb/ vt (pt **robbed**) voler (**sb of sth** qch à qn); (bank, house) dévaliser; (deprive) priver (**of** de). **robber** n voleur/-euse m/f. **robbery** n vol m.
robe /rəʊb/ n (of judge) robe f; (dressinggown) peignoir m.
robin /'rɒbɪn/ n rouge-gorge m.
robot /'rəʊbɒt/ n robot m.
robust /rəʊ'bʌst/ adj robuste.
rock /rɒk/ n roche f; (rock face, boulder) rocher m; (hurled stone) pierre f; (sweet) sucre m d'orge; (Mus) rock m; **on the** ~s (drink) avec des glaçons; (marriage) en crise. ● vt/i (se) balancer; (shake) (faire) trembler; (child) bercer. ~-**climbing** n varappe f.
rocket /'rɒkɪt/ n fusée f.
rocking-chair n fauteuil m à bascule.
rocky /'rɒkɪ/ adj (-**ier**, -**iest**) (ground) rocailleux; (hill) rocheux; (shaky: fig) branlant.
rod /rɒd/ n (metal) tige f; (wooden) baguette f; (for fishing) canne f à pêche.
rode /rəʊd/ ➡**RIDE.**
roe /rəʊ/ n œufs mpl de poisson.
rogue /rəʊg/ n (dishonest) bandit m; (mischievous) coquin/-e m/f.
role /rəʊl/ n rôle m.
roll /rəʊl/ vt/i rouler; ~ **(about)** (child, dog) se rouler; **be** ~**ing (in money)**⊡ rouler sur l'or. ● n rouleau m; (list) liste f; (bread) petit pain m; (of drum, thunder) roulement m; (of ship) roulis m. □ ~ **out** étendre; ~ **over** se retourner; ~ **up** (sleeves) retrousser.
roll-call n appel m.

r

roller /ˈrəʊlə(r)/ n rouleau m. ~ **blade** n patin m en ligne, roller m. ~**-coaster** n montagnes fpl russes. ~**-skate** n patin m à roulettes.

ROM abbr (**read-only memory**) mémoire f morte.

Roman /ˈrəʊmən/ adj & n romain/-e (m/f). ~ **Catholic** adj & n catholique (mf).

romance /rəʊˈmæns/ n (novel) roman m d'amour; (love) amour m; (affair) idylle f; (fig) poésie f.

Romania /rəʊˈmeɪnɪə/ n Roumanie f.

Romanian /rəʊˈmeɪnɪən/ adj roumain. ● n (person) Roumain/-e m/f; (language) roumain m.

romantic /rəʊˈmæntɪk/ adj (love) romantique; (of the imagination) romanesque.

roof /ruːf/ n toit m; (of mouth) palais m. ● vt recouvrir. ~**-rack** n galerie f. ~**-top** n toit m.

room /ruːm/ n pièce f; (bedroom) chambre f; (large hall) salle f; (space) place f; ~ **for manoeuvre** marge f de manœuvre. ~**-mate** n camarade mf de chambre.

roomy /ˈruːmɪ/ adj spacieux; (clothes) ample.

root /ruːt/ n racine f; (source) origine f; **take** ~ prendre racine. ● vt/i (s')enraciner. □ ~ **about** fouiller; ~ **for** (US 🔲) encourager; ~ **out** extirper.

rope /rəʊp/ n corde f; **know the** ~**s** être au courant. ● vt attacher; ~ **in** (person) enrôler.

rose /rəʊz/ n rose f. ● →RISE.

rosé /ˈrəʊzeɪ/ n rosé m.

rosy /ˈrəʊzɪ/ adj (**-ier, -iest**) rose; (hopeful) plein d'espoir.

rot /rɒt/ vt/i (pt **rotted**) pourrir.

rota /ˈrəʊtə/ n liste f (de service).

rotary /ˈrəʊtərɪ/ adj rotatif.

rotate /rəʊˈteɪt/ vt/i (faire) tourner; (change round) alterner.

rotten /ˈrɒtn/ adj pourri; (tooth) gâté; (bad 🔲) mauvais, sale.

rough /rʌf/ adj (manners) rude; (to touch) rugueux; (ground) accidenté; (violent) brutal; (bad) mauvais; (estimate) approximatif. ● adv (live) à la dure.

roughage /ˈrʌfɪdʒ/ n fibres fpl.

roughly /ˈrʌflɪ/ adv rudement; (approximately) à peu près.

round /raʊnd/ adj rond. ● n (circle) rond m; (slice) tranche f; (of visits, drinks) tournée f; (competition) partie f, manche f; (boxing) round m; (of talks) série f; ~ **of applause** applaudissements mpl; **go the** ~**s** circuler. ● prep autour de; **she lives** ~ **here** elle habite par ici; ~ **the clock** vingt-quatre heures sur vingt-quatre. ● adv autour; ~ **about** (nearby) par ici; (fig) à peu près; **go** or **come** ~ **to** (a friend) passer chez; **enough to go** ~ assez pour tout le monde. ● vt (object) arrondir; (corner) tourner. □ ~ **off** terminer; ~ **up** rassembler

roundabout /ˈraʊndəbaʊt/ n (in fairground) manège m; (for traffic) rond-point m (à sens giratoire). ● adj indirect.

round trip n voyage m aller-retour.

round-up n rassemblement m; (of suspects) rafle f.

route /ruːt/ n itinéraire m, parcours m; (Naut, Aviat) route f.

routine /ruːˈtiːn/ n routine f. ● adj de routine.

row[1] /rəʊ/ n rangée f, rang m; **in a** ~ (consecutive) consécutif. ● vi ramer; (Sport) faire de l'aviron. ● vt ~ **a boat up the river** remonter la rivière à la rame.

row[2] /raʊ/ n (noise 🔲) tapage m; (quarrel 🔲) dispute f. ● vi 🔲 se disputer.

rowdy /ˈraʊdɪ/ adj (**-ier, -iest**) tapageur.

rowing /ˈrəʊɪŋ/ n aviron m. ~**-boat** n bateau m à rames.

royal /ˈrɔɪəl/ adj royal. **royalty** n famille f royale; **royalties** droits mpl d'auteur.

RSI abbr (repetitive strain injury) TMS m, trouble m musculo-squelettique.

rub /rʌb/ vt/i (pt **rubbed**) frotter; ~ **it in** insister, en rajouter. ● n friction f. □ ~ **out** (s')effacer.

rubber /ˈrʌbə(r)/ n caoutchouc m; (eraser) gomme f. ~ **band** n élastique m. ~ **stamp** n tampon m.

rubbish /ˈrʌbɪʃ/ n (refuse) ordures fpl; (junk) saletés fpl; (fig) bêtises fpl.

rubble /ˈrʌbl/ n décombres mpl.

r

ruby /'ruːbɪ/ n rubis m.

rucksack /'rʌksæk/ n sac m à dos.

rude /ruːd/ adj impoli, grossier; (improper) indécent; (blow) brutal.

ruffle /'rʌfl/ vt (hair) ébouriffer; (clothes) froisser; (person) contrarier. ● n (frill) ruche f.

rug /rʌg/ n petit tapis m.

rugby /'rʌgbɪ/ n rugby m.

rugged /'rʌgɪd/ adj (surface) rude, rugueux; (ground) accidenté; (character, features) rude.

ruin /'ruːɪn/ n ruine f. ● vt (destroy) ruiner; (damage) abîmer; (spoil) gâter.

rule /ruːl/ n règle f; (regulation) règlement m; (Pol) gouvernement m; as a ~ en règle générale. ● vt gouverner; (master) dominer; (decide) décider; ~ out exclure. ● vi régner. **ruler** n dirigeant/-e m/f, gouvernant m; (measure) règle f.

ruling /'ruːlɪŋ/ adj (class) dirigeant; (party) au pouvoir. ● n décision f.

rum /rʌm/ n rhum m.

rumble /'rʌmbl/ vi gronder; (stomach) gargouiller. ● n grondement m; gargouillement m.

rumour, (US) **rumor** /'ruːmə(r)/ n bruit m, rumeur f; there's a ~ that le bruit court que.

rump /rʌmp/ n (of animal) croupe f; (of bird) croupion m; (steak) romsteck m.

run /rʌn/ vi (pt **ran**; pp **run**; pres p **running**) courir; (flow) couler; (pass) passer; (function) marcher; (melt) fondre; (extend) s'étendre; (of bus) circuler; (of play) se jouer; (last) durer; (of colour in washing) déteindre; (in election) être candidat. ● vt (manage) diriger; (event) organiser; (risk, race) courir; (house) tenir; (temperature, errand) faire; (Comput) exécuter. ● n course f; (journey) parcours m; (outing) promenade f; (rush) ruée f; (series) série f; (for chickens) enclos m; (in cricket) point m; in the long ~ avec le temps; on the ~ en fuite. □ ~ **across** rencontrer par hasard; ~ **away** s'enfuir; ~ **off** (copies) tirer; ~ **down** descendre en courant; (of vehicle) renverser; (production) réduire progressivement; (belittle) dénigrer; ~ **into** (hit) heurter; ~ **out** (be used up) s'épuiser; (of lease) expirer; ~ **out of** manquer de;

~ **over** (of vehicle) écraser; (details) revoir; ~ **through** regarder qch rapidement; ~ **sth through sth** passer qch à travers qch; ~ **up** (bill) accumuler.

runaway /'rʌnəweɪ/ n fugitif/-ive m/f. ● adj fugitif; (horse, vehicle) fou; (inflation) galopant.

rung /rʌŋ/ →RING². ● n (of ladder) barreau m.

runner /'rʌnə(r)/ n coureur/-euse m/f. ~ **bean** n haricot m d'Espagne. ~-**up** n second/-e m/f.

running /'rʌnɪŋ/ n course f à pied; (of business) gestion f; (of machine) marche f; **be in the** ~ **for** être sur les rangs pour. ● adj (commentary) suivi; (water) courant; **four days** ~ quatre jours de suite.

runway /'rʌnweɪ/ n piste f.

rural /'rʊərəl/ adj rural.

rush /rʌʃ/ vi (move) se précipiter; (be in a hurry) se dépêcher. ● vt (person) bousculer; (Mil) prendre d'assaut; ~ **to** envoyer d'urgence à. ● n ruée f; (haste) bousculade f; (plant) jonc m; **in a** ~ pressé. ~-**hour** n heure f de pointe.

Russia /'rʌʃə/ n Russie f.

Russian /'rʌʃn/ adj russe. ● n (person) Russe mf; (language) russe.

rust /rʌst/ n rouille f. ● vt/i rouiller.

rustle /'rʌsl/ vt/i (papers) froisser.

rusty /'rʌstɪ/ adj rouillé.

ruthless /'ruːθlɪs/ adj impitoyable.

rye /raɪ/ n seigle m.

Ss

sabbath /'sæbəθ/ n (Jewish) sabbat m; (Christian) jour m du seigneur.

sabbatical /sə'bætɪkl/ adj (Univ) sabbatique.

sabotage /'sæbətɑːʒ/ n sabotage m. ● vt saboter.

saccharin /'sækərɪn/ n saccharine f.

sack /sæk/ n (bag) sac m; **get the** ~ Ⓘ être renvoyé. ● vt Ⓘ renvoyer; (plunder) saccager. **sacking** n (cloth) toile f à sac; (dismissal Ⓘ) renvoi m.

sacrament /'sækrəmənt/ n sacrement m.

sacred /'seɪkrɪd/ adj sacré.

sacrifice /'sækrɪfaɪs/ n sacrifice m. ● vt sacrifier.

sad /sæd/ adj (**sadder, saddest**) triste.

saddle /'sædl/ n selle f. ● vt (horse) seller.

sadist /'seɪdɪst/ n sadique mf. **sadistic** adj sadique.

sadly /'sædlɪ/ adv tristement; (unfortunately) malheureusement.

sadness /'sædnɪs/ n tristesse f.

safe /seɪf/ adj (not dangerous) sans danger; (reliable) sûr; (out of danger) en sécurité; (after accident) sain et sauf; ~ **from** à l'abri de. ● n coffre-fort m.

safeguard /'seɪfgɑːd/ n sauvegarde f. ● vt sauvegarder.

safely /'seɪflɪ/ adv sans danger; (in safe place) en sûreté.

safety /'seɪftɪ/ n sécurité f. ~**-belt** n ceinture f de sécurité. ~**-pin** n épingle f de sûreté. ~**-valve** n soupape f de sûreté.

saffron /'sæfrən/ n safran m.

sag /sæg/ vi (pt **sagged**) (beam, mattress) s'affaisser; (flesh) être flasque.

sage /seɪdʒ/ n (herb) sauge f.

Sagittarius /sædʒɪ'teərɪəs/ n Sagittaire m.

said /sed/ ⇒SAY.

sail /seɪl/ n voile f; (journey) tour m en bateau. ● vi (person) voyager en bateau; (as sport) faire de la voile; (set off) prendre la mer; ~ **across** traverser. ● vt (boat) piloter; (sea) traverser. **sailing-boat, sailing-ship** n voilier m.

sailor /'seɪlə(r)/ n marin m.

saint /seɪnt/ n saint/-e m/f.

sake /seɪk/ n for the ~ of pour.

salad /'sæləd/ n salade f.

salaried /'sælərɪd/ adj salarié.

salary /'sælərɪ/ n salaire m.

sale /seɪl/ n vente f; for ~ à vendre; on ~ en vente; (reduced) en solde; ~s (reductions) soldes mpl; ~s **assistant**, (US) ~s **clerk** vendeur/-euse m/f.

salesman /'seɪlzmən/ n (pl **-men**) (in shop) vendeur m; (traveller) représentant m.

saline /'seɪlaɪn/ adj salin. ● n sérum m physiologique.

saliva /sə'laɪvə/ n salive f.

salmon /'sæmən/ n inv saumon m.

salon /'sælɒn/ n salon m.

saloon /sə'luːn/ n (on ship) salon m; ~ (**car**) berline f.

salt /sɔːlt/ n sel m. ● vt saler. **salty** adj salé.

salutary /'sæljʊtrɪ/ adj salutaire.

salute /sə'luːt/ n salut m. ● vt saluer. ● vi faire un salut.

salvage /'sælvɪdʒ/ n sauvetage m; (of waste) récupération f. ● vt sauver; (for re-use) récupérer.

same /seɪm/ adj même (as que). ● pron the ~ le même, la même, les mêmes; at the ~ time en même temps; the ~ (thing) la même chose.

sample /'sɑːmpl/ n échantillon m; (of blood) prélèvement m. ● vt essayer; (food) goûter.

sanctimonious /sæŋktɪ'məunɪəs/ adj (pej) supérieur.

sanction /'sæŋkʃn/ n sanction f. ● vt sanctionner.

sanctity /'sæŋktətɪ/ n sainteté f.

sanctuary /'sæŋktʃʊərɪ/ n (safe place) refuge m; (Relig) sanctuaire m; (for animals) réserve f.

sand /sænd/ n sable m; ~s (beach) plage f.

sandal /'sændl/ n sandale f.

sandpaper /'sændpeɪpə(r)/ n papier m de verre. ● vt poncer.

sandpit /'sændpɪt/ n bac m à sable.

sandwich /'sænwɪdʒ/ n sandwich m; ~ **course** cours m avec stage pratique.

sandy /'sændɪ/ adj (beach) de sable; (soil) sablonneux; (hair) blond roux inv.

sane /seɪn/ adj (view) sensé; (person) sain d'esprit.

sang /sæŋ/ ⇒SING.

sanitary /'sænɪtrɪ/ adj (clean) hygiénique; (system) sanitaire; ~ **towel** serviette f hygiénique.

sanitation /sænɪ'teɪʃn/ n installations fpl sanitaires.

sanity /'sænətɪ/ n équilibre m mental; (sense) bon sens m.

S

sank /sæŋk/ ➡SINK.

Santa (Claus) /ˈsæntə (klɔːz)/ n le père Noël.

sapphire /ˈsæfaɪə(r)/ n saphir m.

sarcasm /ˈsɑːkæzəm/ n sarcasme m. **sarcastic** adj sarcastique.

sash /sæʃ/ n (on uniform) écharpe f; (on dress) ceinture f.

sat /sæt/ ➡SIT.

satchel /ˈsætʃəl/ n cartable m.

satellite /ˈsætəlaɪt/ n & adj satellite (m); ~ **dish** antenne f parabolique.

satire /ˈsætaɪə(r)/ n satire f. **satirical** adj satirique.

satisfaction /sætɪsˈfækʃn/ n satisfaction f.

satisfactory /sætɪsˈfæktərɪ/ adj satisfaisant.

satisfy /ˈsætɪsfaɪ/ vt satisfaire; (convince) convaincre.

satphone /ˈsætfəʊn/ n téléphone m satellite.

saturate /ˈsætʃəreɪt/ vt saturer. **saturated** adj (wet) trempé.

Saturday /ˈsætədeɪ/ n samedi m.

sauce /sɔːs/ n sauce f.

saucepan /ˈsɔːspən/ n casserole f.

saucer /ˈsɔːsə(r)/ n soucoupe f.

Saudi Arabia /saʊdɪ əˈreɪbɪə/ n Arabie f saoudite.

sausage /ˈsɒsɪdʒ/ n (for cooking) saucisse f; (ready to eat) saucisson m.

savage /ˈsævɪdʒ/ adj (blow, temper) violent; (attack) sauvage. ● n sauvage mf. ● vt attaquer sauvagement.

save /seɪv/ vt sauver; (money) économiser; (time) gagner; (keep) garder; ~ **(sb) doing sth** éviter (à qn) de faire qch. ● n (football) arrêt m. **saver** n épargnant/-e m/f. **saving** n économie f. **savings** npl économies fpl.

saviour, (US) **savior** /ˈseɪvɪə(r)/ n sauveur m.

savour, (US) **savor** /ˈseɪvə(r)/ n saveur f. ● vt savourer. **savoury** adj (tasty) savoureux; (Culin) salé.

saw /sɔː/ ➡SEE. ● n scie f. ● vt (pt sawed; pp sawn or sawed) scier.

sawdust /ˈsɔːdʌst/ n sciure f.

saxophone /ˈsæksəfəʊn/ n saxophone m.

say /seɪ/ vt/i (pt said) dire; (prayer) faire. ● n have a ~ dire son mot; (in decision) avoir voix au chapitre. **saying** n proverbe m.

scab /skæb/ n croûte f.

scaffolding /ˈskæfəldɪŋ/ n échafaudage m.

scald /skɔːld/ vt (injure, cleanse) ébouillanter. ● n brûlure f.

scale /skeɪl/ n (for measuring) échelle f; (extent) étendue f; (Mus) gamme f; (on fish) écaille f; **on a small** ~ sur une petite échelle; ~ **model** maquette f. ● vt (climb) escalader; ~ **down** réduire. **scales** npl (for weighing) balance f.

scallop /ˈskɒləp/ n coquille f Saint-Jacques.

scalp /skælp/ n cuir m chevelu.

scampi /ˈskæmpɪ/ npl (fresh) langoustines fpl; (breaded) scampi mpl.

scan /skæn/ vt (pt scanned) scruter; (quickly) parcourir. ● n (ultrasound) échographie f; (CAT) scanner m.

scandal /ˈskændl/ n scandale m; (gossip) potins mpl ⊞.

Scandinavia /skændɪˈneɪvɪə/ n Scandinavie f.

scanty /ˈskæntɪ/ adj (-ier, -iest) maigre; (clothing) minuscule.

scapegoat /ˈskeɪpgəʊt/ n bouc m émissaire.

scar /skɑː(r)/ n cicatrice f. ● vt (pt scarred) marquer.

scarce /skeəs/ adj rare. **scarcely** adv à peine.

scare /skeə(r)/ vt faire peur à; **be ~d** avoir peur. ● n peur f; **bomb** ~ alerte f à la bombe. **scarecrow** n épouvantail m.

scarf /skɑːf/ n (pl scarves) écharpe f; (over head) foulard m.

scarlet /ˈskɑːlət/ adj écarlate; ~ **fever** scarlatine f.

scary /ˈskeərɪ/ adj (-ier, -iest) ⊞ qui fait peur.

scathing /ˈskeɪðɪŋ/ adj cinglant.

scatter /ˈskætə(r)/ vt (throw) éparpiller, répandre; (disperse) disperser. ● vi se disperser.

scavenge /ˈskævɪndʒ/ vi fouiller (dans les ordures). **scavenger** n (animal) charognard m.

scene /siːn/ n scène f; (of accident, crime) lieu m; (sight) spectacle m; **behind the ~s** en coulisse. **scenery** n paysage m; (Theat) décors mpl. **scenic** adj panoramique.

scent /sent/ n (perfume) parfum m; (trail) piste f. ● vt flairer; (make fragrant) parfumer.

sceptic /ˈskeptɪk/ n sceptique mf. **sceptical** adj sceptique. **scepticism** n scepticisme m.

schedule /ˈʃedjuːl/, /ˈskedʒʊl/ n horaire m; (for job) planning m; **behind ~** en retard; **on ~** dans les temps. ● vt prévoir; **~d flight** vol m régulier.

scheme /skiːm/ n projet m; (dishonest) combine f; **pension ~** plan m de retraite. ● vi comploter.

schizophrenic /skɪtsəʊˈfrenɪk/ adj & n schizophrène (mf).

scholar /ˈskɒlə(r)/ n érudit/-e m/f.

school /skuːl/ n école f; **go to ~** aller à l'école. ● adj (age, year, holidays) scolaire. **~boy** n élève m. **~girl** n élève f. **schooling** n scolarité f. **~teacher** n (primary) instituteur/-trice m/f; (secondary) professeur m.

science /ˈsaɪəns/ n science f; **teach ~** enseigner les sciences. **scientific** adj scientifique. **scientist** n scientifique mf.

scissors /ˈsɪzəz/ npl ciseaux mpl.

scold /skəʊld/ vt gronder.

scoop /skuːp/ n (shovel) pelle f; (measure) mesure f; (for ice cream) cuillère f à glace; (news) exclusivité f.

scooter /ˈskuːtə(r)/ n (child's) trottinette f; (motor cycle) scooter m.

scope /skəʊp/ n étendue f; (competence) compétence f; (opportunity) possibilité f.

scorch /skɔːtʃ/ vt brûler; (iron) roussir.

score /skɔː(r)/ n score m; (Mus) partition f; **on that ~** à cet égard. ● vt marquer; (success) remporter. ● vi marquer un point; (football) marquer un but; (keep score) marquer les points. **scorer** n (Sport) marqueur m.

scorn /skɔːn/ n mépris m. ● vt mépriser.

Scorpio /ˈskɔːpɪəʊ/ n Scorpion m.

Scot /skɒt/ n écossais/-e m/f.

Scotland /ˈskɒtlənd/ n écosse f.

Scottish /ˈskɒtɪʃ/ adj écossais.

scoundrel /ˈskaʊndrəl/ n gredin m.

scour /ˈskaʊə(r)/ vt (pan) récurer; (search) parcourir. **scourer** n tampon m à récurer.

scourge /skɜːdʒ/ n fléau m.

scout /skaʊt/ n éclaireur m. ● vi **~ around for** rechercher.

scowl /skaʊl/ n air m renfrogné. ● vi prendre un air renfrogné.

scramble /ˈskræmbl/ vi (clamber) grimper. ● vt (eggs) brouiller. ● n (rush) course f.

scrap /skræp/ n petit morceau m; **~s** (of metal, fabric) déchets mpl; (of food) restes mpl; (fight 🄸) bagarre f. ● vt (pl **scrapped**) abandonner; (car) détruire.

scrape /skreɪp/ vt gratter; (damage) érafler. ● vi **~ against** érafler. □ **~ through** réussir de justesse.

scrap: ~-paper n papier m brouillon. **~yard** n casse f.

scratch /skrætʃ/ vt/i (se) gratter; (with claw, nail) griffer; (graze) érafler; (mark) rayer. ● n (on body) égratignure f; (on surface) éraflure f; **start from ~** partir de zéro; **up to ~** à la hauteur. **~ card** n jeu m de grattage.

scrawl /skrɔːl/ n gribouillage m. ● vt/i gribouiller.

scrawny /ˈskrɔːnɪ/ adj (**-ier, -iest**) décharné.

scream /skriːm/ vt/i crier. ● n cri m (perçant).

screech /skriːtʃ/ vi (scream) hurler; (tyres) crisser. ● n cri m strident; (of tyres) crissement m.

screen /skriːn/ n écran m; (folding) paravent m. ● vt masquer; (protect) protéger; (film) projeter; (candidates) filtrer; (Med) faire subir un test de

S

dépistage. **screening** n (cinema) projection f; (Med) dépistage m.

screen: ~**play** n scénario m. ~ **saver** n protecteur m d'écran.

screw /skruː/ n vis f. ● vt visser; ~ **up** (eyes) plisser; (ruin 🔢) cafouiller 🔢. ~**driver** n tournevis m.

scribble /'skrɪbl/ vt/i griffonner. ● n griffonnage m.

script /skrɪpt/ n script m; (of play) texte m.

scroll /skrəʊl/ n rouleau m. ● vt/i (Comput) (faire) défiler. ~ **bar** n barre f de défilement.

scrounge /skraʊndʒ/ 🔢 vt (favour) quémander; (cigarette) piquer 🔢; ~ **money from sb** taper de l'argent à qn. ● vi ~ **off sb** vivre sur le dos de qn.

scrub /skrʌb/ n (land) broussailles fpl. ● vt/i (pt **scrubbed**) nettoyer (à la brosse), frotter.

scruffy /'skrʌfɪ/ adj (-ier, -iest) 🔢 dépenaillé.

scrum /skrʌm/ n (rugby) mêlée f.

scruple /'skruːpl/ n scrupule m.

scrutinize /'skruːtɪnaɪz/ vt scruter. **scrutiny** n examen m minutieux.

scuba-diving /'skuːbədaɪvɪŋ/ n plongée f sousmarine.

scuffle /'skʌfl/ n bagarre f.

sculpt /skʌlpt/ vt/i sculpter. **sculptor** n sculpteur m.

sculpture /'skʌlptʃə(r)/ n sculpture f.

scum /skʌm/ n (on liquid) mousse f; (people: pej) racaille f.

scurry /'skʌrɪ/ vi se précipiter, courir (**for** pour chercher); ~ **off** se sauver.

sea /siː/ n mer f; **at** ~ en mer; **by** ~ par mer. ● adj (air) marin; (bird) de mer; (voyage) par mer. ~**food** n fruits mpl de mer. ~**gull** n mouette f.

seal /siːl/ n (animal) phoque m; (insignia) sceau m; (with wax) cachet m. ● vt sceller; cacheter; (stick down) coller. □ ~ **off** (area) boucler.

seam /siːm/ n (in cloth) couture f; (of coal) veine f.

search /sɜːtʃ/ vt/i (examine) fouiller; (seek) chercher; (study) examiner; (Comput) rechercher. ● n fouille f; (quest) recherches fpl; (Comput) recherche f; **in** ~ **of** à la recherche de. ~ **engine** n (Internet) moteur m de

recherche. ~**light** n projecteur m. ~-**warrant** n mandat m de perquisition.

sea: ~**shell** n coquillage m. ~**shore** n (coast) littoral m; (beach) plage f.

seasick /'siːsɪk/ adj **be** ~ avoir le mal de mer.

seaside /'siːsaɪd/ n bord m de la mer.

season /'siːzn/ n saison f; ~ **ticket** carte f d'abonnement. ● vt assaisonner. **seasonal** adj saisonnier. **seasoning** n assaisonnement m.

seat /siːt/ n siège m; (place) place f; (of trousers) fond m; **take a** ~ asseyez-vous. ● vt (put) placer; **the room** ~**s 30** la salle peut accueillir 30 personnes. ~-**belt** n ceinture f (de sécurité)

seaweed /'siːwiːd/ n algue f marine.

secluded /sɪ'kluːdɪd/ adj retiré.

seclusion /sɪ'kluːʒn/ n isolement m.

second[1] /'sekənd/ adj deuxième, second; **a** ~ **chance** une nouvelle chance; **have** ~ **thoughts** avoir des doutes. ● n deuxième mf, second/-e m/f; (unit of time) seconde f; ~ **s** (food) rab m. 🔢 ● adv (in race) deuxième; (secondly) deuxièmement. ● vt (proposal) appuyer.

second[2] /sɪ'kɒnd/ vt (transfer) détacher (**to** à).

secondary /'sekəndrɪ/ adj secondaire; ~**school** lycée m, école f secondaire.

second-best n pis-aller m.

second-class adj (Rail) de deuxième classe; (post) au tarif lent.

second hand n (on clock) trotteuse f.

second-hand adj & adv (article) d'occasion; (information) de seconde main.

secondly /'sekəndlɪ/ adv deuxièmement.

second-rate adj médiocre.

secrecy /'siːkrəsɪ/ n secret m.

secret /'siːkrɪt/ adj secret. ● n secret m; **in** ~ en secret.

secretarial /sekrə'teərɪəl/ adj (work) de secrétaire.

secretary /'sekrətrɪ/ n secrétaire mf; **S** ~ **of State** ministre m; (US) ministre m des Affaires étrangères.

secrete /sɪ'kriːt/ vt (Med) sécréter; (hide) cacher.

secretive /'siːkrətɪv/ adj secret. **secretly** adv secrètement.

sect /sekt/ n secte f. **sectarian** adj sectaire.

section /ˈsekʃn/ n partie f; (in store) rayon m; (of newspaper) rubrique f; (of book) passage m.

sector /ˈsektə(r)/ n secteur m.

secular /ˈsekjʊlə(r)/ adj (school) laïque; (art, music) profane.

secure /sɪˈkjʊə(r)/ adj (safe) sûr; (job, marriage) stable; (knot, lock) solide; (window) bien fermé; (feeling) de sécurité; (person) sécurisé. ● vt attacher; (obtain) s'assurer; (ensure) assurer.

security /sɪˈkjʊərəti/ n (safety) sécurité f; (for loan) caution f; ~ **guard** vigile m.

sedate /sɪˈdeɪt/ adj calme. ● vt donner un sédatif à. **sedative** n sédatif m.

seduce /sɪˈdjuːs/ vt séduire. **seducer** n séducteur/-trice m/f. **seduction** n séduction f. **seductive** adj séduisant.

see /siː/ vt/i (pt) **saw**; pp **seen** voir; **see you (soon)!** à bientôt!; ~**ing that** vu que. □ ~ **out** (person) raccompagner à la porte; ~ **through** (deception) déceler; (person) percer à jour; ~ **sth through** mener qch à bonne fin; ~ **to** s'occuper de; ~ **to it that** veiller à ce que.

seed /siːd/ n graine f; (collectively) graines fpl; (origin: fig) germe m; (tennis) tête f de série. **seedling** n plant m.

seek /siːk/ vt (pt) **sought** chercher.

seem /siːm/ vi sembler; **he** ~**s to think** il a l'air de croire.

seen /siːn/ ➡SEE.

seep /siːp/ vi suinter. ~ **into** s'infiltrer dans.

see-saw /ˈsiːsɔː/ n tapecul m. ● vt osciller.

seethe /siːð/ vi ~ **with** (anger) bouillir de; (people) grouiller de.

segment /ˈsegmənt/ n segment m; (of orange) quartier m.

segregate /ˈsegrɪgeɪt/ vt séparer.

seize /siːz/ vt saisir; (territory, prisoner) s'emparer de. ● vi ~ **on** (chance) saisir; ~ **up** (engine) se gripper.

seizure /ˈsiːʒə(r)/ n (Med) crise f.

seldom /ˈseldəm/ adv rarement.

select /sɪˈlekt/ vt sélectionner. ● adj privilégié. **selection** n sélection f. **selective** adj sélectif.

self /self/ n (pl **selves**) moi m; (on cheque) moi-même. ~**-assured** adj plein d'assurance. ~**-catering** adj (holiday) en location. ~**-centred**, (US) ~**-centered** adj égocentrique. ~**-confident** adj sûr de soi. ~**-conscious** adj timide. ~**-contained** adj (flat) indépendant. ~**-control** n sangfroid m. ~**-defence** n autodéfense f; (Jur) légitime défense f. ~**-employed** adj qui travaille à son compte. ~**-esteem** n amour-propre m. ~**-governing** adj autonome. ~**-indulgent** adj complaisant. ~**-interest** n intérêt m personnel.

selfish /ˈselfɪʃ/ adj égoïste.

selfless /ˈselflɪs/ adj désintéressé.

self: ~**-portrait** n autoportrait m. ~**-reliant** adj autosuffisant. ~**-respect** n respect m de soi. ~**-righteous** adj satisfait de soi. ~**-sacrifice** n abnégation f. ~**-satisfied** adj satisfait de soi. ~**-seeking** adj égoïste. ~**-service** n & adj libre-service (m).

sell /sel/ vt/i (pt **sold**) vendre; ~ **well** se vendre bien. □ ~ **off** liquider; ~ **out** (items) se vendre; **have sold out** avoir tout vendu.

Sellotape® /ˈseləʊteɪp/ n scotch® m.

sell-out n (betrayal) 🅸 revirement m; **be a** ~ (show) afficher complet.

semester /sɪˈmestə(r)/ n (Univ) semestre m.

semicircle /ˈsemɪsɜːkl/ n demi-cercle m.

semicolon /semɪˈkəʊlən/ n point-virgule m.

semi-detached /semɪdɪˈtætʃt/ adj ~ **house** maison f jumelée.

semifinal /semɪˈfaɪnl/ n demi-finale f.

seminar /ˈsemɪnɑː(r)/ n séminaire m.

semolina /seməˈliːnə/ n semoule f.

senate /ˈsenɪt/ n sénat m. **senator** n sénateur m.

send /send/ vt/i (pt **sent**) envoyer. □ ~ **away** (dismiss) renvoyer; ~ **(away** or **off) for** commander (par la poste); ~ **back** renvoyer; ~ **for** (person, help) envoyer chercher; ~ **up** 🅸 parodier.

senile /ˈsiːnaɪl/ adj sénile.

senior /ˈsiːnɪə(r)/ adj plus âgé (**to** que); (in rank) haut placé; **be** ~ **to sb** être le supérieur de qn. ● n aîné/-e m/f. ~

s

citizen n personne f âgée. ~ **school** n lycée m.

sensation /sen'seɪʃn/ n sensation f. **sensational** adj sensationnel.

sense /sens/ n sens m; (mental impression) sentiment m; (common sense) bon sens m; ~**s** (mind) raison f; **there's no ~ in doing** cela ne sert à rien de faire; **make ~** avoir un sens; **make ~ of** comprendre. ● vt (pres-)sentir. **senseless** adj insensé; (Med) sans connaissance.

sensible /'sensəbl/ adj raisonnable; (clothing) pratique.

sensitive /'sensətɪv/ adj sensible (**to** à); (issue) difficile.

sensory /'sensərɪ/ adj sensoriel.

sensual /'senʃʊəl/ adj sensuel. **sensuality** n sensualité f.

sensuous /'senʃʊəs/ adj sensuel.

sent /sent/ ➡SEND.

sentence /'sentəns/ n phrase f; (punishment: Jur) peine f. ● vt ~ **to** condamner à.

sentiment /'sentɪmənt/ n sentiment m. **sentimental** adj sentimental.

sentry /'sentrɪ/ n sentinelle f.

separate¹ /'separət/ adj (piece) à part; (issue) autre; (sections) différent; (organizations) distinct.

separate² /'sepəreɪt/ vt/i (se) séparer.

separately /'sepərətlɪ/ adv séparément.

separation /sepə'reɪʃn/ n séparation f.

September /sep'tembə(r)/ n septembre m.

septic /'septɪk/ adj (wound) infecté; ~ **tank** fosse f septique.

sequel /'siːkwəl/ n suite f.

sequence /'siːkwəns/ n (order) ordre m; (series) suite f; (in film) séquence f.

Serb /sɜːb/ adj serbe. ● n (person) Serbe mf; (Ling) serbe m.

Serbia /'sɜːbɪə/ n Serbie f.

sergeant /'sɑːdʒənt/ n (Mil) sergent m; (policeman) brigadier m.

serial /'sɪərɪəl/ n feuilleton m. ● adj (Comput) série inv.

series /'sɪəriːz/ n inv série f.

serious /'sɪərɪəs/ adj sérieux; (accident, crime) grave.

seriously /'sɪərɪəslɪ/ adv sérieusement; (ill) gravement; **take ~** prendre au sérieux.

sermon /'sɜːmən/ n sermon m.

serpent /'sɜːpənt/ n serpent m.

serrated /sɪ'reɪtɪd/ adj dentelé.

serum /'sɪərəm/ n sérum m.

servant /'sɜːvənt/ n domestique mf.

serve /sɜːv/ vt/i servir; faire; (transport, hospital) desservir; ~ **as/to** servir de/à; ~ **a purpose** être utile; ~ **a sentence** (Jur) purger une peine. ● n (tennis) service m.

server /'sɜːvə(r)/ n serveur m; **remote ~** téléserveur m.

service /'sɜːvɪs/ n service m; (maintenance) révision f; (Relig) office m; ~**s** (Mil) forces fpl armées. ● vt (car) réviser. ~**area** n (Auto) aire f de services. ~ **charge** n service m. ~ **station** n station-service f.

session /'seʃn/ n séance f; **be in ~** (Jur) tenir séance.

set /set/ vt (pt set; pres p **setting** placer; (table) mettre; (limit) fixer; (clock) mettre à l'heure; (example, task) donner; (TV), (cinema) situer; ~ **fire to** mettre le feu à; ~ **free** libérer; ~ **to music** mettre en musique. ● vi (sun) se coucher; (jelly) prendre; ~ **sail** partir. ● n (of chairs, stamps) série f; (of knives, keys) jeu m; (of people) groupe m; (TV), (radio) poste m; (Theat) décor m; (tennis) set m; (mathematics) ensemble m. ● adj (time, price) fixe; (procedure) bien determiné; (meal) à prix fixe; (book) au programme; ~ **against** sth opposé à; **be ~ on doing** tenir absolument à faire. □ ~ **about** se mettre à; ~ **back** (delay) retarder; (cost 🄸) coûter; ~ **in** (take hold) s'installer, commencer; ~ **off** or **out** partir; ~ **off** (panic, riot) déclencher; (bomb) faire exploser; ~ **out** (state) présenter; (arrange) disposer; ~ **out to do sth** chercher à faire qch; ~ **up** (stall) monter; (equipment) assembler; (experiment) préparer; (company) créer; (meeting) organiser. ~**-back** n revers m.

settee /se'tiː/ n canapé m.

setting /'setɪŋ/ n cadre m; (on dial) position f.

settle /'setl/ vt (arrange, pay) régler; (date) fixer; (nerves) calmer. ● vi (come to rest) (*bird*) se poser; (*dust*) se déposer; (*live*) s'installer. □ ~ **down** se calmer; (*marry etc.*) se ranger; ~ **for** accepter; ~ **in** s'installer; ~ **up** (**with**) régler.

settlement /ˈsetlmənt/ n règlement m (**of** de); (*agreement*) accord m; (*place*) colonie f.

settler /ˈsetlə(r)/ n colon m.

seven /ˈsevn/ adj & n sept (m).

seventeen /sevnˈtiːn/ adj & n dix-sept (m).

seventh /ˈsevnθ/ adj & n septième (mf).

seventy /ˈsevntɪ/ adj & n soixante-dix (m).

sever /ˈsevə(r)/ vt (*cut*) couper; (*relations*) rompre.

several /ˈsevrəl/ adj & pron plusieurs; ~ **of us** plusieurs d'entre nous.

severe /sɪˈvɪə(r)/ adj (*harsh*) sévère; (*serious*) grave.

sew /səʊ/ vt/i (pt **sewed**; pp **sewn** or **sewed**) coudre.

sewage /ˈsuːɪdʒ/ n eaux fpl usées.

sewer /ˈsuːə(r)/ n égout m.

sewing /ˈsəʊɪŋ/ n couture f. ~-**machine** n machine f à coudre.

sewn /səʊn/ ➡SEW.

sex /seks/ n sexe m; **have** ~ avoir des rapports (sexuels). ● adj sexuel. **sexist** adj & n sexiste (mf). **sexual** adj sexuel.

shabby /ˈʃæbɪ/ adj (-**ier**, -**iest**) (*place, object*) miteux; (*person*) habillé de façon miteuse; (*treatment*) mesquin.

shack /ʃæk/ n cabane f.

shade /ʃeɪd/ n ombre f; (*of colour, opinion*) nuance f; (*for lamp*) abat-jour m inv; **a** ~ **bigger** légèrement plus grand. ● vt (*tree*) ombrager; (*hat*) projeter une ombre sur.

shadow /ˈʃædəʊ/ n ombre f. ● vt (*follow*) filer. **S~ Cabinet** n cabinet m fantôme.

shady /ˈʃeɪdɪ/ adj (-**ier**, -**iest**) ombragé; (*dubious*) véreux.

shaft /ʃɑːft/ n (*of tool*) manche m; (*of arrow*) tige f; (*in machine*) axe m; (*of mine*) puits m; (*of light*) rayon m.

shake /ʃeɪk/ vt (pt **shook**; pp **shaken**) secouer; (*bottle*) agiter; (*belief*) ébranler; ~ **hands with** serrer la main à; ~ **one's head** dire non de la tête. ● vi trembler. ● n secousse f; **give sth a** ~ secouer qch. □ ~ **off** se débarrasser

de. ~-**up** n (Pol) remaniement m.

shaky /ˈʃeɪkɪ/ adj (-**ier**, -**iest**) (*hand, voice*) tremblant; (*ladder*) branlant; (*weak*: fig) instable.

shall /ʃæl/ v aux **I** ~ **do** je ferai; **we** ~ **see** nous verrons; ~ **we go. . . ?** si on allait . . . ?

shallow /ˈʃæləʊ/ adj peu profond; (fig) superficiel.

shame /ʃeɪm/ n honte f; **it's a** ~ c'est dommage. ● vt faire honte à.

shampoo /ʃæmˈpuː/ n shampooing m. ● vt faire un shampooing à.

shandy /ˈʃændɪɡæf/ n panaché m.

shan't ➡SHALL NOT.

shanty /ˈʃæntɪ/ n (*shack*) baraque f; ~ **town** bidonville m.

shape /ʃeɪp/ n forme f. ● vt (*clay*) modeler; (*rock*) façonner; (*future*: fig) déterminer; ~ **sth into balls** faire des boules avec qch. ● vi ~ **up** (*plan*) prendre tournure; (*person*) faire des progrès.

share /ʃeə(r)/ n part f; (Comm) action f. ● vt/i partager; (*feature*) avoir en commun. ~**holder** n actionnaire mf. ~**ware** n (Comput) logiciel m contributif.

shark /ʃɑːk/ n requin m.

sharp /ʃɑːp/ adj (*knife*) tranchant; (*pin*) pointu; (*point, angle, cry*) aigu; (*person, mind*) vif; (*tone*) acerbe. ● adv (*stop*) net; (*sing, play*) trop haut; **six o'clock** ~ six heures pile. ● n (Mus) dièse m.

sharpen /ˈʃɑːpən/ vt aiguiser; (*pencil*) tailler.

shatter /ˈʃætə(r)/ vt (*glass*) fracasser; (*hope*) briser. ● vi (*glass*) voler en éclats.

shave /ʃeɪv/ vt/i (se) raser. ● n **have a** ~ se raser. **shaver** n rasoir m électrique.

shaving /ˈʃeɪvɪŋ/ n (*of wood*) copeau m. ● adj (*cream, foam, gel*) à raser.

shawl /ʃɔːl/ n châle m.

she /ʃiː/ pron elle. ● n (*animal*) femelle f.

shear /ʃɪə(r)/ vt (pp **shorn** or **sheared**) (*sheep*) tondre; ~ **off** se détacher.

shears /ʃɪəz/ npl cisaille f.

shed /ʃed/ n remise f. ● vt (pt **shed**; pres p **shedding**) perdre; (*light, tears*) répandre.

sheen /ʃiːn/ n lustre m.

S

sheep /ʃiːp/ *n inv* mouton *m.* ∼**-dog** *n* chien *m* de berger.

sheepish /'ʃiːpɪʃ/ *adj* penaud.

sheepskin /'ʃiːpskɪn/ *n* peau *f* de mouton.

sheer /ʃɪə(r)/ *adj* pur; (steep) à pic; (fabric) très fin. ● *adv* à pic.

sheet /ʃiːt/ *n* drap *m;* (of paper) feuille *f;* (of glass, ice) plaque *f.*

shelf /ʃelf/ *n* (*pl* **shelves**) étagère *f;* (in shop, fridge) rayon *m;* (in oven) plaque *f.*

shell /ʃel/ *n* coquille *f;* (on beach) coquillage *m;* (of building) carcasse *f;* (explosive) obus *m.* ● *vt* (nut) décortiquer; (peas) écosser; (Mil) bombarder.

shellfish /'ʃelfɪʃ/ *npl* (lobster etc.) crustacés *mpl;* (mollusc) coquillages *mpl.*

shelter /'ʃeltə(r)/ *n* abri *m.* ● *vt/i* (s')abriter; (give lodging to) donner asile à.

shelve /ʃelv/ *vt* (plan) mettre en suspens.

shepherd /'ʃepəd/ *n* berger *m;* ∼**'s pie** hachis *m* Parmentier. ● *vt* (people) guider.

sherry /'ʃerɪ/ *n* xérès *m.*

shield /ʃiːld/ *n* bouclier *m;* (screen) écran *m.* ● *vt* protéger.

shift /ʃɪft/ *vt/i* (se) déplacer, bouger; (exchange, alter) changer de. ● *n* changement *m;* (workers) équipe *f;* (work) poste *m;* ∼ **work** travail *m* posté, travail *m* par roulement.

shifty /'ʃɪftɪ/ *adj* (**-ier, -iest**) louche.

shimmer /'ʃɪmə(r)/ *vi* chatoyer. ● *n* chatoiement *m.*

shin /ʃɪn/ *n* tibia *m.*

shine /ʃaɪn/ *vt* (*pt* **shone**) (torch) braquer (**on** sur). ● *vi* (light, sun, hair) briller; (brass) reluire. ● *n* lustre *m.*

shingle /'ʃɪŋɡl/ *n* (pebbles) galets *mpl;* (on roof) bardeau *m.*

shingles /'ʃɪŋɡlz/ *npl* (Med) zona *m.*

shiny /'ʃaɪnɪ/ *adj* (**-ier, -iest**) brillant.

ship /ʃɪp/ *n* bateau *m,* navire *m.* ● *vt* (*pt* **shipped**) transporter. **shipment** *n* (by sea) cargaison *f;* (by air, land) chargement *m.* **shipping** *n* (ships) navigation *f.* ∼**wreck** *n* épave *f;* (event) naufrage *m.*

shirt /ʃɜːt/ *n* chemise *f;* (woman's) chemisier *m.*

shiver /'ʃɪvə(r)/ *vi* frissonner. ● *n* frisson *m.*

shock /ʃɒk/ *n* choc *m;* (Electr) décharge *f;* **in** ∼ en état de choc; ∼ **absorber** amortisseur *m.* ● *adj* (result) choc *inv;* (tactics) de choc. ● *vt* choquer.

shoddy /'ʃɒdɪ/ *adj* (**-ier, -iest**) mal fait; (behaviour) mesquin.

shoe /ʃuː/ *n* chaussure *f;* (of horse) fer *m;* (**brake**) ∼ sabot *m* (de frein). ● *vt* (*pt* **shod;** *pres p* **shoeing**) (horse) ferrer. ∼**lace** *n* lacet *m.* ∼ **size** *n* pointure *f.*

shone /ʃɒn/ →SHINE.

shook /ʃʊk/ →SHAKE.

shoot /ʃuːt/ *vt* (*pt* **shot**) (gun) tirer un coup de; (bullet) tirer; (missile, glance) lancer; (person) tirer sur; (kill) abattre; (execute) fusiller; (film) tourner. ● *vi* tirer (**at** sur). ● *n* (Bot) pousse *f.* □ ∼ **down** abattre; ∼ **out** (rush) sortir en vitesse; ∼ **up** (spurt) jaillir; (grow) pousser vite.

shooting /'ʃuːtɪŋ/ *n* (killing) meurtre *m* (par arme à feu) **hear** ∼ entendre des coups de feu.

shop /ʃɒp/ *n* magasin *m;* (small) boutique *f;* (workshop) atelier *m.* ● *vi* (*pt* **shopped**) faire ses courses; ∼ **around** comparer les prix. ∼ **assistant** *n* vendeur/-euse *m/f.* ∼**-floor** *n* (workers) ouvriers *mpl.* ∼**keeper** *n* commerçant/-e *m/f.* ∼**lifter** *n* voleur/-euse *m/f* à l'étalage.

shopper /'ʃɒpə(r)/ *n* acheteur/-euse *m/f.*

shopping /'ʃɒpɪŋ/ *n* (goods) achats *mpl;* **go** ∼ (for food) faire les courses; (for clothes etc.) faire les magasins. ∼ **bag** *n* sac *m* à provisions. ∼ **centre,** (US) ∼ **center** *n* centre *m* commercial.

shop window *n* vitrine *f.*

shore /ʃɔː(r)/ *n* côte *f,* rivage *m;* **on** ∼ à terre.

short /ʃɔːt/ *adj* court; (person) petit; (brief) court, bref; (curt) brusque; **be** ∼ (**of**) manquer (de); **everything** ∼ **of** tout sauf; **nothing** ∼ **of** rien de moins que; **cut** ∼ écourter; **cut sb** ∼ interrompre qn; **fall** ∼ **of** ne pas arriver à; **he is called Tom for** ∼ son diminutif est Tom; **in** ∼ en bref. ● *adv* (stop) net. ● *n* (Electr) court-circuit *m;* (film) courtmétrage *m;* ∼**s** (trousers) short *m.*

shortage /'ʃɔːtɪdʒ/ *n* manque *m.*

short: ~**bread** n sablé m. ~**-change** vt (cheat) rouler ⊞. ~ **circuit** n court-circuit m. ~**coming** n défaut m. ~ **cut** n raccourci m.

shorten /'ʃɔ:tn/ vt raccourcir.

shortfall /'ʃɔ:tfɔ:l/ n déficit m.

shorthand /'ʃɔ:thænd/ n sténographie f; ~ **typist** sténodactylo f.

short: ~ **list** n liste f des candidats choisis. ~**-lived** adj de courte durée.

shortly /'ʃɔ:tlɪ/ adv bientôt.

short: ~**-sighted** adj myope. ~**-staffed** adj à court de personnel; ~ **story** n nouvelle f. ~**-term** adj à court terme.

shot /ʃɒt/ →SHOOT. ● n (firing, attempt) coup m de feu; (person) tireur m; (bullet) balle f; (photograph) photo f; (injection) piqûre f; **like a** ~ sans hésiter. ~**gun** n fusil m de chasse.

should /ʃʊd/ v aux devoir; **you** ~ **help me** vous devriez m'aider; **I** ~ **have stayed** j'aurais dû rester; **I** ~ **like to** j'aimerais bien; **if he** ~ **come** s'il venait.

shoulder /'ʃəʊldə(r)/ n épaule f. ● vt (responsibility) endosser; (burden) se charger de. ~ **bag** n sac m à bandoulière. ~ **blade** n omoplate f.

shout /ʃaʊt/ n cri m. ● vt/i crier (**at** après); ~ **sth out** lancer qch à haute voix.

shove /ʃʌv/ n **give sth a** ~ pousser qch. ● vt/i pousser; ~ **off!** ⊞ tire-toi! ⊞.

shovel /'ʃʌvl/ n pelle f. ● vt (pt **shovelled**) pelleter.

show /ʃəʊ/ vt (pt **showed**; pp **shown**) montrer; (dial, needle) indiquer; (put on display) exposer; (film) donner; (conduct) conduire; ~ **sb in/out** faire entrer/sortir qn. ● vi (be visible) se voir. ● n (exhibition) exposition f, salon m; (Theat) spectacle m; (cinema) séance f; (of strength) démonstration f; **for** ~ pour l'effet; **on** ~ exposé. □ ~ **off** faire le fier/la fière; ~ **sth/sb off** exhiber qch/qn; ~ **up** se voir; (appear) se montrer; ~ **sb up** ⊞ faire honte à qn.

shower /'ʃaʊə(r)/ n douche f; (of rain) averse f. ● vt ~ **with** couvrir de. ● vi se doucher.

showing /'ʃəʊɪŋ/ n performance f; (cinema) séance f.

show-jumping n concours m hippique.

shown /ʃəʊn/ →SHOW.

show: ~**-off** n m'as-tu-vu mf inv. ⊞ ~**room** n salle f d'exposition.

shrank /ʃræŋk/ →SHRINK.

shrapnel /'ʃræpnl/ n éclats mpl d'obus.

shred /ʃred/ n lambeau m; (least amount: fig) parcelle f. ● vt (pt **shredded**) déchiqueter; (Culin) râper.

shrewd /ʃru:d/ adj (person) habile; (move) astucieux.

shriek /ʃri:k/ n hurlement m. ● vt/i hurler.

shrill /ʃrɪl/ adj (voice) perçant; (tone) strident.

shrimp /ʃrɪmp/ n crevette f.

shrine /ʃraɪn/ n (place) lieu m de pèlerinage.

shrink /ʃrɪŋk/ vt/i (pt **shrank**; pp **shrunk**) rétrécir; (lessen) diminuer; ~ **from** reculer devant.

shrivel /'ʃrɪvl/ vt/i (pt **shrivelled**) (se) ratatiner.

shroud /ʃraʊd/ n linceul m. ● vt (veil) envelopper.

Shrove Tuesday n mardi m gras.

shrub /ʃrʌb/ n arbuste m.

shrug /ʃrʌg/ vt (pt **shrugged**) ~ **one's shoulders** hausser les épaules; ~ **sth off** ignorer qch.

shrunk /ʃrʌŋk/ →SHRINK.

shudder /'ʃʌdə(r)/ vi frémir. ● n frémissement m.

shuffle /'ʃʌfl/ vt (feet) traîner; (cards) battre. ● vi traîner les pieds.

shun /ʃʌn/ vt (pt **shunned**) fuir.

shut /ʃʌt/ vt (pt **shut**; pres p **shutting**) fermer. ● vi (door) se fermer; (shop) fermer. □ ~ **in** or **up** enfermer; ~ **up** ⊞ se taire; ~ **sb up** faire taire qn.

shutter /'ʃʌtə(r)/ n volet m; (Photo) obturateur m.

shuttle /'ʃʌtl/ n (bus) navette f; ~ **service** navette f. ● vi faire la navette. ● vt transporter.

shuttlecock /'ʃʌtlkɒk/ n (badminton) volant m.

shy /ʃaɪ/ adj timide. ● vi ~ **away from** se tenir à l'écart de.

sibling /'sɪblɪŋ/ n frère/sœur m/f.

sick /sɪk/ adj malade; (humour) macabre; (mind) malsain; **be** ~ (vomit)

S

vomir; **be ~ of** 🔲 en avoir assez or marre de 🔲 **feel ~** avoir mal au cœur. **~-leave** n congé m de maladie.

sickly /'sɪklɪ/ adj (**-ier,-iest**) (person) maladif; (taste, smell) écœurant.

sickness /'sɪknɪs/ n maladie f.

sick-pay n indemnité f de maladie.

side /saɪd/ n côté m; (of road, river) bord m; (of hill, body) flanc m; (Sport) équipe f; (TV 🔲) chaîne f; **~ by ~** côte à côte. ● adj latéral. ● vi **~ with** se ranger du côté de. **~ board** n buffet m. **~effect** n effet m secondaire. **~light** n (Auto) feu m de position. **~line** n activité f secondaire. **~show** n attraction f. **~step** vt (pt) **-stepped** éviter. **~street** n rue f latérale. **~track** vt fourvoyer. **~ walk** n (US) trottoir m.

sideways /'saɪdweɪz/ adj (look) de travers. ● adv (move) latéralement; (look at) de travers.

siding /'saɪdɪŋ/ n voie f de garage.

sidle /'saɪdl/ vi s'avancer furtivement (up to vers).

siege /si:dʒ/ n siège m.

siesta /sɪ'estə/ n sieste f.

sieve /sɪv/ n tamis m; (for liquids) passoire f. ● vt tamiser.

sift /sɪft/ vt tamiser. ● vi **~ through** examiner.

sigh /saɪ/ n soupir m. ● vt/i soupirer.

sight /saɪt/ n vue f; (scene) spectacle m; (on gun) mire f; **at** or **on ~** à vue; **catch ~ of** apercevoir; **in ~** visible; **lose ~ of** perdre de vue. ● vt apercevoir.

sightseeing /'saɪtsi:ɪŋ/ n tourisme m.

sign /saɪn/ n signe m; (notice) panneau m. ● vt/i signer. □ **~ on** (as unemployed) pointer au chômage; **~ up** (s')engager.

signal /'sɪɡnl/ n signal m. ● vt (pt) **signalled** (gesture) faire signe (**that** que); (indicate) indiquer.

signatory /'sɪɡnətrɪ/ n signataire mf.

signature /'sɪɡnətʃə(r)/ n signature f; **~ tune** indicatif m.

significance /sɪɡ'nɪfɪkəns/ n importance f; (meaning) signification f. **significant** adj important; (meaningful) significatif. **significantly** adv (much) sensiblement.

signify /'sɪɡnɪfaɪ/ vt signifier.

signpost /'saɪmpəʊst/ n panneau m indicateur.

silence /'saɪləns/ n silence m. ● vt faire taire.

silent /'saɪlənt/ adj silencieux; (film) muet. **silently** adv silencieusement.

silhouette /sɪlu:'et/ n silhouette f. ● vt **be ~d against** se profiler contre.

silicon /'sɪlɪkən/ n silicium m; **~ chip** puce f électronique.

silk /sɪlk/ n soie f.

silly /'sɪlɪ/ adj (**-ier, -iest**) bête.

silver /'sɪlvə(r)/ n argent m; (silverware) argenterie f. ● adj en argent.

SIM card /'sɪmkɑ:d/ n carte f SIM.

similar /'sɪmɪlə(r)/ adj semblable (**to** à). **similarity** n ressemblance f. **similarly** adv de même.

simile /'sɪmɪlɪ/ n comparaison f.

simmer /'sɪmə(r)/ vt/i (soup) mijoter; (water) (laisser) frémir.

simple /'sɪmpl/ adj simple.

simplicity /sɪm'plɪsətɪ/ n simplicité f.

simplify /'sɪmplɪfaɪ/ vt simplifier.

simplistic /sɪm'plɪstɪk/ adj simpliste.

simply /'sɪmplɪ/ adv simplement; (absolutely) absolument.

simulate /'sɪmjʊleɪt/ vt simuler.

simultaneous /sɪml'teɪnɪəs/ adj simultané.

sin /sɪn/ n péché m. ● vi (pt **sinned**) pécher.

---

since /sɪns/

● preposition

····▸ depuis; **I haven't seen him ~ Monday** je ne l'ai pas vu depuis lundi; **I've been waiting ~ yesterday** j'attends depuis hier; **she had been living in Paris ~ 1985** elle habitait Paris depuis 1985.

● conjunction

····▸ (in time expressions) depuis que; **~ she's been working here** depuis qu'elle travaille ici; **~ she left** depuis qu'elle est partie or depuis son départ.

····▸ (because) comme; **~ he was ill, he couldn't go** comme il était malade, il ne pouvait pas y aller.

● adverb

····▸ depuis; **he hasn't been seen ~** on ne l'a pas vu depuis.

sincere /sɪnˈsɪə(r)/ *adj* sincère. **sincerely** *adv* sincèrement. **sincerity** *n* sincérité *f.*

sinful /ˈsɪnfl/ *adj* immoral; ∼ **man** pécheur *m.*

sing /sɪŋ/ *vt/i* (*pt* **sang**; *pp* **sung**) chanter.

singe /sɪndʒ/ *vt* (*pres p* **singeing**) brûler légèrement; (with iron) roussir.

singer /ˈsɪŋə(r)/ *n* chanteur/-euse *m/f.*

single /ˈsɪŋɡl/ *adj* seul; (not double) simple; (unmarried) célibataire; (room, bed) pour une personne; (ticket) simple; **in** ∼ **file** en file indienne. ● *n* (ticket) aller simple *m*; (record) 45 tours *m inv*; ∼**s** (tennis) simple *m.* ● *vt* ∼ **out** choisir. ∼**-handed** *adj* tout seul. ∼**-minded** *adj* tenace. ∼ **parent** *n* parent *m* isolé.

singular /ˈsɪŋɡjʊlə(r)/ *n* singulier *m.* ● *adj* (strange) singulier; (noun) au singulier.

sinister /ˈsɪnɪstə(r)/ *adj* sinistre.

sink /sɪŋk/ *vt* (*pt* **sank**; *pp* **sunk**) (boat) couler; (well) forer; (post) enfoncer. ● *vi* (boat) couler; (sun, level) baisser; (wall) s'effondrer. ● *n* (in kitchen) évier *m*; (wash-basin) lavabo *m.* □ ∼ **in** (news) faire son chemin.

sinner /ˈsɪnə(r)/ *n* pécheur/-eresse *m/f.*

sip /sɪp/ *n* petite gorgée *f.* ● *vt* (*pt* **sipped**) boire à petites gorgées.

siphon /ˈsaɪfn/ *n* siphon *m.* ● *vt* ∼ **off** siphonner.

sir /sɜː(r)/ *n* Monsieur *m*; **Sir** (title) Sir *m.*

siren /ˈsaɪərən/ *n* sirène *f.*

sirloin /ˈsɜːlɔɪn/ *n* aloyau *m.*

sister /ˈsɪstə(r)/ *n* sœur *f*; (nurse) infirmière *f* en chef. ∼**-in-law** *n* (*pl* ∼**s-in-law**) belle-sœur *f.*

sit /sɪt/ *vt/i* (*pt* **sat**; *pres p* **sitting**) (s')asseoir; (committee) siéger; ∼ **(for)** (exam) se présenter à; **be** ∼**ting** être assis. □ ∼ **around** ne rien faire; ∼ **down** s'asseoir.

site /saɪt/ *n* emplacement *m*; **(building)** ∼ chantier *m.* ● *vt* construire.

sitting /ˈsɪtɪŋ/ *n* séance *f*; (in restaurant) service *m.* ∼**-room** *n* salon *m.*

situate /ˈsɪtjʊeɪt/ *vt* situer; **be** ∼**d** être situé. **situation** *n* situation *f.*

six /sɪks/ *adj* & *n* six (*m*).

sixteen /sɪkˈstiːn/ *adj* & *n* seize (*m*).

sixth /sɪksθ/ *adj* & *n* sixième (*mf*).

sixty /ˈsɪkstɪ/ *adj* & *n* soixante (*m*).

size /saɪz/ *n* dimension *f*; (of person, garment) taille *f*; (of shoes) pointure *f*; (of sum, salary) montant *m*; (extent) ampleur *f.* □ ∼ **up** (person) se faire une opinion de; (situation) évaluer. **sizeable** *adj* assez grand.

skate /skeɪt/ *n* patin *m*; (fish) raie *f.* ● *vi* patiner.

skateboard /ˈskeɪtbɔːd/ *n* skateboard *m*, planche *f* à roulettes. ● *vi* faire du skateboard.

skating /ˈskeɪtbɔːd/ *n* patinage *m.*

skeleton /ˈskelɪtn/ *n* squelette *m*; ∼ **staff** effectifs *mpl* minimums.

sketch /sketʃ/ *n* esquisse *f*; (hasty) croquis *m*; (Theat) sketch *m.* ● *vt* faire une esquisse or un croquis de. ● *vi* faire des esquisses.

sketchy /ˈsketʃɪ/ *adj* (**-ier, -iest**) (details) insuffisant; (memory) vague.

skewer /ˈskjuːə(r)/ *n* brochette *f.*

ski /skiː/ *n* ski *m.* ● *adj* de ski. ● *vi* (*pt* **ski'd** or **skied**; *pres p* **skiing**) skier; (go skiing) faire du ski.

skid /skɪd/ *vi* (*pt* **skidded**) déraper. ● *n* dérapage *m.*

skier /ˈskiːə(r)/ *n* skieur/-euse *m/f.*

skiing /ˈskiːɪŋ/ *n* ski *m.*

ski jump *n* saut *m* à ski.

skilful /ˈskɪlfl/ *adj* habile.

ski lift *n* remontée *f* mécanique.

skill /skɪl/ *n* habileté *f*; (craft) compétence *f*; ∼**s** connaissances *fpl.* **skilled** *adj* (worker) qualifié; (talented) consommé.

skim /skɪm/ *vt* (*pt* **skimmed**) écumer; (milk) écrémer; (pass over) effleurer. ● *vi* ∼ **through** parcourir.

skimpy /ˈskɪmpɪ/ *adj* (clothes) étriqué.

skin /skɪn/ *n* peau *f.* ● *vt* (*pt* **skinned**) (animal) écorcher; (fruit) éplucher.

skinny /ˈskɪnɪ/ *adj* (**-ier, -iest**) ⚏ maigre.

skip /skɪp/ *vi* (*pt* **skipped**) sautiller; (with rope) sauter à la corde. ● *vt* (page, class) sauter. ● *n* petit saut *m*; (container) benne *f.*

skipper /ˈskɪpə(r)/ *n* capitaine *m.*

skirmish /ˈskɜːmɪʃ/ *n* escarmouche *f.*

skirt /skɜːt/ *n* jupe *f.* ● *vt* contourner. **skirting-board** *n* plinthe *f.*

S

skittle /ˈskɪtl/ n quille f.

skull /skʌl/ n crâne m.

sky /skaɪ/ n ciel m. **~-blue** adj & n bleu ciel m inv. **~ marshal** n garde m armé (à bord d'un avion.) **~scraper** n gratte-ciel m inv.

slab /slæb/ n (of stone) dalle f.

slack /slæk/ adj (not tight) détendu; (person) négligent; (period) creux. ● n (in rope) mou m. ● vi se relâcher.

slacken /ˈslækən/ vt (rope) donner du mou à; (grip) relâcher; (pace) réduire. ● vi (grip, rope) se relâcher; (activity) ralentir; (rain) se calmer.

slam /slæm/ vt/i (pt **slammed**) (door) claquer; (throw) flanquer; (criticize 🔲) critiquer. ● n (noise) claquement m.

slander /ˈslɑːndə(r)/ n (offence) diffamation f; (statement) calomnie f. ● vt calomnier; (Jur) diffamer. **slanderous** adj diffamatoire.

slang /slæŋ/ n argot m.

slant /slɑːnt/ vt/i (faire) pencher; (news) présenter sous un certain jour. ● n inclinaison f; (bias) angle m. **slanted** adj (biased) orienté; (sloping) en pente.

slap /slæp/ vt (pt **slapped**) (strike) donner une tape à; (face) gifler; (put) flanquer 🔲. ● n claque f; (on face) gifle f. ● adv tout droit.

slapdash /ˈslæpdæʃ/ adj (person) brouillon 🔲; (work) bâclé 🔲.

slash /slæʃ/ vt (picture, tyre) taillader; (face) balafrer; (throat) couper; (fig) réduire (radicalement). ● n lacération f.

slat /slæt/ n (in blind) lamelle f; (on bed) latte f.

slate /sleɪt/ n ardoise f. ● vt 🔲 taper sur 🔲.

slaughter /ˈslɔːtə(r)/ vt massacrer; (animal) abattre. ● n massacre m; abattage m.

slave /sleɪv/ n esclave mf. ● vi trimer 🔲. **slavery** n esclavage m.

sleazy /ˈsliːzɪ/ adj (-ier, -iest) 🔲 (story) scabreux; (club) louche.

sledge /sledʒ/ n luge f; (horse-drawn) traîneau m.

sleek /sliːk/ adj (hair) lisse, brillant; (shape) élégant.

sleep /sliːp/ n sommeil m; **go to ~** s'endormir. ● vi (pt **slept**) dormir; (spend the night) coucher; **~ in** faire la grasse matinée. ● vt loger.

sleeper /ˈsliːpə(r)/ n (Rail) (berth) couchette f; (on track) traverse f.

sleeping-bag n sac m de couchage.

sleeping-pill n somnifère m.

sleep-walker n somnambule mf.

sleepy /ˈsliːpɪ/ adj (-ier, -iest) somnolent; **be ~** avoir sommeil.

sleet /sliːt/ n neige f fondue.

sleeve /sliːv/ n manche f; (of record) pochette f; **up one's ~** en réserve.

sleigh /sleɪ/ n traîneau m.

slender /ˈslendə(r)/ adj (person) mince; (majority) faible.

slept /slept/ ⇒SLEEP.

slice /slaɪs/ n tranche f. ● vt couper (en tranches).

slick /slɪk/ adj (adept) habile; (insincere) roublard 🔲. ● n (oil) ~ marée f noire.

slide /slaɪd/ vt/i (pt **slid**) glisser; **~ into** (go silently) se glisser dans. ● n glissade f; (fall: fig) baisse f; (in playground) toboggan m; (for hair) barrette f; (Photo) diapositive f.

sliding /ˈslaɪdɪŋ/ adj (door) coulissant; **~ scale** échelle f mobile.

slight /slaɪt/ adj petit, léger; (slender) mince; (frail) frêle. ● vt (insult) offenser. ● n affront m. **slightest** adj moindre. **slightly** adv légèrement, un peu.

slim /slɪm/ adj (**slimmer, slimmest**) mince. ● vi (pt **slimmed**) maigrir.

slime /slaɪm/ n dépôt m gluant; (on riverbed) vase f. **slimy** adj visqueux; (fig) servile.

sling /slɪŋ/ n (weapon, toy) fronde f; (bandage) écharpe f. ● vt (pt **slung**) jeter, lancer.

slip /slɪp/ vt/i (pt **slipped**) glisser; **~ped disc** hernie f discale; **~ sb's mind** échapper à qn. ● n (mistake) erreur f; (petticoat) combinaison f; (paper) bout m de papier; **~ of the tongue** lapsus m. □ **away** s'esquiver; □ **into** (go) se glisser dans; (clothes) mettre; □ **up** 🔲 faire une gaffe 🔲.

slipper /ˈslɪpə(r)/ n pantoufle f.

slippery /ˈslɪpərɪ/ adj glissant.

slip road n bretelle f.

slit /slɪt/ n fente f. ● vt (pt **slit**; pres p **slitting**) déchirer; **~ sth open** ouvrir qch; **~ sb's throat** égorger qn.

slither /ˈslɪðə(r)/ vi glisser.

sliver /ˈslɪvə(r)/ n (of glass) éclat m; (of soap) reste m.

slobber /ˈslɒbə(r)/ vi 🔊 baver.

slog /slɒg/ 🔊 vt (pt **slogged**) (hit) frapper dur. ● vi (work) bosser 🔊. ● n (work) travail m dur.

slogan /ˈsləʊgən/ n slogan m.

slope /sləʊp/ vi être en pente; (handwriting) pencher. ● n pente f; (of mountain) flanc m.

sloppy /ˈslɒpɪ/ adj (**-ier, -iest**) (food) liquide; (work) négligé; (person) négligent.

slosh /slɒʃ/ vt 🔊 répandre; (hit 🔊) frapper. ● vi clapoter.

slot /slɒt/ n fente f. ● vt/i (pt **slotted**) (s')insérer.

sloth /sləʊθ/ n paresse f.

slot-machine n distributeur m automatique; (for gambling) machine f à sous.

slouch /slaʊtʃ/ vi être avachi.

Slovakia /sləˈvækɪə/ n Slovaquie f.

Slovenia /sləˈviːnɪə/ n Slovénie f.

slovenly /ˈslʌvnlɪ/ adj débraillé.

slow /sləʊ/ adj lent; be ~ (clock) retarder; in ~ motion au ralenti. ● adv lentement. ● vt/i ralentir. **slowly** adv lentement. **slowness** n lenteur f.

sludge /slʌdʒ/ n vase f.

slug /slʌg/ n (mollusc) limace f; (bullet 🔊) balle f; (blow 🔊) coup m.

sluggish /ˈslʌgɪʃ/ adj (person) léthargique; (circulation) lent.

slum /slʌm/ n taudis m.

slump /slʌmp/ n (Econ) effondrement m; (in support) baisse f. ● vi (demand, trade) chuter; (economy) s'effondrer; (person) s'affaler.

slung /slʌŋ// →SLING.

slur /slɜː(r)/ vt/i (pt **slurred**) (words) mal articuler. ● n calomnie f (on sur).

slush /slʌʃ/ n (snow) neige f fondue. ~ **fund** n caisse f noire.

sly /slaɪ/ adj (crafty) rusé; (secretive) sournois. ● n on the ~ en cachette.

smack /smæk/ n tape f; (on face) gifle f. ● vt donner une tape à; gifler. ● vi ~ of sth sentir qch. ● adv 🔊 tout droit.

small /smɔːl/ adj petit. ● n ~ of the back creux m des reins. ● adv (cut) menu. ~ ad n petite annonce f. ~

business n petite entreprise f. ~ **change** n petite monnaie f. ~**pox** n variole f. ~ **print** n petits caractères mpl. ~ **talk** n banalités fpl.

smart /smɑːt/ adj élégant; (clever 🔊) malin, habile; (restaurant) chic inv; (Comput) intelligent. ● vi (wound) brûler.

smarten /ˈsmɑːtn/ vt/i ~ (**up**) embellir; ~ (**oneself**) up s'arranger.

smash /smæʃ/ vt/i (se) briser, (se) fracasser; (opponent, record) pulvériser. ● n (noise) fracas m; (blow) coup m; (car crash) collision f; (hit record 🔊) tube m. 🔊

smashing /ˈsmæʃɪŋ/ adj 🔊 épatant.

SME abbr (**small and medium enterprises**) PME.

smear /smɪə(r)/ vt (stain) tacher; (coat) enduire; (discredit: fig) diffamer. ● n tache f; (effort to discredit) propos m diffamatoire; ~ (**test**) frottis m.

smell /smel/ n odeur f; (sense) odorat m. ● vt/i (pt **smelt** or **smelled**) sentir; ~ of sentir. **smelly** adj qui sent mauvais.

smelt /smelt/ →SMELL.

smile /smaɪl/ n sourire m. ● vi sourire.

smiley /ˈsmaɪlɪ/ n (Internet) binette f.

smirk /smɜːk/ n petit sourire m satisfait.

smitten /ˈsmɪtn/ adj (in love) fou d'amour.

smog /smɒg/ n smog m.

smoke /sməʊk/ n fumée f; have a ~ fumer. ● vt/i fumer. **smoked** adj fumé. **smokeless** adj (fuel) non polluant. **smoker** n fumeur/-euse m/f. **smoky** adj (air) enfumé.

smooth /smuːð/ adj lisse; (movement) aisé; (manners) onctueux; (flight) sans heurts. ● vt lisser; (process) faciliter.

smoothly /ˈsmuːðlɪ/ adv (move, flow) doucement; (brake, start) en douceur; **go** ~ marcher bien.

smother /ˈsmʌðə(r)/ vt (stifle) étouffer; (cover) couvrir.

smoulder /ˈsməʊldə(r)/ vi (lit) se consumer; (fig) couver.

smudge /smʌdʒ/ n trace f. ● vt/i (ink) (s')étaler.

smug /smʌg/ adj (**smugger, smuggest**) suffisant.

S

smuggle /'smʌgl/ vt passer (en contrebande). **smuggler** n contrebandier/-ière m/f. **smuggling** n contrebande f.

smutty /'smʌtɪ/ adj grivois.

snack /snæk/ n casse-croûte m inv.

snag /snæg/ n inconvénient m; (in cloth) accroc m.

snail /sneɪl/ n escargot m.

snake /sneɪk/ n serpent m.

snap /snæp/ vt/i (pt **snapped**) (whip, fingers) (faire) claquer; (break) (se) casser net; (say) dire sèchement. ● n claquement m; (Photo) photo f. ● adj soudain. □ ~ **up** (buy) sauter sur.

snapshot /'snæpʃɒt/ n photo f.

snare /sneə(r)/ n piège m.

snarl /snɑːl/ vi gronder (en montrant les dents). ● n grondement m. ~-**up** n embouteillage m.

snatch /snætʃ/ vt (grab) attraper; (steal) voler; (opportunity) saisir; ~ sth **from sb** arracher qch à qn. ● n (theft) vol m; (short part) fragment m.

sneak /sniːk/ vi aller furtivement. ● n 🔲 rapporteur/-euse m/f.

sneer /snɪə(r)/ n sourire m méprisant. ● vi sourire avec mépris.

sneeze /sniːz/ n éternuement m. ● vi éternuer.

snide /snaɪd/ adj narquois.

sniff /snɪf/ vt/i renifler. ● n reniflement m.

snigger /'snɪgə(r)/ n ricanement m. ● vi ricaner.

snip /snɪp/ vt (pt **snipped**) couper.

sniper /'snaɪpə(r)/ n tireur m embusqué.

snippet /'snɪpɪt/ n bribe f.

snivel /'snɪvl/ vi (pt **snivelled**) pleurnicher.

snob /snɒb/ n snob mf.

snooker /'snuːkə(r)/ n snooker m.

snoop /snuːp/ vi 🔲 fourrer son nez partout.

snooty /'snuːtɪ/ adj (-**ier**, -**iest**) 🔲 snob inv, hautain.

snooze /snuːz/ n petit somme m. ● vi sommeiller.

snore /snɔː(r)/ n ronflement m. ● vi ronfler.

snorkel /'snɔːkl/ n tuba m.

snort /snɔːt/ n grognement m. ● vi (person) grogner; (horse) s'ébrouer.

snout /snaʊt/ n museau m.

snow /snəʊ/ n neige f. ● vi neiger; **be** ~**ed under with** être submergé de.

snowball /'snəʊbɔːl/ n boule f de neige. ● vi faire boule de neige.

snow: ~**board** n snowboard m. ~**boarding** n surf m des neiges. ~-**bound** adj bloqué par la neige. ~**drift** n congère f. ~**drop** n perce-neige m or f inv. ~**flake** n flocon m de neige. ~**man** n (pl -**men**) bonhomme m de neige. ~-**plough** n chasse-neige m inv.

snub /snʌb/ vt (pt **snubbed**) rembarrer. ● n rebuffade f.

snuffle /'snʌfl/ vi renifler.

snug /snʌg/ adj (**snugger, snuggest**) (cosy) confortable; (tight) bien ajusté.

snuggle /'snʌgl/ vi se pelotonner.

so /səʊ/ adv si, tellement; (thus) ainsi; ~ **am I** moi aussi; ~ **good as** aussi bon que; **that is** ~ c'est ça; **I think** ~ je pense que oui; **five or** ~ environ cinq; ~ **as to** de manière à; ~ **far** jusqu'ici; ~ **long!** 🔲 à bientôt!; ~ **many,** ~ **much** tant (de); ~ **that** pour que. ● conj donc, alors.

soak /səʊk/ vt/i (faire) tremper (**in** dans). □ ~ **in** pénétrer; ~ **up** absorber. **soaking** adj trempé.

soap /səʊp/ n savon m. ● vt savonner. ~ **opera** n feuilleton m. ~ **powder** n lessive f.

soar /sɔː(r)/ vi monter (en flèche).

sob /sɒb/ n sanglot m. ● vi (pt **sobbed**) sangloter.

sober /'səʊbə(r)/ adj qui n'a pas bu d'alcool; (serious) sérieux. ● vi ~ **up** dessoûler.

soccer /'sɒkə(r)/ n football m.

sociable /'səʊʃəbl/ adj sociable.

social /'səʊʃl/ adj social. ● n réunion f (amicale), fête f.

socialism /'səʊʃəlɪzəm/ n socialisme m. **socialist** adj & n socialiste (mf).

socialize /'səʊʃəlaɪz/ vi se mêler aux autres; ~ **with** fréquenter.

socially /'səʊʃəlɪ/ adv socialement; (meet) en société.

social: ~ **security** n aide f sociale. ~ **worker** n travailleur/-euse m/f social/-e.

society /səˈsaɪətɪ/ n société f.

sociological /səʊsɪəˈlɒdʒɪkl/ adj sociologique. **sociologist** n sociologue mf. **sociology** n sociologie f.

sock /sɒk/ n chaussette f. ● vt (hit 🔟) flanquer un coup (de poing) à.

socket /ˈsɒkɪt/ n (for lamp) douille f; (Electr) prise f (de courant); (of eye) orbite f.

soda /ˈsəʊdə/ n soude f; ∼(-water) eau f de Seltz.

sodden /ˈsɒdn/ adj détrempé.

sofa /ˈsəʊfə/ n canapé m. ∼ **bed** n canapé-lit m.

soft /sɒft/ adj (gentle, lenient) doux; (not hard) doux, mou; (heart, wood) tendre; (silly) ramolli. ∼ **drink** n boisson f non alcoolisée.

soften /ˈsɒfn/ vt/i (se) ramollir; (tone down, lessen) (s')adoucir.

soft spot n to have a ∼ for sb avoir un faible pour qn.

software /ˈsɒftweə(r)/ n logiciel m.

soggy /ˈsɒgɪ/ adj (**-ier, -iest**) (ground) détrempé; (food) ramolli.

soil /sɔɪl/ n sol m, terre f. ● vt/i (se) salir.

sold /səʊld/ →SELL. ● adj ∼ **out** épuisé.

solder /ˈsəʊldə(r)/ n soudure f. ● vt souder.

soldier /ˈsəʊldʒə(r)/ n soldat m. ● vi ∼ **on** 🔟 persévérer.

sole /səʊl/ n (of foot) plante f; (of shoe) semelle f; (fish) sole f. ● adj unique, seul. **solely** adv uniquement.

solemn /ˈsɒləm/ adj solennel.

solicitor /səˈlɪsɪtə(r)/ n notaire m; (for court and police work) ≈ avocat/-e m/f.

solid /ˈsɒlɪd/ adj solide; (not hollow) plein; (gold) massif; (mass) compact; (meal) substantiel. ● n solide m; ∼s (food) aliments mpl solides.

solidarity /sɒlɪˈdærətɪ/ n solidarité f.

solidify /səˈlɪdɪfaɪ/ vt/i (se) solidifier.

solitary /ˈsɒlɪtrɪ/ adj (alone) solitaire; (only) seul.

solo /ˈsəʊləʊ/ n solo m. ● adj (Mus) solo inv; (flight) en solitaire.

soluble /ˈsɒljʊbl/ adj soluble.

solution /səˈluːʃn/ n solution f.

solve /sɒlv/ vt résoudre.

solvent /ˈsɒlvənt/ adj (Comm) solvable. ● n (dis)solvant m.

---

some /sʌm, səm/

● determiner

····➤ (unspecified amount) du/de l'/de la/des; **I have to buy** ∼ **bread** je dois acheter du pain; **have** ∼ **water** prenez de l'eau; ∼ **sweets** des bonbons.

····➤ (certain) certains/certaines; ∼ **people say that** certains disent que.

····➤ (unknown) un/une; ∼ **man came to the house** un homme est venu à la maison.

····➤ (considerable amount) **we stayed there for** ∼ **time** nous sommes restés là assez longtemps; **it will take** ∼ **doing** ça ne va pas être facile à faire.

➡️ In front of a plural adjective des changes to de: **some pretty dresses** de jolies robes.

● pronoun

····➤ en; **he wants** ∼ il en veut; **have** ∼ **more** reprenez-en.

····➤ (certain) certains/certaines; ∼ **are expensive** certains sont chers.

● adverb

····➤ environ; ∼ **20 people** environ 20 personnes.

---

somebody /ˈsʌmbədɪ/ pron quelqu'un. ● n be a ∼ être quelqu'un.

somehow /ˈsʌmhaʊ/ adv d'une manière ou d'une autre; (for some reason) je ne sais pas pourquoi.

someone /ˈsʌmwʌn/ pron & n →SOMEBODY.

someplace /ˈsʌmpleɪs/ adv (US) →SOMEWHERE.

somersault /ˈsʌməsɒlt/ n roulade f. ● vi faire une roulade.

something /ˈsʌmθɪŋ/ pron & n quelque chose (m); ∼ **good** quelque chose de bon; ∼ **like** un peu comme.

sometime /ˈsʌmtaɪm/ adv un jour; ∼ **in June** en juin. ● adj (former) ancien.

sometimes /ˈsʌmtaɪmz/ adv quelquefois, parfois.

S

somewhat /'sʌmwɒt/ adv quelque peu, un peu.

somewhere /'sʌmweə(r)/ adv quelque part.

son /sʌn/ n fils m.

song /sɒŋ/ n chanson f; (of bird) chant m.

son-in-law /'sʌnɪnlɔː/ n (pl **sons-in-law**) gendre m.

soon /suːn/ adv bientôt; (early) tôt; **I would ~er stay** j'aimerais mieux rester; **~ after** peu après; **~er or later** tôt ou tard.

soot /sʊt/ n suie f.

soothe /suːð/ vt calmer.

sophisticated /sə'fɪstɪkeɪtɪd/ adj raffiné; (machine) sophistiqué.

sopping /'sɒpɪŋ/ adj trempé.

soppy /'sɒpɪ/ adj (-ier, -iest) 🔲 sentimental.

sorcerer /'sɔːsərə(r)/ n sorcier m.

sordid /'sɔːdɪd/ adj sordide.

sore /sɔː(r)/ adj douloureux; (vexed) en rogne (**at, with** contre). ● n plaie f.

sorely /'sɔːlɪ/ adv fortement.

sorrow /'sɒrəʊ/ n chagrin m.

sorry /'sɒrɪ/ adj (-ier, -iest) (regretful) désolé (**to** de; **that** que); (wretched) triste; **feel ~ for** plaindre; **~!** pardon!

sort /sɔːt/ n genre m, sorte f, espèce f; (person 🔲) type m; **what ~ of?** quel genre de?; **be out of ~s** ne pas être dans son assiette. ● vt **~ (out)** (classify) trier; **~ out** (tidy) ranger; (arrange) arranger; (problem) régler.

so-so /səʊ'səʊ/ adj & adv comme ci comme ça.

sought /sɔːt/ →SEEK.

soul /səʊl/ n âme f.

sound /saʊnd/ n son m, bruit m. ● adj solide; (healthy) sain; (sensible) sensé. ● vt/i sonner; (seem) sembler (**as if** que); (test) sonder; **~ out** sonder; **~ a horn** klaxonner; **~ like** sembler être. **~ asleep** adj profondément endormi. **~ barrier** n mur m du son.

soundly /'saʊndlɪ/ adv (sleep) à poings fermés; (built) solidement.

sound-proof /'saʊndpruːf/ adj insonorisé. ● vt insonoriser.

sound-track /'saʊndtræk/ n bande f sonore.

soup /suːp/ n soupe f, potage m.

sour /'saʊə(r)/ adj aigre. ● vt/i (s')aigrir.

source /sɔːs/ n source f.

south /saʊθ/ n sud m. ● adj sud inv, du sud. ● adv vers le sud.

South Africa n Afrique f du Sud.

South America n Amérique f du Sud.

south-east n sud-est m.

southern /'sʌðən/ adj du sud. **southerner** n habitant/-e m/f du sud.

southward /'saʊθwəd/ adj (side) sud inv; (journey) vers le sud.

south-west n sud-ouest m.

souvenir /suːvə'nɪə(r)/ n souvenir m.

sovereign /'sɒvrɪn/ n & a souverain/-e (m/f).

sow¹ /səʊ/ vt (pt **sowed**; pp **sowed** or **sown**) (seed) semer; (land) ensemencer.

sow² /saʊ/ n (pig) truie f.

soya /'sɔɪə/ n soja m. **~ sauce** n sauce f soja.

spa /spɑː/ n station f thermale.

space /speɪs/ n espace m; (room) place f; (period) période f. ● adj (research) spatial. ● vt **~ (out)** espacer. **~craft** n inv, **~ship** n engin m spatial. **~suit** n combinaison f spatiale.

spacious /'speɪʃəs/ adj spacieux.

spade /speɪd/ n (for garden) bêche f; (child's) pelle f; (cards) pique m. **~work** n (fig) travail m préparatoire.

spaghetti /spə'getɪ/ n spaghetti mpl.

spam /spæm/ n (Comput) multipostage m abusif.

Spain /speɪn/ n Espagne f.

span /spæn/ n (of arch) portée f; (of wings) envergure f; (of time) durée f. ● vt (pt **spanned**) enjamber; (in time) embrasser.

Spaniard /'spænjəd/ n Espagnol/-e m/f.

spaniel /'spænjəl/ n épagneul m.

Spanish /'spænɪʃ/ adj espagnol. ● n (Ling) espagnol m.

spank /spæŋk/ vt donner une fessée à.

spanner /'spænə(r)/ n (tool) clé f (plate); (adjustable) clé f à molette.

spare /speə(r)/ vt (treat leniently) épargner; (do without) se passer de; (afford to give) donner, accorder. ● adj en réserve; (surplus) de trop; (tyre, shoes) de rechange; (room, bed) d'ami; **are there any ~ tickets?** y a-t-il encore des places? ● n **~ (part)** pièce f de rechange. ~ **time** n loisirs mpl.

sparing /ˈspeərɪŋ/ adj frugal. **sparingly** adv en petite quantité.

spark /spɑːk/ n étincelle f. ● vt ~ **off** (initiate) provoquer.

sparkle /ˈspɑːkl/ vi étinceler. ● n étincellement m. **sparkling** adj (wine) mousseux; (eyes) brillant.

spark-plug n bougie f.

sparrow /ˈspærəʊ/ n moineau m.

sparse /spɑːs/ adj clairsemé. **sparsely** adv (furnished) peu.

spasm /ˈspæzəm/ n (of muscle) spasme m; (of coughing, anger) accès m.

spat /spæt/ ➡SPIT.

spate /speɪt/ n a ~ **of** (letters) une avalanche de.

spatter /ˈspætə(r)/ vt éclabousser (**with** de).

spawn /spɔːn/ n frai m, œufs mpl. ● vt pondre. ● vi frayer.

speak /spiːk/ vi (pt **spoke**; pp **spoken**) parler. ● vt (say) dire; (language) parler. □ ~ **up** parler plus fort.

speaker /ˈspiːkə(r)/ n (in public) orateur m; (Pol) président m; (loudspeaker) baffle m; **be a French/a good** ~ parler français/bien.

spear /spɪə(r)/ n lance f.

spearmint /ˈspɪəmɪnt/ n menthe f verte.

special /ˈspeʃl/ adj spécial; (exceptional) exceptionnel.

specialist /ˈspeʃəlɪst/ n spécialiste mf.

speciality, **specialty** /speʃɪˈælətɪ/ n spécialité f.

specialize /ˈspeʃəlaɪz/ vi se spécialiser (**in** en).

specially /ˈspeʃəlɪ/ adv spécialement.

species /ˈspiːʃiːz/ n inv espèce f.

specific /spəˈsɪfɪk/ adj précis, explicite.

specification /spesɪfɪˈkeɪʃn/ n (of design) spécification f; (of car equipment) caractéristiques fpl. **specify** vt spécifier.

specimen /ˈspesɪmən/ n spécimen m, échantillon m.

speck /spek/ n (stain) (petite) tache f; (particle) grain m.

specs /speks/ npl 🄸 lunettes fpl.

spectacle /ˈspektəkl/ n spectacle m. **spectacles** n lunettes fpl. **spectacular** adj spectaculaire.

spectator /spekˈteɪtə(r)/ n spectateur/-trice m/f.

spectrum /ˈspektrəm/ n (pl **-tra**) spectre m; (of ideas) gamme f.

speculate /ˈspekjuleɪt/ vi s'interroger (**about** sur); (Comm) spéculer. **speculation** n conjectures fpl; (Comm) spéculation f. **speculator** n spéculateur/-trice m/f.

speech /spiːtʃ/ n (faculty) parole f; (diction) élocution f; (dialect) langage m; (address) discours m. **speechless** adj muet (**with** de).

speed /spiːd/ n (of movement) vitesse f; (swiftness) rapidité f. ~ **camera** n radar m. ~ **dating®** n rencontres fpl rapides, speed dating m. ● vi (pt **sped**) aller vite; (pt **speeded**) (drive too fast) aller trop vite. □ ~ **up** accélérer; (of pace) s'accélérer.

speedboat /ˈspiːdbəʊt/ n vedette f.

speeding /ˈspiːdɪŋ/ n excès m de vitesse.

speed limit n limitation f de vitesse.

speedometer /spɪˈdɒmɪtə(r)/ n compteur m (de vitesse).

spell /spel/ n (magic) charme m, sortilège m; (curse) sort m; (of time) (courte) période f. ● vt/i (pt **spelled** or **spelt**) écrire; (mean) signifier; ~ **out** épeler; (explain) expliquer. ~**checker** n correcteur m orthographique.

spelling /ˈspelɪŋ/ n orthographe f. ● adj (mistake) d'orthographe.

spend /spend/ vt (pt **spent**) (money) dépenser (**on** pour); (time, holiday) passer; (energy) consacrer (**on** à). ● vi dépenser.

spent /spent/ ➡SPEND. ● adj (used) utilisé; (person) épuisé.

sperm /spɜːm/ n (pl **sperms** or **sperm**) sperme m.

sphere /sfɪə(r)/ n sphère f.

spice /spaɪs/ n épice f; (fig) piquant m.

spick-and-span adj impeccable.

spicy /ˈspaɪsɪ/ adj épicé; piquant.

spider /ˈspaɪdə(r)/ n araignée f.

spike /spaɪk/ n pointe f.

spill /spɪl/ vt (pt **spilled** or **spilt**) renverser, répandre. ● vi se répandre; ~ **over** déborder.

spin /spɪn/ vt/i (pt **spun**; pres p **spinning**) (wool, web) filer; (turn) (faire) tourner; (story) débiter; ~ **out** faire

S

durer. ● *n* (movement, excursion)
tour *m*.

spinach /'spɪnɪdʒ/ *n* épinards *mpl*.

spinal /'spaɪnl/ *adj* vertébral. ~ **cord** *n*
moelle *f* épinière.

spin-drier *n* essoreuse *f*.

spine /spaɪn/ *n* colonne *f* vertébrale;
(prickle) piquant *m*.

spin-off *n* avantage *m* accessoire; (by-
product) dérivé *m*.

spinster /'spɪnstə(r)/ *n* célibataire *f*;
(pej) vieille fille *f*.

spiral /'spaɪərəl/ *adj* en spirale; (staircase) en colimaçon. ● *n* spirale *f*. ● *vi*
(*pt* **spiralled**) (prices) monter (en
flèche).

spire /'spaɪə(r)/ *n* flèche *f*.

spirit /'spɪrɪt/ *n* esprit *m*; (boldness)
courage *m*; ~s (morale) moral *m*;
(drink) spiritueux *mpl*. ● *vt* ~ **away**
faire disparaître. **spirited** *adj* fougueux. ~**-level** *n* niveau *m* à bulle.

spiritual /'spɪrɪtʃʊəl/ *adj* spirituel.

spit /spɪt/ *vt/i* (*pt* **spat** *or* **spit**; *pres p*
spitting) cracher; (of rain) crachiner;
~ **out** cracher; **the** ~**ting image of**
le portrait craché *or* vivant de. ● *n*
crachat(s) *m*(*pl*); (for meat) broche *f*.

spite /spaɪt/ *n* rancune *f*; **in** ~ **of** malgré. ● *vt* contrarier.

splash /splæʃ/ *vt* éclabousser. ● *vi* faire
des éclaboussures; ~ **(about)** patauger. ● *n* (act, mark) éclaboussure *f*;
(sound) plouf *m*; (of colour) tache *f*.

spleen /spliːn/ *n* (Anat) rate *f*.

splendid /'splendɪd/ *adj* magnifique,
splendide.

splint /splɪnt/ *n* (Med) attelle *f*.

splinter /'splɪntə(r)/ *n* éclat *m*; (in finger) écharde *f*. ~ **group** *n* groupe *m*
dissident.

split /splɪt/ *vt/i* (*pt* **split**; *pres p* **split-
ting**) (se) fendre; (tear) (se) déchirer;
(divide) (se) diviser; (share) partager;
~ **one's sides** se tordre (de rire). ● *n*
fente *f*; déchirure *f*; (share [T]) part *f*,
partage *m*; (quarrel) rupture *f*; (Pol)
scission *f*. □ ~ **up** (couple) rompre. ~
second *n* fraction *f* de seconde.

splutter /'splʌtə(r)/ *vi* crachoter;
(stammer) bafouiller; (engine) tousser.

spoil /spɔɪl/ *vt* (*pt* **spoilt** *or* **spoiled**)
(pamper) gâter; (ruin) abîmer; (mar)
gâcher, gâter. ● *n* ~**(s)** butin *m*.

~**-sport** *n* trouble-fête *mf inv*.

spoke[1] /spəʊk/ *n* rayon *m*.

spoke[2], **spoken** ➔SPEAK. /

spokesman /'spəʊksmən/ *n* (*pl* **-men**)
porteparole *m inv*.

sponge /spʌndʒ/ *n* éponge *f*. ● *vt*
éponger. ● *vi* ~ **on** vivre aux crochets
de. ~**-bag** *n* trousse *f* de toilette.
~**-cake** *n* génoise *f*.

sponsor /'spɒnsə(r)/ *n* (of concert)
parrain *m*, sponsor *m*; (surety) garant
m; (for membership) parrain *m*, marraine *f*. ● *vt* parrainer, sponsoriser;
(member) parrainer. **sponsorship** *n*
patronage *m*; parrainage *m*.

spontaneous /spɒn'teɪnɪəs/ *adj*
spontané.

spoof /spuːf/ *n* [T] parodie *f*.

spoon /spuːn/ *n* cuiller *f*, cuillère *f*.

spoonful /'spuːnfʊl/ *n* (*pl* ~**s**) cuille-
rée *f*.

sport /spɔːt/ *n* sport *m*; **(good)** ~ (person [T]) chic type *m*; ~**s car/coat**
voiture/veste *f* de sport. ● *vt* (display)
exhiber, arborer.

sporting /'spɔːtɪŋ/ *adj* sportif; **a** ~
chance une assez bonne chance.

sportsman /'spɔːtsmən/ *n* (*pl* **-men**)
sportif *m*.

sporty /'spɔːtɪ/ *adj* [T] sportif.

spot /spɒt/ *n* (mark, stain) tache *f*;
(dot) point *m*; (in pattern) pois *m*;
(drop) goutte *f*; (place) endroit *m*;
(pimple) bouton *m*; **a** ~ **of** [T] un peu
de; **on the** ~ sur place; (without
delay) sur le coup. ● *vt* (*pt* **spotted**)
[T] apercevoir. ~ **check** *n* contrôle *m*
surprise.

spotless /'spɒtlɪs/ *adj* impeccable.

spotlight /'spɒtlaɪt/ *n* (lamp) projecteur *m*, spot *m*.

spotty /'spɒtɪ/ *adj* (skin) boutonneux.

spouse /spaʊz/ *n* époux *m*, épouse *f*.

spout /spaʊt/ *n* (of teapot) bec *m*; (of
liquid) jet *m*; **up the** ~ (ruined [T])
fichu. ● *vi* jaillir.

sprain /spreɪn/ *n* entorse *f*, foulure *f*.
● *vt* ~ **one's wrist** se fouler le
poignet.

sprang /spræŋ/ ➔SPRING.

sprawl /sprɔːl/ *vi* (town, person) s'étaler. ● *n* étalement *m*.

spray /spreɪ/ *n* (of flowers) gerbe *f*;
(water) gerbe *f* d'eau; (from sea) em-

bruns *mpl;* (device) bombe *f,* atomiseur *m.* ● *vt* (surface, insecticide, plant) vaporiser; (person) asperger; (crops) traiter.

spread /spred/ *vt/i* (*pt* **spread**) (stretch, extend) (s')étendre; (news, fear (se) répandre; (illness) (se) propager; (butter) (s')étaler. ● *n* propagation *f;* (of population) distribution *f;* (paste) pâte *f* à tartiner; (food) belle table *f.* **~-eagled** *adj* bras et jambes écartés. **~sheet** *n* tableur *m.*

spree /spri:/ *n* **go on a ~** (have fun 🅸) faire la noce.

sprig /sprɪg/ *n* petite branche *f.*

sprightly /'spraɪtlɪ/ *adj* (**-ier, -iest**) alerte, vif.

spring /sprɪŋ/ *vi* (*pt* **sprang;** *pp* **sprung**) bondir. ● *vt* **~ sth on sb** annoncer qch de but en blanc à qn. ● *n* bond *m;* (device) ressort *m;* (season) printemps *m;* (of water) source *f.* **~ from** provenir de; **~ up** surgir. **~board** *n* tremplin *m.* **~ onion** *n* oignon *m* blanc.

springy /'sprɪŋɪ/ *adj* (**-ier, -iest**) élastique.

sprinkle /'sprɪŋkl/ *vt* (with liquid) arroser (**with** de); (with salt, flour) saupoudrer (**with** de); (sand) répandre. **sprinkler** *n* (in garden) arroseur *m;* (for fires) extincteur *m* (à déclenchement) automatique.

sprint /sprɪnt/ *vi* (Sport) sprinter. ● *n* sprint *m.*

sprout /spraʊt/ *vt/i* pousser. ● *n* (on plant) pousse *f;* (**Brussels**) **~s** choux *mpl* de Bruxelles.

spruce /spru:s/ *adj* pimpant. ● *vt* **~ oneself up** se faire beau. ● *n* (tree) épicéa *m.*

sprung /sprʌŋ/ **➡SPRING.**

spud /spʌd/ *n* 🅸 patate *f.*

spun /spʌn/ **➡SPIN.**

spur /spɜ:(r)/ *n* (of rider) éperon *m;* (stimulus) aiguillon *m;* **on the ~ of the moment** sous l'impulsion du moment. ● *vt* (*pt* **spurred**) éperonner.

spurious /'spjʊərɪəs/ *adj* faux.

spurn /spɜ:n/ *vt* repousser.

spurt /spɜ:t/ *vi* jaillir; (fig) accélérer. ● *n* jet *m;* (of energy) sursaut *m.*

spy /spaɪ/ *n* espion/-ne *m/f.* ● *vi* espionner. ● *vt* apercevoir.

squabble /'skwɒbl/ *vi* se chamailler. ● *n* chamaillerie *f.*

squad /skwɒd/ *n* (of soldiers) escouade *f;* (Sport) équipe *f.*

squadron /'skwɒdrən/ *n* (Mil) escadron *m;* (Aviat) escadrille *f.*

squalid /'skwɒlɪd/ *adj* sordide.

squander /'skwɒndə(r)/ *vt* (money, time) gaspiller.

square /skweə(r)/ *n* carré *m;* (open space in town) place *f.* ● *adj* carré; (honest) honnête; (meal) solide; (boring 🅸) ringard; (**all**) ~ (quits) quitte; **~ metre** mètre *m* carré. ● *vt* (settle) régler; **~ up to** faire face à.

squash /skwɒʃ/ *vt* écraser; (crowd) serrer. ● *n* (game) squash *m;* (marrow: US) courge *f;* **lemon ~** citronnade *f;* **orange ~** orangeade *f.*

squat /skwɒt/ *vi* (*pt* **squatted**) s'accroupir; **~ in a house** squatteriser une maison. ● *adj* (dumpy) trapu. **squatter** *n* squatter *m.*

squawk /skwɔ:k/ *n* cri *m* rauque. ● *vi* pousser un cri rauque.

squeak /skwi:k/ *n* petit cri *m;* (of door) grincement *m.* ● *vi* crier; grincer.

squeal /skwi:l/ *n* cri *m* aigu. ● *vi* pousser un cri aigu; **~ on** (inform on 🅸) dénoncer.

squeamish /'skwi:mɪʃ/ *adj* (trop) délicat.

squeeze /skwi:z/ *vt* presser; (hand, arm) serrer; (extract) exprimer (**from** de); (extort) soutirer (**from** à). ● *vi* (force one's way) se glisser. ● *n* pression *f;* (Comm) restrictions *fpl* de crédit.

squid /skwɪd/ *n* calmar *m.*

squint /skwɪnt/ *vi* loucher; (with half-shut eyes) plisser les yeux. ● *n* (Med) strabisme *m.*

squirm /skwɜ:m/ *vi* se tortiller.

squirrel /'skwɪrəl/ *n* écureuil *m.*

squirt /skwɜ:t/ *vt/i* (faire) jaillir. ● *n* jet *m.*

stab /stæb/ *vt* (*pt* **stabbed**) (with knife) poignarder. ● *n* coup *m* (de couteau); **have a ~ at sth** essayer de faire qch.

stability /stə'bɪlətɪ/ *n* stabilité *f.* **stabilize** *vt* stabiliser.

stable /'steɪbl/ *adj* stable. ● *n* écurie *f.* **~-boy** *n* lad *m.*

S

stack /stæk/ n tas m. ● vt (~ **up**) entasser, empiler.

stadium /'steɪdɪəm/ n stade m.

staff /stɑːf/ n personnel m; (in school) professeurs mpl; (Mil) état-major m; (stick) bâton m. ● vt pourvoir en personnel.

stag /stæg/ n cerf m.

stage /steɪdʒ/ n (Theat) scène f; (phase) stade m, étape f; (platform in hall) estrade f; **go on the** ~ faire du théâtre. ● vt mettre en scène; (fig) organiser. ~ **door** n entrée f des artistes. ~ **fright** n trac m.

stagger /'stægə(r)/ vi chanceler. ● vt (shock) stupéfier; (payments) échelonner. **staggering** adj stupéfiant.

stagnate /stæg'neɪt/ vi stagner.

stag night n soirée f pour enterrer une vie de garçon.

staid /steɪd/ adj sérieux.

stain /steɪn/ vt tacher; (wood) colorer. ● n tache f; (colouring) colorant m. **stained glass window** n vitrail m.

stainless steel n acier m inoxydable.

stain remover n détachant m.

stair /steə(r)/ n marche f; **the** ~s l'escalier m. ~**case**, ~**way** n escalier m.

stake /steɪk/ n (post) pieu m; (wager) enjeu m; **at** ~ en jeu. ● vt (area) jalonner; (wager) jouer; ~ **a claim to** revendiquer.

stale /steɪl/ adj pas frais; (bread) rassis; (smell) de renfermé.

stalk /stɔːk/ n (of plant) tige f. ● vi marcher de façon guindée. ● vt (hunter) chasser; (murderer) suivre.

stall /stɔːl/ n (in stable) stalle f; (in market) éventaire m; ~s (Theat) orchestre m. ● vt/i (Auto) caler; ~ (**for time**) temporiser.

stallion /'stælɪən/ n étalon m.

stamina /'stæmɪnə/ n résistance f.

stammer /'stæmə(r)/ vt/i bégayer. ● n bégaiement m.

stamp /stæmp/ vt/i ~ (**one's foot**) taper du pied. ● vt (letter) timbrer. ● n (for postage, marking) timbre m; (mark: fig) sceau m. ~ **out** supprimer. ~-**collecting** n philatélie f.

stampede /stæm'piːd/ n fuite f désordonnée; (rush: fig) ruée f. ● vi s'enfuir en désordre; se ruer.

stand /stænd/ vi (pt **stood**) être or se tenir (debout); (rise) se lever; (be situated) se trouver; (Pol) être candidat (for à); ~ **in line** (US) faire la queue; ~ **to reason** être logique. ● vt mettre (debout); (tolerate) supporter; ~ **a chance** avoir une chance. ● n (stance) position f; (Mil) résistance f; (for lamp) support m; (at fair) stand m; (in street) kiosque m; (for spectators) tribune f; (Jur) barre f; **make a** ~ prendre position. ~ **back** reculer; ~ **by** or **around** ne rien faire; ~ **by** (be ready) se tenir prêt; (promise, person) rester fidèle à; ~ **down** se désister; ~ **for** représenter; Ⓣ supporter; ~ **in for** remplacer; ~ **out** ressortir; ~ **up** se lever; ~ **up for** défendre; ~ **up to** résister à.

standard /'stændəd/ n norme f; (level) niveau m (voulu); (flag) étendard m; ~ **of living** niveau m de vie; ~**s** (morals) principes mpl. ● adj ordinaire.

standard of living n niveau m de vie.

standby /'stændbaɪ/ adj de réserve. ● n **be a** ~ être de réserve.

stand-in /'stændɪn/ n remplaçant/-e m/f.

standing /'stændɪŋ/ adj debout inv. ● n réputation f; (duration) durée f. ~ **order** n prélèvement m bancaire.

standpoint /'stændpɔɪnt/ n point m de vue.

standstill /'stændstɪl/ n **at a** ~ immobile; **bring/come to a** ~ (s')immobiliser.

stank /stæŋk/ →**STINK**.

staple /'steɪpl/ n agrafe f. ● vt agrafer. ● adj principal, de base. **stapler** n agrafeuse f.

star /stɑː(r)/ n étoile f; (person) vedette f. ● vt (pt **starred**) (film) avoir pour vedette. ● vi ~ **in** être la vedette de.

starch /stɑːtʃ/ n amidon m; (in food) fécule f. ● vt amidonner.

stardom /'stɑːdəm/ n célébrité f.

stare /steə(r)/ vi ~ **at** regarder fixement. ● n regard m fixe.

starfish /'stɑːfɪʃ/ n étoile f de mer.

stark /stɑːk/ adj (desolate) désolé; (severe) austère; (utter) complet; (fact) brutal. ● adv complètement.

starling /'stɑːlɪŋ/ n étourneau m.

start /stɑːt/ *vt/i* commencer; (*machine*) (se) mettre en marche; (*fashion*) lancer; (*cause*) provoquer; (*jump*) sursauter; (*of vehicle*) démarrer; ~ **to do** commencer *or* se mettre à faire; ~**ing tomorrow** à partir de demain. ● *n* commencement *m*, début *m*; (*of race*) départ *m*; (*lead*) avance *f*; (*jump*) sursaut *m*. □ ~ **off** commencer (**doing** par faire); ~ **out** partir; ~ **up** (*business*) lancer. **starter** *n* (Auto) démarreur *m*; (*runner*) partant *m*; (Culin) entrée *f*.

starting point *n* point *m* de départ.

startle /'stɑːtl/ *vt* (make jump) faire tressaillir; (shock) alarmer.

starvation /stɑː'veɪʃn/ *n* faim *f*.

starve /stɑːv/ *vi* mourir de faim. ● *vt* affamer; (deprive) priver.

stash /stæʃ/ *vt* cacher.

state /steɪt/ *n* état *m*; (pomp) apparat *m*; S~ état *m*; **the S~s** les États-Unis, **get into a** ~ s'affoler. ● *adj* d'état, de l'état; (*school*) public. ● *vt* affirmer (**that** que); (*views*) exprimer; (fix) fixer.

> **State school** Environ 90% des élèves britanniques font leur scolarité dans une *state school* (école publique). l'enseignement y est gratuit et suit le programme scolaire national établi par le gouvernement. À l'entrée dans le secondaire, les élèves intègrent normalement une *comprehensive school*, ou, à l'issue d'un examen d'entrée, une *grammar school*. ▷**PUBLIC SCHOOLS**.

stately /'steɪtlɪ/ *adj* (**-ier, -iest**) majestueux. ~ **home** *n* château *m*.

statement /'steɪtmənt/ *n* déclaration *f*; (of account) relevé *m*.

statesman /'steɪtsmən/ *n* (*pl* **-men**) homme *m* d'état.

static /'stætɪk/ *adj* statique. ● *n* (radio, TV) parasites *mpl*.

station /'steɪʃn/ *n* (Rail) gare *f*; (TV) chaîne *f*; (Mil) poste *m*; (rank) condition *f*. ● *vt* poster, placer; ~**ed at** *or* **in** (Mil) en garnison à.

stationary /'steɪʃənrɪ/ *adj* immobile, stationnaire; (vehicle) à l'arrêt.

stationery /'steɪʃnərɪ/ *n* papeterie *f*.

station wagon *n* (US) break *m*.

statistic /stə'tɪstɪk/ *n* statistique *f*; ~**s** statistique *f*.

statue /'stætʃuː/ *n* statue *f*.

status /'steɪtəs/ *n* (*pl* ~**es**) situation *f*, statut *m*; (prestige) standing *m*.

statute /'stætʃuːt/ *n* loi *f*; ~**s** (rules) statuts *mpl*. **statutory** *adj* statutaire; (holiday) légal.

staunch /stɔːntʃ/ *adj* (friend) loyal, fidèle.

stave /steɪv/ *n* (Mus) portée *f*. ● *vt* ~ **off** éviter, conjurer.

stay /steɪ/ *vi* rester; (spend time) séjourner; (reside) loger. ● *vt* (hunger) tromper. ● *n* séjour *m*. □ ~ **away from** (school) ne pas aller à; ~ **behind** *or* ~ **on** rester; ~ **in** rester à la maison; ~ **up** veiller, se coucher tard.

stead /sted/ *n* **stand sb in good** ~ être utile à qn.

steadfast /'stedfɑːst/ *adj* ferme.

steady /'stedɪ/ *adj* (**-ier, -iest**) stable; (hand, voice) ferme; (regular) régulier; (staid) sérieux. ● *vt* maintenir, assurer; (calm) calmer.

steak /steɪk/ *n* steak *m*, bifteck *m*; (of fish) darne *f*.

steal /stiːl/ *vt/i* (*pt* **stole**; *pp* **stolen**) voler (**from sb** à qn).

steam /stiːm/ *n* vapeur *f*; (on glass) buée *f*. ● *vt* (cook) cuire à la vapeur. ● *vi* fumer. ~**-engine** *n* locomotive *f* à vapeur.

steamer /'stiːmə(r)/ *n* (Culin) cuit-vapeur *m*; (boat) (bateau à) vapeur *m*.

steel /stiːl/ *n* acier *m*; ~ **industry** sidérurgie *f*. ● *vpr* ~ **oneself** s'endurcir, se cuirasser.

steep /stiːp/ *adj* raide, rapide; (price: 🔢) excessif. ● *vt* (soak) tremper; ~**ed in** (fig) imprégné de.

steeple /'stiːpl/ *n* clocher *m*.

steer /stɪə(r)/ *vt* diriger; (ship) gouverner; (fig) guider. ● *vi* (in ship) gouverner; ~ **clear of** éviter.

steering-wheel *n* volant *m*.

stem /stem/ *n* tige *f*; (of glass) pied *m*. ● *vi* (*pt* **stemmed**) ~ **from** provenir de. ● *vt* (*pt* **stemmed**) (check, stop) endiguer, contenir. ~ **cell** *n* cellule *f* souche.

stench /stentʃ/ *n* puanteur *f*.

stencil /'stensɪl/ *n* pochoir *m*. ● *vt* (*pt* **stencilled**) décorer au pochoir.

S

step /step/ *vi* (*pt* **stepped**) marcher, aller. ● *n* pas *m*; (stair) marche *f*; (of train) marchepied *m*; (action) mesure *f*; ~**s** (ladder) escabeau *m*; **in** ~ au pas; (fig) conforme (**with** à). ~ **down** (resign) démissionner; (from ladder) descendre; ~ **forward** faire un pas en avant; ~ **in** (intervene) intervenir; ~ **up** (pressure) augmenter. ~**brother** *n* demifrère *m*. ~**daughter** *n* belle-fille *f*. ~**father** *n* beau-père *m*. ~**ladder** *n* escabeau *m*. ~**mother** *n* belle-mère *f*. **stepping-stone** *n* (fig) tremplin *m*. ~**sister** *n* demi-sœur *f*. ~**son** *n* beau-fils *m*.

stereo /'sterɪəʊ/ *n* stéréo *f*; (record-player) chaîne *f* stéréo. ● *adj* stéréo *inv*.

stereotype /'sterɪətaɪp/ *n* stéréotype *m*.

sterile /'steraɪl/ *adj* stérile. **sterility** *n* stérilité *f*.

sterilize /'sterəlaɪz/ *vt* stériliser.

sterling /'stɜːlɪŋ/ *n* livre(s) *f* (*pl*) sterling. ● *adj* sterling *inv*; (silver) fin; (fig) excellent.

stern /stɜːn/ *adj* sévère. ● *n* (of ship) arrière *m*.

steroid /'stɪərɔɪd/ *n* stéroïde *m*.

stew /stjuː/ *vt/i* cuire à la casserole; ~**ed fruit** compote *f*; ~**ed tea** thé *m* trop infusé. ● *n* ragoût *m*.

steward /stjʊəd/ *n* (of club) intendant *m*; (on ship) steward *m*. **stewardess** *n* hôtesse *f*.

stick /stɪk/ *vt* (*pt* **stuck**) (glue) coller; (put 🔲) mettre; (endure 🔲) supporter. ● *vi* (adhere) coller, adhérer; (to pan) attacher; (remain 🔲) rester; (be jammed) être coincé; **be stuck with sb** 🔲 se farcir qn. ● *n* bâton *m*; (for walking) canne *f*. ~ **at** persévérer dans; ~ **out** *vt* (head) sortir; (tongue) tirer; *vi* (protrude) dépasser; ~ **to** (promise) rester fidèle à; ~ **up for** 🔲 défendre.

sticker /'stɪkə(r)/ *n* autocollant *m*.

sticky /'stɪkɪ/ *adj* **-ier**, **-iest** poisseux; (label, tape) adhésif.

stiff /stɪf/ *adj* raide; (limb, joint) ankylosé; (tough) dur; (drink) fort; (price) élevé; (manner) guindé; ~ **neck** torticolis *m*.

stifle /'staɪfl/ *vt/i* étouffer.

stiletto /stɪ'letəʊ/ *adj & n* ~**s**, ~ **heels** talons *mpl* aiguille.

still /stɪl/ *adj* immobile; (quiet) calme, tranquille; **keep** ~**!** arrête de bouger! ● *n* silence *m*. ● *adv* encore, toujours; (even) encore; (nevertheless) tout de même.

stillborn /stɪlbɔːn/ *adj* mort-né.

still life *n* nature *f* morte.

stimulate /'stɪmjʊleɪt/ *vt* stimuler. **stimulation** *n* stimulation *f*.

stimulus /'stɪmjʊləs/ *n* (*pl* **-li**) (spur) stimulant *m*.

sting /stɪŋ/ *n* piqûre *f*; (of insect) aiguillon *m*. ● *vt/i* (*pt* **stung**) piquer.

stingy /'stɪndʒɪ/ *adj* (**-ier**, **-iest**) avare (**with** de).

stink /stɪŋk/ *n* puanteur *f*. ● *vi* (*pt* **stank** or **stunk**; *pp* **stunk**) ~ (**of**) puer.

stipulate /'stɪpjʊleɪt/ *vt* stipuler.

stir /stɜː(r)/ *vt/i* (*pt* **stirred**) (move) remuer; (excite) exciter; ~ **up** (trouble) provoquer. ● *n* agitation *f*.

stirrup /'stɪrəp/ *n* étrier *m*.

stitch /stɪtʃ/ *n* point *m*; (in knitting) maille *f*; (Med) point *m* de suture; (muscle pain) point *m* de côté; **be in** ~**es** 🔲 avoir le fou rire. ● *vt* coudre.

stock /stɒk/ *n* réserve *f*; (Comm) stock *m*; (financial) valeurs *fpl*; (family) souche *f*; (soup) bouillon *m*; **we're out of** ~ il n'y en a plus; **take** ~ (fig) faire le point; **in** ~ en stock. ● *adj* (goods) courant. ● *vt* (shop) approvisionner; (sell) vendre. ● *vi* ~ **up** s'approvisionner (**with** de). ~**broker** *n* agent *m* de change. ~ **cube** *n* bouillon-cube *m*. **S**~ **Exchange** *n* Bourse *f*.

stocking /'stɒkɪŋ/ *n* bas *m*.

stock market *n* Bourse *f*.

stockpile /'stɒkpaɪl/ *n* stock *m*. ● *vt* stocker; (arms) amasser.

stock-taking *n* (Comm) inventaire *m*.

stocky /'stɒkɪ/ *adj* (**-ier**, **-iest**) trapu.

stodgy /'stɒdʒɪ/ *adj* lourd.

stole, **stolen** ➡STEAL.

stomach /'stʌmək/ *n* estomac *m*; (abdomen) ventre *m*. ● *vt* (put up with) supporter. ~**-ache** *n* mal *m* à l'estomac *or* au ventre.

stone /stəʊn/ *n* pierre *f*; (pebble) caillou *m*; (in fruit) noyau *m*; (weight) 6,350 kg. ● *adj* de pierre; ~**-cold**/**-deaf** complètement froid/sourd. ● *vt* (throw stones) lapider; (*fruit*) dénoyauter.

stony /'stəʊnɪ/ *adj* pierreux.

stood /stʊd/ ➡**STAND.**

stool /stuːl/ *n* tabouret *m.*

stoop /stuːp/ *vi* (bend) se baisser; (condescend) s'abaisser. ● *n* have a ～ être voûté.

stop /stɒp/ *vt/i* (*pt* **stopped**) arrêter (**doing** de faire); (*moving, talking*) s'arrêter; (prevent) empêcher (**from** de); (*hole, leak*) boucher; (*pain, noise*) cesser; (stay I) rester. ● *n* arrêt *m*; (full stop) point *m*;～ (**-over**) halte *f*; (port of call) escale *f.* ～ **off** s'arrêter; ～ **up** boucher.

stopgap /'stɒpgæp/ *n* bouche-trou *m.* ● *adj* intérimaire.

stoppage /'stɒpɪdʒ/ *n* arrêt *m*; (of work) arrêt *m* de travail; (of pay) retenue *f.*

stopper /'stɒpə(r)/ *n* bouchon *m.*

stop-watch *n* chronomètre *m.*

storage /'stɔːrɪdʒ/ *n* (of goods, food) emmagasinage *m.* ～ **heater** *n* radiateur *m* électrique à accumulation.

store /stɔː(r)/ *n* réserve *f*; (warehouse) entrepôt *m*; (shop) grand magasin *m*; (US) magasin *m*; **have in ～ for** réserver à; **set ～ by** attacher du prix à. ● *vt* (for future) mettre en réserve; (in warehouse, mind) emmagasiner. ～**-room** *n* réserve *f.*

storey /'stɔːrɪ/ *n* étage *m.*

stork /stɔːk/ *n* cigogne *f.*

storm /stɔːm/ *n* tempête *f*, orage *m.* ● *vt* prendre d'assaut. ● *vi* (rage) tempêter.

story /'stɔːrɪ/ *n* histoire *f*; (in press) article *m*; (storey: US) étage *m.* ～**-teller** *n* conteur/-euse *m/f.*

stout /staʊt/ *adj* corpulent; (strong) solide. ● *n* bière *f* brune.

stove /stəʊv/ *n* cuisinière *f.*

stow /stəʊ/ *vt* ～ **away** (put away) ranger; (hide) cacher. ● *vi* voyager clandestinement.

straddle /'strædl/ *vt* être à cheval sur, enjamber.

straggler /'stræɡlə(r)/ *n* traînard/-e *m/f.*

straight /streɪt/ *adj* droit; (tidy) en ordre; (frank) franc; ～ **face** visage *m* sérieux; **get sth ～** mettre qch au

clair. ● *adv* (in straight line) droit; (direct) tout droit; ～ **ahead** *or* **on** tout droit; ～ **away** tout de suite; ～ **off** I sans hésiter. ● *n* (Sport) ligne *f* droite.

straighten /'streɪtn/ *vt* (nail, situation) redresser; (tidy) arranger.

straightforward /streɪt'fɔːwəd/ *adj* honnête; (easy) simple.

straight off *adj* I sans hésiter.

strain /streɪn/ *vt* (rope, ears) tendre; (limb) fouler; (eyes) fatiguer; (muscle) froisser; (filter) passer; (vegetables) égoutter; (fig) mettre à l'épreuve. ● *vi* fournir des efforts. ● *n* tension *f*; (fig) effort *m*; (breed) race *f*; (of virus) variété *f*; ～**s** (tune: Mus) accents *mpl.*

strained *adj* forcé; (relations) tendu.

strainer *n* passoire *f.*

strait /streɪt/ *n* détroit *m*; ～**s** détroit *m*; **be in dire ～s** être aux abois. ～**-jacket** *n* camisole *f* de force.

strand /strænd/ *n* (thread) fil *m*, brin *m*; (of hair) mèche *f.*

stranded /'strændɪd/ *adj* (person) en rade; (ship) échoué.

strange /streɪndʒ/ *adj* étrange; (unknown) inconnu. **stranger** *n* inconnu/-e *m/f.*

strangle /'stræŋɡl/ *vt* étrangler.

stranglehold /'stræŋɡlhəʊld/ *n* **have a ～ on** tenir à la gorge.

strap /stræp/ *n* (of leather) courroie *f*; (of dress) bretelle *f*; (of watch) bracelet *m.* ● *vt* (*pt* **strapped**) attacher.

strategic /strə'tiːdʒɪk/ *adj* stratégique. **strategy** *n* stratégie *f.*

straw /strɔː/ *n* paille *f*; **the last ～** le comble.

strawberry /'strɔːbrɪ/ *n* fraise *f.*

stray /streɪ/ *vi* s'égarer; (deviate) s'écarter. ● *adj* perdu; (isolated) isolé. ● *n* animal *m* perdu.

streak /striːk/ *n* raie *f*, bande *f*; (trace) trace *f*; (period) période *f*; (tendency) tendance *f.* ● *vt* (mark) strier. ● *vi* filer à toute allure.

stream /striːm/ *n* ruisseau *m*; (current) courant *m*; (flow) flot *m*; (in school) classe *f* (de niveau). ● *vi* ruisseler (**with** de); (eyes, nose) couler.

streamline /'striːmlaɪn/ *vt* rationaliser. **streamlined** *adj* (shape) aérodynamique.

S

street /striːt/ *n* rue *f*. **~car** *n* (US) tramway *m*. **~ lamp** *n* réverbère *m*. **~ map** *n* indicateur *m* des rues.

strength /streŋθ/ *n* force *f*; (of wall, fabric) solidité *f*; **on the ~ of** en vertu de. **strengthen** *vt* renforcer, fortifier.

strenuous /'strenjʊəs/ *adj* (*exercise*) énergique; (*work*) ardu.

stress /stres/ *n* (emphasis) accent *m*; (pressure) pression *f*; (Med) stress *m*. ● *vt* souligner, insister sur.

stretch /stretʃ/ *vt* (pull taut) tendre; (*arm, leg*) étendre; (*neck*) tendre; (*clothes*) étirer; (*truth*) forcer; **~ one's legs** se dégourdir les jambes. ● *vi* s'étendre; (*person*) s'étirer; (*clothes*) se déformer. ● *n* étendue *f*; (period) période *f*; (of road) tronçon *m*; **at a ~** d'affilée. ● *adj* (fabric) extensible.

stretcher /'stretʃə(r)/ *n* brancard *m*.

strew /struː/ *vt* (*pt* **strewed**; *pp* **strewed** or **strewn**) (scatter) répandre; (cover) joncher.

strict /strɪkt/ *adj* strict.

stride /straɪd/ *vi* (*pt* **strode**; *pp* **stridden**) faire de grands pas. ● *n* grand pas *m*.

strife /straɪf/ *n* conflit(s) *m(pl)*.

strike /straɪk/ *vt* (*pt* **struck**) frapper; (*blow*) donner; (*match*) frotter; (*gold*) trouver. ● *vi* faire grève; (attack) attaquer; (*clock*) sonner. ● *n* (of workers) grève *f*; (Mil) attaque *f*; (find) découverte *f*; **on ~** en grève. □ **~ off** or **out** rayer; **~ up** (*a friendship*) lier amitié (with avec). **striker** *n* gréviste *mf*; (football) attaquant/-e *m/f*. **striking** *adj* frappant.

string /strɪŋ/ *n* ficelle *f*; (of violin, racket) corde *f*; (of pearls) collier *m*; (of lies) chapelet *m*; **the ~s** (Mus) les cordes; **pull ~s** faire jouer ses relations. ● *vt pt* **strung** (thread) enfiler. **stringed** *adj* (instrument) à cordes.

stringent /'strɪndʒənt/ *adj* rigoureux, strict.

stringy /'strɪŋɪ/ *adj* filandreux.

strip /strɪp/ *vt/i* (*pt* **stripped**) (undress) (se) déshabiller; (deprive) dépouiller. ● *n* bande *f*.

stripe /straɪp/ *n* rayure *f*, raie *f*. **striped** *adj* rayé.

strip light *n* néon *m*.

stripper /'strɪpə(r)/ *n* strip-teaseur/-euse *m/f*; (solvent) décapant.

strip-tease *n* strip-tease *m*.

strive /straɪv/ *vi* (*pt* **strove**; *pp* **striven** s'efforcer (**to** de).

strode /strəʊd/ ➔STRIDE.

stroke /strəʊk/ *vt* (with hand) caresser. ● *n* coup *m*; (of pen) trait *m*; (swimming) nage *f*; (Med) attaque *f*, congestion *f*; **at a ~** d'un seul coup.

stroll /strəʊl/ *vi* flâner; **~ in** entrer tranquillement. ● *n* petit tour *m*. **stroller** *n* (US) poussette *f*.

strong /strɒŋ/ *adj* fort; (*shoes, fabric*) solide; **be fifty ~** être fort de cinquante personnes. **~hold** *n* bastion *m*.

strongly /'strɒŋlɪ/ *adv* (greatly) fortement; (with energy) avec force; (deeply) profondément.

strove /strəʊv/ ➔STRIVE.

struck /strʌk/ ➔STRIKE.

structure /'strʌktʃə(r)/ *n* (of cell, poem) structure *f*; (building) construction *f*.

struggle /'strʌɡl/ *vi* lutter, se battre. ● *n* lutte *f*; (effort) effort *m*; **have a ~ to** avoir du mal à.

strum /strʌm/ *vt* (*pt* **strummed**) gratter de.

strung /strʌŋ/ ➔STRING. ● *adj* **~ up** (tense) nerveux.

strut /strʌt/ *n* (support) étai *m*. ● *vi* (*pt* **strutted**) se pavaner.

stub /stʌb/ *n* bout *m*; (counterfoil) talon *m*. ● *vt* (*pt* **stubbed**) **~ one's toe** se cogner le doigt de pied. □ **~ out** écraser.

stubble /'stʌbl/ *n* (on chin) barbe *f* de plusieurs jours; (remains of wheat) chaume *m*.

stubborn /'stʌbən/ *adj* obstiné.

stuck /stʌk/ ➔STICK.● *adj* (jammed) coincé; **I'm ~** (for answer) je sèche. **~-up** *adj* 🔢 prétentieux.

stud /stʌd/ *n* (on jacket) clou *m*; (for collar) bouton *m*; (stallion) étalon *m*; (horse farm) haras *m*. ● *vt* (*pt* **studded**) clouter.

student /'stjuːdnt/ *n* (Univ) étudiant/-e *m/f*; (School) élève *mf*. ● *adj* (restaurant, life) universitaire.

studio /'stjuːdɪəʊ/ *n* studio *m*.

studious /'stjuːdɪəs/ *adj* (person) studieux; (deliberate) étudié.

study /'stʌdɪ/ n étude f; (office) bureau m. ● vt/i étudier.

stuff /stʌf/ n substance f; 🔲 chose (s) f (pl). ● vt rembourrer; (animal) empailler; (cram) bourrer; (Culin) farcir; (block up) boucher; (put) fourrer. **stuffing** n bourre f; (Culin) farce f.

stuffy /'stʌfɪ/ adj (-ier, -iest) mal aéré; (dull 🔲) vieux jeu inv.

stumble /'stʌmbl/ vi trébucher; ∼ **across** or **on** tomber sur. **stumbling block** n obstacle m.

stump /stʌmp/ n (of tree) souche f; (of limb) moignon m; (of pencil) bout m.

stumped /stʌmpt/ adj embarrassé.

stun /stʌn/ vt (pt **stunned**) étourdir; (bewilder) stupéfier.

stung /stʌŋ/ →STING.

stunk /stʌŋk/ →STINK.

stunning /'stʌnɪŋ/ adj (delightful 🔲) sensationnel.

stunt /stʌnt/ vt (growth) retarder. ● n (feat 🔲) tour m de force; (trick 🔲) truc m; (dangerous) cascade f.

stupid /'stju:pɪd/ adj stupide, bête. **stupidity** n stupidité f.

sturdy /'stɜ:dɪ/ adj (-ier, -iest) robuste.

stutter /'stʌtə(r)/ vi bégayer. ● n bégaiement m.

sty /staɪ/ n (pigsty) porcherie f; (on eye) orgelet m.

style /staɪl/ n style m; (fashion) mode f; (sort) genre m; (pattern) modèle m; **do sth in** ∼ faire qch avec classe. ● vt (design) créer; ∼ **sb's hair** coiffer qn.

stylish /'staɪlɪʃ/ adj élégant.

stylist /'staɪlɪst/ n (of hair) coiffeur/-euse m/f.

suave /swɑ:v/ adj (urbane) courtois; (smooth: pej) doucereux.

subconscious /sʌb'kɒnʃəs/ adj & n inconscient (m), subconscient (m.)

subcontract /sʌbkən'trækt/ vt soustraiter.

subdue /səb'dju:/ vt (feeling) maîtriser; (country) subjuguer. **subdued** adj (person, mood) morose; (light) tamisé; (criticism) contenu.

subject[1] /'sʌbdʒɪkt/ adj (state) soumis; ∼ **to** soumis à; (liable to, dependent on) sujet à. ● n sujet m; (focus) objet m; (School,Univ) matière f; (citizen) ressortissant/-e m/f, sujet/-te m/f.

subject[2] /səb'dʒekt/ vt soumettre.

subjective /səb'dʒektɪv/ adj subjectif.

subject-matter n contenu m.

subjunctive /səb'dʒʌŋktɪv/ adj & n subjonctif (m.)

sublet /sʌb'let/ vt sous-louer.

submarine /sʌbmə'ri:n/ n sousmarin m.

submerge /səb'mɜ:dʒ/ vt submerger. ● vi plonger.

submissive /səb'mɪsɪv/ adj soumis.

submit /səb'mɪt/ vt/i (pt **submitted**) (se) soumettre (**to** à).

subordinate /sə'bɔ:dɪnət/ adj subalterne; (Gram) subordonné. ● n subordonné/-e m/f.

subpoena /sə'pi:nə/ n (Jur) citation f, assignation f.

subscribe /səb'skraɪb/ vt/i verser (de l'argent) (**to** à); ∼ **to** (loan, theory) souscrire à; (newspaper) s'abonner à, être abonné à. **subscriber** n abonné/-e m/f. **subscription** n abonnement m; (membership dues) cotisation f.

subsequent /'sʌbsɪkwənt/ adj (later) ultérieur; (next) suivant. **subsequently** adv par la suite.

subside /səb'saɪd/ vi (land) s'affaisser; (flood, wind) baisser.

subsidiary /səb'sɪdɪərɪ/ adj accessoire. ● n (Comm) filiale f.

subsidize /'sʌbsɪdaɪz/ vt subventionner. **subsidy** n subvention f.

substance /'sʌbstəns/ n substance f.

substandard /sʌb'stændəd/ adj de qualité inférieure.

substantial /səb'stænʃl/ adj considérable; (meal) substantiel.

substitute /'sʌbstɪtju:t/ n succédané m; (person) remplaçant/-e m/f. ● vt substituer (**for** à).

subtitle /'sʌbtaɪtl/ n sous-titre m.

subtle /'sʌtl/ adj subtil.

subtract /səb'trækt/ vt soustraire.

suburb /'sʌbɜ:b/ n faubourg m, banlieue f; ∼**s** banlieue f. **suburban** adj de banlieue. **suburbia** n la banlieue.

subway /'sʌbweɪ/ n passage m souterrain; (US) métro m.

succeed /sək'si:d/ vi réussir (**in doing** à faire). ● vt (follow) succéder à.

success /sək'ses/ n succès m, réussite f.

successful /sək'sesfl/ adj réussi, couronné de succès; (favourable) heureux;

S

(in exam) reçu; **be ~ in doing** réussir à faire.

succession /sək'seʃn/ n succession f; **in ~** de suite.

successive /sək'sesɪv/ adj successif; **six ~ days** six jours consécutifs.

successor /sək'sesə(r)/ n successeur m.

such /sʌtʃ/ det & pron tel(le), tel(le)s; (so much) tant(de). ● adv si; **~ a book** un tel livre; **~ books** de tels livres; **~ courage** tant de courage; **~ a big house** une si grande maison; **~ as** comme, tel que; **as ~** en tant que tel; **there's no ~ thing** ça n'existe pas. **~-and-~** adj tel ou tel.

suck /sʌk/ vt sucer. □ **~ in** or **up** aspirer. **sucker** n (rubber pad) ventouse f; (person 🅸) dupe f.

suction /'sʌkʃn/ n succion f.

sudden /'sʌdn/ adj soudain, subit; **all of a ~** tout à coup. **suddenly** adv subitement, brusquement.

sue /suː/ vt (pres p) **suing** poursuivre (en justice).

suede /sweɪd/ n daim m.

suffer /'sʌfə(r)/ vt/i souffrir; (loss, attack) subir. **sufferer** n victime f, malade mf. **suffering** n souffrance(s) f(pl).

sufficient /sə'fɪʃnt/ adj (enough) suffisamment de; (big enough) suffisant.

suffix /'sʌfɪks/ n suffixe m.

suffocate /'sʌfəkeɪt/ vt/i suffoquer.

sugar /'ʃʊɡə(r)/ n sucre m. ● vt sucrer.

suggest /sə'dʒest/ vt suggérer. **suggestion** n suggestion f.

suicidal /suːɪ'saɪdl/ adj suicidaire.

suicide /'suːɪsaɪd/ n suicide m; **commit ~** se suicider.

suit /suːt/ n (man's) costume m; (woman's) tailleur m; (cards) couleur f. ● vt convenir à; (garment, style) aller à; (adapt) adapter.

suitable /'suːtəbl/ adj qui convient (**for** à), convenable. **suitably** adv convenablement.

suitcase /'suːtkeɪs/ n valise f.

suite /swiːt/ n (rooms) suite f; (furniture) mobilier m.

suited /'suːtɪd/ adj (well) **~** (matched) bien assorti; **~ to** fait pour, apte à.

sulk /sʌlk/ vi bouder.

sullen /'sʌlən/ adj maussade.

sultana /sʌl'tɑːnə/ n raisin m de Smyrne, raisin m sec.

sultry /'sʌltrɪ/ adj (-ier, -iest) étouffant, lourd; (fig) sensuel.

sum /sʌm/ n somme f; (in arithmetic) calcul m. ● vt/i (pt **summed**) **~ up** résumer, récapituler; (assess) évaluer.

summarize /'sʌməraɪz/ vt résumer.

summary /'sʌmərɪ/ n résumé m. ● adj sommaire.

summer /'sʌmə(r)/ n été m. ● adj d'été. **~time** n (season) été m.

Summer camps Les camps de vacances sont une composante importante des vacances d'été des jeunes Américains. Souvent situés dans des parcs nationaux, ces camps proposent de multiples activités de plein air (canoë, escalade, équitation, natation, ski nautique, tennis, randonnée, etc.). Des milliers d'étudiants y sont recrutés chaque année en tant que moniteurs.

---

summery /'sʌmərɪ/ adj estival.

summit /'sʌmɪt/ n sommet m; **~ (conference)** (Pol) (conférence f au) sommet m.

summon /'sʌmən/ vt appeler; **~ sb to a meeting** convoquer qn à une réunion; **~ up** (strength, courage) rassembler.

summons /'sʌmənz/ n (Jur) assignation f. ● vt assigner.

sun /sʌn/ n soleil m. ● vt (pt **sunned**) **~ oneself** se chauffer au soleil. **~burn** n coup m de soleil.

Sunday /'sʌndeɪ/ n dimanche m. **~ school** n catéchisme m.

sundry /'sʌndrɪ/ adj divers; **sundries** articles mpl divers; **all and ~** tout le monde.

sunflower /'sʌnflaʊə(r)/ n tournesol m.

sung /sʌŋ/ →SING.

sun-glasses npl lunettes fpl de soleil.

sunk /sʌŋk/ →SINK.

sunken /'sʌŋkən/ adj (ship) submergé; (eyes) creux.

sunlight /'sʌnlaɪt/ n soleil m.

sunny /'sʌnɪ/ adj (-ier, -iest) ensoleillé.

sun: ~rise n lever m du soleil. **~roof** n toit m ouvrant. **~ screen** n filtre m solaire. **~set** n coucher m du soleil.

~**shine** n soleil m. ~**stroke** n insolation f.

sun-tan /'sʌntæn/ n bronzage m. ~
lotion n lotion f solaire. ~ **oil** n huile f
solaire.

super /'suːpə(r)/ adj 🆃 formidable.

superb /suːˈpɜːb/ adj superbe.

superficial /suːpəˈfɪʃl/ adj superficiel.

superfluous /suːˈpɜːflʊəs/ adj superflu.

superimpose /suːpərɪmˈpəʊz/ vt superposer (**on** à).

superintendent /suːpərɪnˈtendənt/ n
directeur/-trice m/f; (of police) commissaire m.

superior /suːˈpɪərɪə(r)/ adj & n
supérieur/-e (m /f).

superlative /suːˈpɜːlətɪv/ adj suprême.
● n (Gram) superlatif m.

supermarket /'suːpəmɑːkɪt/ n supermarché m.

supersede /suːpəˈsiːd/ vt remplacer,
supplanter.

superstition /suːpəˈstɪʃn/ n superstition f. **superstitious** adj superstitieux.

superstore /'suːpəstɔː(r)/ n hypermarché m.

supervise /'suːpəvaɪz/ vt surveiller, diriger. **supervision** n surveillance f.
supervisor n surveillant/-e m/f; (shop)
chef m de rayon; (firm) chef m de
service.

supper /'sʌpə(r)/ n dîner m; (late at
night) souper m.

supple /'sʌpl/ adj souple.

supplement[1] /'sʌplɪmənt/ n supplément m. **supplementary** adj supplémentaire.

supplement[2] /'sʌplɪmənt/ vt compléter.

supplier /səˈplaɪə(r)/ n fournisseur m.

supply /səˈplaɪ/ vt fournir; (equip)
pourvoir; (feed) alimenter (**with** en).
● n provision f; (of gas) alimentation f;
supplies (food) vivres mpl; (material)
fournitures fpl.

support /səˈpɔːt/ vt soutenir; (family)
assurer la subsistance de. ● n soutien
m, appui m; (Tech) support m. **supporter** n partisan/-e m/f; (Sport) supporter m. **supportive** adj qui soutient
et encourage.

suppose /səˈpəʊz/ vt/i supposer; **be
~d to do** être censé faire, devoir

faire; **supposing he comes** supposons
qu'il vienne. **supposedly** adv soi-
disant, prétendument.

suppress /səˈpres/ vt (put an end to)
supprimer; (restrain) réprimer; (stifle)
étouffer.

supreme /suːˈpriːm/ adj suprême.

surcharge /'sɜːtʃɑːdʒ/ n supplément
m; (tax) surtaxe f.

sure /ʃɔː(r)/ adj sûr; **make ~ of** s'assurer de; **make ~ that** vérifier que.
● adv (US 🆃) pour sûr. **surely** adv sûrement.

surf /sɜːf/ n ressac m. ● vi faire du surf;
(Internet) surfer.

surface /'sɜːfɪs/ n surface f. ● adj superficiel. ● vt revêtir. ● vi faire surface;
(fig) réapparaître.

surfer /'sɜːfə(r)/ n surfeur/-euse m/f;
(Internet) internaute m/f.

surge /sɜːdʒ/ vi (waves, crowd) déferler;
(increase) monter.● n (wave) vague f;
(rise) montée f.

surgeon /'sɜːdʒən/ n chirurgien m.

surgery /'sɜːdʒərɪ/ n chirurgie f; (office)
cabinet m; (session) consultation f;
need ~ devoir être opéré.

surgical /'sɜːdʒɪkl/ adj chirurgical. ~
spirit n alcool m à 90 degrés.

surly /'sɜːlɪ/ adj (-ier, -iest) bourru.

surname /'sɜːneɪm/ n nom m de
famille.

surplus /'sɜːpləs/ n surplus m. ● adj en
surplus.

surprise /səˈpraɪz/ n surprise f. ● vt
surprendre. **surprised** adj surpris (**at**
de). **surprising** adj surprenant.

surrender /səˈrendə(r)/ vi se rendre.
● vt (hand over) remettre; (Mil) rendre. ● n (Mil) reddition f; (of passport)
remise f.

surround /səˈraʊnd/ vt entourer; (Mil)
encercler. **surrounding** adj environnant. **surroundings** npl environs mpl;
(setting) cadre m.

surveillance /sɜːˈveɪləns/ n surveillance f.

survey[1] /səˈveɪ/ vt (review) passer en
revue; (inquire into) enquêter sur;
(building) inspecter.

survey[2] /'sɜːveɪ/ n (inquiry) enquête f;
inspection f; (general view) vue f d'ensemble.

S

surveyor /sə'veɪə(r)/ n expert m (géomètre).

survival /sə'vaɪvl/ n survie f.

survive /sə'vaɪv/ vt/i survivre (à). **survivor** n survivant/-e m/f.

susceptible /sə'septəbl/ adj sensible (to à); ∼ **to** (prone to) prédisposé à.

suspect[1] /sə'spekt/ vt soupçonner; (doubt) douter de.

suspect[2] /'sʌspekt/ n & adj suspect/-e (m/f).

suspend /sə'spend/ vt (hang, stop) suspendre; (licence) retirer provisoirement. **suspended sentence** n condamnation f avec sursis.

suspender /sə'spendə(r)/ n jarretelle f; ∼**s** (braces: US) bretelles fpl. ∼ **belt** n porte-jarretelles m.

suspension /sə'spenʃn/ n suspension f; retrait m provisoire.

suspicion /sə'spɪʃn/ n soupçon m; (distrust) méfiance f.

suspicious /sə'spɪʃəs/ adj soupçonneux; (causing suspicion) suspect; **be** ∼ **of** se méfier de. **suspiciously** adv de façon suspecte.

sustain /sə'steɪn/ vt supporter; (effort) soutenir; (suffer) subir.

sustenance /'sʌstɪnəns/ n (food) nourriture f; (nourishment) valeur f nutritive.

swallow /'swɒləʊ/ vt/i avaler; ∼ **up** (absorb, engulf) engloutir. ● n hirondelle f.

swam /swæm/ →SWIM.

swamp /swɒmp/ n marais m. ● vt (flood, overwhelm) submerger.

swan /swɒn/ n cygne m.

swap /swɒp/ vt/i (pt **swapped**) 🔟 échanger. ● n 🔟 échange m.

swarm /swɔːm/ n essaim m. ● vi fourmiller; ∼ **into** or **round** (crowd) envahir.

swat /swɒt/ vt (pt **swatted**) (fly) écraser.

sway /sweɪ/ vt/i (se) balancer; (influence) influencer. ● n balancement m; (rule) empire m.

swear /sweə(r)/ vt/i (pt) swore; pp sworn jurer (**to sth** de qch); ∼ **at** injurier; ∼ **by sth** 🔟 ne jurer que par qch. ∼ **-word** n juron m.

sweat /swet/ n sueur f. ● vi suer.

sweater /'swetə(r)/ n pull-over m.

sweat-shirt n sweat-shirt m.

swede /swiːd/ n rutabaga m.

Swede /swiːd/ n Suédois/-e m/f. **Sweden** n Suède f.

Swedish /'swiːdɪʃ/ adj suédois. ● n (Ling) suédois m.

sweep /swiːp/ vt/i (pt **swept**) (floor) balayer; (carry away) emporter, entraîner; (chimney) ramoner. ● n coup m de balai; (curve) courbe f; (movement) geste m, mouvement m; (for chimneys) ramoneur m. ∼ **by** passer rapidement or majestueusement. **sweeper** n (for carpet) balai m mécanique; (football) libero m.

sweet /swiːt/ adj (not sour, pleasant) doux; (not savoury) sucré; (charming 🔟) gentil; **have a** ∼ **tooth** aimer les sucreries. ● n bonbon m; (dish) dessert m. ∼**corn** n maïs m.

sweeten /'swiːtn/ vt sucrer; (fig) adoucir. **sweetener** n édulcorant m.

sweetheart /'swiːthɑːt/ n petit/-e ami/-e m/f; (term of endearment) chéri/-e m/f.

sweetly /'swiːtlɪ/ adv gentiment.

sweetness /'swiːtnɪs/ n douceur f; goût m sucré.

sweet pea n pois m de senteur.

swell /swel/ vt/i (pt **swelled**; pp **swollen** or **swelled**) (increase) grossir; (expand) (se) gonfler; (hand, face) enfler. ● n (of sea) houle f. **swelling** n (Med) enflure f.

sweltering /'sweltərɪŋ/ adj étouffant.

swept /swept/ →SWEEP.

swerve /swɜːv/ vi faire un écart.

swift /swɪft/ adj rapide. ● n (bird) martinet m.

swim /swɪm/ vi (pt **swam**; pp **swum**; pres p **swimming**) nager; (be dizzy) tourner. ● vt traverser à la nage; (distance) nager. ● n baignade f; **go for a** ∼ aller se baigner. **swimmer** n nageur/-euse m/f. **swimming** n natation f.

swimming pool n piscine f.

swimsuit /'swɪmsuːt/ n maillot m (de bain).

swindle /'swɪndl/ vt escroquer. ● n escroquerie f.

swine /swaɪn/ *npl* (pigs) pourceaux *mpl.* ● *n inv* (person 🔲) salaud *m.*

swing /swɪŋ/ *vt/i* (*pt* swung) (se) balancer; (turn round) tourner; (*pendulum*) osciller. ● *n* balancement *m;* (seat) balançoire *f;* (of opinion) revirement *m* (**towards** en faveur de); (Mus) rythme *m;* **be in full ~** battre son plein. □ **~ round** (*person*) se retourner.

swipe /swaɪp/ *vt* (hit 🔲) frapper; (steal 🔲) piquer. **~ card** *n* carte *f* magnétique, badge *m.*

swirl /swɜːl/ *vi* tourbillonner. ● *n* tourbillon *m.*

Swiss /swɪs/ *adj* suisse. ● *n inv* Suisse *mf.*

switch /swɪtʃ/ *n* bouton *m* (électrique), interrupteur *m;* (shift) changement *m,* revirement *m.* ● *vt* (transfer) transférer; (exchange) échanger (**for** contre); (reverse positions of) changer de place; **~ trains** (change) changer de train. ● *vi* changer. □ **~ off** éteindre; **~ on** mettre, allumer.

switchboard /swɪtʃbɔːd/ *n* standard *m.*

Switzerland /swɪtzələænd/ *n* Suisse *f.*

swivel /swɪvl/ *vt/i* (*pt* swivelled) (faire) pivoter.

swollen /swəʊlən/ →SWELL.

swoop /swuːp/ *vi* (bird) fondre; (police) faire une descente, foncer. ● *n* (police raid) descente *f.*

sword /sɔːd/ *n* épée *f.*

swore /swɔː(r)/ →SWEAR.

sworn /swɔːn/ →SWEAR. ● *adj* (enemy) juré; (ally) dévoué.

swot /swɒt/ *vt/i* (*pt* swotted) (study 🔲) bûcher 🔲. ● *n* 🔲 bûcheur/-euse *m/f*🔲

swum /swʌm/ →SWIM.

swung /swʌŋ/ →SWING.

syllabus /sɪləbəs/ *n* (*pl* ~es) (School, Univ) programme *m.*

symbol /sɪmbl/ *n* symbole *m.* **symbolic (al)** *adj* symbolique. **symbolize** *vt* symboliser.

symmetrical /sɪˈmetrɪkəl/ *adj* symétrique.

sympathetic /sɪmpəˈθetɪk/ *adj* compatissant; (fig) compréhensif.

sympathize /sɪmpəθaɪz/ *vi* **~ with** (pity) plaindre; (fig) comprendre les sentiments de. **sympathizer** *n* sympathisant/-e *m/f.*

sympathy /sɪmpəθɪ/ *n* (pity) compassion *f;* (fig) compréhension *f;* (solidarity) solidarité *f;* (condolences) condoléances *fpl;* (affinity) affinité *f;* **be in ~ with** comprendre, être en accord avec.

symptom /sɪmptəm/ *n* symptôme *m.*

synagogue /sɪnəgɒg/ *n* synagogue *f.*

synonym /sɪnənɪm/ *n* synonyme *m.*

synopsis /sɪˈnɒpsɪs/ *n* (*pl* -opses) résumé *m.*

syntax /sɪntæks/ *n* syntaxe *f.*

synthesis /sɪnθəsɪs/ *n* (*pl* -theses) synthèse *f.*

synthetic /sɪnˈθetɪk/ *adj* synthétique.

syringe /sɪˈrɪndʒ/ *n* seringue *f.*

syrup /sɪrəp/ *n* (liquid) sirop *m;* (treacle) mélasse *f* raffinée.

system /sɪstəm/ *n* système *m;* (body) organisme *m;* (order) méthode *f.* **systematic** *adj* systématique.

systems analyst *n* analysteprogrammeur/- euse *m/f.*

Tt

tab /tæb/ *n* (on can) languette *f;* (on garment) patte *f;* (label) étiquette *f;* (US 🔲) addition *f;* (Comput) tabulatrice *f;* (setting) tabulation *f.*

table /teɪbl/ *n* table *f;* **at (the) ~** à table; **lay** *or* **set the ~** mettre la table. ● *vt* (motion) présenter. **~-cloth** *n* nappe *f.* **~-mat** *n* set *m* de table. **~spoon** *n* cuillère *f* de service.

tablet /tæblɪt/ *n* (of stone) plaque *f;* (drug) comprimé *m.*

table tennis *n* tennis *m* de table; ping-pong® *m.*

taboo /təˈbuː/ *n & a* tabou (*m*).

tacit /tæsɪt/ *adj* tacite.

tack /tæk/ *n* (nail) clou *m;* (stitch) point *m* de bâti; (course of action) voie *f.* ● *vt* (nail) clouer; (stitch) bâtir; (add) ajouter. ● *vi* (Naut) louvoyer.

tackle /'tækl/ *n* équipement *m*; (in soccer) tacle *m*; (in rugby) plaquage *m*.
● *vt* (*problem*) s'attaquer à; (*player*) tacler, plaquer.

tact /tækt/ *n* tact *m*. **tactful** *adj* plein de tact.

tactics /'tæktɪks/ *npl* tactique *f*.

tadpole /'tædpəʊl/ *n* têtard *m*.

tag /tæg/ *n* (label) étiquette *f*. ● *vt* (*pt* **tagged**) (label) étiqueter. ● *vi* ~ **along** ⓘ suivre.

tail /teɪl/ *n* queue *f*; ~**s** (coat) habit *m*; ~**s!** (on coin) pile! ● *vt* (follow) filer. ● *vi* ~ **away** or **off** diminuer. ~**-back** *n* bouchon *m*. ~**-gate** *n* hayon *m*.

tailor /'teɪlə(r)/ *n* tailleur *m*. ● *vt* (*garment*) façonner; (fig) adapter. ~**-made** *adj* fait sur mesure.

take /teɪk/ *vt/i* (*pt* **took**, *pp* **taken**) prendre (**from sb** à qn); (carry) emporter, porter (**to** à); (escort) emmener; (contain) contenir; (tolerate) supporter; (accept) accepter; (*prize*) remporter; (*exam*) passer; (*precedence*) avoir; (view) adopter; ~ **sb home** ramener qn chez lui; **be taken by** or **with** être impressionné par; **be taken ill** tomber malade; **it** ~**s time** il faut du temps pour. ❑ ~ **after** tenir de; ~ **apart** démonter; (fig) descendre en flammes ⓘ; ~ **away** (object) enlever; (person) emmener; (pain) supprimer; ~ **back** reprendre; (return) rendre; (accompany) raccompagner; (*statement*) retirer; ~ **down** (object) descendre; (notes) prendre; ~ **in** (object) rentrer; (include) inclure; (cheat) tromper; ~ **off** (Aviat) décoller; ~ **sth off** enlever qch; ~ **sb off** imiter qn; ~ **on** (task, staff, passenger) prendre; (*challenger*) relever le défi de; ~ **out** sortir; (stain) enlever; ~ **over** *vt* (country, firm) prendre le contrôle de; *vi* prendre le pouvoir; ~ **over from** remplacer; ~ **part** participer (**in** à); ~ **place** avoir lieu; ~ **to** se prendre d'amitié pour; (activity) prendre goût à; ~ **to doing** se mettre à faire; ~ **up** (object) monter; (hobby) se mettre à; (occupy) prendre; (resume) reprendre; ~ **up with** se lier avec. ~**-away** *n* (meal) repas *m* à emporter. ~**-off** *n* (Aviat) décollage *m*. ~**-over** *n* (Pol) prise *f* de pouvoir; (Comm) rachat *m*.

tale /teɪl/ *n* conte *m*; (report) récit *m*; (lie) histoire *f*.

talent /'tælənt/ *n* talent *m*. **talented** *adj* doué.

talk /tɔːk/ *vt/i* parler; (chat) bavarder; ~ **sb into doing** persuader qn de faire; ~ **sth over** discuter de qch. ● *n* (talking) propos *mpl*; (conversation) conversation *f*; (lecture) exposé *m*.

talkative /'tɔːkətɪv/ *adj* bavard.

tall /tɔːl/ *adj* (high) haut; (person) grand.

tame /teɪm/ *adj* apprivoisé; (dull) insipide. ● *vt* apprivoiser; (lion) dompter.

tamper /'tæmpə(r)/ *vi* ~ **with** (lock, machine) tripoter; (accounts, evidence) trafiquer.

tan /tæn/ *vt/i* (*pt* **tanned**) bronzer; (hide) tanner. ● *n* bronzage *m*.

tangerine /'tændʒəriːn/ *n* mandarine *f*.

tangle /'tæŋgl/ *vt/i* ~ **(up)** s'emmêler. ● *n* enchevêtrement *m*.

tank /tæŋk/ *n* réservoir *m*; (vat) cuve *f*; (for fish) aquarium *m*; (Mil) char *m* (de combat).

tanker /'tæŋkə(r)/ *n* (lorry) camion-citerne *m*; (ship) navire-citerne *m*; **oil/petrol** ~ pétrolier *m*.

tantrum /'tæntrəm/ *n* crise *f* (de colère).

tap /tæp/ *n* (for water) robinet *m*; (knock) petit coup *m*; **on** ~ disponible. ● *vt* (*pt* **tapped**) (knock) taper (doucement); (resources) exploiter; (phone) mettre sur écoute.

tape /teɪp/ *n* bande *f* (magnétique); (cassette) cassette *f*; (video) cassette *f* vidéo; (fabric) ruban *m*; (sticky) scotch (r) *m*. ● *vt* (record) enregistrer; ~ **sth to sth** coller qch à qch. ~**-measure** *n* mètre *m* ruban. ~ **recorder** *n* magnétophone *m*.

tapestry /'tæpəstrɪ/ *n* tapisserie *f*.

tar /tɑː(r)/ *n* goudron *m*. ● *vt* (*pt* **tarred**) goudronner.

target /'tɑːgɪt/ *n* cible *f*; (objective) objectif *m*. ● *vt* (city) prendre pour cible; (weapon) diriger; (in marketing) viser.

tariff /'tærɪf/ *n* (price list) tarif *m*; (on imports) droit *m* de douane.

tarmac, Tarmac® /'tɑːmæk/ *n* macadam *m*; (runway) piste *f*.

tarpaulin /tɑːˈpɔːlɪn/ *n* bâche *f*.

tarragon /'tærəgən/ n estragon m.

tart /tɑːt/ n tarte f. ● adj aigrelet.

task /tɑːsk/ n tâche f.

taste /teɪst/ n goût m; (experience) aperçu m. ● vt (eat, enjoy) goûter à; (try) goûter; (perceive taste of) sentir (le goût de). ● vi ~ **of** or **like** avoir un goût de. **tasteful** adj de bon goût.

tattoo /tə'tuː/ vt tatouer. ● n tatouage m.

tatty /'tætɪ/ adj (**-ier, -iest**) 🇫🇷 miteux.

taught /tɔːt/ →TEACH.

taunt /tɔːnt/ vt railler. ● n raillerie f.

Taurus /'tɔːrəs/ n Taureau m.

tax /tæks/ n (on goods, services) taxe f; (on income) impôt m. ● vt imposer; (put to test: fig) mettre à l'épreuve. **taxable** adj imposable. **taxation** n imposition f; (taxes) impôts mpl.

tax: ~ **collector** n percepteur m. ~**-deductible** adj déductible des impôts. ~ **disc** n vignette f. ~**-free** adj exempt d'impôts. ~ **haven** n paradis m fiscal.

taxi /'tæksɪ/ n taxi m. ~ **rank** n station f de taxi.

tax: ~**payer** n contribuable mf. ~ **relief** n dégrèvement m fiscal. ~ **return** n déclaration f d'impôts.

tea /tiː/ n (drink, meal) thé m; (children's snack) goûter m; ~ **bag** sachet m de thé.

teach /tiːtʃ/ vt (pt **taught**) apprendre (**sb sth** qch à qn); (in school) enseigner (**sb sth** qch à qn). ● vi enseigner. **teacher** n enseignant/-e mf; (secondary) professeur m; (primary) instituteur/-trice mf.

team /tiːm/ n équipe f; (of animals) attelage m. ● vi ~ **up** faire équipe (**with** avec).

teapot /'tiːpɒt/ n théière f.

tear[1] /teə(r)/ vt/i (pt **tore**; pp **torn**) (se) déchirer; (snatch) arracher (**from** à); (rush) aller à toute vitesse. ● n déchirure f.

tear[2] /tɪə(r)/ n larme f; **in** ~**s** en larmes. ~**-gas** n gaz m lacrymogène.

tease /tiːz/ vt taquiner. ● n taquin/-e mf.

tea: ~ **shop** n salon m de thé. ~**spoon** n petite cuillère f.

teat /tiːt/ n tétine f.

tea-towel n torchon m.

technical /'teknɪkl/ adj technique.

technician /tek'nɪʃn/ n technicien/-ne mf.

technique /tek'niːk/ n technique f.

techno /'teknəʊ/ n (Mus) techno f.

technology /tek'nɒlədʒɪ/ n technologie f.

technophobe /teknʊ'fəʊb/ n technophobe mf.

teddy /'tedɪ/ adj ~ **bear** ours m en peluche.

tedious /'tiːdɪəs/ adj ennuyeux.

tee /tiː/ n (golf) tee m.

teenage /'tiːneɪdʒ/ adj (girl, boy) adolescent; (fashion) des adolescents. **teenager** n jeune mf, adolescent/-e mf.

teens /tiːnz/ npl **in one's** ~ adolescent.

teeth /tiːθ/ →TOOTH.

teethe /tiːð/ vi faire ses dents.

teetotaller /tiː'təʊtələ(r)/ n personne f qui ne boit pas d'alcool.

telecommunications /telɪkəmjuːnɪ'keɪʃnz/ npl télécommunications fpl.

telecommuting /telɪkə'mjuːtɪŋ/ n télétravail m.

teleconferencing /telɪ'kɒnfərənsɪŋ/ n téléconférence f.

telegram /'telɪɡræm/ n télégramme m.

telegraph /'telɪɡrɑːf/ n télégraphe m. ● adj télégraphique.

telephone /'telɪfəʊn/ n téléphone m. ● vt (person) téléphoner à; (message) téléphoner. ● vi téléphoner. ~ **book** annuaire m. ~ **booth,** ~ **box** n cabine f téléphonique. ~ **call** n coup m de téléphone. ~ **number** n numéro m de téléphone.

telephoto /telɪ'fəʊtəʊ/ adj ~ **lens** téléobjectif m.

telescope /'telɪskəʊp/ n télescope m. ● vt/i (se) télescoper.

teletext /'telɪtekst/ n télétexte m.

televise /'telɪvaɪz/ vt téléviser.

television /'telɪvɪʒn/ n télévision f; ~ **set** poste m de télévision, téléviseur m.

teleworking /'telɪwɜːkɪŋ/ n télétravail m.

telex /'teleks/ n télex m. ● vt envoyer par télex.

tell /tel/ vt (pt **told**) dire (**sb sth** qch à qn); (story) raconter; (distinguish) distinguer; **~ sb to do sth** dire à qn de faire qch; **~ sth from sth** voir la différence entre qch et qch. ● *vi* (*show*) avoir un effet; (*know*) savoir. □ **~ off** Ⓣ gronder.

temp /temp/ *n* intérimaire *mf*. ● *vi* faire de l'intérim.

temper /'tempə(r)/ *n* humeur *f*; (*anger*) colère *f*; **lose one's ~** se mettre en colère.

temperament /'temprəmənt/ *n* tempérament *m*. **temperamental** *adj* capricieux

temperature /'temprətʃə(r)/ *n* température *f*; **have a ~** avoir de la fièvre *or* de la température.

temple /'templ/ *n* temple *m*; (*of head*) tempe *f*.

temporary /'temprəri/ *adj* temporaire, provisoire.

tempt /tempt/ *vt* tenter; **~ sb to do** donner envie à qn de faire.

ten /ten/ *adj & n* dix (*m*).

tenacious /tɪ'neɪʃəs/ *adj* tenace.

tenancy /'tenənsɪ/ *n* location *f*. **tenant** *n* locataire *mf*.

tend /tend/ *vt* s'occuper de. ● *vi* **~ to** (be apt to) avoir tendance à; (look after) s'occuper de. **tendency** *n* tendance *f*.

tender /'tendə(r)/ *adj* tendre; (sore, painful) sensible. ● *vt* offrir, donner. ● *vi* faire une soumission. ● *n* (Comm) soumission *f*; **be legal ~** (money) avoir cours.

tendon /'tendən/ *n* tendon *m*.

tennis /'tenɪs/ *n* tennis *m*. ● *adj* (court, match) de tennis.

tenor /'tenə(r)/ *n* (meaning) sens *m* général; (Mus) ténor *m*.

tense /tens/ *n* (Gram) temps *m*. ● *adj* tendu. ● *vt* (muscles) tendre, raidir. ● *vi* (face) se crisper.

tension /'tenʃn/ *n* tension *f*.

tent /tent/ *n* tente *f*.

tentative /'tentətɪv/ *adj* provisoire; (hesitant) timide.

tenth /tenθ/ *adj & n* dixième (*mf*).

tepid /'tepɪd/ *adj* tiède.

term /tɜːm/ *n* (word, limit) terme *m*; (of imprisonment) temps *m*; (School) trimestre *m*; **~s** conditions *fpl*; **on good/ bad ~s** en bons/mauvais termes; **in the short/long ~** à court/long terme;

come to ~s with sth accepter qch; **~ of office** (Pol) mandat *m*. ● *vt* appeler.

terminal /'tɜːmɪnl/ *adj* (point) terminal; (illness) incurable. ● *n* (oil, computer) terminal *m*; (Rail) terminus *m*; (Electr) borne *f*; **air ~** aérogare *f*.

terminate /'tɜːmɪneɪt/ *vt* mettre fin à. ● *vi* prendre fin.

terminus /'tɜːmɪnəs/ *n* (pl **-ni**) (station) terminus *m*.

terrace /'terəs/ *n* terrasse *f*; (houses) rangée *f* de maisons contiguës; **the ~s** (Sport) les gradins *mpl*.

terracotta /terə'kɒtə/ *n* terre *f* cuite.

terrible /'terəbl/ *adj* affreux, atroce.

terrific /tə'rɪfɪk/ *adj* (huge) énorme; (great Ⓣ) formidable.

terrify /'terɪfaɪ/ *vt* terrifier; **be terrified of** avoir très peur de.

territory /'terətrɪ/ *n* territoire *m*.

terror /'terə(r)/ *n* terreur *f*.

terrorism /'terərɪzəm/ *n* terrorisme *m*. **terrorist** *n* terroriste *mf*.

test /test/ *n* épreuve *f*; (written exam) contrôle *m*; (of machine, product) essai *m*; (of sample) analyse *f*; **driving ~** examen *m* du permis de conduire. ● *vt* évaluer; (School) contrôler; (machine, product) essayer; (sample) analyser; (patience, strength) mettre à l'épreuve. ● *vi* **~ for** faire une recherche de.

testament /'testəmənt/ *n* testament *m*; **Old/New T~** Ancien/Nouveau Testament *m*.

testicle /'testɪkl/ *n* testicule *m*.

testify /'testɪfaɪ/ *vt/i* témoigner (**to** de; **that** que).

testimony /'testɪmənɪ/ *n* témoignage *m*.

test tube *n* éprouvette *f*.

tetanus /'tetənəs/ *n* tétanos *m*.

text /tekst/ *n* texte *m*. ● *vt* **~ sb** envoyer un texto à qn. **~book** *n* manuel *m*. **~ message** *n* texto *m*.

texture /'tekstʃə(r)/ *n* (of paper) grain *m*; (of fabric) texture *f*.

than /ðæn/, /ðən/ *conj* que, qu'; (with numbers) de; **more/less ~ ten** plus/ moins de dix.

thank /θæŋk/ *vt* remercier; **~ you!, ~s!** merci! **thankful** *adj* reconnaissant (for de). **thanks** *npl* remerciements *mpl*; ~**s to** grâce à. **Thanksgiving (Day)** *n* (US) jour *m* d'Action de Grâces.

---

that /ðæt/ *pl* **those**

● *determiner*

····▸ ce, cet, cette, ces; ~ **dog** ce chien; ~ **man** cet homme; ~ **woman** cette femme; **those books** ces livres; **at** ~ **moment** à ce moment-là.

❗ To distinguish **that/those** from **this/these**, you add *-là* to the noun: **I prefer that car** *je préfère cette voiture-là.*

● *pronoun*

····▸ cela, ça, ce; **what's** ~?, **what are those?** qu'est-ce que c'est (que ça)?; **who's** ~? qui est-ce?; ~ **is my brother** c'est *or* voilà mon frère; **those are my parents** ce sont mes parents.

····▸ (emphatic) celui-là, celle-là, ceux-là, celles-là; **all the dresses are nice but I like** ~/**those best** toutes les robes sont jolies mais je préfère celle-là/celles-là.

● *relative pronoun*

····▸ (*for subject*) qui; **the man** ~ **stole the car** l'homme qui a volé la voiture.

····▸ (*for object*) que; **the girl** ~ **I met** la fille que j'ai rencontrée.

❗ With a preposition, use *lequel/laquelle/lesquels/ lesquelles:* **the chair** ~ **I was sitting on** *la chaise sur laquelle j'étais assis.* With a preposition that translates as *à,* use *auquel/à laquelle/ auxquels/auxquelles:* **the girls** ~ **I was talking to** *les filles auxquelles je parlais.* With a preposition that translates as *de,* use *dont:* **the people** ~ **I've talked about** *les personnes dont j'ai parlé.*

● *conjunction* que; **she said** ~ **she would do it** elle a dit qu'elle le ferait.

---

thatched /'θætʃd/ *adj* de chaume; ~ **cottage** chaumière *f.*

thaw /θɔː/ *vt/i* (faire) dégeler; (*snow*) (faire) fondre. ● *n* dégel *m.*

---

the /ðə, ði:/ *determiner*

····▸ le, l', la, les; ~ **dog** le chien; ~ **tree** l'arbre; ~ **chair** la chaise; **to** ~ **shops** aux magasins.

❗ With a preposition that translates as *à:* à + le = au and à + les = aux.

---

theatre /'θɪətə(r)/ *n* théâtre *m.*

theft /θeft/ *n* vol *m.*

their /ðeə(r)/ *adj* leur, *pl* leurs.

theirs /ðeəz/ *pron* le *or* la leur, les leurs.

them /ðem/, /ðəm/ *pron* les; (*after preposition*) eux, elles; (**to**) ~ leur; **phone** ~! téléphone-leur!; **I know** ~ je les connais; **both of** ~ tous/toutes les deux.

theme /θiːm/ *n* **thème** *m.* ~ **park** *n* parc *m* de loisirs (à thème).

themselves /ðem'selvz/ *pron* eux-mêmes, elles-mêmes; (*reflexive*) se; (*after preposition*) eux, elles.

then /ðen/ *adv* alors; (*next*) ensuite, puis; (*therefore*) alors, donc. ● *adj* d'alors; **from** ~ **on** dès lors.

theology /θɪ'ɒlədʒɪ/ *n* théologie *f.*

theory /'θɪərɪ/ *n* théorie *f.*

therapy /'θerəpɪ/ *n* thérapie *f.*

there /ðeə(r)/ *adv* là; (*with verb*) y; (*over there*) là-bas; **he goes** ~ il y va; **on** ~ là-dessus; ~ **is,** ~ **are** il y a; (*pointing*) voilà. ● *interj* ~, ~! allons, allons!

therefore /'ðeəfɔː(r)/ *adv* donc.

thermal /'θɜːml/ *adj* thermique.

thermometer /θə'mɒmɪtə(r)/ *n* thermomètre *m.*

Thermos® /'θɜːməs/ *n* thermos ® *m or f inv.*

thermostat /'θɜːməstæt/ *n* thermostat *m.*

thesaurus /θɪ'sɔːrəs/ *n* (*pl* **-ri**) dictionnaire *m* de synonymes.

these /ðiːz/ ➡**THIS.**

thesis /'θiːsɪs/ *n* (*pl* **theses**) thèse *f.*

they /ðeɪ/ *pron* ils, elles; (emphatic) eux, elles; (people in general) on.

thick /θɪk/ *adj* épais; (stupid) bête; **be 6 cm** ~ avoir 6 cm d'épaisseur.

t

thief /θi:f/ *n* (*pl* **thieves**) voleur/-
euse *m/f.*

thigh /θaɪ/ *n* cuisse *f.*

thin /θɪn/ *adj* (**thinner, thinnest**)
mince; (*person*) maigre, mince;
(*sparse*) clairsemé; (*fine*) fin. ● *vt/i* (*pt*
thinned) ~ (**down**) (*paint*) diluer;
(*soup*) allonger.

thing /θɪŋ/ *n* chose *f;* ~**s** (*belongings*)
affaires *fpl;* **the best** ~ **is to** le mieux
est de; **the (right)** ~ ce qu'il faut (**for**
sb à qn).

think /θɪŋk/ *vt/i* (*pt* **thought**) penser
(**about, of** à); (*carefully*) réfléchir
(**about, of** à); (*believe*) croire; **I** ~ **so**
je crois que oui; ~ **of doing** envisager
de faire. □ ~ **over** bien réfléchir à;
□ ~ **up** inventer.

third /θɜːd/ *adj* troisième. ● *n* troisième
mf; (*fraction*) tiers *m.* **T**~ **World** *n*
tiers-monde *m.*

thirst /θɜːst/ *n* soif *f.*

thirsty /ˈθɜːstɪ/ *adj* **be** ~ avoir soif;
make ~ donner soif à.

thirteen /θɜːˈtiːn/ *adj & n* treize (*m*).

thirty /ˈθɜːtɪ/ *adj & n* trente (*m*).

---

this /ðɪs/*pl* **these**

● *determiner*

····▸ ce/cet/cette/ces; ~ **dog** ce
chien; ~ **man** cet homme; ~
woman cette femme; **these**
books ces livres.

> ❗ To distinguish from **that** and
> **those**, you need to add -*ci*
> after the noun: **I prefer this car**
> je préfère cette voiture-ci.

● *pronoun*

····▸ ce; **what's** ~**?, what are**
these? qu'est-ce que c'est?; **who**
is ~**?** qui est-ce?; ~ **is the**
kitchen voici la cuisine; ~ **is So-**
phie je te *or* vous présente Sophie; **these are your things** ce
sont tes affaires.

····▸ (*emphatic*) celui-ci/celle-
ci/ceux-ci/celles-ci; **all the dresses**
are nice but I like ~/**these best**
toutes les robes sont jolies mais je
préfère celle-ci/celles-ci.

---

thistle /ˈθɪsl/ *n* chardon *m.*

thorn /θɔːn/ *n* épine *f.*

thorough /ˈθʌrə/ *adj* (*detailed*) approfondi; (*meticulous*) minutieux. **thor-**
oughly *adv* (*clean, study*) à fond;
(*very*) tout à fait.

those /ðəʊz/ ➡THAT.

though /ðəʊ/ *conj* bien que. ● *adv*
quand même.

thought /θɔːt/ ➡THINK. ● *n* pensée *f,*
idée *f.* **thoughtful** *adj* pensif; (*kind*)
prévenant.

thousand /ˈθaʊznd/ *adj & n* mille (*m*
inv); ~**s of** des milliers de. **thou-**
sandth *adj & n* millième (*mf*).

thread /θred/ *n* (*yarn & fig*) fil *m;* (*of*
screw) pas *m.* ● *vt* enfiler; ~ **one's**
way se faufiler.

threat /θret/ *n* menace *f.* **threaten** *vt/i*
menacer (**with** de).

three /θriː/ *adj & n* trois (*m*).

threw /θruː/ ➡THROW.

thrill /θrɪl/ *n* frisson *m;* (*pleasure*) plaisir *m.* ● *vt* transporter (de joie); **be**
~**ed** être ravi. ● *vi* frissonner (de joie).

thrive /θraɪv/ *vi* (*pt* **thrived** *or* **thro-**
ve;pp thrived *or* **thriven**) prospérer;
he ~**s on it** cela lui réussit.

throat /θrəʊt/ *n* gorge *f;* **have a sore**
~ avoir mal à la gorge.

throb /θrɒb/ *vi* (*pt* **throbbed**) (*heart*)
battre; (*engine*) vibrer. ● *n* (*pain*) élancement *m;* (*of engine*) vibration *f.*
throbbing *adj* (*pain*) lancinant.

throne /θrəʊn/ *n* trône *m.*

through /θruː/ *prep* à travers; (*during*)
pendant; (*by means of*) au moyen de, out of)
par; (*by reason of*) grâce à, à cause
de. ● *adv* à travers; (*entirely*) jusqu'au
bout. ● *adj* (*train*) direct; **be** ~ (*fin-*
ished) avoir fini; **come** *or* **go** ~ (*cross,*
pierce) traverser; **I'm putting you** ~
je vous passe votre correspondant.

throughout /θruːˈaʊt/ *prep* ~ **the**
country dans tout le pays; ~ **the day**
pendant toute la journée. ● *adv*
(*place*) partout; (*time*) tout le temps.

throw /θrəʊ/ *vt* (*pt* **threw**; *pp* **thrown**)
jeter, lancer; (*baffle*) déconcerter; ~ **a**
party faire une fête. ● *n* jet *m;* (*of*
dice) coup *m.* □ **away** jeter; **off** (*get*
rid of) se débarrasser de; ~ **out** jeter;
(*person*) expulser; (*reject*) rejeter; ~
up (*arms*) lever; (*vomit* ⚊) vomir.

thrust /θrʌst/ *vt* (*pt* **thrust**) pousser.
● *n* poussée *f.*

t

thud /θʌd/ n bruit m sourd.

thug /θʌg/ n voyou m.

thumb /θʌm/ n pouce m. ● vt (book) feuilleter; ~ **a lift** faire de l'autostop. ~**-index** n répertoire m à onglets.

thump /θʌmp/ vt/i cogner (sur); (heart) battre fort. ● n coup m.

thunder /'θʌndə(r)/ n tonnerre m. ● vi (weather, person) tonner. ~**storm** n orage m.

Thursday /'θɜːzdeɪ/ n jeudi m.

thus /ðʌs/ adv ainsi.

thwart /θwɔːt/ vt contrecarrer.

thyme /taɪm/ n thym m.

tick /tɪk/ n (sound) tic-tac m; (mark) coche f; (moment 🔲) instant m; (insect) tique f. ● vi faire tic-tac. ● vt (~ off) cocher. □ ~ **over** tourner au ralenti.

ticket /'tɪkɪt/ n billet m; (for bus, cloakroom) ticket m; (label) étiquette f. ~**-collector** n contrôleur/-euse m/f. ~**-office** n guichet m.

tickle /'tɪkl/ vt chatouiller; (amuse: fig) amuser. ● n chatouillement m.

tidal /'taɪdl/ adj (river) à marées; ~ **wave** raz-de-marée m inv.

tide /taɪd/ n marée f; (of events) cours m.

tidy /'taɪdɪ/ adj (-ier, -iest) (room) bien rangé; (appearance, work) soigné; (methodical) ordonné; (amount 🔲) joli. ● vt/i ~ (**up**) faire du rangement; ~ **sth** (**up**) ranger qch; ~ **oneself up** s'arranger.

tie /taɪ/ vt (pres p **tying**) attacher; (knot) faire; (scarf) nouer; (link) lier. ● vi (in football) faire match nul; (in race) être ex aequo. ● n (necktie) cravate f; (fastener) attache f; (link) lien m; (draw) match m nul. ~ **down** attacher; ~ **in with** être lié à; ~ **up** attacher; (money) immobiliser; (occupy) occuper.

tier /tɪə(r)/ n étage m, niveau m; (in stadium) gradin m.

tiger /'taɪgə(r)/ n tigre m.

tight /taɪt/ adj (clothes, budget) serré; (grip) ferme; (rope) tendu; (security) strict; (angle) aigu. ● adv (hold, sleep) bien; (squeeze) fort.

tighten /'taɪtn/ vt/i (se) tendre; (bolt) (se) resserrer; (control) renforcer.

tights /taɪts/ npl collant m.

tile /taɪl/ n (on wall, floor) carreau m; (on roof) tuile f. ● vt carreler; couvrir de tuiles.

till /tɪl/ n caisse f (enregistreuse). ● vt (land) cultiver. ● prep & conj ➡UNTIL.

timber /'tɪmbə(r)/ n bois m (de construction); (trees) arbres mpl.

time /taɪm/ n temps m; (moment) moment m; (epoch) époque f; (by clock) heure f; (occasion) fois f; (rhythm) mesure f; ~**s** (multiplying) fois fpl; any ~ n'importe quand; **for the** ~ **being** pour le moment; **from** ~ **to** ~ de temps en temps; **have a good** ~ s'amuser; **in no** ~ en un rien de temps; **in** ~ à temps; (eventually) avec le temps; **a long** ~ longtemps; **on** ~ à l'heure; **what's the** ~? quelle heure est-il?; ~ **off** du temps libre. ● vt choisir le moment de; (measure) minuter; (Sport) chronométrer. ~ **limit** n délai m.

timer /'taɪmə(r)/ n minuterie f; (for cooker) minuteur m.

time: ~**-scale** n délais mpl. ~**table** n horaire m. ~ **zone** n fuseau m horaire.

timid /'tɪmɪd/ adj timide; (fearful) peureux.

tin /tɪn/ n étain m; (container) boîte f; ~**(plate)** fer-blanc m. ● vt (pt **tinned**) mettre en boîte. ~**foil** n papier m d'aluminium.

tingle /'tɪŋgl/ vi picoter. ● n picotement m.

tin-opener n ouvre-boîtes m inv.

tint /tɪnt/ n teinte f; (for hair) shampooing m colorant. ● vt teinter.

tiny /'taɪnɪ/ adj (-ier, -iest) tout petit.

tip /tɪp/ n (of stick, pen, shoe, ski) pointe f; (of nose, finger, wing) bout m; (gratuity) pourboire m; (advice) tuyau m; (for rubbish) décharge f. ● vt/i (pt **tipped**) (tilt) pencher; (overturn) (faire) basculer; (pour) verser; (empty) déverser; (give money) donner un pourboire à. □ ~ **off** prévenir.

tiptoe /'tɪptəʊ/ n on ~ sur la pointe des pieds.

tire /'taɪə(r)/ vt/i (se) fatiguer; ~ **of** se lasser de. ● n (US) pneu m.

tired /'taɪəd/ adj fatigué; **be** ~ **of** en avoir assez de.

tiring /'taɪərɪŋ/ adj fatigant.

tissue /'tɪʃuː/ n tissu m; (handkerchief) mouchoir m en papier; ~ **(paper)** papier m de soie.

tit /tɪt/ n (bird) mésange f; **give** ~ **for tat** rendre coup pour coup.

title /'taɪtl/ n titre m. ~ **deed** n titre m de propriété.

---

to /tuː, tə/

● preposition

····▸ à; ~ **Paris** à Paris; **give the book** ~ **Jane** donne le livre à Jane; ~ **the office** au bureau; ~ **the shops** aux magasins.

····▸ (with feminine countries) en; ~ **France** en France.

····▸ (to + personal pronoun) me/te/lui/nous/vous/leur; **she gave it** ~ **them** elle le leur a donné; **I'll say it** ~ **her** je vais le lui dire.

! à + le = au
! à + les = aux.

● in an infinitive

to is not translated (**to go** aller; **to sing** chanter)

····▸ (in order to) pour; **he's gone into town** ~ **buy a shirt** il est parti en ville pour acheter une chemise.

····▸ (after adjectives) à; de; **be easy/difficult** ~ **read** être facile/difficile à lire; **it's easy/difficult to read her writing** c'est facile/difficile de lire son écriture.

➡ For verbal expressions using the infinitive 'to' such as **to tell sb to do sth, to help sb to do sth** ➡**tell, help.**

---

toad /təʊd/ n crapaud m.

toast /təʊst/ n pain m grillé, toast m; (drink) toast m. ● vt (bread) faire griller; (drink to) porter un toast à. **toaster** n grille-pain m inv.

tobacco /tə'bækəʊ/ n tabac m.

tobacconist /tə'bækənɪst/ n marchand/-e m/f de tabac; ~**'s (shop)** tabac m.

toboggan /tə'bɒgən/ n toboggan m, luge f.

today /tə'deɪ/ n & adv aujourd'hui (m).

toddler /'tɒdlə(r)/ n bébé m (qui fait ses premiers pas).

toe /təʊ/ n orteil m; (of shoe) bout m; **on one's** ~**s** vigilant. ● vt ~ **the line** se conformer.

together /tə'geðə(r)/ adv ensemble; (at same time) à la fois; ~ **with** avec.

toilet /'tɔɪlɪt/ n toilettes fpl.

toiletries /'tɔɪlɪtrɪz/ npl articles mpl de toilette.

token /'təʊkən/ n (symbol) témoignage m; (voucher) bon m; (coin) jeton m. ● adj symbolique.

told /təʊld/ →**TELL.**

tolerance /'tɒlərəns/ n tolérance f.

tolerate /'tɒləreɪt/ vt tolérer.

toll /təʊl/ n péage m; **death** ~ nombre m de morts; **take its** ~ faire des ravages. ● vi (bell) sonner.

tomato /tə'mɑːtəʊ/ n (pl ~**es**) tomate f.

tomb /tuːm/ n tombeau m.

tomorrow /tə'mɒrəʊ/ n & adv demain (m); ~ **morning/night** demain matin/soir; **the day after** ~ après-demain.

ton /tʌn/ n tonne f (= 1016 kg); **(metric)** ~ tonne f (= 1000 kg); ~**s of** 🔲 des masses de.

tone /təʊn/ n ton m; (of radio, telephone) tonalité f. ● vt ~ **down** atténuer. ● vi ~ **(in)** s'harmoniser (**with** avec).

tongs /tɒŋz/ npl (for coal) pincettes fpl; (for sugar) pince f; (for hair) fer m.

tongue /tʌŋ/ n langue f.

tonic /'tɒnɪk/ n (Med) tonique m. ● adj (effect, accent) tonique; ~ **(water)** tonic m, Schweppes® m.

tonight /tə'naɪt/ n & adv (evening) ce soir; (night) cette nuit.

tonsil /'tɒnsl/ n amygdale f.

too /tuː/ adv trop; (also) aussi; ~ **many people** trop de gens; **I've got** ~**much/many** j'en ai trop; **me** ~ moi aussi.

took→**TAKE.**

tool /tuːl/ n outil m. ~**bar** n barre f d'outils. ~**box** n boîte f à outils.

toot /tuːt/ n coup m de klaxon®. ● vt/i ~ **(the horn)** klaxonner.

tooth /tuːθ/ n (pl **teeth**) dent f. ~**ache** n mal m de dents. ~**brush** n brosse f à dents. ~**paste** n dentifrice m.

~**pick** n cure-dents m inv.

top /tɒp/ n (highest point) sommet m; (upper part) haut m; (upper surface) dessus m; (lid) couvercle m; (of bottle, tube) bouchon m; (of beer bottle) capsule f; (of list) tête f; **on ~ of** sur; (fig) en plus de. ● adj (shelf) du haut; (step, floor) dernier; (in rank) premier; (best) meilleur; (distinguished) éminent; (maximum) maximum. ● vt (pt **topped**) (exceed) dépasser; (list) venir en tête de; **~ up** remplir; **~ped with** (dome) surmonté de; (cream) recouvert de.

topic /'tɒpɪk/ n sujet m.

topless /'tɒplɪs/ adj aux seins nus.

torch /tɔːtʃ/ n (electric) lampe f de poche; (flaming) torche f.

tore /tɔː(r)/ ➡TEAR¹.

torment /tɔː'ment/ vt tourmenter.

torn /tɔːn/ ➡TEAR¹.

torrent /'tɒrənt/ n torrent m.

tortoise /'tɔːtəs/ n tortue f. **~shell** n écaille f.

torture /'tɔːtʃə(r)/ n torture f; (fig) supplice m. ● vt torturer.

Tory /'tɔːrɪ/ n & a tory (mf), conservateur/-trice (mf).

toss /tɒs/ vt lancer; (salad) tourner; (pancake) faire sauter. ● vi se retourner; **~ a coin**, **~ up** tirer à pile ou face (**for** pour).

tot /tɒt/ n petit/-e enfant m/f; (drink) petit verre m.

total /'təʊtl/ n & a total (m). ● vt (pt **totalled**) (add up) additionner; (amount to) se monter à.

touch /tʌtʃ/ vt toucher; (tamper with) toucher à. ● vi se toucher. ● n (sense) toucher m; (contact) contact m; (of artist, writer) touche f; **a ~of** (small amount) un petit peu de; **get in ~ with** se mettre en contact avec; **out of ~ with** déconnecté de. □ **~ down** (Aviat) atterrir; **~ up** retoucher. **~down** n atterrissage m; (Sport) essai m. **~ line** n ligne f de touche.**~tone** adj (phone) à touches.

tough /tʌf/ adj (negotiator) coriace; (law) sévère; (time) difficile; (robust) robuste.

tour /tʊə(r)/ n voyage m; (visit) visite f; (by team) tournée f; **on ~** en tournée. ● vt visiter.

tourist /'tʊərɪst/ n touriste mf. ● adj touristique. **~ office** n syndicat m d'initiative.

tournament /'tɔːnəmənt/ n tournoi m.

tout /taʊt/ vi **~ (for)** racoler ⬛. ● vt (sell) revendre. ● n racoleur/-euse m/f; revendeur/-euse m/f.

tow /təʊ/ vt remorquer. ● n remorque f; **on ~** en remorque.

toward(s) /tə'wɔːd(z)/ prep vers; (of attitude) envers.

towel /'taʊəl/ n serviette f.

tower /'taʊə(r)/ n tour f. ● vi **~ above** dominer.

town /taʊn/ n ville f; **in ~** en ville. **~ council** n conseil m municipal. **~ hall** n mairie f.

tow: ~ path n chemin m de halage. **~ truck** n dépanneuse f.

toxic /'tɒksɪk/ adj toxique.

toy /tɔɪ/ n jouet m. ● vi **~ with** (object) jouer avec; (idea) caresser.

trace /treɪs/ n trace f. ● vt (person) retrouver; (cause) déterminer; (life) retracer; (draw) tracer; (with tracing paper) décalquer.

track /træk/ n (of person, car) traces fpl; (of missile) trajectoire f; (path) sentier m; (Sport) piste f; (Rail) voie f; (on disc) morceau m; **keep ~ of** suivre. ● vt suivre la trace or la trajectoire de. □ **~ down** retrouver. **~ suit** n survêtement m.

tractor /'træktə(r)/ n tracteur m.

trade /treɪd/ n commerce m; (job) métier m; (swap) échange m. ● vi faire du commerce; **~on** exploiter. ● vt échanger. ● adj (route, deficit) commercial. **~-in** n reprise f. **~ mark** n marque f (de fabrique); (registered) marque f déposée.

trader /'treɪdə(r)/ n commerçant/-e m/f; (on stockmarket) opérateur/-trice m/f.

trade union n syndicat m.

trading /'treɪdɪŋ/ n commerce m; (on stockmarket) transactions fpl (boursières).

tradition /trə'dɪʃn/ n tradition f.

traffic /'træfɪk/ n trafic m; (on road) circulation f. ● vi (pt **trafficked**) faire du trafic (**in** de). **~ jam** n embouteillage m. **~-lights** npl feux mpl (de circulation). ~ **warden** contractuel/-le *m/f.*

trail /treɪl/ *vt/i* traîner; (*plant*) ramper; (*track*) suivre; ~ **behind** traîner. ● *n* (of powder) traînée *f*; (track) piste *f*; (path) sentier *m.*

trailer /'treɪlə(r)/ *n* remorque *f*; (caravan) caravane *f*; (film) bande-annonce *f.*

train /treɪn/ *n* (Rail) train *m*; (underground) rame *f*; (procession) file *f*; (of dress) traîne *f.* ● *vt* (instruct, develop) former; (*sportsman*) entraîner; (*animal*) dresser; (*ear*) exercer; (*aim*) braquer. ● *vi* être formé, étudier; (Sport) s'entraîner. **trained** *adj* (skilled) qualifié; (*doctor*) diplômé. **trainee** *n* stagiaire *mf.* **trainer** *n* (Sport) entraîneur/-euse *m/f.* **trainers** *npl* (shoes) chaussures *fpl* de sport. **training** *n* formation *f*; (Sport) entraînement *m.*

tram /træm/ *n* tram(way) *m.*

tramp /træmp/ *vi* marcher (d'un pas lourd). ● *vt* parcourir. ● *n* (vagrant) clochard/-e *m/f*; (sound) bruit *m.*

trample /'træmpl/ *vt/i* ~ (**on**) piétiner; (fig) fouler aux pieds.

tranquil /'træŋkwɪl/ *adj* tranquille. **tranquillizer** *n* tranquillisant *m.*

transact /træn'zækt/ *vt* négocier. **transaction** *n* transaction *f.*

transcript /'trænskrɪpt/ *n* transcription *f.*

transfer[1] /træns'fɜ:(r)/ *vt* (*pt* **transferred**) transférer; (*power*) céder; (*employee*) muter. ● *vi* être transféré; (*employee*) être muté.

transfer[2] /'trænsfɜ:(r)/ *n* transfert *m*; (of employee) mutation *f*; (image) décalcomanie *f.*

transform /træns'fɔ:m/ *vt* transformer.

transitive /'trænzətɪv/ *adj* transitif.

translate /trænz'leɪt/ *vt* traduire. **translation** *n* traduction *f.* **translator** *n* traducteur/-trice *m/f.*

transmit /trænz'mɪt/ *vt* (*pt* **transmitted**) transmettre. **transmitter** *n* émetteur *m.*

transparency /træns'pærənsɪ/ *n* transparence *f*; (Photo) diapositive *f.*

transplant /træns'plɑ:nt/ *n* transplantation *f*; (Med) greffe *f.*

transport[1] /træns'pɔ:t/ *vt* transporter.

transport[2] /'trænspɔ:t/ *n* transport *m.*

trap /træp/ *n* piège *m.* ● *vt pt* **trapped** (jam, pin down) coincer; (cut off) bloquer; (snare) prendre au piège.

trash /træʃ/ *n* (refuse) ordures *fpl*; (nonsense) idioties *fpl.* ~**-can** *n* (US) poubelle *f.*

trauma /'trɔ:mə/ *n* traumatisme *m.* **traumatic** *adj* traumatisant.

travel /'trævl/ *vi* (*pt* **travelled**, US **traveled**) voyager; (*vehicle, bullet*) aller. ● *vt* parcourir. ● *n* voyages *mpl.* ~ **agency** *n* agence *f* de voyages.

traveller, (US) **traveler** /'trævlə(r)/ *n* voyageur/-euse *m/f*; ~**'s cheque** chèque *m* de voyage.

trawler /'trɔ:lə(r)/ *n* chalutier *m.*

tray /treɪ/ *n* plateau *m*; (on office desk) corbeille *f.*

treacle /'tri:kl/ *n* mélasse *f.*

tread /tred/ *vi* (*pt* **trod**, *pp* **trodden**) marcher (**on** sur). ● *vt* fouler. ● *n* (sound) pas *m*; (of tyre) chape *f.*

treasure /'treʒə(r)/ *n* trésor *m.* ● *vt* (*gift, memory*) chérir; (*friendship, possession*) tenir beaucoup à.

treasury /'treʒərɪ/ *n* trésorerie *f*; **the** T~ le ministère des Finances.

treat /tri:t/ *vt* traiter; ~ **sb to sth** offrir qch à qn. ● *n* (pleasure) plaisir *m*; (food) gâterie *f.* **treatment** *n* traitement *m.*

treaty /'tri:tɪ/ *n* traité *m.*

treble /'trebl/ *adj* triple; ~ **clef** clé *f* de sol. ● *vt/i* tripler. ● *n* (voice) soprano *m.*

tree /tri:/ *n* arbre *m.*

trek /trek/ *n* randonnée *f.* ● *vi* (*pt* **trekked**) ~ **across/through** traverser péniblement; **go** ~**king** faire de la randonnée.

tremble /'trembl/ *vi* trembler.

tremendous /trɪ'mendəs/ *adj* énorme; (excellent) formidable.

tremor /'tremə(r)/ *n* tremblement *m*; (earth) ~ secousse *f.*

trench /trentʃ/ *n* tranchée *f.*

trend /trend/ *n* tendance *f*; (fashion) mode *f.* **trendy** *adj* 🔳 branché 🔳.

trespass /'trespəs/ *vi* s'introduire illégalement (**on** dans). **trespasser** *n* intrus/-e *m/f.*

trial /'traɪəl/ *n* (Jur) procès *m*; (test) essai *m*; (ordeal) épreuve *f*; **go on** ~

passer en jugement; **by ~ and error** par expérience.

triangle /'traɪæŋgl/ n triangle m.

tribe /traɪb/ n tribu f.

tribunal /traɪ'bjuːnl/ n tribunal m.

tributary /'trɪbjʊtərɪ/ n affluent m.

tribute /'trɪbjuːt/ n tribut m; **pay ~ to** rendre hommage à.

trick /trɪk/ n tour m; (dishonest) combine f; (knack) astuce f; **do the ~** 🔲 faire l'affaire. ● vt tromper. **trickery** n ruse f.

trickle /'trɪkl/ vi dégouliner; **~ in/out** arriver or partir en petit nombre. ● n filet m; (fig) petit nombre m.

tricky /'trɪkɪ/ adj (task) difficile; (question) épineux; (person) malin.

trifle /'traɪfl/ n bagatelle f; (cake) diplomate m; **a ~** (small amount) un peu. ● vi **~ with** jouer avec.

trigger /'trɪgə(r)/ n (of gun) gâchette f; (of machine) manette f. ● vt **~ (off)** (initiate) déclencher.

trim /trɪm/ adj (**trimmer, trimmest**) soigné; (figure) svelte. ● vt (pt **trimmed**) (hair, grass) couper; (budget) réduire; (decorate) décorer. ● n (cut) coupe f d'entretien; (decoration) garniture f; **in ~** en forme.

trinket /'trɪŋkɪt/ n babiole f.

trip /trɪp/ vt/i (pt **tripped**) (faire) trébucher. ● n (journey) voyage m; (outing) excursion f.

triple /'trɪpl/ adj triple. ● vt/i tripler. **triplets** npl triplés/-es m/fpl.

tripod /'traɪpɒd/ n trépied m.

trite /traɪt/ adj banal.

triumph /'traɪʌmf/ n triomphe m. ● vi triompher (**over de**).

trivial /'trɪvɪəl/ adj insignifiant.

trod, trodden /trɒd(ən)/ ➡TREAD.

trolley /'trɒlɪ/ n chariot m.

trombone /trɒm'bəʊn/ n (Mus) trombone m.

troop /truːp/ n bande f; **~s** (Mil) troupes fpl. ● vi **~ in/out** entrer/sortir en bande.

trophy /'trəʊfɪ/ n trophée m.

tropic /'trɒpɪk/ n tropique m; **~s** tropiques mpl.

trot /trɒt/ n trot m; **on the ~** 🔲 coup sur coup. ● vi (pt **trotted**) trotter.

trouble /'trʌbl/ n problèmes mpl ; ennuis mpl; (pains, effort) peine f; **be in ~** avoir des ennuis; **go to a lot of ~** se donner du mal; **what's the ~?** quel est le problème? ● vt (bother) déranger; (worry) tracasser. ● vi **~ (oneself) to do** se donner la peine de faire. **~maker** n provocateur/-trice m/f. **~shooter** n conciliateur/-trice m/f; (Tech) expert m.

troublesome /'trʌblsəm/ adj ennuyeux.

trousers /'traʊzəz/ npl pantalon m; **short ~** short m.

trout /traʊt/ n inv truite f.

trowel /'traʊəl/ n (garden) déplantoir m; (for mortar) truelle f.

truant /'truːənt/ n (School) élève mf qui fait l'école buissonnière; **play ~** sécher les cours.

truce /truːs/ n trève f.

truck /trʌk/ n (lorry) camion m; (cart) chariot m; (Rail) wagon m de marchandises. **~driver** n routier m.

true /truː/ adj vrai; (accurate) exact; (faithful) fidèle.

truffle /'trʌfl/ n truffe f.

truly /'truːlɪ/ adv vraiment; (faithfully) fidèlement; (truthfully) sincèrement.

trumpet /'trʌmpɪt/ n trompette f.

trunk /trʌŋk/ n (of tree, body) tronc m; (of elephant) trompe f; (box) malle f; (Auto, US) coffre m; **~s** (for swimming) slip m de bain.

trust /trʌst/ n confiance f; (association) trust m; **in ~** en dépôt. ● vt avoir confiance en; **~ sb with** confier à qn. ● vi **~ in** or **to** s'en remettre à. **trustee** n administrateur/-trice m/f. **trustworthy** adj digne de confiance.

truth /truːθ/ n (pl **-s**) vérité f. **truthful** adj (account) véridique; (person) qui dit la vérité.

try /traɪ/ vt/i (pt **tried**) essayer; (be a strain on) éprouver; (Jur) juger; **~ on** or **out** essayer; **~ to do** essayer de faire. ● n (attempt) essai m; (rugby) essai m.

T-shirt /'tiːʃɜːt/ n tee-shirt m.

tub /tʌb/ n (for flowers) bac m; (of ice cream) pot m; (bath) baignoire f.

tube /tjuːb/ n tube m; **the ~** 🔲 le métro.

t

tuberculosis /tjuːbɜːkjʊˈləʊsɪs/ n tuberculose f.

tuck /tʌk/ n pli m. ● vt (put away, place) ranger; (hide) cacher. ● vi ~ in or into 🄵 attaquer; ~ in (shirt) rentrer; (blanket, person) border.

Tuesday /ˈtjuːzdeɪ/ n mardi m.

tug /tʌɡ/ vt (pt **tugged**) tirer. ● vi ~ at/on tirer sur. ● n (boat) remorqueur m.

tuition /tjuːˈɪʃn/ n cours mpl; (fee) frais mpl pédagogiques.

tulip /ˈtjuːlɪp/ n tulipe f.

tumble /ˈtʌmbl/ vi (fall) dégringoler. ● n chute f. ~-**drier** n sèche-linge m inv.

tumbler /ˈtʌmblə(r)/ n verre m droit.

tummy /ˈtʌmɪ/ n 🄵 ventre m.

tumour /ˈtjuːmə(r)/ n tumeur f.

tuna /ˈtjuːnə/ n inv thon m.

tune /tjuːn/ n air m; **be in** ~/**out of** ~ (instrument) être/ne pas être en accord; (singer) chanter juste/faux. ● vt (engine) régler; (Mus) accorder. ● vi ~ in (to) (radio),TV écouter. □ ~ up s'accorder.

Tunisia /tjuːˈnɪzɪə/ n Tunisie f.

tunnel /ˈtʌnl/ n tunnel m; (in mine) galerie f. ● vi (pt **tunnelled**) creuser un tunnel (into dans).

turf /tɜːf/ n (pl **turf** or **turves**) gazon m; **the** ~ (racing) le turf. ● vt~ **out** 🄵 jeter dehors.

Turk /tɜːk/ n Turc m, Turque f. **Turkey** n Turquie f.

turkey /ˈtɜːkɪ/ n dinde f.

Turkish /ˈtɜːkɪʃ/ adj turc. ● n (Ling) turc m.

turn /tɜːn/ vt/i tourner; (person) se tourner; (to other side) retourner; (change) (se) transformer (**into** en); (become) devenir; (deflect) détourner; (milk) tourner. ● n tour m; (in road) tournant m; (of mind, events) tournure f; **do a good** ~ rendre service; **in** ~ à tour de rôle; **take** ~**s** se relayer. □ ~ **against** se retourner contre; ~ **away** vi se détourner; vt (avert) détourner; (refuse) refuser; (send back) renvoyer; ~ **back** vi (return) retourner; (vehicle) faire demitour; vt (fold) rabattre; ~ **down** refuser; (fold) rabattre; (reduce) baisser; ~ **off** (light) éteindre; (engine) arrêter; (tap) fermer; (of driver) tour-

ner; ~ **on** (light) allumer; (engine) allumer; (tap) ouvrir; ~ **out** vt (light) éteindre; (empty) vider; (produce) produire; vi **it** ~**s out that** il se trouve que; ~ **out well**/**badly** bien/mal se terminer; ~ **over** (se) retourner; ~ **round** (person) se retourner; ~ **up** vi arriver; (be found) se retrouver; vt (find) déterrer; (collar) remonter.

turning /ˈtɜːnɪŋ/ n rue f; (bend) virage m.

turnip /ˈtɜːnɪp/ n navet m.

turn: ~**out** n assistance f. ~**over** n (pie) chausson m; (money) chiffre m d'affaires. ~**table** n (for record) platine f.

turquoise /ˈtɜːkwɔɪz/ adj turquoise inv.

turtle /ˈtɜːtl/ n tortue f (de mer). ~-**neck** n col m montant.

tutor /ˈtjuːtə(r)/ n (private) professeur m particulier; (Univ) (GB) chargé/-e m/f de travaux dirigés.

tutorial /tjuːˈtɔːrɪəl/ n (Univ) classe f de travaux dirigés.

tuxedo /tʌkˈsiːdəʊ/ n (US) smoking m.

TV /tiːˈviː/ n télé f.

tweezers /ˈtwiːzəz/ npl pince f (à épiler).

twelfth /twelfθ/ adj & n douzième (mf).

twelve /twelv/ adj & n douze (m); ~ (o'clock) midi m or minuit m.

twentieth /ˈtwentɪəθ/ adj & n vingtième (mf).

twenty /ˈtwentɪ/ adj & n vingt (m).

twice /twaɪs/ adv deux fois.

twig /twɪɡ/ n brindille f.

twilight /ˈtwaɪlaɪt/ n crépuscule m. ● adj crépusculaire.

twin /twɪn/ n & adj jumeau/-elle (m/f).● vt (pt **twinned**) jumeler.

twinge /twɪndʒ/ n (of pain) élancement m; (of conscience, doubt) accès m.

twinkle /ˈtwɪŋkl/ vi (star) scintiller; (eye) pétiller. ● n scintillement m; pétillement m.

twinning /ˈtwɪnɪŋ/ n jumelage m.

twist /twɪst/ vt tordre; (weave together) entortiller; (roll) enrouler; (distort) déformer. ● vi (rope) s'entortiller; (road) zigzaguer. ● n torsion f; (in rope) tortillon m; (in road) tournant m; (in play, story) coup m de théâtre.

t

twitch /twɪtʃ/ vi (person) trembloter; (mouth) trembler; (string) vibrer.● n (tic) tic m; (jerk) secousse f.

two /tuː/ adj & n deux (m); **in ~s** par deux; **break in ~** casser en deux.

tycoon /taɪˈkuːn/ n magnat m.

type /taɪp/ n type m, genre m; (print) caractères mpl. ● vt/i (write) taper (à la machine). **~face** n police f (de caractères). **~writer** n machine f à écrire.

typical /ˈtɪpɪkl/ adj typique.

typist /ˈtaɪpɪst/ n dactylo mf.

tyrant /ˈtaɪərənt/ n tyran m.

tyre /ˈtaɪə(r)/ n pneu m.

....

Uu

....

udder /ˈʌdə(r)/ n pis m, mamelle f.

UFO /ˈjuːfəʊ/ n OVNI m inv.

UHT abbr **ultra heat treated ~ milk** lait m longue conservation.

ugly /ˈʌɡlɪ/ adj (**-ier, -iest**) laid.

UK abbr ➞**UNITED KINGDOM.**

Ukraine /juːˈkreɪn/ n Ukraine f.

ulcer /ˈʌlsə(r)/ n ulcère m.

ulterior /ʌlˈtɪərɪə(r)/ adj ultérieur; **~ motive** arrière-pensée f.

ultimate /ˈʌltɪmət/ adj dernier, ultime; (definitive) définitif; (basic) fondamental.

ultrasound /ˈʌltrəsaʊnd/ n ultrason m.

umbilical cord /ʌmˈbɪlɪkl kɔːd/ n cordon m ombilical.

umbrella /ʌmˈbrelə/ n parapluie m.

umpire /ˈʌmpaɪə(r)/ n arbitre m. ● vt arbitrer.

umpteenth /ˈʌmptiːnθ/ adj 🄲 énième.

UN abbr (**United Nations**) ONU f.

unable /ʌnˈeɪbl/ adj incapable; (through circumstances) dans l'impossibilité (**to do** de faire).

unacceptable /ʌnəkˈseptəbl/ adj (suggestion) inacceptable; (behaviour) inadmissible.

unanimous /juːˈnænɪməs/ adj unanime. **unanimously** adv à l'unanimité.

unattended /ʌnəˈtendɪd/ adj sans surveillance.

unattractive /ʌnəˈtræktɪv/ adj (idea) peu attrayant; (person) peu attirant.

unauthorized /ʌnˈɔːθəraɪzd/ adj non autorisé.

unavoidable /ʌnəˈvɔɪdəbl/ adj inévitable.

unbearable /ʌnˈbeərəbl/ adj insupportable.

unbelievable /ʌnbɪˈliːvəbl/ adj incroyable.

unbiased /ʌnˈbaɪəst/ adj impartial.

unblock /ʌnˈblɒk/ vt déboucher.

unborn /ʌnˈbɔːn/ adj (child) à naître; (generation) à venir.

uncalled-for /ʌnˈkɔːldfɔː(r)/ adj injustifié, déplacé.

uncanny /ʌnˈkænɪ/ adj (**-ier, -iest**) étrange, troublant.

uncivilized /ʌnˈsɪvɪlaɪzd/ adj barbare.

uncle /ˈʌŋkl/ n oncle m.

> **Uncle Sam** Interprétation ⓘ plaisante des initiales U.S.Am. (United States of America). Personnification du gouvernement ou du peuple des États-Unis représentés par un grand homme maigre avec une barbiche, habillé aux couleurs du drapeau américain. C'est à lui que l'on a recours pour faire appel au patriotisme de la population, mais aussi pour caricaturer les États-Unis.

uncomfortable /ʌnˈkʌmftəbl/ adj (chair) inconfortable; (feeling) pénible; **feel** or **be ~** (person) être mal à l'aise.

uncommon /ʌnˈkɒmən/ adj rare.

unconscious /ʌnˈkɒnʃəs/ adj sans connaissance, inanimé; (not aware) inconscient (**of** de). ● n inconscient m.

unconventional /ʌnkənˈvenʃənl/ adj peu conventionnel.

uncouth /ʌnˈkuːθ/ adj grossier.

uncover /ʌnˈkʌvə(r)/ vt découvrir.

undecided /ʌndɪˈsaɪdɪd/ adj indécis.

under /ˈʌndə(r)/ prep sous; (less than) moins de; (according to) selon. ● adv au-dessous; **~ it/there** là-dessous. **~ age** adj mineur. **~ cover** adj secret. **~cut** vt (pt **-cut**; pres p **-cutting**) (Comm) vendre moins cher que. **~dog** n (Pol) opprimé/-e m/f; (socially) déshérité/-e m/f. **~done** adj pas assez cuit. **~-estimate** vt sous-

estimer. **~fed** adj sous-alimenté. **~go**
vt (pt **-went**; pp **-gone**) subir.
~graduate n étudiant/-e m/f (qui prépare la licence).

underground /'ʌndəgraʊnd/ adj souterrain; (secret) clandestin. ● adv sous
terre. ● n (rail) métro m.

under: **~line** vt souligner. **~mine** vt
saper.

underneath /ʌndə'ni:θ/ prep sous.
● adv (en) dessous.

under: **~pants** npl slip m. **~rate** vt
sous-estimer.

understand /ʌndə'stænd/ vt/i (pt
-stood) comprendre.

understanding /ʌndə'stændɪŋ/ adj
compréhensif. ● n compréhension f;
(agreement) entente f.

undertake /ʌndə'teɪk/ vt (pt **-took**; pp
-taken) entreprendre. **~taker** n entrepreneur m de pompes funèbres.
~taking n (task) entreprise f; (promise) promesse f.

underwater /ʌndə'wɔ:tə(r)/ adj sous-
marin. ● adv sous l'eau.

under: **~wear** n sous-vêtements mpl.
~world n (of crime) milieu m,
pègre f.

undo /ʌn'du:/ vt (pt **-did**; pp **-done**)
défaire, détacher; (wrong) réparer;
(Comput) annuler.

undress /ʌn'dres/ vt/i (se) déshabiller;
get ~ed se déshabiller.

undue /ʌn'dju:/ adj excessif.

unearth /ʌn'ɜ:θ/ vt déterrer.

uneasy /ʌn'i:zɪ/ adj (ill at ease) mal à
l'aise; (worried) inquiet; (situation) difficile.

uneducated /ʌn'edʒʊkeɪtɪd/ adj (person) inculte; (speech) populaire.

unemployed /ʌnɪm'plɔɪd/ adj en chômage. ● npl **the ~** les chômeurs mpl.

unemployment /ʌnɪm'plɔɪmənt/ n
chômage m; **~ benefit** allocations fpl
de chômage.

uneven /ʌn'i:vn/ adj inégal.

unexpected /ʌnɪk'spektɪd/ adj inattendu, imprévu. **unexpectedly** adv
(arrive) à l'improviste; (small, fast)
étonnamment.

unfair /ʌn'feə(r)/ adj injuste.

unfaithful /ʌn'feɪθfl/ adj infidèle.

unfit /ʌn'fɪt/ adj (Med) pas en forme;
(ill) malade; (unsuitable) impropre (**for**

à); **~ to** (unable) pas en état de.

unfold /ʌn'fəʊld/ vt déplier; (expose)
exposer. ● vi se dérouler.

unforeseen /ʌnfɔ:'si:n/ adj imprévu.

unforgettable /ʌnfə'getəbl/ adj inoubliable.

unfortunate /ʌn'fɔ:tʃənət/ adj malheureux; (event) fâcheux.

ungrateful /ʌn'greɪtfl/ adj ingrat.

unhappy /ʌn'hæpɪ/ adj (**-ier, -iest**)
(person) malheureux; (face) triste;
(not pleased) mécontent (**with** de).

unharmed /ʌn'hɑ:md/ adj indemne,
sain et sauf.

unhealthy /ʌn'helθɪ/ adj (**-ier, -iest**)
(climate) malsain; (person) en mauvaise santé.

unheard-of /ʌn'hɜ:dɒv/ adj inouï.

unhurt /ʌn'hɜ:t/ adj indemne.

uniform /'ju:nɪfɔ:m/ n uniforme
m.● adj uniforme.

unify /'ju:nɪfaɪ/ vt unifier.

unintentional /ʌnɪn'tenʃənl/ adj involontaire.

uninterested /ʌn'ɪntrəstɪd/ adj indifférent (**in** à).

union /'ju:nɪən/ n union f; (trade
union) syndicat m; **U~ Jack** drapeau m
du Royaume-Uni.

unique /ju:'ni:k/ adj unique.

unit /'ju:nɪt/ n unité f; (of furniture)
élément m; **~ trust** ≈ SICAV f.

unite /ju:'naɪt/ vt/i (s')unir.

United Kingdom n Royaume-Uni m.

United Nations npl Nations fpl Unies.

United States (of America) npl
États-Unis mpl (d'Amérique).

unity /'ju:nətɪ/ n unité f.

universal /ju:nɪ'vɜ:sl/ adj universel.

universe /'ju:nɪvɜ:s/ n univers m.

university /ju:nɪ'vɜ:sətɪ/ n université f.
● adj universitaire; (student, teacher)
d'université.

unkind /ʌn'kaɪnd/ adj pas gentil,
méchant.

unknown /ʌn'nəʊn/ adj inconnu. ● n
the ~ l'inconnu m.

unleaded /ʌn'ledɪd/ adj sans plomb.

unless /ən'les/ conj à moins que.

unlike /ʌn'laɪk/ adj différent. ● prep
contrairement à; (different from) différent de.

u

unlikely /ʌnˈlaɪklɪ/ adj improbable.

unload /ʌnˈləʊd/ vt décharger.

unlock /ʌnˈlɒk/ vt ouvrir.

unlucky /ʌnˈlʌkɪ/ adj **-ier, -iest** malheureux; (number) qui porte malheur.

unmarried /ʌnˈmærɪd/ adj célibataire.

unnatural /ʌnˈnætʃrəl/ adj pas naturel, anormal.

unnecessary /ʌnˈnesəsrɪ/ adj inutile.

unnoticed /ʌnˈnəʊtɪst/ adj inaperçu.

unofficial /ʌnəˈfɪʃl/ adj officieux.

unpack /ʌnˈpæk/ vt (suitcase) défaire; (contents) déballer. ● vi défaire sa valise.

unpleasant /ʌnˈpleznt/ adj désagréable (**to** avec).

unplug /ʌnˈplʌg/ vt débrancher.

unpopular /ʌnˈpɒpjʊlə(r)/ adj impopulaire; ~ **with** mal vu de.

unprofessional /ʌnprəˈfeʃənl/ adj peu professionnel.

unqualified /ʌnˈkwɒlɪfaɪd/ adj non diplômé; (success) total; **be** ~ **to** ne pas être qualifié pour.

unravel /ʌnˈrævl/ vt (pt **unravelled**) démêler.

unreasonable /ʌnˈriːznəbl/ adj irréaliste.

unrelated /ʌnrɪˈleɪtɪd/ adj sans rapport (**to** avec).

unreliable /ʌnrɪˈlaɪəbl/ adj peu sérieux; (machine) peu fiable.

unrest /ʌnˈrest/ n troubles mpl.

unroll /ʌnˈrəʊl/ vt dérouler.

unruly /ʌnˈruːlɪ/ adj indiscipliné.

unsafe /ʌnˈseɪf/ adj (dangerous) dangereux; (person) en danger.

unscheduled /ʌnˈʃedjuːld/ adj pas prévu.

unscrupulous /ʌnˈskruːpjʊləs/ adj sans scrupules, malhonnête.

unsettled /ʌnˈsetld/ adj instable.

unsightly /ʌnˈsaɪtlɪ/ adj laid.

unskilled /ʌnˈskɪld/ adj (worker) non qualifié.

unsound /ʌnˈsaʊnd/ adj (roof) en mauvais état; (investment) douteux.

unsteady /ʌnˈstedɪ/ adj (step) chancelant; (ladder) instable; (hand) mal assuré.

unsuccessful /ʌnsəkˈsesfl/ adj (result, candidate) malheureux; (attempt) infructueux; **be** ~ ne pas réussir (**in doing** à faire).

unsuitable /ʌnˈsuːtəbl/ adj inapproprié; **be** ~ ne pas convenir.

unsure /ʌnˈʃɔː(r)/ adj incertain.

untidy /ʌnˈtaɪdɪ/ adj (**-ier, -iest**) (person) désordonné; (room) en désordre; (work) mal soigné.

untie /ʌnˈtaɪ/ vt (knot, parcel) défaire; (person) détacher.

until /ənˈtɪl/ prep jusqu'à; **not** ~ pas avant. ● conj jusqu'à ce que; **not** ~ pas avant que.

untrue /ʌnˈtruː/ adj faux.

unused /ʌnˈjuːst/ adj (new) neuf; (not in use) inutilisé.

unusual /ʌnˈjuːʒl/ adj exceptionnel; (strange) insolite, étrange.

unwanted /ʌnˈwɒntɪd/ adj (useless) superflu; (child) non désiré.

unwelcome /ʌnˈwelkəm/ adj fâcheux; (guest) importun.

unwell /ʌnˈwel/ adj souffrant.

unwilling /ʌnˈwɪlɪŋ/ adj peu disposé (**to** à); (accomplice) malgré soi.

unwind /ʌnˈwaɪnd/ vt/i (pt **unwound**) (se) dérouler; (relax 🄸) se détendre.

unwise /ʌnˈwaɪz/ adj imprudent.

unwrap /ʌnˈræp/ vt déballer.

up /ʌp/ adv en haut, en l'air; (sun, curtain) levé; (out of bed) levé, debout; (finished) fini; **be** ~ (level, price) avoir monté. ● prep (a hill) en haut de; (a tree) dans; (a ladder) sur; **come** or **go** ~ monter; ~ **in the bedroom** là-haut dans la chambre; ~ **there** là-haut; ~ **to** jusqu'à; (task) à la hauteur de; **it is** ~ **to you** ça dépend de vous (**to** de); **be** ~ **to sth** (able) être capable de qch; (plot) préparer qch; **be** ~ **to** (in book) en être à; **be** ~ **against** faire face à; ~ **to date** moderne; (news) récent. ● n ~**s and downs** les hauts et les bas mpl.

up-and-coming adj prometteur.

upbringing /ˈʌpbrɪŋɪŋ/ n éducation f.

update /ʌpˈdeɪt/ vt mettre à jour.

upgrade /ʌpˈgreɪd/ vt améliorer; (person) promouvoir.

upheaval /ʌpˈhiːvl/ n bouleversement m.

uphill /ʌpˈhɪl/ adj qui monte; (fig) difficile. ● adv **go** ~ monter.

u

upholstery /ʌpˈhəʊlstərɪ/ n rembourrage m; (in vehicle) garniture f.

upkeep /ˈʌpkiːp/ n entretien m.

up-market adj haut-de-gamme.

upon /əˈpɒn/ prep sur.

upper /ˈʌpə(r)/ adj supérieur; **have the ~ hand** avoir le dessus. ● n (of shoe) empeigne f. **~ class** n aristocratie f. **~most** adj (highest) le plus haut.

upright /ˈʌpraɪt/ adj droit. ● n (post) montant m.

uprising /ˈʌpraɪzɪŋ/ n soulèvement m.

uproar /ˈʌprɔː(r)/ n tumulte m.

uproot /ʌpˈruːt/ vt déraciner.

upset[1] /ʌpˈset/ vt (pt upset; pres p upsetting) (overturn) renverser; (plan, stomach) déranger; (person) contrarier, affliger. ● adj peiné.

upset[2] /ˈʌpset/ n dérangement m; (distress) chagrin m.

upside-down /ʌpsaɪdˈdaʊn/ adv (lit) à l'envers; (fig) sens dessus dessous.

upstairs /ʌpˈsteəz/ adv en haut. ● adj (flat) du haut.

uptight /ʌpˈtaɪt/ adj ⊞ tendu, coincé ⊞.

up-to-date adj à la mode; (records) à jour.

upward /ˈʌpwəd/ adj & adv, **upwards** adv vers le haut.

urban /ˈɜːbən/ adj urbain.

urge /ɜːdʒ/ vt conseiller vivement (**to do** de faire); **~ on** encourager. ● n forte envie f.

urgency /ˈɜːdʒənsɪ/ n urgence f; (of request, tone) insistance f. **urgent** adj urgent; (request) pressant.

urinal /jʊəˈraɪnl/ n urinoir m.

urine /ˈjʊərɪn/ n urine f.

us /ʌs, əs/ pron nous; (**to**) **~** nous; **both of ~** tous/toutes les deux.

US abbr →UNITED STATES.

USA abbr →UNITED STATES OF AMERICA.

use[1] /juːz/ vt se servir de, utiliser. (consume) consommer; **~ up** épuiser.

use[2] /juːs/ n usage m, emploi m; **in ~** en usage; **it is no ~ doing** ça ne sert à rien de faire; **make ~ of** se servir de; **of ~** utile.

used[1] /juːzd/ adj (car) d'occasion.

used[2] /juːst/ v aux **he ~ to smoke** il fumait (autrefois). ● adj **~ to** habitué à.

useful /ˈjuːsfl/ adj utile.

useless /ˈjuːslɪs/ adj inutile; (person) incompétent.

user /ˈjuːzə(r)/ n (of road, service) usager m; (of product) utilisateur/-trice m/f. **~-friendly** adj facile d'emploi; (Comput) convivial. **~name** nom m d'utilisateur.

usual /ˈjuːʒl/ adj habituel, normal; **as ~** comme d'habitude. **usually** adv d'habitude.

utility /juːˈtɪlətɪ/ n utilité f; (public) **~** service m public.

utmost /ˈʌtməʊst/ adj (furthest, most intense) extrême; **the ~ care** le plus grand soin. ● n **do one's ~** faire tout son possible.

utter /ˈʌtə(r)/ adj complet, absolu. ● vt prononcer.

U-turn /ˈjuːtɜːn/ n demi-tour m; (fig) volteface f inv.

Vv

vacancy /ˈveɪkənsɪ/ n (post) poste m vacant; (room) chambre f disponible.

vacant /ˈveɪkənt/ adj (post) vacant; (seat) libre; (look) vague.

vacate /vəˈkeɪt/ vt quitter.

vacation /vəˈkeɪʃn/ n vacances fpl.

vaccinate /ˈvæksɪneɪt/ vt vacciner.

vacuum /ˈvækjʊəm/ n vide m. **~ cleaner** n aspirateur m. **~-packed** adj emballé sous vide.

vagina /vəˈdʒaɪnə/ n vagin m.

vagrant /ˈveɪɡrənt/ n vagabond/-e m/f.

vague /veɪɡ/ adj vague; (outline) flou; **be ~ about** ne pas préciser.

vain /veɪn/ adj (conceited) vaniteux; (useless) vain; **in ~** en vain.

valentine /ˈvæləntaɪn/ n **~ (card)** carte f de la Saint-Valentin.

valid /ˈvælɪd/ adj (argument, ticket) valable; (passport) valide.

valley /ˈvælɪ/ n vallée f.

valuable /ˈvæljʊəbl/ adj (object) de valeur; (help) précieux. **valuables** npl objets mpl de valeur.

valuation /væljʊ'eɪʃn/ n (of painting) expertise f; (of house) évaluation f.

value /'vælju:/ n valeur f; ~ **added tax** taxe f à la valeur ajoutée, TVA f. ● vt (appraise) évaluer; (cherish) attacher de la valeur à.

valve /vælv/ n (Tech) soupape f; (of tyre) valve f; (Med) valvule f.

van /væn/ n camionnette f.

vandal /'vændl/ n vandale mf.

vanguard /'vængɑ:d/ n **in the** ~ **of** à l'avantgarde f de.

vanilla /və'nɪlə/ n vanille f.

vanish /'vænɪʃ/ vi disparaître.

vapour /'veɪpə(r)/ n vapeur f.

variable /'veərɪəbl/ adj variable.

varicose /'værɪkəʊs/ adj ~ **veins** varices fpl.

varied /'veərɪd/ adj varié.

variety /və'raɪətɪ/ n variété f; (entertainment) variétés fpl.

various /'veərɪəs/ adj divers.

varnish /'vɑːnɪʃ/ n vernis m. ● vt vernir.

vary /'veərɪ/ vt/i varier.

vase /vɑːz/ n vase m.

vast /vɑːst/ adj (space) vaste; (in quantity) énorme.

vat /væt/ n cuve f.

VAT abbr (**value added tax**) TVA f.

vault /vɔːlt/ n (roof) voûte f; (in bank) chambre f forte; (tomb) caveau m; (jump) saut m. ● vt/i sauter.

VCR abbr →VIDEO CASSETTE RECORDER.

VDU abbr →VISUAL DISPLAY UNIT.

veal /viːl/ n veau m.

vegan /'viːgən/ adj & n végétalien/-ne (m/f).

vegetable /'vedʒtəbl/ n légume m. ● adj végétal.

vegetarian /vedʒɪ'teərɪən/ adj & n végétarien/-ne (m/f).

vehicle /'vɪəkl/ n véhicule m.

veil /veɪl/ n voile m.

vein /veɪn/ n (in body, rock) veine f; (on leaf) nervure f.

velvet /'velvɪt/ n velours m.

vending-machine /'vendɪŋ mə'ʃiːn/ n distributeur m automatique.

veneer /vɪ'nɪə(r)/ n (on wood) placage m; (fig) vernis m.

venereal /və'nɪərɪəl/ adj vénérien.

venetian /vɪ'niːʃn/ adj ~ **blind** jalousie f.

vengeance /'vendʒəns/ n vengeance f; **with a** ~ de plus belle.

venison /'venɪsn/ n venaison f.

venom /'venəm/ n venin m.

vent /vent/ n bouche f, conduit m; (in coat) fente f. ● vt (anger) décharger (on sur).

ventilate /'ventɪleɪt/ vt ventiler. **ventilator** n ventilateur m.

venture /'ventʃə(r)/ n entreprise f. ● vt/i (se) risquer.

venue /'venjuː/ n lieu m.

verb /vɜːb/ n verbe m.

verbal /'vɜːbl/ adj verbal.

verdict /'vɜːdɪkt/ n verdict m.

verge /vɜːdʒ/ n bord m; **on the** ~ **of doing** sur le point de faire. ● vi ~ **on** friser, frôler.

verify /'verɪfaɪ/ vt vérifier.

vermin /'vɜːmɪn/ n vermine f.

versatile /'vɜːsətaɪl/ adj (person) aux talents variés; (mind) souple.

verse /vɜːs/ n strophe f; (of Bible) verset m; (poetry) vers mpl.

version /'vɜːʃn/ n version f.

versus /'vɜːsəs/ prep contre.

vertebra /'vɜːtɪbrə/ n (pl **-brae**) vertèbre f.

vertical /'vɜːtɪkl/ adj vertical.

vertigo /'vɜːtɪgəʊ/ n vertige m.

very /'verɪ/ adv très. ● adj (actual) même; **the** ~ **day** le jour même; **at the** ~ **end** tout à la fin; **the** ~ **first** le tout premier; ~ **much** beaucoup.

vessel /'vesl/ n vaisseau m.

vest /vest/ n maillot m de corps; (waistcoat: US) gilet m.

vet /vet/ n vétérinaire mf. ● vt (pt **vetted**) (candidate) examiner (de près).

veteran /'vetərən/ n vétéran m; **war** ~ ancien combattant m.

veterinary /'vetrɪnrɪ/ adj vétérinaire; ~ **surgeon** vétérinaire mf.

veto /'viːtəʊ/ n (pl ~**es**) veto m; (right) droit m de veto. ● vt mettre son veto à.

vibrate /vaɪ'breɪt/ vt/i (faire) vibrer.

vicar /'vɪkə(r)/ n pasteur m.

V

vice /vaɪs/ n (depravity) vice m; (Tech) étau m.

vicinity /vɪˈsɪnətɪ/ n environs mpl; **in the ~ of** à proximité de.

vicious /ˈvɪʃəs/ adj (spiteful) méchant; (violent) brutal; **~ circle** cercle m vicieux.

victim /ˈvɪktɪm/ n victime f.

victor /ˈvɪktə(r)/ n vainqueur m. **victory** n victoire f.

video /ˈvɪdɪəʊ/ adj (game, camera) vidéo inv. ● n (recorder) magnétoscope m; (film) vidéo f; **~ (cassette)** cassette f vidéo. **~ game** n jeu m vidéo. **~phone** n vidéophone m. ● vt enregistrer.

videotape /ˈvɪdɪəʊteɪp/ n bande f vidéo. ● vt (programme) enregistrer; (wedding) filmer avec une caméra vidéo.

view /vjuː/ n vue f; **in my ~** à mon avis; **in ~ of** compte tenu de; **on ~** exposé; **with a ~ to** dans le but de. ● vt (watch) regarder; (consider) considérer (as comme); (house) visiter. **viewer** n (TV) téléspectateur/-trice m/f.

view: ~finder n viseur m. **~point** n point m de vue.

vigilant /ˈvɪdʒɪlənt/ adj vigilant.

vigour, (US) **vigor** /ˈvɪgə(r)/ n vigueur f.

vile /vaɪl/ adj (base) vil; (bad) abominable.

villa /ˈvɪlə/ n pavillon m; (for holiday) villa f.

village /ˈvɪlɪdʒ/ n village m.

villain /ˈvɪlən/ n scélérat m, bandit m; (in story) méchant m.

vindictive /vɪnˈdɪktɪv/ adj vindicatif.

vine /vaɪn/ n vigne f.

vinegar /ˈvɪnɪgə(r)/ n vinaigre m.

vineyard /ˈvɪnjəd/ n vignoble m.

vintage /ˈvɪntɪdʒ/ n (year) année f, millésime m. ● adj (wine) de grand cru; (car) d'époque.

viola /vɪˈəʊlə/ n (Mus) alto m.

violate /ˈvaɪəleɪt/ vt violer.

violence /ˈvaɪələns/ n violence f. **violent** adj violent.

violet /ˈvaɪələt/ n (Bot) violette f; (colour) violet m.

violin /vaɪəˈlɪn/ n violon m.

VIP abbr (**very important person**) personnalité f, VIP m.

virgin /ˈvɜːdʒɪn/ n (woman) vierge f.

Virgo /ˈvɜːgəʊ/ n Vierge f.

virtual /ˈvɜːtʃʊəl/ adj quasi-total; (Comput) virtuel. **virtually** adv pratiquement.

virtue /ˈvɜːtʃuː/ n vertu f; (advantage) mérite m; **by ~ of** en raison de.

virus /ˈvaɪərəs/ n virus m.

visa /ˈviːzə/ n visa m.

visibility /vɪzəˈbɪlətɪ/ n visibilité f. **visible** adj visible.

vision /ˈvɪʒn/ n vision f.

visit /ˈvɪzɪt/ vt (pt **visited**) (person) rendre visite à; (place) visiter. ● vi être en visite. ● n (tour, call) visite f; (stay) séjour m. **visitor** n visiteur/-euse m/f; (guest) invité/-e m/f.

visual /ˈvɪʒʊəl/ adj visuel. **~ display unit** n visuel m, console f de visualisation.

visualize /ˈvɪʒʊəlaɪz/ vt se représenter; (foresee) envisager.

vital /ˈvaɪtl/ adj vital.

vitamin /ˈvɪtəmɪn/ n vitamine f.

vivacious /vɪˈveɪʃəs/ adj plein de vivacité.

vivid /ˈvɪvɪd/ adj (colour, imagination) vif; (description, dream) frappant.

vivisection /vɪvɪˈsekʃn/ n vivisection f.

vocabulary /vəˈkæbjʊlərɪ/ n vocabulaire m.

vocal /ˈvəʊkl/ adj vocal; (person) qui s'exprime franchement. **~ cords** npl cordes fpl vocales.

vocation /vəʊˈkeɪʃn/ n vocation f. **vocational** adj professionnel.

voice /vɔɪs/ n voix f. ● vt (express) formuler. **~ mail** n messagerie f vocale.

void /vɔɪd/ adj vide (of de); (not valid) nul. ● n vide m.

volatile /ˈvɒlətaɪl/ adj (person) versatile; (situation) explosif.

volcano /vɒlˈkeɪnəʊ/ n (pl **~es**) volcan m.

volley /ˈvɒlɪ/ n (of blows, in tennis) volée f; (of gunfire) salve f.

volt /vəʊlt/ n (Electr) volt m. **voltage** n tension f.

volume /'vɒljuːm/ n volume m.

voluntary /'vɒləntrɪ/ adj volontaire; (unpaid) bénévole.

volunteer /vɒlən'tɪə(r)/ n volontaire mf. ● vi s'offrir (**to do** pour faire); (Mil) s'engager comme volontaire. ● vt offrir.

vomit /'vɒmɪt/ vt/i (pt **vomited**) vomir. ● n vomi m.

vote /vəʊt/ n vote m; (right) droit m de vote. ● vt/i voter; ~ **sb in** élire qn. **voter** n électeur/-trice m/f. **voting** n vote m (**of** de); (poll) scrutin m.

vouch /vaʊtʃ/ vi ~ **for** se porter garant de.

voucher /'vaʊtʃə(r)/ n bon m.

vowel /'vaʊəl/ n voyelle f.

voyage /'vɔɪɪdʒ/ n voyage m (en mer).

vulgar /'vʌlgə(r)/ adj vulgaire.

vulnerable /'vʌlnərəbl/ adj vulnérable.

Ww

wad /wɒd/ n (pad) tampon m; (bundle) liasse f.

wade /weɪd/ vi ~ **through** (mud) patauger dans. (book: fig) avancer péniblement dans.

wafer /'weɪfə(r)/ n (biscuit) gaufrette f.

waffle /'wɒfl/ n (talk 🇬🇧) verbiage m; (cake) gaufre f. ● vi 🇬🇧 divaguer.

wag /wæg/ vt/i (pt **wagged**) (tail) remuer.

wage /weɪdʒ/ vt (campaign) mener; ~ **war** faire la guerre. ● n (weekly, daily) salaire m; ~**s** salaire m. ~-**earner** n salarié/-e m/f.

wagon /'wægən/ n (horse-drawn) chariot m; (Rail) wagon m (de marchandises).

wail /weɪl/ vi gémir. ● n gémissement m.

waist /weɪst/ n taille f. ~**coat** n gilet m.

wait /weɪt/ vt/i attendre; **I can't** ~ **to start** j'ai hâte de commencer; **let's** ~ **and see** attendons voir; ~ **for** attendre; ~ **on** servir. ● n attente f.

waiter /'weɪtə(r)/ n garçon m, serveur m.

waiting-list n liste f d'attente.

waiting-room n salle f d'attente.

waitress /'weɪtrɪs/ n serveuse f.

waive /weɪv/ vt renoncer à.

wake /weɪk/ vt/i (pt **woke**; pp **woken**) ~ (**up**) (se) réveiller. ● n (track) sillage m; **in the** ~ **of** (after) à la suite de. ~ **up call** n réveil m téléphoné.

Wales /weɪlz/ n pays m de Galles.

walk /wɔːk/ vi marcher; (not ride) aller à pied; (stroll) se promener. ● vt (streets) parcourir; (distance) faire à pied; (dog) promener. ● n promenade f, tour m; (gait) démarche f; (pace) marche f, pas m; (path) allée f; **have a** ~ faire une promenade. □ ~ **out** (go away) partir; (worker) faire grève; ~ **out on** abandonner.

walkie-talkie /wɔːkɪ'tɔːkɪ/ n talkie-walkie m.

walking /'wɔːkɪŋ/ n marche f (à pied). ● adj (corpse, dictionary: fig) ambulant.

walkman® /'wɔːkmən/ n walkman® m, baladeur m.

walk: ~-**out** n grève f surprise. ~-**over** n victoire f facile.

wall /wɔːl/ n mur m; (of tunnel, stomach) paroi f. ● adj mural. **walled** adj (city) fortifié.

> **Wall Street** Cette petite rue new yorkaise est le centre de la finance et des affaires aux États-Unis. *Wall Street* est souvent employé pour désigner la Bourse de New York, également située dans cette rue. _ℹ️_

wallet /'wɒlɪt/ n portefeuille m.

wallpaper /'wɔːlpeɪpə(r)/ n papier m peint. ● vt tapisser.

walnut /'wɔːlnʌt/ n (nut) noix f; (tree) noyer m.

waltz /wɔːls/ n valse f. ● vi valser.

wander /'wɒndə(r)/ vi errer; (stroll) flâner; (digress) s'écarter du sujet; (in mind) divaguer.

wane /weɪn/ vi décroître.

want /wɒnt/ vt vouloir (**to do** faire); (need) avoir besoin de (**doing** d'être fait); (ask for) demander; **I** ~ **you to**

do it je veux que vous le fassiez. ● *vi* ~ **for** manquer de. ● *n* (*need, poverty*) besoin *m*; (*desire*) désir *m*; (*lack*) manque *m*; **for** ~ **of** faute de. **wanted** *adj* (*criminal*) recherché par la police.

war /wɔː(r)/ *n* guerre *f*; **at** ~ en guerre; **on the** ~**path** sur le sentier de la guerre.

ward /wɔːd/ *n* (*in hospital*) salle *f*; (*minor: Jur*) pupille *mf*; (*Pol*) division *f* électorale. ● *vt* ~ **off** (*danger*) prévenir.

warden /'wɔːdn/ *n* directeur/-trice *m/f*; (*of park*) gardien/-ne *m/f*; (**traffic** ~) contractuel/-le *m/f*.

wardrobe /'wɔːdrəʊb/ *n* (*furniture*) armoire *f*; (*clothes*) garde-robe *f*.

warehouse /'weəhaʊs/ *n* entrepôt *m*.

wares /weəz/ *npl* marchandises *fpl*.

warfare /'wɔːfeə(r)/ *n* guerre *f*.

warm /wɔːm/ *adj* chaud; (*hearty*) chaleureux; **be** *or* **feel** ~ avoir chaud; **it is** ~ il fait chaud. ● *vt/i* ~ (**up**) (se) réchauffer; (*food*) chauffer; (*liven up*) (s')animer; (*exercise*) s'échauffer.

warmth /wɔːmθ/ *n* chaleur *f*.

warn /wɔːn/ *vt* avertir, prévenir; ~ **sb off sth** (*advise against*) mettre qn en garde contre qch; (*forbid*) interdire qch à qn.

warning /'wɔːnɪŋ/ *n* avertissement *m*; (*notice*) avis *m*; **without** ~ sans prévenir. ~ **light** *n* voyant *m*. ~ **triangle** *n* triangle *m* de sécurité.

warp /wɔːp/ *vt/i* (*wood*) (se) voiler; (*pervert*) pervertir; (*judgment*) fausser.

warrant /'wɒrənt/ *n* (*for arrest*) mandat *m* (d'arrêt); (*Comm*) autorisation *f*. ● *vt* justifier.

warranty /'wɒrəntɪ/ *n* garantie *f*.

wart /wɔːt/ *n* verrue *f*.

wartime /'wɔːtaɪm/ *n* **in** ~ en temps de guerre.

wary /'weərɪ/ *adj* (**-ier, -iest**) prudent.

W **was** /wɒz, wəz/ →**BE**.

wash /wɒʃ/ *vt/i* (se) laver. (*flow over*) baigner; ~ **one's hands of** se laver les mains de. ● *n* lavage *m*; (*clothes*) lessive *f*; **have a** ~ se laver. ~ **up** faire la vaisselle; (*US*) se laver. ~**basin** *n* lavabo *m*.

washer /'wɒʃə(r)/ *n* rondelle *f*.

washing /'wɒʃɪŋ/ *n* lessive *f*. ~**-machine** *n* machine *f* à laver. ~**-powder** *n* lessive *f*.

washing-up *n* vaisselle *f*. ~ **liquid** *n* liquide *m* vaisselle.

wash: ~**-out** *n* 🄸 fiasco *m*. ~**-room** *n* (*US*) toilettes *fpl*.

wasp /wɒsp/ *n* guêpe *f*.

wastage /'weɪstɪdʒ/ *n* gaspillage *m*.

waste /weɪst/ *vt* gaspiller; (*time*) perdre. ● *vi* ~ **away** dépérir. ● *adj* superflu; ~ **products** *or* **matter** déchets *mpl*. ● *n* gaspillage *m*; (*of time*) perte *f*; (*rubbish*) déchets *mpl*; **lay** ~ dévaster. **wasteful** *adj* peu économique; (*person*) gaspilleur.

waste: ~**land** *n* (*desolate*) terre *f* désolée; (*unused*) terre *f* inculte; (*in town*) terrain *m* vague. ~ **paper** *n* vieux papiers *mpl*. ~**-paper basket** *n* corbeille *f* (à papier).

watch /wɒtʃ/ *vt/i* (*television*) regarder; (*observe*) observer; (*guard, spy on*) surveiller; (*be careful about*) faire attention à. ● *n* (*for telling time*) montre *f*; (Naut) quart *m*; **be on the** ~ guetter; **keep** ~ **on** surveiller. ~ **out** (*take care*) faire attention (**for** à); ~ **out for** (*keep watch*) guetter.

water /'wɔːtə(r)/ *n* eau *f*; **by** ~ en bateau. ● *vt* arroser. ● *vi* (*eyes*) larmoyer; **my/his mouth** ~**s** l'eau me/lui vient à la bouche. ⬜ ~ **down** couper (*d'eau*); (*tone down*) édulcorer. ~**-colour** *n* (*painting*) aquarelle *f*. ~**cress** *n* cresson *m* (de fontaine). ~**fall** *n* chute *f* d'eau, cascade *f*. ~ **heater** *n* chauffe-eau *m*. **watering-can** *n* arrosoir *m*. ~**-lily** *n* nénuphar *m*. ~**-melon** *n* pastèque *f*. ~**proof** *adj* (*material*) imperméable. ~ **shed** *n* (*in affairs*) tournant *m* décisif. ~**-skiing** *n* ski *m* nautique. ~**tight** *adj* étanche. ~**-way** *n* voie *f* navigable.

watery /'wɔːtərɪ/ *adj* (*colour*) délavé; (*eyes*) humide; (*soup*) trop liquide.

wave /weɪv/ *n* vague *f*; (*in hair*) ondulation *f*; (*radio*) onde *f*; (*sign*) signe *m*. ● *vt* agiter. ● *vi* faire signe (de la main); (*move in wind*) flotter.

waver /'weɪvə(r)/ *vi* vaciller.

wavy /'weɪvɪ/ *adj* (*line*) onduleux; (*hair*) ondulé.

wax /wæks/ *n* cire *f*; (*for skis*) fart *m*. ● *vt* cirer; farter; (*car*) lustrer.

way /weɪ/ n (road, path) chemin m (**to** de); (distance) distance f; (direction) direction f; (manner) façon f; (means) moyen m; ~**s** (habits) habitudes fpl; **be in the** ~ bloquer le passage; (hindrance: fig) gêner (qn); **be on one's** or **the** ~ être sur son or le chemin; **by the** ~ à propos; **by the** ~**side** au bord de la route; **by** ~ **of** comme; (via) par; **go out of one's** ~ se donner du mal; **in a** ~ dans un sens; **make one's** ~ **somewhere** se rendre quelque part; **push one's** ~ **through** se frayer un passage; **that** ~ par là; **this** ~ par ici; ~ **in** entrée f; ~ **out** sortie f. ● adv Ⅰ loin.

we /wiː/ pron nous.

weak /wiːk/ adj faible; (delicate) fragile.

weakness /ˈwiːknɪs/ n faiblesse f; (fault) point m faible; **a** ~ **for** (liking) un faible pour.

wealth /welθ/ n richesse f; (riches, resources) richesses fpl; (quantity) profusion f.

wealthy /ˈwelθɪ/ adj (**-ier, -iest**) riche. ● n the ~ les riches mpl.

weapon /ˈwepən/ n arme f; ~**s of mass destruction** armes fpl de destruction massive.

wear /weə(r)/ vt (pt **wore**; pp **worn**) porter; (put on) mettre; (expression) avoir. ● vi (last) durer; ~ (**out**) (s')user. ● n (in use) usage m; (damage) usure f. ~ **down** user; ~ **off** (colour, pain) passer; ~ **out** (exhaust) épuiser.

weary /ˈwɪərɪ/ adj (**-ier, -iest**) fatigué, las. ● vi ~ **of** se lasser de.

weather /ˈweðə(r)/ n temps m; **under the** ~ patraque. ● adj météorologique. ● vt (survive) réchapper de or à. ~ **forecast** n météo f.

weave /wiːv/ vt/i (pt **wove**; pp **woven**) tisser; (basket) tresser; (move) se faufiler. ● n (style) tissage m.

web /web/ n (of spider) toile f; (on foot) palmure f.

Web /web/ n (Comput) Web m. ~**cam** n webcam f. ~**master** n administrateur m de site Internet. ~ **page** n page f Web. ~ **search** n recherche f sur le Web. ~**site** n site m Internet.

wedding /ˈwedɪŋ/ n mariage m. ~**-ring** n alliance f.

wedge /wedʒ/ n (of wood) coin m; (under wheel) cale f. ● vt caler; (push) enfoncer; (crowd) coincer.

Wednesday /ˈwenzdɪ/ n mercredi m.

weed /wiːd/ n mauvaise herbe f. ● vt/i désherber; ~ **out** extirper.

week /wiːk/ n semaine f; **a** ~ **today/ tomorrow** aujourd'hui/demain en huit. ~**day** n jour m de semaine. ~**end** n week-end m, fin f de semaine.

weekly /ˈwiːklɪ/ adv toutes les semaines. ● adj & n (periodical) hebdomadaire (m).

weep /wiːp/ vt/i (pt **wept**) pleurer (**for sb** qn).

weigh /weɪ/ vt/i peser; ~ **anchor** lever l'ancre. ~ **down** lester (avec un poids); (bend) faire plier; (fig) accabler; ~ **up** calculer.

weight /weɪt/ n poids m; **lose/put on** ~ perdre/prendre du poids. ~**-lifting** n haltérophilie f. ~ **training** n musculation f en salle.

weird /wɪəd/ adj bizarre.

welcome /ˈwelkəm/ adj agréable; (timely) opportun; **be** ~ être le or la bienvenu(e), être les bienvenu(e)s; **you're** ~**!** il n'y a pas de quoi!; ~ **to do** libre de faire. ● interj soyez le or la bienvenu(e), soyez les bienvenu(e)s. ● n accueil m. ● vt accueillir; (as greeting) souhaiter la bienvenue à; (fig) se réjouir de.

weld /weld/ vt souder. ● n soudure f.

welfare /ˈwelfeə(r)/ n bien-être m; (aid) aide f sociale. **W**~ **State** n état-providence m.

well[1] /wel/ n puits m.

well[2] /wel/ adv (**better, best**) bien; **do** ~ (succeed) réussir; ~ **done!** bravo! ● adj bien inv; **as** ~ aussi; **be** ~ (healthy) aller bien. ● interj eh bien; (surprise) tiens.

well: ~**-behaved** adj sage. ~**-being** n bien-être m inv.

wellington /ˈwelɪŋtən/ n (boot) botte f de caoutchouc.

well: ~**-known** adj (bien) connu. ~**-meaning** adj bien intentionné. ~ **off** aisé, riche. ~**-read** adj instruit. ~**-to-do** adj riche. ~**-wisher** n admirateur/-trice m/f.

Welsh /welʃ/ adj gallois. ● n (Ling) gallois m.

w

Welsh Assembly L'Assemblée du Pays de Galles a été établie à Cardiff en 1999, à l'issue d'un référendum auprès de la population galloise. À la différence du parlement écossais, elle n'a pas de réel pouvoir législatif, mais ses 60 membres peuvent aménager les lois nationales en fonction des besoins spécifiques des Gallois. ▷SCOTTISH PARLIAMENT.

went /went/ →GO.

wept /wept/ →WEEP.

were /wɜː(r)/ →BE.

west /west/ n ouest m; **the W~** (Pol) l'Occident m. ● adj d'ouest. ● adv vers l'ouest.

western /'westən/ adj de l'ouest; (Pol) occidental. ● n (film) western m. **westerner** n occidental/-e m/f.

West Indies /west 'ɪndiːz/ n Antilles fpl.

westward /'westwəd/ adj (side) ouest inv; (journey) vers l'ouest.

wet /wet/ adj (**wetter, wettest**) mouillé; (damp, rainy) humide; (paint) frais; **get ~** se mouiller. ● vt (pt **wetted**) mouiller. ● n **the ~** l'humidité f; (rain) la pluie f. **~suit** n combinaison f de plongée.

whale /weɪl/ n baleine f.

wharf /wɔːf/ n quai m.

what /wɒt/
● pronoun
••••➤ (in questions as object pronoun) qu'est-ce que?; **~ are we going to do?** qu'est-ce que nous allons faire?
••••➤ (in questions as subject pronoun) qu'est-ce qui?; **~ happened?** qu'est-ce qui s'est passé?
••••➤ (introducing clause as object) ce que; **I don't know ~ he wants** je ne sais pas ce qu'il veut.
••••➤ (introducing clause as subject) ce qui; **tell me ~ happened** raconte moi ce qui s'est passé.
••••➤ (with prepositions) quoi; **~ are you thinking about?** à quoi penses-tu?

● determiner
••••➤ quel/quelle/quels/quelles; **~ train did you catch?** quel train as-tu pris?; **~ time is it?** quelle heure est-il?

whatever /wɒt'evə(r)/ adj **~ book** quel que soit le livre. ● pron (no matter what) quoi que, quoi qu'; (anything that) tout ce qui; (object) tout ce que or qu'; **~ happens** quoi qu'il arrive; **~ happened?** qu'est-ce qui est arrivé?; **~ the problems** quels que soient les problèmes; **~ you want** tout ce que vous voulez; **nothing ~** rien du tout.

whatsoever /wɒtsəu'evə(r)/ adj & pron →WHATEVER.

wheat /wiːt/ n blé m, froment m.

wheel /wiːl/ n roue f; **at the ~** (of vehicle) au volant; (helm) au gouvernail. ● vt pousser. ● vi tourner; **~ and deal** faire des combines. **~barrow** n brouette f. **~chair** n fauteuil m roulant.

when /wen/ adv & pron quand. ● conj quand, lorsque; **the day/moment ~** le jour/moment où.

whenever /wen'evə(r)/ conj & adv (at whatever time) quand; (every time that) chaque fois que.

where /weə(r)/ adv, conj & pron où; (whereas) alors que; (the place that) là où.

whereabouts /weərə'bauts/ adv (à peu près) où. ● n **sb's ~** l'endroit où se trouve qn.

whereas /weər'æz/ conj alors que.

wherever /weər'evə(r)/ conj & adv où que; (everywhere) partout où; (anywhere) (là) où; (emphatic where) où donc.

whether /'weðə(r)/ conj si; **not know ~** ne pas savoir si; **~ I go or not** que j'aille ou non.

which /wɪtʃ/
● pronoun
••••➤ (in questions) lequel/laquelle/lesquels/lesquelles; **there are three peaches, ~ do you want?** il y a trois pêches, laquelle veux-tu?

····➤ (in questions with superlative adjective) quel/quelle/quels/quelles; **~ (apple) is the biggest?** quelle est la plus grosse?

····➤ (in relative clauses as subject) qui; **the book ~ is on the table** le livre qui est sur la table.

····➤ (in relative clauses as object) que; **the book ~ Tina is reading** le livre que lit Tina.

● determiner

····➤ quel/quelle/quels/quelles; **~ car did you choose?** quelle voiture as-tu choisie?

whichever /wɪtʃˈevə(r)/ adj **~ book** quel que soit le livre que or qui; **take ~ book you wish** prenez le livre que vous voulez. ● pron celui/celle/ceux/ celles qui or que.

while /waɪl/ n moment m. ● conj (when) pendant que; (although) bien que; (as long as) tant que. ● vt **~ away** (time) passer.

whilst /waɪlst/ conj ➡WHILE.

whim /wɪm/ n caprice m.

whine /waɪn/ vi gémir, se plaindre. ● n gémissement m.

whip /wɪp/ n fouet m. ● vt (pt **whipped**) fouetter; (Culin) fouetter, battre; (seize) enlever brusquement. ● vi (move) aller en vitesse. □ **~ up** exciter; (cause) provoquer; (meal 🔢) préparer.

whirl /wɜːl/ vt/i (faire) tourbillonner. ● n tourbillon m. **~pool** n tourbillon m. **~wind** n tourbillon m (de vent).

whisk /wɪsk/ vt (snatch) enlever or emmener brusquement; (Culin) fouetter. ● n (Culin) fouet m.

whiskers /ˈwɪskə(r)s/ npl (of animal) moustaches fpl; (of man) favoris mpl.

whisper /ˈwɪspə(r)/ vt/i chuchoter. ● n chuchotement m; (rumour: fig) rumeur f, bruit m.

whistle /ˈwɪsl/ n sifflement m; (instrument) sifflet m. ● vt/i siffler; **~ at** or **for** siffler.

white /waɪt/ adj blanc. ● n blanc m; (person) blanc/-che m/f. **~ coffee** n café m au lait. **~-collar worker** n employé/-e m/f de bureau. **~ elephant** n projet m coûteux et peu rentable. **~ lie** n pieux mensonge m.

W**~ Paper** n livre m blanc.

whitewash /ˈwaɪtwɒʃ/ n blanc m de chaux. ● vt blanchir à la chaux; (person: fig) blanchir.

Whitsun /ˈwɪtsn/ n la Pentecôte.

whiz /wɪz/ vi (pt **whizzed**) (through air) fendre l'air; (hiss) siffler; (rush) aller à toute vitesse. **~-kid** n jeune prodige m.

who /huː/ pron qui.

whoever /huːˈevə(r)/ pron (no matter who) qui que ce soit qui or que; (the one who) quiconque; **tell ~ you want** dites-le à qui vous voulez.

whole /həʊl/ adj entier; (intact) intact; **the ~ house** toute la maison. ● n totalité f; (unit) tout m; **on the ~** dans l'ensemble. **~foods** npl aliments mpl naturels et diététiques. **~-hearted** adj sans réserve. **~meal** adj complet.

wholesale /ˈhəʊlseɪl/ adj (firm) de gros; (fig) systématique. ● adv (in large quantities) en gros; (fig) en masse.

wholesome /ˈhəʊlsəm/ adj sain.

wholly /ˈhəʊllɪ/ adv entièrement.

whom /huːm/ pron (that) que, qu'; (after prepositions and in questions) qui; **of ~** dont; **with ~** avec qui.

whooping cough /ˈhuːpɪŋ kɒf/ n coqueluche f.

whose /huːz/ pron & a à qui, de qui; **~ hat is this?** à qui est ce chapeau?; **~ son are you?** de qui êtes-vous le fils?; **the man ~ hat I see** l'homme dont je vois le chapeau.

why /waɪ/ adv pourquoi; **the reason ~** la raison pour laquelle.

wicked /ˈwɪkɪd/ adj méchant, mauvais, vilain.

wide /waɪd/ adj large; (ocean) vaste. ● adv (fall) loin du but; **open ~** ouvrir tout grand; **~ open** grand ouvert; **~ awake** éveillé. **widely** adv (spread, spaced) largement; (travel) beaucoup; (generally) généralement; (extremely) extrêmement.

widespread /ˈwaɪdspred/ adj très répandu.

widow /ˈwɪdəʊ/ n veuve f. **widowed** adj (man) veuf; (woman) veuve. **widower** n veuf m.

width /wɪdθ/ n largeur f.

W

wield /wiːld/ vt (axe) manier; (power: fig) exercer.

wife /waɪf/ n (pl **wives**) femme f, épouse f.

wig /wɪg/ n perruque f.

wiggle /'wɪgl/ vt/i remuer; (hips) tortiller; (worm) se tortiller.

wild /waɪld/ adj sauvage; (sea, enthusiasm) déchaîné; (mad) fou; (angry) furieux. ● adv (grow) à l'état sauvage.

wildlife /'waɪldlaɪf/ n faune f.

---

will¹ /wɪl/

> present **will**; present negative **won't**, **will not**; past **would**

● auxiliary verb

····▶ (in future tense) **he'll come** il viendra; **it ~ be sunny tomorrow** il va faire du soleil demain.

····▶ (inviting and requesting) **~ you have some coffee?** est-ce que vous voulez du café?

····▶ (making assumptions) **they won't know what's happened** ils ne doivent pas savoir ce qui s'est passé.

····▶ (in short questions and answers) **you'll come again, won't you?** tu reviendras, n'est-ce pas?; **'they won't forget'—'yes they ~'** 'ils n'oublieront pas'—'si'.

····▶ (capacity) **the lift ~ hold 12** l'ascenseur peut transporter 12 personnes.

····▶ (ability) **the car won't start** la voiture ne veut pas démarrer.

● transitive verb **~ sb's death** souhaiter ardemment la mort de qn.

---

will² /wɪl/ n volonté f; (document) testament m; **at ~** quand or comme on veut.

willing /'wɪlɪŋ/ adj (help, offer) spontané; (helper) bien disposé; **~ to** disposé à. **willingly** adv (with pleasure) volontiers; (not forced) volontairement. **willingness** n empressement m (**to do** à faire).

willow /'wɪləʊ/ n saule m.

will-power /'wɪlpaʊə(r)/ n volonté f.

win /wɪn/ vt/i (pt **won**; pres p **winning**) gagner; (prize) remporter; (fame) ac-

quérir, trouver; **~ round** convaincre. ● n victoire f.

winch /wɪntʃ/ n treuil m. ● vt hisser au treuil.

wind¹ /wɪnd/ n vent m; (breath) souffle m; **get ~ of** avoir vent de; **in the ~** dans l'air. ● vt essouffler. **~ farm** n ferme f d'éoliennes. **~ turbine** moteur m éolien.

wind² /waɪnd/ vt/i (pt **wound**) (s')enrouler; (of path, river) serpenter; **~ (up)** (clock) remonter; **~ up** (end) (se) terminer; **~ up in hospital** finir à l'hôpital.

windmill /'wɪndmɪl/ n moulin m à vent.

window /'wɪndəʊ/ n fenêtre f; (glass pane) vitre f; (in vehicle, train) vitre f; (in shop) vitrine f; (counter) guichet m; (Comput) fenêtre f. **~-box** n jardinière f. **~-cleaner** n laveur m de carreaux. **~-dresser** n étalagiste mf. **~-ledge** n rebord m de (la) fenêtre. **~-shopping** n lèche-vitrines m. **~-sill** n (inside) appui m de (la) fenêtre; (outside) rebord m de (la) fenêtre.

windscreen /'wɪndskriːn/ n pare-brise m inv. **~ wiper** n essuie-glace m.

windshield /'wɪndʃiːld/ n (US) **➡WINDSCREEN.**

windsurfing /'wɪndsɜːfɪŋ/ n planche f à voile.

windy /'wɪndɪ/ adj (**-ier, -iest**) venteux; **it is ~** il y a du vent.

wine /waɪn/ n vin m. **~-cellar** n cave f (à vin). **~-glass** n verre m à vin. **~-grower** n viticulteur m. **~ list** n carte f des vins. **~-tasting** n dégustation f de vins.

wing /wɪŋ/ n aile f; **~s** (Theat) coulisses fpl; **under one's ~** sous son aile. **~ mirror** n rétroviseur m extérieur.

wink /wɪŋk/ vi faire un clin d'œil; (light, star) clignoter. ● n clin m d'œil; clignotement m.

winner /'wɪnə(r)/ n (of game) gagnant/-e m/f; (of fight) vainqueur m.

winning /'wɪnɪŋ/ **➡WIN.** ● adj (number, horse) gagnant; (team) victorieux; (smile) engageant. **winnings** npl gains mpl.

winter /'wɪntə(r)/ n hiver m.

wipe /waɪp/ vt essuyer. ● vi **~ up** essuyer la vaisselle. ● n coup m de torchon or d'éponge. □ **~ out** (destroy) anéantir; (remove) effacer.

wire /'waɪə(r)/ n fil m; (US) télégramme m.

wiring /'waɪərɪŋ/ n (Electr) installation f électrique.

wisdom /'wɪzdəm/ n sagesse f.

wise /waɪz/ adj prudent, sage; (look) averti.

wish /wɪʃ/ n (specific) souhait m, vœu m; (general) désir m; **best ~es** (in letter) amitiés fpl; (on greeting card) meilleurs vœux mpl. ● vt souhaiter, vouloir, désirer (**to do** faire); (bid) souhaiter. ● vi **~ for** souhaiter; **I ~ he'd leave** je voudrais bien qu'il parte.

wishful /'wɪʃfl/ adj **it's ~ thinking** c'est prendre ses désirs pour des réalités.

wistful /'wɪstfl/ adj mélancolique.

wit /wɪt/ n intelligence f; (humour) esprit m; (person) homme m d'esprit, femme f d'esprit.

witch /wɪtʃ/ n sorcière f.

with /'wɪð/ prep avec; (having) à; (because of) de; (at house of) chez; **the man ~ the beard** l'homme à la barbe; **fill ~** remplir de; **pleased/ shaking ~** content/frémissant de.

withdraw /wɪð'drɔː/ vt/i (pt **withdrew**; pp **withdrawn**) (se) retirer. **withdrawal** n retrait m.

wither /'wɪðə(r)/ vt/i (se) flétrir.

withhold /wɪð'həʊld/ vt (pt **withheld**) refuser (de donner); (retain) retenir; (conceal) cacher (**from** à).

within /wɪ'ðɪn/ prep & adv à l'intérieur (de); (in distances) à moins de; **~ a month** (before) avant un mois; **~ sight** en vue.

without /wɪ'ðaʊt/ prep sans; **~ my knowing** sans que je sache.

withstand /wɪð'stænd/ vt (pt **withstood**) résister à.

witness /'wɪtnɪs/ n témoin m; (evidence) témoignage m; **to ~** témoigner de. ● vt être le témoin de, voir. **~ box**, **~ stand** n barre f des témoins.

witty /'wɪtɪ/ adj (**-ier**, **-iest**) spirituel.

wives /waɪvz/ →**WIFE**.

wizard /'wɪzəd/ n magicien m; (genius: fig) génie m.

WMD abbr (weapon of mass destruction) ADM f.

woke, woken →**WAKE**.

wolf /wʊlf/ n (pl **wolves**) loup m. ● vt (food) engloutir.

woman /'wʊmən/ n (pl **women**) femme f; **~ doctor** femme f médecin; **~ driver** femme f au volant.

women /'wɪmɪn/ →**WOMAN**.

won /wʌn/ →**WIN**.

wonder /'wʌndə(r)/ n émerveillement m; (thing) merveille f; **it is no ~** ce or il n'est pas étonnant (**that** que). ● vt se demander (**if** si). ● vi s'étonner (**at** de); (reflect) songer (**about** à).

wonderful /'wʌndəfl/ adj merveilleux.

won't /wəʊnt/ →**WILL NOT**.

wood /wʊd/ n bois m.

wooden /'wʊdn/ adj en or de bois. (stiff: fig) raide, comme du bois.

wood: **~wind** n (Mus) bois mpl. **~work** n (craft, objects) menuiserie f.

wool /wʊl/ n laine f. **woollen** adj de laine. **woollens** npl lainages mpl.

woolly /'wʊlɪ/ adj laineux; (vague) nébuleux. ● n (garment 🆃) lainage m.

word /wɜːd/ n mot m; (spoken) parole f, mot m; (promise) parole f; (news) nouvelles fpl; **by ~ of mouth** de vive voix; **give/keep one's ~** donner/tenir sa parole; **have a ~ with** parler à; **in other ~s** autrement dit. ● vt rédiger. **wording** n termes mpl.

word processing n traitement m de texte. **word processor** n machine f à traitement de texte.

wore /wɔː(r)/ →**WEAR**.

work /wɜːk/ n travail m; (product, book) œuvre f, ouvrage m; (building work) travaux mpl; **~s** (Tech) mécanisme m; (factory) usine f. ● vi (person) travailler; (drug) agir; (Tech) fonctionner, marcher. ● vt (Tech) faire fonctionner, faire marcher; (land, mine) exploiter; (shape, hammer) travailler; **~ sb** (make work) faire travailler qn. □ **~ out** vt (solve) résoudre; (calculate) calculer; (elaborate) élaborer; vi (succeed) marcher; (Sport) s'entraîner; **~ up** vt développer, vi (to climax) monter vers; **~ed up** (person) énervé.

workaholic /wɜːkə'hɒlɪk/ n 🆃 bourreau m de travail.

W

worker /ˈwɜːkə(r)/ n travailleur/-euse m/f; (manual) ouvrier/-ière m/f.

work-force n main-d'œuvre f.

working /ˈwɜːkɪŋ/ adj (day, lunch) de travail; **~s** mécanisme m; **in ~ order** en état de marche.

working class n classe f ouvrière. ● adj ouvrier.

workman /ˈwɜːkmən/ n (pl **-men**) ouvrier m.

work: ~out n séance f de mise en forme. **~shop** n atelier m. **~-station** n poste m de travail.

world /wɜːld/ n monde m; **best in the ~** meilleur au monde. ● adj (power) mondial; (record) du monde.

world-wide adj universel.

World Wide Web, **WWW** n World Wide Web m, réseau m des réseaux.

worm /wɜːm/ n ver m. ● vt **~ one's way into** s'insinuer dans.

worn /wɔːn/ →WEAR. ● adj usé. **~-out** adj (thing) complètement usé; (person) épuisé.

worried /ˈwʌrɪd/ adj inquiet.

worry /ˈwʌrɪ/ vt/i (s')inquiéter. ● n souci m.

worse /wɜːs/ adj pire, plus mauvais; **be ~ off** perdre. ● adv plus mal. ● n pire m. **worsen** vt/i empirer.

worship /ˈwɜːʃɪp/ n (adoration) culte m. ● vt (pt **worshipped**) adorer. ● vi faire ses dévotions.

worst /wɜːst/ adj pire, plus mauvais. ● adv (the) **~** (sing) le plus mal. ● n **the ~ (one)** (person, object) le or la pire; **the ~ (thing)** le pire.

worth /wɜːθ/ adj **be ~** valoir; **it is ~ waiting** ça vaut la peine d'attendre; **it is ~ (one's) while** ça (en) vaut la peine. ● n valeur f; **ten pence ~ of** (pour) dix pence de. **worthless** adj qui ne vaut rien. **worthwhile** adj qui (en) vaut la peine.

worthy /ˈwɜːðɪ/ adj (**-ier**, **-iest**) digne (of de); (laudable) louable.

would /wʊd/ v aux he **~ do/you ~ sing** (conditional tense) il ferait/tu chanterais; **he ~ have done** il aurait fait; **I ~ come every day** (used to) je venais chaque jour; **I ~ like some tea** je voudrais du thé; **~ you come here?** voulez-vous venir ici?; **he**

wouldn't come il a refusé de venir. **~-be** adj soidisant.

wound¹ /wuːnd/ n blessure f. ● vt blesser; **the ~ed** les blessés mpl.

wound² /waʊnd/ →WIND².

wove, woven /wəʊv, ˈwəʊvn/ →WEAVE.

wrap /ræp/ vt (pt **wrapped**) **~ (up)** envelopper. ● vi **~ up** (dress warmly) se couvrir; **~ped up in** (engrossed) absorbé dans.

wrapping /ˈræpɪŋ/ n emballage m.

wreak /riːk/ vt **~ havoc** faire des ravages.

wreath /riːθ/ n (of flowers, leaves) couronne f.

wreck /rek/ n (sinking) naufrage m; (ship, remains, person) épave f; (vehicle) voiture f accidentée or délabrée. ● vt détruire; (ship) provoquer le naufrage de. **wreckage** n (pieces) débris mpl; (wrecked building) décombres mpl.

wrestle /ˈresl/ vi lutter, se débattre (with contre).

wrestling /ˈreslɪŋ/ n lutte f; (all-in) **~** catch m.

wriggle /ˈrɪgl/ vt/i (se) tortiller.

wring /rɪŋ/ vt (pt **wrung**) (twist) tordre; (clothes) essorer; **~ out of** (obtain from) arracher à.

wrinkle /ˈrɪŋkl/ n (crease) pli m; (on skin) ride f. ● vt/i (se) rider.

wrist /rɪst/ n poignet m.

write /raɪt/ vt/i (pt **wrote**; pp **written**) écrire. □ **~ back** répondre; **~ down** noter; **~ off** (debt) passer aux profits et pertes; (vehicle) considérer bon pour la casse; **~ up** (from notes) rédiger.

write-off /ˈraɪtɒf/ n perte f totale.

writer /ˈraɪtə(r)/ n auteur m, écrivain m; **~ of** auteur de.

write-up /ˈraɪtʌp/ n compte-rendu m.

writing /ˈraɪtɪŋ/ n écriture f; **~(s)** (works) écrits mpl; **in ~** par écrit. **~-paper** n papier m à lettres.

written →WRITE.

wrong /rɒŋ/ adj (incorrect, mistaken) faux, mauvais. (unfair) injuste; (amiss) qui ne va pas; (clock) pas à l'heure; **be ~** (person) avoir tort (to de); (be mistaken) se tromper; **go ~** (err) se tromper; (turn out badly) mal tourner;

W

465

it is ~ **to** (morally) c'est mal de;
what's ~? qu'est-ce qui ne va pas?;
what is ~ with you? qu'est-ce que
vous avez? ● *adv* mal. ● *n* injustice *f*;
(evil) mal *m*; **be in the ~** avoir tort.
● *vt* faire (du) tort à. **wrongful** *adj* injustifié, injuste. **wrongfully** *adv* à tort.
wrongly *adv* mal; (*blame*) à tort.

wrote /rəʊt/ →WRITE.

wrought iron /rɔːt ˈaɪən/ *n* fer *m*
forgé.

wrung /rʌŋ/ →WRING.

••••••••••••••••••••••••••••

••••••••••••••••••••••••••••

Xmas /ˈkrɪsməs/ *n* Noël *m*.

X-ray /ˈeksreɪ/ *n* rayon *m* X; (photograph) radio (graphie) *f*. ● *vt* radio-
graphier.

••••••••••••••••••••••••••••

••••••••••••••••••••••••••••

yank /jæŋk/ *vt* tirer brusquement. ● *n*
coup *m* brusque.

yard /jɑːd/ *n* (measure) yard *m* (=
0.9144 metre). (of house) cour *f*; (garden: US) jardin *m*; (for storage) chantier *m*, dépôt *m*. ~**stick** *n* mesure *f*.

yawn /jɔːn/ *vi* bâiller. ● *n* bâillement *m*.

yeah /jeə/ *adv* 🄸 ouais.

year /jɪə(r)/ *n* an *m*, année *f*; **school/
tax**~ année scolaire/fiscale; **be ten
~s old** avoir dix ans.

yearly /ˈjɪəlɪ/ *adj* annuel. ● *adv* annuel-
lement.

yearn /jɜːn/ *vi* avoir bien *or* très envie
(for, to do).

yeast /jiːst/ *n* levure *f*.

yell /jel/ *vt/i* hurler. ● *n* hurlement *m*.

yellow /ˈjeləʊ/ *adj* jaune; (cowardly 🄸)
froussard. ● *n* jaune *m*.

yes /jes/ *adv* oui; (as answer to negative
question) si. ● *n* oui *m inv*.

yesterday /ˈjestədeɪ/ *n & adv* hier (*m*).

yet /jet/ *adv* encore; (already) déjà.
● *conj* pourtant, néanmoins.

yew /juː/ *n* if *m*.

yield /jiːld/ *vt* (produce) produire, rendre; (*profit*) rapporter; (surrender)
céder. ● *n* rendement *m*.

yoga /ˈjəʊgə/ *n* yoga *m*.

yoghurt /ˈjɒgət/ *n* yaourt *m*.

yolk /jəʊk/ *n* jaune *m* (d'œuf).

you /juː/ *pron* (familiar form) tu, *pl* vous;
(polite form) vous; (object) te, t', *pl*
vous; (polite) vous; (after prep.) toi, *pl*
vous; (polite) vous; (indefinite) on;
(object) vous; **(to)** ~ te, t', *pl* vous;
(polite) vous; **I gave ~ a pen** je vous
ai donné un stylo; **I know ~** je te
connais *or* je vous connais.

young /jʌŋ/ *adj* jeune. ● *n* (people)
jeunes *mpl*; (of animals) petits *mpl*.

your /jɔː(r)/ *adj* (familiar form) ton, ta,
pl tes; (polite form, & familiar form pl.)
votre, *pl* vos.

yours /jɔːz/ *pron* (familiar form) le tien,
la tienne, les tien(ne)s; (polite form, &
familiar form pl.) le *or* la vôtre, les vô-
tres; ~ **faithfully/sincerely** je vous
prie d'agréer mes salutations les
meilleures.

yourself /jɔːˈself/ *pron* (familiar form)
toimême; (polite form) vous-même;
(reflexive & after prepositions) te, t';
vous; **proud of ~** fier de toi. **yourselves** *pron* vous-mêmes; (reflexive) vous.

youth /juːθ/ *n* jeunesse *f*; (young man)
jeune *m*. ~ **hostel** *n* auberge *f* de
jeunesse.

Yugoslav /ˈjuːgəʊslɑːv/ *adj* yougoslave.
● *n* Yougoslave *mf*.

Yugoslavia /juːgəʊˈslɑːvɪə/ *n* Yougoslavie *f*.

••••••••••••••••••••••••••••

••••••••••••••••••••••••••••

zap /zæp/ *vt* 🄸 (kill) descendre;
(Comput) enlever.

zeal /ziːl/ *n* zèle *m*.

zebra /ˈzebrə/ *n* zèbre *m*. ~ **crossing** *n*
passage *m* pour piétons.

zero /'zɪərəʊ/ *n* zéro *m.*

zest /zest/ *n* (gusto) entrain *m;* (spice: fig) piment *m;* (of orange or lemon peel) zeste *m.*

zip /zɪp/ *n* (vigour) allant *m;* ∼(-fastener) fermeture *f* éclair(r). ● *vt* (*pt* **zipped**) fermer avec une fermeture éclair(r); (Comput) compresser.
Zip code (US) *n* code *m* postal.

zodiac /'zəʊdɪæk/ *n* zodiaque *m.*

zone /zəʊn/ *n* zone *f.*

zoo /zuː/ *n* zoo *m.*

zoom /zuːm/ *vi* (rush) se précipiter.
□ ∼ **off** *or* **past** filer (comme une flèche). ∼ **lens** *n* zoom *m.*

zucchini /zuːˈkiːnɪ/ *n inv* (US) courgette *f.*

French Verbs

1 chanter

Present indicative

je	chante
tu	chantes
il	chante
nous	chantons
vous	chantez
ils	chantent

Present subjunctive

(que)	je	chante
(que)	tu	chantes
(qu')	il	chante
(que)	nous	chantions
(que)	vous	chantiez
(qu')	ils	chantent

Future indicative

je	chanterai
tu	chanteras
il	chantera
nous	chanterons
vous	chanterez
ils	chanteront

Present conditional

je	chanterais
tu	chanterais
il	chanterait
nous	chanterions
vous	chanteriez
ils	chanteraient

Imperfect indicative

je	chantais
tu	chantais
il	chantait
nous	chantions
vous	chantiez
ils	chantaient

Past participle

chanté/chantée

Perfect indicative

j'	ai	chanté
tu	as	chanté
il	a	chanté
elle	a	chanté
nous	avons	chanté
vous	avez	chanté
ils	ont	chanté
elles	ont	chanté

Pluperfect indicative

j'	avais	chanté
tu	avais	chanté
il	avait	chanté
elle	avait	chanté
nous	avions	chanté
vous	aviez	chanté
ils	avaient	chanté
elles	avaient	chanté

2 finir

Present indicative

je	finis
tu	finis
il	finit
nous	finissons
vous	finissez
ils	finissent

Present subjunctive

(que)	je	finisse
(que)	tu	finisses
(qu')	il	finisse
(que)	nous	finissions
(que)	vous	finissiez
(qu')	ils	finissent

Future indicative

je	finirai
tu	finiras
il	finira
nous	finirons
vous	finirez
ils	finiront

Present conditional

je	finirais
tu	finirais
il	finirait
nous	finirions
vous	finiriez
ils	finiraient

Imperfect indicative

je	finissais
tu	finissais
il	finissait
nous	finissions
vous	finissiez
ils	finissaient

Past participle

fini/finie

Pluperfect indicative

j'	avais	fini
tu	avais	fini
il	avait	fini
elle	avait	fini
nous	avions	fini
vous	aviez	fini
ils	avaient	fini
elles	avaient	fini

Perfect indicative

j'	ai	fini
tu	as	fini
il	a	fini
elles	a	fini
nous	avons	fini
vous	avez	fini
ils	ont	fini
elles	ont	fini

3 attendre

Present indicative

j'	attends
tu	attends
il	attend
nous	attendons
vous	attendez
ils	attendent

Future indicative

j'	attendrai
tu	attendras
il	attendra
nous	attendrons
vous	attendrez
ils	attendront

Imperfect indicative

j'	attendais
tu	attendais
il	attendait
nous	attendions
vous	attendiez
ils	attendaient

Perfect indicative

j'	ai	attendu
tu	as	attendu
il	a	attendu
elle	a	attendu
nous	avons	attendu
vous	avez	attendu
ils	ont	attendu
elles	ont	attendu

Present subjunctive

(que)	j'	attende
(que)	tu	attendes
(qu')	il	attende
(que)	nous	attendions
(que)	vous	attendiez
(qu')	ils	attendent

Present conditional

j'	attendrais
tu	attendrais
il	attendrait
nous	attendrions
vous	attendriez
ils	attendraient

Past participle

attendu/attendue

Pluperfect indicative

j'	avais	attendu
tu	avais	attendu
il	avait	attendu
elle	avait	attendu
nous	avions	attendu
vous	aviez	attendu
ils	avaient	attendu
elles	avaient	attendu

4 être

Present indicative

je	suis
tu	es
il	est
nous	sommes
vous	êtes
ils	sont

Future indicative

je	serai
tu	seras
il	sera
nous	serons
vous	serez
ils	seront

Imperfect indicative

j'	étais
tu	étais
il	était
nous	étions
vous	étiez
ils	étaient

Perfect indicative

j'	ai	été
tu	as	été
il	a	été
elle	a	été
nous	avons	été
vous	avez	été
ils	ont	été
elles	ont	été

Present subjunctive

(que)	je	sois
(que)	tu	sois
(qu')	il	soit
(que)	nous	soyons
(que)	vous	soyez
(qu')	ils	soient

Present conditional

je	serais
tu	serais
il	serait
nous	serions
vous	seriez
ils	seraient

Past participle

été (*invariable*)

Pluperfect indicative

j'	avais	été
tu	avais	été
il	avait	été
elle	avait	été
nous	avions	été
vous	aviez	été
ils	avaient	été
elles	avaient	été

5 avoir

Present indicative

j'	ai
tu	as
il	a
nous	avons
vous	avez
ils	ont

Future indicative

j'	aurai
tu	auras
il	aura
nous	aurons
vous	aurez
ils	auront

Imperfect indicative

j'	avais
tu	avais
il	avait
nous	avions
vous	aviez
ils	avaient

Perfect indicative

j'	ai	eu
tu	as	eu
il	a	eu
elle	a	eu
nous	avons	eu
vous	avez	eu
ils	ont	eu
elles	ont	eu

Present subjunctive

(que)	j'	aie
(que)	tu	aies
(qu')	il	ait
(que)	nous	ayons
(que)	vous	ayez
(qu')	ils	aient

Present conditional

j'	aurais
tu	aurais
il	aurait
nous	aurions
vous	aurlez
ils	auraient

Past participle

eu/eue

Pluperfect indicative

j'	avais	eu
tu	avais	eu
il	avait	eu
elle	avait	eu
nous	avions	eu
vous	aviez	eu
ils	avaient	eu
elles	avaient	eu

[6] acheter
1 j'achète 2 j'achèterai 3 j'achetais
4 que j'achète 5 acheté

[7] acquérir
1 j'acquiers, nous acquérons,
ils acquièrent 2 j'acquerrai
3 j'acquérais 4 que j'acquière
5 acquis

[8] aller
1 je vais, tu vas, il va, nous allons,
vous allez, ils vont 2 j'irai 3 j'allais
4 que j'aille, que nous allions, qu'ils
aillent 5 allé

[9] asseoir
1 j'assois, tu assois, il assoit, nous
assoyons, vous assoyez, ils assoient
2 j'assoirai 3 j'assoyais 4 que
j'assoie, que nous assoyions, qu'ils
assoient 5 assis

[10] avancer
1 nous avançons 3 j'avançais

[11] battre
1 je bats, il bat, nous battons
2 je battrai 3 je battais 4 que je
batte 5 battu

[12] boire
1 je bois, il boit, nous buvons,
ils boivent 2 je boirai 3 je buvais
4 que je boive 5 bu

[13] bouillir
1 je bous, il bout, nous bouillons,
ils bouillent 2 je bouillirai

3 je bouillais 4 que je bouille
5 bouilli

[14] céder
1 je cède, nous cédons, ils cèdent
2 je céderai 3 je cédais 4 que je
cède 5 cédé

[15] créer
1 je crée, nous créons 2 je créerai
3 je créais 4 que je crée 5 créé

[16] conclure
1 je conclus, il conclut, nous
concluons, ils concluent 2 je
conclurai 3 je concluais 4 que je
conclue 5 conclu (*but* inclus)

[17] conduire
1 je conduis, nous conduisons,
2 je conduirai 3 je conduisais
4 que je conduise 5 conduit (*but* lui,
nui)

[18] connaître
1 je connais, il connaît, nous
connaissons 2 je connaîtrai
3 je connaissais 4 que je connaisse
5 connu

[19] coudre
1 je couds, il coud, nous cousons,
ils cousent 2 je coudrai 3 je cousais
4 que je couse 5 cousu

[20] courir
1 je cours, il court, nous courons,
ils courent 2 je courrai 3 je courais
4 que je coure 5 couru

1 Present Indicative   2 Future Indicative   3 Imperfect Indicative
4 Present Subjunctive   5 Past Participle

[21] couvrir

1 je couvre 2 je couvrirai 3 je couvrais 4 que je couvre 5 couvert

[22] craindre

1 je crains, il craint, nous craignons, ils craignent 2 je craindrai 3 je craignais 4 que je craigne 5 craint

[23] croire

1 je crois, il croit, nous croyons, ils croient 2 je croirai 3 je croyais, nous croyions 4 que je croie, que nous croyions 5 cru

[24] croître

1 je croîs, il croît, nous croissons 2 je croîtrai 3 je croissais 4 que je croisse 5 crû/crue (*but* accru, décru)

[25] cueillir

1 je cueille 2 je cueillerai 3 je cueillais 4 que je cueille 5 cueilli

[26] devoir

1 je dois, il doit, nous devons, ils doivent 2 je devrai 3 je devais 4 que je doive, que nous devions 5 dû/due

[27] dire

1 je dis, il dit, nous disons, vous dites, ils disent 2 je dirai 3 je disais 4 que je dise 5 dit

[28] dissoudre

1 je dissous, il dissout, nous dissolvons, ils dissolvent 2 je dissoudrai 3 je dissolvais 4 que je dissolve 5 dissous/dissoute

[29] distraire

1 je distrais, il distrait, nous distrayons 2 je distrairai 3 je distrayais 4 que je distraie 5 distrait

[30] écrire

1 j'écris, il écrit, nous écrivons 2 j'écrirai 3 j'écrivais 4 que j'écrive 5 écrit

[31] employer

1 j'emploie, nous employons, ils emploient 2 j'emploierai 3 j'employais, nous employions 4 que j'emploie, que nous employions 5 employé

[32] envoyer

1 j'envoie, nous envoyons, ils envoient 2 j'enverrai 3 j'envoyais, nous envoyions 4 que j'envoie, que nous envoyions 5 envoyé

[33] faire

1 je fais, nous faisons (*say* /fəzɔ̃/), vous faites, ils font 2 je ferai 3 je faisais (*say* /fəzɛ/) 4 que je fasse, que nous fassions 5 fait

[34] falloir (*impersonal*)

1 il faut 2 il faudra 3 il fallait 4 qu'il faille 5 fallu

[35] fuir

1 je fuis, nous fuyons 2 je fuirai 3 je fuyais, nous fuyions 4 que je fuie, que nous fuyions 5 fui

---

1 Present Indicative   2 Future Indicative   3 Imperfect Indicative
4 Present Subjunctive   5 Past Participle

[36] haïr
1 je hais, il hait, nous haïssons,
ils haïssent **2** je haïrai **3** je haïssais
4 que je haïsse **5** haï

[37] interdire
1 j'interdis, vous interdisez
2 j'interdirai **3** j'interdisais
4 que j'interdise **5** interdit

[38] jeter
1 je jette, nous jetons, ils jettent
2 je jetterai **3** je jetais **4** que je jette
5 jeté

[39] lire
1 je lis, il lit, nous lisons **2** je lirai
3 je lisais **4** que je lise **5** lu

[40] manger
1 je mange, nous mangeons
2 je mangerai **3** je mangeais
4 que je mange, que nous mangions
5 mangé

[41] maudire
1 je maudis, il maudit, nous
maudissons **2** je maudirai
3 je maudissais **4** que je maudisse
5 maudit

[42] mettre
1 je mets, tu mets, nous mettons
2 je mettrai **3** je mettais **4** que je
mette **5** mis

[43] mourir
1 je meurs, il meurt, nous mourons
2 je mourrai **3** je mourais **4** que je
meure **5** mort

[44] naître
1 je nais, il naît, nous naissons
2 je naîtrai **3** je naissais **4** que je
naisse **5** né

[45] oublier
1 j'oublie, nous oublions, ils
oublient **2** j'oublierai **3** j'oubliais,
nous oubliions, vous oubliiez
4 que nous oubliions, que vous
oubliiez **5** oublié

[46] partir
1 je pars, nous partons **2** je partirai
3 je partais **4** que je parte **5** parti

[47] plaire
1 je plais, il plaît (*but* il tait), nous
plaisons **2** je plairai **3** je plaisais
4 que je plaise **5** plu

[48] pleuvoir *(impersonal)*
1 il pleut **2** il pleuvra **3** il pleuvait
4 qu'il pleuve **5** plu

[49] pouvoir
1 je peux, il peut, nous pouvons,
ils peuvent **2** je pourrai **3** je pouvais
4 que je puisse, que nous puissions
5 pu

[50] prendre
1 je prends, il prend, nous prenons
2 je prendrai **3** je prenais **4** que je
prenne **5** pris

---

1 Present Indicative **2** Future Indicative **3** Imperfect Indicative
4 Present Subjunctive **5** Past Participle

[51] prévoir

1 je prévois, il prévoit, nous prévoyons, ils prévoient **2** je prévoirai **3** je prévoyais, nous prévoyions **4** que je prévoie, que nous prévoyions **5** prévu

[52] recevoir

1 je reçois, il reçoit, nous recevons, ils reçoivent **2** je recevrai **3** je recevais **4** que je reçoive, que nous recevions **5** reçu

[53] résoudre

1 je résous, il résout, nous résolvons, ils résolvent **2** je résoudrai **3** je résolvais **4** que je résolve **5** résolu

[54] rire

1 je ris, nous rions, ils rient **2** je rirai **3** je riais, nous riions **4** que je rie, que nous riions **5** ri

[55] savoir

1 je sais, il sait, nous savons, ils savent **2** je saurai **3** je savais **4** que je sache, que nous sachions **5** su

[56] suffire

1 il suffit, ils suffisent **2** il suffira **3** il suffisait **4** qu'il suffise **5** suffi (*but* frit)

[57] suivre

1 je suis, il suit, nous suivons **2** je suivrai **3** je suivais **4** que je suive **5** suivi

[58] tenir

1 je tiens, il tient, nous tenons, ils tiennent **2** je tiendrai **3** je tenais **4** que je tienne, que nous tenions **5** tenu

[59] vaincre

1 je vaincs, il vainc, nous vainquons, ils vainquent **2** je vaincrai **3** je vainquais **4** que je vainque **5** vaincu

[60] valoir

1 je vaux, il vaut, nous valons **2** je vaudrai **3** je valais **4** que je vaille, que nous valions **5** valu

[61] vêtir

1 je vêts, il vêt, nous vêtons **2** je vêtirai **3** je vêtais **4** que je vête **5** vêtu

[62] vivre

1 je vis, il vit, nous vivons, ils vivent **2** je vivrai **3** je vivais **4** que je vive **5** vécu

[63] voir

1 je vois, nous voyons, ils voient **2** je verrai **3** je voyais, nous voyions **4** que je voie, que nous voyions **5** vu

[64] vouloir

1 je veux, il veut, nous voulons, ils veulent **2** je voudrai **3** je voulais **4** que je veuille, que nous voulions **5** voulu

---

1 Present Indicative   **2** Future Indicative   **3** Imperfect Indicative
4 Present Subjunctive   **5** Past Participle

• •

What are the equivalent tenses in English

Present indicative
je chante = I sing, I'm singing

Future indicative
je chanterai = I will sing

Imperfect indicative
je chantais = I was singing

Perfect indicative
j'ai chanté = I sang, I have sung

Pluperfect indicative
j'avais chanté = I had sung

Present subjunctive
bien que je chante = although I sing

Present conditional
si je pouvais, je chanterais
= if I could, I would sing

Past participle
chanté/chantée = sung

How to conjugate a reflexive verb

Present indicative and other simple tenses

je me lave
tu te laves
il se lave
elle se lave
nous nous lavons
vous vous lavez
ils se lavent
elles se lavent

Perfect indicative and other compound tenses
*(always with auxiliary **être**)*

je me suis lavé
tu t'es lavé
il s'est lavé
elle s'est lavée
nous nous sommes lavés
vous vous êtes lavés
ils se sont lavés
elles se sont lavées

in the negative form

je ne me lave pas
tu ne te laves pas
il ne se lave pas
elle ne se lave pas
nous ne nous lavons pas
vous ne vous lavez pas
ils ne se lavent pas
elles ne se lavent pas

in the negative form

je ne me suis pas lavé
tu ne t'es pas lavé
il ne s'est pas lavé
elle ne s'est pas lavée
nous ne nous sommes pas lavés
vous ne vous êtes pas lavés
ils ne se sont pas lavés
elles ne se sont pas lavées

Verbes irréguliers anglais

Infinitif	Prétérit	Participe passé	Infinitif	Prétérit	Participe passé
be	was	been	**drive**	drove	driven
bear	bore	borne	**eat**	ate	eaten
beat	beat	beaten	**fall**	fell	fallen
become	became	become	**feed**	fed	fed
begin	began	begun	**feel**	felt	felt
bend	bent	bent	**fight**	fought	fought
bet	bet, betted	bet, betted	**find**	found	found
			flee	fled	fled
bid	bade, bid	bidden, bid	**fly**	flew	flown
bind	bound	bound	**freeze**	froze	frozen
bite	bit	bitten	**get**	got	got, gotten *US*
bleed	bled	bled	**give**	gave	given
blow	blew	blown	**go**	went	gone
break	broke	broken	**grow**	grew	grown
breed	bred	bred	**hang**	hung, hanged	hung, hanged
bring	brought	brought			
build	built	built	**have**	had	had
burn	burnt, burned	burnt, burned	**hear**	heard	heard
			hide	hid	hidden
burst	burst	burst	**hit**	hit	hit
buy	bought	bought	**hold**	held	held
catch	caught	caught	**hurt**	hurt	hurt
choose	chose	chosen	**keep**	kept	kept
cling	clung	clung	**kneel**	knelt	knelt
come	came	come	**know**	knew	known
cost	cost, costed (*vt*)	cost, costed	**lay**	laid	laid
			lead	led	led
cut	cut	cut	**lean**	leaned, leant	leaned, leant
deal	dealt	dealt			
dig	dug	dug	**learn**	learnt, learned	learnt, learned
do	did	done			
draw	drew	drawn	**leave**	left	left
dream	dreamt, dreamed	dreamt, dreamed	**lend**	lent	lent
			let	let	let
drink	drank	drunk	**lie**	lay	lain

Infinitif	Prétérit	Participe passé	Infinitif	Prétérit	Participe passé
lose	lost	lost	**spend**	spent	spent
make	made	made	**spit**	spat	spat
mean	meant	meant	**spoil**	spoilt,	spoilt,
meet	met	met		spoiled	spoiled
pay	paid	paid	**spread**	spread	spread
put	put	put	**spring**	sprang	sprung
read	read	read	**stand**	stood	stood
ride	rode	ridden	**steal**	stole	stolen
ring	rang	rung	**stick**	stuck	stuck
rise	rose	risen	**sting**	stung	stung
run	ran	run	**stride**	strode	stridden
say	said	said	**strike**	struck	struck
see	saw	seen	**swear**	swore	sworn
seek	sought	sought	**sweep**	swept	swept
sell	sold	sold	**swell**	swelled	swollen,
send	sent	sent			swelled
set	set	set	**swim**	swam	swum
sew	sewed	sewn, sewed	**swing**	swung	swung
shake	shook	shaken	**take**	took	taken
shine	shone	shone	**teach**	taught	taught
shoe	shod	shod	**tear**	tore	torn
shoot	shot	shot	**tell**	told	told
show	showed	shown	**think**	thought	thought
shut	shut	shut	**throw**	threw	thrown
sing	sang	sung	**thrust**	thrust	thrust
sink	sank	sunk	**tread**	trod	trodden
sit	sat	sat	**under-**	under-	understood
sleep	slept	slept	**stand**	stood	
sling	slung	slung	**wake**	woke	woken
smell	smelt,	smelt,	**wear**	wore	worn
	smelled	smelled	**win**	won	won
speak	spoke	spoken	**write**	wrote	written
spell	spelled,	spelled,			
	spelt	spelt			

Numbers/Les nombres

Cardinal numbers/ Les nombres cardinaux

0	zero **zéro**
1	one **un**
2	two **deux**
3	three **trois**
4	four **quatre**
5	five **cinq**
6	six **six**
7	seven **sept**
8	eight **huit**
9	nine **neuf**
10	ten **dix**
11	eleven **onze**
12	twelve **douze**
13	thirteen **treize**
14	fourteen **quatorze**
15	fifteen **quinze**
16	sixteen **seize**
17	seventeen **dix-sept**
18	eighteen **dix-huit**
19	nineteen **dix-neuf**
20	twenty **vingt**
21	twenty-one **vingt et un**
22	twenty-two **vingt-deux**
30	thirty **trente**
40	forty **quarante**
50	fifty **cinquante**
60	sixty **soixante**
70	seventy **soixante-dix**
80	eighty **quatre-vingt**
90	ninety **quatre-vingt-dix**

100	a hundred **cent**
101	a hundred and one **cent un**
110	a hundred and ten **cent dix**
200	two hundred **deux cents**
250	two hundred and fifty **deux cent cinquante**
1,000	one thousand **mille**
1,001	one thousand and one **mille un**
2,000	two thousand **deux mille**
10,000	ten thousand **dix mille**
100,000	a hundred thousand **cent mille**
1,000,000	a million **un million**

Ordinal numbers/ Les nombres ordinaux

1st	first	**premier**
2nd	second	**deuxième**
3rd	third	**troisième**
4th	fourth	**quatrième**
5th	fifth	**cinquième**
6th	sixth	**sixième**
7th	seventh	**septième**
8th	eighth	**huitième**
9th	ninth	**neuvième**
10th	tenth	**dixième**
11th	eleventh	**onzième**
12th	twelfth	**douzième**
13th	thirteenth	**treizième**
14th	fourteenth	**quatorzième**
15th	fifteenth	**quinzième**

. . . .

16th   sixteenth **seizième**

17th   seventeenth **dix-septième**

18th   eighteenth **dix-huitième**

19th   nineteenth **dix-neuvième**

20th   twentieth **vingtième**

21st   twenty-first **vingt et unième**

22nd   twenty-second **vingt-deuxième**

30th   thirtieth **trentième**

40th   fortieth **quarantième**

50th   fiftieth **cinquantième**

60th   sixtieth **soixantième**

70th   seventieth **soixante-dixième**

80th   eightieth **quatre-vingtième**

90th   ninetieth **quatre-vingt-dixième**

100th   hundredth **centième**

101st   hundred and first **cent unième**

110th   hundred and tenth **cent dixième**

200th   two hundredth **deux centième**

250th   two hundred and fiftieth **deux cent cinquantième**

1,000th   thousandth **millième**

1,001st   thousand and first **mille et unième**

2,000th   two thousandth **deux millième**

10,000th   ten thousandth **dix millième**

100,000th   hundred thousandth **cent millième**

1,000,000th   millionth **millionième**

Fractions/Les fractions

½   a half **un demi**

⅓   a third **un tiers**

¼   a quarter **un quart**

¹⁄₁₀   a tenth **un dixième**

⅔   two-thirds **deux tiers**

⅝   five-eighths **cinq huitièmes**

¹⁄₁₀₀   one hundredth **un centième**

1½   one and a half **un et demi**

2¼   two and a quarter **deux et un quart**

Decimals/Les décimaux

0.1   point one **zéro virgule un**

0.25   point two five **zéro virgule vingt-cinq**

1.2   one point two **un virgule deux**

1.46   one point four six **un virgule quarante-six**

Percentages/Pourcentages

25%   twenty-five per cent **vingt-cinq pour cent**

50%   fifty per cent **cinquante pour cent**

100%   a hundred per cent **cent pour cent**

365%   three hundred and sixty-five per cent **trois cent soixante-cinq pour cent**

4.25%   four point two five per cent **quatre virgule vingt-cinq pour cent**